Oracle® Forms Developer's Handbook

Oracle Forms Developer's Handbook

Albert Lulushi

Prentice Hall PTR
Upper Saddle River, NJ 07458
www.phptr.com

Library of Congress Cataloging-in-Publication Data

Lulushi, Albert.
Oracle forms developer's handbook/Albert Lulushi.
p. cm.
ISBN 0-13-030754-8
1. Oracle (Computer file) 2. Application software—Development. I. Title.

QA76.76.A65 L85 2000
005.75'85—dc21 00-063711

Acquisitions editor: *Tim Moore*
Cover designer: *Anthony Gemmellaro*
Cover design director: *Jerry Votta*
Manufacturing manager: *Maura Zaldivar*
Editorial assistant: *Allison Kloss*
Marketing manager: *Debby van Dijk*
Project coordinator: *Anne Trowbridge*
Compositor/Production services: *Pine Tree Composition, Inc.*

Prentice-Hall, Inc.
Upper Saddle River, New Jersey 07458

Prentice Hall books are widely used by corporations and government agencies for training, marketing, and resale.

The publisher offers discounts on this book when ordered in bulk quantities. For more information contact:

Corporate Sales Department
Phone: 800-382-3419
Fax: 201-236-7141
E-mail: corpsales@prenhall.com

Or write:

Prentice Hall PTR
Corp. Sales Dept.
One Lake Street
Upper Saddle River, New Jersey 07458

Printed in the United States of America
10 9 8 7 6 5 4 3 2

ISBN 0-13-030754-8

Prentice-Hall International (UK) Limited, *London*
Prentice-Hall of Australia Pty. Limited, *Sydney*
Prentice-Hall Canada Inc., *Toronto*
Prentice-Hall Hispanoamericana, S.A., *Mexico*
Prentice-Hall of India Private Limited, *New Delhi*
Prentice-Hall of Japan, Inc., *Tokyo*
Pearson Education Asia Pte. Ltd.
Editora Prentice-Hall do Brasil, Ltda., *Rio de Janeiro*

For Enit, Alex, and Anna

Contents

PREFACE

Oracle Forms is the most important tool used to create client/server and World Wide Web applications that run against Oracle databases. *Oracle Forms Developer's Handbook* is a complete reference guide for those who use Forms to build sophisticated database systems rapidly and productively. The book covers in detail all the aspects, features, and functionality of Oracle Forms. It also focuses on how modern application development concepts, such as client/server computing and object-oriented programming, are applied in the Oracle Forms environment.

ORGANIZATION OF THE BOOK

Oracle Forms Developer's Handbook is divided into five parts. They can be read sequentially or independently, depending on the your familiarity with Oracle Forms. The following paragraphs describe these parts:

- **Part One.** This part introduces readers to Oracle Forms programming. Following the detailed instructions provided in this part, you build and run your first form. In the process, I present important concepts of Form Builder and Runtime environments. At the end of this part, you will have completed the first form and become familiar with terms and concepts that will be encountered throughout the rest of the book.

- **Part Two.** This part equips you with the necessary tools to create, design and enhance forms. It begins with an overview of Oracle Developer suite and then focuses on the Form Builder and its components: Object Navigator, Layout Editor, Property Palette, Menu Editor, Object Library Editor and PL/SQL Editor. Separate chapters discuss the purpose, access methods, components and usage of each tool. Rapid Application Development (RAD) and object reusability with Oracle Forms are also covered in this part. The final three chapters discuss the elements of the Standard Query Language (SQL) used in Oracle applications, the Oracle's own programming language—PL/SQL—as well as object-relational features introduced by Oracle8 that affect Oracle Forms programming.
- **Part Three.** This part presents the Form Builder as an object-oriented and event-driven programming environment. It explains the features and functionality of its objects, including data blocks, items, windows, record structures, and menus. It also discusses events associated with each object, triggers they fire, and how you can use them to enhance Forms applications.
- **Part Four.** This part covers advanced programming with Oracle Forms. It begins with debugging techniques and activities. Then it discusses the integration of Forms with other Oracle Developer tools such as Report Builder and Graphic Builder. I dedicate an entire chapter to the reusable components provided by Oracle Developer and the benefits you draw by including them in your applications. Another important subject I cover in this part is the development and deployment of Forms applications on the Web in a three-tier architecture. In a separate chapter, I present tips and techniques to simplify Forms development and installation using the Project Builder. I conclude this part discussing the use of Oracle Designer in creating, maintaining, and generating Form Builder modules.
- **Part Five.** This part focuses on the integration of Oracle Forms with other Microsoft Windows applications through Dynamic Data Exchange (DDE) and Microsoft's COM-based technologies, including OLE Documents, Automation, and ActiveX controls. I also cover here the implementation of user exits and the extension of Oracle Developer applications' functionality using the PL/SQL interface to foreign functions.

AUDIENCE

Oracle Forms Developer's Handbook is intended primarily for software engineers whose mission is to create database applications for the Oracle DBMS. As such, this book addresses the needs of this group of IT professionals. Because of the way the material is organized, the book can be used by application developers at all levels of proficiency.

The first part is for newcomers to the Oracle Forms environment. This part explains important Form Builder and Runtime concepts, which benefit not just the beginner, but also end-users of Oracle applications.

The second part addresses the needs of intermediate programmers who do not have a vast experience with Oracle Forms. The chapters in this part are organized to serve as reference materials for the main components of the Form Builder, where most of the development activities occur.

The third part explains fundamental concepts that every serious Oracle Forms developer should know and master. The material covered in this part is for programmers dedicated to creating applications conforming with object-oriented principles, Multiple-Document Interface (MDI) paradigm and well-established GUI principles.

The last two parts of the book provide information for advanced programmers who go the extra mile to deliver integrated and user-friendly applications. The focus in Part Four is the integration of Oracle Forms modules with others Oracle design and development tools—Oracle Designer, Oracle Developer tools, and Oracle Developer reusable components. Part Five targets developers familiar with Microsoft Windows programming techniques and shows them how to integrate them in the Form Builder environment.

Here is a list of the most important benefits this book offers to you:

- Clear and concise explanation of all the features of Oracle Forms.
- Presentation of important aspects of Oracle Forms programming in the context of building Oracle-based enterprise applications.
- Gradual introduction of concepts and techniques that allows readers to build on their existing knowledge and increase their Oracle Forms proficiency level.
- Detailed instructions on how to perform the major development activities in Oracle Forms.
- A number of hands-on activities that allow readers to apply the concepts discussed in the book.
- A companion software downloadable from the Internet that contains all the software modules discussed in the book. The software provides readers with a chance to execute these modules and explore for themselves the code segments that implement the features discussed in the book.

THE COMPANION SOFTWARE

Oracle Forms Developer's Handbook is first and foremost a hands-on guide to application development with Oracle Forms, and you should read it as such. I strongly urge you to follow the discussion of different topics in the book by performing the activities with one or more application systems in your environment. In order to help you with these activities, I have provided a number of Oracle Forms modules that you can use in your environment. These modules will enable you to follow the discussion of different topics in the book by performing the activities described there. These software assets are very important because they allow you to start from any chapter in the book and follow the hands-on activities discussed in that chapter. They also serve as reference items that can be used to explore the implementation of the features discussed in the book. Oracle Developer version 6 was used to produce the application systems and record the movies.

The software provided is configured for Microsoft Windows operating systems. You can browse the contents by using your Web browser. Simply point to the file D2KFORMS.HTM on the root directory and then follow the hyperlinks to different assets provided. For questions, comments, or an updated list of contents, point your Web browser at http://www.belacorp.com/OracleForms.

The software items provided are organized by chapters of the book. At the end of each chapter there is a list of software assets discussed in that chapter as well as instructions on how to access these assets. The following is a list of the applications covered in the book that you will find in the companion software:

- **Equipment Tracking System application.** This is the application discussed in Chapters 1, 2, and 3.
- **Movie Rental Database objects.** These are tables you can use to test the SQL statements discussed in Part Two.
- **MRD application.** This is the application system developed throughout Part 3 and, partly, in Part 4.
- **Form Builder modules integrated with Oracle Developer reusable components.** These are the modules discussed in chapter 22 in which I have integrated Oracle Developer reusable controls, such as a calendar, hierarchy navigator, wizard dialog box, and so on to your Forms applications.
- **Form Builder modules implementing DDE.** These are the modules discussed in chapter 26 that allow you to integrate Form Builder with Microsoft Excel, Word and Program Manager through Dynamic Data Exchange.
- **Form Builder modules implementing COM-based technologies.** These are the modules discussed in chapters 27 and 28 implement OLE documents, Automation, and ActiveX controls in the Form Builder environment.

INSTALLING THE DATABASE OBJECTS

All the commands to create the database objects discussed in the book and populate them with the necessary data are provided in SQL*Plus files in the folder Software\SQL of the companion software. The instructions to run these commands are provided online as part of the assets of the companion software.

TYPOGRAPHIC CONVENTIONS

This book uses the following typographic conventions to make your reading and understanding of the material easier:

- Selection from menu items is presented in the following format:
  `File | Open, File | Save As…, or Edit | Copy.`
- Everything you should type in order to set a property is shown enclosed in single quotes as in this example:
  `Set the property Hint to 'The purchase date of the item.'`
- Any code used in the Form Builder is shown in Courier font, as in the following example:

```
BEGIN
  SELECT order_date
  INTO v_order_date
  FROM ORDERS
  WHERE
    order_number = v_order_number;
END;
```

- Tips offered throughout the book appear in boxes like the following one:

> **Tip**
>
> Tips are hints or suggestions you may follow to enhance the way you work with Oracle Forms.

- Warnings raised throughout the book appear in boxes like the following one:

> **Warning**
>
> Warnings are situations about which you need to be careful. They may potentially turn into problematic situations.

- Cautions discussed throughout the book appear in boxes like the following one:

> **Caution**
>
> These are situations that may have catastrophic consequences for your environment. Avoid them at any cost.

QUESTIONS AND COMMENTS

I welcome any questions or comments you may have about *Oracle Forms Developer's Handbook*. You can email them at albert.lulushi@belacorp.com. I strongly suggest that you periodically visit URL http://www.belacorp.com/OracleForms. There you will find answers to the most frequently asked questions about *Oracle Forms Developer's Handbook*, as well as a list of updated software assets of the CD as they become available.

Part I

Introduction to Developer/2000 Forms

He who has begun has half done. Dare to be wise; begin!
—Horace

Chapter 1

DEVELOPING THE FIRST FORM

Look with favor upon a bold beginning.
—Virgil

- The Equipment Tracking System
- Creating the First Form
- The Object Navigator
- Creating a Data Block with the Data Block Wizard
- The Layout Wizard
- Adding a Detail Block
- Compiling the Module
- Summary

In this chapter, you will develop the first Developer Forms application to solve a real-life problem. Before beginning the development activities, you will analyze the structure of entities, attributes, and database objects involved in this application.

Next, you will create a data entry form for the application. In the process, important elements of the Form Builder, such as the Object Navigator, toolbar, and message bar, will be discussed. The chapter also introduces basic Forms development techniques such as creating base table blocks, using master/detail relationships, and saving and generating modules.

1.1 THE EQUIPMENT TRACKING SYSTEM

Print and Press is a small desktop publishing company in Suburbia that prints everything, from *The Suburban Sentinel,* to postcards, to wedding invitations. It has a dozen employees, including Mrs. White, the general manager, and Mr. Brown, the receptionist. They all use desktop computers that run different software applications. In addition, the print shop has three scanners, two photocopying machines, and several printers.

1.1.1 STATEMENT OF THE PROBLEM

Mrs. White has hired you to put in order her bills and receipts for hardware and software purchases. Mr. Brown currently stores them in a file folder each time a new item is purchased. The problem is that, periodically, someone has to go through all the receipts in order to figure out the status of the assets as well how much money was spent on hardware and on software. You assess the situation, interview some of the employees who need these data the most, and decide to create a small Oracle Developer Forms application to solve their problem.

Before going any further, you should come up with a name for your application. Just like a sound bite, this name should convey as much information about the system as possible. The core functionality of the application should come across in no more than three or four words. The use of acronyms is acceptable, but you should be very careful to choose one that is easy to pronounce and remember. So, call the new application the Equipment Tracking System, or ETS for short.

1.1.2 DEFINING THE DATABASE OBJECTS FOR ETS

The main objects in the ETS application are the entities *Hardware Asset* and *Software Asset*. The first entity represents information about any electronic equipment purchased and located in the premises of *Print and Press,* that is used in the daily activity of the employees. Examples of hardware assets would by a personal computer (PC), a monitor, a scanner, or a printer. The entity Software Asset stores data about any software package that is installed and runs on a particular piece of hardware. Examples of software assets are Windows NT, Microsoft Office, and other programs installed on Mr. Brown's PC. The relationship between the entities Hardware Asset and Software Asset is shown graphically in Figure 1.1. This diagram is created in the Oracle Designer's Entity Relationship Diagrammer, although many other tools are available to create such diagrams.

Each block in this diagram represents an entity. The line connecting the entities represents the relationship between the instances each entity may contain. From left to right, it can be read as follows: "Each Hardware Asset may be a location for one or more Software Assets." It can also be read right to left, and, in that case, it becomes: "Each Software Asset must be installed on one and only one Hardware Asset."

Identifying the entities of an application and the relationships among them is called entity modeling or data modeling. It is one of the most important activities in the process of designing information systems because it identifies the main facts and data elements, which the systems will create and maintain. Entities contribute directly to the definition and properties of the principal database objects for these systems. In the case of ETS, the tables HW_ASSETS and SW_ASSETS correspond directly to the entities Hardware Asset and Software Asset. Graphically, the tables that are part of a database system are presented in data diagrams similar in layout and purpose to the entity relationship diagrams. Figure 1.2 shows the data diagram for ETS created in the Oracle Designer's Design Editor.

Besides the main objects of ETS and the relationship between them, this diagram also shows the columns and constraints for each table. The most important property of a column is its data type. Depending on the kind of data the column stores, its data type can be one of the predefined alphanumeric, numeric, date, or binary types. Object-relational versions of the Oracle Server, starting with Oracle8, support columns based on user-defined object types as well.

Alphanumeric columns represent character string data. The alphanumeric data types supported by the Oracle Server database include CHAR for fixed-length strings, and VARCHAR2 for variable-length strings, which is also the most flexible and frequently used alphanumeric data type. Numeric attributes have, in general, NUMBER data type and represent virtually any fixed and floating point numeric data, with up to 38 digits of precision. Attributes of DATE data type represent dates

FIGURE 1.1 The entity relationship diagram for ETS.

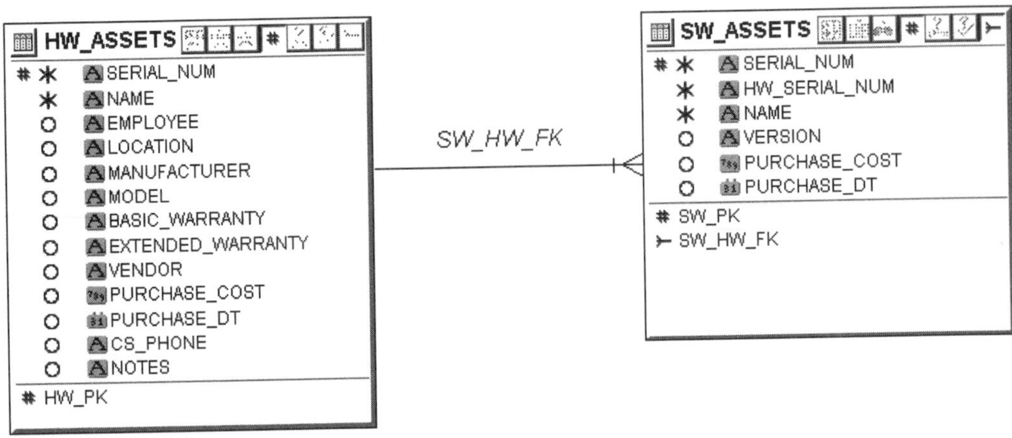

FIGURE 1.2 The data diagram for ETS.

in a flexible format that includes century, year, month, day, hours, minutes, and seconds. If the attribute will represent binary data up to 2000 bytes long, then RAW data type is used. For larger binary objects (up to 2 GB) such as graphics, bitmaps, and images, Oracle7 uses the LONG RAW data type. Oracle8 provides a more complete support for such objects through the large object (LOB) types, including CLOB for character objects and BLOB for binary objects.

A primary key (PK) constraint is made up of one or more columns that uniquely identify an instance of the database table. For example, the column SERIAL_NUM uniquely identifies each record in the table HW_ASSETS. A foreign key (FK) constraint on a table contains one or more columns that point to the columns that make up the primary key of another table. The foreign key provides reference integrity that guarantees that the values in that key match the values in the primary key of another table. For example, the foreign key constraint SW_HW_FK shown in the ETS data diagram contains the column HW_SERIAL_NUM. In the definition of the constraint, this column is associated with the primary key SERIAL_NUM of the table HW_ASSETS.

Every foreign key represents a relation between records in two tables. More precisely, it describes the dependence or child/parent relationship between the table that owns the foreign key on the table pointed at by the key. In the ETS application, the foreign key SW_HW_FK represents the fact that a software item is dependent on a hardware unit on which the software is installed.

Analyzing properties of attributes offers a good opportunity to identify the rules that data items will obey in the application. For example, in the ETS application, it is reasonable to ask that data satisfy the following rules:

- Names of hardware and software assets must be specified, hence they should not be NULL.

- The purchase cost of any hardware or software asset should be a positive value not to exceed $100,000.
- All dollar values should be specified in dollars and cents.

Some of these requirements, such as the first one, will be enforced at the database level. The rest of them could be implemented there as well, but you will enforce them in the application you are about to develop. Properties that determine whether the column of a table is a primary key, a foreign key, or the data it represents must not be NULL, must be unique, or obey other rules such as the ones described above, are also known as *constraints*. Often the constraints are represented visually in data diagrams, as in the case of the primary key and NOT NULL constraints for the tables HW_ASSETS and SW_ASSETS. As you can see in Figure 1.2, the required columns in the diagram are preceded by the asterisk (*) to set them apart from the optional ones which are preceded by a small "o" (for optional). The icon (#) identifies the columns that make up the primary key constraint of each table. Figure 1.3 lists the columns of the table HW_ASSETS and their properties.

COLUMN	DATA TYPE	LENGTH	CONSTRAINTS	DESCRIPTION
Serial Number	CHAR	6	PK, fixed length	Internal tracking number
Name	VARCHAR2	30	Not NULL	The name of the asset
Employee	VARCHAR2	30		The employee responsible for this asset
Location	VARCHAR2	30		The location of the asset
Manufacturer	VARCHAR2	30		The name of manufacturing company
Model	VARCHAR2	20		Model name and number
Basic Warranty	VARCHAR2	30		Manufacturer warranty on the asset
Extended Warranty	VARCHAR2	30		Ant additional warranty on the asset
Vendor	VARCHAR2	30		The name of vending company
Purchase Cost	NUMBER	8, 2	Between $0.00 and $100,000.00	Cost of purchase for the asset
Purchase Date	DATE			Date when asset was purchased
CS Phone	VARCHAR2	10		Customer support phone number
Notes	VARCHAR2	255		A brief description of the asset

FIGURE 1.3 Columns for table HW ASSETS and their properties.

ATTRIBUTES	DATA TYPE	LENGTH	CONSTRAINTS	DESCRIPTION
Serial Number	CHAR	6	PK, fixed length	Internal tracking number
Hardware Serial Number	CHAR	6	FK; points to HW ASSETS.SERIAL NUM	Equipment where software is installed
Name	VARCHAR2	30	Not NULL	The name of the asset
Version	VARCHAR2	10		Version of the software program
Purchase Cost	NUMBER	8, 2	Between $0.00 and $100,000.00	Cost of purchase for the asset
Purchase Date	DATE			Date when asset was purchased

FIGURE 1.4 Columns for table SW_ASSETS and their properties.

Figure 1.4 lists the columns of the table SW_ASSETS and their properties.

1.1.3 CREATING THE DATABASE OBJECTS FOR ETS

In order to follow the development activities discussed in the rest of this chapter and in the following two chapters, you must create the ETS tables in your database and load sample data in them. The section *Installation of ETS Database Objects* in the Preface provides the necessary instructions to complete this task. Please follow these instructions before continuing to the next section.

1.2 CREATING THE FIRST FORM

After creating the database tables, you are ready to begin developing the form for the ETS application. First, create a separate directory in your hard disk to store it. The remainder of this chapter will assume that this directory is C:\ETS. Now, launch the Form Builder following these steps:

1. Click the Start button in the Windows task bar.
2. Select Programs | Oracle Developer | Form Builder.

At this point, the Form Builder is started. If this is the first time you launch this application or you have not changed its default settings, you will be presented with the dialog box Welcome to the Form Builder shown in Figure 1.5. This dialog is a helpful utility when you are new to the Form Builder environment. It allows you to quickly begin the design of a new form by selecting one of the four

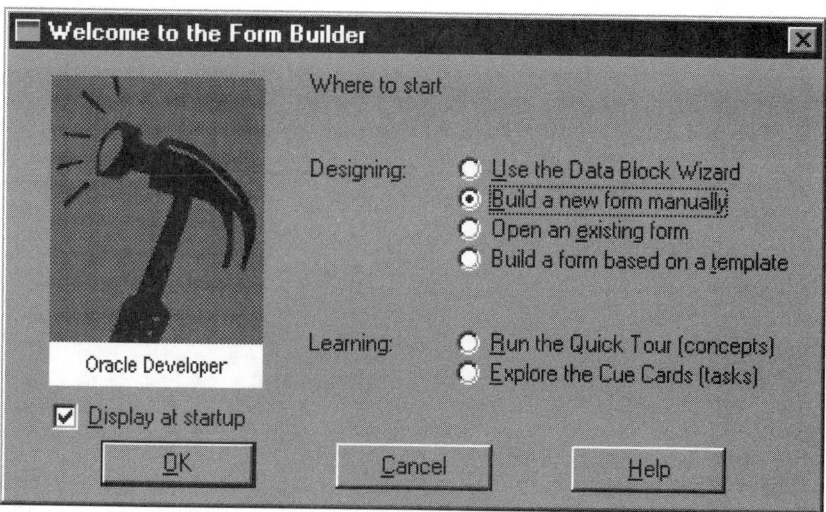

FIGURE 1.5 The Welcome to the Form Builder dialog box.

options in the Designing radio group. From here you can also access the Form Builder online help content. All the tasks that can be jump-started from the Welcome to the Form Builder dialog box are accessible from within the Form Builder. Once you become familiar with the Form Builder environment, you will want to stop this dialog from appearing each time you start the Form Builder. To achieve this, simply deselect the check box Display at startup under the Oracle Developer icon. To continue with the creation of the form, select the option Build a new form manually and click OK.

1.2.1 NAMING THE FORM

When the Form Builder is initially launched, it creates a new form module to help you get started with the development activities. This module is represented by the node MODULE1 in the hierarchy tree of objects shown in the Object Navigator window. Typically, you want to replace this name with another one that better represents the purpose of the module. The following steps allow you to rename the newly created module:

1. Click the MODULE1 entry in the list, if it is not already selected.
2. Click the same node again. Notice that the text of the node is selected.
3. Type "ETS" as the name of the new module.
4. Press ENTER when done.

1.2.2 SAVING THE FORM

The following are the actions required to save the form in the C:\ETS directory:

1. Select File | Save from the menu. Because this is a new module, the Windows' standard Save As dialog box appears.

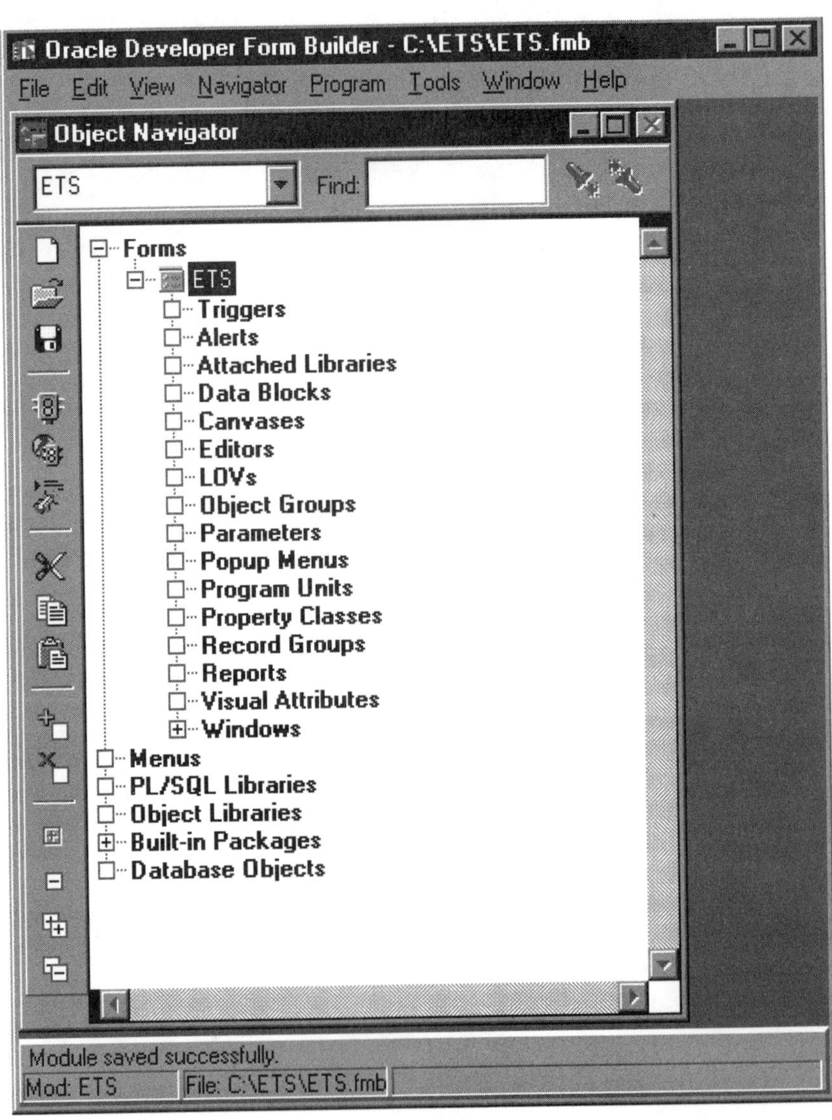

FIGURE 1.6 The Form Builder after saving the ETS module.

2. Do not modify the proposed name of the file or its type. This way, the module will be saved under the file ETS.fmb.
3. In the list box that displays the folder where the new file will be saved, select the folder C:\ETS.
4. Click Save.

At this point, the Form Builder saves the form according to your specifications. Your desktop should look similar to Figure 1.6. Notice in this figure that the name of file you just saved is shown in the status bar as well as in the title bar of the Form Builder window.

1.2.3 CONNECTING TO THE DATABASE

In order to proceed with the development of the ETS application, you need to connect to the database schema in which you created the tables HW_ASSETS and SW_ASSETS. These are the steps to connect:

1. Select File | Connect . . . from the menu. The Connect dialog box appears (see Figure 1.7).
2. Enter User Name and Password. The user name should be the Oracle account used to create the ETS tables, for example FORMS_DEV.
3. Enter the Database Service Name, SID or database alias, as it may apply to your environment. This entry uniquely identifies the database instance where the ETS tables reside.
4. Click Connect.

When the connection is established, the little icon to the left of the node Database Objects shows the expansion indicator "+." If you click it, you will see all the database users whose objects you can access. By further expanding the nodes in the hierarchy tree, you can browse the database objects as shown in Figure 1.8. In this figure, account FORMS_DEV owns several tables that you will encounter as you read the rest of this book. Among them, you can see the table HW_ASSETS,

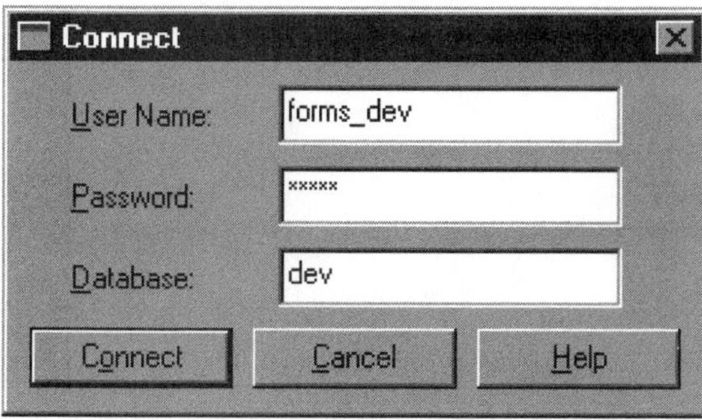

FIGURE 1.7 The Connect dialog box.

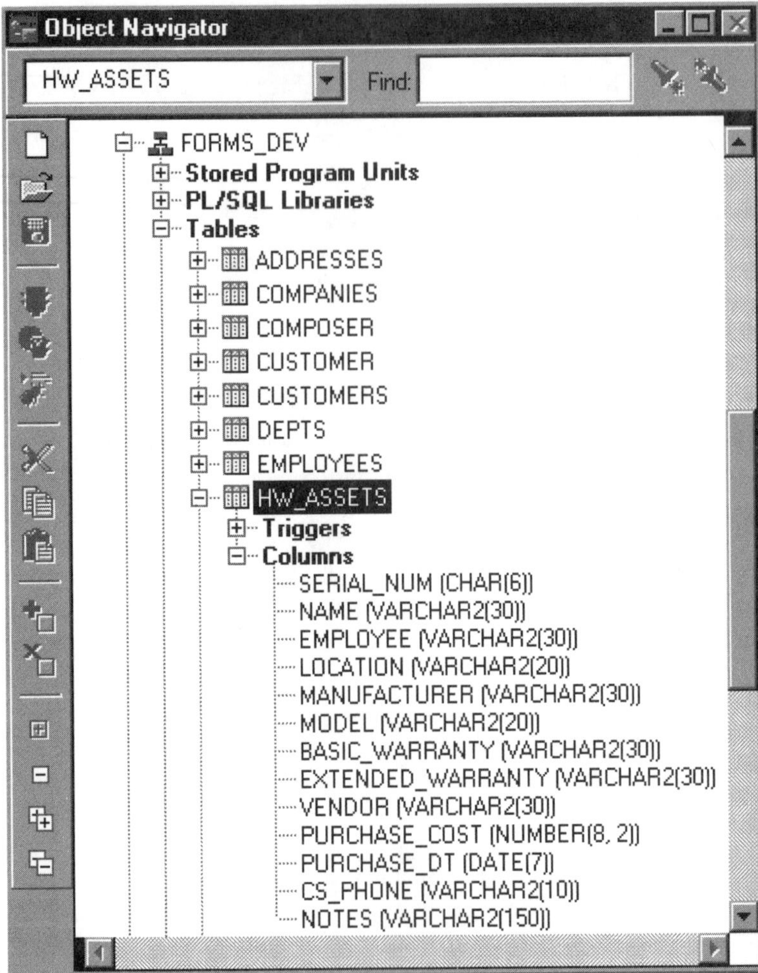

FIGURE 1.8 Viewing database objects in the Object Navigator.

which is expanded to show its columns. The data type of each column is shown in parentheses.

1.3 THE OBJECT NAVIGATOR

The window you have been working on so far is the Form Builder's Object Navigator. The Object Navigator is the heart of not only the Form Builder, but also all the other Oracle Developer components. From here you can display, access, and

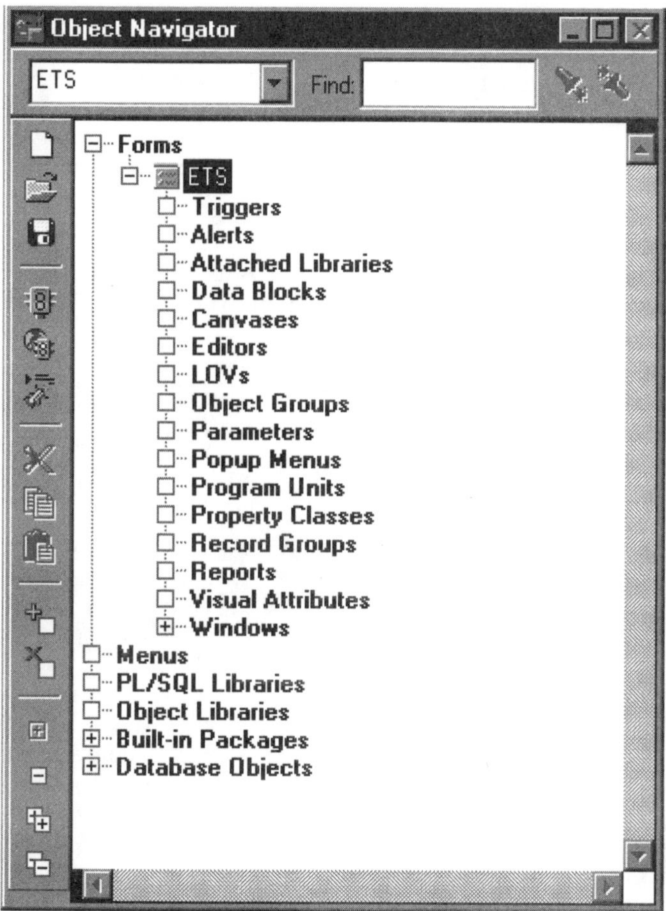

FIGURE 1.9 The Form Builder Object Navigator.

edit just about every object in an application. Figure 1.9 represents the Object Navigator.

The most important part of the Object Navigator is the hierarchy tree of objects that make up the application. The entries in the list are grouped and organized based on the type of each Form Builder object. As you can see from Figure 1.9, a form module can have objects such as triggers, alerts, and data blocks. Do not allow names such as "LOVs" or "Canvases" discourage you. As cryptic as they may seem now, you will see that they are really easy to use and manipulate.

Entries in the hierarchy tree are also called nodes. Small icons precede the label of each node. These icons play a very important informational and navigational role. The "empty square" icon means that the object type is not instantiated. In other words, there are no objects of that type in the application yet. To create one, double-click the icon. If the icon has the indicator "+" inside the square, then there is at least one object of that type in the application. To see all the objects of a particular object type, click the "+" icon or, as it is often said, *expand* the node. When the node is expanded, the indicator "+" is replaced by the indicator "–." All the instances of that object type are listed beneath, indented to the right of the object type node. To hide them, click the "–" icon, or *collapse* the node.

Along the left border of the Object Navigator window is a vertical toolbar. The buttons listed here allow fast access to often-used commands such as Open, Save, Cut, Paste, Expand, and Collapse. The bitmaps incorporated in these buttons clearly describe their purpose. However, you do not have to memorize the meaning of all these icons. Developer/2000 Forms uses popup help to assist you identifying and selecting the right button. To display a brief description of an icon, place the mouse on the icon and do not move it for an instant. A little box will pop up on the side, displaying the icon's name.

1.4 CREATING A DATA BLOCK WITH THE DATA BLOCK WIZARD

Ultimately, any Form Builder application is a collection of interface items and boilerplate objects that allow users to visually access and modify data from the database. The interface items may correspond to columns in database objects, or may represent derived or computed data. All items in a form are grouped in a higher level of abstract objects, based on their meaning and functionality. These objects are called blocks. Blocks are often associated with database objects, in which case they are called data blocks. Blocks that are not associated with any particular database object are called control blocks. In the ETS application you will create two blocks that will interface with the tables HW_ASSETS and SW_ASSETS.

The process of creating a data block in the Form Builder can be summarized in the following steps:

1. Select the database object upon which the new block will be based (normally a table or view).
2. Specify the data bound items that will be part of the block (normally related to the columns of the selected database object).
3. Define the GUI layout of the block.

As you will see in the following two sections, the Data Block Wizard helps you complete the first two of these steps. The Layout Wizard, covered in Section 1.5, helps you accomplish the last step. Both these wizards, and other wizards encountered in the Form Builder, follow the metaphor for accomplishing multi-step tasks introduced and popularized by the Microsoft Windows graphical user interface (GUI). A wizard is essentially a dialog box with multiple panes attached to it. Each pane allows you to accomplish a specific activity required for the task. You can move between activities by clicking the buttons Next or Back. When you have completed all the required activities and are ready to complete the task, click Finish. At any time, you can exit the wizard by clicking Cancel or request help specific to the current activity by clicking Help.

To invoke the wizard, select Tools | Data Block Wizard from the menu. By default, the first pane of the wizard is a welcome pane that summarizes the main purpose and functionality of the wizard. Deselect the check box at the center of the pane if you do not want to see this pane the next time you invoke the wizard.

1.4.1 DEFINING THE DATA BLOCK TYPE

Essentially, a data block may be based either on a database table or view, or on a set of PL/SQL procedures stored in the Oracle RDBMS Server. In the ETS application all your data blocks will be based on database tables. You can convey this to the Data Block Wizard by selecting the radio button Table or View on the first pane of the wizard, as shown in Figure 1.10. After selecting this radio button, click Next to proceed to the second step.

1.4.2 DEFINING THE DATA ITEMS OF THE DATA BLOCK

The new block will present data from the table HW_ASSETS. Follow these steps to let the Wizard know about this.

1. Click the Browse button to the right of the text item Table or view. The Tables dialog box is displayed (see Figure 1.11). The checked items in this dialog mean that the Wizard will display only those tables that are owned by the current user. Depending on the application, you may want to display other types of objects that you or other users own. Select the appropriate check boxes to accomplish this.
2. Select the table HW ASSETS from the list of available tables.
3. Click OK to close the dialog box and return to the Data Block Wizard.

At this point, the name of the selected table is entered in the text item Table or view. Notice that the list control Available Columns is populated with the all the columns of the HW_ASSETS table. In order to include an item in the new block for each of these columns, click the button with the label ">>." The visual effect of this action is that all the columns will be transferred from the list box Available Columns to the list box Database Items on the right. At this point, the

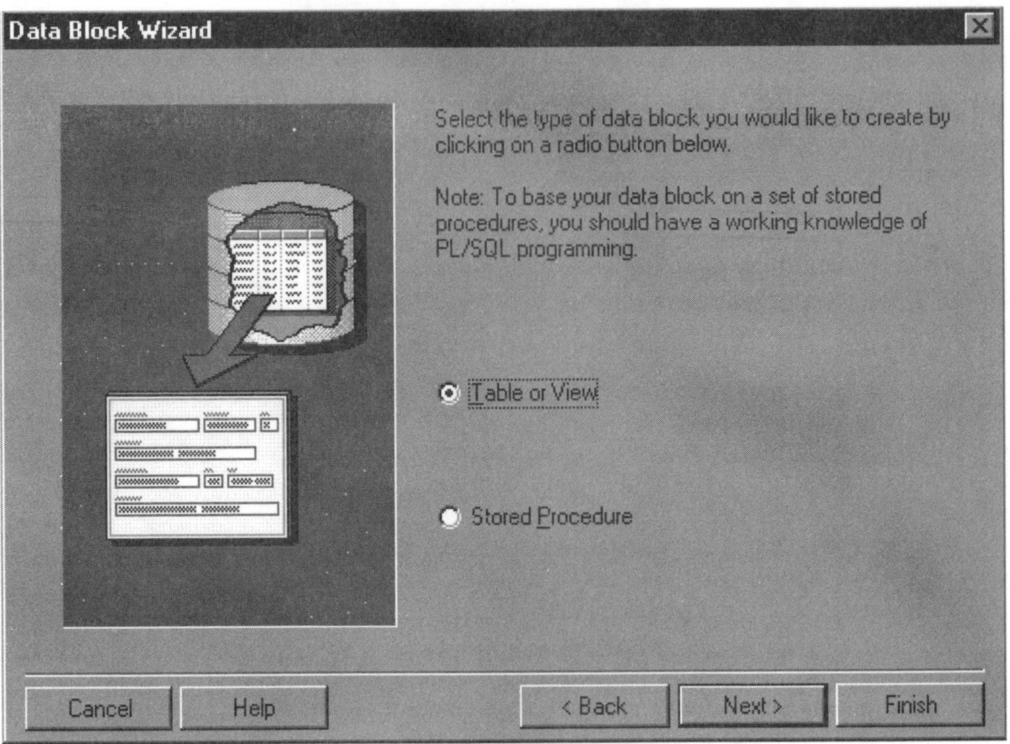

FIGURE 1.10 The Type pane of the Data Block Wizard.

Data Block Wizard should look like Figure 1.12. Click Finish to complete the creation of the first block.

1.5 THE LAYOUT WIZARD

The Data Block Wizard helps you define the database items that will be part of the new block. These items will ultimately be displayed to the users in the GUI interface. While from the database interaction perspective all items are grouped in blocks, from the user interface perspective items may be grouped in frames. Each frame can be associated with only one block and a block may not have more than one frame.

The Layout Wizard is used to adjust the visible interface and GUI properties of items in a frame. Since they work hand-in-hand to create a new block, the Form Builder invokes the Layout Wizard as soon as the Data Block Wizard completes its task. In general, you can invoke the Layout Wizard independently by

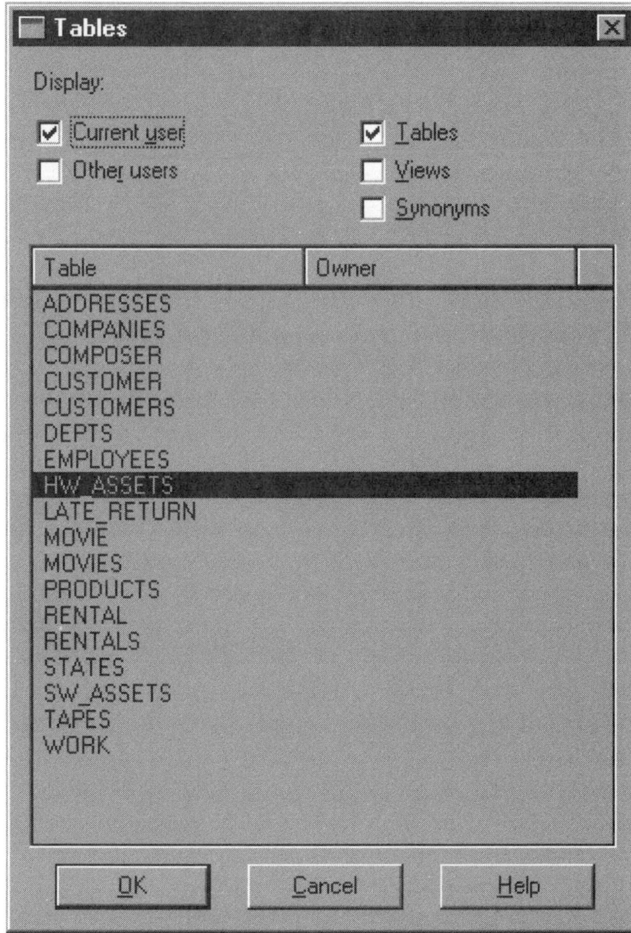

FIGURE 1.11 The Tables dialog box.

selecting Tools | Layout Wizard from the menu. As with the other wizard, deselect the check box in the Welcome pane if you do not want to see this pane the next time you invoke the wizard.

In Forms Builder applications, all the interface items are placed on objects of a special type called canvases. A canvas is then attached to a window frame and ultimately displayed to the user when the application is run. The first pane in the Layout Wizard allows you to specify the canvas object for the data block items and its type. Since there are no canvases previously created in the module, the only available option in the list box Canvas is (New Canvas), as shown in Figure 1.13. With the settings shown in this figure, the Layout Wizard will place the items of the new block on a new content canvas.

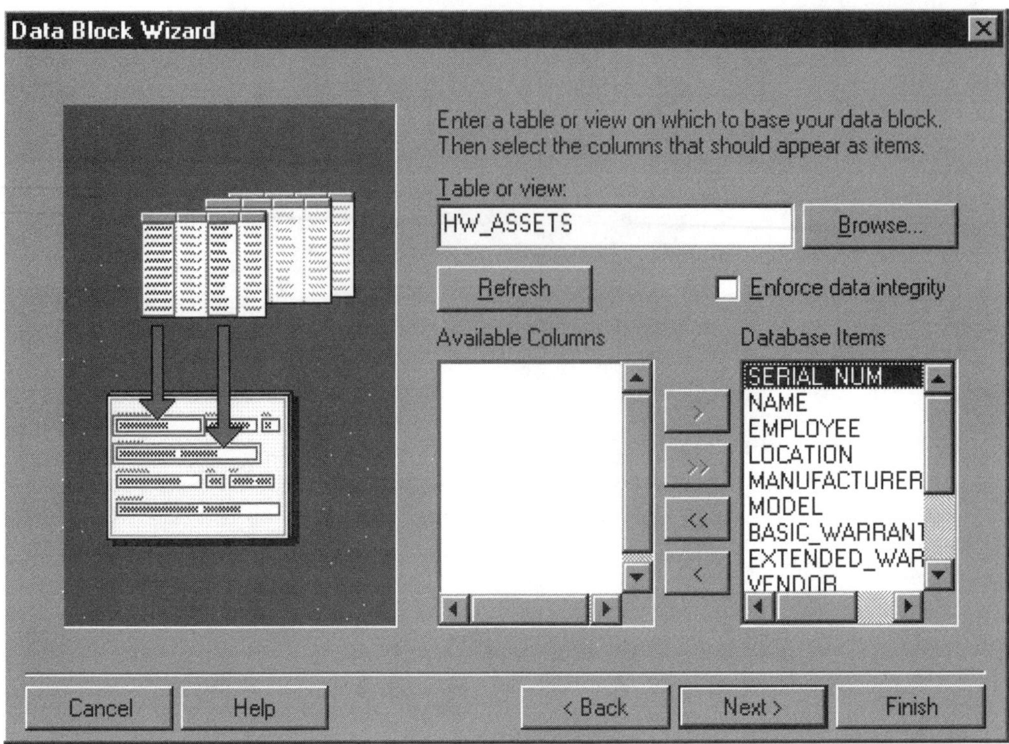

FIGURE 1.12 The Table pane of the Data Block Wizard.

The next pane helps you define which items from the block HW_ASSETS will be displayed to the users. The list control Available Items in this pane is populated with the all the items of block. In order to display all the items, click the button with the label ">>." This will cause all the items to be transferred to the Displayed Items list box.

The next pane in the Layout Wizard helps you define the prompt that will accompany each displayed item, as well as the width and height. Based on the properties of the database column, such as the name and length, the wizard proposes settings for these properties. You can override these settings if necessary. As an example, you can change the prompt of the item SERIAL_NUM replacing the default setting "Serial Num" with "Serial Number," and reduce the Width of the item Notes to 200, as shown in Figure 1.14. Click Next when you are ready to continue to the next step.

Now specify layout settings for the frame. The items in the HW_ASSETS block will be displayed in form style, therefore keep the radio button Form selected and click Next. In the new pane, type "Hardware Assets" in the Frame

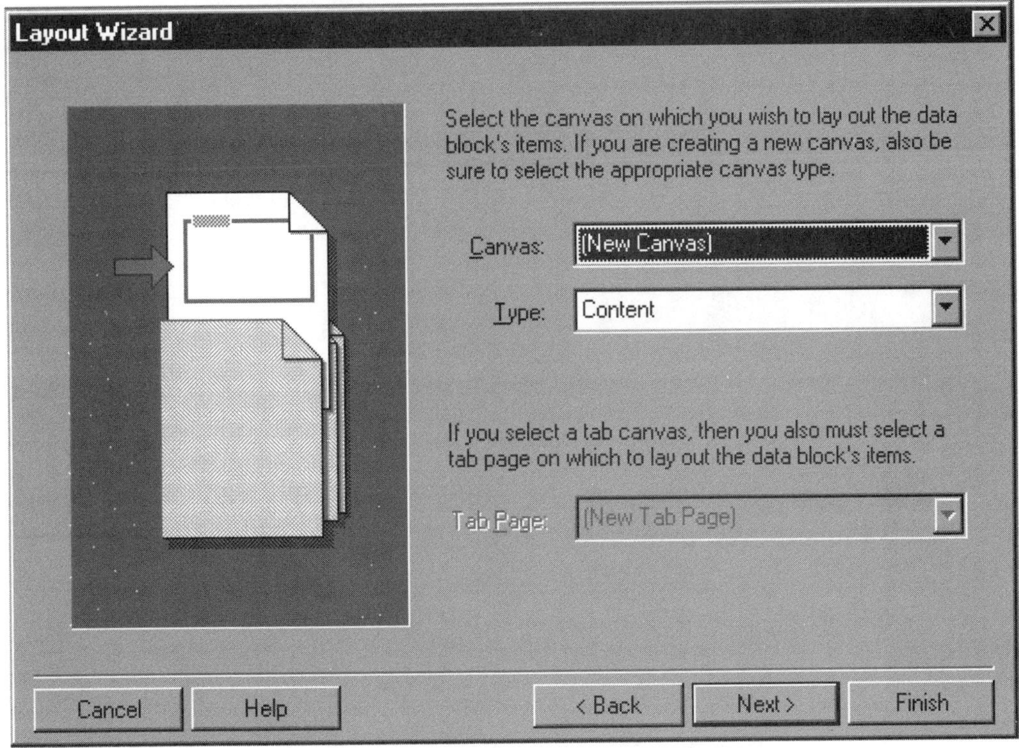

FIGURE 1.13 The Canvas pane of the Layout Wizard.

Title text item; leave the other properties unchanged. Figure 1.15 shows the state of the current pane.

At this point, you are ready to complete the layout design of the HW_ASSETS block. Click Finish to close Layout Wizard. The Form Builder creates the frame Hardware Assets and brings up the Layout Editor containing the results of actions taken by the wizard.

1.6 ADDING A DETAIL BLOCK

In this section you will create a block that will interface with data in the SW_ASSETS table. The ETS users are mainly interested to know which software products are installed and run on their hardware equipment. You want the application to reflect this. In other words, if Mr. Brown's PC is displayed in the HW_ASSETS block, the SW_ASSETS block should list all the programs installed

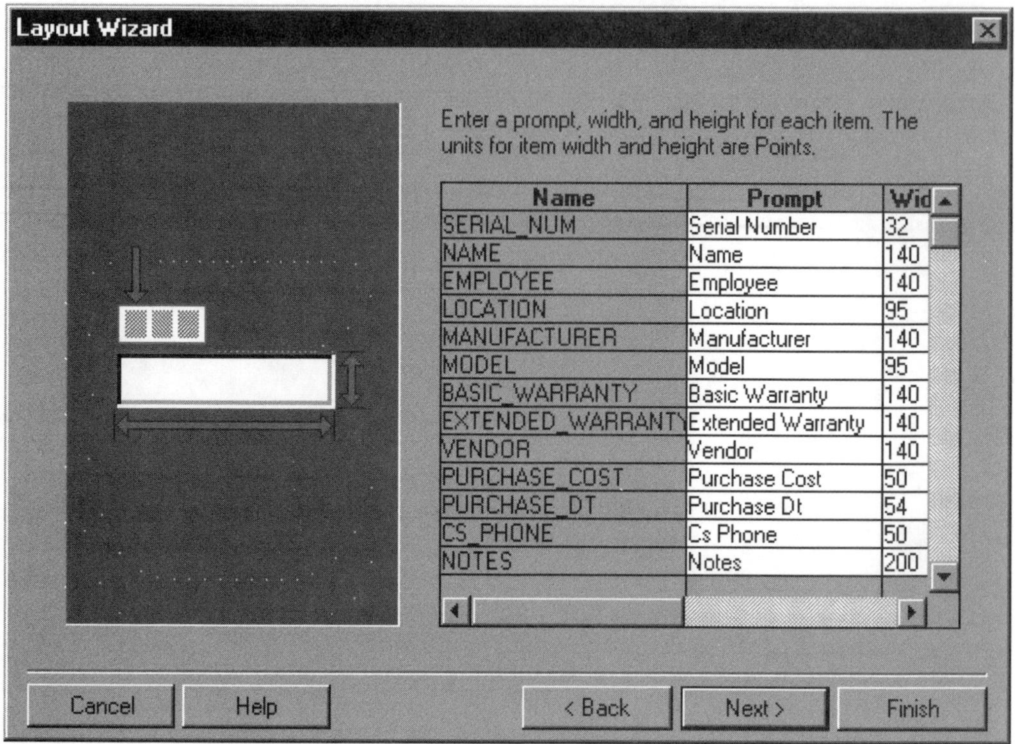

FIGURE 1.14 The Items pane of the Layout Wizard.

there. If Mrs. White's PC is displayed, the software items should change accordingly.

In Form Builder, this type of coordination is implemented by defining a *master-detail* relationship between the HW_ASSETS and SW_ASSETS blocks. The HW_ASSETS block will be the master block, because it will drive the information displayed in the other block. The SW_ASSETS block will be the detail one, because it will supply additional information about the master record currently displayed in the HW_ASSETS block.

The process of creating any data block is very similar to what you did in Sections 1.4 and 1.5. Therefore, this section will not provide detailed instructions on how to create the SW_ASSETS block or define its layout. Instead, here is a list of the main steps you can execute:

1. Invoke the Data Block Wizard and request to create a block based on a table or view.

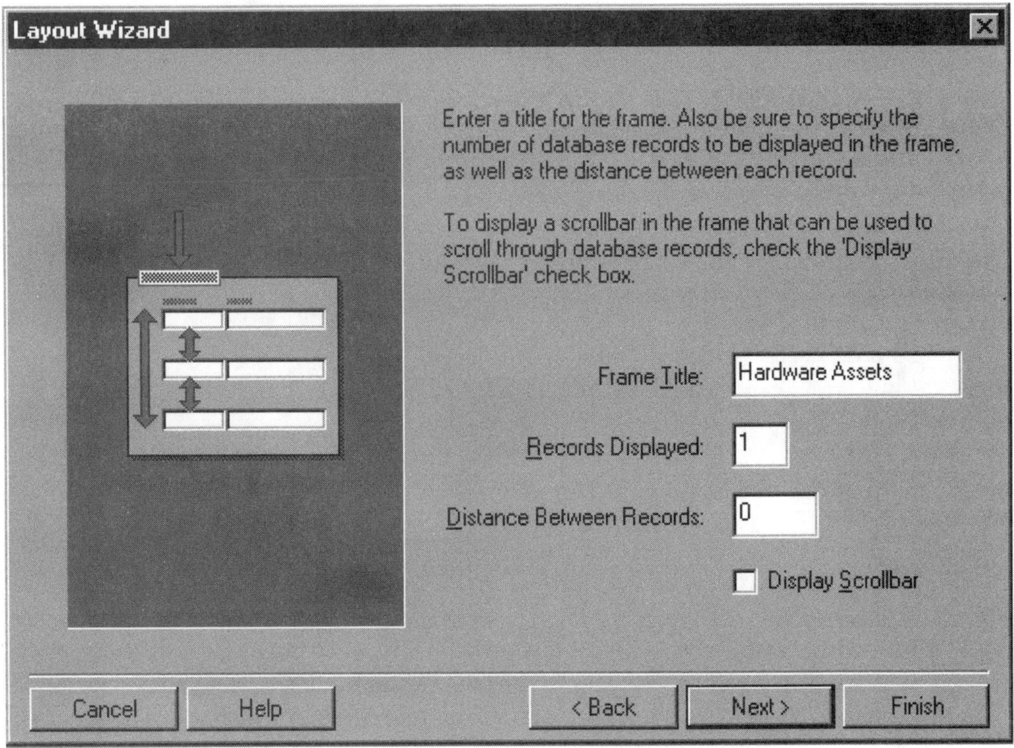
Layout Wizard
Enter a title for the frame. Also be sure to specify the number of database records to be displayed in the frame, as well as the distance between each record.
To display a scrollbar in the frame that can be used to scroll through database records, check the 'Display Scrollbar' check box.
Frame Title:
Hardware Assets
Records Displayed:
1
Distance Between Records:
0
Display Scrollbar
Cancel
Help
< Back
Next >
Finish

FIGURE 1.15 The Rows pane of the Layout Wizard.

2. Select SW_ASSETS as the base table for the new block, and include all its columns as database items in the block. At this point, the Data Block Wizard presents a new pane that you did not see when you created the HW_ASSETS block. This pane allows you to create a master-detail relationship between the blocks.
3. Click the Create Relationship button. The ETS: Data Blocks dialog box appears.
4. Select HW_ASSETS from the list and click OK to close the dialog box. The wizard intelligently supplies the join condition, as shown in Figure 1.16, based on column, primary key and foreign key definitions for both tables.
5. Click Finish to complete work with the Data Block Wizard and invoke the Layout Wizard.
6. Accept the selection of the existing canvas as the one where the items of the new block will be created.

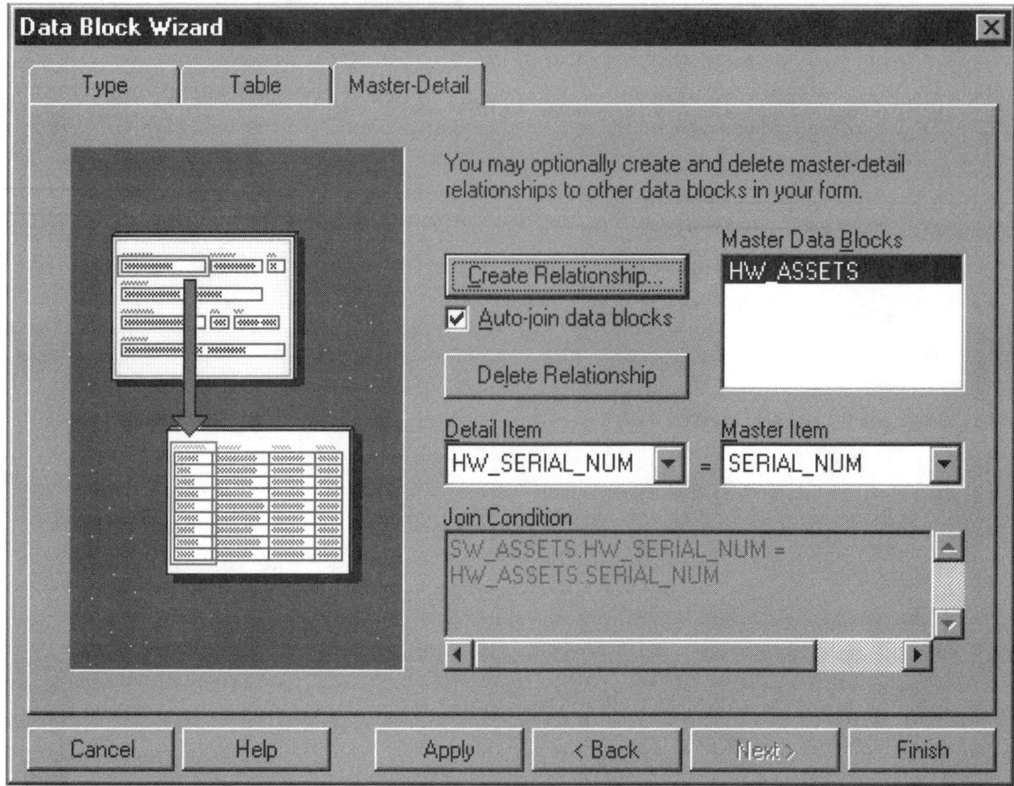

FIGURE 1.16 The Master-Detail pane of the Data Block Wizard.

7. Select to display all the database items except for HW_SERIAL_NUM.
8. Choose a tabular layout of the frame for the SW_ASSETS block.
9. Set the Frame Title to "Software Asset"; set Records Displayed to "5" and select the check box Display Scrollbar.
10. Click Finish to complete the creation of the second block.

Once again, the Layout Wizard builds the layout of the specified block and displays the results in the Layout Editor. Save the work done so far by taking any of the following actions:

- Select File | Save from the menu.
- Press CTRL+S from the keyboard.
- Click the Save icon in the toolbar.

1.7 COMPILING THE MODULE

As in other programming environments, in order to run the newly created module, an executable file must be compiled first. During the compiling process, the Form Builder checks and validates all the objects in the module, their property settings, and the code attached to them. If conflicts are found, the appropriate error messages are generated and displayed to the user. The error messages are also written to a file that has the same name as the form module, and the extension ".ERR." For example, if errors are encountered during the compilation of ETS.FMB module, they are written to the file ETS.ERR. The error file is created under the same directory as the binary file.

1.7.1 COMPILING FROM THE FORM BUILDER

There are two ways to generate a module that is open in the Form Builder:

- ❑ Select File | Administration | Compile File from the menu.
- ❑ Press CTRL+T from the keyboard.

If the compilation is successful, an executable file with the extension .FMX is created under the same directory as the binary file. For example, the executable file of the ETS.FMB module will be ETS.FMX.

1.7.2 SETTING FORM BUILDER PREFERENCES

In the Form Builder, like in other programming environments, the application development process repeats the following basic sequence of actions:

1. Change the application by adding to or modifying its functionality.
2. Create the new executable version by compiling.
3. Execute or run the application to assess the effects of additions and modifications.

Because it is so customary to generate the executable version of a module before running it, a setting in the Form Builder Preferences allows you to bypass Step 2 in the sequence above. When developing a form, you simply work with the application and then run it to see the effect of the modifications. The Form Builder automatically compiles the new executable before running it.

The setting for this and other options of the Form Builder can be accessed and modified in the Preferences dialog box. You can access this dialog by selecting Tools | Preferences . . . from the menu. Figure 1.17 shows the default settings for the General tab of this dialog box.

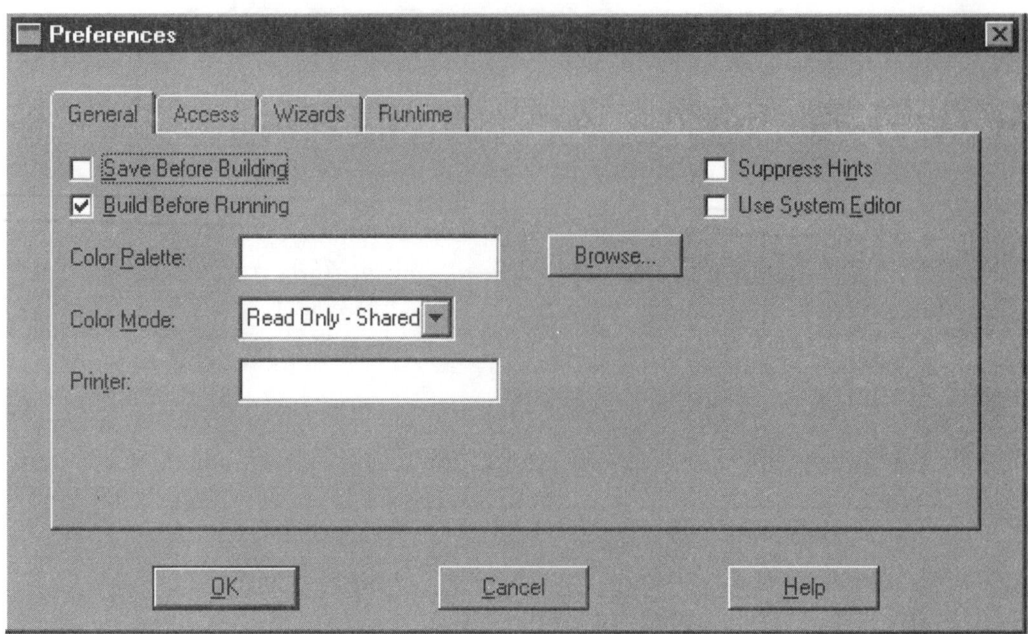

FIGURE 1.17 The General tab of the Preferences dialog box.

As you can see from this figure, if you set the Save before Building check box, you can skip the step of saving the form before generating and running it. Once an option is set, the setting will remain in effect until you change or reset it.

1.7.3 USING THE DEVELOPER FORM COMPILER

The methods described above compile a module from within the Form Builder, while you develop the application. There are instances when you may want only to compile a module, without doing any other design activities. These situations are mostly encountered when you upgrade from older versions of Oracle Developer or when you port your application from one platform to another. In these cases, you may use the Form Compiler tool to speed the process of creating new executables. The Form Compiler takes as input the binary files (.FMB) created in the Form Builder. If the generation process is successful, the executable (.FMX) is created. Follow these steps to invoke and use the Form Compiler:

1. Click the Start button in the Windows task bar.
2. Select Programs | Oracle Developer | Form Compiler. The Form Compiler Options window appears (see Figure 1.18).
3. Enter the name of the form module you want to compile, as shown in Figure 1.18. Click Browse to select the appropriate module if necessary.

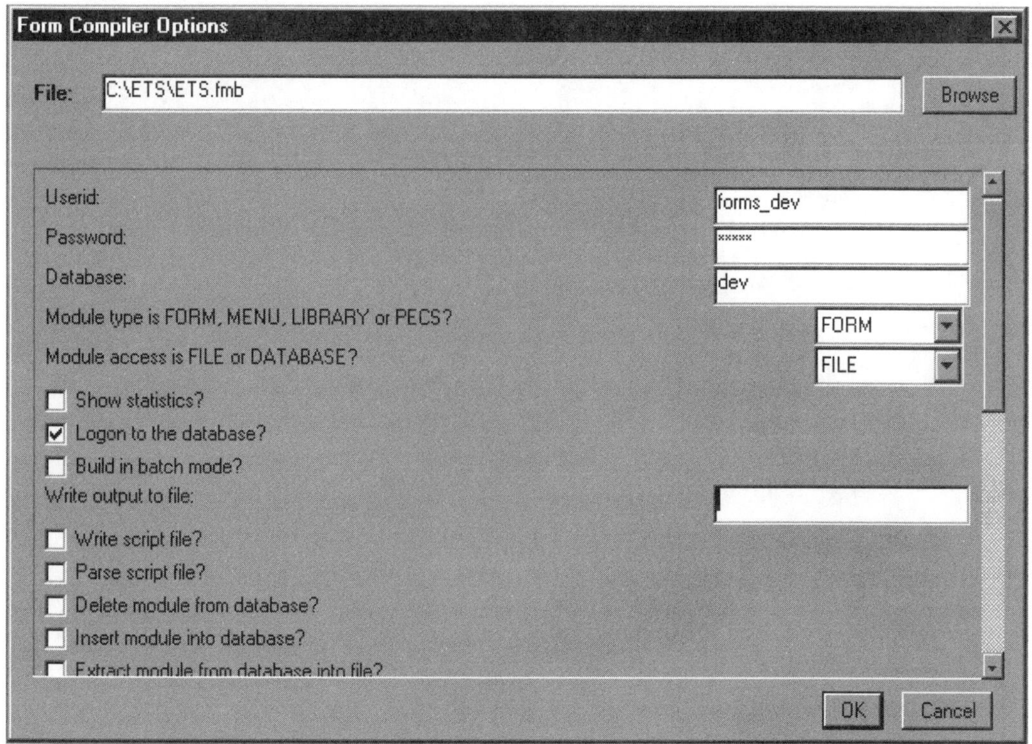

FIGURE 1.18 The Form Compiler Options utility.

4. Fill in the Userid, Password, and Database text items according to your environment.
5. Click OK.

If you do not supply the full name and location of the module, Forms Generate will search only the BIN folder of the Oracle Home folder of your environment. For example, if this folder is C:\ORACLE, then the directory searched by the compiler default is C:\ORACLE\BIN.

1.8 SUMMARY

This chapter introduced you to a simple application and guided you through the process of creating the first Form Builder module. Some of the most important concepts discussed here were:

- **The Equipment Tracking System**
  - Statement of the Problem
  - Defining the Database Objects for ETS
  - Creating the Database Objects for ETS
- **Creating the First Form**
  - Naming the Form
  - Saving the Form
  - Connecting to the Database
- **The Object Navigator**
- **Creating a Data Block with the Data Block Wizard**
  - Defining the Data Block Type
  - Defining the Data Items of the Data Block
- **The Layout Wizard**
- **Adding a Detail Block**
- **Compiling the Module**
  - Compiling from the Form Builder
  - Setting Form Builder Preferences
  - Using the Form Compiler

The following table describes the software assets that were discussed in this chapter. From the main HTML page of the software utilities provided with the book follow the links *Software* and *Chapter 1* to access these assets:

ASSET NAME	DESCRIPTION
CH01.FMB	The ETS module created in this chapter.

Chapter 2

RUNNING THE FIRST FORM

O young artist, you search for a subject—everything is a subject.
—Eugène Delacroix

- Running Modules Within the Form Builder
- Developer Forms Runtime Window
- Querying the Database
- Normal Mode and Query Mode
- Manipulating the Database
- Transactions in Developer/2000 Forms
- Multi-User Applications and Record Locking
- What Is Missing in ETS?
- Summary

In this chapter you will run the form created in the previous chapter and, in the process, learn about some important features of the Developer Forms Runtime. If you just completed reading Chapter 1, the module ETS.FMB should be open in the Form Builder, and the compiled executable ETS.FMX ready to run.

2.1 RUNNING MODULES WITHIN THE FORM BUILDER

The Form Builder supports three modes of running a form: client-server, Web, and debug. The first two correspond to the two modes in which Form Builder modules can be deployed to the user community. They allow you to assess the functionality and interface of the modules you are developing in the native environment in which they will run. In order to run a module from within the Form Builder, the module needs to be opened and compiled.

2.1.1 RUNNING MODULES IN CLIENT-SERVER MODE

In order to run a module within the Form Builder in client-server mode, you can issue either one of the following commands:

- Select Program | Run Form | Client/Server from the menu.
- Click the icon Run Form Client/Server in the toolbar.
- Click CTRL+R in the keyboard.

As a result, the module will be displayed in the Oracle Developer Forms Runtime window as shown in Figure 2.1.

2.1.2 RUNNING MODULES IN WEB MODE

When you deploy a Form Builder application over the Web, your users will access it by following a URL link that you provide. In order to test the module in this environment from within the Form Builder, you need to run it in Web mode. Any of the following commands can be used to run a module in this mode:

- Select Program | Run Form | Web from the menu.
- Click the icon Run Form Web in the toolbar.
- Click CTRL+E in the keyboard.

As a result, the module will be displayed in the Oracle Developer Forms Runtime-Web window as shown in Figure 2.2. Notice the similarities between the client-server and Web interfaces.

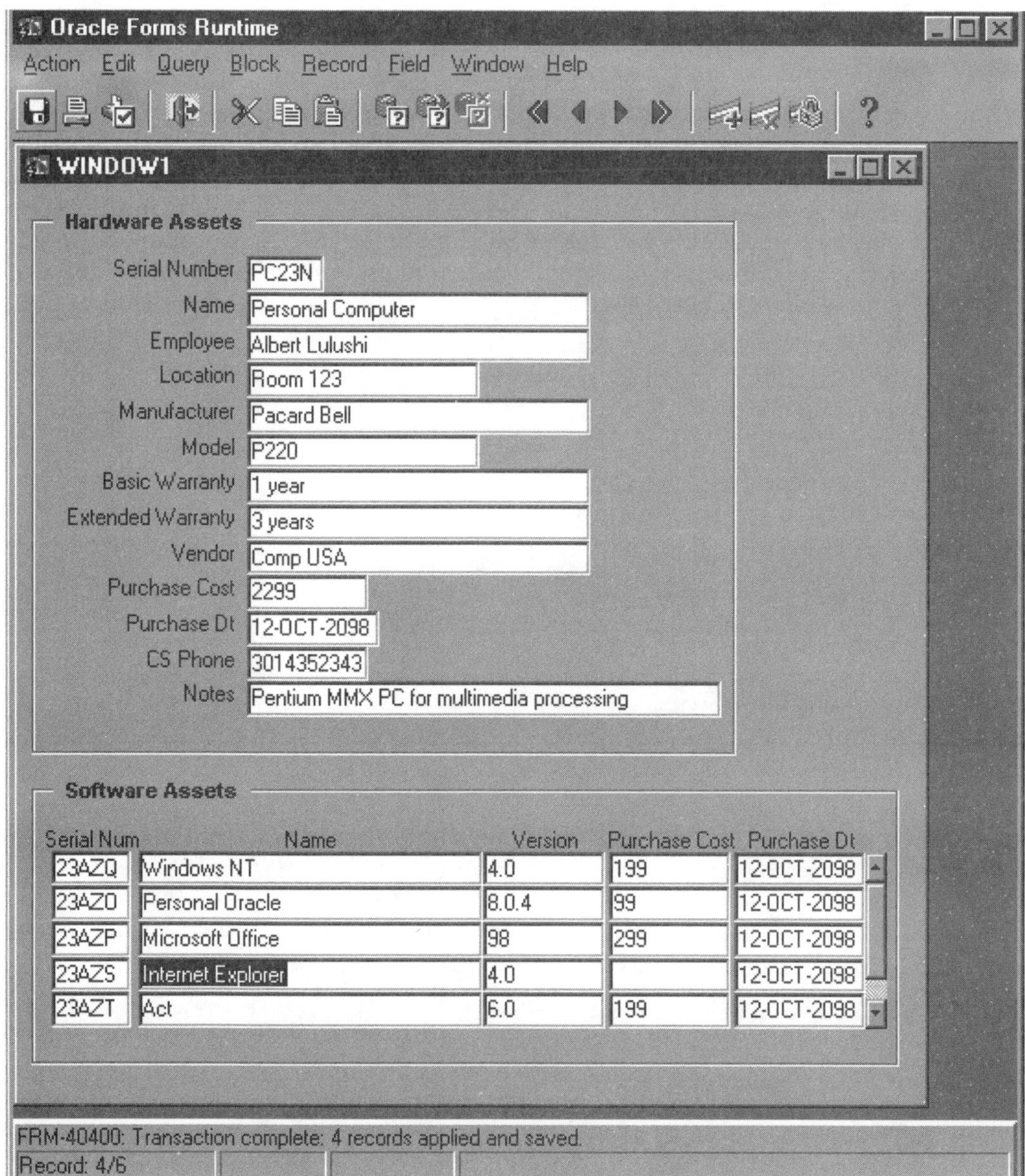

FIGURE 2.1 Running a module in client-server mode.

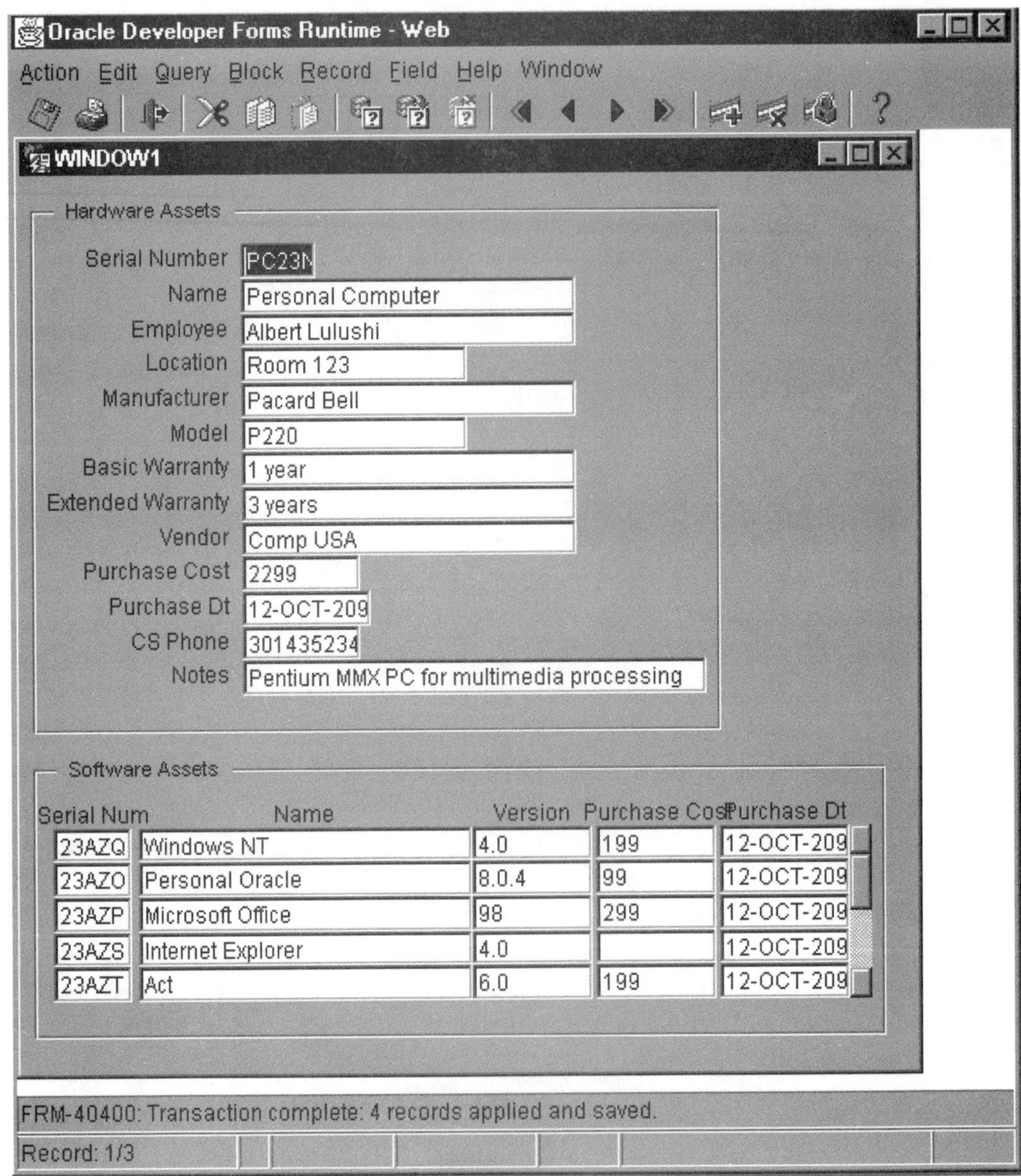

FIGURE 2.2 Running a module in Web mode.

2.1.3 RUNNING MODULES IN DEBUG MODE

As you develop a form in the Form Builder, you also debug it. During this process, you try to identify two categories of errors. The first category includes logical or design errors. Bugs of this category are identified in close interaction with the application users, during joint review sessions of the application. The second category includes the more traditional bugs, hidden in the PL/SQL code. The Forms Debugger is a tool incorporated in the Form Builder that facilitates the discovery of this type of bugs. You can invoke it by running the module in the debug mode. The following actions may be taken to run a module in the debug mode:

- Select Program | Run Form | Debug from the menu.
- Click the icon Run Form Debug in the toolbar.
- Click SHIFT+CTRL+R in the keyboard.

Figure 2.3 shows an example of the Forms Debugger window.

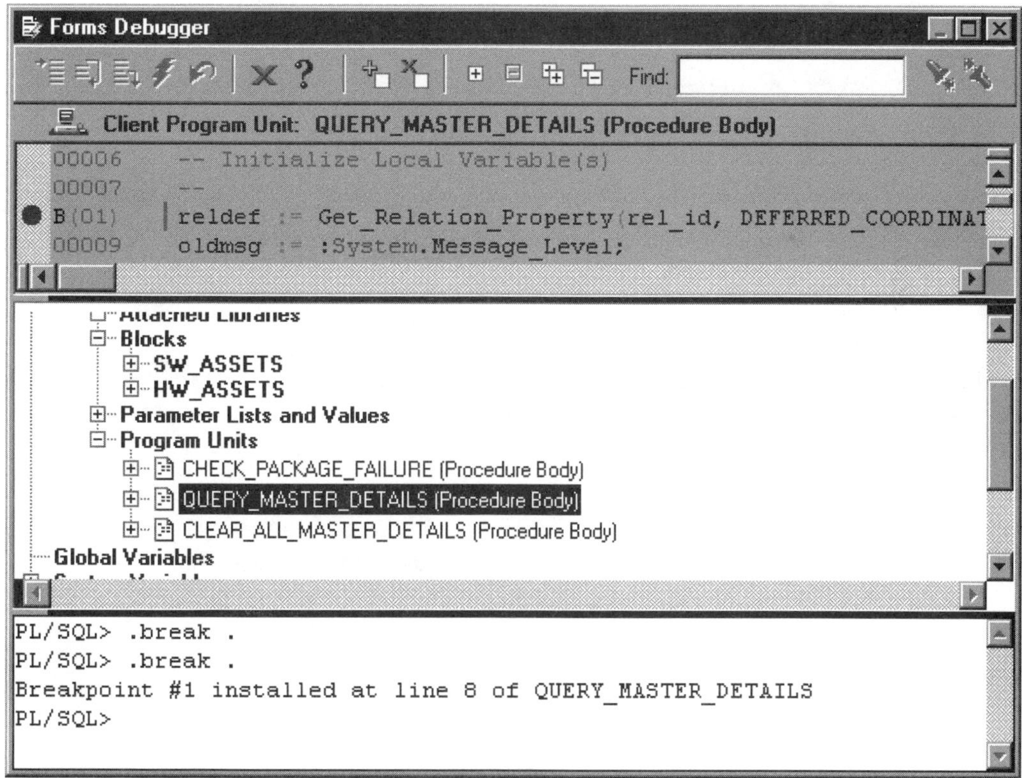

FIGURE 2.3 Running a module in debug mode.

2.2 DEVELOPER/2000 FORMS RUNTIME WINDOW

Whether you decide to run the ETS module in client-server or Web mode, the module is displayed within the Runtime window (see Figure 2.1 or Figure 2.2). There are three important components of this window:

- **Working area.** This is the normal MS Windows application workspace. All the interface objects of a form are located in this area. The chapters to come will discuss in detail how to make the application workspace as user-friendly and productive as possible.
- **Menu and toolbar.** The form has a complete menu and toolbar, although you did not create one explicitly. These are the Developer Forms default menu and toolbar. They can be attached to any module you create and provide easy access to useful commands such as navigating to blocks and items, specifying and executing queries, manipulating data, and editing text.
- **Status bar.** This bar, located at the bottom of the Runtime window, is very similar in form and purpose to the Form Builder's message bar. This is also known as the application's console. The first line in the message bar displays useful processing information to the users. This information can be generated internally by Forms, or created programmatically at runtime. The second line contains several fields, which provide context and navigational information. The message shown in Figure 2.2, for example, indicates that the focus of the application is in the first record of a block that contains three records in total.

2.3 QUERYING THE DATABASE

Retrieving data that already exist in the database, or querying, is the simplest way to use your application. In this section, you will use the ETS form to perform several queries against the database. These data are inserted in the tables by the SQL*Plus script that creates them, provided with the companion software.

2.3.1 UNRESTRICTED QUERIES

First, click inside any text item in the HW_ASSETS block, if the cursor is not already there.

1. Select Query | Enter from the menu or click the icon Enter Query in the toolbar.

2. Select Query | Execute from the menu or click the icon Execute Query in the toolbar.

In both cases, Forms performs a search for *all* the records from the HW_ASSETS table. The hardware records are displayed one at a time. There are a variety of ways to navigate between records in an application. Some of the alternatives are listed below:

- Scroll up and down by simply pressing the arrow keys.
- Click the icons Previous Record or Next Record.
- Select Record | Previous or Record | Next from the menu.

As you can notice, each time the form displays a new hardware record, the records in the SW_ASSETS block change to reflect the software items installed on that hardware equipment. This is the master/detail coordination at work. When the SW_ASSETS block was created, you simply stated that it should be a detail block of the master block HW_ASSETS. The Data Block Wizard interpreted this and generated the code to automatically refresh the contents of the SW_ASSETS block when the focus in the HW_ASSETS block moves to a different record.

In the previous example, you retrieved all the records from the HW_ASSETS table. This type of query should be avoided as much as possible. The reason is very simple. Imagine the ETS application being used by a company with 1,000 employees. Its inventory contains 40,000 to 50,000 hardware items. It is not wise to query all those records, if probably only a few are needed. The issue is particularly important in applications deployed over a wide-area network or over the Internet, which are very sensitive to network traffic and congestion. In the scenario presented above, each time this query is issued and users scroll through the records, a large quantity of data will be moved across the network, between the database server and the clients.

2.3.2 QUERY-BY-EXAMPLE INTERFACE

To avoid the situation described in the previous section, the number of records retrieved by queries should be restricted. Developer Forms offers different methods to narrow the scope of queries. The most popular one is the query-by-example interface. The meaning of the term is that users can enter query criteria on the same screen in which they enter or manipulate data. They are not required to know any of the SQL language constructs to access the data. For example, suppose you want to know how many monitors there are in the database.

1. Click the icon Enter Query in the toolbar.
2. Click inside the text item Name in the HW_ASSETS block.

3. Type "Monitor."
4. Click the icon Execute Query in the toolbar.

The query retrieves the records that match the criterion entered. This is called an exact match query, because Forms retrieves only those hardware records whose name is exactly as you typed it.

2.3.3 RELAXING QUERIES USING WILDCARDS

Often, exact matches are too restrictive. They may not return all the necessary data. The inconsistency of data is one reason why this situation occurs. Sometimes, users of a database application will find compelling reasons to enter *MONITOR, Mntr., Monit.*, etc., when all they mean to enter is *Monitor*. Of course, if they want to see all the monitors in their system, the previous query will not work. A more flexible query is needed. Fortunately, Developer Forms offers different ways to relax queries.

Using wildcards is one method. The wildcards used in the Oracle products, both database and tools, are the ones specified in the ANSI standard of SQL language: "%" and "_". The wildcard "_" stands for any single character, whereas "%" stands for any number of characters, including no characters at all. For example, "HO_SE" will represent "HORSE" or "HOUSE," but neither "HORTICULTURE COURSE" nor "HOSE." "HO%SE" on the other hand, will represent all of the above.

1. Click the icon Enter Query.
2. Click inside the text item Name in the HW_ASSETS block.
3. Type "M%."
4. Click the icon Execute Query.

The query returns all the desired records.

2.3.4 RELAXING QUERIES USING SQL STATEMENTS

For users who are familiar with the syntax of SQL language, Forms provides ways to further restrict or customize a query. For example, suppose you want to retrieve all the hardware items that were purchased for $300 or more. At the same time, you want all the items manufactured by Dell or Compaq corporations regardless of the price. All the records should be ranked in descending order, based on the purchase price. The following steps show how to specify this rather complicated query in the HW ASSETS block.

1. Click the icon Enter Query.
2. Click inside the Manufacturer text item and type ":manufacturer." The colon indicates that you will provide a variable rather than a static value for your query.
3. Click inside the Purchase Cost text item and type ":cost."

4. Click the icon Execute Query. The Query/Where dialog box appears (see Figure 2.4).
5. Enter your query criteria as shown in Figure 2.4.
6. Click OK.

Forms executes the query according to your specifications.

If you need to enter only ORDER BY criteria, the process becomes simpler.

1. Click the icon Enter Query.
2. Click any text item in the block and type "&."
3. Click the icon Execute Query. The Query/Where dialog box appears.
4. Enter the ORDER BY statement, for example, "ORDER BY purchase cost." Do not prefix colons to the database column names. They are used only for variables or parameters.
5. Click OK.

The retrieved records will be ordered according to your statement. Notice that, in both cases, you do not have to specify a full-length SQL statement. Forms supplies most of it; you supply only the search or ordering criteria.

2.3.5 COUNTING QUERY HITS

A particularly useful feature in Developer/2000 Forms is being able to count the query hits, or the number of records the query will return, without actually returning these records to the user. This allows users to carefully use computer

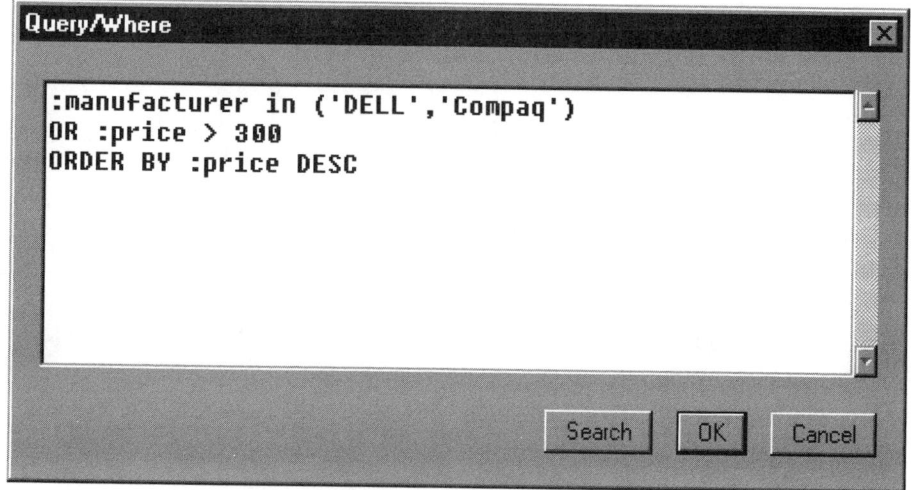
Query/Where
:manufacturer in ('DELL','Compaq')
OR :price > 300
ORDER BY :price DESC
Search
OK
Cancel

FIGURE 2.4 Query/Where dialog box.

FIGURE 2.5 Response of a Count Query Hits command.

resources. If a query will return thousands of records, there is no reason to load the database server and client machines with the burden of retrieving and sending these records to the requesting form. You can specify additional, more restrictive, query criteria that will retrieve the data faster and cheaper. Use the Count Query feature in your form as follows:

1. Click the icon Enter Query.
2. Select Query | Count Hits from the menu. A message similar to Figure 2.5 will be displayed in the message bar.

   Now, restrict the query criteria.

1. Click the Manufacturer text item and type "D%."
2. Select Query | Count Hits again. The number of records the query will retrieve is now smaller.
3. Either execute, or cancel the query.

2.4 NORMAL MODE AND QUERY MODE

You may wonder why you must always select Query | Enter before specifying search criteria and executing queries. Developer/2000 Forms has two modes of operations: Normal mode and Enter Query mode. The former is the default state. This is where records are created, deleted, or updated. Most of a form's life is spent in this mode. The Enter Query mode is used to specify criteria for retrieving records. These records are retrieved when the query is executed. After that, the form returns to Normal mode. If the query is canceled, Forms returns to Normal mode without further action. The transition diagram between these two states is presented in Figure 2.6. As the diagram shows, Forms can navigate out of a block only if it is in Normal mode. If the block is in Enter Query mode, the query must be executed or canceled before users are allowed to go to another block.

It is important to mention that all the functionality described in this section is available and can be used programmatically. This allows developers to design their own query interface, when the default interface is not sufficient to meet the application's requirements. As you read this book and become more familiar with Developer/2000 Forms, you may decide to do the same, thus providing

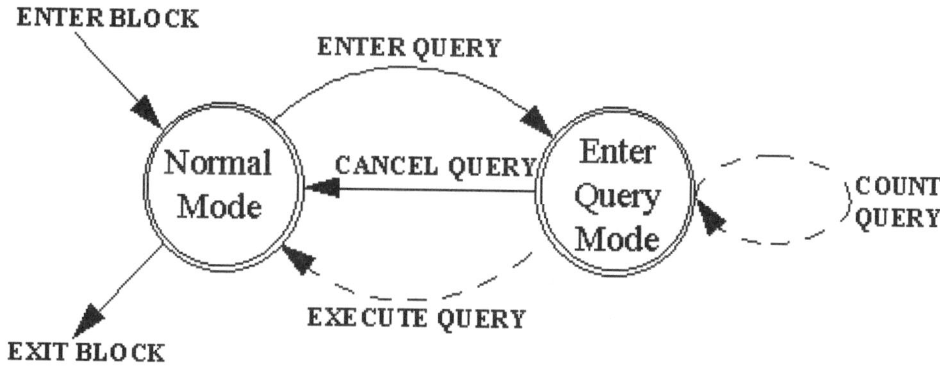

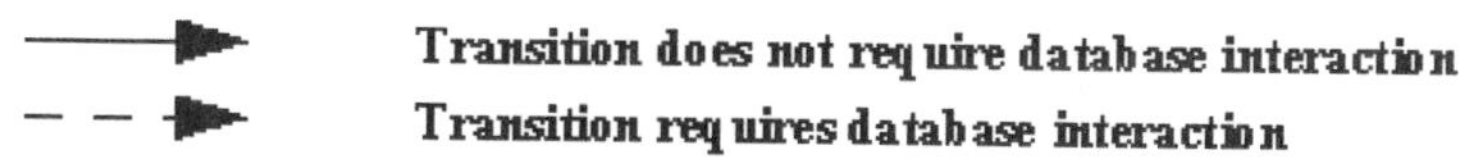

FIGURE 2.6 State transition diagram between Normal mode and Enter Query mode.

your application with better, more flexible, and powerful queries. However, keep in mind the state transition diagram presented in Figure 2.6. If the custom-designed query interface follows the same model, your queries will be easier to understand, easier to use, and consistent with the Forms querying paradigm.

2.5 MANIPULATING THE DATABASE

So far, you have used your application rather passively, only to query data that already exist in the database. It is time to assume a more active role and start modifying the data by entering new records, or updating and deleting existing ones. Before proceeding with the activities discussed in this section, keep in mind the following two points:

- Forms allows you to manipulate data only if it is in Normal mode. If you are in Enter Query mode, either execute, or cancel the query to return to Normal mode.
- While you use an application to manipulate data, Developer/2000 Forms buffers the changes in its internal memory structures. It is not until you save, or commit, that these changes are sent to the database. Only at this point do the database transactions occur. If, for some reason, you clear or

leave the block without saving to the database, your work since the last commit will be lost.

2.5.1 INSERTING

First, insert a new record. There is an easy way to do this is, as described by the following steps:

1. Click the icon Insert Record or select Record | Insert from the menu. Forms creates a blank record.
2. Enter data in the newly created record.
3. Click the icon Save or select Action | Save from the menu to insert the record into the database.

You can also navigate to the last record and press the down-arrow key to move to a new record, but this is somewhat confusing to the users. It is preferable to create records with clearly defined actions such as selecting from a menu or clicking a button. Therefore, the navigation of Forms to a new record from the last one in the list is usually disabled. In the next chapter, you will implement this feature programmatically, together with other enhancements to the ETS form.

In order to facilitate the process of entering similar data in the database, Developer Forms offers duplicating functionality, which can be used at the record level or at the item level. Suppose three identical PCs have been received by Print and Press. You are assigned the task to enter these data into the database. Obviously, you can use the brute force approach and enter the same data three times. But you can also use the Forms Duplicate Record functionality, as described below.

1. Insert a new record as described above.
2. Enter data for the first computer as shown in Figure 2.7.
3. Create a new blank record for the next entry.
4. Select Record | Duplicate from the menu.

The newly created record is filled with information from the previous record. Enter a unique Serial Number for the second PC. Repeat the last two steps as many times as necessary. Commit the newly entered records to the database.

Suppose now that you are entering software data for one of the new PCs. This computer has the Windows NT operating system and Microsoft Office installed in it. The purchase date for both packages is the same. Enter data for the first software record as shown in Figure 2.8. When you are ready to enter the Purchase Date for Microsoft Office, do not retype its value. Instead, select Field | Duplicate from the menu. Forms will automatically fill the item with content from the corresponding item in the previous record.

Hardware Assets

Serial Number	PC23N
Name	Personal Computer
Employee	Albert Lulushi
Location	Room 123
Manufacturer	Packard Bell
Model	T324
Basic Warranty	1 year
Extended Warranty	3 years
Vendor	Comp USA
Purchase Cost	2299
Purchase Dt	12-OCT-1998
CS Phone	3014352343
Notes	Pentium MMX PC for multimedia processing

FIGURE 2.7 Sample data to illustrate the duplicate record functionality.

2.5.2 DELETING

If you want to delete a record, navigate to that record and click the icon Remove Record or select Record | Remove. Forms will remove the record from the block and flag it for delete processing during the next database commit. Now, delete a few records from the ETS database.

1. Go to HW ASSETS block and query the monitor with serial number 98-N69.

Software Assets

Serial Num	Name	Version	Purchase Cost	Purchase Dt
23AZQ	Windows NT	4.0	199	12-OCT-1998
23AZP	Microsoft Office	98	299	

FIGURE 2.8 Sample data to illustrate the duplicate item functionality.

2. Select Record | Remove from the menu. The record is removed from the block.
3. Commit the delete action.

Now delete a PC.

1. Query the hardware item with serial number 95-N45.
2. Select Record | Remove from the menu.

The action cannot be completed! The status bar displays the message "Cannot delete master record when matching detail records exist." Once again, this is the master-detail relationship at work. Forms is protecting software records from becoming orphans, after their parent hardware record is deleted. To be able to delete this PC, you must first delete all the software items associated with it, and then commit the changes.

Of course, this is not a nice way to treat the users of your application. What you need here is a way to delete the master and all its detail records in one step. This process is also known as *cascade delete*. In the chapters that follow, you will learn how to implement cascade deletes in Oracle Developer applications.

There is an item under the Record menu, called Clear. Visually, Record | Clear and Record | Remove are similar. They both flush the current record from the block. But they are fundamentally different actions. Record | Remove requires interaction with the database. When a record is removed, it will be deleted from the database during the next commit and will no longer be available to this or any other application. When a record is cleared, it is flushed *only* from the working set of records buffered by Forms internally. It is not deleted from the database and can be retrieved again when needed.

2.5.3 UPDATING

Updating data in Developer/2000 Forms is as easy as performing the changes, whether by typing or any other action, right in the screen. The Forms will flag the record for update. The actual update of the record in the database will occur during the next commit process.

2.6 TRANSACTIONS IN DEVELOPER/2000 FORMS

The previous sections emphasized the fact that changes made through inserts, deletes or updates will not be permanently written to the database unless a commit command is issued. In fact, the history of a database system is only a repetition of the basic cycle presented in Figure 2.9.

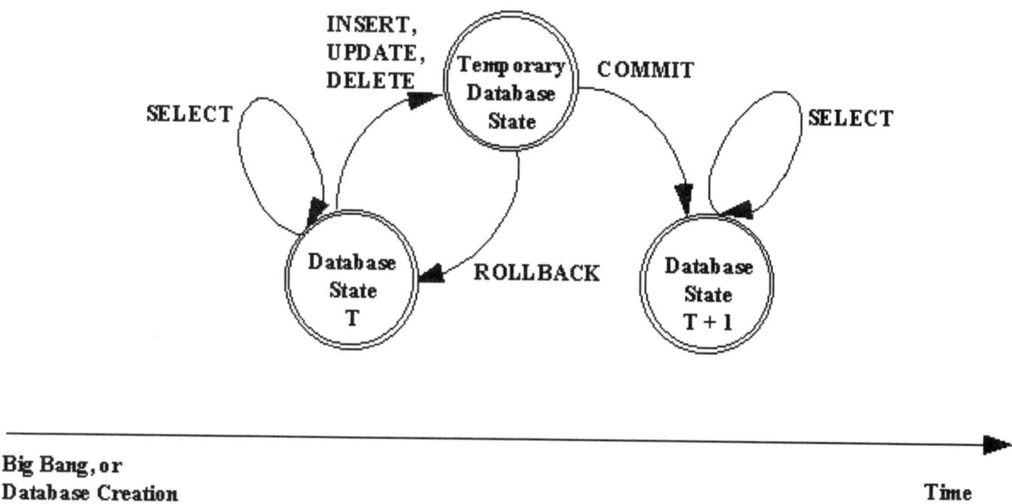

FIGURE 2.9 Basic cycle in the life of a database system.

When users initially open a session and establish a connection to the database, the database is in a consistent state, shown in Figure 2.9 as *Database State T*. By selecting data from the database objects, they do not change the state of the database. However, it is by modifying data, that is, by inserting, deleting, and updating, that a database can become a really useful repository of information. When INSERT, DELETE, and UPDATE statements are issued, the changes users make are not applied to the database immediately. Instead, they are written to temporary structures such as the Developer Forms internal memory buffers, or Oracle Server rollback segments.

In a situation like this, the user initiating the changes looks at a picture of data that is different from what other users may see. In fact, this user will see the changes while he or she is making them; the picture offered to him or her is the *Temporary Database State.* The other users will only see data as they were before the changes began; the picture offered to them is still the *Database State T*. This state of affairs gives users more flexibility and more control over their actions. It also protects them from unwanted accidental modifications of data. Users can roll back the changes, and go to the state they were in before any of the commands were issued. In that case, everybody will again look at the data in *Database State T*. They can also issue the COMMIT command that makes the changes permanent. In that case, the database will move to a new consistent state, the *Database State T+1*.

All the commands issued in the scenario presented in Figure 2.9 form a transaction. If the COMMIT command is issued, it is said that the transaction is committed; if the ROLLBACK command is issued, it is said that the transaction is rolled back. In both cases, these commands end the current transaction. The first command issued after these statements initiates a new transaction.

2.7 MULTI-USER APPLICATIONS AND RECORD LOCKING

Applications being developed today are used by multiple users at the same time. This eventually leads to situations where more than one user attempts to update or delete the same data, simultaneously. If the database application would allow that, then users would be overwriting each other's data inadvertently and chaotically. Data being modified by a user could be changed by another user before the first one had completed his or her transaction. In fact, imagine the following situation in the Print and Press print shop.

When the record for the PC with serial number 98-N60 was created in the ETS application, the Model name and Purchase Cost were not at hand, and therefore not entered in the database. At a later date, Tom finds the Model information in the back of the computer, pulls the record up on the screen, and begins entering the new information. At the same time, Linda finds the price in the shipping receipt. She also retrieves the record and supplies the Purchase Cost data. Next, Tom commits his changes and goes to lunch. Then, Linda commits her changes. Being the last one to commit, her record will overwrite Tom's record. Thus, the database will contain a record for PC 98-N60 that has a Purchase Cost but not a Model name. Tom is in for a surprise when he comes back from lunch!

For the database, letting this situation occur is as disastrous as leaving a busy intersection without traffic lights during rush hours. In order to preserve and guarantee the consistency of data, some mechanism must be in place to manage the competing requests for the same data, also known as data contention.

Every serious multi-user database package today uses *locking* to supervise the requests for updates and deletes of data. There are as many different implementations of locking as there are database vendors. The Oracle Server follows this approach:

1. Place a lock on the resource when a user first modifies it.
2. From that moment, until the lock is released, do not allow other users to modify the resource.
3. Allow other users to query the locked resource. To maintain consistency, the view offered is that of the resource when the lock was placed, but not any of the changes that may have occurred since that event.
4. Release the lock when the user commits or rolls back the transaction.

Although all the back-end database packages use some form of locking to protect the data, very few front-end development tools have a locking mechanism of their own. Developer Forms not only provides this mechanism as part of its default processing, but also integrates it tightly with the locking mechanism implemented in the Oracle Server database. The following sequence of figures shows how Developer Forms and Oracle Server interact to handle the scenario presented at the beginning of this section.

In Figure 2.10, Tom has retrieved the PC with serial number 98-N60 and is entering the Model name. Automatically, Forms has sent an instruction to the database server to place an exclusive lock on the record in the HW ASSETS table. This event occurred as soon as Tom started modifying the record.

The meaning of exclusive lock is that other users, such as Linda, can select the record, but cannot modify it. As Figure 2.10 shows, the record that Linda sees is the same as the one stored and locked in the database. Neither of them reflects

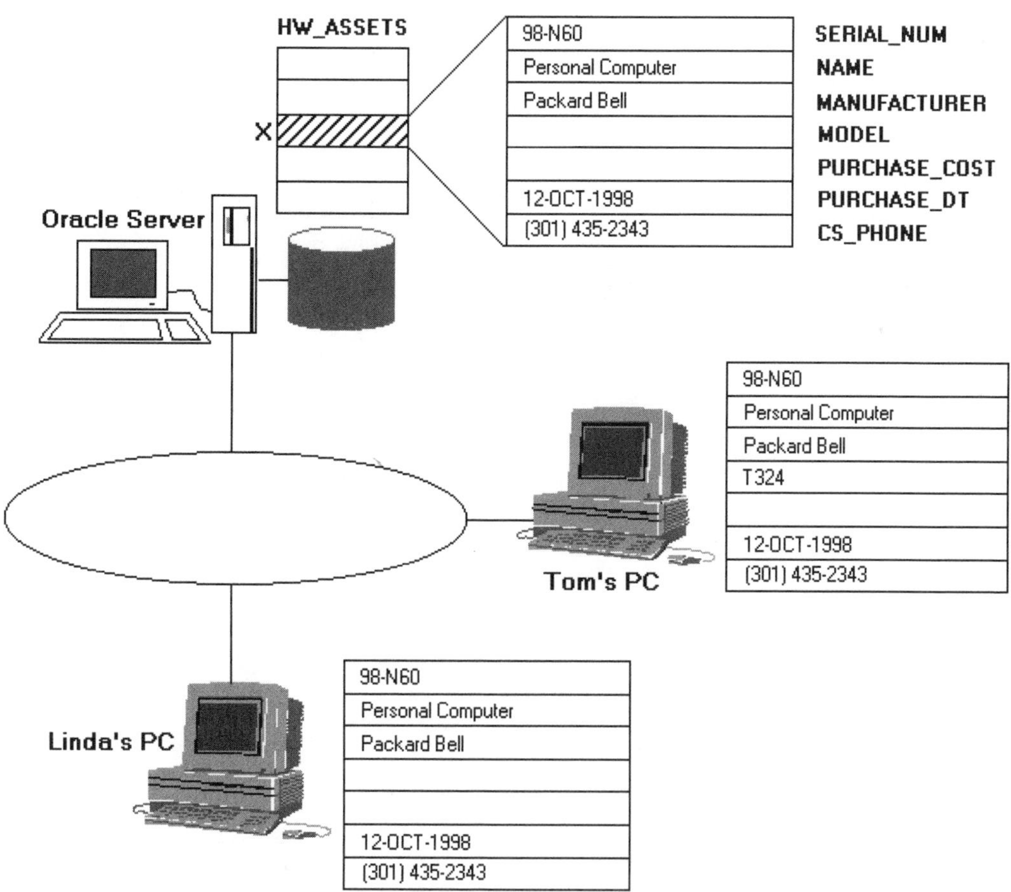

FIGURE 2.10 Locking and transaction processing in Developer Forms.

any of the changes Tom is making. These changes are visible only to Tom and are maintained by the application instance running in his machine. In this case, if Linda attempts to enter the Purchase Cost on her screen, Forms will display the message "FRM-40501: ORACLE error: unable to reserve the record for update or delete." She will have to wait until the lock on the record is released to proceed with her changes.

In Figure 2.11, Tom has finished entering the Model name. When he commits, Developer/2000 Forms sends the changes over to the database server. This, in turn, applies the changes, and releases the lock from the record. Now the view of data offered to Tom is consistent with what the database actually stores. Linda's view however is outdated, and her instance of Forms has an elegant way to find this out. If she attempts to do anything with the record displayed on her

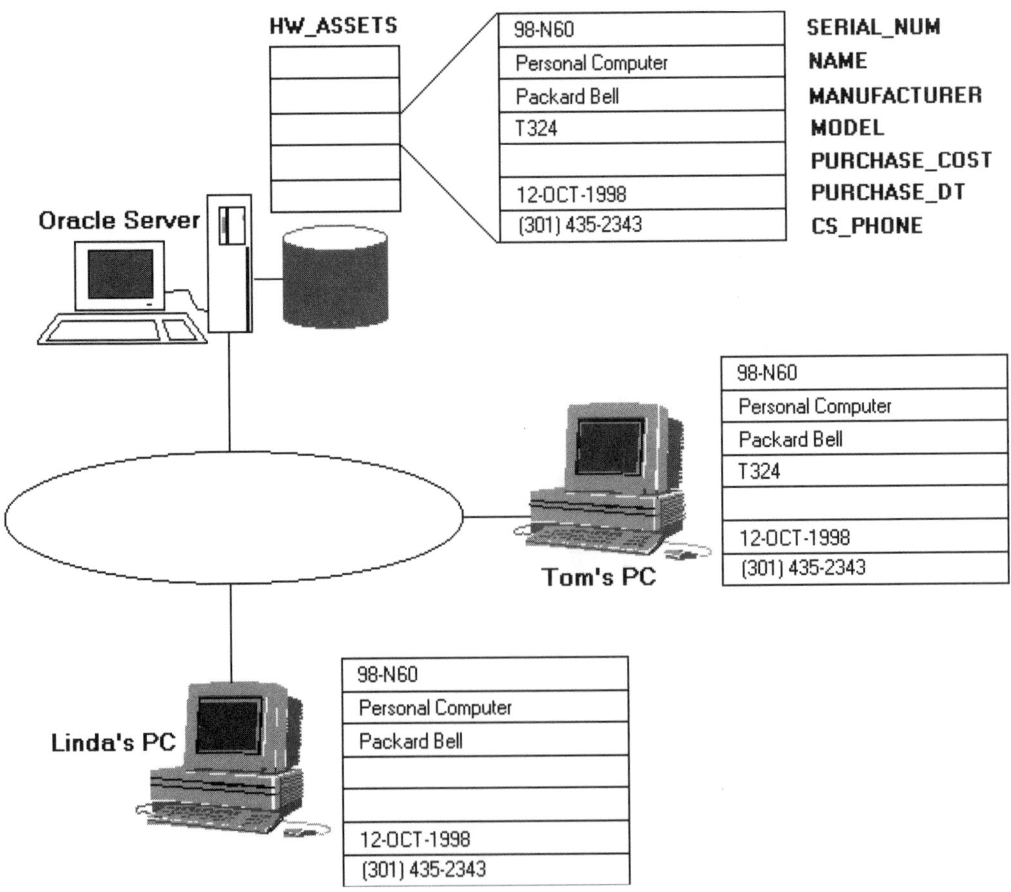

FIGURE 2.11 Locking and transaction processing in Developer Forms (Continued).

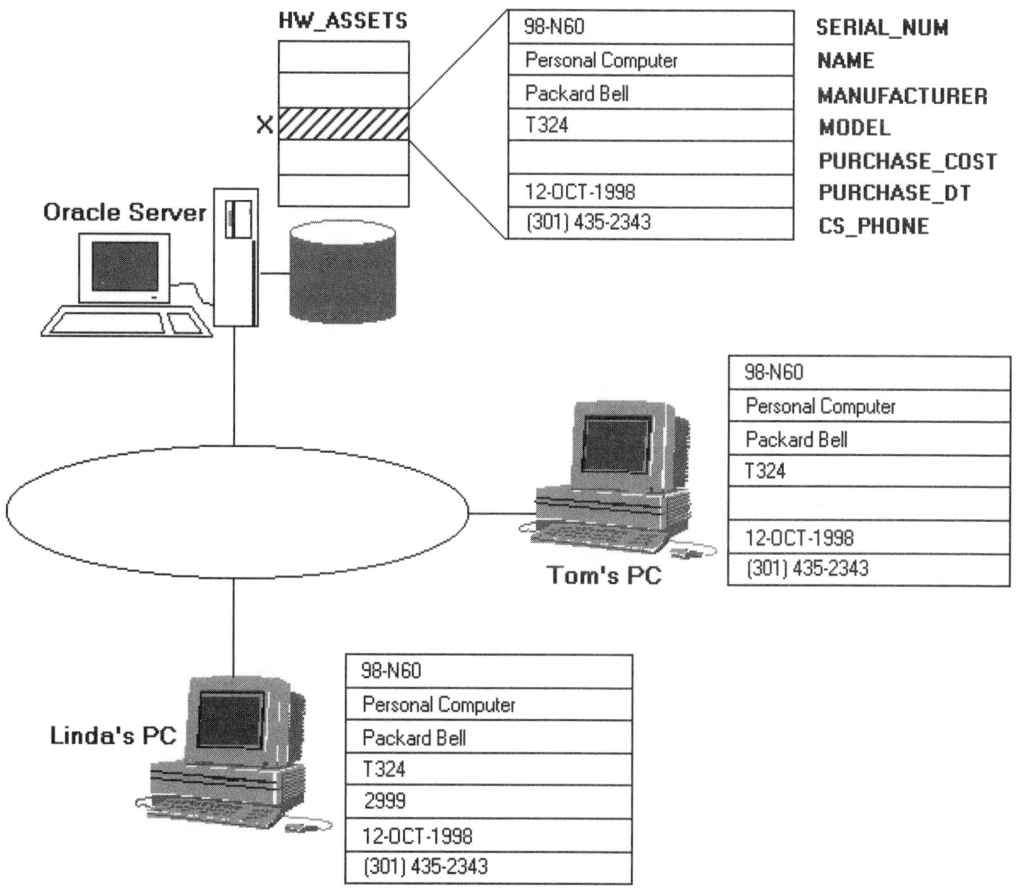

FIGURE 2.12 Locking and transaction processing in Developer Forms (Continued).

screen, she will get the message "FRM-40654: Record has been updated by another user. Re-query to see changes."

In the scenario presented in Figure 2.12, Linda has re-queried the database, retrieved the record with the Model name that Tom entered, and now is entering the purchase price. Now she holds a lock on the record in the HW_ASSETS table, and it is Tom's turn to wait for her to commit and release the lock, if he wants to modify that record.

As said above, locks on records are held until the Forms operator commits or cancels his or her actions. It is not difficult to realize that if Tom goes to lunch before committing his changes, Linda will have to wait until he comes back in order to complete her job. This is not a good situation to occur, especially in heavily used applications. From an application developer's perspective there are two things you can do to avoid it.

First, educate your users. Teach them not just what keystrokes to press or actions to take when using your application, but also fundamental concepts behind the screens and windows they work with. Explain to them why they should commit their work regularly and often, and make them aware of the problems that may arise by not doing so.

Second, tailor your application to avoid unnecessary long transactions. It is not difficult to keep a count of records being modified and, when this count exceeds a certain threshold, you may remind the users to commit the changes. You can also create a timer that starts ticking when the first modification of data occurs. Then, if data are not committed within a certain interval of time, say five minutes, users are prompted to save their changes. Later in the book, you will learn how to build both these features in your applications.

2.8 WHAT IS MISSING IN ETS?

The development of any Forms application, no matter how complicated or extensive it is, usually proceeds in two stages. Initially, you use the Object Navigator and a number of Form Builder wizards to lay out the framework for the application. You create the module, connect to the database under the appropriate account, and use the default functionality to quickly create the data blocks and items the application will require. Then, you move on to fill the details and make the form a more robust, user-friendly application. In this second stage, you use the Layout Editor to enhance and fine-tune the form's interface, set objects' properties, and modify or extend the form's functionality by using PL/SQL triggers and program units.

In Chapter 1, you took the ETS module through the first stage. This provided you with a usable application, and allowed you to explore some of the default features of two components of Developer/2000 Forms: Form Builder and Forms Runtime. However, the functionality of the application could be improved. For example, you may want to enforce some data standards with your form. One of them could be that users enter all their data in uppercase. You may also want the dollar sign to precede the value in Purchase Cost items. These values must be positive, but should not exceed $100,000. In the next chapter, you will implement these and other features that will make ETS not only fully functional, but also a user-friendly database application.

2.9 SUMMARY

In this chapter, you became familiar with the Oracle Developer Forms Runtime and how to operate a Forms application. Some of the basic concepts discussed here included the following:

- **Running Modules within the Form Builder**
  - Running Modules in Client-Server Mode
  - Running Modules in Web Mode
  - Running Modules in Debug Mode
- **Developer/2000 Forms Runtime Window**
- **Querying the Database**
  - Unrestricted Queries
  - Query-by-Example Interface
  - Relaxing Queries Using Wildcards
  - Relaxing Queries Using SQL Statements
  - Counting Query Hits
- **Normal Mode and Query Mode**
- **Manipulating the Database**
  - Inserting
  - Deleting
  - Updating
- **Transactions in Developer/2000 Forms**
- **Multi-User Applications and Record Locking**

The following table describes the software assets that were discussed in this chapter. From the main HTML page of the software utilities provided with the book, follow the links *Software* and *Chapter 2* to access these assets:

ASSET NAME	DESCRIPTION
CH02.FMB	The ETS module created in Chapter 1. You need to compile and run this module in order to perform the actions described in this chapter.
CH02.FMX	The ETS module created in Chapter 1 compiled for Win32 (Windows NT and 95) platforms.

Chapter 3

ENHANCING THE FIRST FORM

Behold, I have refined thee...
—Isaiah 48:10

In this chapter, you will enhance the ETS form and add on to the default functionality that was created by the Form Builder when the form was created in Chapter 1. You will be introduced to important components of the Form Builder, such as the Layout Editor and the Property Palette. You will arrange the items in a tabbed control where each tab will contain a small number of related items from the tables HW_ASSETS and SW_ASSETS. You will enhance the appearance of the objects and add some boilerplate objects to the existing form. You will also write your first triggers to improve the validation of data by your form. By the end of this chapter, the ETS application will look like Figure 3.1.

The starting point for this chapter is the form you created in Chapter 1. Start Form Builder and open the module ETS.FMB from your working directory. You can also copy the form CH03.FMB provided in the companion software and rename it to ETS.FMB using any of the standard utilities of your environment. The companion software also includes a copy of what the ETS form should look like at the end of this chapter, named CH03_F.FMB. Consult with it any time during the chapter if you feel you need to do so.

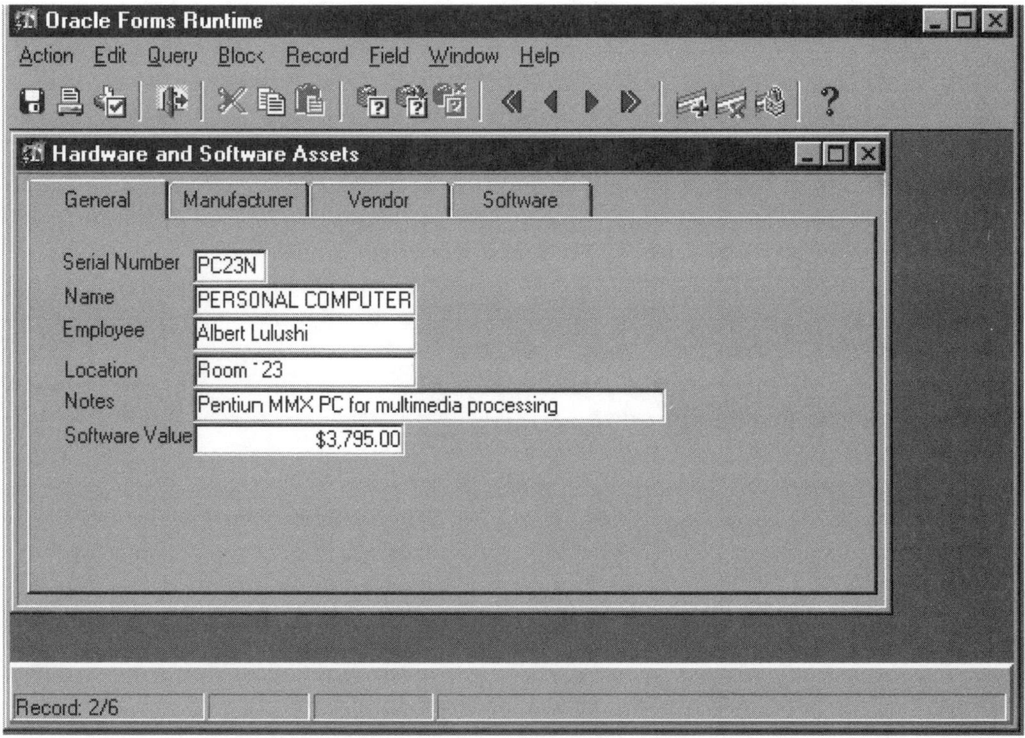

FIGURE 3.1 Completed version of the ETS application.

3.1 TRANSFORMING THE FORM INTO A TABBED LAYOUT

Begin now enhancing the display of the ETS form. As you may have noticed from the work done in Chapter 1, when database items are created, they are grouped in a frame and "painted" on a canvas. This canvas in turn is assigned to a window and shown to the user at runtime. In order to modify the visual appearance of the application, you must "paint" on the canvas. The Layout Editor is the Form Builder component that offers drawing tools, rulers, colors, and other utilities you may need in the process. In the following sections, you will organize the items in the ETS form in a window with four tabbed folders.

3.1.1 REENTERING THE LAYOUT WIZARD

The first step towards rearranging the layout of items in your form is to invoke the Layout Wizards again. It is characteristic of this and all the other wizards in the Form Builder that they are reentrant. That is, you can invoke them at any point during the design of a form to rearrange the user interface of the form. The following steps help you create a tab canvas object in the ETS form, create the first tab and populate this tab with four database items from the block HW_ASSETS:

1. Expand the node Data Blocks in the Object Navigator and select HW_ASSETS.
2. Choose Tools | Layout Wizard from the menu.
3. Select the option (New Canvas) from the list box Canvas. This option will make the wizard create a new canvas object.
4. Select the option Tab from the list box Type. By default, the wizard creates content canvases. This step instructs the wizard to create a tab canvas instead. Note that when you set the list box Type as described in this step, the list box Tab Page is enabled and the option (New Tab Page) is selected to indicate that the wizard will also create the first page on the tab canvas.
5. Click Finish.

If you want, before clicking Finish, walk through all the steps of the wizard by clicking the button Next. You will notice that all the database items from the block HW_ASSETS will be displayed in a form layout. Optionally, you could provide a title for the new frame, as you did in Chapter 1. However, the layout of items in tabbed pages will make the use of the frame superfluous. Therefore, as you will see in the following section, you will delete this frame.

When the Wizard completes its job, you will see the new canvas displayed in the Layout Editor. The layout of the items is almost identical to the original layout, except that now the canvas contains one tab page, as shown in Figure 3.2.

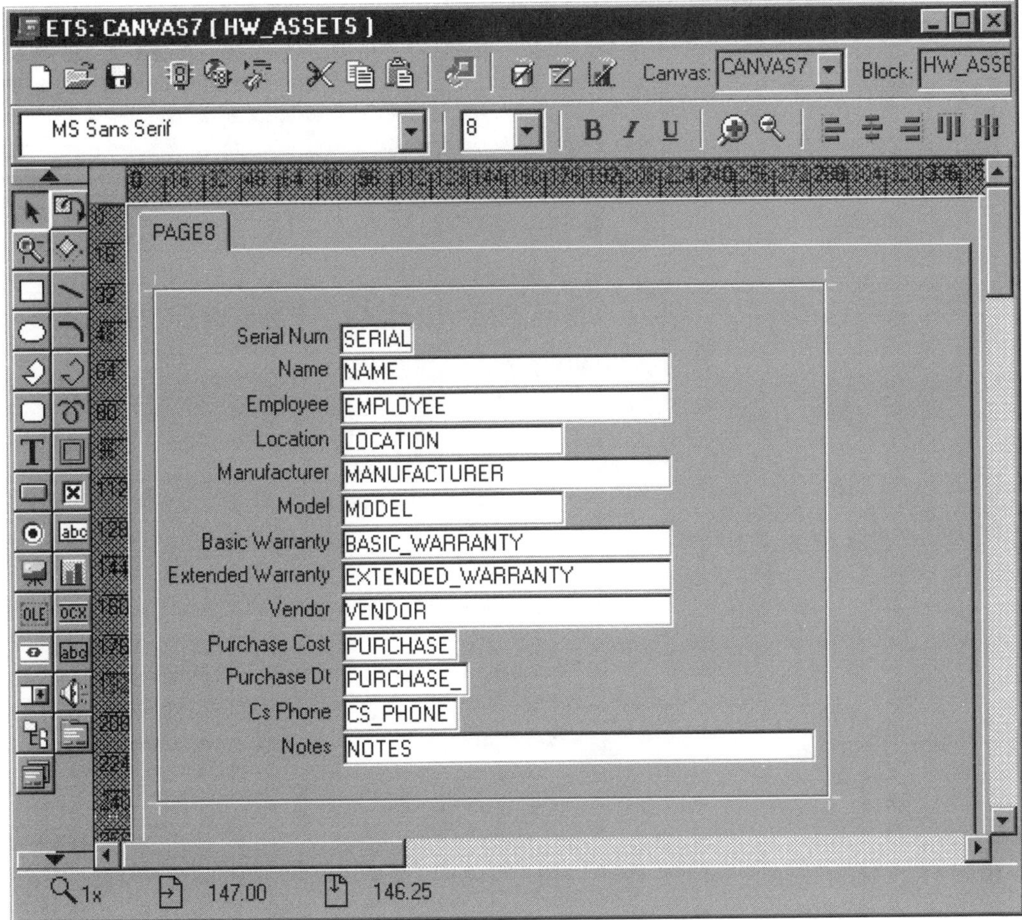

FIGURE 3.2 The tab page created by the Layout Wizard.

3.1.2 DELETING OBJECTS IN THE LAYOUT EDITOR

By default, the Layout Editor creates a frame object that binds together all the database items for a given block. In the ETS form, you will split the items of the block HW_ASSETS across three tab pages; therefore the frame associated with this block is not very useful. The following steps help you delete this frame from the form:

1. Click the frame in the Layout Editor to select it. Visually, the frame is presented as a rectangle enclosing all the items of the HW_ASSETS block, as shown in Figure 3.2.
2. Press DELETE.

The ETS module contains another frame associated with the block HW_ASSETS. This frame was created by the Layout Wizard when you created the block in Chapter 1 and is located in the content canvas of the module. To delete this frame, display the canvas in a Layout Editor window and follow the two steps listed above. To display the content canvas in the current Layout Editor window, select its name from the list box Canvas in the first horizontal toolbar of the window. To display the canvas on a new Layout Editor window, simply double-click it in the hierarchy tree of the Object Navigator.

3.1.3 CREATING NEW OBJECTS IN THE OBJECT NAVIGATOR

Turn now the attention to the Object Navigator window of the Form Builder. By expanding the node Canvases, you can see two canvas objects, similar to the ones shown in Figure 3.3. The first one is the canvas from the first version of the form; the second one is the canvas the Layout Wizard just created. The new canvas contains one tab page created earlier, which, in the case of Figure 3.3 is called PAGE7. The Form Builder assigns default names to any object you create in the module for which you do not provide an explicit name. These default names follow the pattern <OBJECT_TYPE><COUNTER>, where COUNTER is incremented for each new object created in the form. CANVAS6, FRAME8, or PAGE7 are examples of such default names. Depending on other objects you may have created in the module, the sequence-generated numbers that follow the default names of canvases and pages may not be exactly the same as the ones described in this section.

In order to create three more tabs in the tab canvas created earlier, follow these steps:

1. Select the node that represents the existing tab page in the Navigator. In the case of Figure 3.3, this node is called PAGE7.
2. Click the icon Create in the Navigator's vertical toolbar. You will see a new page object created; assume that the label of the new tab is PAGE9.
3. Repeat Step 2 two more times to create PAGE10 and PAGE11.

It helps the development and maintenance of the application if you provide more meaningful names to these objects, whenever necessary. Figure 3.4 pro-

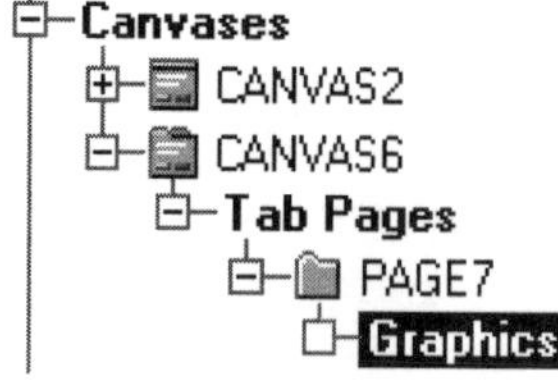

FIGURE 3.3 Canvas objects in the ETS module.

DEFAULT NAME	SUGGESTED REPLACEMENT	ROLE IN THE ETS MODULE
CANVAS6	EQUIPMENT	Store all interface items for ETS module
PAGE7	GENERAL	Contain general hardware properties.
PAGE9	MANUFACTURER	Contain hardware properties related to the manufacturer.
PAGE10	VENDOR	Contain hardware properties related to the vendor.
PAGE11	SW_ASSETS	Contain properties of software items installed in the current hardware equipment.

FIGURE 3.4 Suggested names for the canvas and tab pages of the ETS module.

vides a list of the default names for the canvas and tab pages of the ETS module and suggested values to rename these objects. A brief description of the role that these objects will provide in the ETS module is provided as well.

The steps to rename an object in the Navigator were discussed in Chapter 1. They are listed here for your convenience:

1. Click the node you want to rename in the hierarchy tree.
2. Click the same node again. Notice that the text of the node is selected.
3. Type the new name of the object.
4. Press ENTER when done.

3.1.4 SETTING PROPERTIES IN THE PROPERTY PALETTE

The names of the objects are used internally by Form Builder to identify these objects. Users of the application will identify the objects by their display properties and labels. These and all the other properties of an object can be viewed and modified in the Property Palette. The following steps describe the process of setting the property Label of the tab GENERAL in the ETS form:

1. Select the tab GENERAL in the Object Navigator.
2. Right-click and select Property Palette from the popup menu.
3. In the Property Palette window that appears, click the property Label in the Functional category. The setting of the property is selected.
4. Type "General" and press ENTER.

The Property Palette of this tab now should look like the one shown in Figure 3.5. Similarly, you can set the labels of the other tabs to "Manufacturer," "Vendor," and "Software."

The Property Palette allows you to view and maintain the properties not only of a single object but also those of multiple objects at the same time. You can

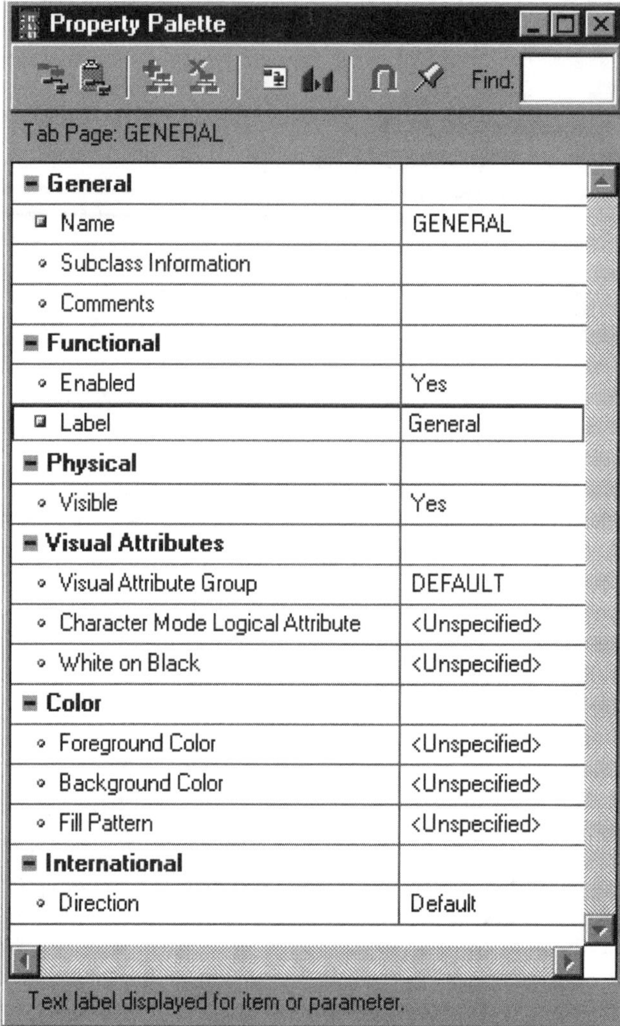

FIGURE 3.5 The Property Palette for the tab GENERAL.

use this feature to move the items of the ETS module to their respective tabs as a group rather than one by one. The following steps allow you to move the items MANUFACTURER, MODEL and BASIC_WARRANTY of the block HW_ASSETS onto the tab MANUFACTURER:

1. Expand the following nodes in the Object Navigator: Data Blocks, HW_ASSETS, and Items.

2. Click the item MANUFACTURER.
3. SHIFT+CLICK the item BASIC_WARRANTY. The items MANUFACTURER, MODEL and BASIC_WARRANTY will be selected.
4. Select Tools | Property Palette from the menu.
5. Scroll down the list of properties until you see the category Physical.
6. Click the text item to the right of the property Tab Page. Notice that a list box replaces the text item.
7. Select the tab MANUFACTURER from the list.

If you display the canvas EQUIPMENT in the Layout Editor, you will notice that the three items whose property you modified have been moved from the tab GENERAL to the tab MANUFACTURER. With similar actions, you can move the items VENDOR, EXTENDED_WARRANTY, PURCHASE_COST, PURCHASE_DT, and CS_PHONE to the tab VENDOR.

Finally, you need to move all the items of the block SW_ASSSETS to the tab SW_ASSETS of the canvas EQUIPMENTS. To achieve this, you could set the property Canvas to EQUIPMENTS and then the property Tab Page to SW_ASSETS for all the items in the block. In addition, you will need to set the property Scroll Bar Canvas to EQUIPMENTS and then the property Scroll Bar Tab Page to SW_ASSETS for the block SW_ASSETS itself. These properties are located in the Scrollbar category of the block's Property Palette.

As you can see, several steps are required to transfer all the items of the block and its scrollbar from one canvas to the other. These steps are dramatically reduced if, instead of moving each individual object you move the object that ties them all together in one logical group—the frame of the data block. The following are the steps that allow you to move the block SW_ASSSETS to the tab SW_ASSETS of the canvas EQUIPMENTS using the frame:

1. In the Object Navigator expand the original canvas that still holds the block SW_ASSETS.
2. Expand the node Graphics. You will see only one frame object that corresponds to the block SW_ASSETS. Recall that the frames that correspond to the block HW_ASSETS were deleted in Section 3.1.2.
3. Expand the canvas EQUIPMENT and the node Tab Pages.
4. Drag the frame that corresponds to the block SW_ASSETS and drop it on the tab SW_ASSETS.
5. Display the canvas EQUIPMENT on the Layout Editor and switch to the tab SW_ASSETS.

At this point, the frame appears in the lower half of the tab, preserving the position it had in the content canvas. Simply drag it upward until the frame and all its items come in close to the top of the page. In the following section, you will properly organize the items and enhance the layout of the other tabs of the canvas EQUIPMENT.

3.2 ARRANGING ITEMS IN THE LAYOUT EDITOR

In the following sections, you will perform several activities in the Layout Editor, such as resizing, moving, and aligning objects in each tab. Although these activities focus on arranging the layout of the tab GENERAL, similar steps should be followed to enhance the layout of the other two tabs: MANUFACTURER and VENDOR.

3.2.1 RESIZING OBJECTS

It is a good practice to set the length of an item that corresponds to a database column to the length of the column itself. This saves your application from truncation errors that may occur if data from the database are fetched to items that are not long enough to hold them. But the length of an item is one thing, and the space it occupies on the canvas is another. The item EMPLOYEE, for example, is thirty characters long, but most employee names your form will handle will be no more than twenty characters. There is no reason why this item should take more space than that on the window. To resize the item follow these steps:

1. Select the item by clicking it.
2. Drag the handle in the middle of the vertical right edge of the item to approximately two-thirds of the original length.
3. Release the mouse button. The item is resized.

3.2.2 SETTING OBJECTS TO THE SAME SIZE

Your application will have a more uniform look and feel if items from the same tab have similar sizes. For example, in the tab GENERAL, the items NAME and LOCATION could have the same size as EMPLOYEE. However, you do not have to resize each item individually. Use the following steps instead.

1. Click EMPLOYEE to select it, if it is not already selected.
2. CTRL+CLICK the items NAME and LOCATION. Now all three items are selected.
3. Select Arrange | Size Objects from the menu. The Size Objects dialog box appears.
4. Click radio button Smallest in radio group Width.
5. Click OK.

The Layout Editor sets the width of the selected objects to the width of the smallest one, EMPLOYEE.

3.2.3 MOVING OBJECTS

In the current layout, the items are spread inconsistently on each tab. You want to move them to better locations on the tab. The following actions allow you to move an item:

1. Click the item on the Layout Editor to select it.
2. Drag the item to the desired location on the tab. Alternatively, use the arrow keys from the keyboard to move the item.

Note that when you move an item, the associated text label accompanies the item to the new position. Following these steps, move the items on the GENERAL tab so that they form a vertical column beginning with SERIAL_NUM, followed by NAME, EMPLOYEE, LOCATION, and NOTES. Do not worry if the items are not properly aligned or if the distance between adjacent items is not the same. The following section will show you a quick way to fix these problems.

3.2.4 ALIGNING OBJECTS

When arranging objects on the canvas, it is not difficult to lose the alignment between them. It is important though to offer users applications in which the items and text labels are neatly aligned with dividing space uniformly distributed. To align the objects on the tab GENERAL, you should follow these steps:

1. Click on the tab higher up and further to the left than the item SERIAL_NUM.
2. Drag the mouse diagonally, down and to the right. You will notice a virtual rectangle being drawn as you drag the mouse.
3. When the rectangle includes all the items, release the mouse button. All the items on the tab are selected.
4. Choose Arrange | Align Objects from the menu. The dialog box Align Objects appears.
5. Select the radio item Align Left from the group Horizontally. With this option set, the Layout Editor will align all the items to the left.
6. Select the item Distribute from the radio group Vertically. With this option set, the Layout Editor will distribute the items equally in the space between the top-most and the bottom-most item.
7. Click OK. All the items are aligned.

Similar steps can be used to align the text labels that correspond to the database items. As a shortcut, after selecting all the labels at the end of step 3, select Align | Repeat Alignment from the menu or press CTRL+L from the keyboard. With this command, the Layout Editor will align the selected objects using the options you set in the dialog box Align Objects.

3.2.5 CHANGING THE TAB ORDER OF OBJECTS

The tab order of items on the screen is the sequence in which the application focus moves from item to item when users press the TAB key. To obtain an intuitive user interface of your application, it is important to set the tab order so that it reflects the layout and grouping of items on the screen. In the case of the GENERAL tab, for example, because the item NOTES is underneath LOCATION it is natural to expect the focus to land on NOTES when the TAB key is pressed on LOCATION.

In the Form Builder, the tab order is the sequence of items within the data block in the Object Navigator. If you take a look at the current order, you will notice that NOTES is at the bottom of the list, far removed from LOCATION. The following are the actions required to change the position of NOTES in the Object Navigator:

1. Select the item NOTES.
2. Drag the item NOTES and drop it between LOCATION and MANUFACTURER.

This technique can be used in general to re-sequence any objects in the Object Navigator.

3.2.6 RESIZING THE CANVAS AND WINDOW OBJECTS

Now that the items of the ETS form have been rearranged, it is time to reset the dimensions of the canvas and window objects that will be used to display these items to the users. The canvas object can be resized on the Layout Editor, just like any other object displayed there. However, it is easier to coordinate the dimensions of the canvas with those of the window where this canvas will be "attached" using the Property Palette. The following are the steps to set the dimensions in the ETS form:

1. Right-click the canvas EQUIPMENT in the Object Navigator and select Property Palette from the popup menu.
2. Set the properties Viewport Width to 360 and Viewport Height to 180. Both these properties are located in the Viewport category.

3. Switch to the Object Navigator, select the window WINDOW1, and display its properties in the Property Palette.
4. Set the properties Width to 360 and Height to 180. These properties are located in the Physical category.

As a bonus feature here, you may want to set the property Title of the window to a string that describes the purpose of the window, for example "Hardware and Software Assets." This property is located in the Physical group of the Property Palette.

It is a good moment now to save the work done so far, regenerate the module and run it in order to view the changes. At this point, the tabs in your form should look approximately like the ones shown in Figure 3.6, Figure 3.7, Figure 3.8, and Figure 3.9.

3.3 ENHANCING THE GUI INTERFACE

In this section, you will modify properties of several items in the form. The goal is to improve the GUI interface of the form by presenting certain data elements according to a predefined format and by providing helpful hints to the users.

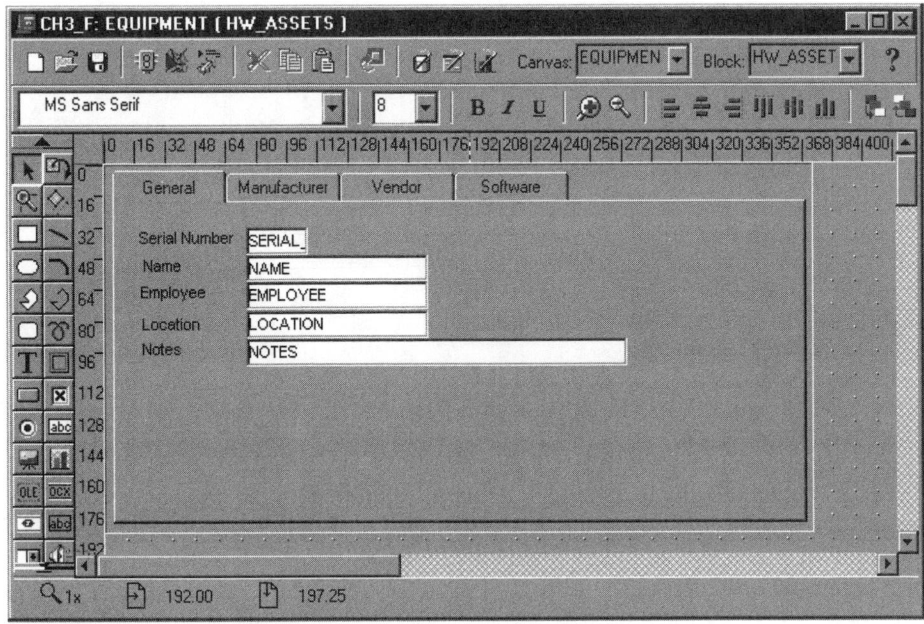

FIGURE 3.6 Final layout of the GENERAL tab.

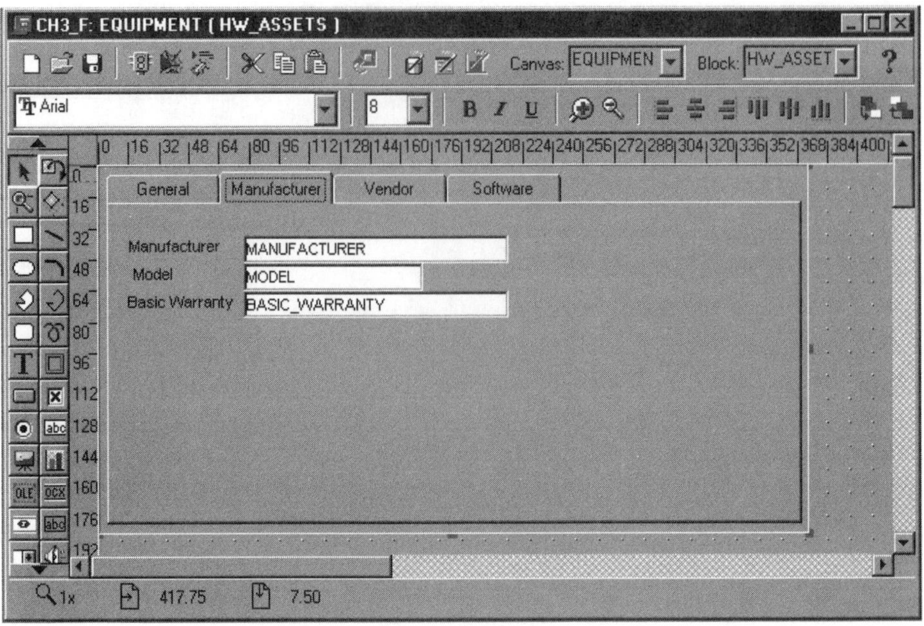

FIGURE 3.7 Final layout of the MANUFACTURER tab.

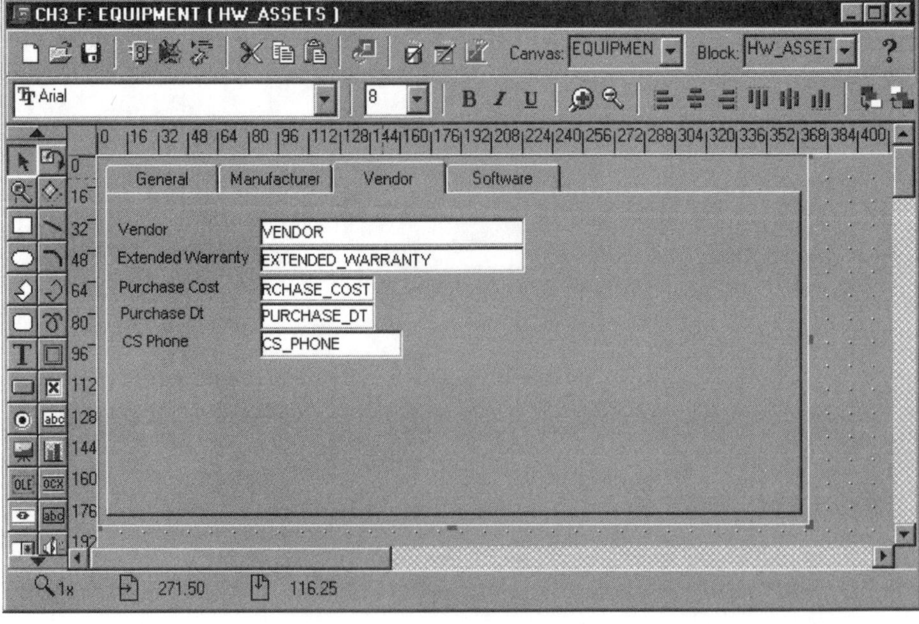

FIGURE 3.8 Final layout of the VENDOR tab.

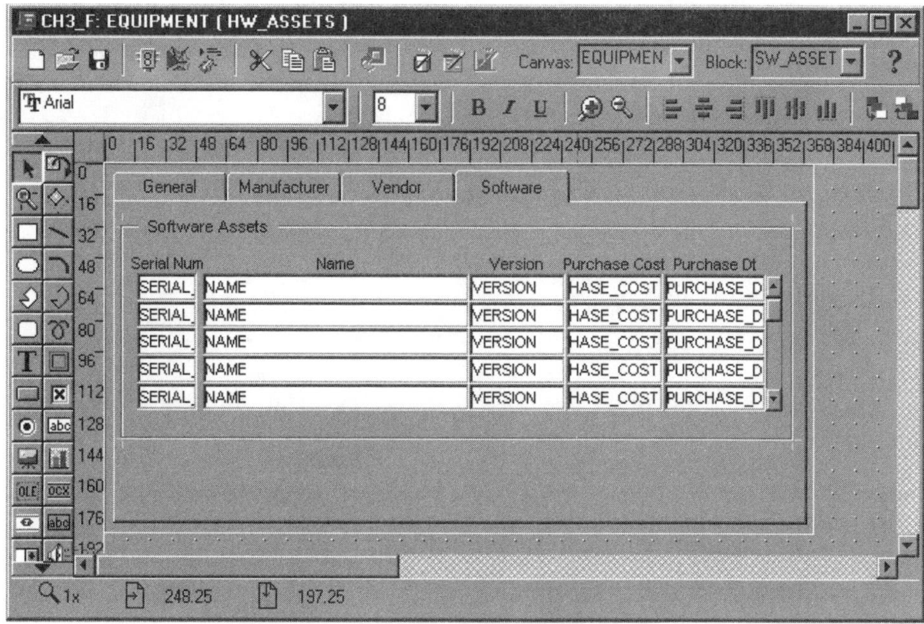

FIGURE 3.9 Final layout of the SW_ASSETS tab.

3.3.1 SETTING PROPERTIES OF TEXT ITEMS

Modify now some of the item properties in your form. The following change may apply to a number of items in HW_ASSETS and SW_ASSETS blocks, including NAME, MANUFACTURER, MODEL, and VENDOR. As a preliminary step, select them in the Object Navigator and switch to the Property Palette.

You want all the selected items to accept and display data in uppercase characters. This will standardize data across the application. (Remember that SQL language, and, therefore, Oracle considers "Personal Computer" and "PERSONAL COMPUTER" as two different data values, although in real life they may mean the same thing.)

1. In the Property Palette, select the property Case Restriction, located in the Functional category. Its current setting is "Mixed."
2. Select the option "Upper" from the list.

A better way to standardize values of data elements such as NAME or MANUFACTURER is to use lists of values. These lists can be static, with members that do not change during the life of the application. But they can also be dynamic lists maintained by users at runtime. Later in the book you will learn how to incorporate lists of values of both types in your applications.

Another beneficial feature you can add to your form is the ability to display a hint message to the users, prompting them to enter the value for the current item whenever they navigate to that item.

1. Select all the items in the blocks HW_ASSETS and SW_ASSETS.
2. Switch to the Property Palette.
3. Scroll down the list of item properties until you see the property Hint in the Help category. Currently, this property is not set.
4. Type "Enter the value for this item" in the property Hint.
5. Set the property Display Hint Automatically to "Yes."

If you find this hint message too generic or want to provide some additional information to the users, set it on an item-by-item basis.

Another property that you may want to set for each item is Tooltip in the Help group. The setting of this property will be shown to the users as a popup message when the mouse moves over the item. Although the tooltips are very common for toolbar icons and other GUI controls, they may be used for text items as well.

3.3.2 SETTING FORMAT MASKS

Turn your attention now to items that display currency values. According to established GUI standards, you want them to be indented to the right. You also want the currency symbol to precede these values, but users should not be required to enter it. Finally, you want to enforce the business rule that values must be non-negative and not to exceed $100,000.

The following steps apply equally well to the item PURCHASE_COST in the HW_ASSETS block or PURCHASE_COST in the SW_ASSETS block. Select both items and display the Property Palette.

1. Set the property Justification in the Functional category to "Right."
2. Scroll down until you see the property Format Mask in the Data category.
3. Set the property to $999,999.99. With this setting, users need to enter only the numeric value of the item, for example 1199.99. Forms will automatically display it as $1,199.99.
4. Set the property Lowest Allowed Value immediately below to 0.
5. Set the property Highest Allowed Value immediately below to 100,000.

With the property Format Mask set as described in Step 3, you save a few keystrokes to your users for each record they enter. This may seem like a small detail, but it is very relevant for applications intensely used for data entry and manipulation. In such applications, every keystroke spared the users may translate in significant increase in their productivity. Good candidates for setting the Format Mask property are fixed length numeric items with embedded characters in them such as telephone numbers or Social Security numbers. With the goal of minimizing data entry time in mind, set the properties of the CS_PHONE item by following these steps:

1. Select the item and switch to the Properties Palette.
2. Set the Format Mask property to "("999") "999"-"9999.
3. Set the property Maximum Length to 14. The setting of this property needs to be increased by 4 characters to accommodate the extra formatting characters introduced by the format mask. The property Maximum Length is located in the Data category, just like Format Mask.
4. Scroll down until you see the property Width in the Physical category. This property controls the width of the displayed items on the screen, It is currently wide enough to display ten characters.
5. Set the Width property to 75 to account for the extra characters introduced by the format mask.

With these settings, users need to enter only the ten digits that make up the phone number, for example 8005254567. The application will format the entry to look like (800) 525-4567.

Finally, implement another business rule of the ETS application. It was mentioned in Chapter 1 that the serial numbers in Print and Press are all six characters long. This means that your application should not allow users to enter NT-98 as a serial number either for hardware or software assets. Since the serial numbers will be of fixed length, it would be nice if you make the application navigate to the next item as soon as the operators enter them. This way they do not have to explicitly navigate out of these items. The following steps can be used with the item SERIAL_NUM in the block HW_ASSETS or SW_ASSETS.

1. Select SERIAL_NUM and switch to the Property Palette.
2. Set the property Fixed Length in the Data category to "Yes." This setting will require the users to enter the full length of the serial number.
3. Set the property Automatic Skip in the category Functional to "Yes." This setting will cause the application to navigate to the next item as soon as the user has entered the serial number.

Save the changes made so far in the ETS application before moving on to the next section.

3.4 ADDING CALCULATED ITEMS

Besides database items, a form may also contain items whose values are derived from other items or calculated according to a certain formula. In this section, you will add one such item on the GENERAL tab. This item will display the sum of purchase cost for all the software items installed in the current hardware asset. The following steps describe the process of creating such an item.

1. Double-click the tab GENERAL in the Object Navigator to display it in the Layout Editor.
2. Select "SW_ASSETS" from the list box Blocks in the toolbar.
3. Click the icon Display Item on the vertical toolbar of the Editor. Notice how the mouse cursor becomes a cross hair when the mouse moves over the canvas.
4. Click on the tab page under the item NOTES. The display item is created on the tab. Because of Step 2, the new item will be part of the SW_ASSETS block, although it is presented together with items from the HW_ASSETS block. A visual indicator of this fact is that the item appears as five stacked items, one for each record displayed in the SW_ASSETS block.

Display items are a special type of text items in the Developer Forms environment. For all intents and purposes, they can be considered as read-only text items. Their value cannot be entered directly by the users, although it can be set programmatically. In order to transform the newly created item into the desired summary item, you need to set a number of properties as described in the following steps:

1. Double-click the display item and switch to its Property Palette.
2. In the General category of properties, set Name to "SW_COST."
3. In the Functional category of properties, set Justification to "Right."
4. In the Data category of properties, set Data Type to "Number"; set Format Mask to $999,999.99.
5. In the Calculation category, set Calculation Mode to "Summary"; set Summary Function to "Sum"; set Summarized Block to "SW_ASSETS"; and set Summarized Item to "PURCHASE_COST."
6. In the Records category, set Number of Items Displayed to 1. By default, this property is set to 0, which means that its actual setting is derived from the number of records the block will display.
7. In the Physical category set Width to 90 and Height to 14.
8. In the Prompt category set Prompt to "Software Value."
9. Arrange the layout of the tab GENERAL if necessary.

In order to complete the creation of the calculated item, you need to set two more properties of the block SW_ASSETS.

1. Double-click the node SW_ASSETS in the Object Navigator and switch to its Property Palette.
2. In the Records category set Query All Records to "Yes." Because the summary will be performed in the client side, it is important for the Forms Runtime to have all the available records at hand, hence the need to set this property.

At this point, you can save the changes made so far in the ETS application, compile and run it to see the effect of the actions you have take so far.

3.5 ENHANCING THE FUNCTIONALITY OF APPLICATIONS WITH PL/SQL CODE

By carefully setting properties of items as described in the previous sections, you make your application enforce a great deal of data validation and business rules, without any explicit coding. If, however, more complicated rules must be implemented or additional actions will be performed, then PL/SQL code is written and organized in triggers, functions, procedures, and packages. This section guides you through some activities performed in this stage.

In your application, HW_SERIAL_NUM is the primary key for the HW_ASSETS table. The Oracle database will not allow more than one hardware record to exist in the table with the same serial number. To see how this works, follow these steps:

1. Generate and run the ETS form.
2. Retrieve the hardware record with serial number 98-N45. (If for some reason this record does not exist, create one and commit it to the database.)
3. Select Record | Insert from the menu to create a new record.
4. Select Record | Duplicate from the menu to make the new record an identical copy of the 98-N45 record.

If you try to commit the new record you will get the error message "FRM-40508: ORACLE error: unable to INSERT record." Exit the ETS form you were running and return to the Form Builder.

This type of behavior could be acceptable if users would commit each record when they insert or modify it. But, if they enter five more records before requesting the commit, the whole transaction will fail, even if only one record violates the uniqueness constraint. Because the message above does not identify the violator, users have to go through each individual record to identify the problem.

3.5.1 WRITING THE FIRST TRIGGER

You can improve the situation described above by checking for existing serial numbers when the record is validated. Later in the book, you will see in more detail when this event occurs. At this point, it is sufficient to say that the record will be validated whenever users navigate out of it, or commit. This event fires a trigger called WHEN-VALIDATE-RECORD for the particular block where the event occurs. You will place the code that does the check in this trigger, attached to the HW_ASSETS block. The steps to create this trigger are as follows:

1. In the Object Navigator, right-click the node HW_ASSETS.
2. Select Smart Triggers | WHEN-VALIDATE-RECORD from the popup menu.
3. A PL/SQL Editor window will be displayed (see Figure 3.10).

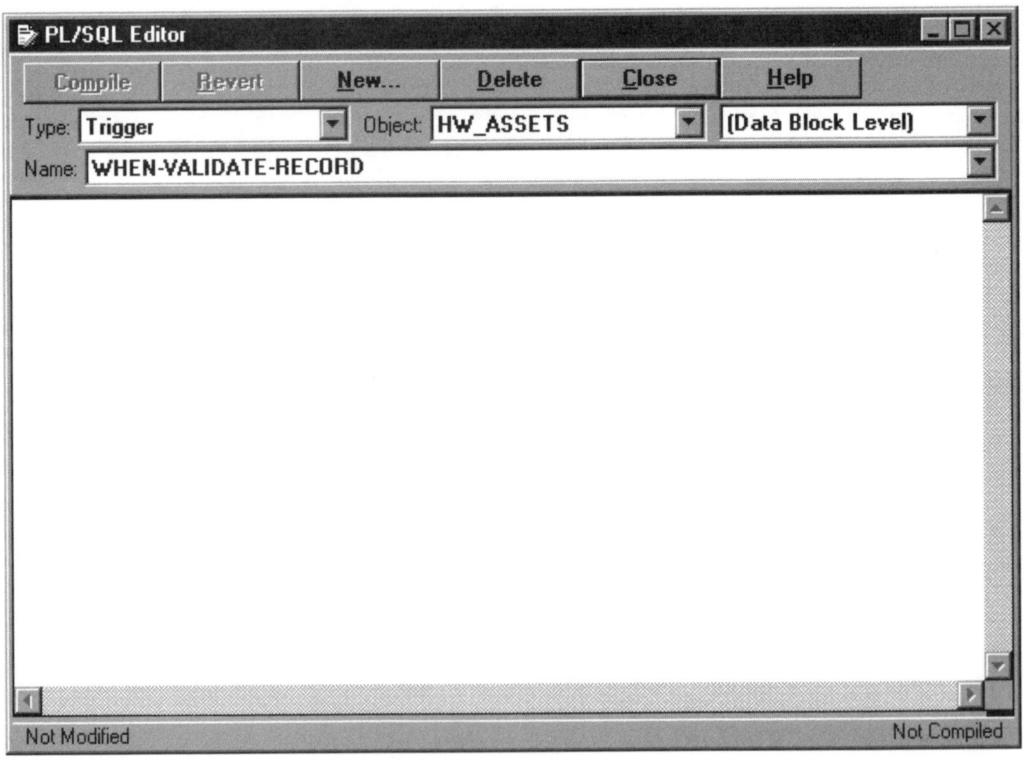

FIGURE 3.10 PL/SQL Editor window.

The text pane of the window is blank, and the cursor is positioned in its upper-left-hand corner, waiting for your input. You also see that the Compile push button is disabled and the status bar at the bottom of the window displays the status lamps Not Modified to the left and Not Compiled to the right. Enter the text shown in Figure 3.11.

Notice that as you enter the text, the Compile button is enabled and the status lamps of the trigger change to Modified and Not Compiled. When you are finished entering the text, click the Compile button. If you did not make any typing mistakes, the trigger compiles successfully and its status lamps become Not Modified and Successfully Compiled. Notice also that the editor window uses different colors for different areas of the text you enter. The words displayed in blue are Oracle and PL/SQL keywords. These include DECLARE, BEGIN, END, IF, THEN, END IF, and so on. Text in quotes appears in cyan. If you had comments in the code, they would appear in green letters. The PL/SQL Editor uses this color scheme to help you enter the code quickly and without mistakes.

What you just entered in the PL/SQL Editor window is called a PL/SQL block. The following paragraphs briefly explain its components and the meaning of the PL/SQL statements that are part of it.

- Line 2 declares a variable of data type NUMBER, called counter. This is a local variable whose value can be accessed only in this block of code. All the

```
1   DECLARE
2     counter NUMBER;
3   BEGIN
4     IF :SYSTEM.RECORD_STATUS = 'INSERT' THEN
5       SELECT COUNT(*)
6       INTO counter
7       FROM HW_ASSETS
8       WHERE SERIAL_NUM = :HW_ASSETS.SERIAL_NUM;
9       IF counter <> 0 THEN
10        BELL;
11        MESSAGE('Item with this serial number already
          exists.');
12        RAISE FORM_TRIGGER_FAILURE;
13      END IF;
14    END IF;
15  END;
```

FIGURE 3.11 Contents of WHEN-VALIDATE-RECORD trigger for HW_ASSETS block.

declarations of local variables are made in the declaration section of the PL/SQL block, which begins with the keyword DECLARE (Line 1) and ends with the keyword BEGIN (Line 3).

- The statements enclosed between the keywords BEGIN and END (lines 3 through 15) are known as the executable part of the block. They are executed only if the record is a new record that will be inserted into the database. The status of the record is stored in the system variable SYSTEM.RECORD_STATUS and is tested in line 4. These statements between lines 5 and 13 are responsible for the actions that will occur when the record is a newly created one. There are basically two such actions.
- Lines 5 through 8 require the database to count all the records in the HW_ASSETS table in which the value of column SERIAL_NUM equals the value stored in the Forms item HW_ASSETS.SERIAL_NUM. The value retrieved is held in the variable counter. If there are no such records, the value of counter will be 0; otherwise, counter will hold the number of these records. In the context of the ETS application, if counter is 0, the serial number entered in the form is a new one and, therefore, valid; otherwise, it is invalid because it is duplicating the serial number of another record.
- Line 9 decides what to do next, based on the value stored in variable counter. If it is 0, everything is fine, and the trigger ends with no further action. But if counter is not 0, lines 10, 11, and 12 will be executed.
- Line 10 attracts the attention of the user by sounding the PC's bell. The built-in procedure BELL serves this purpose.
- Line 11 informs the user on what happened. The built-in procedure MESSAGE sends its argument string to the application's console.
- Line 12 prevents Forms from taking any further processing steps. A built-in named exception, FORM_TRIGGER_FAILURE is raised to stop the operations.

3.5.2 REUSING CODE IN THE SW_ASSETS BLOCK

The process of implementing the same functionality for the SW_ASSETS block is very similar. You can easily do it on your own, by adopting the approach described above. The following paragraph presents a technique that you may find useful when creating and working with your triggers. It takes advantage of the fact that you already have created the WHEN-VALIDATE-RECORD for the HW_ASSETS block. In the process, you will also learn how to copy and paste objects in the Object Navigator.

1. Expand the nodes Data Blocks, HW_ASSETS, and Triggers in the Object Navigator.
2. Select the node WHEN-VALIDATE-RECORD and press CTRL+C to copy the trigger.

3. Select the block SW_ASSETS and click CTRL+V to paste the trigger. Notice that the Form Builder appropriately places the new object in the right position in the tree.

These steps create a new WHEN-VALIDATE-RECORD trigger for the block SW_ASSETS with the same contents as the trigger in HW_ASSETS. In order to complete the functionality for SW_ASSETS, you need to modify only a few lines that will be different between the two triggers. Double-click the trigger WHEN-VALIDATE-RECORD for block SW_ASSETS and edit its contents to look like Figure 3.12.

The copy and paste approach described in this section has two advantages. On one hand, it saves you the effort of creating a new trigger from scratch. On the other, users will see similar reactions for similar errors. Put in more academic terms, you will reduce the application development time, and create a consistent user interface. These are two basic principles for code sharing in software projects.

3.5.3 WRITING A PROCEDURE

It was mentioned in Chapter 2 that you may want to write some code that will disallow users to move to a new record from the last record in a block. This functionality would hold for any block, including HW_ASSETS and SW_ASSETS. At

```
DECLARE
 counter NUMBER;
BEGIN
 IF :SYSTEM.RECORD_STATUS = 'INSERT' THEN
  SELECT COUNT(*)
  INTO counter
  FROM SW_ASSETS
  WHERE HW_SERIAL_NUM = :SW_ASSETS.HW_SERIAL_NUM AND
     SERIAL_NUM = :SW_ASSETS.SERIAL_NUM;
  IF counter <> 0 THEN
   BELL;
   MESSAGE('Item with this serial number already exists.');
   RAISE FORM_TRIGGER_FAILURE;
  END IF;
 END IF;
END;
```

FIGURE 3.12 Contents of WHEN-VALIDATE-RECORD trigger for SW_ASSETS block.

the same time, it will be invoked by at least two events. One is when users try to navigate to the next record. The trigger fired in this case is KEY-NXTREC. The other event is when users press the downarrow key. The trigger fired in this case is KEY-DOWN.

In cases where the same code is invoked in several places in the application, it is advisable to place it in a procedure and issue calls to this procedure from the different triggers. In this section, you will create the procedure Move_Next_Record to implement the functionality mentioned here. You can create the procedure from the Layout Editor window by following these steps:

1. Select "Program Unit" from the Type list box in the PL/SQL Editor window list.
2. Click the New . . . button to create a new program unit. The New Program Unit dialog box appears. This dialog allows you to specify the name and the type of the new program unit. The type 'Procedure' is already selected.
3. Enter "Move_Next_Record" in the Name text item.
4. Click OK.

At this point the control returns to the PL/SQL Editor window. A template for the procedure is already entered in the source code pane. Enter the contents of the procedure as shown in Figure 3.13. In this procedure you are using the value stored in the system variable SYSTEM.LAST_RECORD to decide whether the current record is the last record in the block or not. If not, the built-in procedure NEXT_RECORD is used to navigate to the next record. Otherwise, the operation is halted in a way similar to the two previous triggers.

```
PROCEDURE Move_Next_Record IS
BEGIN
 IF :SYSTEM.LAST_RECORD <> 'TRUE' THEN
   NEXT_RECORD;
 ELSE
 – No more records to move to.
  BELL;
  MESSAGE('At last record.');
  RAISE FORM_TRIGGER_FAILURE;
 END IF;
END;
```

FIGURE 3.13 Contents of procedure Move_Next_Record.

3.5.4 WRITING FORM-LEVEL TRIGGERS

Now that you have written the procedure Move_Next_Record, you should place calls to it from the form-level triggers KEY-NXTREC and KEY-DOWN. By creating these triggers at the form level rather than at each individual block level, you reduce the amount of code to create and maintain. To create the trigger KEY-NXTREC form the PL/SQL Editor window follow these steps:

1. Select "Trigger" from the Type list box in the PL/SQL Editor window. The Object list box displays the entry (Form Level).
2. Click the New . . . button to create a new trigger. A List of Values dialog box with the names of all the trigger types appears.
3. Type "K." The list is narrowed to those triggers that begin with "KEY."
4. Type "N." The list now contains only five entries from which it is easy to identify the trigger type you want to create.
5. Select KEY-NXTREC and click OK. The List of Values dialog box is closed, a new form-level KEY-NXTREC trigger is created and the control returns to the PL/SQL Editor window.
6. Enter the text of the trigger as follows:
   ```
   Move_Next_Record;
   ```

To create the trigger KEY-DOWN form the PL/SQL Editor window follow these steps:

1. Click the New . . . button to create a new trigger.
2. From the List of Values dialog box with the names of the triggers, select KEY-DOWN.
3. Enter the text of the trigger as follows:
   ```
   Move_Next_Record;
   ```

> **TIP**
>
> You may have noticed that there exists a form-level trigger called ON-CLEAR-DETAILS in the application. This trigger and the procedures CHECK_PACKAGE_FAILURE, QUERY_MASTER_DETAILS, and QUERY_ALL_MASTER_DETAILS are created by the Form Builder to implement the master/detail relationship between HW_ASSETS and SW_ASSETS blocks.

Now, you can say that you have a complete application, full of functionality but also with a nice interface. Save and generate it, and feel free to use it to master the concepts discussed in Chapter 2.

3.6 DEPLOYING THE ETS APPLICATION

After completing the development process on your form, you should provide access to it to those employees that will need to use the application. You can deploy Oracle Developer applications in client-server mode or on the Web. This section discusses how you can deploy the ETS form in client-server mode. Later in the book, you will learn more about the Web-enabled architecture of the Oracle Developer tools and how to deploy your applications over the Web. In the meanwhile, you can get a feel for how the application will run over the Web by running it from within the Form Builder in Web mode. Chapter 2 discussed how you can run a form in Web mode from within the Form Builder.

It is assumed here that you have installed at least the Developer/2000 Forms Runtime software either on each individual client PC, or on a shared directory in a file server. It is also assumed that you have installed and configured the software required to connect to the database. To install the ETS application on a PC follow these steps:

1. Create a directory, for example C:\ETS, where the executable ETS.FMX will reside.
2. Copy in C:\ETS the file ETS.FMX from your development environment.
3. Right-click on the desktop area and choose New | Folder from the popup menu.
4. Type "Equipment Tracking System" as the name of the new folder.
5. Double-click the new folder.
6. Select File | New | Shortcut from the menu. The Create Shortcut Wizard appears.
7. Fill the Command Line text item with the location and name of the Forms Runtime executable followed by the location and name of ETS.FMX. If, for example, Forms Runtime is installed in C:\ORANT\BIN, then the Command Line for the new shortcut would be "C:\ORANT\BIN\ifrun60.exe C:\ETS\ETS.FMX."
8. Provide the name of the shortcut, for example, "ETS Form." Windows creates the shortcut in the folder.

Now the ETS application is ready to be used.

3.7 WHAT IS THE REST OF THE BOOK ABOUT?

If you followed the material presented so far, you have a good start in your Oracle Developer programming efforts. You know the basic components of Form Builder and Forms Runtime. You have been exposed to concepts of database applications development. You have an understanding of the principal stages in which the development of a form evolves. What's more important, you just finished a useful application that rewards your work and places you among those software engineers that can develop in Form Builder.

In order to learn more about Oracle Developer, you need to follow the rest of this book. The following is a summary of what's ahead:

- **Part II** equips you with the necessary tools to create, design, and enhance forms. The purpose, access methods, components and usage of important tools such as the Object Navigator, Layout Editor, Property Palette, Menu Editor, Object Library Editor, and PL/SQL Editor, are discussed in detail. This part also covers Rapid Application Development (RAD) and object reusability with Developer/2000 Forms. The final three chapters in Part II discuss the elements of the Standard Query Language (SQL) used in Oracle applications, the Oracle's own programming language—PL/SQL—as well as object-relational features introduced by Oracle8 that affect Form Builder programming.
- **Part III** presents Form Builder as an object-oriented and event-driven programming environment. It explains the features and functionality of its objects, including data blocks, items, windows, record structures and menus. It also discusses events associated with each object, triggers they fire, and how you can use them to enhance Forms applications.
- **Part IV** covers advanced programming with Form Builder. It begins with debugging techniques and activities. Then, it discusses the integration of Forms with other Oracle Developer tools, such as Report Builder and Graphic Builder. An entire chapter is dedicated to the reusable components provided by Oracle Developer and the benefits you draw by including them in your applications. Another important subject covered in this part is the development and deployment of Forms applications on the Web in a three-tier architecture. A separate chapter presents tips and techniques to simplify Forms development and installation using the Project Builder. The final two chapters of this part discuss the use of Oracle Designer in creating, maintaining and generating Form Builder modules.
- **Part V** focuses on to the integration of Form Builder applications with other Microsoft Windows applications through Dynamic Data Exchange (DDE), and Microsoft's COM-based technologies, including OLE Documents,

Automation, and ActiveX controls. I also cover here the implementation of user exits and the extension of Developer/2000 applications' functionality using the PL/SQL interface to foreign functions.

3.8 SUMMARY

In this chapter, you turned the ETS form in a user-friendly GUI application. To achieve this, you worked to enhance the layout of the form in the Layout Editor and to customize the properties of its objects in the Property Palette. You also enhanced the application functionality by writing some PL/SQL code in the form of triggers and procedures. Among important concepts discussed in this chapter were:

- **Transforming the Form into a Tabbed Layout**
  - Reentering the Layout Wizard
  - Deleting Objects in the Layout Editor
  - Creating New Objects in the Object Navigator
  - Setting Properties in the Property Palette
- **Arranging Items in the Layout Editor**
  - Resizing Objects
  - Setting Objects to the Same Size
  - Moving Objects
  - Aligning Objects
  - Changing the Tab Order of Objects
  - Resizing the Canvas and Window Objects
- **Enhancing the GUI Interface**
  - Setting Properties of Text Items
  - Setting Format Masks
- **Adding Calculated Items**
- **Enhancing the Functionality of Applications with PL/SQL Code**
  - Writing the First Trigger
  - Reusing Code in the SW_ASSETS Block
  - Writing a Procedure
  - Writing Form-Level Triggers
- **Deploying the ETS Application**

The following table describes the software assets that were discussed in this chapter. From the main HTML page of the software utilities provided with the book follow the links *Software* and *Chapter 3* to access these assets:

ASSET NAME	DESCRIPTION
CH03.FMB	The ETS module created in Chapter 1.
CH03_F.FMB	The ETS module created in Chapter 1 and enhanced in this chapter.
CH03_F.FMX	The final version of the ETS module compiled for Win32 platforms.

Part II

FORMS DEVELOPER TOOLBOX

The tools we use have a profound influence on our thinking habits, and, therefore, on our thinking abilities.

—Edsger W. Dijkstra

Chapter 4

ORACLE DEVELOPER FORM BUILDER

Every tool carries with it the spirit by which it has been created.
—Werner Karl Heisenberg

- Overview of Oracle Developer
- Components of Oracle Developer
- Overview of the Form Builder
- Working with Modules
- Storing Modules in the Database
- Summary

This chapter offers a brief overview of Oracle Developer and its components and focuses primarily on the characteristics of the Form Builder.

4.1 OVERVIEW OF ORACLE DEVELOPER

Oracle Developer is an application development suite of tools that was first introduced in January 1995 under the name of Cooperative Development Environment 2—CDE2. It was a major improvement of its predecessor, CDE. It not only offered a sophisticated Graphical Users Interface (GUI), but it also combined powerful forms, reports, and graphics into large, complex, and scaleable client/server applications. Each subsequent release of the product has introduced significant improvements aimed at increasing its support for different database engines, for deploying the applications on the Web, and for taking advantages of the latest achievements in the field of object-relational database packages. This section lists and briefly describes some of the main characteristics of Oracle Developer tools.

4.1.1 POWERFUL DEVELOPMENT SUITE FOR ORACLE DATABASES

Oracle Developer is considered the most powerful application development environment for the Oracle Relational Database Management System (RDBMS) databases, because it is tailored around and supports extensively its functionality. Many other programming tools can be used to create applications that run against Oracle databases. Oracle Developer offers a clear advantage over them because it shares the same programming language with the Oracle Server database—PL/SQL. This means that, if you are well versed in writing stored functions or procedures for the Oracle Server database, you can easily create functions and procedures in the Oracle Developer application that run in a Forms module or the Oracle RDBMS. In addition, data blocks in the forms created with Oracle Developer can be based on a set of stored procedures. One of the principal components of every tool in the Oracle Developer package, the Object Navigator, allows you to view and manipulate the code of your application in one window, no matter whether it resides in the client module or is stored in the database server. In the Navigator, you can move the routines from the client to the server, and vice versa, with a simple drag-and-drop action. This process, also known as partitioning of application logic, enables you to optimize the distribution of your code based on the specific environment where the application will run.

Initially, Oracle Developer was intended to be a tool for developing client-server applications working with an Oracle RDBMS at the back-end. However, as the technology has evolved, so has the tool and its offerings. Today, applications created with Oracle Developer may work with multiple database servers and can be deployed in a multi-tiered architecture composed of a thin 100 percent Java

GUI client as the front tier, an application server in the middle tier and one or more database servers in the back-end tier.

4.1.2 POWERFUL SUPPORT FOR SQL

Structured Query Language (SQL) has become the standard language for interacting with relational database management systems. Its non-procedural structure allows users to specify what they want done, without specifying how to do it. Its English-like syntax makes it relatively easy to understand and learn. Although not the inventor, Oracle Corporation implemented the first commercial version of SQL, in 1979. Since then, it has always played a leading role in defining and refining the language. The Oracle RDBMS and Oracle Developer tools utilize supersets of SQL compliant with the standards defined by the American National Standards Institute (ANSI), International Standards Organization (ISO), and the U.S. federal government. PL/SQL is the programming language used by both Oracle Developer and Oracle RDBMS. It expands the SQL commands with procedural capabilities such as loops, conditional checks, and procedural calls.

4.1.3 RAPID APPLICATION DEVELOPMENT TOOLS

Rapid Application Development (RAD) is an approach to building high-quality and low-cost information systems in a significantly short amount of time. Under well-defined methodology principles, RAD combines Computer-Aided System Engineering (CASE) tools, highly skilled professionals, user-driven prototyping, and rigorous delivery time limits in a winning formula that has proved to guaranty success in the development of information systems. Oracle Developer offers a number of features and components that enable you to create applications according to RAD principles. These include a number of wizards, the support for object libraries, and the ability to reduce development time and enforce standards through the use of templates. When combined with another set of Oracle tools—Oracle Designer, Oracle Developer provides a complete solution for the design, prototyping, development, and documentation of database systems according to RAD principles and methodology.

4.1.4 GRAPHICAL USERS INTERFACE TOOLS

Applications developed with Oracle Developer can utilize all the features of a GUI environment such as Multiple Documents Interface (MDI) paradigm, mouse support, radio groups, check boxes, buttons, and dynamic lists. They also offer powerful visual and graphical representation of data through interactive charts, boilerplate drawings, colors, patterns, and fonts. Each object developed with Oracle Developer can be used in windows platforms such as Microsoft Windows, Macintosh and X Window System as well as being portable to the Network Computing Architecture (thin client). It will automatically adapt to the native look of the underlying environment, thus enabling you to deploy your application in multiple platforms.

Oracle Developer also supports environment-specific features, For example, in Microsoft Windows and Macintosh environments, you can take advantage of Object Linking and Embedding (OLE) and Dynamic Data Exchange (DDE); in the different Windows operating systems you can embed ActiveX controls; you can also access functions developed in other languages such as C or C++, and compiled in the form of Windows Dynamic Link Libraries (DLL). Oracle Developer also supports the Java programming language and Java Bean technology because it allows you to embed and interact with modules developed in Java and encapsulated in the form of Java Bean components.

4.1.5 OBJECT-ORIENTED PROGRAMMING ENVIRONMENT

Oracle Developer is an object-oriented application development environment. It is built around concepts such as object abstraction, event-driven control, inheritance structures, encapsulation and reusability of data and processes. Operations such as creation and storage of objects in object libraries for further reuse, the compilation of reusable code in PL/SQL libraries which are loaded dynamically during runtime and the combination of logically related data, functions and procedures in packages, provide much of the power, capabilities and flexibility of object-oriented programming in the Oracle Developer tools. The support of Oracle Developer for objects is further increased due to its integration with the Oracle8 object-relational database. A combination of Oracle Developer and the Objects option of Oracle8 allow you to build applications that create and manage objects in a GUI front-end and store them in an object-aware database back-end.

4.2 COMPONENTS OF ORACLE DEVELOPER

Oracle Developer is built around three main components: Forms, Reports, and Graphics. To further support you in the process of creating applications, other utilities such as Procedure Builder, Schema Builder, and Query Builder, are included as both independent tools and are integrated into Oracle Forms and Reports. When you install the software, several program folders are created in your desktop.

- **Oracle Developer.** This folder contains all the executables that are needed to design, generate, and execute the applications. This is the program group accessed the most during development activities with Oracle tools.
- **Oracle Developer Documentation.** This folder contains reference manuals, developer guides, user guides, message and error manuals. All this information is provided in the form of HTML documents. Most of the informa-

tion contained in these documents is also accessible from within Oracle Developer tools as standard Help files.

- **Oracle Developer Demos.** This folder contains applications developed by Oracle Corporation to demonstrate features and functionality of Forms, Reports, and Graphics. It also contains program items that create or drop the database objects required by these applications.
- **Oracle Developer Administration.** This folder contains program items that create or drop the database objects required to store Oracle Developer modules in the Oracle RDBMS.

The two folders, Oracle Forms 6I and Oracle Forms & Reports 6i, bundle together the utilities that will be used most often in this book. Figure 4.1 and Figure 4.2 shows the program items included in these groups. They are not necessarily created in this order during the installation process, but are arranged for the sake of clarity.

From this picture, you can see that Oracle Developer contains a number of "builders." These are the tools used by the developers to design and develop their applications. They can be used to create and modify most of the components that make up a database application, from the back-end database objects to the front-end modules. The following list provides a brief description of these tools.

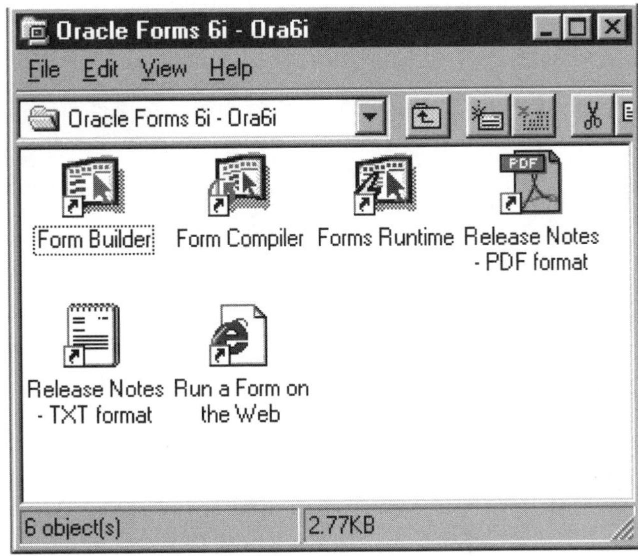

FIGURE 4.1 Components of Forms 6i program group.

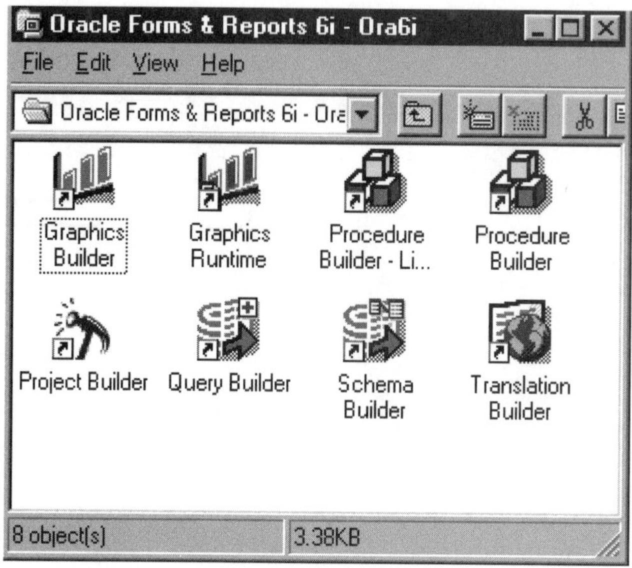

FIGURE 4.2 Components of Developer Forms & Reports program group.

- **Form Builder.** This is the tool where most of the Oracle Developer programming occurs. It is used to create GUI interfaces that allow users to create and maintain the data stored in the database. The Form Builder is the principal subject of this book and will be covered in detail in the pages that follow.
- **Report Builder.** This tool is used to extract data out of the database and present it in a variety of reporting formats. The reports that can be created with the tool range in complexity from trivial ones to reports with extensive computations and multiple levels of detail.
- **Graphics Builder.** This tool is use to present data in graphical format. It can be used as a stand-alone tool, although typically, the charts developed with it become part of Form Builder or Report Builder modules.
- **Schema Builder.** This tool helps you view and maintain the objects in one or more database schemas. It is especially useful in cases when you are developing the software system without a more powerful tool, such as Oracle Designer where you can maintain the design and structure of the database schema and all the software modules involved.
- **Query Builder.** This tool helps you perform ad hoc queries against one or more database schemas, which you can access. It can come handy when designing the queries for your applications. A subset of Query Builder is also used within Forms to help build SQL for LOV's, etc.

- **Procedure Builder.** This tool is used to create, maintain, and debug PL/SQL programming objects. These objects can be stored in the Oracle RDBMS or in the file system as PL/SQL libraries.
- **Project Builder.** This tool is very helpful for development efforts that involve a number of software assets that need to be bundled together. For example, a number of forms, reports and charts, together with their online help files, images and icons, need to be developed as part of one project and deployed to the users as part of the same application. Project Builder helps you maintain the relations and dependencies of all these files.

In addition to the "builders," Oracle Developer has runtime components for forms, reports, and graphics. The runtime components are used by the end users to execute the finished applications. When these applications are deployed in client/server mode, the users access the runtime components directly, either from their desktops, or from a shared location in the network. When the Form Builder applications are deployed over the Web, the Forms Runtime and Applications reside in the Middle Tier Web server and users use their Web browser to access their applications via the Forms Server Listener.

In order to facilitate the process of porting forms and reports from one platform to another (client/server to Web, for example) or upgrading them from earlier releases, Oracle Developer provides the Form Compiler and the report Compiler. Both these tools take source binary files created in the respective builders as input and create executables that can be run form the runtime components.

4.3 OVERVIEW OF THE FORM BUILDER

Form Builder allows you to create, access, modify, save, debug, and compile your form-based application. Form Builder operates on objects, which it organizes according to certain rules of hierarchy and ownership.

Each object within Form Builder has a set of Properties. Modules are the objects at the highest level of the hierarchy. In Form Builder, you work with form, menu, PL/SQL library, or object library modules. Each module contains objects, which, in turn, may contain other objects. Objects may occur once in a module, or they may be stored in object libraries for potential reuse in multiple forms. PL/SQL objects are written by programmers to carry out the functionality of the applications. As with other objects, they can be incorporated in the form or menu modules. They can also be packaged and grouped together in the form of PL/SQL library modules, similar to object libraries, but restricted only to PL/SQL objects. Those of you with C++ and Java backgrounds should note that the objects referred to here are not in strict conformance to with every object standard used in those pure object-oriented environments.

Although forms, menus, and libraries share the highest level in the hierarchy of objects, from a runtime perspective, there is some ranking even among them. When users run a Forms application, they will first execute a form module. This form may have attached to it a menu from which the users can select available options. Depending on the situation and the functionality of the application, this menu can be replaced by another menu. The first form may call another form as well. A PL/SQL library may be attached to the menus, the forms, or even another library.

4.3.1 FORM BUILDER COMPONENTS

The Object Navigator and Property Palette are central to most activities performed in Form Builder. For each category of objects (form, menu, PL/SQL library, or object library), Form Builder has *editors* specialized to work with these objects. In the Form Builder, you encounter the Layout Editor, the PL/SQL Editor, the Menu Editor, and the Object Library Editor. Furthermore, activity-driven components like Data Block Wizard, Layout Wizard, LOV Wizard and Chart Wizard, help you accomplish better and faster important tasks in your development effort. The following paragraphs will briefly explain each of these components. The next six chapters provide detailed information about their functionality and use.

- **Object Navigator.** This component is the heart of the Form Builder. It allows you to create the modules that will become part of your applications and browse the hierarchy of objects in these modules. The Object Navigator is the only component that is always available and used during a Form Builder working session. From this component, you can access all the other components.
- **Layout Editor.** This component allows you to visually control the layout of a form and monitor its look and feel at design and development time. In order to optimize the developers time, it offers a numerous functions for arranging, adding, deleting and formatting objects in the form layout.
- **Property Palette.** This component offers access to all the property settings of one or more objects in the Form Builder. Other methods exist to maintain selected properties of objects in selected editors. For example, you can change an object's name in the Object Navigator or its position and dimensions in the Layout Editor. However, the Property Palette offers the most generic and all-encompassing method to view and set the properties of objects.
- **PL/SQL Editor.** This component is used to create and maintain the contents of PL/SQL objects. It is integrated with the PL/SQL engine of Form Builder and provides a number of compiling and text management utilities.

- **Menu Editor.** This component helps you create and maintain the structure of menu modules in your application. It similar to the Layout Editor in that it is used to visually manipulate the layout and structure of the menu at design time.
- **Object Library Editor.** This component is used to maintain and organize objects stored in object library modules.
- **Data Block Wizard.** This component facilitates the process of creating a data block. It can be used to create new data block definitions or modify existing data blocks. It is "database aware" and is the fastest and simplest way to create a data block. As with wizards in general, it is a step by step procedure which organizes the information requirements into logical blocks.
- **Layout Wizard.** This component helps you take a first-cut at the layout of the data block of form modules. It can be especially useful when prototyping forms for the purpose of requirement gathering and definition. If you have not manually modified the layout of a block, it can be used to modify an existing block.
- **Chart Wizard.** This component helps you add a chart item to your form module.

4.3.2 FORM BUILDER MENUS

As you move from one component to the other in the Form Builder the menu options change fit each component. Each menu contains at least five submenus: File, Edit, Tools, Window, and Help. The functionality accessed through these submenus either applies to the entire module, as in the case of the File menu, or is used throughout a Form Builder session, as in the case of the remaining menus. The contents of these submenus are discussed in the following list:

- **File.** The File submenu controls functions that apply to the entire module. These include, creating a new module, opening, closing, or saving an existing module, connecting or disconnecting from the database, and exiting Form Builder.
- **Edit.** The Edit submenu provides all the usual GUI editing operations such as Undo, Cut, Copy, Paste, and Clear. Of special interest in this submenu, is the item SmartClasses. This item allows you to apply properties of SmartClass objects to one or more selected objects. SmartClass objects are stored in an Object Library module to encourage other objects to inherit properties from them. They will be discussed in more detail in Chapter 7.
- **Tools.** The Tools submenu is used to access the Form Builder components discussed in the previous section. It also provides access to the dialog box where Form Builder and Forms Runtime preferences are maintained. The Form Builder enables and disables these menu items according to the con-

text of the application. For example, if the current context is a form module, items like Layout Editor or Data Block Wizard, unique to forms, are enabled. Items like Menu Editor or Report Builder are disabled.

- **Window.** The Window submenu allows you to manage the display of different Form Builder windows that may be open at any one time, as well as to navigate to any of these windows.
- **Help.** The Help submenu provides access to the Form Builder's online help content. This is organized in the form of standard Windows Help files, with a table of contents for browsing, and index for searching, as well as with a Find utility for more detailed searches. If you want on-line help for a particular component of the Form Builder, select the context to that component and press F1 from the keyboard. The Help submenu allows you to access other sources of information, such as a quick tour of Form Builder's features, multimedia cue cards for major development activities with Form Builder, as well as the online manuals.
- **Popup.** When you are working in the Object Navigator, Layout Editor or Menu Editor windows, you can also click the right mouse button to display a popup menu. This menu provides access to frequent actions, like cut and paste, navigate to other Form Builder components, creating PL/SQL triggers, or inheriting properties from shared objects.

Depending on which component of the Form Builder you are using, additional submenus are added between the Edit and Tools submenus. These submenus handle functionality that applies to the particular component, but not to the rest of the application. The content and functionality of these submenus will be explained in the following six chapters, in the context of their associated components.

4.4 WORKING WITH MODULES

As mentioned above, Form Builder follows a modular approach to building an application. Every object and piece of code is created, organized and maintained in form, menu, PL/SQL or object library modules. By default, modules are saved as local files on your computer..

4.4.1 TYPES OF MODULES

Each module can be in one of the following three formats:

- **Binary modules.** These are binary files that can be read only by the Form Builder. When you create and save a module, Form Builder saves it as a binary file. When you open the module for later modifications, the Form Builder will ask you to specify a binary file. The extension for binary forms is .FMB, for menus .MMB, for PL/SQL libraries .PLL, and for object libraries .OLB. The binary modules you create are portable from one platform to another. In other words, you can develop a form in MS Windows, and then open that very same form in the Macintosh version of Oracle Developer and continue working with it.

- **Executable modules.** These are files in machine-readable format that are created when the modules are compiled. The default extensions for forms is .FMX, for menus is .MMX and for PL/SQL libraries is .PLX.Object libraries are not compiled and remain in the binary format. From within the Form Builder, you can generate the module by selecting File | Administration | Compile File from the menu, or by pressing CTRL+T from the keyboard. You can also compile a module using the Form Compiler utility as explained in Chapter 1. Forms Runtime executes .FMX files and, implicitly, uses the .MMX, and .PLL (or .PLX) files, if menus or PL/SQL libraries are attached to the form or if there are objects subclassed from other objects stored in an object library. While Form Builder binary files are portable across platforms and operating systems, the same is not true for the executable files. You need to compile the binary modules in each platform where you intend to deploy the module, in order to create a valid executable file.
- **Text modules.** These are text files that contain the information about the module in a complicated but human-readable format that can be displayed in a text editor such as Notepad. The extension for forms is .FMT, for menus .MMT, for PL/SQL libraries .PLD, and for object libraries .OLT. One reason to convert a module to a text format is to place it under the control of a software version control utility for configuration management purposes.

The following sections describe some of the common actions performed on modules.

4.4.2 CREATING MODULES

To create a new module follow these steps:

1. Select File | New form the Form Builder menu. This displays the submenu of module types.
2. Select the type of module you want to create. It can be a form, menu, PL/SQL library, or object library.

The Form Builder creates the new module and assigns it a default name. Note that when you launch the Form Builder, it creates a new form module by default, ready for you to use. If you want to work with an existing module, this default module is removed from the module list in the Navigator as soon as you open the other module.

4.4.3 OPENING MODULES

To open an existing module, select File | Open from the Form Builder menu, or click the Open icon in the Object Navigator toolbar, or press CTRL+O from the keyboard. The standard Open dialog box will be displayed (see Figure 4.3). In this dialog box you can specify the drive, directory and file name of the module you want to open. For the selected directory, you can list only the form modules (.FMB), menu modules (.MMB), PL/SQL modules (.PLL), or object library modules (.OLB).

4.4.4 SAVING MODULES

To save an existing file, select File | Save from the menu, click the Save icon, or press CTRL+S from the keyboard. To save a new file or to save an existing file under a new name, select File | Save As from the menu. A dialog box very similar to the one shown in Figure 4.3 appears. The only difference between these dialog boxes is the title bar. It is 'Open' or 'Save As,' depending on the command you are issuing. Specify the location and the name of the file you want to save, and click OK.

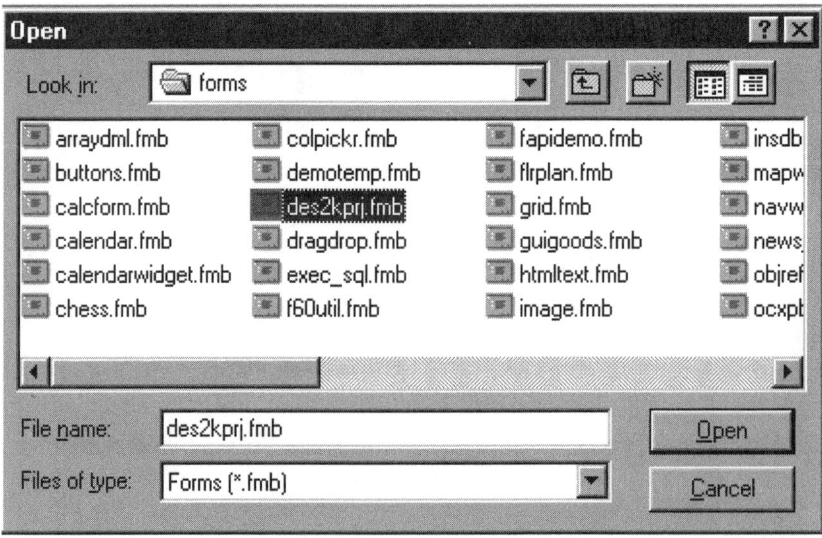

FIGURE 4.3 Open dialog box.

4.4.5 CLOSING MODULES

To close a module select File | Close from the menu or press CTRL+W form the keyboard. If there are unsaved changes in the module, you will be prompted to save them. If you choose to save a newly-created module, the Save As dialog box appears, where you can specify the name of the module.

4.4.6 REVERTING MODULES

If you want to throw away all changes made on a module since the last save, choose File | Revert from the menu. This is a shortcut to closing the module without saving and then opening it again.

4.4.7 CONVERTING MODULES

The following are the steps required to convert a module:

1. Select File | Administration | Convert... from the menu. The Convert dialog box appears (see Figure 4.4).
2. Select the module type. This can be 'Form,' 'Menu,' 'PL/SQL Libraries,' or 'Object Libraries.'
3. Enter the name of the module. If you want to search the directory tree for the module name, click the Browse button.
4. Specify the direction of conversion. It can be either 'Binary-to-Text' or 'Text-to-Binary.'
5. Click Convert. The module is converted according to your specifications.

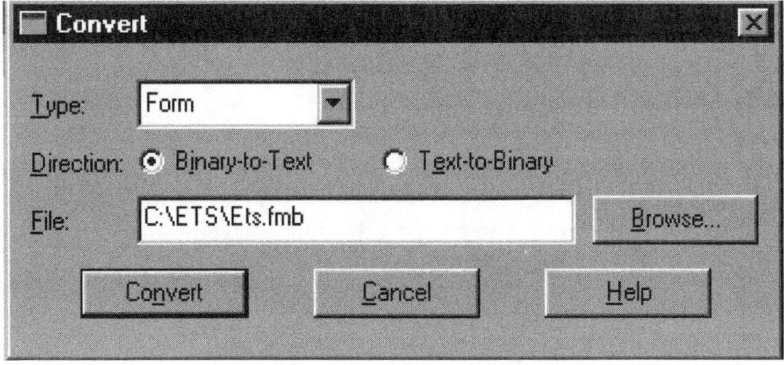

FIGURE 4.4 Convert dialog box.

4.5 STORING MODULES IN THE DATABASE

By default, modules are stored as files on your local systems hard drive. However, Form Builder and all the other Oracle Developer tools have a rather unique feature that allows you to store the modules in the Oracle RDBMS. This section explains how to store and access the modules in the database.

4.5.1 PREPARING THE DATABASE TO STORE MODULES

Together with the Oracle Developer software, Oracle Corporation provides the necessary SQL scripts to create the appropriate database objects that will store the information about modules. These scripts are located in the Oracle Developer Admin program group. The first step you need to take is to create the Oracle Developer common database objects. These objects are used to store Oracle Developer Forms, Reports, and Graphics modules. To create these objects follow these actions:

1. Click Start | Oracle Developer Admin | Oracle Developer Build program item. The program invokes SQL*Plus.
2. Supply the password for SYSTEM as prompted by the program.
3. Supply the database connect string as it applies to your environment.

After this, the program executes the script and exits SQL*Plus.

The next step is to grant access to these objects to all users that will need to store the modules in the database. The following are the actions required to perform these grants:

1. Click Start | Oracle Developer Admin | Oracle Developer Grant program item. The program invokes SQL*Plus.
2. Supply the password for SYSTEM as prompted by the program.
3. Supply the database connect string as it applies to your environment.
4. Enter the user name to whom you want to grant access. If you want to grant the privilege to several users, supply their names, separated by commas. This script will grant access to the common Oracle Developer objects to the users you specify and then prompt you again for a user name. After you provide a name, the script will grant access to the form-specific objects for this user. The same events will be repeated for Reports and Graphic Objects.

4.5.2 SETTING MODULE ACCESS OPTIONS

As mentioned earlier, by default modules are stored and accessed from the file system. To change this default behavior, select Tools | Preferences... from the

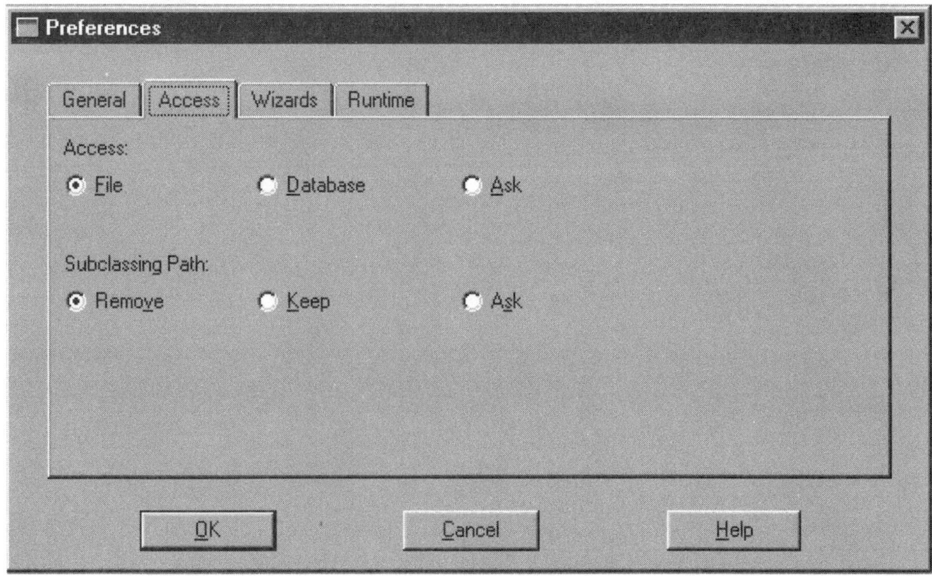

FIGURE 4.5 The Access tab of the Preferences dialog box.

menu. When the Preferences dialog box is displayed, switch to the Access tab shown in Figure 4.5.

The three radio items in the Access group are the options you want to set. By default, File is checked. If you check Database, modules can be opened from and saved to the database only. If you select Ask, each time you open or save a module, you will see the Filter dialog box shown in Figure 4.6. Here you can specify whether you want to work with file or database modules.

4.5.3 OPENING AND SAVING

Everything that was said in the Sections 4.4.3 and 4.4.4 about opening and saving modules in the file system applies here as well, with one exception. When work-

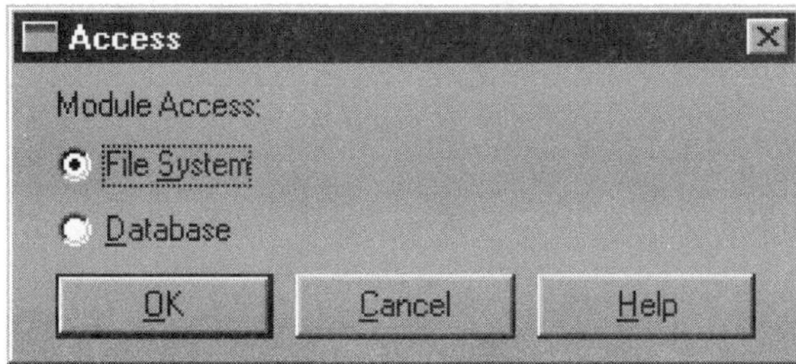

FIGURE 4.6 The Filter dialog box.

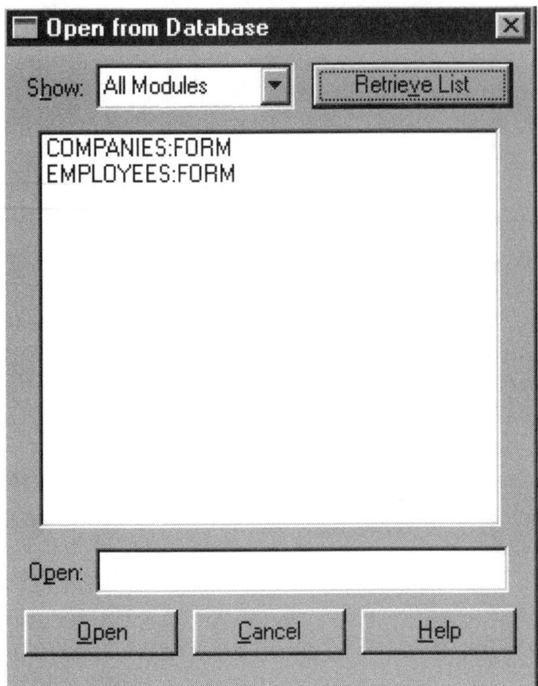

FIGURE 4.7 The Open from Database dialog box.

ing with database modules, the standard Windows dialog boxes are replaced with dialog boxes similar to the one shown in Figure 4.7.

This dialog box is displayed when you attempt to open a module. To retrieve a list of modules stored in the database that you can open, click the Retrieve List button. Then, select the desired module from the list and click Open button.

The dialog box that is displayed when you try to save a module to the database is similar to the one shown in Figure 4.7. The only difference is the title of the dialog, which now is Save in Database. The name of the text field where you specify the module name and of the button you click to perform the action is now 'Save' instead of 'Open'.

4.5.4 DELETING AND RENAMING

When working with modules stored in files, deleting and renaming are carried out by operating system commands, outside the Form Builder. For example, you can use the Windows Explorer to delete or rename modules. To delete a module from the *database* follow these steps:

1. Choose File | Administration | Delete from the menu. A dialog box similar to Figure 4.7 appears. In this case, the text label 'Open' is replaced by 'Delete.'
2. Locate the module you want to delete using the Retrieve command if necessary.
3. Click the Delete button.

To rename a module follow these steps:

1. Select File | Administration | Rename from the menu. The Rename in Database dialog box is displayed (see Figure 4.8).
2. Provide the name of the module to rename in the Old text field. Use the Retrieve functionality if necessary.

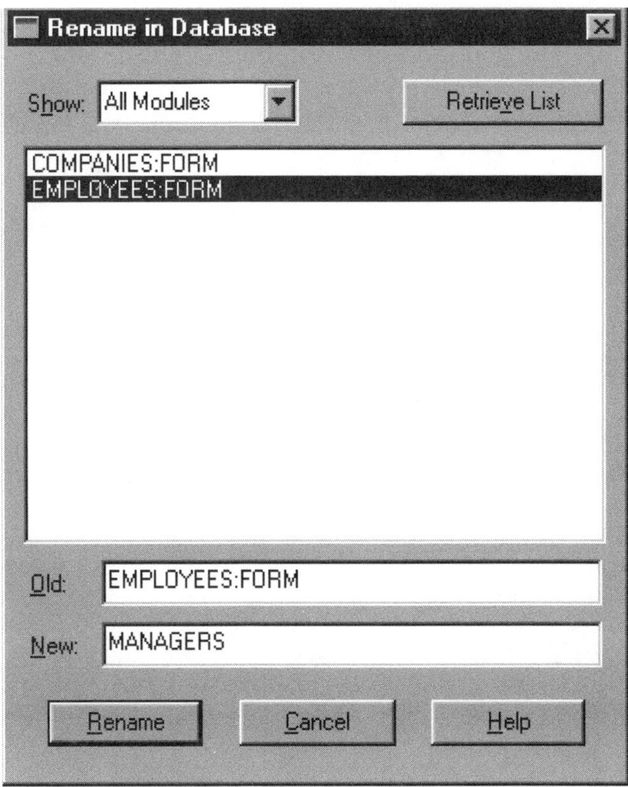

FIGURE 4.8 Rename in Database dialog box.

3. Enter the new name of the module in the New text field.
4. Click Rename button to proceed with the action.

4.5.5 GRANTING AND REVOKING ACCESS TO MODULES

If other users need to work with a module that you have stored in the database under your account, you must grant them access to it. When they are done with it, you may want to revoke their privileges. To grant or revoke access to your module follow these steps:

1. Select File | Administration | Module Access from the menu. The Grant Module dialog box appears (see Figure 4.9).
2. Specify the name of the module in the Module text field. Use the retrieve functionality if necessary.
3. Enter the name of user in the User text field.
4. Check the radio button at the top of the window that describes the action you want to perform: Grant or Revoke.
5. Click OK to perform the action.

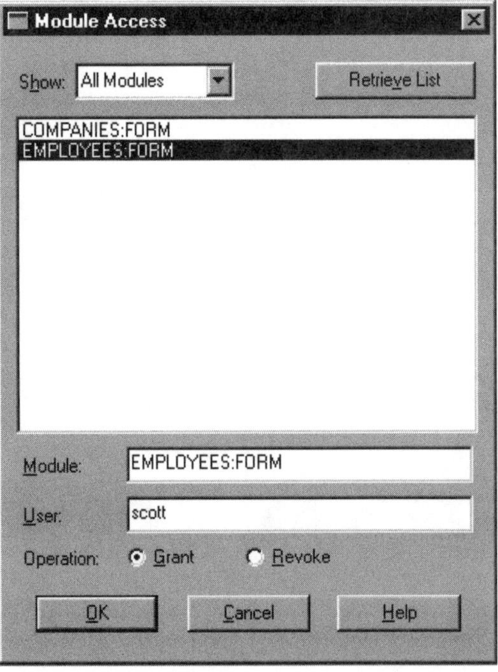

FIGURE 4.9 The Grant Module dialog box.

Unfortunately, there is not an easy way to grant access to multiple users with one single command, or to see which users have been granted access to the module. In order to administer effectively the privileges that other users have on your modules, you must rely on other forms of documentation for your application.

4.6 SUMMARY

This chapter offered an overview of Oracle Developer components, the Form Builder, and issues related to working with modules in the Form Builder. Main topics discussed were:

- **Overview of Oracle Developer**
  - Powerful Development Suite for Oracle Databases
  - Powerful Support for SQL
  - Rapid Application Development Tools
  - Graphical Users Interface Tools
  - Object-Oriented Programming Environment
- **Components of Oracle Developer**
- **Overview of the Form Builder**
  - Form Builder Components
  - Form Builder Menus
- **Working with Modules**
  - Types of modules
  - Creating Modules
  - Opening Modules
  - Saving Modules
  - Closing Modules
  - Reverting Modules
  - Converting Modules
- **Storing Modules in the Database**
  - Preparing the Database to Store Modules
  - Setting Module Access Options
  - Opening and Saving
  - Deleting and Renaming
  - Granting and Revoking Access to Modules

Chapter 5

OBJECT NAVIGATOR

Learn of the little nautilus to sail,
Spread the thin oar, and catch the driving gale.
—Alexander Pope

- Accessing the Object Navigator
- Components of Object Navigator
- Form Builder Object Types and Object Instances
- Getting Around Object Navigator
- Manipulating Objects in Object Navigator
- Different Views of Objects in Object Navigator
- Customizing the Object Navigator
- Summary

The Object Navigator is used to browse and manage the objects that make up a Form Builder application. These objects are organized hierarchically by object type. At the top level of the hierarchy are the main groups of objects: Forms, Menus, PL/SQL Libraries, Object Libraries, Built-in Packages, and Database Objects. Each of these groups can be expanded to several levels, thus allowing you to view all the child objects you need at a particular moment during your development activity. The Object Navigator provides ways to quickly search for and locate the objects contained in an application. From the Object Navigator, you can create new objects or delete existing ones, access and modify all their properties. You can also create or change PL/SQL code associated with an object. This chapter presents the Object Navigator and its functionality.

5.1 ACCESSING THE OBJECT NAVIGATOR

The Object Navigator is always present when the Form Builder is running. It is the first window to come up and the last one to go. However, as you work with other editors, it may be temporarily hidden from view. In these cases, there are three ways to display the Object Navigator window, as listed below:

- Select Tools | Object Navigator... from the Form Builder menu.
- Select Window | Object Navigator from the Form Builder menu.
- Press F3 on the keyboard.

5.2 COMPONENTS OF OBJECT NAVIGATOR

Figure 5.1 represents a typical Object Navigator window. The main part of it is occupied by an area where all the objects are displayed. This area will be called the Node Display area. Sometimes, it is also referred to as the application object tree, because it offers a hierarchical view of all the form, menu, PL/SQL library, or object library modules currently open. The horizontal toolbar of the Object Navigator contains the Context List and the Fast Search control. Along the left side of the window, there is a vertical toolbar. The following sections provide additional information about these four components.

The Object Navigator window is equipped with a horizontal and a vertical scroll bar. These allow you to display those areas of the window that contain objects but extend beyond the boundaries of the window at a particular moment. On top of the vertical scroll bar, there is the horizontal split pane bar. To the left of the horizontal scroll bar, you can see the vertical split pane bar. Split pane bars allow you to split the Object Navigator window in up to eight horizontal or verti-

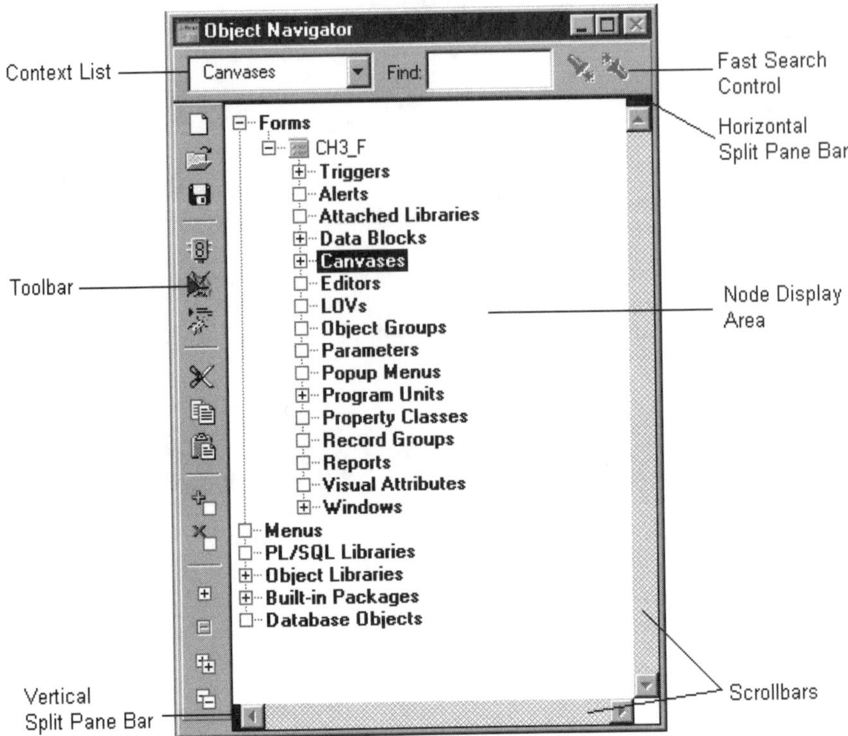

FIGURE 5.1 Components of the Object Navigator window.

cal panes that can display the information independently. Section 5.7.1 later in this chapter discusses the functionality of split pane bars.

5.2.1 NODE DISPLAY AREA

The Node Display area, as the name suggests, is the part of the Object Navigator window where all the objects accessible in the current Form Builder development session are listed. As Figure 5.1 shows, these objects belong to forms, menus, PL/SQL libraries, and object libraries. In addition, built-in program units and database objects can be displayed and accessed from here.

Each entry in the list is called a node. A node may represent an object type such as Forms, Data Blocks, and Triggers; or it may represent a user-created object instances such as ETS form, HW_ASSETS block, or MANUFACTURER item. Section 5.3 discusses in detail objects and their types in the Form Builder environment.

5.2.2 FAST SEARCH CONTROL

The Fast Search control enhances the search capabilities of Object Navigator. It is made up of a text field where search criteria are entered, and two iconic buttons that specify the direction of search. The Search Forward icon searches forward, from the current cursor position downward; whereas the Search Backward icon searches backwards. By default, the hierarchy tree is searched from top down, or forward. When the bottom of the list is reached, the search resumes from the top. To search backwards enter the search string and press Search Backwards icon. The search stops at the first entry in the tree that satisfies the search criteria. This entry is selected and highlighted by the Object Navigator.

The Fast Search control implements two powerful features that make it a very effective navigational tool. First, the objects are searched as you type. If, for example, T is entered in the text field, the search engine will locate the first object in the direction of search that begins with T. As more characters are typed in, the selection moves to entries of the tree that match the additional criteria. If the current selection does not change as you type, then there are no objects whose names match the string being entered. Second, the Object Navigator performs a depth-first search on all the nodes in the direction of search. For each node, all its children, and their children are searched recursively, even if they are not displayed in the Object Navigator in expanded state. When a match occurs, all the parent and ancestor nodes of the newly found entry are expanded as necessary.

5.2.3 CONTEXT LIST

The Context List displays all the modules currently open in the Object Navigator. If the name of a module is selected from the list, the Navigator jumps to the node that represents that module in the hierarchy tree. The Context List also displays the name of the object currently selected in the Navigator. This is the reason why it is often referred to as the Location Indicator. Together with the currently selected object, the Context List displays its parent and ancestors, indented based on their relationship to the object. Figure 5.2 shows typical information provided by the Context List.

In this example, the current object is WHEN-MOUSE-CLICK trigger, associated with CS_PHONE item. This item is a member of HW_ASSETS block, and they are all part of ETS form module. In the situation shown in Figure 5.2, two other modules are open in the Navigator: MAIN_MENU and STANDARDS.

The Context List becomes really advantageous if long lists of objects are displayed in the Navigator. For example, suppose you are working in a module and you want to use the built-in function CREATE_GROUP. You want to look up its syntax, so you click inside the Fast Search control and start typing the function's name. After you have typed the second letter, the search utility locates the function. At this point, there are several dozens of nodes between your original location in the object tree and the method CREATE_GROUP located in the STAN-

FIGURE 5.2 Context List.

DARD package, under the node Built-in Packages. As explained in the previous section, on the way to locate the method, the search utility has expanded all its parents.

Now, you want to navigate back to your module and continue work. If you decide to use the vertical scroll bar, it may take you a while to reach your destination. Use instead the Context List to navigate immediately to your module, as described by the following steps:

1. Click inside Context List field or on the list button to its right. The drop-down list displays all the open modules and the function CREATE_GROUP.
2. Select the module to which you want to navigate from the list.

The Navigator will select the module automatically. From there, it is not difficult to navigate to your location prior to the function lookup.

> **TIP**
>
> For simple functions such as CREATE_GROUP you can just enter your desired code. For more complex functions, though, you may discover that by the time you return to the initial location, you have forgotten some small detail in their specification. The Object Navigator allows you to paste the name or the arguments of the PL/SQL object directly in your code by selecting Navigator | Paste Names or Navigator | Paste Arguments from the menu. These menu items are enabled only if there is a PL/SQL Editor window open in the application.

5.2.4 TOOLBAR

On the left-hand side of the Object Navigator window, is a list of iconic buttons, also known as the Navigator toolbar. The toolbar allows you to access often-used functionality with a click of the mouse. The buttons are grouped by functionality in five segments. The first one contains buttons that create, open and save modules. The Run Form Client/Server, Run Form Web, and Debug buttons in the second segment facilitate the process of developing and testing applications. The third segment of buttons offers editing functionality such as cut, paste, and copy of objects. The buttons in the fourth segment are used to create or delete objects in the Navigator. Finally, the last four buttons that make up the fifth segment expand or collapse entries in the hierarchy tree.

The first three groups in the toolbar cover functionality that is available and accessible throughout the development process in the Form Builder. These buttons are available in other editors such as Layout Editor or Menu Editor. The last two segments of the toolbar cover functionality that is exclusive to the Object Navigator.

5.3 FORM BUILDER OBJECT TYPES AND OBJECT INSTANCES

As mentioned earlier, each entry listed in the Object Navigator's hierarchy tree is called a node. There are two kinds of nodes: object types and user created object instances. The following sections provide details for each of them.

5.3.1 FORM BUILDER OBJECT TYPES

The object types are names of categories of objects that can be used in Forms applications. Because each actual object falls under one of these categories, object type nodes are often called headings. Each object type node has the following format:

```
[Expand/Collapse Status Indicator] [Object Type Name]
```

The Expand/Collapse Status Indicator can have one of the following icons:

⊞ Indicates that this category of objects is already populated. There is at least one object of that type in the application. Clicking the icon expands the object heading and displays the objects of that type. For clarity, the objects are indented below the corresponding object type node.

☐ Indicates that there are no objects of this category in the application yet. Double-clicking the icon creates a new object of that type. This action is equivalent to clicking the Create icon in the toolbar, or to selecting Navigator | Create from the menu.

⊟ Indicates that the object category is already expanded. All the objects of that category are listed below the node, indented according to the hierarchy level. Clicking the icon collapses the object category and hides its instances from sight.

The Object Type Name is preset in the Form Builder, and cannot be changed during development activities. These names are typically in plural. Some examples of object types are: Forms, Data Blocks, Items, Menus, Menu Items, Attached Libraries, and Windows. Feel free to explore the Object Navigator and see all the other types of objects not mentioned here.

5.3.2 FORM BUILDER OBJECT INSTANCES

The object instances represent actual objects created and used in the application. Figure 5.3 shows a typical listing of object types and object instances in the Object Navigator. The module used here is a copy of the module ETS.FMB developed in Part I. It is provided in the companion CD-ROM under the name CH05.FMB.

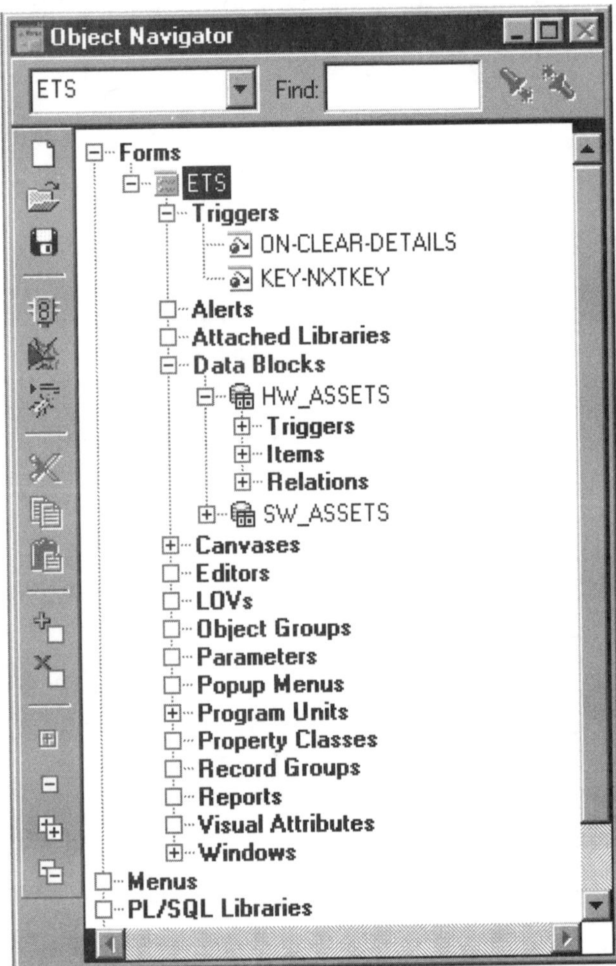

FIGURE 5.3 Object types and object instances.

In this figure, HW_ASSETS is an instance of object type Blocks. HW_ASSETS, like any block, may own three other types of objects: triggers, items, and relations. Because the expand/collapse status indicators of nodes Triggers, Items and Relations under HW_ASSETS contain the + indicator, you can conclude that this block contains at least one object of each these types.

Each object instance node has the following format:

```
[Expand/Collapse Status Indicator] [Object Type Icon]
[Object Name]
```

The Expand/Collapse Status Indicator can have one of the following states:

⊞ Indicates that this object may own other objects. Clicking the icon expands the object and displays the types of objects it may own. These types may be populated or not, depending on the particular application.

⊟ Indicates that the object is already expanded. Clicking the icon collapses the object and hides its children.

For objects that cannot have any descendants in the object hierarchy tree, the expand/collapse status indicator is not present. Such objects are also called atomic objects. In the example shown in Figure 5.3, the trigger ON-CLEAR-DETAILS is an atomic object. No other objects depend on it.

The Object Type Icon serves as a visual indicator of an object's type. Double-clicking this icon brings up the Property Palette for most of the objects, except for the following situations:

- Double-clicking the icon of canvases or any other dependent objects brings up a Layout Editor window for that canvas.
- Double-clicking the icon of PL/SQL objects, including triggers and program units brings up the PL/SQL Editor for the object.
- Double-clicking the icon of menus or any dependent objects brings up the Menu Editor.
- Double-clicking the icon of object libraries or any dependent objects brings up the Object Library editor.

The Object Name uniquely identifies the instance of an object in the application. For each newly created object, the Form Builder generates a name automatically. This name is formed by concatenating the object type or an abbreviation of it with a sequence-generated number. The sequence is set to 1 when the module is created. For each object created subsequently, the number increments by 1. Examples of such names are MODULE1, BLOCK2, ITEM10, WINDOW12, and LIB_029. Obviously, these names are not very helpful during development and application maintenance activities. You can easily change them to more descriptive names to facilitate your module development and maintenance.

5.4 GETTING AROUND OBJECT NAVIGATOR

Earlier in the chapter, you learned how to use the Context List and Fast Search utilities to locate and move to target objects in the Navigator. The following sections provide additional information about navigating, selecting, expanding, collapsing, and marking objects.

5.4.1 NAVIGATING AND SELECTING OBJECTS

The easiest way to navigate to and select an object is to click it in the area of the node list where the object is displayed. In order to do this, the target object must be visible in the hierarchy tree of the Object Navigator. If this is not the case, scrolling up and down the node list may be necessary. If the desired object is in a level of the hierarchy tree that is currently collapsed, expand the parent objects as necessary and then select the object. Expanding and collapsing are explained in Section 5.4.3. The Fast Search utility of the Object Navigator is very useful in locating target objects. This utility was discussed earlier in the chapter.

You can also use the arrow keys to navigate and select nodes in the Object Navigator. The up-arrow key navigates to the node immediately above the current node; the down-arrow key to the one immediately below.

5.4.2 SELECTING MULTIPLE OBJECTS

Using the mouse to select objects is not only easy but also powerful. This method allows selection of single or multiple objects. In order to better understand the process, perform the actions in the module CH5.FMB provided in the companion CD-ROM.

First, expand the blocks HW_ASSETS and SW_ASSETS so that their items are. Now select all the items that belong to HW_ASSETS block with the following actions.

1. Click the item SERIAL_NUM. It is selected.
2. SHIFT+CLICK the item CS_PHONE. All the items between SERIAL_NUM and CS_PHONE are selected.

This type of object selection is called range selection. In a range selection, all the entries between the initial and final selection points must be objects of the same type. When objects of a different type are included in the range, then only the objects of the same type that are in the same segment of the node list as the initial object are selected. As an example, try to select all the items of HW_ASSETS and SW_ASSETS blocks.

1. Click the item SERIAL_NUM in the HW_ASSETS block. The item is selected.
2. SHIFT+CLICK the item PURCHASE_DT in the SW_ASSETS block.

All the items in the HARDWARE block are selected, but none from the SOFTWARE block is included in the range. In order to select objects that are not adjacent, the CTRL key is used in conjunction with mouse clicks. For example, to select the items NAME, MODEL and PURCHASE_DT of the HW_ASSETS block, you would take the following steps:

1. Click the item NAME in the HW_ASSETS block. The item is selected.
2. CTRL+CLICK first MODEL then PURCHASE_DT. They are selected as you click.

If you want to de-select an already selected object, simply CTRL+CLICK the item. For obvious reasons, the selecting methods described above are also known as Shift-clicking and Control-clicking. The two methods can be combined to provide more flexible and powerful selecting capabilities. For example, using Shift- and Control-clicking, you can select all the items from HW_ASSETS and SW_ASSETS blocks with the following actions:

1. Click the item SERIAL_NUM in HW_ASSETS block. The item is selected.
2. SHIFT+CLICK CS_PHONE in HW_ASSETS block. All the items in this block are selected.
3. CTRL+CLICK SW_COST in the SW_ASSETS block. The item is added to the already selected items from HW_ASSETS block.
4. SHIFT+CLICK PURCHASE_DT in SHW_ASSETS block. All the items in the HW_ASSETS and SW_ASSETS blocks are now selected.

Once the objects are selected, you can perform group operations on them such as moving them to another module, deleting, or setting common properties. As a matter of fact, performing these types of operations is the main purpose for selecting multiple objects.

5.4.3 EXPANDING AND COLLAPSING NODES

In order to better manage and organize the information about the many objects involved in an application, the Form Builder provides expanding and collapsing services. These services include the expand/collapse status indicators that show the state of a node and commands to actually expand or collapse nodes in the Navigator. The different status indicators were explained earlier in the chapter. The rest of this section deals only with the commands to perform these operations.

There are four commands to expand or collapse nodes in the Object Navigator. The Expand command displays all the subnodes at the hierarchical level immediately below the currently selected object. It can be accessed in one of the following three equivalent methods:

- ❑ Click the Indicator icon on the left of the node.
- ❑ Click the Expand icon on the toolbar.
- ❑ Select Navigator | Expand from the menu.

The Collapse command hides the subnodes immediately below the currently selected object. Any of the following commands will collapse a node in the Navigator:

- ❑ Click the Indicator icon on the left of the node.
- ❑ Click the Collapse icon on the toolbar.
- ❑ Select Navigator | Collapse from the menu.

The commands Expand and Collapse act upon nodes that are in the hierarchy level immediately below that of the current node. In cases when you need to display or hide the whole hierarchical tree of objects below a certain object, you can use the commands Expand All and Collapse All.

The Expand All command displays all the subnodes at every hierarchical level below the currently selected object. It expands recursively to the atomic level each node under the current node. It can be accessed in one of the following equivalent methods:

- ❑ Shift-click the Indicator icon on the left of the node.
- ❑ Click the Expand All icon on the toolbar.
- ❑ Select Navigator | Expand All from the menu.

The Collapse All command hides all the subnodes below the currently selected object. It collapses all the hierarchies under the current node. To perform this action in the Navigator issue one of the following commands:

- ❑ Shift-click the Indicator icon on the left of the node.
- ❑ Click the Collapse All icon in the toolbar.
- ❑ Select Navigator | Collapse All from the menu.

It was mentioned earlier that up-arrow and down-arrow keys can be used to navigate between nodes. Left and right arrow keys combine navigational and expand/collapse functionality. The left-arrow key navigates to the parent node of the currently selected object and collapses it. The right-arrow key expands the current node and moves the focus to the first node immediately below it.

5.4.4 BOOKMARKING OBJECTS

Bookmarks are very helpful when you want to access Form Builder objects quickly. You can place a bookmark on any node in the hierarchy tree by selecting the node and choosing Navigator | Add Bookmark from the menu. Once a node is bookmarked, the Form Builder can navigate to it from any position on the Navigator window or any other Editor window. To navigate to a bookmarked object, select Navigator | Go to Bookmark from the menu. If the target node is collapsed, the Object Navigator will expand the object tree as necessary.

You can set only one bookmark in each Object Navigator pane. Later in the chapter you will see what the panes are and how to use multiple panes. A bookmark remains effective until one of the following events occur:

- A new object is bookmarked, thus overriding the current bookmark.
- The bookmarked object is deleted.
- The module that contains the bookmarked object is closed.
- Form Builder application terminates.

5.5 MANIPULATING OBJECTS IN OBJECT NAVIGATOR

The Object Navigator not only allows you to navigate to, search for, and select objects, but also gives you the possibility to act upon these objects. Actions such as create, delete, copy, and paste, can be accessed from other specialized editors, as well. For example, items can be created and modified in the Layout Editor, triggers and program units in the PL/SQL Editor, and menu items in the Menu Editor. But, with its unified view of all the application objects, the Navigator gives uniformity and coherence to these actions. With its graphical view of the hierarchy tree, Navigator also facilitates a great deal the process of placing an object in the appropriate position in the application object tree.

5.5.1 CREATING OBJECTS

Before creating an object, you must decide the location of that object in the Navigator's hierarchy. This location depends on the type of the object. Form-dependent objects such as alerts, data blocks, canvases, or program units, go right under the respective object type nodes. If the new object depends from objects other than the modules, than the parent object must be selected first. For example, before adding an item you must decide the block where that item will go; before creating a trigger you must first select the object to which the trigger will be attached.

If there are no objects of the same type as the object you want to create, the expand/collapse status indicator of the object type node will be the "empty box" icon. As it was explained earlier, double-clicking this icon creates a new object.

If objects of the same type exist, select the object type node or one of the existing objects to indicate the location where the new object will be created. Then, take any of the following actions to create the new object:

- Click the Create icon on the toolbar.
- Select Navigator | Create from the menu.

5.5.2 DELETING OBJECTS

You can delete one or more selected objects with one of the following commands:

- Press DELETE on the keyboard.
- Click the Delete icon on the toolbar.
- Select Edit | Clear from the menu.

In all cases, the Navigator will prompt you to confirm that you want to delete the selected objects. If you decide to proceed with the operation, the Navigator will remove the selected object from the tree. If the delete operation is performed on an object type node, then all the objects underneath the node will be deleted. The only exception to this is when the selected node is a module. In that case, the operation closes the module.

ALERT

Be careful when you delete objects in the Object Navigator, since this command is not reversible. If the deleted object existed before the last File | Save command, either issue a Revert command, or close the module without saving, and reopen it to get the object back. Of course, in the process you will lose all the work since the last time the module was saved. That's why saving your work periodically and frequently protects you from accidental losses of precious work efforts.

5.5.3 CUTTING AND COPYING OBJECTS

A milder form of deleting an object is to cut it. Cutting places the object in the clipboard—a memory buffer that temporarily stores the last copied or cut object. Once cut, the object will remain in the clipboard until the next cut operation. It can be pasted in the original position, or in as many other locations in the application as necessary. The following are several ways to cut selected objects:

- ❑ Press CTRL+X on the keyboard.
- ❑ Click the Cut icon on the toolbar.
- ❑ Select Edit | Cut from the menu.

If you want to place objects in the clipboard, but not remove them from their current position in the hierarchy tree, then select the desired objects and copy them. The ways to copy a selection are

- ❑ Press CTRL+C on the keyboard.
- ❑ Click the Copy icon on the toolbar.
- ❑ Select Edit | Copy from the menu.

5.5.4 PASTING AND DUPLICATING OBJECTS

Certain applications may contain objects that have identical or similar properties. To reduce development efforts, the Form Builder allows you to duplicate objects or copy and paste them to the desired location. To duplicate an object first select it, then choose Edit | Duplicate from the menu. Alternatively, you may press CTRL+D from the keyboard. A duplicate copy is created immediately below the current selection.

To paste an object to the desired location, first place it in the clipboard by either copying or cutting it. Then click where you want to insert the new object and paste the contents from the clipboard in one of the following ways:

- ❑ Press CTRL+V on the keyboard.
- ❑ Click the Paste icon on the toolbar.
- ❑ Select Edit | Paste from the menu.

When pasting objects, the Navigator ensures that they are inserted in appropriate locations, according to their types. For example, items can be pasted only under data blocks, but not under windows or alerts. Copying and duplicating conserves the hierarchy and ownership of objects as well. If the original object contains children, its copy will have exactly the same children. Thus, if you copy a block, you will copy all the triggers and items associated with it.

5.5.5 MOVING OBJECTS

Often there is a need to move objects from one location to another in the Navigator. For example, you want to rearrange the TAB order of items in a certain block, or you want to move well-performing program units between modules and the database. One way to achieve this is to cut and paste. Another way is to use the drag-and-drop functionality that the Navigator provides. As with copying and pasting, Navigator will ensure that the drag-and-drop actions do not conflict with object types. It will not allow you, for example, to move triggers under alerts or windows under blocks. In addition, if you want to move multiple objects with one action, they must all be of the same type. In other words, you may move items or block-level triggers from one block to another separately, but you cannot mix and match the types.

5.5.6 RENAMING OBJECTS

When new objects are created, the Object Navigator assigns them automatically a name. These names indicate the type of the object (alert, data block, item, and so on.). They are appended with digits generated internally by the Form Builder to enforce their uniqueness. While assuring the consistency and robustness of the application, names such as BLOCK2 and ITEM13, do not add any value to its readability and maintainability. The need for informative and mnemonic names becomes crucial for applications developed by teams of programmers. Especially in such cases, you should select names that describe the purpose and functionality of the application objects clearly and concisely. One way to rename an object is to follow these steps:

1. Select the object to be renamed.
2. Click the name of the object again. Be careful not to double-click the object, as this will open the Property Palette or another editor.
3. The cursor is placed inside the name field and the current name is selected.
4. Edit the object's name as needed.

When renaming objects, additional checking must be done to ensure that there are no referencing conflicts in the application. Frequently, triggers, functions and procedures reference objects by name. If the object's name changes, the new name should be propagated in all the statements that use it throughout the application. Unfortunately, this process may be very tedious at times. Therefore, it is important to establish naming conventions for the application early in the development stage, before any extensive coding is done. Another way to avoid these situations is to write object-independent code. This is code in which the objects are not referenced directly by their name, but indirectly. In the chapters to come you will see several examples of such statements.

> **WARNING**
>
> Be particularly careful when renaming names of items. If an item represents a database column, its name must be exactly like that of the column name, otherwise the form will not compile.

5.6 DIFFERENT VIEWS OF OBJECTS IN OBJECT NAVIGATOR

In all the examples presented thus far, you have used the Object Navigator in its default and most common state. Other ways to view the objects of an application exist as well. The following sections discuss each of them.

5.6.1 OWNERSHIP VIEW

This is the default and most comprehensive view offered by the Navigator. It allows you to look at all the objects in an application, organized by ownership hierarchy. The position and indentation of objects in the hierarchical tree clearly indicate who their parent objects are and what other objects they own. This hierarchy represents the internal ordering of objects used by the Form Builder, and was discussed throughout this chapter.

5.6.2 VISUAL VIEW

Sometimes, it is helpful to organize objects in an application from a visual perspective. In other words, display only the objects that will be visible in the user interface, and hide the remaining objects. For this purpose, you can use the Visual view of the Object Navigator. To switch to Visual view, select View | Visual View radio item from the menu. To switch back to Ownership view, select View | Ownership View radio item from the menu. Figure 5.4 represents the module CH5.FMB in Visual View.

As you can see from this figure, the Visual view displays only visual attributes, windows, canvases, tab pages (when present) and items. In this mode, items are no longer owned by blocks, but by the canvases or tab pages on which they are located. The fictitious canvas NULL_Canvas owns items that are not assigned to a canvas. Each canvas, is owned by the window to which it is attached. The virtual window named NULL_Window owns canvases that are not assigned to any window. Note here that if a canvas is assigned to multiple windows, the Visual view of the Object Navigator will display it under each of these windows. The information is repeated in the display, although the canvases and their items are not replicated in the module. Once again, this is what the windows will contain when users will see them.

5.6.3 DISPLAYING ONLY OBJECTS THAT CONTAIN PL/SQL CODE

Sometimes, it is useful to display only PL/SQL objects and the application objects to which they may be attached. This feature becomes important especially in the stage of the development where the layout and interface design are more or less completed. The main activities now are coding and debugging triggers, proce-

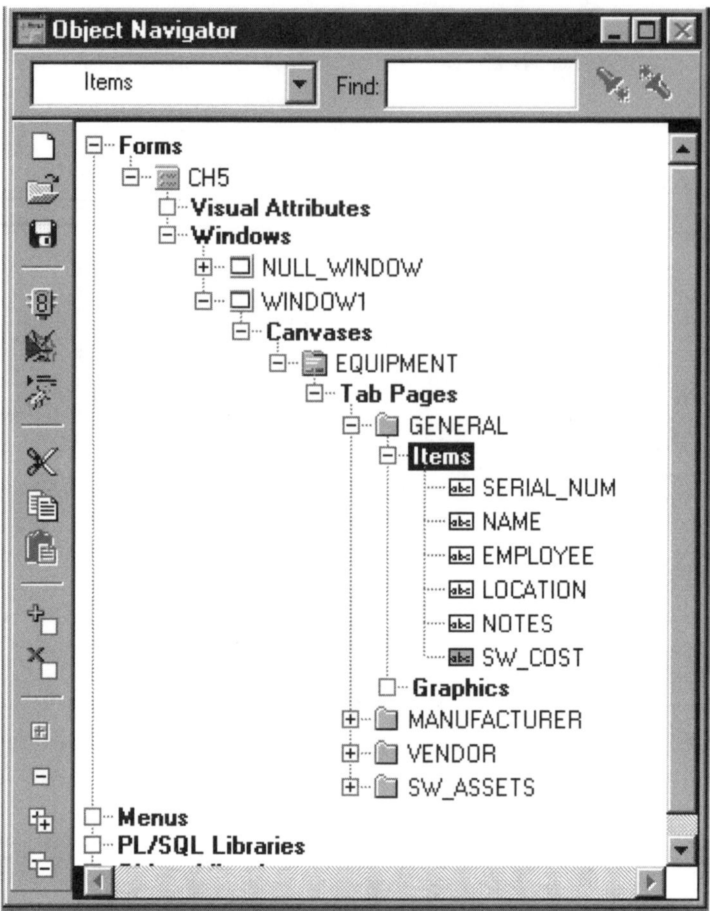

FIGURE 5.4 Visual View of Object Navigator.

dures, and functions. It may be convenient to keep around in the Navigator only those objects that are directly involved in these activities.

Objects that may contain PL/SQL code are triggers, attached libraries, blocks and their items, program units, and property classes. To view only these objects check the item View | Show PL/SQL only from the Form Builder menu. By default, this option is not set. This option can be set in both Ownership and Visual views, but it has effect only in the Ownership view. As mentioned earlier, the Visual view displays visual attributes, canvases, items, and windows. Figure 5.5 shows the Ownership view of CH5.FMB with the option 'Show PL/SQL only' set.

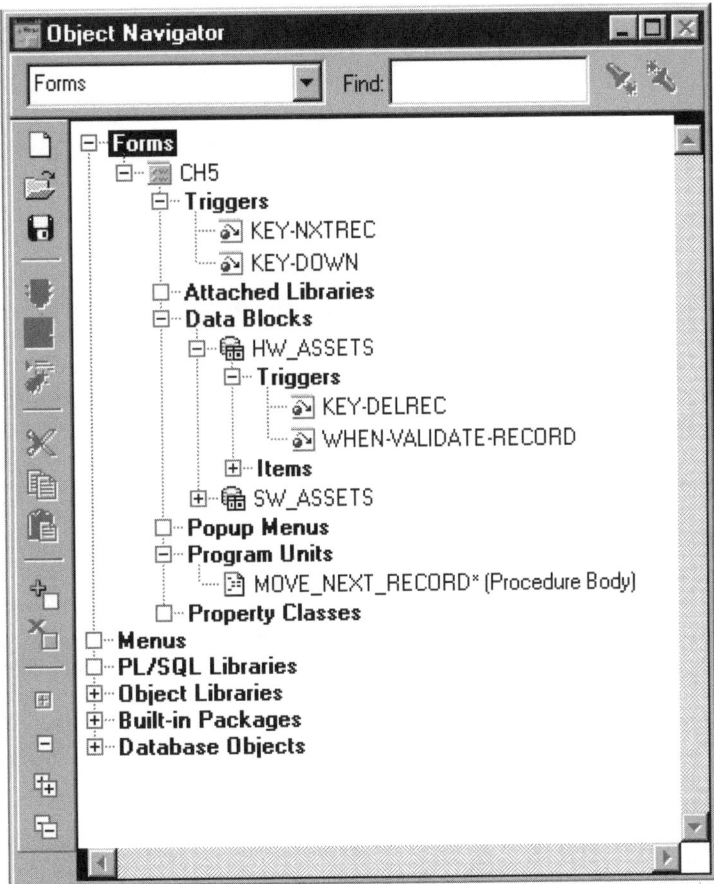

FIGURE 5.5 Ownership View of Object Navigator with Only Objects with PL/SQL option set.

5.7 CUSTOMIZING THE OBJECT NAVIGATOR

When working with the Object Navigator, you may want to further customize its behavior. The following two sections describe how to set up multiple panes of the Navigator and how to synchronize other open editors with the Navigator.

5.7.1 WORKING WITH MULTIPLE PANES

Form Builder applications can be made up of a large number of objects, resulting in long lists of entries in the Navigator's hierarchy tree. During the development process, you may need to view objects located in remote locations in this tree.

Rather than scrolling up and down each time you need to access these objects, you can use multiple panes in the Object Navigator. Each pane is an identical view of the Navigator, which can be scrolled independently of views in other panes. There can be up to eight panes in the Navigator window. This window can be split either in horizontal or vertical panes. Examples in this section will focus on vertical panes. Splitting the Navigator in horizontal panes is a similar process that you can easily practice on your own. Figure 5.6 represents the form CH5.FMB displayed in two vertical panes.

Split bars are used to divide the Navigator window in different panes. They are thick black lines attached to the scroll bars of the Navigator window. The horizontal split bar is on top of the vertical scroll bar, and the vertical split bar is on the left of the horizontal scroll bar. If the Navigator window is not large enough, one split bar, or both of them, may be hidden. To display them, simply enlarge or maximize the window. When the mouse moves on top of split bars, it changes shape to the horizontal split indicator, or the vertical split indicator, as the case may be.

Use the horizontal split bars to divide the Navigator window in two panes, similar to Figure 5.6. Open the module CH5.FMB in the Form Builder and follow these steps:

1. Move the cursor on the vertical split bar to the left of the horizontal scroll bar of the Navigator window. The mouse shape changes to the vertical split indicator.
2. Hold down the mouse button. The thick black line of the split bar now extends all the way across the screen to the top of the Navigator window.
3. Holding the button down, drag the mouse to the right. The long vertical split line follows the mouse movement across the window.
4. Drop the split line in the middle of the Navigator window. A new pane is created.

Once a pane is created, you can grab the split bar with the mouse, and adjust the size of each pane to your preference. Expand objects as necessary and scroll up and down each pane to obtain a picture of the Navigator similar to Figure 5.6.

To remove an existing pane, grab the pane's split handle and move it outside the pane area. For example, to remove the vertical pane you just created, grab the vertical split bar and move it all the way either to the left or to the right of the Navigator window.

5.7.2 SYNCHRONIZING CONTENTS OF EDITORS

Objects in Form Builder can be accessed not only from the Object Navigator, but also from other editors such as the Layout Editor, or the Menu Editor. All these editors may be open at the same time during the development process. It is un-

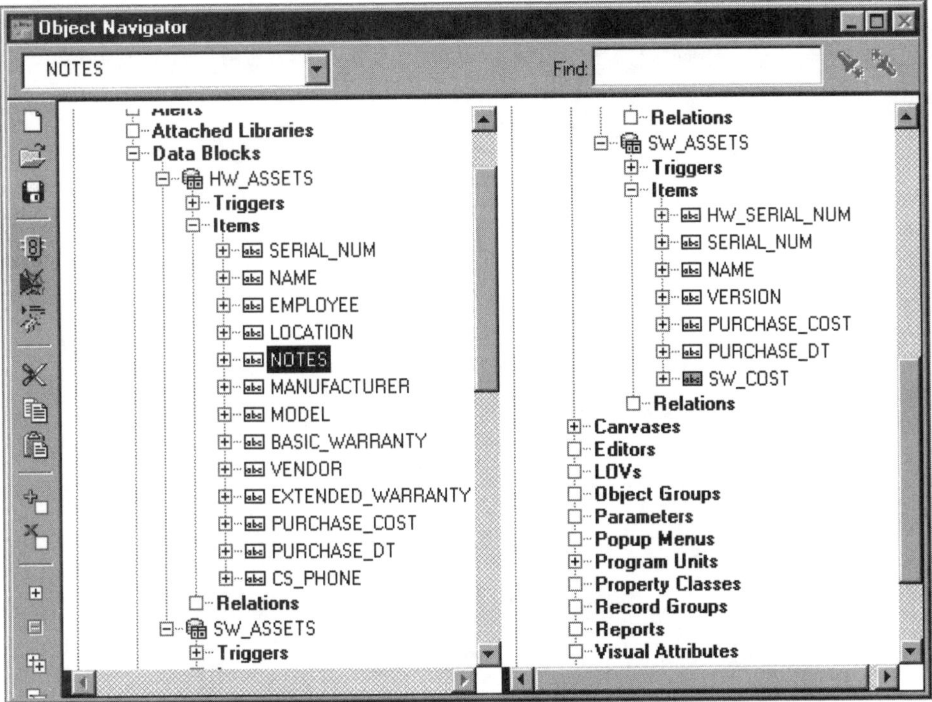

FIGURE 5.6 Vertical panes of the Object Navigator.

derstandable and convenient to require that if an object is selected, say, in the Layout Editor, the corresponding entry in the Object Navigator will be automatically selected, and vice versa. The Object Navigator has a property that allows you to synchronize the contents of these editors with the selections in the Navigator. When the Synchronize property is set, selecting any item in the Navigator simultaneously selects that item in the other editors.

To set the Synchronize property, select Navigator | Synchronize from the menu. This is a check menu item. If it is checked, synchronizing is on, otherwise it is off. If the Synchronize property is off, then the selections in the Navigator are independent of those in the Layout and Menu Editors.

Most of the time you are likely to want the synchronization on, but there are occasions when it comes handy to turn it off. Suppose, for example, that you have selected several items in the Layout Editor for alignment and resizing purposes. Suddenly you realize that you need to look up the properties of another item that is displayed in the Navigator window. If the Synchronize property is on and you click the item in the Navigator, that item will be selected in the Layout Editor, thus de-selecting all your previous items. This does not occur if Synchronize is off.

5.8 SUMMARY

This chapter explained the components and properties of the Object Navigator. It also focused on the different actions that you can perform in this environment. Some key concepts covered were:

- **Accessing the Object Navigator**
- **Components of Object Navigator**
  - Node Display Area
  - Fast Search Control
  - Context List
  - Toobar
- **Form Builder Object Types and Object Instances**
  - Form Builder Object Types
  - Form Builder Object Instances
- **Getting Around Object Navigator**
  - Navigating and Selecting Objects
  - Selecting Multiple Objects
  - Expanding and Collapsing Nodes
  - Bookmarking Objects
- **Manipulating Objects in Object Navigator**
  - Creating Objects
  - Deleting Objects
  - Cutting and Copying Objects
  - Pasting and Duplicating Objects
  - Moving Objects
  - Renaming Objects
- **Different Views of Objects in Object Navigator**
  - Ownership View
  - Visual View
  - Displaying only Objects that Contain PL/SQL Code
- **Customizing the Object Navigator**
  - Working with Multiple Panes
  - Synchronizing Contents of Editors

The following table describes the software assets that were discussed in this chapter. From the main HTML page of the software utilities provided with the book follow the links *Software* and *Chapter 5* to access these assets:

ASSET NAME	DESCRIPTION
CH05.FMB	A copy of the ETS module created in Part I.

Chapter 6

Layout Editor

Right now a moment of time is fleeting by! Capture its reality in paint!
—Paul Cézanne

- Accessing the Layout Editor
- Components of the Layout Editor
- Working with Objects in Layout Editor
- Setting Visual Attributes in Layout Editor
- Customizing the Layout Editor
- Customizing Graphics Options
- Customizing Color Palettes
- Summary

The Layout Editor allows you to graphically view, access and modify the interface objects of your applications. These objects establish and maintain the communication of users with their data stored in database structures. When creating a landscape, artists paint on a canvas. When the work is completed, the canvas is framed and exhibited to viewers. Metaphorically, creating a Developer/2000 Forms application is a similar process. The Layout Editor provides you with the tools to create and manipulate different objects on a canvas. The canvas then is "framed," or attached to a window. It is through these windows that users can access the objects of the application at runtime. This chapter will explain the components and functionality of the Layout Editor.

6.1 ACCESSING THE LAYOUT EDITOR

You can access the Layout Editor in one of the following ways:

- Select Tools | Layout Editor from the Form Builder menu.
- Select Layout Editor from the popup menu displayed by a right-button mouse click.
- In Object Navigator, double-click the canvas you want to edit or one of its components.

If there are no canvases in the form, the Layout Editor will create one when invoked. If there is only one canvas, the Layout Editor automatically displays it. If there is more than one canvas, and the Layout Editor is not launched when one of them is selected, the Form Builder displays a list of canvases first, from which one can be chosen for editing. When a canvas is loaded in a Layout Editor window, the name of the canvas becomes part of the title of that layout window. If you want to return to that layout window, simply find it in the list of open windows under the Window menu displayed at the top of your screen.

Each instance, or window, of the Layout Editor displays exactly one canvas. In situations where you need to work with multiple canvases simultaneously, you can display each canvas in its own Layout Editor window. However, it is a good habit to close a window when you finish editing the canvas. You will free precious system resources and make them available for other activities in your environment.

6.2 COMPONENTS OF THE LAYOUT EDITOR

Figure 6.1 represents a Layout Editor window. This window is made up of several components. The most important one is the layout work area, where objects are created, arranged and edited. Each window has a horizontal toolbar and a

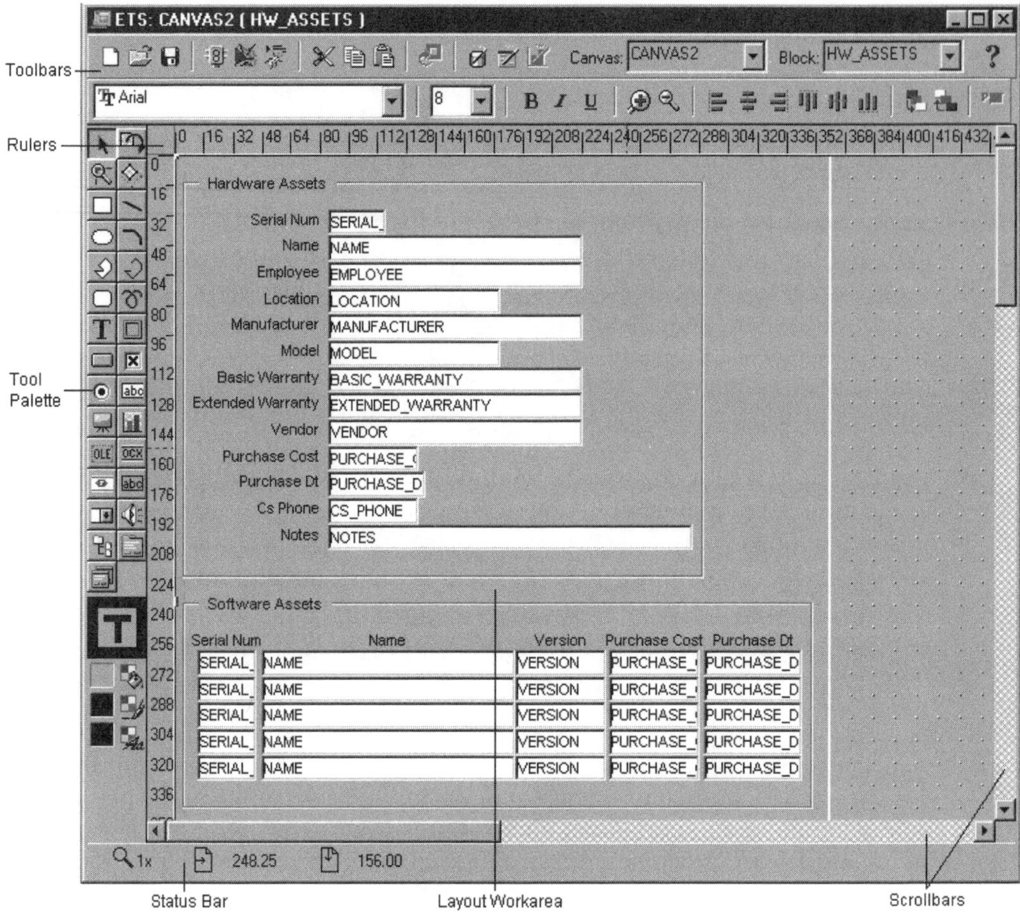

FIGURE 6.1 Components of the Layout Editor window.

vertical toolbar, called tool palettes. At the bottom of the window, the status bar displays important information such as the mouse position and the magnifying level. The following sections provide detailed information for each of these components.

6.2.1 LAYOUT WORK AREA

The layout work area allows you to access all the objects on a canvas. Its size does not depend on the size of the Layout Editor window. If this window is not large enough to display the whole canvas, vertical and horizontal scrollbars may be used to navigate to the parts, which will not fit on the screen.

The canvas displayed in the layout work area is itself an object that is displayed by default. You can hide it by unchecking the View | Show Canvas from the Layout Editor menu. Another basic object that is always present in the Layout Editor window is the View of the canvas. The view is the area of the canvas that is shown to users when they run the application. Form Builder operates with five types of canvases: content, horizontal toolbar, vertical toolbar, stacked, and tab canvases. Stacked canvases are the only ones that are not attached to a window. For this type of canvases, views have a real effect in what the users can see; for the other types of canvases, the view object is irrelevant and superseded by the window object. By default the view is hidden, but it can be displayed if needed. To display the view of a stacked canvas check the View | Show View menu item from the Layout Editor menu. This menu item is enabled only when the Layout Editor window displays a stacked canvas.

On top and along the left side of the Layout Editor window there are two rulers, also shown in Figure 6.1. These rulers form a system of coordinates for the window. Its origin is the top left corner of the canvas and the unit of measurement can be expressed in inches, centimeters, points, or character cells. Point is the default unit. Section 6.5.1 later in this chapter explains how to change the measurement unit. By expressing the distance of the current mouse position from the origin of coordinates, the rulers assist you in the process of sizing and moving objects. Rulers are displayed by default, but can be hidden by unchecking the View | Rulers menu item.

The current position of the cursor is projected on the rulers in the form of two markers. These are small lines that slide alongside both rulers as the mouse moves in the layout work area. They are hidden or displayed together with the rulers. To further assist you in the process of creating, sizing and moving objects, the Layout Editor provides horizontal and vertical ruler guides. These are dashed lines that can be very useful especially when aligning objects in the work area. To create a ruler guide, click either the horizontal or the vertical ruler, and, holding the mouse button down, drag the ruler to the desired location. Multiple ruler guides can be created and used. When you don't want to use a guide any longer, simply drag it over the respective ruler to remove it. Ruler guides can also be hidden without being removed. To do this, uncheck the View | Ruler Guides menu item. All the guides will be hidden from sight. When you check the View | Ruler again, the guides appear in the previous positions.

To help positioning objects in the work area, the Layout Editor provides a grid. The grid is a set of horizontal and vertical lines that cover the whole work area. The distance between the lines, also known as the grid density, is specified in the units used by the ruler, and is set in the Ruler Settings dialog box. In Section 6.5.2 you will see how to use the Ruler Settings dialog box. The grid can be hidden from view by unchecking View | Grid menu item. If the canvas is visible, as in Figure 6.1, it will cover the grid.

6.2.2 TOOLBAR

On top of the layout work area, there is the Layout Editor toolbar. It is shown separately in Figure 6.2. The toolbar is made up of two rows of icons and controls that provide quick access to often-used functionality within the Layout Editor. The first row contains a number of icons that can also be found in other Form Builder windows such as the Object Navigator and Menu Editor. The first three buttons are used to create, open, and save modules. The next three buttons run the form in client/server, Web or debug mode. The following three icons offer editing functionality for objects such as cut, copy and paste. The tenth icon on the toolbar allows you to update the layout of the canvas after object properties that affect it have been modified in other Form Builder components. And the last three icons in this toolbar invoke the Data Block, Layout, and Chart wizards. The first horizontal toolbar ends with two list boxes. The first one contains a list of all the canvases in the module and allows you to replace the canvas currently displayed in the Layout Editor with another canvas. The second list box maintains all the blocks in the application and it is used to set the context of the Form Builder to a particular block when you create items in the Layout Editor window.

The second row of icons in the toolbar facilitates the setting of visual attributes of objects as well as the alignment of these objects on the canvas. The meaning and use of these icons will be discussed in the remainder of this chapter.

6.2.3 TOOL PALETTE

Along the left side of the Layout Editor window there is a group of iconic buttons, commonly known as the tool palette. These buttons allow application developers to create new objects on a canvas, and modify the appearance of existing ones. Figure 6.3 shows the tool palette of the Layout Editor.

The Select icon is used to select objects in the Layout Editor. It is maybe the most often used tool because you must select an object first, before moving, resizing, changing properties, or perform any other action on it. This is also the default tool of the Layout Editor.

The Magnify icon is used to modify the view size of the objects. Its functionality is duplicated and complemented by the Zoom In, Zoom Out, Normal Size and Fit to Window menu items of View menu.

FIGURE 6.2 The Layout Editor toolbar.

FIGURE 6.3 Layout Editor tool palette.

Based on the functionality they provide, the remaining tools can be classified in the following groups:

- **Tools that create new boilerplate objects on the canvas.** This group includes the following tools: Rectangle, Line, Ellipse, Arc, Polygon, Polyline, Rounded Rectangle, Freehand Object, Text, and Frame.
- **Tools that create new items on the canvas.** There is one icon for each item type: Push Button, Check Box, Radio Button, Text Item, Image Item, Chart Item, OLE Container, ActiveX Control, Java Bean, Display Item, List Item, Sound Item, and Hierarchical Tree control. This category often includes two more icons, Tab Canvas and Stacked Canvas, although they do not create new items but canvases of a special type.

- **Tools that modify visual properties of existing objects.** There are five tools that make up this group: Rotate, Reshape, Fill Color, Line Color, and Text Color.

To activate any of these tools, simply click it. This allows the functionality associated with the activated tool to be executed only once. If the tool must be used repeatedly, double-click on it and perform the operation as many times as necessary. Double-clicking a tool sets it in a pinned state. Visually, a red pin appears across the tool button. The tool remains pinned until another tool is selected. If the Layout Editor window is not big enough to display the whole tool palette, handles appear on top and on the bottom of the palette, as shown in Figure 6.3. Use these handles to scroll the tool palette as necessary.

6.2.4 STATUS BAR

At the bottom of the Layout Editor window there is a status bar that displays information that may come in handy when creating, sizing, moving and rotating objects in the Layout Editor. The information is presented in the form of small icons followed by digits. When coordinates or dimensions are measured, the digits are units as defined in the ruler settings. Angles are measured in degrees ranging from 0 to 360. The horizontal direction is an angle of 0 degrees. The leftmost icon, which is always present, expresses the current magnification level as a factor of the normal size. A factor of 2x means that the displayed size of objects is 200 percent of their actual size. A factor of 1/2x means that the currently displayed objects are 50 percent of their actual size.

The content of the status bar is different for different actions on different objects. Figure 6.4 shows some typical information displayed in the status bar. In addition to the above information, the status bar also displays brief information about the iconic buttons in the tool palette. For this, the mouse should be positioned above any of the buttons, and held steady momentarily. The Form Builder displays popup help on the side of the button and a longer description of the tool in the status bar. For example, if the mouse is positioned on top of the Select button, the status bar will display the message "Selects objects on the layout."

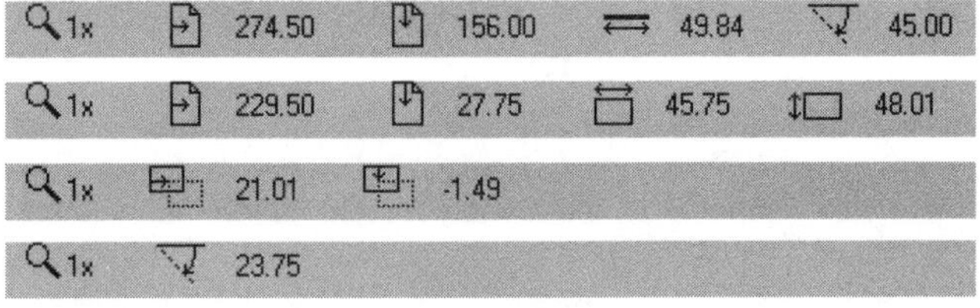

FIGURE 6.4 Sample information displayed by the Layout Editor status bar.

6.3 WORKING WITH OBJECTS IN LAYOUT EDITOR

This section describes the main actions that can be performed in the Layout Editor. These include creating different types of objects, selecting, reshaping, moving them around, and so on.

6.3.1 UNDOING CHANGES

Before moving further in the discussion, focus for a minute on the Undo command. It reverses the last action performed in the Layout Editor. It is a very helpful command that protects the application from accidental and unwanted actions. It is important to understand that Form Builder implements only a one-level Undo command. This means that if you want to undo something, you should do so immediately after the action or command is executed, without performing anything else in between.

The two ways to invoke the Undo utility are listed below:

- Select Edit | Undo from the Form Builder Menu.
- Press CTRL+Z from the keyboard.

In both cases your last action is reversed. When you issue the Undo command, the Undo menu item in the Edit menu changes to Redo. Like any other command, you can undo the Undo command as well. In other words, the action you wanted to undo can be redone. You can perform the Redo command only if nothing else has happened since your last Undo. To redo an undone command, take any of the following steps:

- Select Edit | Redo from the Form Builder Menu.
- Press CTRL+Z from the keyboard.

6.3.2 CREATING OBJECTS

Creating objects in the Layout Editor is simply a matter of drawing them where you want on the canvas. All Forms items and most of the boilerplate objects can be created with an easy two-step procedure.

1. Activate the tool icon in the tool palette that corresponds to the type of object you want to create. The cursor changes shape to the crosshair icon +.
2. Click on the canvas where you want to create the object.

When you release the mouse button a new object is created. The Form Builder assigns default dimensions to newly created objects. But it also allows you to specify their dimensions when you create them. To do this, follow the additional Step 3.

3. While holding the mouse button down, draw the object to the desired size.

A rectangle that will include the new object helps you estimate its size. The width and height of the object are displayed on the status bar.

The procedure to create lines, polygons, polylines, freehand, and text objects is slightly different. To create a line, you need to follow these steps:

1. Activate the Line icon in the tool palette.
2. Click on the canvas where you want the line to begin.
3. Hold the mouse button down and move the mouse towards the terminal point of the line. To guide you in the process, Form Builder draws a virtual line and displays its length and angle on the status bar.
4. Release the mouse button when the other extremity of line is reached. The line is created.

To create polygons or polylines, follow these steps:

1. Activate the Polygon icon or Polyline icon in the tool palette.
2. Click on the canvas where you want the first vertex of the object to be.
3. Click on the canvas where you want each subsequent vertex to be. Note that you do not need to keep the mouse button pressed. As each edge is drawn, Form Builder displays it on the canvas, and its angle on the status bar.
4. Double-click when the final vertex is reached.

At this point, the polyline is complete. For the polygon, Form Builder automatically draws the last edge between the last and first vertices.

To draw a freehand object, follow these steps:

1. Activate the Freehand Object icon in the tool palette.
2. Click on the canvas where you want the drawing to begin.
3. Hold the mouse button down and draw the object.
4. Release the mouse button when done.

To create a text object on the boilerplate follow these objects:

1. Activate the Text icon in the tool palette.
2. Click on the canvas where you want to create the text object. A box is created and the cursor is positioned inside the box waiting for input.
3. Type the text. The rectangle around the text objects is expanded as needed.
4. When done, click anywhere outside the text object to exit text edit mode.

To help you create objects of regular shapes, the tools in the Layout Editor can be used in Constraint mode. In this mode, rectangles become squares, ellipses become circles, and lines of any direction become horizontal, vertical or 45-degree-angle lines. To use a tool in Constraint mode, activate the tool and hold down SHIFT while using it.

Objects you create on the Layout Editor window can be either data block items or boilerplate objects. The former are responsible for the interaction of users with the data sources of the application; the later enhance the user interface and the layout of the application. The Object Navigator lists all the items under the data blocks to which they belong. The boilerplate objects are listed under the node Graphics of the canvas that contains them. Figure 6.5 shows the example of a canvas object and a number of boilerplate objects as they appear on the Object Navigator window.

6.3.3 SETTING THE CONTEXT OF LAYOUT EDITOR

An important fact that must be kept in mind when creating items in the Layout Editor is that items are owned by data blocks and cannot exist outside them. It is very common for items from different blocks to share the same canvas or tab page. For example, in the ETS application you developed in Part One, the tab page GENERAL contains items that belong to two different blocks: HW_ASSETS and SW_ASSETS. Since a canvas can contain items from different blocks, it is important to set the context of the Layout Editor to the block that will own an item before creating that item.

The context is displayed in the title bar of the Layout Editor window. It can also be seen in the list of open windows under Window menu. Its format is

```
FORM_NAME:CANVAS_NAME(BLOCK_NAME)
```

In the case of Figure 6.1, the Layout Editor context in the ETS form is the ETS canvas and HW_ASSETS block. Therefore, the window title is ETS:ETS (HW_ASSETS). To change the block context of the Layout Editor simply select the new block from the list box Blocks on the toolbar. Be aware that any items

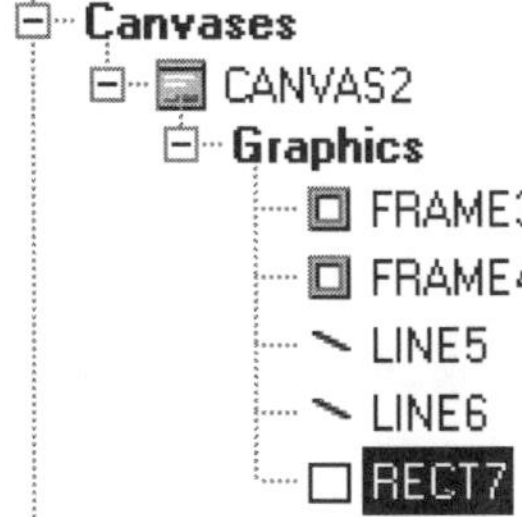

FIGURE 6.5 A canvas and its boilerplate objects on the Object Navigator window.

selected in the canvas will be transferred automatically to the new block. To replace the canvas currently displayed in the Layout Editor window with a different canvas from the same form, select its name from the list box Canvas.

6.3.4 SELECTING OBJECTS

As mentioned earlier, selecting is probably the most common action in the Layout Editor. Before moving, resizing, cutting, pasting, aligning, or performing any other action with an object, you must first select it. To select an object, just move the mouse on the object and click. When the object is selected, handles appear around it. Handles are dark gray boxes on the corners and middle points of the virtual rectangle that encircles and object.

Often, there is the need to select more than one object. Layout Editor provides two ways to select multiple objects. The first one selects one object at a time.

1. Select the first object.
2. Hold down either SHIFT or CTRL, and select each additional object.

This method allows you to select only those objects you need, anywhere on the canvas. But, it can be tedious if the number of objects to be selected is large. The second method, referred to as "rubber banding," is used in this case.

1. Place the mouse cursor further to the left and higher up than any object.
2. Holding the mouse button down, draw a virtual selection rectangle large enough to enclose entirely all the objects to be selected.

When you release the mouse button, all the objects completely inside the selection rectangle are selected. Selecting objects this way is particularly helpful if the objects are adjacent or near each other. However, it may happen that other objects are selected together with the desired objects. If this is the case, deselect any unwanted objects. These are the steps to deselect an object:

1. Hold down SHIFT or CTRL key.
2. Click the selected object.

As you can see, selecting multiple objects is similar in the Layout Editor and Object Navigator. The only difference is that the concept of range selections does not exist in the Layout Editor. Therefore SHIFT+CLICK and CTRL+CLICK are synonymous actions here, but different in the Navigator.

Sometimes, there may be a need to select all the objects on the current canvas. Any of the following two commands can be used to achieve this.

- ❑ Select Edit | Select All from the menu.
- ❑ Press CTRL+A from the keyboard.

In either case, all the objects on the canvas are selected.

6.3.5 MOVING, RESIZING, AND RESHAPING OBJECTS

As discussed in Section 6.3.2, the Layout Editor allows you to place new objects you create where you want on the canvas. It also allows you to size the object as you create it. Nevertheless, after an object is created, or later, when the application's look is fine-tuned, you may need to move and resize objects. You can perform these actions on individual objects or multiple objects simultaneously. Multiple objects will be moved as a group and, when resized, their dimensions will change proportionally. To move an object after it is selected, follow these steps:

1. Click anywhere inside the object and hold the mouse button down. Make sure not to click one of the handles.
2. Drag the object to the position you want on the canvas. The status bar displays the distance of the current position from the original one.
3. Release the button when you are satisfied with the new position.

You can also use the arrow keys to move an object. Each time the arrow key is pressed, the object moves one unit in the direction of the arrow. If the Grid Snap property is on, the unit is as specified in the Number of Snap Points Per Grid Spacing text item of the Ruler Settings dialog box. Refer to Section 6.5.2 later in this chapter for more details about this dialog box. If the Grid Snap property is not set, the unit of movement equals the ruler unit specified in Ruler Settings dialog box.

To resize an object after it is selected, you click and drag its handles until the object has reached the desired size. If only the width of the object needs to be changed, handles on the vertical edges of the selecting rectangle are used. Handles on horizontal edges are used to adjust the object's height. The handles on all four vertices of the selecting rectangle are used to resize an object horizontally and vertically at the same time.

The Layout Editor allows you to change the *shape* of three boilerplate objects: polygons, polylines and freehand drawings. This action is different from resizing, because it allows you to change proportions and position of single vertices or parts of these objects, rather than change them proportionally, as a whole. To reshape an already selected polygon, polyline, or freehand object follow these steps:

1. Click the Reshape icon in the tool palette. The selecting rectangle around the object is replaced by selecting handles in each vertex of the object.
2. Click the desired handle and drag it to the new position.
3. Repeat these steps as necessary.

You can reshape only one object at a time. If you attempt to use the Reshape tool when multiple objects are selected, you will get the Oracle Forms message "VGS-206: More than one object selected." If the Reshape tool is used with any of the other objects on the canvas, it simply resizes the object.

6.3.6 ALIGNING OBJECTS

When objects are moved around the canvas, it is difficult to keep them aligned and spaced properly. Although these may seem superfluous issues, not directly related to the main functionality of the application, they are known to affect users' reactions to the interface of the application. The Layout Editor provides several alignment settings for objects on a canvas. The alignment process itself is simple and is described by the following steps:

1. Select the objects to align.
2. Select Arrange | Align Objects from the menu. The Alignment Settings dialog box appears (see Figure 6.6).
3. Specify the alignment settings according to your application needs.
4. Click OK.

The selected objects are aligned according to the settings you specified.

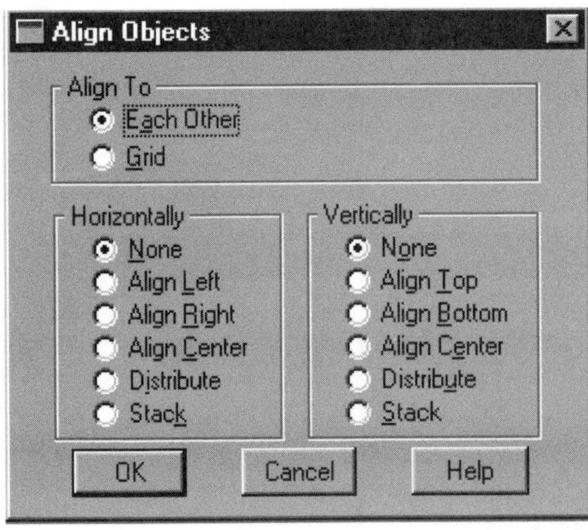

FIGURE 6.6 Alignment Settings dialog box.

If you want to align other objects using the same settings:

1. Select the objects to align.
2. Select Arrange | Repeat Alignment from the menu, or press CTRL+L from the keyboard.

Once set, the alignment settings will remain in effect for the canvas until they are reset, or the module is closed. The settings will remain in effect even if the Layout Editor window holding that canvas is closed. The Alignment Settings dialog box has two mutually exclusive modes of aligning objects: Align to Each Other and Align to Grid.

Align to Each Other mode aligns objects with respect to each other. Two or more objects must be selected for this mode to be active. Objects can be aligned vertically or horizontally. For each direction, a set of six exclusive options can be specified. Four of these options—None, Align Center, Distribute, and Stack—are common for both directions. The following paragraphs describe the distinct alignment options you can set in the Alignment Settings dialog box.

- **None** is chosen by default for both horizontal and vertical alignments, meaning that by default no alignment occurs. If you want to align objects, some settings must be specified beforehand.
- **Align Left** means that the left side of each selected object will be aligned with the left side of the left-most object. This option applies only to horizontal alignments.
- **Align Right** means that the right side of each selected object will be aligned with the right side of the right-most object. Like the previous option, this one applies only to horizontal alignments.
- **Align Top** means that the top of each selected object will be aligned with the top of the upper-most object. This option applies only to vertical alignments.
- **Align Bottom** means that the bottom of each selected object will be aligned with the bottom of the lower-most object. Like the previous option, this one applies only to vertical alignments.
- **Align Center** aligns the middle-point handles of selected objects on a common centerline between them.
- **Distribute** spreads three or more selected objects in the horizontal or vertical direction so that there is an equal distance between them. The left-most and right-most objects are not moved for the Horizontally Distribute option. The top and bottom objects are not moved for the Vertically Distribute option.
- **Stack** aligns objects so that there is no space between them in the respective direction. Combined with other options, Stack can be used to create adjacent rows or columns of objects.

As mentioned earlier, each of the six horizontal alignment settings can be combined with any of the six vertical ones. Therefore, there are thirty-six different ways to align a group of selected objects with respect to each other. You may want to practice your aligning skills by experimenting with each of them. Despite the large number of options available, practice has shown that only a few of them are used over and over. For the six most-frequently used alignment options, the Layout Editor provides the following icons on the second row of controls of the toolbar:

- **Align Left**: Aligns objects horizontally to the left.
- **Align Center**: Aligns horizontally the middle points of the selected objects.
- **Align Right**: Aligns objects horizontally to the right.
- **Align Top**: Aligns objects vertically on top.
- **Align Center**: Aligns vertically the middle points of the selected objects.
- **Align Bottom**: Aligns objects vertically to the bottom.

Align to Grid mode allows you to align one or more objects with respect to the grid lines. For example, Align Left will move the selected object so that its left side falls in the closest vertical grid line. Align Top will snap the topside of an object to the closest horizontal line. Similar actions result from Align Right and Align Bottom settings. Align Center will place the center handles of the object on the closest horizontal or vertical grid line.

Align to Grid affects each object individually. Even if multiple objects are selected, each of them will be moved to the closest grid line, according to specified settings. If View | Grid Snap property is set, the Align to Grid settings do not result in any position changes, because the sides of objects are already along grid lines. However, this mode of alignment is independent from Grid Snap settings.

6.3.7 SETTING OBJECTS TO SAME SIZE

As said earlier, alignment of canvas objects plays an important role in the overall look and feel of an application. Setting objects to the same size is equally important. Modern GUI development practices emphasize the use of standards across applications. One of these important standards is that the size of identical or similar objects should be the same. The Form Builder provides extended functionality to help developers size objects uniformly. To set objects to the same size, follow these steps:

1. Select the desired objects.
2. Select Arrange | Size Objects from the menu. The Size Objects dialog box appears (see Figure 6.7).

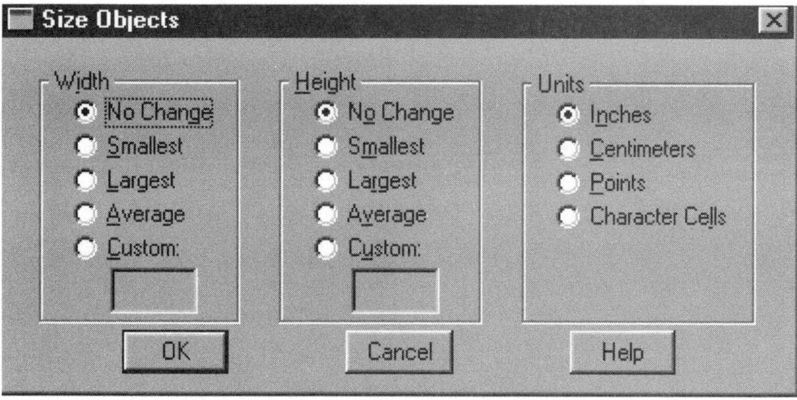

FIGURE 6.7 Size Objects dialog box.

3. Specify the sizing settings according to your needs.
4. Click OK.

The selected objects are sized according to the settings you specified.

If you want to size other objects using the same settings, follow these steps:

1. Select the objects to size.
2. Select Arrange | Repeat Sizing from the menu.

Once set, the sizing settings will remain in effect for the canvas until they are reset, or the module is closed. The settings will remain in effect even if the Layout Editor window with that canvas is closed. The Size Objects dialog box allows you to set the width and height of selected objects. For each of the dimensions, one setting can be chosen out of five available options. By default, No Change is selected. If Smallest is set, the width or height of all selected objects will be set to that of the object with the smallest dimension. Largest option sets the dimension to the highest value of dimensions for all selected objects. If Average is selected, then Form Builder computes an arithmetic average of the appropriate dimension for all selected objects and sets this dimension to the computed average.

You can also specify exactly how many units of measurements the dimensions for each object will be. To do this, click the Custom radio button and enter the size or width or height in the field below. The units of measurement are those of the Layout Editor grid. You can specify them in the Units column to the right. Inches are the default unit. The Size Objects dialog box allows you to set these units in any case, but they are meaningful only if custom width or height dimension settings are specified.

6.3.8 DELETING OBJECTS

To delete objects in the Layout Editor, you must first select them. Then, issue one of these commands:

- ❑ Press Delete key on the keyboard.
- ❑ Select Edit | Clear from the menu.

In both cases, the objects will be removed from the canvas and, simultaneously, from the Object Navigator's hierarchy tree. The effects of accidentally issuing the Delete command in the Layout Editor are not as severe as in the Object Navigator. Fortunately, there is the Undo that saves the day. As long as you do not perform any other actions since the accidental delete, the Undo command will restore the objects unintentionally deleted on the canvas. Remember that you cannot do this if the objects are deleted from the Object Navigator.

6.3.9 CUTTING AND COPYING OBJECTS

Cutting and copying in the Layout Editor is very similar to the same actions in the Navigator. A copy of the object will be placed in the clipboard and will remain there until the next Windows cut or copy operation. One of the following commands allows you to cut an object or group of objects from the canvas:

- ❑ Press CTRL+X.
- ❑ Click the Cut icon on the toolbar.
- ❑ Select Edit | Cut from the menu.

Selected objects will be removed from the canvas and the Navigator object tree and placed in the clipboard. If you want to place just a copy of the objects in the clipboard, without removing them from the existing position in the form, then use the Copy command. To copy an already selected object or group of objects, issue one of these commands:

- ❑ Press CTRL+C.
- ❑ Click the Copy icon on the toolbar.
- ❑ Select Edit | Copy from the menu.

6.3.10 PASTING AND DUPLICATING OBJECTS

To duplicate an object in the Layout Editor, first select it, then press CTRL+D or choose Edit | Duplicate from the menu. A duplicate copy is created beside the current selection. Duplicate will replicate the selected object on the same canvas as the original one. For a more flexible replication scheme, a combination of cut or copy and paste is used.

To paste an object to a target location, first place it in the clipboard by either copying or cutting it. If you want to copy the object to a different canvas, switch to the Layout Editor window that contains that canvas, if it is already loaded, or open a new window to display it. Paste the objects from the clipboard in one of the following ways:

- Press CTRL+V.
- Click the Paste icon on the toolbar.
- Select Edit | Paste from the menu.

Pasted objects will be placed in exactly the same location on the canvas as their original versions. If pasting within the same canvas, the objects will overlap, with the new object immediately on top of the existing one. You will have to move the newly pasted object to the desired location. If pasting to a different canvas, and the position of the new object falls outside the canvas's boundaries, the Form Builder will display the message "One or more Object will extend off the canvas."

Finally, to close this section, note that when items are created, whether new from scratch or copied from existing objects, the Layout Editor will assign them generic names. To change these names to more meaningful ones, either rename the items in the Object Navigator, or double-click the object to display its property palette, and change its name there. The following chapter provides detailed information about the Property Palette Editor.

6.3.11 GROUPING AND UNGROUPING OBJECTS

Often, during the process of laying out a form, it may be convenient to treat several separate objects as one single object. For example, after certain items are aligned and sized, you would want to move them together, with one single operation, rather than moving each one separately, and then having to repeat the realignment process. Grouping is the process that combines two or more selected objects into one larger entity that includes these objects. To perform this operation, select the objects that will be grouped. Then, issue one of these commands:

- Select Arrange | Group from the menu.
- Press CTRL+G.

Visually, you will notice that all the selecting handles around individual objects will disappear and will be replaced by handles of a selecting rectangle that includes all the grouped objects. This rectangle will represent the newly grouped objects. It can be considered as a single object, and you can perform on it moving, sizing, cutting, pasting, or any other actions that you want to perform on each individual member of the group.

To select a group, click any of its members once. Selecting handles will appear around the virtual rectangle that includes all objects in the group. If you need to select a particular member of the group, click that object a second time.

If an object is already selected and you want to know its parent group, choose Arrange | Group Operations | Select Parent from the Form Builder menu. If the object is already grouped, its parent group will be selected. If a group is already selected and you need to select all its children as individual objects, choose Arrange | Group Operations | Select Children from the Form Builder menu. Selecting handles will appear around each group member.

To add new objects to an existing group, follow these steps:

1. Select the group.
2. SHIFT+CLICK or CTRL+CLICK each object to be added to the group.
3. Choose Arrange | Group Operations | Add to Group from the menu.

Step 3 above can be replaced by either of the following steps:

- ❑ Choose Arrange | Group from the menu, or
- ❑ Press CTRL+G from the keyboard.

In all cases, the resulting group will be expanded to include the new members.

Objects bundled together in a group can be ungrouped as well. The following steps help you remove one or more objects from an existing group:

1. Select the group.
2. Select the objects to be removed from the group.
3. Choose Arrange | Group Operations | Remove from Group from the Form Builder menu.

Ungrouping is another way to break up the structure of an existing group. To ungroup, first select the desired group. Then, issue one of these commands:

- ❑ Select Arrange | Ungroup from the menu.
- ❑ Press SHIFT+CTRL+G from the keyboard.

Like other boilerplate objects, the Object Navigator represents groups as nodes under the canvas that owns them. In the example shown in Figure 6.5 earlier, the canvas contains a number of boilerplate objects and a group that contains a line and a rectangle. The actions of adding or removing items from the group in the Object Navigator are much simpler. To add an object to the group, simply drag it over the group node; to remove it from the group, drag it outside the group.

6.3.12 ROTATING OBJECTS

It was mentioned earlier that boilerplate objects are used to enhance the look of Forms applications. To increase the variety of shapes and objects that can be built on a canvas, the Layout Editor allows rotating these objects to any angle form the original position. To rotate a boilerplate object or group of objects, first select them. Then, perform these actions:

1. Select the Rotate icon from the tool palette.
2. Click any of the handles and hold the mouse button down.
3. While holding the mouse down, drag the handle to the new position.
4. When the object is rotated as desired, release the mouse button.

During rotating operations, Form Builder displays a virtual rectangle that encircles the selected object or group of objects, and follows your mouse movements. Form Builder also displays a line connecting the current clicked handle and the center of this rectangle. The status bar displays the current rotation angle in degrees. If during rotation part of the selected object falls outside the layout work area, the Form Builder will display the message "One or more objects will extend off the canvas. Operation disallowed."—and will cancel the action.

6.3.13 WORKING WITH OVERLAPPING OBJECTS

The Layout Editor allows developers to create several basic drawing objects. But creative use of these objects allows for a variety of designs to be created on the canvas. Overlapping objects form a stack. You see only the view from the top of this stack. Objects can be moved around in the stack to create different images or visual illusions. Four operations help you in the process:

- **Bring to Front.** This command moves the selected object to the top of the stack, above every other overlapping object. Any of the following actions allow you to bring to front an already selected object or group of objects:
  - Press F5 from the keyboard.
  - Click Bring to Front icon on the toolbar.
  - Select Arrange | Bring to Front from the menu.
- **Send to Back.** This command moves the selected object at the bottom of the stack, immediately above the canvas. To send to back an already selected object or group of objects, perform one of these actions:
  - Press F6 from the keyboard.
  - Click Send to Back icon on the toolbar.
  - Select Arrange | Send to Back from the menu.
- **Move Forward.** This command moves the selected object one level up the stack, above the object that was immediately overlapping it. To move for-

ward an already selected object or group of objects, issue one of these commands:
- ❑ Press F7 from the keyboard.
- ❑ Select Arrange | Move Forward from the menu.

❑ **Move Backward.** This command moves the selected object one level down the stack, under the object it was overlapping. Use one of these commands to move backward an already selected object or group of objects:
- ❑ Press F8 from the keyboard.
- ❑ Select Arrange | Move Backward from the menu.

6.4 SETTING VISUAL ATTRIBUTES IN THE LAYOUT EDITOR

Each object in the Layout Editor has a variety of properties. Some of these properties define its functionality and behavior; others define the appearance of the object. Properties of the first type are called functional properties. Only items can have functional properties. Properties of the second type are known as visual attributes of an object. All objects on a canvas, items and boilerplate objects, have visual attributes. Visual attributes are the text, color and pattern properties of an object. This section discusses how to set and modify them in the Layout Editor.

6.4.1 FONT ATTRIBUTES

Font attributes include the font name, size, and style. By default all text items and labels on the canvas are created using the default Windows font, MS Sans Serif, but you can change the font settings for any item or boilerplate object. To do this:

1. Select the object or group of objects that you want to modify.
2. Choose Format | Font from the menu. Font dialog box appears (see Figure 6.8).
3. Specify font settings such as name, type, style, size, and special effects.
4. Click OK.

Font attributes of the selected objects will change according to your specifications.

The main components of the Font dialog box are the lists of options from which attributes settings can be selected. The list on the left displays all the fonts available to your application. Windows TrueType fonts are preceded by the TT indicator 𝕋. TrueType fonts have enough variety and scalability to meet virtually all the needs of your applications. They allow you to set different sizes and styles for text items on the canvas, thus making the applications look better and feel more user-friendly. Some fonts used frequently are Arial, `Courier New`, and

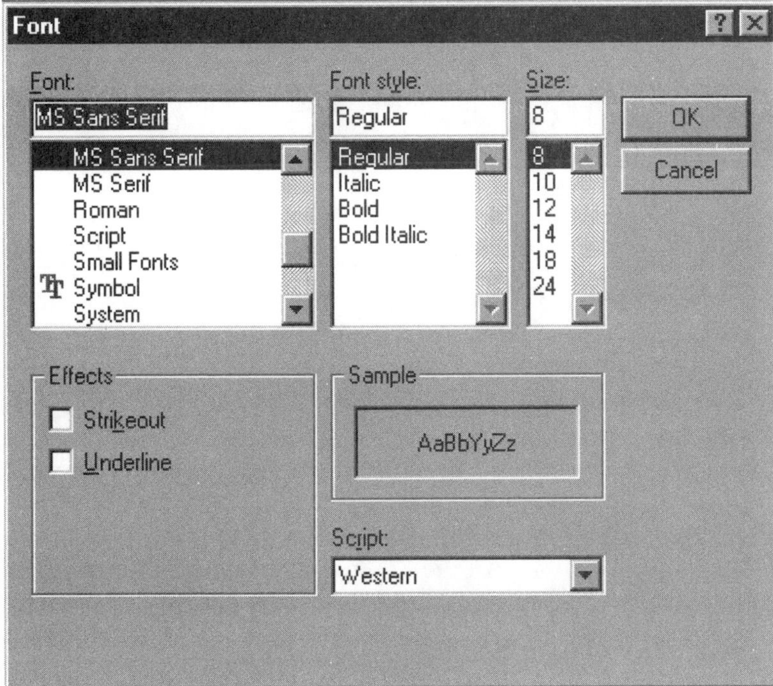

FIGURE 6.8 The Font dialog box.

Times New Roman. You can add additional TrueType fonts to further enhance your Windows applications. Care must be taken with non-standard fonts to insure that they will be acceptable in all the environments where your applications may run.

The list in the middle of the dialog box allows you to select the font style. It can be regular, **bold**, *italic* or ***bold italic.*** The list to the right allows you to specify the size of the chosen font. Usually, only TrueType fonts support different sizes of their characters. For example, MS Sans Serif font shown in Figure 6.8 supports a whole range of font sizes, but System font, which is not TrueType, supports only characters of size 10.

Some fonts may be specific to the installation of the operating system in your machine, which may be different from what the users have. Furthermore, the appearance and size of non-TrueType fonts depends on the resolution of the Windows desktop (640 × 480, 800 × 600, 1024 × 768, and so on.). Therefore it is important that you develop your applications in those fonts and resolutions that are available and used by the user-community.

On the lower-left corner of the Font dialog box you can specify two additional font attributes: Underline and Strikeout. If the check boxes are marked, then the text will have underline and ~~strikeout~~ effects, respectively. The Font dialog box offers you a chance to see the outcome of your selections in the Sample field. In this field, you can see how the text objects you are modifying will look like, before actually making the changes.

> **TIP**
>
> As with other functional areas, the most often used commands for setting the font attributes can be accessed from controls and icons in the Layout Editor's toolbar. In particular, you can set the font and font size by selecting from the respective list boxes; you can control the bold, italic, or underline properties of text by clicking the corresponding icons B, I, U.

6.4.2 SPACING AND JUSTIFICATION SETTINGS

Besides setting font attributes, you can also specify spacing and alignment settings for text labels on the canvas. Spacing applies only to boilerplate text objects, and it does not have any effect on text items. It affects the distance between lines of text; therefore, it will have a visual effect only on multi-line text labels. To set the text spacing, follow these steps:

1. Select the object or group of objects that you want to modify.
2. Choose Format | Text Spacing from the menu. A list of radio button menu items appears (see Figure 6.9).
3. Select the setting that meets your needs.

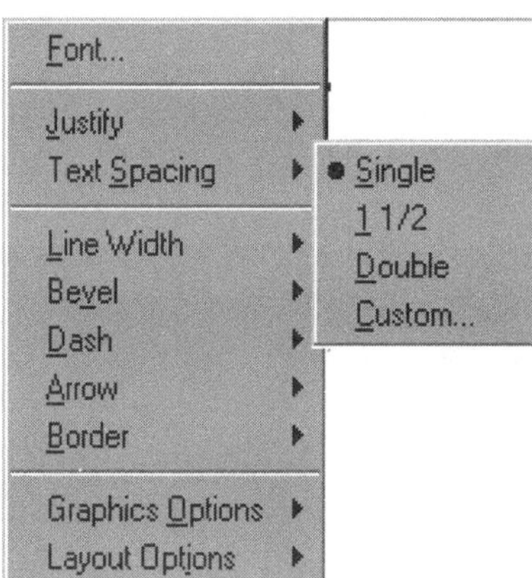

FIGURE 6.9 The items of Format | Text Spacing menu.

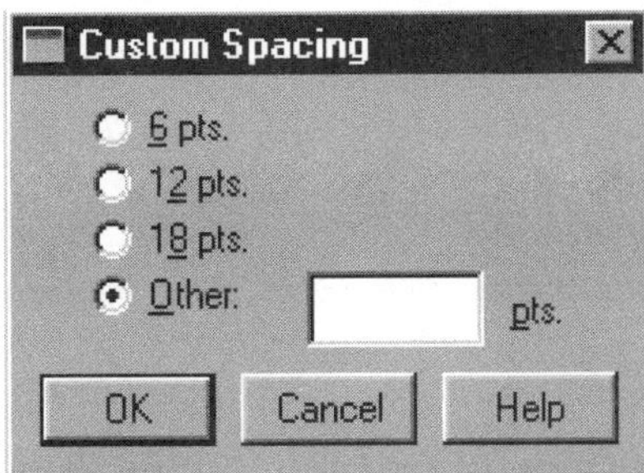

FIGURE 6.10 The Custom Spacing dialog box.

By default, text is single-spaced. Form Builder allows you to quickly space text at 1.5 lines and double lines. If you are not satisfied with these settings, you can specify custom spacing parameters. To do so, follow Steps 1 and 2 above, and select Custom from the menu items of Format | Spacing. Custom Spacing dialog box will appear (see Figure 6.10).

You can set the distance between lines of text to 6, 12, or 18 points. You can also check Other radio button and specify any number of points in the field to the right. Specifying 0 points is equivalent to Format | Spacing | Single; 6 points to Format | Spacing 1 _; and 12 points to Format | Spacing | Double.

Justification settings control whether the boilerplate text objects or text items display text aligned to the left, center or right. Other forms of text on the canvas such as labels for radio button or check box items are not affected visually by the justification settings. By default, Form Builder justifies text to the left. These are the steps required to set the justification:

1. Select the object or group of objects whose text you want to align.
2. Choose Format | Justify from the menu. A list of radio button menu items appears (see Figure 6.11).
3. Select the appropriate option.

To conclude this section, note that settings for fonts, spacing and alignment not only apply to the currently selected objects, but also become the default setting for objects that you create thereafter.

6.4.3 COLOR ATTRIBUTES

The Layout Editor allows you to change the color of borderlines, background, and text of objects. The tools that perform these operations are located in the bottom part of the tool palette. Before modifying the color settings of an object, you must first select it. To change the background color and pattern, click the Fill Color icon ; to change the borderline color, click Line Color icon ; finally, to

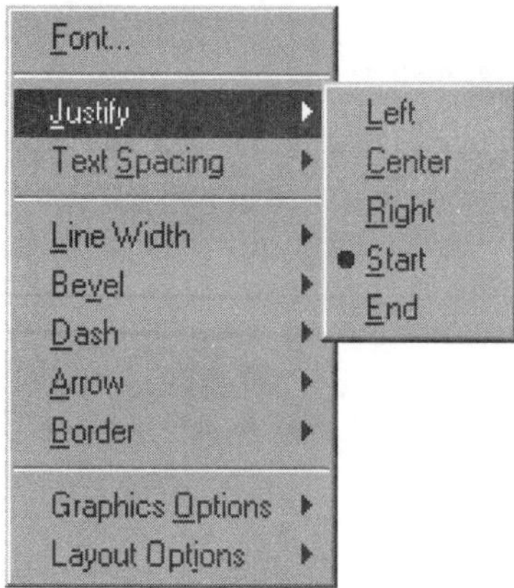

FIGURE 6.11 Items of Format | Justify menu.

change the text color, click Text Color icon. In all cases, a color palette will appear, similar to the Fill Color palette shown in Figure 6.12.

Move the mouse pointer around the palette to search for the color you want. As you do so, the colored box to the left of the button you clicked will display the color. The sample square on top will also update its color with the color currently pointed at by the mouse. Once you find a good color that you like, click on it. The fill, line or text color will change according to your specifications.

From the Fill Color palette, you can also change the background pattern of the selected object. To do so, click the Patterns menu item. The Fill Pattern Palette dialog box will appear (Figure 6.13).

Selecting a pattern here is similar to selecting a color from the color palette. By default, the pattern is black on white. If you wan to change it click the drop down list buttons. This action displays the color palette from which you can select a replacement for these colors. When satisfied with your changes, close the dialog box.

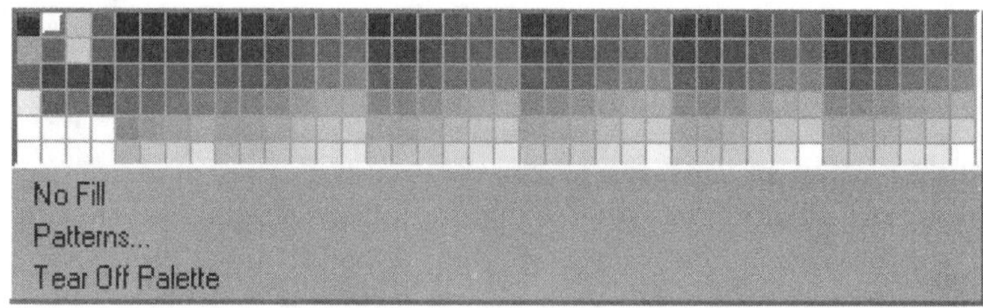

FIGURE 6.12 The Fill Color palette.

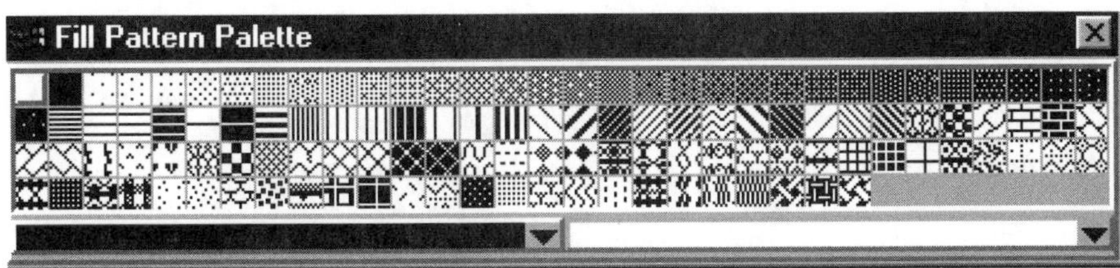

FIGURE 6.13 The Fill Pattern palette.

For Fill Color you can also specify the No Fill option. In this case, the background will not have a fill color. Similarly, for Line Color you can specify the No Line option, which removes the borderline from the object. This option is meaningless for the Text Color tool, therefore it is not available.

By default, the color palettes for all three tools pop up when the tool icon is clicked and are closed by the next mouse click, no matter whether a color selection was made or not. To keep the color palette displayed until you decide to dismiss it, select Tear Off Palette menu item, which is present in all the palettes. This places the palette in a dialog box like the Fill Pattern Palette dialog box shown in Figure 6.13. As with fonts, spacing and alignment settings, color settings discussed in this paragraph will apply to all the objects that will be created subsequently, after the changes take effect.

> **TIP**
>
> Like fonts, colors may vary from workstation to workstation. The first 4 × 4 grid on the color palette represents the basic 16 colors that are found in virtually every configuration. The purity of other colors will depend on the workstation setup. It is important that you know the configuration of your users' environment.

6.4.4 LINE AND BORDER ATTRIBUTES

The Layout Editor provides additional functionality that developers can use to enhance the image of boilerplate objects. The features presented in this section apply only to borders of boilerplate objects and objects created with the line, polyline and freehand tools. They do not apply to items. First, borderlines of these objects can have different thickness. To change the width of the lines, you need to take the following steps:

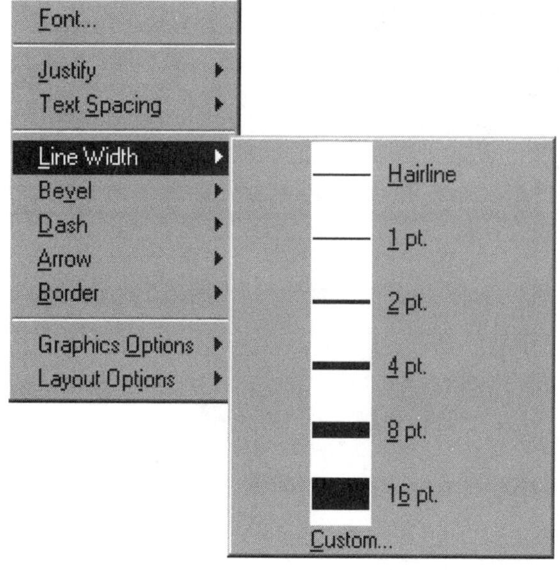

FIGURE 6.14 The Items of Format | Line Width menu.

1. Select the object or group of objects whose borderlines you want to change.
2. Choose Format | Line Width from the menu. A list of radio button menu items appears (see Figure 6.14).
3. Select the appropriate setting for the width of selected lines.

Form Builder lists six commonly used width settings, from which you can choose one that suits your needs. You can also directly set the line width by choosing Custom option from the above menu. The Custom Line Width dialog box appears (see Figure 6.15). Here you can specify the line width in inches, centimeters or points. The process of changing the width of lines, polylines and freehand objects is identical.

Rectangles and frames you create on the canvas can have a 3D-look if their bevel property is set. The following steps show how to set this property:

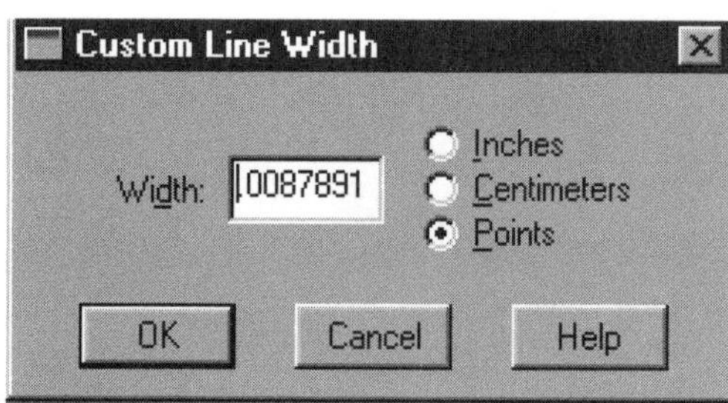

FIGURE 6.15 The Custom Line Width dialog box.

1. Select the object on the canvas.
2. Choose Format | Bevel from the menu. A list of radio button menu items appears.
3. Select the appropriate bevel for the rectangle.

As mentioned earlier, bevel settings can be specified only for frames and rectangles. Nevertheless, using overlapping techniques discussed in Section 6.3.13, 3D rectangles can be used as background for other boilerplate objects and items that do not have a 3D-look inherently. Items such as text items, radio buttons, and check boxes, come by default beveled. Modifying their properties in the Property Palette can change their bevel settings.

By default, borders of boilerplate objects, as well as lines, polylines and freehand drawings are solid lines. The Layout Editor allows you to use a variety of dashed lines as well. The following are the steps required to set this property:

1. Select the object you want to modify
2. Choose Format | Dash from the menu. A list of radio button menu items appears (see Figure 6.16).
3. Select the appropriate dashed line.

Note that dashed lines must have default width. Also, note that objects with dashed borderlines cannot have bevel settings specified.

The Layout Editor also allows drawing arrows of different types. Only line objects can be transformed in arrows by following these steps:

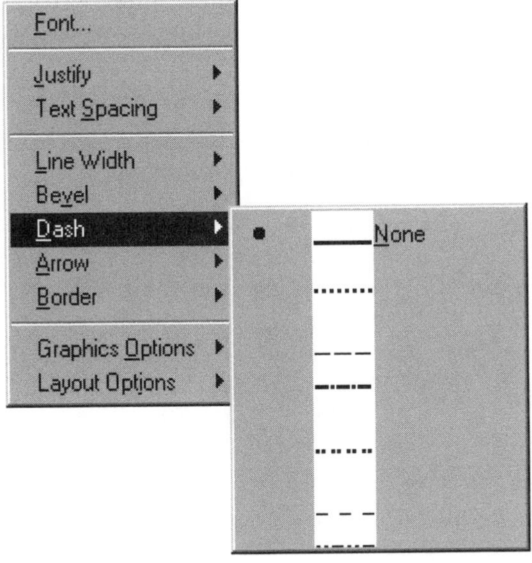

FIGURE 6.16 The items of Format | Dash menu.

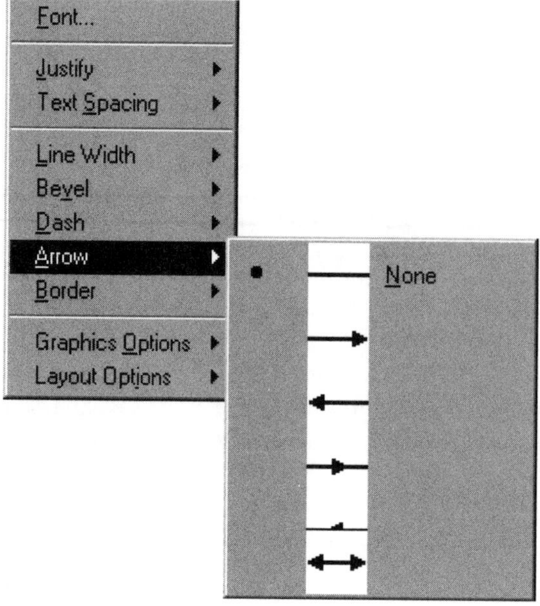

FIGURE 6.17 The items of Format | Arrow menu.

1. Select the line to be transformed into arrow.
2. Choose Format | Arrow from the menu. A list of radio button menu items appears (see Figure 6.17).
3. Select the appropriate arrow type.

As with other settings explained in the previous two paragraphs, border and line settings discussed here not only apply to the selected objects, but will be default setting for all the objects that will be created in the future until you close the Layout Editor.

6.4.5 MAINTAINING PROPERTIES IN THE PROPERTY PALETTE

Sections 6.4.1 through 6.4.4 showed how you could change the properties of boilerplate items by using menu and toolbar commands. A common thread to this approach is that once you change the properties of one item, for example the font setting, the new setting will apply to all the items that you create subsequently. Some properties such as font setting remain the default when leaving and reactivating the Layout Editor. Others such as line settings return to their original default settings. To modify the visual attributes of an item without affecting the default settings of the Layout Editor, you can double-click the item on the canvas or the Object Navigator to display its Property Palette. Here you can view and change all the properties that are applicable for the particular item. Figure 6.18 shows the example of the Property Palette for a line boilerplate object.

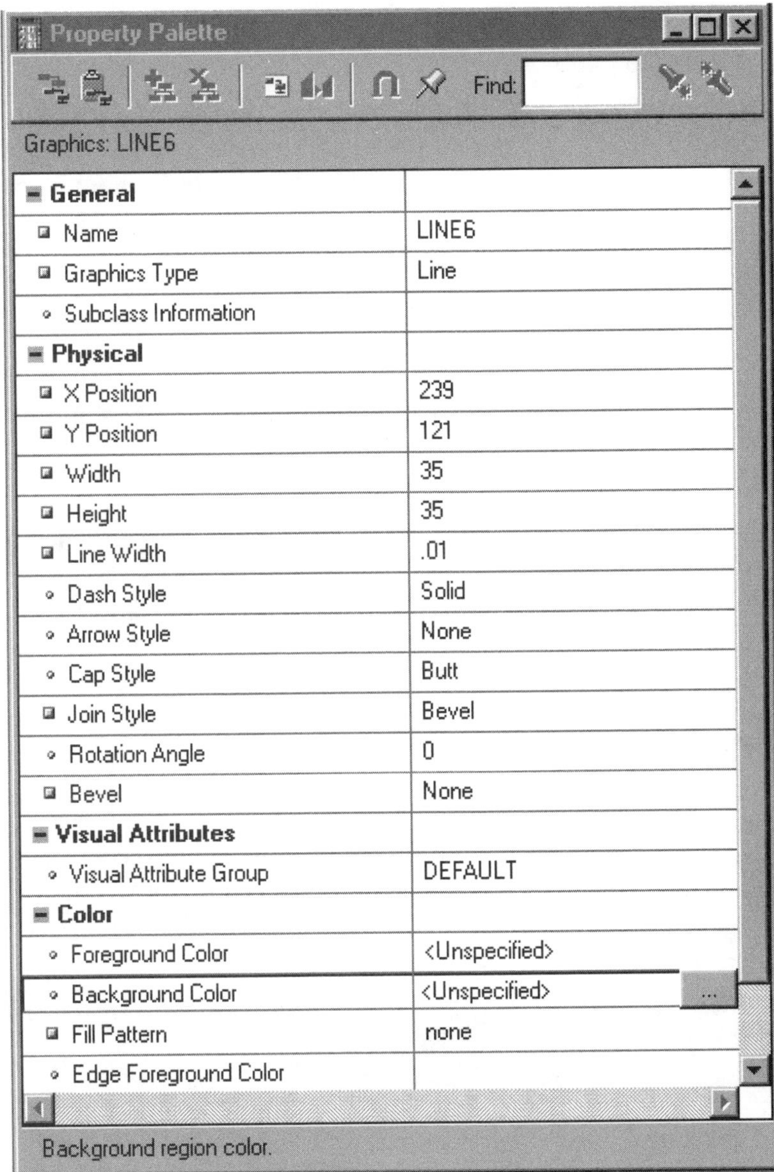

FIGURE 6.18 The Property Palette for a line boilerplate object.

6.5 CUSTOMIZING THE LAYOUT EDITOR

Once you become familiar with the Layout Editor, you may want to customize some of its settings. The following sections explain the main activities you can perform to make this editor better suit the needs of your application.

6.5.1 CUSTOMIZING LAYOUT WORK AREA

There are two parameters of the Layout work area that can be customized: Size and Page Direction. The size is the height and width of the work area, expressed in inches or centimeters. The page direction instructs the File | Print command to print pages left to right or top to bottom. To change the Layout work area settings select Format | Layout Options | Layout from the menu. The Layout Settings dialog box appears (see Figure 6.19).

This dialog box displays the current Size and Page Direction settings. The default size of the Layout work area is 15 inches wide by 20 inches long. The default Page Direction is top to bottom. When changing the dimensions of the work area, make sure that all the existing objects will fit in the newly sized canvas. The Layout Editor will not move them automatically if they fall outside boundaries, and their behavior and properties may be unpredictable.

6.5.2 CUSTOMIZING RULER SETTINGS

The settings you can customize for rulers are the unit of measurement, the grid spacing and the number of snap points per grid. To view or change these settings, choose the Format | Layout Options | Rulers item from the Layout Editor menu. The Ruler Settings dialog box appears (see Figure 6.20). It shows the current settings of the parameters for the canvas displayed in the Layout Editor.

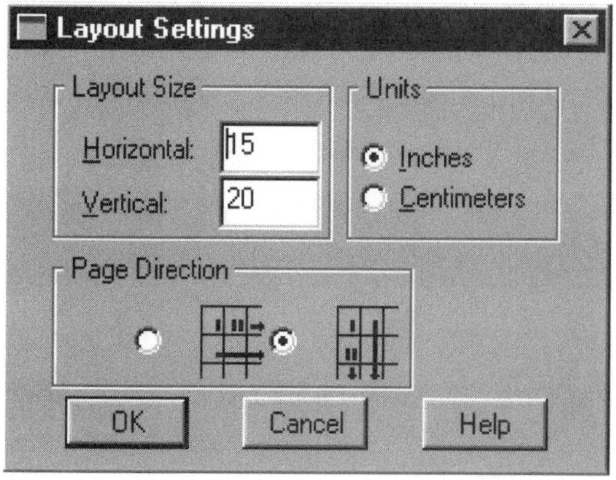

FIGURE 6.19 Layout Settings dialog box.

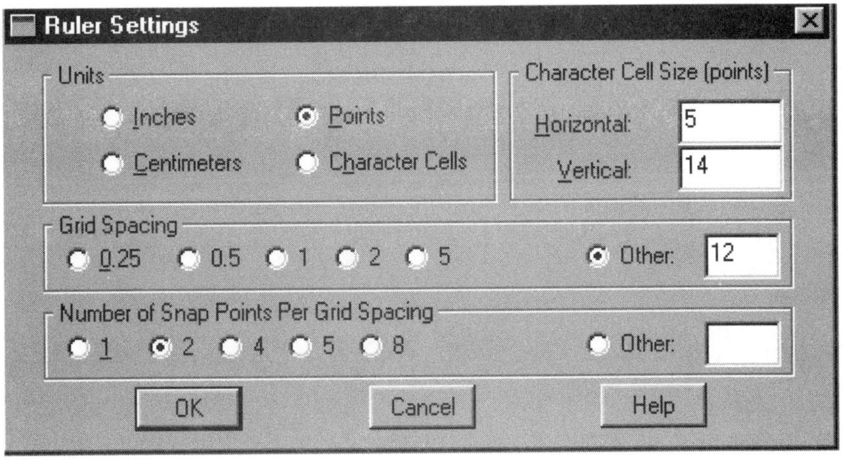

FIGURE 6.20 Ruler Settings dialog box.

The upper part of the Ruler Settings dialog box is where the rulers' units are specified. They can be inches, centimeters, points, or character cells. If the last unit is used, then the controls in the group Character Cell Size on the right are used to specify the size of each character cell in points. The default settings for units and character cell size are derived from the property Coordinate Information of the form module.

The middle part of the Ruler Settings dialog box is where you specify the grid spacing, or the distance between grid lines. You can choose any of the five predetermined settings on the left. Or you can enter any value you desire by clicking the radio button Other and entering the value in the field to its right. In the case of Figure 6.20, the grid lines will be 12 points apart.

The lower part of the Ruler Settings dialog box allows you to set the number of snap points allowed between the grid lines. If the Grid Snap property of the canvas is set, then the ratio between the Grid Spacing and Number of Snap Points per Grid Spacing becomes the basic unit of measurement. If for example, the ruler unit is inches, the grid spacing is 1 inch, and the number of snap points is 4, then the smallest distance an object can be moved in any direction is 1/4 of an inch (grid spacing divided by number of snap points per grid spacing). Similarly, the smallest dimension of any newly created object will be 1/4 of an inch. Distances and dimensions will now be multiples of 1/4 of an inch. In other words, a line can be 1/2 inch or 2.75 inches long, but not 2 1/3 inches long. Thus, when Grid Snap is on, the ratio between grid spacing and number of grid points per grid spacing defines a new virtual coordinate system, or grid, that is coarser than the base system. When the Grid Snap property is not set, then the previous settings do not affect the dimensions of, or distances between objects in the Layout Editor. The menu item View | Snap to Grid controls the setting of this property.

6.5.3 CUSTOMIZING THE APPEARANCE OF THE LAYOUT EDITOR

The Layout Editor can be used at different magnification levels: the higher the magnification level, the larger will the objects look on the screen. To increase the magnification level of the Editor perform these actions:

1. Select the Magnify icon in the tool palette.
2. Click anywhere on the canvas.
3. The current size of the layout is doubled.

An alternate way to magnify the current layout is to click the icon Zoom In on the toolbar or to select View | Zoom In from the Editor's menu. To reduce the magnification level of the Layout Editor click the icon Zoom Out on the toolbar or choose View | Zoom Out from the menu. Each zoom out reduces the layout size in half.

If you get too much carried away zooming in and out and lose track of the original size of the objects, then select View | Normal Size from the menu. If you select View | Fit to Window from the menu, the whole layout work area is reduced to fit in the current Layout Editor window. Remember that the size of this area is defined in Layout Settings dialog box (see Figure 6.19).

You also have the option to hide and display certain components of the Layout Editor window such as the tool palette, status bar, canvas, and view, which are displayed by default. Check menu items under the View menu control their display status. For example, to hide the tool palette, deselect View | Tool Palette.

6.5.4 CUSTOMIZING GRAPHICS OPTIONS

You can change the way objects are drawn in general, and the way arcs, rounded rectangles, and text objects are created, in particular. You can also change the way images are treated by the Form Builder.

- **General Graphics Options.** To view or modify general graphics options select Format | Graphics Options | General from the Layout Editor menu. In the General Drawing Options dialog box that appears you can specify how end points of lines should be rendered, how corners of rectangles should be rendered, and how objects will be created.
- **Arc Graphics Options.** To view or modify arc graphics options, choose Format | Graphics Options | Arc from the menu. In the Arc Drawing Options dialog box that appears you can specify which part of the canvas region defined by the arc will be the fill region for the arc, and how the borderlines will be drawn.
- **Text Graphics Options.** To view or modify text graphics options, choose Format | Graphics Options | Text from the menu. In the Text Drawing Options dialog box that appears you can control the alignment of the text labels, and whether the text box is adjusted dynamically or not.

- **Round Rectangle Graphics Options.** To view or modify round rectangle graphics options, choose Format | Graphics Options | Rounded Rectangle from the menu. In the Rounded Rectangle Drawing Options dialog box that appears, you can specify the radius of the rounded corners.
- **Image Graphics Options.** To view or modify image graphics options, choose Format | Graphics Options | Image from the menu. In the Image Drawing Options dialog box that appears you can control the quality of images imported on the canvas. The higher the image quality, better it will appear on the screen. The drawback to this is that the screen drawing process will be more resource intensive, and, therefore, slower. Applications to be deployed across slower networks such as the Internet are especially sensitive to image size.

Another way to save some precious computing resources when working with boilerplate images is to reduce their resolution. Resolution is the amount of detail provided for each image. The resolution of an image is proportional to its quality, but also to the resources it consumes, and the time it takes to be displayed on the screen. Often, an acceptable compromise is reached, and low-resolution images that are easier to manipulate are used. To reduce the resolution of an image follow these steps:

1. Select the image to modify.
2. Select Format | Graphics Options | Reduce Image Resolution from the menu.

You can reduce the resolution only for one image at a time. The reverse action is not available; the resolution of an image cannot be increased. This may result in loss of image's details. For example, consider an image that is imported on the canvas, and its size is reduced. If the image resolution is reduced, the quality of the image will deteriorate. Because of the image's small size, this deterioration may not be noticeable. But, if the image is restored to its original size, degradation of its quality will be noticeable.

> **TIP**
>
> As with other settings of boilerplate objects, the options described in these sections affect the properties of selected objects and become the default properties that the Layout Editor will use for other objects created in the future. If you want to modify the properties of only one object, without affecting the default settings of the Layout Editor, double-click the object on the canvas or the Object Navigator and set the properties in the Property Palette.

6.6 CUSTOMIZING COLOR PALETTES

Earlier in the chapter, it was explained how you can change fill, line and text colors of objects in the Layout Editor. A color palette like the one in Figure 6.12 is used. This color palette contains 228 cells. Each of the cells represents a different combination of red, green and blue (RGB) levels, which make up a distinct color or nuance on the palette. Each form can use one color palette, which most often is the Form Builder's default palette. However, if the application requires special colors that do not exist in the palette, the Layout Editor gives you the ability to create these colors and save them as color palettes in the file system or to the database. A session of the Form Builder can use only one color palette. If the default palette is not used, its name is specified in the General tab of the Preferences dialog box, as shown in Figure 6.21. If the Color Palette field of this dialog box is blank, the default palette is in use. Recall that you can access the Preferences dialog box by selecting Tools | Preferences from the Form Builder menu.

In the Preferences dialog box, the Color Mode list box specifies one of the ways to use this color palette: Read-Only—Shared, Read-Only—Private, or Editable. When custom palettes are used, it is important, especially in team development efforts, that all developers use the same baseline palette in read-only shared mode. This ensures that the color scheme used by all the forms in the application

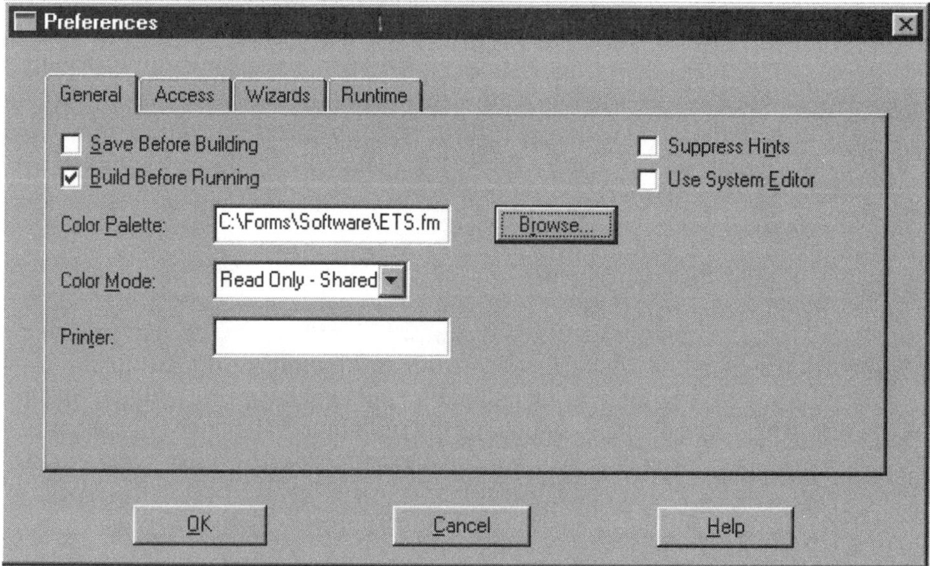

FIGURE 6.21 The General tab of the Preferences dialog box where a custom color palette is defined.

is independent from individual programmers, and protected from accidental changes. If the settings of the color palette options are changed, the Form Builder must be restarted for the changes to take effect.

> **WARNING**
>
> Make sure to never edit the default color palette. This should be used as a baseline for the colors in your application. Follow the discussion presented in the following sections with a copy of your default palette. The palettes provided by Developer/2000 are located in the folder Tools\Common of the Oracle Home folder of your installation. To make a copy of the default palette, copy the file Col256.pal from this folder to a working folder, for example C:\ETS, and rename it to ETS.PAL.

6.6.1 EDITING COLOR PALETTES

If you want to edit the color palette, you must load it in edit mode. The following steps are required to do this:

1. Select Tool | Preferences from the menu. The Preferences dialog box appears (see Figure 6.21).
2. Enter the name of the color palette to be edited in the Color Palette field. Note that you must enter the full path and name of the files as shown in Figure 6.21.
3. Choose "Editable" from the Color Mode list box.
4. Click OK.
5. Exit and restart the Form Builder so that the new preference settings may take effect.

When the Form Builder is restarted you may modify the color palette according to your needs. As a first step open a Layout Editor window and select Format | Layout Options | Color Palette from the Layout Editor menu. The Color Palette dialog box appears (see Figure 6.22). Note that this menu item is enabled only if the current color palette is editable.

The central part of the Color Palette dialog box displays the colors defined in the current palette. The Palette Name field under it displays the name of the palette. Each color in the palette can be selected for editing by clicking its cell. The color cell currently selected has a raised bevel status, and its name is displayed in the Current Color item. In the default palette, sixteen colors in the 4 × 4 cells square in the upper left corner of the palette use descriptive English names such as *black, green, magenta,* or *darkgrey*. Eight cells underneath them are named

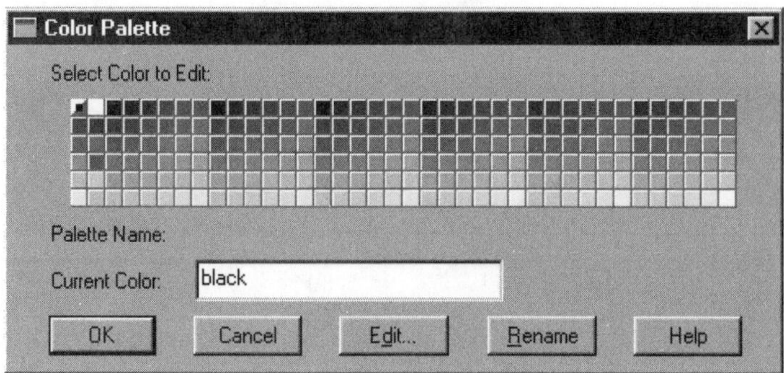

FIGURE 6.22 The Color Palette dialog box.

custom1 through *custom8*. In the default palette, they are blank. These are additional colors that you can create, besides editing the existing ones. The rest of the colors have names such as r100g25b100 that describe their saturation level of red, green and blue.

If you want to rename a selected color, follow these steps:

1. Click inside the Current Color text item.
2. Type the new name.
3. Click Rename button on the Color Palette dialog box.

The color now assumes the new name. To edit an already selected color, or to add a custom color to the palette, click Edit button on the Color Palette dialog box. The Select Color dialog box appears (see Figure 6.23).

You could select any of the forty-eight basic colors on the upper left quarter of the window as your new color. However, since they are already defined in the color palette, you will end up with duplicate cells. What you want to do instead, is use the basic colors to define a custom color, as described here:

1. Click one of the sixteen rectangles in the Custom Color group. You will fill this rectangle with the color that you will define in the following steps.
2. Click the Basic Color rectangle that resembles the most the color you want to create.
3. Refine the color by dragging the cross hair icon around the big color spectrum box on the right half of the window. You may also drag the white triangle up and down the vertical bar further right, or directly enter numeric values from 0 to 255 in the fields under the box.
4. Click the Add to Custom Colors button, when you have defined the color

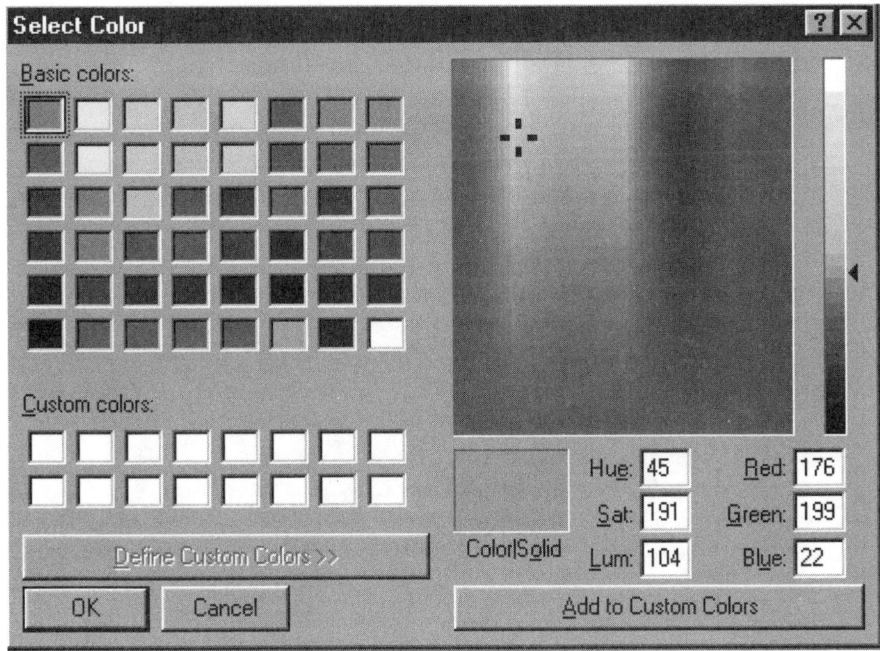

FIGURE 6.23 Select Color dialog box.

you want. The newly defined color is placed in the Custom Color rectangle selected in Step 1.

You can specify up to sixteen different Custom Colors. To use one of them in the color palette, select it, and click OK in the Select Color dialog box. The control is returned to the Color Palette dialog box. The cell that was selected before Edit button was pressed, now displays the new color.

If you are finished editing colors or creating new ones, click OK to dismiss the Color Palette dialog box. Export the new palette to the file system or the database, if you need to distribute it to other developers. The next section provides instructions on how to export and import a color palette. It is very important not to proceed with Forms development with the tool palette in Editable mode. Set its mode to Read Only—Shared with the following actions:

1. Select Tools | Preferences from the menu. The Preferences dialog box appears.
2. Choose Read Only—Shared from the Color Mode drop-down list.
3. Click OK.
4. Restart the Form Builder for the changes to take effect.

6.6.2 EXPORTING AND IMPORTING COLOR PALETTES

If an application needs a customized color palette, you must ensure that all the forms are being developed using the same palette. It would be unwise to ask each developer to change the color palette and to expect these palettes to be the same. Instead, only one color palette must be modified. Then, it is exported either as a file or as an object in the database. This exported palette is and should be treated like any other resource or component of the application. It must be protected from accidental damages, backed up regularly, and made available, in read-only shared mode, to all those programmers that need it. To use the master color palette, the programmers, in turn, import it in their environment. The following steps allow you to export a color palette:

1. Open the Layout Editor if not already opened.
2. Select File | Export | Color Palette from the menu. The Export dialog box appears (see Figure 6.24). The Color Palette menu item is enabled only if a Layout Editor window is opened and currently selected.
3. Specify where to export the color palette and under which name.
4. Click OK. The color palette is exported according to your specifications.

To help you specify the destination of the exported color palette, the export dialog box offers a browse utility. If you choose to export to the file system, clicking Browse button will display a standard Save As dialog box. Form Builder will prompt you to save the file in the same directory and with the same name as the current module. The extension of an exported color palette is PAL.

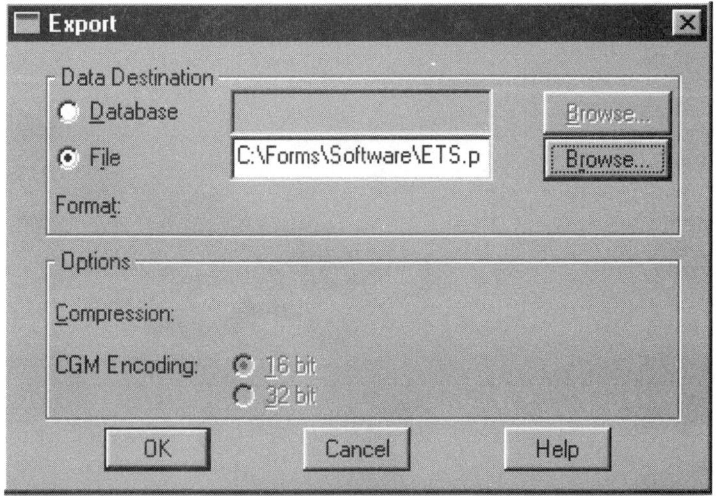

FIGURE 6.24 The Export dialog box.

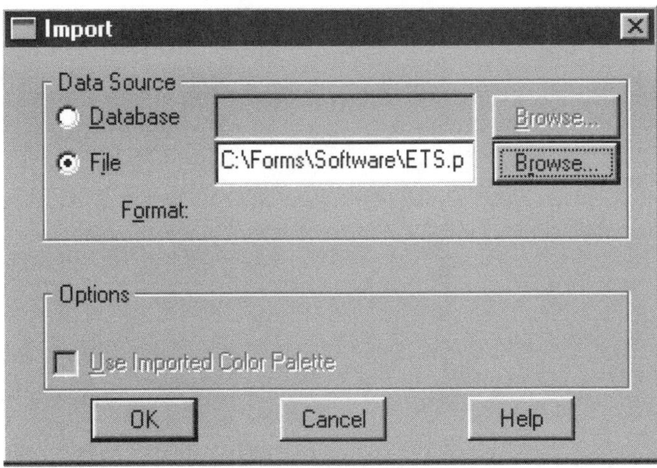

FIGURE 6.25 The Import dialog box.

To import a color palette, follow these steps:

1. Open the Layout Editor if not already opened.
2. Select File | Import | Color Palette from the menu. The Import dialog box appears (see Figure 6.25). The Color Palette menu item is enabled only if a Layout Editor window is selected and the Form Builder's color palette mode is set to Editable.
3. Specify the location and file name of the palette file to be imported.
4. Click OK. The color palette is imported from the file or database object you specified.

To help you locate the color palette, the import dialog box offers a browse utility. If you chose to import a file, clicking Browse button will display a standard Open dialog box. If you are importing the palette form the database, clicking Browse button displays a dialog box almost identical to the one shown in Figure 4.7 in Chapter 4. The only difference is that the title is Import from Database. Select the palette from the list, and click OK to return to the Import dialog box.

6.7 SUMMARY

This chapter provided information about one of the most important components of Oracle Forms Form Builder: the Layout Editor. The main concepts discussed were

- **Accessing the Layout Editor**
- **Components of the Layout Editor**
  - Layout Work area
  - Toolbar
  - Tool Palette
  - Status Bar
- **Working with Objects in Layout Editor**
  - Undoing Changes
  - Creating Objects
  - Setting the Context of Layout Editor
  - Selecting Objects
  - Moving, Resizing, and Reshaping Objects
  - Aligning Objects
  - Setting Objects to Same Size
  - Deleting Objects
  - Cutting and Copying Objects
  - Pasting and Duplicating Objects
  - Grouping and Ungrouping
  - Rotating
  - Working with Overlapping Objects
- **Setting Visual Attributes in the Layout Editor**
  - Font Attributes
  - Spacing and Justification Settings
  - Color Attributes
  - Line and Border Attributes
  - Maintaining Properties in the Property Palette
- **Customizing the Layout Editor**
  - Customizing Layout Work area
  - Customizing Ruler Settings
  - Customizing the Appearance of the Layout Editor
- **Customizing Graphics Options**
  - General Graphics Options
  - Arc Graphics Options
  - Text Graphics Options
  - Round Rectangle Graphics Options
  - Image Graphics Options
- **Customizing Color Palettes**
  - Editing Color Palettes
  - Exporting and Importing Color Palettes

The following table describes the software assets that were discussed in this chapter. From the main HTML page of the software utilities provided with the book follow the links *Software* and *Chapter 6* to access these assets:

ASSET NAME	DESCRIPTION
CH06.PAL	A copy of the Form Builder default palette.

Chapter 7

Property Palette, Menu Editor, and Object Editor

We must learn to explore all the options and possibilities that confront us in a complex and rapidly changing world.

—James William Fulbright

- The Property Palette
- Components of Property Palettes
- Using the Property Palette
- The Menu Editor
- Components of Menu Editor
- Using the Menu Editor
- The Library Editor
- Components of the Library Editor
- Using the Library Editor
- Summary

As you saw in Chapter 4, the Form Builder has several components used for special tasks and functions in the design and development process. The previous two chapters discussed in detail two of them: the Object Navigator and the Layout Editor. This chapter focuses on three other components: the Property Palette, the Menu Editor, and the Object Editor.

7.1 THE PROPERTY PALETTE

The behavior and functionality of objects in Form Builder applications is determined by their properties. Upon creation, each object is assigned a set of default properties, which can be changed and reset based on the needs of the application. The Property Palette is the Form Builder component that allows you to access and modify properties of one or more objects. There is a variety of ways to access the Property Palette in the Form Builder.

- From anywhere in the application, you can press F4 on the keyboard or select Tools | Property Palette from the menu. This command will display a Property Palette window as long as the Form Builder's focus is on at least one object instance. If there are no objects selected when the command is issued, the menu item is disabled.
- In the Object Navigator, Layout Editor, or Menu Editor you can also right-click to display the popup menu, and select Property Palette from this menu.
- Another way to access the properties of most objects displayed in the Object Navigator is to double-click the object type icon to the left of the object's name. The only exception to this would be canvases, menus and PL/SQL objects. Double-clicking their icons brings up the Layout Editor, Menu Editor, and PL/SQL Editor, respectively. If you are in a Layout Editor or Menu Editor window, double clicking displays the properties of objects on the Property Palette.

All the actions above will open a Property Palette window if none has been opened up to that point. If there is a Property Palette already open, these actions will make that window the current window in the Form Builder. Often, there is a need to compare properties of objects while developing applications. To do this, you can display each of them in its own Property Palette. To open additional Property Palettes, keep the SHIFT key pressed while double-clicking the object whose properties you want to display.

If a Property Palette is already open and you want to navigate to it, you can select it from the list of currently open windows accessible from the Window menu of the Form Builder. Unfortunately, the title of the window is simply Property Palette, without any reference to the name of the object, which may not be very helpful if more than one Property Palette is open.

7.2 COMPONENTS OF PROPERTY PALETTES

Figure 7.1 displays the Property Palette for a trigger in the ETS application. There are three major components on this window. The toolbar allows access to common commands related to properties; the context bar provides information about the type and name of the currently selected object; the property sheet contains all the properties that apply to the current selection of objects, and their settings. The rest of this section discusses in detail each of these components.

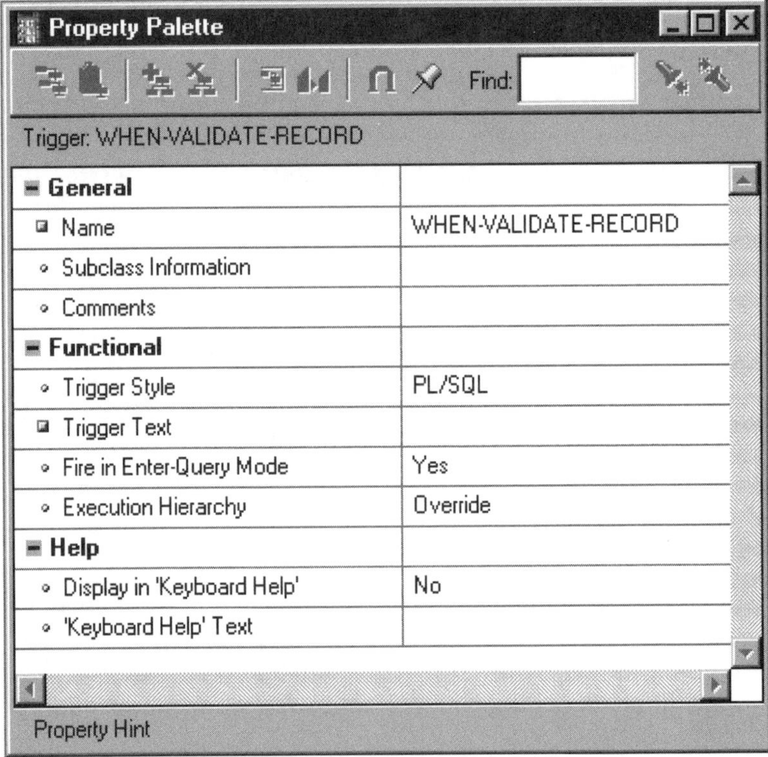

FIGURE 7.1 Components of the Property Palette.

7.2.1 TOOLBAR

Like the Object Navigator and the Layout Editor, the Property Palette comes with a toolbar that allows you to access quickly commands often used in this window. The toolbar is displayed horizontally, right under the window's title bar. The commands invoked by a number of these icons are also accessible from the submenu Property of the Property Palette. The following is a list of all the icons on the toolbar accompanied by their names and a brief description for each of them. The corresponding menu items are shown wherever they exist.

- **Copy Properties.** Use this icon to copy the properties settings displayed in the Property Palette. Alternatively, select Property | Copy Properties from the menu.
- **Paste Properties.** Use this icon to paste property settings in the current Property Palette. Alternatively, select Property | Paste Properties from the menu.
- **Add Property.** Use this icon to add a property to the property class displayed in the Property Palette. Alternatively, select Property | Add Property from the menu. Both the icon and the menu item are disabled if the Property Palette does not contain properties of a property class.
- **Delete Property.** Use this icon to remove the selected property from the property class displayed in the Property Palette. Alternatively, select Property | Delete Property from the menu. Both the icon and the menu item are disabled if the Property Palette does not contain properties of a property class.
- **Property Class.** Use this icon to create a property class based on the properties displayed in the Property Palette.
- **Inherit.** Use this icon to set the currently selected property to its default value.
- **Intersect.** This icon indicates that the Property Palette is in Intersect mode. In this mode, only the common properties of the selected objects are displayed. Clicking the icon toggles the Property Palette's mode to Union.
- **Union.** This icon indicates that the Property Palette is in Union mode. In this mode, all the properties of the selected objects are displayed. Clicking the icon toggles the Property Palette's mode to Intersect.
- **Unfreeze.** This icon indicates that the Property Palette is in Unfreeze mode; its content is updated each time a new object is selected to reflect properties of the current selection. Clicking the icon toggles the Property Palette's mode to Freeze. The same effect can be achieved by checking the item Property | Freeze Properties from the menu.
- **Freeze.** This icon indicates that the Property Palette is in Freeze mode; it displays the properties of only one object, and is not synchronized with ob-

jects selected in the Navigator and other editors. Clicking the icon or deselecting the item Property | Freeze Properties from the menu toggles the Property Palette's mode to Unfreeze.

In addition to the icons listed above, the Property Palette's toolbar contains a Fast Search control very similar in use and behavior to the same control in the Object Navigator's toolbar. It is made up of a text field where search criteria are entered, and two iconic buttons that specify the direction of search. The Fast Search control enhances the search of properties for objects with a long list of properties. Its auto-reduction feature helps you locate properties displayed in the Palette by typing the first few characters of their name. Refer to Section 5.2.2 in Chapter 5 for more information on the Fast Search control.

7.2.2 CONTEXT BAR

The context bar is located immediately below the toolbar and displays information that identifies the object whose properties are currently displayed in the window. The type and name of the object define the context of the window. In Figure 7.1 for example, the Property Palette shows information about the trigger WHEN-VALIDATE-RECORD. When more than one object is selected, the context bar displays the message "Multiple selection." When no objects are selected, the message displayed becomes "No selection."

7.2.3 THE PROPERTY SHEET

The property sheet occupies most of the Property Palette window. It has the form of a two-column table. The left column contains the names of properties and the right one the setting for each property. The length of this list depends on the object or group of objects selected.

The properties in the list are grouped by functionality. Each functional group begins with a header entry in bold typeface. All objects have one common group, General, with at least three properties in it: Name, Subclass Information, and Comments. The reason is simple: each object must have a name, its property settings may be inherited (or subclassed) from another object or property class, and its behavior and functionality may be documented and commented.

Other groups of properties may be added to the list based on the type and number of selected objects and based on the Intersection mode of the Property Palette. The property groups can be expanded and collapsed by double-clicking their name on the property sheet or by selecting Property | Expand and Property | Collapse from the Property Palette menu. You also have the option to expand or collapse all the groups on the property sheet by selecting Property | Expand All and Property | Collapse All from the menu. By default, the Property Palette expands all the groups of properties.

When more than one object is selected, the properties displayed in the properties list depend on the mode of the Property Palette. If it is in Intersect mode, which is also the default mode, only common properties are listed. If the Property Palette is in Union mode, all the properties of selected objects are listed. If the selected objects share a common property, the actual value of its setting is displayed only if it is the same for all of objects. If at least one object contains a different setting, the right column of the property list will display the string "*****." The name of the property on the left column will be preceded by a question mark as an indicator of this situation.

7.3 USING THE PROPERTY PALETTE

This section explains how to use the Property Palette to set properties, copy and paste them.

7.3.1 SETTING PROPERTIES OF OBJECTS

When you are viewing properties in the Property Palette, their settings appear in the tabular format similar to the one shown in Figure 7.1. In order to modify the setting of a property, you need to select the row that represents the property and then click the right-hand column of the row. Depending on the type of property, the cell on the property sheet is transformed in one of the following controls:

- **Text item.** If the property setting can be specified by a text string or a digit, the property setting cell is a text item, in which you can type the desired value. If the property is already set, the text in the text item is selected when you click, so that it can be typed over more easily.
- **Text item with Text Editor button.** If the text for the property setting can be particularly long, a button is displayed at the end of the text item. Clicking this button brings up the Form Builder's text editor, where you can type and edit the text more easily.
- **List box.** If the property setting must be chosen from a list of pre-defined values, the property setting cell becomes a list box. This list contains the valid settings for the property, from which one must be chosen. When appropriate, this list allows you to set the property to NULL by selecting the option <Null> or <Unspecified> from the list.
- **Text item with List of Values button.** When the number of options is larger than what a list box handles, the Form Builder uses List of Values controls to help you set the property. Visually, the cell appears as a text item followed by a button. Clicking this button displays the List of Values control, from which you can select the desired value for the property. For this type of property, you can directly type text in the text field. For most of the prop-

erties, the Form Builder will validate your entry against the List of Values. If the test fails, you will not be allowed to continue without entering a valid value. However, for a few properties such as Font Name for text items, the validation test is not done until the form is generated.

- **Button More...** . If setting a property requires more complicated actions, then the property setting cell displays the More button. Clicking on the button displays a dialog box in which you can specify the settings accordingly. For properties whose setting is PL/SQL code, such as the property Trigger Text, clicking More button launches the PL/SQL Editor for that trigger.

There are instances, especially when multiple objects are selected, when you cannot set a property. For example, you cannot set the name of multiple objects with one command. In these cases, the Form Builder disables the property-setting bar.

If more than one object is selected, setting a property will store the setting in all the objects that contain that property. The action will overwrite any existing settings of that property. This can be especially helpful when creating applications with objects that share a consistent look and interface such as text font, color schemes, and style. There is a caveat here, though. The Form Builder does not warn you about overwritten properties. Nor does it allow you to undo a property setting action. Therefore you should be careful not to lose precious work when setting properties this way.

7.3.2 COMPARING PROPERTIES OF OBJECTS

A quick way to compare the properties of two or more objects is to select them and navigate to a Property Palette in Intersect (default) mode. The properties displayed in the property list are the ones the objects share. If the settings have a value displayed, all objects share that value; if the setting displays "*****," at least one object has a different setting for that property.

For a more detailed comparison, you need to display each object in its separate Property Palette. Earlier in the chapter you learned how to open more than one of these windows. By default, each Property Palette is synchronized with the Object Navigator, Layout Editor and Menu Editor. This means that it will display the properties of the current selection in one of these windows. If they are left in this default state, all the Property Palette windows in the Form Builder will contain exactly the same information.

In order to display the properties of two or more objects simultaneously in separate windows, you must break this synchronization. To do this, toggle the state of the Property Palette window to Freeze as explained in Section 7.2.1. In this state, the properties of the object are "pinned" to the window and will remain displayed there even after you select another object in the other components of Form Builder. You can navigate to a second Property Palette and display side-by-side the properties of different objects.

7.3.3 COPYING AND PASTING PROPERTIES OF OBJECTS

Form Builder extends the concept of copying and pasting objects to that of copying and pasting their properties. The commands Copy Properties and Paste Properties can be accessed from the Property Palette toolbar and Property menu. The following actions are needed to copy properties:

1. Select the object or group of objects whose properties you want to copy.
2. Click Copy Properties icon from the window's toolbar or choose Property | Copy Properties from the menu.

The Form Builder places the property settings in the clipboard, ready to be pasted onto another object. If you are copying properties of multiple objects, only the common properties of these objects are copied. This means that property settings that look like '*****' in the Property Palette will not be copied to the clipboard.

To paste properties, follow these steps:

1. Select the object or group of objects on which you want to paste the properties
2. Click Paste Properties icon from the window's toolbar or choose Property | Paste Properties from the menu.

The objects where you paste the properties need not be of the same type as the objects from which these properties were copied. When issuing a Paste Properties command, Form Builder will paste only those properties that have a meaning for the target object. This feature allows you, for example, to copy the properties of an item in a form module and paste them on a menu item. Only shared attributes such as Font Name, Font Size, and Font Style, will be applied to the menu item.

You should be cautious when copying and pasting properties, because these commands act upon all the properties of the selected objects. If, for example, you copy the properties of an item and paste them onto another item, *all* their properties, except name, will become identical. Thus, you will end up with two overlapping items that have the same functionality. A better way to share common properties of similar objects is to create property classes and visual attributes. The subclassing mechanism can be used to set the properties of objects based on property classes or properties of other objects. The benefits and features of this mechanism are explained in Chapter 8.

7.4 THE MENU EDITOR

The Menu Editor is a tool that facilitates the visual development of menus for Form Builder applications. It is tightly integrated with the functionality of the Object Navigator. In many aspects, it is the counterpart of the Layout Editor in menu development activities. By graphically displaying the menu while it is being designed, the Menu Editor allows application developers to get a real picture of its behavior at runtime.

In order to access the Menu Editor, at least one menu module must be open in the Object Navigator. Chapter 4 provides instructions on how to open or create new modules in the Form Builder. There are different ways to access the Menu Editor. The most generic one launches a Menu Editor window from the Object Navigator when you perform these actions:

1. Click anywhere in the hierarchy tree of the menu module you want to display in the editor.
2. Select Tools | Menu Editor from the Navigator menu. The Menu Editor window appears.

A menu module usually contains more than one menu object. The Menu Editor window displays only one menu object at a time. When invoked with the steps listed above, the Editor will display the menu that is on top of the menu hierarchy for the current module. If you want to work with a different menu object in that module, select its name from the list box Display Menu on the Menu Editor's toolbar.

Alternatively, expand the hierarchy of menu objects in the Object Navigator until you see the desired menu and its characteristic icon. This action opens a Menu Editor window and displays the selected menu in it. If there is an editor window already open for that module, double-clicking the icon of any menu object simply sets the Form Builder's focus to that window; it does not replace the menu displayed in the Menu Editor window with the new object.

7.5 COMPONENTS OF MENU EDITOR

Figure 7.2 presents a typical Menu Editor window, with a sample menu in it. The main component of this window is the work area in which menus and menu items are displayed, created, modified, or deleted. Like other Form Builder components, the Menu Editor comes with a toolbar that allows you to quickly display a different menu in the work area, or to perform frequently used commands. The following sections describe these components.

7.5.1 THE MENU EDITOR WORK AREA

This is the heart of the Menu Editor, where all the menu design activities occur. It allows you to visualize the structure of the menu being created, and to access the properties of all the objects that are part of it. There are no size limits for the work area. It will accommodate as many objects as necessary. If they extend beyond the

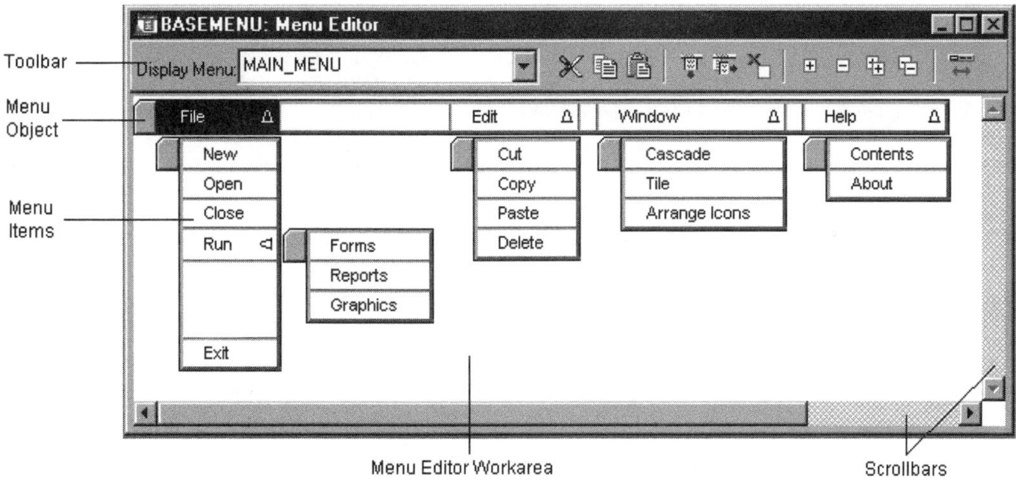

FIGURE 7.2 Components of Menu Editor window.

limits of the Menu Editor window, vertical and horizontal scroll bars can be used to navigate to them. The orientation of the objects in the work area can be switched from horizontal to vertical, depending on your preference. Later in the chapter you will see how to do this.

There are two types of objects displayed in the Menu Editor work area: menus and menu items. Although they look similar, they are fundamentally different. Menus own menu items and organize them, and the functionality they make available, in a logical, user-friendly fashion. Menu items carry out the actual actions in the application such as connecting, disconnecting, saving, cutting and pasting. Visually, menus are represented by menu handles ▯, whereas menu items by rectangular boxes. For example, in Figure 7.2, the rectangles displayed horizontally, containing the labels File, Edit, Window, and Help are the menu items of the MAIN_MENU menu object. This menu itself is represented by the gray-colored box at the left of menu item File. Similarly, the FILE menu is represented by the handle on the left of the New menu item, and all its items are listed vertically underneath.

7.5.2 TOOLBAR

The toolbar for the Menu Editor is a group of iconic tools that make often-used actions and commands as easy as one mouse click. For clarity, it is shown separately in Figure 7.3. The first control on the toolbar is the list box Display Menu. It displays the name of the menu object currently loaded in the work area. The Display Menu list box makes the process of switching from one menu to another in the Editor very simple. All you have to do is select the menu you want to work

FIGURE 7.3 Menu Editor Toolbar.

with from this list. The Menu Editor replaces the menu currently displayed in the work area with the one you selected.

The first group of icons on the toolbar is also present in the Object Navigator and Layout Editor windows. The icons here provide quick access to commands for cutting, copying and pasting objects in the Menu Editor. The next three buttons are used to create or delete menu objects in the editor. The next four icons are used to expand and collapse the branches of menus. Finally, the last icon, Switch Orientation, is used to toggle the menu display between horizontal and vertical orientation. Its corresponding menu item is Menu | Switch Orientation.

7.6 USING THE MENU EDITOR

This section explains how to use the Menu Editor to design and create menus for Form Builder applications. Unlike the Layout Editor, where the Undo command protects the application from accidents and errors, in the Menu Editor you cannot undo commands. However, before accomplishing potentially destructive tasks such as deleting or replacing objects, the Menu Editor will warn you and prompt you to confirm the action.

To better understand the features and techniques explained in this section, use the menu module CH7.MMB provided with the companion software. Open the module, launch the Menu Editor, and display the menu named MAIN_MENU in the work area, as explained earlier in this chapter.

7.6.1 SELECTING AND NAVIGATING

In the Menu Editor you work with either menu objects or menu items. A variety of techniques is used to navigate to and select each of them. It the object you want to navigate to is visible, clicking it moves the Form Builder's focus on the object and selects it. To select a menu item, simply click the rectangle that represents it on the window. To select a menu, click the menu handle to its left. In both cases, the coloration of the object is reversed, thus, clearly marking it as selected. If you need to select more than one object, use either SHIFT+CLICK or CTRL+CLICK techniques similar to the ones used for the same purpose in the Object Navigator.

When the Synchronize property of the Object Navigator is on, each object you select in the Menu Editor will be automatically selected in the Navigator, and vice versa. This means that, besides the Menu Editor, you can use the Navigator to select the menu objects you want to work with.

Each submenu has an expand/collapse status indicator to the right of its label. The icon ▼ indicates that the menu is collapsed; the icon △ indicates that the menu is expanded. There are three ways to expand a menu. The simplest one is to click its ▼ icon. You can also select the menu to expand and then click the Expand icon on the toolbar, or choose Menu | Expand from the menu. The Expand command acts upon objects that are only one level below the current menu in the hierarchy. To expand all the menu levels below the current menu, click the Expand All icon from the toolbar, or choose Menu | Expand All from the menu.

In the Menu Editor, as in the Object Navigator, the opposite action of expanding the menu hierarchy is collapsing it. The quickest way to collapse a menu is to click its expand/collapse indicator . You may also select the menu you want to collapse and click the Collapse icon from the toolbar, or choose Menu | Collapse from the Form Builder menu.

The Menu Editor remembers the status of the hierarchical tree under the menu even after you collapse it. This means that, when a menu with several levels underneath is collapsed and then expanded again, the hierarchy view will be exactly as it was before it was collapsed. To collapse all the submenus under the current menu, Click the Collapse All icon on the toolbar, or choose Menu | Collapse All from the menu.

7.6.2 CREATING MENUS AND MENU ITEMS

In the Menu Editor you can create menus and menu items quickly and easily. To experience this, in this section you will build a menu similar to the menu provided in CH8.FMB. First create and save a new menu module that will be used during this section.

1. Start Form Builder.
2. Create a new menu module in the Object Navigator.
3. Replace the module's default name assigned by the Navigator with a more meaningful one, for example BASEMENU.
4. Save the newly created module to an appropriate directory in your file system.

Now you are ready to create the new menu. Launch the Menu Editor as explained in Section 7.4. The Form Builder creates and displays a menu called MAIN_MENU and a menu item labeled <New_Item>, which is selected and waiting for you to type over.

1. Type "File" over the <New_Item> label.
2. Click the Create Right icon on the toolbar or select Menu | Create Right from the menu. The editor creates a new item to the right of File.
3. Type "Edit" in the label of the new item.
4. Repeat steps 2 and 3 to create the items Window and Help for the MAIN_MENU.

If your Navigator has the Synchronize property on, you will see that the new menu items fall in the appropriate location in the Navigator's object tree as you create them. At this point, you have created the top-level menu. Its items could be terminal nodes that execute a command, or open a window; however, in a full-fledged application, they usually call other menus to offer more options to the user. To create the submenu of the File menu, perform these actions:

1. Select the File menu item.
2. Click the Create Down icon on the toolbar, or select Menu | Create Down from the menu. The editor creates a new menu and a <New_Menu> item for this menu. The File item in the MAIN_MENU is now linked to the newly created menu.
3. Type "New" over <New_Item> label.
4. Click the Create Down icon on the toolbar or select Menu | Create Down from the menu. This time, the editor creates a new menu item under New.
5. Label the new item "Open."
6. Repeat Step 3 and 4 to create the menu items Close, Run, Print, and Exit.

If you look at the Object Navigator window, you will notice that Form Builder has created a new menu and named it FILE_MENU. Its items are listed underneath as you created them. Furthermore, in the MAIN_MENU, the Form Builder has set the property Submenu Name of the item FILE to point to the menu FILE_MENU that you created. When users will run the application and select File from the menu, FILE_MENU will appear.

As you see, the Menu Editor allows you to draw this relationship in the work area. To practice your skills, create submenus for Edit, Window, and Help items, following the instructions above. They should contain the same items as the menu in Figure 7.2.

You can use the Layout Editor to create as many submenus as your application needs, all in one screen. For example, to create a submenu under the Run menu item of FILE_MENU, follow these steps:

1. Select the Run menu item.
2. Click the Create Right icon on the toolbar, or select Menu | Create Right from the menu. The editor creates a new submenu to the right of Run. The

Edit, Window, and Help submenus are shifted right to make room for the new submenu. The Object Navigator inserts this new submenu in the object tree and names it RUN_MENU.

3. Label the first item of this submenu "Forms."
4. Click the Create Down tool on the toolbar, or select Menu | Create Down from the menu. Each time this action is executed, the editor creates a new item for the RUN_MENU.
5. Follow Steps 3 and 4 above create menu items labeled "Reports" and "Graphics."

When finished, your menu should look like the one shown in Figure 7-4. Save the module, because you will use it later in the chapter. As you see, it takes only a few minutes to create the frame for the menu of an application. Its functionality must be embellished, and useful actions attached to each menu item. Issues related to this process are discussed in Chapter 17. By making the process of creating the menu simple and easy, the Form Builder allows you to focus the attention on this functionality. Technicalities such as linking or naming menu objects become transparent and are handled automatically by the Menu Editor.

7.6.3 DELETING MENUS AND MENU ITEMS

You can delete one menu item at a time or a selection of them by following these steps:

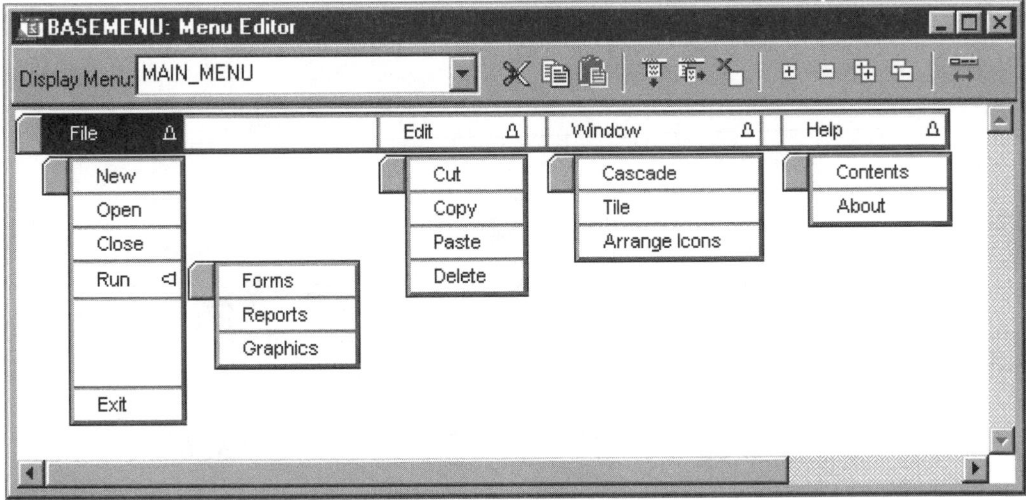

FIGURE 7.4 Base menu.

1. Select the item or items you want to delete.
2. Press DELETE from the keyboard or click the Delete icon on the toolbar. An alert box is displayed (see Figure 7.5). It wants you to confirm that you want to delete.
3. Click Yes if you want to proceed with the delete, or No to cancel the operation.

While the Form Builder allows you to delete multiple menu items at a time, menu objects can be deleted only one at a time. To delete a menu object, follow these steps:

1. Click the menu handle of the object you want to delete.
2. Press DELETE from the keyboard or click the Delete icon on the toolbar.

Depending on the selected object several things may happen here. If you selected to delete the top-level menu, you will be prompted to confirm the action with the same alert as in Figure 7-5. If the menu does not have any submenus attached to it, clicking Yes removes it from the current module. But, if the menu has submenus attached, clicking Yes will bring up the alert shown in Figure 7.6.

Clicking Yes in this alert box will delete the selected menu and all its submenus. Clicking No will delete only the current menu, but leave the submenus attached to it intact. Clicking Cancel rolls back the whole delete action. If, on the other hand, you selected to delete a submenu of the top-level menu, you will see the alert shown in Figure 7.7.

Clicking Detach will simply break the link between the selected menu and the menu item that owns it in the parent menu. The menu itself will not be removed from the current module. Clicking Delete will proceed with the deletion. Again here, if the selected menu has submenus attached to it, you will be prompted to delete the submenus or not, as discussed previously.

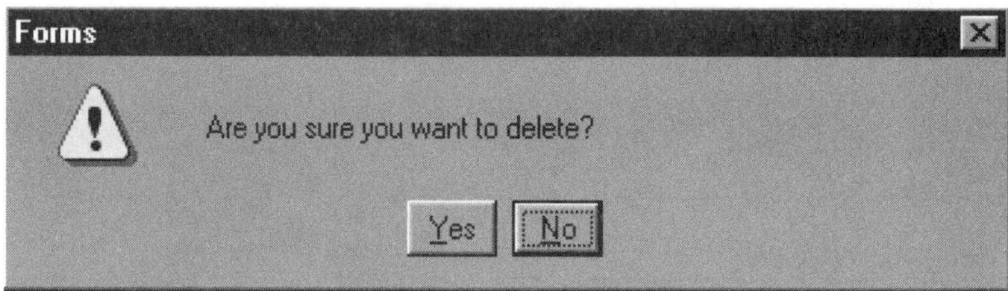

FIGURE 7.5 The Delete confirmation alert.

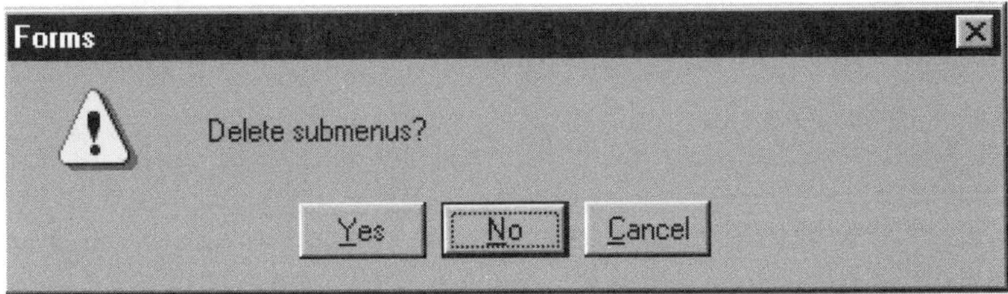

FIGURE 7.6 The Delete submenus confirmation alert.

7.6.4 CUTTING, COPYING, PASTING AND MOVING

As in other Form Builder editor, cutting in the Menu Editor is a safer alternative to deleting, because you can always paste the object from the clipboard. Cutting removes the object from the current module and places it in the Windows clipboard, where it will remain until another object is placed there. To cut, follow these steps:

1. Select the object or objects you want to cut.
2. Press CTRL+X from the keyboard or click the Cut icon on the toolbar.

As with deleting, you can cut several menu items together, but only one menu object at a time. To place the object in the clipboard without removing it from the Menu Editor, use the copy command. To copy, follow these steps:

1. Select the object or objects you want to copy.
2. Press CTRL+C from the keyboard or click the Copy icon on the toolbar.

Again here, copying works for more than one menu item, but only for one menu object at a time. Once an object is placed in the clipboard, you can paste it to another location in the menu. Follow these steps to paste:

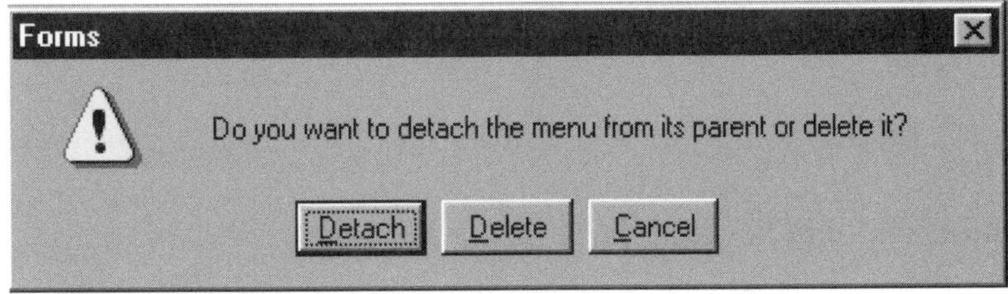

FIGURE 7.7 The Detach confirmation alert.

1. Click in the menu location where you want to paste the object.
2. Press CTRL+V from the keyboard or click the Paste icon on the toolbar.

The Menu Editor will execute the paste command only if you clicked a menu item. If the object in the clipboard is another menu item, then it is added to the right or below the current selection, as yet another item in the parent menu. But, if the object in the clipboard is a menu, then this is not only copied to the new location, but also attached to the selected item.

Cut and paste operations can be used to move objects from one window of the Menu Editor to another. If you want to move objects to a location within the window, you can simply drag and drop them to the new location. To move menu items:

1. Select the item or items you want to move.
2. Drag the selection to the new location. When the cursor moves outside the selected item, it changes shape to visually indicate that you are dragging an object.
3. Drop the selection on the new location.

The Menu Editor provides visual cues to help you move an item to the appropriate location. When the mouse moves on menu items, indicator bars appear along the borderlines of these items. They show the position where the objects being dragged will be inserted if you release the mouse button. These indicator bars appear along vertical edges of menu items for horizontally-displayed menus, and along horizontal edges for vertically-displayed ones.

Using drag-and-drop techniques with menus is slightly different than with menu items. First of all, as with other commands in this section, you cannot move multiple menus with one action. If you attempt to move more than one menu, Form Builder will display the error message "FRM-15205: Cannot drag more than one menu item at once."

Dragging the menu handle and dropping it to a new location, detaches the menu from the original menu item, and attaches it to the new item, but does not affect the menu itself. If during the move, the mouse cursor navigates inside an item to which this menu can be attached, that item is highlighted. If the menu item is not highlighted, then attaching the menu to that item is not allowed. For example, you cannot attach the menu to an item of its own.

When a menu is moved around and attached to another menu item, the Command Type property of that item is set to "Menu." If the previous setting for this property was "PL/SQL," and there is PL/SQL code attached to the menu item, the Menu Editor helps you prevent accidental loss of code when Command Type changes to "Menu." You will be prompted with the alert shown in Figure 7.8. If you do not want to save the code currently attached to the item, click

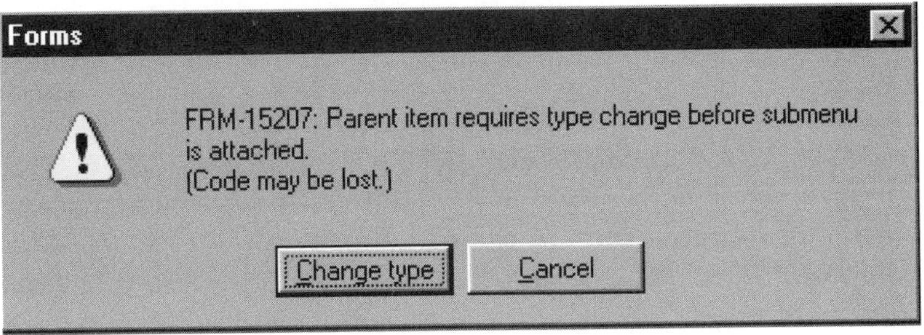

FIGURE 7.8 The Replace confirmation alert.

Change type button. Otherwise click Cancel and take the necessary steps to save the code. If another submenu is already attached to the item, an alert will appear and you can choose to either replace it with the selected menu, or cancel the operation.

As you can see, drag-and-drop in its simple form does not create any new menus in the module; it simply detaches and attaches existing ones to different items. But by using the CTRL key you can make drag-and-drop replicate and expand the functionality of copy and paste. To do this keep the CTRL pressed while performing the actions described earlier. The following steps describe this functionality:

1. CTRL+CLICK the menu handle of the menu you want to drag and hold the mouse button down.
2. Drag the menu to the new location while holding the key CTRL pressed.
3. Release the mouse button to drop the menu to the new location. At this point, the alert box shown in Figure 7.9 appears.

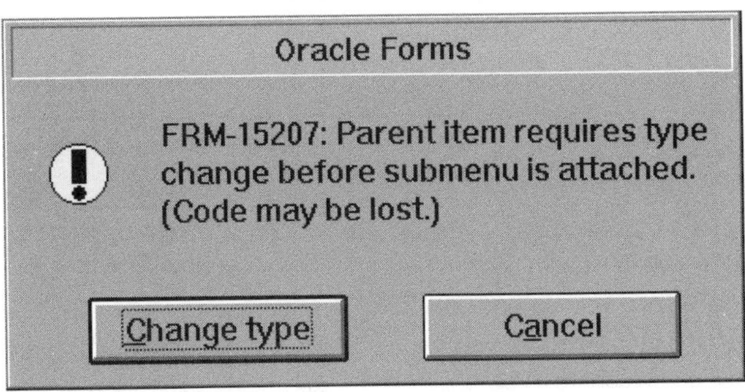

FIGURE 7.9 Duplicate Confirmation alert.

Clicking Duplicate will create a new menu with the same items as the original one, attached to the target item. The original menu is still in its place. Thus, this action is identical to a copy-and-paste action. Clicking Reuse button, will not create a new object. A pointer to the original menu is created, instead. The menu handle for both instances changes to the icon that indicates that there are multiple instances of that menu. Not all the instances of a multiple-instance menu may be visible at any given moment in the Menu Editor. If one instance is displayed, and you want to locate the other instances, select Menu | Next Instance from the menu. This command moves in circular fashion among all the instances of a menu object.

7.6.5 HORIZONTAL AND VERTICAL ORIENTATION

By default, the Menu Editor will display the top-level menu horizontally. However, there may be the need to switch the orientation and display the menu vertically. To experiment with this feature, continue working with the File menu from the BASEMENU module you created earlier in the chapter.

1. Select FILE_MENU from the Display Menu drop-down list box in the tool bar. The menu is displayed vertically in the Layout Editor window.
2. Click the Switch Orientation icon or select Menu | Switch Orientation from the menu.

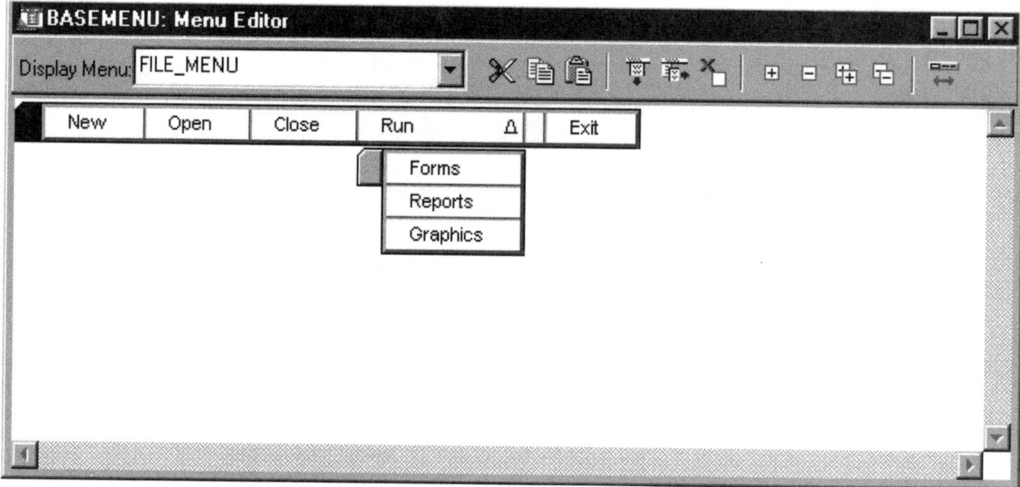

FIGURE 7.10 Vertical orientation of a menu in the Menu Editor.

Expand the FILE_MENU. You should see something similar to Figure 7.10. Click the icon Switch Orientation or select Menu | Switch Orientation again to return to the original view of the editor.

7.7 THE LIBRARY EDITOR

The Library Editor is the Form Builder component that helps you create and maintain object libraries. Object libraries, as the name indicates, are collections of objects stored in OLB library files. Members of an object library may be simple objects or object groups. The first type is used primarily to enforce standard settings of properties for similar objects. For example, a text item in an object library may be used to control the visual properties of all the items in your application. The second type of member is used to bundle together complex objects and functionality for the purpose of dropping it in modules. For example, a calendar control may be implemented using a number of Form Builder objects. Reusing it in several modules becomes trivial once these objects are grouped in an object group and stored in an object library. Chapter 8 will cover in detail the benefits and techniques of object reusability. The following sections only describe the Library Editor and the most important actions you can perform with it.

To invoke the Library Editor simply select Tools | Object Library from the menu. If an object library module is open in the Object Navigator, the editor loads its objects; otherwise, a new object library is created. Another way to invoke the Library Editor for an object library module currently open is to double-click the node type icon of any of its members in the Object Navigator.

7.8 COMPONENTS OF THE LIBRARY EDITOR

Figure 7.11 shows an object library displayed in the Library Editor. The main components of this editor are the tabbed work area in which the objects are organized and a toolbar that allows you to quickly access the most common commands of the Library Editor. The following sections describe these two components.

7.8.1 THE TABBED WORK AREA

The number of objects in an object library can be quite large. To help you view and organize these objects, the Object Library implements its work area in the form of a tabbed control. Each tab may contain several objects listed in it. As you

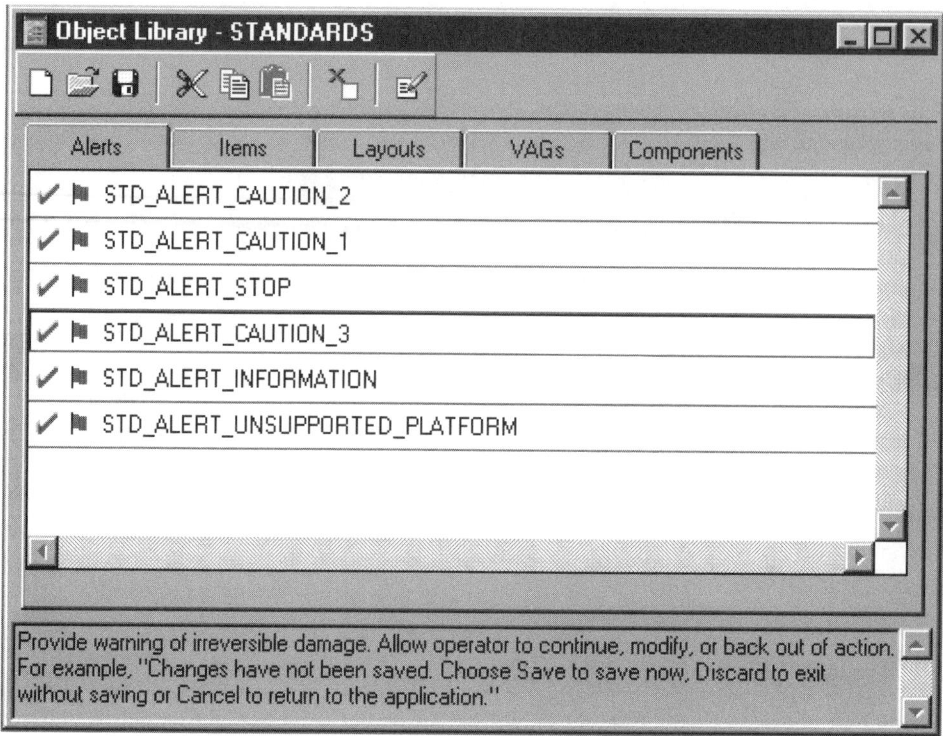

FIGURE 7.11 Components of Library Editor window.

can see from Figure 7.11, the work area displays the names of the objects inside the tab and any comments associated with them underneath the tabbed control.

7.8.2 TOOLBAR

The toolbar for the Library is shown in Figure 7.12. As in the Object Navigator or the Layout Editor, this toolbar provides icons to create, open, or save a module, as well as those to cut, copy and paste objects in the Library Editor. The next two icons (Create Tab and Delete Tab) are used to create or delete tabs in the library. The same actions can be performed by selecting Object | Create Tab and Object | Delete Tab from the menu. The last two icons on the toolbar are used to delete an object from the library and to edit the comments for a given object. The following

FIGURE 7.12 Library Editor Toolbar.

section explains in more detail the activities you can accomplish with the Library Editor.

7.9 USING THE LIBRARY EDITOR

This section explains how to use the Library Editor to create and maintain library tabs and to add and remove objects in these tabs. To better understand the features and techniques explained in this section, use the menu module CH7.OLB provided with the companion software. Open the module and launch the Library Editor.

7.9.1 MAINTAINING LIBRARY TABS

As explained earlier, object libraries organize their object in tabs. The Library Editor allows you to create and delete tabs from the library. To create a tab, follow these steps:

1. Select the tab after which the new tab will be located.
2. Click the icon Create Tab on the toolbar or select Object | Create Tab from the menu.

The Library Editor assigns default values to the properties Name and Label of the new tab. To replace these settings with more meaningful ones, display the Property Palette for the tab object and set these properties as explained in Section 7.3.1. To delete a tab from the library, select it and click the icon Delete Tab on the toolbar or select Object | Create Tab from the menu.

7.9.2 ADDING OBJECTS

The tabs of an object library serve as mere containers for holding objects. These objects are created and maintained in their original environment—a form or menu module. This means that in order to add an object to a library, the object must be created elsewhere in the Form Builder environment. To add an object from another module into an object library, perform these actions:

1. Open the Library Editor and select the tab that will host the new object.
2. Switch to the Object Navigator window and resize it so that it does not obfuscate the Library Editor window.
3. Select the object in the hierarchy tree.
4. Drag the object and drop it on the Library Editor window.

These actions create a copy of the object from the source module into the object library. To move the object from the module into the object library, hold the SHIFT key pressed while dragging it. If the object library contains already an object of the same type and name as the object you are trying to add, the Editor will inform you about this and ask whether you want to replace the existing object with the new one.

It is a good practice to provide a brief description of the objects you add to a library. This will help the other developers that will use this library to understand the meaning and purpose of the object. The following are the steps required to add comments to an object:

1. Select the object on the Library Editor.
2. Click the icon Edit Comment on the toolbar or select Object | Edit Comment from the menu.
3. Enter the description of the object in the Comment dialog box that appears.
4. Click OK.

7.9.3 REUSING LIBRARY OBJECTS

There are two fundamental ways in which you can reuse the objects of an object library in other modules: copying and subclassing. Copying simply creates a copy of the object in the target module; subclassing, in addition to this, maintains the reference of the object in the target module to the object in the object library. With subclassing, when properties of objects in the object library are changed the property changes of subclassed objects take place in the form module the next time it is brought up in Form Builder. Chapter 8 will provide more details about these two operations. The following are the steps to execute them:

1. Switch to the Object Navigator window and open the module where you want to add the new object.
2. Open the Library Editor and select the tab that hosts the object to be reused.
3. Resize the Library Editor window so that it does not obfuscate the Object Navigator.
4. Drag the object and drop it on the Library Editor window.

These actions create a subclassed version of the object in the object library. To create a copy of it in the target module, hold the CTRL key pressed while dragging the object. To move the object out of the object library and into the target module, hold the SHIFT key pressed while dragging it.

In order to simplify the process of subclassing objects from reusable objects, the Form Builder uses the concept of smart classes. These are special objects that appear under the item SmartClasses of the Edit menu or the popup menu of the

Form Builder. A condition that the smart classes appear under these menu items is that the object library in which they reside must be open in the Object Navigator. The following steps allow you to qualify objects in the library as smart classes:

1. Select the object in the Library Editor.
2. Choose Object | SmartClass from the menu.

When an object is tagged as a smart class, a check mark appears in front of the object's icon in the Library Editor, as seen in Figure 7.11.

7.9.4 MAINTAINING LIBRARY OBJECTS

As mentioned earlier, the properties of objects cannot be modified within the object library. The following is a roadmap for editing the properties of an object from the library:

1. Open or create a module in which the object can reside.
2. Copy the object from the library onto the module.
3. Edit the properties of the object as necessary.
4. Move the object back in the library and choose to replace the old copy of the object.
5. Save the library.

If you want to remove an object from the library, select it and press DELETE or click the icon Delete Object on the toolbar.

7.10 SUMMARY

The Menu Editor is the Form Builder's tool to create the menu modules for your applications. This chapter explained the components of the Menu Editor and how to use it effectively. Basic concepts covered in this chapter were:

- **The Property Palette**
- **Components of Property Palette**
  - Toolbar
  - Context Bar
  - The Property Sheet
- **Using the Property Palette**

- Setting Properties of Objects
- Comparing Properties of Objects
- Copying and Pasting Properties of Objects

- **The Menu Editor**
- **Components of Menu Editor**
  - The Menu Editor Work area
  - Toolbar
- **Using the Menu Editor**
  - Navigating and Selecting
  - Creating Menus and Menu Items
  - Deleting Menus and Menu Items
  - Cutting, Copying, Pasting and Moving
  - Horizontal and Vertical Orientation
- **The Library Editor**
- **Components of the Library Editor**
  - The Tabbed Work area
  - Toolbar
- **Using the Library Editor**
  - Maintaining Library Tabs
  - Adding Objects
  - Reusing Library Objects
  - Maintaining Library Objects

The following table describes the software assets that were discussed in this chapter. From the main HTML page of the software utilities provided with the book follow the links *Software* and *Chapter 7* to access these assets:

ASSET NAME	DESCRIPTION
CH7.MMB	The menu module that you can use to perform the actions discussed in sections 7.4, 7.5, and 7.6.
CH7.OLB	A copy of the Form Builder standard object library that you can use with sections 7.7, 7.8, and 7.9.

Chapter 8

RAD AND OBJECT REUSABILITY

High quality, lower cost and rapid development go hand-in-hand if an appropriate development methodology is used. We use the term RAD, Rapid Application Development, to refer to such a methodology.

—James Martin

Rapid Application Development (RAD) is a methodology that, when followed and applied consistently, shortens the development process and improves your chances to complete development efforts on time and within budget. Oracle Developer is a set of tools that facilitate RAD projects. Combined with Oracle Designer, it offers a complete solution to software engineers that want to design, develop, and deploy systems following the RAD methodology. This chapter offers an overview of the RAD methodology and its principles and focuses on the Form Builder objects that enable you to use them. These objects include object library and template modules, object groups, visual attribute groups and property classes. This chapter also covers reusable components—Oracle Designer constructs intended to increase the reusability of Oracle Developer objects in your projects.

8.1 OVERVIEW OF RAPID APPLICATION DEVELOPMENT

Software engineering is a business activity whose ultimate goal is the production and implementation of high-quality software systems and applications on schedule and within allocated budgets. Although newer, software engineering shares many characteristics with older and more established engineering disciplines, like mechanical, electrical, or construction engineering. In particular, it produces its outputs by using and converting resources from the following four categories:

- **Business Community.** Software engineering is a business activity whose products solve one or more business problems. As such, it is closely related to the business community. This community supplies software engineers with two important resources: problems to solve, and money to reach the solutions.
- **Science.** Like any other engineering discipline, software engineering resides upon solid scientific foundations. The science that provides software engineers with methodology, tools, and algorithms to solve business problems is Computer Science.
- **Software Engineers.** Despite the high degree of automation that software engineering employs, people remain a very important factor in every solution designed and implemented by the discipline. As software engineering becomes more and more mature, the level of skills of the people who practice it, the software engineers, increases constantly. The most successful projects today are carried out by SWAT (Skilled, With Advanced Tools) teams of software engineers.
- **Management.** A software engineering project cannot succeed without a strong and committed management team. Like the coach of a successful sport team, the manager of a software engineering team provides guidelines

and direction to the team during its effort to build successful software systems.

Figure 8.1 shows a diagram that represents the relationships between software engineering and these four important factors that influence its results.

Since the early stages, software engineers have identified a number of tasks, activities, and processes that must be completed in order to produce a successful software product. They are presented in Section 8.1.1. In general, software engineers of all schools recognize the need for these tasks and activities. How to accomplish them is where debate exists. Such debates have lead to the formulation of a number of methodologies, some competing and some complementing each other. Section 8.1.2 presents a brief overview of one such methodology: Rapid Application Development (RAD).

8.1.1 PROCESSES IN THE SOFTWARE DEVELOPMENT LIFE-CYCLE

Several tasks need to be completed in order to create a software product successfully. These tasks vary from project to project, depending on the type of software to be developed, on the resources available, and on the composition of the development team. Because of such variations, there are no two projects with identical tasks or work activities. However, practice has shown that these tasks can be grouped in high-level processes, which, in turn, are common across projects. These processes are described in the following paragraphs:

- **Requirement Definition.** This process aims at identifying the business requirements that justify the software system. It normally requires that analysts review existing business processes and identify which activities in

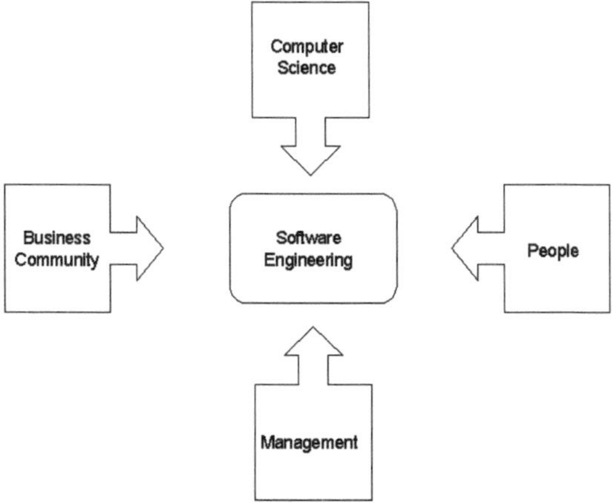

FIGURE 8.1 Relationships between software engineering and influencing factors.

these processes would benefit from the software solution. It is very common during this process to identify fundamental problems with the way an organization implements its business processes. In such situations, analysts may identify and propose improvements of these processes or new processes altogether. Therefore, the reengineering of business processes is often a byproduct of the requirement definition process. Once the business needs are identified, they are translated in requirements on the software system or its components, including the user interface, network layout, system availability, hardware and software configuration, and so on.

- **Technical Architecture.** This process builds the foundation upon which the software solution will be built. It uses input from the Requirements Definition process to quantify the current and future needs of the system, including those for disk space, memory, network bandwidth, CPU power. Based on such needs, the system architect identifies the hardware, software, and network configuration that best meets these needs. In this process, the architect identified components from the existing IT architecture that can be reused and the new components that must be procured. If the new system will interface with other system—and most of them do—the interfaces between these systems are defined as part of the technical architecture, as well.
- **System Design.** This process includes the design of the database schema and all the software modules that the system requires to implement its functionality. These subprocesses are so important in themselves that often they are presented and considered as separate processes. The system design is based on the requirements of the system as well as on its technical architecture.
- **System Development.** This is the process of building the application code and functionality based on the design specifications of the system. It is one of the most important processes in the software life cycle because it materializes the solution in a form that users can touch and feel and, therefore, provide feedback about its usability and effectiveness. Just as System Design, this process often is divided in activities related to the database and those related to the other software modules. However, in development environments that support moving of the code from the database to the client software layer, the distinction between these activities is blurred. For example, developing a PL/SQL package may be considered part of the database development effort as well as an Oracle Developer development activity.
- **Testing.** This process validates that the system designed and developed meets the needs of users as identified by the Requirements Definition process. There is a number of activities that may occur during this process, including functionality testing, stress testing, usability testing. Typically, these activities are concluded by the user acceptance testing during which the sponsors of the software project certify that the system is built according to their specifications.
- **Documentation.** This process includes all the activities required to produce

textual information that describes the system. Such information typically includes on-line and context-sensitive instructions that users can review as they use the system as well as more formal publications that document the behavior and functionality of the software.

- **Training.** This process includes activities that aim at educating primarily two categories of people. First, users of the software who need to know how to accomplish the tasks that their job requires with the new system. Second, administrators of the system who need to know how to install and maintain it over time. Based on the type of project and resources available, training may range from informal exchanges of information between the development team and the two groups mentioned above, to computer-based training (CBT) packages, to formal courses taught by professional trainers.
- **Deployment.** This process includes all the activities needed to make the newly-developed software available to its users. The distribution of the software can be simple enough to be handled by the end-users; or it can be fully automated as in the case of Internet and intranet applications; or it can be fairly complex and require configuration of hardware and software, migration of legacy data, and transitioning from old systems to the new one.
- **Maintenance and Support.** The activities in this process ensure that the system will function well after the deployment. They include monitoring the system's performance, providing for backup and recovery of the data, upgrading the software, and providing support to users experiencing problems.

The sequence in which the processes above are presented resembles that in which they are executed in practice. However, several of the tasks in these processes may occur in parallel and overlap with one another. Each of these processes requires a well-defined set of skills from the members of the development team. These skills define the roles that these members play in the development of the software product. Some of these roles are system analyst, business analyst, system architect, database designer, software developer, tester, technical writer, trainer, customer support specialist, and so on. In general, different individuals play these roles, although it is becoming customary nowadays to have professionals with varied skills that enable them to transition from one role to the other during the life of the software project.

8.1.2 RAPID APPLICATION DEVELOPMENT METHODOLOGY

As said at the beginning of this section, the processes listed above apply to one extent or another to every software development effort, no matter how large or small. Different methodologies do not argue about whether these processes should occur but on how to execute them in order to develop high-quality software systems on time and within resources. Much is said and written about the definition of a high-quality software system. In general, a software system is considered of good quality if it displays the following characteristics:

- It meets the business needs of the user community.
- It meets or exceeds the requirements of its users for performance, reliability, and availability.
- It is easy to learn and use.
- It requires minimal maintenance during its life.

In addition to having good quality, software systems need to be delivered on time and within budget. RAD is the methodology that defines the road map for implementing high-quality software systems within time and at reasonable cost. The methodology was defined in early 1990s by James Martin—who also coined the term RAD— in his classic work Rapid Application Development (Macmillan Publishing Company, 1991). The methodology provides the principles that allow highly skilled professionals using advanced software engineering tools to develop information systems successfully. One of the features of RAD that sets it apart from other methodologies is that it considers essential the participation of end-users in the requirements gathering and system design activities. Joint requirement definition (JRP) workshops, joint application design (JAD) sessions and user-driven prototypes to validate the requirements and refine the design are considered essential for the success of a RAD project.

Like engineers from other disciplines who face similar choices, software engineers today have at their reach a variety of tools that they use to build their products. In their origins, these tools were called computer-assisted software engineering (CASE) tools. They were helpful in defining and documenting the requirements of a software system, often in the form of diagrams that were easy to build and understand. They also enforced a system-wide dictionary of terms and facilitated the task of cross-checking and discovering inconsistencies in the system's requirements. The next generation of software engineering tools were the integrated CASE (I-CASE) tools. They extended the capabilities of CASE tools and allowed software engineers to convert the requirements of their systems into software modules generated automatically by the tool. The latest generation of integrated CASE tools, which includes Oracle Designer and Oracle Developer, extend these capabilities with a number of features that automate almost all the software engineering processes described in Section 8.1.1. Therefore these tools are essential for developing an application system following RAD principles.

8.1.3 ENABLING RAD THROUGH OBJECT REUSE

As mentioned in the previous section, one of the characteristics of RAD projects is that the requirements and the design are defined, validated, and finalized through a number of user-driven prototypes. In order to develop these prototypes and the ultimate software product within the time frame that RAD promises, it is essential to use prepackaged objects that have been created and tested previously. While a traditional software project typically involves a lot of custom-written code and modules developed from scratch, a RAD project achieves a good part of its functionality by assembling objects and components and building the new functionality upon them. Therefore, in order to implement a RAD project successfully, it is essential that the development tool you choose allow you to reuse objects defined previously. Form Builder contains a number of objects and features that allow you to reuse the code for future software projects. They include:

- **Object library modules.** After creating and refining objects, you can store them in libraries. From that point on, the objects can be copied or subclassed into other modules as needed. Developer Forms users can create and maintain Object libraries. In addition, Object libraries are very important in the process of generating Oracle Developer modules from specifications held in the Oracle Designer Repository.
- **Object groups.** Object groups bundle together objects of different types into higher-level building blocks. They are very useful if you want to reuse a number of related objects without having to maintain their relationship to each other.
- **Property classes.** In earlier versions of Form Builder, property classes were very important to achieve object reuse. Nowadays, the ability to subclass properties from an object has diminished their role in object reusability. However, they are still used when you want to inherit properties of objects of different types from a common source.
- **Visual attribute objects.** These objects bundle together settings for visual attribute properties such as font, color, and pattern properties. They are used to provide your form and menu modules with a consistent interface.
- **Template modules.** These modules contain a number of objects that are typically found in most of the modules you develop. In general, they are not functional modules and serve as a starting point for new modules. They are important in the process of generating Oracle Developer modules from Oracle Designer.
- **PL/SQL libraries.** They allow you to store program units that implement reusable application logic in one module and reference it from as many modules as necessary.

The following sections provide additional information on increasing object reusability through these objects.

8.2 OBJECT REUSE IN ORACLE DEVELOPER

Form Builder allows you to reuse objects through a simple two-step process:

1. Store the object with potential for reuse in an object library module.
2. Copy or subclass the object from the object library module into a new module.

Chapter 7 described how you can use the Library Editor to create, populate, and maintain objects in an object library. The following two sections will focus on the concept of subclassing and the differences between copying and subclassing objects.

8.2.1 UNDERSTANDING SUBCLASSING

In the object-oriented model of the world, object types are represented by object classes. Instances of an object class may enter in a number of relationships with instances of other classes. A special category of relationships is inheritance, often called the "is a kind of" relationship. If Person and Student are two object classes, than the fact that a student has all the characteristics of a person is expressed as "Student is a kind of Person" or as "Student inherits from Person." While an instance of class Student may inherit a number of characteristics from class Person, it also has other characteristics that set it aside, or specialize it, from instances of class Person. In such situations, it is said that Student is a subclass of Person. Thus, in object-oriented terminology, B is subclass of A if it enjoys the following two properties:

- **Inheritance.** Class B has the capability to inherit the characteristics of class A, which is also called the based class.
- **Specialization.** Class B has the capability to override the properties of its base class.

Subclassing is one of the pillars of object-oriented programming. Inheritance techniques give programmers the capability to create new objects in an application based on a set of previously defined objects. It not only cuts significantly the development time, but also creates applications which share a common and consistent look and behavior.

For example, in a financial application, you may want to align fields that contains dollar values right, rather than left, which is the default alignment setting for text items. You may also want to display them in the currency format, preceded by the dollar sign and expressed as dollars and cents. Furthermore, negative values may be presented differently from non-negative ones to attract the attention of the user. A method, or trigger, must be attached to the text item field which checks the current value stored there, and based on it, changes the font, color, or any other visual attribute considered appropriate.

In traditional programming environments, each time a text field that displays dollar values is added to the application, the programmer must specify its size, format, alignment settings, and replicate the code that sets its attributes based on the value of the item. Programming applications this way is a lengthy, costly, and very tedious process. Maintaining them is not easy either. If there is a slight change in the requirements, programmers need to go and apply the change to all the dollar value items in their modules.

In object-oriented environments, an object class is created instead. General attributes and methods are specified for this class. Then, each time the application needs a dollar value item, that item is subclassed from the base class. No additional programming is needed to set its format, or create the check method. If, in the future, the requirements change, attributes or methods need to be modified in only one place, the base class. All the objects subclassed from this class will automatically inherit the new settings with no further effort from the developers.

If you are implementing the financial application in Form Builder, you need to create and embellish only one currency item. Then, you can save this object in an object library so that you can easily access it when needed. From that moment on, each time a new currency item needs to be created, it can be subclassed from this class. Of course, any of the inherited properties can be overwritten if necessary. However, those that are not overwritten are maintained in one single object—the base class. Any changes to them will be automatically propagated to all the subclassed objects.

8.2.2 BENEFITS OF SUBCLASSING

From the description of subclassing in the previous section, you can easily identify a number of benefits that this technique provides. Some of them are:

- Subclassing allows you to create exact copies of an object.
- You can alter the properties of the subclassed object inherited form the base class, effectively specializing it.
- You can add dependent objects to the subclassed object. This feature is important if the subclassed object is a composite one, containing other objects. For example, a subclassed data block may contain a number of items inherited from its base class block. You can add additional items to the subclassed block, provided that they all go after the subclassed items in the Object Navigator.
- Through the inheritance mechanism, changes to the base class properties are propagated automatically and instantaneously to all the subclassed objects.

Finally, a note on the relationship between object library modules, subclassing, and object reuse. In order to subclass an object, the base class does not need to reside in an object library. It can be in any module and even within the same module as the subclassed object. Object libraries however help organize and catalog the objects you want to reuse. They serve as containers of objects set aside exclusively for the purpose of reuse. Therefore, they reduce the need for housekeeping and tracking the location of these objects, thus allowing you to focus on their properties and features rather than on their whereabouts.

8.2.3 SUBCLASSING OBJECTS

One way to subclass an object is to create a new reference to the base class in the desired module. As explained earlier, dragging the base class and dropping it in the target module allows you to create a new subclass object. But there may be cases when the object you want to sublcass already exists in the target module. These are the steps to subclass such objects in this situation:

1. Display the Property Palette for the object to be subclassed.
2. Click the button More… associated with the property Subclass Information. The dialog box Subclass Information appears (see Figure 8.2). By default, the radio button Object is selected.
3. Select the module that owns the base class from the list box Modules. This list is populated with the names of all the modules currently open in the Forms Builder.
4. Select the base class from the list Object Name. This list is populated with objects from the base module of the same type as the object you are subclassing. At this point, the dialog box Subclass Information should be similar to the one shown in

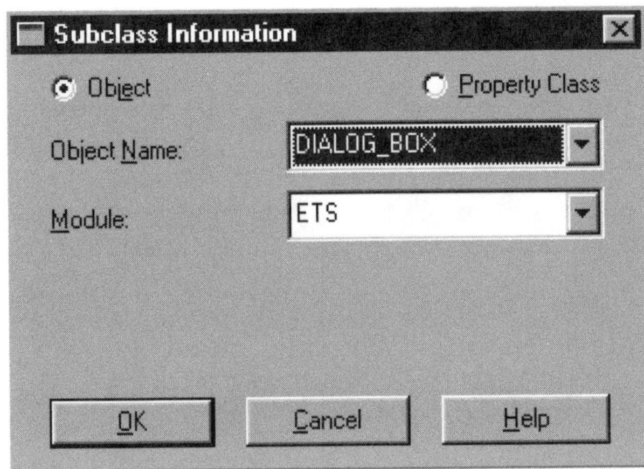

FIGURE 8.2 The Subclass Information dialog box for the case of objects.

An object that serves as a base class to a subclassed object, like any other object in Form Builder, can in turn be subclassed from another object, thus leading to multiple levels of subclassing. In the scenario introduced in Section 8.2.1, if your financial application needs to display currencies other than dollars, you can create a new subclassed object that inherits all the properties and triggers from the object used in dollar values text items. Then, necessary adjustments such as format and currency symbol, are made to this object. Text items subclassed from it will share common characteristics with other currency items, while preserving their differences.

8.3 OBJECT GROUPS

The objects you need to reuse across different modules are often related with one another. For example, a data block and all its items, a number of triggers and program units, a canvas, and a window may be required to implement a dialog box. These objects need to be copied or subclassed together. In order to facilitate the process of reusing related objects from one module to another, Oracle Developer Forms provides a special type of objects, called object groups. Object groups serve as containers in which you can store pointers to any objects within the module. The object groups have no other purpose than to bundle in one package objects that should be reused from one module to the other. You create them like any other object in the Navigator, and populate them by simply dragging the desired object and dropping it in the group. All the members of a group appear under the node Object Group Children. You can remove an object from the group by selecting under this node and deleting it.

> **TIP**
>
> Object groups contain only references to objects in the module but no actual instances of objects. Therefore, adding objects to a group does not duplicate their instances. Deleting objects from the group simply removes the references to their instances but does not delete the instances themselves. If you want to access or modify the properties of members of an object group, you have to use their corresponding instances in the module.

In order to practice the process of creating and populating object groups, follow these steps:

1. Launch the Form Builder and open the module CH8_1.FMB.
2. Create a new object group and name it MDI_WINDOWS_GROUP.

3. Expand the node Property Classes. The property classes MDI_SHEET, MDI_DIALOG_BOX, and MDI_MODELESS_DIALOG_BOX are displayed.
4. Select these property classes and drag them over to the object group MDI_WINDOWS_GROUP. You will notice that they will appear under the node Object Group Children.
5. Repeat steps 3 and 4 for alerts INFO_ALERT, WARNING_ALERT, and CRITICAL_ALERT.
6. Repeat steps 3 and 4 for triggers PRE-FORM and WHEN-WINDOW-CLOSED.
7. Save module CH8_1.FMB.

Now you are ready to reuse the objects added to the object group by following these steps:

1. Open the module CH8_2.FMB in the Form Builder.
2. Select the object group MDI_WINDOWS_GROUP in the module CH8_1.FMB and drag it in the Navigator until the mouse pointer is on the Object Groups node of the module CH8_2.FMB.

   You may notice that, as you drag the object group, the cursor's shape will give you a visual cue about the right position where you can drop the object in the Navigator. It will have the shape of the Stop sign as it moves over nodes of any type other than Object Groups.
3. Drop the object group in its place in the module CH8_2.FMB. Form Builder asks you whether you want to copy the object or subclass it.
4. Click the Subclass button.

Once you do that, the subclassing action is completed. The beauty of object groups is that they preserve the hierarchical position of their members. You can notice that the properties classes in this group went under the Properties Classes node in the Navigator, the alerts under the Alert node, and the form-level triggers PRE-FORM and WHEN-WINDOW-CLOSED went to their appropriate location.

8.4 PROPERTY CLASSES

Before Form Builder could support subclassing as described in Section 8.2, property classes were the only way to implement inheritance in Oracle Developer applications. However, since the incorporation of object reusability functions in Form Builder, the role of property classes in object reuse has lost significant ground. Nevertheless, they are still important in cases when the properties you want to set and inherit cross the boundaries of object types. The following sections provide information on how to create and maintain property classes in the Form Builder.

8.4.1 CREATING PROPERTY CLASSES

Property classes are objects in a module; therefore, they can be created in the Object Navigator like any other object. After you create the new class, you need to populate it with the necessary attributes. If an object that will serve as model for the properties settings in the class already exists, the class can be created directly from the content of the Property Palette for this object. The following are the steps to do this:

1. Display the Property Palette for the object.
2. Control+Click the properties you want to include in the new class. They will all be selected in the Property Palette.
3. Click the icon Property Class from the window toolbar. The Form Builder displays a message of the form "Creating property class PROPERTY_CLASS2."
4. Click OK.
5. Rename the newly created property class in the Navigator.

This is the most common way to create a property class because it allows you to specify quickly the properties included in the class. Most, if not all of them, are already present in the Property Palette. All you have to do to bring the class to the state you want is to add or delete just a few properties.

8.4.2 ADDING AND DELETING PROPERTIES IN A PROPERTY CLASS

Once a property class is created, it may need some adjustments in its content. To change the content of a property class, display it in a Property Palette. Here you can change their settings, as you would normally do with any other object. You can also add or delete other properties in the existing list. To add a property to the class follow these steps:

1. Click the icon Add Property from the toolbar. The Properties List of Values dialog box appears (see Figure 8.3).
2. Select the property you want to add. Remember to use the auto-reduction and search features of this List of Values.
3. Click OK.

The property is added and set to its default value. The Form Builder places the new property in its own place under the appropriate functional category. If

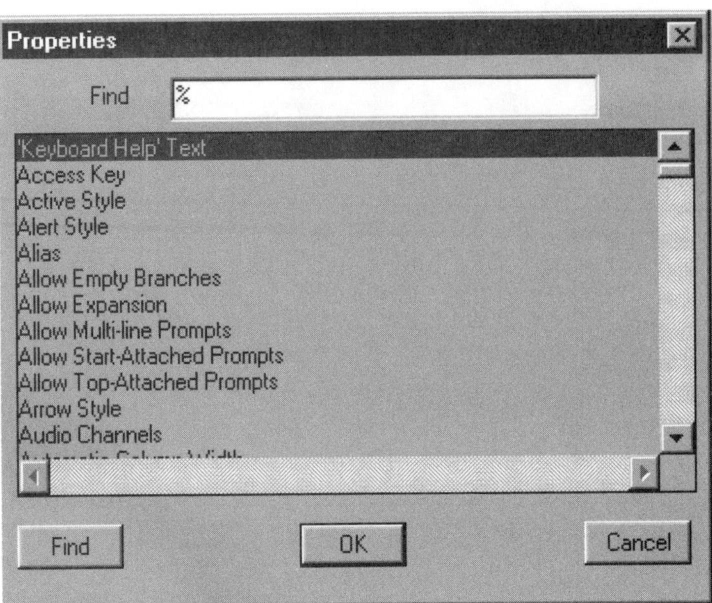

FIGURE 8.3 The Properties List of Values dialog box.

the category is not present in the list, it is automatically created when one of its properties is added to the class.

Another way to quickly add multiple properties to an existing class is to use the Copy Properties and Paste Properties commands discussed in earlier chapters. You copy the properties of the source object and then paste them in the target property class window. If the class already contains any of the properties of the source, their settings will be overwritten; all the other properties will be added to the class.

To delete a property from the class follow these steps:

1. Select the property you want to delete from the list.
2. Click Delete Property icon from the toolbar.

The selected property is deleted. Note that you can add or delete only one property at a time.

8.4.3 INHERITING PROPERTIES FROM PROPERTY CLASSES

Once a property class is created, it can be used to define the properties of other objects in the application. To inherit properties of an object from an existing class:

1. Display the Property Palette for that object.
2. Click the button More... associated with the property Subclass Information. The dialog box Subclass Information appears.
3. Select the radio button Property Class. Notice how the label for the first list box changes to "Property Class Name."
4. Select the module that owns the property class from the list box Modules. This list is populated with the names of all the modules currently open in the Forms Builder.
5. Select the property class from the list Property Class Name from which the properties will be inherited. At this point the dialog box Subclass Information should be similar to the one shown in Figure 8.4.

An object can inherit properties from only one class at any one time. To inherit properties from another property class, simply change the setting of the lists Module and Property Class Name in the Subclass Information dialog box.

Inheriting an object's properties from a class affects only those properties that are included in the class. Visually, they are distinguished from the rest of the property sheet by an arrow-like icon that precedes their name. Properties of the object that are not included in the class remain unchanged.

Settings of inherited properties can be changed in two different ways. If the change applies to only one object, set the property of that object in the Property Palette. The arrow icon will now appear with a red mark across to indicate that the link is broken and the property is no longer inherited. If you want to apply the change to all the objects that inherit their properties from the same class, modify the setting at the class level. The Form Builder will automatically apply the change to all objects inherited from that class.

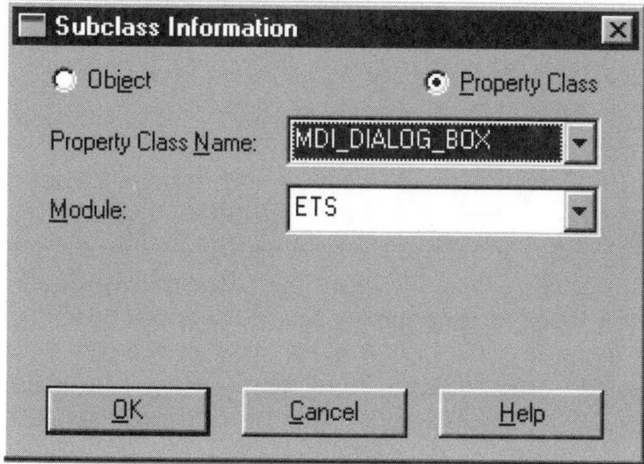

FIGURE 8.4 The Subclass Information dialog box.

If you change the setting of an inherited property, you also break the link between this property and its setting in the property class. If settings for that property are modified in the property class, the changes will not be applied to the object. To reestablish this link and reset a modified property to the value specified in the property class, use the Inherit command in the Property Palette.

1. Select the property to reset.
2. Click the Inherit icon from the toolbar.

The inheritance indicator reappears to the left of the property. You can use the Inherit command even if the property is not inherited. In this case, clicking the Inherit icon sets the property to its value within the default object maintained by the Form Builder.

8.5 VISUAL ATTRIBUTE GROUPS

Visual attribute groups, in a sense, are an explicit type of property class, managed as separate objects by the Form Builder. The basic functionality that can be achieved using visual attribute groups, can also be implemented with property classes. However, your application will benefit and gain in clarity if properties that regulate only the visual appearance of objects are grouped separately in the form of visual attribute groups.

The characteristic properties of a visual attribute group are part of the Font & Color functional group. They include Font Name, Font Size, Font Style, Font Weight, and Font Spacing; Foreground Color and Background Color; Fill Pattern, Character Mode Logical Attribute, and White on Black. You can create and name a visual attribute group like any other object in the Navigator. You can specify the settings of a visual attribute group as you would for any object in the Property Palette.

Each interface object has some, if not all, the font, color, and pattern properties specified above. The settings of these properties are controlled by the object's Visual Attribute Group property. If this property is set to "DEFAULT," then the visual attributes will be the Form Builder default attributes. If any of these attributes is modified, either in the Property Palette or the Layout Editor, the Forms Runtime engine will use the specified settings rather than the default ones.

To base the attributes of an existing object on a visual attribute group, you simply set the property Visual Attribute Group of the object to the name of the group. Form Builder places the arrow-like inheritance indicator in front of all the visual attributes set in the visual attribute group. Only properties that are meaningful for the object being modified are applied to the selected object. Thus, setting attributes based on a visual attributes group is similar to inheriting properties from a property class.

The one and only purpose of visual attribute groups is to control the visual appearance of other objects in an application. Therefore, it is reasonable that they have precedence over property classes, which may specify these and other properties. If an object inherits some visual properties from a class, and, at the same time its Visual Attribute Group property is set to a visual attribute group, the settings specified in the visual attribute group override the settings of the property class.

Another difference between visual attribute groups and property classes is that the assignment of a named visual attribute group to an object can be changed programmatically at runtime, whereas the subclassing information, including the property class, is specified at design time and cannot be changed programmatically. On the other hand, property classes can contain all the properties contained in visual attribute groups and other additional ones. What is more important, they allow PL/SQL triggers to be associated with the class and then inherited to all the objects derived from the class.

It is difficult to say when it is more advantageous to use visual attribute groups or property classes. Clearly, a combination of the functionality from both types would provide more benefits, power and flexibility than each of them separately. In the following section, you create visual attribute groups and property classes that can be used in the financial application described earlier in this chapter.

8.6 PRACTICAL EXAMPLES

In this section, you will work with form CH8_2.FMB provided with the companion software. It contains a finished version of the ETS application that you developed in Part I. The final version of this form, which includes the work performed in this section, is provided in module CH8_3.FMB. Open the module CH8_2.FMB in the Form Builder. In Chapter 3 you modified the visual attributes, alignment settings and format mask for the currency value items. Here you will take advantage of that effort.

Start by creating two visual attribute groups that will be used in this section. They will be called NON_NEGATIVE and NEGATIVE. The properties of the visual attribute group NON_NEGATIVE will have the default settings of the From Builder. The properties of the visual attribute group NEGATIVE will be similar to NON_NEGATIVE, except for the Foreground Color, which will be set to "red." These are the steps to create these objects:

1. Create a new visual attribute object in the Object Navigator, and name it "NEGATIVE."
2. Create a second visual attribute object in the Object Navigator, and name it "NON_NEGATIVE."
3. Double-click the visual attribute group "NEGATIVE" to display its Property Palette.

4. Display the Colors List of Values dialog box associated with the property Foreground Color property.
5. Select "red" from the list.

Now, create a property class that will contain properties characteristic for currency value items. Once again you will use the settings of the item HW_ASSETS.PURCHASE_COST. The following are the steps to create the new class based on these settings:

1. Double-click the PURCHASE_COST item to display its Property Palette.
2. Control+Click the following properties to select them in the Property Palette: Item Type, Comments, Justification, Data Type, Format Mask, Lowest Allowed Value, Highest Allowed Value, Hint, Display Hint Automatically, and Tooltip.
3. Click the icon Property Class on the toolbar to create a new Property Class object with the properties selected in the previous step.
4. Rename the newly created property class to US_CURRENCY.
5. Set the property class US_CURRENCY as shown in Figure 8.5.

Finally, add a trigger to this property class. The trigger will fire during the validation of any item that inherits its properties from the US_CURRENCY class. Based on the value stored in the item, the trigger will set the Visual Attribute Group of the item to "NON_NEGATIVE" or "NEGATIVE."

1. Expand the US_CURRENCY node in the Object Navigator, and select the node Triggers underneath it.
2. Click the Create icon on the toolbar. The LOVs dialog box with trigger names appears.
3. Select WHEN-VALIDATE-ITEM form the list of trigger names. The new trigger is created and a PL/SQL Editor window is displayed.
4. Enter the text of the trigger as shown in Figure 8.6, compile it and close the PL/SQL Editor window.

In this trigger, if a negative value is entered in the item, that item is assigned the visual attribute 'NEGATIVE.' On the other hand, if a non-negative value is entered, the visual attribute for the item becomes 'NON-NEGATIVE.' The value of the item is stored in the system variable SYSTEM.CURSOR_VALUE, the name of the item is retrieved from the system variable SYSTEM.CURSOR_ITEM, and the visual attribute is replaced using the built-in procedure SET_ITEM_PROPERTY.

Now, whenever you will need money items in your forms, you can inherit their characteristic properties from the US_CURRENCY class created here. As an example, inherit the properties of item PURCHASE_COST in blocks HW_AS-

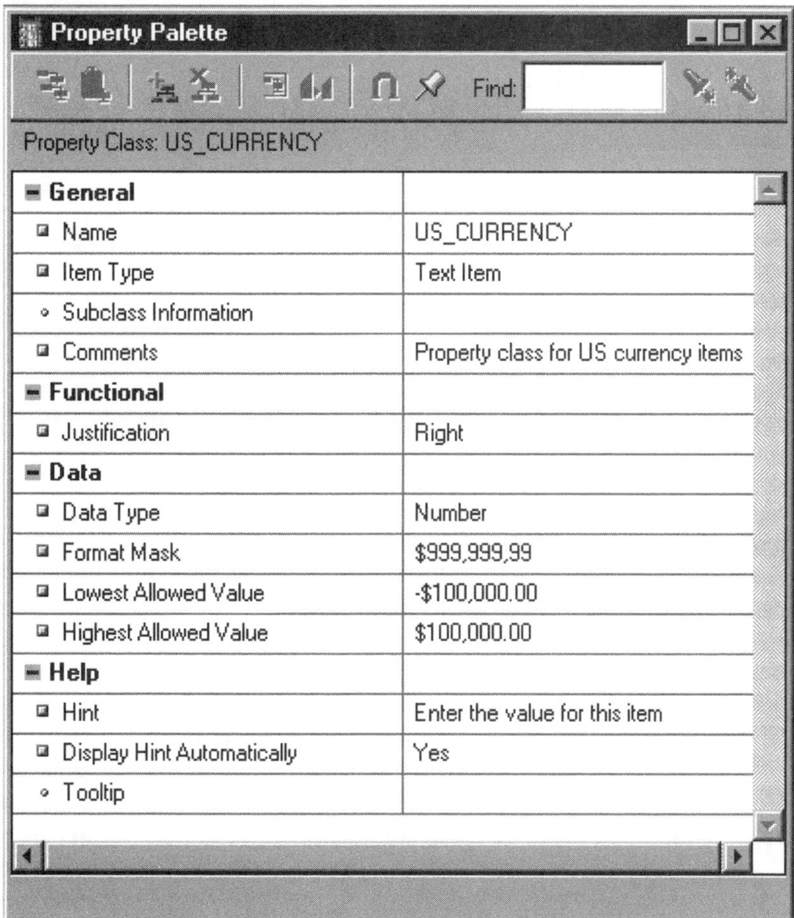

FIGURE 8.5 Settings of the property class US_CURRENCY.

SETS and SW_ASSETS from US_CURRENCY and execute the application to see how the visual attributes are replaced when non-negative dollar amounts are replaced by negative ones and vice versa.

> **TIP**
>
> The code you have written in this trigger cannot be dependent on the particular item that will inherit it. The use of system variables such as SYSTEM.CURSOR_ITEM (that returns the name of the item at runtime) and SYSTEM.CURSOR_VALUE (that returns the value stored in that item) enables you to write the trigger in an object-independent fashion.

```
IF :SYSTEM.CURSOR_VALUE < 0 THEN        – Negative value
                                          entered
– Attach NEGATIVE visual attribute to item
  SET_ITEM_PROPERTY(:SYSTEM.CURSOR_ITEM,
VISUAL_ATTRIBUTE, 'NEGATIVE');
ELSE                                    – Non-negative value
                                          entered
– Attach NON_NEGATIVE visual attribute to item
  SET_ITEM_PROPERTY(:SYSTEM.CURSOR_ITEM,
VISUAL_ATTRIBUTE, 'NON_NEGATIVE');
END IF;
```

FIGURE 8.6 Adding a trigger to a properties class.

8.7 ORACLE DESIGNER REUSABLE COMPONENTS

In many areas of industry, assembling existing objects or components into higher-level objects or products is typical. In recent years this concept has found wide acceptance in software engineering as well. The component-based development paradigm essentially means building application systems by assembling reusable components. The popularity of ActiveX and COM on one hand and JavaBeans and CORBA technologies on the other has pushed component-based development into the mainstream.

While software component technologies focus on the development and reuse of software, a higher level of thinking of components is to come up with reusable design objects—encapsulations of data structures and software module layouts that can be reused over and over in new applications. The reusable module components are the technology provided by Oracle Designer to allow you to componentize important design concepts in such a way that you can easily reuse them in different modules. You have two ways to create a reusable module component in the Design Editor:

- ❑ Use the Module Component Data Wizard. Make sure that the context is not a module when you invoke the tool.
- ❑ In the Design Navigator, switch to the tab Modules, select the node Reusable Module Components, and click the icon Create.

Reusable module components and specific components are no different as far as the way the properties are set and the elements included in them. What sets apart these two types of modules is the property Module Component Type, which is set to "Re-usable" or "Specific." You can access this property in the Property Palette of a module component. In order to include a reusable component in an existing module, you can take one of the following actions:

- In the Design Navigator, drag the reusable module component and drop it on the module where you want to add it.
- If the module is shown already in the Data Diagrammer, click the icon Include Reusable Component, and click the module in the diagram. From the list of reusable module components defined in the repository, select the component you want to add and click OK.

The properties of reusable module components included in a particular module cannot be modified. Technically speaking, these components are read-only references of the source component in the body of the module. So if you have included the same reusable module component in multiple modules, you need to modify and maintain the properties in only one place. The reference mechanism implemented by Designer/2000 will ensure that the properties are propagated at each instance. Thus, reusable module components extend the inheritance concept of object-oriented programming into the design world.

In order to break the link between a reusable module component and its use in a module, you need to switch the property Module Component Type from "Re-usable" to "Specific." To be able to do so, the reusable component must be used by only one module. When the property setting is modified, the component becomes an element of the module. Conversely, you can promote any specific module component to a reusable component by setting the property Module Component Type to "Re-usable."

The data diagram of a module is very helpful for understanding and visualizing the elements and layout of modules. The Design Editor allows you to display reusable module components in module diagrams although these components do not represent complete modules. To display a reusable component in the Module Diagrammer, select it in the Design Editor and issue one of the following commands:

- Select Tools | Reusable Component Graphical Editor.
- Right-click the component and select the item Show On Diagram from the popup menu that appears.

The Diagrammer window for a reusable module component is the same as the Diagrammer for regular modules in all aspects, except that it lacks all the tools that are meaningful for modules but not for reusable components, such as the ability to create new module components or windows.

8.8 SUMMARY

Rapid Application Development has become nowadays the preferred methodology for developing application systems. Its principles allow for the completion of software projects on time and within budget. Development tools that allow the reuse objects and software components and that are tightly integrated with advanced CASE tools are essential in the success of a RAD project. Oracle Developer has a number of features that make it an ideal tool to develop systems following the RAD methodology. This chapter focused on these features. Its topics included:

- **Overview of Rapid Application Development**
  - Processes in the Software Development Life-Cycle
  - Rapid Application Development Methodology
  - Enabling RAD through Object Reuse
- **Object Reuse in Oracle Developer**
  - Understanding Subclassing
  - Benefits of Subclassing
  - Subclassing Objects
- **Object Groups**
- **Property Classes**
  - Creating Property Classes
  - Adding and Deleting Properties in a Property class
  - Inheriting Properties from Property Classes
- **Visual Attribute Groups**
- **Practical Examples**
- **Oracle Designer Reusable Components**

The following table describes the software assets that were discussed in this chapter. From the main HTML page of the software utilities provided with the book follow the links *Software* and *Chapter 8* to access these assets:

ASSET NAME	DESCRIPTION
CH8_1.FMB	A module provided to allow you to practice creating and populating object groups.
CH8_2.FMB	A copy of the ETS application created in Part I.
CH8_3.FMB	An enhanced version of the ETS application that implements currency items using visual attribute groups and a property class.
CH8_3.FMX	The enhanced version of the ETS application the compiled for Win32 platforms.

Chapter 9

INTRODUCTION TO SQL

God never sent a messenger save with the language of his folk, that he might make the message clear for them.

—The Koran

SQL, an abbreviation for Structured Query Language, forms the foundations of all relational database systems. It is an English-like computer language that makes the process of interacting with relational databases simple and consistent. For traditional and historical reasons, its name is pronounced "sequel," although a more recent way to say it is "es-que-el," claimed by some to be the standard one. This chapter provides and overview of SQL, its most important commands, and their implementation by Oracle Server and Oracle Developer. In order to simplify the coverage of this large topic, this chapter presents generic concepts and syntactic structures of SQL that apply to the relational and object-relational implementations of the Oracle Server. Chapter 10 will focus on the extensions of SQL required to support the object-relational features of Oracle8.

9.1 BRIEF HISTORY OF SQL LANGUAGE

SQL and relational database management systems originate in an article titled "A Relational Model of Data for Large Shared Data Banks," published in June 1970 in *Communications of the Association for Computing Machinery* (CACM) *Journal*. Its author, Dr. Edgar F. Codd was a researcher at the IBM Research Laboratory in San Jose, California. Using concepts and results of branches of mathematics such as set theory and Boolean algebra, Codd laid the foundations of what would become the most widespread type of databases in the computer industry today.

Other researchers at the IBM San Jose Research Laboratory concentrated their efforts in implementing the ideas of Codd. In the mid-1970s, a number of languages were designed, based on his abstract relational model. One of these languages, known as Structured English QUEry Language (SEQUEL), was used in an IBM prototype called SEQUEL-XRM. In 1976, IBM launched the efforts for a second prototype of its relational database system under the code name System R. System R used a subset of the original SEQUEL language, called SQL.

The warm reception of System R in those IBM sites where it was deployed clearly showed that relational databases using SQL had a bright future. Other vendors began to move even faster than IBM and develop their own products. At least one of them, Relational Software, Inc., from Belmont, California, created in 1979 the first commercially available relational database called ORACLE. Based on the popularity of its product, the company later changed its name to Oracle Corporation. It is today the leading relational database vendor and the third largest software company worldwide. IBM and other vendors followed with their own SQL products. DB2 was introduced in 1983 and SYBASE in 1986.

Because of the large number of SQL-based products and the WIDESPREAD use of SQL with relational database technologies, there has been a persisting need to standardize the language. The first SQL standard was approved by the American National Standards Institute (ANSI) in 1986. This standard was adopted by the International Standards Organization (ISO) in 1987. In late 1992, both ANSI and ISO approved a revised and greatly expanded standard of SQL under the name "International Standard ISO.IEC 9075:1992, *Database Language SQL.*"

9.2 MOVIE RENTAL DATABASE

This chapter will discuss a number of SQL commands and functions. A small application provided with the software utilities that accompany this book will help you follow the examples presented here. This application consists of only three tables: CUSTOMER, MOVIE, and RENTAL. They contain information that a hypothetical movie rental store can find useful in keeping track of its business activities. The CUSTOMER table stores data about individual customers such as name, telephone number, date of birth, and membership date. The MOVIE table stores information about the movies that the video store rents out to its customers. Such information includes the movie title, year of production, rating, and number of copies available. A customer may rent several movies, and a movie may be rented by more than one customer at any one time. The RENTAL table records every such transaction. The data stored in this table include the customer and movie identification numbers, rental date, return date, and rental rate. Figure 9.1 represents the entity relationship diagram of the Movie Rental Database, which, from now on, will be called MRD.

The relationship between the entities CUSTOMER and RENTAL on the left side of the picture can be interpreted as follows: "A Customer may be initiator of one or more Rental transactions, during which he or she rents a movie. A Rental transaction must be initiated by one and only one customer." The relationship between the entities Movie and Rental to the right states: "A Movie may be rented zero or more times during a Rental transaction by a custom. A Rental transaction must be for one and only one movie." Figure 9.2, Figure 9.3, and Figure 9.4 list the columns of tables CUSTOMER, MOVIE, and RENTAL and their properties.

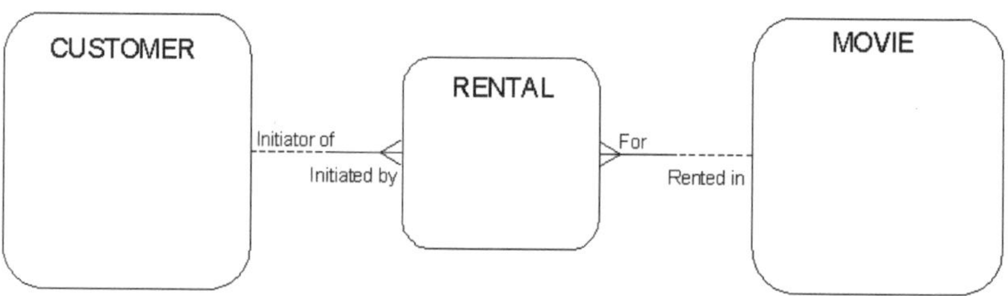

FIGURE 9.1 The Entity Relationship Diagram for Movie Rental Database.

COLUMN	DATA TYPE	LENGTH	CONSTRAINTS	DESCRIPTION
ID	NUMBER	6	PK (Primary Key)	Internal tracking number
Last Name	VARCHAR2	30		The last name.
First Name	VARCHAR2	30	Not NULL	The first name.
Phone Number	VARCHAR2	14		The telephone number.
Date of Birth	DATE			The telephone number.
Membership Date	DATE			The membership date.

FIGURE 9.2 Columns for table CUSTOMER and their properties.

The MRD database schema with which you will work in this chapter and the next is simplified in order to allow you to focus on the elements of the SQL and PL/SQL languages rather than on the complexity of a data modeling problem. Part Three expands on the problem of the neighborhood video rental store. The chapters in this part analyze, design and build Oracle Developer application to solve this problem. The companion software provided with this book installs a SQL*Plus script to create these tables and load sample data in them. Instructions to execute this script against your Oracle Server database are provided in the section *Installing the Companion Software* in the Preface.

At this point you are ready to follow the topics discussed in the rest of this chapter. It will be assumed that you are using the Oracle Corporation's SQL*Plus plus program to execute the commands discussed here. Start SQL*Plus and log on to the database with the user account used to run the script mentioned in the previous paragraph.

COLUMN	DATA TYPE	LENGTH	CONSTRAINTS	DESCRIPTION
ID	NUMBER	6	PK	Internal tracking number
Title	VARCHAR2	50	Not NULL	The title.
Director Name	VARCHAR2	30		The name of movie's director.
Main Actor	VARCHAR2	30		The name of movie's lead actor.
Main Actress	VARCHAR2	30		The name of movie's lead actress.
Rating	VARCHAR2	8		The rating of the movie.

FIGURE 9.3 Columns for table MOVIE and their properties.

COLUMN	DATA TYPE	LENGTH	CONSTRAINTS	DESCRIPTION
Customer ID	NUMBER	6	PK, FK	ID of customer renting a movie.
Movie ID	NUMBER	6	PK, FK	ID of movie rented by the customer.
Rent Date	DATE		PK	The date of transaction.
Return Date	DATE			The date when movie was returned.
Daily Rate	NUMBER	4, 2		The daily rental rate.

FIGURE 9.4 Columns for table RENTAL and their properties.

9.3 CATEGORIES OF SQL COMMANDS

The SQL language in itself tries to avoid complicated syntactic structures or a large number of commands. The intentions of its designers were to allow a large number of users to access and manipulate data stored in database structures easily. The idea was to provide users of SQL with a way to ask for the data they needed, without specifying how these data were to be retrieved. It is customary to classify the commands in the SQL language in four categories.

- **Data Retrieval Command.** This category contains only one command: SELECT. This command is a cornerstone of SQL and allows users to query necessary data from the database. Because of its importance and widespread usage, if is often considered in a separate category of its own.
- **Data Manipulation Language (DML) commands.** Commands in this category allow you to manipulate data in existing database objects. The most popular commands in this category are INSERT, UPDATE, and DELETE. Often it is necessary to use the SELECT command to specify the set of data that should be updated or deleted. This is the reason why SELECT sometimes is included in the DML category.
- **Data Definition Language (DDL) commands.** Commands in this category modify the structure of the database by creating, replacing, altering or dropping objects such as tables, indexes, and views.
- **Data Control Language (DCL) commands.** This category includes commands that protect the integrity of the database and the consistency of data by controlling and managing the access to the database structures. These commands are often divided in transaction control commands, session control commands, and system control commands.

A full discussion of SQL and all the categories of commands introduced above would be beyond the scope of this book. They are discussed thoroughly in other books and manuals. This chapter will discuss only those SQL commands that are most commonly used in Oracle Developer applications. They belong to the first two categories and are SELECT, INSERT, UPDATE, and DELETE.

9.4 DATA RETRIEVAL WITH SELECT

A SELECT command is a query expression optionally followed by an ORDER BY clause. The first part of the command retrieves the data from the database according to the query specifications. If the ORDER BY clause is specified, the set of records is sorted, or ordered, according to the clause. Figure 9.5 shows two select commands, and the data they return.

The first command contains only the query expression; the second command, in addition, contains ordering instructions, which affect the order in which the records retrieved by the query are displayed. The following is a list of conventions that will be used throughout this chapter when representing the SQL commands:

- SQL language keywords like SELECT, FROM, WHERE and ORDER BY will always be shown capitalized. Nothing would change in the outcome of these statements if lowercase letters were used, because SQL is not a case-sensitive language. The purpose of this convention is to clearly distinguish the language constructs from database objects.
- If you type the statements shown in Figure 9.5 at the SQL prompt, each time you press ENTER to move to a new line, SQL*Plus will precede the line with a line number. You do not have to type the line numbers in this and all other examples.
- The outcome of a statement will be shown only when it helps understanding the statement.
- Throughout the chapter the SQL statements will be executed against the MRD tables. In general, these statements may be executed against other types of objects. For example, in Oracle8, SELECT statements may be issued against tables, object tables, views, object views, or snapshots. In order to keep the discussion simple, schema objects other than tables will be mentioned explicitly only when it will be necessary to highlight important differences.
- Breaking SQL statements in multiple lines is done primarily for clarity and ease of understanding. It is not a requirement of the language syntax. The statements shown in Figure 9.6 are equivalent, but more obscure and difficult to follow than the ones in Figure 9.5.

```
SQL> SELECT last_name, first_name
  2 FROM customer
  3 WHERE member_dt > '01-JAN-97'

LAST_NAME                          FIRST_NAME
--------------------------------   ----------------------------
Smith                              Robert
Richard                            Joanne
Moore                              Suzanne
Moore                              Karla
Campbell                           Michael
Andrews                            Rebecca
Milton                             Henry
Baker                              Paul
Johnson                            Michelle

SQL> SELECT last_name, first_name
  2 FROM customer
  3 WHERE member_dt > '01-JAN-97'
  4 ORDER BY last_name

LAST_NAME                          FIRST_NAME
--------------------------------   ----------------------------
Andrews                            Rebecca
Baker                              Paul
Campbell                           Michael
Johnson                            Michelle
Milton                             Henry
Moore                              Suzanne
Moore                              Karla
Richard                            Joanne
Smith                              Robert
```

FIGURE 9.5 Examples of SELECT commands.

```
SELECT last_name, first_name FROM
customer WHERE member_dt > '01-JAN-97';

SELECT last_name, first_name FROM customer WHERE
member_dt > '01-JAN-97' ORDER BY last_name;
```

FIGURE 9.6 Examples of obscure SELECT statements.

9.4.1 SELECTING ALL ROWS FROM A TABLE

As a minimum, every query expression must contain a SELECT clause and a FROM clause. The SELECT clause defines the columns that must be retrieved from the query. The FROM clause specifies the one or more table, view, or snapshot from which the data will be retrieved. A query that contains only the SELECT and FROM clauses retrieves all the rows in the specified tables. A third clause, the WHERE clause, must be added to supply restrictive criteria that reduce the number of rows returned by the query.

Depending on the content of the SELECT clause, the query may retrieve one, more than one, or all the columns of data in a table. To retrieve just one column from a table, simply provide the name of the column after the SELECT command, as shown in Figure 9.7.

To retrieve more than one column, provide their name after the SELECT keyword. The name of each column, except for the last must be followed by a comma to separate it from the others. The query shown in Figure 9.8 selects the First Name, Last Name, and Membership Date from the Customer table.

When the query returns the data from the database, the columns will be listed in the order specified in the SELECT statement. In the previous example, FIRST_NAME is followed by the LAST_NAME for each customer, despite the fact that the data in the table definition is defined in the reverse order.

There are two ways to retrieve all the columns from a table. The first one uses the same format as the SELECT statement shown in Figure 9.8. You specify the names of all the columns, instead of just three. Obviously, this method requires you to know the names of all the columns beforehand, and may involve

```
SQL> SELECT title
 2 FROM movie;

TITLE
_________________________
Pulp Fiction
Jefferson in Paris
Howard's End
The Remains of the Day
A Walk in the Clouds
Something to Talk About
Scent of a Woman
When a Man Loves a Woman
Amadeus
The Silence of the Lambs
```

FIGURE 9.7 One column SELECT command.

```
SQL> SELECT first_name, last_name, member_dt
  2 FROM customer

FIRST_NAME               LAST_NAME                MEMBER_DT
------------------------ ------------------------ ---------
John                     Moore                    27-MAR-96
Karen                    Campbell                 14-NOV-96
Robert                   Smith                    01-SEP-97
Joanne                   Richard                  25-JUL-97
Suzanne                  Moore                    24-MAR-97
Karla                    Moore                    30-JUL-97
Michael                  Campbell                 19-AUG-97
```

FIGURE 9.8 Multiple column SELECT command.

extensive typing, especially for tables with many columns. The advantages though are that you get exactly those data elements you ask for, in the order you specify. This type of statement is mostly used in applications that use SQL and embedded SQL statements. A shortcut to this method is to use the asterisk symbol * after the SELECT keyword. An example of this is the following statement:

```
SELECT * FROM customer;
```

When the query returns data from the database, the columns are listed in the same order as they are stored in the physical structure of the table. This type of query is usually used in interactive sessions such as a SQL*Plus session.

9.4.2 FILTERING ROWS WITH THE WHERE CLAUSE

Queries discussed in the previous section retrieve all the rows from the tables specified in the FROM clause. In systems with scarce computing resources and high number of users, or in client/server environments, queries like these affect negatively the performance of the applications, and of the database system as a whole. On the other hand, very few applications require all the records of a table to be queried and retrieved. In most database systems, users need only a small subset of the large number of records that may be stored in tables.

In order to select only certain rows from a table, the WHERE clause is added to the previous query statements immediately after the FROM clause. This clause filters out rows that do not meet the needs of users and that would be otherwise returned by the query. Rows are included or excluded based upon the value of the condition specified by the WHERE clause. For every row in the table, if the condition is evaluated to TRUE, the row is returned by the query. If it is evaluated to FALSE or UNKNOWN the row is not returned. A query statement now has the following form:

```
SELECT <clause>
FROM <clause>
WHERE <condition>;
```

9.4.3 SQL OPERATORS

In its most simple form, a condition uses an operator to compare data in a column with a character literal, numerical expression or data in another column. If the column being compared has an alphanumeric data type, the character literal it is being compared with must be enclosed in quotes.

Figure 9.9 lists some of the logical operators used the most in SQL statements. The first column contains the form of the condition if the operator is used. The second column states in which case the condition evaluates TRUE. The following paragraphs present some examples that use these operators in SELECT statements against tables of the Movie Rental Database.

- **Equality Operator.** This operator is used to retrieve rows with a certain column value. The following statement retrieves all the movies in the database directed by Spielberg:

```
SELECT title
FROM movie
WHERE director = 'Spielberg';
```

CONDITION ...	... EVALUATES TRUE IF ...
A = B	A is equal to B
A != B, A <> B	A is not equal to B
A > B; A >= B	A is greater than B; A greater than or equal to B
A < B; A <= B	A is smaller than B; A is smaller than or equal to B
A IN (List_Item_1, ... , List_Item_N)	A is equal to any member of the list
A BETWEEN x AND y	Value of A is between values x and y, inclusive
A LIKE y	A matches the pattern specified by y
A IS NULL	Value of A is not specified
NOT	Reverses the truth value of any of the preceding four operators

FIGURE 9.9 Frequently used logical operators in SQL

- **Inequality Operators.** These operators are used to retrieve all those rows that do not contain a certain column value. The following statement returns all the movies that are not rated R:

```
SELECT title
FROM movie
WHERE rating <> 'R';
```

- **Greater Than/Less Than Operators.** These operators retrieve rows for which the value of the specified column is greater than or less than a particular value, respectively. The conditions can be relaxed in both cases by adding the equality operator "=". The following statement retrieves all the records of Rental transactions for which the customers have paid $1.99 or more every day:

```
SELECT *
FROM rental
WHERE daily_rate >= 1.99;
```

  Oracle adjusts the behavior of these operators to the data type of the column being compared. Indeed, if the column's data type is alphanumeric, the condition `column_name > value` retrieves all the rows for which the value of the column ranks behind the given value in alphabetic order. The following statement lists all the customers whose last name begins with 'L' and beyond:

```
SELECT first_name, last_name
FROM customer
WHERE last_name >= 'L';
```

  If the data type of the column is date, then the equality or inequality operators compare the dates. For example, retrieve all the customers that have joined the club on or after January 1, 1997:

```
SELECT first_name, last_name
FROM customer
WHERE member_dt >= '01-JAN-97';
```

  The ability of the same operator (or function) to perform differently depending, among others, on the data type of parameters passed into it, is called overloading.

- **IN Operator.** The general syntax of this operator is `column IN (item_1, ... item_N)`. It selects only those rows whose column value is one of the list items included in parentheses. For example, select all the movies rated as PG-13 and R:

```
SELECT title
FROM movie
WHERE rating IN ('PG-13', 'R');
```

When the operator IN is preceded by the operator NOT, the query selects all those rows whose column value is not one of the list items. The following statement retrieves all the movies that are not rated PG-13 or R:

```
SELECT title
FROM movie
WHERE rating NOT IN ('PG-13', 'R');
```

- **BETWEEN Operator.** The syntax for this operator is `column BETWEEN value_1 AND value_2`. This operator selects all rows whose column value is greater than or equal to `value_1` and smaller than or equal to `value_2`. Again here Oracle uses overloading to implement the operator with different data types. The following query retrieves all the rental transactions for which the customers paid between $1.25 and $1.99 per day:

```
SELECT *
FROM rental
WHERE daily_rate BETWEEN 1.25 AND 1.99;
```

The following query retrieves all the customers that joined the video rental club on the first ten days in July 1998:

```
SELECT first_name, last_name
FROM customer
WHERE member_dt BETWEEN '01-JUL-98' AND '10-JUL-98';
```

When the operator BETWEEN is preceded by the operator NOT, the query retrieves rows whose column value is less than `value_1` or greater than `value_2`. The following query retrieves all the customer records that were not retrieved by the previous one:

```
SELECT first_name, last_name
FROM customer
WHERE member_dt NOT BETWEEN '01-JUL-98' AND '10-JUL-98';
```

- **LIKE Operator.** The general syntax of this operator is `column LIKE pattern`. It selects all those rows whose column value matches the character pattern specified by `pattern`. The column data type in this case must be either CHAR or VARCHAR2. When the equality operator is used, Oracle does an exact match of the values in the table column. But, when the LIKE operator is used, the query can be less restrictive thanks to the use of two wildcard symbols "%" and "_" in the character pattern specification. The wildcard "%" is used to represent zero or more characters in the pattern string. The following query searches for the names of the directors of ROCKY and all its sequels in the database:

```
SELECT director
FROM movie
WHERE title LIKE 'ROCKY%';
```

The wildcard "_" represents one and only one character in the exact position in the string where the wildcard is used. The following query selects the directors of ROCKY II and ROCKY IV, but not the director of the initial movie itself or of ROCKY III:

```
SELECT director
FROM movie
WHERE title LIKE 'ROCKY__';
```

Once again, the operator NOT can be used to negate logically the outcome of the LIKE operator. For example, the following query selects all the customers, except for those that live in Washington, D.C., where the area code of telephone numbers is 202:

```
SELECT first_name, last_name
FROM customer
WHERE phone NOT LIKE '(202)%';
```

- **IS NULL Operator.** The syntax of this operator is `column IS NULL`. It selects all those rows whose specified column does not contain any value at all. To select the columns that do contain any value the IS NOT NULL operator is used. The following query retrieves all the movies that are not rated:

```
SELECT title
FROM movie
WHERE rating IS NULL;
```

The statement below retrieves the movies that are rated:

```
SELECT title
FROM movie
WHERE rating IS NOT NULL;
```

9.4.4 BOOLEAN OPERATORS

You can specify multiple conditions in the WHERE clause. These conditions can be combined with the Boolean operators AND and OR, which are explained in the following paragraphs:

- **AND.** This logical operator returns TRUE if both its operands evaluate to TRUE. It returns FALSE if at least one of the operands evaluates to FALSE. A query whose WHERE clause looks like:

  `WHERE Condition_A AND Condition_B`

  will return only those rows that satisfy both `Condition_A` and `Condition_B`. For example, the following query retrieves all the customers whose last name begins with 'S' and who have been club members since January 1, 1997:

```
SELECT first_name, last_name
FROM customer
WHERE last_name LIKE 'S%'
AND member_dt >= '01-JAN-97';
```

- **OR.** This logical operator returns TRUE if at least one of the operands evaluates to TRUE. It returns FALSE only if both of them evaluate to FALSE. A query whose WHERE clause looks like:

  `WHERE Condition_A OR Condition_B`

  will return those rows that satisfy `Condition_A` or `Condition_B`. The following query selects all the movies in which Tom Hanks or Sharon Stone play the leading role:

```
SELECT title
FROM movie
WHERE actor = 'Tom Hanks'
OR actress = 'Sharon Stone';
```

Figure 9.10 displays the results of these operations when the operands take different truth values. In Boolean algebra, this is known as a truth table.

The operators NOT, AND and OR can be combined to form complicated search criteria. In such cases, the truth value of the conditions is evaluated according to precedence rules. The NOT operator is highest in the hierarchy, then comes AND, and finally, the OR operator. For example, the following query retrieves all the customers whose last name begins with 'S' and have the phone number in the database; it also selects all the customers born after January 1, 1975 whether they meet the previous criteria or not:

```
SELECT first_name, last_name, phone, dob
FROM customer
WHERE last_name LIKE 'S%'
AND phone IS NOT NULL
OR dob >= '01-JAN-75';
```

9.4.5 USING PARENTHESES IN LOGICAL EXPRESSIONS

When several conditions are combined in a WHERE clause, the expression may become complicated and difficult to read. It is easy to introduce errors in such expressions and it is difficult to debug them. I recommend that you use parentheses in order to simplify the appearance of complicated logical expressions. Parentheses can also be used to override the default precedence rules of logical operators. Every expression enclosed in parentheses is evaluated before other expressions to its right or left. After this, the evaluation of the expression proceeds according to the precedence rules mentioned before. The query in Figure 9.11 selects all the rental transactions for movies *The Remains of the Day* (Movie ID is 203) or *Amadeus* (Movie ID is 208) that occurred during the first ten days of July 1998:

If the parentheses are omitted, the outcome of the query is different, as Figure 9.12 shows. In the statement presented here, the operator AND takes precedence over OR. Therefore, the query will retrieve all the transactions for the movie *The Remains of the Day* regardless of the rent date, and the transactions for movie *Amadeus* during first ten days in July 1998:

A	B	A AND B	A OR B
TRUE	TRUE	TRUE	TRUE
TRUE	FALSE	FALSE	TRUE
FALSE	TRUE	FALSE	TRUE
FALSE	FALSE	FALSE	FALSE

FIGURE 9.10 Truth table for Boolean operators AND and OR.

```
SQL> SELECT *
FROM rental
WHERE (movie_id = 203
OR movie_id = 208)
AND rent_dt BETWEEN '01-JUL-98' AND '10-JUL-98';

CUSTOMER_ID   MOVIE_ID RENT_DT   RETURN_DT DAILY_RATE
----------- ---------- --------- --------- ----------
         70        203 02-JUL-98 04-JUL-98        .99
         70        208 02-JUL-98 04-JUL-98       1.99
         60        208 02-JUL-98 04-JUL-98       1.99
         40        203 02-JUL-98 04-JUL-98        .99
```

FIGURE 9.11 Importance of parentheses in logical expressions.

```
SQL> SELECT *
FROM rental
WHERE movie_id = 203
OR movie_id = 208
AND rent_dt BETWEEN '01-JUL-98' AND '10-JUL-98';

CUSTOMER_ID   MOVIE_ID RENT_DT   RETURN_DT DAILY_RATE
----------- ---------- --------- --------- ----------
         70        203 02-JUL-98 04-JUL-98        .99
         70        208 02-JUL-98 04-JUL-98       1.99
         60        208 02-JUL-98 04-JUL-98       1.99
         40        203 02-JUL-98 04-JUL-98        .99
         30        203 12-JUN-98 13-JUN-98        .99
         60        203 21-NOV-98 23-NOV-98        .99
         20        203 21-AUG-98 22-AUG-98        .99
         10        203 22-AUG-98 23-AUG-98        .99
         50        203 24-AUG-98 26-AUG-98        .99
         30        203 23-AUG-98 24-AUG-98        .99
         60        203 23-AUG-98 24-AUG-98        .99
```

FIGURE 9.12 Importance of parentheses in logical expressions (Continued)

9.4.6 GROUP BY CLAUSE

Often, there exists a need to group data returned from a query and display summary information for that group of data. The GROUP BY clause allows the SELECT statement to meet this requirement. The general syntax of this clause is `GROUP BY column`. The SELECT statement with a GROUP BY clause will return only one row displayed for each unique value of the column whose name is specified in the clause. The query presented in Figure 9.13 calculates how many rental transactions have occurred between August 20 and August 24, 1998 for movies *The Remains of the Day* (Movie ID is 203) or *Amadeus* (Movie ID is 208). The GROUP BY clause ensures that one record is displayed for each day, with the total number of the above movies rented in that time period.

The GROUP BY clause can be used with more than one column. In the example above, you do not have a way to tell exactly how many copies of these two movies were rented each day. To retrieve the total of movies rented for each movie, for each day, you expand the GROUP BY clause as shown in Figure 9.14. Now you can tell that on August 21 and 22 both movies rented equally well. On August 23, *The Remains of the Day* rented one copy more than *Amadeus*. The situation was the reverse on August 24.

9.4.7 HAVING CLAUSE

When selecting rows from a table, you filter the unwanted ones by specifying restricting criteria in the WHERE clause. Similarly, when using the GROUP BY clause, you may need to filter out some of the grouped rows. In this case, the HAVING clause is used. The general format of this clause is `HAVING condition`, where `condition` is a logical expression that evaluates to TRUE or FALSE like the conditions in the WHERE clause. The following query is a slight modifi-

```
SQL> SELECT rent_dt, count(*)
  FROM rental
  WHERE movie_id IN (203, 208)
  AND rent_dt BETWEEN '21-AUG-98' AND '24-AUG-98'
  GROUP BY rent_dt;

RENT_DT       COUNT(*)
---------     --------
21-AUG-98            2
22-AUG-98            2
23-AUG-98            3
24-AUG-98            3
```

FIGURE 9.13 GROUP BY clause.

```
SQL> SELECT rent_dt, movie_id, count(*)
FROM rental
WHERE movie_id IN (203, 208)
AND rent_dt BETWEEN '21-AUG-98' AND '24-AUG-98'
GROUP BY rent_dt, movie_id;


RENT_DT       MOVIE_ID    COUNT(*)
----------- ----------- ----------
21-AUG-98          203           1
21-AUG-98          208           1
22-AUG-98          203           1
22-AUG-98          208           1
23-AUG-98          203           2
23-AUG-98          208           1
24-AUG-98          203           1
24-AUG-98          208           2
```

FIGURE 9.14 GROUP BY clause with multiple columns.

cation of the statement shown in Figure 9.14. The query lists on a day-by-day basis all the movies that have rented more than five copies per day during the specified period of time:

```
SELECT rent_dt, movie_id, count(*)
FROM rental
WHERE rent_dt BETWEEN '21-AUG-98' AND '24-AUG-98'
GROUP BY rent_dt, movie_id
HAVING count(*) >=5;
```

In a SELECT statement that contains WHERE, GROUP BY, and HAVING clauses, the records that do not fulfill the WHERE conditions are discarded first. Then, the remaining records are bundled together as specified in the GROUP BY clause. Finally, the HAVING clause removes those groups that do not meet its conditions. Obviously, you want to remove as much records in the first filtering performed by the WHERE clause. Therefore, the HAVING clause conditions should be designed to operate only on data that depend on the grouping of rows, but not on each individual record in the table.

9.4.8 JOINS

In the examples presented so far, you have queried data from single tables. One of the strongest features of SQL is the ease and flexibility it provides in selecting data from multiple tables. When data from more than one table are selected and displayed by the query as one logical record, it is said that the tables are joined. The easiest way to join two tables is to specify their column names in the SELECT clause, and their names in the FROM clause of the query. However, this is not a type of query that should occur often, if at all. The reason is that it generates a Cartesian product of the rows in each table, or in other words, it matches each row in one table with all the rows in the second table, thus resulting in a large, often too large, number of records returned by the query.

Suppose, for example that the Customer table has 100 records and the Movies table 1000 records, and you issue the following query:

```
SELECT last_name, first_name, title
FROM customer, movie;
```

In response to this statement, Oracle would return $100 \times 1000 = 100{,}000$ records from the database. This is certainly not needed or necessary and rarely meaningful.

The join that is used most frequently is the simple join (also called equi-join or inner-join). In this type of join, records from tables are joined based on the equality of data in columns from the respective tables. Obviously, similar data are compared together. The comparing occurs in the WHERE clause, or the HAVING clause if the GROUP BY clause is present. For example, the following query retrieves the names of customers and the dates they rented movies from the video store:

```
SELECT first_name, last_name, rent_dt
FROM customer, rental
WHERE customer.id = rental.customer_id;
```

The condition for joining records from tables CUSTOMER and RENTAL is that the values in the columns ID and CUSTOMER_ID must be the same. In order to avoid any ambiguity that arises when columns with the same name but from different tables are used in a SQL statement, the names of these columns must be prefixed by the table name, as shown in the example above.

You can join records from more than two tables. Be careful though to avoid a Cartesian product of rows, which has the undesired results explained earlier. The following example selects the movies rented by each customer, together with rental dates and prices paid:

```
SELECT first_name, last_name, title, daily_rate
FROM customer, rental, movie
WHERE customer.id = rental.customer_id
AND movie.id = rental.movie_id;
```

In the last two queries the condition in the WHERE clause is responsible for joining data from different tables in a logical manner, but does little to further restrict the number of records returned by the queries. Additional conditions should be added to the statements as discussed in the previous sections. For example, the following statement returns the customers whose last name begins with A, B, or C and the dates in which they rented movies. It is a more restrictive version of a similar statement shown earlier in this section which does not place any restrictions on which customers are returned:

```
SQL> SELECT first_name, last_name, rent_dt
  2  FROM customer, rental
  3  WHERE customer.id = rental.customer_id
  4  AND last_name < 'D';

FIRST_NAME                LAST_NAME                 RENT_DT
------------------------  ------------------------  ---------
Karen                     Campbell                  12-NOV-98
Karen                     Campbell
21-AUG-98
Karen                     Campbell                  21-AUG-98
Michael                   Campbell                  02-JUL-98
Michael                   Campbell                  02-JUL-98
Paul                      Baker                     11-MAR-97
Paul                      Baker                     11-MAR-97
Paul                      Baker                     28-FEB-97
```

The way this statement is written, its return set will contain only those records for which the join condition is satisfied. But it will not return any customers who have not rented any movies, since their ID will not be present in the column RENTAL.CUSTOMER_ID. In situations where you want to return not only the records in the CUSTOMER table that meet the equality condition but also those that have no matching records in the RENTAL table, you need to define the join condition as an *outer join* using the outer join operator (+). The following statement uses the outer join operator for the same query shown above. This statement returns the customer Rebecca Andrews who has not rented any movies:

```
SQL> SELECT first_name, last_name, rent_dt
  2  FROM customer, rental
  3  WHERE customer.id = rental.customer_id (+)
  4  AND last_name < 'D';

FIRST_NAME                LAST_NAME                 RENT_DT
------------------------  ------------------------  ---------
Karen                     Campbell                  12-NOV-98
Karen                     Campbell                  21-AUG-98
Karen                     Campbell                  21-AUG-98
Michael                   Campbell                  02-JUL-98
Michael                   Campbell                  02-JUL-98
Rebecca                   Andrews
Paul                      Baker                     11-MAR-97
Paul                      Baker                     11-MAR-97
Paul                      Baker                     28-FEB-97
```

Finally, let us mention that when multiple table names are involved in the query, the typing of their names can become cumbersome. To avoid the inevitable mistakes that can be made, pseudonyms or aliases can be used instead of the full names of tables. The following example is another version of the previous query, where aliases are used:

```
SELECT first_name, last_name, rent_dt
FROM customer C, rental R
WHERE C.id = R.customer_id (+)
AND last_name < 'D';
```

9.4.9 ORDER BY CLAUSE

What has been silently accepted in all the examples above is the fact that the records returned by the queries so far do not appear in a particular order. In fact, records in relational databases are not stored in any particular order. However, the ORDER BY clause allows you to sort the outcome of a query based on the values of columns or expressions that will be returned by the query. For example, the following query lists the customers that have joined the video club during 1997, ordered alphabetically by LAST_NAME.

By default, SQL sorts the records in the ascending order, as shown in Figure 9.15. If you want to sort them in the descending order, add the keyword DESC at the end of the ORDER BY clause. Figure 9.16 shows a query that retrieves the same data as the query in Figure 9.15, but sorts them by LAST_NAME in descending order.

```
SQL> SELECT last_name, first_name
  2 FROM customer
  3 WHERE member_dt >= '01-JAN-97'
  4  AND member_dt < '01-JAN-98'
  5 ORDER BY last_name;

LAST_NAME                                FIRST_NAME
---------------------------------------- --------------------
Andrews                                  Rebecca
Baker                                    Paul
Campbell                                 Michael
Johnson                                  Michelle
Milton                                   Henry
Moore                                    Suzanne
Moore                                    Karla
Richard                                  Joanne
Smith                                    Robert
```

FIGURE 9.15 ORDER BY clause.

```
SQL> SELECT last_name, first_name
  2 FROM customer
  3 WHERE member_dt >= '01-JAN-97'
  4  AND member_dt < '01-JAN-98'
  5 ORDER BY last_name DESC;

LAST_NAME                                FIRST_NAME
---------------------------------------- --------------------
Smith                                    Robert
Richard                                  Joanne
Moore                                    Suzanne
Moore                                    Karla
Milton                                   Henry
Johnson                                  Michelle
Campbell                                 Michael
Baker                                    Paul
Andrews                                  Rebecca
```

FIGURE 9.16 ORDER BY clause in descending order.

The output of a query can be ordered based on the data from more than one column. To do this, the additional columns are specified in the ORDER BY statement, separated by a comma. In a situation like this, the records are first sorted based on the value of the first column in the ORDER BY clause. Then, each set of records with the same value for the first column is sorted based on the second column, and so on. For example, the following query displays all the movies in the video rental database. The movies are sorted first based on the name of the leading actress, then actor, and, finally, title:

```
SELECT actress, actor, title
FROM movie
ORDER by actress, actor, title;
```

The columns to order by can be specified by supplying their name, as in all the examples presented here. They can currently also be specified by giving their position in the list of columns that appear in the SELECT clause. This is particularly useful when, instead of table columns, long expressions are evaluated. The following query is similar to another query encountered before. For each date between the specified dates, it calculates the number of the movies rented. It displays only those movies that have rented more than five copies each day, starting from the best rentals. This query sorts by the value calculated by the function COUNT, which is the third one in the SELECT clause:

```
SELECT rent_dt, movie_id, count(*)
FROM rental
WHERE rent_dt BETWEEN '21-AUG-97' AND '24-AUG-97'
GROUP BY rent_dt, movie_id
HAVING count(*) > 5
ORDER BY 3 DESC;
```

9.5 EXPANDING QUERIES WITH SET OPERATIONS

It was mentioned earlier that the relational database model and SQL language are founded upon the mathematical theory of sets. For the purposes of this chapter, a set is a collection of items that share some common characteristics. These items are called elements of a set. Conventionally, sets are denoted with uppercase letters, whereas elements of a set are denoted with lowercase characters, sometime followed by subscripts. Curled brackets are used to present a set and its elements—or a part thereof. For example the following represents the set of days of the week:

```
WEEK = {Sunday, Monday, Tuesday, Wednesday, Thursday,
Friday, Saturday}
```

Two constraints placed on the elements of a set are that a set cannot contain duplicate elements, and the set cannot be considered as an element of itself. The need for the first one is fairly obvious. Weeks that contain two Mondays are not particularly helpful. The second constraint is less evident, but it should be sufficient to note that the Mathematics entered a deep crisis at the turn of the century, simply because mathematicians were not aware of the importance of this constraint.

TIP

The blind alley the mathematicians of the early years of this century found themselves in is known as the Russell's paradox, after the great English mathematician and philosopher Lord Bertrand Russell (1872–1970). This paradox is often described in the popular literature as the barber's paradox.

Question: How would you define the barber of a village?

Answer: He shaves those who do not shave themselves.

Question: Who shaves the barber, then?

Answer: (Scratching the head) Well, there is no other barber to go to, since he's the only one in the village. But, he cannot shave himself either, because, being a barber, he must shave only those who do not shave themselves!

There are three basic operations defined in set theory that allow for creation of new sets by combining elements of existing sets. These operations are UNION, INTERSECT, and MINUS. The UNION operation results in a set that contains elements that are in either set. It is denoted usually as $A \cup B$, or $A + B$. The INTERSECT operation results in a set that contains elements that are in both sets. It is denoted usually as $A \cap B$, or $A \bullet B$, or, simply, AB. The MINUS operation results in sets with elements that are part of the first set, but are not part of the second one. It is denoted usually as A / B, or $A - B$. Figure 9.17 visually displays the results of these operations.

In relational databases, records returned by a query, or SELECT statement, form a set. Each individual record is an element of this set. The SQL language implements the three set operations described above, thus allowing you to further extend your ability to retrieve data from the database. The general syntax of statements that use set operators is

```
QUERY_1 <Set Operator> QUERY_2.
```

As an example, let QUERY_1 be the statement that selects all the movies where Anthony Hopkins plays the leading role:

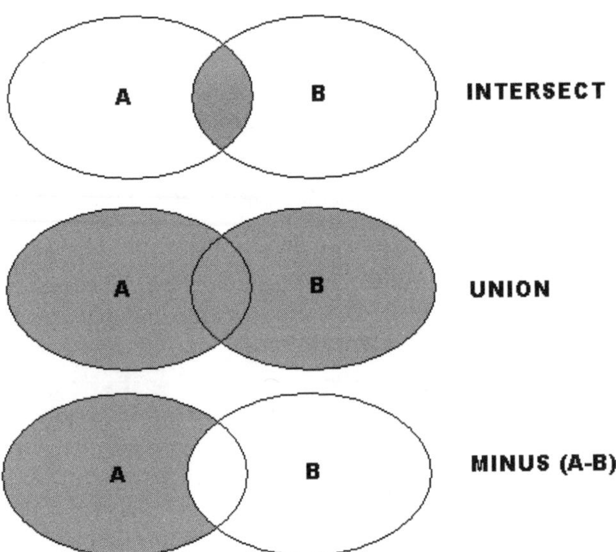

FIGURE 9.17 Visual representation of set operations.

```
SELECT title
FROM movie
WHERE actor = 'Anthony Hopkins';
```

Let QUERY_2 be the statement that selects all the movies where Emma Thompson plays the leading role:

```
SELECT title
FROM movie
WHERE actress = 'Emma Thompson';
```

Then, the following statement (Figure 9.18) selects the movies in which Anthony Hopkins or Emma Thompson plays a leading role:

Note that movies *Howard's End* and *The Remains of the Day* appears only once in the list, despite the fact that they are returned by both QUERY_1 and QUERY_2. This is how SQL implements the set theory constraint that elements in a set must be unique. However, in practice there may be instances when returning only the distinct rows of two queries is not desirable. To address this problem, SQL uses the operator UNION ALL, an extension of UNION, which simply merges the output of the two queries, without worrying about returning only the distinct rows.

```
SQL> SELECT title
FROM movie
WHERE actor = 'Anthony Hopkins'
UNION
SELECT title
FROM movie
WHERE actress = 'Emma Thompson';

TITLE
_______________________
Howard's End
Much Ado About Nothing
The Remains of the Day
The Silence of the Lambs
```

FIGURE 9.18 Using UNION in queries

Figure 9.19 shows the same two queries joined by the operator INTERSECT. The query returns all the movies in which the two actors play together.

Figure 9.20 shows QUERY_1 and QUERY_2 joined by the operator MINUS. The query returns the movies where Anthony Hopkins plays but not Emma Thompson.

The outcome of operators UNION, UNION ALL, and INTERSECT does not depend on the order in which the individual queries are listed. It is said that these operators are commutative. You can convince yourself by reversing the order of the queries in the first three statements. The operator MINUS however does not

```
SQL> SELECT title
FROM movie
WHERE actor = 'Anthony Hopkins'
INTERSECT
SELECT title
FROM movie
WHERE actress = 'Emma Thompson';

TITLE
______________________
Howard's End
The Remains of the Day
```

FIGURE 9.19 Using INTERSECT in queries.

```
SQL> SELECT title
FROM movie
WHERE actor = 'Anthony Hopkins'
MINUS
SELECT title
FROM movie
WHERE actress = 'Emma Thompson';

TITLE
------------------------------------
The Silence of the Lambs
```

FIGURE 9.20 Using MINUS in queries.

enjoy this property. Its outcome depends on the order in which the queries are executed. The query shown in Figure 9.21 uses the same individual queries as the one in Figure 9.20, but in reverse order. The different results are to be expected. The second query returns the movies where Emma Thompson plays without Anthony Hopkins.

To conclude this section, a note on multiple uses of set operators. The examples shown previously use only two individual queries, but statements can be written where several queries can be combined using one or more set operators. In set theory, the operator INTERSECT has the highest precedence of all. This means that $A \cup B \cap C$ is evaluated according to the following two steps:

1. $D = B \cap C$
2. $E = A \cup D$

```
SQL> SELECT title
FROM movie
WHERE actress = 'Emma Thompson'
MINUS
SELECT title
FROM movie
WHERE actor = 'Anthony Hopkins';

TITLE
------------------------------------
Much Ado About Nothing
```

FIGURE 9.21 MINUS is not commutative.

However, in the Oracle implementation of SQL language, all the set operators have the same precedence. Therefore, set expressions are evaluated left to right. Here, the same statement $A \cup B \cap C$ is evaluated as:

1. $D = A \cup D$
2. $E = D \cap C$

Oracle will enforce the precedence rules of set operators in its upcoming versions. In the meantime, to ensure that SQL statements written today will return the same data in the future, resolve any potential ambiguity by using parentheses. For example, implement the previous statements as $(A \cup (B \cap C))$.

9.6 DATA MANIPULATION LANGUAGE COMMANDS

The next four sections will explain how to add, modify, or delete data from the database. The SQL commands that perform these tasks, INSERT, UPDATE, and DELETE are simple and straightforward. They form a category of SQL statements, called Data Manipulation Language (DML). DML statements are slightly different from the SELECT command. SELECT is a passive command in the sense that it only displays data that already exist in the database. The content of the database does not change when a SELECT statement is issued. But, when a DML statement is issued, the content of the database changes.

9.6.1 COMMIT AND ROLLBACK

However, these changes do not occur instantaneously. The actual procedure that the Oracle RDBMS undertakes is complicated but from the users point of view the following sequence occurs. As DML statements are issued, Oracle stores the data they modify in internal structures, known as rollback segments. At the same time, Oracle places locks on modified data, so that other users may not change them. Only when a COMMIT command is issued are these statements applied to the database, thus making the changes effective and available to all other users. At COMMIT time, the locks on data are released as well. In order to ensure the integrity of the database, Oracle issues an implicit COMMIT command each time Data Definition Language statements such as a CREATE, ALTER or DROP commands, are issued.

If you decide you want to undo the actions of DML commands issued during the current transaction, issue the ROLLBACK command. ROLLBACK throws away all changes made to data since the last COMMIT. Sometime, you may want to rollback just part of the transaction, but not the entire changes, since the last COMMIT. In such case, *savepoints* can be created in the transaction. Think of a savepoint as a picture of the database taken at the moment the savepoint is created. If at any time after that moment, you are not happy with the outcome of some statement, you can undo the changes and move to the database state captured by the picture, or the savepoint. To achieve this, you issue a ROLLBACK TO SAVEPOINT statement. By doing so, you do not lose the modifications made since your last COMMIT up to the savepoint. Obviously, the next time you commit, everything will be written to the database. The savepoints are no longer valid and are automatically discarded.

Figure 9.22 illustrates the COMMIT, ROLLBACK and SAVEPOINT concepts in a typical database session.

9.6.2 INSERT

The SELECT command is important because it allows you to view what is stored in the database. However, at some point, somebody needs to enter those records in the database. SQL provides a simple command to insert data in a database. The INSERT command can be used to enter records one at a time. When combined with the SELECT command, it can insert multiple records from data structures that already exist in the database. The general syntax of the command is:

```
INSERT INTO table_name (column_1, column_2, ... column_N)
VALUES (value_1, value_2, ... value_N);
```

There must be a one-to-one relationship between the columns in the INSERT clause and the values provided in the VALUES clause; the data types must also match. Here is a typical INSERT statement:

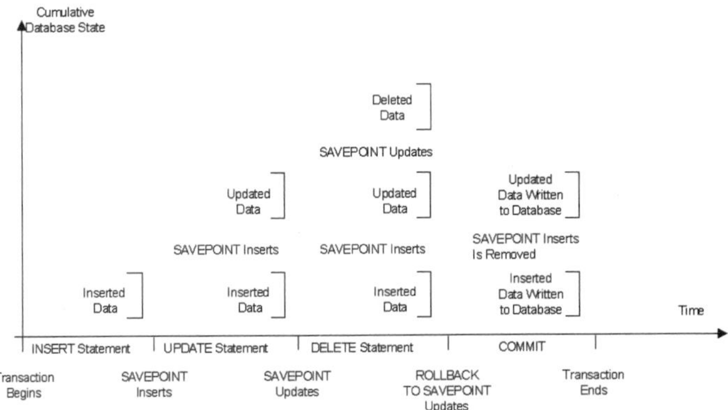

FIGURE 9.22 Commit, Rollback and Savepoint concepts in a database transaction.

```
INSERT INTO movie (id, title, director, actor, actress,
rating)
VALUES (211, 'The Piano', 'Jane Campion', 'Harvey
Keitel', 'Holly Hunter', 'R');
```

Alphanumeric and DATE values are always enclosed in single quotes, but the quotes are not needed if the values are of NUMBER data type. If data is missing for a particular column, specify the keyword NULL. However, the INSERT statement will fail with an error if you do not provide a value for a column with the NOT NULL database constraint enabled. The order of the columns in the INSERT statement is not important as long as specified values follow the same order.

The INSERT statement can be used without column specifications. In this case, the database assumes that all the columns in the table will be entered in the order in which they are stored in the physical table structure. The following example inserts a new customer in the database with this type of statement:

```
INSERT INTO customer
VALUES (122, 'Collins', 'David', NULL, '31-MAR-63', '05-
SEP-98');
```

This statement relies too much on your knowledge of the database at a given point in time. For applications that access tables whose structure may change, commands like the one above are not flexible and may lead to errors and inability of users to insert data. The first type of INSERT statement is more flexible because the columns to be inserted are fixed.

The INSERT command followed by the VALUES clause allows you to insert data one record at a time. When data are retrieved from other existing tables, the INSERT statement can be combined with the SELECT clause to insert multiple records in a table with one command. To see an example for this type of statement, you will use an additional table called LATE_RETURN. This table records the customers that do not return their movies within one month from the rental date. Figure 9.23 shows the SQL statement used to create this table.

The table was created together with the other three tables of the Movie Rental Database, but it does not contain any records. You will populate it with the names and phone numbers of customers that have a gap of one month or more between the rental and return dates. You also want to store the title of the movie they have rented. The following query retrieves all the records that meet these requirements:

```
CREATE TABLE late_return (
 customer_id      NUMBER,
 last_name        VARCHAR2(30),
 first_name       VARCHAR2(30),
 phone            VARCHAR2(14),
 title            VARCHAR2(30),
 rent_dt          DATE,
 return_dt        DATE
);
```

FIGURE 9.23 SQL statement to create the table LATE_RETURN.

```
SELECT customer.id, first_name, last_name,
phone, title, rent_dt, return_dt
FROM customer, movie, rental
WHERE customer.id = rental.customer_id
 AND movie.id = rental.movie_id
 AND MONTHS_BETWEEN (return_dt, rent_dt) >= 1;
```

To insert these records into the table LATE_RETURN, simply add the INSERT clause before the SELECT clause as shown in the following statement:

```
INSERT INTO late_return
SELECT customer.id, first_name, last_name,
phone, title, rent_dt, return_dt
FROM customer, movie, rental
WHERE customer.id = rental.customer_id
 AND movie.id = rental.movie_id
 AND MONTHS_BETWEEN (return_dt, rent_dt) >= 1;
```

This statement uses the fully qualified name (tablename.column) for columns that are encountered in more that one table. The SQL function MONTHS_BETWEEN will be discussed in Section 9.7.2 later in the chapter.

9.6.3 UPDATE

Once you have entered records in the database, you need to be able to alter that data. The UPDATE command provided by the SQL language allows for updates on one or more columns, and one or more rows in a table. The general syntax for this statement is

```
UPDATE table
SET column = value [, column = value]
WHERE <condition>;
```

It instructs the database to set the data of each column in the SET clause to the specified value for all rows in the table mentioned in the UPDATE clause that satisfy the WHERE clause. The following example updates the telephone number of customer Karen Campbell.

```
UPDATE customer
SET phone = '8002344323'
WHERE last_name = 'Campbell'
 AND first_name = 'Karen';
```

If the statement updates more than one column, they are separated by commas in the SET clause, as the following example shows.

```
UPDATE customer
SET phone = '8004567890', dob = '13-FEB-64'
WHERE last_name = 'Collins'
 AND first_name = 'David';
```

The WHERE clause in the UPDATE statement is very important because it decides which rows will be updated. If no WHERE clause is defined, all the rows in the table will be updated. The following statement can be issued when customer David Collins (CUSTOMER_ID = 112) returns the movie *Amadeus* (MOVIE_ID = 203).

```
UPDATE rental
SET return_dt = SYSDATE
WHERE customer_id = 112
 AND movie_id = 203
 AND return_dt IS NULL;
```

SYSDATE is another SQL function that returns the current date (and time) as maintained by the database. In the query shown above, you know the CUSTOMER_ID and the MOVIE_ID beforehand. If only the customer name or the movie title are known, the tables CUSTOMER and MOVIE must be queried to retrieve the ID numbers. A SELECT statement, may be used in the WHERE clause to enable you to specify the records to be updated. This type is SELECT statement is called a Subquery. The following query registers the return of the movie *Pulp Fiction* by Karen Campbell without explicitly using, or requiring you to know, ID numbers of the movie or the customer:

```
UPDATE rental
SET return_dt = SYSDATE
WHERE customer_id IN (
  SELECT id FROM customer
  WHERE last_name = 'Campbell' AND first_name = 'Karen')
 AND movie_id IN (
  SELECT id FROM movie
  WHERE title = 'Pulp Fiction')
 AND return_dt IS NULL;
```

The indentation of the subqueries is for readability purpose only, and it does not affect the syntax of the query itself.

9.6.4 DELETE

The DELETE statement allows you to delete data from a table. Its general syntax is:

```
DELETE FROM table
WHERE <condition>;
```

The following example purges the Rental table by deleting records for movies that were returned before January 1, 1987.

```
DELETE FROM rental
WHERE return_dt < '01-JAN-87';
```

The WHERE clause is very important because it specifies which records should be deleted from the table. If the clause is not present, *all* the records from the table will be deleted. As with the UPDATE statement, a SELECT command can be combined with the WHERE clause of a DELETE statement to better identify the records that should be removed. The following statement deletes from the table LATE_RETURN the records for those customers that returned their movies.

```
DELETE FROM late_return
WHERE customer_id NOT IN (
 SELECT DISTINCT customer_id FROM rental
 WHERE return_dt IS NULL);
```

The subquery in this statement retrieves the ID of those customers that have not returned their movies. Note here the significance of the keyword DISTINCT in the subquery. It ensures that the SELECT statement return only one customer ID, despite the fact that the customer may have several movies to return. The condition in the WHERE clause singles out for delete those customers that are not in the group identified by the subquery, that is, the customers that have returned their movies.

9.7 SQL FUNCTIONS

As some of the examples discussed previously show, the data can be actively manipulated in SQL statements through arithmetic operators. But the SQL language itself and its implementation by Oracle also provide a large number of functions that help perform computations that are beyond the scope of simple arithmetic expressions. Depending on the way they act upon records, the functions can be classified as single-row, or scalar functions, and group or aggregate functions.

Scalar functions act upon each row returned by the query. They can be placed in the SELECT clause, thus performing calculations of data returned by the query; or in the WHERE clause, thus enabling the query to specify more precise and sophisticated retrieval criteria. Depending on the parameters they take, and values they return, these functions are classified as character functions, date functions, and mathematical functions. A fourth category of miscellaneous functions such as those responsible for data conversion from one type to the other, or NULL value substitution, can also be considered separately.

The standard ANSI SQL language defines only the following functions: AVG, COUNT, MAX, MIN, and SUM. They are all group functions. This means that all the other functions discussed in this section are specific to the Oracle implementation of SQL. This is not to say that implementations of SQL by other database vendors do not have these, or similar functions. Functions ROUND and TRUNC, for example, are implemented identically by INFORMIX SQL and Oracle SQL.

The following sections discuss the different types of SQL functions and provide examples of such functions for each type.

9.7.1 SCALAR CHARACTER FUNCTIONS

Scalar character functions take alphanumeric data as arguments. Some of them return alphanumeric values, but a few return numeric values. Among the most important functions in this category are the case conversion functions (INITCAP, LOWER, UPPER), concatenation function (CONCAT), and substring function (SUBSTR).

- **Case conversion functions.** These functions transform the case of the input character string. INITCAP returns the input string with the first character of each word in uppercase; LOWER returns all the characters in the input string in lower case; UPPER returns all the characters in the input string in upper case. Figure 9.24 shows a statement that uses all these three functions to display the last name of a customer in different formats.
- **The concatenation function.** The syntax of this function is `CONCAT (string_1, string_2)`. As the name suggests, it returns the input strings concatenated together. The following is an example of the use of this function:

```
SELECT CONCAT(first_name, last_name)
FROM customer
WHERE customer_id = 20;
```

Note that you can achieve the same result with the concatenation operator `||`, as shown in the following statement:

```
SELECT first_name||last_name
FROM customer
WHERE customer_id = 20;
```

Sometimes, especially when concatenating multiple strings, the concatenation operator `||` is easier to write and read than multiple calls to the CONCAT function. Consider first the following statement that uses the CONCAT function:

```
SELECT CONCAT (CONCAT(title, ' was directed by '),
director)
FROM movie
WHERE movie_id = 208
```

```
SQL> SELECT INITCAP(last_name), UPPER(last_name),
LOWER(last_name)
 2 FROM customer
 3 WHERE id = 20;

INITCAP(LAST_NAME)  UPPER(LAST_NAME)       LOWER(LAST_NAME)
------------------  --------------------   ----------------
Campbell            CAMPBELL           8    campbell
```

FIGURE 9.24 Case conversion SQL functions.

Now compare it with the following statement, which uses the concatenation operator:

```
SELECT title || ' was directed by ' || director
FROM movie
WHERE movie_id = 208;
```

They both result in the same string concatenated, but the second one is much more natural and easier to understand.

- **The substring function.** The syntax of this function is `SUBSTR(input_string, n, m)`, where `input_string` is the string from which you want to strip out a substring, `n` is the position in `input_string` from which you want to begin stripping the substring, and `m` is the number of characters to be included in the substring. Both `n` and `m` are integers. Value of `m` cannot be smaller than one. If `n` is positive, the substring will begin `n` positions starting from the beginning of `input_string`. If `n` is negative, the substring will begin `n` positions starting from the end of `input_string`.

```
SELECT SUBSTR (title, 5, 7) First, SUBSTR(title, -3, 3)
Second
FROM movie
WHERE movie_id = 203;
```

In this statement, the first call to SUBSTR function returns string 'Remains'—seven characters starting from position 5 in string 'The Remains of the Day'. The second call returns substring 'Day'—three characters, starting three positions from the end of title.

- **Character functions that return numeric values.** Among the most important functions in this group are INSTR and LENGTH. The syntax of the first function in `INSTR(string_1, string_2, n, m)`. It searches `string_1`, starting from character `n` for the `m`-th occurrence of `string_2`. The function returns the initial position of `string_2` with respect to the beginning of `string_1`. The function returns 0 if the `m`-th occurrence of `string_2` does not occur starting from the `n`-th position of `string_1`. If the value of `n` is positive, `string_1` is searched from the beginning; if the value of `n` is negative, the search of `string_1` begins from the end.

```
SELECT INSTR (title, 'he', 2, 2)
FROM movie
WHERE movie_id = 203;
```

The statement above returns 17, which is the position in which the second occurrence of substring 'he' begins in string 'The Remains of the Day.'

The syntax of function LENGTH is `LENGTH(input_string)`. It returns the length of the `input_string` in characters. The following statement returns 22, which is the length in bytes of string 'The Remains of the Day:'

```
SELECT LENGTH (title)
FROM movie
WHERE movie_id = 203;
```

9.7.2 SCALAR DATE FUNCTIONS

Scalar date functions take as input date values. They all return date values, except for the MONTHS_BETWEEN function, which returns the number of months between two dates. Other important functions in this category are ADD_MONTHS, LAST_DAY, NEXT_DAY and SYSDATE. The following paragraphs describe these functions:

- **SYSDATE.** This function requires no arguments and returns the current system date and time.
- **ADD_MONTHS.** The syntax of this function is `ADD_MONTHS(in_date, number_of_months)`. It adds the specified number of months to the input date, and returns the new date. For example, in order to rent movies rated R, customers must be seventeen years or older. The following query displays the seventeenth birthday of the customer Karen Campbell. She cannot rent any movies rated R until that date:
- **MONTHS_BETWEEN.** The general syntax of this function is `MONTHS_BETWEEN(date_1, date_2)`. The function returns the months between the two input dates. The following query makes it easier for the clerk to decide whether to rent R rated movies to Karen Campbell. It calculates her age in

```
SQL> SELECT ADD_MONTHS(dob, 17*12)
 2 FROM customer
 3 WHERE first_name = 'Karen'
 4  AND last_name = 'Campbell';

ADD_MONTH
---------
09-APR-99
```

FIGURE 9.25 ADD_MONTHS SQL function.

months, and then divides it by 12 to display it in years. As you can see from this example, the age of Karen, as returned by this statement is a decimal number.

```
SELECT MONTHS_BETWEEN(SYSDATE, dob)/12 Age
FROM customer
WHERE first_name = 'Karen' AND last_name = 'Campbell';

AGE
----------
15.8674693
```

- **NEXT_DAY.** The syntax of this function is `NEXT_DAY(input_date, day)`. It returns the date of the first occurrence of the specify day of the week since the input date. The variable `day` can take any of the following values: "MONDAY," "TUESDAY," "WEDNESDAY," "THURSDAY," "FRIDAY," "SATURDAY," "SUNDAY."

Suppose that during the week a clerk wants to post a notice about the video rental store being closed the coming Monday. The following query supplies the needed date, and can be executed any of the week-days the store is open without requiring any changes:

```
SELECT NEXT_DAY (SYSDATE, 'MONDAY')
FROM DUAL;
```

DUAL is a 'dummy' table that will be discussed in Section 9.8 of this chapter.

9.7.3 SCALAR MATHEMATICAL FUNCTIONS

Scalar mathematical functions take numeric values as input and return numeric values. Oracle provides functions for basic mathematical functions such as exponential, logarithmic, trigonometric, hyperbolic, and other functions. This section provides an example for the function TRUNC. Its general syntax is `TRUNC(input_number, m)`. It truncates the `input_number` to `m` decimal places. The parameter m is optional. If it is omitted, the function will display only the whole part of the `input_number`. If m is positive, the function truncates the `input_number` to `m` digits after the decimal point. If `m` is negative, the function makes zero `m` digits before the decimal point. The following query displays the age of Karen Campbell, but this time only as a whole number. The age of Karen as shown by this statement is an integer and not a decimal number as in the similar example in the previous section:

```
SELECT TRUNC (MONTHS_BETWEEN (SYSDATE, dob)/12) Age
FROM customer
WHERE first_name = 'Karen' AND last_name = 'Campbell';

AGE
-----
       15
```

9.7.4 CONVERSION AND MISCELLANEOUS FUNCTIONS

An important group of functions are those that convert data from one type to another. The most important functions in this group are TO_CHAR, TO_DATE, and TO_NUMBER. The general format of these functions is `conversion_function(data_to_be_converted, fmt)`. Each function takes the input data, converts them to the appropriate type and displays them in the specified format `fmt`. In all these functions, the format parameter `fmt` is optional. If not specified, a default format for the data type in question is supplied during the SQL processing. The following paragraphs describe each of these functions:

- **TO_CHAR.** This function converts DATE data type to VARCHAR2. The following query uses this function with three formats. First, the default Oracle format is used, then two custom formats are invoked with the function:

  The function TO_CHAR can be used to convert NUMBER to VARCHAR2 data type, as well. The following query displays dollar values stored as numbers in the database. The first column displays the data using Oracle's default format; the second column displays the same data according to the format '$0.99':
- **TO_DATE.** This function converts alphanumeric CHAR and VARCHAR2 data types to DATE data type. It is usually used in INSERT and UPDATE

```
SQL> SELECT dob,
  2  TO_CHAR(dob, 'DD MONTH YYYY') format_one,
  3  TO_CHAR(dob, 'Month DD, YYYY') format_two
  4 FROM CUSTOMER
  5 WHERE first_name = 'Karen' AND last_name = 'Campbell';

DOB       FORMAT_ONE          FORMAT_TWO
--------- ------------------- ------------------
09-APR-80 09 APRIL    1980    April   09, 1980
```

FIGURE 9.26 Using TO_CHAR SQL function to convert dates.

```
SQL> SELECT daily_rate def, TO_CHAR(daily_rate, '$0.99')
frmt
 2 FROM rental;

DEF          FRMT
----------   ------
      1.99   $1.99
       .99   $0.99
      1.99   $1.99
       .99   $0.99
```

FIGURE 9.27 Using TO_CHAR SQL function to format numbers.

operations to populate DATE columns of a table. It is also used to convert the data type of input values to date functions. If no format is specified, the input string must be a valid date in the default Oracle format specified for the database. The default date format may also vary with the local language defined.

- **TO_NUMBER.** This function is used to convert alphanumeric CHAR and VARCHAR2 data types CHAR and VARCHAR2 to NUMBER data type. Similar to TO_DATE, the function TO_NUMBER is used to specify numeric values in INSERT and UPDATE statements, or to convert the data type of input values for mathematical functions.
- **NVL.** This is another important function in the miscellaneous category. NVL stands for NULL Value Substitution. The general syntax of this function is `NVL(parameter_1, parameter_2)`. This function returns `parameter_1` if it is not NULL. When this parameter is NULL, rather than not displaying anything at all, the function NVL returns `parameter_2`. The following statement selects the return date of the movies. If the return date is NULL, the movie is not returned yet; therefore the query displays the string 'Not Returned.'

```
SELECT customer_id, NVL (TO_CHAR (return_dt), 'Not
Returned')
FROM rental;
```

Note that the function NVL can be overloaded. Its parameters can be of NUMBER, CHAR, VARCHAR2, DATE, or BOOLEAN. However, they must both be of the same data type. This is the reason why in the previous example you must convert the DATE column RETURN_DT using the function TO_CHAR.

- **DECODE.** The general syntax of this function is `DECODE(input_value, S1, R1, S2, R2, ... Sn, Rn, default_value)`. When this function is invoked, it compares the `input_value` with `S1`. If a match occurs, `R1` is returned. Otherwise, `input_value` is compared with `S2`. If a match occurs, `R2` is returned. Otherwise, the matching process continues. If the last search parameter `Sn` does not produce a match, the value `default_value` is returned. If `default_value` is not specified, DECODE returns NULL. The number of parameters in this function may vary, but cannot go beyond 255. The following statement selects the movie titles and a description for their rating from the database. If the movie is rated R the string 'Restricted' is displayed; if the movie is rated G the string 'General' is displayed; for all other cases the string 'Other' is displayed:

```
SELECT title, DECODE (rating, 'R', 'Restricted', 'G',
'General', 'Other')
FROM movie;
```

If you are familiar with procedural languages such as Pascal, C, or PL/SQL, you can easily conclude that DECODE is a way of implementing IF ... THEN ... ELSE statements, or CASE statements in SQL. Indeed, the following IF ... ELSE statement in a pseudo-language would result in the same outcome as the previous DECODE statement.

```
IF rating = 'R' THEN
 display 'Restricted'
ELSE IF rating = 'G' THEN
 display 'General'
ELSE
 display 'Other'
END IF
```

The following statements using SWITCH and CASE produce the same result:

```
SWITCH (rating)
 CASE 'R'
  display 'Restricted'
 CASE 'G'
  display 'General'
 DEFAULT
  display 'Other'
```

9.7.5 GROUP FUNCTIONS

While scalar functions operate on a record-per-record basis, the group functions operate on groups of records. The group functions include AVG, COUNT, MAX, MIN, STDDEV, SUM, and VARIANCE. All of these functions take numeric values as input, except for COUNT, MAX, and MIN that can take input of any data type. The statement shown in Figure 9.28 provides examples of use of each of these functions:

This example analyzes the data for DAILY_RATE fees. First, the function COUNT returns the number of different daily rates stored in the database. Then, the maximum, minimum, and average rates are computed using functions MAX, MIN, AVG. Finally, two important statistical parameters, the standard deviation and variance of daily rentals are computed using the functions STDDEV and VARIANCE.

All the previous functions, except for COUNT, operate on *all* the records as a group. Sometime, it is necessary to perform actions based only on distinct values in the set of records. In this case, the DISTINCT keyword is specified inside parentheses, before any other parameters are specified. In the example above, the keyword DISTINCT guaranties that the function COUNT retrieves the number of distinct daily rates. If it were omitted it would return the number of rental transactions recorded in the table.

Any NULL value in the set of records on which the functions act upon will be ignored. The only exception to this rule is the function COUNT when the syntax COUNT(*) is used. Under this condition, the function returns the number of all records that are returned by the query, including records that contain NULL values.

```
SQL> SELECT COUNT(DISTINCT daily_rate) count,
MAX(daily_rate) max,
   MIN(daily_rate) min, AVG(daily_rate) avg,
   STDDEV(daily_rate) stddev, VARIANCE(daily_rate) var
  FROM rental;

   COUNT        MAX        MIN        AVG        STDDEV        VAR
--------- ---------- ---------- ---------- ------------- ---------
        2       1.99        .99       1.47    .509901951       .26
```

FIGURE 9.28 Using group functions.

9.8 DUAL TABLE

Sometimes it is necessary to use a certain function, or perform a certain calculation without having to query a table from the database. For example, you may want to display the system date, or select the next value from a sequence, or simply display a text string. For these instances, Oracle provides a construct called DUAL table. It is a table with only one column, DUMMY, and only one row, 'X', in it. It is owned by the user SYS, but every user of the database can select from it. Obviously, every table can be used to compute an expression by selecting from it, but the expression will be returned as many times as there are rows in the table. DUAL, by having only one row, guaranties that the calculated expression or constant will be returned only once. The following query selects the current system date:

```
SELECT SYSDATE FROM DUAL;
```

The following query selects the next value from a sequence:

```
SELECT internal_id_seq.NEXTVAL from DUAL;
```

Finally, the next query simply selects a text string:

```
SELECT 'This is the last statement for this chapter.'
FROM DUAL;
```

9.9 SUMMARY

This chapter introduces elements of the Structured Query Language that you will need as you develop your Oracle Developer applications. These are some of the highlights of this chapter:

- **Brief History of SQL Language**
- **Movie Rental Database**
- **Categories of SQL Commands**
- **Data Retrieval with SELECT**
  - Selecting all Rows from a Table
  - Filtering Rows—The WHERE Clause
  - SQL Operators

- Boolean Operators
- Using Parentheses in Logical Expressions
- GROUP BY Clause
- HAVING Clause
- Joins
- ORDER BY Clause

- **Expanding Queries with Set Operations**

- **Data Manipulation Language Commands**
  - COMMIT and ROLLBACK
  - INSERT
  - UPDATE
  - DELETE

- **SQL Functions**
  - Scalar Character Functions
  - Scalar Date Functions
  - Scalar Mathematical Functions
  - Miscellaneous Functions
  - Group Functions

- **DUAL Table**

The following table describes the software assets that were discussed in this chapter. From the main HTML page of the software utilities provided with the book follow the links *Software* and *Chapter 9* to access these assets:

ASSET NAME	DESCRIPTION
CH9.SQL	A SQL*Plus script that creates and populates with data the tables CUSTOMER, MOVIE, and RENTAL discussed in this chapter.

Chapter 10

INTRODUCTION TO PL/SQL

High thoughts must have high language.
—Aristophanes

PL/SQL is Oracle Corporation's procedural language (PL) that extends the Structured Query Language (SQL) with procedural capabilities such as program units, loops, and conditional statements. If your applications are being developed using Oracle's development tools, such as Form Builder, Report Builder, and Web Application Server, PL/SQL is the main programming language you will use to implement business logic. However, even if applications will be developed using other tools, such as Visual Basic or Java, the business logic implemented in the Oracle Server will normally be programmed in PL/SQL. This chapter offers an overview of the major features and constructs of PL/SQL that you will encounter in your work with Oracle Designer tools.

10.1 OVERVIEW OF PL/SQL

The following four sections present a brief history of the PL/SQL language, an overview of the functionality of the PL/SQL engine in Form Builder and Oracle Server, the major structural components of PL/SQL blocks, and the most important manipulation statements used in PL/SQL Blocks.

10.1.1 BRIEF HISTORY OF THE PL/SQL LANGUAGE

One major innovation of SQL as a programming language is its simple syntax, which allows users to focus on the data they need without worrying about how to access the data or how to process them after they are retrieved from the database. Another innovation of SQL is that it is non-procedural and state-independent. This means that each operation does not depend on the one before it. By design, SQL lacks features of other programming languages such as language control structures, subroutines, arguments, and so on. From the early days of relational databases, the fact became clear that incorporating these features into extensions to the language would increase the advantages of SQL as a result-oriented language.

A solution offered initially was to open up existing procedural languages such as C, COBOL, FORTRAN, and others to syntactic structures of SQL. This marked the birth of embedded SQL and pre-compilers. Early development tools, such as SQL*Forms V2, used a rudimentary scripting language, which was tedious to program and did not support much functionality. The increasing needs of data processing systems could be met only with a full-fledged programming language that would combine all the benefits of procedural languages with the non-procedural characteristics of the SQL language.

The response of Oracle Corporation to this need was PL/SQL (Procedural Language/Structured Query Language). Its first version was introduced in 1990 with Oracle products such as SQL*Forms Version 3.0 and Oracle RDBMS Version 6.0. Every subsequent release of these products included enhanced versions of

PL/SQL. A series of development tools, such as Form Builder, Graphics, Reports, and Procedure Builder, are built with PL/SQL engines embedded in them. The Oracle RDBMS contains its own PL/SQL engine to process and execute programming constructs stored in the database server.

The fact that PL/SQL is a language shared by the Oracle database server and all the tools in the Oracle Developer suite, including Form Builder, Report Builder and Graphics Builder, has several advantages. First, mastering programming in PL/SQL in any of these environments enables you to become proficient in all the other areas of systems development where PL/SQL is used. Second, the sharing of code between the database server and the front-end tools becomes a trivial task. The same PL/SQL procedure can be called from a form, report, or graphic. It can also be stored in the database and be used by other front-end development tools. Finally, the application code can be tuned and distributed easily between client and server to maximize performance.

10.1.2 FUNCTIONALITY OF PL/SQL ENGINES

Despite the differences in the implementation of PL/SQL in the development tools and the database server, the PL/SQL engines contain similar functionality. Figure 10.1 presents graphically the workflow of the PL/SQL engine in one of the front-end development tools, such as Form Builder.

This engine breaks up objects that contain PL/SQL code, such as triggers, functions, and procedures, in smaller units called PL/SQL blocks. Each of these PL/SQL blocks is processed separately. Its statements are divided into three

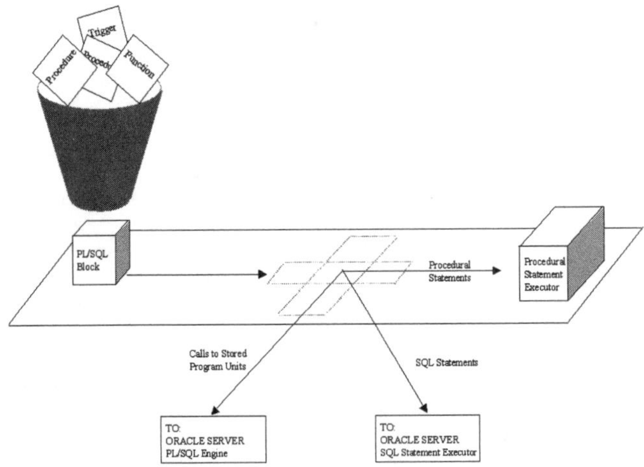

FIGURE 10.1 A graphical representation of the PL/SQL engine in Form Builder.

major categories. Procedural statements such as IF ... THEN ... ELSE, or LOOP statements, are handled internally by the Procedural Statement Executor. SQL statements such as SELECT, INSERT, UPDATE, and DELETE statements are stripped out and sent to the Oracle Server's SQL Statements Executor. Any calls to functions and procedures stored in database structures, also known as *stored program units,* are sent to the PL/SQL engine of the Oracle Server. The PL/SQL engine in the Oracle Server proceeds in a similar fashion. Its functionality is presented in Figure 10.2.

If the database server receives a call for one of its stored program units, the called object is retrieved and handed out for processing to the PL/SQL engine. Like its counterpart in Form Builder, this engine breaks up the stored unit in PL/SQL blocks, which then are processed individually. For each block, procedural statements are separated from SQL statements. The former are sent to the Procedural Statement Executor, the latter to the SQL Statement Executor. SQL statements from Form Builder pass through this engine as well.

10.1.3 STRUCTURAL ELEMENTS OF PL/SQL BLOCKS

As the discussion in the previous paragraph showed, no matter how complicated a PL/SQL program unit is, it is ultimately broken up into units of code called PL/SQL blocks. Figure 10.3 represents a typical PL/SQL block used in Form Builder applications.

Following SQL language conventions, a semicolon must terminate each statement in a PL/SQL block. The statement may be on one line or span multiple lines. The PL/SQL parser will process all the lines up to the semicolon as one statement. Multiple statements can reside on one line as well.

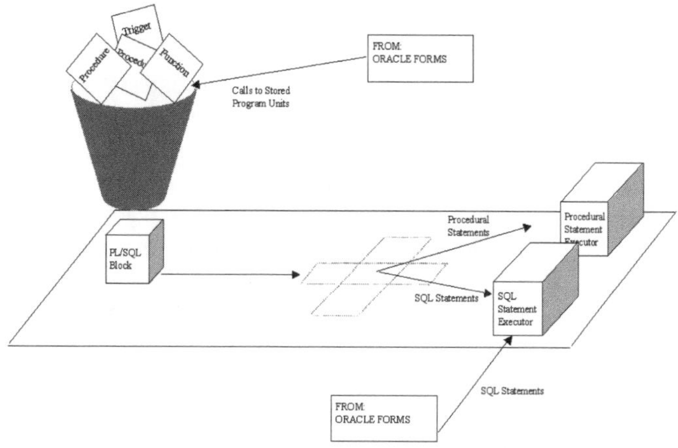

FIGURE 10.2 A graphical representation of the PL/SQL engine in Oracle Server.

```
DECLARE
  f_name VARCHAR2(30);
  l_name VARCHAR2(30);
BEGIN
  SELECT first_name, last_name
  INTO f_name, l_name
  FROM customer
  WHERE id = :RENTAL.CUSTOMER_ID;

  IF (f_name IS NULL) AND (l_name IS NULL) THEN
    :RENTAL.CUSTOMER_NAME := 'Missing Name';
  ELSE
    f_name := UPPER(f_name);
    l_name := UPPER(l_name);
    :RENTAL.CUSTOMER_NAME := f_name ||' '||l_name;
  END IF;
EXCEPTION
  WHEN TOO_MANY_ROWS THEN
    MESSAGE('Duplicate customer records.');
    RAISE FORM_TRIGGER_FAILURE;
  WHEN OTHERS THEN
    MESSAGE('Error retrieving Customer Name.');
    RAISE FORM_TRIGGER_FAILURE;
END;
```

FIGURE 10.3 A typical PL/SQL block used in Form Builder applications.

A PL/SQL block may have up to three distinct sections: declaration, execution, and exception. The declaration section begins with the keyword DECLARE. Variables that will be used in the block are declared and initialized here. Constants and other PL/SQL constructs such as cursors and user-defined exceptions are defined in this section as well.

The execution section contains statements that perform the core functionality of the PL/SQL block. Here is where all the data are selected and manipulated. In general, the execution section is preceded by the declaration section and followed by the exception section. The keyword BEGIN separates the declaration section from the execution section, as shown in Figure 10.3. The execution section must be always present in the block. Sometimes it can be the only section in it. Figure 10.4 shows a PL/SQL block that contains only the execution section. In the general case though, the execution section is preceded by the declaration section, and followed by the exception section.

```
PROCEDURE Move_Next_Record IS
BEGIN
  IF :SYSTEM.LAST_RECORD <> 'TRUE' THEN
    NEXT_RECORD;
  ELSE
  – No more records to move to.
    BELL;
    MESSAGE('At last record.');
    RAISE FORM_TRIGGER_FAILURE;
  END IF;
END;
```

FIGURE 10.4 Example of a PL/SQL block that contains only the execution section.

The exception section protects the application from unexpected events or failures. In the example presented in Figure 10.3, the SELECT statement retrieves the first name and last name of the customers based on the CUSTOMER_ID stored in the RENTAL block. Many things can go wrong during the execution of this statement. In the example of Figure 10.3, you explicitly handle the situation where the query returns no records. If any other error occurs, a generic message is displayed. The exception section is optional, but I strongly suggest it. The keyword EXCEPTION marks the beginning of this section. The keyword END marks the end of the PL/SQL block. The keywords BEGIN and END must always be in matching pairs.

In every application development environment, documenting the code is important. A program unit that is well documented is much easier to maintain or modify without adversely affecting the rest of the application. PL/SQL allows you to write comments on one line or across multiple lines. The symbol '—' comments out everything until the end of the line. The symbols '/* ... */' comment out everything enclosed between them, even if it spans several lines.

10.1.4 MANIPULATING DATA IN PL/SQL BLOCKS

Data in PL/SQL blocks can be selected and manipulated using the following SQL language statements: SELECT, INSERT, UPDATE, DELETE, COMMIT, and ROLLBACK. These are also the only SQL commands that can be used in a PL/SQL block. DDL statements such as CREATE and DROP or Data Control Language (DCL) statements such as GRANT and REVOKE cannot be used directly. (However, PL/SQL engines implemented in Oracle Developer tools and the Oracle Server provide standard packages, which allow you to execute such commands indirectly.)

Structurally, SELECT statements in PL/SQL are similar to their counterparts in the SQL language. They may contain clauses like SELECT, FROM, WHERE, GROUP BY, and ORDER BY. A new clause that is always required for PL/SQL SELECT statements is the INTO clause, which immediately follows the SELECT clause. The reason for this clause is simple and reflects one of the main reasons for the existence of PL/SQL as a supplement of SQL. SQL is originally designed as an interactive language. You type a statement at the command prompt and wait to see the results on the screen. PL/SQL, though, being a procedural language, aims at not just displaying the data, but also processing the information and making decisions based on its content. This task is greatly facilitated if data retrieved from the database is stored in memory locations that can be easily accessed and manipulated. These memory locations are represented by PL/SQL variables, and the redirection is done by the INTO clause.

The PL/SQL block shown in Figure 10.3 contains the example of a SELECT statement in a PL/SQL program. This example shows that for each column or expression in the SELECT clause, a PL/SQL variable must be in the INTO clause to store the value returned from the SELECT statement.

In general, the SELECT statement may return zero, one, or more rows returned from the database. In SQL, this behavior does not cause any problems. However, in PL/SQL, SELECT … INTO queries must be tailored so that they return one record, at most. The normal outcome of a SELECT statement in PL/SQL is to return only one row. If the query retrieves no rows, the exception NO_DATA_FOUND is raised; if more than one row is returned, the exception TOO_MANY_ROWS is raised.

The fact that the SELECT ... INTO statement should raise an exception if more than one row is found is an ANSI standard. To conform with this standard, whenever the first row of a query is returned, the PL/SQL engine makes another trip to the database to see whether the query returned more rows. If not, everything is fine; otherwise, the TOO_MANY_ROWS exception is raised. In any event, the second trip is superfluous. In the best case, it returns little needed information (additional records are returned by the query but not retrieved by the PL/SQL engine); in the worst case, it is a waste of computing time and resources (the extra trip to the database just to find out that the row you have already is the only one retrieved by the query). To remedy this behavior of the SELECT … INTO statement, PL/SQL cursors are used. Section 10.4 discusses the structure and functionality of PL/SQL cursors.

Little difference exists between SQL INSERT, UPDATE, and DELETE statements and their counterparts in PL/SQL blocks. The only novelty is that PL/SQL variables can be used to supply the values and expressions required by each statement. An example will be provided for each statement.

The following PL/SQL statement inserts a record into the table LATE_RETURN.

```
INSERT INTO late_return(customer_id, last_name, title,
rent_dt)
VALUES (:customer.id, :customer.last_name, :movie.title,
:movie.rent_dt);
```

The following statement updates the description of a record in LATE_RETURN:

```
UPDATE late_return
SET first_name = :customer.first_name, phone =
:customer.phone
WHERE customer_id = :customer.id;
```

The following statement deletes the record from the table PRODUCTS:

```
DELETE FROM late_return
WHERE customer_id = :customer.id;
```

What was said in the previous chapter about the COMMIT and ROLLBACK commands in SQL applies to PL/SQL programming as well. Be aware though that Form Builder also keeps track of the status of its data blocks. If after a statement like the ones presented above you add the statement COMMIT, Form Builder will commit not just the statement you issued, but also the changes that exist in these data blocks. (The Forms built-in COMMIT is a different command than the database COMMIT.)

All the SQL functions discussed in the previous chapter can be used in SQL statements of PL/SQL blocks as well. It is easy to locate the names and the parameters of these functions in the Form Builder. They are all listed under the STANDARD built-in package, the last one in the list of Built-in Packages in the Form Builder. Do not confuse this with the STANDARD Extensions built-in package that contains all the Form Builder built-in functions and procedures, and is the first one in the list of Built-in Packages. As explained in Chapter 5, you can use the commands Navigator/Paste Name and Navigator/Paste Arguments from the menu to add the specifications of these built-ins in your PL/SQL program units.

10.2 PROCEDURAL CONSTRUCTS OF PL/SQL

Procedural statements allow PL/SQL to control the flow of program execution. They include conditional branching statements such as the IF … THEN ... ELSE clause, loop statements such as LOOP, WHILE, or FOR clause, and the unconditional branching statement GOTO.

10.2.1 IF STATEMENT

The simplest form of this statement is shown here:

```
IF <condition> THEN
  <PL/SQL statements>;
ELSE
  <PL/SQL statements>;
END IF;
```

When this statement is executed, the logical condition `<condition>` between the keywords IF and THEN is first evaluated. If its value is TRUE, then the statements in the IF clause are executed. If it is FALSE or UNKNOWN, then statements in the ELSE clause are executed. The ELSE clause is not required, and it can be omitted if no action should be taken when the condition is not fulfilled. Multiple IF statements can be nested inside each clause. A typical nested IF statement appears below:

```
IF <condition> THEN
  <PL/SQL statements>;
  IF <condition> THEN
    <PL/SQL statements>;
  END IF;
ELSE
  <PL/SQL statements>;
END IF;
```

When the condition may have more than just a TRUE/FALSE outcome, the IF ... ELSE statements can be nested. The following template can be used to check for a three-values condition:

```
IF <condition> THEN
  <PL/SQL statements>;
ELSE
  IF <condition> THEN
    <PL/SQL statements>;
  ELSE
    <PL/SQL statements>;
  END IF;
END IF;
```

This representation can be tedious and difficult to understand, especially when multiple conditions are evaluated. To simplify this situation, PL/SQL allows the use of the ELSIF keyword. Now the previous construct is simplified as follows:

```
IF <condition> THEN
  <PL/SQL statements>;
ELSIF condition THEN
  <PL/SQL statements>;
ELSE
  <PL/SQL statements>;
END IF;
```

Multiple ELSIF clauses can be specified if necessary. However, only one ELSE clause and only one END IF statement are needed.

10.2.2 LOOPING STATEMENTS

Loops perform actions repetitively. The iteration they control continues until a certain condition evaluates to TRUE, or while a certain condition holds TRUE, or a specific number of times. Based on these three different situations, you can distinguish three types of loops.

The first type repeats the loop statements until the exit condition evaluates to TRUE. Its general syntax is:

```
LOOP
  <PL/SQL statements>;
  EXIT WHEN <condition>;
  <PL/SQL optional statements>;
END LOOP;
```

The PL/SQL statements within this loop are executed at least once. If the exit condition evaluates to FALSE or NULL, the loop will repeat its iteration. Only when the exit condition evaluates to TRUE, the loop stops and control is passed to the rest of the statements outside the loop.

The second type of loop executes the statements only if and while the entry loop condition is TRUE. Its general syntax is:

```
WHILE <condition> LOOP
 <PL/SQL statements>;
END LOOP;
```

In this loop, the PL/SQL statements may be executed zero or more times. The execution will occur only if the loop entry condition evaluates to TRUE and stops as soon as the condition evaluates to FALSE or NULL.

The third type of loop is used when the iterations will be performed a certain number of times. Its general syntax is:

```
FOR <counter> IN <lower_bound>..<upper_bound> LOOP
 <PL/SQL statements>;
END LOOP;
```

The loop counter is declared internally as an integer, meaning that you do not need to declare it explicitly. The value of the counter can be assigned to other variables inside the loop. However, because the counter is maintained internally, you cannot assign a value to it or change its existing value. Therefore, the counter will faithfully increment by one unit, starting from the lower bound of its range values all the way up to the upper bound.

The implicit handling of the loop counter by the PL/SQL engine protects the loop from accidentally becoming an infinite loop. You do not have to worry about incrementing the loop counter in each iteration. PL/SQL will make sure that the loop executes exactly the number of times allowed by its range.

10.2.3 UNCONDITIONAL BRANCHING

For backward compatibility and traditional reasons, more than for its usefulness, PL/SQL continues to support unconditional jumps to labels in the code using the command GOTO. This command rarely provides any functionality that is not already implemented better and more elegantly by other constructs. Therefore, I will not discuss it to any extent.

10.3 DATA TYPES AND VARIABLES

Like any other programming language, PL/SQL uses variables as placeholders of information needed by program units. The data stored in variables are transient in nature. They exist as long as the scope of the execution remains within the block in which the variables are declared, but are wiped out of memory as soon as the execution of the program moves out of the block. This section will discuss how to declare and use variables in PL/SQL programs.

10.3.1 PL/SQL DATA TYPES

An important characteristic of variables is their data type. PL/SQL comes with a large number of predefined data types, which can be grouped in three categories: scalar, composite, and reference data types. Scalar data types allow you to manipulate numeric, alphanumeric, date, and Boolean variables. The first release of PL/SQL provided support only for a limited number of scalar data types, such as

NUMBER, CHAR, DATE, and BOOLEAN. The next major upgrade of the language (version 2.0) introduced a number of new data types, such as BINARY_INTEGER, and PLS_INTEGER. In addition, it extended the language to include two composite data types, RECORD and index-by TABLE, whose behavior and functionality are similar to structures and arrays in C or PASCAL. Version 2.3 of the language, released with Oracle7 Server version 7.3, introduced in PL/SQL the concept of pointers through the first reference data type, REF CURSOR. Last, but not the least, the introduction of object-relational features in Oracle8 and PL/SQL8, expanded the language to support abstract data types (ADT), objects, collections, and a number of other object-oriented features that will be covered in detail in the next chapter.

The data types in PL/SQL can also be classified into base types and subtypes. All the data types mentioned above are base types. Subtypes derive their properties from a base data type, but add a restriction to the base type. For example, NATURAL is a predefined PL/SQL subtype whose base type is BINARY_INTEGER. NATURAL variables allow you to manipulate only non-negative BINARY_INTEGER values. In addition to predefined subtypes, PL/SQL allows you to define your own subtype data types. The following statement defines a new subtype based on the scalar base type NATURAL:

```
DECLARE
  SUBTYPE LoopCounter IS NATURAL;
  k LoopCounter;
BEGIN
  ...
END;
```

The following statement defines a new data type as a VARCHAR2 base type that can hold up to 240 bytes of data:

```
DECLARE
  vc_descr              VARCHAR2(240);
  SUBTYPE Description IS vc_descr%TYPE;
  movie_description     Description;
BEGIN
  ...
END;
```

10.3.2 PL/SQL VARIABLES

As mentioned above, variables are declared in the declaration section of a PL/SQL block. Each variable must be assigned a data type upon declaration. At the same time, an initial value may be assigned to the variable. If the variable is not initialized explicitly, PL/SQL initializes it to NULL, which represents the absence of data. The following statements represent several examples of declaring and initializing scalar data type variables:

```
DECLARE
  vn_movie_id      PLS_INTEGER;
  vc_movie_descr   VARCHAR2(240);
  vc_rating        VARCHAR2(10)  := 'PG-13';
  vn_revenue       NUMBER(8,2) NOT NULL := 0.0;
  vb_discount      BOOLEAN DEFAULT TRUE;
BEGIN
 ...
END;
```

From the statements above, two remarks can be made about the declaration and initialization of variables. First, to assign an initial value to a variable, you can use the standard assignment operator ':=' or the keyword DEFAULT. Note, however, that this place is the only one in a PL/SQL program where DEFAULT can be used to assign a value to a variable. Second, you can declare a variable to be a required one in the program by specifying the keywords NOT NULL after the data type. A required variable must always be initialized in the DECLARE section.

Another way to specify the data type of a variable is to reference the %TYPE attribute of another variable that is already defined. In the following example, the first line defines a variable named `price`. The second line then defines a second variable, `discount_price` of the same type as `price`.

```
DECLARE
  price            NUMBER;
  discount_price   price%TYPE;
BEGIN
  ...
END;
```

This type definition has a clear advantage. If the definition of `price` changes in the future, the change will automatically propagate to the variable `discount_price`, or any other variable defined based on the type of `price`. You do not have to change the type definition of the derived variables. The technique is especially useful when variables are declared based on the data type of a table column in the database. In the following example, both `price` and `discount_price` are declared using the definition of the column MSRP in the table PRODUCTS.

```
DECLARE
  price            RENTAL.DAILY_RATE%TYPE;
  discount_price   RENTAL.DAILY_RATE %TYPE;
BEGIN
  ...
END;
```

Defining the data type of variables as shown here assures that the database structure will always be synchronized with the application code. If the requirements change in the future, the only place where you need to change the type definition is the database. The application will automatically reflect the change.

10.3.3 PL/SQL CONSTANTS

Variables can be assigned values throughout the life of the PL/SQL program. Constants, on the other hand, may be assigned values only during the initialization phase. During the execution of the program unit, the constants preserve this value and cannot be assigned a different value. When you are declaring a constant, you may specify the keyword CONSTANT immediately before the data type. The following statements provide an example of how to declare and use a PL/SQL constant.

```
DECLARE
  VA_TAX                  CONSTANT NUMBER := 0.045; –
                          Virginia state tax
  vn_subtotal            NUMBER(8,2) := 100.00;
  vn_taxed_subtotal      NUMBER(8,2);
BEGIN
  vn_taxed_subtotal := vn_subtotal(1 + VA_TAX);
END;
```

10.3.4 PL/SQL RECORDS

PL/SQL records are used to create record-like data types in PL/SQL program units. They allow you to bundle together a number of fields of different data types. The RECORD data type extends the functionality of the attribute %ROWTYPE of database tables, which has existed in PL/SQL since the early versions of the language. Records created using the %ROWTYPE attribute are bound to the structure of the corresponding table. Their elements contain exactly the same fields and data types as the columns in that table. Using the RECORD data type, you are not bound to one table anymore. Columns from different tables can be combined with non-database fields in one structure. Furthermore, records can be nested into definitions of more complex record structures.

In order to use records in your program units, you must first declare a user-defined data type for the record and then declare an object of that data type. The following statements contain examples of declaring RECORD data types:

```
DECLARE
  TYPE LocationType IS RECORD (
    region          VARCHAR2(80),
    area            VARCHAR2(80),
    name            VARCHAR2(80));

  TYPE SalesDataType IS RECORD (
    rental_total  RENTAL.DAILY_RATE%TYPE := 0.0,
    category      MOVIE.RATING%TYPE,
    location      LocationType);

  city            LocationType;
  daily_sales     SalesDataType;
  daily_total     RENTAL.DAILY_RATE %TYPE;

BEGIN
  ...
END;
```

The first record type groups data used to describe a geographic location, including the region, area, and name of that location. The second record type expands the first one by adding to the location placeholders for the total revenue generated by rental transactions from customers that rent movies in a particular rating category. As you can see from this example, the components of a record can be initialized upon declaration.

Structures of the RECORD data type can be referenced using the usual dot notation. The following two statements are examples of how you can assign a value to, or retrieve a value from, a field of a record. These statements use the variables defined above and could reside in the execution part of the PL/SQL block shown above.

```
city.name   := 'Washington D.C.';
city.region := 'East Coast';
city.area   := 'Mid-Atlantic';
daily_total := 10000.00;
```

```
daily_sales.location    := city;
daily_sales.order_total := daily_total;
daily_sales.industry    := 'Small Business';
```

You can also assign values to several or all fields of a record, by making them part of the INTO clause of a SELECT ... INTO statement that retrieves data that match these fields. Cursors can be used as well. If you want to transfer data from one record to another, you can use a statement like the following:

```
record_1 := record_2;
```

This technique can be used only if both records are of the same record type. Two records are considered of the same type only if their data types are derived from the same record type. If the data types are different record types, the records are considered different, even if their parent data types contain exactly the same fields.

10.3.5 INDEX-BY TABLES

The PL/SQL data type TABLE is a composite data type that allows you to implement in PL/SQL programs functionality similar to that of arrays in other programming languages. Like arrays, index-by tables are indexed by a number, in this case a number of data type BINARY_INTEGER. In addition, each indexed position in the table allows you to store and access data of another data type. The components of index-by tables are often referred to as the primary key and the columns, for analogy with the terminology that describes regular tables.

The data stored in index-by tables may be of scalar data type, declared using any of the base data types, pre-defined subtypes, or user-defined subtypes, as discussed earlier in the chapter. The following statements show two examples of index-by tables with elements of scalar data types:

```
DECLARE
  TYPE CustNameType IS TABLE OF VARCHAR2(80) NOT NULL
  INDEX BY BINARY_INTEGER;

  TYPE MovieTitleType IS TABLE OF MOVIE.TITLE%TYPE
  INDEX BY BINARY_INTEGER;

  customer_names CustNameType;
  movie_titles   MovieTitleType;
BEGIN
  ...
END;
```

The first table type CustNameType will store alphanumeric strings up to 80 characters long and will not allow NULL elements in the table. The second table inherits the data type properties for its element from those of the column TITLE in the table MOVIE.

PL/SQL also allows you to store in tables elements of RECORD data types. The definition of these records may be derived from database tables or specified by you in a user-defined data type. Examples of tables with elements of RECORD data types appear below:

```
DECLARE
  TYPE CustomerType IS TABLE OF CUSTOMER%ROWTYPE
  INDEX BY BINARY_INTEGER;

  TYPE LocationType IS RECORD (
    region          VARCHAR2(80),
    area            VARCHAR2(80),
    name            VARCHAR2(80));

  TYPE LocationTableType IS TABLE OF LocationType
  INDEX BY BINARY_INTEGER;

  customers_tab   CustomerType;
  cities_tab      LocationTableType;
BEGIN
  ...
END;
```

The first table type CustomerType will hold records whose properties are inherited from the columns of the database table CUSTOMER. The second table type LocationTableType will contain elements whose data type is determined by the user-defined record LocationType.

After a table is declared, its elements can be populated or accessed through the index of the table, like usual arrays. For example, to store the name Michelle Johnson in the fifth position of the table customer_names of data type CustNameType defined earlier, you would use this statement:

```
customer_names(5) := 'Michelle Johnson';
```

The index of the table can be any integer in the range of a BINARY_INDEX data type, including negative numbers. So if the name John Michael is stored in position –5 of the table customer_names, the following statement assigns its value to the pre-declared variable current_customer, which has the same data type as the element of the table.

```
current_customer := customer_names(-5);
```

The structure of the table does not enforce any bounds or cohesion between its indices. So the table can contain elements in positions –2, 5, and 155, and these can be the only three elements of it. If the program references any other table elements, the exception NO_DATA_FOUND will be raised. In order to prevent the exception from being raised, you can use the index-by table method EXISTS, as in the following example:

```
IF customer_names.EXISTS(-5) THEN
  current_customer := customer_names(-5);
ELSE
  current_customer := NULL:
END IF;
```

PL/SQL defines additional methods for table objects that enhance the features and functionality of Index-by tables and make them truly useful data types for your program units. The methods FIRST and LAST allow you to get the index of the first and last entries in the table; the method COUNT returns the number of entries in the table; the methods NEXT and PRIOR return the index of the next or previous row in the table from a given position within the table, if they exist. In addition, the method DELETE can remove a single entry, a range of entries, or all the entries from a table.

10.4 CURSORS IN PL/SQL

When the Oracle RDBMS receives a SQL statement for execution, it makes sure that it is a valid SQL statement and that the user issuing it has the appropriate privileges to issue that statement. If both these checks are successful, a chunk from the database server memory, called the *private SQL area,* is allocated to the statement. If this time is the first that the statement has been issued against the database, Oracle will parse the statement and store its parsed version in another memory structure, called the *shared SQL area.* The shared and private SQL areas reside within the Library Cache, which is part of the Shared Pool. The shared SQL area uses caching algorithms to avoid reparsing the SQL. If the entire shared pool has already been allocated, Oracle will deallocate items from the pool using a modified least recently used algorithm. The shared SQL area will also contain the plan that Oracle will follow in order to execute the statement. Finally, the statement will be executed.

This division of the information contained within the SQL statements allows Oracle to bypass the parsing phase the next time the same statement is issued. In such a case, the private SQL area for the statement is still created, but when Oracle realizes that a parsed version of the statement is present in the library cache of the shared SQL area, it proceeds directly with the execution of this parsed representation. This chain of events will hold true even if the statement is issued by a different connection in the database established by a different user of your application.

The private SQL area contains information about the statement that can be divided into two categories. The first one is static and permanently attached to the statement. This includes, for example, the table and column names that the statement affects and the binding information between them and the bind variables in the statement. The second category is dynamic, and its size changes, depending on the actual values of the bind variables when the statement is issued. This part of the private SQL area is known as *runtime area,* because it expands and shrinks in size and content as the statement is executed. If, for example, the statement is a SELECT that returns 20 rows, the runtime area will be expanded to accommodate those records. Figure 10.5 shows graphically how the SQL Statement Executor manages the SQL statements.

This figure assumes that `Statement A` is sent prior to `Statement B`. When `Statement A` is received, Oracle binds the value '01-SEP-96' for MEMBER_DT to the bind argument :1, and records the column names in the private SQL area of this statement—in its persistent part, to be exact. Then the statement is parsed and stored in the shared SQL area of the library cache. The execution plan that Oracle will follow is stored here as well. Finally the statement is executed to retrieve the data. When `Statement B` is received, the process is similar, except that the statement is not parsed again. After binding, `Statement A` and `Statement B` are the same. Therefore, the SQL Statement Executor proceeds directly with the retrieval of data. The data returned from each query are stored in the runtime part of each statement's private SQL area.

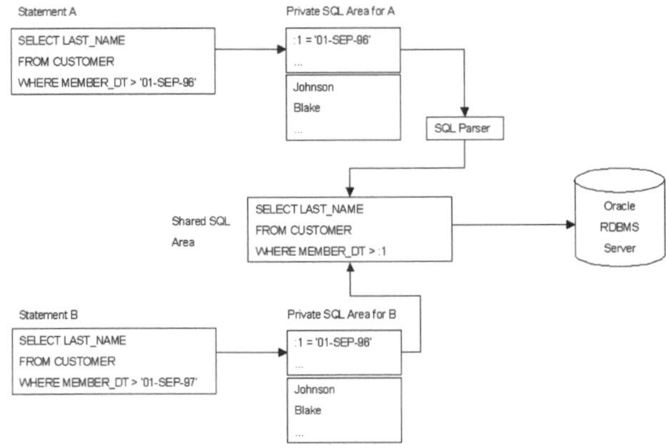

FIGURE 10.5 The execution of SQL statements by the Oracle Server.

A cursor is nothing but a name, or a *handle,* for the memory location of the private SQL area of a statement that allows you to access the information stored there from within PL/SQL blocks.

10.4.1 DECLARING EXPLICIT CURSORS

Explicit cursors are PL/SQL objects built upon SELECT statements that allow you to better manipulate records returned by queries. They can also be used to create complex queries in a more procedural fashion, and in certain instances improve the performance of the application. Cursors are declared in the DECLARE part of a PL/SQL block following the syntax:

```
CURSOR <cursor_name> IS <select_statement>;
```

The SELECT statement in a cursor declaration should not contain the INTO clause that is normally used in PL/SQL. As you will see in the Section 10.4.2, the storage of the retrieved data into PL/SQL variables is done as a separate step with cursors. However, this statement defines the number and data type of the columns that each record returned by the query in the cursor's runtime area will have. The following statements contain two examples of cursor declaration:

```
DECLARE
  CURSOR c_movie_rental_101 IS
    SELECT rental.customer_id, rental.rent_dt,
rental.return_dt
    FROM rental
    WHERE rental.movie_id = 101;

  CURSOR c_movie_rentals (movieId NUMBER) IS
    SELECT rental.customer_id, rental.rent_dt,
rental.return_dt
    FROM rental
    WHERE rental.movie_id = movieId;
BEGIN
  ...
END;
```

In both these examples, the runtime area will contain records with fields of the same data type as the columns CUSTOMER_ID, RENT_DT, and RETURN_DT of table RENTAL. The cursor presented in the first example is not very useful because of the static nature of its SELECT statement. The cursor will contain only those records from the table RENTAL that correspond to the movie with a specific value of MOVIE_ID. The cursor becomes really effective and usable if its SELECT statement is free of any hard-coded values, as in the second example. In this case, the cursor uses an argument in its statement much the same way a procedure or a function would use it.

10.4.2 METHODS AND ATTRIBUTES OF EXPLICIT CURSORS

Explicit cursors, being names of a particular work area allocated to the SQL statements, are considered a special kind of object in PL/SQL. As such, they have their attributes and methods to access and manipulate their stored information.

After the cursor is declared, you can use the statement `OPEN cursor_name` to execute the query contained in the cursor, and store the records in the runtime part of the private SQL area. If the declaration of the cursor contains parameters, the value of these parameters is specified in the OPEN statement. So the statements that open the cursors shown in the previous section will be:

```
OPEN c_movie_rentals_101;
OPEN c_ movie_rentals (movieId);
```

The attribute %ISOPEN keeps track of the state of the cursor. If the cursor is opened, this attribute evaluates to TRUE; otherwise, its value will be FALSE. Since the predefined exception CURSOR_ALREADY_OPEN will be raised if the OPEN statement is issued against a cursor that is already open, checking for the state of the cursor before opening it is always a good idea.

Opening the cursor only identifies the records that the query will return. However, none of these records is returned to the calling environment until the FETCH command is issued explicitly. When the cursor is opened, a pointer is placed on the first record retrieved by the query. When the first FETCH statement is issued, this record is returned to the calling environment, and the pointer is advanced to the next record. This process will continue until all the records in the runtime area are returned. The pointer to the current record can only be advanced by one record at a time. So, for example, the second FETCH will return only the second record, if it exists. No way exists to advance the pointer so that the fifth record is returned before its predecessors, or to set it back so that the first record is returned again.

When you use the FETCH statement, you must always follow it with an INTO clause, which will place the data from the fetched record into the variables of the routine that will use them. To avoid any runtime errors, these variables must have the same data type and size as the data being fetched. One way to ensure this is to declare the data type of these variables using the %TYPE attribute of the corresponding table columns.

The number of the records fetched is stored in another attribute of the cursor, called %ROWCOUNT. Whenever the cursor is opened, this attribute is set to zero; after the first record is fetched, it is set to one; and after each FETCH operation, it is incremented by one unit. The value of this attribute can be useful if you want to retrieve only a certain number of records from the set of all the records that the cursor may contain. For example, to retrieve only the first three records, the FETCH command is issued within a loop until the %ROWCOUNT evaluates to three.

As I said earlier, the FETCH statement returns the current record of the cursor to the calling environment. But what happens if the last record is fetched and another FETCH is issued? Or when the cursor contains no records and the first FETCH is issued? To help you deal with these situations, cursors are equipped with two more attributes: %FOUND and %NOTFOUND. They are Boolean attributes that complement each other. They are both set to NULL when the cursor is opened. Then, after each FETCH, the values of these attributes are set according to the outcome of the statement. If the record was fetched successfully, %FOUND is set to TRUE and %NOTFOUND is set to FALSE. If all the records of the cursor are fetched, the next fetch will not return a valid row, %FOUND will be set to FALSE, and %NOTFOUND to TRUE.

These attributes are used as exit conditions for loops that should retrieve all the records of a cursor and stop safely after the last one is fetched. For these loops, the exit condition should be tested immediately after the FETCH statements and should follow this format:

```
EXIT WHEN cursor_name%NOTFOUND;
```

In this case, during the iteration after the one that fetches the last record, the FETCH statement will fail, thus setting the %NOTFOUND attribute to TRUE. This result causes the iteration to stop and the control of the program to jump outside the loop.

Note, however, that this exit condition relies on the cursor to contain at least one record. If the query that populates the cursor returns no records, the FETCH statement is not executed. Therefore, the attribute %NOTFOUND remains set to the original value NULL. Because the exit condition of the loop does not evaluate to TRUE, its iterations will continue forever. In order to handle the case when the cursor may not have records to fetch, you can add an additional check in the exit condition of the loop for NULL values of the attributes %FOUND and %NOTFOUND. Two examples of using each of these attributes follow:

```
LOOP
  FETCH c_movie_rentals INTO custID, rentDt, returnDt;
  EXIT WHEN (c_ movie_rentals%NOTFOUND
          OR c_ movie_rentals%NOTFOUND IS NULL);
  ...
END LOOP;
```

```
LOOP
  FETCH c_movie_rentals INTO custID, rentDt, returnDt;
  IF c_ movie_rentals%FOUND OR
     c_ movie_rentals%FOUND IS NULL THEN
  ...
  ELSE
    EXIT;
  END IF;
END LOOP;
```

After the record is opened and used, you should close it to release the database resources it occupies. For this action, you issue the CLOSE statement followed by the name of the cursor to close, as in:

```
CLOSE c_movie_rentals;
```

When you have to process some of the records from the set of all the records that are returned by a query, you must construct your code around the statements described above. In order to avoid runtime errors that may occur if the statements are not issued in the proper context, follow the steps below:

1. Declare the cursor in the DECLARE part of the PL/SQL block or program unit.
2. Open the cursor.
3. Create a loop with the appropriate EXIT condition that will scroll sequentially through the records of the cursor and process each record according to your needs.
4. Close the cursor.

Figure 10.6 shows an example of a PL/SQL block that manipulates a cursor following these steps.

10.4.3 USING THE FOR LOOP WITH EXPLICIT CURSORS

Many of the steps described in the previous section, and the possibility of mixing them up, can be avoided by using the FOR loop with the cursor. The PL/SQL block shown in Figure 10.7 contains the same functionality as the one in Figure 10.6.

No comments are needed to point out the significant gains in simplicity that this technique represents. You do not have to explicitly open the cursor, fetch the rows in variables declared previously, and close it when finished. The FOR loop will inherently open the cursor with the appropriate input variables that you

```
DECLARE
  CURSOR c_movie_rentals (movieId MOVIE.ID%TYPE) IS
    SELECT customer_id, rent_dt, return_dt
    FROM rental
    WHERE movie_id = movieId;
  custID    CUSTOMER.ID%TYPE;
  rentDt    RENTAL.RENT_DT%TYPE;
  returnDt RENTAL.RETURN_DT%TYPE;
BEGIN
  OPEN c_movie_rentals (121);
  LOOP
    FETCH c_movie_rentals INTO custId, rentDt, returnDt;
    EXIT WHEN c_movie_rentals%NOTFOUND
           OR c_movie_rentals%NOTFOUND IS NULL;
    /* Processing statements go here.    */
  END LOOP;
  CLOSE c_movie_rentals;
END;
```

FIGURE 10.6 An example of correct usage of cursors.

```
DECLARE
  CURSOR c_movie_rentals (movieId MOVIE.ID%TYPE) IS
    SELECT customer_id, rent_dt, return_dt
    FROM rental
    WHERE movie_id = movieId;
  custID    CUSTOMER.ID%TYPE;
  rentDt    RENTAL.RENT_DT%TYPE;
  returnDt RENTAL.RETURN_DT%TYPE;
BEGIN
  FOR current_rental IN c_movie_rentals (121) LOOP
    custID   := current_rental.ID;
    rentDt   := current_rental.RENT_DT;
    returnDt := current_rental.RETURN_DT;
    /* Processing statements go here.    */
  END LOOP;
END;
```

FIGURE 10.7 An explicit cursor in a FOR loop.

specify. The index of the loop will be automatically declared of the same data type as the records that the cursor contains. The FOR loop will fetch in this index each record until the last one, unless you exit before the last record is fetched. For each iteration, you can access the data fetched by referencing the fields of the record that is also the iterator of the loop. Finally, when the loop is exited, either because the last record was retrieved or because you chose to terminate it, the cursor is closed automatically.

Using the cursor FOR loop, you can even declare the cursor on the fly. For example, you could write the following statement, which inherently declares a cursor, opens it, fetches each record in the index `current_rental`, and closes the cursor at the end of the loop.

```
FOR current_rental IN (SELECT * FROM rental) LOOP
  /* Processing statements go here.*/
END LOOP;
```

10.4.4 CURSOR VARIABLES

In the examples used so far, the SELECT statement that populates a cursor with data is specified when the cursor is declared, meaning that if two or more program units need to manipulate data from the same cursor, each of them will have to declare, open, fetch, and close the cursor. Starting from version 2.2 of PL/SQL, released with Oracle7 RDBMS version 7.2, cursors can be declared and manipulated like any other PL/SQL variable. The cursor variables are references or handles to static cursors. They allow you to pass references to the same cursor among all the program units that need access to that cursor. With cursor variables, the SELECT statement is bound to the cursor dynamically, at runtime. The same cursor variable can be bound to more than one SELECT statement, thus adding flexibility to your PL/SQL programs. Figure 10.8 shows an example of how you could use cursor variables in PL/SQL programs. In general, follow these steps:

1. Declare a composite data type for the cursor variable of type REF CURSOR. You may, but are not required to, provide the structure of the records that will be returned by cursor variables of this cursor data type. Not providing the structure is especially useful when the cursors will return records of different structure, as in the case shown in Figure 10.8.
2. Declare one or more cursor variables of the reference cursor data type declared in the previous step.
3. Instantiate each cursor variable using the method OPEN. In this step, the SELECT statement is bound to the cursor variable and executed in the database server. From this point, until the cursor variable is instantiated as another cursor, it can be used as a regular cursor.

```
DECLARE
  TYPE custCursorType IS REF CURSOR;
  TYPE custShortRecType IS RECORD (
    id           CUSTOMER.ID%TYPE,
    name         VARCHAR2(80));

    custCursor   custCursorType;
    custShortRec custShortRecType;
    custFullRec  CUSTOMER%ROWTYPE;
BEGIN
  OPEN custCursor FOR SELECT ID, FIRST_NAME, LAST_NAME
FROM CUSTOMERS;
  FETCH custCursor INTO custShortRec;
  CLOSE custCursor;

  OPEN custCursor FOR SELECT * FROM CUSTOMER;
  FETCH custCursor INTO custFullRec;
  CLOSE custCursor;
  /* Process data in custShortRec and custFullRec.   */
END;
```

FIGURE 10.8 An example of the use of cursor variables in PL/SQL.

4. Fetch the data from the cursor in local variables.
5. Close the cursor when finished.

10.4.5 IMPLICIT CURSORS

Oracle uses a cursor for every SELECT ... INTO statement that is not referenced by an explicit cursor. It also uses cursors for all INSERT, UPDATE, or DELETE statements that it processes. These are called *implicit cursors* to distinguish them from the ones you declare and manipulate explicitly. Although they are created and managed internally by the RDBMS, you do have a way to check the attributes of the last implicit cursor used by Oracle. This cursor can be addressed with the name SQL, and its attributes can be accessed like any other explicit cursor you create.

Of the four cursor attributes discussed in Section 10.4.2, %ISOPEN is what you will probably never use for implicit cursors. The simple reason is that when the control returns from the DML statement, the cursor is already closed by the RDBMS. Therefore, this attribute for implicit cursors will always be FALSE.

The attributes %FOUND and %NOTFOUND find out whether the DML statement affected any records at all. The example shown in Figure 10.9 inserts a

```
BEGIN
  INSERT INTO MOVIE (ID, TITLE)
  VALUES(121, 'The Piano');
  IF SQL%FOUND THEN
    INSERT INTO RENTAL(CUSTOMER_ID, MOVIE_ID, RENT_DT,
DAILY_PRICE)
    VALUES(34, 121, '21-JUL-98', 0.99);
    COMMIT;
  END IF;
END;
```

FIGURE 10.9 Checking the attributes of the SQL cursor.

record in the table MOVIE. Then it inserts a rental transaction initiated by the customer with ID=34 for this movie in the table RENTAL. Clearly, if the first INSERT fails, the second statement should not be issued, because the referential integrity of the data will be violated. The attribute %FOUND checks the outcome of the first statement and, depending on this outcome, either proceeds with the second one or not.

The attribute %ROWCOUNT returns the number of rows affected by the DML statement. Structuring your code in a fashion similar to Figure 10.9, you can use the value stored in SQL%ROWCOUNT to take certain actions that depend on the number of the records affected by your statement.

TIP

Recall that if a SELECT ... INTO statement returns no records, the predefined exception NO_DATA_FOUND is raised. If the statements returns more than one record, the exception TOO_MANY_ROWS is raised. You can use these exceptions instead of directly checking the %FOUND, %NOTFOUND, or %ROWCOUNT attributes of the implicit cursor associated with that statement.

In fact, in the second case, the %ROWCOUNT attribute will not contain the number of the records returned by the query. Oracle raises the exception TOO_MANY_ROWS and sets this attribute to 1 whenever the query returns more than one record.

10.5 PL/SQL PROGRAM UNITS

The material presented so far has discussed concepts and features of PL/SQL language in the context of anonymous blocks. These blocks may be executed interactively from the SQL*Plus prompt or stored in Oracle Developer development tools components, such as in Form Builder triggers.

PL/SQL code in Form Builder applications can be written in triggers and menu items. Triggers are attached to either a form, a block, or an item. Their code is executed upon the occurrence of the specific event for which they are written. The code associated with a menu item is executed when the users select that menu item at runtime.

The code written in triggers or menu items is in the form of anonymous PL/SQL blocks. However, whenever some functionality will be executed more than once and across development environments, the code can be organized into PL/SQL program units such as functions and procedures. Logically related functions and procedures can be grouped together with related data in larger PL/SQL objects called *packages*. Form Builder provides a large number of built-in program units that can be used in its programmatic structures. These built-ins implement actions and functionality that occur so often that they have become standards in Forms applications. You can define your own program units, as well. The user-defined functions and procedures are separate Form Builder objects that belong to the form or menu module. They are listed under the Program Units node of the Object Navigator. This section will provide an overview of functions, procedures, and packages in PL/SQL.

10.5.1 COMPONENTS OF PROGRAM UNITS

In PL/SQL, as in other programming languages, procedures are defined as objects that perform certain actions, whereas functions are objects that must return a value. The syntax rules of PL/SQL do not prohibit procedures from returning values to the calling environment, or functions from performing tasks. However, the code is clearer if these two criteria are followed. In order to discuss the components of functions and procedures, a typical function and procedure are provided. Figure 10.10 contains the definition of the function `Days_Between`.

Figure 10.11 contains the definition of the procedure `Set_Cust_Phone`.

Each program unit has a specification part and a body. The specification for a procedure is made up of the keyword `PROCEDURE`, the name of the procedure, and the argument list enclosed in parentheses. The specification for a function is made up of the keyword `FUNCTION`, the name of the function, the argument list enclosed in parentheses, and the `RETURN` clause, which defines the data type of the value returned by the function. The argument definition list contains the name, mode, and data type of each argument.

```
FUNCTION Days_Between(first_dt IN DATE, second_dt IN
DATE)
RETURN NUMBER IS
  dt_one NUMBER;
  dt_two NUMBER;
BEGIN
  dt_one := TO_NUMBER(TO_CHAR(first_dt, 'DDD'));
  dt_two := TO_NUMBER(TO_CHAR(second_dt, 'DDD'));

  RETURN(dt_two - dt_one);
END;
```

FIGURE 10.10 An example of a function.

The body of the program unit begins with the keyword `IS`. If local variables will be used, they must be declared between this keyword and the keyword `BEGIN`, as in the case of function `Days_Between`. Named program units do not use the keyword `DECLARE` to indicate the beginning of the declaration section. The executable statements followed by the `EXCEPTION` section are placed between the keywords `BEGIN` and `END`, which are mandatory for named functions and procedures.

10.5.2 ARGUMENTS IN PROGRAM UNITS

The arguments (also called parameters) defined in the header of a program unit and used in its body are called *formal arguments*. For example, the argument `cust_id` in Figure 10.10 or `first_dt` in Figure 10.11 are formal arguments. The

```
PROCEDURE Set_Cust_Phone (cust_id IN OUT NUMBER,
          cust_phone IN OUT VARCHAR2) IS
BEGIN
  UPDATE customers
  SET phone = cust_phone
  WHERE customer_number = cust_id;
EXCEPTION
  WHEN OTHERS THEN
    RAISE_APPLICATION_ERROR(-20001, 'Internal error
occurred.');
END;
```

FIGURE 10.11 An example of a procedure.

values passed to the program unit when it is called are called *actual arguments.* The actual arguments can be passed using positional notation or named notation. The following statements show how you can use the function and procedure discussed here with arguments in the positional notation:

```
days := Days_Between(order_dt, delivery_dt);
Set_Cust_Phone(cust_id, new_phone);
```

The following statements show how you can use the same program units to obtain the same results, but this time using arguments in the named notation. In the named notation, the association operator => associates the formal variable to the left with the actual variable to the right. As you can see from the second of these statements, the order in which arguments are passed to a program unit is not important when the named notation is used:

```
days := Days_Between(first_dt => rent_dt, second_dt =>
return_dt);
Set_Cust_Phone(cust_phone => new_phone, cust_id =>
customer_id);
```

The mode of arguments can be IN, OUT, or IN OUT. It defines the way the program unit handles the data passed to it through these arguments. IN arguments are used to pass a value that should not be changed by the program unit. In the program unit's body, an IN argument behaves like a constant whose value cannot be modified by assignment statements. If not specified otherwise, an argument is by default an IN mode argument. OUT arguments allow modification of the value of the actual argument in the calling environment. An OUT argument acts like an uninitialized variable, in that its value cannot be assigned to another variable or reassigned to itself. The value of an OUT actual parameter before the call, is no longer available when the control returns back to the calling environment. The program unit must assign a value to each its OUT arguments; otherwise, their value after the unit's execution completes is undetermined. The only operation allowed on the OUT arguments is to assign it a value. IN OUT arguments allow the calling environment to pass values to a program unit. In its body, they are treated like normal variables. The program unit may modify the value of the argument, and this modification is visible to the outside environment.

10.5.3 PL/SQL PACKAGES

Functions and procedures are important PL/SQL objects that allow you to group together and modularize the PL/SQL statements that are necessary to perform the functionality of the application. Packages are PL/SQL objects that take this process one step further. They bundle together in one object data and program units that access and modify the data.

Packages provide the PL/SQL implementation of several fundamental concepts of object-oriented programming, such as encapsulation of data with the operations performed on the data, code reusability, dynamic binding of data types, and data hiding. They are a close equivalent of the concept of classes in object-oriented programming languages, such as C++ or Java.

Structurally, a package is divided in two parts: the specification and the body. The specification part holds the data, functions, and procedures that will be freely accessible by all the other routines that will use the package. This part also contains the specification for those program units that other programs may call but that they do not need to see implemented. Thus, in a sense, the specification of a package is the communication protocol of the package with the outside environment.

The body part of the package contains private information that cannot be seen or accessed by the routines outside the package. The functions and procedures in the body are a direct implementation of the program units declared in the specification part of the package. But the body part may also contain functions and procedures that are not declared in the specification part. They will not be accessible by program units other than those within the body. Figure 10.12 shows a graphical representation of the package object. It is also known as the Booch diagram of the packages, after Grady Booch, one of the founders of object-oriented programming.

In the example shown in Figure 10.12, the pseudo-package `PACKAGE` contains some data declaration `Data`, a function specification `Function_A`, and a

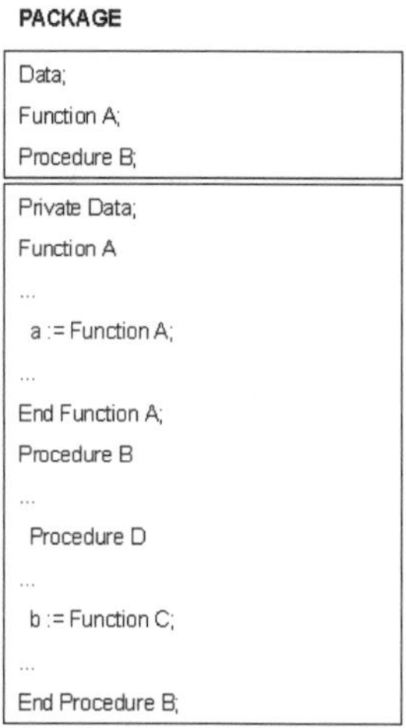

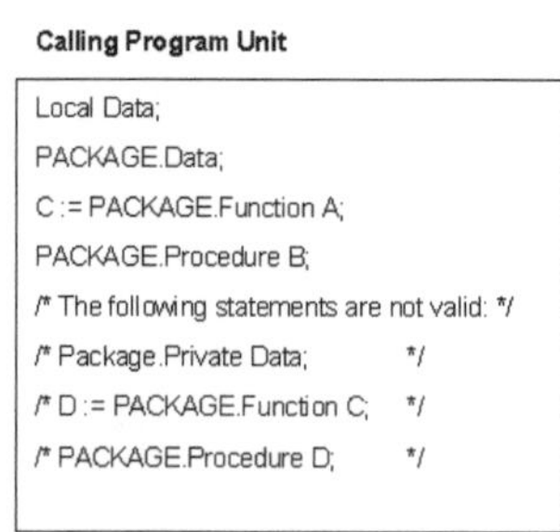

FIGURE 10.12 A graphical representation of a package.

procedure specification `Procedure_B`. The body of the package, represented by the shaded area, contains some data declarations that are strictly local to the body, and the implementation for `Function_A` and `Procedure_B`. `Function_A` in its body calls `Function_C`, and `Procedure_B` calls `Procedure_D` and `Function_C`. The definitions for both these program units are within the package body.

The programs outside can access and use only what is available in the specification part. The program unit shown in the box to the right can access the public data and functions using the syntax `PACKAGE.Data`, `PACKAGE.Function_A`, or `PACKAGE.Procedure_B`. Implicitly, through this interface, this program unit is using `Function_C` or `Procedure_D` only because these program units are used by `Function_A` or `Procedure_B`. However, it cannot access these objects directly. In fact, if `Function_A` inside the package's body is modified to implement a different algorithm, or data structure, the calling program would have no way of knowing about the modification.

10.5.4 BENEFITS OF PACKAGES

Even from this graphical presentation, packages clearly encapsulate in one object the data elements and the operations or methods that manipulate them. The advantage of this approach versus the more traditional one is that it represents the world that the application describes more naturally, as a continuum of objects that interact with each other.

Also, Figure 10.12 very clearly shows how a package can achieve the hiding of code and implementation details. The benefit of hiding the code from the outside routines is that the application becomes more robust as a whole. Because the outside routines do not know how the internals of the public components of the package are implemented, no risk exists that they will become wired into the details of this package. As long as the interface, or specification, of the package remains unchanged, modifications inside the body will not force the calling routines to change their behavior or have to be recompiled.

Another great usage of the information-hiding capability of packages is when designing and prototyping the application. In the top-down design approach, you define the high-level objects and routines first, and then move on to the detailed implementation. When you are still at the high-level phase, you can place all the functions and procedures declarations in the specification of a package. Then the rest of the application can continue to be developed independently. The calls to the package are made according to its specification. They will compile and execute successfully, although not much functionality exists behind them. Meanwhile, as the implementation of the package progresses, the rest of the development team does not have to modify and constantly change their code. All this work happens in the gray area of Figure 10.12, which, as I said, is invisible to the rest of the world.

Finally, the other object-oriented programming feature of packages is the dynamic binding of data types, also known as *overloading*. Inside a package, you can create functions and procedures that have the same name but take arguments of different data types. For the outside routines, the fact becomes transparent that different program units are executed when different arguments of different data types are used. The package intelligently selects which routine to invoke when it receives a call, thus removing the burden of the programmers to make that selection themselves, based on the data type of the arguments.

When cursors are declared in packages, you have the choice of dividing the SELECT statement of the cursor definition from its body. In the package specification, you could place statements like these:

```
/* Specifications of other public package components may
   go here.                                              */
CURSOR c_movie_rentals (movieId MOVIE.ID%TYPE)
RETURN RENTAL.DAILY_RATE%TYPE;
/* Specifications of other public package components may
   go here.                                              */
```

As you can see, you must provide the data types and the number of data elements of records that the SELECT statements of the cursor will return. Then in the package body you specify the actual SELECT statement, as shown in the following example:

```
/* Body of other package components may go here.     */
CURSOR c_movie_rentals (movieId MOVIE.ID%TYPE)IS
  SELECT customer_id, rent_dt, return_dt
  FROM RENTAL
 WHERE movie_id= movieId;
/* Body of other package components may go here.     */
```

Implementing cursors this way draws all the benefits that packages bring into PL/SQL programming, as I discussed above. In particular, it allows you to change the WHERE clause of the select statement, if need be, without affecting the programs that will use the cursor.

10.6 EXCEPTION HANDLING

When discussing the components of a PL/SQL block, I also mentioned the purpose and usage of exceptions in PL/SQL code. They are abnormal conditions in the PL/SQL environment, associated with a warning or error of which the user of the application must be aware. When any of these abnormal conditions occur, an exception is raised. The execution flow of the program is interrupted. The control jumps to the EXCEPTION part of the block, which the programmer should be careful to include. The exception section of the PL/SQL block is where you write the code that gracefully handles the error condition, or takes measures to correct it.

Two types of exceptions can occur in an Oracle application. The first category includes all the exceptions that the PL/SQL engine raises automatically when the abnormal condition occurs. These are called *internal exceptions.* The second category includes *user-specified exceptions.* They are not Oracle processing errors, but rather situations in the application to which the user's attention must be attracted.

10.6.1 INTERNAL EXCEPTIONS

Each internal exception is associated with an Oracle Server error number. The group of internal exceptions is further divided into *named* and *unnamed exceptions.* The named internal exceptions are a number of exceptions that occur most frequently and are defined in the PL/SQL engine. Figure 10.13 lists some of these exceptions that you are likely to encounter the most in your development practice.

Examples provided in this chapter, such as the PL/SQL block in Figure 10.3, show how to handle these exceptions. The majority of internal errors are not named explicitly, although they automatically raise an exception when they occur. However, in order to trap and handle them appropriately, the code of these errors must be associated with an exception that you have declared ahead of time. The pragma EXCEPTION_INIT associates an error number with the user-defined exception. In PL/SQL, a *pragma* is a directive that instructs the PL/SQL compiler to bind the internal error number to the specified exception

EXCEPTION NAME	ORACLE ERROR	DESCRIPTION
NO_DATA_FOUND	ORA-01403	SELECT ... INTO statement returns no rows
TOO_MANY_ROWS	ORA-01427	SELECT ... INTO statement returns more than one row
ZERO_DIVIDE	ORA-01476	Numeric value is divided by zero
VALUE_ERROR	ORA-01403	Error occurred during a computation or data conversion
STORAGE_ERROR	ORA-06500	No sufficient memory available, or memory is corrupted
PROGRAM_ERROR	ORA-06501	Internal error of PL/SQL

FIGURE 10.13 Examples of named internal exceptions.

name. Whenever the error occurs, the name can handle the exception. Figure 10.14 shows how to handle an unnamed internal exception.

In this case, you assume that a check constraint in the table RENTAL does not allow the daily rate for a rental transaction to be above $3.00. If the record sent for INSERT to the database contains a higher value for the column DAILY_RATE, the statement will violate the check constraint defined in the table RENTAL. The error raised by the database server will be ORA-02290. The internal value of this error and all other internal Oracle errors has a negative sign. In the PL/SQL block shown in Figure 10.14, this error is associated with the user-declared exception `check_constraint_violated` using the pragma EXCEPTION_INIT.

10.6.2 USER-DEFINED EXCEPTIONS

Some abnormal situations in an application are not due to a failure or error of the database engine, but to a violation of the requirements or logic of the application. In that case, a user-specified exception may be used to trap and handle the situation. The following example (Figure 10.15) is an improvement on the previous

```
DECLARE
– Declare a name for the constraint
 check_constraint_violated    EXCEPTION;
– Bind the constraint to an Oracle error code
 PRAGMA EXCEPTION_INIT (check_constraint_violated, -
2290);
BEGIN
 INSERT INTO rental (customer_id, movie_id, rent_dt,
daily_rate)
 VALUES (:main.customer_id, :main.movie_id,
:main.rent_dt, :main.daily_rate);
 – INSERT fails if daily_rate > $3.00
 – Violation of check constraint raises ORA-02290
 – In such case control jumps to EXCEPTION section
 COMMIT;
EXCEPTION
 WHEN check_constraint_violated THEN
 MESSAGE('Excessive daily rate.')
 WHEN OTHERS THEN
 MESSAGE('Internal error occurred.');
END;
```

FIGURE 10.14 Using unnamed internal exceptions.

```
DECLARE
– Declare a name for the constraint
  check_constraint_violated  EXCEPTION;
  vn_daily_rate NUMBER := 0.75;
BEGIN
  IF (:main.daily_rate > 3) THEN
    RAISE check_constraint_violated;
  END IF;

  – If control comes here, discount is less then 70
percent
  INSERT INTO rental (customer_id, movie_id, rent_dt,
daily_rate)
  VALUES (:main.customer_id, :main.movie_id,
:main.rent_dt, :main.daily_rate);
  COMMIT;
EXCEPTION
  WHEN check_constraint_violated THEN
    MESSAGE('Excessive discount.')
  WHEN OTHERS THEN
    MESSAGE('Internal error occurred.');
END;
```

FIGURE 10.15 An example of a user-named exception.

code, because it does check the value of DISCOUNT before the record is sent for insertion into the database.

The difference between unnamed internal exceptions and user-named exceptions is that the second type must be raised explicitly when the abnormal condition occurs. The RAISE statement in a sense serves as a GOTO statement, because the program execution is interrupted and the flow jumps to the exception. However, using the RAISE command makes the code more uniform and consistent with other situations. A user-defined exception that is declared in the built-in package STANDARD of the Form Builder is FORM_TRIGGER_FAILURE. You can raise this exception any time you want to halt the processing of any Form Builder trigger.

10.6.3 ERROR-REPORTING FUNCTIONS

A known fact in the information technology environment is that the number of things that could potentially go wrong with an application is proportional to the functionality of the application. However, a recognized trend is that the systems developed today are more robust and protected than systems developed in the past, because of great improvements in hardware and software development tools and to better preparation of programmers to handle different situations that a system can face. But expecting an application to handle every error that can occur is unrealistic. The developer must decide which errors can and must be corrected when they occur, and which ones may simply be reported and taken care of later.

In PL/SQL programs, a good place to put error-reporting code is in the OTHER clause of the EXCEPTION section. Whenever an error occurs, Oracle provides the number of that error and a brief descriptive message. They can both be retrieved and further manipulated by the functions SQLCODE and SQLERRM. These are PL/SQL-specific functions that cannot be used in a SQL statement. SQLCODE returns the error number, and SQLERRM returns the error message. Figure 10.16 expands the functionality of the PL/SQL block in Figure 10.15 by adding error-reporting functionality.

```
DECLARE
  err_code NUMBER;
  err_text VARCHAR2(255);
  – Declare a name for the constraint
  check_constraint_violated  EXCEPTION;
BEGIN
  IF (:main.daily_rate > 3) THEN
    RAISE check_constraint_violated;
  END IF;

  – If control comes here, discount is less then 70
percent
  INSERT INTO rental (customer_id, movie_id, rent_dt,
daily_rate)
  VALUES (:main.customer_id, :main.movie_id,
:main.rent_dt, :main.daily_rate);
  COMMIT;
EXCEPTION
  WHEN check_constraint_violated THEN
    MESSAGE('Excessive discount.')
  WHEN OTHERS THEN
    err_code := SQLCODE;
    err_text := SQLERRM;
    MESSAGE('Error '||TO_CHAR(err_code)||' - '||
err_text);
END;
```

FIGURE 10.16 Using the functions SQLCODE and SQLERRM.

10.6.4 PROPAGATION OF EXCEPTIONS

When an exception is raised, Form Builder looks for a handler clause for that exception in the PL/SQL block where the exception occurs. If one is found, the instructions contained in that handler are executed. If no handler exists, then the exception is passed to the parent block, if it exists. The same check for an exception handler occurs here. The exception continues to propagate upward until it reaches the upper programmatic layer. Figure 10.17 represents the diagram of a trigger that contains a call to `Procedure_A` and `Function_B` in its body. `Procedure_A` in turn issues a call to `Function_C`, and `Function_B` to `Procedure_D`. The diagram identifies the checkpoints an exception has to pass through when raised.

Any exception raised in `Function_C` can be handled in the EXCEPTION part of this function. If it is not trapped here, the exception will propagate to `Procedure_A`, where it can be handled by its EXCEPTION section, labeled as Trap 3 in the figure. If no handler is defined in `Procedure_A`, the exception will be propagated to the body of the calling trigger. The EXCEPTION section of this trigger, Trap 5, is the last chance to handle the raised exception. If it is not handled even here, the trigger will fail. If in any of these steps, a handler for the exception OTHERS is used, none of the exceptions raised in the block and all its enclosing blocks will be propagated outside the block. For example, if you place the WHEN OTHERS clause in Trap 4, all the exceptions that can be raised by `Procedure_D` or `Function_B` that are not handled by explicit handlers will be trapped and handled by the statements in this clause.

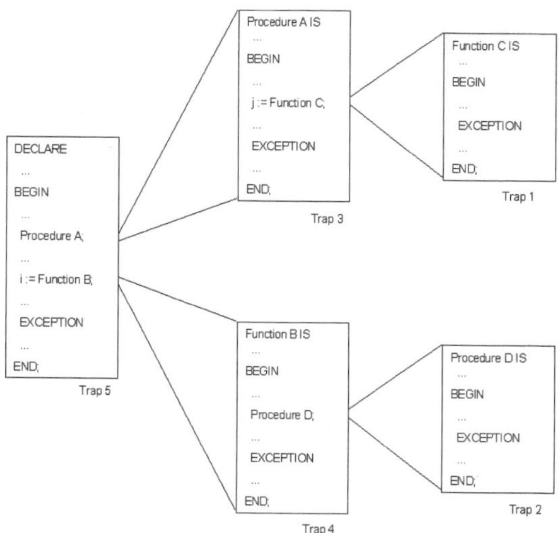

FIGURE 10.17 Trapping exceptions in a database trigger.

10.7 PL/SQL IN FORM BUILDER

As any other programming language, PL/SQL uses variables as placeholders of information or data. In the PL/SQL blocks presented so far you have seen the use of different kinds or variables such as local variables, Forms objects and database columns. This section will provide more details for each of them.

10.7.1 LOCAL AND GLOBAL VARIABLES

Form Builder uses global and local variables. Local variables are accessible only within the PL/SQL block in which they are declared. Global variables are accessible from every object, trigger, function and procedure in the running module. While local variables can be declared only in the declaration section of a PL/SQL block, global variables can be declared anywhere in the application. However, it is an established practice to declare these variables when a form is first accessed, usually in a PRE-FORM trigger. The reason for this is that in Forms a variable must be declared before being used. Normally, a global variable is used in more than one piece of code. Given the unpredictability and randomness with which pieces of code are executed—a characteristic for all GUI applications, it may happen that Forms runs into a global variable before executing the code in which it is declared. In this case a runtime error will occur. On the other hand, the code of the PRE-FORM trigger is executed in the initial moments of the forms' existence, before any thing else happens. By declaring global variables in this trigger, you protect the application from these runtime errors.

Another difference between local and global variables in Form Builder, is the way the memory allocated to them is handled. For a local variable, the memory is allocated when the focus moves inside the PL/SQL block. As soon as the execution of that block of code ends, the memory for the variable is released. For a global variable, the memory is allocated when the variable is declared, and remains allocated until the form is closed, or the global is explicitly destroyed, whichever comes first. It is important to understand this fact. In the case of large applications that keep multiple forms open, using a large number of global variables may consume too much memory resources and affect performance especially in the Windows environment. It is common to release the memory taken by global variables when a form is exited. This is usually done in a POST-FORM trigger, which is the last one to be executed in a Forms module.

The names of all global variables must be in the format `GLOBAL.<name>`, as in `GLOBAL.first_name`, or `GLOBAL.cost`. Note that PL/SQL, like SQL, is not case-sensitive. However, as in the previous chapter, keywords and other language constructs will be used in uppercase letters to distinguish them from the rest of the code.

10.7.2 DATA TYPES OF VARIABLES IN FORM BUILDER

An important characteristic of variables is their data type. For the sake of simplicity, the data types of Form Builder variables will be divided in two groups. The first group includes all the data types defined and used by the PL/SQL language. These data types were covered in Section 10.3.1. It is important here to emphasize that the generic data types, specific to the PL/SQL language, can be used in all the Oracle tools that support the PL/SQL syntax. PL/SQL code that utilizes only these data types has the greatest potential for portability. Such code can be written in Forms, and, with no modifications required, can run on the database as a stored procedure, can be included in an Oracle Reports or Oracle Graphics trigger, or can be executed from SQL*Plus.

In order to increase the efficiency of the code in a particular environment, PL/SQL allows data types specific to that environment. These data types normally correspond to the types of objects used by the tools. So, in Form Builder you have variables of type WINDOW, ITEM, and BLOCK that store internal identifiers for these objects; in Oracle Graphics you have variables of type OG_LAYER or OG_RECTANGLE that store information about layers or rectangles. The data types used to represent Form Builder objects will be referred to as Forms-specific data types.

Declaring a Forms-specific data type variable is similar to declaring a generic data type variable. Indeed, both the following statements are equally valid:

```
score           NUMBER;
help_win        WINDOW;
```

However, assigning values to them is a slightly different process. Generic data type variables can be assigned a value directly, as in the following statement:

```
score := 25;
```

To assign a value to a Forms-specific data type variable, you must use the built-in function FIND that corresponds to the object of that data type. There are fourteen such functions that correspond to as many objects categories in Form Builder. The general syntax of these functions is `FIND_object('object_name')`, where the object name is the name in the Form Builder of a form, data block, item, alert, canvas, window, and so on. They return a unique identifier for the object with the specified `object_name`, if it exists. Otherwise they return NULL. This unique identifier is called the object ID and its value is assigned and maintained internally by the Forms. The object ID has the Forms-specific data type that corresponds to the particular object. In the example being discussed here, the variable `help_win` can be assigned a value with this statement:

```
help_win := FIND_WINDOW('MAIN_HELP');
```

If there is a window named MAIN_HELP in the module, its object ID will be stored in the variable `help_win`. You can use `help_win` to access and modify all the properties of MAIN_HELP window. If the module does not contain a window called MAIN_HELP, `help_win` will be NULL. To protect the application from unexpected failures, you must check that FIND_WINDOW returned a non-NULL value to variable `help_win`, before proceeding with the actions mentioned above. Form Builder provides the function ID_NULL that helps you test the existence of any object with the ID returned by the FIND functions. This function returns TRUE if there is an object in the runtime environment with the ID passed in as the function's argument; it returns FALSE otherwise. Figure 10.18 presents a way to handle the situation described here.

10.7.3 FORMS ITEMS AND DATABASE COLUMNS

Form Builder items can be used just like any PL/SQL variable in an application. They can be assigned values, which then can be further manipulated. To access the values stored in Form Builder items, their names must be preceded by the colon character ":". When items are created in the module, Form Builder ensures that there are no naming conflicts among them. You should be equally careful in your code in avoiding these conflicts. The best provision for this is to use the fully qualified names of the items. You should make it a habit to always reference items using their fully qualified name following this pattern:

```
<BLOCK_NAME>.<ITEM_NAME>
```

```
DECLARE
  help_win WINDOW;
  – Other declarations go here
BEGIN
  help_win := FIND_WINDOW('MAIN_HELP');
  IF ID_NULL(help_win) THEN
  – MAIN_HELP does not exist.
  – Remedy for the situation
  ELSE
  – Manipulate the window
  END IF;
  – Other statements go here
END;
```

FIGURE 10.18 Using Forms-specific data type variables.

Suppose for example that you are working with a data entry form for the MRD application. The form contains three database blocks to interact with the Customer, Movie, and Rental tables. You try to add the following statement to a trigger:

```
:ID := 155;
```

Under these conditions, you will get an error when you compile the module. Form Builder cannot decide whether you are trying to set the ID in CUSTOMER block or MOVIE block, and will inform you about the ambiguity of your statement. The situation gets worse if you have a statement like the following one:

```
GO_ITEM('ID');
```

Here, you are instructing Forms to jump from the current location to the item ID. The problem is Form Builder does not look inside the single quotes during the compilation; it compiles the statement with the understanding that the address of the item will be resolved and will be available at runtime. Thus, you have an application that compiles with no errors but will certainly fail when this statement will be executed. The address of the item ID as specified above cannot be resolved.

Eliminate these problems by referring to the item ID using the name of the block to which this item belongs. If you are working with CUSTOMER block, you can solve all ambiguities by instructing Forms to set the value of this item to 155 and to navigate to it using the following statements:

```
:CUSTOMER.ID := 155;
GO_ITEM('CUSTOMER.ID');
```

Looking at the statements above, you may wonder why in the first one the item name is preceded with a colon, but in the second one not only it is not, but it is also enclosed in quotes. The two notations don't just happen to be different. In fact, they denote different objects. A notation like `CUSTOMER.ID` references the object, the place where some data resides. The value of the data per se is referenced by the notation `:CUSTOMER.ID`. Therefore, the statement `:CUSTOMER.ID := 155;` in reality means that the value stored in the object `CUSTOMER.ID` should become 155. Of course, this is often abbreviated as `CUSTOMER.ID` is 155.

Database columns in PL/SQL can be used only in SQL statements. To avoid any conflicting names, it is good to fully qualify column names by preceding them with the table name. If ambiguities still exist, the name of the table owner can be added.

10.8 THE PL/SQL EDITOR

The PL/SQL Editor is a tool that facilitates the process of creating, modifying, compiling and saving PL/SQL objects in a Form Builder application. These objects include triggers, functions, procedures and packages. In the Form Builder object hierarchy triggers can be attached to forms, blocks, or items. Functions, procedures and packages are all listed under the Program Units heading in the Object Navigator.

10.8.1 INVOKING THE PL/SQL EDITOR

If you create a trigger or a program unit, the Form Builder will automatically invoke a PL/SQL Editor window. The following are the steps required to create a new program unit in the Form Builder:

1. Select the node Program Units in the Object Navigator.
2. Click the icon Create in the Navigator's toolbar. The New Program Unit dialog box shown in Figure 10.19 appears.
3. Specify the name of the program unit and its type.
4. Click OK.

The process of creating a trigger is slightly different. As I have already mentioned, triggers belong to other Form Builder objects. Thus, you need to identify

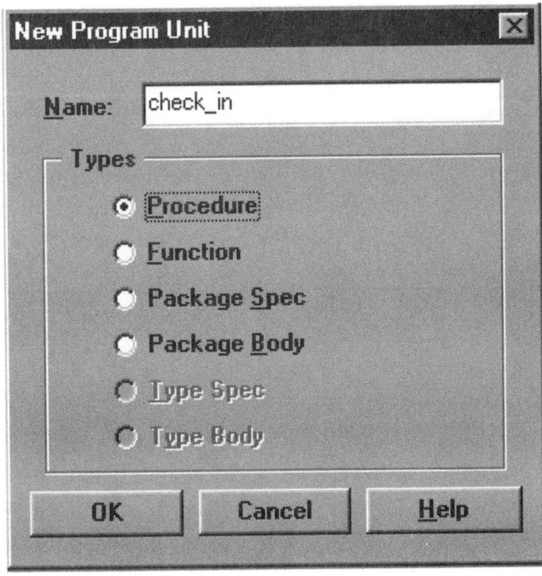

FIGURE 10.19 New Program Unit dialog box.

the object that will own the trigger first. After accomplishing this, you can follow these steps:

1. Expand the node Triggers for the object.
2. Click the icon Create in the Navigator's toolbar. The List of Values control with all the possible trigger names appears. As a replacement of Steps 1 and 2, you may right-click the object on the Object Navigator or the Layout Editor and select PL/SQL Editor from the popup menu.
3. Select the desired trigger name using the auto-restrict features of the dialog box.
4. Click OK.

The List of Values control will always contain the names of all the triggers that you may potentially create in your form. However, certain triggers are typical for certain categories of objects. These triggers are called 'Smart Triggers' in the Form Builder world. You can create a smart trigger for an object by issuing these simple commands:

1. Right-click the object on the Object Navigator or the Layout Editor.
2. Expand the menu item SmartTriggers from the popup menu.
3. Select the desired trigger from the list. Click Other to invoke the list of all trigger names if the one you want is not defined as a smart trigger.

In all these situations, Form Builder opens a PL/SQL editor window and provides a template that you can use to create the new program unit. Use the editor as described in the following section to define and compile the newly created function or procedure. If you want to edit the contents of an existing PL/SQL object, select it in the Navigator and use any of the following commands:

- Double-click the trigger icon or program unit icon to the left of the object name.
- Select the object and choose Tools | PL/SQL Editor... from the Form Builder menu.
- Right-click the object and select PL/SQL Editor from the popup menu.

Figure 10.20 shows a typical PL/SQL editor window. Its components are the source code pane, the messages pane, the context definition area and button palette. At the bottom of the window, you can see a status bar. The window also has a vertical scroll bar that allows navigating to hidden part of it.

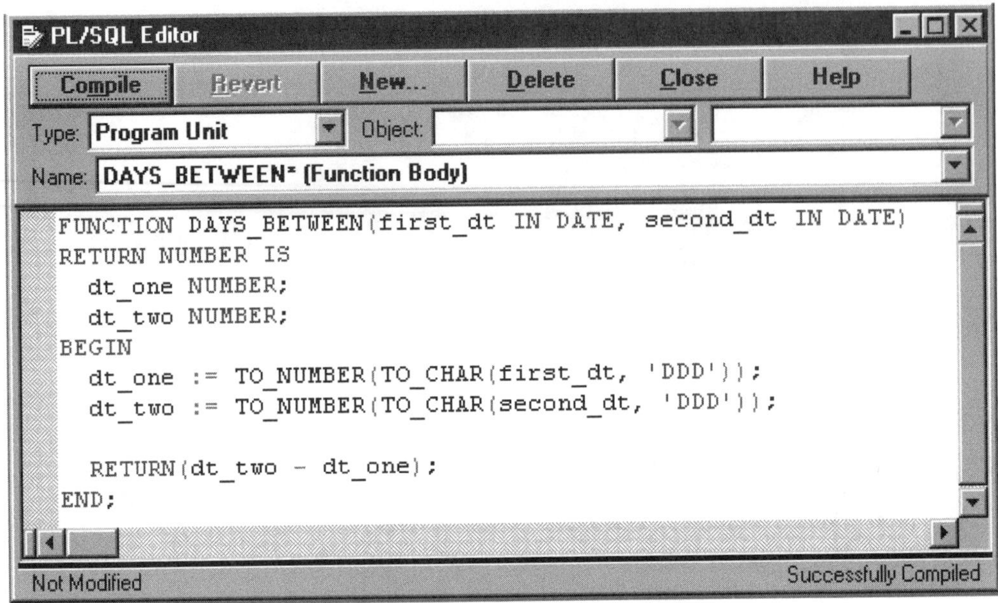

FIGURE 10.20 PL/SQL Editor window.

10.8.2 EDITING TEXT

In the source code pane you can use all the standard text editing functions. Namely, you can cut, copy, paste, and delete by either choosing the corresponding menu items from the Edit menu, or by pressing the hot keys from the keyboard. In the editing area, you can also search for a specific string or replace it with a new string. To search for or replace a string in the PL/SQL object currently displayed in the window:

1. Select Edit | Find and Replace… from the menu. The Search/Replace dialog box appears (see Figure 10.21).
2. Enter the string to search for in the Find What text item. If you want to replace it with another string, enter the new string in the Replace With text item.
3. Check the respective boxes if you want to perform a case-sensitive search, or to search regular expressions.
4. Click Find Next to find the first occurrence of the string, or Replace to substitute the first occurrence of the string, or Replace All to substitute all the occurrences of the string.
5. Click Cancel when done.

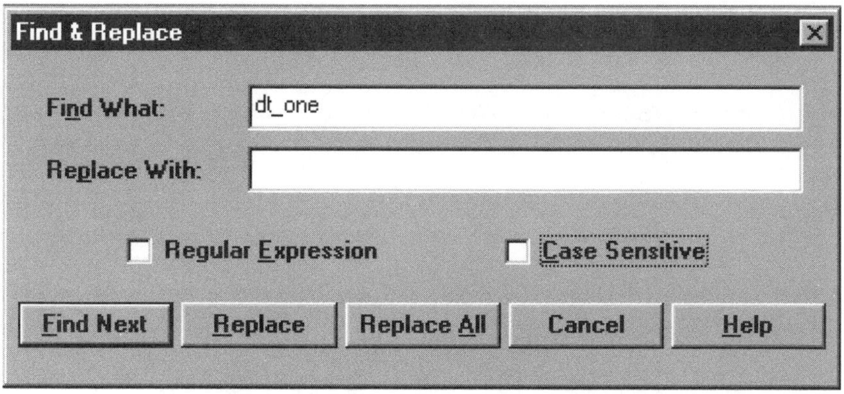

FIGURE 10.21 Search/Replace dialog box.

When you click the Search, Replace, or Replace All buttons, the editor will search forward, starting from the current position of the cursor. If it reaches the end of the code, and no occurrences of the string are found, you will be asked if you want to continue searching from the beginning.

The PL/SQL editor allows you to perform global search-and-replaces on all the PL/SQL objects in the module. To accomplish this task follow the steps listed above, but invoke the Search/Replace dialog box by selecting Program | Search/Replace PL/SQL... menu item, instead of Edit | Search/Replace. The rest is the same. When the editor reaches the end of a program unit, it asks you whether you want to continue search to the next program unit.

> **TIP**
>
> The names of the Search/Replace menu items may lead to some confusion. They both search and replace PL/SQL code. However, Search/Replace... works with one object at a time, and Search/Replace PL/SQL... acts upon all the triggers, functions, and procedures in the current module.

10.8.3 EXPORTING AND IMPORTING TEXT

The PL/SQL editor also allows you to move the text in the source code area from the Form Builder to a file in the directory tree and vice-versa. To export the contents of a PL/SQL object to a file follow these steps:

1. Select File | Export Text... A standard Save As dialog box appears.
2. Specify the name and the location of the file.
3. Click OK.

To import the content of a text file into the source code area of a PL/SQL editor, follow these steps:

1. Select Edit | Import Text... . A standard Open dialog box appears.
2. Specify the name and the location of the file you want to import.
3. Click OK.

The content of the file will be loaded starting from the current cursor position.

10.8.4 COMPILING CODE

After you enter code in the source pane you need to compile it. To do so, click the Compile button in the button palette. If the compilation is successful, the status bar of the window will display the `Compiled Successfully` status indicator to the right. If the PL/SQL engine encounters any syntax errors, the status indicator will be `Compiled with Errors`, and the errors will be displayed in the message pane as shown in Figure 10.20. If you click at the line number of the error, the editor places the cursor in the source code pane at the line where the error occurred. You can drag the bar that divides the panes to rearrange the sizes of the two panes. If you move it all the way to the bottom of the window, the message pane will be hidden.

You can compile PL/SQL objects from the Object Navigator as well. If you select the Program | Compile Incremental from the menu, only those objects that are not in a successfully compiled state will be processed. If you want the compile the whole module, including those PL/SQL objects that were compiled successfully earlier, select Program | Compile | All from the menu. In both cases, a dialog box similar to Figure 10.22 will be displayed.

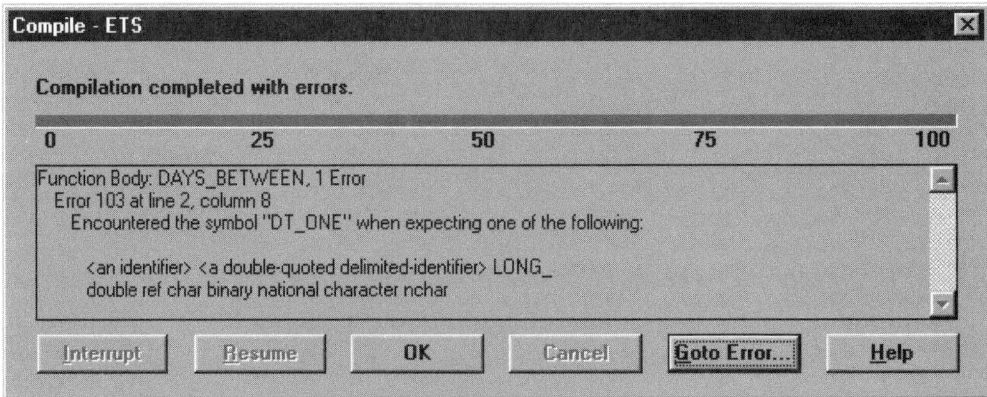

FIGURE 10.22 The Compile dialog box.

The line across the window shows the percentage of the code compiled. It is filled dynamically during the compilation. At this time, you also can stop the process by clicking the Interrupt button. Click Resume when you are ready to continue compiling the rest of the code. The button Goto Error..., opens a PL/SQL editor window and places the cursor at the line where the error occurred.

> **TIP**
>
> When the module is generated all the PL/SQL objects are compiled as well. If errors occur, they are displayed in a scrollable window and, at the same time, written to a file with the extension .ERR.

10.8.5 CONTEXT AREA

The context area of the PL/SQL Editor window is where the name and type of the object are defined. In the case of triggers, the type of trigger and the object they are attached to are displayed here as well. The context area is a combination of four list boxes on top of the window. The first one, up and to the left, shows the type of the object currently loaded in the editor. Its value can be Program Unit, Trigger, or Menu Item Code. The two other drop-down lists to its right are enabled only if the type of object is Trigger or Menu Item Code. They define the form object (form, block, or item) that owns the trigger or the menu item that contains the PL/SQL block. The list box in the second row displays the name of the PL/SQL object. Figure 10.23 shows samples of the five possible context definitions that can be used in an application.

If the object type is Program Unit, the Object drop-down list boxes are disabled. If the PL/SQL object is a form-level or block-level trigger, or a menu item PL/SQL block, the first one of them displays either (Form Level), or the name of the block that owns the trigger, or the name of the menu item; the last list box is disabled. By selecting different entries from the list boxes described above, you can quickly navigate to the PL/SQL objects you want to work with. Suppose, for example that you just finished work with the function ADD_MONTHS (see Figure 10.23 a); you want to call this function from the trigger WHEN-NEW-ITEM-INSTANCE attached to item DAILY_RATE of block RENTAL (see Figure 10.23 d).

1. Select the option 'Trigger' from the list box Type. The context switches to the first trigger in the module hierarchy. In the case of Figure 10.23 b, it happens to be the form-level trigger PRE-FORM. The first list box in the Object group is now enabled.
2. Select the block RENTAL from the first list box in the Object group. At this

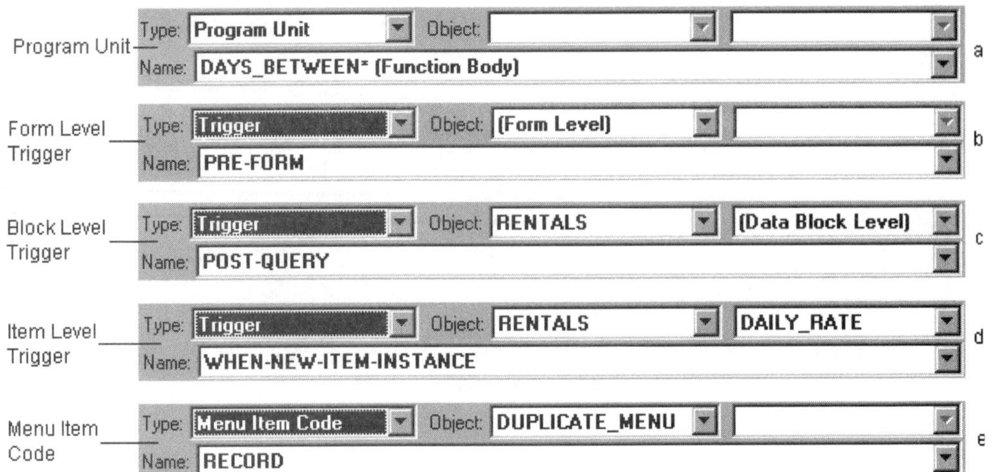

FIGURE 10.23 Five context settings of the PL/SQL Editor window.

point, the second list box in the Object group is enabled. This list box helps you further focus on items within the block RENTAL.

3. Select the item DAILY_RATE from the second list box in the Object group.
4. Select WHEN-NEW-ITEM-INSTANCE from the list box Name (see Figure 10.23 d).

10.9 SUMMARY

PL/SQL is the programming language used by a number of development tools produced by the Oracle Corporation, including Oracle Developer, Oracle WebDB and Oracle Application Server. In addition, all the business units implemented in the Oracle RDBMS in the form of stored program units and database triggers are programmed in PL/SQL. This chapter is an overview of the major syntactic structures and concepts of PL/SQL. Major topics of this chapter included:

- **Overview of PL/SQL**
  - Brief History of the PL/SQL Language
  - Functionality of PL/SQL Engines
  - Structural Elements of PL/SQL Blocks
  - Manipulating Data in PL/SQL Blocks

- **Procedural Constructs of PL/SQL**
  - IF Statement
  - Looping Statements
  - Unconditional Branching
- **Data Types and Variables**
  - PL/SQL Data Types
  - PL/SQL Variables
  - PL/SQL Constants
  - PL/SQL Records
  - Index-by Table
- **Cursors in PL/SQL**
  - Declaring Explicit Cursors
  - Methods and Attributes of Explicit Cursors
  - Using the FOR Loop with Explicit Cursors
  - Cursor Variables
  - Implicit Cursors
- **PL/SQL Program Units**
  - Components of Program Units
  - Arguments in Program Units
  - PL/SQL Packages
  - Benefits of Packages
- **Exception Handling**
  - Internal Exceptions
  - User-Defined Exceptions
  - Error-Reporting Functions
  - Propagation of Exceptions
- **PL/SQL in Form Builder**
  - Local and Global Variables
  - Data Types of Variables in Form Builder
  - Forms Items and Database Columns
- **The PL/SQL Editor**
  - Invoking the PL/SQL Editor
  - Editing Text
  - Exporting and Importing Text
  - Compiling Code
  - Context Area

Chapter 11

Object-Relational Oracle8 and PL/SQL8

Civilization advances by extending the number of important operations which we can perform without thinking about them.
—Alfred North Whitehead

Chapter 9 and Chapter 10 presented an overview of the traditional SQL and PL/SQL languages, as they have existed and been used with the Oracle Server database before the release of version 8. This release pushed the Oracle Server technology in three major directions:

- ❑ **Scaleability.** Improvements in this direction were aimed at increasing the support of the Oracle Server database for data warehouses and very large database (VLDB) applications.
- ❑ **Openness.** Improvements in this area were aimed at making the Oracle Server the centerpiece of Oracle Corporation's Network Computing Architecture (NCA).
- ❑ **Object-Relational technology.** Developments in this area expanded the traditional relational framework of Oracle and added support for user-defined object types and collections.

This chapter will focus on the major concepts introduced by Oracle8 and its versions of SQL and PL/SQL to support the object-relational technology.

11.1 OVERVIEW OF THE OBJECT-RELATIONAL TECHNOLOGY

As discussed in Chapter 9, the relational model was defined in the 1970s and commercial applications of it started being implemented in the 1980s. Throughout that decade and in the early to mid-1990s, relational databases grew up and hosted a large percentage of the data corporations cared about. The simplicity of the relational world (expressed in a short list of steps known as the normalization rules), the straightforward implementations of SQL by all the database vendors, and a number of data modeling and database design tools helped IT professionals put order in their data universe and build robust relational database applications.

The relational model, as defined and described in its latest standard (SQL2), considers the data to be organized in fields and records. The data stored in each of these fields may be described by a data type from a (short) list of predefined data types. By the mid-1990s, an increasing number of IT professionals began realizing that what was considered a virtue of the relational model—its simplicity—was quickly becoming a liability. The fast-paced improvements in hardware, software, and communication technologies enabled corporations to address much more complex structures and relations in their data. The relational model by itself was no longer optimal for storing and handling this complexity. There were two alternatives from which system designers and application developers could choose in order to address the shortcomings of the relational databases:

- ❑ **Build an object-oriented layer on top of the pure relational model.** This approach placed the burden on the application developers and increased the complexity of applications by introducing a middle-layer in the code whose purpose was to abstract and encapsulate the relational storage of data.

- **Migrate the data from a relational database to an object-oriented database.** This approach required abandoning the investments on relational database products, and its success depended on the migration of legacy data to the new environments.

Clearly, none of these approaches was very satisfying. By the mid-1990s, all the stakeholders in the relational world, including database vendors, standards' committees, designers, and developers, agreed that the relational model and SQL had to be extended with object-oriented features. In Oracle8, the Oracle Corporation introduced a set of features that enabled designers and developers to natively implement and support objects in the Oracle Server. These features are collectively known as the Objects Option of Oracle8 and are grouped in the following categories:

- **Object types.** They are also known as user-defined or abstract data types. Object types allow you to represent the structure (attributes) and the behavior (methods) of entities as they appear in the real world.
- **References.** They are handles to instances of object types, which allow you to represent the relations among objects in a way that optimizes the storage of these objects.
- **Collections.** They allow you to group data in an ordered or unordered way for efficient and optimized access. These are two categories of collections in Oracle8 Objects Option: variable-length arrays, often abbreviated as VARRAYs, and nested tables.
- **Object storage.** Oracle8 with Objects Option allows you not only to define objects from the previous three categories, but also to store them in the Oracle Server. Extensions to SQL allow you to manipulate these objects just like the pre-defined data types. Furthermore, object views allow you to build object definitions upon purely relational structures and are very important when migrating applications into the object-relational world.

In the remainder of this chapter, I will discuss each of these categories of features in detail. From now on, I will use the expression Oracle8 to mean Oracle8 with Objects Option, unless otherwise noted.

11.2 OBJECT TYPES AND OBJECT INSTANCES

The world around us is made up of objects that we see, touch, and interact with constantly. These objects are materialized in the form of a number of attributes and operations you perform with them. A simple object like a door has attributes such as weight, material, color, dimensions, and price. Some operations you can perform on a door are open, close, mount, lock, and break. Depending on who you are and your intentions, you may be interested in different attributes of doors and perform different operations on them. If you are a homeowner considering purchasing a door for your bedroom, you may want to know its dimensions and price, as well as how to open, close, or lock it. But, if you are a contractor hired to install a door, you need to know its weight and material, as well as how to mount it.

One of the major advantages that object-oriented languages brought to software engineering is the ability to model, design, and build applications using the familiar object paradigm with which we all are familiar. These languages allow you to distinguish between the actual objects and the templates that describe the structure and methods of a group of objects. In a number of OO languages, like C++ and Java, these templates are called object classes, or simply classes. Class instances created and manipulated during the life of the application are the actual objects with which users interact.

In Oracle8, the templates that describe the attributes and methods of a category of objects are called object types. They are defined using DDL commands and are considered part of the schema objects defined in the Oracle Server data dictionary. The actual objects are called instances of the object type and can be stored temporarily in PL/SQL program units or persistently in the Oracle Server database structures. Object instances can be created and maintained using SQL DML commands and PL/SQL syntactic structures.

In a sense, PL/SQL and Oracle have offered similar constructs even before Oracle8. In fact, any language offers a number of "object types" called data types. For example, the PL/SQL data types VARCHAR2 or NATURAL define the attributes of their instance variables, such as alphanumeric strings no longer than 2000 characters or positive integers. They also define the allowed operations on each of these variables: NATURAL numbers can be added and multiplied, whereas VARCHAR2 strings cannot. Complex data types in PL/SQL, such as records and index-by tables discussed in the previous chapter, allow you to extend the predefined scalar data types with complex data types that are associated with a number of predefined methods, like NEXT and PRIOR in the case of index-by tables. Finally, packages in PL/SQL have allowed for a long time the association and encapsulation of data (attributes) with methods. The Objects Option in Oracle8 unifies and extends these features in the following aspects:

- ❑ **Support for abstract data types (ADT).** The object types created in Oracle8 can be of any level of complexity. They may contain a large number of attributes (up to 1000) and methods. Each of these attributes may be of a predefined or another abstract data type.
- ❑ **Centralized storage of ADT definitions.** By storing the definitions and properties of the object types as part of the schema, Oracle8 enables you to access and use them at any level in your application architecture. You can use them at the database level or, through PL/SQL at the application layer.

Furthermore, mechanisms provided by other Oracle Corporation's tools, such as Designer/2000, allow you to derive class definitions in languages such as C++ from object type definitions stored in the Repository.

11.2.1 DEFINING OBJECT TYPES

As I mentioned earlier, object types are defined as part of the schema in the Oracle Server using DDL statements. The structure of object types is very similar to that of the packages discussed in the previous chapter. Like packages, object types are made up of a mandatory specification and an optional body part. The specification part contains the attributes and the method specifications for the object type. The body part contains the implementation of these methods. However, unlike packages, object types cannot contain private attributes or methods implemented in the body but not defined in the specification. Structurally, each object type may contain one or more attributes and zero or more methods. More details on attributes and methods are provided in the following section. The SQL statement shown in Figure 11.1 creates the specification for the object type `point_t` used to store information about points in the two-dimensional real plan. This object type definition allows you to store the coordinates of the point and provides a method for computing its distance from the origin of coordinates:

The statement shown in Figure 11.2 creates the corresponding body of the object type `point_t`.

11.2.2 ATTRIBUTES AND METHODS

The attributes in an object type describe the placeholders in which object instances will store data. As you can see from the examples at the end of the previous section, attributes are defined in a way similar to the way variables are defined in a PL/SQL program unit. However, certain differences exist, as detailed in the following list:

- Attributes cannot be initialized in the object type specification.
- Attributes cannot be constrained in the object type specification other than by the data type and length (or precision, for numeric data types that support it).

```
CREATE TYPE point_t AS OBJECT (
  x NUMBER,
  y NUMBER,
  MEMBER FUNCTION GetDistance RETURN NUMBER
);
```

FIGURE 11.1 A simple example of an object type definition.

```
CREATE TYPE BODY point_t AS
  MEMBER FUNCTION GetDistance RETURN NUMBER IS
  BEGIN
    RETURN SQRT(x*x + y*y);
  END;
END;
```

FIGURE 11.2 The implementation of the object type `point_t`.

- Most of the Oracle's predefined data types can be used as an attribute's data type. Some exceptions are the data types LONG, LONG RAW, BOOLEAN, RECORD, and BINARY_INTEGER.

On the other hand, an attribute may be assigned any user-defined object type stored in the Oracle Server schema. This mechanism allows you to create complex objects with attributes defined as other nested objects. The statements shown in Figure 11.3 contain the specification and body for the object type `circle_t`. As you can see from this example, the center of the circle is an object of type `point_t` defined at the end of the previous section.

The object type definitions shown so far contain only one simple method. However, methods are not required to define an object type. In this case, the body of the type definition is not required and the object type resembles a structure in languages like C. Obviously, the benefits of encapsulating data with operations are realized when the attributes are followed by a number of interesting

```
CREATE OR REPLACE TYPE circle_t AS OBJECT (
  center   point_t,
  radius   NUMBER,
  MEMBER FUNCTION GetArea RETURN NUMBER
);

CREATE OR REPLACE TYPE BODY circle_t AS
  MEMBER FUNCTION GetArea RETURN NUMBER IS
    pi CONSTANT NUMBER := 3.14;
  BEGIN
    RETURN (pi*radius*radius);
  END;
END;
```

FIGURE 11.3 A simple example of a nested object type definition and its implementation.

```
CREATE OR REPLACE TYPE point_t AS OBJECT (
  x  NUMBER,
  y  NUMBER,
  MEMBER FUNCTION GetDistance RETURN NUMBER,
  MEMBER FUNCTION GetDistance (p point_t) RETURN NUMBER,
  MEMBER FUNCTION GetMidPoint RETURN point_t,
  MEMBER FUNCTION GetMidPoint (p point_t) RETURN point_t,
  MEMBER FUNCTION AddPoint (p point_t) RETURN point_t,
  MEMBER FUNCTION SubtractPoint (p point_t) RETURN
point_t
);
```

FIGURE 11.4 The complete definition of the object type `point_t`.

methods in the object type definition. The statement contained in Figure 11.4 extends the definition of the object type `point_t` with a number of methods that implement operations with point on the Real plane.

The corresponding body of this object type is shown in Figure 11.5. From the contents of this figure, you can see that the methods of an object type are defined and implemented just like regular functions and procedures in a PL/SQL package. In particular, the specification of the method resides within the object type specification, whereas its implementation resides in the object type body. Furthermore, methods can be overloaded as in the example of the methods `GetDistance`. Based on the arguments passed to these methods, a client application is able to compute the distance of a point from the origin of the coordinate system or from another point on the plane. Similarly, the first method `GetMidPoint` allows you to compute the coordinates of the point in the middle of the segment that joins the given point with the origin of coordinates. The second method computes the midpoint of the segment that connects the point with any other point on the plane.

The implementations of the methods for the object type `point_t` shown in Figure 11.5, highlight a few special characteristics of them, which are described in the following list:

- **Constructor method.** The implementation of the last four methods contains a call to the method `point_t`, which was never defined explicitly. This is a special method, called a constructor method, provided automatically by Oracle for every object type you define. The constructor allows you to create an object instance and, in the process, initialize all its data attributes. Structurally, the constructor method is a function with the same name as the object type, which takes as formal arguments all the attributes of the object

```
CREATE OR REPLACE TYPE BODY point_t AS
  MEMBER FUNCTION GetDistance RETURN NUMBER IS
  BEGIN
    RETURN SQRT(x*x + y*y);
  END;

  MEMBER FUNCTION GetDistance (p point_t) RETURN NUMBER IS
  BEGIN
    RETURN SQRT((x-p.x)*(x-p.x) + (y-p.y)*(y-p.y));
  END;

  MEMBER FUNCTION GetMidPoint RETURN point_t IS
    new_p point_t := point_t(NULL,NULL);
  BEGIN
    new_p.x := x/2;
    new_p.y := y/2;

    RETURN new_p;
  END;

  MEMBER FUNCTION GetMidPoint (p point_t) RETURN point_t IS
    new_p point_t := point_t(NULL,NULL);
  BEGIN
    new_p.x := (x + p.x)/2;
    new_p.y := (y + p.y)/2;

    RETURN new_p;
  END;

  MEMBER FUNCTION AddPoint (p point_t) RETURN point_t IS
    new_p point_t := point_t(NULL,NULL);
  BEGIN
    new_p.x := SELF.x + p.x;
    new_p.y := SELF.y + p.y;

    RETURN new_p;
  END;

  MEMBER FUNCTION SubtractPoint (p point_t) RETURN
point_t IS
    new_p point_t := point_t(NULL,NULL);
  BEGIN
    new_p.x := x - p.x;
    new_p.y := y - p.y;

    RETURN new_p;
  END;
END;
```

FIGURE 11.5 The complete implementation of the object type `point_t`.

type in the order in which they are defined, and returns an object instance of that type.

- **SELF.** A method may have to operate with instances of the same object type, as it is the case with the methods `Add` or `Substract`. How does PL/SQL distinguish in such cases the members of the object instance whose method was called from those of the other objects? PL/SQL provides each object instance with a reference to itself, called SELF. SELF is not an object instance in itself; it is passed to each method as an implicit argument, and therefore it can be accessed from within the method just like any other object, as shown in the case of the method `Add`. If you are familiar with object-oriented languages like C++ or Java, you will notice that SELF is very similar to the reference `this` in these languages. One more point of similarity is that SELF is not required to reference the members of an object within a method. As shown in the case of function `Subtract`, an attribute or method without an object reference is implicitly considered as a member of the object instance whose method is invoked.

TIP

In most cases, SELF is passed to the method implicitly, by the PL/SQL engine. However, PL/SQL allows you to pass the SELF reference explicitly, as well, as the first formal parameter of a method. Practically, the only time you may want to pass the reference SELF explicitly is when you want to change its mode. By default, the mode of this parameter is IN for functions and IN OUT for procedures. Changing this mode is rarely necessary and should be questioned seriously.

By default, PL/SQL allows you to compare two instances of the same object type in the sense that it can tell you whether these instances are equal or not. In addition, you can also add the ability to sort these objects just as you sort objects of basic data types, such as DATE, NUMBER, or VARCHAR2. In order for Oracle to be able to sort object instances, the object type must contain either one of the following two methods:

- **MAP method.** This method is a function that maps the object instance to a hash value, which then is used to sort the object. The data type of the return value of the map function can be DATE, NUMBER, or VARCHAR2. The keyword MAP should precede the mapping function in the object type definition and body. Figure 11.6 shows the object type `point_t` discussed earlier, in which the function `GetDistance` is defined as a MAP function. Given the implementation of this function, you can easily see that point objects will be ordered based on their distance from the origin of the coordinate system.

```
CREATE TYPE point_t AS OBJECT (
  x  NUMBER;
  y  NUMBER;
  MAP MEMBER FUNCTION GetDistance RETURN NUMBER,
  MEMBER FUNCTION GetDistance (p point_t) RETURN NUMBER,
  MEMBER FUNCTION GetMidPoint RETURN point_t,
  MEMBER FUNCTION GetMidPoint (p point_t) RETURN point_t,
  MEMBER FUNCTION AddPoint (p point_t) RETURN point_t,
  MEMBER FUNCTION SubtractPoint (p point_t) RETURN
point_t
);
```

FIGURE 11.6 The object type `point_t` with a MAP function.

- **ORDER method.** An alternative way to sort objects is to define a method that compares the object with another object. This method is preceded by the keyword ORDER and returns a negative number, zero, or a positive number if the object whose method is invoked is less than, equal, or greater than the input object. Figure 11.7 shows the definition of the object type `point_t` with the ORDER method `Compare`. Figure 11.8 shows the simple, one-line implementation of this method. When sorting a set of objects using the ORDER method, Oracle needs to compare them individually. For large sets, this may degrade the performance of the operation, therefore you should consider using the MAP function.

The discussion so far could apply to any language that supports objects. However, what is special about the Object Option in Oracle8 is that object in-

```
CREATE TYPE point_t AS OBJECT (
  x  NUMBER;
  y  NUMBER;
  MEMBER FUNCTION GetDistance RETURN NUMBER,
  MEMBER FUNCTION GetDistance (p point_t) RETURN NUMBER,
  MEMBER FUNCTION GetMidPoint RETURN point_t,
  MEMBER FUNCTION GetMidPoint (p point_t) RETURN point_t,
  MEMBER FUNCTION AddPoint (p point_t) RETURN point_t,
  MEMBER FUNCTION SubtractPoint (p point_t) RETURN
point_t
  ORDER MEMBER FUNCTION Compare (p point_t) RETURN NUMBER
);
```

FIGURE 11.7 The object type `point_t` with an ORDER function.

```
ORDER MEMBER FUNCTION Compare(p point_t) RETURN NUMBER IS
  selfDistance NUMBER;
  pDistance NUMBER;
BEGIN
  selfDistance := x*x + y*y;
  pDistance := p.x*p.x + p.y*p.y;
  RETURN (selfDistance - pDistance);
END;
```

FIGURE 11.8 The implementation of the ORDER method Compare of the object type `point_t`.

stances may be closely associated with objects stored in the database. Therefore, the methods defined in the object type could be part of SQL statements, like SELECT, INSERT, or UPDATE. In order for these statements to be executed successfully, the member methods have to follow a small number of rules aimed at limiting their references to and dependency from other schema objects, like tables and stored packages. For example, a method cannot be invoked from a SQL statement if it inserts, updates, or deletes data from one or more tables. You can enlist the PL/SQL compiler to help you define and implement such methods. The pragma RESTRICT_REFERENCES indicates to the compiler a method and the level of restrictions placed on it. When the compiler compiles this method, it uses the pragma definition to verify that the method is not violating any of the rules defined by the pragma. Figure 11.9 shows how you can inform the compiler that the function `GetArea` should read no database state (RNDS), write no database state (WNDS), read no package state (RNPS), and write no package state (RNPS).

11.2.3 WORKING WITH OBJECT INSTANCES

In order to create instances of objects in PL/SQL program units or even store them in database objects, you must first create their object types in the schema as described in the previous two sections. Then you can declare and initialize ob-

```
CREATE TYPE circle_t AS OBJECT (
  center   point_t,
  radius   NUMBER,
  MEMBER FUNCTION GetArea RETURN NUMBER,
  PRAGMA RESTRICT_REFERENCES(GetArea, RNDS, WNDS, RNPS,
WNPS)
);
```

FIGURE 11.9 Using the pragma RESTRICT_REFERENCES.

jects, and access their attributes and methods. Figure 11.10 shows the contents of a Developer/2000 PL/SQL procedure which takes as arguments the coordinates of two points on the plane (X1, Y1, X2, and Y2). The procedure calculates the coordinates of the midpoint and displays them in the message line.

The declaration section of this procedure declares three instances of object type `point_t`. The first two instances are also initialized using the default constructor of the object type and the values passed by the arguments. The body of the trigger first compares the two points. If they are equal, the situation is trivial and the message 'The points are not distinct' is displayed to the user. Recall that two objects are equal if and only if their attributes are mutually equal. If the points are not equal, the method `GetMidPoint` on object A is invoked. The object B is passed as an argument to this method and the object C is returned. This object contains the coordinates of the midpoint which are displayed to the users in the message line. As you can see, the familiar "dot" notation is used to access the attributes of an object as well as to invoke any of the methods you have defined.

Let us revisit now the object type `circle_t` defined in Figure 11.3 earlier in the chapter. This object contains an object of type `point_t` that describes the center of the circle. Suppose now that you are developing an application that deals with a large number of concentric circles, that is, circles that have a common point on the plane as their center. There are two disadvantages with the current definition of `circle_t`. First, for each circle, you will create a `point_t` object instance to hold the coordinates of the center. Obviously, you will consume memory locations to store identical object instances for these circles. Second, suppose your users want to move the center of these circles to a new point on the plane.

```
PROCEDURE MidPoints(X1 NUMBER, Y1 NUMBER, X2 NUMBER, Y2
NUMBER) IS
  A point_t := point_t(X1, Y1);
  B point_t := point_t(X2, Y2);
  C point_t := point_t(NULL,NULL);
BEGIN
  IF (A = B) THEN
    MESSAGE('The points are not distinct.');
ELSE
    C := A.GetMidPoint(B);
    MESSAGE('MidPoint coordinates are: X=['||C.x||'],
Y=['||C.x||'].');
END IF;
END;
```

FIGURE 11.10 Using object instances in a PL/SQL program unit.

```
CREATE TYPE circle_t AS OBJECT (
  center    REF point_t;
  radius    NUMBER;
  MEMBER FUNCTION GetArea RETURN NUMBER
);
```

FIGURE 11.11 Using REF modifiers in the object type definition.

You application will have to assign the new coordinates to the center objects of each circle.

Clearly what you need here is a way to create only one instance for the center point and refer to it from all the circles that need it. This way, you will not store multiple instances of the same object and you will have only one object to maintain. In PL/SQL, references or pointers to objects are called *refs*. Figure 11.11 shows the revised definition of the object type `circle_t` in which the attribute circle is a reference to an object of data type `point_t`.

For each object instance created, Oracle generates a universally unique identifier, called the Object Identifier, or simply OID. Attributes or variables that reference another object are assigned the OID of an object instance. The PL/SQL block shown in Figure 11.12 declares one `point_t` object `A`, a reference to it `A_ref`, and two `circle_t` objects `C1` and `C2`. The first statement of the block stores the reference to the object `A` in the variable `A_ref`. Then the point is initialized to the origin of coordinates. After that, two circles are initialized. These circles share the same origin pointed at by the OID of the center point. Their radii are 10 and 20 units, respectively.

As the example shown in Figure 11.12 hints, the OID of an object is not directly accessible. Similarly, the reverse operation, that is getting the actual object

```
DECLARE
  A point_t := point_t(NULL, NULL);
  A_ref REF point_t;
  C1 circle_t := circle_t(NULL, NULL);
  C2 circle_t := circle_t(NULL, NULL);
BEGIN
  SELECT DEREF(A_ref) INTO A FROM DUAL;
  A := point_t(0, 0);
  C1 := circle_t(A_ref, 10);
  C2 := circle_t(A_ref, 20);
END;
```

FIGURE 11.12 Assigning object references to REF attributes.

referenced by the OID, is not yet available in PL/SQL. A workaround to both these problems is to use the SQL operator DEREF. This operator must be used in a SELECT statement and returns the value of the object in a predefined variable. Typically, the SELECT statement is issued against the dummy table DUAL as in Figure 11.12.

Figure 11.13 expands the PL/SQL block presented in Figure 11.12 in the form of a procedure that takes as arguments the coordinates of two points on the plane (X1, Y1, X2, and Y2). First, the procedure initializes the circles C1 and C2 to the point (X1, Y1). Then, the center of the objects is moved to the point (X2, Y2). Finally, the centers of the circles are dereferenced and their coordinates are printed in the message console of the Developer/2000 Forms application.

The examples used here have been very simple in order to allow you to focus on the concepts rather than on implementation details. However, the real power of concepts such as referencing and dereferencing is realized only when large and complex objects are stored persistently in database structures. The following section will cover details on this topic and will show you how to insert and manipulate objects instances using SQL statements.

```
PROCEDURE MoveCircles(X1 NUMBER, Y1 NUMBER, X2 NUMBER, Y2
NUMBER) IS
  A point_t;
  B point_t;
  A_ref REF point_t;
  C1 circle_t;
  C2 circle_t;
BEGIN
  SELECT DEREF(A_ref) INTO A FROM DUAL;
  A := point_t(X1, Y1);
  C1 := circle_t(A_ref, 10);
  C2 := circle_t(A_ref, 20);
  A := A.AddPoint(point_t(X2,Y2));
  SELECT DEREF(C1.center) INTO B FROM DUAL;
  MESSAGE('C1 new coordinates are:
X=['||B.x||'],Y=['||B.y||'].');
  SELECT DEREF(C2.center) INTO B FROM DUAL;
  MESSAGE('C2 new coordinates are:
X=['||B.x||'],Y=['||B.y||'].');
END;
```

FIGURE 11.13 Accessing referenced objects with the DEREF operator.

11.3 STORING OBJECTS IN THE ORACLE8 DATABASE

In the examples shown in the previous section, the object types you defined were used as data types for attributes of other objects or as data types for PL/SQL variables. Oracle8 allows you to use these object types as data types for columns in a table object. It also allows you to create tables that will store instances of a defined data type. Figure 11.14 shows the definition of two the object types `movie_t` and `address_t` from the MRD application. Figure 11.15 shows three tables that use these definitions. The table MOVIES is an object table that stores instances of `movie_t`. The table CUSTOMERS is like the other tables you have seen so far, except that one of its columns, ADDRESS is of data type `address_t`. And finally, the table RENTALS contains the column MOVIE_OID that references a movie stored in the object table MOVIES.

11.3.1 SELECTING OBJECTS

When selecting objects from the database, you use their attributes in any of the clauses of the SELECT statement. Two examples of such statements are shown below:

```
SELECT m.title, m.rating
FROM movies_obj m
WHERE m.actor = 'Anthony Hopkins';
SELECT c.address.zip, count(*)
FROM customers_obj c
WHERE c.address.state = 'VA'
GROUP BY c.address.ZIP;
```

There are two operators that are closely related to the use of objects in SELECT statements. They are VALUE and REF. The first operator returns the value of an object. The second operator returns the reference to a particular object instance. Recall from the discussion about refs in Section 11.2.3 that the SQL operator DEREF is used to return the object pointed to by a reference value. The statements shown in Figure 11.16 use each of these operators. The first one uses VALUE to select an object from table MOVIES with a given ID. The second one uses REF to return the OID of the movie object retrieved by the first statement. And the last statement returns the same object but this time by dereferencing the OID returned by the second statement.

11.3.2 INSERTING OBJECTS

You can use the standard INSERT statement discussed in Chapters 9 and 10 to insert records in object tables or in tables that contain object columns. The following

```
CREATE TYPE movie_t AS OBJECT (
  id        NUMBER,
  title     VARCHAR2(30),
  director  VARCHAR2(30),
  actor     VARCHAR2(30),
  actress   VARCHAR2(30),
  rating    VARCHAR2(8)
);

CREATE TYPE address_t AS OBJECT (
  street    VARCHAR2(30),
  city      VARCHAR2(30),
  state     VARCHAR2(2),
  zip       VARCHAR2(10)
);
```

FIGURE 11.14 Two object type definitions from the MRD application.

```
CREATE TABLE movies OF movie_t;

CREATE TABLE customers (
  id         NUMBER,
  last_name  VARCHAR2(30),
  first_name VARCHAR2(30),
  phone      VARCHAR2(14),
  dob        DATE,
  member_dt  DATE,
  address    address_t
);

CREATE TABLE rentals (
  customer_id NUMBER,
  movie_OID  REF movie_t,
  rent_dt    DATE,
  return_dt  DATE,
  daily_rate NUMBER(4, 2)
);
```

FIGURE 11.15 Database table objects that use object type definitions.

```
DECLARE
  m_obj movie_t;
  m_ref REF movie_t;
BEGIN
  SELECT VALUE(m)
  INTO m_obj
  FROM movies_obj m
  WHERE ID = '121';

  SELECT REF(m)
  INTO m_ref
  FROM movies_obj m
  WHERE ID = '121';

  SELECT DEREF(m_ref)
  INTO m_obj
  FROM DUAL;
END;
```

FIGURE 11.16 Using the operators VALUE, REF, and DEREF.

statements insert two records in the tables MOVIES_OBJ and CUSTOMERS_OBJ, respectively:

```
INSERT INTO movies_obj
VALUES (123, 'Speed', NULL, NULL, 'Sandra Bullock', 'PG-
13');

INSERT INTO customers_obj
VALUES (21, 'Johnson', 'Michelle', NULL, NULL, NULL,
       address_t('123 Commerce Street', 'Springfield',
'VA', '22152'));
```

As you can see from the second statement, the default constructor method provided by Oracle must be used in order to insert data in a columns that contains object instances. If the table is a table of objects, the constructor is not required, as the first example shows.

When inserting object references, you may find very handy the RETURNING clause of the INSERT statement. This clause returns the reference to the newly inserted object to a PL/SQL variable. This reference can than be used for further processing without the need to query the database for it. Figure 11.17

```
DECLARE
movie_ref REF movie_t;
BEGIN
  INSERT INTO movies_obj m
  VALUES (movie_t(123, 'Speed', NULL, NULL, 'Sandra
Bullock', 'PG-13'))
  RETURNING REF(m) INTO movie_ref;

  INSERT INTO RENTALS_obj
  VALUES (21, movie_ref, '02-SEP-98', NULL, 0.99);
END;
```

FIGURE 11.17 Inserting object references using the RETURNING clause.

shows a PL/SQL anonymous block that inserts an object in the table MOVIES and then records a rental transaction for the new object in the table RENTALS.

You can also insert objects in an object table that are returned by a query. Assuming that a table called R_MOVIES has been created, the following statement inserts in this table all the movies rated R from the object table MOVIES. Notice in this statement the operator VALUE which returns the value of the objects retrieved by the subquery. Alternatively, you could have used the familiar SELECT * form of the subquery.

```
INSERT INTO R_movies
  SELECT VALUE(m) FROM MOVIES_OBJ m
    WHERE m.rating = 'R';
```

11.3.3 UPDATING OBJECTS

As with the INSERT statement, you can use the traditional version of the UPDATE statement or one that uses the constructor of an object type. The following statements update the ZIP_CODE of the customer with ID 21. Notice that when you use the constructor method, you need to provide the correct values for all the attributes of the object and not only the ones that you want to modify.

```
UPDATE customers_obj c
  SET c.address.zip = '22153'
  WHERE c.ID = 21;

UPDATE customers_obj
  SET address = address_t('123 Commerce Street',
'Springfield', 'VA', '22153')
  WHERE ID = 21;
```

11.3.4 DELETING OBJECTS

The process of deleting objects from the database is very simple. Here are only two statements for you to inspect:

```
DELETE FROM customers_obj c
WHERE c.address.state = 'VA';

DELETE FROM movies_obj
WHERE movies_obj.actress = 'Sandra Bullock';
```

Notice however that the table RENTALS_OBJ may contain records which reference the movie you just deleted in the second statement above. The record inserted in the statements of Figure 11.17 is one example. For object references, Oracle does not enforce the same referential integrity mechanism similar to the foreign key constraints defined in the relational model. Instead, it leaves the reference dangling. Since at runtime, dangling references always cause errors and unexpected exceptions, you should be careful to nullify all the references to an object that you delete. Thus, the following UPDATE statement should append the DELETE statement shown above:

```
UPDATE rentals
  SET movie_OID = NULL
  WHERE movie_OID IS DANGLING;
```

11.4 COLLECTIONS

Chapter 10 discussed index-by tables as a data type that allows you to introduce array-like structures in you PL/SQL program units. Index-by tables were introduced in version 2 of PL/SQL that came along with Oracle7. Oracle8 expands your ability to define customized tabular structures by introducing nested tables and variable-size arrays (VARRAY). The features of these collection types will be the subject of this section. In the remainder of this section, I will use the term *varray* to denote an object of type VARRAY.

11.4.1 OVERVIEW OF COLLECTIONS

Nested tables and varrays are PL/SQL structures that resemble one-dimensional arrays in the sense that they organize objects of the same data type based on the values of a subscript. These values always begin at 1, unlike array structures in other languages in which the subscript of the first element is 0. Using the subscript, you can access an element in these structures using the subscript. Nested tables and varrays have a number of similarities with objects in Oracle8. Some of them are listed here:

- You need to define a collection (nested table or varray) type before initializing any instances of these collections. However, while object types can be defined only using DDL statements and are stored as part of the schema, collection types may be defined as part of the schema as well as in any PL/SQL program unit. Figure 11.18 shows the DDL statements to create a varray and nested table type in the Oracle8 schema. Figure 11.19 shows how you can define the same types in the DECLARE section of a PL/SQL block.
- Oracle8 allows you to initialize a collection using a constructor method similar to the one used to initialize object instances. Figure 11.19 shows examples of how you declare two collection variables and initialize them.
- Collection types may be the data type of PL/SQL variables as well as object attributes and table columns. Figure 11.18 shows a revised definition of the object `movie_t` introduced in Figure 11.14. In the new object type `movies_t` the attributes DIRECTOR, ACTOR, and ACTRESS are of the var-

```
CREATE TYPE people_t AS VARRAY(10) OF VARCHAR2(30);

CREATE TYPE rental_t AS OBJECT (
  customer_id NUMBER,
  rent_dt     DATE,
  return_dt   DATE,
  daily_rate  NUMBER(4, 2)
);

CREATE TYPE rental_tab_t AS TABLE OF rental_t;

CREATE TYPE movies_t AS OBJECT (
  id       NUMBER,
  title    VARCHAR2(30),
  director people_t,
  actor    people_t,
  actress  people_t,
  rating   VARCHAR2(8)
);
```

FIGURE 11.18 Defining nested table and varray types with DDL scripts.

```
DECLARE
  TYPE people_t IS VARRAY(10) OF VARCHAR2(30);
  TYPE rental_tab_t IS TABLE OF rental_t;

  actors people_t := people_t('Anthony Hopkins', 'Tom
Hanks', 'Robin Williams', 'Gene Hackman');
  Piano_rentals rental_tab_t;
BEGIN
  SELECT customer_id, rent_dt, return_dt, daily_fee
  INTO Piano_rentals
  FROM rental
  WHERE movie_id = '121';
  – Other statements may go here.
END;
```

FIGURE 11.19 Declaring and initializing collection instances in a PL/SQL block.

ray data type `people_t`. This allows you to store up to ten names in each of these attributes rather than just one as in the previous definition.

As you will see in the following section, the similarities between nested tables and varryas extend beyond the ones listed above. They include the way you work with them and the methods defined for each collection type. However, there are also important differences between nested tables and varrays. You need to be aware of them in order to select the appropriate collection in a given situation. The following is a list of these differences:

- For nested tables, the upper bound of the subscript is practically unlimited ($2^{32} - 1$) whereas the upper bound of varrays is fixed at the time of the type declaration.
- Varrays are always compact, with no gaps between their elements, whereas nested tables, like index-by tables, allow you to delete elements from them without compacting the entire structure.
- When stored in database structures, varray data are located in the same database block as the data from the other fields of the table record. The nested table data, on the other hand, are stored in a separate table (hence the term nested table) whose records reside in separate data blocks and may be located in a different tablespace.
- The varray elements are maintained as a block, at the varray level. This means that in order to select, insert, update, or delete an element in the varray, you have to perform the operation on the entire structure, carrying with

you all the other elements, as well. Nested tables on the other hand offer more flexibility and granularity. They allow you to access and manipulate individual records within the table just as you would do with records in a regular Oracle table.

Finally, I conclude this section with a few differences between nested tables and index-by tables:

- The subscript of nested tables is a positive number ranging from 1 to $(2^{32} - 1)$, whereas the subscript of index-by tables may be anywhere in the range $-(2^{32} - 1)$ to $(2^{32} - 1)$, including negative integers.
- Index-by tables are intended to be used in PL/SQL program units and cannot be manipulated with SQL statements. In nested tables, on the other hand, you can use the SQL commands, like SELECT, INSERT, UPDATE, and DELETE, as you would do with a standard Oracle table.
- There is a list of data types that elements of nested tables cannot have but are allowed for in index-by tables. These include BOOLEAN, LONG, LONG RAW, and BINARY_INTEGER.
- Index-by tables are unbounded in the sense that you can store elements in them anywhere in the range of their subscript. Nested tables have a lower bound because their subscript cannot be smaller than 1. Although they have no upper bound, you need to extend them until they include or surpass the desired value of the subscript before storing an element in that position. For example, to store the first element in a nested table, you need to extend it at least by one and then store the element in the first position in the table.
- Typically, nested tables are compact initially and may become sparse as you delete elements from them. Index-by tables on the other hand are sparse to begin with and may be filled in certain regions with elements.

11.4.2 WORKING WITH COLLECTIONS

This section presents examples of the major operations you perform with collection objects. The objects that will be used in this section are shown in Figure 11.20. The statements to create these objects are provided in the file CH11_3.SQL with the companion software. You are already familiar with the varray `people_t` and nested table `rental_tab_t` defined in the previous section. In addition, Figure 11.20 shows the structure of the table MOVIES_TABLE, which will store the values of the columns DIRECTOR, ACTOR, and ACTRESS as in-line varrays and all the rental transactions for a given movie in the out-of-line table RENTALS_TABLE.

Two situations may arise when you work with collections stored in the database. The first one is when you consider them as "black-boxes" and manipulate them like any other data fields in the table record. Figure 11.21 shows a

```
CREATE TYPE people_t AS VARRAY(10) OF VARCHAR2(30);

CREATE TYPE rental_t AS OBJECT (
  customer_id NUMBER,
  rent_dt     DATE,
  return_dt   DATE,
  daily_rate  NUMBER(4, 2)
);

CREATE TYPE rental_tab_t AS TABLE OF rental_t;

CREATE TABLE movies_table (
  id        NUMBER,
  title     VARCHAR2(30),
  director  people_t,
  actor     people_t,
  actress   people_t,
  rating    VARCHAR2(8),
  rentals   rental_tab_t)
NESTED TABLE rentals STORE AS rentals_table;
```

FIGURE 11.20 Definitions of collection types and of a table object.

PL/SQL block with operations from this scenario. In the statements shown in this figure, you insert a movie in the database, update its ACTRESS column, and then select the new record from the database.

The most interesting situation is the one in which you want to access the collection at a more granular level and work with its individual elements. For example, each time a new rental transaction occurs, you will want to insert a new record in the nested table stored in the column RENTALS of the movie in question. When the movie is returned, you want to update the transaction record with the return date; you may also want to see the number of all the transactions generated for a movie on a given date; and finally you may want to delete a transaction from the nested table. Figure 11.22 shows a PL/SQL block with statements that manipulate the records in the nested table along these lines.

Notice that these statements differ from the regular statements you issue against an Oracle table only by the way you define the table name. Normally in clauses like `INSERT INTO <table>`, `UPDATE <table>`, `SELECT ... FROM <table>`, or `DELETE <table>`, you specify the name of a given table from the schema. When the statements are issued against a nested table, you need to use the operand THE to specify the table object. This operand works with a subquery which must return exactly one nested table object. In the examples shown in Fig-

```
DECLARE
  actors     people_t := people_t('Tom Cruise', 'Ed Harris');
  actresses people_t := people_t('Holly Hunter', 'Jeanne
             Tripplehorn');
  rental_trx rental_tab_t := rental_tab_t(
                             rental_t(212, '02-SEP-98', NULL,
                               0.99),
                             rental_t(213, '03-SEP-98', NULL,
                               0.99),
                             rental_t(541, '06-SEP-98', NULL,
                               1.49));
  movie_id NUMBER;
BEGIN
  INSERT INTO movies_table (id, title, actor, rentals)
  VALUES(189, 'The Firm', actors, rental_trx);

  UPDATE movies_table SET actress = actresses WHERE id = 189;

  SELECT id, actor, actress, rentals
  INTO movie_id, actors, actresses, rental_trx
  FROM movies_table
  WHERE id = 189;
END;
```

FIGURE 11.21 Working with collection objects at the object level.

ure 11.22, this subquery returns the nested table stored in the column RENTALS of the movie record with ID 189.

When I listed the differences between nested tables and varrays in the previous section, I mentioned that nested tables allow you to manipulate their elements individually but varrays do not. In the examples shown so far in this section, you have seen how easy it is to select, insert, update, or delete a single element from nested tables. The programming is more involved if you want to perform similar tasks with varray columns. The following is a list of steps you need to follow to accomplish these tasks:

1. Retrieve the varray object into a PL/SQL variable of the same type. If you intend to modify the value on any elements within the object, place a database lock on the record.
2. If you are planning to insert a new element, extend the collection.
3. Loop through all the varray elements until you find the element you want

```
DECLARE
  trx_countNUMBER;
BEGIN
  INSERT INTO THE ( SELECT rentals FROM movies_table
WHERE id=189)
  VALUES ( rental_t(543, '07-SEP-98', NULL, 1.49));

  UPDATE THE ( SELECT rentals FROM movies_table WHERE
id=189)
  SET return_dt = '09-SEP-98'
  WHERE customer_id = 543 and return_dt IS NULL;

  SELECT COUNT(*)
  INTO trx_count
  FROM THE ( SELECT rentals FROM movies_table WHERE
id=189)
  WHERE rent_dt = '07-SEP-98';

  DELETE THE ( SELECT rentals FROM movies_table WHERE
id=189)
  WHERE rent_dt > '01-JAN-90';
END;
```

FIGURE 11.22 Accessing elements of nested tables.

```
DECLARE
  actors   people_t;
  j        INTEGER;
BEGIN
  SELECT actor INTO actors FROM movies_table WHERE id =
158
  FOR UPDATE OF actor;

  actors.EXTEND(2);
  j := actors.LAST - 1;
  actors(j) := 'Gene Hackman';
  actors(j + 1) := 'Hal Holbrook';

  UPDATE movies_table SET actor = actors WHERE id = 158;
END;
```

FIGURE 11.23 Accessing elements of varray objects.

to select, update, or delete, or until you find the place where you want to insert the new element.

4. Perform the desired operation with the selected element.
5. Update the table with the new value of the varray object.

The PL/SQL block shown in Figure 11.23 shows how you could follow these steps in order to add an actor to the list of actors in the movie *The Firm* created in Figure 11.21.

11.5 SUMMARY

The Objects Option of Oracle8 allows you to define abstract data types that encapsulate data attributes with operations on those attributes. It also extends the previous support for collections by introducing nested tables and variable-size arrays. This chapter highlights the major features of objects and collections. Its main topics included:

- **Overview of the Object-Relational Technology**
- **Object Types and Object Instances**
  - Defining Object Types
  - Attributes and Methods
  - Working with Object Instances
- **Storing Objects in the Oracle8 Database**
  - Selecting Objects
  - Inserting Objects
  - Updating Objects
  - Deleting Objects
- **Collections**
  - Overview of Collections
  - Working with Collections

The following table describes the software assets that were discussed in this chapter. From the main HTML page of the software utilities provided with the book follow the links *Software* and *Chapter 11* to access these assets:

ASSET NAME	DESCRIPTION
CH11_1.SQL	SQL files with the statements that create the objects discussed in Section 11.2 of the chapter.
CH11_2.SQL	SQL files with the statements that create the objects discussed in Section 11.3 of the chapter.
CH11_3.SQL	SQL files with the statements that create the objects discussed in Section 11.4 of the chapter.

Part III

DEVELOPER FORMS OBJECTS

When you strip away all the politics, rhetoric and other baggage ..., you find that an object is an instance of some class in which that object is anything that supports three fundamental notions:

- *Encapsulation*
- *Polymorphism*
- *Inheritance*

—Kraig Brockschmidt

Chapter 12

Object-Oriented Analysis and Design

Once the whole is divided, the parts need names.

—Lao Tsu

This chapter returns and expands on the problem of the neighborhood video rental store, which was used in the previous three chapters for the purpose of learning the syntax of SQL and PL/SQL languages. The statements issued and executed in those chapters help you create an idea about the problems that the employees in the store face in their everyday activities. This chapter will analyze in more detail these problems and design the application that will be developed in the coming chapters. The approach taken here is not the one taken traditionally in the analysis and design of database systems with Developer Forms. Because of the many object-oriented features incorporated in the software with the recent and upcoming releases, the more modern and increasingly more popular methodology of object-oriented analysis (OOA) and design (OOD) is used.

12.1 MOVIE RENTAL DATABASE PROBLEM RESTATED

Movie Rental Database (MRD) is an application that will serve the needs of a neighborhood video store. The jobs that employees perform there can be grouped in two broad groups. The first group is the one you are most familiar with, because you interact with it each time you rent or return a movie. The employees fulfilling duties included in this category stay behind counters and serve the customers. The range of services they provide is very broad. Not all of them require the use of the MRD application. Informing a customer about the business hours of the store is such a service. However, most of the functions in this job category will be greatly facilitated by your system. Such duties would be opening a new account for a customer, checking out videos, and responding to customers' inquiries about certain movies, actors, or other information in the system.

The second group includes functions that occur behind the counters, not necessarily in interaction with the customers. Some of these actions are simple such as making sure that videos are in good working condition and rewound when they are returned. Others are more complex such as analyzing the revenue generated by different movies and making decisions on what to buy next based on this analysis.

Your application will accommodate functionality from both groups.

12.2 OBJECT-ORIENTED TERMINOLOGY

The purpose of this section is to explain some of the terms frequently used in object-oriented analysis, design and programming. It also attempts to shed some light on the concepts they represent, and how they apply to Developer Forms programming. You should not consider this section conclusive in nature. As you will see, you will return to concepts mentioned here later in the chapter when you will use them to design the MRD application. You will put to practice these concepts in the chapters to come where the application will be developed.

12.2.1 OBJECTS, CLASSES, AND INSTANCES

The word *object* in the everyday life means something that we can touch, feel, or conceive intellectually. In software engineering, an object is something that the user can see and feel on the screen, click on with the mouse, drag from one point, and drop into another. The object in software engineering is an abstract representation of the real world. For example, in the real world, we consider videos as objects. But in the MRD application videos are represented by a set of data items on the screen. Through the power of intellectual abstraction, we establish one or more conventional rules similar to this. In other words, we define the objects involved in the application. The purpose of this analysis is to establish some order and to group the amount of information that the system will process.

The colloquial language that we use at home, workplace, or school contains a considerable amount of fuzziness. When we refer to a table in our conversation, in some circumstances we may be thinking of a particular coffee table, and in other circumstances about all the tables as a category of objects. The marvelous information processing machine that is in our heads, the brain, is able to use a whole range of other inputs from the context or the situation and establish the appropriate meaning of the word. In software systems, where we tend to discard information deemed to be irrelevant to the problem, some additional conventions must be established in order to avoid this fuzziness. Thus, the concepts class and instance are introduced.

A class is the generalization of the characteristics that a group of objects have in common. The class Table would represent all the tables in the world, and the class Customer would represent all the customers that do business with our video rental store. The instance, on the other hand, is specific information about a particular object in the class. The coffee table in your living room is an instance of class Table; Mary Jones is an instance of class Customer.

> **TIP**
>
> The concepts described above are encountered, under different names, in more traditional approaches to software engineering. In relational databases for example, the concept of entity could substitute the concept of class to a great extent. When the database is physically implemented, tables represent these entities, or classes. Each table is populated with records, or instances of the entity. On the front-end, if the application is implemented in Developer Forms, the entities are represented by blocks. Each record displayed in the block is an instance of the entity.

12.2.2 ATTRIBUTES

From what I said above, you can conclude that common characteristics of similar objects can be grouped together in an abstract class. These characteristics are called attributes of the class. Each object instance derived from that class will, by definition, have the same attributes as the parent class. Imagine for a moment an Developer Forms block that represents the class Customer on the screen. Attributes of this class such as data type of FIRST_NAME, or maximum length of LAST_NAME, will be the same for all the instances or records of that class.

The concept of variables is introduced with the attributes. Settings that do not change from instance to instance are called class variables. They are given a value when the class is created and this value remains the same during the life of the class. There is a second type of variables called instance variables, whose value changes from instance to instance. In the example above, the contents of data items such as FIRST_NAME and LAST_NAME, are instance variables. Their values will generally change from record to record.

12.2.3 METHODS

In real life, objects are not a static picture of data, frozen in time. They interact with and constantly act upon each other. We buy and drive cars, rent and watch videos, take exams, or pass tests. This dynamic scenario of our life is reflected in the software systems we create. These systems perform actions upon data, from the simplest to the most complicated ones. Every computer system, whether it is programmed according to structured methodology principles or using object-oriented tools and approach must fulfill this requirement. The innovative approach that object-oriented programmers introduced in software engineering is not in what can be done as much as in how intuitively this can be done. The object-oriented methodology premise is that the computer models you create will be closer to reality and easier to manipulate if they reflect this reality faithfully. Since objects and actions go hand-in-hand in real life, that's how they must be implemented in a software system.

An object-oriented application bundles in one class not only the attributes and data that the class represents, but also actions to be performed upon these data. These actions are known as methods associated with the object class. These methods, when executed, manipulate the data encapsulated in the class structure. They may also initiate actions on other objects. True object-oriented programming languages allow access to the methods of a class only through that class. The methods cannot be called directly like functions or procedures in structured programming. In Oracle applications, methods associated with objects are called triggers.

12.2.4 MESSAGES

In the structured methodology, programmers are in the driver's seat. They establish a flow in the internal logic of the program, which users must follow in order to perform the actions they need. Users are offered a very limited choice of options, and typically are reduced to answering Yes/No type of questions. The object-oriented approach is different. Programmers no longer control the flow of the application. In fact, there is no deterministic way in which an application is executed. At any point in time, users have a variety of places to click on, windows to browse, lists to select from, etc. It is very unusual here to find long subroutines with several levels of calls to other routines. What you have instead is objects and small pieces of code attached to them. These objects patiently wait for the user to interact with them. The interaction can take several aspects. It can be a mouse-click, a change in the value of the data item, request for validation of the data entered, creation of a new record, etc. Whenever this happens, it is said that the object received a message. Another way to express this is that an event occurred for the object. Each object has a certain number of events, or messages, that can serve as a wake-up call. These events, commonly known as the protocol of the object, are mostly predefined, based on the type of object, but can also be defined by the programmer.

When the object receives a message that is part of its protocol, it checks to see if there is a method or trigger associated with it. In case there is one, the method is executed; otherwise, the object does not react to the message. In Developer Forms, the number of messages an object can receive can be quite large, but most of them are ignored or handled by the default functionality. For example, it is typical for push buttons to respond to the mouse click, but not to dozens of other actions the user may try to do. Chapter 19 will discuss in larger detail the events and triggers in Developer Forms applications.

12.2.5 INHERITANCE

Inheritance is the object-oriented programming principle that allows you to reuse object classes developed and tested previously. It reflects the gradual changes between reality objects that share similar characteristics, but have differences in a limited number of attributes or methods. Imagine, for example, a class of objects called Clothes. Some of its attributes may be Size, Price, Date of Purchase. Some methods associated with it could be Wash and Iron. Pants is a new class that inherits all the attributes and methods of class Clothes. This class may have additional attributes added to it such as Length and Seam. If there is a need to add more specific instructions for washing and ironing pants, the methods inherited from the parent class can be modified or overridden.

In the current version of Developer Forms you can create classes based on properties of objects. Triggers may be attached to these classes as well. These classes are used to assign the set of properties and associated methods to an object using the inheritance mechanism.

12.2.6 ENCAPSULATION

As mentioned earlier, encapsulation is a method to group logically related data together with the methods that access and modify them. It is also a method to protect the data in the class from unwanted and potentially destructive access. A class is truly encapsulated in an object-oriented sense if its attributes are modifiable only through the methods of the class. The interface offered by this class to the outside application must be limited to the specifications of these methods. It is not necessary for the rest of the application to know how the methods are implemented internally, and to rely on or utilize this implementation. If that were allowed, a minor change in the body of the method could result in modifications throughout the application. If, on the other hand, the implementation of the method is hidden, the changes will be transparent to the rest of the application. PL/SQL offers a solid implementation of encapsulation through packages. These objects will be discussed in Chapter 19 as well.

12.2.7 POLYMORPHISM

Polymorphism is the object-oriented technique that allows the same message to generate different responses in different objects. The concept of polymorphism is encountered frequently in everyday life. Suppose, for example, that there is a conference of Developer Forms developers scheduled in three months. The organizing committee issues a call for papers to all the professionals in its mailing list. At this point, the committee does not care how each individual will react to the message. Some may prepare a demo, some may prepare a presentation, some may ignore the message altogether. The fact remains that the same message will generate different responses in different persons. Or take another example. Each year, the federal government announces the date in April when taxes are due. Different people will react differently to the message. Some will prepare the taxes themselves, some will hire an accountant, some will buy a tax preparation software package, etc. Again, the same message makes different people react differently.

In Developer Forms, the polymorphism can be seen and used in several instances. For example, the built-in routine CREATE_RECORD will always create an empty record in any base table block, despite the number of items in the block, or the structure of the block itself. Furthermore, PL/SQL allows you to create program units with the same name, but that take variables of different data types. Based on these variables, different actions can be taken, but these differences remain transparent to the application that issues the call to the function.

12.3 STRUCTURED DESIGN VERSUS OBJECT-ORIENTED DESIGN

The process of analyzing the requirements for a software system follows a certain sequence of steps, recommended by the particular methodology you are following. The design of a system according to structured programming methodology will proceed following the steps listed below.

1. Define the data used by the application. In this step, software engineers define the entities used in the application, their attributes, and the type of relations they form with each other. Based on this analysis, a logical design for the database is prepared and stored in the system's knowledge repository. The logical database design includes, among others, entity-relationship diagrams, data dictionaries, and business rules that affect data items.
2. Create the physical database design model. Based on the logical database design, database specialists define the physical database structures that will store the information contained in the system. This step more or less concludes the design of the back-end, or the database side of the application.
3. Identify and describe each function that the future system will perform. Complex functions are divided into simpler subfunctions until a satisfactory level of simplicity is reached. For each function, systems analysts define its input and output data, and outline its functionality. The outcome of this step is the function hierarchy diagram of the system.
4. Define and describe the dependency among processes in the system. In other words, define how, and under what conditions processes will pass the control to other processes. The outcome of this step is the process-flow diagrams, also known as data-flow diagrams. The last two steps often are merged together during system design sessions.
5. Design modules, procedures and functions of the system to reflect the analysis performed in the previous two steps. This step also includes designing screens, windows, menus, and other user-interface elements of the front-end application.

As you can see, the attention of the structured methodology shifts from the data objects (Steps 1 and 2) to the actions or processes that occur in the system (Steps 3, 4, and 5). The function hierarchy diagrams and data-flow diagrams, when implemented by the software engineers, will inherently define the logical flow of the application. Users are often restricted to follow the system in order to perform the business transactions implemented there.

Object-oriented programming on the other hand, keeps the designers' attention focused on the objects. The first two steps of the traditional approach are still preserved, although different terminology may be used in each of them. The next steps though are quite different.

3. Visualize the conduct of each object when it interacts with the users and specify the methods associated with it. As explained in the previous section, these methods maintain a low profile in the application. They are services that the object offers to the users only when they request them. Users request these services by sending messages to the objects. The number of methods that can be associated with an object is practically unlimited. However, a well-designed object has only a few pertinent methods explicitly defined. The rest of them are handled by the implicit default processing of the application. In Developer Forms for example, to create a new record in a block, you may simply invoke the method CREATE_RECORD, without having to implement it.
4. Define the protocol of the object, or the messages that will activate each method. Messages can be generated by users' actions, by methods of other objects, by internal processes such as navigation, data validation, database interactions, etc. However, as in the previous step, you do not identify every message that the object can intercept, but only the few ones that need special attention. These two steps are often performed together. The results are presented in a unified table known as the control-by-message matrix of the application. The first row of the matrix contains the objects involved in the system; the first column lists the messages that they can intercept. The matrix cell at the intersection of an object column with a message row contains the method of that object that is activated by the message. For an example of a control-by-message matrix see Figure 12.8 later in the chapter.
5. Design screens, windows, menus, and other user-interface elements of the application to reflect the object-oriented design. The layout of the application should make the process of activating the methods associated with objects clear, easy, and intuitive. In this step, you also identify objects that will benefit from inheritance, or that will respond differently to the same message.

Some debate exists in the IT community about the effectiveness of object-oriented techniques in applications that use relational databases. Object-oriented purists require that object class structures and their instances be stored in object-oriented databases. The advent of object-relational databases, including Oracle8, has allowed developers to take a more pragmatic approach to this problem by using the best that both sides have to offer. These databases utilize the extensive functionality, robustness, and maturity that relational database systems have achieved and enhance it with object-oriented features. In general, applications nowadays use these databases for the back-end implementation of the system. The front-end applications are designed and implemented following object-oriented principles. This is a *modus vivendi* reached in many modern data processing centers today.

12.4 DESIGNING THE MRD APPLICATION

In this section, I will apply the steps described in the previous section to design the Movie Rental Database Application.

12.4.1 OBJECTS DEFINITION AND ENTITY-RELATIONSHIP DIAGRAMS

By carefully analyzing the business process of the video store, it is not difficult to conclude that the main entities of this application are Customer, Movie, Tape, and Rental. Customer represents the typical clients of the store who open an account and rent tapes for a limited amount of time. Movie is a play, story, or event in the form of a motion picture. A movie can be seen in movie theaters, television, etc., but, for the purpose of this application, it is copied in one or more tapes and rented to customers. Tape is a magnetic tape used to record pictures of a movie. Customers in the MRD application rent one or more tapes to watch the movies they contain. Finally, Rental is the object that represents the transaction between a customer and the video store in which a tape is rented for one or more days.

The definitions provided above contain inherently the relationships between the objects in the MRD application. Nevertheless, they need further clarification. Relationships, or relations, are significant associations or forms of interactions between objects. On both sides of a relation reside entities. Depending on the number of objects from one entity that can be associated with objects from the other entity, several types of entity relationships are distinguished. These types are shown and explained in Figure 12.1.

Figure 12.2 represents the entity-relationship diagram for the MRD application. There are three relationships between the entities of this application. They can be worded as follows:

1. Each Customer may initiate zero or more Rental transactions. Each Rental transaction must be initiated by one and only one Customer.
2. Each Tape may be part of zero or more Rental transactions. Each Rental transaction must include one and only one Tape.
3. Each Movie may be stored in one or many Tapes. Each Tape must contain one and only one movie.

After the main entities of the application are defined, each entity is analyzed in detail to identify their attributes. As in other examples in this book, the characteristics of attributes that you try to capture in this stage are name, data type, length, referential integrity constraints such as primary key, foreign key and uniqueness.

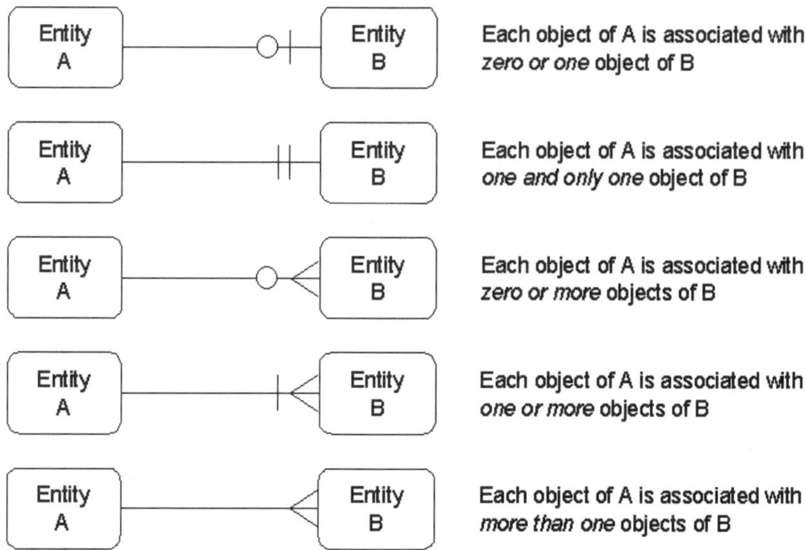

FIGURE 12.1 Types of entity relationships.

Figure 12.3 shows the attribute definitions for entity Customer. Figure 12.4 shows the attribute definitions for entity Tape. Figure 12.5 shows the attribute definitions for entity Movie. Finally, Figure 12.6 shows the attribute definitions for entity Rental.

The next step after the logical design of the database is the physical design. In this phase, the database package is selected, and its particular features utilized. Each entity identified in the logical design is mapped to a table in the physical design. The tables for the MRD application will be CUSTOMERS, TAPES, MOVIES, RENTALS. Note that it is customary to use the plural of an entity's name as the name of its corresponding table. The storage parameters for each table are defined based on the analysis of data volume for each entity.

Other structures designed in this phase are sequence number generators, indexes, stored program units, and database triggers. The MRD application will use a sequence to generate the internal identification numbers for instances of the entities defined above. Oracle Server automatically creates indexes for all the columns of a table that are part of the primary key. These indexes will be sufficient for the needs of your application, given the modest size of the MRD database. The program units and database triggers are part of the application logic placed on the back-end rather than the front-end application. They are considered methods associated with the database objects. The following section defines the methods of the MRD application in general, and the stored program units in particular.

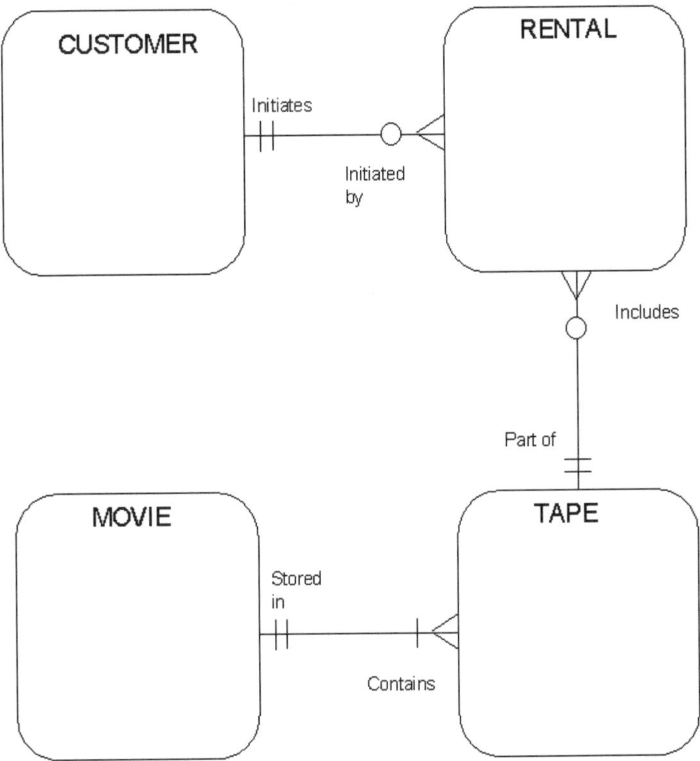

FIGURE 12.2 Entity relationship diagram for Movie Rental Database.

In order to follow the development activities discussed in the following chapters, you must create the MRD tables in your database and load sample data in them. The section *Installation of MRD Database Objects for Part III* in Appendix B provides the necessary instructions to complete this task.

12.4.2 METHODS AND MESSAGES

This section defines the methods that will be encapsulated together with the data attributes of the entities in the MRD application. At the same time, the messages or events that activate these methods will be specified. It is important to point out that at this stage you identify only the most important methods and messages in the highest level of the application. As you progress further in the development process, you will identify and document additional methods attached to objects in lower levels of the hierarchy of objects.

Figure 12.7 presents graphically the MRD objects and the specifications of their methods.

ATTRIBUTES	DATA TYPE	LENGTH	CONSTRAINTS	DESCRIPTION
Customer Id	NUMBER	6	PK, fixed length	Membership Number
First Name	VARCHAR2	30	Not NULL	
Last Name	VARCHAR2	30	Not NULL	
Gender	CHAR	1	(M)ale, (F)emale	
Date Of Birth	DATE			
Membership Date	DATE			
Status	VARCHAR2	1	(A)ctive; (G)ood Credit; (B)ad Credit	
Address Line	VARCHAR2	50		
City	VARCHAR2	30		
State	CHAR	2		
Zip Code	VARCHAR2	10		
Day-time Telephone Number	VARCHAR2	10		
Evening Telephone Number	VARCHAR2	10		
Comedy	CHAR	1	Y if Preferred, NULL otherwise	
Drama	CHAR	1	Y if Preferred, NULL otherwise	
Mystery	CHAR	1	Y if Preferred, NULL otherwise	
Foreign	CHAR	1	Y if Preferred, NULL otherwise	

FIGURE 12.3 Attributes for entity Customer

ATTRIBUTES	DATA TYPE	LENGTH	CONSTRAINTS	DESCRIPTION
Tape Id	NUMBER	6	PK, fixed length	Internal Tracking Number
Movie Id	NUMBER	6	PK. FK; points to MOVIE.ID	Movie Id Contained in tape
Status	CHAR	1		(A)vailable; (R)ented; Re(T)urned

FIGURE 12.4 Attributes for entity Tape

ATTRIBUTES	DATA TYPE	LENGTH	CONSTRAINTS	DESCRIPTION
Movie Id	Number	6	PK, fixed length	Internal Tracking Number
Title	VARCHAR2	30	Not NULL	Not NULL
Status	CHAR	1		(A)vailable; (N)ot Available
Director Name	VARCHAR2	30		
Main Actor	VARCHAR2	30		
Main Actress	VARCHAR2	30		
Producer	VARCHAR2	30		
Producing Company	VARCHAR2	30		
Start Date	DATE			Date when Rentals Began
End Date	DATE			Date when Movie Is Discontinued
Rating	CHAR	1		1 = NR, 2 = PG-13, 3 = R, 4 = NC-17

FIGURE 12.5 Attributes for entity Movie.

Here is a brief description of the methods associated with object Customer.

- **New.** Invoked by the internal event CreateRecord. Creates a new record, and assigns a unique identification number to the customer. Customer status is set to Active.
- **Validate.** Invoked by the internal event ValidateRecord. If the record is newly-entered, check the database to see if the new customer was member before.

ATTRIBUTES	DATA TYPE	LENGTH	CONSTRAINTS	DESCRIPTION
Customer Id	NUMBER	6	PK, fixed length	Customer renting the tape
Tape Id	NUMBER	6	PK, FK; references TAPE.ID	Tape rented by the customer
Rent Date	DATE		PK	
Return Date	DATE			
Daily Rate	NUMBER	4	Between $0.00 and $10.00	

FIGURE 12.6 Attributes for entity Rental.

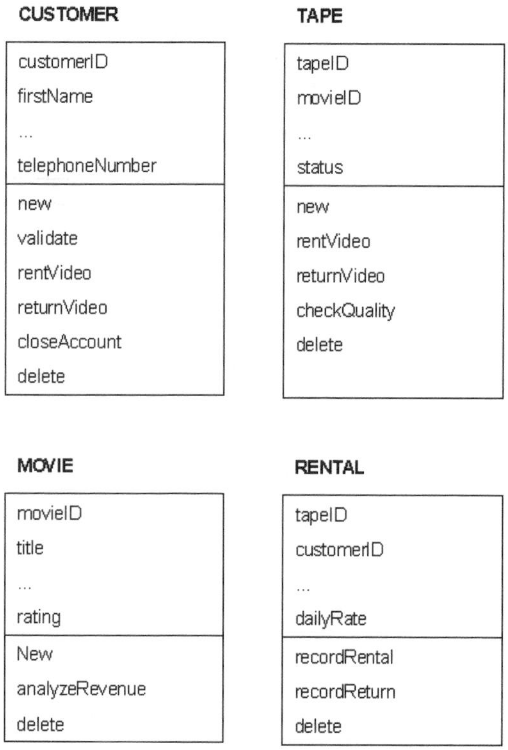

CUSTOMER
customerID
firstName
...
telephoneNumber
new
validate
rentVideo
returnVideo
closeAccount
delete

TAPE
tapeID
movieID
...
status
new
rentVideo
returnVideo
checkQuality
delete

MOVIE
movieID
title
...
rating
New
analyzeRevenue
delete

RENTAL
tapeID
customerID
...
dailyRate
recordRental
recordReturn
delete

FIGURE 12.7 Data and methods encapsulated in Movie Rental Database objects.

- **RentVideo.** Invoked by the user-defined event RentVideo. Check the credit status of the customer
- **ReturnVideo.** Invoked by the user-defined event ReturnVideo. Update the credit status if necessary.
- **CloseAccount.** Invoked by the user-defined event CloseAccount. If the customer has no tapes to return, set the status to Good Credit; otherwise, set the status to Bad Credit.
- **Delete.** Invoked by the internal event DeleteRecord. Sends DeleteRecord(Customer.CustomerId) message to object Rental to delete all the rental transactions initiated by this customer, and deletes current record from Customer.

The following is a list of methods encapsulated with object Movie.

- **New.** Invoked by the internal event CreateRecord. Enter a new movie record, and sent the message CreateRecord to Tape to create one or more tape records for the new movie.

- **AnalyzeRevenue.** Invoked by the user-defined event AnalyzeRevenue. Displays the revenue generated for the specified period.
- **Delete.** Invoked by the internal event DeleteRecord. Sends DeleteRecord(Movie.MovieId) message to object Tape to delete all the tapes for the movie, and deletes the current record from Movie.

The methods of object Tape are listed below.

- **New.** Invoked by the internal event CreateRecord. Enter a new tape for a movie.
- **RentVideo.** Invoked by the user-defined event RentVideo. Set status of tape to Rented.
- **ReturnVideo.** Invoked by the user-defined event ReturnVideo. Set status of tape to Returned. Broadcast the CheckQuality message.
- **CheckQuality.** Invoked by the user defined message CheckQuality. Manually check the tape for problems and rewind it, if necessary. If the tape is in good working conditions, display it in the shelves and set the status to Available. Otherwise, issue DeleteRecord message and discard the tape.
- **Delete.** Invoked by the internal event DeleteRecord. Sends DeleteRecord (Tape.TapeId) message to object Rental to delete all the rental transactions for this tape, and deletes current record from Tape.

Finally, here is a description of the methods of object Rental.

- **RecordRental.** Invoked by the user-defined event RentVideo. Creates a new rental record for the particular customer and tape.
- **RecordReturn.** Invoked by the user-defined event ReturnVideo. Sets the return date to the current date. The appropriate fee is collected from the customer.
- **Delete.** Invoked by the internal event DeleteRecord. Deletes current record from Rental.

Figure 12.8 summarizes the information presented so far in the form of a matrix. The first row of this matrix contains the objects in the MRD application: Customer, Movie, Video, and Rental. The first column of the matrix contains the events or messages generated in the application. The intersection cell of an object with an event contains the name of the method activated in that object by the corresponding event.

	CUSTOMER	MOVIE	VIDEO	RENTAL
CreateRecord	new	new	new	
ValidateRecord	validate			
DeleteRecord	delete	delete	delete	delete
CloseAccount	closeAccount			
RentVideo	rentVideo		rentVideo	recordRental
ReturnVideo	returnVideo		returnVideo	recordReturn
CheckQuality			checkQuality	
AnalyzeRevenue		analyzeRevenue		

FIGURE 12.8 Object-Oriented Matrix for MRD Application.

12.5 USER INTERFACE DESIGN AND CONVENTIONS

At this point, you have an idea about what data entities and business rules the MRD application will cover. The next step before moving to the actual development activities is to create a high-level design of the user interface. Without worrying too much about the implementation details, you identify here the menu structure, types of windows, and any other relevant components that will be part of the application.

12.5.1 THE MDI FRAME

When the users will execute the application, they will first land in a window that does not contain any data items, except for the main menu of the application attached to it. The window will serve as the MDI frame for the MRD application. Its title will be "Movie Rental Database," and the message bar will display information to help users in their data processing activities. The MDI frame window will also contain the application menu. In addition, a vertical and horizontal toolbar will be displayed and available to provide access to the main commands with a click of the mouse. At different points during the use of the application, some menu items may not be available. Upon such conditions, the logic of the application will disable these items by graying them out, as in other Windows applications. Figure 12.9 shows a prototype of the MDI frame for the MRD application.

12.5.2 THE APPLICATION MENU

The menu of the application will contain File, Edit, Tools, Data, Window, and Help submenus. The following paragraphs describe each of these menus:

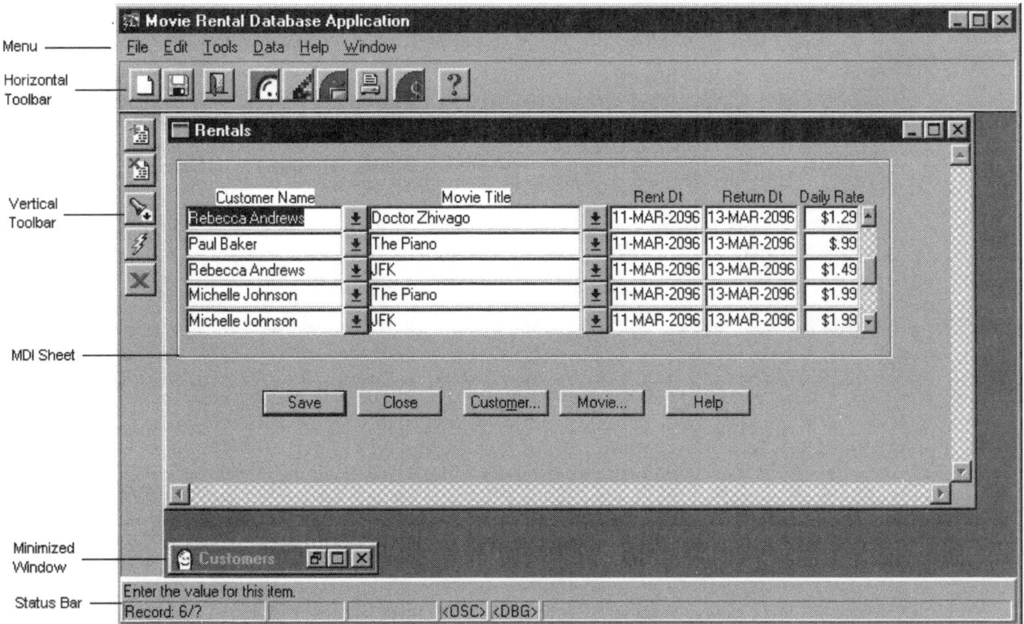

FIGURE 12.9 MDI frame for the MRD application.

- **File.** This menu contains only three items. File | Clear sets the whole application in a clean state, as it is when it is first loaded. File | Save commits changes to the database. File | Exit closes all the open windows and exits the application. These menu items correspond to the first three items of the horizontal toolbar of the MDI frame.
- **Edit.** This menu contains the standard text editing menu items, including Cut, Copy, Paste, and Clear.
- **Tools.** This menu contains menu items that invoke all the other windows in the application. The ellipses ... after the label indicates that a window will appear when the menu item will be selected. The iconic buttons located at the center of the horizontal toolbar will duplicate the functionality of these items.
- **Data.** This menu contains menu items used for database interaction. The first group of these items allows users to insert, duplicate, and delete data in the current block. The second group controls the querying of the database. Items in this menu, except for Duplicate, correspond to the vertical toolbar icons under the editing buttons.

- **Window.** This is the standard MDI menu that allows cascading, and tiling of all open windows, or arranges the icons of minimized ones. The second part of it lists the windows currently open.
- **Help.** This menu displays online help available for the application. The last item, About..., will display a copyright notice and the version of the application.

12.5.3 GUI STANDARDS FOR APPLICATION WINDOWS

As in every MDI application, all the windows and dialog boxes in the MRD application will be displayed and manipulated within the boundaries of the MDI frame window. These windows, also known as MDI sheets, will all share the following characteristics:

- Each window will contain data to support only one business function.
- Windows will have Resize, Minimize, and Maximize capabilities.
- The background color for the windows will be gray.
- All the controls (items, buttons, etc.) will have a 3D look.
- The title bar of the window will be a two- to three-word description of the business function accomplished by the window.
- An appropriate icon must be displayed if the window is in Minimized state (see Figure 11.9). The icon title must be the same as the window title.
- Each window will have at least two standard push buttons: Save and Close. Save will commit changes to the database, and leave the window open. Close will prompt the user to save any uncommitted changes and close the window.
- Text items will have white background color and black text color. Text will be in MS Sans Serif font, size 8.
- Text labels will have gray background color (to match windows background) and black text color. Text will be in MS Sans Serif font, size 8.
- Each navigable item, including any push buttons on the window must have micro-help displayed in the message bar.
- The window must be sized and populated so that horizontal or vertical scrollbars will not be needed to view or access its objects.

Note that these are only suggested standards. You may modify or add to them if you find it necessary during the development process. The main point here is that, whatever the standards are, they must exist, discussed and agreed upon in close interaction with the owners and users of the application. The issue is especially important when developing enterprise-wide applications using several software engineers to create the windows and screens.

12.5.4 WINDOWS AND DIALOG BOXES

This section describes in general terms the layout of each window in the MRD application.

- **Customer.** This window will display data about customers one record at a time. This format will allow users to view all information about a particular customer in the window. This window will be used to enter, update, delete, and query customer records.
- **Movie.** The layout of this window is similar to that of Customer window. The upper part will display the movies in the MRD database one record at a time. The lower part will display the tapes for the current movie. The tapes that are currently available will be displayed first, and those that are already rented will follow.
- **Rental.** Front-desk clerks will use this window to record or update a rental transaction. The upper-left quarter of the window will serve as a retrieval block for the customer; the upper-right one for the movie. Remember that both these entities must be present when a tape is rented or returned. The lower half of the window will display by default the videos that the customer has not returned. Based on the number of the unreturned videos, additional requests for rentals may be turned down. Here the application users may also issue additional queries to review the customer's renting history.
- **Mailing Labels.** This window will be used to generate mailing labels for different groups of customers.
- **Analyze.** There will be two such windows that will be used to analyze the revenue generated by the store. One of them will be display the amount of money customers spend on movie rentals ion a given period of time, summed by zip code. The second window will display the amount in revenue generated by movies that the stores rents, based on their rating category.

Each of these windows can be invoked from the MDI frame by either clicking an iconic button in the toolbar, or by selecting the appropriate menu item. Users will be free to navigate from window to window while they are open. In addition, from the Customer and Movie window, users will be able to open or activate the Rental window to record a particular renting transaction that may occur. Vice versa, from the Rental window, they will be able to navigate to the Customer and Movie windows, in order to retrieve additional information that may be required. In such a case, the contents of the three windows will be synchronized accordingly. Push button items will be created in the respective windows to implement this functionality.

In addition to the windows above, the MRD application will also contain application modal dialog boxes that will supply additional information or will perform specific tasks related to a business function. While these dialog boxes are open, users cannot perform any other activity in the application. However, their ability to run other applications will not be affected. A special type of dialog boxes, Developer Forms' Lists of Values, will be used to enter the appropriate state code in the address of a customer.

The layout of dialog boxes will follow the same guidelines as the ones presented earlier in the chapter. The only difference is that the push button Save will be replaced with OK, or another label that better describes the task accomplished in the dialog box. Activating this button will save the users' settings and close the dialog box.

12.5.5 APPLICATION SECURITY

The users of the applications will be divided in two security groups, according to the job description and their need to view, access, and edit data. The members of the first group will be primarily the employees of the movie rental store that interact with the customers during the business hours of the store. They will have access to Customers, Movie, and Rental windows. They will also be able to print Mailing Labels for the Customers, but will be restricted from accessing the Analyze window. The second group will have unrestricted access on all the windows of the application, including the Analyze window. Members of this group will be the managers and the financial analysts of the movie rental store. The logic of the application will decide in which group a user belongs upon logging to the database. Menu items and iconic buttons in the toolbar will be enabled and disabled accordingly.

12.6 SUMMARY

This chapter presented an overview of object-oriented analysis and design techniques, and how they apply to the Movie Rental Database problem. Some important concepts discussed in this chapter were:

- **Movie Rental Database Problem Restated**
- **Object-Oriented Terminology**
  - Objects, Classes, and Instances
  - Attributes
  - Methods
  - Messages
  - Inheritance

  - Encapsulation
  - Polymorphism
- **Structured Design versus Object-Oriented Design**
- **Designing the MRD Application**
  - Objects Definition and Entity-Relationship Diagrams
  - Methods and Messages
- **User Interface Design and Conventions**
  - The MDI Frame
  - The Application Menu
  - GUI Standards for Application Windows
  - Windows and Dialog Boxes
  - Application Security

The following table describes the software assets that were discussed in this chapter. From the main HTML page of the software utilities provided with the book follow the links *Software* and *Chapter 12* to access these assets:

ASSET NAME	DESCRIPTION
CH12_1.SQL	A SQL*Plus file with statements that create the database objects needed for the MRD application.

Chapter 13

DATA BLOCKS, FRAMES, AND RELATIONS

Go play with the towns you have built of blocks. . . .
—Stephen Vincent Benét

- Types of Blocks
- Creating and Maintaining Data Blocks
- Defining and Maintaining the Layout of Blocks
- Maintaining Block Properties in the Form Builder
- Maintaining Block Properties Programmatically
- Frames
- Relations
- Blocks and Relations for the MRD Application
- Summary

Blocks group together data elements based on the logical relationships that exist among them. In the front-end application, they implement object types or entities manipulated by the middle-tier or back-end layers. In Developer Forms, blocks are not only the means to bundle data, but also define and contain the methods that access and manipulate these data. For example, the block CUSTOMER in the MRD application will be used as a container of data attributes related to the entity CUSTOMER, and, at the same time, will allow you to enter, modify, and maintain these attributes for each customer.

An instance of the data object represented by the block is called a record. In the Form Builder, the term has a broader meaning than the same term used in the context of a relational database. In general, a record may not represent data from just one table. As a matter of fact, it is common to have calculated data items in a block, which are not stored in the database. While a block is an object represented by a node in the Navigator hierarchy tree, records are objects maintained internally by Forms. Their properties and methods can be accessed at runtime by built-in program units. This chapter will discuss in detail the properties and features of blocks and records.

13.1 TYPES OF BLOCKS

Blocks in a Form Builder module may be classified based on a number of criteria. For example, based on the source of the data they display and manipulate, they can be data blocks and control blocks. Data blocks may be master blocks or detail blocks whose records are always coordinated with the record in the master record. Based on the number of records they display to the users, blocks may be single-record or multi-record ones. The following sections discuss each of these types of blocks.

13.1.1 DATA BLOCKS AND CONTROL BLOCKS

As mentioned above, blocks are logical containers of data items in a form. Based on the source of data for these items, blocks are divided into data blocks and control blocks. Data blocks are those blocks whose underlying data source is a database object, a table, a view, a number of stored procedures, or transactional triggers. For such blocks, at least one item in the block is directly linked with a database object. Understandably, the items that correspond to database objects are called data items. Items that do not represent data from database objects are referred to as control items. If all the items in a block are control items, then the block is a control block. There are a few interesting facts that should be noted for base table and control blocks. They are listed in the following paragraphs.

A data block may not share the same name with the database object upon which the block is based. However, base table items in a block based on a table or view must have the same name as the corresponding columns. For example, later in this chapter you will create a multi-record block that will display data from the table CUSTOMERS in the RENTAL window. You will name it CUST_RENT, a different name from the database table. But you will still keep the column names for the items of the block.

A data block may be based on one database table or view at most. However there are situations in which an application needs to display and manipulate data from more than one table. You have two options available in such situations. The first one is to select the table or view that drives the other data and base the block on it. Then, you implement the items that correspond to the remaining columns as control items within the same block. The logic of the application must ensure that these control items communicate correctly with their counterparts in the database. As an example, in the MRD application, the RENTAL block will need to display data from three tables: CUSTOMERS, TAPES, and RENTALS. Because the main functionality of this block is to describe a rental transaction, most of the database interaction will be handled by items that are derived from RENTALS table. For this reason, you will base the block upon this table. Then, programmatically, through triggers, functions, and procedures, you will complete the picture with detailed data about the customer and the video.

The second alternative is to base the block on stored program units that select, insert, update, delete, or lock the data items in the block. These program units operate with index-by table structures. The function that populates the block with data, for example, performs all the queries needed to populate the block items and stores them in an index-by table. When Form Builder needs to query the block, it calls this function and gets all the data from the returned index-by table. Triggers and other front-end application logic objects are no longer needed to return the data from the other tables. As you can notice, no matter which implementation method you decide to use, the block will represent the data in the association in which they occur in real life, although this may not necessarily be the way they are stored in the database.

Data blocks allow you to automatically inherit many of the database object properties when the blocks are created. Data type and length of items are the most trivial ones. In addition, data integrity constraints such as primary keys, foreign keys, required values, and unique values are inherited, if you choose to enforce these constraints when the block is created. When a design and modeling tool like Oracle Designer is used, you may set these and a number of other properties once in the Repository and use the tool to apply them to the database objects or to the module components.

Finally, data blocks greatly reduce the amount of SQL statements you must write in order to retrieve and manipulate the data. Consider, for example, the following scenario:

The database contains a table THE_TABLE with only one column, THE_COLUMN. Two blocks are defined in a Form module. The first one is based on THE_TABLE, and the second one is not. They are called BASE_TABLE and

CONTROL respectively. Your task is to insert a new row in the table, then query the database to redisplay it. Figure 13.1 shows the steps to carry out the tasks with a data block. Figure 13.2 shows the steps to carry the same task with a control block.

As you can see from this picture, the amount of code required in control blocks can be significantly larger than that in data blocks. The task becomes even more complicated if the block displays and manipulates multiple records simultaneously. Keeping track of the status for each record—whether it is newly-inserted, updated, deleted, and so on—is overwhelming for control blocks, but is part of the default functionality of the data block. Naturally, in the applications you will develop, data will be manipulated through data blocks. Control blocks, as the name suggests will be used to further coordinate and enhance the default functionality of Form Builder.

13.1.2 MASTER AND DETAIL BLOCKS

The Master-Detail relationship is a very common one in database applications and reflects the dependency of one or more records (detail records) from a master record. The simplest implementation of such a relationship is a form with one master and one detail block. The Form Builder allows you to create more complex and interesting applications, such as forms with Master-Detail/detail blocks, forms with one master and several detail blocks, and forms with more than one master block driving a single detail block. Relations are the Form Builder objects that allow you to implement relationships among blocks. Section 13.7 later in the chapter will provide more details on relations and how you can use them to implement complex relationships in a form module.

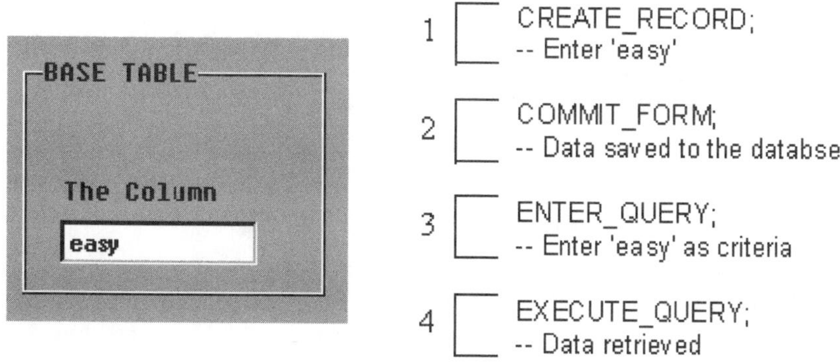

FIGURE 13.1 Data blocks use effectively the default functionality of Form Builder.

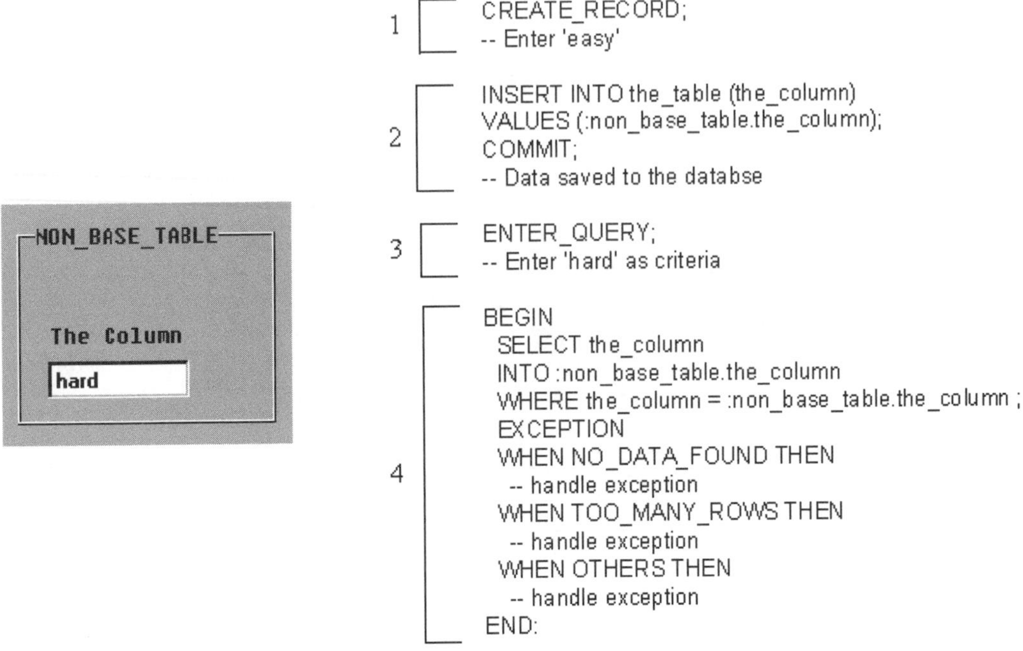

NON_BASE_TABLE
The Column
hard
1
CREATE_RECORD;
-- Enter 'easy'
2
INSERT INTO the_table (the_column)
VALUES (:non_base_table.the_column);
COMMIT;
-- Data saved to the databse
3
ENTER_QUERY;
-- Enter 'hard' as criteria
4
BEGIN
SELECT the_column
INTO :non_base_table.the_column
WHERE the_column = :non_base_table.the_column ;
EXCEPTION
WHEN NO_DATA_FOUND THEN
-- handle exception
WHEN TOO_MANY_ROWS THEN
-- handle exception
WHEN OTHERS THEN
-- handle exception
END;

FIGURE 13.2 Control blocks usually require additional programming.

13.1.3 SINGLE-RECORD AND MULTI-RECORD BLOCKS

All data blocks in a form module provide a buffer mechanism that allows you to use them as containers for any number of records in your application. Thus, in a sense, all blocks are multi-record blocks. The distinction between single-record and multi-record blocks applies only to the user interface that they offer. The first type of blocks allows users to view only one record at a time; the second type may display multiple records at any one moment.

Typically, single-record blocks have a form layout with their items filling the available screen space based on Form Builder layout algorithms or based on the work of the developer at design time. Multi-record blocks have a tabular layout and display the data in matrix format.

13.2 CREATING AND MAINTAINING DATA BLOCKS

The process of creating a block in the Form Builder can be essentially summarized in the following steps:

1. Define the data items that will be part of the block.
2. Define the layout of the items on the screen.

The complexity of these steps may range throughout the entire spectrum, depending on the type of block you are creating. To assist you in the process of creating and maintaining blocks, Form Builder provides two tools: the Data Block Wizard and the Layout Wizard. The following sections cover the purpose and use of these wizards.

13.2.1 INVOKING THE DATA BLOCK WIZARD

The first wizard, as the name indicates, facilitates the process of creating data blocks; the second one helps you define and maintain the layout of the data and control blocks. There is a number of ways in which you can access the Data Block Wizard. By default, when the Form Builder is launched, it displays the dialog box Welcome to the Form Builder. If the radio item Use the Data Block Wizard is selected as shown in Figure 13.3, when you click OK, Form Builder will create a new module and invoke the wizard. When you are in the Form Builder, you can always invoke the wizard by selecting Tools | Data Block Wizard from the menu. If the Form Builder focus is not in a block or dependent object, this action allows you to create a new data block. Otherwise, the context of the Data Block Wizard will be set to the block in question and the wizard can be used to maintain the data-related properties of the block. Using the Data Block Wizard for this purpose is known as re-entering the wizard. This is the reason why the Data Block

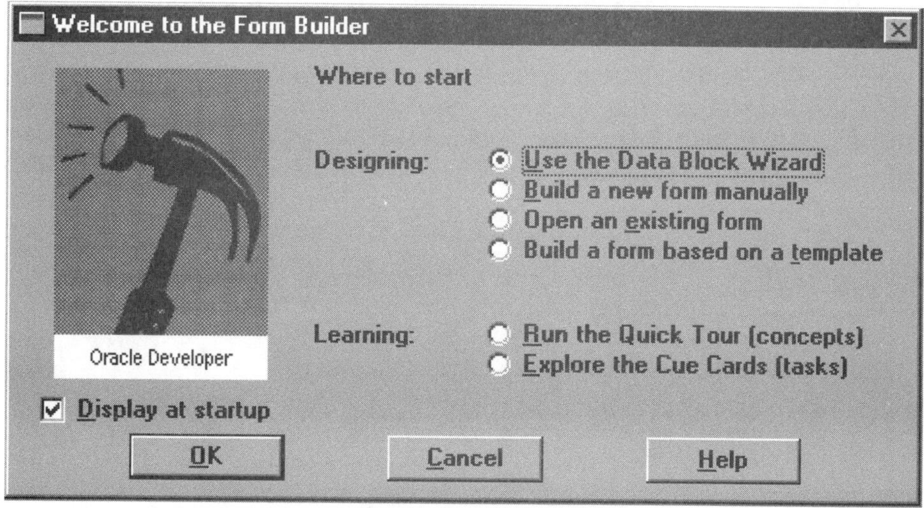

FIGURE 13.3 The Welcome to the Form Builder dialog box.

Wizard is considered as a re-entering wizard. You can also create a block in the Object Navigator by selecting the node Data Blocks and issuing one of the commands used in the Navigator to create a new object. In this case, the dialog box New Data Block appears (Figure 13.4). By selecting the option Use the Data Block Wizard and clicking OK, you will invoke the wizard. If you select the other option and click OK, the Form Builder will create a new block in the Navigator. Note that this second option is the only way in which you can create a new control block.

The Data Block Wizard is composed of a number of screens that correspond to the activities performed when creating or maintaining a data block. When you create the block, these screens are displayed as you complete each step and click the button Next. When you maintain the block, the same screens are displayed in a dialog box. The following four sections will show these screens as they appear in the tabbed dialog box.

13.2.2 DEFINING THE BLOCK TYPE

As mentioned earlier in the chapter, a data block may be based on database objects like tables and views or on a set of PL/SQL procedures stored in the Oracle Server database. The screen Type of the wizard allows you to define the category of the data block. As you can see from Figure 13.5, each of the categories is represented by a radio item. The screens that the wizard displays for the other steps depend on the option selected in the screen Type.

13.2.3 DEFINING THE DATABASE ITEMS

If the data block is based on a table or view, the screen Table of the wizard allows you to identify this object among the other schema objects you can access as well as to select the columns that will become data items. Figure 13.6 shows an example of this screen. If you know the name of the object, enter it directly in the text item Table or View. If not, click the Browse button to its right. You will be presented first with a filter dialog box, called Tables. Here you inform the wizard about the objects you want to look up—tables, views, or synonyms—and whether these objects are owned by you or by other users. After entering the fil-

FIGURE 13.4 The New Data Block dialog box.

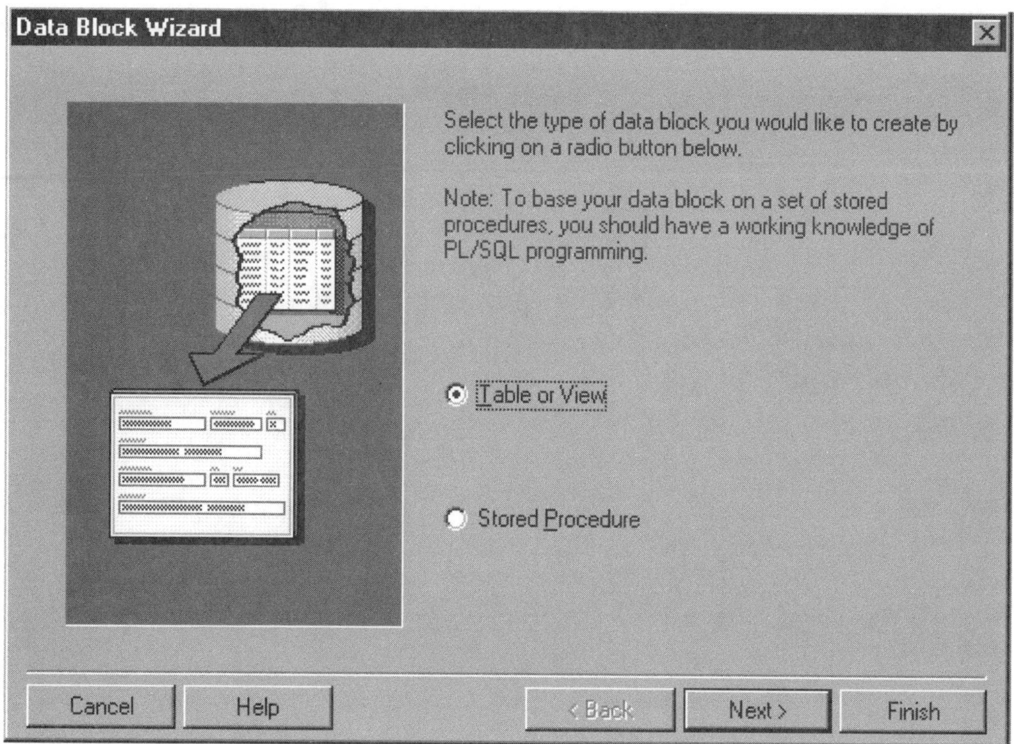

FIGURE 13.5 The Type screen of the Data Block Wizard.

tering criteria, you will see a List of Values dialog box with the same title Tables. This dialog box will allow you to select the desired object. Remember to use the auto-reduction functionality of LOVs, if the number of entries in the list is large.

> **TIP**
>
> Be cautious when setting filtering criteria in the Tables dialog box to values other than Tables for Current User. The wizard will retrieve the object names for all the schemas, including SYS and SYSTEM. This could result in a long list of entries in the LOVs dialog box.

After selecting the table or view on which to base the block, you need to select the columns that will become database items for the block. The list of columns defined in the data dictionary for the object is displayed in the list box Available Columns. Click the button Refresh to populate this list. In order to create a database item that corresponds to a particular column, move the column

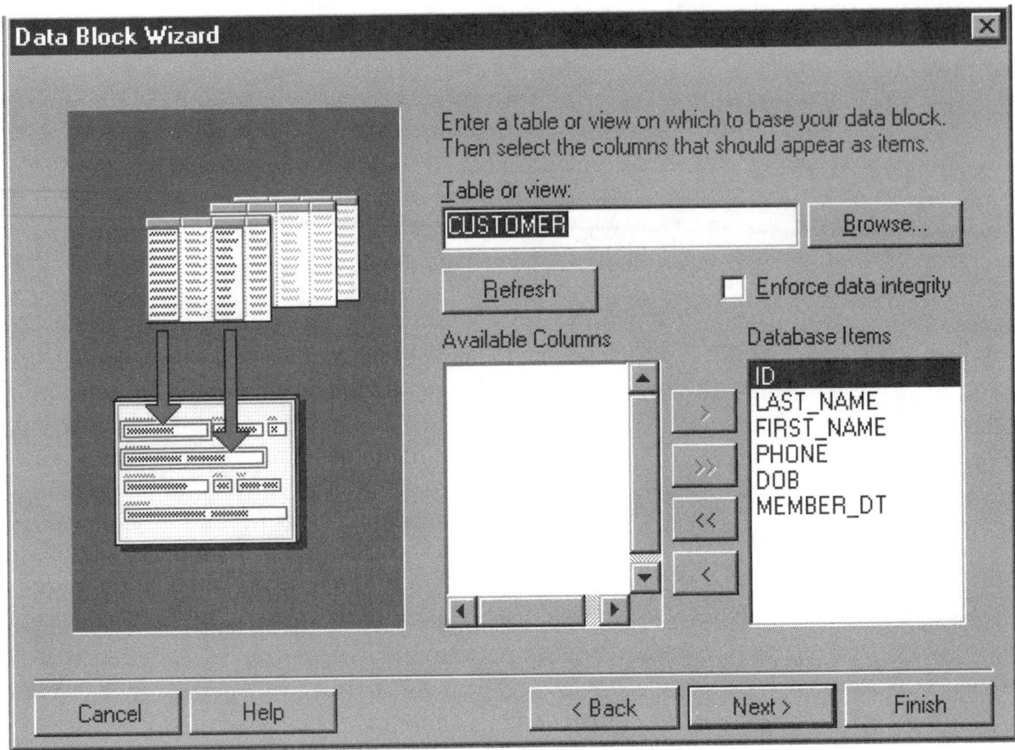

FIGURE 13.6 The Table screen of the Data Block Wizard.

from the list Available Columns to the list Database Items. You can easily move items between the two lists in the Table screen by using the four buttons displayed between the controls or by simply dragging the desired items from one list and dropping them onto the other. By transferring elements between these list controls, you can add or remove database items from the block even after the block is initially created. However, keep in mind the following two points:

- When you move an item from the Database Items list back to the Available Columns list, the wizard will not delete the item from the block; it will simply set its property Database Item to "No." This means that the item will remain in the block, but as a control item.
- When you move a column from the list Available Columns to the list Database Items, the wizard will create a new item if the block does not already contain another item with the same name. If the block contains an item with the same name as the column being moved, the wizard will set its property Database Item to "Yes," thus making it a database item.

If the check box Enforce data integrity is selected, the wizard will query the database dictionary for the constraints defined on the table and the columns that will be part of the block. Constraints such as primary key, foreign key, unique or required values, are transferred directly from the table definition to the item properties. If there are check constraints defined for a particular column or table, the wizard will convert them to triggers that fire when the item or the record is validated in the form. Suppose, for example, that the check constraint (ID > 10) is defined on column ID of table CUSTOMERS. The Oracle RDBMS database stores this constraint in the data dictionary. If you create a block called CUSTOMER based on this table with the option Enforce data integrity checked, the wizard will create a WHEN-VALIDATE-ITEM for item ID of that block. The contents of this trigger are shown in Figure 13.7.

The trigger may need some customization such as a more informative message for the user. However, the wizard implements automatically the business rule defined at the database level. If the check constraint is defined for the table, rather than for a particular column, the wizard will place the validation rule in a WHEN-VALIDATE-RECORD trigger.

If this is the first data block in your form, pressing the Next button will take you to the Congratulations Screen as shown in Figure 13.8. You may then exit the wizard or continue into the Layout Wizard.

13.2.4 CREATING MASTER DETAIL RELATIONS BETWEEN BLOCKS

The Master-Detail screen (see Figure 13.9) allows you to define a Master-Detail relationship between two data blocks in the module. In cases when the base tables in the database are associated through foreign key constraints, you can take advantage of the definition of these keys in the Oracle Server data dictionary. The following are the conditions that must be met in order to use derive Master-Detail relationships from foreign key constraints in the Data Block Wizard.

1. The master block must be a data block already created in the module.
2. A foreign key constraint must be defined in the base table of the detail block. This key must reference the primary key of the master block base table.

```
if not (:CUSTOMER.ID > 10 ) then
  message('WHEN-VALIDATE-ITEM trigger failed on field - '
          || :system.trigger_field);
  raise form_trigger_failure;
end if;
```

FIGURE 13.7 Trigger created when the Data Block Wizard enforces integrity constraints upon creation of block.

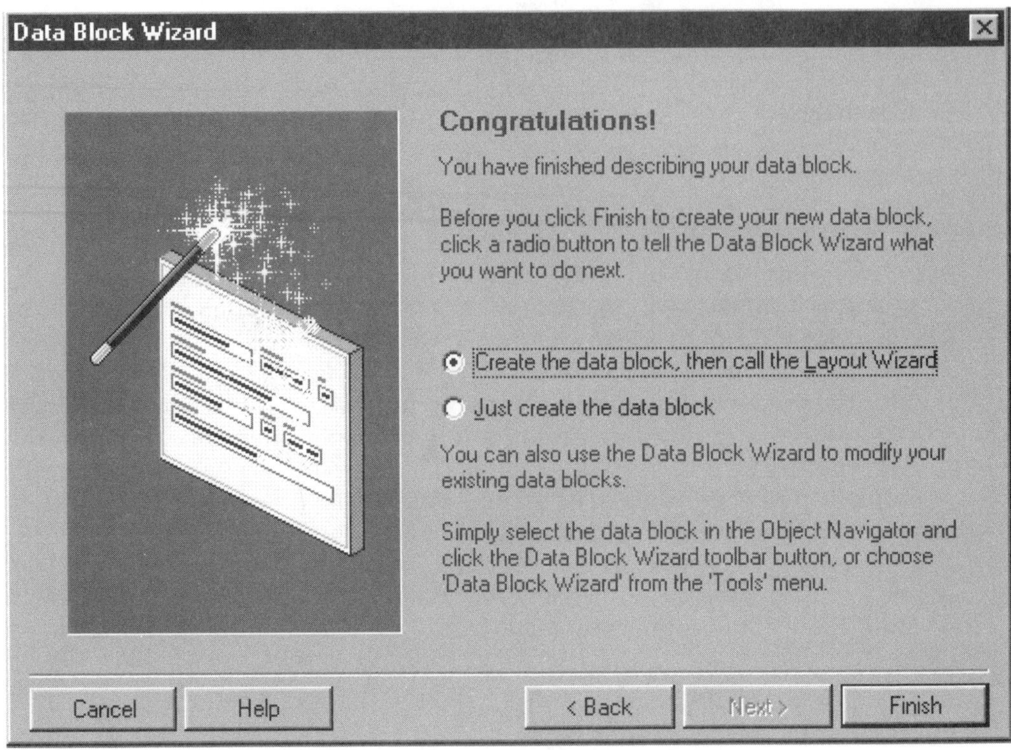

FIGURE 13.8 The Congratulations Screen

3. The check box Auto-join data blocks in the Master-Detail screen of the wizard must be selected.

Under these conditions, you must click the button Create Relationship to display a LOVs dialog box with the names of blocks that could be candidates for the master block position. The following is the list of steps that the wizard performs internally in order to populate the LOVs dialog box.

1. Get the base table name of the detail block from the Table tab.
2. Query the database data dictionary for all the foreign key constraints of this table. If no foreign key is defined or enabled, the operation stops. The block cannot become part of a Master-Detail relation at this time.
3. Compile a list of tables referenced by the foreign keys of the detail table.
4. Query the module for those blocks that are based on the tables defined in the previous step. The operation stops if no such blocks exist.
5. Populate the LOVs dialog box with block names from the previous step.

Once you select the name of a block, the wizard closes the LOVs dialog box and fills in the join condition that will govern the Master-Detail relationship between the two blocks. An example is shown in Figure 13.9. By default, this condition is an equi-join derived from the definition of the foreign key that corresponds to the relationship. You can further restrict this condition with additional equality criteria by selecting items from the list boxes Detail Item and Master Item. The additional criteria will be ANDed to the default condition. To remove one of these criteria, select the element (No Join) from the list Master Item. To delete a relationship altogether, and hence break the master-detail coordination of the blocks, select the desired block from the list Master Data Blocks and click Delete Relationship.

There are cases when your application may benefit from a master-detail coordination of its blocks even though the underlying database objects are not associated through foreign key constraints. In order to create these relations in the Master-Detail screen of the Data Block Wizard you should first clear the checkbox Auto-join data blocks. Under this condition, the wizard will populate the list of blocks that are candidates for master block with all the blocks in the form.

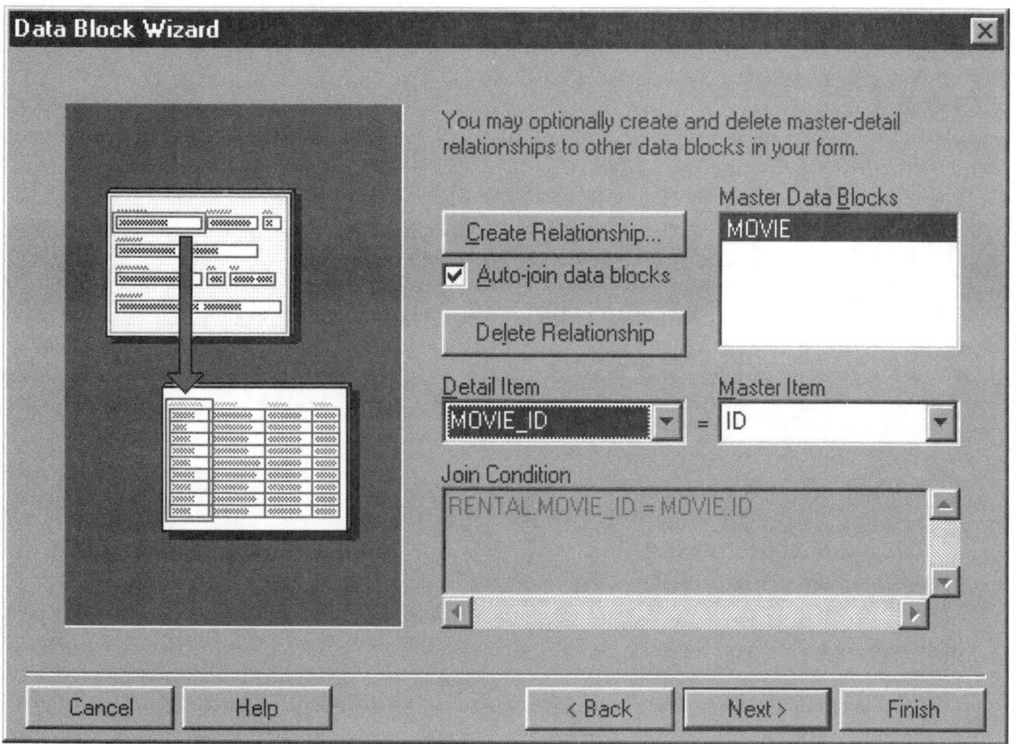

FIGURE 13.9 The Master-Detail screen of the Data Block Wizard.

After you select one of these blocks, you need to define the join conditions by selecting from the list boxes Detail Item and Master Item, as described in the previous paragraph.

When the detail block is created, the Data Block Wizard creates a series of additional objects that are responsible for the coordination of the two blocks. The most important of them is the relation object that describes the relationship between the blocks. The default name of this relation is `MasterBlockName_DetailBlockName`, for example MOVIE_TAPE. Then, there are a number of triggers and procedures that coordinate the querying, and deleting of data between blocks. The last sections of this chapter will provide more details about relations. At this point, it is sufficient to mention that you do not need to worry about the content of these PL/SQL objects. The Form Builder allows you to visually modify the properties of the relation object in its Property Palette or through the Data Block Wizard. The code of the triggers is updated automatically, in order to reflect the new settings of these properties. If you decide you want to break the

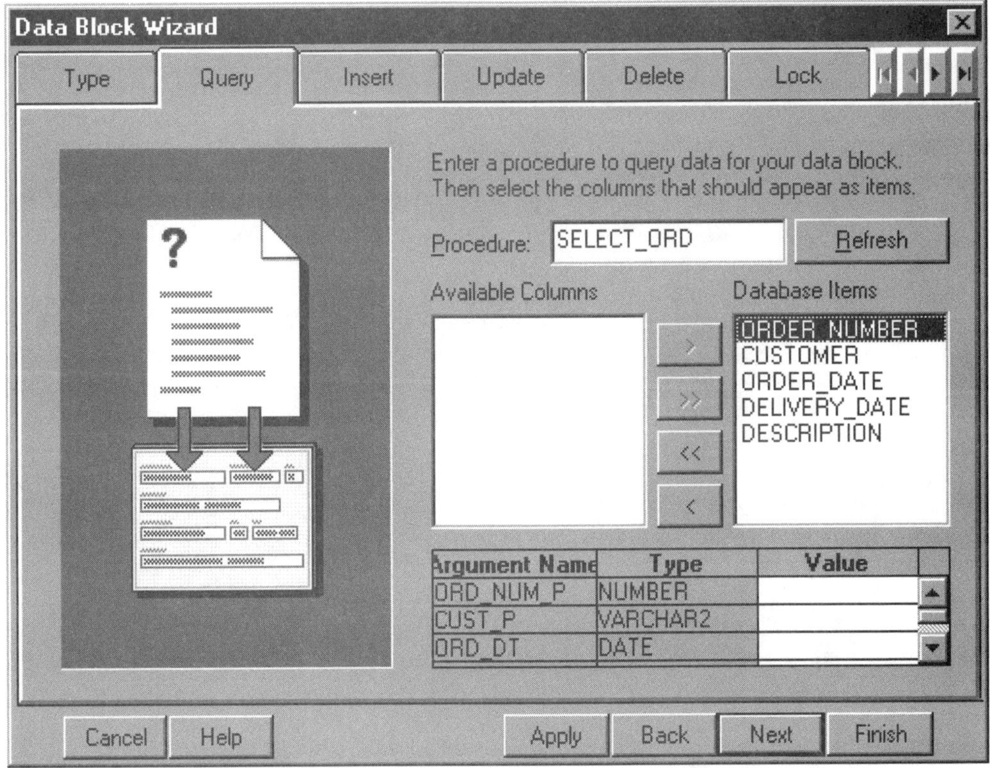

FIGURE 13.10 The Query screen of the Data Block Wizard for a block based on stored procedures.

Master-Detail relationship between blocks, the Form Builder will also delete the PL/SQL objects associated with it.

13.2.5 DEFINING BLOCKS BASED ON STORED PROCEDURES

When the data block is based on stored procedures, you may specify up to five procedures that select, insert, update, delete, or lock data in the database. These procedures may not necessarily operate with data from one single object. They may perform joins among a number of tables, computations, and any other operation allowed by SQL and PL/SQL. The only restriction is that the select procedure should return the selected records in the form of an index-by table, table or REF cursor object. The structure of this table defines the database items of the block. Figure 13.10 shows the screen of the Data Block Wizard in which you define the procedure that queries data to populate the block. The name of the procedure is entered in the text item Procedure and should refer to any procedure accessible by you, whether it is stand-alone or part of a PL/SQL package. The list items Available Columns and Database Items have the same meaning and are used exactly like the corresponding control in the Table tab, discussed in Section 13.2.3. The lower part of the screen contains a listing of the arguments for the procedure and is used to define any values that are passed to the procedure by default.

13.3 DEFINING AND MAINTAINING THE LAYOUT OF BLOCKS

Associating the data items of a block with source database objects is an important activity in the process of creating and maintaining a data block. Another equally important activity is to define and maintain the layout if these items on the screen. The Layout Wizard is the Form Builder utility that helps you perform all the steps in this activity. Rather than maintaining the layout properties of individual items, the Layout Wizard creates and maintains frame objects. As you will see in Section 13.6, frames are Form Builder objects that help you define the layout properties of all the visible items in a block as a group.

13.3.1 INVOKING THE LAYOUT WIZARD

You can invoke the Layout Wizard only if the form module contains at least one block object. Under this condition, you can invoke the utility from anywhere in the module by selecting Tools | Layout Wizard from the menu or by displaying the popup menu and selecting the Layout Wizard item. Like a typical wizard tool in Microsoft Windows, the Layout Wizard presents you with a screen in each step of the process. You can move between these steps by clicking the buttons Next and Back. From any tab, you can complete the activity by clicking the button Finish or cancel any modification you have performed by clicking Cancel. The following sections describe each step in the process of using the Layout Wizard.

13.3.2 DEFINING THE CANVAS PROPERTIES

Use the first screen of the Layout Wizard to define the canvas object on which the frame and the data items will be placed. Figure 13.11 shows an example of this tab. The list box Canvas allows you to select an existing canvas and designate it as the placeholder for the data items. By selecting the option (New Canvas) you can also instruct the wizard to create a new canvas object in the module. When creating a new canvas, set its type by selecting one of the options from the list box Type. If the canvas is a tabbed canvas, you can designate which of the screens will contains the data items and the frame of the block by selecting its name from the list Tab Page. If the page does not exist, select the option (New Tab Page) to create a new one.

In the hierarchy of Form Builder objects, frames are dependent on canvases. The Layout Wizard allows you to initially allocate the frame under a specific canvas. After that, if you want to move the frame to a different canvas, you should use the commands available in the Object Navigator. The Layout Wizard cannot be used to move the frame object to a different canvas or tab page. Therefore, the canvas shown in Figure 13.11 does not appear when the wizard is invoked to maintain the properties of an existing frame.

13.3.3 DEFINING THE ITEM LAYOUT PROPERTIES

The Layout Wizard contains two screens you can use to maintain the layout properties of items. The first one is shown in Figure 13.12. It allows you to select the block for which you will maintain the layout from the list Data Block. The combination of list boxes Available Items and Displayed Items is used to define those items that will be displayed in the GUI. In the situation shown in Figure 13.12, all the items in the block CUSTOMER will be displayed except for the item ID. By default, all the items in a form module are text items. However, you can use the list Item Type to set the item to another type, such as check box, radio group, or display item. Selecting the right type of GUI control for an item is a process that requires careful thinking and design of the application's GUI. Given the nature of the Layout Wizard—a tool that helps you quickly define the layout of your blocks—I recommend that that you leave the item type unchanged. Later, in the Layout Editor, you can easily convert the item to the appropriate GUI control.

The Item Layout screen is used primarily to define which items should be displayed and which ones not. For the displayed items, you can use the Items screen of the Layout Wizard to review and modify the properties Prompt, Width, and Height. Typically, I use this screen to define the prompt labels that associate each item on the canvas. The wizard proposes such prompts based on the name of the items, which in itself is derived from the database column name. Often, be-

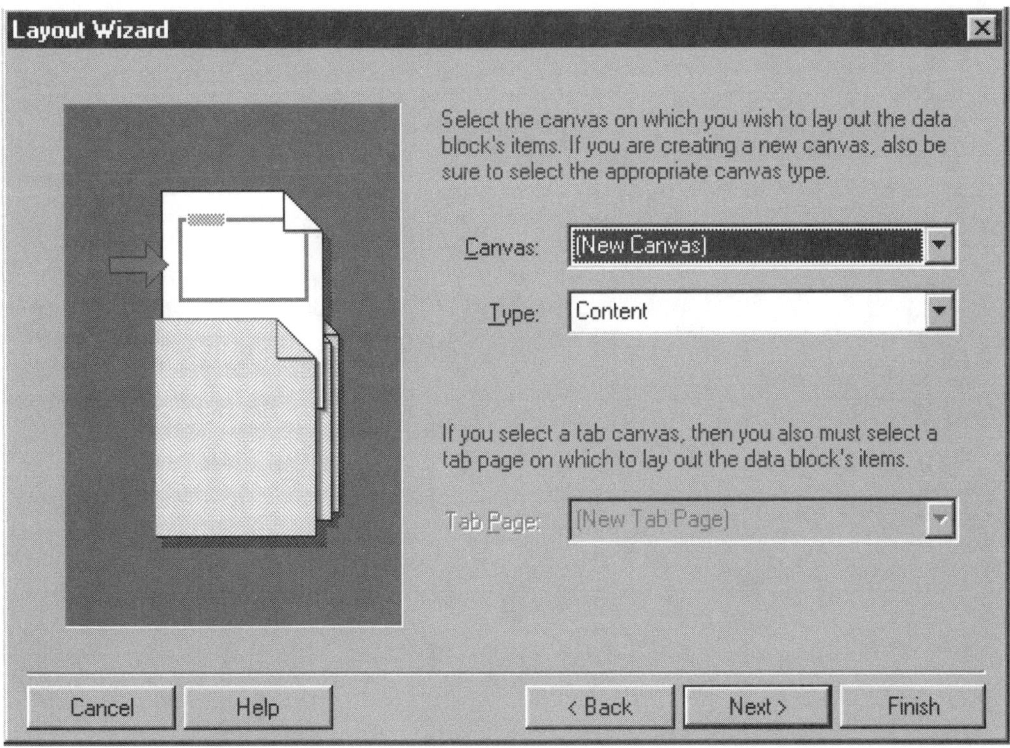

FIGURE 13.11 The Canvas screen of the Layout Wizard.

cause these names are not intended to be displayed to the users, the computed prompts are not too user friendly. In such cases, you can enter the prompts you desire on the Items tab. Figure 13.13 shows an example of this screen in which the labels of the last two items have been manually modified. The prompts initially proposed by the wizard were "Dob," and "Member Dt."

13.3.4 DEFINING THE LAYOUT STYLE

The items in a data block can be organized essentially in two styles: Form and Tabular layout. In form layout, items fill the space on the canvas from top down and from left to right. This layout is generally used to display more details about an entity one record at a time. In tabular layout, items and records in a block are organized in a matrix format. The displayed items form the columns of the matrix; the records displayed on the frame form the rows of the matrix. The tabular style is used primarily to display multiple records simultaneously. These block usually display only those data elements that are sufficient to identify an instance of the entity. For example, in a tabular CUSTOMER block, you would display the

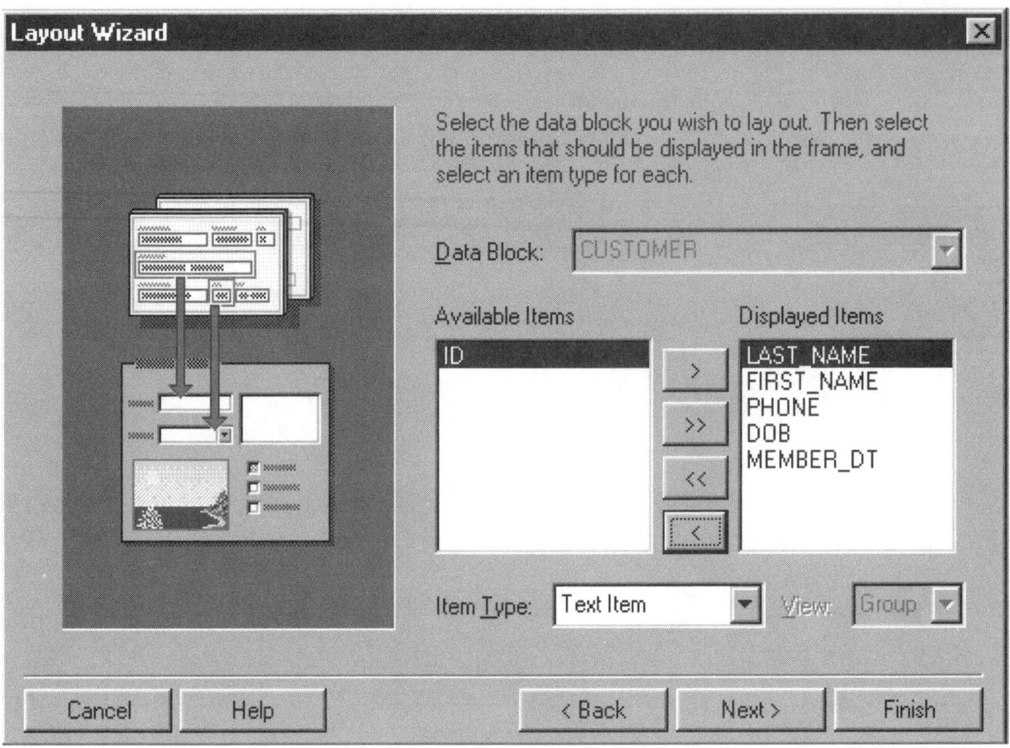

FIGURE 13.12 The Item screen of the Layout Wizard.

first name, last name, and telephone number for each individual, but not the address. All the data items about the address would be more suitable in a form style block. The layout style of the frame is defined in the Layout Style canvas. This canvas has only two radio items which represent each of the styles.

The layout of the frame is closely related with the settings of other frame properties maintained in the Frame screen of the Layout Wizard. An example of this screen is shown in Figure 13.13. As you can see, this screen allows you to set the title of the frame, which is displayed as a text label on the upper left-hand corner of the rectangle that represents the frame on the canvas. By setting other controls in this screen you can also specify the maximum number of records displayed in the frame at any one time, the distance between records, and whether a scrollbar should be displayed to facilitate the navigation of users through the records.

Normally, frames with form layout display only one record in the GUI. If multiple records are displayed, their number is kept to a minimum, usually not more than three records per screen. This is done to conserve and better utilize the working area of the window that a form-style block displaying multiple records

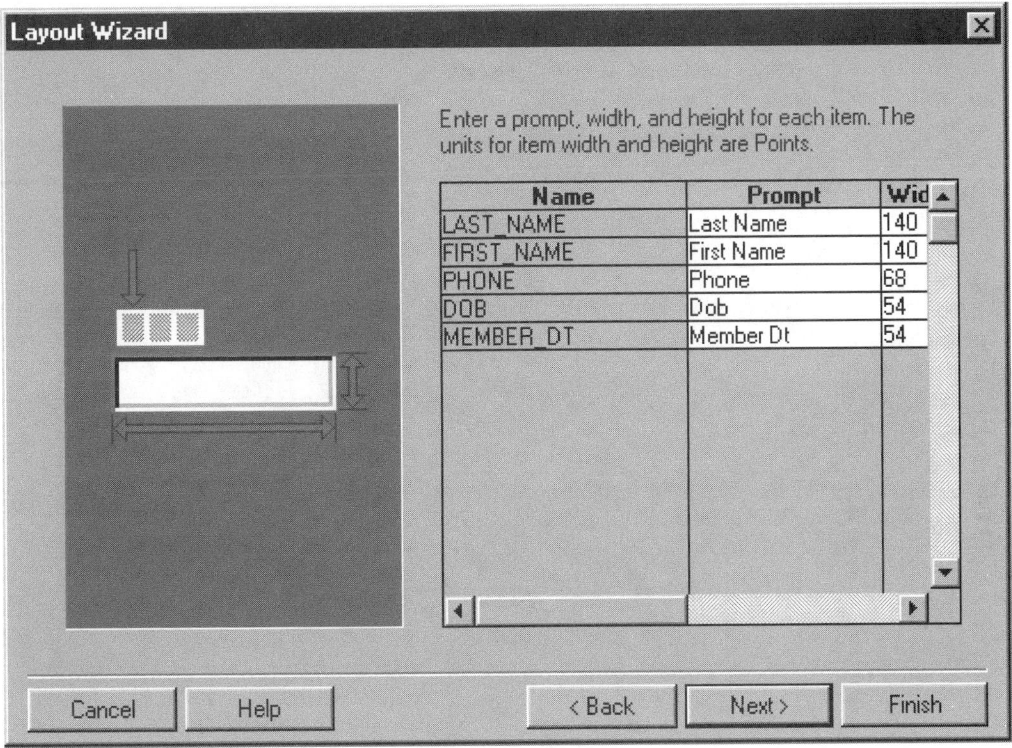

FIGURE 13.13 The Item Layout screen of the Layout Wizard.

would otherwise occupy. The distance between records is relevant only when more than one record is displayed. These frames do not display a scrollbar either.

Tabular frames on the other hand typically display several records with a scrollbar to help navigating through them. The distance between records is kept to 0 to maintain the matrix effect, but it may be increased. It is very unusual to see tabular-style records that display less than five records at a time. In fact, the purpose of these blocks is to present as much information as possible in the least amount of screen area. The number of records displayed in tabular blocks should not be greater than ten to twelve. In cases when the number is expected to be large, users should be provided with ways to quickly navigate through and search the records displayed.

The Data Block Wizard or the Data Layout Wizard are helpful tools that allow you to set a number of block properties upon creation and to maintain them throughout the life of the application. However, in the development process you may need to access the block properties at a more granular level of detail than the wizards offer. If your application is to be really flexible, you may want to change some block properties dynamically as well. In the following sec-

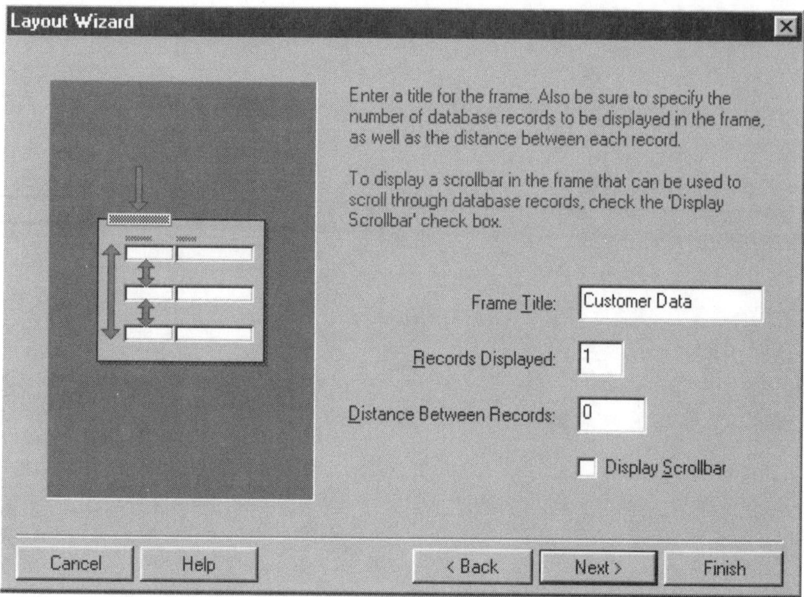
Layout Wizard
Enter a title for the frame. Also be sure to specify the number of database records to be displayed in the frame, as well as the distance between each record.
To display a scrollbar in the frame that can be used to scroll through database records, check the 'Display Scrollbar' check box.
Frame Title: Customer Data
Records Displayed: 1
Distance Between Records: 0
Display Scrollbar
Cancel
Help
< Back
Next >
Finish

FIGURE 13.14 The Frame screen of the Layout Wizard.

tion, I discuss how you set and maintain the properties of blocks in the Form Builder. Section 12.5 explains how you can set these properties programmatically.

13.4 MAINTAINING BLOCK PROPERTIES IN THE FORM BUILDER

In the Form Builder, you can access and modify the properties of a block in its Property Palette. These properties are organized in a number of groups. The group General contains the properties Name, Subclass Information, and Comments, available for every object in the Form Builder. The following sections describe the most important properties in the other groups.

13.4.1 NAVIGATION PROPERTIES

The properties under the Navigation group are used primarily in character-mode applications, where users must move from item to item sequentially. GUI applications offer the flexibility to navigate to the desired destination by simply clicking there. However, even for these applications, good keyboard navigation features are signs of serious programming efforts, and may save the day if the mouse driver or hardware fail. The following is a list of properties in this group.

- **Navigation Style.** This property defines the behavior of Forms when users are in the block's last item and try to navigate to the next item by pressing the TAB key. If the property is set to "Same Record," the focus will move to the first item within the same record; if the setting is "Change Record," Forms will jump to the first item of the next record; if the setting is "Change Data Block," the cursor will land in the first navigable item in the next block.
- **Next Navigation Data Block and Previous Navigation Data Block.** These properties define which block is considered the next block and which one is considered the previous block relative to the given block. If these properties are not set, the sequence ID, or the ordering of the blocks in the Object Navigator, defines the navigation order. This default sequence can be overridden by setting these properties to the names of other blocks in the current module. If you do not want the users to navigate outside the block using the keyboard or the built-in procedures NEXT_BLOCK or PREVIOUS_BLOCK, set these properties to the name of the block itself.

13.4.2 RECORDS PROPERTIES

This group contains properties that control the way the block displays records and more importantly the way queries populate the block with records. Careful settings of these properties may have a significant influence in the overall performance of the application. The following list describes the most important of these properties.

- **Number of Records Displayed.** This property controls the maximum number of records the block displays at any one time. Recall that this property may be set in the Frame screen of the Layout Wizard as well.
- **Number of Records Buffered.** The setting of this property is the number of records that Forms keeps in its internal memory structures at any one time. By default, this number is three units larger than the number specified in the Number of Records Displayed property. In other words, if the block displays seven records, Forms will buffer ten records in memory. The setting of Records Displayed serves as a minimum boundary for the setting of Records Buffered. In the scenario above, if you set Records Buffered to anything less than seven, at compile time the Form Builder will display the message "FRM-30033: Records buffered must be greater than records displayed."
- **Query Array Size.** When a query is executed, Form Builder does not retrieve all the records in one trip to the database. Instead, the number of trips, or fetches, depends on the setting of the Query Array Size property. By default this property has the same setting as the property Number of Records Displayed. Assuming that this property is set to 7 and that a query

returns 20 records, the first fetch will bring over only the first seven records. When users are at the seventh record and try to navigate to the next record, Forms will fetch the next seven records, and so on.

Forms does not display the records in the block until the whole set is fetched from the database. Therefore, a large setting of the Query Array Size may slow down the process of populating the block with the query results. On the other hand, a low setting may result in frequent calls to the database. This situation occurs often when blocks have a form layout that displays only one record and their default setting of the property Query Array Size is not increased. In such conditions, the application will fetch the records one at a time as the users navigate to them. The overhead cost of sending these bursts of information may degrade the performance in Local Area Network (LAN) and Wide Area Network (WAN) environments, and especially of applications deployed on the Web.

- **Query All Records.** By default, this property is set to "No." Setting it to "Yes" causes Forms to fetch all the records back to the block after the query. This setting is equivalent to disabling the fetching of queried records in arrays. Applications deployed on the Web may benefit from such a setting, provided you can guarantee that the number of the records ever returned by a query will not be large. Otherwise, the wait time of the users for the first record of the query to be displayed may be significant. One way to guarantee that the query will always return a reasonable number of records is to set the property Maximum Records Fetched in the Database group. The meaning of this property is explained in the following sections.
- **Current Record Visual Attribute Group.** This property is used to automatically assign a named visual attribute object to the current record. This attribute could be used to highlight the current selection in a multi-record block.

> **CAUTION**
>
> The way the Property Palette displays default settings of number-valued properties like Number of Records Buffered, may be misleading. If not set manually, these settings are NULL (default values). However, they appear as 0, which is not consistent with the way alphanumeric properties set to NULL are presented (<Null>).

13.4.3 DATABASE PROPERTIES

The Database group contains properties that control the basic interaction of the block with the database. Obviously, these properties are meaningful only for data blocks. For control blocks, the only property worth noting in this group is Database

Data Block, which is set to "No" and invalidates the settings of all the other properties. The following list describes the most important properties in this group.

- **Query Data Source Properties.** There are four such properties that allow you to define the data source that will populate the block with records during a query. Query Data Source Type is usually set to "Table" but it can also be set to "Procedure," "Transactional Triggers," or "FROM Clause Query." Query Data Source Name contains the name of the object that serves as the query data source, for example, the name of a table, view, or stored procedure. Query Data Source Columns allows you to maintain the columns from the data source object that serve as data items for the block. Query Data Source Arguments is used only in case the query data source for the block is a stored procedure that needs some parameters to be executed. Note that the Data Block Wizard allows you to set these properties from a much friendlier interface.
- **CRUD Operation Properties.** The properties in this category include Delete Allowed, Insert Allowed, Query Allowed, and Update Allowed. By default, they are all set to "Yes," which means that users can perform all these four operations in the block. To disable any of these operations, set the corresponding property to "No." These four operations are also known as Create, Retrieve, Update, and Delete, hence the acronym CRUD.
- **WHERE Clause and ORDER BY Clause.** These are two more properties that can help you customize the queries issued from a data block. They allow you to enter query and ordering criteria in addition to those entered by the users in the query-by-example interface of your block. For example, if you want to create a block that will display only the active customers, you may set the WHERE Clause to "STATUS = A." Whenever users execute a query in this block, Form Builder will prepare the SELECT statement based on the criteria they specify, and, in addition, will append the condition "AND STATUS = A" to the WHERE clause of the statement. Setting the property ORDER BY Clause works in an entirely similar fashion. You do not need to add the keywords WHERE or ORDER BY when setting these properties.
- **Performance Optimization Properties.** In this category, I include four properties whose settings may affect the performance of the application. These are Optimizer Hint, Maximum Query Time, Maximum Records Fetched, and Update Changed Columns Only. The property Optimizer Hint is used to pass a hint to the Oracle Server optimizer together with the SQL statement that selects data for the block. The purpose of the hint is to help the optimizer choose an execution plan. The setting of the property Maximum Query Time serves as a threshold for the time allowed for a query to complete its execution. When this property is set, Forms will time out any query that is not executed within the allocated time. The setting of the property Maximum Records Fetched serves as the upper limit of the number of

records fetched by a query. Queries that return more records than this threshold are aborted.

> **TIP**
>
> The properties Maximum Query Time and Maximum Records Fetched can be set at the module level. Consider setting them at the block level only if you need to override these settings.

The three properties discussed in the previous paragraph help you optimize the queries of data blocks. The property Update Changed Columns Only may have an impact on the performance of UPDATE statements issued by the application. By default, this property is set to "No." With this setting, during the commit of a changed record, Forms will construct an UPDATE statement that will include all the columns in the block, even those whose value did not change. This saves some processing time and improves the performance of the server. The improvements result from the way the Oracle Server executes SQL statements. The first time the statement is encountered, for example an UPDATE statement, the SQL Statement Executor will parse it to identify the table and columns being updated. Then, the variables will be bound to the actual values passed in the statements, and, finally, the statement will be executed. After that, each time the same statement is issued, the database server will bypass the parsing step, because the table and column names do not change. The statements are considered the same if they are exactly the same, byte per byte. An extra white space, or a character in the opposite case are enough to make the statements different.

However, there are situations when it is desirable to set the property Update Changed Columns Only to "Yes." Imagine, for example, that for each movie in the database you store twenty seconds of video clips in a column of LONG RAW data type in Oracle7 or BLOB data type in Oracle8. This video clip will be played at the customer's request, but almost never edited. Other data for the movie though, will be updated frequently. If the property in question is set to "No," each time a column value is updated, the whole movie record, together with several megabytes of the video clip will be sent across the network to the database for update. If, on the other hand, Update Changed Columns Only is set to "Yes," only the modified data will be sent for update.

13.4.4 ADVANCED DATABASE PROPERTIES

Most of the properties in this group are used to specify the name, columns, and arguments of the stored procedures used to insert, delete, update, and lock records in a block. Obviously, such properties are set only for those data blocks that rely on stored procedures for DML operations. One property in this group that may improve the performance of DML operations in applications deployed on the Web is DML Array Size. By default, this property is set to 1. When users insert five new records and then commit, the application issues five INSERT statements. The overhead of network traffic may be reduced by increasing the size of the DML array. In this case, the records to be inserted are bundled in the array and sent as a block, rather than individually.

13.4.5 SCROLLBAR PROPERTIES

The properties in this group govern the appearance of the scrollbar associated with a block. An important property in the this group is Show Scroll Bar. Its value is "No" if the block does not have a scroll bar attached to it. When this property is set to "Yes" the Form Builder will add a scroll bar to the block. The location, position, size, orientation, and functionality of the scroll bar is determined by the settings of the other properties. Some of them are described in the following list:

- **Scroll Bar Canvas.** This property allows you to specify the canvas on which the scroll bar will reside. If this setting is <Null>, you will not be able to see the scroll bar even if the property Show Scroll Bar is set to "Yes." If the canvas is a tab canvas, use the property Scroll Bar Tab Page to select the page on which the scroll bar will appear.
- **Scroll Bar Orientation.** By default, scroll bars are vertical ones, but you can set the Scroll Bar Orientation property to "Horizontal" to obtain a horizontal scroll bar.
- **Position and Dimension Properties.** The properties Scroll Bar X Position, Scroll Bar Y Position, Scroll Bar Width, and Scroll Bar Height allow you to set the position and dimensions of the scroll bar. The scroll bar is initially positioned on the upper left-hand corner of the canvas, but you can drag and resize it in the Layout Editor to the desired location and dimension. This is much easier than setting the properties in the Property Palette.

13.4.6 MISCELLANEOUS PROPERTIES

Block objects have properties in three more groups: Font & Color, Character Mode, and International. The properties in the Font & Color group have a visual effect only on the scroll bar of the block, when it is displayed. If, for example, you set the property Background Color to red, then the bar in the scroll bar will appear red. The two properties in the Character Mode group are useful only in applications developed for character-based environments. Form Builder maintains internally a list of block names that can be displayed to the users and allows them to navigate to the desired block. Although Forms documentation calls this a block menu, it is nothing more than a LOVs dialog box (see Figure 13.15). You can dis-

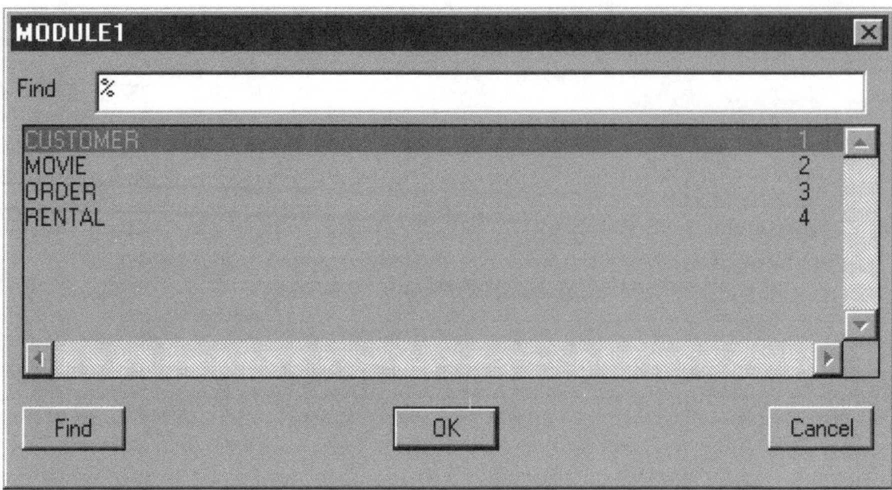

FIGURE 13.15 Form Builder Block menu.

play this menu programmatically by invoking the BLOCK_MENU built-in procedure, or by pressing [Block Menu] key on the keyboard.

If the property Listed in Data Block Menu is set to "No," the block will not appear in the menu. If it is set to "Yes" and the property Data Block Description is NULL, the block will not appear in the menu. The only time the block is displayed, is when the property Listed in Data Block Menu is set to "Yes" and the property Data Block Description contains a string value. The contents of Data Block Description will appear in the block menu.

13.5 MAINTAINING BLOCK PROPERTIES PROGRAMMATICALLY

In order to make the application flexible and responsive to the user's actions, it may be necessary to retrieve or modify the setting of some block properties at runtime. The location and situation for which you place the code to perform these actions varies widely. However, certain steps must be followed in the trigger, function, or procedure where you plan to access or change the block properties.

In order to retrieve the setting for a particular property, you must first know the data type of this setting. For example, the setting of the property Query Data Source Name is a character string that stores the base table name for the block. But the setting for the property Number of Records Displayed is a number that indicates how many records can be displayed in the block.

After you define the data type of the property setting, you must declare a variable of the same data type that will store the value of that setting. The function GET_BLOCK_PROPERTY is used to place the value of the property in the variable you declared.

The process of setting the value of a property is similar. Here you first declare a variable with the appropriate data type, and store the new setting in it. Then, the procedure SET_BLOCK_PROPERTY is used to complete the action. Let us see some examples that follow the steps described above.

Figure 13.16 shows a function that returns the status of a block whose name is passed as an input argument. The property STATUS is a property that exists only at runtime. You cannot access or set it in the Property Palette of the Form Builder. The status of a block is QUERY if the block contains only queried records. It is NEW if the block contains only one record that has just been created. It is CHANGED if at least one record in the block has been modified. If records are initially queried, and then new records are created, the status of the record is also CHANGED.

The next example implements some security features for the MRD application. You can think of the users of this application as divided in three categories, according to their job functions. Each category is represented by a database account, and their names are "CLERK", "STAFF", or "MANAGER." Employees who interact with customers at the counter log on the system as "CLERK"; those that maintain the inventory in the back of the store use the 'STAFF' account; supervisors and managers log on as 'MANAGER'. The account 'MANAGER' does not have any restrictions. This account can query, insert, update, and delete records in all the blocks. Front-desk clerks cannot delete records in any blocks. They can insert, update, and delete in blocks CUSTOMER and RENTAL, but only query in MOVIE and TAPE. Maintenance staff cannot delete any records as well. They are limited to just viewing data in blocks CUSTOMER and TAPE, but can insert, update, and delete from CUSTOMER and RENTAL. Figure 13.17 shows the procedure that could be used to implement the business rules described above.

The previous program units are fairly easy to write and understand. However, they are vulnerable to errors. In both these routines you assume that there are no mistakes in specifying the block name. But, if one such error occurs, the code is not protected from the failure of the built-in routines GET_BLOCK_PROPERTY or SET_BLOCK_PROPERTY. To remedy for this prob-

```
FUNCTION Get_Block_Status (block_name VARCHAR2)
RETURN VARCHAR2 IS
 block_status VARCHAR2(20) :=NULL;
BEGIN
 block_status := GET_BLOCK_PROPERTY(block_name, STATUS);
 RETURN block_status;
END Get_Block_Status;
```

FIGURE 13.16 Retrieving the status of a block at runtime.

```
PROCEDURE Set_Block_Security (username VARCHAR2) IS
BEGIN
 IF username = 'CLERK' THEN
  SET_BLOCK_PROPERTY('CUSTOMER',DELETE_ALLOWED,PROPERTY_FALSE);
  SET_BLOCK_PROPERTY('RENTAL',DELETE_ALLOWED,PROPERTY_FALSE);
  SET_BLOCK_PROPERTY('MOVIE',DELETE_ALLOWED,PROPERTY_FALSE);
  SET_BLOCK_PROPERTY('MOVIE',INSERT_ALLOWED,PROPERTY_FALSE);
  SET_BLOCK_PROPERTY('MOVIE',UPDATE_ALLOWED,PROPERTY_FALSE);
  SET_BLOCK_PROPERTY('TAP',DELETE_ALLOWED,PROPERTY_FALSE);
  SET_BLOCK_PROPERTY('TAPE',INSERT_ALLOWED,PROPERTY_FALSE);
  SET_BLOCK_PROPERTY('TAPE',UPDATE_ALLOWED,PROPERTY_FALSE);
 ELSIF username = 'STAFF' THEN
  SET_BLOCK_PROPERTY('CUSTOMER',DELETE_ALLOWED,PROPERTY_FALSE);
  SET_BLOCK_PROPERTY('CUSTOMER
',INSERT_ALLOWED,PROPERTY_FALSE);
  SET_BLOCK_PROPERTY('CUSTOMER
',UPDATE_ALLOWED,PROPERTY_FALSE);
  SET_BLOCK_PROPERTY('RENTAL',DELETE_ALLOWED,PROPERTY_FALSE);
  SET_BLOCK_PROPERTY('RENTAL',INSERT_ALLOWED,PROPERTY_FALSE);
  SET_BLOCK_PROPERTY('RENTAL ',UPDATE_ALLOWED,PROPERTY_FALSE);
  SET_BLOCK_PROPERTY('MOVIE',DELETE_ALLOWED,PROPERTY_FALSE);
  SET_BLOCK_PROPERTY('TAPE',DELETE_ALLOWED,PROPERTY_FALSE);
 END IF;
END Set_Block_Security;
```

FIGURE 13.17 Controlling users' access to blocks programmatically.

lem, you must guarantee that the block is present before using any of the above built-ins.

The procedure `Set_Block_Security` has a performance problem, as well. As mentioned earlier, Forms assigns unique identifiers to objects in a module. These identifiers are used to access the object internally. If, in your code you refer to an object by its name, Forms has to perform a look up in its internal structures to find the ID of the object with that name. In this procedure, Forms must query the IDs of blocks MOVIE and TAPE three times. You could certainly improve the performance by retrieving the block ID and then issuing the call to SET_BLOCK_PROPERTY as many times as it is necessary. Figure 13.18 contains the modified and improved version of function `Get_Block_Status`.

A new version of the procedure `Set_Block_Security` that incorporates the same feature would be similar. You would declare four variables of data type Block and store the internal ID for each block in them using the FIND_BLOCK function. Then the SET_BLOCK_PROPERTY procedure is invoked as in Figure 13.18, but this time you use the ID rather than the name of the block.

```
FUNCTION Get_Block_Status (block_name VARCHAR2)
RETURN VARCHAR2 IS
 block_status VARCHAR2(20) :=NULL;
 block_id   BLOCK;
BEGIN
 block_id := FIND_BLOCK(block_name);
 IF NOT ID_NULL(block_id) THEN
  block_status := GET_BLOCK_PROPERTY(block_name, STATUS);
 ELSE
  MESSAGE('Block ' || block_name || ' does not exist.');
  RAISE FORM_TRIGGER_FAILURE;
 END IF;

 /* If control comes here, no errors occurred. */
 RETURN block_status;
END Get_Block_Status;
```

FIGURE 13.18 Internal identifiers improve the application's robustness and performance.

It is worth noting here that you will use the same layout of code when accessing or modifying properties of other object in Forms. The general steps you will follow are:

1. Use the object-specific FIND function to get the internal ID for the object, based on its name. Examples of this function are FIND_BLOCK, FIND_ITEM, and FIND_WINDOW.
2. Use the IS_NULL function to ensure that the ID is valid.
3. Use the object-specific GET function to retrieve the setting for a property. Examples of such functions are GET_BLOCK_PROPERTY, GET_ITEM_PROPERTY, and GET_WINDOW_PROPERTY.
4. Use the object-specific SET procedure to set a property. Examples of such procedures are SET_BLOCK_PROPERTY, SET_ITEM_PROPERTY, and SET_WINDOW_PROPERTY.

13.6 FRAMES

Up to this point, frames have been discussed in the context of blocks and their GUI layout. It is time to take a closer look at the properties and usage of these objects in your Form Builder applications. In general, you can maintain the GUI layout of a block by arranging each item individually. The Layout Editor provides for simple ways to align and group items on the canvas. Wouldn't it be nice though to define the layout of all the items in a block as a group, without having to maintain each of them individually? Frames are objects used to achieve exactly that. Like all the other objects in the Form Builder, they have a number of properties that you can view and maintain in the Property Palette. Some of the properties influence the rendering and display of the frame object itself. However, what sets frames apart from other objects in the Form Builder is that a good number of their properties influence other objects. More precisely, they directly affect the layout of items in the block associated with the frame.

The fact that you can influence the layout of all the items in the block by modifying the properties of one single object—the frame—is in itself a big step saver and highlights one of the most important advantages that frames provide. In addition, frames, like any other Form Builder object, can be included in object library modules and referenced from a number of modules in your application. This way, you can ensure that the layout of your blocks will be consistent even though different developers create and maintain them in different modules.

13.6.1 CREATING FRAMES

The easiest way to create a new frame and associate it with a block is to use the Layout Wizard. A number of properties you set in the screens of this wizard apply to the properties of the frame object. Section 13.3 explained in details the use and properties of the Layout Wizard. Frames can also be created manually in the Layout Editor. The following steps describe the process of creating a frame in this editor and associating it with a block:

1. Open a Layout Editor window and display the canvas in which you want to create the frame.
2. Click the Frame icon on the Tool Palette and draw the new frame in the desired location and with the desired dimensions on the canvas. You can also move and resize the frame object just like any other graphic on the canvas.
3. Display the Property Palette for the frame object.
4. Set the property Layout Data Block to the name of the block you want to associate with the frame. Notice how all the items with the property Visible set to "Yes" are arranged within the boundaries of the frame.

In addition to associating the visible items of a block with the new frame, you also need to set a number of other properties of the frame. The following section will highlight the most important properties of frames.

13.6.2 PROPERTIES OF FRAMES

As you have already seen, frames are nothing but special types of graphic objects owned by Canvas or Tab Page objects in the Form Builder. From the visual perspective, they are composed of a rectangle object and a text label. The properties of these objects can be maintained just like the properties of any rectangle or text object in the Layout Editor. In particular, all the commands discussed in Chapter 6 for setting the dimensions, position, line style, color, and font of graphic objects in the Layout Editor can be used with a frame object. These properties may also be modified in the Property Palette of the frame object where they are located in the following groups: Physical, Font & Color, and Frame Title Font & Color. In the following paragraphs, I will describe only the properties that are specific to frames.

- **Frame layout properties.** In this category, I include first and foremost the property Layout Style. The effects of its settings—"Form" or "Tabular"—were discussed in the Section 13.3.4. This property can also be set in the Style tab of the Layout Editor. Two other properties that fall in this category are Allow Expansion and Shrinkwrap. The first one can be used to allow the dimensions of the frame to be increased if additional items are included in the block; the second one, when set to "Yes," will cause the frame to adjust its size so that any extra blank space on the canvas is trimmed out. All the properties mentioned so far are located in the Layout Frame group of the Property Palette.

  Other properties that have directly influenced the layout of the frame are those included in the groups Frame Title, Records, and Scroll Bar of the Property Palette. The properties in the Frame Title group allow you to maintain the contents of the text label that describes the frame on the canvas, as well as its alignment with respect to the frame's rectangle and the offset of the label from the corners of the rectangle. The properties most commonly changed in this group are Frame Title, Frame Title Alignment, and Frame Title Offset. The properties in the Records group allow you to maintain the number of records displayed within the frame and the distance between these records, in cases when more than one record is displayed. And the properties in the Scroll Bar group are used to display or hide the block's scroll bar, and, in cases when it is displayed, to define its width and its position with respect to the frame's rectangle. Note that the properties Frame Title, Number of Records Displayed, Distance Between Records, and Show Scroll Bar are accessible from the screen Rows of the Layout Wizard dialog box as well.

TIP

Some properties, such as Number of Records Displayed, Show Scroll Bar, and Scroll Bar Width, can be set for blocks as well as for frames. When a frame is first associated with a block the settings of the shared properties for the frame object override those for the block. After that, you can maintain these properties in any object and the modifications will be reflected in the companion object.

- **Item layout properties.** This category includes properties that govern the way items are organized within the frame. Frame Alignment controls the alignment of items within the frame. By default, this property is set to "Column" and causes all the text labels to be aligned right in one columns and all the data items to be aligned left in a second column. Other settings often used are "Start" and "End," which aligns all the items left or right, respectively.

  The properties Horizontal Margin and Vertical Margin control the position of the items and text labels with respect to the upper left hand corner of the frame's rectangle. If, for example, these properties are set to 5 and 15, respectively, then the first object within the frame will be located 5 points to the right and 15 points below the upper left-hand corner of the rectangle. The properties Horizontal Object Offset and Vertical Object Offset are also important because they allow you to control the distances between objects on the canvas. Typically, the Vertical Object Offset has more effect visually because it allows you to arrange the items in horizontal lines with consistent distances between the lines.
- **Frame refresh properties.** The only property in this category is Update Layout. Nevertheless, I have set it aside as a special category so that I can describe the process in which the layout of the frame is updated. Normally, the property Update Layout is set to "Automatically." This causes all the objects within the frame to be laid out on the canvas each time you modify one of the frame's properties in the Property Palette, or move or resize it on the Layout Editor. Upon this act, the Layout Editor computes the position of each item based on the number and size of items and based on the settings of the frames' properties of the that I have been discussing so far. When the property is set to "Manually" none of the actions above triggers the layout update. Instead, you have to click the icon Update Layout on the Layout Editor's toolbar or select Arrange | Update Layout from the menu. Finally, you do not want the frame to influence the layout of the items on the canvas, set the property Update Layout to "Locked." With this setting, the only modifications to the items' layout can happen by changing their properties individually in the Property Palette or on the Layout Editor.

TIP

Understanding the implications of each setting for the property Update Layout and applying them at different points during the development life-cycle may be the key to successfully using frames in Form Builder. My recommendation is that you set the property to "Automatically" when you initially define the block's layout. This will allow you to delineate the major features of the layout for the particular block. After that, you may need to modify a number of properties of the frame object in order to fine-tune its layout. To avoid unnecessary refreshing of the layout each time you change one of these properties, set the property Update Layout to "Manually." Finally, if you manually arrange the position or dimensions of the items and do not want the Layout Editor to override these changes by running its algorithm, set the property to "Locked."

- **Item prompt properties.** The properties in this category influence the way the prompts associated with the items are laid out on the canvas. Such properties are Start Prompt Alignment and Top Prompt Alignment, which allow you to align the prompt with the item's horizontal and top edges. The first property is used mostly for form style frames, whereas the second one is used for tabular frames. The properties Start Prompt Offset and Top Prompt Offset define the distance between the prompt and the item. They have effect for form and tabular frames, respectively, as well. Finally, another property that is often set in this category is Allow Multi-line Prompts. When this property is set to "Yes," the prompts are split in multiple lines whenever possible to conserve the canvas space. All the properties in this category are part of the Layout Frame group in the Property Palette.

13.7 RELATIONS

As mentioned previously, blocks in a Form Builder module correspond to logical groups of data in the world that the application is describing. When the system is designed, the relationships between these groups of data are discovered. It is natural to expect the application to reflect such relationships in its interface.

The Form Builder has a separate class of objects, called Relations, to administer the coordination of blocks that represent related data. On one side of the relation object resides the master block. On the other side is the detail block. There may be zero or more records in the detail block that correspond to each record in the master block. The condition that records from each block must meet in order for them to be considered related is called a join condition. The join condition is typically an equality condition. The value stored in the foreign key of the relation block must be equal to the value of the primary key in the master block.

13.7.1 CREATING RELATIONS AND SETTING THEIR PROPERTIES IN THE FORM BUILDER

Up to now, I have explained how you create default Master-Details relations using the Data Block Wizard. As you saw in Section 13.2.4 this wizard helps you create relations whether or not the relationship is already defined at the database level, in the form of a foreign key constraint. An alternative method is to create the relations in the Object Navigator. Relations are objects that in the hierarchy tree of the Object Navigator belong to blocks, or, more precisely, to the master block in the relation. In order to create a relation, you must follow these steps:

1. Identify the master block and the detail block that will be joined by the relation.
2. Expand the master block node in the Navigator, and create a new Relation object. The New Relation dialog box appears (see Figure 13.19).
3. Set the properties for the new relation according to your needs. The meaning of these settings is discussed in the rest of this section. An example is shown in Figure 13.19.
4. Click OK.

The New Relation dialog box allows you to set the properties of a relation at creation time. The name of the relation is specified in the Name text field. It corre-

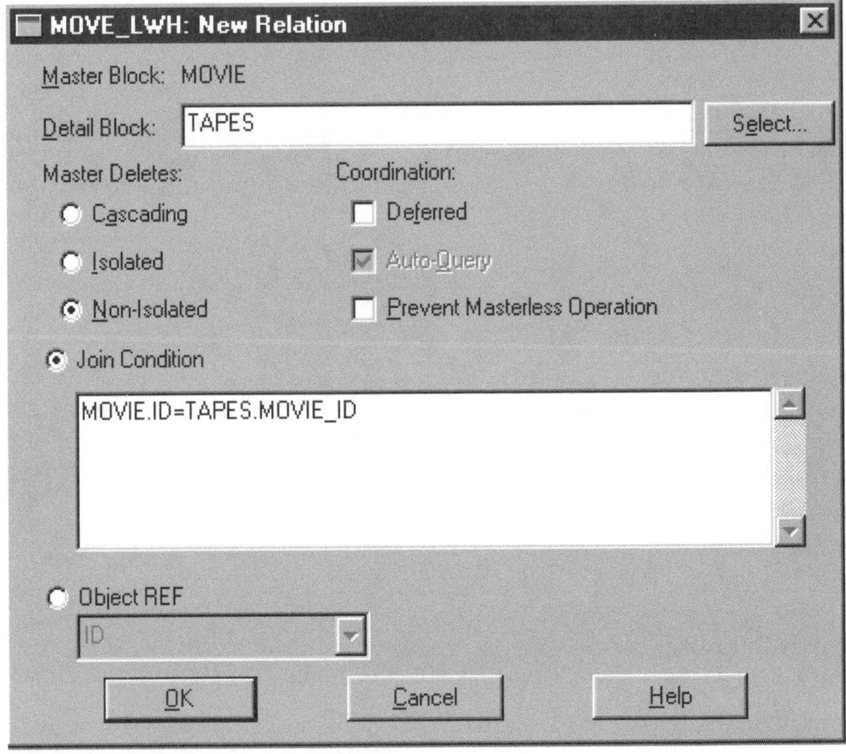

FIGURE 13.19 New Relation dialog box.

sponds to the Name property of the relation and it can be any valid Form Builder name. However, it is customary to concatenate the name of the master block followed by the name of the detail block, as shown in Figure 13.19. If you know which blocks you want to connect, supply their names directly in the Master Block and Detail Block text fields. You can also click the Select buttons to their right to display a LOVs dialog box from which you can choose the block name. When the New Relation dialog box is displayed, the Master Block text field contains the name of the block from where the operation originated. Nevertheless, you can supply any other block name in the field. When the relation is created, the object will be placed under the hierarchy of the block you specify as master.

Under the name fields is a group of three radio buttons called Master Deletes. Its settings correspond to the property Delete Record Behavior in the Property Palette of the relation. The options you can choose here control if, when, and how detail records will be deleted if the master record is deleted. The "Non-Isolated" option is the default setting of the Delete Record Behavior property. When this option is set, records in the master block cannot be deleted if the detail block contains records. This behavior may be too restrictive at times. If, for example, the database contains twenty copies of a movie that is being taken off the shelves, you would want to delete the movie record and have the application ensure that the tape records that depend on it are deleted as well. At the application level, you can implement this functionality by selecting the Cascading radio button from the Master Deletes group, thus effectively setting the property Delete Record Behavior to "Cascades."

Depending on the particular environment for each application, you may choose to place the cascade delete logic in the database server, or in client application. At the database level you may define foreign key constraints with the ON DELETE CASCADE option. For example, the table RENTALS that will be used in the MRD application has the following two constraints defined:

```
CONSTRAINT rentals_cust_id_fk FOREIGN KEY (customer_id)
           REFERENCES customers
           ON DELETE CASCADE
CONSTRAINT rentals_tape_id_fk FOREIGN KEY (tape_id)
           REFERENCES tapes
           ON DELETE CASCADE
```

With these constraints enabled, each time a record is deleted in the table CUSTOMERS or TAPES, Oracle will automatically delete records in RENTALS associated with it. If for some reason the foreign key constraints are found to be too restrictive, the same functionality can be implemented by defining database triggers in tables MOVIES and CUSTOMERS, which fire each time a record is deleted, and remove all the related records from table RENTALS.

Whichever approach you take, you must not duplicate the effort by implementing the same feature at both levels. The "Isolated" option is the least restrictive from all the possible settings of the Delete Record Behavior property. This allows users to delete records in the master block independently from the records displayed in the detail block.

To the right of the Master Deletes radio group is a check-box group called Coordination. Each member of this group corresponds to a relation property. The settings of the check boxes under this group control the display of records in the detail block when a coordination event occurs in the master block. A coordination event is any action that causes moving of the focus from one record in the block to another record in that block. Examples of coordination events are moving to the next or previous record, creating a new record, or deleting an existing one. Moving to another item within a record, changing an item, or committing changes to the database do not constitute coordination events.

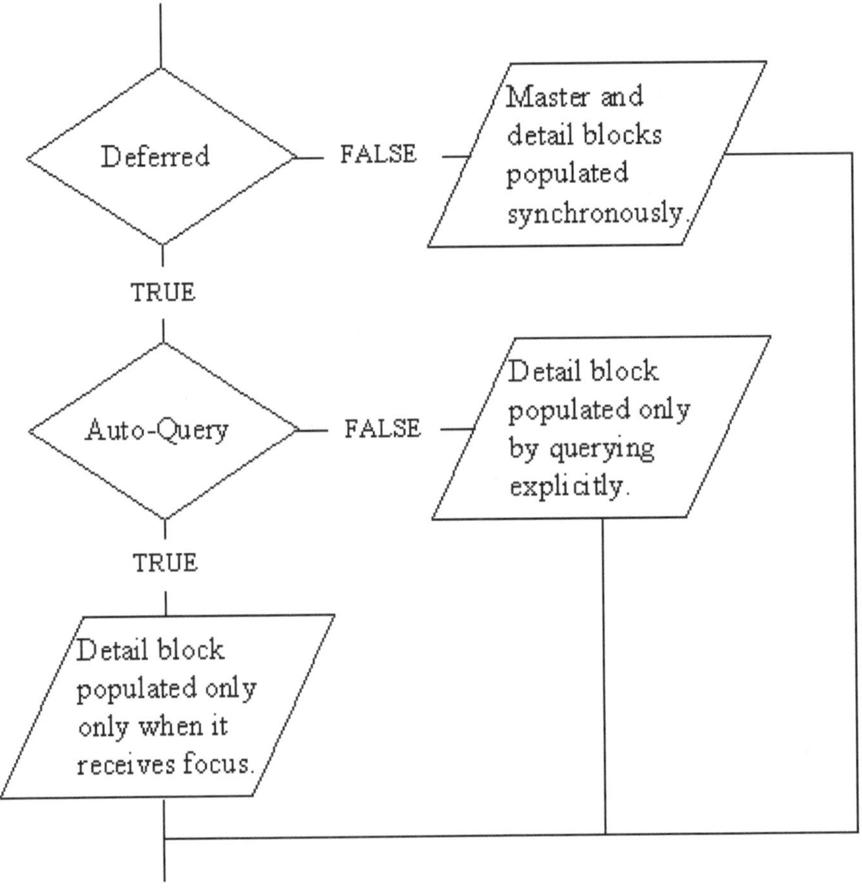

FIGURE 13.20 Meaning of Deferred and Auto-Query Relation Properties.

The effects of selecting the check boxes in this group, the wording of the text labels, and the micro-help messages associated with them can be quite confusing and, at times, obscure. Therefore, we will go through them carefully and explain each combination separately.

The first two options are closely related to each other. If the Deferred option is not checked, Forms will populate the detail block as soon as a coordination event occurs in the master block. But, if the Deferred option is checked, then the retrieval of records in the detail block is postponed, or deferred, in two ways. If Auto-Query is checked, the detail records are queried as soon as the focus navigates in the detail block. If the Auto-Query is not checked, the detail records are retrieved only if the users explicitly query the detail block. Figure 13.20 presents graphically the meaning of these options. By default, the Deferred property is turned off, thus resulting in an automatic and synchronized coordination of the blocks.

The third check box, Prevent Masterless Operations, does not depend on the setting of the previous two properties. If the option is set, the records in the detail block could be queried even when there are no records present in the master block. If the option is not set, which is also the default behavior, Forms cannot navigate to the detail block if the master contains no records.

The multi-line text field Join Condition is where you specify the condition that establish the coordination of the block. In general terms, this condition specifies the data items in the detail and master blocks whose values must match. Usually, the join condition is fully qualified, as in Figure 13.20. However, if the items in both blocks share the same name, simply providing that common name will work equally well. In the example of Figure 13.20, the join condition could have simply been `MOVIE_ID`.

Once a relation is created its properties can be modified at design time in the Property Palette for the relation. The properties for a relation object are divided in two main groups. The Functional group includes the properties Detail Data Block, Join Condition, Delete Record Behavior, and Prevent Masterless Operations. The Coordination group includes the properties Deferred and Automatic Query. The settings of these windows in the Property Palette have the same meaning as in the New Relation dialog box.

13.7.2 SETTING THE PROPERTIES OF RELATIONS AT RUNTIME

The Form Builder built-ins routines FIND_RELATION, ID_NULL, GET_RELATION_PROPERTY, and SET_RELATION_PROPERTY allow you to manipulate the properties of a relation programmatically. The function shown in Figure 13.21 takes as input variable the name of a relation and returns the coordination state between the related blocks. The logic of the function follows the meaning of Deferred and Automatic Query properties explained earlier, and the flowchart diagram presented in Figure 13.20. The function `Get_Coordination_Status` returns SYNCHRONOUS if Deferred property is "No," DEFERRED_AUTOMATIC if Deferred property is "Yes" and Automatic Query is "Yes"; and DEFERRED_MANUAL if Deferred property is "Yes" and Automatic Query is "No."

It is worth mentioning that the properties for relations, and all the other objects in Form Builder have two names. The first one is what you see in the Properties Window at design time. For example, the names for two properties of records are Deferred and Automatic Query. The second name is what you should use

```
FUNCTION Get_Coordination_Status (rel_name VARCHAR2)
RETURN VARCHAR2  IS
 deferred_status VARCHAR2(20) :=NULL;
 autoquery_status      VARCHAR2(20) :=NULL;
 coordination_status   VARCHAR2(20) :=NULL;
 rel_id            RELATION;
BEGIN
 rel_id := FIND_RELATION(rel_name);
 IF NOT ID_NULL(rel_id) THEN
  deferred_status := GET_RELATION_PROPERTY(rel_id,
DEFERRED_COORDINATION);
  autoquery_status := GET_RELATION_PROPERTY(rel_id,
AUTOQUERY);
 ELSE
  MESSAGE('Relation ' || rel_name || ' does not exist.');
  RAISE FORM_TRIGGER_FAILURE;
 END IF;

 /* If control comes here, the relation exists in the
module. */
 IF deferred_status = 'TRUE' THEN
  IF autoquery_status = 'TRUE' THEN
   coordination_status := 'DEFERRED_AUTOMATIC';
  ELSE
   coordination_status := 'DEFERRED_MANUAL';
  END IF;
 ELSE
  coordination_status := 'SYNCHRONOUS';
 END IF;

 RETURN coordination_status;
END Get_Coordination_Status;
```

FIGURE 13.21 Defining the coordination state of a relation at runtime.

with the object-specific built-in routines GET and SET to manipulate the settings of these properties at runtime. The names for the properties mentioned above are DEFERRED_COORDINATION and AUTOQUERY. In this book, you will see both names used according to the context.

The procedure shown in Figure 13.22 takes as input variable the name of a relation and a character string that represents the coordination state between the related blocks. If this string is SYNCHRONOUS, the procedure `Set_Coordination_Status` will set the property Deferred to "No"; if it is DEFERRED_AUTOMATIC, the properties Deferred and Automatic Query are set to "Yes"; and if it is

```
PROCEDURE Set_Coordination_Status ( relation_name VARCHAR2,
                                    status VARCHAR2) IS
 relation_id      RELATION;
BEGIN
 relation_id := FIND_RELATION(relation_name);
 IF NOT ID_NULL(relation_id) THEN
  IF status = 'SYNCHRONOUS' THEN
   SET_RELATION_PROPERTY(relation_id, DEFERRED_COORDINATION,
                                               PROPERTY_FALSE);
  ELSIF status = 'DEFERRED_AUTOMATIC' THEN
   SET_RELATION_PROPERTY(relation_id, DEFERRED_COORDINATION,
                                               PROPERTY_FALSE);
   SET_RELATION_PROPERTY(relation_id, AUTOQUERY,
      PROPERTY_TRUE);
  ELSIF status = 'DEFERRED_MANUAL' THEN
   SET_RELATION_PROPERTY(relation_id, DEFERRED_COORDINATION,
                                               PROPERTY_FALSE);
   SET_RELATION_PROPERTY(relation_id, AUTOQUERY,
      PROPERTY_TRUE);
  ELSE
   MESSAGE(UPPER(status) || ' is not a valid coordination
      status.');
   RAISE FORM_TRIGGER_FAILURE;
  END IF;
 ELSE
  MESSAGE('Relation ' || relation_name || ' does not exist.');
  RAISE FORM_TRIGGER_FAILURE;
 END IF;
END Set_Coordination_Status;
```

FIGURE 13.22 Setting the coordination state of a relation at runtime.

DEFERRED_MANUAL, the Deferred property is set to "Yes" and Automatic Query to "No."

You can use both these program units to give users the flexibility and ability to decide at runtime how the detail blocks in the application will be populated, rather than making a decision for them at design time.

The Join Condition of a relation specifies that two or more data items in the master and detail blocks will have the same values. If an item that is part of the relation's foreign key in the detail block is accessible, users may override its value, thus breaking the link with the master record. Usually this situation must not occur, therefore, you may consider hiding the item by setting its Visible property to "No." The item is still part of the detail block, but it is simply hidden from the users.

13.7.3 PL/SQL OBJECTS ASSOCIATED WITH RELATIONS

When you create a new relation, Form Builder automatically creates a series of triggers and program units that control the coordination between the master and detail blocks. The type of triggers will depend on the setting of the properties for the relation.

If at least one relation exists in the form, Form Builder creates the form-level trigger ON-CLEAR-DETAIL. This trigger fires when the focus moves from one record to another in the master block. It simply issues a call to the CLEAR_ALL_MASTER_DETAIL procedure, which is created and updated as relations are created. The purpose of this procedure is to go through the list of all the blocks that serve as detail blocks for the block being cleared, and to clear them from existing records.

The trigger ON-POPULATE-DETAIL is created for each relation. It is attached to the master block of a relation and is responsible for the way the records in the detail block are queried. This trigger fires when the focus of the forms lands inside the record in the master block.

If the record is not committed to the database, or the item that is part of the *Join Condition* is NULL, the trigger does not act in any manner. This behavior is to be expected, since both conditions mean that the master record cannot have any detail records associated with it in the database.

If the master record already exists in the database and the *Join Condition* item is not NULL, the trigger invokes the procedure QUERY_MASTER_DETAILS, which is created and maintained automatically by the Form Builder when relations are created. The settings of the Coordination properties define the actions this procedure can perform. If the property Deferred is "No," QUERY_MASTER_DETAIL issues a query in the detail block that synchronizes its contents with the record that has the focus in the master block. If Deferred is "Yes," the only action of QUERY_MASTER_DETAIL is to set the COORDINATION_STATUS property of the detail block to NON_COORDINATED. If, during the execution of the application, users navigate to the detail block, this setting prompts Forms Runtime engine to act according to the setting of the property Automatic Query. If it is "Yes," a query is issued to refresh the contents of the block; otherwise, no action occurs.

If the property Delete Record Behavior of the relation is set to "Isolated," these are the only triggers created by Form Builder. If this property is set to "Non Isolated," Form Builder creates the trigger ON-CHECK-DELETE-MASTER, in addition to the other two. This trigger is attached to the master block and fires when users attempt to delete a record in it. The trigger allows the delete process to continue only if there are no detail records in the database. Otherwise, it displays the message "Cannot delete master record when matching detail records exist." You have already seen this message in the ETS application that you created in Part One.

If the property Delete Record Behavior is set to "Cascading," a PRE-DELETE trigger is created in addition to ON-CLEAR-DETAILS and ON-POPULATE-DETAILS triggers. This trigger is also attached to the master block, and fires just before the DELETE statement for the master record is sent to the database. Its functionality is to delete the detail records.

In addition to the triggers and procedures mentioned here, Form Builder also creates a procedure called CHECK_PACKAGE_FAILURE that halts any further processing if the last action in the form is not successful.

If you are a little confused by all the functionality that these program units perform, be assured that, with all likelihood, you will never have to edit them. Your task in the process of defining a relation is as simple as setting the properties of the relation in the Data Block Wizard, in the New Relation dialog box, or in the Property Palette. Form Builder will read these settings and create or edit the PL/SQL objects accordingly. Here are a few actions that Form Builder will perform in order to maintain the code of these objects for you:

1. If a block enters in several complicated relations with other blocks, Form Builder will expand the triggers and procedures mentioned above to reflect the position of the block as master or detail in all the relations it takes part.
2. If a relation is deleted, the PL/SQL objects will be edited according to the new relationship structure. If no longer needed, they will be removed altogether.
3. If the property Delete Record Behavior of a relation changes, Form Builder will create, modify, or delete triggers according to the setting of the property. For example, if you change the setting from "Non-Isolated" to "Cascading," Form Builder will delete the ON-CHECK-DELETE-MASTER trigger and create a PRE-DELETE trigger.
4. If you place code in the triggers mentioned here (ON-CLEAR-DETAILS, ON-POPULATE-DETAILS, ON-CHECK-DELETE-MASTER, and PRE-DELETE), Form Builder will preserve your code. The code necessary for the Master-Detail coordination will be appended to or removed from existing triggers, depending on the situation.

The elegant handling of all the code creation and maintenance activities, and the fact that relations in Form Builder represent purely logical connections between data elements, free from constraints specified in the database, makes them a powerful tool in Forms development activities.

13.8 BLOCKS AND RELATIONS FOR THE MRD APPLICATION

Before creating the blocks that will be part of the MRD application, perform these preliminary steps:

1. Create a subdirectory that will hold all the code for the MRD application, for example, C:\MRD.
2. Launch Form Builder and connect to the database with the account used to create the MRD database objects.
3. Replace the default name of the Forms module with MRD.
4. Save the module to the C:\MRD directory.

Now you can use the Data Block Wizard followed by the Layout Wizard to specify the initial properties of the data blocks. The following steps contain the recommended settings for the properties that you will change. The rest of the properties may retain their default values.

1. Create the block CUSTOMERS based on the table CUSTOMERS and include all the columns from this table. In the Layout Wizard, select the (New Canvas) option to create a new canvas for the block. Choose to display all the items and set the layout style of the frame to "Form." Do not provide a name for the new frame. Rename the newly-related canvas to "CUSTOMERS."
2. Create the block MOVIES based on the table MOVIES. Include all the columns from this table and display them all on a new canvas in form layout. Do not provide a name for the new frame and rename the new canvas to "MOVIES."
3. Create the block TAPES based on the table TAPES. In the Data Block Wizard, include all the items in the block and select MOVIES as the master block of the new block. In the Layout Wizard, place the frame for this block on the canvas "MOVIES," display the items ID and STATUS, select the tabular layout style, set Frame Title to "Tapes for Movie," set Records Displayed to "5," and check the check box Display Scrollbar.
4. Create the block RENTALS based on the table RENTALS. Create this block on a new canvas and rename this canvas "RENTALS." Display all the items of the block, set the layout style to "Tabular," Frame Title to "Rental Trans-

actions," Records Displayed to "5," and select the check box Display Scrollbar.

Wrap up the work by saving and generating the module. Module CH13_2.FMB provided with the companion software contains the final version of the MRD form at the end of this chapter.

13.9 SUMMARY

This chapter discussed the properties of blocks and relations in Form Builder. Important concepts of this chapter were:

- **Types of Blocks**
  - Data Blocks and Control Blocks
  - Master and Detail Blocks
  - Single-Record and Multi-Record Blocks
- **Creating and Maintaining Data Blocks**
  - Invoking the Data Block Wizard
  - Defining the Block Type
  - Defining the Database Items
  - Creating Master Detail Relations between Blocks
  - Defining Blocks Based on Stored Procedures
- **Defining and Maintaining the Layout of Blocks**
  - Invoking the Layout Wizard
  - Defining the Canvas Properties
  - Defining the Item Layout Properties
  - Defining the Layout Style
- **Maintaining Block Properties in the Form Builder**
  - Navigation Properties
  - Records Properties
  - Database Properties
  - Advanced Database Properties
  - Scrollbar Properties
  - Miscellaneous Properties
- **Maintaining Block Properties Programmatically**
- **Frames**
  - Creating Frames
  - Properties of Frames

- **Relations**
  - Creating Relations and Setting Their Properties in the Form Builder
  - Setting the Properties of Relations at Runtime
  - PL/SQL Objects Associated with Relations
- **Blocks and Relations for the MRD Application**

The following table describes the software assets that were discussed in this chapter. From the main HTML page of the software utilities provided with the book follow the links *Software* and *Chapter 13* to access these assets:

ASSET NAME	DESCRIPTION
CH13_1.FMB	A template Form Builder module that contains the program units discussed in this chapter
CH13_2.FMB	The MRD application with the blocks and relations created in this chapter.
CH13_2.FMX	The executable version of the MRD application created in this chapter compiled on Win32 platforms.

Chapter 14

ITEMS AND DATA ITEMS

We're making the users do more and more programming,
but they don't know it.
—Dan Bricklin

- Types of Items
- Creating Items
- Generic Properties of Items
- Setting Properties of Items at Runtime
- Validation of Items
- Text Items and Display Items
- Calculated Items
- Events of Text Items
- GUI Guidelines for Data Items
- Data Items in the MRD Application
- Summary

Items are the most basic and, at the same time, the most important element of an application's user interface. It is by entering data into, or selecting from items that users establish links to the repository of data. In the object hierarchy of the Form Builder, items must exist within blocks. Items must also lie on a canvas. If users will interact directly with the items, the canvas is a named one. If items will be used to facilitate the internal processing, and will not need to be displayed to the users they are "placed" on a virtual canvas, called the NULL canvas. This chapter discusses in detail the types of items that can be used in Form Builder applications, and their properties.

14.1 TYPES OF ITEMS

In general, items in Form Builder applications allow users to interact with data that reside in persistent storage devices. They are a bridge between the back-end and the front-end parts of an application. This dichotomy displays itself in the classification of items. Based on the origin of data, items are divided in data and control items. Based on the way the data are presented to users in a GUI environment, items are classified as data-entry items and GUI controls. Data-entry items include text and display items. GUI controls include push buttons, radio buttons, check boxes, and list boxes. In addition, applications developed Form Builder can use image items, sound items, charts from Developer Graphics, OLE containers, ActiveX Controls, and Java Beans.

14.1.1 DATA ITEMS AND CONTROL ITEMS

Data items can only be part of data blocks. They are directly mapped to database columns—part of tables or views upon which blocks may be based or part of PL/SQL tables for blocks based on stored procedures. When a query is executed, data from these columns appear directly in the corresponding items. When a record is created or updated, data supplied in the items will be sent to the corresponding database columns and handled appropriately.

Control items, on the other hand, do not directly map to database columns. They can be part of both data and control blocks. When used in data blocks, control items usually display data derived from other items in the block. For example, a control item may calculate the total revenue generated by a customer, based on the amount of money paid over a period of time to rent videos. Another popular use of control items in data blocks is to retrieve and display data based on values of data items in the block. For example, in a block based on table RENTALS, you would like to display the full name of the customer renting a movie, rather than just the ID stored in this table. The name item in the block will be a control item, and it will be populated from the CUSTOMERS table, based on the value of CUSTOMER_ID for each particular rental transaction. Such items are often called lookup items. Finally, a third use of control items is to enhance the interaction of users with the application. Items in this category typically include button or toolbar icons that used to invoke different actions in the application.

> **TIP**
>
> During the analysis and design phase of the application, an important activity is normalizing data entities and relations, or making sure that all the data elements of an entity depend on the entity's primary key, the whole key, and nothing but the key. The purpose of this activity is to create a clear understanding of the data involved, and the rules that govern their relations and interaction. During the development phase, in order to represent the data in a way that is familiar and understandable to the users, some of the data entities are merged, in a process known as denormalization of the data model. At a certain level the denormalization happens at the database. But another form of denormalization happens during the application development when control items represent related data that are not stored in the data items of a block.

14.1.2 GUI INTERFACE ITEMS

As mentioned before, the interface between users and the database is maintained by data-entry items and controls such as buttons, radio buttons, check boxes, and list boxes. Figure 14.1 shows the example of a form that contains items from each

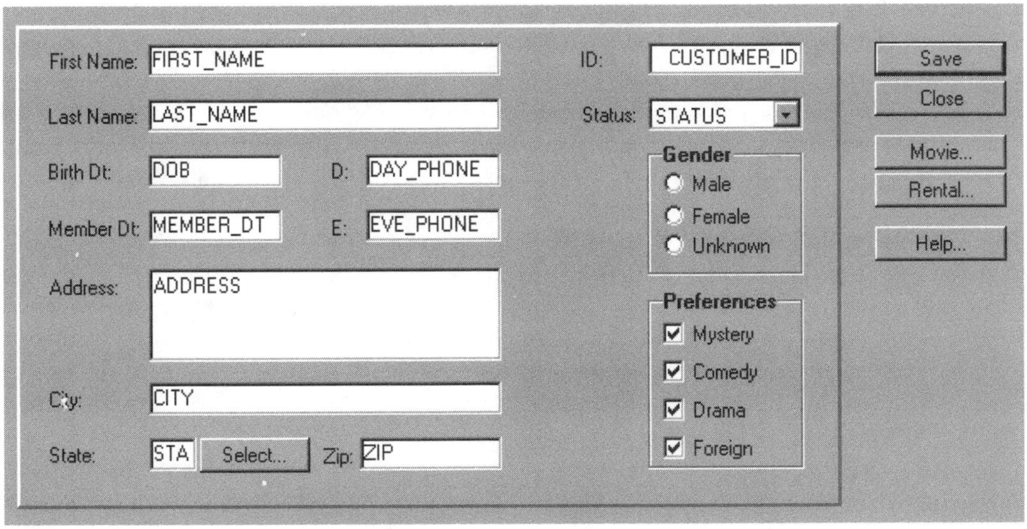

FIGURE 14.1 Major GUI categories of items.

of these categories. The term data-entry item is used for traditional and historical reasons. Usually, in GUI standards and reference guides, this term is used for single-line or multi-line text fields, like those shown in Figure 14.1.

Buttons are control items that usually initiate an action such as saving to the database or opening a dialog box where additional information is processed. Iconic buttons found primarily in toolbars are a special form of buttons. Radio buttons are used to select only one choice from a short list of options. Check boxes are used to select more than one choice from a short list of options. If the number of options to choose from is large, list boxes are used to improve the readability of the application. Single-selection list boxes expand the functionality of radio groups; multi-selection list boxes expand the functionality of check boxes.

The rest of this chapter will discuss issues related to the creation and use of items, and their generic properties. The second part of the chapter will focus on text and display items. The next chapter will discuss the GUI control items: buttons, radio buttons, check boxes, and lists. Chapter 15 will provide the necessary information multimedia items and controls such as image items, Developer Graphics charts, sound items, OLE containers, ActiveX controls, and Java Beans.

14.2 CREATING ITEMS

For data blocks, the number of data items you can create is limited by the number of columns in the tabular structure upon which the block is based. If not all these columns are included as items in the block, you can easily add the additional items in the Table tab of the Data Layout Wizard for the corresponding block. By default, the items you create are text items. You can transform them into radio group, check box, or any other type of item, by invoking the Data Layout Wizard. Recall from the previous chapter that in the tab Data Block of this wizard you can set the type of any displayed item by selecting from the list box Item Type. However, since additional editing is still required, it is easier to create the block with text items, and then change the Item Type property in the Property Palette of the item.

You can add new items to an existing block by creating them either in the Object Navigator, or in the Layout Editor. It is preferable to create items in the Layout Editor, since it is much easier to place and size them on the canvas. The context of the Editor when the item is created defines the block and the canvas that will own the item. You must ensure that the context is set appropriately before the item is created.

When data items are created using the Data Block Wizard, Form Builder inherits a number of their properties from the columns' properties as they are recorded in the data dictionary. Such properties include at least Name, Data Type, and Maximum Length. If the check box Enforce data integrity is checked in the Table tab of the wizard, additional formatting and validation information is transferred from the database to the items. When items are created in the Navigator or Layout Editor, Form Builder does not query the database for any of the data dictionary definitions mentioned above. You must manually set all the properties of the new item according to the needs of the application. If the item is a data item, make sure that its name matches the column name in the table. You must also make sure that the data type and length of the new item do not conflict with the database settings. By default, an item created in the Navigator or the Layout Editor is a thirty-character alphanumeric item. If its database counterpart has settings different from the above, the application will be prone to several kinds of error. Some of the errors that may occur are listed below:

- ❑ If the column data type is different from the item data type, you cannot perform any database actions. If, for example, you try to query the database, you will get the error message "FRM-40505: ORACLE error: unable to perform query," followed by "ORA-00932: Inconsistent data types."
- ❑ If the column is longer than the item, truncation may occur when records are fetched from database queries. Forms will display the message "FRM-40831: Truncation occurs: value too long for field FIELD_NAME."
- ❑ If the column is shorter than the item, you may not be able to insert or update records in the database. If, for example, the UPDATE command fails, Forms will display the error message "FRM-40509: ORACLE error: unable to UPDATE record," followed by "ORA-01401: INSERTED value too large for column."

> **TIP**
>
> You may retrieve some of the information required to create a new data item in the Object Navigator. Expanding the Database Objects node to an appropriate level, you can display the name and data type for each column in any table. For more detailed information, you must rely either on the database design and data dictionary documentation, or use other tools provided by the Oracle Corporation or third party vendors. Better yet, if you are maintaining the design of your system in the Oracle Designer Repository, a number of properties can be set and shared between database objects and software module objects.

Given all the different steps you must take to add a data column to an already-created block, it is natural to conclude that you should consider the structure of the blocks carefully before you create them. You should spend some time discussing and finalizing all the database columns that will be included in the block in order to avoid the extra effort required to add a column at a later date.

As a final note in this section, keep in mind that the type of block defines also the type of items created within that block in the Object Navigator or the Layout Editor. When creating an item for a data block, the Database Item property for that item will be set to "Yes." If you are creating a control item for the block, you must remember to set this property to "No."

14.3 GENERIC PROPERTIES OF ITEMS

Like other objects in Form Builder, the properties of items in the Property Palette are grouped in categories based on their use and functionality. The General group contains the omnipresent Name, Subclass Information, and Comments properties. The property Item Type, whose setting determines the GUI type of the item, is found in this group as well. The other properties are grouped in categories to facilitate the process of viewing and modifying their settings. The number of these categories is quite large and it varies with the type of item. For example, all the items that can interact with the database have properties in the following categories: Functional, Navigation, Data, Records, Database, Physical, Font & Color, Prompt, Prompt Font & Color, and Help. This includes text, display, check box, radio group, image, ActiveX Controls, Java Beans, and OLE Container items. Push button items do not contain any properties in the Data or Database groups, because their purpose is to initiate some action and not to display or modify data. Similarly, chart items, used to store Graphics Builder displays in the form, and report items, used to invoke Report Builder reports from the form, do not have properties in these two groups. Instead, they contain properties in the group Dev Integration and Chart or Report.

Figure 14.2 presents the distribution of property groups by item types in a tabular format. The following sections describe the most important groups of properties shared by items of all types.

14.3.1 FUNCTIONAL PROPERTIES

The Functional group includes the property Enabled that is common for all types of items. By default, this property is set to "Yes," thus allowing users to access the item's data. If you set the property to "No," users have no way to access the item. Triggers associated with events in a disabled item will not be executed, since none of these events occurs. Data displayed in the field will appear grayed out to indicate its unavailability.

Another Functional property shared by all the item types is Popup Menu. This property allows you to associate a specific item with a menu displayed by right-clicking the item. Pop-up menus can be defined at the canvas level or for each item individually. Chapter 18 provides more details on this type of Form Builder objects.

	TEXT ITEM	DISPLAY ITEM	LIST ITEM	CHECK BOX	RADIO GROUP	PUSH BUTTON	SOUND, IMAGE	CHART, REPORT	OLE CONTAINER	ACTIVEX CONTROL	JAVA BEAN
General	√	√	√	√	√	√	√	√	√	√	√
Functional	√	√	√	√	√	√	√	√	√	√	√
Navigation	√	√	√	√	√	√	√	√	√	√	√
Data	√	√	√	√	√		√		√	√	√
Calculation	√	√	√	√	√				√	√	√
Records	√	√	√	√	√	√	√	√	√	√	√
Database	√	√	√	√	√		√		√	√	√
List of Values (LOV)	√										
Editor	√										
Physical	√	√	√	√	√	√	√	√	√	√	√
Font & Color	√	√	√	√	√	√	√	√	√	√	√
Prompt	√	√	√	√		√	√	√	√	√	√
Prompt Font & Color	√	√	√	√		√	√	√	√	√	√
Help	√	√	√	√	√	√	√	√	√	√	√
International	√	√	√	√	√	√					

FIGURE 14.2 Distribution of property groups by item types.

The Functional group contains a number of other properties that are specific to each item type. Functional properties of text and display items will be discussed later in the chapter. Functional properties of push buttons, radio groups, check boxes, and lists will be explained in the Chapter 14. Functional properties of images, charts, sound items, ActiveX controls, Java Bean, and OLE Container items will be discussed in Parts Four and Five.

14.3.2 NAVIGATION PROPERTIES

The Navigation group includes the properties Keyboard Navigable, Mouse Navigate, Next Navigation Item and Previous Navigation Item. The property Keyboard Navigable controls the access to enabled items using the keyboard navigation keys. If the property is set to "Yes," users can use the keyboard keys to navigate to the item. If the property is set to "No," the keyboard keys will not be able to place the form's focus inside the item.

Clicking the mouse on items such as check boxes, radio groups, list items, push buttons, charts, ActiveX controls, Java Beans, and OLE containers, is done primarily to perform an action rather than to navigate to them. To avoid placing the Forms focus on these items, set their Mouse Navigate property to "No." This will still cause all the appropriate events to occur when the mouse is clicked, but will not move the focus from where it currently is to the clicked item.

Finally, the Next Navigation Item and Previous Navigation Item properties, if set, indicate the item where Forms should navigate when users press the TAB or SHIFT+TAB keys from the keyboard, or the NEXT_ITEM or PREVIOUS_ITEM built-ins are issued programmatically. If these properties are not set, the default tab order for the item is specified by the order of items in the Object Navigator.

14.3.3 DATA PROPERTIES

The Data group properties control data-related aspects of items such as length, data type, and default value. As mentioned earlier, some items, like chart and push button items do not have any properties in this group. For the remaining types, some of the properties may not be meaningful, and therefore, absent. For example, OLE Container and image items do not have properties such as data type or length. The following paragraphs describe the most important properties in this group:

- **Data Type.** This property specifies what kind of data is represented by the item. The property is meaningful only for text, display, radio group, check box, and list items. The fundamental data types are CHAR, DATE, and NUMBER, and LOB. CHAR data type is used for items that manipulate up to 2 Kb of character data. DATE is used for items that contain date and time information. NUMBER is used to represent numeric data. LOB data type is used for large binary objects. For backward compatibility reasons, text items

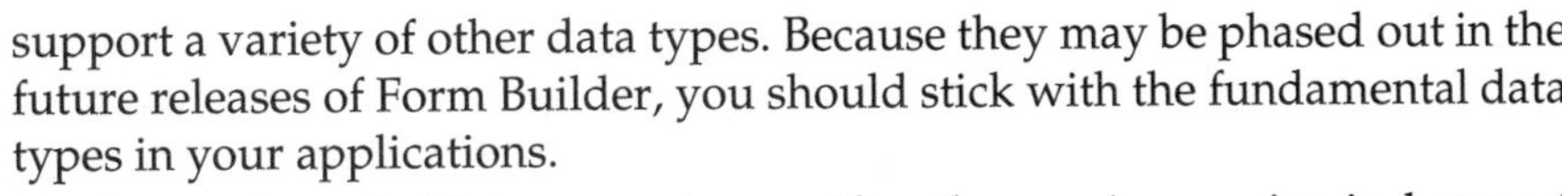

support a variety of other data types. Because they may be phased out in the future releases of Form Builder, you should stick with the fundamental data types in your applications.

- **Maximum Length.** This property specifies the maximum size in bytes of data that can be manipulated by the item. It is important to set this property in a way that information is not truncated and can be retrieved from the database. Note that the Maximum Length property does not interfere with the size of the item on the canvas, defined by the Width and Height properties in the Physical group.
- **Initial Value.** This property is used to fill the item with data when the record is first created. If carefully thought out and properly set, this property can reduce significantly the data-entry time and effort. If there is a value that is common for the majority of records in the database, you may want to specify it as the default value for the item. The rule of thumb is that if users pick a value more than fifty percent of the time, that should become the default value for the item. There are several goals you may achieve by setting the Default Value property of an item. Some of them are listed below:
    - Provide a hard-coded value such as `5`, or `Active`, that users will enter frequently. To do this, set the property to that value in the Property Palette.
    - Populate the item with numbers generated by a sequence. You could use this approach in the MRD application to supply ID numbers for customers and movies stored in the database. In this case, the setting of Default Value property should be:

      ```
      :SEQUENCE.MRD_SEQ.NEXTVAL
      ```

    - Supply dates in the application, rather than having users type them in. In the MRD application, many records will bear a creation date stamp on them. For customer records this will be the MEMBER_DT, for rental records it will be RENT_DT. When the application is first loaded, you will store the system date in a global variable, called `GLOBAL.Sysdate`. Then, the Default Value for the items mentioned above will be set to `:GLOBAL.Sysdate`.
- **Synchronize with Item.** This property can be set for all items except OLE containers. It allows you to create mirrored instances of an item within the same block. All these instances will display synchronously the same data. Modifying one instance propagates the change in all the other instances. You can use this property if you need to display the same data item in different contexts within the block.
- **Copy Value from Item.** The setting of this property indicates that the value of the current item must be initially copied from another item in the form, as indicated by its setting. When a master-detail relation is created, Form

Builder sets the Copy Value from Item property of the foreign key in the detail block to the primary key of the master block. The following example explains this. Consider the relation MOVIE_TAPE, in which MOVIE is the master and TAPE is the detail block. The property Copy Value from Item of item MOVIE_ID in TAPE block is set to MOVIE.MOVIE_ID.

The property Copy Value from Item is different from the property Synchronize with Item in two ways:

- ❑ The setting for Copy Value from Item can be any item in the current module. The setting for Mirror Item can be only an item within the same block.
- ❑ Copy Value from Item property populates the item with data, but after that does not maintain the source and the destination of data synchronized. Synchronize with Item, on the other hand, ensures that both the source and destination items will contain the same data at any one moment.

14.3.4 RECORDS PROPERTIES

The Records group contains the following three properties: Current Record Visual Attribute Group, Distance Between Records, and Number of Items Displayed. Recall from the previous chapter that these properties are defined for block objects as well. However, setting them at the item level overrides the block-level settings and has many interesting implications, especially for multi-record blocks. Suppose, for example, that you want to include the scanned picture of each customer in a multi-record block that displays other biographical data about them. You can conserve screen space and computing resources by displaying only one image at a time. To do this set the Number of Items Displayed property to 1 at the item level. Note that the default value for this property is zero. It means that the item will be displayed according to the setting of block-level property Records Displayed. Likewise, if you want the visual attributes of a particular item to differ from them of the entire record when the record is currently selected, set the property Current Record Visual Attribute Group to point to a visual attribute object different from the one selected for the block property.

14.3.5 DATABASE PROPERTIES

The main properties included in this group are Database Item, Query Only, Primary Key, Insert Allowed, Query Allowed, and Update Allowed. The property Database Item is set to "Yes" for data items and to "No" for control items. The meaning of this property was discussed earlier in the chapter.

The Query Only property is set to "No" by default, thus allowing users not only to query, but also insert or update the data managed by the item. Although this property appears in the Form Builder, and its value can be set in the Property

Palette of an item, the setting specified at design time does not have any effects on its functionality at runtime. The default setting for this property can be overridden only programmatically.

The properties Insert Allowed, Query Allowed, and Update Allowed control the ability of users to include the item in the respective database transactions. By default, they are all set to "Yes." Setting Insert Allowed to "No" does not allow users to enter data in the item when a new record is created. This feature can be used for example to populate items from sequence generators, and prevent users from overriding the generated numbers. Finally, if Update Allowed is "No" users can retrieve data for the item from the database, but cannot modify it. This feature can be used to protect sensitive data from unauthorized modifications. Setting Query Allowed to "No" prevents users from navigating to the item when the block is in Enter Query mode.

Chapter 2 explained how Form Runtime locks a record in the database as soon as an item in that record is changed by the user. For the locking to be done automatically, the item must be a data item. All too often, control items are used in conjunction with data items in a block. To have the locking process kick in automatically when a control item is modified, set its Lock Record property to "Yes." By default, the property is set to "No." This is the only property in the Database group of properties that is meaningful for control items.

14.3.6 DISPLAY PROPERTIES

The properties that influence the ways the items are displayed on the GUI are organized in two categories. The following paragraphs describe these groups and the major properties in each of them.

- **Physical.** The properties in this group control the position and the dimensions of the item on the GUI. The property Canvas contains the name of the canvas on which the item resides. If the item is located on a tab canvas, the property Tab Page indicates the page in which the item is located. Setting these properties to NULL removes the item from any canvas displayed on the Layout Editor and hides it from the users of the application. Thus, it effectively renders the item invisible both in the Form Builder and at runtime. Set the property Visible to 'No,' if you want an item to be displayed on a canvas at design time but remain invisible to users at runtime. The Physical group also includes properties that control the position (X Position, Y Position), size (Width, Height), and appearance of the border (Bevel) for items on the canvas. These properties are more easily set on the Layout Editor, but for finer-tuning of their setting you may use the Property Palette.
- **Font & Color.** As is the case with other Form Builder objects, properties in this group allow you to set different font and color properties of items, such as Font Name, Font Size, Font Style, Foreground Color and Background

Color. Although you can set each of these properties individually, I strongly recommend that you use visual attribute objects to maintain display properties of objects. Set the property Visual Attribute Group to the desired visual attribute object to inherit all its properties.

14.3.7 PROMPT PROPERTIES

Each item is associated with a text label that describes the item's name on the canvas. This text label, called prompt, is considered as part of the item and its properties are maintained in the categories Prompt and Prompt Font & Color. The following paragraphs describe these categories:

- **Prompt.** The properties in this group control the text of the label (Prompt) and its justification (Prompt Justification). An interesting property to mention is Prompt Display Style, which can be set to "All Records," "First Record," or "Hidden." The first setting is normally used with form layout styles and causes the prompt to appear by the item for each displayed record. (Obviously, this setting is relevant when the number of displayed records is greater than one.) The second setting is typically used with tabular style blocks. The third setting hides the prompt's contents from view at runtime, although you can view and manipulate it on the canvas at design time. Other prompt properties include Prompt Attachment Edge which can be set to one of the four item's edges to which the prompt is attached. Prompt Attachment Offset determines the distance in points between the prompt and the edge. Prompt Alignment determines the alignment of the prompt text with respect to this edge.

> **TIP**
>
> Settings for a number of properties in the Prompt group are determined by or derived from settings of properties of the frame objects in which the item is included. If the property Update Layout of the frame is set to "Automatically" any changes you make at the item level will be overwritten by the frame's properties. If you use a frame object to determine the layout of your block and want to set properties like Prompt Attachment Edge and Prompt Attachment Offset for an individual item, make sure to set the property Update Layout of the frame to "Locked."

- **Prompt Font & Color.** The properties in this group allow you to set the font properties as well as the text color of the text label that makes up the prompt. As in the case of similar properties of other objects, you should minimize individual settings of such properties. For a consistent interface and maximal reuse of effort, consider setting these properties in a visual attribute object and then setting the property Prompt Visual Attribute Group to that object.

14.3.8 HELP PROPERTIES

This group contains a number of properties that help you implement context-sensitive help for items in your applications. All items, except for display and chart items, contain the properties Hint and Display Hint Automatically. The setting for Hint is a message that can be displayed in the micro-help line of the MDI frame when the focus is on the current item. The message is displayed only if the property Display Hint Automatically is set to "Yes." It is a good programming practice to always provide micro-help to the users of your application. The combination of the properties Display Hint Automatically and Hint offers a satisfactory solution for character-based applications. In these applications, users can be only at one item at any given time. In GUI-based applications, while the input focus of the form is still in only one item, users can move the mouse around to point at different items on the screen. It would be useful to display some information about the item as the mouse rests on the item. The following section explains how you can display the contents of the property Hint in the micro-help message line when the mouse is over the item, without requiring users to place the focus of the form in the item itself.

Another way to display information when the mouse is on an item is to use tooltips. Tooltips are text boxes that pop up when the mouse remains on an item for more that half a second. The text displayed is specified in the property Tooltip. By default, the visual attributes of the tooltip are the same as the ones of the corresponding item. Use the property Tooltip Visual Attribute Group to change these properties. Tootips are a required feature for iconic buttons displayed on toolbars or elsewhere in the application. For regular items, they should be used with moderation and in cases when the item's prompt is not clear enough or cannot be displayed. It is also a good idea to offer the users the option to display and hide the tooltips at their discretion. This allows users that have just started using your application to get familiar with it and, once they reach the desired level of proficiency, to turn off the display of tooltips. The following section explains how you can dynamically turn tooltips on or off at runtime.

14.4 SETTING PROPERTIES OF ITEMS AT RUNTIME

By carefully setting the properties of items in the Form Builder, you can enhance a great deal the look and the functionality of the your application. You can also set them at runtime, thus making the form more dynamic and responsive to the changes that occur in the data. Programmatically, you can retrieve and store in PL/SQL variables the settings of any property, and specify new settings for almost any property. The general steps followed in the process are presented in Figure 14.3. Note that the two parts of this pseudo-routine may be located in different PL/SQL objects. In one place you may just get the property of an item. In another place you may only set that property.

Figure 14.4 shows the procedure that retrieves the hint message of the item whose name is passed as input variable, and displays it in the form of a micro-help message.

In order to display the hint when the user moves the mouse over an item, as promised at the end of Section 14.3.8, all you need to do, is add the following line in a form-level WHEN-MOUSE-ENTER trigger:

```
Display_Hint(:SYSTEM.MOUSE_ITEM);
```

This trigger will fire whenever the mouse moves inside an item. The system variable `SYSTEM.MOUSE_ITEM`, stores the name of the item, which is passed to `Display_Hint` for processing. Figure 14.5 shows an enhancement of the proce-

```
PROCEDURE Generic_Item_Routine (item_name VARCHAR2) IS
 item_id                ITEM;
 property_setting       VARCHAR2;

BEGIN
 /* FIND_ITEM returns the appropriate item ID.                     */
 item_id := FIND_ITEM(item_name);

 IF NOT ID_NULL(item_id) THEN
  /* PROPERTY_NAME will depend on the particular item type.  */
  property_setting := GET_ITEM_PROPERTY(item_id,
     PROPERTY_NAME);

 /* Additional processing may occur here                         */

  /* PROPERTY_NAME will depend on the particular item type.  */
  SET_ITEM_PROPERTY(item_id, PROPERTY_NAME, property_setting);
 ELSE
  MESSAGE('Item '||item_name||' does not exist.');
  RAISE FORM_TRIGGER_FAILURE;
 END IF;
END Generic_Item_Routine;
```

FIGURE 14.3 Guidelines for retrieving and setting properties of items at Runtime.

```
PROCEDURE Display_Hint (item_name VARCHAR2) IS
 item_id     ITEM;
 item_hint   VARCHAR2(80);

BEGIN
 IF item_name IS NOT NULL THEN
 /* FIND_ITEM returns the appropriate item ID. */
  item_id := FIND_ITEM(item_name);

  IF NOT ID_NULL(item_id) THEN
   item_hint := GET_ITEM_PROPERTY(item_id, HINT_TEXT);
   MESSAGE(item_hint, NO_ACKNOWLEDGE);
  ELSE
   MESSAGE('Item'||item_name||' does not exist.');
   RAISE FORM_TRIGGER_FAILURE;
  END IF;
 END IF;
END Display_Hint;
```

FIGURE 14.4 Procedure to display the micro-help message for an item.

dure `Display_Hint`. This version takes a second argument called `show_tooltip`. If the value of the argument is 'Y,' then the procedure sets the Tooltip property to the string stored in the Hint property.

In your form application, you can use a global variable, for example `GLOBAL.Show_Tooltip` to store the user preference. The value of this variable could be set from a menu item or from a check box item in the application. Under these conditions, the statement in the form-level WHEN-MOUSE-ENTER trigger now looks is as follows:

```
Display_Hint(:SYSTEM.MOUSE_ITEM, :GLOBAL.Show_Tooltip);
```

This trigger will fire whenever the mouse moves inside an item. The system variable `SYSTEM.MOUSE_ITEM`, stores the name of the item, which is passed to `Display_Hint` for processing.

If you want to see another example of getting and setting properties of items, run the module CLICKME.FMB provided with the companion software. This is a form with only one push button item. Your task is to click the button with the mouse. You will see that the button will jump sideways to a new position each time you click the mouse on it. Once you get tired or bored with the game, choose File | Exit from the menu to close the application.

```
PROCEDURE Display_Hint (item_name VARCHAR2, show_tooltip
VARCHAR2) IS
 item_id    ITEM;
 item_hint  VARCHAR2(80);

BEGIN
 IF item_name IS NOT NULL THEN
 /* FIND_ITEM returns the appropriate item ID. */
  item_id := FIND_ITEM(item_name);

  IF NOT ID_NULL(item_id) THEN
   item_hint := GET_ITEM_PROPERTY(item_id, HINT_TEXT);
   MESSAGE(item_hint, NO_ACKNOWLEDGE);
   IF (show_tooltip = 'Y') THEN
     SET_ITEM_PROPERTY(item_id, TOOLTIP_TEXT, item_hint);
   END IF;
  ELSE
   MESSAGE('Item'||item_name||' does not exist.');
   RAISE FORM_TRIGGER_FAILURE;
  END IF;
 END IF;
END Display_Hint;
```

FIGURE 14.5 Procedure to display the micro-help message for an item.

Now run the module CLICKME1.FMB from the same location. This module is very similar to the first one except that the upper part of its window contains some informative data to help you understand how the application works (see Figure 14.6).

As soon as the mouse enters the push button area, the trigger WHEN-MOUSE-ENTER calls the functions that populate the items in the upper part of the window with the current coordinates and dimensions of the item. This trigger also computes the new position where the item will jump to, if the mouse is clicked. Figure 14.7 shows the code for the function that retrieves the X coordinate of the item.

The functions that return the Y coordinate, width, and height of the button are entirely similar. Instead of returning the value of property X_POS, they return the setting for properties Y_POS, WIDTH, and HEIGHT, respectively.

Based on the current coordinates and dimensions of the item, on the dimensions of the canvas, and on the current position of the mouse, the functions `Com-`

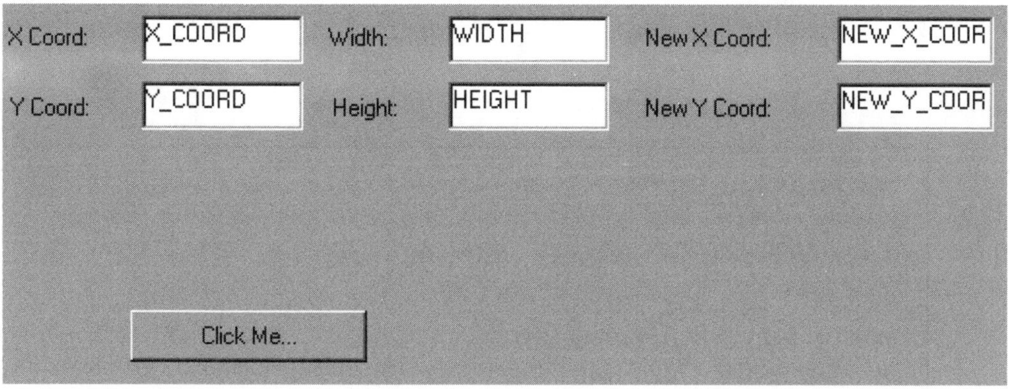

FIGURE 14.6 Manipulating the position of an item on the canvas at runtime.

pute_New_X and Compute_New_Y compute the new position of the item in a way that when the mouse is clicked, the item escapes out of the reach of the mouse. For a detailed explanation of the algorithm used to compute the new coordinates, refer to the comments in the body specification of the program units in modules CLICKME.FMB or CLICKME1.FMB.

```
FUNCTION Get_X_Coord (item_name VARCHAR2)
RETURN VARCHAR2 IS
 item_id   ITEM;
 x_coord   VARCHAR2(10);

BEGIN
 IF item_name IS NOT NULL then
 /* FIND_ITEM returns the appropriate item ID. */
  item_id := FIND_ITEM(item_name);

  IF NOT ID_NULL(item_id) THEN
   x_coord := GET_ITEM_PROPERTY(item_id, X_POS);
  ELSE
   MESSAGE('Item'||item_name||' does not exist.');
   RAISE FORM_TRIGGER_FAILURE;
  END IF;
  RETURN x_coord;
 END IF;
END Get_X_Coord;
```

FIGURE 14.7 Retrieving the coordinates of items at runtime.

```
PROCEDURE Set_X_Coord (item_name VARCHAR2,
                       x_coord   NUMBER) IS
 item_id   ITEM;

BEGIN
 IF item_name IS NOT NULL then
 /* FIND_ITEM returns the appropriate item ID. */
  item_id := FIND_ITEM(item_name);

  IF NOT ID_NULL(item_id) THEN
   SET_ITEM_PROPERTY(item_id, X_POS, x_coord);
  ELSE
   MESSAGE('Item'||item_name||' does not exist.');
   RAISE FORM_TRIGGER_FAILURE;
  END IF;
 END IF;
END Set_X_Coord;
```

FIGURE 14.8 Setting the coordinates of items at runtime.

The procedures that place the item in the new position are `Set_X_Coord` and `Set_Y_Coord`. Figure 14.8 shows the implementation of the procedure `Set_X_Coord`.

The code for `Set_Y_Coord` resembles that of `Set_X_Coord`, except that here the `y_coord` input variable is used to set the property Y_POS. Both these procedures are called from the WHEN-MOUSE-DOWN trigger, which fires when the event MouseDown occurs. The choice of this event is not casual. In the Form Builder mouse event protocol, a MouseClick event is a combination of a MouseDown and a MouseUp that occur sequentially. If you do not want the users to click the button, then you should move it to a new location before the event occurs. Placing the movement code in the WHEN-MOUSE-DOWN moves the item when the users begin to click (with a MouseDown), but before completing the action (with a MouseUp).

CAUTION

If you look closely at the implementation of function Get_X_Coord and procedure Set_X_Coord shown in Figure 14.7 and Figure 14.8, you will notice that the built-in function GET_ITEM_PROPERTY returns the setting of X_POS as a character value. However, the built-in procedure SET_ITEM_PROPERTY requires the setting for the same property to be a number.

14.5 VALIDATION OF ITEMS

The validation of items is the event that checks the conformity of the data they contain with the requirements set fourth for these items. If the validation process is successful, items can be sent safely to the database for storage. The time when the validation occurs depends on the setting of the property Validation Unit for the current module. For GUI environments, the validation event will occur as soon as the users try to navigate out of the item.

At any given point during the execution of an application, its items can be in one of the following states: NEW, CHANGED or VALID. When a new record is created, all its items are NEW. As soon as users begin entering data in one of the items, the state of this item and all other items in the block becomes CHANGED. When users request to commit the record, each item and the record itself are validated. If the validation process is successful, the state of each item is set to VALID. A record is sent to the database only if all its items are VALID. When, on the other hand, records are brought in the application from a database query, the status of all their items is VALID. If one of the items in the record is modified, the status for all the items in that record is set to CHANGED. They must all be validated during the next database commit. Figure 14.9 shows the states of items and the actions that cause the transition from one state to the other.

The requirements specified for an item can be as simple as the data type or the length of data they represent. They are usually handled by appropriately setting different properties of the items. However, they can also be complicated business rules that the application must enforce upon data. In this case, these

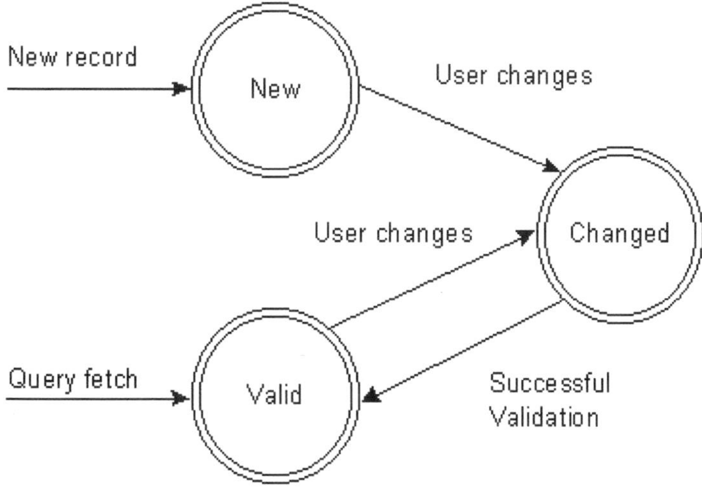

FIGURE 14.9 Transition diagram for the states of an item.

rules are implemented using PL/SQL and are placed in a method or trigger that fires when the ValidateItem event occurs. The name of the trigger is WHEN-VALIDATE-ITEM.

14.6 TEXT ITEMS AND DISPLAY ITEMS

Text items are, by far, the most common items in a Form Builder application, because of their ease of use, flexibility, and extended functionality. They can be used to retrieve, display, and manipulate data of several types, sizes, and formats. Display items can be used only for the purpose of displaying data. Users cannot navigate to or modify the information presented by display items. Because of the reduced functionality, display items also use less system resources. In addition to generic properties discussed earlier in the chapter, text and display items have other properties that are specific to them. The following sections discuss some of the most important properties of text and display items.

14.6.1 BEVEL AND RENDERED PROPERTIES

Two properties that are worth mentioning in the Physical group are Bevel and Rendered. Bevel controls the display of the item's border. By default, its setting is "Raised." If you set it to "None," the border will not be visible. This setting is useful if you use display items for dynamic text labels in the form.

In order to understand the meaning of the property Rendered, you must understand how Form Runtime manages the display of items. Visually, you get the impression that there are as many containers of data on the screen as there are items. In reality, this is not exactly true. By default, there is only up to one such container at any one moment. The real container is the text or display item where the current focus of Forms is located. All the other items and widgets on the screen are just drawings on the boilerplate. To clarify the discussion, Figure 14.10 presents the state of a form at runtime.

Here, the focus is initially on Item A. Forms Runtime uses Physical properties of items such as X Position, Y Position, Width, and Height, to divide the boilerplate in context-sensitive areas. If the focus of the application is placed on an item, say Item B (by clicking it, tabbing into it, or by internal navigation), Forms Runtime initially retrieves the boilerplate position of this item. Then, it queries its internal structures to retrieve the context-sensitive information for that screen location. If this information indicates that the target is another text or display item, the data contained in the item are transferred from the internal structures of Forms Runtime into the container that is created for the item, and made available to the user for processing. Meanwhile, if the Rendered property of Item A is set to "Yes," the boilerplate drawing that represents the item is updated, and the con-

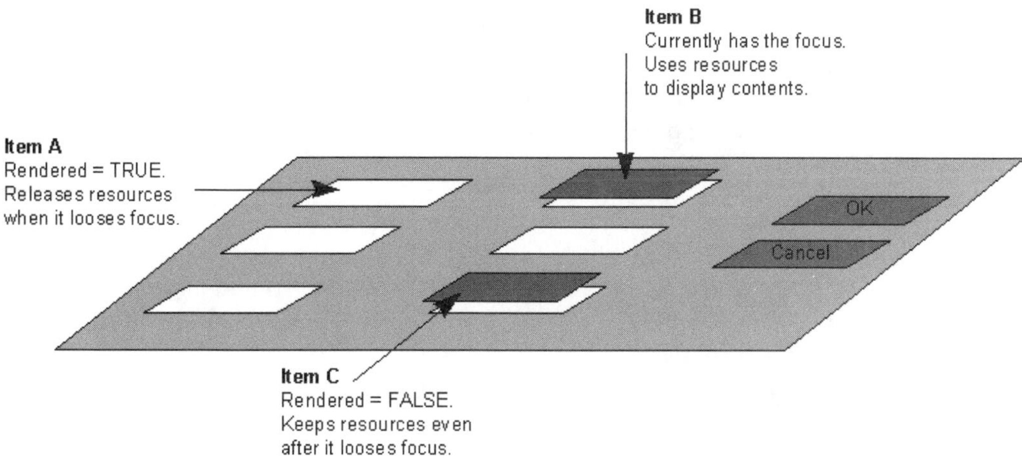
Item B
Currently has the focus.
Uses resources
to display contents.
Item A
Rendered = TRUE.
Releases resources
when it looses focus.
OK
Cancel
Item C
Rendered = FALSE.
Keeps resources even
after it looses focus.

FIGURE 14.10 Forms Runtime renders its items by default.

tainer of data for that item is erased from memory, thus releasing the system resources it occupies. If this property is set to "No," as in the case of Item C, Forms Runtime maintains the container attached to the item. In order to complete the discussion on the rendering of items, the following points should be further clarified:

- There is no visual difference between an item that has the current focus, and other items with similar properties. The fact that Forms Runtime renders these items, or treats them as boilerplate drawings, does not affect their appearance.
- Only text or display items need a container around them to manage the information they contain. Other items such as push buttons, check boxes, or radio buttons, change their contents due to actions performed on them.
- If the Rendered property of a text or display item is set to "No," the item will continue to occupy resources even when it no longer has the focus of Forms Runtime.
- If the Rendered property of a text or display item is set to "Yes," there will be some processing overhead each time the item receives the focus. This additional processing is needed to create and populate the container that will display the item's data.
- The benefits of setting Rendered property to "Yes," measured in saved system resources, clearly surpass the cost of overhead processing that will occur each time the item receives focus.

14.6.2 DATA PROPERTIES OF TEXT ITEMS

In addition to generic properties discussed in Section 14.3.3, text items have other useful properties in the Data group. Proper settings of these properties allow you to better display the data, and to facilitate the task of entering the information in the database.

If the Required property is set to "Yes," users cannot leave the item without entering a value in it. Items based on NOT NULL database columns that are created with the Data Block Wizard have the Required property set to "Yes" automatically. For other items that are manually created, the default setting of the property is "No." If they need this restriction, you must change the default setting in the Property Palette.

The Format Mask property is used to display data according to a certain predefined pattern. The variety of format masks that can be specified here is overwhelming. Being unable to cover all of them here, this section provides some examples that create a good idea about format masks.

1. If you want your users to enter only the digits of a dollar amount, but display it in the ordinary business format, set Format Mask to `$999,999.99PR`. Now, when users enter 1223.89, Forms will display the item as $1,223.89. When they enter –1223.83, the amount will be displayed as <$1,223.89>. (It is a common accounting practice to represent negative values in parentheses rather than preceded by the minus sign.)
2. If you want to embed characters inside numeric strings, enclose them in double-quotes in the Format Mask setting. Among the most common format masks are `"("999")"999"-"9999` used for telephone numbers and `999"-"99"-"9999` used for Social Security Numbers.
3. If you want to display the date in the format `12/05/2000`, set Format Mask to `DD"/"MM"/"YYYY`.

To spare users the effort of typing the extra characters included in the format mask, put the FM indicator in front of it. If, for example the Format Mask is specified as `FM"("999")"999"-"9999`, users need to type only `2220001111`, and the input will be formatted as `(222)000-1111`. However, for date formats the FM indicator does not have the same effect. Users must enter the item as required by the format.

If the data of a particular item will be within a range of values, you can set the properties Lowest Allowed Value or Highest Allowed Value to the lower and upper bounds of the range. Forms will automatically ensure that the data entered do not extend beyond the allowed range.

14.6.3 DATABASE PROPERTIES OF TEXT ITEMS

Besides the generic properties from this group discussed in Section 14.3.5, text items have two additional properties that are used in the query-by-example interface of Forms Runtime. The Query Length property controls the length of query criteria that can be entered in the item when the block is in Enter Query mode. By default, the setting of Query Length equals that of Maximum Length property. It can be higher than Maximum Length, but never smaller. In Form Builder messages or documentation you will often see stated that this setting can be zero. Like other numeric settings of properties, a zero setting for the Query Length indicates that the property has its default value, which is Maximum Length.

The advantage of setting Query Length to a higher value than Maximum Length, is that it allows users to enter more flexible criteria in Enter Query mode. For example, the default setting for these two properties for date items is 11—the length of Oracle's default data format DD-MON-YYYY. Suppose that you keep these settings for the item MEMBER_DT in the block CUSTOMER of the application. Your users will be able to retrieve customers that became members of the video store on a certain date. However, by setting the Query Length to 13, you can offer them a more flexible way to query the table. Now they will be able to query the database for all the customers that opened an account on or after a certain date, simply by entering `>=DD-MON-YYYY` in the MEMBER_DT item. A variety of other queries can be issued using the operators <>, <, and <=.

The property Case Insensitive Query is set to "No" by default. This means that Developer Forms will construct the query using criteria exactly as you enter them. If, for example, you enter `SMITH` in the item LAST_NAME of block CUSTOMER and issue a query, the WHERE clause of the SELECT statement sent to the database will contain the following criteria:

```
LAST_NAME = 'SMITH'
```

The query will return only the customers whose last name is SMITH. But, what if your data is not consistent, and you have customers whose names are entered as 'SMITH,' 'Smith,' or 'smith'? Despite the typing discrepancies, you still want the users to retrieve all these records by entering 'SMITH' in the form in Enter Query mode. To achieve this, you simply set the property Case Insensitive Query to "Yes." Assuming that the only query criteria for a query is the one entered in the LAST_NAME item, the following is the WHERE clause of the statement issued by the form against the database at runtime:

```
WHERE UPPER(LAST_NAME) = 'SMITH' AND
   (LAST_NAME LIKE 'Sm%' OR LAST_NAME LIKE 'sM%' OR
    LAST_NAME LIKE 'SM%' OR LAST_NAME LIKE 'sm%');
```

The statement above is not just rich in functionality. It is also efficient from the database performance perspective. Indeed, an alternative WHERE clause to the one shown above is the following:

```
WHERE UPPER(LAST_NAME) = 'SMITH';
```

Although this statement looks simpler than the first one it contains the conversion function UPPER, which prevents the optimizer from using any index that may exist on the column LAST_NAME. If the number of records is large, a full scan of the table may slow down the query significantly. The first statement on the other hand, uses the index to resolve the second condition:

```
(LAST_NAME LIKE 'Sm%' OR LAST_NAME LIKE 'sM%'
OR LAST_NAME LIKE 'SM%' OR LAST_NAME LIKE 'sm%')
```

The records that satisfy this condition are then compared against the second condition using an exact match.

> **TIP**
>
> As you can see from the SQL statement compiled by Forms Runtime, the case in which users provide their input is significant for the results of the query. You can help users here by changing the default setting of the property Case Restriction in the Functional group from "Mixed" to "Upper." A bonus feature that you get by setting this property is that the case of the new data entered by the users will be consistent.

As mentioned in Section 14.3.5, the property Update Allowed controls the users' ability to update the data. If the property is set to "No," the information presented in the item cannot be updated. This restriction can be relaxed a little by setting the property Update Only If NULL to "Yes." In this case, users can supply data if the item does not contain any information.

14.6.4 FUNCTIONAL PROPERTIES OF TEXT ITEMS

The Case Restriction property can be used to enforce a particular case for the data entered in the item. For example, to enter data in uppercase letters, set this property to "Upper." Note that this property converts the case only if information is entered through the item. If a value is stored in lowercase characters in the database, it will be displayed that way when retrieved by a query.

Another property that is useful for data entry tasks is Automatic Skip. When the property is set to "Yes," the focus of the form at runtime automatically navigates to the next item as soon as the user enters all maximum characters allowed in the item.

The Justification property defines the alignment of data in the item. By default, items are justified to the left. If your application displays monetary data, you may want to justify these items to the right by setting this property.

If you want to protect the data at the item level, you may set the property Conceal Data to "Yes." With this setting, the item will display the data as a sequence of asterisk characters '*.' Because the property can be set dynamically, you can use it to hide certain data elements from unauthorized users.

If the data displayed in the item is too long to fit in a single-line item, you may display the item as a multi-line item. To achieve this, set the property Multi-Line to "Yes" and adjust the size of the item on the canvas to span across multiple lines. If the amount of data in the item will make scrolling necessary, you can add a vertical scroll bar to the item by setting the property Vertical Scroll Bar in the Physical group to "Yes." By default, when Developer Forms navigates inside an item, it places the cursor at the beginning of the item. Especially for multi-line text items, it may be helpful to place the cursor where it was when users navigated out of the item. Forms will automatically do this for you, if the property Keep Cursor Position is set to "Yes." Finally, another property that is mostly useful for multi-line items is Word Wrap. It defines how the lines are broken when the entire text does not fit in one line and, by default, is set to "Word."

14.7 CALCULATED ITEMS

As mentioned earlier, control items are used to display data derived or computed from other items. Form Builder provides a number of properties that facilitate the definition of such items. These properties are located in the Calculation group of the Property Palette and are described in the following paragraphs:

- **Calculation Mode.** There are essentially two types of calculated items in a Forms application: summary and formula items. Summary items, derive their value from all the values of an item in a given block. One of the SQL group functions is used to compute the value of summary items. Formula items get their value from a PL/SQL expression that can use any of the valid PL/SQL operators, functions, and constructs. The settings "Summary" or "Formula" of the property Calculation Mode help you differentiate these two types of calculated items. If the item is not calculated this property is set to "None."
- **Formula.** This property is set to the PL/SQL expression that serves as formula for computing the value of a calculated item. Forms Runtime uses this expression only if Calculation Mode is set to "Formula." The variables used in the expression can be any PL/SQL variables available in Form Builder, including global variables, system variables, module parameters, and form items. In the formula, you can use any non-restricted built-in or user-defined program units.
- **Summary Item Properties.** The properties Summary Function, Summarized Block, and Summarized Item are used to compute the value of an item

whose Calculation Mode is set to "Summary." The first property is set to any of the Oracle SQL group functions. Recall from Chapter 8 that these functions are COUNT, SUM, MIN, MAX, AVG, STDDEV, and VARIANCE. The block and item whose values are summarized are stored in the properties Summarized Block, and Summarized Item.

In order to implement calculated items successfully in your applications, you need to understand how Forms Runtime computes their value as well restrictions in their use. The following list contains some of these restrictions:

- Forms Runtime assigns the value of calculated items internally. You cannot assign a value to such items using programmatic constructs and the users cannot enter the values in these items. Given this situation, display items are the best implementation of calculated items.
- Calculated items are control items. If you accidentally set the property Calculation Mode to anything but "Formula" or "Summary," Forms Runtime will ignore any properties in the Database group, such as Database Item, Query Allowed, Insert Allowed, and Update Allowed.
- The data type of calculated items should be set so that it does not conflict with the return value of the formula of summary function. If you are using a mathematical summary function, such as COUNT, AVG, SUM, STDDEV, or VARIANCE, the data type should be NUMBER. But if you are computing the earliest data of an event using the function MIN, then the data type should be DATE.
- Summary items may reside either in the same block as the item they summarize or in a control block with the property Single Record set to "Yes."
- If the block contains at least one summarized item, Forms Runtime will need to know all the values for this item in order to populate the summary item with the correct value. You can achieve this by setting the property Query All Records to "Yes," thus effectively fetching all the records from the server to the client. In order to prevent this potential inefficient use of network resources, set Precompute Summaries to "Yes." This allows Forms to populate the summary item with the correct value even if not all the records are fetched from the database.

14.8 EVENTS OF TEXT ITEMS

There are three basic events that occur in a text item: EnterItem, ValidateItem and LeaveItem. The final outcome of the EnterItem event is to place the focus of the form inside the target item. In the process, Forms Runtime executes the PRE-TEXT-ITEM trigger, if it is specified. When the EnterItem event is completed and the cursor lands inside the item, the WHEN-NEW-ITEM-INSTANCE trigger is fired.

Once inside the item, users can enter and edit data for that item. As soon as they do this the status of the item is set to CHANGED. If no changes are made to the contents of the item, its status remains the same as prior to entering the item.

> **TIP**
>
> Any action that modifies the data sets the item status to CHANGED, even if the final outcome of the item is the same as at the beginning. In other words, even if you cut and paste the contents of a text item, without any other action, its status will be CHANGED.

When the users initiate the LeaveItem event, Forms Runtime decides whether to validate the item or not. If the item's status in NEW or CHANGED, the validation event occurs. If the ValidateItem event is successful, the event LeaveItem proceeds to completion. The trigger POST-TEXT-ITEM is fired during this event. The ValidateItem event may be initiated programmatically from within the item, without necessarily having to wait for the LeaveItem event to occur. The built-in procedure ENTER is used for this purpose.

For text items, the validation event is more extended than for other types of items. Depending on the settings of different properties for the item, each of the following checks may occur:

1. Check the value's format mask if the Format Mask property is set.
2. Check that value is not NULL if properties Required and Input Allowed are both set to "Yes."
3. Check that the length of entered value equals the item's Maximum Length if Fixed Length is set to "Yes."
4. Check that the value's data type does not conflict with the setting of Data Type property.
5. Check that the value is within the settings of properties Lowest Allowed Value and Highest Allowed Value, if they are defined.
6. Fire the WHEN-VALIDATE-ITEM trigger if it is defined at the item, block, or form level.

Failure to satisfy any of the checks stops the validation process. If any of the first five checks fails, the focus of the form cannot leave the item. If the WHEN-VALIDATE-ITEM trigger fails, users will not be able to leave the item if the exception FORM-TRIGGER-FAILURE is raised. The status of the item is set to VALID only if all the checks that are applicable to that particular item are successful.

If the status of an item is NEW, that is, the record is just created, the only validation check will be Rule 2 in the list above. This is often very restrictive, as the following scenario demonstrates. Imagine that you just created a new record in the block CUSTOMER and the focus of the form is in a required item such as ID. However you want to enter the new customer's name first. You will discover that you cannot navigate to any other item in that record, before entering some value for the item CUSTOMER.ID.

To avoid this situation, you may shift the checking for NULL values from Rule 2 to Rule 6. In other words, set the Required property to "No," and write code in the WHEN-VALIDATE-ITEM trigger that does not allow users to leave the item if it is NULL. The drawback to this approach is that it will add an extra level of complexity to the WHEN-VALIDATE-ITEM trigger for the item, and must be done for each item with the Required property set to "No."

A more elegant solution is to set the form module property DEFER_REQUIRED_ENFORCEMENT to "Yes." This is a property that can be set only programmatically. For example, to set it for the MRD module, you would use the following statement in a trigger that fires when the form module is initially launched such as PRE-FORM or WHEN-NEW-FORM-INSTANCE:

```
SET_FORM_PROPERTY('MRD', DEFER_REQUIRED_ENFORCEMENT,
PROPERTY_TRUE);
```

With this setting, Forms Runtime will not apply the Rule 2 until the ValidateRecord event occurs. In other words, users are allowed to move freely among items of the same block, even if they do not enter values for required items. They will be asked to provide these values only when they will try to move outside the record.

> **CAUTION**
>
> In earlier versions of Form Builder, the POST-CHANGE trigger fires right before the WHEN-VALIDATE-ITEM trigger fires. This trigger is still available for backward compatibility reasons, but its use is not recommended.

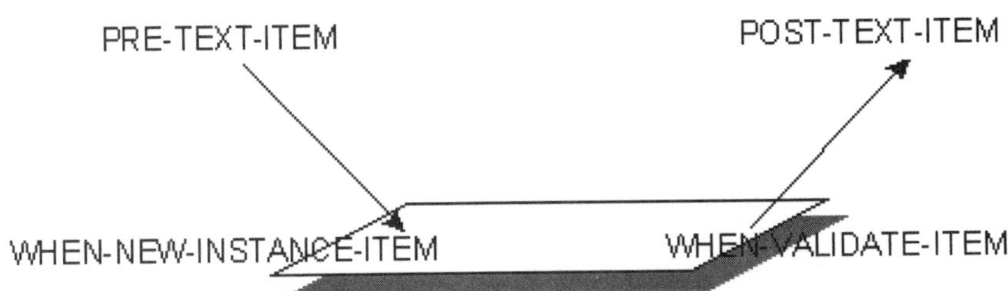

FIGURE 14.11 Triggers of text items in Developer Forms.

Figure 14.11 graphically summarizes the item-related events and triggers in Developer Forms.

14.9 GUI GUIDELINES FOR DATA ITEMS

There are two goals that you must have in mind when creating applications for GUI.

- **Be consistent.** Every screen you design must have a look and feel that is standard across the entire application, and possibly, in a wider range, across all the applications used by your organization.
- **Don't show off.** The screens you create must not be used neither to display your talent as painter or designer, nor your latest ideas on color combination.

The application must not attract the users' attention, or distract them from the main purpose they have when using it: To access and manipulate their data in the most productive and efficient manner. With all the new and fancy programming tools that proliferate in the market, the temptation to put all kinds of bells, whistles and flashing lights in the application can be satisfied easily. But you must learn to overcome that temptation. Whenever the subject comes up, I like to quote one of the Microsoft Word Tips of the Day: "Plaid shirts and striped pants rarely make a positive fashion."

This section will discuss some guidelines to follow in the development of forms in GUI platforms. The topic will come up in the discussion about control items, windows, dialog boxes, and menus, in their respective chapters.

14.9.1 COLORS

By default, a screen in a Form Builder application uses three basic colors. Light gray is used as background color for the canvas. White is used as background color for text items. Black is used as text color for text and display items, and for text labels on the canvas. Use very sparingly additional colors, if you think you will need them.

If you decide to use other colors, do so for very specific situations, and choose colors that are associated with a cultural meaning. For example, use red to express urgency, or danger; use yellow to caution the users; or blue to simply inform them about an event. Sticking with the basic colors has another advantage. It will save system resources and reduce the time it takes your video driver and Forms Runtime to draw the screen.

Use colors to get the attention of users about very specific situations. Do not use them to simply draw fancy-looking boxes on the screen. They will wear out your users' patience very quickly. However, do not rely too much on your users reacting to the colors. A considerable number of people are color-blind. The phenomenon is particularly common among men fifty years or older.

14.9.2 TEXT

By default, text in Form Builder applications is displayed in the font that is typical for your system. In Microsoft Windows environments, for example, the font is MS Sans Serif of size eight. Sans Serif fonts like MS Sans Serif and Arial are widely used, because the items and labels take less space on the canvas. However, there may be people among your users that may have problems with any font smaller than ten points.

Do not use colors or other visual effects such as italics, strikeout, or underline. If you want to emphasize certain text items or labels, use bold typeface.

Avoid multi-line items that cannot display all the data they may contain. It was explained earlier in the chapter how to add scroll bars to help users view the text in these items. However, it is desirable to display all the data in one large dialog box. Form Builder comes to your aid in these types of situations, because it provides an editor window, sizable to your specifications, that can be displayed anywhere on the screen. This editor provides standard text editing utility and will be discussed in greater extent in Chapter 16.

14.9.3 TEXT ITEMS AND TEXT LABELS

Text items should have white background, visible border, and should present the text in black color. Display items should have a light gray background that matches the background color of the canvas if they will serve as dynamic text labels. They may or may not have a border.

Text items must provide users with visual clues about the size of the data that they contain. If the average length of data in an item is fifty characters long, it is not a good idea to present it on the screen as ten characters long. If items are of similar size set them to the same size. Use the properties of frames to initially lay out the items and then use the Size Objects and Align Objects utilities of the Layout Editor to reduce to a minimum the different margins on the screen. See Figure 14.1 at the beginning of this chapter for an example of a form that contains very few margins.

In the process of rearranging the layout, it may be necessary to move some data items around the screen. Make sure that data elements that are logically related are visually grouped together. Do not overlook the tab order of the items on the screen either, even if the mouse and not the keyboard will be the primary mean of interface between the users and the application. Remember that this order is defined by the sequence of items in the Object Navigator.

Each item must have a brief but descriptive text label associated with it. In frames with form layout style, the text labels are to the left of the data item they describe. It is good if they can be aligned to the left. In frames with tabular layout, text labels stay on top of the data items and their bottoms are aligned horizontally.

14.10 DATA ITEMS IN THE MRD APPLICATION

At this point, you are ready to go back to the MRD application you started developing in the previous chapter. In this section you will organize and set the properties of text items in the form. You may use the form you created in the last chapter, or open the form CH14_1.FMB, provided with the companion software to follow the discussion here.

14.10.1 REUSING VISUAL ATTRIBUTE GROUPS AND PROPERTY CLASSES

As explained in Chapter 8, there are many reasons why you should always consider reusing objects in your applications. The benefits of this approach are even clearer in the MRD form, which contains a considerable number of items with common properties. In this chapter you will reuse the property class US_CURRENCY and the visual attribute groups NEGATIVE and NON_NEGATIVE created in Chapter 8. For your convenience, these objects are provided in module CH14_2.FMB with the companion software. Follow these steps to include these objects in the MRD module:

1. Open the module CH14_2.FMB in the Object Navigator.
2. Drag the property class US_CURRENCY and drop it in the MRD form. Choose to subclass or copy the object.
3. Drag the visual attribute groups NEGATIVE and NON_NEGATIVE and drop them in the MRD form. Choose to subclass or copy the objects.

In addition, perform the following actions to create a property class for text items that display telephone numbers:

1. Create a new property class named US_PHONE_ITEM in the MRD form and display its Property Palette.
2. Add the property Width to the class and set it to "60."
3. Add the property Maximum Length to the class and set it to "12."
4. Add the property Format Mask to the class and set it to "FM"("999") "999"-"9999."

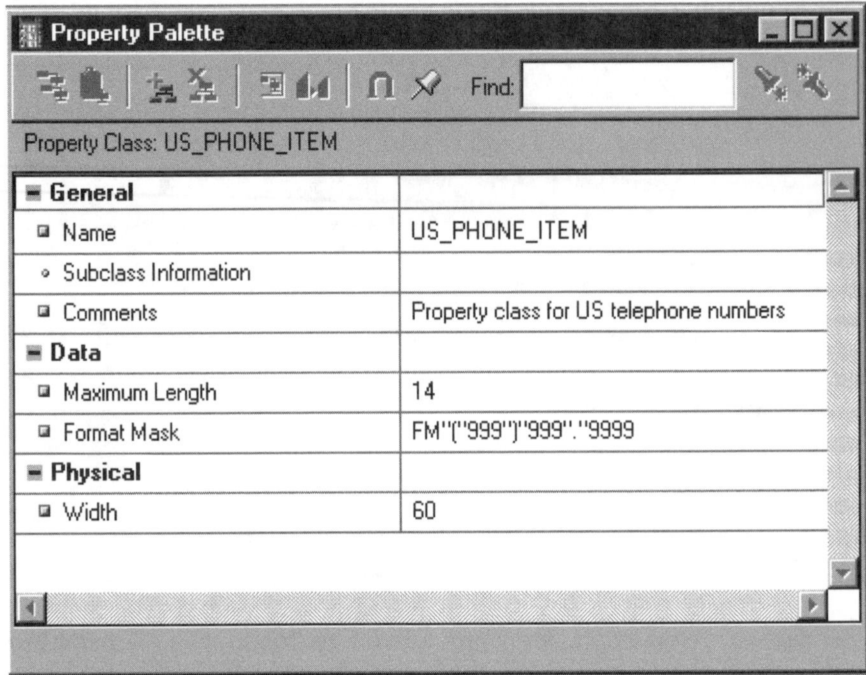

FIGURE 14.12 Contents of property class US_PHONE_ITEM.

At this point, the Property Palette of the US_PHONE_ITEM class should be as shown in Figure 14.12.

14.10.2 ARRANGING THE CUSTOMERS CANVAS

First, double-click the CUSTOMERS canvas in the Object Navigator to display it in a Layout Editor window. Then set the properties of items in the block CUSTOMERS as follows:

1. For the items ID set Item Type to "Display Item." This will prevent users from manually entering or updating this item.
2. For the items that will display telephone numbers, DAY_PHONE and EVE_PHONE, derive their properties from the class US_PHONE_ITEM. To accomplish this task display the dialog box Subclass Information associated with the property of the same name, select the radio item Property Class and select "US_PHONE_ITEM" from the list box Property Class Name.
3. For the item ADDRESS, set the property Multi-Line to "Yes."

4. For the item STATE, set the properties Case Restriction to "Upper," Automatic Skip to "Yes," and Fixed Length to "Yes."

Now arrange the items of the block CUSTOMERS on the canvas. As a first step, turn off the automatic refreshing of the frame's layout by setting the property Update Layout to "Locked." Then align and size the items following the GUI guidelines discussed earlier for the alignment and sizing of text items and labels. Do not worry too much at this point about the following items: STATUS, GENDER, MYSTERY, COMEDY, DRAMA, and FOREIGN. In the next chapter you will convert them to other types of items. Simply set them aside, out of the way. When finished, the CUSTOMER canvas should look similar to Figure 14.13. Notice that the item ADDRESS is expanded across multiple lines.

14.10.3 ARRANGING THE MOVIES CANVAS

Display the MOVIES canvas in the Layout Editor and set the property Update Layout to "Locked" for the frame of the MOVIES block. Then hide the item ID in the block MOVIES by setting the properties Canvas to "<Null>" and Displayed to "No." In the next chapter you will convert RATING, STATUS for block MOVIE and STATUS for block TAPE to different types of items, therefore leave them as they are for the moment being. Finally, arrange the items on the canvas to look like Figure 14.14.

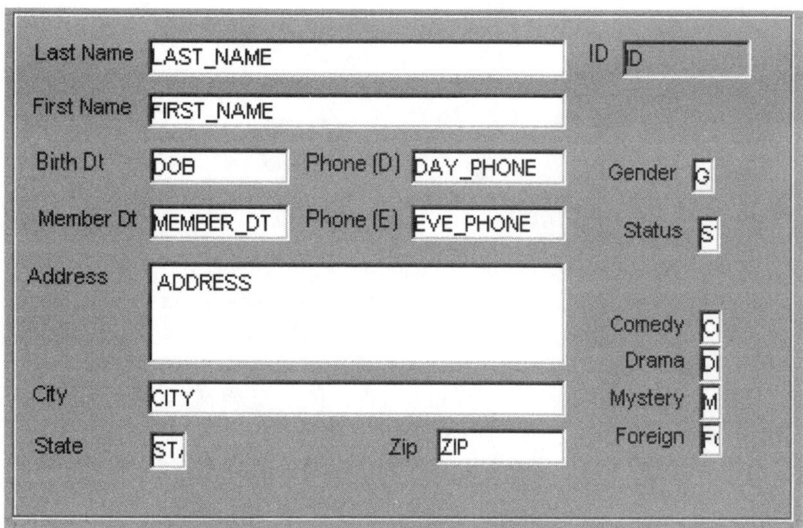

FIGURE 14.13 The CUSTOMERS canvas after text items are arranged.

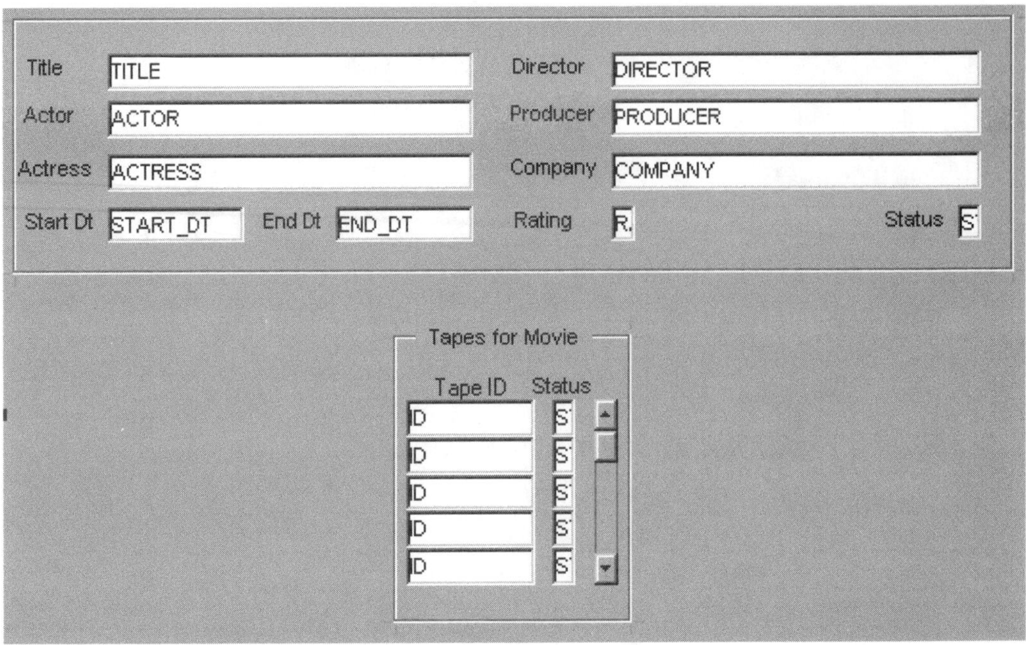

FIGURE 14.14 The MOVIES canvas after text items are arranged.

14.10.4 ARRANGING THE RENTALS CANVAS

Display the RENTALS canvas in the Layout Editor and set the properties of items in the RENTALS block as follows:

1. Set the properties Visible to "No" and Canvas to "<Null>" for the items CUSTOMER_ID and TAPE_ID.
2. Set the properties of the item DAILY_RATE by inheriting from the property class US_CURRENCY.
3. Create a new text item in the block RENTAL and set the properties Name to "CUSTOMER_NAME," Maximum Length to "65," Database Item to "No," Width to "90," Height to "14," and Prompt to "Customer Name." This item will display the name of the customer renting the movie.
4. Copy and paste the item CUSTOMER_NAME . For the new text item set the properties Name to "MOVIE_TITLE," Width to "120" and Prompt to "Movie Title." This item will display the title of the movie in the rented tape.
5. Arrange the tab order of the items in the Object Navigator as follows: CUSTOMER_NAME, MOVIE_TITLE, RENT_DT, RETURN_DT, and DAILY_RATE.

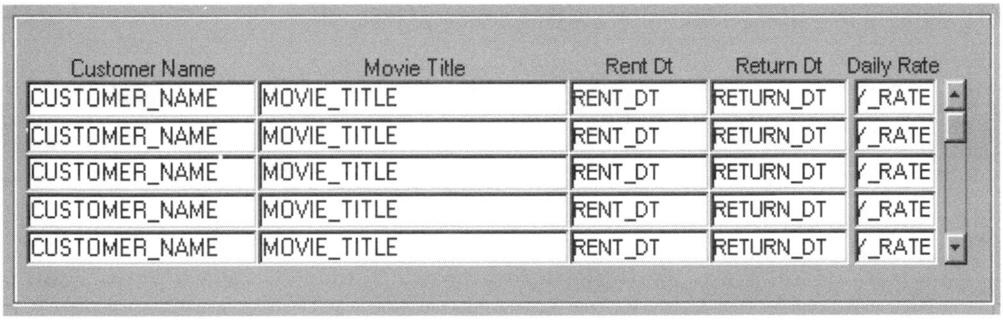

FIGURE 14.15 The RENTALS canvas after text items are arranged.

Finally, arrange, resize, and align the items on the canvas until it looks similar to Figure 14.15. The quickest way to achieve this is to let the frame of the RENTALS block update the layout automatically. For this, modify one of the properties of the frame, for example, resize the frame in the Layout Editor window.

When you are finished, save, compile and execute the form to get a feel for the changes you performed in this chapter. Consult with module CH14_3.FMB for any questions regarding the actions discussed above.

14.11 SUMMARY

This chapter discusses the Developer Forms items, their properties and events. The first part of the chapter deals with generic properties of items of all types and the second part sets its focus on text items in particular. Major concepts of this chapter were:

- **Types of Items**
  - Data Items and Control Items
  - GUI Interface Items
- **Creating Items**
- **Generic Properties of Items**
  - Functional Properties
  - Navigation Properties
  - Data Properties
  - Records Properties
  - Database Properties
  - Display Properties

- Prompt Properties
- Help Properties

- **Setting Properties of Items at Runtime**
- **Validation of Items in Developer Forms**
- **Text Items and Display Items**
  - Bevel and Rendered Properties
  - Data Properties of Text Items
  - Database Properties of Text Items
  - Functional Properties of Text Items
- **Calculated Items**
- **Events of Text Items**
- **GUI Guidelines for Data Items**
  - Colors
  - Text
  - Text Items and Text Labels
- **Data Items in the MRD Application**
  - Creating Visual Attributes and Property Classes
  - Arranging Canvas CUSTOMER
  - Arranging Canvas MOVIE
  - Arranging Canvas RENTAL

The following table describes the software assets that were discussed in this chapter. From the main HTML page of the software utilities provided with the book follow the links *Software* and *Chapter 14* to access these assets:

ASSET NAME	DESCRIPTION
CH14_1.FMB	The MRD application completed in the last chapter. Use this module as a starting point for the activities discussed in this chapter.
CH14_2.FMB	A Form Builder module that contains the property class US_CURRENCY and visual attribute groups NEGATIVE and NON-NEGATIVE.
CH14_3.FMB	The MRD application as it should be at the end of this chapter.
CH14_3.FMX	The executable version of the MRD application as it should be at the end of this chapter. It is compiled for Win32 platforms.
CLICK_1.FMB	A Form Builder module that demonstrates how you can get and set item properties dynamically.
CLICK_2.FMX	The executable version of CLICK_1.FMB compiled for Win32 platforms.
CLICK_2.FMB	A more interactive version of CLICK_1.FMB.
CLICK_1.FMX	The executable version of CLICK_2.FMB compiled for Win32 platforms.

Chapter 15

GUI Control Items

I think the real challenge is to design software that is simple on the outside but complex on the inside.

—John Page

- Push Buttons
- Radio Groups and Radio Buttons
- Check Boxes
- List Boxes
- GUI Guidelines for Controls
- Controls in the MRD Application
- Summary

Control items are the principal tools that users have to express their intentions, to initiate actions, or to influence the flow of the application. The Form Builder supports four types of GUI controls: push buttons, list boxes, radio buttons, and check boxes. This chapter discusses the properties and implementation of these controls.

15.1 PUSH BUTTONS

Push buttons are always used to initiate an action. Typical actions triggered by clicking buttons are to commit changes to a database, cancel an operation, close a dialog box, initiate internal navigation such as to a different block or initiate external navigation such as to another module. Based on their appearance, push buttons are divided into label and iconic push buttons. Label push buttons contain a text label that clearly states their functionality such as Save, Cancel, or Print. If these buttons open other windows or dialog boxes, the label's text should end with an ellipsis. This is a well-established industry standard that you should observe in your applications. Label buttons are used primarily in windows and dialog boxes, to indicate and perform the main functions associated with them. They should be placed prominently in such a way that users can immediately tell by looking at the window what functions they can performs there, or what to do next.

Iconic buttons contain an icon on their face instead of a label. The icon presents graphically the functionality of the button. This type of buttons is used mainly in toolbars, but it is not unusual to find them in windows and dialog boxes, as well.

Because of their nature, push buttons can only be control items in a Forms module. They cannot display any data, and, therefore, do not contain any properties in the Data or Database groups, usually associated with other types of items. For the same reason, they can be created only from the Object Navigator of the Layout Editor, but not from the Data Block Wizard, like other types of items in the Form Builder.

15.1.1 FUNCTIONAL PROPERTIES OF PUSH BUTTONS

Most of the generic properties of Form Builder items discussed in the first part of Chapter 14 apply to push buttons as well. This section will discuss only their Functional properties.

The Label property contains the string of characters that will appear on the face of the button. To allow users to access the button from the keyboard, without using the mouse, you can set the property Access Key to one character from the label string. Forms Runtime will underline the first character of the label string that matches the access key. Users can select the button by pressing ALT and the access key simultaneously. For example, if the button's label is Close and the access key is C, the label will appear to the users as Close. They can navigate to it by pressing ALT+C, and then press the space bar to push the button.

One button per block can be activated by the users from anywhere on the screen by pressing ENTER. This is known as the default button and can become such by setting the Default Button property to "Yes." At runtime, as long as no other push button is selected, the default button will maintain the selection border around it. This means that the button is always ready to fire, whenever ENTER is pressed. Because there is no need to navigate to the button in order to push it, default buttons do not need access keys.

> **CAUTION**
>
> The possibility of pressing default buttons inadvertently is high. Therefore, do not use them to perform destructive actions such as deleting records from the database or exiting the form without commiting database changes.

The Iconic property of push buttons controls whether they are iconic or label buttons. When it is set to "Yes," the button is an iconic button; when it is set to "No," the button is a label button. For an iconic button, you must also specify the name of the icon that will be displayed on top of the button. This is done by setting the property Icon Filename to the name of the file that contains the icon. There are two things you should be careful about when specifying the name of an icon.

- Forms Runtime expects the file to be with the appropriate extension—for example, .ICO—in the file system, and wants you to specify only the file name in the Icon Filename property. If you add the extension of the file, Forms will not be able to attach it to the button. For example, if the icon file name is CUSTOMER.ICO, set the Icon Filename property only to "CUSTOMER." Forms Runtime will not be able to attach it to the button, even if you specify a fully qualified path for the icon file.
- The location of the icon file must be in one of the directories specified in the environment variable TKxx. The characters "xx" ('60' for version 6.0) in the name of the variable stand for two digits representing the version of Oracle Developer installed in your environment. In Microsoft Windows platforms, this variable is located in the folder HKEY_LOCAL_MACHINE\SOFTWARE\ORACLE of the registry.

15.1.2 EVENTS OF PUSH BUTTONS

There are two major events that happen in the life of a push button: ActivateButton, and PressButton. They can originate from the keyboard, or from mouse clicks. The only way to activate a button without pressing it is to use the TAB or SHIFT+TAB keys, also known in the Form Builder terminology as [Next Item] and [Previous Item] until the focus navigates to the button. This requires that the Keyboard Navigable property of the button is set to "Yes." Once the button is activated, there are several ways to press it.

- Press the space bar from the keyboard.
- Press ENTER from the keyboard.
- Click the button with the mouse.

When the mouse or the keyboard access keys are used, activating and pressing the button occur in rapid succession and are often considered as one event: PressButton.

You can associate the method WHEN-NEW-ITEM-INSTANCE with the ActivateButton event, and the method WHEN-BUTTON-PRESSED with the PressButton event. Usually, the second one is used to perform the functionality that the button is designed to do.

> **TIP**
>
> By setting the property Mouse Navigate to "No," it is possible to fire the PressButton event without the ActivateButton event, because the focus cannot be placed on the button.

15.2 RADIO GROUPS AND RADIO BUTTONS

Radio buttons offer users a way to choose only one option from a list of mutually exclusive options. A label and a radio button on the side of the label that indicates whether the option is currently selected represent each of the options. The radio buttons that represent all the choices available for a particular situation form a radio group. Form Builder items can be represented by radio groups. Those few data options that are allowed for the radio group item are the radio buttons that make up the group.

The easiest way to implement an item as a radio group is to change the Item Type in the Property Palette from, say, "Text Item" to "Radio Group." When you do this, you will notice that a number of properties from the Physical group, properties such as Visible, X Position, Y Position, Width, and Height, disappear from the list of item's properties. Because the radio group itself is not displayed on the screen, these properties do not have any meaning for this type of item.

However, the properties Canvas and Tab Page remain in effect, and its setting will determine where the members of that radio group will be displayed.

If you expand the radio group item in the hierarchy tree, you will see that besides Triggers, this type of item also owns Radio Buttons. You must create radio button objects under the radio group item to represent the different choices that users have on the screen. You can create these objects in the Object Navigator or from the Layout Editor. If you create radio buttons from the Layout Editor, you will be presented with a list of radio groups in the current block. From this list, you choose the group that will become the parent of the newly created button.

15.2.1 PROPERTIES OF RADIO GROUPS AND RADIO BUTTONS

The most important properties of radio buttons are Radio Button Value, Label, and Access Key. The following paragraphs describe these properties:

- **Radio Button Value.** This property is the value that the radio button will pass to the parent group if users select it. It is also the value that must be fetched by a query or stored programmatically in the radio group item in order to select the radio button. For example, suppose that the item GENDER in the block CUSTOMER of the MRD application is implemented as a radio group. Two radio buttons, MALE and FEMALE, are members of this group. Their property Radio Button Value is set to "M" and "F," respectively. Each time the users will click the button Female on the screen, F will be the value assigned to the item GENDER. If the record of a customer is queried from the database, and the value of GENDER is F, the button Female will be selected.
- **Label.** This property is the text that users will see on the side of the radio button. It should explain the meaning of the option clearly and concisely.
- **Access Key.** This property has the same meaning here as in push buttons. It is a character that users can type from the keyboard in conjunction with the ALT key and that allows them to select the radio button without clicking it with the mouse.

Radio buttons also have properties in the Physical group, including Visible, X Position, Y Position, Width, and Height. These properties control their appearance, position and dimensions on the canvas.

Among the properties of radio groups, one worth special consideration is Mapping of Other Values in the Functional group. You can use this property to make the handling of the data by the radio group more robust. The default setting of the property is NULL. With such a setting, the block will reject all the queried records that do not contain any of the values assigned to the radio buttons in their radio group item. In the case presented above, if the query returns a customer whose GENDER is not set to M or F, the record will not be allowed to appear in the block. Sometimes, this way of handling inconsistent data may be too restrictive. If you build an application on top of these data for the purpose of standardizing them, the default setting of Mapping of Other Values will not allow you to view the erratic data items that you are trying to fix. In such situations, you may set this property (either its name, or its value) to one of the radio buttons in the group. After that, whenever a non-conforming record is queried, the radio button specified in the Mapping of Other Values property will be selected. The fact that radio buttons make one choice out of a number of mutually exclusive options implies that a choice is always made. In other words, if an item is implemented as radio group, it will always contain a value as specified by the radio buttons. The value can be NULL if the property of one of the buttons is set as such.

Finally, although radio groups are not represented visually on the canvas, you should give the idea that their radio buttons are grouped together. Usually a rectangle is drawn around the buttons and a text label placed on top of the box describes their functionality.

15.2.2 EVENTS OF RADIO GROUPS

The events that are associated with radio group items are ActivateRadioGroup and ChangeRadioGroupSelection. The first event occurs when users navigate to the group using the keyboard, or when they click on the radio button that is currently selected. At the successful completion of this event, the trigger WHEN-NEW-ITEM-INSTANCE will fire. The Keyboard Navigable property of the radio group item must be set to "Yes," if the keyboard will be used to activate the item; the Mouse Navigate property must be set to "Yes," if the mouse will be used for the same purpose. The selection of the radio group can be changed in one of two ways:

- ❑ Click the appropriate radio button.
- ❑ Press simultaneously the ALT key and the character specified in the Access Key property, if it exists.

Any of these actions causes the event ChangeRadioGroupSelection, which, in turn fires the trigger WHEN-RADIO-CHANGED. You can use this trigger to perform any actions that should be taken if the selection of the radio button changes. It is interesting to note that when the selection of the radio group changes, the first event to occur is ChangeRadioGroupSelection, followed by ActivateRadio-Group. The navigation to the item itself is completed after this event. Thus, the trigger WHEN-RADIO-CHANGED will fire before the trigger WHEN-NEW-ITEM-INSTANCE. Keep in mind this sequence if you are placing code in both triggers.

As with other controls, if the Mouse Navigate property of the radio group item is set to "No," you can click a radio button without moving the focus of the form to the radio group itself. In this case, only the trigger WHEN-RADIO-CHANGED will fire if the selection of the radio button is changed.

15.3 CHECK BOXES

Like radio buttons, check boxes are used to choose among some options, but unlike radio buttons, the choices that check boxes represent are not mutually exclusive. In other words, if your users need to make multiple selections out of a number of options, check boxes must be used to represent these options. But if the user must choose only one of these options, you should use radio buttons.

Check box items are created either by converting the Item Type property of an existing item to "Checkbox," or by creating the item from scratch in the Layout Editor. When you do so, the object type icon in the Object Navigator will change to a check box.

15.3.1 PROPERTIES OF CHECK BOXES

When you convert an existing text item to a check box, most properties are carried over to the new type, except for properties in the Functional group and a few other properties specific to text items, such as Bevel. Physical properties, such as the position and dimensions of the check box, are inherited from those of the original text item. This may require you to adjust the dimension of the check box, if its label is not fully visible, and to delete the text label previously associated with the text item.

From the properties in the Functional group, Label and Access Key properties have the same meaning as the respective properties for radio buttons. The property Value when Checked contains the value that the item should contain if users check the box on the screen. If the item is populated with this value either by a query, or programmatically, the status of the check box on the canvas will be Checked. The property Value when Unchecked is set to the value that must be placed in the item if the check box is not checked. If this value is assigned to the item internally, the status of the box becomes unchecked.

> **TIP**
>
> The properties Value when Checked and Value when Unchecked must have different settings for the check box to be considered valid. If the properties are not set to different values, you will get the following error when generating the module: "FRM-30174: Checked and unchecked values must be distinct."

As an example, consider the preferences a customer may have for movies. If the customer has interest in Mystery movies, the MYSTERY column in the database will store the value Y; otherwise, no values will be stored. If you implement the item MYSTERY in block CUSTOMER as a check box, you would assign Y to its Value when Checked property, and leave blank the property Value when Unchecked. Now users can check the box to express the fact that the customer is interested in Mystery movies, instead of entering `Y` in a text item. When the record is retrieved from the database, the Mystery item will be checked if the column contains Y, or unchecked if it contains no values at all.

The property Checkbox Mapping of Other Values has the same meaning as the property Mapping of Other Values for radio groups. It handles the case when the value stored in the database does not match the setting of the properties Value when Checked and Value when Unchecked. By default, this property is set to "Checked," and sets the status of the box to Checked if such values are returned from a query or assigned to the item programmatically. You can set it to "Unchecked" to reverse the effect, or to "Not Allowed" to reject records that contain inconsistent values.

15.3.2 CHECK BOX EVENTS

Two events associated with a check box are activating and changing the check status of the item. You can activate the check box by using TAB or SHIFT+TAB keys to navigate to them. When this event is complete, the trigger WHEN-NEW-ITEM-INSTANCE fires. The ActivateCheckbox event occurs only when the property Keyboard Navigable of the item is "Yes." Once the item is activated, you can change its state by pressing the space bar on the keyboard. This causes the event ChangeCheckBox, which, in turn, activates the trigger WHEN-CHECKBOX-CHANGED.

If you click the check box or its label, both events will occur in rapid succession. The event that takes precedence in this case is changing the status of the check box. Therefore, WHEN-CHECKBOX-CHANGED trigger will fire before WHEN-NEW-ITEM-INSTANCE trigger. The effect of clicking the check box with the mouse can be replicated from the keyboard by pressing at the same time the ALT key and the access key, if one is defined.

As is the case with push buttons and radio buttons, if the property Mouse Navigate property is set to "No," you can change the setting of the check box without placing the focus on the item itself. In such case, only the event CheckboxChanged will occur, and therefore, only the trigger WHEN-CHECKBOX-CHANGED will fire.

At the conclusion of this section, recall that it is important that logically related check boxes be grouped visually on the canvas. In this case, as with radio buttons, you should draw a rectangle around the items and place a text label on top of it that summarizes the purpose or the functionality of these items.

15.4 LIST BOXES

Given the amount of space they occupy on the screen, it is recommended that you limit the number of radio items or check boxes to five or fewer per group. If your application requires choosing from a larger number of options, then selection lists should be used. Single-selection lists have more functionality than radio buttons in the sense that they allow users to pick only one entry from a list of options presented to them. Multi-selection lists allow users to choose several options at the same time, and, therefore are functionally similar to a group of check boxes. The Form Builder runtime, by default, supports only single-selection lists. Multi-selection lists can be implemented programmatically. In the rest of this section, referring to lists will mean single-selection lists.

To convert an existing item to a list, simply set its Item Type property to "List Item." If you are converting a text item to a list, you will notice that the new items will inherit all the other properties of the original item, with the exception of properties in the Functional group and the properties Bevel and Rendered.

15.4.1 TYPES OF LISTS

There are three types of lists used in GUI environments and in Form Builder applications: drop-down list boxes, text lists, and combo boxes. The type of list is controlled by the property List Style under the Functional group.

- **Drop-down list boxes.** The List Style property for these objects is set to 'Poplist,' hence the alternate name used to identify them. When they are not in use, poplists look like text items. To their right, they have an arrow button, which, when activated, displays the elements of the list. If the number of options is larger than ten, a scrollbar will appear to help users navigate to the other items not displayed in the list. When users pick one option, the list folds back to its normal state, and the selection appears in the text area of the list. By default, when a list is created, it is a drop-down list box.
- **Text lists.** The List Style property for these objects is set to "Tlist." In their normal state, they are rectangular boxes where the list items are displayed. The size of the box is defined in the Layout Editor, when you create the list. If the list contains more items than can fit in the box, a scroll bar to the right of the box can be used to scroll the list.
- **Combo boxes.** With the two previous types of lists, users can only select one value that already exists and is displayed by the list. There are occasions when they must be allowed to enter a value that is not in the list. Combo boxes combine the benefits of using a list of predefined data elements to populate an item with the flexibility to enter additional data that

are not in the list. Visually, combo boxes are similar to drop-down list boxes. Functionally, users can click the list button to display the list of available options, and pick an option from the list to fill the text item. They can also type directly in the text item as they would with any other text item in the Form. The combo box will not record automatically the new data as elements of the list. If the application must update the list of options with the new data, the feature must be implemented programmatically. Later in the chapter, you will see how to do this. To implement a list as a combo box, set its List Style property to "Combo Box."

Figure 15.1 shows examples of the same item implemented using the styles of lists described above.

15.4.2 SETTING LIST PROPERTIES AT DESIGN TIME

The principal property of a list used in the Form Builder is the property Elements in List. This property defines the options that users will see when they activate the list at runtime. This property is set in the List Items Elements dialog box that is displayed if you double-click it or if you click the More button displayed in the properties settings bar (see Figure 15.2).

There are two parts in this dialog box. The List Elements text list is where you define the items that users will see when accessing your list. The List Item Value field is where you specify the value that will correspond to the list element in form item. In the example shown in Figure 15.2, the current element is Comedy, and the item value that corresponds to it is C. This means that, if users select Comedy from the list, the CATEGORY item in the form will be assigned the value C. If a query or programmatic assignment places the value C in the CATEGORY item, Comedy will become the selected element in the list.

The List Item Elements dialog box does not provide a way to sort the elements of the list in any order. If you want to sort them, you must populate the list dynamically via a SELECT statement that contains an ORDER BY clause. Inserting or deleting entries in the text list is not a very intuitive process either. In order

FIGURE 15.1 Three types of lists in Form Builder applications.

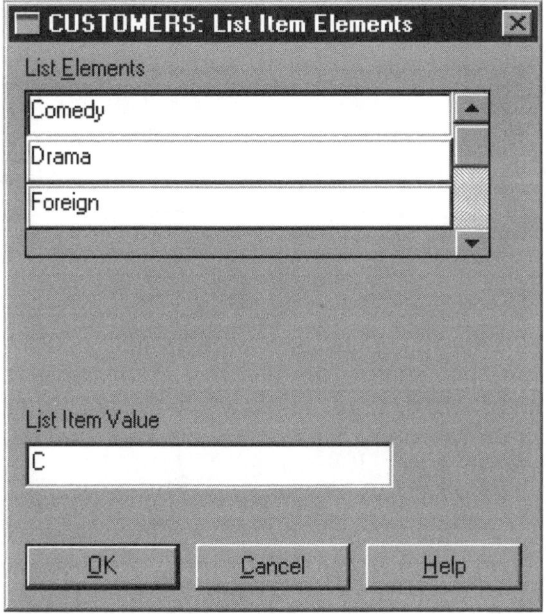

FIGURE 15.2 List Item Elements dialog box.

to figure out the right key combination for these actions, press CTRL+K from the keyboard to display the list of keys that can be used in this dialog box. There, you can see that to insert an element you must press SHIFT-CTRL+> and to delete it SHIFT-CTRL+<. Once you enter all the elements of the list, you can click the OK button, to accept the changes.

The property Mapping of Other Values in the Functional group of list items has exactly the same meaning as the corresponding property for radio group items. It can be set to either a list element such as Comedy, or to the list item value that corresponds to that element, for example C.

15.4.3 EVENTS OF LISTS

As with other controls discussed in this chapter, the two most important events in the life of a list are activating it and changing its selection. Both events can be initiated by keystrokes, or by mouse clicks. The Keyboard Navigable property must be set to "Yes" to be able to access the list using the keyboard.

The ActivateList event occurs if the TAB or SHIFT+TAB keys are used to navigate to the list. At the completion of this event, the focus of the form is placed on the list, its current value is highlighted, and the WHEN-NEW-ITEM-INSTANCE trigger fires.

When drop-down list boxes or the combo boxes are activated, you must press the down-arrow key to display the list members. Once these types of lists are unfolded, you can scroll their elements to search for the choice you want. To pick one of the list items, highlight it and press ENTER. At this point, the Change-List event occurs and the trigger WHEN-LIST-CHANGED fires. At the conclusion of this event, the lists are folded back to their initial state.

When text lists are activated, the current list value will be selected. Scrolling the elements of the list will cause the event ChangeList and the trigger WHEN-LIST-CHANGED to fire.

The easiest way to activate or change the value of a list is to use mouse clicks. If you click drop-down list boxes, the list elements will appear. The ActivateList event occurs, and the WHEN-NEW-ITEM-INSTANCE trigger fires only if the Mouse Navigate property is set to "Yes." From the list of options available, you can click one to change the value of the list. If the option you pick is different from the current value of the list, the ChangeList occurs; otherwise, nothing happens.

For text lists, their elements are displayed in the list box. If the focus is not on the list, and you click one of its elements, the ChangeList and ActivateList events will occur one after the other in this order. Again here, if the Mouse Navigate property is "No," the ActivateList event does not occur.

Text lists have two aspects in their behavior that are different from the other types of lists.

- ❑ If the currently selected list element is clicked, the element will be deselected. Visually, the selection box around the element disappears. Internally, the value stored in the list item is set to NULL.
- ❑ Forms recognizes double-clicking an element of the list as a separate event. This event triggers the WHEN-LIST-ACTIVATED method to fire.

The method is meaningful only for text list items. Because the ChangeList event occurs before DoubleClickListElement, the new value of the list item is available in the WHEN-LIST-ACTIVATED trigger, and can be used to initiate actions such as display a dialog box or perform a computation. You will utilize this feature of text lists to programmatically implement a multiple selection list in Chapter 17.

The Mouse Navigate property of combo boxes is always "Yes." If you set it to "No," the Form Builder will display a warning when the module is generated, and the setting will be ignored at runtime. If you click inside the text field of the combo box, the current selection will be highlighted and the cursor will be placed inside the field. The same thing happens when the list button of the combo box is clicked, but, in addition, the list elements will be displayed like in a drop-down list box. At this point, you can either pick another element from the list, or type a new entry over the current selection. In both cases, the ChangeList event will occur. The new selection will be available to the trigger WHEN-LIST-CHANGED that fires in response to this event.

> **CAUTION**
>
> If the value of a combo box is changed via a mouse-click, the ChangeList event will fire only once. However, if a new entry is typed in the text field, the ChangeList event will occur each time a character is typed. As a consequence, the WHEN-LIST-CHANGED trigger will fire as many times as you hit the keyboard. Be very careful with the code you place in this trigger for combo boxes.

15.4.4 MANIPULATING LISTS PROGRAMMATICALLY

Besides creating list items at design time, you can also use a series of built-in functions and procedures to maintain them at runtime. In this section you will implement the COMPANY item in block MOVIE of the MRD application as a combo box list that will be populated by the users as the application is being used. In the process of implementing this functionality, you will understand the meaning of the built-in program units that you will use.

You can follow the discussion in this section with the MRD module you are creating as you are reading this book. You can also use the module CH15.FMB provided in the companion disk, which contains the MRD application, as it should have been at the end of Chapter 14.

Open the module, navigate to the MOVIE block, select the item COMPANY, and display its properties in a Property Window. Then:

1. Set Item Type to "List Item."
2. Set List Style in the Functional group to "Combo Box."

In order for Forms Runtime to be able to initialize the list item, you must specify at least one element in the list.

1. Double-click the property Elements in List to display the List Item Elements dialog box.
2. Create a list element that will represent a movie-making company, for example MIRAMAX.
3. Set the list item value for that element to the same value as the label, that is MIRAMAX.
4. Enter additional companies if you wish.
5. Click OK when done.

Save and generate the form module before moving to the programmatic implementation of the functionality of COMPANY combo box.

As mentioned earlier in the chapter, combo boxes are "memoryless." They allow users to enter data that are not elements of the list, but do not incorporate the new entries in the list automatically. In order to make combo boxes record the new data elements you will capture the value of the list item when the event ActivateList occurs—in the WHEN-NEW-ITEM-INSTANCE trigger. Then, during the event ValidateItem—in the WHEN-VALIDATE-ITEM trigger—you will compare the final value of the list item with the original value. If there is a change, the new value is a candidate to become an element of the list. You will decide whether to add this new value or not to the list by comparing it with the existing elements in the list.

TIP

The initial impulse would be to place this functionality in the WHEN-LIST-CHANGED trigger. However, if the users pick several choices before making up their mind, or if they type in a new value this trigger will fire multiple times. In your implementation, you will let the users pick and choose as much as they like. When they decide to leave the item, the value stored there will be validated, and here you will decide whether a new element must be added to the list or not.

You will store the initial value of the list in a global variable, which will be declared when the form module is first created. The safest place to declare global variables is a PRE-FORM form-level trigger. Thus, expand the existing PRE-FORM trigger in your module with the following statement that declares the variable `GLOBAL.original_value`:

```
:GLOBAL.original_item := NULL;
```

To implement the desired functionality you have to complete two steps. First, store the current value of the list item in the variable `GLOBAL.original_value` when the list is activated. Then, during the ValidateItem event, compare the new value entered by the user with the original one. If they are different and if the new value is not already an element in the list, then expand the list to include the new value.

The following steps allow you to assign the old value of the list to the variable `GLOBAL.original_value`.

1. In the Object Navigator, right-click the item COMPANY in the MOVIES block.
2. Choose the item SmartTriggers from the pop-up menu and then select the trigger WHEN-NEW-ITEM-INSTANCE.

3. Enter the following line in the PL/SQL Editor:

```
:GLOBAL.original_item := :MOVIES.COMPANY;
```

4. Compile the trigger and close the PL/SQL Editor window.

To implement the second step create a WHEN-VALIDATE-ITEM trigger for item COMPANY. Enter the text shown in Figure 15.3 in the body of the trigger.

The first action this trigger performs is to check whether the list selection has changed. If the current value of the list item is different from the initial value stored in `GLOBAL.original_item`, then the trigger uses the function `Element_Label_Exists` to check whether the new item is an item already present in the list. The outcome of the check is stored in the Boolean variable `IsTextinList`. If the new value is not in the list, then the user has just typed a new item. The procedure `Insert_Element` is invoked to add the value and the label of a new element to the list. In the implementation of COMPANY as a combo box both the label of the new element and its value match the string that the operator entered. Therefore the argument passed to the procedure `Insert_Element` are `'MOVIES.COMPANY'`, `:MOVIES.COMPANY`, and `:MOVIES.COMPANY`, respectively.

In the present state of the form, the trigger will not compile successfully, because neither the function `Element_Label_Exists` nor the procedure `Insert_Element` are declared. However, the PL/SQL Editor allows you to create the trigger even if its contents are not compiled. This feature can be used to prototype the high-level functionality of the trigger, and then move on to a lower programming level where all the implementation details are clarified.

```
DECLARE
  IsTextinList BOOLEAN;
BEGIN
  IF (:GLOBAL.original_item <> :MOVIES.COMPANY) THEN
    IsTextinList := Element_Label_Exists(list_name =>
'MOVIES.COMPANY',
                                              label     =>
:MOVIES.COMPANY);
    IF NOT IsTextinList THEN
      Insert_Element(list_name => 'MOVIES.COMPANY',
                     label     => :MOVIES.COMPANY,
                     value     => :MOVIES.COMPANY);
    END IF;
  END IF;
END;
```

FIGURE 15.3 Trigger that inserts a new list item if it does not already exist.

From the PL/SQL editor window, create the function `Element_Label_Exists`, as shown in Figure 15.4. The first lines of this function are familiar. You retrieve the internal ID of the list item and make sure that it exists before proceeding any further. The built-in function GET_LIST_ELEMENT_COUNT is used to retrieve the number of elements in the list. This number serves as an upper bound of the FOR loop that checks whether the input label equals any of the existing elements' labels. As you loop through the elements of the list, the function GET_LIST_ELEMENT_LABEL is used to return the label for the current element of the list.

```
FUNCTION Element_Label_Exists (list_name VARCHAR2,
                                label VARCHAR2)
RETURN BOOLEAN IS
  list_id         ITEM;
  list_count            NUMBER;
  found           BOOLEAN := FALSE;
  current_label   VARCHAR2(50);

BEGIN
  /* FIND_ITEM returns the appropriate item ID.*/
  list_id := FIND_ITEM(list_name);

  IF NOT ID_NULL(list_id) THEN
    list_count := GET_LIST_ELEMENT_COUNT(list_id);

    FOR i IN 1..list_count LOOP
      current_label := GET_LIST_ELEMENT_LABEL(list_id,
i);
      IF label = current_label THEN
        found := TRUE;
        EXIT;
      END IF;
    END LOOP;
  ELSE
    MESSAGE('List Item '||list_name||' does not exist.');
    RAISE FORM_TRIGGER_FAILURE;
  END IF;

  RETURN found;

END Element_Label_Exists;
```

FIGURE 15.4 Searching a list for a given value.

If a match is found, the input label exists already in the list. The variable `found` is set to TRUE and the FOR loop is interrupted. If the loop searches all the list elements and finds no matches, the value of the variable `found` remains FALSE, as it was initialized at the beginning of the function. If successfully completed, the function returns this variable.

> **TIP**
>
> With a minor modification, this function can be used to search for matches between the input argument and list elements' values. Instead of the built-in function GET_LIST_ELEMENT_LABEL, you would use the function GET_LIST_ELEMENT_VALUE to retrieve the value of the current list element.

Once you edit and compile the function `Element_Label_Exists`, create procedure `Insert_Element`, as shown in Figure 15.5. The only new thing in this procedure is the use of the built-in procedure ADD_LIST_ELEMENT. This procedure takes four input arguments. The first one is the internal ID of the list item. The second parameter is the position in the list where the new item will be

```
PROCEDURE Insert_Element (list_name VARCHAR2,
                          label VARCHAR2,
                          value VARCHAR2) IS
  list_id         ITEM;
  list_count      NUMBER;

BEGIN
  /* FIND_ITEM returns the appropriate item ID.*/
  list_id := FIND_ITEM(list_name);

  IF NOT ID_NULL(list_id) THEN
    list_count := GET_LIST_ELEMENT_COUNT(list_id);
    /* Add new element at the bottom of the list.     */
    ADD_LIST_ELEMENT(list_id, list_count + 1, label,
value);
  ELSE
    MESSAGE('List Item '||list_name||' does not exist.');
    RAISE FORM_TRIGGER_FAILURE;
  END IF;
END Insert_Element;
```

FIGURE 15.5 Inserting a new element in a list.

inserted. The procedure `Insert_Element` places the new elements at the bottom of the list. If you pass the number 1 in this argument, the elements will always be added at the top of the list. The third parameter is the label associated with the new element, and the last parameter is its value.

> **TIP**
>
> If you need to delete an element from the list, you can use the built-in procedure DELETE_LIST_ELEMENT. This procedure takes as input parameters the internal ID of the list item and the position of the element in the list.

> **TIP**
>
> All the built-in program units that have been discussed in this section can take the list item internal ID or name as a parameter. The use of the internal ID after making sure that it exists increases the robustness of your application.

15.4.5 WRITING OBJECT-INDEPENDENT CODE

The MRD application has several items that could benefit from the functionality you just added to item COMPANY. In order to avoid repeating the same actions for these items, you should create a property class based on some properties of COMPANY.

1. In the Object Navigator, create a duplicate copy of property class TEXT_ITEM and name it UPDATEABLE_COMBO.
2. Set property Item Type to 'List Item.'
3. Add property List Style and set it to 'Combo Box.'

Now select the triggers WHEN-NEW-ITEM-INSTANCE and WHEN-VALIDATE-ITEM attached to item COMPANY and drag them onto the property class UPDATEABLE_COMBO.

The code for these triggers explicitly uses information about item COMPANY, which would not be very helpful in a property class that you intend to use generically. Edit the contents of WHEN-NEW-ITEM-INSTANCE trigger, and replace the existing code with the following line:

```
:GLOBAL.original_item := :SYSTEM.CURSOR_VALUE;
```

SYSTEM.CURSOR_VALUE is a system variable that records the value of the item where the cursor is currently.

Edit the contents of WHEN-VALIDATE-ITEM trigger as shown in Figure 15.6.

```
DECLARE
  IsTextinList BOOLEAN;
  item_name    VARCHAR2(80);
  item_value   VARCHAR2(80);

BEGIN
  item_name := :SYSTEM.CURSOR_ITEM;
  item_value := :SYSTEM.CURSOR_VALUE;
  IF (:GLOBAL.original_item <> item_value) THEN
    IsTextinList := Element_Label_Exists(list_name =>
item_name,
                                         label     =>
item_value);
    IF NOT IsTextinList THEN
      Insert_Element(list_name => item_name,
                     label     => item_value,
                     value     => item_value);
    END IF;
  END IF;
END;
```

FIGURE 15.6 Generic trigger that inserts a new element in a list item.

In this trigger, SYSTEM.CURSOR_ITEM is the system variable that records the name of the item where the cursor is currently located.

Save and generate the form. In Section 15.6.2 later in this chapter, COMPANY and other items in the MOVIE block will inherit these triggers from the property class UPDATEABLE_COMBO.

There is a major caveat in the way this section implements the dynamic management of lists. Users will be able to enter new elements in the list and will see the new entries as long as they do not exit the application. However, because the inserted elements are maintained in temporary memory structures of Forms Runtime, as soon as the application is terminated, the modifications will be discarded. In order to make this functionality really productive and useful, you need to record these changes in permanent structures that last between sessions. Chapter 16 will explain how to use record groups to populate list items with data from the database.

15.5 GUI GUIDELINES FOR CONTROLS

As discussed in the previous chapter, when developing a GUI application you strive for a uniform and standard look of all the screens, and also for compliance with other successful applications. Remember that the goal is to be noticed the least possible. The software applications you develop should be considered as utilities, tools in the hands of users that help them accomplish their business goals. Users should notice these applications as much as they notice the telephone set when they place or receive a call. At the same time, they should find them as reliable and easy to use as their telephone.

Establishing and following standards is as important for controls as for text items in the interface of the application.

15.5.1 PUSH BUTTONS

The position and size of buttons play an important role in the ability of users to notice and use them. Depending on the orientation of the window, buttons can be placed either on the upper right-hand corner of the window or centered at the bottom of it. If the buttons are placed up and to the right of the window, they must all have the same size and be vertically aligned. If they are placed at the bottom, they must be aligned horizontally, and share the same height. It is good if they can have the same width, but this is not required.

The dimensions of the buttons should be set so that the whole text label is completely inside the margins. It is not a bad idea to add a little extra space if running in varied enviroments since font sizes may vary. Buttons whose labels fall off the margins give the impression of an application put together in haste.

The buttons should be grouped together by functionality. The distance between groups should be larger than the distance between buttons of the same group. The button that is likely to be used the most by the users, usually the OK or Save button, should always be the first button from the top for vertically-aligned buttons, or from the left for horizontally aligned buttons. This button should also have the *Default Button* property set to "Yes." The Cancel or Close button should be placed immediately next to this button. If the window contains a Help button, it should be the last one, positioned at the opposite side of the default button.

Limit the number of buttons in a window to no more than five.

If iconic buttons are used, they should have the same size as the icon displayed on them. Because of differences in their dimensions, text label buttons should not be mixed with iconic buttons. Use one type or the other consistently across the window. It is an effective GUI technique to place iconic buttons in toolbars attached to the sides of the window.

15.5.2 RADIO BUTTONS AND CHECK BOXES

Given the similarity in appearance between radio buttons and check boxes, you should follow the same guidelines when working with them. The following paragraphs list some of these guidelines:

- Radio buttons and check boxes must be aligned vertically. Each button or box must have a label to its right that briefly but clearly describes the option represented by the object. In addition, all the options that are related must be grouped visually, and a label should be placed on top of the group.

- Do not place more than six to eight radio buttons or check boxes in a group. If the number of options is higher, replace radio buttons with single-selection lists, and implement programmatically multi-selection lists to replace the check boxes.
- I do not recommended the use of check boxes that, when checked, select all the other options in the group. The functionality can by better implemented programmatically with a multi-selection list and a push button that selects all the elements of the list.

15.5.3 LISTS

Lists are controls that should replace radio buttons or check boxes in the following situations:

- There are more than six to eight options in the group.
- The space or the layout of the window does not allow the use of radio buttons or check boxes. In this case, drop-down list boxes and combo boxes should be considered.
- The options in the group are likely to change. In this case, lists that can be updated and expanded dynamically should be used.

Drop-down list boxes and combo boxes created in Form Builder applications can display up to ten items at a time. You have more control in the number of elements displayed in text lists. Limit that number to no more than ten.

Each list box must be labeled like any other item on the window. If the list is very long, and users will search it frequently, consider adding auto-restriction capabilities that filter the possible matches as users type the element label in a text field. Excellent examples of lists with these features are the List of Values dialog box and the MS Windows Help search utility.

15.6 CONTROLS IN THE MRD APPLICATION

This section concludes the design of the principal canvases in the MRD application by adding some of the controls discussed in this section. You can continue to work with the module you used in Sections 15.4.4 and 15.4.5, or you can open the module CH15_3.FMB provided with the companion software. This module contains the MRD application as it should have been at the end of Chapter 14. In addition, it also contains the property class that was defined in these sections.

15.6.1 CONTROLS IN THE CUSTOMERS CANVAS

Display the canvas CUSTOMERS in the Layout Editor. First, change the item STATUS into a list box. Display its properties in the Property Palette and follow these steps:

1. Set the property Item Type to "List Item."
2. Set Width to 60.
3. Double-click the property Elements in List and enter the following list elements: Active, Good Credit, and Bad Credit. The list item values should be A, G, and B, respectively.
4. Set the property Initial Value to "A" or "Active."

Now change the Item Type of GENDER from "Text Item" to "Radio Group." You will see that it will disappear from the canvas.

1. Use the Radio Button tool in the Layout Editor tool palette to create a radio button approximately where GENDER was located. The Radio Group dialog box will appear (see Figure 15.7).
2. Click OK to add the new radio button to the Gender radio group.
3. Set the properties Name and Label of this radio item to "Male"; set Radio Button Value to "M."
4. Repeat steps 1 to 3 to create the radio button FEMALE. Set Radio Button Value for this button to "F."
5. Repeat Steps 1 to 3 to create the radio button UNKNOWN (in the sense that data are not available). Leave the property Radio Button Value for this button unset.
6. Group and align vertically the radio buttons and create the text label Gender on top of them.

Depending on the settings of visual attribute properties of the Layout Editor, the objects you create, including the radio items and the text label, may not have color properties that are consistent with the rest of your application. To avoid this problem, display the Property Palette of the violating object and set the properties in the Font & Color group to the Form Builder default settings.

The items MYSTERY, COMEDY, DRAMA, and FOREIGN will all be implemented as check boxes. These are the actions you need to take to convert them:

1. Select all the items in question and display the Property Palette.
2. Set the properties Item Type to "Check Box," Value when Checked to "Y" and Prompt Attachment Edge to "End." The setting of this last property will display the prompts to the right of the check boxes rather than to their left.

FIGURE 15.7 Radio Groups dialog box.

3. Group and align vertically the check boxes and create the text label Preferences on top of them.
4. Align vertically and set the widths of the items ID and STATUS, radio group GENDER and check box group Preferences to minimize the vertical margins of the objects on the canvas.

Now use the Button icon from the toolbar to create five push buttons in the upper-right corner of the canvas

1. Name the buttons COMMIT_FORM, CLOSE, MOVIE, RENTAL, and HELP.
2. Set the Label property to "Save," "Close," "Movie...," "Rental...," and "Help," respectively.
3. Set the Access Key property to the initial letter of each button, except for COMMIT_FORM.
4. Set the Default Button property to "Yes" for the button COMMIT_FORM.
5. Set the Width property to 14 for all the buttons.

6. Align the buttons vertically. Group COMMIT_FORM and CLOSE together and MOVIE and RENTAL together.

In order to wrap things up with the CUSTOMERS canvas, reduce its dimensions to just a few pixels larger than the area occupied by the text items and controls of the CUSTOMERS block. In the Object Navigator reset the tab order of items to reflect the flow of data on the screen. At this point, the CUSTOMERS canvas should look like Figure 15.8. Save the module before moving to the next section.

15.6.2 CONTROLS IN THE MOVIES CANVAS

As a preliminary step, open the canvas MOVIES in the Layout Editor. In the block MOVIES, you will use the property class UPDATEABLE_COMBO to set the following items as combo boxes that expand dynamically during the session: ACTOR, ACTRESS, DIRECTOR, PRODUCER, and COMPANY. These are the steps to set properties of the item ACTOR based on the property class UPDATEABLE_COMBO:

1. Display the Property Palette window for the item.
2. Display the dialog box Subclass Information associated with the property of the same name.
3. Select the radio item Property Class and select "UPDATEABLE_COMBO" from the list Property Class Name.
4. Click OK to dismiss the dialog box Subclass Information.

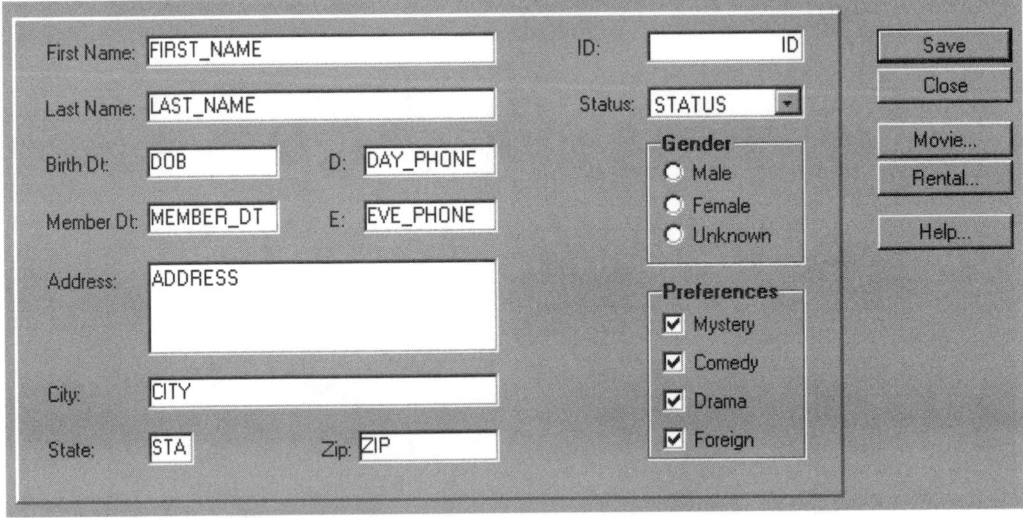

FIGURE 15.8 The CUSTOMERS canvas with all the controls in place.

Follow similar steps to set the properties of the items ACTRESS, DIRECTOR, PRODUCER, and COMPANY. As said earlier, Forms will not be able to initialize the lists at runtime if no elements are defined for them in the Form Builder. Therefore, you must enter at least one element in the List Item Elements dialog box for each of the above items. One common entry you can use for all the items is an element with label "<Unspecified>" and no value associated with it. Add this element to all the combo box items discussed here.

Now convert the items MOVIES.RATING and TAPES.STATUS from text items to list boxes. Set the property Width for both items to 50. Populate the lists as follows:

1. RATING should have four list elements: "NR," "PG-13," "R," and "NC-17." The list item values will be "1," "2," "3," and "4," respectively. Set the properties Initial Value and Mapping of Other Values to "2."
2. STATUS in the block TAPE should have the following list elements: "Available," "Rented," and "Returned." The list item values will be "A," "R," and "T," respectively. Set the properties Initial Value and Mapping of Other Values to "A."
3. Resize the TAPES frame so that the layout of the block is automatically refreshed.

Convert the STATUS item in the block MOVIES to a check box item by setting the Item Type property to "Check Box." Set its properties as follows:

1. Set the property Label to "Available?"
2. Set the properties Value when Checked and Initial Value to "A."
3. Set the property Value when Unchecked to "N."
4. Clear the setting of the property Prompt; currently it is set to "Status."

Create five push buttons in block MOVIES similar to the ones you added in the block CUSTOMERS. A quick way to add these buttons is described here:

1. In the Object Navigator, select the buttons COMMIT_FORM, CLOSE, MOVIE, RENTAL, and HELP in the block CUSTOMERS.
2. Copy the selected objects.
3. Expand the block MOVIES and select the last item on the block.
4. Paste the previously selected buttons. The new buttons, being a copy of the old ones, will be created on the canvas CUSTOMERS.
5. Display the Property Palette for all the selected objects and set the property Canvas to "MOVIES."
6. For the button MOVIE change its properties Name to "CUSTOMER," Label to "Customer...," and Access Key to "C."

7. In the Layout Editor window align the buttons horizontally on the canvas MOVIES, as shown in Figure 15.9.

As a final step, adjust the size of the MOVIES canvas according to the layout of the items on it. Arrange the tab order of items in MOVIES block to reflect the screen layout.

15.6.3 CONTROLS IN THE RENTALS CANVAS

The only controls that will be added to the RENTALS canvas are push buttons, similar to the ones you added on the MOVIES canvas. The process of adding these buttons is also similar and is briefly described as follows:

1. In the Object Navigator, expand the block MOVIES, select the five push button items, and copy them.
2. Expand the block RENTALS, select the last item in it, and paste the buttons.
3. With the new buttons in the RENTAL block still selected, display the Property Palette.
4. Set the properties Canvas to "RENTALS" and Number of Items Displayed to "1."
5. For the button RENTAL change its properties Name to "MOVIE," Label to "Movie...," and Access Key to "M."

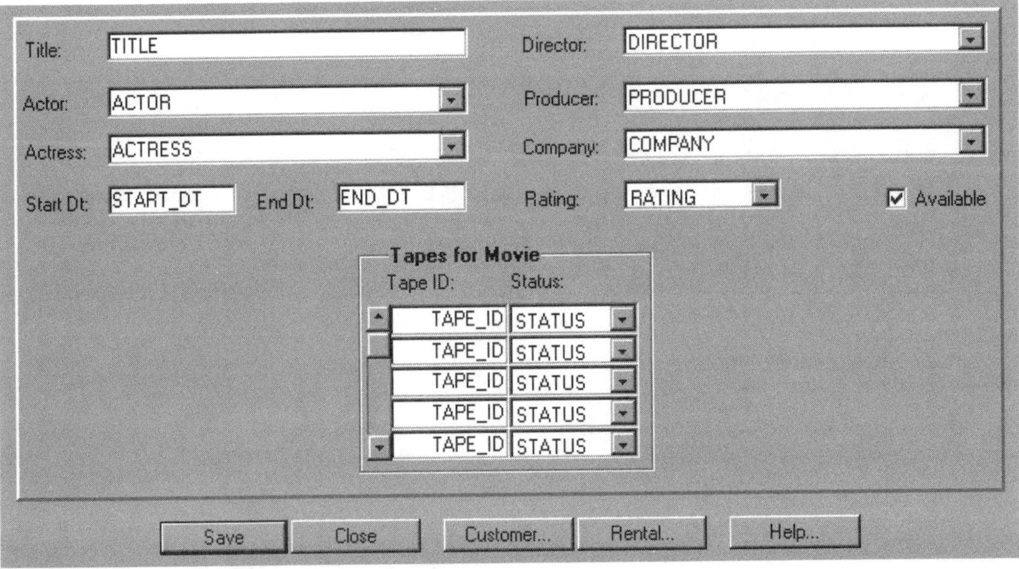

FIGURE 15.9 The MOVIES canvas with all the controls in place.

FIGURE 15.10 The RENTALS canvas with all the controls in place.

At this point, set the property Update Layout of the RENTALS frame to "Locked" and arrange the position of the new buttons on the canvas and the dimensions of the canvas itself. At the end, the RENTALS canvas should look like Figure 15.10.

15.7 SUMMARY

This chapter provided information about Form Builder GUI controls, their properties, and functionality. Important concepts in this chapter were

- **Push Buttons**
  - Functional Properties of Push Buttons
  - Events of Push Buttons
- **Radio Groups and Radio Buttons**
  - Properties of Radio Groups and Radio Buttons
  - Events of Radio Groups

- **Check Boxes**
  - Properties of Check boxes
  - Events of Check boxes
- **List Boxes**
  - Types of Lists
  - Setting List Properties at Design Time
  - Events of Lists
  - Manipulating Lists Programmatically
  - Writing Object-Independent Code
- **GUI Guidelines for Controls**
  - Push Buttons
  - Radio Buttons and Check Boxes
  - Lists
- **Controls in the MRD Application**
  - Controls in the CUSTOMERS Canvas
  - Controls in the MOVIES Canvas
  - Controls in the RENTALS Canvas

The following table describes the software assets that were discussed in this chapter. From the main HTML page of the software utilities provided with the book follow the links *Software* and *Chapter 15* to access these assets:

ASSET NAME	DESCRIPTION
CH15_1.FMB	The MRD application completed in the last chapter. Use this module as a starting point for the activities discussed in this chapter.
CH15_2.FMB	The MRD application with the activities discussed in Sections 15.4.4 and 15.4.5. Use this module as a starting point for the activities discussed in Section 15.6.
CH15_3.FMB	The MRD application with all the activities discussed in this chapter.
CH15_3.FMX	The executable version of CH15_3.FMB compiled for Win32 platforms.

Chapter 16

Windows, Canvases, and Dialog Boxes

The windows of my soul I throw
Wide open to the sun.
—John Greenleaf Whittier

- Properties of Windows
- Developing MDI Applications with Form Builder
- Alerts
- Canvases
- Canvas Use Cases
- Windows and Dialog Boxes in the MRD Application
- Summary

All the data-entry and interface items with which users interact during the lifetime of a GUI application are placed in windows. In applications such as the ones you develop with Form Builder, multiple windows can be available, open, and visible at any time. In addition, several dialog boxes may be used to get and display data or perform specific actions.

In Form Builder applications, items and controls are placed on canvases, which then in turn are attached to windows and, through them, displayed to users at runtime. This chapter discusses the types and properties of windows, dialog boxes, canvases, and a special type of built-in dialog boxes, the alerts.

16.1 PROPERTIES OF WINDOWS

Each window has the fundamental properties of every other object in the Form Builder, such as Name, Subclass Information, and Comment. When a window object is created in the Object Navigator, the Form Builder assigns it a default name. This name should be set to a more meaningful one that expresses the window's main functionality. This name also becomes the default window label. You can rename a window like any other object in the Navigator, or in the Property Palette, by setting its Name property. If the window is subclassed from another window or property class, the property Subclass Information contains information about this object and the module in which it resides. Later in this chapter you will create two property classes based on the properties of windows that you can use to implement MDI sheets and dialog boxes. The Comment property may be used by programmers to document the window object on-line.

Windows have several properties that govern the way they are presented to users during the execution of the application. These properties can be set in the Property Palette for the window object. They can also be set programmatically, using the Forms built-in SET_WINDOW_PROPERTY. Figure 16.1 represents a typical window developed in the Form Builder.

A great number of properties for a window at runtime can be changed directly by the users through basic and standard Windows actions such as clicking the Minimize and Maximize icons, selecting from or double-clicking the windows control menu, dragging and positioning the window on the screen or dragging its borders and corners until the window reaches a desired size.

The properties of windows are grouped in two major categories: Functional and Physical. Not all the properties that you may see in the Property Palette apply to window objects. For example, in the group Font & Color you can see properties related to visual attributes such as Visual Attribute Name, Font Name, and Font Size. In Microsoft Windows and Macintosh environments, these window properties do not have any meaning and you can ignore them. The same can be said for the property Bevel in the Physical group. The following section will

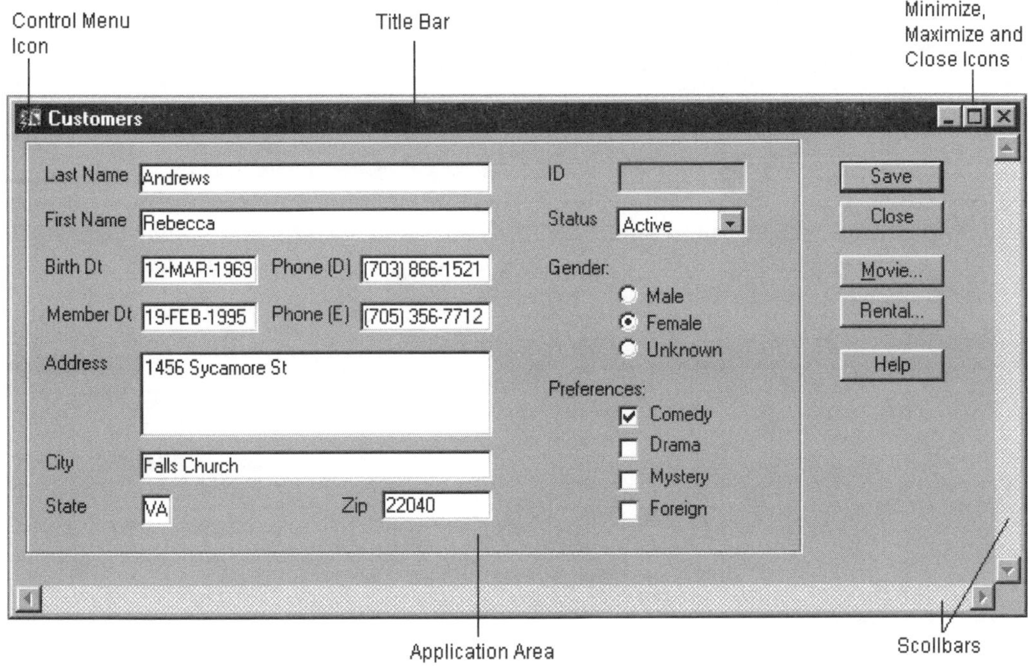

FIGURE 16.1 GUI components of a window.

discuss the most important properties of windows, and how you can set them in the Form Builder.

16.1.1 SETTING WINDOWS PROPERTIES IN THE FORM BUILDER

Each window has a title bar, which can summarize the functionality, or the data displayed on the window. You can set this title bar by entering a string of characters in the Title property. If you do not provide an explicit title for the window, Forms Runtime will use its name to fill the contents of the title bar.

The position of the window is defined by the X and Y coordinates of its upper left-hand corner. In the Form Builder, you can set the properties X Position and Y Position to specify where on the screen the window should be displayed when users access it for the first time. After the window is displayed on the screen, users can move it around by dragging the window's title bar or by choosing the Move item from its control menu. This is a standard feature of every application, and should not be repressed. However, if you want to prevent users from moving the window, set the property Move Allowed in the Functional group to "No." This setting will also remove the Move item from the control menu of the window.

The initial size of the window can be set by providing values for the Width and Height properties. It is acceptable and to be expected that users will resize the window by dragging any of its borders or corners, or by selecting the Size menu item from the window's control menu. When the size of the window is reduced, it is probable that the application's work area may not be able to fit entirely inside the window. It is very important that you equip these windows with vertical and horizontal scrollbars so that users can view the hidden parts of the work area. To do this, set the properties Show Horizontal Scrollbar and Show Vertical Scrollbar to "Yes." They are both members of the Functional group. By default, the properties Show Horizontal Scrollbar and Show Vertical Scrollbar are set to "No." In order to avoid the problem described above, you must change these settings to "Yes" for any window that will be resizable. You can still keep the default settings if the window will not be resizable, and its dimensions are such that all the data items and controls of the window are visible.

If you do not want the users to be able to resize the window, set the property Resize Allowed to "No." This setting will hide the item Size from the control menu. The borders and the corners of the window will also disappear.

In the Form Builder you can also specify whether or not users will be able to change the state of the window at runtime. A window can be in one of three states: Normal, Minimized, and Maximized. The position and size of a window in Normal state are defined by the properties X Position, Y Position, Width and Height, as described above. This is the default state in which a window is displayed. The window shown in Figure 16.1 is in Normal state.

At runtime, users can minimize a normal window by clicking the Minimize icon or by choosing Minimize from the control menu. When the window is minimized, it is displayed in the form of an icon. For this reason, the terms "Minimize" and "Iconify" are used interchangeably when speaking about windows. Once in Minimized state, the window can be restored to its Normal state by double-clicking its icon, or by choosing Restore from the control menu. Users can also maximize the window by selecting Maximize from the control menu.

The ability of users to minimize and maximize windows in Forms Runtime is controlled by the properties Minimize Allowed and Maximize Allowed. By default, the property Minimize Allowed is set to "Yes," which means that users can minimize the window at runtime. By setting the Minimize Allowed property to "No," you will not allow users to minimize the window. In this case, the window will not contain a Minimize icon, and its control menu will not have the Minimize item.

When the window is iconifiable, it is always good to attach an icon to the window, and a title that will be displayed under this icon. Both the title and the icon should represent the functionality of the window. They are defined by setting the properties Minimized Title and Icon Filename. If these properties are not set explicitly, when this window is minimized, Forms Runtime will use its own icon and the title bar of the window as visual identifiers of the window in the desktop.

> **TIP**
>
> When setting the Icon Filename property of a window you should keep in mind the same guidelines presented in Chapter 15 for iconic buttons. Namely:
>
> - Enter only the name of the icon file, for example CUSTOMER, without the path or the extension.
> - The icon file must be in one of the directories specified in the UI_ICON environment variable.

The default setting of the property Maximize Allowed is "Yes," which allows users to set their windows to Maximized state. If you set it to "No," the maximize icon in the upper right-hand corner of the window and the Maximize item in the control menu will not appear.

The property Close Allowed is a little different from the other properties discussed in this section. Setting it to "No" will remove the ability to close the window with any of the standard Microsoft Windows commands: double-clicking the window's control menu box, or pressing CTRL+F4 from the keyboard. However, setting the property to "Yes" will not enable your users to close the window with the above commands, either.

A window is an object that communicates with the environment through messages. When users issue any of the two commands mentioned above, they send a message to the window that should cause it to close. If Close Allowed property is set to "No," this message is not part of the messages recognized by the window. Therefore, it causes no events to occur. If the property is set to "Yes," the message is recognized by the window, and causes the event CloseWindow. Any actions that should be taken when this event occurs must be placed in the WHEN-WINDOW-CLOSED trigger. In order to close the window, you must place PL/SQL statements that perform this or any other actions associated with closing the window. The following section shows an example of how to do this.

The Functional group of properties for windows contains other properties, besides the ones discussed in this section. Their meaning is related with the types of windows that can be used in Form Builder applications. The discussion about them will be postponed until Sections 16.2.2 and 16.2.4.

16.1.2 CONTROLLING WINDOWS PROGRAMMATICALLY

The properties of windows can be accessed and modified at runtime, using several built-in procedures and functions. The most important players in this process are the functions FIND_WINDOW, ID_NULL, GET_WINDOW_PROPERTY, and the procedure SET_WINDOW_PROPERTY.

FIND_WINDOW is used to retrieve the internal ID of a window, based on its name. The value that this function returns must be stored in a variable of type WINDOW. The function ID_NULL checks for the existence of a window based on its internal ID. The function GET_WINDOW_PROPERTY retrieves the current setting for a number of properties discussed in the previous section, such as title, position, and dimensions of the window. It can also be used to retrieve the current state of the window. The procedure SET_WINDOW_PROPERTY is used to set the same properties, except for the windows title.

Figure 16.2 shows a PL/SQL procedure that, with little modifications, can be used to retrieve or set the properties of a window object.

There is one property of windows that exists only at runtime. This is the VISIBLE property, and it can be used to hide or display the window programmatically. If a window is not opened yet by the application, its VISIBLE property is set to "No." If you activate the application's Window menu, the title of the window does not appear under the list of currently-open windows. But if the window has already been accessed by the application, its VISIBLE property is set to "Yes," and its title appears in the Window menu.

To display a window, you need to set its VISIBLE property to "Yes." To close it, set the same property to "No." The generic procedure displayed in Figure 16.2 can be used for this purpose. Form Builder provides you with two additional built-in procedures that can be used for the same purpose. They are called SHOW_WINDOW and HIDE_WINDOW.

The companion software that comes with this book includes the module WINDYNM.FMB to demonstrate the process of dynamically showing and hiding windows in Forms. Load this application in the Form Builder and run it. Initially you will see a toolbar with four push buttons in it. If you click one of the buttons, for example the one labeled First, a window with the same name in the title bar will appear (see Figure 16.3)

Up to three windows can be opened in the application. The first two windows contain two push buttons each. The Close button closes the window in both cases. The other buttons display the window with the same title as the button's label. The third window serves to demonstrate the fact that you can display a window even if there are no data items or controls in it.

This application uses two procedures that take advantage of the built-ins SHOW_WINDOW and HIDE_WINDOW. The first procedure, called `Open_Window`, takes as parameter the window name, ensures that this window exists, and then, it displays it. Figure 16.4 shows the contents of this procedure.

The procedure `Close_Window` takes as input parameter the name of the window to close, and after it makes sure that the window exists and is currently visible, it closes it. The contents of this procedure are very similar to the procedure shown in Figure 16.4. The only difference is that the later uses the built-in HIDE_WINDOW.

```
PROCEDURE Generic_Window_Routine (window_name VARCHAR2)
IS
 window_id          WINDOW;
 property_setting VARCHAR2(80);
 Window_Not_Found EXCEPTION;
BEGIN
 /* FIND_WINDOW returns the appropriate window ID.     */
 window_id := FIND_WINDOW(window_name);
 IF ID_NULL(window_id) THEN
  RAISE Window_Not_Found;
 END IF;
 /* If control comes here, window ID exists.           */
 /* PROPERTY_NAME can be POSITION, WINDOW_SIZE,
WINDOW_STATE, etc. */
 property_setting := GET_WINDOW_PROPERTY(window_id,
PROPERTY_NAME);

 /* Additional processing may occur here               */

 /* PROPERTY_NAME can be POSITION, WINDOW_SIZE,
WINDOW_STATE, etc. */
 SET_WINDOW_PROPERTY(window_id, PROPERTY_NAME,
property_setting);

EXCEPTION
 WHEN Window_Not_Found THEN
  MESSAGE('Window '||window_name||' does not exist.');
  RAISE FORM_TRIGGER_FAILURE;
 WHEN OTHERS THEN
  MESSAGE('Internal error occurred.');
  RAISE FORM_TRIGGER_FAILURE;
END Generic_Window_Routine;
```

FIGURE 16.2 Template program unit to access and modify properties of windows at Runtime.

`Open_Window` and `Close_Window` reduce to just one line the contents of WHEN-BUTTON-PRESSED triggers for the push buttons in this application. The trigger for the button Close in the window FIRST, for example, contains the following statement:

```
Close_Window('FIRST');
```

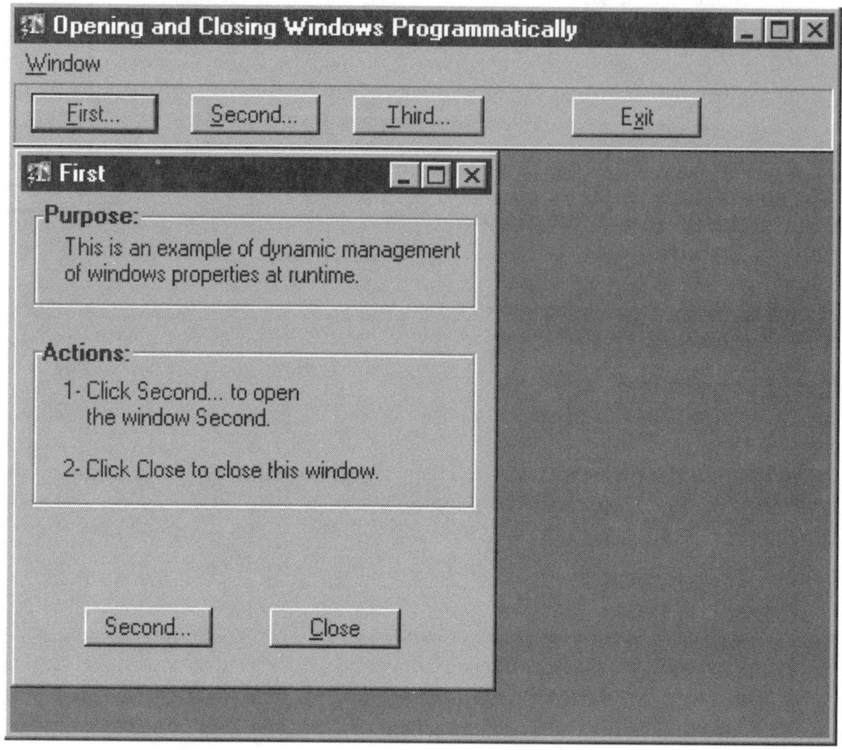

FIGURE 16.3 Hiding and displaying windows programmatically.

The statement in the trigger attached to any of the push buttons labeled Second is as follows:

```
Open_Window('SECOND');
```

In Forms Runtime, displaying a window does not necessarily mean that the focus of the application will move to that window. Setting the VISIBLE property to "Yes" or using the procedure SHOW_WINDOW does not raise the window on top of the stack of other open windows if the focus of Forms Runtime is on an item in one of these windows. In order to better understand this, you can use the module WINDYNM1.FMB provided in the companion disk. This module is identical to WINDYNM.FMB except for an additional text item in block FIRST. (This module is also closer to what you eventually develop because it contains data items and control items in several windows.) After opening the module in the Form Builder, follow these steps:

```
PROCEDURE Open_Window (window_name VARCHAR2) IS
 window_id          WINDOW;
 Window_Not_Found EXCEPTION;

BEGIN
 window_id := FIND_WINDOW(window_name);
 IF ID_NULL(window_id) THEN
  RAISE Window_Not_Found;
 END IF;

 SHOW_WINDOW(window_id);

EXCEPTION
 WHEN Window_Not_Found THEN
  MESSAGE('Window '||window_name||' does not exist.');
  RAISE FORM_TRIGGER_FAILURE;
 WHEN OTHERS THEN
  MESSAGE('Internal error occurred in Open_Window.');
  RAISE FORM_TRIGGER_FAILURE;
END Open_Window;
```

FIGURE 16.4 Showing a window dynamically.

1. Run the module WINDYNM1.FMB.
2. Open the windows FIRST and SECOND by clicking the respective buttons in the toolbar.
3. Click inside item Focus. This action places the focus of Forms Runtime in an item in block FIRST.

At this point, clicking the button Second does not activate the corresponding window any more—the title bar of this window is not highlighted. To make this fact more noticeable, resize the window FIRST so that it completely covers the window SECOND. Now, clicking the button Second has no visual effect because the window SECOND will not appear on top if FIRST as you would expect. The only way to activate window SECOND in this situation is to select its title from this list of windows currently open maintained by the Window menu. Thus, in order to have a full functional activation of the window, you must not only set its VISIBLE property to 'Yes,' but also navigate to a navigable item inside of it.

Another side of this discussion is to see what happens if you close the window FIRST after placing the focus of Forms on the item Focus. Follow these steps:

1. Click the Close button in window FIRST. The window will be hidden from view.
2. Display either window SECOND or THIRD by clicking the appropriate button in the toolbar.

Contrary to what you expect, the window FIRST appears and the item where the focus was before closing it is selected.

The discussion and the examples in this section may help you understand a little better the concept of the focus in Forms Runtime. You can think of the focus as a state in which Forms activates an item for input and positions the screen cursor within the item. Navigating to an item in a window, will place the focus of the form on the item, activate the window, and raise it on top of the stack of other open windows. As long as the focus is in an item of the window, the window will be the functionally active window of the application. You can show other windows, but they will not be active unless the focus moves away form the current window as a result of mouse and keyboard navigation, or programmatic statements such as GO_BLOCK, or GO_ITEM.

Similarly, you cannot close the window if the focus continues to be an item in that window. The only way to safely hide the window is to move the focus of Forms Runtime away first, and then set its Visible property to "No," or call the procedure HIDE_WINDOW.

16.1.3 EVENTS OF WINDOWS

Four events are recognized by windows in Form Builder applications. These are ActivateWindow, DeactivateWindow, ResizeWindow, and CloseWindow.

The ActivateWindow event occurs when the window becomes the application's active window. In response to this event, Forms fires the trigger WHEN-WINDOW-ACTIVATED. As I explained earlier, activating a window does not necessarily mean navigating to it. In order to place the focus on the window, you must navigate to an item there.

If a window is already active and there is an attempt to activate another window, the event DeactivateWindow occurs in the first window. This event causes the trigger WHEN-WINDOW-DEACTIVATED to fire.

If a window is resized, either because users drag its borders or corners, or because its Width and Height properties are set programmatically, the event ResizeWindow occurs. As a result of this event, the trigger WHEN-WINDOW-RESIZED will fire. If the property Resize Allowed of the window is set to "No," the event ResizeWindow cannot occur.

Finally, when users close the window using one of the window's manager commands, such as double-clicking the control menu box, or pressing CTRL+F4 from the keyboard in Microsoft Windows, the event CloseWindow occurs. For this event to happen, the window must have its property Close Allowed set to "Yes." This event fires the trigger WHEN-WINDOW-CLOSED where you can place the code that actually closes the window.

The name of the window for which the last of these events occurred, is stored in the system variable SYSTEM.EVENT_WINDOW. Because windows and their events are not related functionally to blocks or items, the four triggers described above are always defined as form-level triggers.

You can find some examples of using these triggers in the module WINDYNM.FMB. Run this module and after selecting each window try to resize it. You will notice that although the borders or corners of the windows can be dragged to any size, when the mouse is released, instead of being resized, they return to the original size. The steps to implement this functionality are as follows:

1. Declare two global variables `GLOBAL.Win_Width`, and `GLOBAL.Win_Height` in a form-level PRE-FORM trigger. They will hold the dimensions of a window.
2. In the trigger WHEN-WINDOW-ACTIVATED, use the procedure `Get_Window_Size` to store the dimensions of the current window in the global variables. The name of the current window is stored in SYSTEM.EVENT_WINDOW variable.
3. In the trigger WHEN-WINDOW-RESIZED, use the procedure `Set_Window_Size` to set the resized window to its original dimensions that were stored in the global variables in the previous step. Since this trigger will fire when the users complete the resizing action, they will be able to drag the window's borders and corners, but, as soon as they release the mouse button, the window will snap to its original position.

If you take a look at the contents of the procedures `Get_Window_Size` and `Set_Window_Size`, you will see that they are straight forward examples of how to use the function GET_WINDOW_PROPERTY, and the procedure SET_WINDOW_PROPERTY. The procedure RESIZE_WINDOW can be used as an alternative to SET_WINDOW_PROPERTY to set the dimensions of a window. Thus the statements:

```
SET_WINDOW_PROPERTY(window_id, WIDTH, win_width);
SET_WINDOW_PROPERTY(window_id, HEIGHT, win_height);
```

are equivalent to:

```
RESIZE_WINDOW(window_id, win_width, win_height);
```

16.2 DEVELOPING MDI APPLICATIONS WITH FORM BUILDER

Multiple Document Interface (MDI) applications are developed following the paradigm and standards established by widely successful desktop software packages such as Microsoft Word and Excel. The paradigm applies only to the Microsoft Windows and Macintosh environments.

An MDI application allows users to open and maintain ready for use multiple windows at any one time. Each window corresponds to a specific task or functional part of the application. For example, in the MRD application, a window could be used for entering and editing data about customers, another one for movies and tapes received by the store, and yet another one to record the rental transactions that occur.

There are four basic types of windows in a MDI application: the MDI frame, MDI sheets, dialog boxes, and message boxes. The following sections explain the functionality of each type of window, and how to implement them in Form Builder applications.

16.2.1 MDI FRAME WINDOW

The MDI frame is often called the application window, because it is the initial window that is opened when the application is launched. All the other components of the application will be either attached to or placed inside the MDI frame. Figure 16.5 shows the main components of the MDI frame window.

The title bar of the MDI frame window displays the name of the application. Under the title bar, there is the application menu. Depending on the functionality of the application, several menus may be used, but all of them are attached to the MDI frame. The MDI frame serves as a placeholder for the application's toolbars as well. Horizontal toolbars go under the menu; vertical toolbars are attached along the MDI frame's left margin.

In environments or applications that do not follow the MDI paradigm, toolbars can be attached to any window. Form Builder allows you to attach toolbars to windows by setting the properties Vertical Toolbar or Horizontal Toolbar to the names of the desired toolbars.

The MDI frame also contains a console, or message bar, at the bottom, which is used to display micro-help messages and other useful processing information. The area limited by the MDI frame borders, the application's console, and its toolbar or menu is called the application's client area. It is here that all the other windows of the application will be displayed. The size of the MDI frame window directly defines the size of the client work area.

The MDI frame enjoys all the generic properties that any window has. In particular, you can specify its title, position, size, and state. Users at runtime can change the position, size and state of the window. However, the MDI frame window is not an object that you can access, or whose properties you can set in the

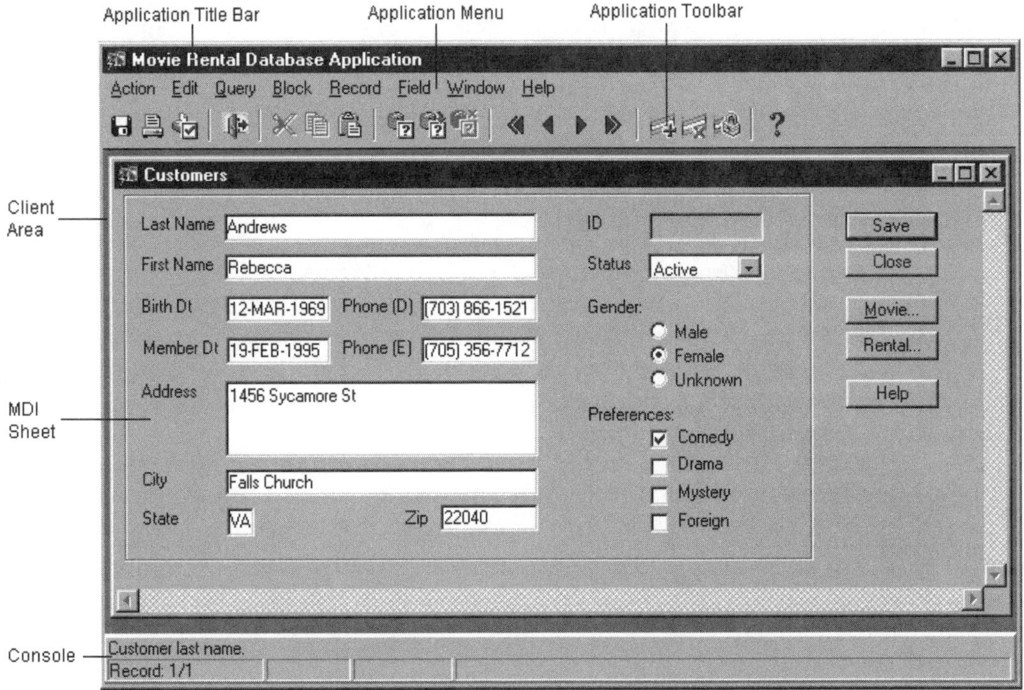

FIGURE 16.5 Components of the MDI frame.

Form Builder. You need to use the built-in constructs discussed in Section 16.1.2 to set these properties at runtime. In order to address the MDI frame object, you must use the internally defined constant FORMS_MDI_WINDOW. Figure 16.6 shows excerpts from the trigger WHEN-NEW-FORM-INSTANCE of module WINDYNM.FMB.

The first line sets the title of the window to the string enclosed in the single quotes. The second line sets the size of the window to the specified arguments (in points). The following statements can be used to set the initial position of the MDI frame or its state, respectively.

```
SET_WINDOW_PROPERTY (FORMS_MDI_WINDOW, POSITION, 5, 5);
SET_WINDOW_PROPERTY (FORMS_MDI_WINDOW, WINDOW_STATE,
MAXIMIZED);
```

These are the only properties you can change in an MDI frame. Given its special purpose in the application, other properties that you would normally set

```
SET_WINDOW_PROPERTY(FORMS_MDI_WINDOW, TITLE,
         'Opening and Closing Windows Programmatically');
SET_WINDOW_PROPERTY(FORMS_MDI_WINDOW, WINDOW_SIZE, 570, 220);
```

FIGURE 16.6 Setting the properties of the MDI frame window.

for a window, cannot be changed. Specifically, the MDI frame can always be moved, resized, minimized, maximized, restored, closed, and it always displays scrollbars if needed. The only actions that affect this window are double-clicking its control menu box or pressing ALT+F4. Both these actions cause the event CloseApplication to occur. This event always invokes the method EXIT_FORM, which terminates the application.

Chapter 18, which discusses the process of creating menus and toolbars for an application, will explain how to attach them to the MDI frame window.

16.2.2 MDI SHEETS

MDI sheets are where most of the life of an application is spent and where most of its functionality is located. These windows can be opened as a result of users choosing options from the menu or the toolbar, or clicking controls in other windows. A window must have several characteristics in order to be considered a MDI sheet. They are listed in the following paragraphs:

- First and foremost, the MDI sheet can never appear outside the MDI frame client area. All the sizing and moving actions initiated by users or programmatically by the application's event must not cause the window to leave this area, even if it has to be hidden partially or completely from the view.
- When the window is minimized, its icon must be placed inside the client area of the MDI frame.
- When the window is maximized, it should be maximized to the full size of the MDI frame window. Its title should appear in parentheses appended to the application's title.
- When the MDI sheet is initially opened, the application's focus must also navigate to one navigable item on the window, if one exists.
- While the MDI sheet remains open, its title should always appear in the Window menu of your application. Users can activate the window by picking it from the list of currently open windows.
- The MDI sheet should be closed if, and only if the users or the application send an explicit Close message to the window. Simply deactivating the window should not close it.

16.2.3 IMPLEMENTING MDI SHEETS

Three properties are essential for obtaining the MDI sheet functionality in your window. They are Window Style, Modal, and Hide on Exit. Setting the Window Style to "Document" will ensure that the window is displayed within the MDI frame client area. Setting the Modal property to "No" will allow users to perform other actions in the application besides the ones contained in the window. Setting the property Hide on Exit to "No" will not hide the window if the users activate another window. The settings described here are the default ones for these three properties.

Other default settings you should consider preserving for your MDI sheets are the properties Close Allowed, Minimize Allowed, Move Allowed, and Maximize Allowed. These properties are all set to 'Yes,' thus allowing users to close, minimize, maximize, and move the window at Runtime. At the same time, do not forget to specify settings for the properties Minimized Title and Icon Filename for each individual MDI sheet.

You should also consider allowing users to resize the window by keeping the property Resize Allowed set to "Yes." In conjunction with this setting, the properties Show Horizontal Scrollbar and Show Vertical Scrollbar must be set to "Yes." This way, users will be able to scroll to hidden parts of your application if they reduce the size of the window.

As you can see, default windows created in the Form Builder are very close to being MDI sheet type of windows. The settings they have fulfill almost all the requirements presented in the previous section. However, their functionality must be enhanced in order to avoid the idiosyncrasies pointed out in Section 16.1.2, and to give them the full features of MDI sheets. In particular, the following things must be added programmatically:

- ❑ When the window is opened, the application must navigate to a navigable item inside the window, if one exits.
- ❑ When the window is closed, the application must first navigate to an item that is outside the window being closed. Then, the VISIBLE property of this window must be set to "No," thus effectively closing the window.

In order to help you in the process of creating standard MDI sheets, the companion disk contains a module called WINPROPS.FMB. There are several objects in this module that you can use to implement MDI sheets in your applications. These objects are described in the following paragraphs:

- ❑ **The property class MDI_SHEET.** You can use this class to inherit properties for any window that will be a MDI sheet window. For individual windows, you will need to override some of the properties inherited from this class, like Title, Primary Canvas, Minimized Title, and Icon Filename.
- ❑ **Form-level trigger PRE-FORM.** This trigger declares the global variable

GLOBAL.Home_Item, and assigns it the item name returned by the function Get_Home_Item (explained next). You can override the setting with the name of any item in the module that you choose to be the home item. Since Forms needs to navigate to this item, make sure its property Enabled is set to "Yes."

The home item is a single unified point where Forms will place the focus each time an MDI sheet is closed. As said earlier, Forms cannot hide a window properly if an item on it has the focus. Therefore the home item must be in a window that will remain open throughout the application's life. This could be an MDI sheet that, based on the application's design, will not be closed by the users. An example of such a window is the Object Navigator in the Form Builder. However, the ideal place for a home item would be the MDI frame, which is available as long as the application is running. Items cannot be placed directly on the MDI frame, but they can be arranged on a toolbar, which in turn is attached to the MDI frame. Therefore, to obtain the highest flexibility, you should create a toolbar and use one of the items there as home item. This should not be viewed as a restriction, since most serious GUI applications today should have a toolbar with it.

- **Function `Get_Home_Item`.** This function returns the name of an item that will serve as a home item for the application. Figure 16.7 shows the PL/SQL code for this function as implemented in module WINPROPS.FMB.

  In this particular implementation, the home item is the first item of the first navigable block in the module. The call to the function GET_APPLICA-

```
FUNCTION Get_Home_Item RETURN VARCHAR2 IS
 home_item          VARCHAR2(80);
 form_module        VARCHAR2(80);
 first_block        VARCHAR2(80);
 last_item          VARCHAR2(80);
BEGIN
 form_module :=
GET_APPLICATION_PROPERTY(CURRENT_FORM_NAME);
 first_block := GET_FORM_PROPERTY(form_module,
FIRST_NAVIGATION_BLOCK);
 home_item    := GET_BLOCK_PROPERTY(first_block,
FIRST_ITEM);
 home_item    := first_block||'.'||home_item;

 RETURN home_item;
END;
```

FIGURE 16.7 Typical implementation of the home item.

TION_PROPERTY retrieves the name of the form module. Then, the function GET_FORM_PROPERTY is used to get the name of the block where the current form will navigate to when it is initially started. Finally, GET_BLOCK_PROPERTY returns the name of the first item in that block. By convention and agreement among developers of your team, this item can be designed to be the application's home item.

- **Procedure `Open_Window(window_name VARCHAR2, block_name VARCHAR2)`.** This procedure displays the window `window_name`, and then navigates to block `block_name`. No navigation occurs if `block_name` is NULL.
- **Procedure `Close_Window(window_name VARCHAR2)`.** This procedure places the Forms focus on the application's home item and closes the window `window_name`.
- **Trigger WHEN-WINDOW-CLOSED.** This is the form-level trigger that is fired by the event CloseWindow. The body of this trigger contains only one line:

  ```
  Close_Window(:SYSTEM.EVENT_WINDOW);
  ```

  Here, `Close_Window` is the function described in the previous point.

The following is a list of generic steps to follow in order to implement MDI sheets in Form Builder applications:

1. Create the block that contains the data items and controls that will be displayed in the dialog box on a separate canvas.
2. Create a new window object and subclass it from the object MDI_SHEET. Set the property Primary Canvas of the new window to the canvas where the block is created.
3. Invoke the procedure `Open_Window` from the appropriate locations in the application.
4. Implement the functions that will be handled by the MDI sheet.

In Section 16.6 of this chapter, you will use these objects to implement MDI sheets in the MRD application. You can use the steps discussed there to incorporate them in any other modules you will create in the future.

16.2.4 DIALOG BOXES

The purpose of dialog boxes is to accept information from users in order to perform a specific task, or to provide them with the outcome and results of a certain action. Usually, when a dialog box is called, users must either complete or cancel the task that can be performed there. In most of the cases, they cannot do anything else in the application until the dialog box is dismissed. However they can switch to another application and do something there. These dialog boxes are called modal dialog boxes. A typical modal dialog box is the Open dialog box that you can access by choosing File | Open... from the Form Builder menu.

There are also dialog boxes that allow users to perform other activities in the application, besides the ones related to the task that the dialog box carries out. These dialog boxes are known as nonmodal, or modeless dialog boxes. A typical example of modeless dialog boxes is the PL/SQL Search/Replace utility accessible by selecting Program | Search/Replace PL/SQL... from the Form Builder menu.

Dialog boxes can be displayed in response to a request from the users for a specific functionality. Several methods can be used to provide users with ways to express their request. The most popular methods in GUI environments are selecting menu items, clicking iconic tools in the toolbar, and clicking push buttons. In MDI applications, the dialog boxes have the following properties:

- ❑ Perform a specific task or function that complements the larger functionality of the application in general, or an MDI sheet in particular.
- ❑ Cannot be minimized or maximized.
- ❑ Can be moved outside the client area of the MDI frame. This is fundamentally different from the MDI sheets which are always bound by this frame.
- ❑ Cannot be resized by the users.
- ❑ Contain always at least two push buttons. The first one, when pressed, performs the primary task assigned to the dialog box. This is usually the default button for the dialog box, unless a destructive action will originate from pressing it. A generic name for this button is OK; a name that is better related to the task being performed such as Print or Save, is preferable. The second button should allow users to close the dialog box without performing the task. This is usually labeled as the Cancel button. It has become a standard, if not a requirement, that the dialog boxes provide a Help button, in addition to the first two ones. By clicking this button, users can access context-sensitive help about the task supported by the dialog box.

16.2.5 IMPLEMENTING DIALOG BOXES

The module WINPROPS.FMB, mentioned in the previous section, contains a property class, called MDI_DIALOG_BOX, that you can use to develop your standard dialog boxes. By inspecting the property class MDI_DIALOG_BOX you will notices that it includes the same properties as the class MDI_SHEET. Some of these properties even have the same settings. However, given the different flavor of these two types of windows, fundamental properties in dialog boxes have the opposite settings of MDI sheets.

In particular, what makes the difference between a dialog box and a MDI window is the Window Style property, which is set to "Dialog" for the former and to "Document" for the later. The property Modal can be set to "Yes" to obtain a modal dialog box. For a modeless dialog box, the Modal property must be set to "No." In the module WINPROPS.FMB you can find the property class MDI_MODELESS_DIALOG_BOX, which you may use whenever you will need to implement modeless dialog boxes. The properties of this class are all inherited from the class MDI_DIALOG_BOX, except for the Modal property, which is set to "No."

In addition, the properties Show Horizontal Scrollbar and Show Vertical Scrollbar are set to "No" for dialog boxes. Usually you define the dimensions of these windows so that users do not need to scroll on hidden areas of the window. Because dialog boxes do not have scrollbars, the property Resize Allowed must be set to "No." You do not want the users to reduce the dialog box and then be unable to see some of the items in it. Finally, so that the dialog boxes cannot be minimized and maximized, the properties Minimize Allowed and Maximize Allowed should be set to "No," as well.

The module WINPROPS.FMB also contains the procedure `Open_Dialog_Box(window_name VARCHAR2, block_name VARCHAR2)`, which you can use to open dialog box windows. This procedure differs from `Open_Window` discussed in the previous section because it computes the position of the dialog box before displaying it and navigating to a block in that window. The computation of the coordinates is based on the dimensions of the MDI frame and those of the dialog box itself and aims at displaying the dialog box at the center of the MDI frame. The code shown in Figure 16.8 is an excerpt from this procedure; it shows how to compute the coordinates after these dimensions are stored in the variables `mdi_width`, `mdi_height`, `win_width`, and `win_height`.

```
IF ( mdi_width > win_width ) THEN
 x_coord := (mdi_width - win_width) / 2;
ELSE
 x_coord := 0;
END IF;
IF ( mdi_height > win_height ) THEN
 y_coord := (mdi_height - win_height) / 2;
ELSE
 y_coord := 0;
END IF;
```

FIGURE 16.8 Computing Coordinates of Dialog Boxes.

> **CAUTION**
>
> MDI sheet windows do not need to have a navigable block on them in order to be displayed. In modules WINDYNM.FMB and WINDYNM1.FMB the window THIRD does not contain any navigable items, but you can still display it because the Window Style property is set to "Document." If this property is set to "Dialog," the window cannot be displayed unless there is a navigable item on it.

When implementing dialog boxes, you should follow this sequence of steps:

1. Create the block that contains the data items and controls that will be displayed in the dialog box on a separate canvas.
2. Create at least two push buttons. Their labels should be OK (or a more descriptive label) and Cancel. A Help button could be provided, especially for dialog boxes with complex functionality.
3. Create a new window object and subclass it from the objects MDI_DIALOG_BOX or MDI_MODELESS_DIALOG_BOX. Set the property Primary Canvas of the new window to the canvas where the block is created.
4. Invoke the procedure `Open_Dialog_Box` from the appropriate locations in the application.
5. Create program units that will populate the data items of the dialog box. To improve performance these routines should be invoked only when the dialog box is displayed, possible immediately after the procedure `Open_Dialog_Box` is invoked.
6. Create WHEN-BUTTON-PRESSED triggers for the buttons in the dialog box. These triggers are responsible for the functionality of the dialog box.

16.2.6 MESSAGE BOXES

Message boxes are used to give users feedback about events and processes that occur in the application. It is important to keep users informed about what is happening in the application, to warn them about potentially destructive actions, or about critical situations that have already occurred. A good reason to display a message to the users is also when queries or any other actions will last for more than a few seconds, or longer than what the users would normally expect.

Depending on the kind of information displayed, the messages can be classified as micro-help messages, informative, warning, and critical messages. The users can see the messages either in the message bar, or in specially crafted dialog boxes, or in special objects called alerts.

The built-in procedure MESSAGE is used to display messages in the message bar. This procedure takes as parameter a string of up to two hundred characters. By default, when two messages are issued consecutively, Forms will display the first one in an alert-like box and will wait until users acknowledge it before displaying the second one in the message bar. You can take advantage of this fact to display your messages in alert-like boxes. The following two lines provide an example of how you could do this:

```
MESSAGE ('This message will be displayed in an alert
box.');
MESSAGE (' ');
```

This approach is good only if you want to display your messages in Stop alert boxes with only one OK button. If you want to display the message simply at the micro-help line, use the procedure MESSAGE with the argument NO_ACKNOWLEDGE, as in this example:

```
MESSAGE ('This message will not be acknowledged',
NO_ACKNOWLEDGE);
```

The message bar is also used to display the text string specified in the Hint property of the item. If you set the Display Hint Automatically property of an item to "Yes," the hint message will be displayed when users navigate to it. However, this alone is not sufficient in every case. There are items such as display items, or those with the Keyboard Navigable property set to "No," to which users cannot navigate. In addition, you should provide users with help without requiring them to navigate to the item itself. In GUI applications, the micro-help message for an item or control is usually displayed when the mouse cursor moves over the item. You can easily this functionality as a Tooltip popup by entering your message in the Tooltip property of an item. Your message will then appear in a small box when the mouse cursor enters the item. An alternate way to implement this functionality is to place the statements shown in Figure 16.9 in a

```
DECLARE
 item_hint VARCHAR2(200);
BEGIN
 item_hint := GET_ITEM_PROPERTY(:SYSTEM.MOUSE_ITEM,
HINT_TEXT);
 MESSAGE(item_hint, NO_ACKNOWLEDGE);
END;
```

FIGURE 16.9 Displaying micro-help messages.

WHEN-MOUSE-ENTER trigger that will fire whenever the mouse enters the sensitive area of an item or control.

In this trigger, the system variable SYSTEM.MOUSE_ITEM is used to access the name of the item on top of which the mouse cursor currently is. Then, the string defined for the Hint property is retrieved and displayed in a message. Note that the code presented in Figure 16.9 assumes that the text in the property Hint is no longer than 200 bytes. In order to have this trigger fire for all the items in the form, create it at as a form-level trigger.

In some situations, you would want to display more than just a string of characters in your message. For example, you may want to add a bitmap or use some colors to convey the message better to the users. In these situations, you can build a modal dialog box in which you place text, pictures, and everything else you need. Although the line that divides dialog boxes and message boxes is not clear, you can think of the first type of objects as windows where users access some functionality of the application by clicking one of several buttons, and of the second types as windows where they just see some information displayed. A typical message box is the About dialog box which displays information, such as the version of the application, credits, and copyright notes. You will see this in almost every application by choosing Help | About... from the menu.

16.3 ALERTS

Alerts are internal objects that when invoked at runtime are displayed as modal dialog boxes. Every other operation in the application is halted until the alert is dismissed. The alert can be dismissed by pressing one of its buttons and sometimes by just closing the window. Every alert must have at least one button, and may have up to three buttons. You may create alerts like any other object in the Object Navigator by selecting the node Alerts in the Node Display area of the Navigator and issuing any of the following commands:

- ❑ Click the icon Create from the toolbar.
- ❑ Select Navigator | Create from the menu.

Form Builder creates the new object and names it using the default conventions. You can rename the alert after it is created.

16.3.1 SETTING PROPERTIES OF ALERTS IN THE FORM BUILDER

After you create an alert, you can set its properties in the Property Palette of the Form Builder. Note that as in the case of window objects, the properties in the Font & Color group do not have any effects on the alerts. Although you can set all the visual attributes properties of an alert in the Property Palette, these properties in reality are determined by the window manager. Therefore, the following paragraphs will discuss only the properties in the Functional group.

- **Title.** The setting of this property determines the text that appears on the alert's title bar. If Title is not set, the alert will show the string "Developer/2000 Forms" in its title bar.
- **Alert Style.** This property determines the type of alert object. It can be set to "Note," "Caution," or "Stop." The Note alert is used for informative messages. The Caution alert is used to warn users about actions they take that may result in considerable or irreversible loss of data. The Stop alert is used to inform users about critical errors that occurred at the Forms Runtime, Oracle Server, or operating system level, but not as a result of users actions.
- **Button label properties.** The properties Button 1 Label, Button 2 Label, and Button 3 Label are used to specify the buttons displayed in the alert and their labels. Internally, Forms assigns an access key to the labels you enter in these properties. Normally the access key is the first letter of the label, or the first letter that does not conflict with an existing label. Usually, informative and critical alerts have only one button labeled OK. Warning alerts should have at least two buttons, one to proceed with the halted operation, the other to cancel it. For warning and critical alerts, a third button can be included to allow users to invoke the application's on-line help that explains why the application was halted and what to do in order to proceed safely. If you have a help button, be sure to reactivate the alert to allow the proper user choice. The first button of the alert is the default button activated when pressing ENTER from the keyboard. You can replace it with any of the other two buttons by setting the property Default Alert Button. Figure 16.10 shows an example of each type of alert. Module WINPROPS.FMB contains three alerts that were used to implement them. They are INFO_ALERT, WARNING_ALERT, and CRITICAL_ALERT.
- **Message.** The message you want to display in the alert can be specified in the Message property. The string you enter here can be of any length, however Forms Runtime will display only up to the first two hundred characters in the alert.

16.3.2 MODIFYING PROPERTIES OF ALERTS AT RUNTIME

Your application may need to display a considerable number of messages that at runtime. It will be a waste of programming resources if separate alerts were built for each message. The approach taken usually is to identify the types of alerts that will be used, and create one alert object for each of these types. Then PL/SQL code is written to dynamically retrieve the alert object that will be needed for a particular message. The built-in functions FIND_ALERT and ID_NULL are used for this purpose. The properties of this alert are set according to the situation or

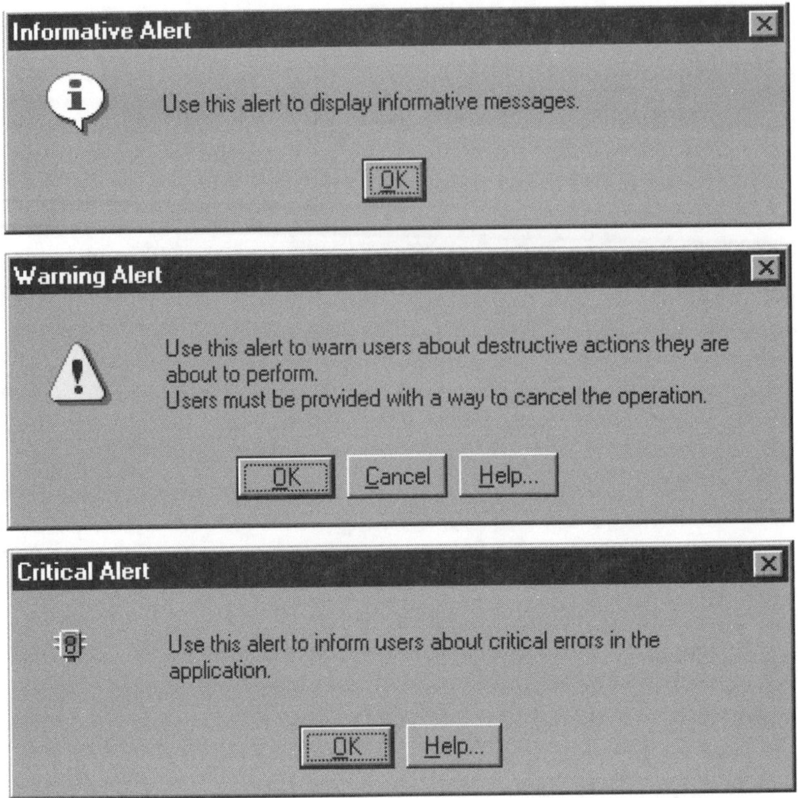

FIGURE 16.10 Example of an informative, warning, and critical alert.

the message to be displayed. The procedure SET_ALERT_PROPERTY is used to override the title to the message properties of the alert. The procedure SET_BUTTON_PROPERTY is used to replace the button labels, if it is necessary. The alert then is displayed using the function SHOW_ALERT, which returns the button pressed by the users to dismiss the alert. Based on this button, you decide what action to take next.

Figure 16.11 presents the contents of the trigger that displays the warning alert shown in Figure 16.10. It is an example of how you would use the built-in procedures and functions discussed here.

The first part of this procedure finds the internal ID of the alert WARNING_ALERT and ensures that all the subsequent invocations of alert related built-in procedures will act upon a valid object. Then, the title and the message of the alert are set using the procedure SET_ALERT_PROPERTY. The procedure SET_ALERT_BUTTON_PROPERTY is used to set the labels of the buttons. Finally, the alert is displayed to the users by the function SHOW_ALERT.

```
DECLARE
 alert_id          ALERT;
 alert_msg         VARCHAR2(200);
 button_pressed    NUMBER;
 Alert_Not_Found   EXCEPTION;

BEGIN
 alert_id := FIND_ALERT('WARNING_ALERT');
 IF ID_NULL(alert_id) THEN
  RAISE Alert_Not_Found;
 END IF;

 SET_ALERT_PROPERTY(alert_id, TITLE, 'Warning Alert');

 alert_msg := 'Use this alert to warn users about
destructive actions they are about to perform. Users must
be provided with a way to cancel the operation.';
 SET_ALERT_PROPERTY(alert_id, ALERT_MESSAGE_TEXT,
alert_msg);

 SET_ALERT_BUTTON_PROPERTY(alert_id, ALERT_BUTTON1,
LABEL, 'OK');
 SET_ALERT_BUTTON_PROPERTY(alert_id, ALERT_BUTTON2,
LABEL, 'Cancel');
 SET_ALERT_BUTTON_PROPERTY(alert_id, ALERT_BUTTON3,
LABEL, 'Help...');

 button_pressed := SHOW_ALERT(alert_id);
 IF button_pressed = ALERT_BUTTON1 THEN
   MESSAGE('First button was pressed.');
 ELSIF button_pressed = ALERT_BUTTON2 THEN
   MESSAGE('Second button was pressed.');
 ELSIF button_pressed = ALERT_BUTTON3 THEN
   MESSAGE('Third button was pressed.');
 END IF;

EXCEPTION
 WHEN Alert_Not_Found THEN
  MESSAGE('Alert WARNING_ALERT does not exist.');
  RAISE FORM_TRIGGER_FAILURE;
 WHEN OTHERS THEN
  MESSAGE('Internal error occurred.');
  RAISE FORM_TRIGGER_FAILURE;
END;
```

FIGURE 16.11 Setting properties of alerts dynamically.

Despite the flexibility and the ease of use that the alerts provide, there are some problems that you need to be aware of when deciding to utilize them in your application.

- You cannot display more than two hundred characters in the message. This includes any non-printable characters such as TAB or carriage returns.
- There does not seem to be an easy way to break the message text in several lines. In order to display the contents of the message in two lines as in Figure 16.10, white spaces were inserted between the two sentences.
- If your application uses fonts other than the Forms Runtime defaults, the alerts will have a different look than the rest of the application.

However, the amount of work required to programmatically create message boxes with the same simplicity and flexibility that the alerts provide may not justify the benefits you will draw from them.

16.4 CANVASES

Canvases are a special type of objects in Form Builder that serve as place-holders or containers for all the data items, controls, text labels, drawings, and bitmaps that the users will see in the application. You can also think of canvases as the background for each of the windows in the application. You can create canvases like any other object in the Navigator, but you can also create them together with frames in the Layout Wizard.

16.4.1 TYPES OF CANVASES

There are four types of canvases in Form Builder: content, toolbar, tab, and stacked canvases. The property Canvas Type in the General group of properties determines the type of the canvas object. The following paragraphs offer an overview of each type:

- **Content canvases.** This is the basic type of canvases in Form Builder applications. You have used content canvases in the examples discussed so far and will continue to use them to a large extent in the future. Content canvases are essentially simple objects. All you have to do is store items and boilerplate objects on them and set a few properties discussed in Section 16.4.2.
- **Toolbar canvases.** These canvases are further divided in horizontal and vertical toolbar canvases. They provide the applications you develop with tool-

bars. In an MDI application, the toolbars are attached to the MDI frame. The horizontal toolbar goes right under the menu; the vertical toolbar is attached along the left border of the MDI frame. The modules WINDYNM.FMB and WINDYNM1.FMB used earlier in the chapter to discuss the dynamic management of windows use a horizontal toolbar. Chapter 19 will provide detailed information about toolbar canvases.

- **Tab canvases.** You use these canvases to implement tabbed dialog boxes like the ones you have seen so far in the Form Builder and in a vast number of other Windows applications. They are very useful in situations where you cannot fit comfortably all the items of the dialog box within the content canvas due to their number or size. Cases when the major activity in the dialog requires several distinct steps to complete are excellent candidates for using tabbed dialogs as well. In all these cases, you can group items in several tab pages, which then are attached as tab folders to the dialog box. At runtime, users can click the tab index of a given page and interact with its items.
- **Stacked canvases.** These canvases are attached to the same window object as another canvas. They store items and graphics just like any other canvas but enjoy a special property. When displayed at runtime, they appear stacked on top of the other canvas objects already displayed. The ability to control the display of these canvases programmatically makes them ideal in cases when you want to give users the impression that the canvas layout is modified dynamically. Section 16.5.3 will explain how to use stacked canvases to allow users to scroll areas of a content canvas without actually scrolling the window.

16.4.2 SETTING PROPERTIES OF CANVASES IN THE FORM BUILDER

In order to display the Property Palette for any canvas object in the Form Builder, you must select the object either in the Object Navigator or in the Layout Editor. Then, use one of the following actions:

- Select Tools | Property Palette from the Form Builder's menu.
- Right-click the object and select Property Palette from the pop-up menu.

Besides the ubiquitous properties in the General group—Name, Subclass Information, Comments, and Content Type—all the other principal properties of canvases are stored in the groups Functional, Physical, and Font & Color. Tab and stacked canvases contain an additional group of properties, Viewport, specific to them. In this section I describe the properties shared by all the canvas types.

- **Visible.** This property determines whether the canvas is viewable by the users at runtime. By default, it is set to "Yes."

- **Popup menu.** Chapter 13 discussed how you can attach a pop-up menu object with one or more items in a form. By setting the property Popup Menu of the canvas, you enable users to display this menu by right-clicking anywhere on the canvas. When implementing pop-up menus into your applications, I recommend that you attach them to the canvas objects. Only if you need to display different pop-up menus based on different context items you should attach these menus to the items.
- **Window.** This property specifies the window that will manage the display of the canvas. In general, I recommend that you attach each content and tab canvas to its own MDI frame or dialog box window.
- **Stacking order of canvases.** In general, it is possible to attach more than one canvas to the same window. When implementing stacked canvases, you will always attach more than one canvas to a window object. All the canvases attached to a window form a stack. What the users will see within the window at runtime is determined by the view of this stack from the top. The order in which the canvases are stored in the stack determines to a great extent this view. If, for example, a canvas larger than all the other canvases on the stack is placed on top of the stack, users will not be able to see any of the other underlying canvases. The initial order of canvases in the stack is determined by their position in the Object Navigator. Canvases listed first in the hierarchy tree are closer to the bottom of the stack. The last canvas in the Navigator occupies the top of the stack.
- **Raise on Entry.** The initial default order of the stack is modified at runtime when a given canvas is raised on top of the stack, either programmatically or due to the navigation of users to items within the canvases. The property Raise on Entry determines when the canvas will be raised on top of all other displayed canvases. If the property is set to "Yes," the canvas will move on top of the stack as soon as the Forms Runtime places its focus in any item on the canvas. If the property is set to "No," the canvas will maintain its position in the stack of canvases as long as the focus is in an item that is visible. If the focus moves to an item that is hidden by one or more canvases, the canvas will jump on top of the stack.
- **Visual attributes.** The group Font & Color contains properties that control the color and pattern of the canvas. By default, each canvas is created with a solid pattern and gray background color. This type of background is recommended by all GUI standards and should be satisfactory for the windows and screens of your applications. However, if you need to change these settings, you may set the properties Foreground Color, Background Color, and Fill Pattern in the Property Palette to the desired values. As in other situations, the recommended way to modify these properties is to create a named visual attribute object and set the property Visual Attribute Group for the canvas to its name.

- **Dimensions of canvases.** The easiest way to adjust the dimensions of a canvas is to display it in a Layout Editor window and resize it by dragging its handles. If more precision is necessary, you can set the properties Width and Height in the Property Palette of the canvas. It is important to set such dimensions so that all the objects on the canvas fit entirely within its borders. Not all the types of canvases have these properties. For example, vertical toolbars do not have the property Height and vertical toolbars do not have the property Width. This is due to the fact that toolbar canvases can be limited only in one dimension. Furthermore, tab canvases do not have the properties Width and Height at all. The dimensions of such canvases are determined by those of the viewport object, as explained in the following section.

16.4.3 VIEWS OF A CANVAS AND VIEWPORTS

The dimensions of a canvas may be such that not all the objects are visible at any one time. The area of the canvas that is displayed to users at any one time is called the view on the canvas. The frame of this view is called the viewport.

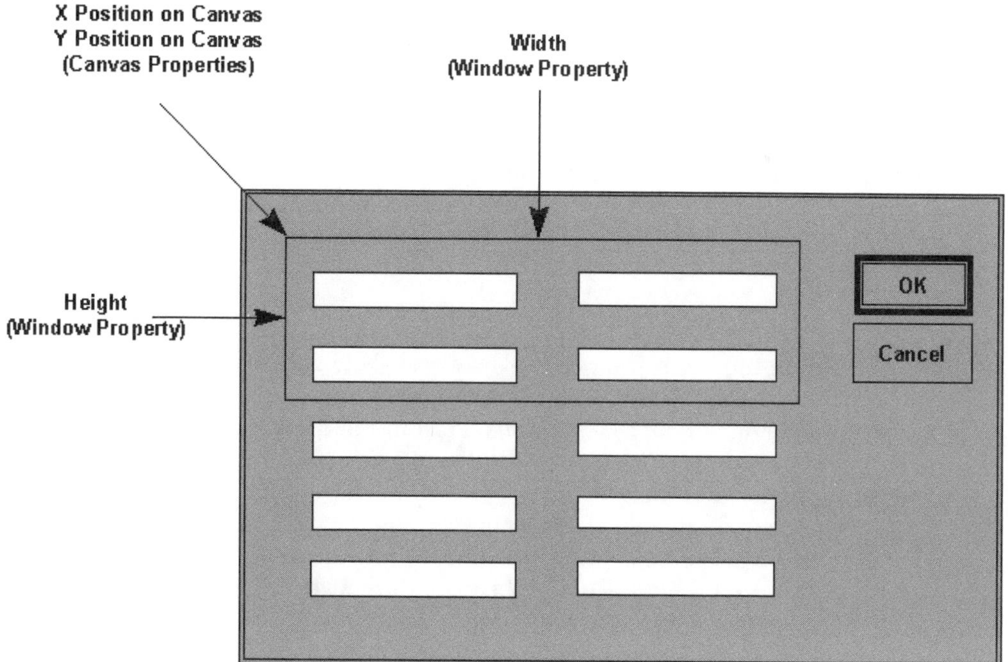

FIGURE 16.12 Views in Form Builder applications.

Think of the viewport as a rectangular box placed on top of the canvas, which governs the part of the canvas that is displayed to the users. In Figure 16.12, the large rectangle with double-lined borders represents a canvas in the Layout Editor, and the single-line rectangle around the first four objects represents the viewport object.

For content and toolbar canvases, the dimensions of the viewport object are determined by the dimensions of the window to which the canvas is attached. As the users minimize, maximize, or resize the window, the area of the canvas they see will be modified accordingly. For content canvases only, you can also specify the position of the upper left-hand corner of the viewport with respect to the upper left-hand corner of the canvas by setting the properties Viewport X Position on Canvas and Viewport Y Position on Canvas in the Physical group, as shown in Figure 16.12.

As mentioned earlier, the properties in the Viewport group apply only to stacked and tab canvases. The properties Viewport Width and Viewport Height determine the size of the view in the case of stacked canvases or the size of the tabbed folder in the case of tab canvases. The properties Viewport X Position and Viewport Y Position determine the location of the stacked canvas on top of the content canvas attached to the same window or the location of the tabbed folder with respect to the upper left hand corner of the window displaying the canvas.

The fact that stacked canvas can be displayed anywhere on the content canvas and that you can control exactly how much of it can be shown to the users is used to implement GUI interfaces in which users view a fixed number of items on the screen and a variable number of other items that do not fit in the screen but can be viewed by scrolling the stacked canvas. To allow users to scroll to items in the stacked canvas view that are outside the boundaries of its view, and therefore invisible, you can equip the viewport with scrollbars by setting the properties Show Horizontal Scrollbar or Show Vertical Scrollbar to "Yes."

16.4.4 MODIFYING PROPERTIES OF CANVASES AT RUNTIME

Although in the Form Builder canvases and their views are represented as unified objects, Forms Runtime considers them as two distinct types of objects. You may already have realized this division from the discussion of the properties of viewports in the previous section. It becomes clear when you consider modifying these properties at Runtime.

There are four built-in program units used to retrieve and modify settings of canvases' properties. They are the functions FIND_CANVAS, ID_NULL, GET_CANVAS_PROPERTY, and the procedure SET_CANVAS_PROPERTY. The size and the visual attribute name are the only properties you can modify for a canvas. Figure 16.13 shows a procedure that changes the visual attribute property of a canvas dynamically.

The program units that retrieve and modify the properties of views are

```
PROCEDURE Set_Canvas_Visual_Attr (canvas_name VARCHAR2,
                                  va_name     VARCHAR2) IS
 canvas_id       CANVAS;
 Canvas_Not_Found EXCEPTION;
BEGIN
 /* FIND_CANVAS returns the appropriate canvas ID.     */
 canvas_id := FIND_CANVAS(canvas_name);
 IF ID_NULL(canvas_id) THEN
  RAISE Canvas_Not_Found;
 END IF;
 /* If control comes here, canvas ID exists.           */
 SET_CANVAS_PROPERTY(canvas_id, VISUAL_ATTRIBUTE,
va_name);

EXCEPTION
 WHEN Canvas_Not_Found THEN
  MESSAGE('Canvas '||canvas_name||' does not exist.');
  RAISE FORM_TRIGGER_FAILURE;
 WHEN OTHERS THEN
  MESSAGE('Internal error occurred.');
  RAISE FORM_TRIGGER_FAILURE;
END Set_Canvas_Visual_Attr;
```

FIGURE 16.13 Program unit that replaces the visual attribute of a canvas at runtime.

used primarily with stacked canvas views, since their properties tend to change dynamically. FIND_VIEW, ID_NULL, GET_VIEW_PROPERTY, and SET_VIEW_PROPERTY serve the same purpose for views as the program units that correspond to canvases, windows, items, and other Form Builder objects. FIND_VIEW returns the internal identifier of the view object, which is of data type Viewport. In addition, you can use the procedures SHOW_VIEW to display a view to the users, HIDE_VIEW to remove a view from the visible area of the application and SCROLL_VIEW to scroll the viewport rectangle horizontally or vertically along the canvas.

Figure 16.14 shows a procedure that can be used to display any stacked canvas where users click the mouse. The coordinates of the clicked point are retrieved from the system variables SYSTEM.MOUSE_X_POS and SYSTEM.MOUSE_Y_POS. They are used to set the coordinates of the upper left-hand corner of the stacked canvas right before the canvas is displayed.

```
PROCEDURE Show_Canvas_Where_Clicked (view_name VARCHAR2)
IS
 view_id         VIEWPORT;
 x_coord         NUMBER;
 y_coord         NUMBER;
 View_Not_Found  EXCEPTION;
BEGIN
 view_id := FIND_VIEW(view_name);
 IF ID_NULL(view_id) THEN
  RAISE View_Not_Found;
 END IF;
/* If control comes here, view ID exists.*/
 x_coord := TO_NUMBER(:SYSTEM.MOUSE_X_POS);
 y_coord := TO_NUMBER(:SYSTEM.MOUSE_Y_POS);

 SET_VIEW_PROPERTY(view_id, DISPLAY_X_POS, x_coord);
 SET_VIEW_PROPERTY(view_id, DISPLAY_Y_POS, y_coord);

 SHOW_VIEW(view_id);
EXCEPTION
 WHEN View_Not_Found THEN
  MESSAGE('View '||view_name||' does not exist.');
  RAISE FORM_TRIGGER_FAILURE;
WHEN OTHERS THEN
  MESSAGE('Internal error occurred.');
  RAISE FORM_TRIGGER_FAILURE;
END Show_Canvas_Where_Clicked;
```

FIGURE 16.14 Program unit that displays a stacked canvas-view with balloon help for a given item.

16.5 CANVAS USE CASES

The following three sections will outline the steps required to associate canvases and windows, as well as two use cases of tab and stacked canvases.

16.5.1 STEPS TO ASSOCIATE CONTENT CANVASES WITH WINDOWS

As said earlier, if your goal is to create MDI applications with minimal programming efforts, you should rely mostly on content canvases attached to MDI frame or dialog box windows. In such a case, the process of associating data items and controls with canvases and windows can be summarized as follows:

1. Create a content canvas where the interface object will reside. If you need to change the default background color and fill pattern of your future window, you may do this by setting the properties of the canvas that will be attached to the window.
2. Add objects on the canvas. This activity may be completed at the same time as the previous one if the Layout Wizard is used to create and set the properties of frames.
3. Create a window that will serve as the frame where the canvas will be attached. Set the properties of this window so that the window is a MDI sheet or a dialog box, depending on the needs of your application.
4. Set the property Window of the canvas to the name of the window. If you need to display the window programmatically, by using the built-in SHOW_WINDOW, rather than by the users' navigational actions, you should also set the property Primary Canvas of the window to the name of the canvas. This property should be set in cases when other canvases, such as stacked canvases, are attached to the same window object.
5. Size, arrange and align objects on the canvas based on the layout requirements of your application. Adjust the dimensions of the canvas if necessary.
6. Set the properties Width and Height of the window to values equal or larger than the same properties for the canvas object. This will ensure that the users will view all the items on the canvas when the window is initially displayed.

> **TIP**
>
> If the window is an MDI sheet, try to fit all the objects on the canvas inside the window. And make sure you don't forget the window scrollbars, since users may want to change the initial dimensions of the window. If the window is a dialog box—they usually are not sizable or scrollable—everything must fit inside the window. If this is not possible, consider redesigning the functionality of the dialog box. It is probably too large and may be divided in two or more dialog boxes.

16.5.2 IMPLEMENTING TABBED DIALOG BOXES

In Section 16.2.5, I outlined the most important properties of windows that you have to set in order to make them behave like dialog boxes. In order to implement tabbed dialog boxes, the steps discussed there should be combined with tab canvases. There are two ways in which you can implement tabbed pages in the Form Builder:

- **Convert an existing content canvas to a tab canvas.** This option is suitable in situations when all the items you need to display will fit in one of the pages of the tab canvas. You can easily implement it by setting the property Canvas Type to "Tab." The converted canvas will contain one page and all the items on it will be transferred to this page.

- **"Embed" a tab canvas on a content canvas.** This option can be used when some items on the tabbed dialog box need to reside outside any of the pages. Typically, these are items that apply to the entire dialog box and not to a particular page. In order to implement this interface, you need to display the content canvas on the Layout Editor, then click the icon Tab Canvas and draw the tab object to the appropriate location and size. A tab canvas with two tab pages will be created on the content canvas. No items from the content canvas will be transferred to any of these pages.

Once a tab canvas has been created, you can use in the Object Navigator to add or delete tab pages from it. The order of the page objects in the hierarchy tree defines the order in which appear on the screen. Among the properties of pages, probably the only one you will need to change is Label. This defines the string that users will see in the index of the tab. The property Enabled is set to "Yes" by default and allows users to access the tab. In order to prevent users from accessing it, set this property to "No." The property Visible determines whether the tab page is displayed to the users at runtime or not. Note that typically these two properties are toggled at runtime, based on the security level of the users. There are a number of visual attribute properties that you can set in the Font & Color group. However, I do not recommend that you set any of these at the tab level. Instead, set them for the canvas object, so that all the tabs within the canvas inherit the same settings.

It has been already mentioned that the properties Visible and Enabled are usually manipulated at runtime based on different factors, such as the privileges of the user. Figure 16.15 shows a program unit that hides the tab FINANCIAL of the canvas EMPLOYEES if the user is member of the group "DATA_ENTRY"; it disables the tab if the user is in the group "MANAGER"; and, finally, it sets the properties Visible and Enabled and displays the tab if the user is in the group "PAYROLL."

16.5.3 IMPLEMENTING SCROLLABLE STACKED CANVASES

It has been mentioned a few times that one of the typical uses of stacked canvases is to implement an interface in which users can scroll to items initially invisible without scrolling the entire window. In this section, you will be guided you through the process adding such an interface to the MRD application. You can follow the discussion in this section with the module you have been developing so far. You can also use the module CH16_1.FMB provided with the companion software as a starting point.

Issue the following commands to create a data block based on the table CUSTOMERS:

```
PROCEDURE Show_Tab_To_User (user_group VARCHAR2) IS
 tab_page_id            TAB_PAGE;
 Tab_Page_Not_Found     EXCEPTION;
BEGIN
 tab_page_id := FIND_TAB_PAGE('EMPLOYEES.FINANCIAL');
– IF ID_NULL(tab_page_id) THEN
–   RAISE Tab_Page_Not_Found;
– END IF;
/* If control comes here, tab page ID exists.  */
 IF (user_group = 'DATA_ENTRY') THEN
   SET_TAB_PAGE_PROPERTY(tab_page_id, VISIBLE,
PROPERTY_FALSE);
 ELSIF (user_group = 'MANAGER') THEN
   SET_TAB_PAGE_PROPERTY(tab_page_id, ENABLED,
PROPERTY_FALSE);
 ELSIF (user_group = 'PAYROLL') THEN
   SET_TAB_PAGE_PROPERTY(tab_page_id, VISIBLE,
PROPERTY_TRUE);
   SET_TAB_PAGE_PROPERTY(tab_page_id, ENABLED,
PROPERTY_TRUE);
   SET_CANVAS_PROPERTY('EMPLOYEES', TOPMOST_TAB_PAGE,
'FINANCIAL');
 END IF;
EXCEPTION
 WHEN Tab_Page_Not_Found THEN
  MESSAGE('Tab Page EMPLOYEES.FINANCIAL does not
exist.');
  RAISE FORM_TRIGGER_FAILURE;
WHEN OTHERS THEN
  MESSAGE('Internal error occurred.');
  RAISE FORM_TRIGGER_FAILURE;
END Show_Tab_To_User;
```

FIGURE 16.15 Program unit that displays a stacked canvas-view with balloon help for a given item.

1. Invoke the Data Block Wizard.
2. Select the option to create a new block based on a table.
3. Select the table CUSTOMER as the object on which the new block will be based.
4. Select all the available columns to become database items for the new block.
5. Click Finish.

Define the layout of the new block by following these steps:

1. Invoke the Layout Wizard if it is not launched automatically when you click Finish in the Data Block Wizard.
2. Select to create the new frame on a new content canvas.
3. Select all the available items to be displayed except for ID.
4. Choose the tabular layout style for the frame.
5. Display eight records and the scrollbar on the frame.
6. Click Finish.

At this point, the layout of the block looks as shown partially in Figure 16.16. Rename the newly created canvas object to "CUST_MATRIX." Do not modify the default name CUSTOMER1 that the Data Block Wizard assigns to the new block.

In the following paragraphs, you will modify the layout properties of the items within the frame. In order for these manual changes to persist even after you modify the frame, set the property Update Layout of the frame to "Locked." The following are the steps required to create the stacked canvas:

1. Display the content canvas CUST_MATRIX in the Layout Editor.
2. Select the icon Stacked Canvas from the tool palette and draw a rectangle that includes the items GENDER, DOB, MEMBER_DT, STATUS, and ADDRESS and their text labels, but does not intersect the rectangle of the frame. To the left of the rectangle you should see the items LAST_NAME and FIRST_NAME.
3. Rename the new canvas to "CUST_MATRIX_STACKED."

Id	Last Name	First Name	Phone
ID	LAST_NAME	FIRST_NAME	PHONE
ID	LAST_NAME	FIRST_NAME	PHONE
ID	LAST_NAME	FIRST_NAME	PHONE
ID	LAST_NAME	FIRST_NAME	PHONE
ID	LAST_NAME	FIRST_NAME	PHONE
ID	LAST_NAME	FIRST_NAME	PHONE

FIGURE 16.16 Initial layout of the CUSTOMER1 block.

At this point, you have created a stacked canvas and have set a number of its properties. Right-click the object and switch to the Property Palette to view some of these properties. Notice that the action of drawing the stacked canvas on top of the content canvas sets the viewport properties of the new object. Furthermore, by resizing and moving the viewport object on the content canvas, you can adjust its position as desired. Based on the settings of the drawing tools in the tool palette, the viewport may be displayed with colors other than the ones of the content canvas. The intention here is to hide from users the fact that they are seeing a different canvas on the screen; therefore you should apply the Form Builder default settings to any Font & Color properties, including Foreground Color and Background Color. The easiest way to achieve this is to select the desired property and click the button Inherit in the Property Palette.

Now you are ready to move the items in the stacked canvas. This can be easily achieved by selecting all the items in the CUSTOMER1 block except for LAST_NAME and FIRST_NAME, displaying their properties in the Property Palette, and setting the property Canvas to "CUST_MATRIX_STACKED." While the items are still selected, open a Layout Editor window for the stacked canvas and move all the items to the left so that their left edge is aligned with the left border of the canvas. Expand the CUST_MATRIX_STACKED canvas so that all the items just moved on it are placed completely within its bounds.

Switch to the Layout Editor window that contains the content canvas and notice that the items GENDER, DOB, MEMBER_DT, STATUS, and ADDRESS appear on this canvas thorough the view of the stacked canvas. The other items are hidden. At this point, you may have to align the items on the CUST_MATRIX_STACKED canvas with the items LAST_NAME and FIRST_NAME on the content canvas CUST_MATRIX. The process is simple and consists of the following steps:

1. Select all the items on the CUST_MATRIX_STACKED canvas.
2. Display the CUST_MATRIX canvas on the Layout Editor.
3. Without loosing the selection of objects, move them using the arrow keys move them until all the visible items are aligned.

In order to complete the layout of the form, the following additional steps are required:

1. Bring the scrollbar associated with the CUSTOMER1 block close to the right edge of the stacked canvas' viewport.
2. Resize the frame associated with the CUSTOMER1 block to reflect the new layout of objects on the content canvas.
3. Display the Property Palette of the stacked canvas.
4. Set the property Bevel to "None" and the property Show Horizontal Scrollbar to "Yes."

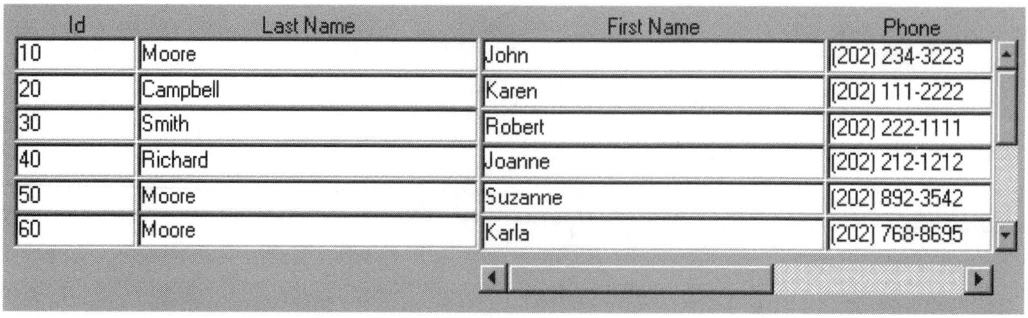

Id	Last Name	First Name	Phone
10	Moore	John	(202) 234-3223
20	Campbell	Karen	(202) 111-2222
30	Smith	Robert	(202) 222-1111
40	Richard	Joanne	(202) 212-1212
50	Moore	Suzanne	(202) 892-3542
60	Moore	Karla	(202) 768-8695

FIGURE 16.17 The layout of the CUSTOMER1 block with a scrollable stacked canvas.

At this point, you can convert a number of items in the block CUSTOMER1 into list boxes and checkboxes by following the guidelines provided in Section 15.6.1. Figure 16.17 shows the layout of the block now that the scrollable stacked canvas is implemented. The module CH16_2.FMB in the companion software contains a version of the MRD module with the CUSTOMER1 block implemented.

> **TIP**
>
> If you execute the module CH16_2.FMB you will notice that the stacked canvas appears with each block. You need to move to the CUSTOMER1 block in order to view a picture similar to the one shown in Figure 16.17. The reason for this behavior is that the application at this point contains only one window object to which all the canvases you have developed so far are attached. Since the stacked canvas CUST_MATRIX_STACKED is also attached to this window, it will appear with the other canvases. You will fix this problem when you will create additional windows in the module as explained in the following section.

The example discussed is this section is fairly simple. In more complex applications, forms usually contain a number of data blocks and canvases. There may be occasions when the module may require a number of stacked canvases as well. In such cases, the default stacking order of the canvases may not be sufficient to display the canvases appropriately, based on the context. Programmatically, you need to ensure that all the related canvases are maintained and displayed together. In the following paragraphs, I will outline a strategy for achieving this and will show sample code of the critical steps. The actions to manage dynamically stacked canvases are as follows:

1. Divide the canvases in your module in groups of related canvases. Each group should contain canvases that form one stack viewable by the users at

runtime. The group typically contains only one content canvas and a number of stacked canvases associated with it. Furthermore, all the canvases in the group are usually associated with their own window object.

2. In a control block, create an invisible text item for each of these groups. This item will store the comma-separated names of all the canvases in the group in the order in which they should be raised. These items may be created in any block of the module, however, I recommend that you set aside a control block that owns all accessory items like these used to enhance the module programmatically.
3. In a PRE-FORM trigger, initialize the items to the canvas names as described in the step above. The following statement shows an example of how you do this.

   ```
   :CTRL.STACK1:= 'CANVAS1,CANVAS3,CANVAS7,CANVAS4';
   ```

4. Identify the blocks into which users can enter each of these canvas groups. Usually, these blocks are located on the content canvas of the group.
5. In WHEN-NEW-BLOCK-INSTANCE triggers for these blocks write logic that raises all the canvases in the proper order. By encapsulating the statements in a program unit, you increase their reuse and simplify the contents of the WHEN-NEW-BLOCK-INSTANCE triggers. Assuming that this program unit is a procedure called `Display_Canvases`, these trigger that displays the canvases of the first stack, stored in the item CTRL.STACK1, contains only the following statement:

   ```
   DISPLAY_CANVASES(:CTRL.STACK1);
   ```

The procedure `Display_Canvases` is fairly straightforward. It takes as an argument the list of canvases to be displayed. It extracts the name of each canvas from the list and then displays it to the users. Figure 16.18 shows the contents of this procedure. Notice here the usage of the PL/SQL functions INSTR and SUBSTR to locate the current canvas from the list of canvases. Once located, this canvas is removed from the string using the function REPLACE. The separating comma is dropped from the current canvas using the function RTRIM. And, finally, the canvas is displayed by setting its property VISIBLE.

16.6 WINDOWS AND DIALOG BOXES IN THE MRD APPLICATION

At this point, you are ready to add windows to the MRD application. Either continue with the module you have been using all along or start with CH16_2.FMB provided with the companion software. In this section you will use a number of

```
PROCEDURE Display_Canvases (p_canvas_list VARCHAR2) IS
 canvases         VARCHAR2(255) := p_canvas_list;
 current_canvas   VARCHAR2(80);
 comma_position   NUMBER;
BEGIN
   WHILE (canvases IS NOT NULL) LOOP
      comma_position := INSTR(p_canvas_list, ',');
      current_canvas := SUBSTR(p_canvas_list, 1,
comma_position);
      canvases := REPLACE(canvases, current_canvas);
      current_canvas := RTRIM(current_canvas, ',');
      SET_VIEW_PROPERTY(current_canvas, VISIBLE,
PROPERTY_TRUE);
   END LOOP;
EXCEPTION
  WHEN OTHERS THEN
      MESSAGE('Internal error occurred.');
      RAISE FORM_TRIGGER_FAILURE;
END Display_Canvases;
```

FIGURE 16.18 The layout of the CUSTOMER block with a scrollable stacked canvas.

objects from the module WINPROPS.FMB. To facilitate the process of reusing these objects, they are all bundled in the object group MDI_WINDOWS_GROUP. With both the modules opened in the Object Navigator, drag the object group MDI_WINDOWS_GROUP from the module WINPROPS.FMB onto the MRD module. Choose to copy or subclass the members of the object group. To complete these preliminary steps, edit the contents of the PRE-FORM trigger in the MRD module and add the following line:

```
:GLOBAL.Home_Item := Get_Home_Item;
```

Now, set the properties of the MDI frame so that when the application is started, the window is maximized and the title bar shows the string "Movie Rental Database Application."

1. Create a form-level WHEN-NEW-FORM-INSTANCE trigger.
2. Enter the contents as shown below.

```
SET_WINDOW_PROPERTY(FORMS_MDI_WINDOW, TITLE,
          'Movie Rental Database Application');
SET_WINDOW_PROPERTY(FORMS_MDI_WINDOW, WINDOW_STATE,
MAXIMIZE);
```

There is only one window currently in the application. Set its properties according to these instructions:

1. Inherit its properties from the property class 'MDI_SHEET,' and set the properties Name, Title, and Primary Canvas to "CUSTOMERS."
2. Display the Property Palette for the canvas CUSTOMERS and set the property Window to "'CUSTOMERS."
3. Select the properties Width and Height and click the icon Copy Properties on the toolbar.
4. Display the Property Palette for the window CUSTOMERS and click the icon Copy Properties on the toolbar. This will set the dimensions of the canvas and its associated window to the same values.

Now, create three more windows, and follow similar steps to create a one-to-one correspondence between the second window and the MOVIES canvas, between the third window and the RENTALS canvas, and between the fourth window and the CUST_MATRIX canvas. For the CUST_MATRIX, set the Title to "Customers in Matrix Layout." In addition, set the property Window to "CUST_MATRIX" for the stacked canvas CUST_MATRIX_STACKED.

Save and generate the application, and run it if you want to take a quick look at the way the windows look. The window CUSTOMER will be initially displayed. Since the module still uses the default menu, you can choose Block | Next from this menu to navigate to block MOVIE. This action will automatically display the window MOVIE. In this window, you can select Block | Next once again to move to block RENTAL and open the window where it resides. Note that the Window menu will display the titles of the open windows, and that you can close the windows by double-clicking their control menu box. Exit the runtime and return to the Form Builder when ready to proceed with the development.

The next step is to associate WHEN-BUTTON-PRESSED triggers with push buttons that will govern the navigation from window to window.

For the CLOSE buttons in all three windows, the statement in the trigger will be

1. Close_Window(window_name); where window_name will be 'CUSTOMERS,' 'MOVIES,' and 'RENTALS,' respectively.

2. For the MOVIE buttons in the CUSTOMER and RENTAL windows, the single line in the trigger's body will be

```
Open_Window('MOVIES', 'MOVIES');
```

3. For the RENTAL buttons in the CUSTOMER and MOVIE windows, the trigger should contain the line:

```
Open_Window('RENTALS', 'RENTALS');
```

4. For the CUSTOMER button in the MOVIE and RENTAL windows the statement of the trigger will be

```
Open_Window('CUSTOMERS', 'CUSTOMERS');
```

Create also a dialog box that will be displayed when users will select About... from the Help menu.

1. Create a new canvas and name it ABOUT.
2. Create a new window, inherit its properties from the property class MDI_DIALOG_BOX, and set its Name, Title, and Primary Canvas properties to "ABOUT."
3. For the canvas ABOUT, set the property Window to "ABOUT."
4. Create a new block, name it CONTROL, and set the property Database Data Block to "No."
5. Display the canvas ABOUT in the Layout Editor and create a button that is part of the CONTROL block. Rename it to CLOSE_ABOUT and set its Label property to "Close."
6. Attach a WHEN-BUTTON-PRESSED trigger to the new item with this line in the body:

```
Close_Window('ABOUT');
```

7. Create a text box and put anything you would normally see in a dialog box of this kind. See Figure 16.19 for an example.
8. Set the dimensions of the canvas and the window to equal values.

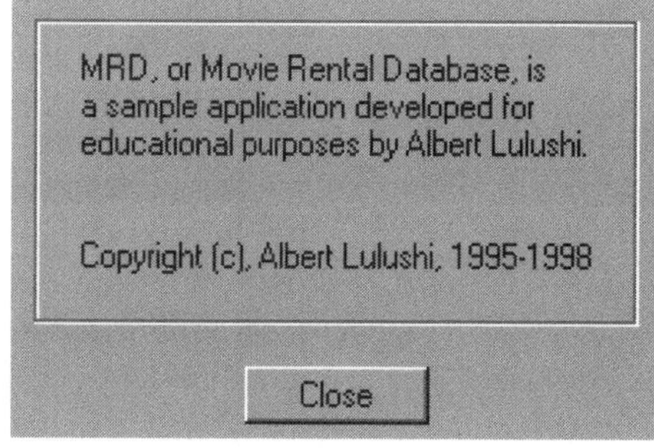

FIGURE 16.19 Sample About dialog box.

You should notice the fact that each of the three main windows contains two push buttons to access the other windows. Thus, in total there are six buttons, when you need only three, one for each window. These buttons must be prominently placed so that are not obscured by the working windows of the application. The best place would be a toolbar, like the one you used in the WINDYNM.FMB module. Only here you will do better. You will create iconic toolbars for the principal functionality of the application. Chapter 18 will discuss the process of creating menus and toolbars for Form Builder applications.

16.7 SUMMARY

This chapter discussed windows, their properties, and objects associated with them. Important concepts in this chapter were

- **Properties of Windows**
  - Setting Windows Properties in the Form Builder
  - Controlling Windows Programmatically
  - Events of Windows
- **Developing MDI Applications with Form Builder**
  - MDI Frame Window
  - MDI Sheets
  - Implementing MDI Sheets
  - Dialog Boxes
  - Implementing Dialog Boxes
  - Message Boxes
- **Alerts**
  - Setting Properties of Alerts in the Form Builder
  - Modifying Properties of Alerts at Runtime
- **Canvases**
  - Types of Canvases
  - Setting Properties of Canvases in the Form Builder
  - Views of a Canvas and Viewports
  - Modifying Properties of Canvases at Runtime
- **Canvas Use Cases**
  - Steps to Associate Content Canvases with Windows
  - Implementing Tabbed Dialog Boxes
  - Implementing Scrollable Stacked Canvases
- **Windows and Dialog Boxes in the MRD Application**

The following table describes the software assets that were discussed in this chapter. From the main HTML page of the software utilities provided with the book follow the links *Software* and *Chapter 16* to access these assets:

ASSET NAME	DESCRIPTION
WINDYNM.FMB	A Form Builder module that demonstrates how you show and hide windows dynamically.
WINDYNM.FMX	The executable version of WINDYNM.FMB compiled on Win32 platforms.
WINDYNM1.FMB	A version of WINDYNM1.FMB that shows how the Form Builder focus influences the management of windows in your applications.
WINDYNM1.FMX	The executable version of WINDYNM1.FMB compiled on Win32 platforms.
WINPROPS.FMB	A Form Builder module that contains a number of property classes and program units that allow you to implement MDI sheets and dialog boxes in your applications.
CH16_1.FMB	The MRD application completed in the last chapter. Use this module as a starting point for the activities discussed in this chapter.
CH16_2.FMB	The MRD application with the implementation of the CUSTOMER1 block in a stacked canvas.
CH16_2.FMX	The executable version of CH16_2.FMB compiled for Win32 platforms.
CH16_3.FMB	The MRD application with all the activities discussed in this chapter.
CH16_3.FMX	The executable version of CH16_3.FMB compiled for Win32 platforms.

Chapter 17

Record Structures and Other Objects

Yea, from the table of my memory
I'll wipe out all trivial fond records . . .
—William Shakespeare

- Records in Form Builder Applications
- Record Groups
- Lists of Values
- Text Editors
- Parameters and Parameter Lists
- Summary

Materials presented up to this point discuss the principal structural and user interface objects in Form Builder applications. In these applications you can use other objects to add to and enhance the functionality of blocks, data items, controls, windows, and dialog boxes. One of these objects, the record, is a virtual object that exists only at runtime. However, it is very important to understand its properties, and especially the events that affect its status. Others, like record groups, editors, List of Values dialog boxes, and parameter lists are objects that can be used to implement several features in the application such as tabular structures, selection and validation of data from lists, and text editing capabilities. This chapter discusses the process of creating and manipulating these objects.

17.1 RECORDS IN FORM BUILDER APPLICATIONS

When the requirements of a system are analyzed, you identify the object classes or entities that will take part in the system. They represent the general characteristics of a group of data items. Each individual occurrence of these data items forms an instance of the entity. For example, the entity Movie is considered as a group of data that includes a title, main actors, producers, rating, and so on. The movie *The Piano* is an instance of this entity, where all the data items have a particular value.

In the Oracle RDBMS, entities are implemented by tabular structures, such as tables, views, and PL/SQL tables. The instances of these entities are stored as rows in these structures. In Form Builder applications, entities are implemented by data blocks and each individual occurrence becomes a record. Records are not objects that you can access and manipulate in the Form Builder. At runtime, they can be created, modified, and deleted according to the needs of the application. From an object-oriented programming perspective, since the records are instances of a block-class, the events that affect them are events that affect the class. This is the reason why, usually, triggers fired by these events are implemented as block-level triggers.

17.1.1 STATES OF RECORDS, BLOCKS, AND FORMS

The state of a record defines whether and how it will be processed by several internal events of Forms Runtime, such as validation or database processing. It also affects the state of the parent block and through it the state of the form module.

A record can be in one of the following states: NEW, INSERT, QUERY, and CHANGED. The record status is NEW, if the event CreateRecord has just occurred, and no values have been entered in any of the items in the record. The status of all the items in a NEW record is also NEW. As soon as some data is entered in one item—either by users or as a result of programmatic assignments—

the status of that item and all the other items in the record becomes CHANGED. The record switches to the state INSERT. As the users continue entering data the status of the record will remain INSERT. When the record is committed, Forms Runtime will ensure that the record is valid, and will send an INSERT statement to the database. If the insertion is successful, the record in the Forms module becomes an identical copy of the record stored in the database. Its status now becomes QUERY. A record is in this state if it is retrieved by a query against the database as well. The state of all the items in a QUERY record is VALID. As long as users or the application do not change any of them, the record remains in this state. However, as soon as a change is made, the status of the record and all its items becomes CHANGED. When the next CommitForm event occurs, Forms takes the records throughout the validation check first, and, if the record is valid, it prepares and sends an UPDATE statement to the database. If the transaction is completed successfully, the record status will become QUERY once again. Figure 17.1 represents the state transition diagram of a record, which summarizes what was said in this paragraph.

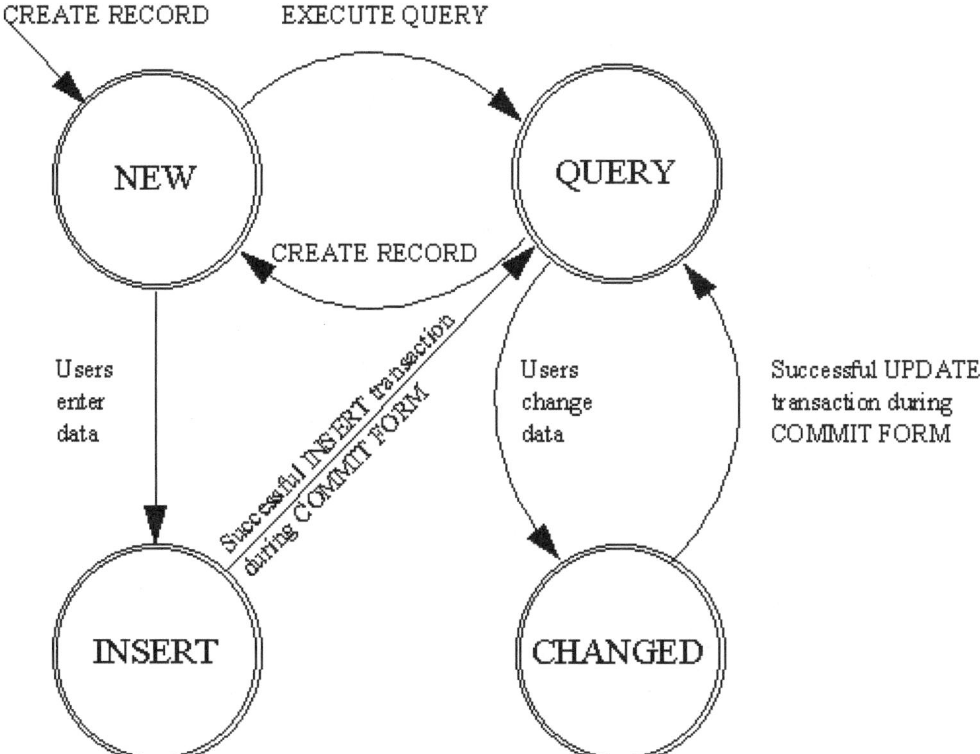

FIGURE 17.1 Transition diagram for the states of a record.

The status of different records in a block defines the status of that block. The status of different blocks in the form define the status of that module. Forms and blocks can have one of the three status: NEW, CHANGED, and QUERY. If a block contains only one record in the NEW state, the status of the block is NEW. If at least one record in the block is in state QUERY, the state of the block is QUERY, even if there is a newly-created record in the state NEW. If the status of at least one record in the block is INSERT or CHANGED, the block will be in the CHANGED state.

The relation between the states of blocks and the state of its parent form is similar. The form is in state NEW if and only if all its blocks are in that state. If one block switches to state QUERY, while the others are still NEW, the status of the form becomes QUERY. And, if the status of at least one block becomes CHANGED, the parent form will be in that state as well.

As you can see, objects in Form Builder applications influence the state of other objects in two directions: from top down, and from bottom up. Figure 17.2 explains this concept better. This figure shows the hierarchical organization of blocks, records, and items in a module.

When the application is first launched or when the ClearForm event occurs, the state of the module is set to NEW. This state is propagated to all the subordinate nodes one level down the tree, in other words to all the blocks in that module. When the state of a block is set to NEW, either from a message received by its parent, or because the ClearBlock event occurs, the block will create a single NEW record. When the state of the block is set to QUERY, because the Execute-Query event occurs, the status of all the records retrieved by the query in this block is set to QUERY. When the status of the record is NEW, either because the parent block is in this state, or because the CreateRecord event occurs in the block, the status of all the items in this record is NEW. Similarly, when the record status is QUERY, the status of all its items will become VALID.

The users do not see any of the hierarchy levels shown in Figure 17.2, except for the lowest one. On their application screens, they enter data in items or click controls to perform their job. When users modify an item, thus setting its status to CHANGED, the state is propagated all the way up to the top of the hierarchy. If,

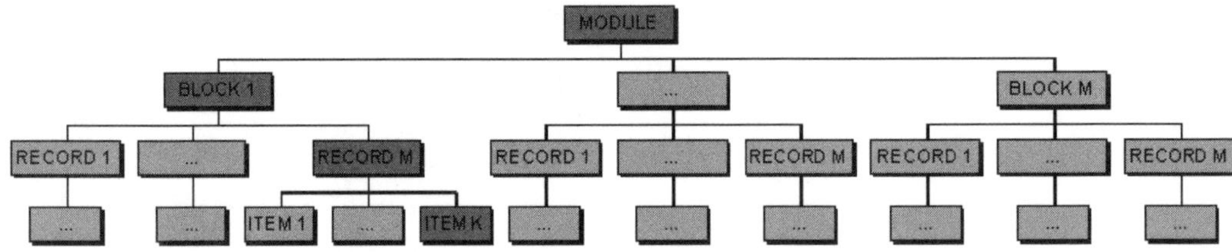

FIGURE 17.2 Hierarchy tree of objects in Form Builder applications.

in the example of Figure 17.2, Item K is changed, it will send the message up to its parent record. This message causes the record to switch to the INSERT state if it was previously in NEW, or CHANGED if it was previously in QUERY. When the state transition occurs, the record sends a signal to its parent block, which immediately sets its state to CHANGED. The block finally transmits the message to the module, thus putting it in the CHANGED state as well.

Then, when the CommitForm event occurs, the process of passing status information and messages begins again, this time from the top all the way down to each item. The life of Form Builder application is nothing more than a constant flow of messages and state transitions as explained here.

Forms Runtime allows you to inspect the status of the form, any of its blocks, or any of their records. The information for the objects where the cursor is currently located is stored in the systems variables SYSTEM.FORM_STATUS, SYSTEM.BLOCK_STATUS, and SYSTEM.RECORD_STATUS, respectively. You can also use the function GET_RECORD_PROPERTY to get the status of any record in any block within the application, of use the function GET_BLOCK_PROPERTY to retrieve the status of any block in your form. There is not a way to inspect the status of an item programmatically.

The companion software includes a form that uses the system variables to retrieve the status of the form, current block and current record at any time during the form's life. This module, called STATUS.FMB, contains two base table blocks, which you can use to query and manipulate data from the tables CUSTOMERS and MOVIES. The horizontal toolbar of the application contains three text items and a push button. When the push button is clicked, these items will display the status of the current record, block and form. Use this application to better understand the concepts discussed in this section.

17.1.2 EVENTS OF RECORDS

In the previous section, while discussing the status of records, mentioned briefly some of the events related to them. This section reviews these events in more detail. The main events that affect a record's life are EnterRecord, LeaveRecord, CreateRecord, RemoveRecord, ChangeRecordItems, and ValidateRecord.

- **EnterRecord.** This event occurs when the users navigate to an item in the record from an item that either is in a different record within the block, or is in another block altogether. Navigating from one item to the other within the same record does not constitute an EnterRecord event. If Forms can place its focus on the item within the record where users have chosen to navigate, right before entering the record, the trigger PRE-RECORD will fire. When the EnterRecord event completes successfully, the WHEN-NEW-RECORD-INSTANCE will fire.

- **LeaveRecord.** This event occurs when users navigate to an item that is in another record within the same block, or on another block. This event will cause the event ValidateRecord to occur. Depending on how the ValidateRecord event will treat items that do not pass the validation test, the LeaveRecord event may not be completed if the validation fails. However, if it is completed successfully, the trigger POST-RECORD will fire right after Forms navigates out of the record.
- **CreateRecord.** This event occurs when the built-in CREATE_RECORD is invoked, either programmatically or by pressing the [CREATE RECORD] key. During this event, Forms leaves the current record, creates a new record immediately after it, and places the focus on a new record. The trigger that fires during this event is WHEN-CREATE-RECORD. Understandably, this trigger is sandwiched between the POST-RECORD trigger fired when Forms leaves the original record, and the PRE-RECORD trigger fired when Forms is about to enter the new record. The CreateRecord event also occurs when Forms initially navigates to a new block. At the end of this event the status of the record is NEW.
- **RemoveRecord.** This event occurs either when the current block is deleted using the built-in DELETE_RECORD, or when it is cleared from the block using the built-in CLEAR_RECORD. As explained earlier in the book, these actions are different in that the first one results in the record being marked for delete by the next commit transaction, and the second one simply flushes the record from the internal structures of the block. In both cases, when the record is removed, the WHEN-REMOVE-RECORD trigger is fired.
- **ChangeRecordItems.** This event occurs whenever users change the value of a base table item in the record. As the result of this change, the record is flagged either for an INSERT or for an UPDATE during the next commit event. In response to this event, the trigger WHEN-DATABASE-RECORD will fire. At the end of the event, the status of all the items in the record is CHANGED. The status of the record is either INSERT or CHANGED, depending on the status prior to the event. This event occurs even if a control text item is changed as long as the block is a data block and the property Lock Record in the Database group of properties of that item is set to "Yes."
- **ValidateRecord.** This event occurs only if the record is in INSERT or CHANGED state, and either LeaveRecord or CommitForm event is initiated. If the record's status is NEW, or QUERY, the record is considered valid by Forms Runtime, therefore no validation occurs. When the ValidateRecord event occurs, the record triggers the ValidateItem event for all its dependent items. If any of these events is not successful, the ValidateRecord event itself will fail. If all the items pass the validation test, the WHEN-VALIDATE-RECORD trigger is fired. Its outcome defines the success or failure of the ValidateRecord item.

17.1.3 EVENTS OF RECORDS IN THE MRD APPLICATION

In this section, you will implement some of the functionality of the MRD application in the form of block-level triggers associated with record events. Begin the process by opening the most current version of the MRD module, which you saved at the end of the previous chapter. You may also use the module CH17_1.FMB provided with the companion software, which contains all the work done so far in the application.

There are three internal identifiers in the MRD application that will be populated with values from a sequence number generator when the records are created. These items are ID in blocks CUSTOMER, MOVIE, and TAPE. The values for these items will come from the sequence MRD_SEQ created together with the other database objects of the application. Create first a function that returns the value from this sequence. The contents of this function are shown in Figure 17.3.

Next, create WHEN-CREATE-RECORD triggers for the blocks CUSTOMERS, MOVIES, TAPES, and CUSTOMERS1. Each trigger should populate the respective ID item with a call to this function. The contents of the trigger in the block CUSTOMERS, for example, are:

```
:CUSTOMER.ID := Get_Sequence_Id;
```

When records are created in the block RENTALS, the values for CUSTOMER_ID and TAPE_ID will be populated from LOV dialog boxes. In a WHEN-CREATE-RECORD trigger for this block set the RENT_DT to the current date as shown in the following line:

```
SELECT SYSDATE INTO :RENTALS.RENT_DT FROM DUAL;
```

Now use the AfterQuery event for the block RENTALS to populate the control items CUSTOMER_NAME and MOVIE_TITLE based on the values of the

```
FUNCTION Get_Sequence_Id RETURN NUMBER IS
 seq_id    NUMBER;
BEGIN
 SELECT MRD_SEQ.NEXTVAL
 INTO seq_id
 FROM DUAL;

 RETURN seq_id;
END;
```

FIGURE 17.3 Function that Return the Next Value from a Sequence.

data bound items CUSTOMER_ID and TAPE_ID. Create a POST-QUERY trigger at the block level that will fire for each record returned by the query and execute the following statements:

```
SELECT FIRST_NAME||' '||LAST_NAME
INTO :RENTALS.CUSTOMER_NAME
FROM CUSTOMERS
WHERE ID = :RENTALS.CUSTOMER_ID;

SELECT TITLE
INTO :RENTALS.MOVIE_TITLE
FROM MOVIES
WHERE ID =
   (SELECT MOVIE_ID
    FROM TAPES
    WHERE ID = :RENTALS.TAPE_ID);
```

Populating lookup items with values in POST-QUERY triggers increases significantly the bandwidth of conversation between the Form client and the database server. Indeed, in the scenario discussed here, each record fetched to the client generates two additional queries sent back to the server for execution. Thus, with POST-QUERY trigger implementation, the number of queries that the

```
DECLARE
 cust_id   VARCHAR2(20);
BEGIN
 IF :SYSTEM.RECORD_STATUS = 'INSERT' THEN
  SELECT COUNT(*)
  INTO cust_id
  FROM CUSTOMERS
  WHERE LAST_NAME = :CUSTOMER.LAST_NAME
   AND FIRST_NAME = :CUSTOMER.FIRST_NAME
   AND MEMBER_DT = :CUSTOMER.MEMBER_DT;
  IF cust_id <> '0' THEN
   BELL;
   MESSAGE('This customer already exists.');
   RAISE FORM_TRIGGER_FAILURE;
  END IF;
 END IF;
END;
```

FIGURE 17.4 Checking for uniqueness of new records.

database server executes is proportional to the number of records fetched to the client. This situation may seriously compromise the performance of your applications, especially when they are deployed over wide-area networks or on the Web. Chapter 24 will show how you can avoid the network bottleneck by querying the data for the block using a PL/SQL stored procedure.

Next use the ValidateRecord event to ensure the quality of data that will be inserted in the system. Create a WHEN-VALIDATE-RECORD trigger for the CUSTOMER block and enter its contents as shown in Figure 17.4. The same trigger should be added to the CUSTOMER1 block with references to its items.

Similarly, create a WHEN-VALIDATE-RECORD trigger for block MOVIE and check for the uniqueness of new records based on the items TITLE and DIRECTOR. In addition, make sure in this trigger that the date items START_DT and END_DT are always specified in the right order (END_DT should always be after START_DT). This constraint should be enforceable for new and existing records, therefore you should place it outside the IF statements that checks the uniqueness of movies.

Finally, create a WHEN-VALIDATE-RECORD for block RENTAL that will ensure that the RENT_DT and RETURN_DT dates are specified in the appropriate order. Save the work done so far and compile the module.

> **TIP**
>
> In the WHEN-VALIDATE-RECORD trigger for blocks CUSTOMERS, CUSTOMERS1, and MOVIES you are enforcing the uniqueness of data only for newly-inserted records. For records that already exist in the database, the IF statement will not be processed since the status of these records is no longer "INSERT." Thus, there is a possibility to create data that violate the uniqueness constraints. In this situation, you should not allow users to update the items that are part of the check. Therefore set the property "Update Allowed" to "No" for FIRST_NAME, LAST_NAME, and MEMBER_DT in the CUSTOMERS and CUSTOMERS1 blocks and for TITLE in the MOVIES block.

17.2 RECORD GROUPS

Record groups are objects that provide the functionality of tabular data structures in Form Builder applications, similar to the arrays of structures in C or index-by tables in PL/SQL. They allow you to combine items of alphanumeric, numeric, and date data types in records that can be accessed based on the value of an index. Depending on how they get populated with data, record groups are divided in query and non-query record groups.

Query record groups are created by a SQL SELECT statement. The columns in the SELECT clause of this statement become the columns of the record group, and the records returned by the query become its rows. This is the most flexible and usable record group. It can be created from the Form Builder at design time and also dynamically at runtime thus allowing for dynamic manipulation of the data. The non-query record groups are created by explicitly specifying the columns they will contain. If created at runtime, they may also be populated with data and their rows can be added or deleted programmatically. However, if created at design time, their structure and values must be specified in the Form Builder and remain fixed throughout their life. For this reason, non-query record groups created at design time are called static record groups.

In this section you will create record group structures that will be used in the MRD application. You will begin by creating three static record groups. One of them will be populated with values in this chapter; the other two in the next chapter. Then, you will create several query record groups that will complete the functionality of the updateable combo boxes created in Chapter 15. You will also see how record groups can be used to implement multiple-selection list boxes in Form Builder applications. Continue work with the module you were using in the previous section or open the module CH17_2.FMB provided with the companion software.

17.2.1 STATIC RECORD GROUPS

At design time, object groups can be created and renamed in the Object Navigator. When you create an object group with any of the standard commands of the Navigator, you will first see the New Record Group dialog box shown in Figure 17.5. In this dialog box you can choose the type of record group you want to create. The radio box at the bottom is checked, which means that query record groups are created by default. In this case, you need to enter a SELECT statement in the Query Text field, which will create and populate the record group. If you want to create a static group, click the Static Values radio button.

From the Navigator, create a static record group that will be used to store the names of the windows in the application. This will enable you to write code that closes all the windows in the application with one single command. After selecting the type of the record group click OK in the New Record Group dialog box. The Column Specification dialog box appears (see Figure 17.6). Define here the structure of the record group WINDOWS and populate it with values using the following steps:

1. Enter WINDOW_NAME in the first record of the multi-record Column Names block. Leave the data type and length of this column set to its default values.
2. Click inside Column Values detail block, and enter the names of the MDI sheet windows in the MRD module, as shown in Figure 17.6.

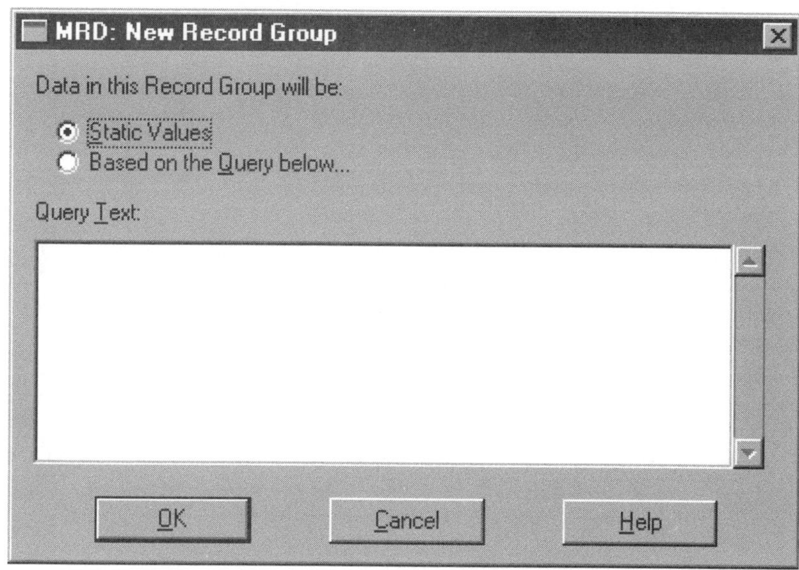

FIGURE 17.5 New Record Group dialog box.

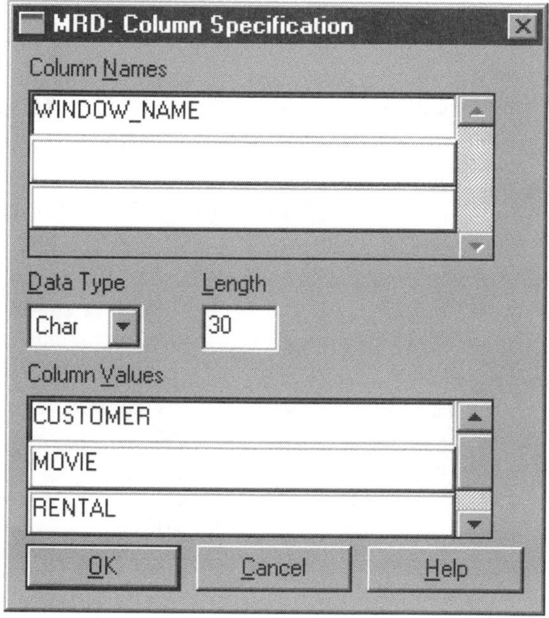

FIGURE 17.6 Column Specification dialog box for record groups.

3. Click OK.
4. Rename the group to "WINDOWS."

If you wanted to add another column to the record group, then you could insert its name under WINDOW_NAME, and provide its values in the Column Values list.

17.2.2 QUERY RECORD GROUPS

As I mentioned earlier, query record groups are created and populated by a SQL SELECT statement. If the record group is created in the Form Builder, the structure of the record group is defined at design time and the population of the group occurs at runtime. You can also create and populate the record groups with one single step at runtime. To create a query record group in the Form Builder, you must follow these steps:

1. Create the record group using any of the standard commands in the Navigator.
2. In the New Record Group dialog box, make sure the second radio button is checked. This button is followed by the label Based on the Query Below.
3. Enter the SELECT statement in the Query Text field. This can be any valid SQL SELECT command.
4. Click OK.
5. Rename the new object group according to your needs.

In the Property Palette for the newly created object, you can see that the property Record Group Type in the Functional group now is "Query," and your statement is in the property Record Group Query. If you display the Column Specification dialog box, you will notice that the Column Values area of the window, which you could see and access for static record groups, is now hidden. Another property whose setting may have an impact on the performance of query record groups is Record Group Fetch Size. This property determines the number of records fetched from the database when the query group is populated. Its default setting is 20 and may increased to reduce the amount of network traffic or decreased to increase the initial response of the application.

With the SELECT statement in hand, you can also create the record group at runtime. The built-in function CREATE_GROUP_FROM_QUERY takes as input parameter the SELECT statement, and returns the internal ID of the newly created group.

17.2.3 ACCESSING DATA OF RECORD GROUPS AT RUNTIME

In order to access the values stored in the cell of a record group, you must follow these steps:

1. Get the internal ID of the record group, based on its name, and make sure that it is a valid one. The functions FIND_GROUP and ID_NULL are used for this purpose.
2. Get the internal ID of the column where the cell is located, based on its name, and make sure that it is a valid one. The functions FIND_COLUMN and ID_NULL serve this purpose.
3. Get the number of records currently stored in the group. The function GET_ROW_COUNT returns this number.
4. Initiate a loop with the number retrieved in the previous step as the upper bound. The loop retrieves the value stored in the current cell of each record, as the iterator goes down the rows. Depending on the data type of the column, one of the following functions is used to retrieve the value stored in the current cell: GET_GROUP_CHAR_CELL, GET_GROUP_NUMBER_CELL, or GET_GROUP_DATE_CELL.
5. Use the value retrieved as required by the particular situation and the needs of your application.

In a procedure that counts all the open windows in the application, you would loop through the record group WINDOWS, get the name of each window, and check the setting of the VISIBLE property for that window. If it is True, an internal counter is incremented by one unit. Obviously, at the and of the loop this counter will hold the number of the open windows. Figure 17.7 contains the implementation details of the function `Count_Open_Windows` that accomplishes this functionality.

17.2.4 POPULATING LIST ITEMS WITH RECORD GROUPS

In Chapter 14, you implemented several items in the block MOVIE as updateable combo lists. But a major problem with the implementation was that the lists could grow and remember the data entered by users only during one session of the application. Record groups created at runtime offer an elegant way to fix this problem with your lists.

Figure 17.8 shows the contents of the procedure `Get_Movie_Lists_Values`. This procedure retrieves the values stored in the database columns for an item implemented as a combo box in the block MOVIE. The name of the list item is passed to the procedure as an argument, which makes it usable for any combo list item in the MRD module.

```
FUNCTION Count_Open_Windows (group_name VARCHAR2,
                        group_column VARCHAR2)
RETURN NUMBER IS
 rows                 NUMBER;
 rec_group_id         RecordGroup;
 column_id            GroupColumn;
 window_id            WINDOW;
 window_name          VARCHAR2(80);
 counter              NUMBER := 0;
BEGIN
-Find ID for record group.
 rec_group_id := FIND_GROUP(group_name);
 IF ID_NULL(rec_group_id) THEN
  Message('Record Group '||group_name||' does not exist.');
  RAISE FORM_TRIGGER_FAILURE;
 END IF;
-Find ID for column of record group.
 column_id := FIND_COLUMN(group_name||'.'||group_column);
 IF ID_NULL(column_id) THEN
  Message('Column '||group_column||' does not exist in record
group '||group_name||'.');
  RAISE FORM_TRIGGER_FAILURE;
 END IF;
-Find number of rows in record group.
 rows := GET_GROUP_ROW_COUNT(rec_group_id);
 -Loop through the records to get the window name
 FOR i IN 1..rows LOOP
  window_name := GET_GROUP_CHAR_CELL( column_id, i );
  window_id := FIND_WINDOW( window_name );
  IF ID_NULL(window_id) THEN
    Message('Window '||window_name||' does not exist.');
  RAISE FORM_TRIGGER_FAILURE;
  END IF;
  IF GET_WINDOW_PROPERTY(window_id, VISIBLE) = 'TRUE' THEN
    counter := counter+1;
  END IF;
 END LOOP;
 RETURN counter;
EXCEPTION
 WHEN OTHERS THEN
  MESSAGE('Internal error occurred in Count_Open_Windows.');
  RAISE FORM_TRIGGER_FAILURE;
END;
```

FIGURE 17.7 Counting the number of open windows in an application.

```
PROCEDURE Get_Movie_Lists_Values (list_name VARCHAR2) IS
 list_id      ITEM;
 col_name     VARCHAR2(80) := SUBSTR(list_name,
INSTR(list_name, '.')+1);
 sql_stat     VARCHAR2(2000);

BEGIN
—Find ID for list item.
 list_id := FIND_ITEM(list_name);
 IF ID_NULL(list_id) THEN
  MESSAGE('List Item '||list_name||' does not exist.');
  RAISE FORM_TRIGGER_FAILURE;
 END IF;

—Build the SQL statement.
 sql_stat := 'SELECT DISTINCT '||list_name||',
'||list_name||
         ' FROM MOVIES ORDER BY 1';

 Populate_the_List(list_id, sql_stat);

EXCEPTION
 WHEN OTHERS THEN
  MESSAGE('Internal error occurred in
Get_Movie_Lists_Values.');
  RAISE FORM_TRIGGER_FAILURE;
END Get_Movie_Lists_Values;
```

FIGURE 17.8 Procedure that populates list items dynamically.

The first part of the procedure retrieves the internal ID of the list item, and the second part build the SQL SELECT statement which will populate the list with elements. The list items in the MRD module are specified in the format `<Block Name>.<Item Name>`. The names of the data items corresponds to the column name in table MOVIES, from which the data will be retrieved. This name is retrieved and stored in variable `col_name` using the SQL functions SUBSTR and INSTR. This column name is used to build the SQL statement which is then passed as an argument to the procedure `Populate_the_List`.

The SQL functions INSTR and SUBSTR were discussed in Chapter 9. INSTR is used to find the position in the string of the dot that separates the block name from the item name. Then the function SUBSTR returns the substring of the original string that begins from the character after the dot. This is also the name of the database column. Note the following features of the SELECT statement built in the procedure `Get_Movie_Lists_Values`:

- You need to select the same column twice because the first value will serve as the list element value and the second as its label.
- In order to avoid duplicate entries in the list, the DISTINCT keyword is included in the SELECT statement.
- Populating the list dynamically gives you a chance to order the list, which you cannot easily do with static lists.
- Using lookup tables to populate your list will allow the list to be changed later without changing the program as is required with a static list. Only the data in the table will need to be changed.

After the SELECT statement is prepared, it is passed together with the list ID to the procedure `Populate_the_List`, which will create the list elements based on the query. The contents of this procedure are shown in Figure 17.9.

This procedure is generic and can be used to populate any list item with elements returned by the SQL statement passed as a parameter. The record group `List_Elements` is created as a temporary container of the records returned by the query, using the function CREATE_GROUP_FROM_QUERY. After creating the group, the function POPULATE_GROUP adds the rows retrieved into the group. If this function completes successfully, it returns the value zero. This is why other statements are processed only if the variable `outcome` is zero.

Once the rows returned by the SELECT statement are in the group, the procedure POPULATE_LIST transfers them in the list item. Finally, the temporary record group `List_Elements` is destroyed by invoking the procedure DELETE_GROUP. This last step is very important for two reasons:

1. It returns the memory resources to the pool of available resources, when they are no longer needed.
2. Ensures that the next call to this function will be as successful as the first one. The function CREATE_GROUP_FROM_QUERY will fail if a record group with the name `List_Elements` already exists.

In order to add the functionality described in this section to the MRD application, create the procedures shown in Figure 17.8 and Figure 17.9. Then, append the following statements to the form-level WHEN-NEW-FORM-INSTANCE trigger:

```
Get_Movie_Lists_Values('MOVIES.ACTOR');
Get_Movie_Lists_Values('MOVIES.ACTRESS');
Get_Movie_Lists_Values('MOVIES.DIRECTOR');
Get_Movie_Lists_Values('MOVIES.COMPANY');
Get_Movie_Lists_Values('MOVIES.PRODUCER');
```

```
PROCEDURE Populate_the_List (  list_id ITEM,
                               sql_stat VARCHAR2) IS
 group_id    RecordGroup;
 outcome     NUMBER;

BEGIN
—Create temporary record group.
 group_id := CREATE_GROUP_FROM_QUERY('List_Elements,'
sql_stat);
 IF ID_NULL(group_id) THEN
  MESSAGE('Record Group could not be created in
Populate_the_List.');
  RAISE FORM_TRIGGER_FAILURE;
 END IF;

—Populate record group.
 outcome := POPULATE_GROUP(group_id);
 IF outcome <> 0 THEN
  MESSAGE('Record Group could not be populated in
Populate_the_List.');
  RAISE FORM_TRIGGER_FAILURE;
 END IF;

—Populate list item
 POPULATE_LIST(list_id, group_id);

—Destroy the temporary record group to release resources
 DELETE_GROUP(group_id);

EXCEPTION
 WHEN OTHERS THEN
  MESSAGE('Internal error occurred in Populate_the_List.');
  RAISE FORM_TRIGGER_FAILURE;
END Populate_the_List;
```

FIGURE 17.9 Using record groups to populate lists dynamically.

If the application will be used only by a single user at any one time, populating the list when the form is initialized is satisfactory for your needs. The fact that you get an initial snapshot of the elements of the list, coupled with the functionality added to the property class UPDATEABLE_COMBO in Chapter 15, will guarantee that your user will see all the current members of the list. However in an intensive multi-user data-entry application, there may be a need to refresh the content of the list frequently. The built-in procedure CLEAR_LIST could be used to clear the contents of the current list, and the procedure `Populate_the_List` could be called again to take the most up-to-date snapshot of the list. It is difficult to offer a general rule about how often you should refresh the list. It is a decision that you will have to make depending on the load of your database server and on the traffic in your network. The type of functionality implemented here should be limited to lists of no more than twenty entries or so. If you expect the lists to grow larger, you may have to add some filtering capabilities that will allow your users to narrow the scope of the query before actually executing it.

> **TIP**
>
> If the contents of the list are likely to change frequently during one session, you may need to refresh it each time the list is accessed. A simple way to do this is to attach a List of Values dialog box to the text item. Section 17.3 discusses the properties of LOVs.

17.2.5 IMPLEMENTING MULTI-SELECTION LISTS WITH RECORD GROUPS

As discussed in Chapter 14, multiple-selection lists are an extension of check box items. They allow your users to select several options from a long list of choices. This section discusses the process of creating a multi-selection list. There are several methods to implement multi-selection lists in your applications, and you can be as inventive as you want. However, there are a few standard functions that each multi-select list should have.

1. Usually, the list of available options appears on the left, and a list of choices made is shown to the right.
2. Some explicit action, such clicking a button or double-clicking an item selects it.
3. When users select an item, they must have a visual cue that the item is selected. Normally, the selection is removed from the list of available items and transferred to the list of selected options.
4. If users select an item, they must also be able to de-select it.
5. It is desirable sometimes to select, or deselect, all the choices in an option list.

In this section, you will create a multi-selection list that will allow the users of the MRD application to pick several or all the customers from the list of the active customers for the purpose of printing their addresses in envelopes. The list will have all the functionality described above. Follow these steps to create the necessary data items, controls and windows for the multi-select list in the MRD form:

1. Create a control block, a canvas, and a window, all called MAIL.
2. Set the properties of the window MAIL based on the property class MDI_DIALOG_BOX and set its Title property to "Print Envelopes."
3. Create a one-to-one correspondence between the canvas and the window by setting the Window property of the canvas to 'MAIL' and the Primary Canvas property of the window to "MAIL."
4. Display the canvas MAIL on the Layout Editor and create two text list items in the block MAIL. Call them AVAILABLE and SELECTED. Set the property Prompt to "Available Customers" and "Selected Customers," respectively. Set the properties Prompt Attachment Edge to "Top" and Prompt Attachment Offset to "3" for both items.
5. Create one element for each list with label and value NULL. You can do this by completely erasing the default entries in the List Elements and List Elements Values fields of the List Item Elements dialog box.
6. Create five push buttons and name them PRINT, CLOSE_MAIL, HELP_MAIL, SELECT, SELECT_ALL, DESELECT, and DESELECT_ALL.
7. Set the properties Width to "48" and Height to "14" for the buttons PRINT, CLOSE_MAIL, HELP_MAIL.
8. Set the properties Width to "14" and Height to "14" for the buttons SELECT, SELECT_ALL, DESELECT, and DESELECT_ALL.
9. Set PRINT to be the default button.
10. Arrange and align the items on the canvas to obtain a layout similar to the one shown in Figure 17.10.

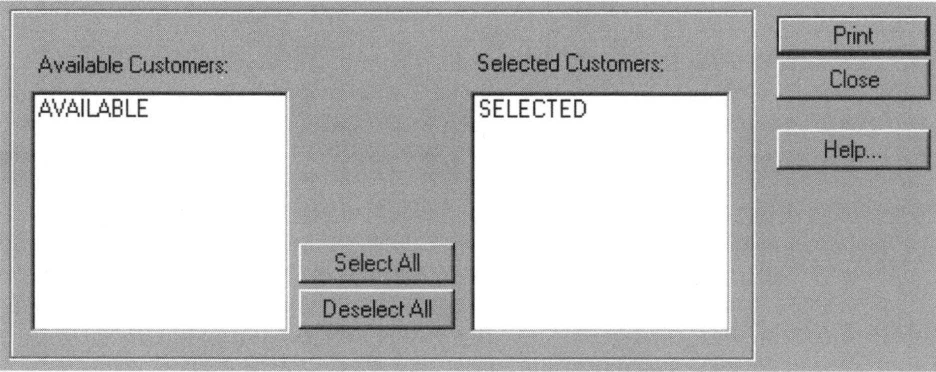

FIGURE 17.10 Multi-select lists.

Now create the program units that will implement the functionality of the multi-select list. First, create a procedure, called `Get_Customers`, that will populate any of the lists with the names of all active customers in the database. This procedure is almost identical to the procedure `Get_Movie_Lists_Values` shown in Figure 17.8. It ensures that the list name is a valid item's name, creates a SELECT statement, and invokes the procedure `Populate_the_List` to add the rows returned by the query to the list.

The only difference between the procedures `Get_Customers` and `Get_Movie_Lists_Values` is the SELECT statement that will populate the lists. This statement for `Get_Customers` is shown in Figure 17.11.

The first name and the last name of each customer are concatenated—with a space in between—and form the list elements' labels. The customer ID numbers are retrieved as character values and form the list elements' values. When the list will be populated from the record group created from this query, the names will be displayed on the screen, while the customer IDs will be the values of the list item behind the scene. In general, record groups can be created with columns of data types other than CHAR. However, if these record groups will populate lists, they must have exactly two columns of CHAR data type, of which the first will provide the list elements with labels and the second with values. This is the reason why the column ID of numeric data type is converted to an alphanumeric string in the select statement of the procedure `Get_Customers`.

The statement shown in Figure 17.11 demonstrates two simple techniques that are often used to build dynamic SQL statements at runtime:

1. To store a single quote in the string precede it with another single quote as in the WHERE clause of the statement.
2. If a character string is too long to fit in the PL/SQL Editor window, you can split it in pieces, which are joined together by the concatenation operator `||`.

The statement in Figure 17.11 is broken in several lines for the sake of clarity but also to give you a hint. The components of this statement such as the WHERE clause or ORDER BY clause, need not be hard-coded; they can be other character strings as well. In fact you can provide the users with a dialog box in which they

```
sql_stat := 'SELECT FIRST_NAME||'' ''||LAST_NAME,
TO_CHAR(ID) '||
      'FROM CUSTOMERS '||
      'WHERE STATUS = ''A'' '||
      'ORDER BY 1';
```

FIGURE 17.11 Constructing SQL statements at Runtime.

can enter their query or ordering criteria at runtime. These criteria are bundled in separate strings, which then are concatenated to form the complete SELECT statement. This technique—dynamic SQL—allows you to write very generic, flexible, and situation-independent routines.

The procedure `Get_Customers` should clear both list items and populate the list AVAILABLE when the dialog box is first accessed. This functionality can be implemented by following these steps:

1. Create a WHEN-NEW-BLOCK-INSTANCE trigger for the block MAIL.
2. In the body of the trigger add the following statements:

```
CLEAR_LIST('MAIL.AVAILABLE');
CLEAR_LIST('MAIL.SELECTED');
Get_Customers('MAIL.AVAILABLE');
```

The procedure `Get_Customers` will also be used to select or deselect all the items in the list. The code will be executed whenever the users press any of the SELECT_ALL and DESELECT_ALL push buttons. These are the actions required to implement the functionality for the button SELECT_ALL:

1. Create a WHEN-BUTTON-PRESSED trigger for button SELECT_ALL.
2. Enter the statements in the body of the trigger as follows:

```
CLEAR_LIST('MAIL.AVAILABLE');
Get_Customers('MAIL.SELECTED');
GO_ITEM('MAIL.SELECTED');
```

To implement the functionality for the button DESELECT_ALL, follow these steps:

1. Create a WHEN-BUTTON-PRESSED trigger for button DESELECT_ALL.
2. Enter the statements in the body of the trigger as follows:

```
CLEAR_LIST('MAIL.SELECTED');
Get_Customers('MAIL.AVAILABLE');
GO_ITEM('MAIL.AVAILABLE');
```

When the SELECT_ALL button is pressed, the trigger clears the list AVAILABLE, populates the list SELECTED, and navigates to that list. The visual effect of this would be that all the customer names will move from the list box Available to the list box Selected. Pressing the DESELECT_ALL button performs the same actions but in the reverse order of lists.

Now, create the code that will move a list element from one list to the other when users double-click it. Recall from Chapter 14 that text lists have a particular trigger, WHEN-LIST-ACTIVATED, that is fired when an element in the list is double-clicked. In this trigger you will place the code that removes the element double-clicked in one list and inserts it in the other list. The procedure `Move_Current_Element` implements such a functionality. This procedure takes as arguments the name of the list item where the element currently is and the name of the list item where this element will be inserted. The value of the element that was clicked is stored in a local variable using the built-in function NAME_IN. The procedure basically loops through the list that was double-clicked until it finds the element that was clicked. When this element is found, its label is retrieved using the list function GET_LIST_ELEMENT_VALUE. An element with the label and the value of the clicked element is inserted into the target list using the procedure ADD_LIST_ELEMENT. The argument 1 passed to this procedure indicates the index of the element to be added in the list. The element itself is deleted from the original list using the built-in DELETE_LIST_ELEMENT and the loop is terminated. Figure 17.12 contains all the details you need to create this procedure.

The fact that the procedure `Move_Current_Element` is generic and does not depend on the particular list items with which it is used, allows you to implement the trigger WHEN-LIST-ACTIVATED at the block level. Figure 17.13 shows the body of the trigger WHEN-LIST-ACTIVATED. The system variable SYSTEM.TRIGGER_ITEM in this trigger is used to capture the name of the button pressed that causes the trigger to fire.

A similar approach can be used to create a block-level WHEN-BUTTON-PRESSED trigger that will fire when the buttons SELECT and DESELECT are pressed. The following statements show the contents of this trigger:

```
DECLARE
 button_activated VARCHAR2(50) := :SYSTEM.TRIGGER_ITEM;

BEGIN
 IF button_activated = 'MAIL.SELECT' THEN
   Move_Current_Element('MAIL.AVAILABLE',
'MAIL.SELECTED');
 ELSIF button_activated = 'MAIL.DESELECT' THEN
   Move_Current_Element('MAIL.SELECTED',
'MAIL.AVAILABLE');
 END IF;
END;
```

```
PROCEDURE Move_Current_Element (from_list_name VARCHAR2,
                                to_list_name  VARCHAR2) IS
 list_id          ITEM;
 list_count NUMBER;
 current_value    VARCHAR2(50);
 clicked_value    VARCHAR2(50) :=
NAME_IN(from_list_name);
 clicked_label    VARCHAR2(80);

BEGIN
 list_id := FIND_ITEM(from_list_name);
 IF ID_NULL(list_id) THEN
  MESSAGE('List Item '||from_list_name||' does not
exist.');
  RAISE FORM_TRIGGER_FAILURE;
 END IF;
 list_count := GET_LIST_ELEMENT_COUNT(list_id);

 FOR i IN 1..list_count LOOP
  current_value := GET_LIST_ELEMENT_VALUE(list_id, i);
  IF clicked_value = current_value THEN
    clicked_label := GET_LIST_ELEMENT_LABEL(list_id, i);
    ADD_LIST_ELEMENT(to_list_name, 1, clicked_label,
clicked_value);
    DELETE_LIST_ELEMENT(list_id, i);
    EXIT;
  END IF;
 END LOOP;

EXCEPTION
 WHEN OTHERS THEN
  Message('Internal error occurred in
Move_Current_Element.');
  RAISE FORM_TRIGGER_FAILURE;
END Move_Current_Element;
```

FIGURE 17.12 Implementing multi-selection lists.

```
DECLARE
 list_activated VARCHAR2(50) := :SYSTEM.TRIGGER_ITEM;

BEGIN
 IF list_activated = 'MAIL.SELECTED' THEN
   Move_Current_Element('MAIL.SELECTED',
'MAIL.AVAILABLE');
 ELSIF list_activated = 'MAIL.AVAILABLE' THEN
   Move_Current_Element('MAIL.AVAILABLE',
'MAIL.SELECTED');
 END IF;
END;
```

FIGURE 17.13 Moving elements from one list to the other.

You can now save and generate the module, and run it to see the functionality of the list. Select Block | Next or Block | Previous form the menu until the focus navigates to the block MAIL. Try selecting and deselecting several customers. Test also the Select All and Deselect All functionality.

TIP

In this case, you replaced triggers of the same type (WHEN-LIST-ACTIVATED) for two objects, with a trigger of the same type, but attached to the parent of these objects. This approach allows you to reduce the number of PL/SQL objects to edit and maintain at any one time, and makes the application's logic more compact. It also makes the application leaner and more efficient at runtime. The approach can be used very successfully during the prototyping phase of the application as well. You can create the screens you need, and place the necessary data items and controls there. Then you create triggers in the upper levels of the hierarchy that contain a few calls to modularized functions and procedures. These program units need not be implemented in detail in the prototyping stage. For example, the procedure Move_Current_Element could simply display a message like: "Will move element from list A to list B. Development in process." As you develop the prototype to an operational system, the messages in the program units bodies are replaced by the working PL/SQL statements, but the trigger will not need to be modified.

17.3 LISTS OF VALUES

Lists of Values (LOVs) are a special type of single selection lists that can be used very effectively and with little effort to display data to the users and allow them to pick the desired element. LOVs are a combination of modal dialog boxes, lists and record groups, therefore they have characteristics from each of these type of objects. The following paragraphs list some of these characteristics:

- LOVs are modal dialog boxes. They will prevent users from accessing any other areas of the application as long as they are displayed. Users must dismiss them by making a selection, or by canceling the operation altogether in order to be able to proceed with their work.
- LOVs can be used to simply present data, but they are primarily used to pick a value and store it into a text item, and, from there, into a database column. Because they come packaged with a search engine and Automatic-reduction features, they could replace very effectively list items that need to display a large number of elements. Furthermore, because the LOVs can build the list of elements they display each time they are invoked, they guarantee that the users will see the most up-to-date version of the list.
- LOVs are built on top of record groups. In general, associating lists with record groups is a relatively easy process. However, the association of LOVs with their underlying record groups is even easier, and almost transparent for you.

17.3.1 CREATING LISTS OF VALUES

In the MRD application, you will use the LOVs in two blocks:

- **CUSTOMERS.** In this block, you will display, populate and validate data entered in the STATE item of the address of a customer using a LOV dialog box.
- **RENTALS.** In this block, you will display and populate the customers renting a movie and the movie being rented.

This section explains in detail how you add LOV functionality to the STATE item. Using a similar approach you can easily implement the other two instances of this functionality. The lookup data that will be used to implement the STATE LOV are stored in the table STATES. This table is created by the script that installed the database objects for the MRD application. It has only two columns and fifty rows. Each row contains the abbreviated postal code and the full name for each state in the United States. In this section, you will implement the following functionality:

1. There will be a push button to the right of the STATE item that the users can click if they want to display the LOVs dialog box.
2. Users can enter the value of a state directly in the STATE item. If they enter a valid value, they will be allowed to proceed; otherwise, the LOVs dialog box will be displayed to allow users to pick the right value.
3. The LOVs will display the full names of the states, but the values stored in the item will be the abbreviated postal codes to conserve storage space.

To create a new LOV object select Tools | LOV Wizard from the menu. As said earlier, under each LOVs there is a record group. The first screen of the LOV Wizard gives you the opportunity to select a record group that already exists or to create a new one. Simply select one of the radio buttons shown in Figure 17.14 to determine which path you want to proceed.

If the record group already exists, you can choose the second radio button in the list and then select it from the list of the record groups currently defined in the module. The record groups upon which the LOV object will be based can be

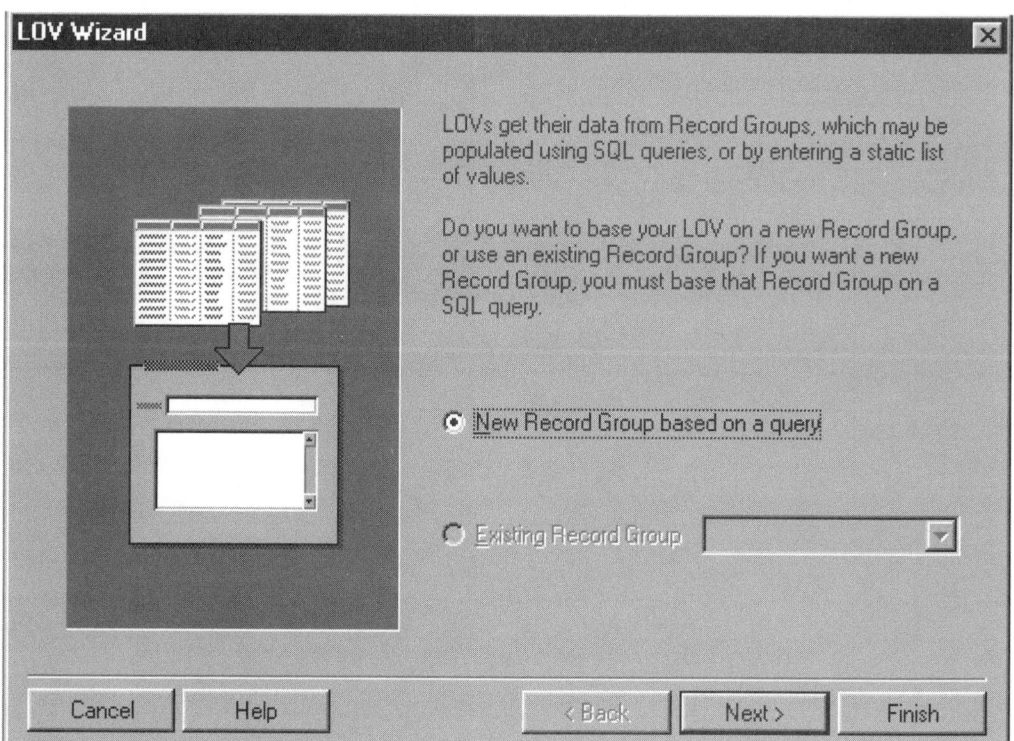

FIGURE 17.14 LOV Wizard Starting Screen.

created on the fly in the next screen by entering the SELECT Statement in the SQL Query Statement, as in the example of Figure 17.15. If you select the Build SQL Query button, you will be taken to a Query Builder function. The third option is to import the SQL query from a text file.

After specifying the query statement, click next to display the screen shown in Figure 17.16. In this screen you choose which columns will show in the LOV.

The column properties can be adjusted in the next screen of the LOV wizard as shown in Figure 17.17. You can also specify the return item for the LOV at this stage. If you click the Lookup Return Item Button, a Return Items Dialog Box appears and allows you to choose any item in the form as shown in Figure 17.18.

The next screen in the LOV Wizard allows you to specify the Title of the LOV, the size and screen position as shown in Figure 17.19.

Clicking the Next button shows the Advanced properties of the LOV, shown in Figure 17.20. If the data to be shown in the LOV rarely changes you can uncheck the Refresh record group data before displaying LOV button to get quicker display of the LOV.

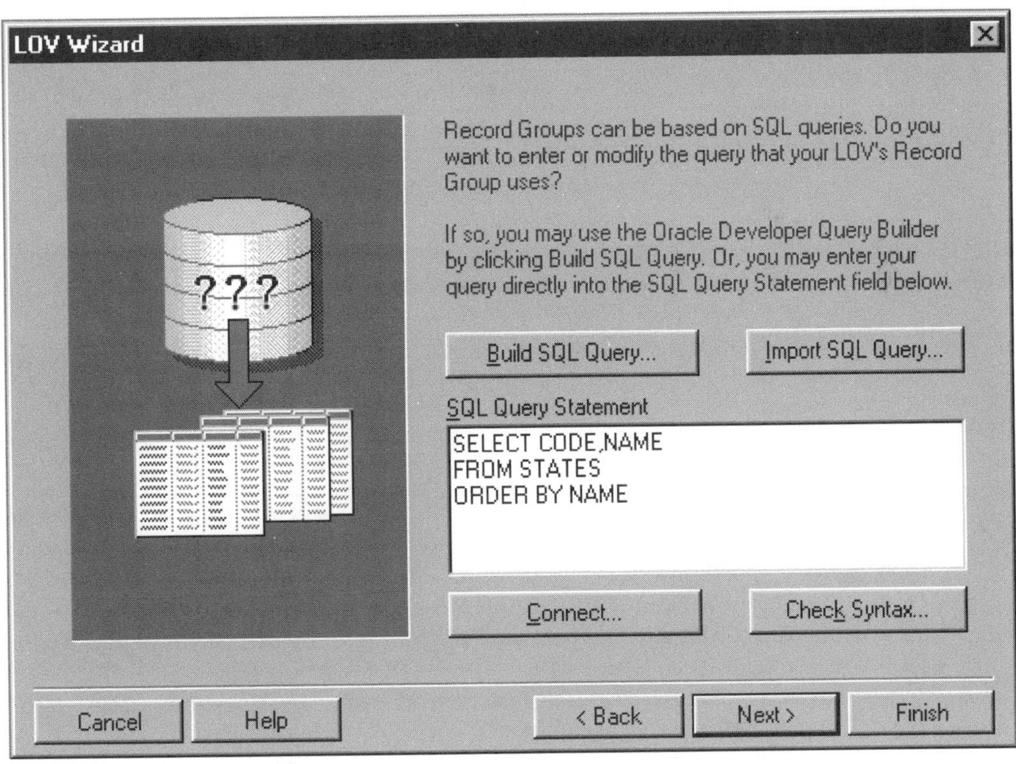

FIGURE 17.15 LOV Wizard Record Group Screen

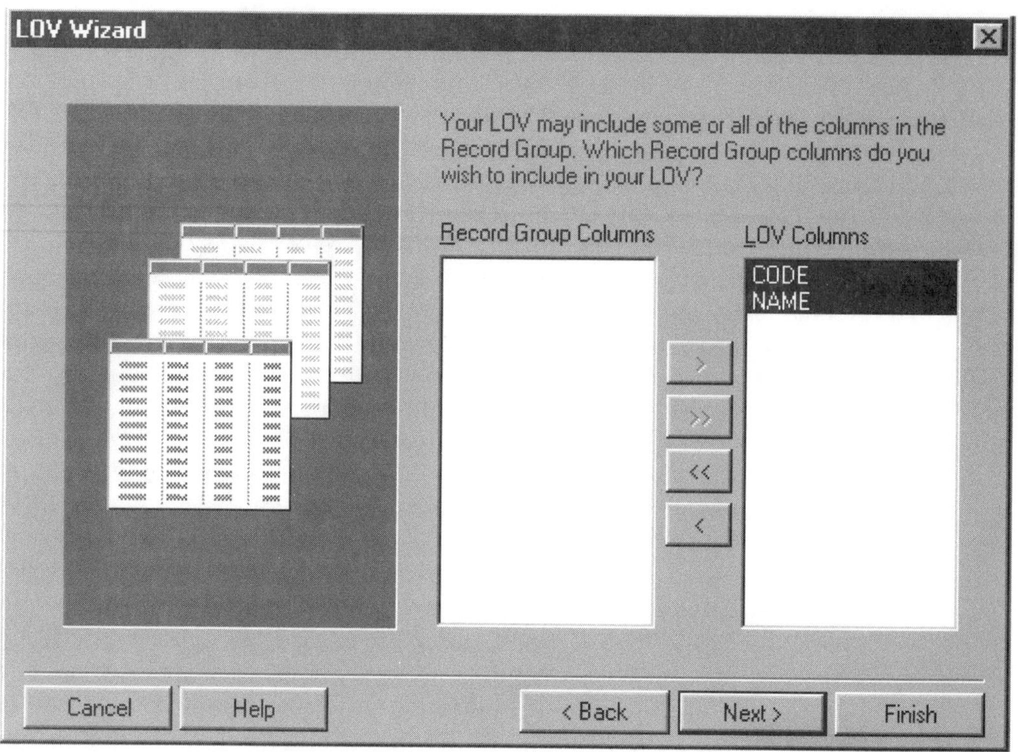

FIGURE 17.16 Record Group Columns Screen.

If you have chosen return item(s), you can move the Return Items to be Assigned Items column as shown in Figure 17.21. This inserts the name of the LOV in the List of Values property of that item but does not set the Validate from List property to "YES" for that item. Most of the time you will want to set the Validate from List property to "YES" after you finish the LOV Wizard. If you click Finish on any of the Screens the LOV Wizard will use default values for the rest of the information required. If it is missing any required information you will be prompted to enter the information. When you click Finish the LOV will be created and named LOVxxx where xxx is a number. A record group is also be created with the same name. You will probably want to rename the LOV and Record Group to something meaningful such as STATE in our example.

If you have an existing LOV selected in the Object Navigator and choose TOOLS | LOV Wizard, the Wizard will display as one screen with tabs. This format allows you to quickly make modifications to the LOV without stepping through all of the screens. You have access to the same parameters as when building a new LOV.

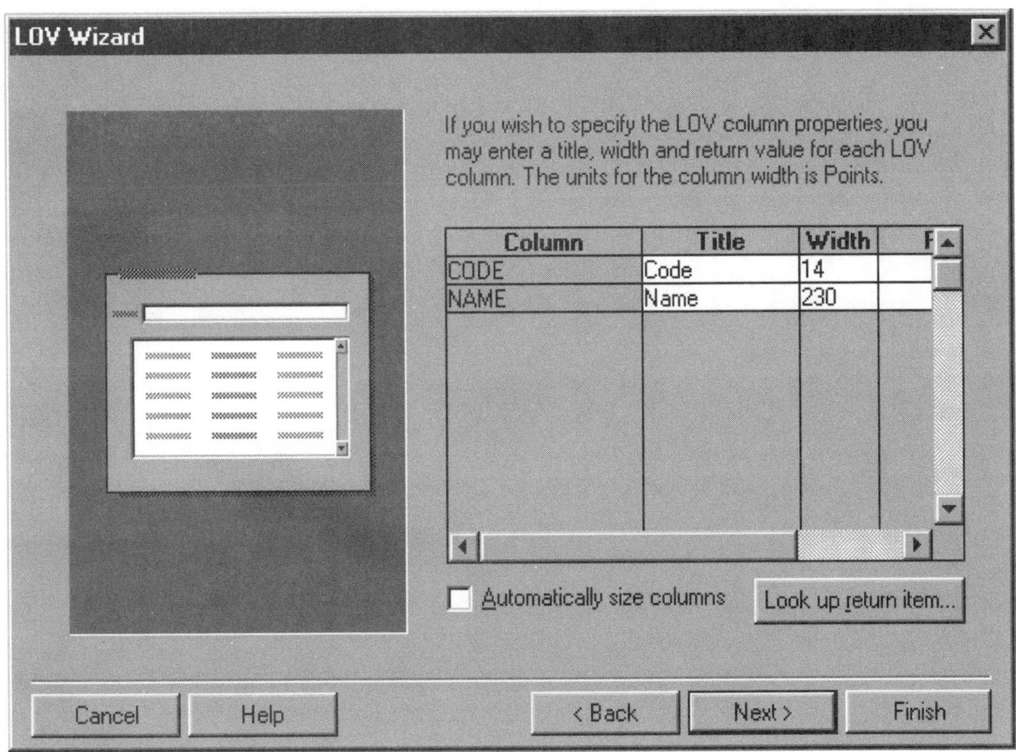

FIGURE 17.17 LOV Wizard Column Properties.

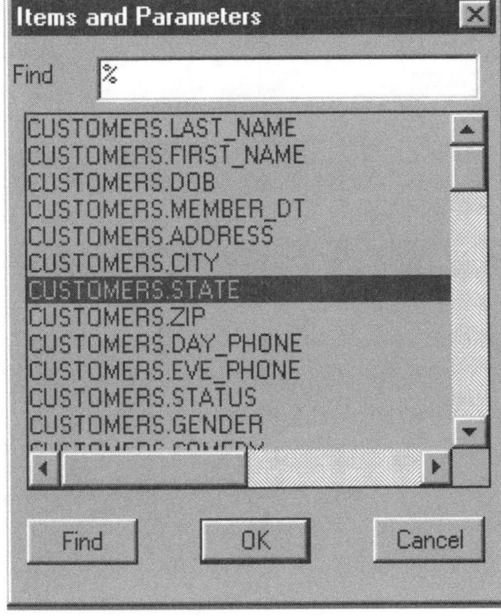

FIGURE 17.18 Return Items Dialog Box.

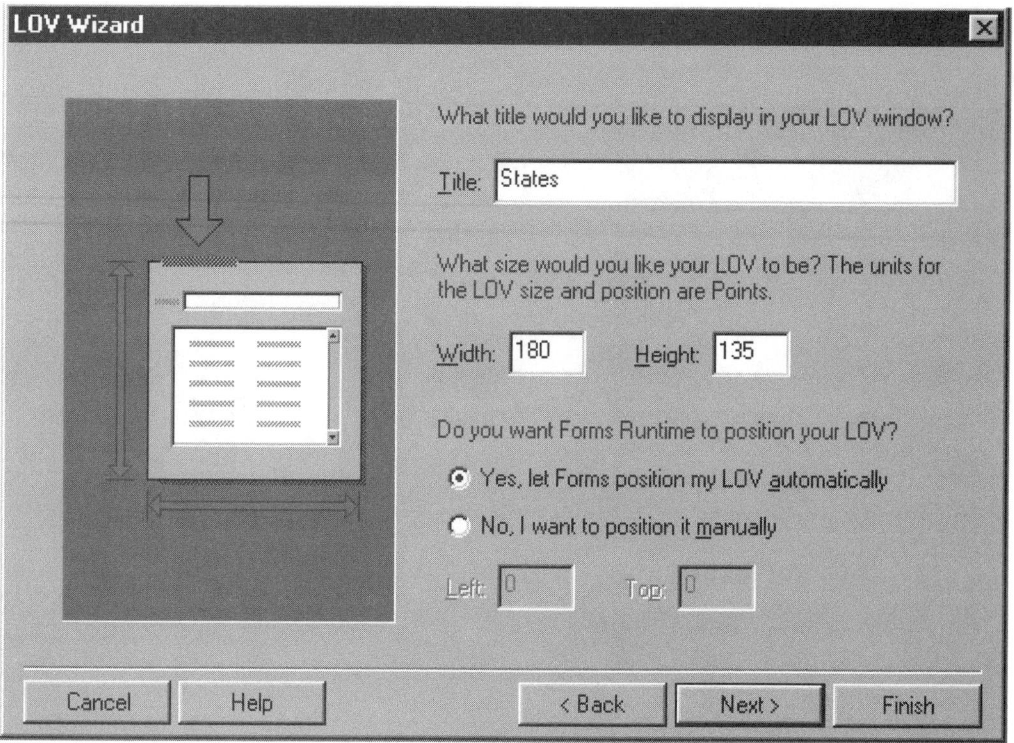

FIGURE 17.19 LOV Wizard Title and Size screen.

After you have created the STATE LOV as shown above, you can create a LOV that displays the first and last names of customers and another one that displays the titles of movies stored in tapes. The following statements should serve as the SELECT statements upon which these LOVs and their record groups are based:

```
SELECT ID, FIRST_NAME||' '||LAST_NAME
FROM CUSTOMERS
ORDER BY 2

SELECT TAPES.ID, MOVIES.TITLE
FROM MOVIES, TAPES
WHERE MOVIES.ID = TAPES.MOVIE_ID
ORDER BY 2
```

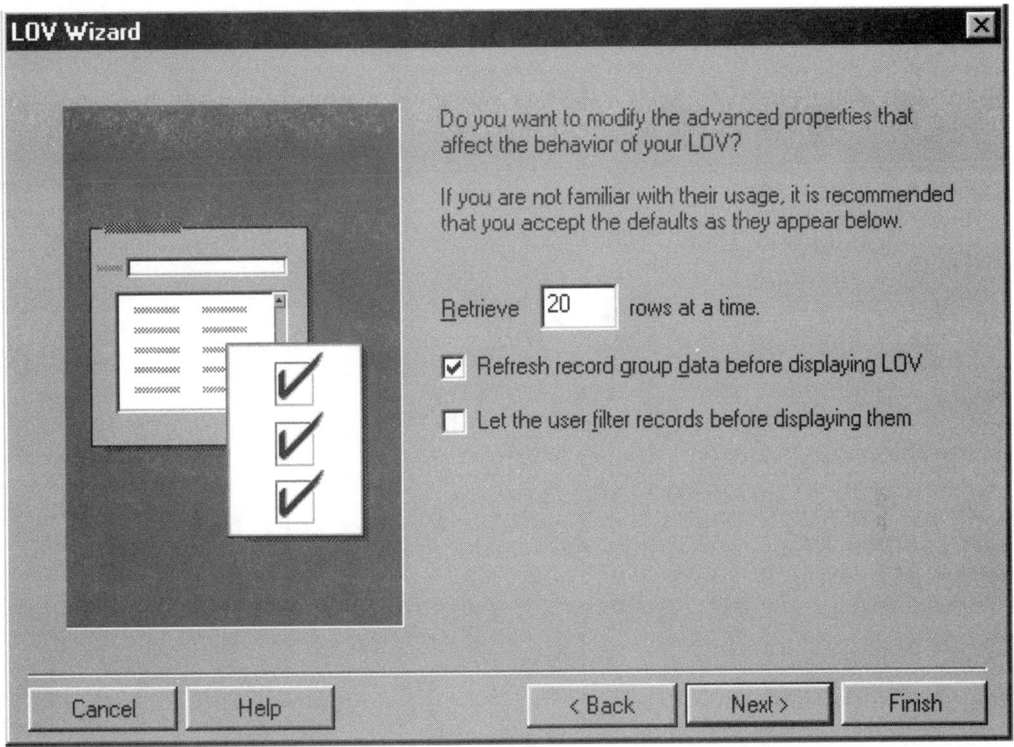

FIGURE 17.20 LOV Wizard Advanced Properties.

Now, you can set the other properties of the newly created LOVs. The connection between the LOV object and the STATE text item in the CUSTOMER block is established in the LOV Column Mapping dialog box (see Figure 17.22). This dialog box is displayed by double-clicking the property Column Mapping Properties in the Functional group of the LOV Property Palette.

Click the CODE column in the Column Names list, and set the Return Item field to CUSTOMER.STATE, and the Display Width to zero, as shown in Figure 17.22. With these settings, Forms Runtime will not display the column CODE in the LOV window, but, if an element is selected from the list, the value in column CODE will be stored in the STATE item. Because this column will not be displayed, the setting of the Column Title is not important in this case. For the NAME column, the Return Item will be NULL This means that no item in the form will receive this value. Set the Display Width to 180 and change the Column Title to "States." Use a similar approach to set the properties of the other two LOVs.

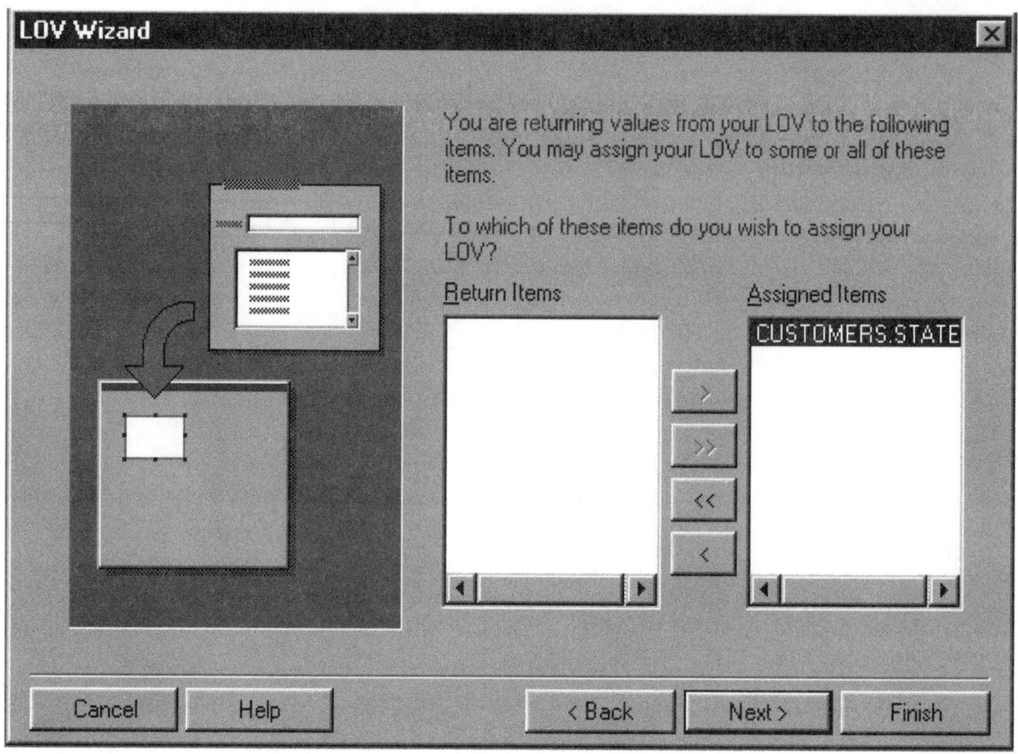

FIGURE 17.21 LOV Wizard Return Items Screen.

17.3.2 PROPERTIES OF LISTS OF VALUES

There are several properties that govern the behavior of the LOV object at runtime. You can set them in the Property Palette. The visual attributes of the LOV dialog box are located in the group Font & Color. As for other objects, they are best maintained using a named visual attribute object as a setting for the property Visual Attribute Group. Although you have the flexibility to define the visual attributes for each object, I recommend that you set these properties to match the look and feel of the other canvases in your applications.

Like any other window in your application, you want to set the coordinates, dimensions, and title of the LOV dialog box, as well. The properties that control the dimensions and the location of the dialog box on the screen are part of the Physical group. As with other windows, setting properties like Width, Height, X Position and Y Position at design time affects only the initial display of the LOV dialog box. Users then can resize and move the window around as they want. For the LOV object being discussed here set both Width and Height to 200. Rather

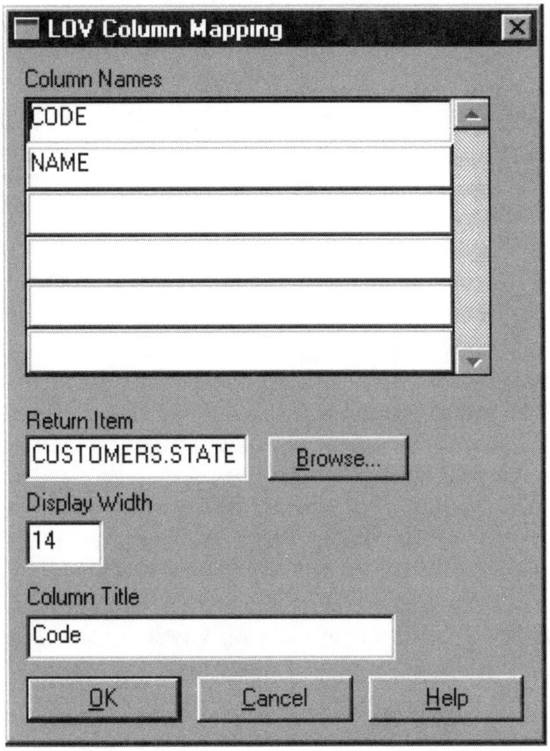

FIGURE 17.22 LOV Column Mapping dialog box.

than specifying the position of the window by setting the properties X Position and Y Position, I recommend that you leave them at their default settings and, instead, set the property Automatic Position to "Yes." This property is located in the Functional group and, when set, displays the dialog box close to the item from which the LOV is invoked. I prefer this approach over the first one because it makes the display of your application more flexible and more responsive to the actions of users at runtime. A third approach is to determine the position of the LOV at runtime and display it dynamically. The following section shows an example of how you implement this approach. The Functional group contains one more property that affect the display of the LOV window at runtime. This is Title and it controls the string displayed in the title bar of the window. For the LOV being implemented, set Title to "List of States," "List of Customers," and "List of Movies."

The Functional group contains a number of other properties that control the behavior of the LOV dialog box. They are described in the following paragraphs:

- **Automatic Select.** This property defines the behavior of the control when the list is reduced to a single element through the automatic reduction process. If it is set to "Yes," that element is picked automatically without the users having to confirm the selection. By default, it is set to "No."

- **Automatic Display.** If this property is set to "Yes," each time the Forms focus is on the item to which the LOV is attached, the LOV dialog box will be displayed. The default setting for both these properties is "No." Setting this property to "Yes" may have some advantages, especially for data-entry applications. However, experience has shows that users get really annoyed when dialog boxes, such as this one, are displayed automatically, without an action more explicit than just focusing on the item.
- **Automatic Refresh.** This property is set to "Yes" by default. This means that each time the LOV dialog box will be invoked, the query through which its record group is populated will be executed. If the property is set to "No," the query is executed only the first time the LOV is invoked. Setting this property requires balancing the need to have the most up-to-date version of the list with the cost of performing a query and fetching data across the network each time the LOV control is accessed. In cases when the list items do not change frequently, as in the STATES example, set this property to "No." At runtime, the query to populate the list will be performed only once, the first time the LOV's dialog box is invoked. After that, Forms will cache the data and display them from the cache rather than re-executing the query when the dialog box needs to be displayed again.
- **Filter Before Display.** Recall from the discussion about blocks that Forms uses array processing mechanisms to limit the number of those records returned by a query that are actually fetched to the client application. Unfortunately, LOVs do not utilize a similar control. They will fetch all the data to the client when invoked. However, by setting the property Filter Before Display to "Yes," each time the LOV's dialog box is invoked, a preliminary filter is displayed were the users can display additional criteria to narrow the scope of the query. By default this property is set to "No."
- **Automatic Skip.** This property is set to 'No' by default. With this setting, the cursor lands on the item from which the LOV's dialog box was invoked, when a selection is made. Set this property to "Yes" to save the users the extra keystroke to navigate outside this item. In such a case, when the selection is made, the focus moves to the next item.

For the LOVs STATE preserve the default settings of all the properties except for Automatic Refresh which should be set to "No," and Automatic Skip which should be set to "Yes." The reason for the setting of Automatic Refresh is that the list of States will practically never change, therefore it can be populated only once when the LOV is invoked for the first time. However, for the other two LOVs keep Automatic Refresh set to "No." In order to display the LOV dialog boxes close to the items, set their property Automatic Position to "Yes."

17.3.3 MODIFYING PROPERTIES OF LISTS OF VALUES AT RUNTIME

Properties of LOVs can be retrieved and modified dynamically using the functions FIND_LOV, ID_NULL, GET_LOV_PROPERTY and the procedure SET_LOV_PROPERTY. The function SHOW_LOV is used to display a LOV dialog box explicitly. This function returns the Boolean value TRUE if the users select an item from the list, or FALSE if they cancel the dialog box.

There is little difference in they way you use these program units for LOVs from the way you use them for other Form Builder objects discussed up to now. Figure 17.23 contains the implementation of the function `Show_Centered_LOV`. This function is an enhancement to the built-in SHOW_LOV because it displays the LOVs dialog box in a central position with respect to the MDI frame of the application. Add the function `Show_Centered_LOV` in the module MRD since it will be used to display the LOV STATE created earlier.

17.3.4 ATTACHING LISTS OF VALUES TO TEXT ITEMS

Now attach the LOVs STATE to the item CUSTOMER.STATE by following these steps:

1. Display the Property Palette for this item.
2. Set the property List of Values in the List of Values (LOV) group to "STATE."
3. Set the property Validate from List to "Yes."

This last setting will guarantee that each value entered by the users will be checked against the LOV. If the entry does not match a state code, the LOV's dialog box will be displayed. The entry in the item serves as a criterion to reduce the number of elements displayed in the list.

Note that the properties List X Position and List Y Position in the List of Values (LOV) group are one more place to determine the location of the LOV's dialog box at runtime. With all the options you have to determine the position of this window, you may rightly wonder which one to use. In order to help you find the appropriate place to set these properties, keep in mind that Forms Runtime determines the position of the LOV's dialog box by following these steps:

1. If the properties List X Position and List Y Position for the item are not set to 0, their settings determine the position of the dialog box.
2. Else, if the property Automatic Position is set to "Yes,"' display the LOV's dialog box close to the associated item.
3. Else, display the dialog box according to the values of properties X Position and Y Position for the LOV object.

```
FUNCTION Show_Centered_LOV (LOV_name VARCHAR2)
RETURN BOOLEAN IS
 LOV_id           LOV;
 x_coord          NUMBER := 0;
 y_coord          NUMBER := 0;
 LOV_width        NUMBER;
 LOV_height       NUMBER;
 mdi_width        NUMBER;
 mdi_height       NUMBER;
 cell_height      NUMBER;
 current_form     VARCHAR2(80);
 LOV_Not_Found    EXCEPTION;
BEGIN
 LOV_id := FIND_LOV(LOV_name);
 IF ID_NULL(LOV_id) THEN
  RAISE LOV_Not_Found;
 END IF;

 mdi_width := GET_WINDOW_PROPERTY(FORMS_MDI_WINDOW,WIDTH) ;
 mdi_height := GET_WINDOW_PROPERTY(FORMS_MDI_WINDOW,HEIGHT) ;
 current_form := GET_APPLICATION_PROPERTY(CURRENT_FORM_NAME);
 cell_height := GET_FORM_PROPERTY(current_form,
CHARACTER_CELL_HEIGHT);
 mdi_height := mdi_height - 1.35*cell_height;

 LOV_width  := GET_LOV_PROPERTY(LOV_id, WIDTH);
 LOV_height  := GET_LOV_PROPERTY(LOV_id, HEIGHT);

 IF ( mdi_width > LOV_width ) THEN
  x_coord := (mdi_width - LOV_width) / 2;
 END IF;
 IF ( mdi_height > LOV_height ) THEN
  y_coord := (mdi_height - LOV_height) / 2;
 END IF;

 SET_LOV_PROPERTY(LOV_id, POSITION, x_coord, y_coord);

 RETURN (SHOW_LOV(LOV_id));
EXCEPTION
 WHEN LOV_Not_Found THEN
  MESSAGE('List of Values '||LOV_name||' does not exist.');
  RAISE FORM_TRIGGER_FAILURE;
 WHEN OTHERS THEN
  MESSAGE('Internal error occurred in Show_LOV.');
  RAISE FORM_TRIGGER_FAILURE;
END;
```

FIGURE 17.23 Retrieving and Modifying Properties of List of Values Dynamically.

Save, generate and execute the form and see for yourself how the LOV's dialog box will help your users enter and validate your data. When the cursor is in the item STATE you will see the status lamp `<LOV>` appear in the message bar. This serves as an indicator to the users that there is a list of values associated with the item. As long as you are inside the STATE item, you will be able to display the LOV at any time by pressing the [LIST OF VALUES] key. When you press the [LIST OF VALUES] key, you will see the LOV STATE displayed close to the location of the item STATE. The reason is that Forms will perform the checks listed in the previous paragraph, it will arrive at step 2 and it will display the dialog box according to this step. In order to use the function `Show_Centered_LOV`, attach the trigger KEY-LISTVAL to the item state and enter its contents as shown in Figure 17.24.

Users in a GUI platform would expect to be able to display the LOV with a mouse click as well. For this reason you should create a push button that will serve the purpose.

1. Create a push button in the block CUSTOMERS and name it STATE_LOV.
2. Set the properties Iconic to "Yes," Icon Filename to "listval," Width to 14 and Height to 14. Note that the file listval.ico is provided by the Form Builder.
3. Align the button horizontally with the text item STATE.
4. Set the property Keyboard Navigable to "No." Users do not need to place the focus on this button. Just clicking it will be sufficient.
5. Create a WHEN-BUTTON-PRESSED trigger that will display the LOV dialog box. Enter the contents of the trigger as shown below.

```
GO_ITEM('CUSTOMERS.STATE');
DO_KEY('LIST_VALUES');
```

```
DECLARE
 ok_button BOOLEAN;
BEGIN
 ok_button := Show_Centered_LOV('STATE');
END;
```

FIGURE 17.24 Displaying a List of Values programmatically.

17.4 TEXT EDITORS

There may be occasions, when you will need to create or maintain long strings of characters in your application. If users need to access these data items often, they may find it very cumbersome having to scroll through a single-line item to read its contents. The first thing to try in these occasions is to implement such items as multi-line text items. If it is necessary, a scroll bar can be added to them. However, depending on the size of the data, even this approach may not offer the desired results. In addition, when working with large amounts of text, users may expect to have some basic editing tools such as search and replace, or cut and paste.

The solution to these situations is to display the contents of the text item in a text editor and let the users benefit from its functionality. To implement this solution, you can use the Forms Runtime internal text editor, or a system editor such as Notepad. The MRD application may need a text editor to display and edit the customer's address in the block CUSTOMER1.

A good way to implement the editor functionality for a text item, is the approach used in the Property Palette to give you access to properties such as Comment, that may contain long strings of text. You will place an iconic button by the side of the ADDRESS item. This button will display the editor when pressed.

1. Display the canvas CUST_MATRIX_STACKED in the Layout Editor and reduce the item ADDRESS.
2. Create a push button in the block CUSTOMERS1 between the items ADDRESS and CITY and name it ADDRESS_EDIT.
3. Set the properties Iconic to "Yes," Icon Filename to "edit," Width to 14 and Height to 14. Note that the file edit.ico is provided by the Form Builder.
4. Align the button horizontally with the text item ADDRESS.
5. Set the property Keyboard Navigable to "No." Users do not need to place the focus on this button. Just clicking it will be sufficient.
6. Create a WHEN-BUTTON-PRESSED trigger for this button, and place these statements in its body:

```
GO_ITEM('CUSTOMERS1.ADDRESS');
EDIT_TEXTITEM;
```

Generate and run the form and query some customer records. Click the push button you created and you will see something like Figure 17.25.

The Forms Runtime editor will adjust its size automatically, depending on the amount of text it will display. If you want to define the size, and dimensions

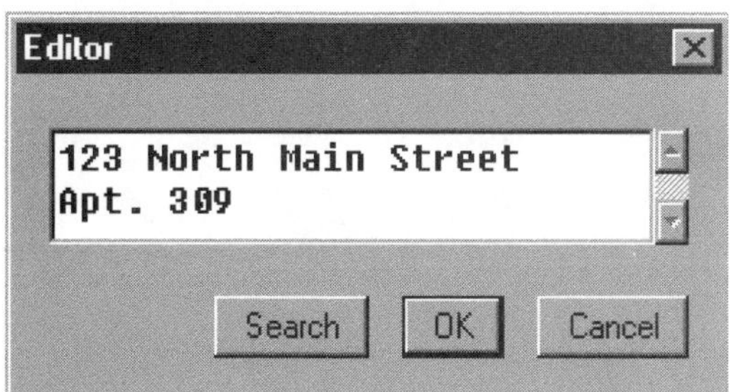

FIGURE 17.25 Forms Runtime default text editor.

of the window, then you replace the previous call to the EDIT_TEXTITEM in the WHEN-BUTTON-PRESSED trigger with a statement like this one:

```
EDIT_TEXTITEM (100, 100, 150, 150);
```

The first two arguments of this statement define the position, and the other two the width and height of the editor dialog box. As you can see from Figure 17.25, the visual attributes used by the default editor are the default attributes of Forms Runtime. If you want to make it look consistent with the rest of your application, or if you want to display your own title on the message box, then you can create an editor object in the Navigator and set its properties in the Property Palette.

1. Create an editor in the Object Navigator and name it ADDRESS_EDITOR.
2. Set its Title to "Address Editor," Font Name to "MS Sans Serif," X Position to 100, and Y Position to 100. Note here that you can also specify a bottom title for the dialog box or whether you want vertical and horizontal scroll bars.
3. Now, display the Property Palette for item ADDRESS, and set its Editor property to "ADDRESS_EDITOR." Here you could override the default position of the editor, by setting the properties Editor X Position and Editor Y Position.

Generate and run the module. When you display the editor again you will see something like Figure 17.26.

The custom editors have an additional feature that may be useful sometime. You can use the procedures SHOW_EDITOR not only to display the editor at the location you want, but also to specify the source of text, and the destination of the contents of the dialog box, when the users dismiss it by pressing OK. In addition, this procedure sets a Boolean variable to True if the users accept the dialog or False if they cancel out of it. This procedure may come handy in occasions when you want to keep more than one version of the text item values. However, typi-

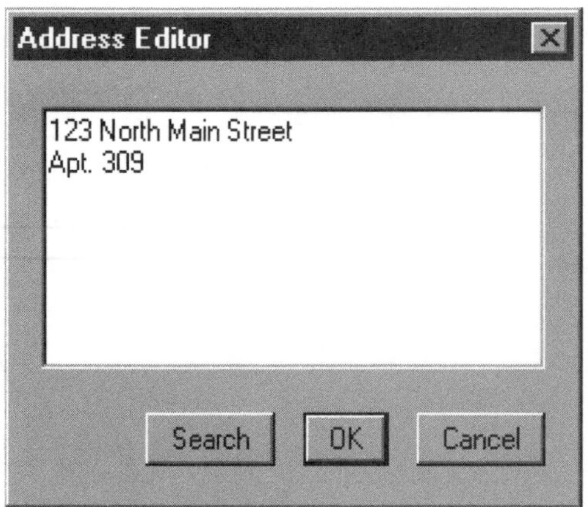

FIGURE 17.26 Forms Runtime custom text editor.

cally the source and the destination of the text will be the same text item in the form.

Besides the internal and custom-made editors, you can also use the system editor in Form Builder applications. In MS Windows, this is the Notepad editor. To use the system editor in your application, set the Editor property of the ADDRESS item to "SYSTEM_EDITOR." Make sure that the WHEN-BUTTON-PRESSED trigger of the button ADDRESS_EDIT still contains the lines:

```
GO_ITEM('CUSTOMERS1.ADDRESS');
EDIT_TEXTITEM;
```

Now generate and run the form. When you click the Editor... button, you will see the Notepad come up. A temporary file is open and it displays the contents of the item ADDRESS. The application in the background is disabled, and will not be available until you close the Notepad window.

17.5 PARAMETERS AND PARAMETER LISTS

Within one module, variables can have a local scope, or be global variables. The scope and visibility of local variable does not extend beyond the program unit in which they are defined. The global variables are visible throughout all the active modules and accessible from all their objects. Parameters implement a different flavor of visibility and accessibility of certain data items across the boundaries of the module. They are objects that are used to pass data between modules, for example when a form calls another, or between products, for example when a Report Builder report is executed from inside Forms Runtime.

There are two types of parameters: text and data. Text parameters are simple text strings of up to 255 bytes. They are used to pass data in and out the forms. Data parameters are also strings, but they contain the name of a record group which is already defined in the module. They are used to pass the data that are stored in the record group to Report Builder and Graphics Builder modules.

Parameters are not passed to other modules or products individually. They are packaged in a larger object, called a parameter list. Only the internal ID of this list is passed on the other side. Based on this ID, the module or product which receives the list, locates it, traverses it and retrieves each individual parameter and its value.

In this section, you will further extend the functionality of the MAIL block, which is used to print mailing labels for customers. In Section 17.2.5, you enabled the users to select multiple customers from the list of all the active customers. Now, you will implement the functionality that is behind the mouse click on the button Print. The strategy here is as follows:

1. Go through the list of selected customers and record all the ID values.
2. Build the WHERE clause of a SELECT statement that retrieves the address data only for those customers that have their ID in the set created in the previous step.
3. Hand this clause over to a Report Builder module that will do the actual retrieval of the data, based on the WHERE clause passed by the forms.

This strategy is implemented in the body of the trigger WHEN-BUTTON-PRESSED for the button Print (see Figure 17.27).

This trigger creates a parameter list, called `Report_PL` using the built-in function CREATE_PARAMETER_LIST. If the parameter list is created successfully, this function returns a non-NULL internal ID, which is stored in the variable `param_list_id` of data type ParamList.

After the parameter list is created, the function `Build_Where_Clause` goes through the list MAIL.SELECTED and builds the WHERE clause that will retrieve the address of the selected customers. This is the value of the parameter that will be passed to Reports. In the report module, there will be a parameter called WHERE_CLAUSE which will receive this value. Figure 17.28 provides the implementation details of this function. The ADD_PARAMETER procedure establishes the connection between the name of the parameter and its value. Because you are passing a simple character string, the type of this parameter is TEXT_PARAMETER. If you were to pass a record group instead, the parameter would be specified as DATA_PARAMETER.

When the WHERE clause is prepared, the report is executed using the built-in procedure RUN_PRODUCT. The meaning of the actual arguments passed to this procedure in Figure 17.20 is as follows:

```
DECLARE
 param_list_id   ParamList;
 param_list_name VARCHAR2(20) := 'Report_pl';
 sql_stat        VARCHAR2(255);

BEGIN
—Make sure that parameter list does not exist.
 param_list_id := GET_PARAMETER_LIST(param_list_name);
 IF NOT ID_NULL(param_list_id) THEN
  MESSAGE('Parameter_list '||param_list_name||' already
exists.');
  RAISE FORM_TRIGGER_FAILURE;
 END IF;

—Create the parameter list.
 param_list_id := CREATE_PARAMETER_LIST(param_list_name);
 IF ID_NULL(param_list_id) THEN
  MESSAGE('Parameter_list '||param_list_name||' cannot be
created.');
  RAISE FORM_TRIGGER_FAILURE;
 END IF;

—Build the WHERE clause.
 sql_stat := Build_Where_Clause('MAIL.SELECTED');

—Add the WHERE clause to the parameter list.
 ADD_PARAMETER(param_list_id, 'WHERE_CLAUSE',
TEXT_PARAMETER, sql_stat);

—Run the report that prints the label.
 RUN_PRODUCT(REPORTS, 'MRDLABEL', ASYNCHRONOUS,
         BATCH, FILESYSTEM, param_list_id, NULL);

—Destroy Parameter List
 DESTROY_PARAMETER_LIST(param_list_id);

EXCEPTION
 WHEN OTHERS THEN
  Message('Internal error occurred in WHEN-BUTTON-
PRESSED.');
  RAISE FORM_TRIGGER_FAILURE;
END;
```

FIGURE 17.27 Creating and populating parameter lists.

- **REPORTS.** This value indicates that you will execute a Report Builder module. The name of this module is `MRDLABEL` and it is passed as the second argument.
- **ASYNCHRONOUS.** This flag instructs Forms to kick off the report and not wait for it to finish. Instead, the control is returned to the user, who can continue working with other tasks in the form.
- **BATCH.** This flag indicates that the Reports Runtime window will not appear to the user.
- **param_list_id.** This is the internal ID of the parameter list you created. When Reports Runtime receives this ID, it will use it to find the memory location where the beginning of the parameter list is. Then, it will go through the individual parameters in the list to get their names and values. If the name of a parameter in the list matches the name of a pre-defined parameter, in your case WHERE_CLAUSE, Oracle Reports will pass the value from the parameter list to the internal parameter.

The last argument in the call to RUN_PRODUCT is always NULL if a report is executed. However, if a Graphics Builder display is being retrieved in a Forms item, the name of the chart item is stored there. You will see an example of this in Part Four of this book.

As a last step in the trigger WHEN-BUTTON-PRESSED, the parameter list is destroyed after the report is executed in order to release the system's resources to other tasks. The purpose of the function `Build_Where_Clause` was mentioned several times. Figure 17.28 provides the implementation details of this function.

Conceptually, this function does not present anything new to you. It simply loops through the elements of a list, and retrieves the value of each element. The only trick, if you can call it such, is how the WHERE clause is constructed. First you start with the following string:

```
ID IN (
```

Then, each iteration of the loop appends the value of the current element in the list, which is the ID, followed by a comma. So, for example, after the second iteration the string could look like this:

```
ID IN ('102', '234',
```

Before each new iteration the length of the string is tested. Since text parameters cannot contain more than 255 bytes of data, the loop is interrupted when this threshold is reached. When the loop terminates, the list will have a comma at the end. You need to remove this final comma and replace it with the matching

```
FUNCTION Build_Where_Clause (list_name VARCHAR2)
RETURN VARCHAR2 IS
 list_id   ITEM;
 list_count      NUMBER;
 sql_stat  VARCHAR2(255) := 'WHERE ID IN (';
 current_idVARCHAR2(50);
 sql_stat_len    NUMBER;

BEGIN
—Get a valid list ID.
 list_id := FIND_ITEM(list_name);
 IF ID_NULL(list_id) THEN
  MESSAGE('List Item '||list_name||' does not exist.');
  RAISE FORM_TRIGGER_FAILURE;
 END IF;

—Get the numeber of elements in the list.
 list_count := GET_LIST_ELEMENT_COUNT(list_id);

 FOR i IN 1..list_count LOOP
   sql_stat_len := LENGTH(sql_stat);
   EXIT WHEN sql_stat_len > 254;
   current_id := GET_LIST_ELEMENT_VALUE(list_id, i);
  —Add a comma after each Customer_ID.
   sql_stat := sql_stat||current_id||,'';
 END LOOP;

—Remove the comma that follows the last Customer ID.
 sql_stat_len := LENGTH(sql_stat);
 sql_stat := SUBSTR(sql_stat, 1, sql_stat_len - 1);
—Finish the string with the closing parenthesis.
 sql_stat := sql_stat||')';

 return sql_stat;
EXCEPTION
 WHEN OTHERS THEN
  MESSAGE('Internal error occurred in
Build_Where_Clause');
  RAISE FORM_TRIGGER_FAILURE;
END Build_Where_Clause;
```

FIGURE 17.28 Building the WHERE clause for a report.

right parentheses. If, in the previous example, the list contains only two elements, the final WHERE clause will be:

```
ID IN ('102', '234')
```

After creating the trigger and the procedure as discussed in this section, generate and save the module. Chapter 21 will discuss in more details the integration of Form Builder, Report Builder, and Graphics Builder components. In that chapter you will also see the example of passing a record group as a parameter to Graphics.

I conclude this section with a note. The limitation of text parameters to 255 bytes would not make this approach a feasible solution for a real life situation where hundreds of customer labels may be printed. In that case data parameters should be considered. Another alternative is to write the full SQL SELECT statement to a text file during the preparatory phase of the label printing process. Form Builder allows you to write data from the application program units into text files using the built-in package TEXT_IO. You would follow a similar looping approach as in Figure 17.21, but, instead of building only the WHERE clause in a local variable, you would write the whole SQL statement to the file. The Reports module, on the other hand, should be designed based on a query from an external file—the same file you write from within Form Builder. Thus, on the Forms side of the application you write the SQL statement to a file, whereas on the Reports side you query the database based on this file, format the data, and print the labels. Chapter 21 contains an example of how the package TEXT_IO can be used to write and read text files.

17.6 SUMMARY

This chapter discussed record structures in Form Builder applications such as runtime records, record groups and list of values. In addition it explained how you can use text editors, parameters and parameter lists. Important topics of this chapter are

- **Records in Form Builder Applications**
  - States of Records, Blocks, and Forms
  - Events of Records
  - Events of Records in the MRD Application
- **Record Groups**
  - Static Record Groups
  - Query Record Groups

- Accessing Data of Record Groups at Runtime
- Populating List Items with Record Groups
- Implementing Multi-Selection Lists with Record Groups

- **Lists of Values**
  - Creating Lists of Values
  - Properties of Lists of Values
  - Modifying Properties of Lists of Values at Runtime
  - Attaching Lists of Values to Text Items

- **Text Editors**

- **Parameters and Parameter Lists**

The following table describes the software assets that were discussed in this chapter. From the main HTML page of the software utilities provided with the book follow the links *Software* and *Chapter 17* to access these assets:

ASSET NAME	DESCRIPTION
STATUS.FMB	A Form Builder module that allows you to see how the status of form, block, and record objects changes as you use the module.
CH17_1.FMB	The MRD application completed in the last chapter. Use this module as a starting point for the activities discussed in this chapter.
CH17_2.FMB	The MRD application with the implementation of record events discussed in Section 17.1.3.
CH17_2.FMX	The executable version of CH17_2.FMB compiled for Win32 platforms.
CH17_3.FMB	The MRD application with all the activities discussed in this chapter.
CH17_3.FMX	The executable version of CH17_3.FMB compiled for Win32 platforms.

Chapter 18

MENUS AND TOOLBARS

We all know sensual pleasures taken to excess are a curse . . . it's the same with menus.

—Bob Carr

- Form Builder Menus
- Toolbars
- Pop-up Menus
- Summary

A key objective that should be always in the back of your mind when developing an application is to make it as accessible for the users as possible. You can write the best piece of software, but if it will take users several steps to get to it, nobody will be thrilled by it and many will not even notice it. On the other hand, you do not want to open everything up as soon as the application is started. Instead users should be in charge. They should decide which parts of the application to keep available and accessible at any one moment.

The bottom line is that your application needs structure. The functionality must be organized logically in a fashion that is natural for the business processes described by the application. Menus and toolbars are used to turn the multitude of objects and pieces of code that make up an application, into an organized and well-thought-out tool to access and manipulate the data. This chapter discusses the process of equipping your Form Builder applications with menus and toolbars.

18.1 FORM BUILDER MENUS

In Form Builder applications, menus can be created, edited, generated, and saved in the Menu Editor. The menu modules exist independently from forms, but they cannot be used unless they are attached to a form. One menu module is always attached to any form you create. This is the default menu that you have seen used in the application developed in Part One.

Chapter 7 explained how to use the Menu Editor to create the skeleton of a menu. This section will discuss in more detail the objects that are part of a menu module and their properties. You will also create the menu for the MRD application.

18.1.1 CREATING THE MENU FOR THE MRD APPLICATION

The general steps you must follow when creating a menu are listed here:

1. Design the menu so that it reflects the most natural and efficient way for users to access the components of the application.
2. In the Menu Editor, lay out the structure of the menu according to the design.
3. For each menu item that users will ultimately select, define its properties according to its purpose and functionality.
4. Save and generate the menu module.
5. Attach the menu to the form module that will use it.
6. Save, generate and run the form to test the new menu's functionality.

If necessary, these steps may be repeated more than once. For the MRD application, you have already completed the first step. From Chapter 7, you also know how to build the structural frame of the menu in the Menu Editor. Here the focus will be on the remaining steps of the process. Before you begin, follow these preliminary steps:

1. Create a new menu module in the Form Builder, and name it MRD.
2. Double-click the menu type icon to its left to bring up the Menu Editor window.
3. Use the icons Create Right Create Down in the Menu Editor's toolbar to quickly create the menu structure as shown in Figure 18.1. If you experience any problems, refer to the steps you followed in Chapter 7 for a similar process.
4. Save the module.

18.1.2 PROPERTIES OF MENUS

There are a few things to note here. First, as you can see from Figure 18.1, there is no need to create a Window submenu. Every form, even if no menu module is attached to it, will have the menu Window attached to its MDI frame. If a menu module is attached to the form, the Window menu will position itself in conformance with GUI standards of the platform. In the case of the MRD application, it will be inserted between the Data and Help menu items in the MAIN_MENU.

Second, the labels you enter in the Menu Editor are what the users will see when they will use the menu. Therefore, proper care must be taken when they are set. In order to provide an access key for the menu item you precede one of

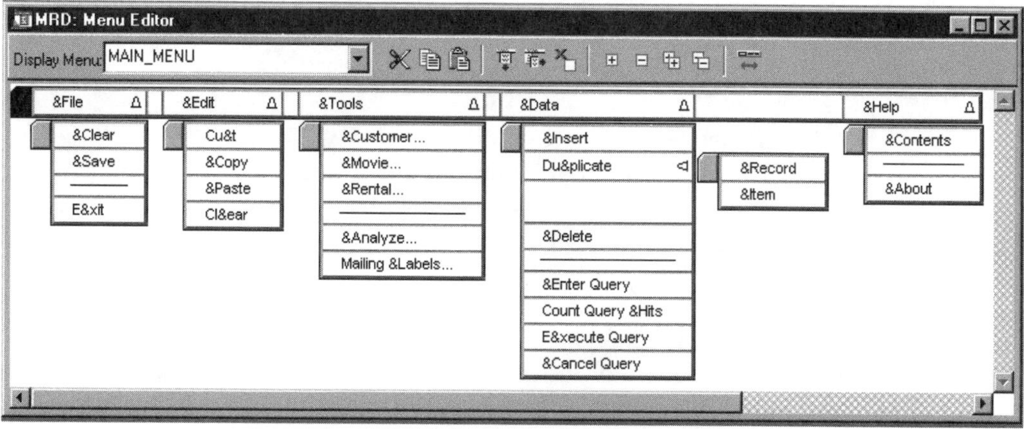

FIGURE 18.1 Structure of MRD menu.

the letters in its label with the ampersand sign &. When the menu will be executed at runtime, this letter will be underlined. If the users are in the parent menu already, they can select the item by typing the access key from the keyboard. When specifying the access keys for a menu, you should be careful not to specify the same key for two items within the same menu. Note also that the label of those menu items that will invoke windows or dialog boxes should terminate with an ellipsis.

Finally, in order not to interrupt the process of laying out the menu as shown in Figure 18.1, you do not want to stop at each and every one of them to set their properties. Instead, you proceed with the creation process keeping in mind that you will return at a later moment to fine-tune the properties of each item.

Notice for example that there are several menu items in Figure 18.1 labeled `separator`. These labels serve as reminders that these items will have no other purpose than separating the items of the respective menus. After you have created the menu, you can assign this functionality to all of them.

1. CTRL-CLICK each menu item labeled `separator` in order to select them all.
2. Choose Tools | Property Palette to display the Property Palette for the selected items.
3. Set the property Menu Item Type to "Separator." This property is part of the Functional group of properties.

You will see that all the selected items will be changed into separating lines. By default, the property Menu Item Type is set to "Plain" for every menu item you create. Plain items are the type that you will encountered the most in the menus you develop. Besides "Plain" and "Separator," the property Menu Item Type can be set to "Magic," "Radio," and "Check." When the type of a menu item is "Magic," you can assign a built-in command or function to the item such as Cut, Copy, or Paste. Using this information, follow these steps to implement the items of the Edit menu in your application:

1. Select all the items in the menu Edit.
2. Set their property Menu Item Type to "Magic," and deselect the items.
3. For each individual item, set the property Magic Item to the setting that corresponds to its name. For example, Magic Item will be "Cut" for the menu item Cut.

The advantage of using magic items is that Forms Runtime will handle the text editing functionality and decide about its availability. Forms internally will check the context for every situation and turn on or off the appropriate menu items that can be used in that situation.

Two other special types of menu items are Radio and Check menu items.

Their purpose and use is very similar to that of radio and check box items in the Forms module. Check menu items are used typically in a View submenu such as the one used in the Forms Builder, to hide and display certain objects in the application. Radio menu items are very unusual for a menu, and are used to set an application to a single state from a number of possible choices that make up the menu radio group. Functionally, this type of menu items does not provide anything that cannot be implemented with Plain items, or that cannot be set in an Options dialog box.

Keeping in mind the GUI rule that your applications should be simple, consistent and not flashy—you should use primarily Plain menu items. Occasionally you may use check items, and you should almost never use radio menu items. However, should you choose to implement any of these types of menu items in your application, set the menu item type appropriately and follow the same steps that you would normally follow for Plain menu items. These steps are explained in this section.

Menu items can utilize a series of visual attribute properties related to fonts. These properties are located in the group Font & Color of the Property Palette. As with other objects, if you intend to modify any properties in this group, consider doing so through a named visual attribute object. However, while it is justifiable to customize the visual attributes of Forms items, you should never do this for menu items. The default settings of the windows manager are typically used universally across all the applications and you should not deviate from this path.

Two other properties that you should never have to set are Icon in Menu and Icon Filename. The first one controls whether a menu item is accompanied by an icon on the menu bar. If this property is set to "Yes," then the property Icon Filename contains the name of the icon to display. Like iconic buttons or windows, this property is set to just the name of the icon file. At runtime, the icon is displayed to the left of the menu item's label. Setting these two properties is one more of those things that you can but should not do, since iconic menus are not seen in any other application. In your applications, you should represent the menu items as string labels. Iconic toolbars may be attached to the MDI frame to offer access to often-used commands.

Besides the properties Menu Item Type and Label, other important properties of menu items are Command Type, Menu Item Code, and Accelerator. The Command Type must be set to "Null" for menu items that will serve as separators. If the Menu Item Type is set to "Magic," the setting of the property Magic Item rules the behavior of the item itself and ignores the setting of the property Command Type. If, for example, a menu item is set to be the Magic item Cut, it will cut selected text no matter what the setting of its Command Type is.

For the rest of menu items—Plain, Check, and Radio—the Command Type can be "Menu," "PL/SQL," "Plus," "Forms," and "Macro." From these settings, the first two are the only one used. The rest are included for backward compatibly reasons with SQL*Menus, the team mate of SQL*Forms in the Oracle's character-based application development tools.

If the Command Type of a menu item is set to "Menu," at runtime, when users will select this menu item, a submenu will appear. The name of this submenu, is stored in the Menu Item Code property. If, on the other hand, the Command Type is set to "PL/SQL," the Menu Item Code property contains the statements that are executed when the menu item is selected. You can access the Menu Item Code property by double-clicking it in the Property Palette, or by double clicking the menu object or menu item icons in the Object Navigator. When editing the Menu Item Code of a Menu type item, a system editor dialog box will appear; when editing a PL/SQL menu item, the PL/SQL Editor window will be displayed.

When you create the menu in the Menu Editor, the Form Builder defines whether the property Command Type should be set to "Menu" or "PL/SQL." In the case of the MRD menu, as you were clicking the Create Right icon to create items of the MAIN_MENU such as File, Edit, and Data, the Form Builder was setting the command of these items to PL/SQL type. When you started using the Create Down icon to create the submenus, the Form Builder automatically changed the command type of the previous menu items to Menu, and assigned the names of the new menu objects to the property Menu Item Code.

The Menu Item Code property is maintained by a plain text editor, with no PL/SQL editing capabilities when its setting is not "PL/SQL." However, it the Command Type is set to "PL/SQL," the text editor is replaced by the PL/SQL editor. This allows you to compile and check your PL/SQL statements to avoid runtime errors. In a sense, the code that you attach to each PL/SQL menu item is like a WHEN-BUTTON-PRESSED trigger attached to a push button. It will be executed when the users choose that menu item.

Another menu item property that should not be overlooked is the Hint property. As in items, the Hint property may contain a brief description about the function of the menu item. When the users select the item, its hint is displayed in the message line of the console at the bottom of the frame.

18.1.3 USING PL/SQL IN MENUS

Using different PL/SQL commands, you can initiate a variety of actions from your menu items. Some of these actions may correspond to Form Builder built-in procedures. For example, in the MRD application, all the menu items in the Data submenu correspond to built-in procedures. The property Menu Item Code for these items may be as simple as the name of this procedure. So, for the menu item Data | Insert the command could be:

```
CREATE_RECORD;
```

The commands executed by a menu module may also be accessible from within the Form Builder module. They may be part of different triggers in the form. This variety of ways to performs the same action, while being very beneficial to the users, may cause configuration management nightmares for the application developers. Imagine for example how users will create records in your applications. They could press [create record], or choose Data | Insert from the menu, or click the CREATE_RECORD button that you will provide for them in the toolbar. Each of these different actions, will normally invoke different PL/SQL methods. Pressing [create record] from the keyboard will invoke the KEY-CREREC trigger, or, in its absence, will execute the CREATE_RECORD built-in procedure. Selecting Data | Insert from the menu will fire the code placed in its Menu Item Code property; and finally, clicking the iconic button in the toolbar will fire the WHEN-BUTTON-PRESSED trigger associated with it.

The problem gets even more complicated in forms with several blocks. In the MRD form, for example, the process of inserting records in the MOVIE block or in the CUSTOMER block could be different. In the form module, this problem is solved by bringing the KEY-CREREC down one level in the hierarchy. In other words, from a form level KEY-CREREC trigger, you create two block level triggers that will handle the different functionality for the two blocks. But now, in the code triggered by selecting the Insert menu item or clicking the button in the toolbar, you must distinguish first in which block the event occurred, and then act according to the situation.

It is natural to look for a way to place the code in only one place and reference it from the other two locations. An elegant solution is to place the code in the key triggers, and invoke these key triggers from the menu or the toolbar button. This solution will guarantee that the same piece of code gets executed each time. It will allow you to maintain the code in only one place. And finally, the code to be executed will be decided by the key trigger placed at the appropriate level in the objects hierarchy. To reference the code of a key trigger, or the built-in procedure that corresponds to it, you use the built-in DO_KEY. This procedure takes as input the name of the Form Builder built-in whose functionality is to be invoked. Following this approach, the Menu Item Code for the Menu | Insert menu item will be:

```
DO_KEY('CREATE_RECORD');
```

Now, whenever the menu item is selected, if there is a KEY-CREREC defined for the block or the module, that trigger will fire; otherwise, the built-in procedure CREATE-RECORD will be executed. In the light of this discussion, set the Menu Item Code for the menu items shown in the first column of Figure 18.2 to the commands specified on the second column. Note that when these commands will be implemented as iconic buttons in the toolbar, their WHEN-BUTTON-PRESSED triggers should also use these statements.

Understandably, it is desirable to take the same approach for items in the menu that do not map directly to Form Builder built-ins. Even for these items, you would still want to create and maintain the code in one location, and reference it from both the WHEN-BUTTON-PRESSED triggers and the Menu Item

MENU ITEM	MENU ITEM CODE PROPERTY
File I Clear	DO_KEY('CLEAR_FORM');
File I Save	DO_KEY('COMMIT_FORM');
File I Exit	DO_KEY('EXIT_FORM');
Data I Insert	DO_KEY('CREATE_RECORD');
Data I Duplicate I Item	DO_KEY('DUPLICATE_ITEM');
Data I Duplicate I Record	DO_KEY('DUPLICATE_RECORD');
Data I Delete	DO_KEY('DELETE_RECORD');
Data I Enter Query	DO_KEY('ENTER_QUERY');
Data I Count Query Hits	DO_KEY('COUNT_QUERY');
Data I Execute Query	DO_KEY('EXECUTE_QUERY');

FIGURE 18.2 Menu Item Code property settings for menu items in the MRD module.

Code property of the menu items. There are several ways to achieve this functionality. The first method follows the same strategy as the one used to take advantage of the Form Builder built-ins and the KEY triggers. For example, to access the CUSTOMER block data you would follow these steps:

1. Create a user-named trigger, for example CUSTOMER_SELECTED, that handles the navigation to the block.
2. Set the Menu Item Code property of Tools | Customer to:
   ```
   EXECUTE_TRIGGER('CUSTOMER_SELECTED');
   ```
3. The WHEN-BUTTON-PRESSED trigger for the Customer iconic button will contain the same statement:
   ```
   EXECUTE_TRIGGER('CUSTOMER_SELECTED');
   ```

However, creating and maintaining user-named triggers is not recommended. This feature, useful in earlier versions of SQL*Forms, is superseded by the ability to create and use functions and procedures in later versions. The second approach is to create a procedure that would take as parameter the name of the button pressed and, based on that name, decide which window to display, or, more generally, what action to take. However, there is a problem with this approach. Because the menu and the form are separate modules the procedure must be present in both the modules. When the menu items will be selected, the procedure in the menu module will be executed; when the toolbar button will be clicked, the Forms procedure will be executed. Again, you are faced with the problem of having to maintain the same code in two different locations.

The third approach is to create a procedure as discussed above and store it in a PL/SQL library module together with every other program unit that will be shared between the menu and the form. This library is attached to the form and the menu modules, thus making its member objects available and accessible to both of them. This is the most elegant and efficient solution, because not only allows you to maintain the code in one single point, but also to reference it from every other form or menu module that may need it. By removing the PL/SQL objects from the body of the form or menu and replacing it with a pointer to a library, you also reduce the size of these modules, thus making the application run faster. The following chapter will discuss in more detail the advantages of PL/SQL libraries in Form Builder applications. In that chapter you will also create the function that will be called when users select the menu item Data | Cancel Query, or any of the menu items in submenus Tools, and Help. For the moment being you can place the following line in their Menu Item Code property:

```
MESSAGE('Feature to be implemented.');
```

Another place where you can put PL/SQL statements in a menu is the startup code. This is a method that is fired every time a menu is loaded into memory. It is used primarily to set the initial state of the menu items. For example, in your application, you may want users to select the last three items of the Data menu (Count Query Hits, Execute Query, and Cancel Query) only if the application enters the Query mode. In the startup code you could place statements that set the ENABLED property of these items to False. Retrieving and setting properties is a similar process for menu items and other objects that you have seen so far. The example of the procedure that would be used to disable the properties of a menu item is shown in Figure 18.3.

```
PROCEDURE Disable_Menu_Item (menu_item_name VARCHAR2) IS
 menu_item_id    MenuItem;
BEGIN
– Find ID for menu item
 menu_item_id := FIND_MENU_ITEM(menu_item_name);
 IF ID_NULL(menu_item_id) THEN
  MESSAGE('Menu item ' || menu_item_name || ' does not
exist.');
  RAISE FORM_TRIGGER_FAILURE;
 END IF;

 SET_MENU_ITEM_PROPERTY(menu_item_id, ENABLED,
PROPERTY_FALSE);
END;
```

FIGURE 18.3 Changing menu item properties programmatically.

Using this procedure the contents of the startup code for the menu would be:

```
Disable_Menu_Item('DATA.COUNT_QUERY');
Disable_Menu_Item('DATA.EXECUTE_QUERY');
Disable_Menu_Item('DATA.CANCEL_QUERY');
```

Note however that there exist two built-in procedures that are not documented in the Form Builder documentation. These are ENABLE_ITEM and DISABLE_ITEM. They both take the name of the menu as a first parameter, and the name of the item in that menu as a second parameter. Using these functions, the startup code of the menu would be:

```
DISABLE_ITEM('DATA', 'COUNT_QUERY');
DISABLE_ITEM('DATA', 'EXECUTE_QUERY');
DISABLE_ITEM('DATA', 'CANCEL_QUERY');
```

Once you disable these items, there should be a point in the application where you enable them again. In general, the enabled state of items needs to be toggled based on the context of the application. In such cases, you should group the statements that enable and disable the menu items in procedures that can be called whenever the appropriate events occur. Chapter 18 shows an example of how you can toggle the ENABLED status of menu items and toolbar buttons in your applications.

18.1.4 ENFORCING THE SECURITY OF THE APPLICATION IN MENUS

In Form Builder applications you can use the definition of roles in the database to restrict the access of users to part of the system they may not be authorized to see. A role is an object defined in the Oracle Server database that is made up of a list of database users to which a set of privileges is assigned. All the privileges assigned to the role will automatically be transferred to the members of that role. Discussing the subject of roles in the administration of Oracle databases stretches outside the topic or this book. Therefore it is assumed that the database you are using to follow the examples of this book contains two roles already: MRD_OPERATOR, and MRD_MANAGER.

In order to use the roles to restrict access to different parts of the menu, you must first make them available to the menu module as a whole. These are the steps required to achieve this:

1. Display the Property Palette for the menu module.
2. Set the property User Security to 'Yes.'

FIGURE 18.4 Menu Module Role dialog box.

3. Double-click the property Module Roles. The Menu Module Roles dialog box will appear (see Figure 18.4).
4. Enter the names of the roles as shown in Figure 18.4.
5. Click OK.

The actions have supplied the menu module with a list of available roles and instructed it to enforce the security based on these roles. Under these conditions, the menu will not allow access to any role. You must explicitly set the properties of each item so that they become available to the roles. All of the items, except for Tools | Analyze..., will be available for both roles. Therefore the quickest way to complete the task is to do a global assignment for all of them, and then limit the access to Tools | Analyze... only for the role MRD_MANAGER.

1. Combining SHIFT+CLICK and CTRL+CLICK to select all the menu items.
2. Display the Property Palette for the selection.
3. Double-click the property Item Roles under the Menu Security group. The Menu Item Roles dialog box will be displayed (see Figure 18.5). Initially, none of the roles displayed in the list is selected.
4. Click MRD_MANAGER and SHIFT+CLICK MRD_OPERATOR to select them both.
5. Click OK.

Now, follow these steps to remove MRD_OPERATOR from the list of roles that have access to the menu item Tools | Analyze.

FIGURE 18.5 Menu Item Role dialog box.

1. Select the menu item Menu | Analyze and display its Property Palette.
2. Double-click the property Item Roles under the Menu Security group. The Menu Item Roles dialog box will be displayed (see Figure 18.5). Both roles assigned to this item are selected.
3. CTRL+CLICK MRD_OPERATOR to deselect it.
4. Click OK.

Make sure that the setting for the property Display without Privilege of this menu item is "Yes." This setting will make the menu item Analyze be always displayed, but unavailable for those users that are not part of the MRD_MANAGER role.

18.1.5 ATTACHING A MENU TO A FORM

At this point, you are ready to connect the menu module developed so far with the MRD form. Save and generate the menu module and open the MRD form that you were working with at the end of the last chapter. You may also choose to work with the modules CH18_1.FMB and CH18_1.MMB provided with the companion software. The first one contains the MRD application with the features discussed so far. The second one is the menu built in the previous sections.

1. Display the Property Palette for the MRD module.
2. Set the Menu Module to the name of the menu you just saved followed by the extension .MMX, for example MRD.MMX.

You do not need to change any of the other settings of the menu-related properties. The Menu Style in Windows is always 'Pull-down'; you will access the menu from the file system, therefore Menu Source must remain set to 'File.' If the menu had multiple levels of hierarchy, you could set the Initial Menu property to the name of a menu other than the MAIN_MENU. This will display only those menu objects and items that are dependent on this menu in the tree.

3. Save, generate, and run the MRD module to see the attached menu.

Forms Runtime looks for the menu module in the directories specified in the environmental variable FORMSxx_PATH of your machine's registry—where xx indicates the version of Form Builder, as in FORMS50, FORMS60, and so on. If your working directory is not added to FORMSxx_PATH and you run the MRD module from the Form Builder, you will receive the error message "FRM-10221: Cannot read file mrd." Specifying the complete path of the menu module will solve the problem, but only temporarily. Hard-coded file names are not flexible when distributing your application to the users' environment. Another solution to this problem is to place the menu module under the same directory as the form module executable and create a program item with working directory the one where these executables are located.

18.2 TOOLBARS

Toolbars group together iconic buttons and help users access functionality that is used frequently and across multiple windows. The toolbars are attached to the MDI frame either horizontally, under the menu, or vertically along the left border of the window. In this section you will create a horizontal toolbar that will be available throughout the application and will allow users to save their data, exit the application, navigate to the major parts of the application and invoke the online help system. You will also create a vertical toolbar that will be available only when users will be working with base table blocks. The iconic buttons here will allow them to access functions typical for these blocks such as inserting, deleting, or querying records from the database.

18.2.1 STEPS TO IMPLEMENT A TOOLBAR IN FORM BUILDER APPLICATIONS

There is very little that you do not know about creating toolbars in Form Builder applications. Although you were ready to complete the task a couple of chapters earlier, it makes more sense to discuss it in this chapter. The reason is that toolbars usually go hand-in-hand with menus. Their iconic buttons represent the major functions of the system that can be selected from the menu. The process of creating toolbars in Form Builder applications can be summarized in the following steps.

1. Create a control block that will own the iconic buttons in the toolbar.
2. Create a canvas, and define its type as Horizontal Toolbar, or Vertical Toolbar, according to the type of toolbar you are creating.
3. Create each control that will be part of the toolbar. Usually, the controls are iconic buttons, but it is not uncommon to see drop-down lists boxes in toolbars as well.
4. Adjust the size of the canvas.
5. Attach the toolbar canvas to the MDI frame of the application.
6. Implement the functionality that each toolbar button will provide through PL/SQL triggers, functions, and procedures.

In the next section, you will follow these steps to create the toolbars for the MRD applications.

18.2.2 CREATING TOOLBARS FOR THE MRD APPLICATION

As always, you may follow the discussion here with the form you are developing, or by opening the module CH18_2.FMB, which contains the work done so far. In this section you will create iconic buttons for the toolbar. The icons are provided in the directory \ICONS of the companion disk. Recall form Chapter 15 that, in order for Forms Runtime to be able to attach the icon files to the buttons, the name of this directory must be specified in the UI_ICON environment variable of the registry. As a preliminary step, append the directory \ICONS to the UI_ICON variable. Now, follow these steps to create the block and the canvas that will contain the iconic buttons.

1. Create a control block and name it TOOLBAR. This block will own all the iconic buttons of the toolbars.
2. Make this block the first one in the list of blocks in the Object Navigator.
3. Create a canvas and name it H_TOOLBAR. The buttons for the horizontal toolbar will reside on this canvas.
4. Set the property Canvas Type to "Horizontal Toolbar."

All the buttons you will create will have similar properties. Rather than setting these properties on an individual basis, you can subclass each object from the iconic button objects that the Form Builder provides in its STANDARD object library. Make sure this library is open in the Object Navigator before proceeding with the creation of the first button of the toolbar. Then,

1. Display the canvas H_TOOLBAR in the Layout Editor.
2. Create a push button and place it in the upper left-hand corner of the canvas. Make sure that the context for the canvas is set to the block TOOLBAR before you create the button.
3. Right-click the button on the canvas to display its pop-up menu.
4. Select STD_BUTTON_ICONIC_SMALL from the SmartClasses menu item. All the characteristic properties of iconic buttons will be inherited from this object.
5. Display the Property Palette for the button and set the properties Name to "CLEAR_FORM," Icon Name to "new," Label to "Clear," and Hint "Clear the application."

At this point, you should have on the canvas a button like this icon . Now create eight more push buttons. Select them all and subclass them from the STD_BUTTON_ICONIC_SMALL object. For each individual button, set the button-specific properties according to Figure 18.6.

Now position the buttons so that they appear grouped by functionality. The criteria you should use are:

1. If the menu items that correspond to the buttons are adjacent, the buttons should be one pixel apart.
2. If there is a separator line, but the menu items are still within the same submenu, the buttons should be three pixels apart.
3. If the menu items are on different menus, the buttons should be six pixels apart.

NAME	ICON NAME	LABEL AND TOOLTIP	HINT
CLEAR_FORM	clearfrm	Clear	Clear the application.
COMMIT_FORM	save	Save	Save the application.
EXIT_FORM	exit	Exit	Exit the application.
CUSTOMER	customer	Customer Data	Enter and edit customer data.
MOVIE	movie	Movie Data	Enter and edit movie data.
RENTAL	rent	Rental Data	Enter and edit rental data.
ANALYZE	analyze	Analyze Trends	Analyze revenue from movie rentals.
MAIL	maill	Print Labels	Print mailing labels.
HELP	help	Help	Invoke on-line help.

FIGURE 18.6 Individual settings for properties of buttons in the horizontal toolbar.

Align the buttons horizontally, and group them by selecting Arrange | Group, so that in the future they all move together as one object. Now you can reduce the height of the canvas. Because the horizontal toolbar canvas will be attached to the MDI frame, its size will condition the height of the client area where all the MDI sheets will be displayed. Therefore it is important that this type of canvases do not take more space than they need.

Finally, your horizontal toolbar should look similar to Figure 18.7.

In principle, creating the vertical toolbar is the same process.

1. Create another canvas and call it V_TOOLBAR.
2. With the context set to the block TOOLBAR, create five push buttons.
3. Inherit their common properties from the TOOLBAR_BUTTON property class.
4. Set their individual properties according to the specification in Figure 18.8.

After grouping and aligning vertically the buttons, and reducing the width of the canvas to an appropriate value, your vertical canvas should be similar to Figure 18.9.

18.2.3 INTEGRATING TOOLBARS WITH WINDOWS MANAGEMENT FUNCTIONALITY

Among other things, Chapter 16 discussed the process of opening and closing windows in MDI applications. Recall that your application would use a home item, where the focus will land each time a window is closed. Implementing the home item in Chapter 16 requires that it be the first item of the first block in the module. It is natural to elect one of the buttons in the horizontal toolbar as the home item for the application. The toolbar, being attached to the MDI frame, will be available as long as the application is running and will not depend on any application window. From the buttons in the horizontal toolbar, the EXIT_FORM button will always be available, to allow users to quit the application. This would be a good choice for home item. Another one would be the button that invokes the online help.

The following steps designate EXIT_FORM as the home item of the MRD module.

1. In the Object Navigator, drag the block TOOLBAR in the first position in the list of blocks.

FIGURE 18.7 Horizontal toolbar for MRD module.

NAME	ICON NAME	LABEL AND TOOLTIP	HINT
CREATE_RECORD	crerec	Create	Create new record.
DELETE_RECORD	delrec	Delete	Delete current record.
ENTER_QUERY	enterqry	Enter Query	Enter query mode.
EXECUTE_QUERY	execqry	Execute Query	Execute query.
CANCEL_QUERY	canclqry	Cancel Query	Cancel query.

FIGURE 18.8 Individual settings for properties of buttons in the vertical toolbar.

2. Drag the button EXIT_FORM in the first position among items in the block TOOLBAR.
3. Set the property Keyboard Navigable for this button to "Yes." This step is necessary to allow Forms Runtime to navigate to the button.

Of course, you could have chosen the short path, by directly entering the following statement in the PRE-FORM trigger of the module:

```
:GLOBAL.Home_Item := 'TOOLBAR.EXIT_FORM';
```

Either of them is acceptable, as long as the application is well documented, and everyone in the development team is aware of the convention.

18.2.4 ATTACHING TOOLBARS TO FORMS MODULES

Now you are ready to attach the toolbar to the MDI frame of the application.

1. Display the Property Palette for the module MRD.
2. Scroll down to the Physical group and set the property Form Horizontal Toolbar Canvas to "H_TOOLBAR."
3. Set the property Form Vertical Toolbar Canvas to "V_TOOLBAR."

FIGURE 18.9 Vertical toolbar for MRD module.

That will do it! You can save, generate and run the module now to take a look at the new toolbars.

18.2.5 ADDING FUNCTIONALITY TO THE MRD TOOLBAR

In this section, you will dress up the iconic buttons in the horizontal and vertical toolbars with the functionality that the users will invoke by clicking each of them. This functionality will be carried out by PL/SQL statements attached to these buttons. According to their functionality, the iconic buttons in the toolbars of the MRD module can be grouped as follows:

1. Buttons that navigate to different windows and dialog boxes of the module. These are the buttons CUSTOMER, MOVIE, RENTAL, ANALYZE, and MAIL.
2. Buttons that will require special consideration. The only button in this category would be the HELP, which will invoke the on-line help for the application.
3. Last but not least, buttons that invoke Form Builder built-in procedures. These are all the remaining buttons in the horizontal or vertical toolbars.

As discussed in the previous section, your goal in the process of implementing functionality programmatically is to modularize and concentrate the code in as few places as possible. To achieve this, create a procedure that takes the name of the button pressed as an argument and, based on that name, executes the appropriate statements. Figure 18.10 shows contents of this procedure.

From the contents of this procedure you can appreciate the choice of names for the iconic buttons in the toolbars. Those buttons that will take the users to a particular window in the application are named after the block in the target window that will serve as landing point for the focus of Forms. This allows you to handle the navigation to all the functional areas of the application with only one line of code:

```
Click_Button(button_name);
```

Those buttons that will correspond to Form Builder built-in routines, are named after the particular routine they will invoke. The one line statement `DO_KEY(button_name)` makes it possible to invoke these routines, or the corresponding key triggers, if they exist, independently of the name of the button.

It is worth discussing the particular situation when the button CANCEL_QUERY is pressed. The Form Builder built-in that can be used to cancel a query is EXIT_FORM. However, you need to be sure that the form is in Query mode, before issuing the call to this procedure. (If the form is in Normal mode, EXIT_FORM closes the application entirely.) The system variable SYS-

```
PROCEDURE Click_Button (button_name IN VARCHAR2) IS
BEGIN
IF button_name IN ('CUSTOMER', 'MOVIE', 'RENTAL') THEN
  Open_Window(button_name, button_name);
 ELSIF button_name IN ('MAIL', 'ABOUT') THEN
  Open_Dialog_Box(button_name, button_name);
 ELSIF button_name IN ('ANALYZE','HELP') THEN
  MESSAGE('Feature not yet implemented.');
 ELSIF button_name = 'CANCEL_QUERY' AND
 :SYSTEM.MODE = 'ENTER-QUERY' THEN
  EXIT_FORM;      — EXIT_FORM takes application
                  — from Enter Query to Normal mode
 ELSE
   DO_KEY(button_name);
 END IF;
 IF NOT FORM_SUCCESS THEN
   MESSAGE('Internal error occurred in Click_Button.');
   RAISE FORM_TRIGGER_FAILURE;
 END IF;
END;
```

FIGURE 18.10 Generic procedure for toolbar icons.

TEM.MODE holds the value for the state of a form when the procedure is invoked.

Note also another way used in this procedure to check the successful completion of any action by Forms Runtime. The FORM_SUCCESS is a function defined in the STANDARD package of Form Builder built-ins. This function returns the Boolean value TRUE if the last action of the form was successful, and FALSE if a problem occurred. There are two other similar functions, FORM_FAILURE and FORM_FATAL, which return TRUE if the last action taken by Forms failed, or resulted with a fatal error. The distinction between a failure and a fatal error is vague, therefore, if you want to check the outcome of an action, you should use the function FORM_SUCCESS, as in the example shown in Figure 18.10.

The function `Click_Button` enables you to invoke the functionality of any button, as long as you know the name of that button. This function can be called from several locations. For example, you could create a WHEN-BUTTON-PRESSED trigger, and call the function with the name of the button hard-coded in it. The trigger for the button CLEAR_FORM, for example, would contain the following line:

```
Click_Button('CLEAR_FORM');
```

You could also define the WHEN-BUTTON-PRESSED trigger at the block level, rather than for each individual button. However, it is not hard to notice that most of the functionality accessible from the toolbars is also accessible from several push buttons created in earlier chapters. You should take advantage of the work done in this section and of the carefully planned naming standards followed previously.

In this context then, it is more appropriate to create the WHEN-BUTTON-PRESSED trigger at the form level. As in other similar situations, in such a trigger you want your code to be object-independent. Therefore, you should find a way to retrieve the name of the button. The system variable SYSTEM.TRIGGER_ITEM contains the name of the item that activated the trigger. This variable stores the fully qualified name of the item, in the form BLOCK_NAME.ITEM_NAME. To strip only the item name from this string, you can use a combination of the SQL functions INSTR and SUBSTR. A similar technique was discussed in Chapter 17. INSTR is used to find the position in the string of the dot that separates the block name from the item name. Then the function SUBSTR returns the substring of the original string that begins from the character after the dot. This is also the name of the item that you pass to the procedure `Click_Button`. Figure 18.11 shows the contents of the trigger WHEN-BUTTON-PRESSED that you should create at the form level.

After creating the form-level trigger, delete the item-level WHEN-BUTTON-PRESSED triggers for all the buttons in blocks CUSTOMER, MOVIE, and RENTAL, except for the buttons that close the windows. Now, when the event ButtonPressed occurs in one of these buttons, for example CUSTOMERS.RENTAL or MOVIES.COMMIT_FORM, Forms Runtime will execute the WHEN-BUTTON-PRESSED trigger defined for the form module. However, if the event occurs for a button that has a proper trigger attached such as CUSTOMERS.CLOSE, the item-level trigger will fire.

```
DECLARE
 block_item      VARCHAR2(80);
 item_name       VARCHAR2(50);
 dot_pos         NUMBER;
BEGIN
 block_item := :SYSTEM.TRIGGER_ITEM;
 dot_pos    := INSTR(block_item, '.', 1, 1);
 item_name  := SUBSTR(block_item, dot_pos + 1 );
 Click_Button(item_name);
END;
```

FIGURE 18.11 Generic trigger to activate an iconic button.

18.2.6 ENABLING AND DISABLING TOOLBAR BUTTONS AND MENU ITEMS DYNAMICALLY

When users will launch the application, they will initially see only the MDI frame, with its menu and toolbars. Not all of the iconic buttons or menu items can be used at this time. For example, users cannot create, or delete, or save any records unless a window is open and they are on a base table block. In fact, if they try to click one of the icons in the vertical toolbar, or select any item from the Data menu, Forms Runtime will return the error message "FRM-41003: This function cannot be performed here."

It is necessary to disable some of the toolbar buttons and menu items whose functionality is not accessible upon the application's startup. However, as soon as a window with a base table block in it becomes active, the buttons and the menu items should return to their normal state. If during the processing users close all the windows, these windows and menu items should be disabled once again. To facilitate the process of enabling and disabling objects, you need to create the following procedures:

- **Toggle_Menu_Item.** This procedure, shown in Figure 18.12, toggles the ENABLED property of a menu item whose name is passed as an argument.
- **Toggle_Item.** This procedure, shown in Figure 18.13, is very similar to the previous one and toggles the ENABLED property of an item whose name is passed as an argument.

```
PROCEDURE Toggle_Menu_Item (menu_item_name VARCHAR2) IS
 menu_item_id     MenuItem;
BEGIN
– Find ID for menu item
 menu_item_id := FIND_MENU_ITEM(menu_item_name);
 IF ID_NULL(menu_item_id) THEN
  MESSAGE('Menu item ' || menu_item_name || ' does not
exist.');
  RAISE FORM_TRIGGER_FAILURE;
 END IF;

 IF GET_MENU_ITEM_PROPERTY(menu_item_id,ENABLED) = 'TRUE' THEN
  SET_MENU_ITEM_PROPERTY(menu_item_id,ENABLED,PROPERTY_FALSE);
 ELSE
  SET_MENU_ITEM_PROPERTY(menu_item_id,ENABLED,PROPERTY_TRUE);
 END IF;
END Toggle_Menu_Item;
```

FIGURE 18.12 Procedure that toggles the ENABLED property of a menu item.

```
PROCEDURE Toggle_Item (item_name VARCHAR2) IS
 item_id   ITEM;
BEGIN
– Find ID for item
 item_id := FIND_ITEM(item_name);
 IF ID_NULL(item_id) THEN
  MESSAGE('Item ' || item_name || ' does not exist.');
  RAISE FORM_TRIGGER_FAILURE;
 END IF;

 IF GET_ITEM_PROPERTY(item_id,ENABLED) = 'TRUE' THEN
  SET_ITEM_PROPERTY(item_id,ENABLED,PROPERTY_FALSE);
 ELSE
  SET_ITEM_PROPERTY(item_id,ENABLED,PROPERTY_TRUE);
 END IF;
END Toggle_Item
```

FIGURE 18.13 Procedure that toggles the ENABLED property of an item.

With these two procedures in hand, you can create the procedure that disables the right menu items and iconic buttons at form startup or when all MDI sheets are closed and enables them when one of the MDI sheets is open. The contents of this procedure are shown in Figure 18.14.

You also need the global variable `GLOBAL.Toggle_State` to hold the toggle state of the application. When the form is initially loaded, the procedure `Toggle_Enable_Property` disables the menu items and the toolbar icons. At the same time, `GLOBAL.Toggle_State` must be set to "DISABLED." When the first of the MDI sheet window is opened, the buttons and menu items must be set to normal state and `GLOBAL.Toggle_State` should be set to "ENABLED." To add this functionality to the MRD module follow these steps:

1. Declare the variable `GLOBAL.Toggle_State` in the PRE-FORM trigger.
2. Create the form-level trigger WHEN-WINDOW-ACTIVATED, and add to it the following statements:

It is clear from these statements that when any of the MDI sheets is activated, and the status of the menu items and toolbar buttons is still disabled, the procedure `Toggle_Enable_Property` will be executed and will enable the objects. The flag `GLOBAL.Toggle_State` will be set the "ENABLED" as well. This will guarantee that when the next window is activated, this procedure does not get executed again. The only time when the procedure `Toggle_Enable_Prop-`

```
PROCEDURE Toggle_Enable_Property IS
BEGIN
 Toggle_Menu_Item('FILE.CLEAR_FORM');
 Toggle_Menu_Item('FILE.SAVE');
 Toggle_Menu_Item('DATA.INSERT');
 Toggle_Menu_Item('DATA.DUPLICATE');
 Toggle_Menu_Item('DATA.DELETE');
 Toggle_Menu_Item('DATA.ENTER');
 Toggle_Item('TOOLBAR.CLEAR_FORM');
 Toggle_Item('TOOLBAR.COMMIT_FORM');
 Toggle_Item('TOOLBAR.CREATE_RECORD');
 Toggle_Item('TOOLBAR.DELETE_RECORD');
 Toggle_Item('TOOLBAR.ENTER_QUERY');
END;
```

FIGURE 18.14 Procedure that enables and disables menu items and iconic buttons.

`erty` should run again is when the users close all the windows in the application. In this case, the menu items and toolbar buttons in question should no longer be accessible, and therefore, their ENABLE property must be set to False. The global variable `GLOBAL.Toggle_State` should once again be set to "DISABLED." The question is what would be the appropriate event that should make you check and see if all the windows are closed, and, if so, perform these actions.

The MRD application uses a special object as the home item where the focus should return after the window is closed. When the focus is placed on an item, the trigger WHEN-NEW-ITEM-INSTANCE fires. Thus, for all purposes, each time a window is closed, this trigger for the home item EXIT_FORM will be activated. The code that disables the objects if no windows are open should be placed in this trigger.

The best way to decide whether all the windows are closed or there is at least one still open, is to use the function `Count_Open_Windows` that returns the number of open windows in the application. Recall that this function was imple-

```
IF :GLOBAL.Toggle_State = 'DISABLED' AND
  :SYSTEM.EVENT_WINDOW <> 'ABOUT' THEN
  Toggle_Enable_Property;
  :GLOBAL.Toggle_State := 'ENABLED';
END IF;
```

FIGURE 18.15 Enabling menu items and iconic buttons.

```
IF Count_Open_Windows('WINDOWS', 'WINDOW_NAME') = 0 THEN
 Toggle_Enable_Property;
 :GLOBAL.Toggle_State := 'DISABLED';
END IF;
```

FIGURE 18.16 Disabling menu items and iconic toolbars.

mented in Chapter 16. Now you can create the trigger WHEN-NEW-ITEM-INSTANCE for the iconic button EXIT_FORM as shown in Figure 18.16. Note that this trigger will handle the initial disabling of the objects as well.

This concludes the work you have to do with the toolbar for the MRD application. Note that although you implemented the functionality for icons CUSTOMER, MOVIE, RENTAL, ANALYZE, MAIL, and HELP, you still have to add it to the menu items. You could do it at this point, by copying the procedure `Click_Button` discussed earlier over to the menu module and setting the Menu Item Code for each menu item using this procedure. For example, the Menu Item Code for Tools | Customer... would be

```
Click_Button('CUSTOMER');
```

The next chapter will discuss the PL/SQL libraries. There, you will create a library with code that is shared by both the form and the menu, and attach the library to each module. From that moment on, the code will be maintained in the PL/SQL library and referenced by the form or the menu.

18.2.7 ADDING BALLOON HELP TO TOOLBARS

While working with the Form Builder, you have seen how you can display pop-up help, also known as balloon help, for iconic buttons in toolbars of the Object Navigator, Layout Editor, Property Palette, and Menu Editor. You would like your applications to contain a similar functionality as well. Since Chapter 13 explained how to implement pop-up help for items in general, this section will just summarize the steps, since this kind of utility is used primarily with toolbar buttons. Here are the steps necessary to add balloon help to your toolbar icons:

1. Display the Property Palette for the desired icon.
2. Set the property Tooltip to a keyword that describes the action invoked by the icon.
3. Optionally, set the property Visual Attribute Group to point to the named visual attribute object. You should use the same object to control the display properties of all the tooltip messages.

18.3 POP-UP MENUS

Pop-up menus have become ubiquitous in GUI applications nowadays. They allow you to associate a number of actions and commands with particular areas or even single items on the screen. In Form Builder applications, pop-up menus are objects created and maintained in the hierarchy of a module, under the node Popup Menus in the Object Navigator. The structure of these menus is maintained in the Menu Editor. There is no difference whether you are using this editor to create a pop-up menu or a menu object in a menu module. The properties of pop-up menu items are very similar with those of items in a menu module, as well. The most often used ones include Label, Menu Item Type, Command Type, and Menu Item Code. Since these properties were discussed in detail in Section 18.1, they will not be covered here. The following are some of the properties of items in menu modules that do not apply to items in pop-up menus.

- **Menu Security properties.** The items in pop-up menus are available to the users of your applications independently of their roles. Unlike menu modules that enforce role-based security automatically, for pop-up menus you need to maintain the enabled status programmatically.
- **Font & Color properties.** As mentioned in Section 18.1.2, setting properties in this group is not a good idea anyway. For pop-up menus, these properties are not available at all.
- **A number of Functional properties.** If you compare the properties in the Functional group, you will notice that pop-up menu items do not have a number of properties, such as Keyboard Accelerator, Icon in Menu, or Icon Filename. They simply do not apply to this type of menus.

Once a menu object is created, you can assign it to a canvas object or an item by simply setting the property Pop-up Menu of the object. Note that although you can assign pop-up menus at the item level, it is usually more intuitive to associate them with canvases.

18.4 SUMMARY

This chapter covered the properties, functionality and usage of menus and toolbars in Form Builder applications. Among major concepts explained here were:

- **Form Builder Menus**
  - Creating the Menu for the MRD Application

- Properties of Menus
- Using PL/SQL in Menus
- Enforcing the Security of the Application in Menus
- Attaching a Menu to a Form

- **Toolbars**
  - Steps to Implement a Toolbar in Form Buider Applications
  - Creating Toolbars for the MRD Application
  - Integrating Toolbars with Windows Management Functionality
  - Attaching Toolbars to Forms Modules
  - Adding Functionality to the MRD Toolbar
  - Enabling and Disabling Toolbar Buttons and Menu Items Dynamically
  - Adding Balloon Help to Toolbars

- **Popup Menus**

The following table describes the software assets that were discussed in this chapter. From the main HTML page of the software utilities provided with the book follow the links *Software* and *Chapter 18* to access these assets:

ASSET NAME	DESCRIPTION
CH18_1.MMB	The MRD menu module created in Section 18.1.
CH18_1.MMX	The executable version of CH18_1.MMB compiled for Win32 platforms.
CH18_1.FMB	The MRD application completed in the last chapter. Use this module as a starting point for the activities discussed in this chapter.
CH18_2.FMB	The MRD application with the menu CH18_1.FMB attached. Make sure that the folder where you save the modules CH18_1.MMB or CH18_1.MMX is in the variable FORMSxx_PATH of your machines registry.
CH18_2.FMX	The executable version of CH18_2.FMB compiled for Win32 platforms.
CH18_3.FMB	The MRD application with all the activities discussed in this chapter.
CH18_3.FMX	The executable version of CH18_3.FMB compiled for Win32 platforms.

Chapter 19

PL/SQL OBJECTS

One event happeneth to them all.
—The Holy Bible, Ecclesiastes

- Events and Triggers in Form Builder Applications
- PL/SQL Libraries
- Creating a Package for the MRD Application
- Stored Program Units and Database Triggers
- Oracle Designer Server API
- Summary

So far in this book, you have used procedures and functions, and have written several triggers to implement the functionality of the MRD application. This chapter takes a closer look at these and other PL/SQL objects used in Form Builder applications. In particular, it looks at different events that occur in these applications and how they activate different PL/SQL objects. It also discusses other PL/SQL objects such as stored procedures, database triggers, and packages. PL/SQL libraries, used to group together the code of PL/SQL objects, are also introduced as a way to ensure code reusability in your applications.

19.1 EVENTS AND TRIGGERS IN FORM BUILDER APPLICATIONS

While discussing different objects used in Form Builder applications such as blocks, data items, controls, and records, previous chapters have also discussed the events that occur in these objects, the triggers associated with these events, and how you can place PL/SQL code in these triggers to make your application react to the events in the desired way.

19.1.1 TYPES OF EVENTS AND TRIGGERS

A Form Builder application is the middle ground where its users meet their data stored in the database. Users are the major players that define the events that occur in the life of a form. The events that originate from their interaction with the application are called *interface events*. Some events are clicking a mouse, pressing a push button, changing the state of a check box, selecting a radio button, or selecting from a list. When Form Builder (called SQL*Forms) was a character-based application environment, users could act on the application by pressing keyboard keys only. Therefore, events were mapped to a variety of keys, primarily function keys. Pressing one of these keys, for example F6, would cause a certain event to happen. Programmers would place their code in the key trigger associated with that event, and, probably add a cryptic label on the boilerplate such as `F6 -> Cust. Info`. Today, there is no need for such techniques. As examples discussed in this part have demonstrated, a push button on the window or an iconic button on the toolbar would be the object that users click to initiate a function or navigate to an area in the application. However, the events associated with pressing keyboard keys and the KEY triggers are still available in the Form Builder.

The triggers associated with user interface events are typically named after the event that fires them, in the format WHEN-*Event-Occurred*. Example of such triggers are WHEN-MOUSE-CLICK, WHEN-MOUSE-DOUBLE-CLICK, WHEN BUTTON-PRESSED, and WHEN-RADIO-CHANGED. You have already used a variety of these triggers in the MRD application.

The triggers activated by pressing function keys are named KEY-*Function*. For example, in regular Windows environments KEY-COMMIT is fired when users press F10 and KEY-CREREC is fired when they press F6. An important trigger in this category is KEY-OTHERS. This is fired whenever one of the predefined keys is pressed and no explicit trigger is associated with it. By placing the statement NULL; in this trigger, you will effectively turn off the ability of users to generate the default functionality of these keys. I recommend that you take this action in GUI applications, where all the functionality of the system must be accessible from the menu, toolbar, or the controls of the application, and not mysteriously hidden behind a key stroke or two.

The events that are caused by the response by the database to the application's requests for information, or desire to act on the data, are called *database transaction events*. Such events are logging in and out of the database, querying data, inserting, deleting, updating, and committing. Forms Runtime divides most of these events in three phases, or subevents. The first phase is right before the transactional event occurs. The second phase is the event itself occurring. And the third phase comes immediately after the event.

The triggers associated with these subevents are called PRE-*Event*, ON-*Event*, and POST-*Event*. Examples of such triggers are PRE-QUERY, ON-QUERY, and POST-QUERY, fired when the DatabaseQuery event occurs; or PRE-INSERT, ON-INSERT, and POST-INSERT, fired when the DatabaseInsert event occurs. This state of affairs allows you to take certain actions in preparation for an event, when the event actually occurs, or after the event has occurred. For example, the PRE-QUERY trigger is typically used to add additional conditions in the SELECT statements of a base table block, based on the query criteria that users have entered in the query-by-example interface of the form. The POST-QUERY trigger on the other hand, is used to retrieve additional data, based on values stored in designated items for each record returned by the query. The ON-*Event* triggers are used only if you want to override the way Forms Runtime handles the event. For example, if the application is running against a non-Oracle database, triggers such as ON-INSERT, ON-DELETE, and ON-COMMIT, must contain the necessary statements to perform the task in these databases. If an application will not need to access the database, you can place the statement `NULL;` in the ON-LOGON trigger, to bypass the logon screen that Forms Runtime displays by default, when the form is launched. The ON-*Event* triggers that are used the most, however are the ON-ERROR and ON-MESSAGE. These are fired when Forms Runtime sends messages generated internally to the user, and can be used to trap, silence, or modify these messages.

Then, there is the gray area of events that are not caused directly by an action of the users, or a transaction with the database. These events occur internally as Forms responds to any of the events described before. The major categories of these events are *navigation events* and *validation events*. The basic navigation events are entering the object, preparing the object for input, and leaving the object. The trigger PRE-*Object* is fired when Forms enters an object. When Forms

Runtime prepares an object for input, the trigger WHEN-NEW-*Object*-INSTANCE is fired. And, when Forms leaves an object, the POST-*Object* trigger is activated. In all these cases, the object can be a form, a block, a record, or a text item. The validation event occurs only for items and records, and the triggers fired during these events are WHEN-VALIDATE-ITEM and WHEN-VALIDATE-RECORD, respectively.

19.1.2 FIRING ORDER OF TRIGGERS

In order to place the code effectively in the key points of your application, it is very important to understand the sequence in which the events described above and their corresponding triggers fire. Given the large number of events and situations that can occur in a Forms application, describing the firing sequence of triggers associated with them extends far beyond the scope of this book. This section will focus only on the sequence of triggers that fire during navigational events. To help you understand how Form Runtime navigates from one item to the other, Figure 19.1 shows graphically the hierarchy of objects in a module.

The objects in a Form Builder application form a connected graph. This means that if the current focus of the form is on Item 1.1.1 and the user clicks Item 2.2.1, the focus does not immediately jump to that item. Internally, Forms Runtime follows the connecting lines to navigate to the clicked item. This means that the form will first go up the tree. It will leave Item 1.1.1, Record 1.1, and Block 1. At this point, there is a line connecting the current block with the block of the target item. Forms will move to this block and navigate down the tree. It will enter Block 2, Record 2.2, and Item 2.2.1. Finally, the target block, record, and item are prepared to receive input from the users.

All the triggers associated with these events, if they exist, will fire in the sequence the events occur. Assuming that both items are text items, the sequence of triggers fired is: POST-TEXT-ITEM, POST-RECORD, POST-BLOCK when Forms is going up the tree; PRE-BLOCK, PRE-RECORD, PRE-TEXT-ITEM when Forms

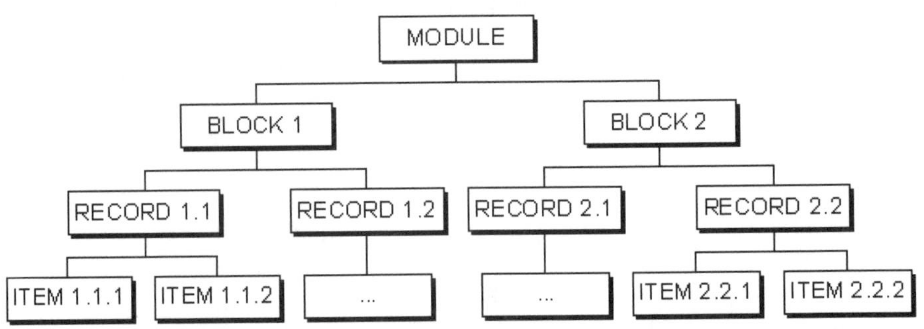

FIGURE 19.1 Hierarchy tree of objects in Form Builder applications.

is going down the tree; and WHEN-NEW-BLOCK-INSTANCE, WHEN-NEW-RECORD-INSTANCE, WHEN-NEW-ITEM-INSTANCE when the objects are prepared for input.

As it can be seen from Figure 19.1, the number of nodes traversed, and therefore triggers fired, will depend on the location of the current focus and of the target item. If from Item 1.1.1 users want to go to Item 1.1.2, only the triggers POST-ITEM, PRE-ITEM and WHEN-NEW-ITEM-INSTANCE would fire. However, it the navigation target is an item in Record 1.2, then the record-related triggers will fire as well.

The validation occurs during the process of leaving the item or the record. The validation of items will occur if their status is not VALID. A record will be validated every time its status is not QUERY. When the record is validated, all its items are validated as well.

19.1.3 TRIGGERS AS METHODS THAT ASSOCIATE OBJECTS WITH EVENTS

A form is built by drawing together resources from the pool of available objects, and the pool of available events. You start by creating objects and then program the way they behave when certain events occur. The association between an object and an event is established by a trigger attached to the object that is fired the event occurs. Thinking of objects and events as entities, triggers are the entity introduced to resolve the many-to-many relationship that exists between them (see Figure 19.2).

Given the number of objects that can be part of a form and the number of events that Forms Runtime recognizes, it would be an overwhelming and impossible task to create triggers that govern the behavior of each object for each event. Fortunately, you do not have to do this. The default functionality of Forms Runtime takes most of the load off your shoulders. For example, very little explicit programming is required and done for database transaction events; applications mostly rely on the handling of these events by Forms. This sharing of responsibilities allows you to focus the attention where most of the programming occurs. That is the user-friendly design of the application and the handling of the user interface and validation events.

Even when you have to explicitly code triggers for an event, you can take advantage of the fact that Forms propagates events in its hierarchy of objects. If a push button is pressed, for example, Forms will look to see if there is a WHEN-BUTTON-PRESSED trigger at the button level. If there is none, it will move up to the block level in search for a trigger with that name attached to the block. If none is found, it will move up to the form level for the same purpose. By default, the first trigger encountered in this traversal from the bottom to the top of the hierarchy will be executed. This behavior allows you to modularize the code, make it more compact, and move it higher in the hierarchy of a module. The advantage here is that the number of triggers to create and maintain can be reduced signifi-

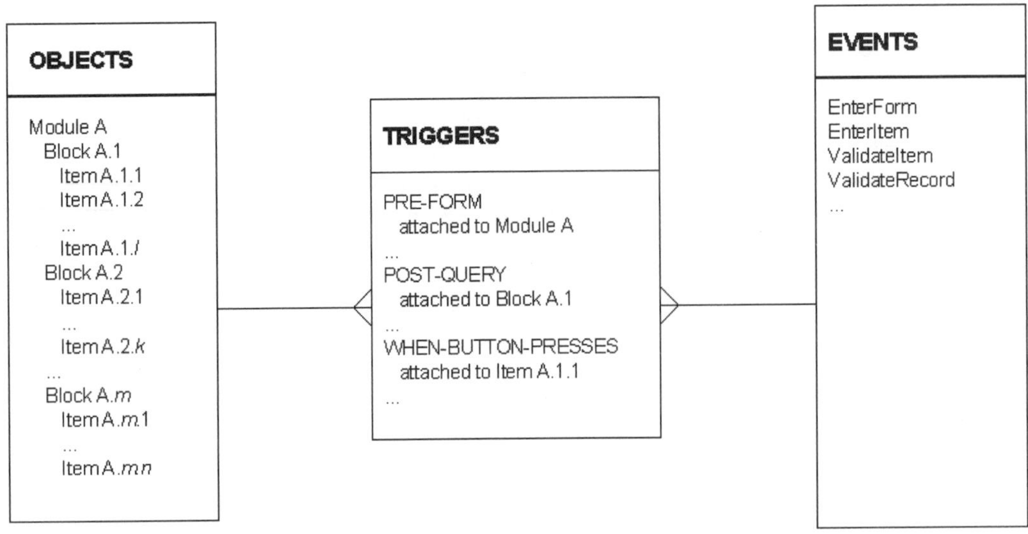

FIGURE 19.2 Relationship between objects, events, and triggers in Form Builder applications.

cantly. If, for example, a block contains several push buttons, instead of having that many WHEN-BUTTON-PRESSED triggers, you could move the code up at the block level, and concentrate it in one single trigger that will fire each time a button in the block is pressed.

Triggers can be attached to property classes as well. Objects that inherit properties from these classes will also inherit the triggers. Forms Runtime will execute only the class triggers, even if triggers of the same type are attached to the objects or their parents.

19.1.4 OVERRIDING THE DEFAULT FIRING ORDER OF TRIGGERS

In some instances, when the behavior of an item in reaction to an event is slightly different from the way all its peers behave. You would still want to execute the main code that is associated with that event, and, in addition, the code that characterizes this special behavior. In such cases, you can still create and maintain the general functionality in a block-level trigger. Then, an item-level trigger is created for the same event and attached to the item that needs special attention. As said earlier, when the event occurs for this item, the default behavior of Forms Runtime is to fire the item-level trigger and stop there. By changing the property Execution Hierarchy for the trigger object, you can make both triggers fire.

The property Execution Hierarchy may be set to "Override," "Before," or "After." "Override" is the default setting, and will cause Forms to execute the first trigger found going up from the item level to block and to form level. If the property is set to "After," the trigger in the parent object will fire first and then the trigger in the current object will be executed. This sequence is reversed when Execution Hierarchy is set to "Before."

Of course, the property can be set recursively. For example, if there is a WHEN-BUTTON-PRESSED defined at the item, block, and form level, and you want to fire the form-level trigger first, then the block-level one, and, finally, the item-level trigger, you could set the Execution Style property for both block and item level triggers to "After." If you want the triggers to fire from the bottom up, the Execution Style should be set to 'Before.'

In the case when you inherit a trigger for an object from a properties class, the trigger defined in the property class will always be the only trigger to fire. Although you may set its Execution Style property to "After" or "Before," these settings do not affect the default firing of the trigger.

Besides Execution Hierarchy, the only other property that you may ever have to set for a trigger is Fire in Enter-Query Mode. By default, this property is set to "Yes," which means that all the triggers you create will fire both in Normal and Enter Query mode. In occasions when you want to fire the trigger only in Normal mode, set this property to "No."

19.1.5 RESTRICTED BUILT-IN PROGRAM UNITS

The built-in functions and procedures that come with the STANDARD package of Form Builder are divided in two groups: restricted and unrestricted built-ins. Restricted built-ins are those functions and procedures that affect the Forms Runtime navigation such as GO_BLOCK, GO_ITEM, CREATE_RECORD, and DELETE_RECORD. They are called restricted because their use is not allowed in triggers that fire as a result of navigational events. Examples of triggers in this category are PRE-*object* and POST-*object* triggers, such as PRE-BLOCK, POST-BLOCK, PRE-TEXT-ITEM, and POST-TEXT-ITEM.

This restriction is placed to avoid circular references and infinite loops in Form Builder applications. Indeed, imagine a situation in which you are allowed to use the restricted procedure CREATE_RECORD in a navigational trigger such as PRE-RECORD. You could easily create a block-level PRE-RECORD trigger which contains a call to CREATE_RECORD. At runtime, when users navigate to a record in the block the following sequence of actions will occur:

1. EnterRecord event fires PRE-RECORD trigger.
2. PRE-RECORD trigger invokes CREATE_RECORD procedure.
3. CREATE_RECORD procedure creates a new record in the block and attempts to navigate to this new record.
4. The navigation attempt causes the event EnterRecord.
5. EnterRecord event fires PRE-RECORD trigger.
6. ...(Cycle is repeated)

Clearly, this is an infinite loop. Restricted procedures can be used from any other types of triggers such as WHEN-NEW-*Object*-INSTANCE, or WHEN-*Event-Occurred*.

Unrestricted procedures, on the other hand, can be used in any type of trigger. Among the most important program units in this group are all those that retrieve and set the properties of objects such as FIND_*Object*, GET_*Object*_PROPERTY, and SET_*Object*_PROPERTY. The Form Builder documentation contains a complete listing of all the built-ins, together with their restricted or unrestricted type.

19.1.6 SMART TRIGGERS

The discussion about triggers is concluded with a brief discussion about smart triggers. In order to assist you in the process of associating triggers with objects, the Form Builder maintains a list of the most popular trigger for each type of object. These are called smart triggers and are displayed in the popup menu activated by right-clicking the object. Examples of smart triggers for a form module are WHEN-NEW-FROM-TRIGGER, PRE-FORM, and POST-FORM; for a text item WHEN-NEW-INSTANCE, WHEN-VALIDATE-ITEM, PRE-TEXT-ITEM, and POST-TEXT-ITEM; for a push button WHEN-NEW-ITEM-INSTANCE and WHEN-BUTTON-PRESSED; and so on. The popup menu item always contains the option Other which allows you to create a trigger any other type not included in the list of the object's smart triggers.

19.2 PL/SQL LIBRARIES

As you have been adding functionality to your application, the list of functions and procedures that implement this functionality has been growing longer and longer. You also have faced the need to implement the same functionality in multiple modules. For example, Chapter 17 raised the problem of having to keep duplicate copies of code in the form and menu modules, in order to implement the same functionality for the iconic buttons and the menu items.

These two problems point out the need for a repository where the program units of a module should reside. This repository should not simply group functions and procedures together, but should also be accessible from all the other modules that may need any of these program units. PL/SQL Library (PLL) modules are a special type of Form Builder modules that serve exactly the purpose of a central repository for all the program units of an application. The major advantage of PLL modules is that they allow reuse of the code over and over across all the Oracle application development tools. In a library, you may store PL/SQL objects that can be accessed from and used in any form or menu module, but also in reports, and displays developed with Report Builder and Graphics Builder.

19.2.1 CREATING AND POPULATING LIBRARIES

Chapter 4 explained how you create, save and compile PLL modules. This section will discuss the process of populating them with objects, and attaching PLL libraries to a form or menu module. You will follow the material introduced here as you work to create PLL libraries for the MRD application. As a preliminary step, open the MRD module you are working with, or the module CH18.FMB from the companion software, which contains all the features you have put in the application so far.

1. In the Object Navigator, double-click the node PL/SQL Libraries to create a new library.
2. Save the newly created library in the same directory where the form MRD.FMB is located. Give it the name MRDMENU.PLL.
3. Create another library and name it LISTS.PLL.
4. Create a third library and name it WINDOWS.PLL.

The first library will store only those program units that must be shared between the MRD form and menu modules. The second library will contain the PL/SQL objects developed to implement the functionality of lists. The third library will be the repository for the windows-related functions and procedures. There are several reasons to split the existing program units in different libraries. Some of them are discussed in the following paragraphs:

- First, saying that libraries are repositories of program units does not mean they are dumpsites where these program units are piled up with no order or organization. There must be some organization and logical unity between the members of a library.
- Second, by splitting the program units by the functional area in which they are used, you increase the chance for the reusability of the code. If in another module you need to implement some list features, but will have only one window that will stay open all the time, all you need to reference is the library LISTS.PLL. If, on the other hand, the application has multiple windows but none of the list features included in LISTS.PLL, you would want to attach only WINDOWS.PLL to that module.
- The last reason, related with the previous one, has to do with the way Forms Runtime uses libraries. When you attach a library to a module, Forms, internally creates a tabular structure with the names of the program units in the library, and the name and location of the library itself. At runtime, when one of these units is called, Forms will retrieve from the table the location of the PLL module where the program unit is stored and will load the entire module in the memory. It is understandable that larger the library is, more memory it is going to occupy when it is loaded. For this reason, you should strive to keep

the size of the libraries as small as possible without affecting its functional completeness. If the menu module will share only one or two procedures with the form, there is no reason to include other functions or procedures that are not functionally related with the original ones.

Now, move the program units from the MRD module to the newly created libraries. You can select and cut the desired program units, and then paste them in the Program Units node of the target library. Or even easier, just drag the objects to move and drop them in the target library. One way or another, move the procedures as described by these steps:

1. Move Click_Button, Toggle_Menu_Item, Toggle_Item, and Toggle_Enable_Property over to MRDMENU.PLL.
2. Move the function Element_Label_Exists and procedures Insert_Element, Move_Current_Element, and Populate_The_List over to module LISTS.PLL.
3. Move the functions Count_Open_Windows and Show_Centered_LOV, and the procedures Close_Window, Open_Window, and Open_Dialog_Box over to module WINDOWS.PLL.

After moving the PL/SQL program units to the appropriate libraries, delete the objects in the MRD module. You should not move any of the master-detail procedures created by Form Builder to synchronize the relations in your module. They are maintained internally, and may change if the properties of relations change.

You should not move the procedures `Get_Customer` and `Get_Movie_Lists_Values`, or the functions `Get_Home_Item`, `Build_Where_Clause` and `Get_Sequence_Id`, either. They are too specific to the MRD module and would not justify their being in any of the three libraries or in a library of their own.

19.2.2 COMPILING PL/SQL LIBRARIES

The next step after creating and populating a PLL library is to compile it. This is an important step, because if the library contains program units that are not compiled, Forms Runtime will not be able to load them. The following are several ways to compile a PLL library:

- Compile each individual program unit by selecting it in the hierarchy tree and then choosing Program | Compile Selection from the menu. You may also display the contents of the program units in the PL/SQL Editor and compile them there.
- Compile only those PL/SQL objects whose status is "Compiled with Errors" or "Not Compiled" by choosing Program | Compile | Incremental from the Form Builder menu.

- ❑ Compile all the PL/SQL objects in the library, even those successfully compiled previously, by selecting Program | Compile | All... from the Form Builder menu.

If you try to compile the library WINDOWS.PLL, you will see a Compile dialog box similar to Figure 19.3. The compilation will stop with error. Clicking the button Goto Error, will place the cursor at the line where the error is located. The line is in the procedure Close_Window and contains a direct reference to the global variable GLOBAL.Home_Item. A second direct reference to that variable occurs a few lines below in the same procedure.

19.2.3 REFERENCING VARIABLES INDIRECTLY IN PL/SQL LIBRARIES

In form modules, you can refer to the value stored in an item as :<BLOCK_NAME>.<ITEM_NAME>, or in a system variable as :SYSTEM.<VARIABLE_NAME>, or in a global variable as :GLOBAL.<VARIABLE_NAME>, or in a parameter as :PARAMETER.<PARAMETER_NAME>. Because these objects are internal to the form module, their values can be referenced directly. However, a PLL library is a separate module, independent of the form. It cannot and should not have any knowledge about objects that are internal to the form. Therefore you cannot reference directly the values of these types of variables.

Similarly, menu modules are separate modules that do not recognize their objects. The same error described at the end of the previous section would have occurred if you had copied the procedure Click_Button in the menu module MRD.MMB, and tried to compile it from there.

In order to reference the value of an item, system variable, global variable, or parameter outside a form module, you should use the built-in function NAME_IN. By replacing the direct reference :GLOBAL.Home_Item with the

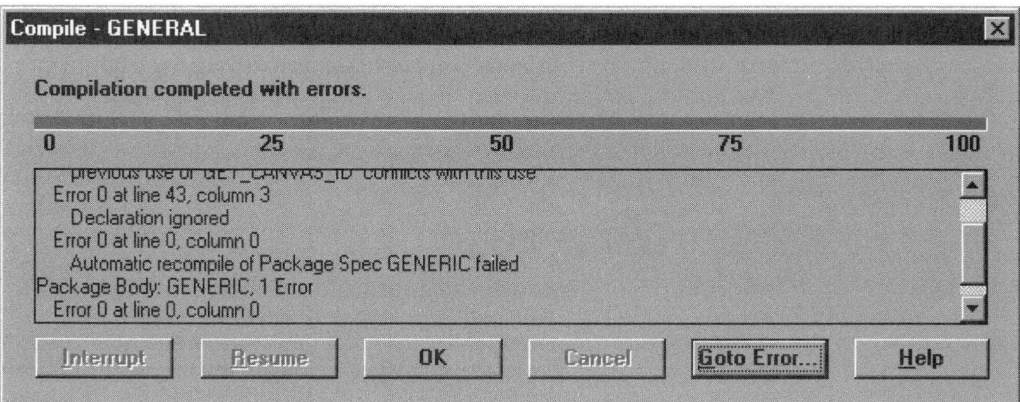

FIGURE 19.3 Compile dialog box.

string NAME_IN('GLOBAL.Home_Item'), you still get the value of the global variable, if it exists, and, at the same time create a generic program unit that can stand on its own, independently from the form module. For the same reason, you cannot assign values directly to any of the four types of variables mentioned above. The following statement will be invalid in PLL or menu modules:

```
:CUSTOMER.FIRST_NAME := 'John';
```

The built-in procedure COPY is used to assign values to variables without referencing them directly. The previous statement should be replaced with this statement:

```
COPY ('John', 'CUSTOMER.FIRST_NAME');
```

After you remove the direct reference to the variable GLOBAL.Home_Item from both locations, you will be able to compile the whole WINDOWS.PLL library successfully. When trying to compile the library MRDMENU.PLL, you will notice a similar problem with the procedure Click_Button. Here, it is the system variable SYSTEM.MODE that is referenced directly. Replace the direct reference with the indirect reference to its value as shown in this statement:

```
NAME_IN('SYSTEM.MODE');
```

The procedure Click_Button will still compile with errors because it contains references to the procedures Open_Window and Open_Dialog_Box, which now are located in module WINDOWS.PLL. You will fix this problem in the following section by attaching the library WINDOWS.PLL to MRDMENU.PLL.

The module LISTS.PLL will compile without any errors. All the code here is generic and will not cause any conflicts. Save the changes you made in all three modules and move to the next section where you will learn how to attach these libraries to the other modules.

19.2.4 ATTACHING PL/SQL LIBRARIES

You can attach a library to a form, menu, or another library module in order to make its member program units available to other modules. The process is the same and does not depend on the type of module to which the PL/SQL library will be attached. Follow these steps to attach the library WINDOWS.PLL to the module MRDMENU.PLL:

1. In the Object Navigator create a new object under the node Attached Libraries for module MRDMENU.PLL. The Attach Library dialog box will be displayed (see Figure 19.4).

FIGURE 19.4 Attach Library dialog box.

2. In the Library field specify the path and name of MRDMENU.PLL. You may click Browse... to open a dialog box that allows you to find the file easier.
3. Click Attach.

When you click the button Attach, an alert is displayed. It informs you that the attached library name you selected contains a non-portable directory path. It is referring to the directory where the library file is located. It also asks you to remove the path or not. If you do not remove the path, at runtime, Forms will search for the library in only one location: that specified by the path shown in the alert box. If you remove the path, then Form will store just the name of the library in its internal reference table. At runtime, when the library must be loaded, Forms will search the current directory from which the form was loaded and those directories specified in the environment variable FORMSxx_PATH. This environment variable is defined in your machine's registry.

Usually, attaching the libraries with the full path specified leads to errors during the deployment of the application. Even more so when the client machines where the application will be installed do not share the same directory structure. It is safer to remove the path when attaching the library, place all the PLL files in one designated directory, and specify the path to this directory in the FORMSxx_PATH variable.

In your case, you can choose to remove the path and then add the working directory to the registry. However, for the new FORMSxx_PATH to take effect, you must restart the Form Builder. When you click the button Yes in the Alert box, you will see the library added under the node Attached Libraries. If you expand its node, you will see the specifications of the members of this library. Note, however that you cannot edit the functions or procedures here. The only point where you can edit these functions from now on is the library module. This is the reason why unstable program units, whose structure or contents may change during the development of the system, are usually kept around in the module.

Only after the program units are mature and do not need to be changed frequently, should they be moved to a library.

After attaching the library WINDOWS.PLL, you can compile successfully the module MRDMENU.PLL. With similar actions you can attach the libraries MRDMENU.PLL and LISTS.PLL to the form module MRD.FMB. Notice how, because the library WINDOWS.PLL is attached to MRDMENU.PLL, all its members become available to the module MRD.FMB as soon as you attach MRDMENU.PLL to it. At the end, generate, save and close the form.

TIP

If you compare the size of the modules before and after the separation of program units in PL/SQL libraries you will notice that the binary file MRD.FMB shrinks by 45 percent and the executable MRD.FMX by 15 percent when PL/SQL objects are grouped in libraries attached to the form. This means that the module will be more efficient at Runtime, but also that it will be easier to work with it in the Form Builder.

Now it is time to attach the library MRDMENU.PLL to the menu module, and complete the settings for the property Menu Item Code of those items that were not implemented in Chapter 18. The following steps guide you through this process:

1. Open the menu module MRD.MMB created in Chapter 18 or CH19.MMB provided in the companion software.
2. Attach the library MRDMENU.PLL to the menu module.
3. Set the property Menu Item Code for the menu items as shown in Figure 19.5.
4. Generate, save and close the menu module.

19.3 CREATING A PACKAGE FOR THE MRD APPLICATION

Functions and procedures are important PL/SQL objects that in a form module can be invoked from the body of triggers and in a menu module from the property Menu Item Code. They allow you to group together and modularize the PL/SQL statements that are necessary to perform the functionality of the application. As Chapter 10 explained, packages are PL/SQL objects that take this process one step further. They bundle together in one object data and program units that access and modify the data. The major benefits of packages are

MENU ITEM	MENU ITEM CODE PROPERTY
File I Clear	`Click_Button ('CLEAR_FORM');`
File I Save	`Click_Button ('COMMIT_FORM');`
File I Exit	`Click_Button ('EXIT_FORM');`
Tools I Customers...	`Click_Button ('CUSTOMER');`
Tools I Movie...	`Click_Button ('MOVIE');`
Tools I Rental...	`Click_Button ('RENTAL');`
Tools I Analyze...	`Click_Button ('ANALYZE');`
Tools I Mailing Labels...	`Click_Button ('MAIL');`
Data I Insert	`Click_Button ('CREATE_RECORD');`
Data I Duplicate I Record	`Click_Button ('DUPLICATE_RECORD');`
Data I Duplicate I Item	`Click_Button ('DUPLICATE_ITEM');`
Data I Delete	`Click_Button ('DELETE_RECORD');`
Data I Enter Query	`Click_Button ('ENTER_QUERY');`
Data I Count Query Hits	`Click_Button ('COUNT_QUERY');`
Data I Execute Query	`Click_Button ('EXECUTE_QUERY');`
Data I Cancel Query	`Click_Button ('CANCEL_QUERY');`
Help I Contains	`Click_Button ('HELP');`
Help I About	`Click_Button ('ABOUT');`

FIGURE 19.5 Command Text property settings for menu items in the MRD module.

- They allow you to hide the code and implementation details of the public methods.
- They increase the potential for reusing code.
- They allow you to overload PL/SQL methods.

In order to understand the great potential that packages have to offer for code reusability, I will critique the program units developed so far for the MRD application. Several instances of them access or set properties of objects. All the GET and SET built-ins utilized can take as a parameter the name of the object. However, it was agreed from the beginning that code written that way is inefficient and prone to runtime errors that cannot be detected by the compiler at design time. Thus, it was decided that each time there was a need for one of these functions, you would use the appropriate FIND function to get the internal ID of the object, and, only if you were certain of the existence of the object, you would proceed with the other statements. This convention was followed faithfully, but, tracing back the steps now, you can find inconsistencies in the implementation of the code. Figure 19.6 shows excerpts from function `Close_Window` and Figure 19.7 from `Count_Open_Windows`. Both these functions retrieve the internal ID

```
window_id := FIND_WINDOW(window_name);
IF ID_NULL(window_id) THEN
  Message('Window '||window_name||' does not exist.');
  RAISE FORM_TRIGGER_FAILURE;
END IF;
```

FIGURE 19.6 Excerpts from Count_Open_Windows.

of a window object based on its name, and handle the case when the object does not exist.

The problem here is not just the fact that you had to code multiple times the same functionality, but that there is a great potential for discrepancies and errors. Imagine what would have been the situation in a large development team working on multiple modules in parallel. In the next section you will create a package, which will contain among other routines the function `Get_Window_Id`, which, given the name of the window, will return its internal ID if it exists, or halt the operations, if not. Then, all those lines of code in your program units will be replaced with a single call to this member of the package. Because the code in this package is generic, you could use it not just in the MRD module, but in all the other forms you will develop in the future.

An excellent example of overloading a routine is the function ID_NULL that has been used over and over with all the object types of Form Builder. This function is part of the STANDARD Extensions package of built-in that come with Forms. If you expand the node of this package in the Object Navigator, you can see many other examples of overloading in the Form Builder built-in functions and procedures.

```
window_id := FIND_WINDOW(window_name);
IF ID_NULL(window_id) THEN
  RAISE Window_Not_Found;
END IF;

/* Other statements are here */

EXCEPTION
/* Other statements are here */
WHEN Window_Not_Found THEN
  MESSAGE('Window '||window_name||' does not exist.');
  RAISE FORM_TRIGGER_FAILURE;
/* Other statements are here */
```

FIGURE 19.7 Excerpts from Close_Window.

You can create a package anywhere you can create program units, including form, menu, and PL/SQL library modules. As an initial effort, create a package in a separate library.

1. Create a new library, and save it to the file system under the name GENERAL.PLL.
2. Create a new program unit for the library in the Object Navigator.
3. In the New Program Unit dialog box enter `Generic` in the Name field, and select the Package Spec radio button to create the package specification.
4. Click OK.

The Form Builder opens a PL/SQL editor and creates a template for the package. Enter the definitions of functions and procedures for this package as shown in Figure 19.8.

The first procedure in the package will handle an error number and string passed by a program unit. The second procedure will process any error that occurred in the program unit. Note that overloading is used here to implement the same procedure with different arguments. The function `Get_Window_Id` will return the internal ID, if the window `object_name` exists, or will stop any further processing in the object does not exist. The package shown in Figure 19.8 does not use any public variables. If you had to use any of them, you would declare them between the header and the first program units specification.

```
PACKAGE Generic IS
 /* Handle the error raised, and passed by the program
unit.*/
 PROCEDURE Handle_Error(prog_unit VARCHAR2,
                         error_num NUMBER,
                         error_msg VARCHAR2);

 /* Handle the error raised by the program unit.       */
 PROCEDURE Handle_Error(prog_unit VARCHAR2);

 /* Return window ID if it exists. Halt operation
otherwise. */
 FUNCTION Get_Window_Id(object_name VARCHAR2)
 RETURN Window;

END Generic;
```

FIGURE 19.8 Specification part of package Generic.

Creating the package body is a very similar process and is described by the following steps:

1. Create a new program unit for the library in the Object Navigator.
2. In the New Program Unit dialog box enter `Generic` in the Name field, and select the Package Body radio button to create the package specification.
3. Click OK.

In the PL/SQL editor window enter the contents of the procedures and function of the package as shown in Figure 19.9.

The first version of procedure `Handle_Error` does nothing more than display two messages, of which the last one is the error number and message passed as arguments. The second and overloaded version of procedure `Handle_Error` uses the PL/SQL functions SQLCODE and SQLERRM to retrieve the number and the text of the error that occurred. Then, these are displayed to the user together with the name of the program unit where the error occurred. The function `Get_Window_Id` retrieves the internal ID for a window based on its name. The only difference between this and previous versions of the same functionality is the way the exception OTHERS is handled. Rather than just displaying a general message, you invoke the procedure `Handle_Error` which will display the error number and message.

Compile the library GENERAL.PLL and attach it to the PL/SQL library WINDOWS.PLL. Now you may replace the old code with the new statements from the package.

1. Display the procedure `Open_Window` in the PL/SQL editor.
2. Replace the lines that retrieve the internal ID for a window with the single statement:
   ```
   Generic.Get_Window_Id(window_name);
   ```
3. Replace the lines for the exception OTHERS with the statement:
   ```
   Generic.Handle_Error('Open_Window');
   ```
4. Repeat Steps 1, 2 and 3 for the procedure `Close_Window` and the function `Count_Open_Windows`.

It is evident that the effort you did to create the package, not only reduces the size and improves the readability of each program unit in this library, but also standardizes the behavior of these program units.

The next step is to expand the package `Generic`. You should create a function for each Form Buikder object similar to function `Get_Window_Id`. The task is simply laborious and contains nothing worth discussing here. To save the effort, you may copy the library GENERIC.PLL provided in the companion disk.

```
PACKAGE BODY Generic IS
 /* Handle the error raised and passed by the program
unit.      */
 PROCEDURE Handle_Error(prog_unit VARCHAR2,
                        error_num NUMBER,
                        error_msg VARCHAR2)IS
 BEGIN
   MESSAGE('Error in '||prog_unit||'.', NO_ACKNOWLEDGE);
   MESSAGE(TO_CHAR(error_num)||': '||error_msg||'.');
 END;

 /* Handle the error raised by the program unit.
*/
 PROCEDURE Handle_Error(prog_unit VARCHAR2)IS
  error_numNUMBER;
  error_msgVARCHAR2(540);
 BEGIN
   error_num := SQLCODE;
   error_msg := SQLERRM;
   MESSAGE('Error in '||prog_unit||'.', NO_ACKNOWLEDGE);
   MESSAGE(TO_CHAR(error_num)||': '||error_msg||'.');
 END;

/* Returns window_ID if exists. Halts operation
otherwise. */
 FUNCTION Get_Window_Id(object_name VARCHAR2)
 RETURN Window IS
 object_id Window;
 BEGIN
  object_id := FIND_WINDOW(object_name);
  IF ID_NULL(object_id) THEN
    MESSAGE('Window '||object_name||' does not exist.');
    RAISE FORM_TRIGGER_FAILURE;
  END IF;
  RETURN(object_id);
 EXCEPTION
  WHEN OTHERS THEN
   Handle_Error('Get_Window_Id');
 END Get_Window_Id;
END Generic;
```

FIGURE 19.9 Body part of package Generic.

This library, in addition to the program units shown in Figure 19.9, contains Get_*Object*_Id functions for all the objects that you encounter in Form Builder applications.

In order not to edit the rest of the libraries the way you edited WINDOWS.PLL, you may also copy the libraries LISTS.PLL and MRDMENU.PLL. These libraries have attached to them the library GENERIC.PLL, and no path is stored, therefore you must place them all under a directory that is declared in FORMSxx_PATH. Finally, PL/SQL objects in the form module MRD.FMB need some modifications of the same kind and the library GENERIC.PLL must be attached to it as well. You may do these modifications yourself, as explained earlier, or copy module CH18A.FMB over to your directory and rename it MRD.FMB.

At this point in the development process, the MRD application involves several files and modules. This is one of those situations where the configuration management of the software becomes as important as the development of new programs or the maintenance of existing ones. To help you organize and double-check that you have all the files and links you need, Figure 19.10 contains a diagram of the modules in the system and the connections among them.

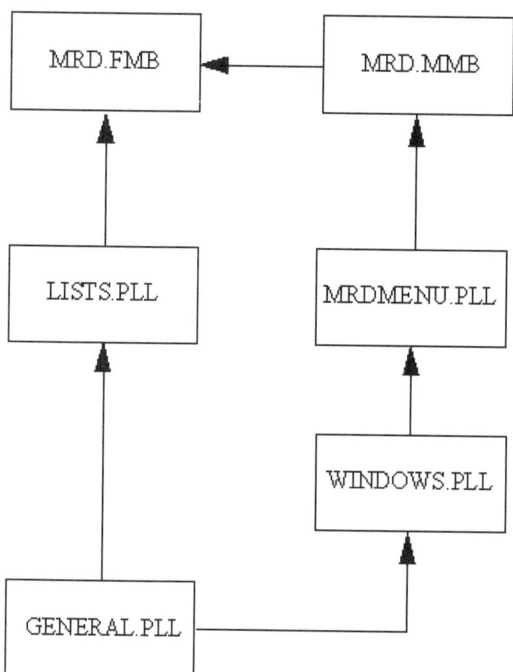

FIGURE 19.10 Software module configuration for MRD application.

19.4 STORED PROGRAM UNITS AND DATABASE TRIGGERS

In database systems today the load of computing and processing the information is divided between the database server and the clients that run the front-end application. Initially databases were little more than receptacles for data. The application developers had to create almost all of the system's logic and functionality in the client side. Today, all the major database packages support the ability to create application logic in the database server. In the Oracle RDBMS for example, you can create stored program units, including functions, procedures, and packages. You can also attach triggers with three major events that occur in a table: INSERT, DELETE, UPDATE.

The application development tools obviously have kept up with these new features. With one level of complication or another, they all support invoking remotely the stored program units in the database. However, in integrating the logic of the client and the server side of a system, and using it seamlessly, the combination of Oracle Server–Form Builder has the following two advantages:

- First, the programming language in Oracle Developer tools and Oracle Server is PL/SQL. This means that a developer working in the front-end application can easily create some program units stored in the database server, when needed. If another development tool is chosen, it will be more difficult for the front-end developers to reach the level of proficiency required to develop efficient and well-performing routines in PL/SQL for the Oracle database and in the programming language used by the application development tool. Normally, in these applications, an additional person that is fluent in PL/SQL is needed to create and maintain the stored logic.
- Second, it would make sense and benefit the system if the logic of the application can be shifted from one side to the other without any disruption or difficulty. This is known as Application Partitioning. Form Builder is the only development tool that reaches that level of integration with the Oracle RDBMS. As you will see later in this section, creating program units for storage in the database is similar to creating program units for the form, menu, or Library modules. Furthermore, using the Form Builder, the program units can be moved easily between the client application and the database server. You simply drag the PL/SQL object from one side and drop it on the other. The Form Builder buffers you from all the details of creating or dropping these units in the database.

19.4.1 STORED PROGRAM UNITS

As was hinted earlier, creating stored program units in the Form Builder is not any different from creating regular program units. In this section you will create a stored function that will be used in the ANALYZE module of the MRD application. You have seen the contents of the first function in Chapter 10. It is called `Days_Between` and returns the number of days between two dates passed as input arguments. Before creating this function, bring up the Form Builder and connect to the database. Then proceed as follows:

1. Expand the node Database Objects in the Navigator. You will initially see the list of database schemas where you can create new database objects, or view existing ones. The length of this list will depend on the privileges you have on other schemas. Normally you will be able to create stored procedures only in your schema.
2. Expand the node that contains the name of your schema. Four subnodes are displayed. They represent the types of objects owned by a schema that can be viewed or accessed from the Designer.
3. Use any of the Navigator's commands to create a new stored program unit. The familiar New Program Unit dialog box will appear.
4. Enter `Days_Between` in the Name field and select the Function radio button.
5. Click OK. A PL/SQL Editor window comes up with a template for your function.
6. Enter the contents of the function as shown in Figure 19.11.

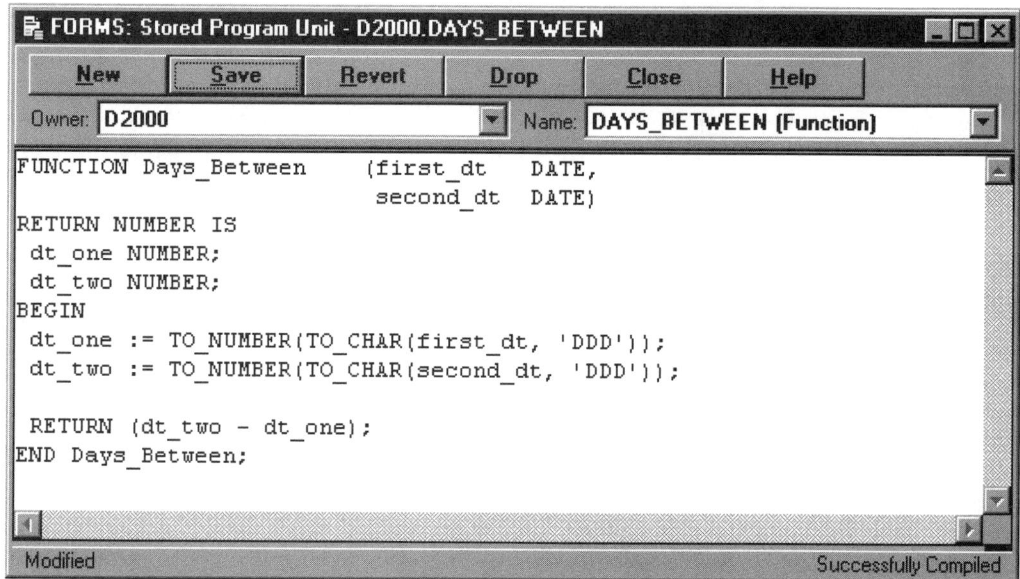

FIGURE 19.11 Stored Program Unit PL/SQL Editor.

7. Click Save. The status lamps at the bottom of the window will be set as in Figure 19.11.

19.4.2 STORED PROGRAM UNIT PL/SQL EDITOR

The context area of the PL/SQL Editor for stored program units is a little different from that of the regular program units. It contains only the Owner and Name drop-down list boxes. The reason for this is that stored program units are objects owned by the schema, much like tables, indexes, or views. In forms, menus or PLL modules, it is the module itself that owns the objects.

The button bar of this editor is a little different from the regular PL/SQL editor as well. Even here, the differences reflect the fact that stored program units are objects in the database. They are dropped rather then deleted, and their contents are saved to the database, rather than to a module. When the stored program unit is saved to the database, the Oracle Server PL/SQL engine compiles it before performing the Save action. The unit is saved only if no errors are encountered.

Except for these minor differences, everything else looks as usual. However, in the background, the Form Builder wraps together the code you enter in the editor, and sends it to the database with the request to create a stored program unit according to your specification. You do not have to do the process manually.

Despite all the likeliness between creating stored program units or regular ones, you must understand clearly that the processes are functionally different. The fact that the PL/SQL engine of the server compiles the unit, for example, is very important. This means that in stored program units you cannot use forms or menu object types such as Item, or MenuItem. They are unknown data types for the server. Thus, the partitioning of the application's logic can be done easily as long as you use only the fundamental data types of PL/SQL recognized by both versions.

One good candidate for moving between the front-end application and the database server is the function `Get_Sequence_Id` that you created in Chapter 16 to retrieve the next value from the sequence MRD_SEQ. This function can effectively reside in either side of the application. If you want to remove it from the MRD module and store it in the database, simply drag the function in the Object Navigator and drop it under the Stored Program Units node of your schema.

19.4.3 DATABASE TRIGGERS

The concept of database triggers is similar to the concept of triggers in form modules. With each table in the database, you can associate methods of PL/SQL code that will be executed when the event for which the method is defined occurs. The events for which you can write database triggers are Insert, Update, and Delete.

Using database triggers enforces a business rule about the data at the database level. It ensures that all the applications that will access the database objects will follow the rule consistently and precisely as it is defined in the object itself. Database triggers associate the flexibility of the relational model with the advantages of object-oriented programming. If the data should follow certain rules, you attach these rules to the table that will hold the data. This is the only place where the rule is coded. Each application that uses the table, from that moment on will not need to recode the rule. The trigger associated with the table will wait patiently until appropriate event occurs. When this happens, the appropriate trigger will fire and execute its statements. .

In the MRD application there are several rules that you could enforce globally, using database triggers. One example would be to provide the ID columns in the application with sequence-generated numbers just before they are inserted in the database. In earlier chapters, you populated the ID items during the CreateRecord event. However, it is more efficient to get the sequence numbers when the new records arrive at the database, rather than move them back and forth across the network.

19.4.4 USING DATABASE TRIGGERS TO POPULATE COLUMNS WITH SEQUENCE-GENERATED NUMBERS

This is where you will begin your work with database triggers. You want to create a trigger that will provide sequence numbers for the column CUSTOMER_ID of new records inserted in table CUSTOMER. Begin by performing these two preliminary steps:

1. Delete the block-level trigger WHEN-RECORD-CREATED in block CUSTOMER, which currently performs this task.
2. Cut the function `Get_Sequence_Id` from the module MRD.FMB and paste it under the Stored Program Units node.

In the Object Navigator, expand the node Tables to display all the tables you currently own. Then expand the node Customer. The nodes Triggers and Columns will be displayed underneath.

1. Create a new object for the node Triggers. The Database Triggers PL/SQL Editor appears (see Figure 19.12). Most of the objects on this window are currently disabled.
2. Click the push button New, to create a new database trigger. You will notice that the objects of the editor will be enabled now.
3. Enter the specifications for the trigger as shown in Figure 19.12. The meaning of the settings is explained in the paragraph that follows.
4. Click Save to have the Oracle Server PL/SQL engine compile and store the trigger in the database.

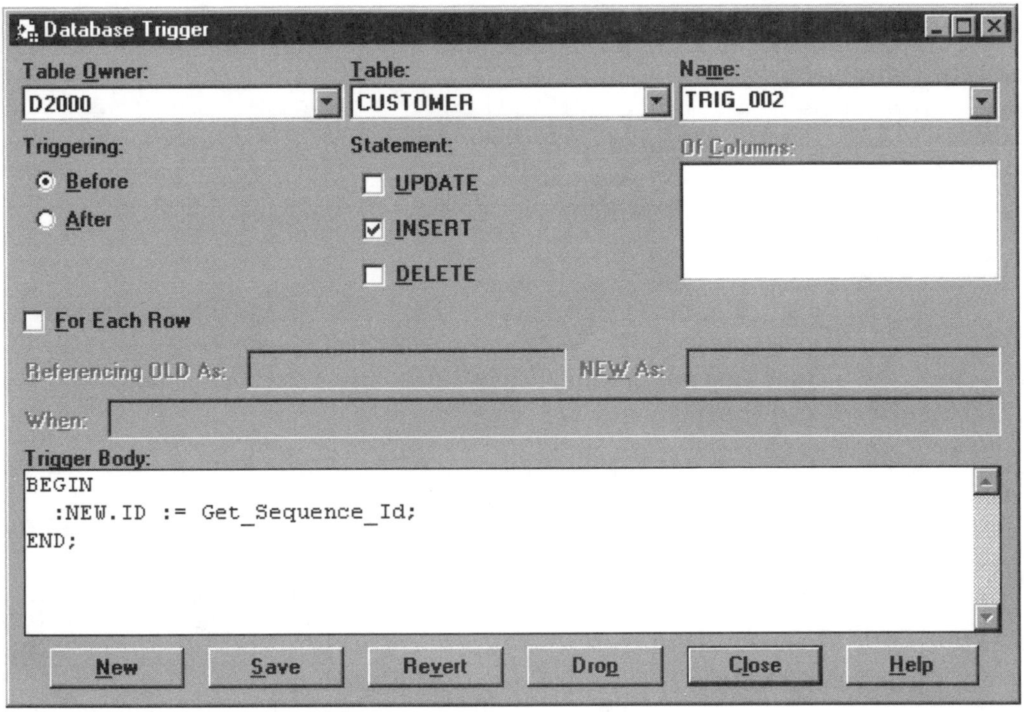

FIGURE 19.12 Database Trigger PL/SQL Editor.

19.4.5 DATABASE TRIGGER PL/SQL EDITOR

There are several things to explain about the settings of the database trigger shown in Figure 19.12. Let us go through them from the top of the window down. The list boxes on the top define the context of the trigger. If you have the appropriate privileges to create triggers on tables owned by other schemas, you can use the Table Owner drop-down list box to select the schema name. You can also select the table where the trigger will be attached using the list Table. The combo box Name is used to specify the name of the trigger. When you create a new trigger, Oracle will provide you with a default name, but you should change it to a more descriptive and meaningful one for your application.

The check-box group Statement defines the event that can activate the trigger. It can be seen here that only INSERT, UPDATE, and DELETE statements can fire a database trigger. In your case, you want the trigger to fire only when records are inserted. Therefore, the check box INSERT is checked. If the trigger should fire for more than one event, you can check more than one check box in this group. The text list Of Columns to the right is enabled only if one of the statements that will fire the trigger is UPDATE. In that case, all the columns of the table will be displayed in the list, sorted alphabetically. By default, the trigger will fire when any of these columns are updated. If you want the trigger to fire only when some specific columns are updated, you can CTRL+CLICK to select them in the list.

The radio group Triggering controls the timing of the trigger in relation to the event that causes the trigger. The database trigger can fire either before or after the statement that caused it is executed by the database. In your case, you want to put the new sequence number in the CUSTOMER_ID before the record is inserted in the table.

The check box For Each Row governs the frequency of the trigger, or how many times it will fire when the statement that causes it is executed on the table. If the check box is unchecked, the trigger will fire only once. Triggers with this setting are also called table-level triggers. If the check box is checked, the trigger will be executed for each record that the statement will affect. These triggers are also called record-level triggers. In your case, the check box is checked because you want the sequence to populate the CUSTOMER_ID for each record.

The state of the check box For Each Row influences the availability, and the contents of the remaining fields in the window as well. If the box is not checked, the fields Referencing OLD As, NEW As, and When are disabled. They have a meaning only for record-level triggers. In this case, in the Trigger Body field, you must reference the components of the record by their column name, as defined in the table.

TIP

Given all the possible settings of these three properties, it is easy to conclude that for any table in the database, there can be up to twelve triggers associated with it. By checking multiple check boxes in the STATEMENT group, you can collapse up to three triggers in one, but this will not enable you to fill the free slots with other triggers. In other words, if you create a trigger that will fire "After Each Row is Inserted, Updated, or Deleted," you can no longer create a trigger that will fire "After Each Row is Inserted."

When triggers fire for each row, Oracle keeps two copies of each record affected by the statement. The state of the record in the database, before the statement is executed, is referred to as OLD. The version of that record after the statement is executed can be referenced as the NEW record. Understandably, when a record is being inserted, its OLD version contains NULL values for all the columns. The reason for this is that the record does not exist in the database until the INSERT statement is executed, and the snapshot that creates OLD is taken before this event. For a similar reason, the NEW version of a deleted record contains

NULL columns. (After the DELETE is completed, the record no longer exists in the table.) If the statement is UPDATE, both NEW and OLD versions of the record will contain some values.

Both versions of the record are accessible in all the triggers. However, you cannot set the columns of the NEW record in an After trigger. Recall that this trigger will fire after the triggering statement is executed. Therefore, the NEW version of the record is created and set before the trigger enters in action. OLD and NEW are also called correlation names. Inside the Trigger Body they must be preceded by the colon, as shown in Figure 19.12. In the very rare event when you will need to create a database trigger for a table named OLD or NEW, the correlation names OLD or NEW will conflict with the name of the table. Only in these cases, you will need to override the default correlation names. You can do this in the Referencing fields. If, for example, the table is named OLD, then you could replace the setting of Referencing OLD As with OLD_RECORD. Then, throughout the trigger, you could use OLD_RECORD to address the version of the record prior to the execution of the triggering statement.

With the settings discussed so far, the triggers can fire only in two extreme cases: either only once, or for every single row affected by the system. There can be occasions where trigger should fire only for a particular set of the records affected by the statement. Imagine, for example, that there is another application besides yours, that is using the MRD database. While you are implementing the generation of identification numbers at the database, the developers of the other application are using a fancy algorithm to come up with a unique number, based on some biographical data provided by the customer. By creating a database trigger, you are enforcing the rule globally. In other words, when a record goes for INSERT in the table CUSTOMERS, the trigger will not check to see which application is sending it—yours or theirs. It will simply enforce your rule and override the value placed in the CUSTOMER_ID by the other application.

In order to restrict the number of records that a record-level trigger will affect when fired, a Boolean condition can be specified in the When field. The trigger will be fired only for those records which evaluate the condition to TRUE. To avoid raising some eyebrows in the scenario presented above, you could set the When field as follows:

```
NEW.CUSTOMER_ID IS NULL
```

With this property, the trigger will get the sequence number only for those records that are sent to the table with an unspecified CUSTOMER_ID value. Note that in this field you do not need to put the colon character in front of the correlation name.

Following similar steps, you can create on your own triggers that will populate the columns MOVIE_ID, and TAPE_ID for tables MOVIE and TAPE with numbers generated from the sequence MRD_SEQ. Make sure to delete the triggers WHEN-CREATE-RECORD for these blocks in order to avoid duplicating the functionality.

19.5 ORACLE DESIGNER SERVER API

When the back end of your application system is implemented in the Oracle RDBMS, you may take advantage of support that Oracle Designer provides for implementing a number of business rules and constraints in the form of a series of PL/SQL program units known commonly as the *Server Application Programmatic Interface (API)*. Implementing the business rules at the database level provides certain advantages, highlighted especially in a thin-client application architecture. Some of these advantages are listed below:

- The business rules are implemented consistently and independently of the particular application system.
- The business rules are maintained centrally. Modifications and updates of these rules do not require massive updates of the applications installed on the client machines.
- The business rules are enforced consistently, and the front-end application is no longer responsible for ensuring that they are implemented.
- The level of code reuse is increased significantly. The business rule is implemented once; its implementation is reused by any application system that needs it. The advantage is even greater when a power tool like Oracle Designer ensures a consistent implementation of similar business rules.

The Server API components generated by Oracle Designer are grouped into two categories:

- **Table API.** For each database table, Oracle Designer generates a package and a set of database triggers that may be installed in the database when the table object is created. The methods of this package may be invoked by any application environment that supports calls of PL/SQL stored procedures, including Oracle Developer tools, Visual Basic, and Oracle WebServer.
- **Database triggers.** For each table, Oracle Designer may also generate a set of database triggers, which are used to enforce the business rules implemented by the table API when records are manipulated by an external application.
- **Module Component API.** This API is used only for Form Builder modules. It allows you to implement query and data manipulation statements through PL/SQL procedures, rather than through the regular Form Builder interface. The module APIs generate module components with the proper-

ties Datasource Type and Datatarget Type set to "View" or "PL/SQL Procedure."

Sections 24.2.1 to 24.2.3 provide details on the APIs in each category and show how you can customize them to add your programmatic logic structures.

19.5.1 TABLE API

For each table in your Repository, Oracle Designer allows you to generate an application programmatic interface (API) composed of methods that allow you to interact with these tables programmatically rather than from a SQL interface. These methods are encapsulated in packages, also known as *table handlers.* One package is available for each table, and its name is `cg$<table_name>`, as in `cg$ORDERS` or `cg$LINE_ITEMS`. The following is a list of the major methods supported by this package:

- ❑ **INS.** Insert a record into the table.
- ❑ **UPD.** Update a record identified by the primary key value.
- ❑ **DEL.** Delete a record identified by the primary key value.
- ❑ **LCK.** Lock a record.
- ❑ **SLCT.** Select a record based on the value of its primary key.

In addition, based on the properties defined for the table object in the Repository, this package provides methods to validate constraints, to populate columns associated with sequences with values from those sequences, and to populate columns for which you have set the property Autogen Type. If you have requested that journaling be performed for the table, methods to populate the journal tables are part of this package as well.

Oracle Designer allows you to define in the Repository your own processing instructions that are executed before or after the generated part of the methods INS, UPD, DEL, and LCK. The Generate Table API utility combines, into the body of the procedure, the user-defined application logic with the statements created based on the properties of the table. Figure 19.13 shows the typical structure of these procedures. In this figure, EVENT stands for one of the event names: Insert, Update, Delete, or Lock.

The following are the steps required to add your own application logic to the table API procedures.

1. Switch to the tab DB Objects of the Design Navigator and expand the table to which you want to add the programming logic.
2. Select the node Table API/Trigger Logic, and click Create. The dialog box Create Trigger/API Code appears (see Figure 19.14).
3. Select the event to which you want to add programmatic logic, and click

```
BEGIN
--  Application_logic Pre-<EVENT> <<Start>>
      -- User-defined logic
—  Application_logic Pre-<EVENT> << End >>

--  Oracle Designer generated logic

--  Application_logic Post-<EVENT> <<Start>>
      -- User-defined logic
--  Application_logic Post-<EVENT> << End >>
END;
```

FIGURE 19.13 A typical structure of a table API method.

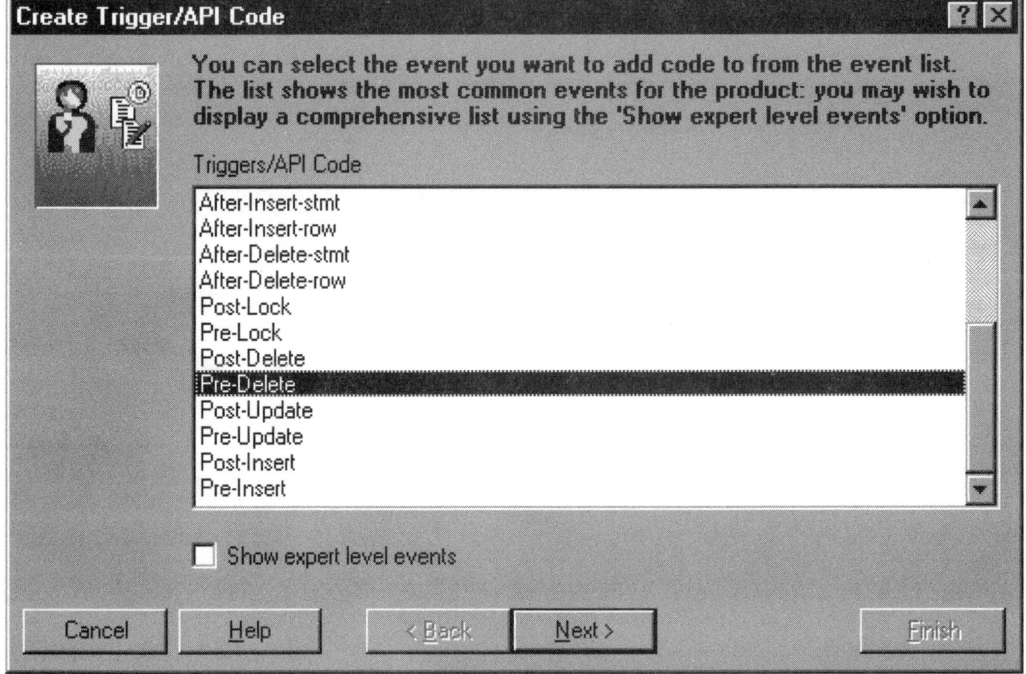

FIGURE 19.14 The Create Trigger/API Code dialog box.

Next. The events whose programmatic statements are inserted in the table API procedures are the last eight events at the bottom of the list.

4. Enter a brief description of the programmatic logic you are about to add to this event in the text field Name. A longer description may be entered in the text box Comment.
5. Click Finish to complete the process.

As in the other cases discussed in this section, the actual statements that make up the logic must be implemented in the Logic Editor of Oracle Designer.

19.5.2 DATABASE TRIGGERS

In combination with the characteristic package, the Generate Table API utility creates a set of twelve database triggers that cover all the possible events for which a trigger may be defined. In a number of these triggers, Oracle Designer creates its own programmatic logic. For example, the triggers Before Insert Row, Before Update Row, and Before Delete Row invoke the procedures INS, UPD, and DEL from the table handler, as well as a number of other methods through which the triggers validate arc constraints, foreign key constraints, and domain rules defined for the table.

> **TIP**
>
> The names of the generated triggers are formed by concatenating the following strings:
>
> - CG$
> - The first letter of the time when the trigger fires: B for Before and A for After
> - The first letter of the event that activated the trigger: I for Insert, U for Update, and D for Delete
> - The first letter of the level where the trigger fires: R for Row level and S for Statement level
> - The table alias or name
>
> Thus, the Before Delete Row trigger for table ORDERS will be named CG$BDR_ORDERS.

All the triggers allow you to add your own logic to them. The Generate Table API utility coordinates your statements with those it generates based on the properties of the table. The steps to add a user-defined logic object to the table triggers are similar to those described in the previous section. The only difference resides in the type of event you select in the dialog box Create Trigger/API. For the case of triggers, select one of the first twelve events in the list.

Because the database triggers that are part of the Table API invoke the table handler procedures and because you can place user-defined logic in the triggers and procedures, be careful not to replicate the logic in these objects. You can avoid the replication if you understand well the flow of execution of the statements in the generated triggers and procedures. To help form this understanding, Figure 19.15 presents a diagram of the code segments that may be executed when the event Before Insert Row occurs. This event is handled by the table API trigger `CG$BIR_<TABLE>`, which contains a set of statements defined by you and another set generated by Oracle Designer. Part of the second set of statements is a call to the table handler procedure `CG$<TABLE>.INS`. This procedure contains application logic generated by Oracle Designer and around it, the statements defined by you in the Pre-Insert and Post-Insert event. As you can see from this diagram, you may define up to three distinct units of logic for this event. You need to make sure that the statements in these units do not conflict with or replicate statements in the other units, generated by you or Oracle Designer.

19.5.3 MODULE COMPONENT API

The module component API is a package characteristic for the module component that provides methods to query a table and return the data in a PL/SQL table, or insert, update, delete, and lock the records in the base table of the mod-

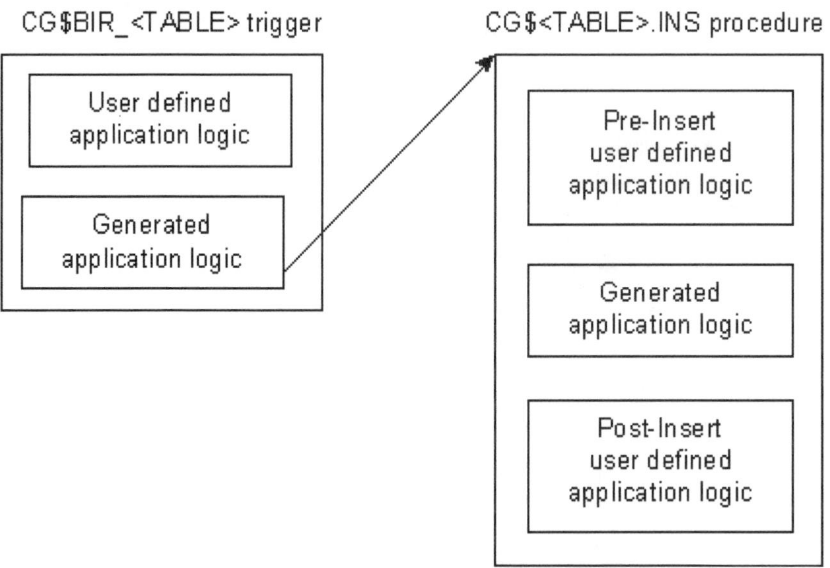

FIGURE 19.15 A diagram of code segments executed during a typical Before Insert Row event.

ule component. For similarity with the table API, this package is often called the *module component handler.* As in the case of the table API, you may specify your own application logic to be executed before or after the operations Insert, Update, Delete, and Lock take place. The following is the procedure to create these objects:

1. Switch to the tab Modules and find the module component to which you want to add the programming logic. This may be a reusable component or a specific one, implemented in a module.
2. Expand the node that represents the module and select API Logic.
3. Click Create . The dialog box Create Module Component API Code appears.
4. Select the event to which you want to add programmatic logic and click Next.
5. Enter a brief description of the programmatic logic you are about to add to this event in the text field Name. A longer description may be entered in the text box Comment.
6. Click Finish to complete the process.

The module component API is built on top of the table API for the base table of the module component. The methods for inserting, updating, deleting, and locking the module component handler perform these operations by invoking the corresponding methods from the table handler. As in the case of database triggers, know the execution sequence of your logic objects and those created by Oracle Designer. Take careful steps to avoid conflicting statements in these handlers.

19.6 SUMMARY

The focus of this chapter was PL/SQL objects used in Form Builder applications. Previous chapters have provided information about triggers, functions, and procedures. This chapter summarized concepts related to them and expanded on additional objects such as PL/SQL libraries, packages, stored program units, and database triggers. Major concepts discussed in this chapter were

- **Events and Triggers in Form Builder Applications**
  - Types of Events and Triggers
  - Firing Order of Triggers
  - Triggers as Methods that Associate Objects with Events

- Overriding The Default Firing Order Of Triggers
- Restricted Built-In Program Units
- Smart Triggers

- **PL/SQL Libraries**
  - Creating and Populating Libraries
  - Compiling PL/SQL Libraries
  - Referencing Variables Indirectly in PL/SQL Libraries
  - Attaching PL/SQL Libraries
- **Creating a Package for the MRD Application**
- **Stored Program Units and Database Triggers**
  - Stored Program Units
  - Stored Program Unit PL/SQL Editor
  - Database Triggers
  - Using Database Triggers to Populate Columns with Sequence-Generated Numbers
  - Database Trigger PL/SQL Editor
- **Oracle Designer Server API**
  - Table API
  - Database Triggers
  - Module Component API

The following table describes the software assets that were discussed in this chapter. From the main HTML page of the software utilities provided with the book follow the links *Software* and *Chapter 19* to access these assets:

ASSET NAME	DESCRIPTION
CH19_1.MMB	The MRD menu module completed in the last chapter.
CH19_2..MMB	The MRD menu module with all the enhancements discussed in this chapter.
CH19_2..MMX	The executable version of CH19_2.MMB compiled for Win32 platforms.
CH19_1.FMB	The MRD application completed in the last chapter. Use this module as a starting point for the activities discussed in this chapter.
CH19_2.FMB	The MRD application with the library attachments discussed in Section 19.2.
CH19_2.FMX	The executable version of CH19_2.FMB compiled for Win32 platforms.
CH19_3.FMB	The MRD application with the library attachments and enhancements discussed in Section 19.3.
CH19_3.FMX	The executable version of CH19_3.FMB compiled for Win32 platforms.
MRDMENU.PLL	The initial version of the library MRDMENU created in Section 19.2.

ASSET NAME	DESCRIPTION
MRDMENU_1.PLL	The enhanced version of the library MRDMENU completed in Section 19.3.
WINDOWS.PLL	The initial version of the library WINDOWS created in Section 19.2.
WINDOWS_1.PLL	The enhanced version of the library WINDOWS completed in Section 19.3.
LISTS.PLL	The initial version of the library LISTS created in Section 19.2.
LISTS_1.PLL	The enhanced version of the library LISTS completed in Section 19.3.
GENERAL.PLL	The library that contains the package GENERIC created in Section 19.3.

Part IV

BUILDING INTEGRATED DEVELOPER APPLICATIONS

Behold, how good and how pleasant it is for brethren to dwell together in unity!
—Bible, Psalms 133:1

Chapter 20

DEBUGGING

What cruel fate! What torture the bugs will this day put me to!
—Aristophanes

No matter how good your programming abilities are, every software system you develop will be associated with a certain probability of failure. It is said that a system fails when an error occurs somewhere in one of its software modules. In general, an error is the inability of the system to exhibit the functionality that users expect from it. Testing is the process that aims at identifying the discrepancies between the systems developed and the true requirements of the customers. Identifying errors in the system and removing them is known as debugging.

There are three levels of debugging. One is high-level debugging, to ensure that the system meets the overall expectations of the customers and contains all the functionality they expect. The second is done at the application code level to ensure that functions are passed the right parameters, loops are repeated only as many times as necessary, data sent to the database is in the appropriate format, and so on. The third is based on the Form Runtime Diagnostic where information is written into a log file for later study.

This chapter will discuss the second- and third-level of debugging. In particular, you will learn how to run a form in the debug mode, and how to perform several debugging tasks with the Developer Debugger, including tracing a program unit step by step, examining and modifying the contents of variables and memory locations, and modifying the code at runtime.

20.1 ACCESSING THE DEBUGGER

In order to access the Debugger, you must first enable the Debug Mode on the Form Builder, and then run the module you want to debug. There are three ways to toggle the Debug Mode on and off.

- In the Object Navigator click the Debug Mode button in the vertical toolbar of the window. The Debug Mode is enabled if the icon is . The Debug Mode is disabled if the icon is 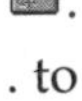 .
- Choose Tools | Preferences . . . to display the Preferences dialog box. In this dialog box, click the Runtime tab to display the options that you can set for your application at runtime. The second check box on the left is labeled Debug Mode. When it is checked, the Debug Mode is enabled.
- Select the menu item Program | Debug Mode to enable debugging, or deselect it to disable debugging.

It is important that before you run a module for debugging purposes you generate it with the Debug Mode enabled. When the module is generated with Debug Mode enabled, the executable contains source code symbols that are accessible and editable from the Debugger. If the module is generated with the

Debug Mode disabled, the Debugger will not be able to display any information about the source code being executed.

You can run a module in Debug Mode using the Form Runtime engine as well. In the command line, simply add the parameter `debug=YES`. For example, if you want to debug the module C:\MRD\MRD.FMX, the command line in the program item will be:

```
IFRUN60.EXE C:\MRD\MRD.FMX DEBUG=YES
```

When you run a module and the Debug Mode is enabled, the first thing that will appear is the Debugger window. This allows you to create any debugging actions that you will need as will be discussed later in the chapter. However, in order to proceed with the execution of the module, you must close the Debugger window. Click the Close iconic button from the Debugger toolbar to dismiss this window.

Now you can run your module as usual. The Debugger will not be displayed until Form Runtime either encounters the built-in BREAK, which serves as a predefined breakpoint in any of your program units. This is important to emphasize because if you want to use the Debugger at some point during the execution of the module, you must explicitly create a breakpoint that will interrupt the normal flow of the application and will pass control to the Debugger.

In order to help you locate the trigger from which an error may occur, Form Runtime has an additional parameter, called `debug_messages`. If you want to run the module mentioned above with this option set, you would use the following command line:

```
IFRUN60.EXE C:\MRD\MRD.FMX DEBUG_MESSAGES=YES
```

Whenever you run the module with this parameter set to YES, Forms Runtime displays a message upon executing each trigger in the module. This message displays context information about the trigger such as its name and the object to which it is attached. A typical message displayed by this utility is "FRM-42400: Performing event trigger WHEN-BUTTON-PRESSED in field CUSTOMER.OK."

Thus, the steps to utilize the Developer Debugger can be summarized as follows:

1. Identify the trigger, program unit or PL/SQL block that you want to debug. You can do this from the Form Builder, if you have an idea where the error may be occurring. You can also run the module using Form Runtime with the parameter `DEBUG_MESSAGES=YES`.
2. Create a breakpoint using the built in procedure BREAK.
3. Generate the module with the Debug Mode option enabled.
4. Run the module until the breakpoint is reached.

> **TIP**
>
> The Debugger is a utility displayed in a modal window. As long as it is active, you will not be able to access or manipulate the application running in the background other than through the Debugger actions.

20.2 COMPONENTS OF THE DEBUGGER

Figure 20.1 represents a typical Debugger window and its components. As you can see from this figure, the Debugger window may have up to three panes displayed at any one time. The Source Pane displays a read-only copy of the program unit currently being executed. The Navigator Pane contains a hierarchical listing of the objects you can access in the Debugger. The Interpreter pane is a

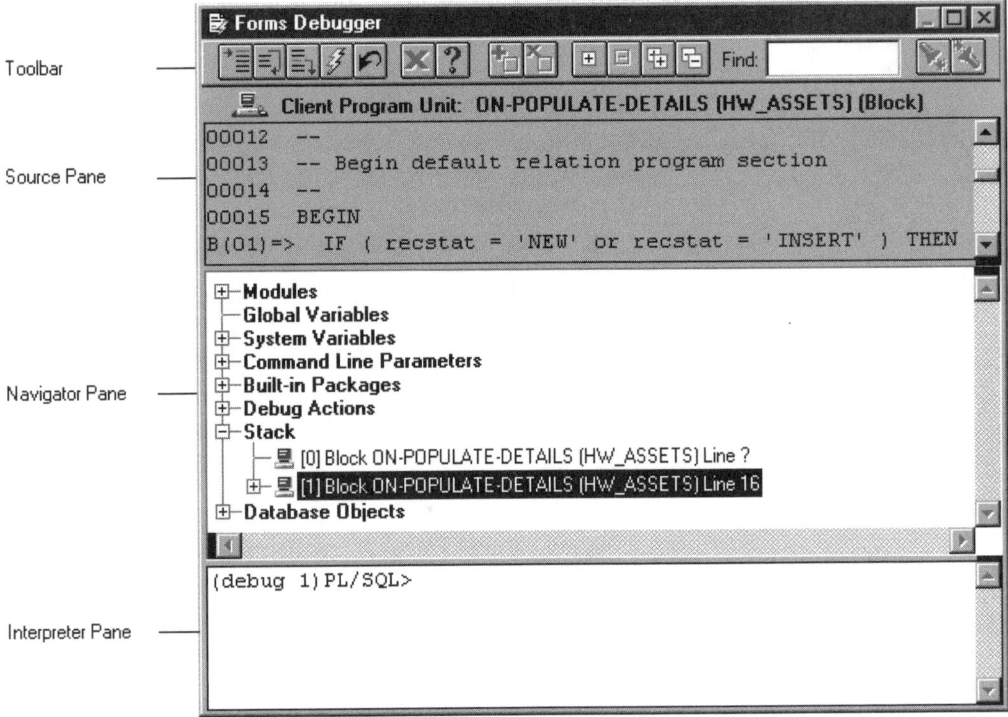

FIGURE 20.1 Components of Debugger window.

command line that allows you to enter statements and debug commands. Each of these panes can be sized and scrolled independently.

The Debugger window contains a toolbar with icons that correspond to the most frequently used commands. In addition, the Debugger has a menu of its own, with four items—View, Navigator, Program, and Debug—which is inserted in the menu of your application, if one is being used.

20.2.1 SOURCE PANE

The Source Pane displays a copy of the program unit that is being currently executed in the Debugger. You can use it to see what are the contents of the program as it is being executed. As said earlier, this is a read-only copy of the statements. You cannot edit the code in the Source Pane.

Each line in the Source Pane is preceded by a line number. If a breakpoint is defined for that line, then the line number is replaced by a symbol like B(n), where n is the internal identifier of the breakpoint. In Figure 20.1, the breakpoint defined in the last line visible in the source pane is indicated by the symbol B(01). Similarly, if a trigger is defined for a particular line, the line number is replaced with the symbol T(n), where n is the sequence number for the trigger.

The Source Pane is displayed by default. If you want to hide it, de-select the menu item View | Source Pane.

20.2.2 NAVIGATOR PANE

The Navigator Pane allows you to list, browse, create, and delete objects that are available in the Debugger interface. You use it in exactly the same way as you would use the Object Navigator in the Form Builder. You can use the Navigator Pane to create PL/SQL program units, attach PLL libraries, and even create database stored procedures and triggers. The purpose of creating these program units is to invoke their functionality from debug triggers that you may want to create.

However, the most important practical use of the Navigator Pane is to inspect and set the values of data items, variables, global variables, system variables, and parameters that are used in the application. If you want to see the current values of global variables, systems variables, or Runtime parameters, simply expand the nodes Global Variables, System Variables, or Command Line Parameters, respectively.

If you want to view and edit data for objects related to modules, then expand the node Modules and its dependent nodes. For modules, you can display and change the contents of items, triggers, program units, and parameter lists. You can also attach PLL libraries while the application is running in Debugger. Figure 20.2 shows the nodes of the Navigator Pane expanded to show the items of module ETS. The data item Location in block HW_ASSETS is selected and is ready to be edited. The effects of changing its contents are the same as if you entered the new data in the item when the application runs in normal mode.

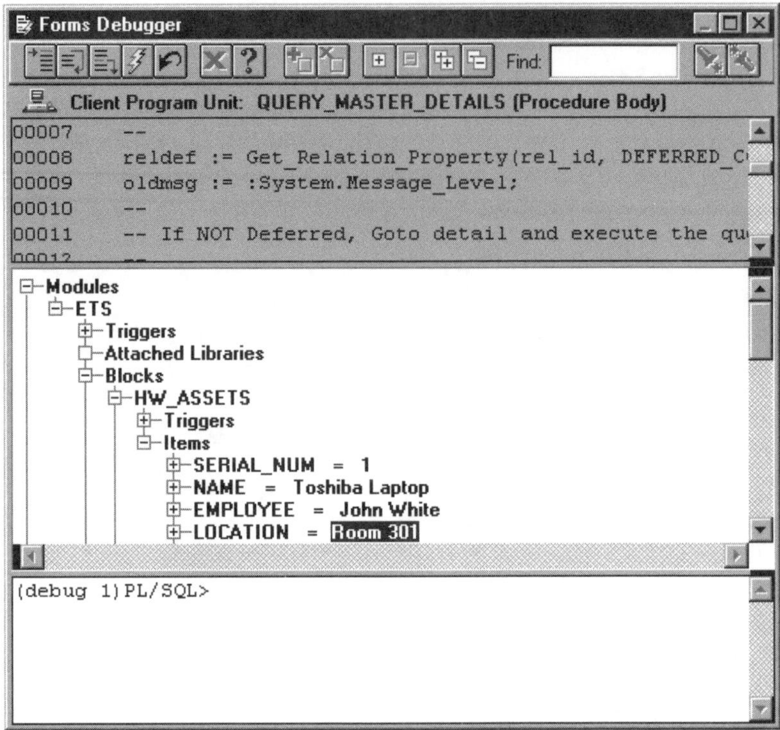

FIGURE 20.2 Changing values of items in the Debugger's Navigator pane.

Keep in mind that all the changes that you make in the structure of the module are temporarily stored in the memory structures of Form Runtime. This means that if you edit the contents of a trigger, create a new procedure, or attach a library to the module, these changes will not be permanently recorded in the source code of your module. If you achieve your objective with these changes, you must go back in the Form Builder and apply them to the source module.

As you will see in Section 20.3, the Navigator Pane is also used to view and maintain debug actions as well as inspect the contents of the execution stack. The Navigator is displayed by default, but you can hide it by de-selecting the menu item View | Navigator.

20.2.3 INTERPRETER PANE

The Interpreter Pane is a command line interface that enables you to enter Debugger commands from the PL/SQL prompt. At the same time, the Interpreter

Pane echoes back the command line equivalents of actions that you may perform in the Navigator Pane.

For example, if you want to delete the breakpoint 1, you could enter the following statements at the PL/SQL> prompt:

```
.DELETE BREAKPOINT 1
```

Like the other two panes, this pane is visible by default, but can be hidden by de-selecting the menu item View | Interpreter Pane.

20.2.4 TOOLBAR

The toolbar of the Debugger is shown in Figure 20.3. The icons in this toolbar can by grouped in two categories. The first one includes icons used to carry out debugging commands. The following paragraphs describe each of them:

- **Step Into** . This icon is used to step inside a program unit if the current statement is a call to a function or procedure; otherwise, it just executes the command.
- **Step Over** . This command bypasses the call to a subroutine.
- **Step Out** . This icon executes all the statements until the end of the current program unit.
- **Go** . This command resumes the execution of the program until a breakpoint is reached or there are no statements left to execute.
- **Reset** . This command abandons the execution of the current program unit and returns the control to an outer level in the Debugger.

The second group of icons allows access to commands that affect the Navigator Pane. They are very similar to the same commands issued against the Object Navigator in the Form Builder. Therefore, I will only briefly describe them here. You click the Create and Delete icons to add or remove object from the hierarchy tree. You can click the icons in the Expand/Collapse group to expand or collapse a node one level at a time or all the way to the end of the hierarchy tree. The Find utility with its Search Forward and Search Backward buttons is used to quickly locate entries in the list. The commands provided by these icons are also available from the Navigator menu of the Debugger.

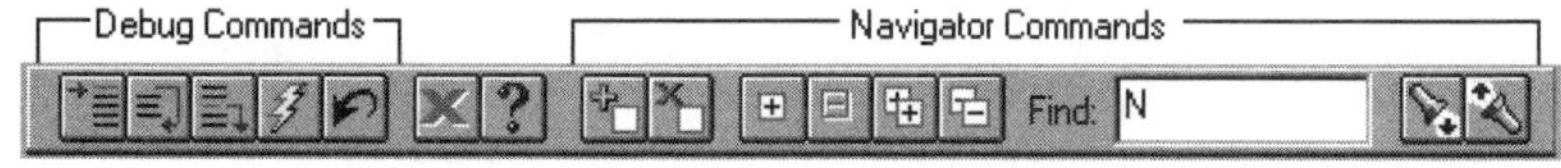

FIGURE 20.3 Developer Forms Debugger toolbar.

20.3 MANAGING DEBUG ACTIONS

There are two types of objects that you can create and use during a debugging session. These are breakpoints and debug triggers, both of which fall under the category of debug actions.

Breakpoints are the most common debug action you take. They are associated with a particular line of code that the PL/SQL engine will execute, and cause the program flow to be interrupted right before this line is reached. Debug triggers are blocks of code that you may associate with the program units being debugged. They can be executed each time the Debugger is invoked, or when a particular line of code is reached. You may even create debug triggers that fire when each statement is executed.

This section explains how to create and manage debug actions. You will use the module MRD that you have developed in previous chapters. As a preliminary step, open this module in the Form Builder and generate it with the Debug Mode enabled. (The companion software provides a copy of this module named CH20_1.FMB.)

20.3.1 CREATING DEBUG ACTIONS

In this section, you will create a breakpoint and a debug trigger in the form-level trigger WHEN-BUTTON of the module.

1. Run the module with the Debug Mode enabled. Before the module is initialized, the Debugger window appears.
2. In the Navigator Pane, expand the necessary nodes in order to select the trigger WHEN-BUTTON-PRESSED defined the property class PUSH_BUTTON. (These nodes are Modules, MRD, Property Classes, PUSH_BUTTON, and Triggers.) When the trigger is selected, its contents appear in the Source Pane.

Now you are ready to create the breakpoint and the debug trigger. To create a breakpoint on line 7 of the trigger, click anywhere inside the line in the Source Pane. Then follow any of these steps:

- ❑ Double-click the line.
- ❑ Enter the command .BREAK in the Interpreter Pane.
- ❑ Select Debug | Break... from the Debugger menu. The PL/SQL Breakpoint dialog box will appear (see Figure 20.4).

The first two commands will create and enable a breakpoint attached with the particular line in the source pane. The third command is more sophisticated,

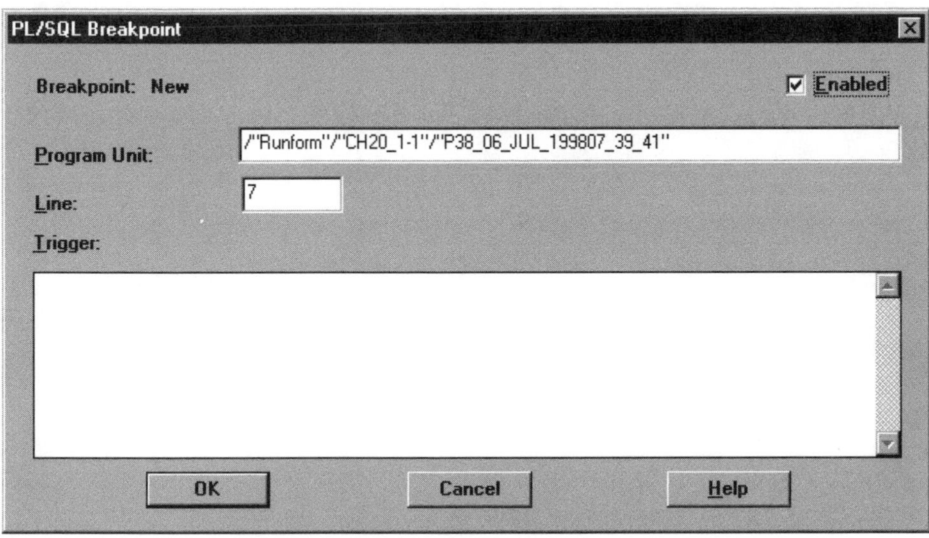

FIGURE 20.4 PL/SQL Breakpoint dialog box.

because it allows you to control the Enabled/Disabled status of the breakpoint by selecting or de-selecting the check box Enabled. At the same time, you can associate a trigger with the breakpoint, by entering the statements in a PL/SQL block in the Trigger pane of the dialog box.

The process of creating a trigger is similar. To create a debug trigger on a given line in the source code, click anywhere inside this line in the Source Pane. Then perform these steps:

1. Select Debug | Break... from the Debugger menu. The PL/SQL Breakpoint dialog box will appear (see Figure 20.5).
2. Enter the body of the trigger in the Trigger Body pane and click OK.

Note that the PL/SQL statements that you enter in the Trigger Body must form a complete PL/SQL block. While in Form Builder triggers you could enter just the IF statement, here you must enclose it between the keywords BEGIN and END.

Another object that should attract your attention is the list box Location, which allows you to define the context of the trigger just created. By default, the value of this list is Program Unit. In this case, the text items Program Unit and Line define the context in which this trigger will fire. If you select Debug Entry from the list, the trigger will fire each time the Debugger is activated due to a breakpoint, or each time one of the debug actions Step Into, Step Over, Step Out,

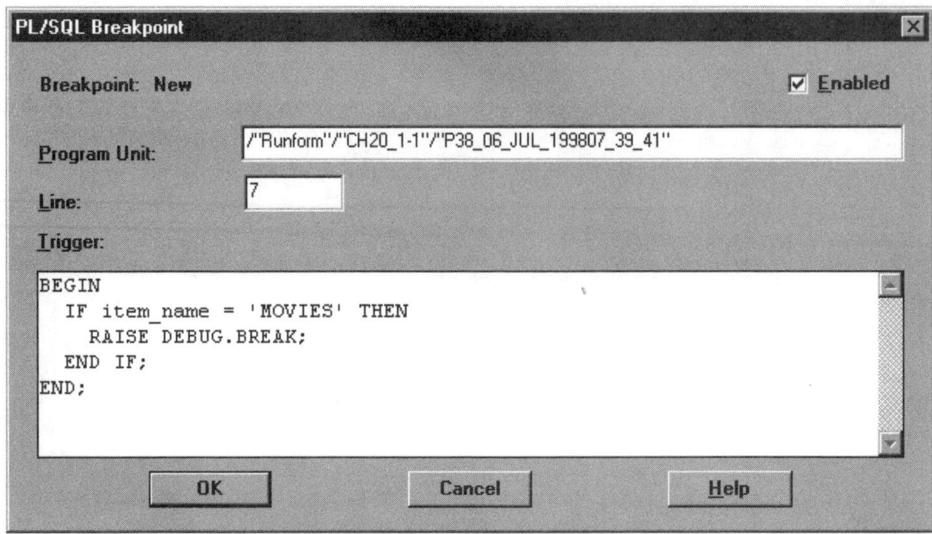

FIGURE 20.5 PL/SQL Trigger dialog box.

Go, and Reset occur. If you select Every Statement, then the trigger will be executed for each statement processed by the Debugger.

Using the PL/SQL Trigger dialog box is the easiest way to create a debug trigger. However, you can also create them from the command line of the Interpreter Pane. Figure 20.6 shows the commands that create the same debug trigger in the three contexts discussed above.

The first of these statements creates a trigger associated with line 10 of WHEN-BUTTON-PRESSED trigger. The second statement creates a trigger equivalent with the one you would create by choosing Debug Entry in the Location list of the dialog box PL/SQL Trigger. The third statement creates a debug trigger that will be executed for each statement.

As discussed earlier, all the breakpoints or debug triggers you create in the Debugger are available throughout the current session of Forms Runtime. However, they will not be available the next time you run the module. In order to create breakpoints that last between session, you should add the statement `BREAK;` before the line that will at which you want the break to occur. When the form is executed in Debug Mode, this built-in procedure passes the control to the Debugger.

For more complicated debug actions such as creating a complex trigger or program unit, you may save a transcript of your actions to a text file. As an example, I will explain how you create and use a log file that records the commands to create the debug trigger discussed previously. Exit the runtime application and run it again. When the initial debug window appears, perform the following steps:

```
PL/SQL> .TRIGGER IS
   +> BEGIN
   +>  IF item_name = 'OK' THEN
   +>   RAISE DEBUG.BREAK;
   +>  END IF;
   +> END;
Trigger #1 installed at line 10 of WHEN-BUTTON-PRESSED-80
PL/SQL> .TRIGGER DEBUG IS
   +> BEGIN
   +>  IF item_name = 'OK' THEN
   +>   RAISE DEBUG.BREAK;
   +>  END IF;
   +> END;
Trigger #2 installed at interpreter entry
PL/SQL> .TRIGGER * IS
   +> BEGIN
   +>  IF item_name = 'OK' THEN
   +>   RAISE DEBUG.BREAK;
   +>  END IF;
   +> END;
Trigger #3 installed at every statement
```

FIGURE 20.6 Creating debug triggers from in the Interpreter Pane.

1. In the command line of the Interpreter Pane enter the following statement:

   `.LOG FILE C:\MRD\DEBUG.LOG`

   This will open a file where all the subsequent commands and Debugger responses will be logged. In the example above, this file will be created in the C:\MRD directory; you can obviously provide a different location.
2. In the Navigator Pane, select the trigger WHEN-BUTTON-PRESSED attached to the property class PUSH_BUTTON. The contents of the trigger are displayed in the Source Pane.
3. In the Source Pane, click inside line 10 of the trigger.
4. Select Debug | Break... from the Debugger menu. The PL/SQL Breakpoint dialog box will appear (see Figure 20.4).
5. Enter the body of the trigger in the Trigger Body pane and click OK.
6. In the command line of the Interpreter Pane enter the following statement:

   `.LOG OFF`

This command will save and close the log file C:\MRD\DEBUG.LOG. The file can be used after you exit the application to retrieve the contents of the trigger and incorporate them with the rest of the application in the Form Builder. If, in subsequent runs you want to append the initial log file, you need to open it with the following statement:

```
.LOG FILE C:\MRD\DEBUG.LOG APPEND
```

When a log file is open, you can view its contents by selecting View | Interpreter Log... from the menu. Figure 20.7 shows an example of the PL/SQL Interpreter Log dialog box that appears. In this window you can scroll the contents of the log file. The buttons Disable and Off are used to suspend or completely turn off the logging. Unfortunately, you cannot copy the contents of this window and paste them in the Command Interpreter, which would save you from reentering long statements each time the Debugger is initialized.

20.3.2 EDITING DEBUG ACTIONS

After you create debug actions, you can go back and edit them at a later time. All the debug actions are listed in the Navigator Pane, under the Debug Actions entry. Figure 20.8 shows an example of such entries.

As you can see from the figure, the information displayed contains the type of debug action, and all the relevant context information such as the program unit name, line number, and trigger type. If the debug action is disabled, as in the case of the last trigger in Figure 20.8, an asterisk sign will appear to the right of the action's identifier.

To edit any of this information, you can double-click the icons that represent the type of the debug action. Depending on the debug action, you may also choose Debug | Break... or Debug | Trigger... from the menu. Either the PL/SQL Breakpoint or PL/SQL Trigger dialog box will appear (see Figure 20.4 and Figure 20.5). In these dialog boxes, you can modify the debug actions according to your needs. For example, you can change the Enabled status of the debug action, its line number, and program unit name. For triggers, you can modify the body and

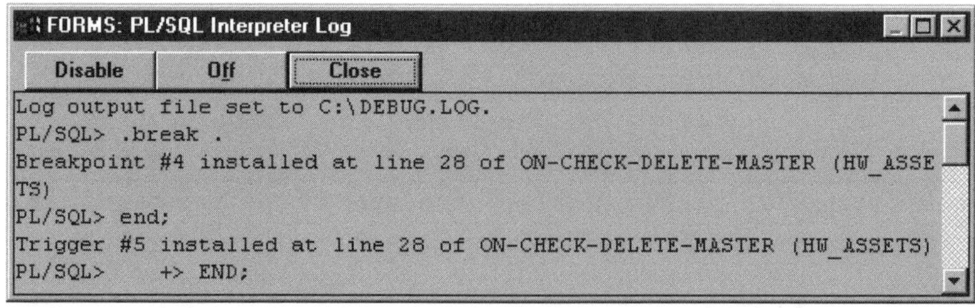

FIGURE 20.7 The PL/SQL Interpreter Log dialog box.

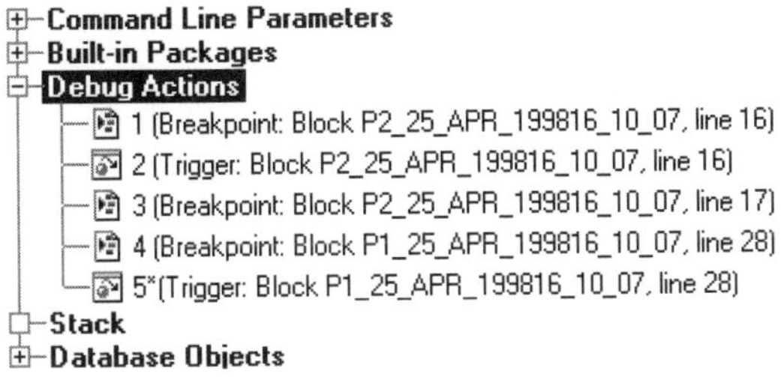

```
+-Command Line Parameters
+-Built-in Packages
-- Debug Actions
   |-- 1 (Breakpoint: Block P2_25_APR_199816_10_07, line 16)
   |-- 2 (Trigger: Block P2_25_APR_199816_10_07, line 16)
   |-- 3 (Breakpoint: Block P2_25_APR_199816_10_07, line 17)
   |-- 4 (Breakpoint: Block P1_25_APR_199816_10_07, line 28)
   `-- 5*(Trigger: Block P1_25_APR_199816_10_07, line 28)
 -Stack
+-Database Objects
```

FIGURE 20.8 Debug actions.

the context as well. If you want to delete the debug action altogether, simply click the Delete icon in the toolbar, or select Navigator | Delete from the menu.

I conclude this section by mentioning that some of the editing of debug actions can be done from the command line of the Interpreter Pane. Figure 20.9 shows three statements issued in the Interpreter that disable the trigger first, then display its status, and finally delete it.

20.3.3 EDITING PROGRAM UNITS AND TRIGGERS

The Debug menu contains a menu item labeled Edit... . This is used to edit the program unit currently displayed in the Source Pane. When you choose this item, the PL/SQL Editor window appears (see Figure 20.10). This editor allows you to edit the contents of the program unit as you would do in the Form Builder.

However, there are two major differences in the window layout between this editor and the regular PL/SQL Editor in the Form Builder.

The absence of the Revert and Delete push buttons reflects the fact that the changes you make here will not be permanently stored in the module.

```
PL/SQL> .DISABLE TRIGGER 2
Disabling debug action 2...
PL/SQL> .DESCRIBE TRIGGER 2
Trigger: 2
 Program Unit: Block WHEN-BUTTON-PRESSED-75
 Line: 6
 Enabled: NO
PL/SQL> .DELETE TRIGGER 2
Removing debug action 2...
PL/SQL>
```

FIGURE 20.9 Editing debug actions in the Interpreter Pane.

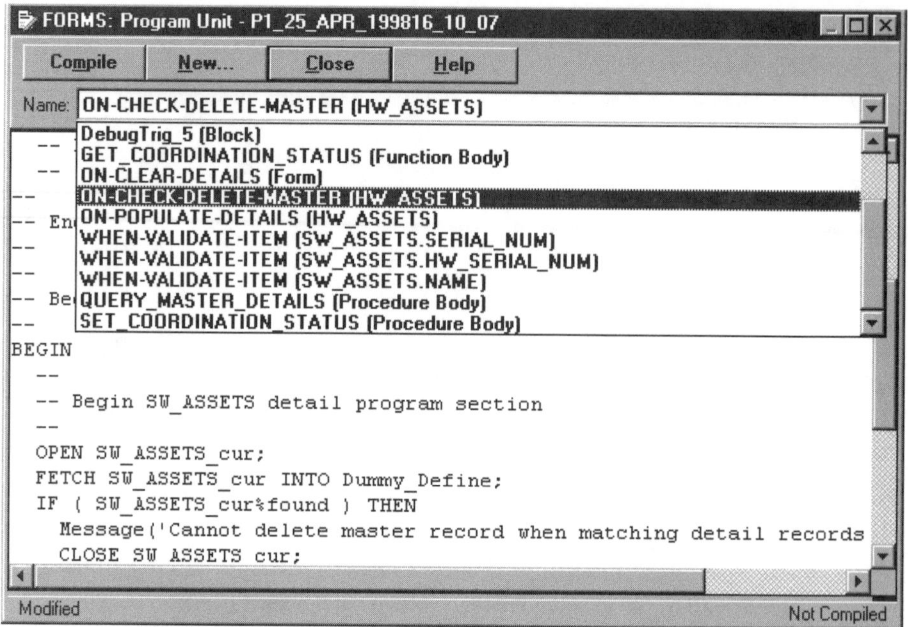

FIGURE 20.10 PL/SQL Editor window for the Debugger.

The box under the buttons bar of the window contains all the program unit names of this module. Different from the context area of the Form Builder's PL/SQL Editor, this list is a unified and alphabetically sorted view of all the triggers and program units in the module. To avoid naming conflicts, the name of each trigger in the list is supplemented with the name of the object where the trigger is attached.

In addition to editing existing program units, you can also create program unit from scratch, either by clicking the push button New... in the Debugger's PL/SQL Editor, or by creating a new object under the Program Units node in the Navigator Pane. You can also attach PL/SQL libraries to the Debugger environment. The process is identical to attaching libraries in the Form Builder.

> **TIP**
>
> When creating or modifying program units in the Debugger, you may want to insert debug actions in them the same way you would insert these actions in regular program units. When the Debugger reaches such a breakpoint or

debug trigger, a nesting in the levels of debugging occurs. The levels of debugging are numbered. The topmost level is assigned the number 0. When the debugging level is zero, Forms Runtime executes the code in the normal fashion and no debugging activities can occur. When a breakpoint is reached, Forms moves to debugging level one. If during the execution of statements in this level another breakpoint is encountered, Forms will move to debugging level two, and so on. The command line in the Interpreter Pane displays the current debug level. The statements in Figure 20.6 and Figure 20.9 are all issued at the debug level zero. If they were issued in the level one, the prompt in the Interpreter Pane would be (debug 1)PL/SQL>.

20.3.4 INSPECTING THE APPLICATION STATE

When the Runtime engine encounters a breakpoint, the flow of the program is interrupted, and control is passed to the Debugger. This gives you an opportunity to inspect the state of your application and to monitor this state at any point during the execution of the application. The Navigator Pane is where most of the actions related to this topic occur.

To inspect the values of system variables and command line parameters, expand the nodes with the same names in the Navigator. You cannot change the values of any of these variables, but you can view and modify the values of global variables, Forms items, and parameter lists by following these steps:

1. Expand the appropriate node.
2. Click the value of the desired object.
3. Type over the new value.

You can also inspect and modify values of variables local to the program units that are currently being executed. The names of these program units, together with the names and values of their variables are kept under the Stack node of the Navigator Pane (see Figure 20.11).

The nodes under Stack are the PL/SQL blocks that Forms Runtime is executing. Because the execution stack grows downward, the program unit that is at the bottom of the stack is the one being currently executed. The one immediately above it is the program unit that called the current subroutine, etc. In the case of Figure 20.11, procedure CLICK_BUTTON is the current program unit, and this procedure is called from the trigger WHEN-BUTTON-PRESSED.

Each program unit in the stack is also called a frame and is identified by the number in square brackets. To select a frame, you simply click its node in the Navigator. You will notice that the Source Pane will be refreshed with the contents of the program unit that the frame represents. If there are local variables de-

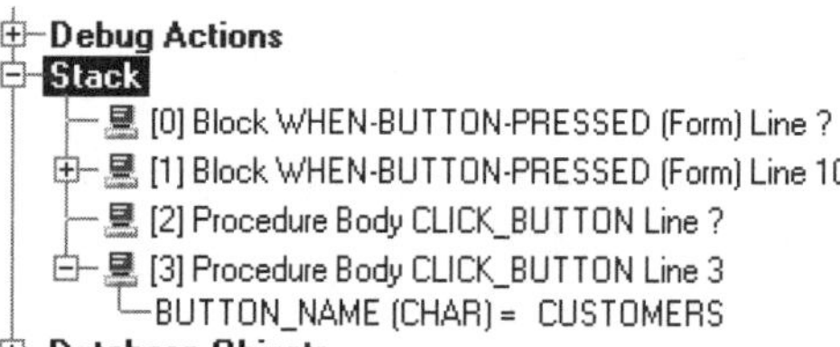

FIGURE 20.11 Viewing the Execution Stack in the Navigator Pane.

clared in this program unit, they will be listed under the frame. You can change their current values, by clicking and typing over the new values.

You can also change the frame of the stack and the contents of local variables from the command line of the Interpreter Pane. The following statement sets the scope of the Debugger to frame 1 of the stack:

```
(debug 1)PL/SQL> .SET SCOPE FRAME 1
```

The following statement overwrites the value of the local variable BUTTON_NAME in the current scope with the string 'MOVIES':

```
(debug 1)PL/SQL> DEBUG.SETC ('BUTTON_NAME','MOVIES');
```

The second command uses the package DEBUG, which will be discussed in greater detail in Section 20.3.6.

20.3.5 RESUMING THE APPLICATION EXECUTION

After the program flow is interrupted and you have inspected or modified the application state, you will eventually decide to resume the execution. At that point, you have three choices:

- **Resume the execution freely.** Forms Runtime will attempt to execute all the program units that are currently stored in the stack. If no other breakpoints are encountered, at the end of the process, the execution stack will be empty, and the Debugger window will be hidden. If Forms Runtime encounters a breakpoint in the execution path, the flow of the program is interrupted again. In order to resume free execution of the program, perform any of the following actions:
  - Click the Go icon in the toolbar.
  - Choose Debug | Go from the menu.
  - Enter the following statement in the Interpreter Pane:

    ```
    (debug 1)PL/SQL> .GO
    ```
- **Terminate the execution of the statements in the stack.** This action is also

called resetting the debug level. In this case, Oracle Forms will not execute any further statements in the current execution thread, but will return to the next higher debug level. At the same time, the message bar will display a message similar to "FRM-40748: Trigger WHEN-BUTTON-PRESSED terminated by reset command."

To reset the execution to a higher debug level, follow any of these steps:

- ❑ Click the Reset icon in the toolbar.
- ❑ Choose Debug | Reset from the menu.
- ❑ Enter the following statement in the Interpreter Pane:

```
(debug 1)PL/SQL> .RESET
```

❑ **Step through the statements in the stack.** This is probably the action that you will perform the most, because it allows you to execute only one or a few statements at a time. When these statements are executed, the control returns to the Debugger to allow you to assess their effects on the application. The most general command for stepping through the code is to choose Debug | Step... menu item from the Debugger's menu. The PL/SQL Step dialog box will appear (see Figure 20.12). The contents of these dialog box reflect the parameters that the STEP command may take.

The radio buttons in this dialog box control the mode in which the statements are executed; the value entered in the Count field controls the number of statements that will be executed in each step. By default, only one statement is executed at each step. Clicking the Apply button will issue the Step command without dismissing the dialog box, at which point you can enter a new mode or target to step to. Clicking the OK button issues the command and dismisses the dialog box. Clicking the Cancel dialog will dismiss the dialog box without any further action.

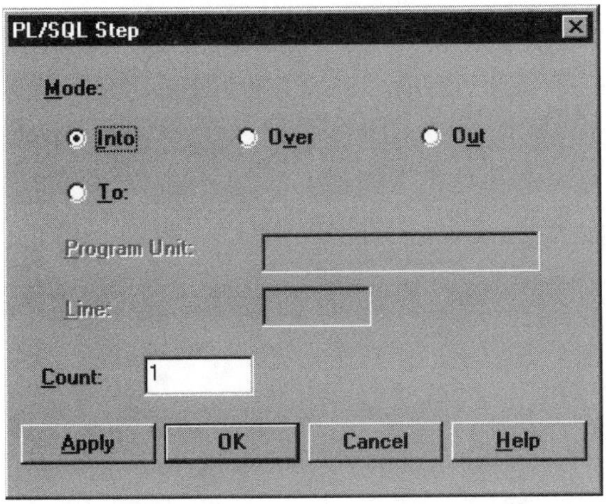

FIGURE 20.12 PL/SQL Step dialog box.

According to the settings of the Mode radio buttons, the Debugger may Step Into, Step Over, Step Out, or Step To a target program unit. In Step Into mode, the Debugger will execute the number of statements specified in Count. If any of these statements is a call to a subroutine, Debugger will descend in the subroutine. In Step Over mode, the Debugger will execute the number of statements specified, but if it encounters a subroutine call the subroutine will be executed but no debugging information will be produced. In Step Out mode, the Debugger will execute all the statements until the end of the current program unit and will pause when the control returns to the calling program unit. The value of Count is irrelevant for this command. When you select the To radio button, the data items Program Unit and line are enabled. You can use them to enter the target program unit and line number. Debugger will execute all the statements until it reaches the specified target.

Although the PL/SQL Step dialog box offers the Step functionality in the most general level, you will rarely use it in practice. The most common Step commands, Step Into, Step Over, and Step Out, are accessible from the Debuggers toolbar. You can issue these commands by clicking the Step Into icon, the Step Over icon, and the Step Out icon.

You may also use the command line in the Interpreter Pane for the purpose of stepping through the program units. For example, to step into the next statement, you would use this command:

```
(debug 1)PL/SQL> .STEP INTO
```

The commands to step over or step out are similar, but the parameter INTO is replaced by the parameter OVER or OUT, respectively.

20.3.6 USING THE DEBUG PACKAGE

When you create debug triggers in the Debugger, you may take advantage of the functions, procedures and exceptions defined in the package DEBUG. This is a special package because it can be accessible only at runtime, from PL/SQL code that you create in the Debugger. You have already seen two instances of using components of this package. In Figure 20.5 the exception DEBUG.BREAK is raised to instruct Form Runtime to stop the execution of the program unit and to pass control to the Debugger. At the end of Section 20.3.4 the procedure DEBUG.SETC is used to set the value of an item.

This procedure is part of a larger group of four procedures that can be used to set values of variables, parameters, or items. The procedure DEBUG.SETC is used to set values of alphanumeric variables; DEBUG.SETN is used for integer variables; DEBUG.SETI is used to set values of PLS_INTEGER variables; and DEBUG.SETD is used with date variables.

If you want to retrieve the values of such variables, you can use four functions that correspond to the procedures above. DEBUG.GETC returns the value of an alphanumeric variable; DEBUG.GETN returns the value of a numeric variable; DEBUG.GETI returns the value of a PLS_INTEGER variable; and DEBUG.GETD returns the value of a date variable.

Finally, if you want to suspend the execution of the debug trigger, use the procedure DEBUG.SUSPEND.

20.4 FORMS RUNTIME DIAGNOSTICS (FRD)

Developer Forms 6.0 offers FRD, a runtime, event-based logging system designed to help you debug your application. You can activate the FRD for the MRD module as follows:

```
IFRU8N60.EXE C:\MRD\MRD.FMX RECORD=COLLECT
[LOG=mylog.log]
```

If the LOG parameter is not specified, forms will write the logging information to the current working directory with the name: collect_<process ID>. Although generally large, you can analyze the output log file with a text editor. You can expect the log to contain the following types of messages:

Triggers

Information about triggers is recorded in the following format:

```
<trigger_name> Trigger Fired:
Form: <form_name>
Block: <block_name>
Item: <item_name>
```

The level of the trigger corresponds to the last item in the list. A trigger on the Form level, therefore, would have only the form name listed below the trigger name. A state delta will be written to the log following a trigger fire. A state delta is a dump of all internal state information that has changed since the occurrence of the previous state delta. The first state delta will dump the entire forms state to the log.

Built-ins

When a PL/SQL Forms built-in is executed, the diagnostic output should appear as follows:

```
Executing <built-in name> Built-In:
In Argument 0 -Type: <type> Value: <value>
```

```
In Argument 1 -Type: <type> Value: <value>
...
Out Argument 0 -Type: <type> Value: <value>
...
```

Argument 0 generally represents the function return value.

Messages

Messages are logged as follows:

```
Error Messages: <message>
```

Unhandled Exceptions

Unhandled Exceptions are logged as follows:

```
Unhandled Exception: <exception_name>
```

20.5 SUMMARY

Debugger is Developer component that allows you to debug PL/SQL code in your applications and analyze the flow of your program. This chapter explained its features and functionality. Major topics discussed here were

- **Accessing the Debugger**
- **Components of the Debugger**
  - Source Pane
  - Navigator Pane
  - Interpreter Pane
  - Toolbar
- **Managing Debug Actions**
  - Creating Debug Actions
  - Editing Debug Actions
  - Editing Program Units and Triggers
  - Inspecting the Application State
  - Resuming the Application Execution
  - Using the DEBUG Package
- **Using Forms Runtime diagnostics**
  - Activating the diagnostics
  - Interpreting the log file

The following table describes the software assets that were discussed in this chapter and are provided with the companion software. From the main page of the companion software, follow the links *Software* and *Chapter 20* to access these assets:

ASSET NAME	DESCRIPTION
CH20_1.FMB	A version of the MRD application developed in Part 3.
CH20_1.FMX	The executable version of CH20_1.FMB compiled on Win32 platforms.

Chapter 21

Creating Integrated Developer Applications

He chose to include things
That in each other are included, the whole,
The complicate, the amassing harmony.
—Wallace Stevens

The Form Builder is a development tool that allows you to incorporate many useful features in your database applications. It is also a flexible tool because it can be integrated effectively with development tools from the Developer family and other environments. This chapter discusses the integration of Form Builder with the other two important components of Developer, Report Builder and Graphic Builder.

21.1 CREATING MULTIPLE-FORM APPLICATIONS

Form Builder easily supports creating applications with dozens of blocks, windows, and extended functionality. Nevertheless, there are often occasions when the functionality of a system must be split into different subsystems. Each of these subsystems may be further divided in smaller systems, which are implemented as separate Forms modules. In development efforts for large enterprise systems, developed by many programmers working in parallel, the creation and maintenance of separate modules which are then are integrated in larger systems is the rule more than the exception. In these systems, a module that represents the most important part of functionality is usually launched first. The other modules can be invoked by the users as and when they are needed. There are three basic ways in which a form can invoke another form in a multi-form application:

- ❑ Use the built-in procedure OPEN_FORM to open a form that is independent from calling form.
- ❑ Use the built-in procedure NEW_FORM to replace the calling form with the new form.
- ❑ Use the built-in procedure CALL_FORM to deactivate the calling form and invoke the new form as a modal application.

In this section, you will try out each scenario by integrating the MRD module developed in previous chapters with the module ANALYZE.FMB provided in the companion disk. The MRD module will continue to implement the main functionality of the MRD application. When users will want to analyze the income generated by customers and movies for the movie rental store, the module ANALYZE.FMB will be activated.

Recall that the ANALYZE functionality is invoked from the menu item Tool | Analyze of the MRD menu module, or by clicking the respective icon on the toolbar of the MRD form. In both cases, a call to the procedure `Click_Button('ANALYZE')` is issued. This procedure is defined in the PL/SQL library MRDMENU.PLL, which is attached to both the menu and the form module mentioned previously.

In this chapter, you can continue to work with the form and library modules you developed in Part III; or you can rename the modules CH21_1.FMB and

MRDMENU.PLL provided with the companion software and use them as the starting point for the activities to follow. The module ANALYZE is provided with the companion software, as well. As a preliminary step, open the library MRD-MENU.PLL, and the modules MRD.FMB and ANALYZE.FMB in the Form Builder.

21.1.1 PASSING VALUES TO CALLED MODULES

When invoking a new module from an existing form, you may often need to pass values from the current environment to the new one. One way of doing this is to use global variables. These variables are visible across all the modules and are used primarily for constant sharing of data between them. If you only need to initialize some values upon new form's startup, you can pass these values using parameter lists. Chapter 17 explained how you can create and populate parameter lists. This section lists only a few features of parameter lists that are specific to the Form Builder environment.

1. Each Form Builder module contains a parameter list called DEFAULT, which can be used like any other custom-created parameter lists to transfer values from the calling to the called form.
2. In general, parameter lists may contain text parameters or data parameters. This last type of parameters, formed of record groups, cannot be used to invoke a new form.
3. All the parameters passed by the calling form must have been defined at design time in the called form.
4. All the parameter values passed with parameter lists are of CHAR data type, whereas the parameters in the called form may be of other data types such DATE or NUMBER. In such case, care must be taken to populate the parameters in the calling form with values that are convertible to the data type of the parameter in the called form. In other words, if the parameter in the called form is of DATE data type, the calling form must pass a value in one of Oracle's recognized DATE formats, for example 'DD-MON-YYYY.' If the variable in the calling program is of type DATE, it must be converted to type CHAR to be passed as a parameter. This is usually done using the TO_CHAR function.

21.1.2 OPENING INDEPENDENT MODULES WITH OPEN_FORM

The built-in procedure OPEN_FORM is used to open a new module independently from the calling module. The only required argument of this procedure is the name of the form. To see the effects of this procedure take the following actions:

1. Open the procedure `Click_Button` in the PL/SQL Editor window. This procedure is part of the PL/SQL library MRDMENU.PLL.
2. Create a new ELSIF clause for the button ANALYZE with contents as follows:

   ```
   OPEN_FORM ('ANALYZE.FMX');
   ```
3. Compile and save the module MRDMENU.PLL.

For simplicity and portability reasons, this example specifies only the name of the new form module. When developing for deployment in the users' environment, you will define a working directory for your application. The example above will work if the module that will be accessed resides in this working directory.

If the module must reside in a directory other than the working directory of the application, in order to avoid hard-coding path names in the call to OPEN_FORM, you should add this directory in the specification of the environmental variable FORMSxx_PATH.

Now you can run the MRD module. Open one or two windows of this module, then call the ANALYZE module. You will notice that the Form Builder focus will be placed immediately on the new form. At the same time, the toolbar and the menu of the MRD module are replaced by those of the ANALYZE module. However, it is not difficult to notice that the windows of the MRD module are still open. They are listed under the WINDOW menu item and can be activated at any moment either by choosing their name from this list, or by directly clicking on the target window. You will notice that each time you click the window of a different module, the MDI frame of the application will replace the menu and the toolbars with those of attached to the clicked module.

As you see, when OPEN_FORM is invoked with the form name as the only argument, the new form receives focus immediately. If you want to open a form, but maintain the focus in the current form, use the following statement:

```
OPEN_FORM ('ANALYZE.FMX', NO_ACTIVATE);
```

This second parameter is also called the `activation_mode`. The other value it can take is ACTIVATE, which is also the default value of the argument.

As you use this application, you may question yourself about the benefit of opening a separate module to access the ANALYZE functionality of the MRD system. The only thing that is different from the single-form environment that you have used previously is that the menus and toolbars are replaced as you move the focus from one module to the other. There are two advantages in breaking down the application functionality in multiple modules following this approach.

The first advantage is generally valid for every software application you develop. The practice has shown that is much easier to develop, maintain, and upgrade modular systems than monolithic applications. If there is a problem with the ANALYZE subsystem of the MRD application, the subsystem can be maintained without directly affecting the rest of the application.

The second advantage, which is specific to Form Builder applications is that invoking new modules with the procedure OPEN_FORM allows you to establish separate sessions with the database for each subsystem. This is another of those situations when the tight integration of Form Builder with the Oracle Server database displays its benefits. The Oracle RDBMS implements all the transaction management functionality such as obtaining, holding and releasing locks, commits and rollbacks, at the session level rather than at the user level. The fact that Forms allows you to have multiple sessions with the database means that you can issue transactions independently in each session. In other words, you can insert some records in the MRD module, and, without having to complete the transaction with a commit or a rollback, you can move on to the ANALYZE module and initiate a new transaction there. Committing the transaction in this second module will not commit the changes you made in the first module, because they are maintained in a separate transaction by a different session.

By default however, OPEN_FORM opens the new module with the same database session as the calling module. To create a new independent session for the module you must complete these two steps:

1. Set the following environment variable `FORMSxx_SESSION` to TRUE. Like other environment variables, this variable can be set in the Registry in Microsoft Windows installations of Developer. Here, the characters 'xx' denote the version of the Form Builder (45, 50, and so on.)
2. Use the following statement to open the new form:

   ```
   OPEN_FORM ('ANALYZE.FMX', ACTIVATE, SESSION);
   ```

   The third parameter in this statement is called `session_mode`. Its default setting is NO_SESSION.

Obviously, the same way you can open multiple modules independently, you can also open the same form module multiple times. Combining this with the fact that you can keep the sessions for each module separate allows you to maintain several transactions for the same block within the application, if this is necessary.

Finally, when parameters in the new form will be populated with values from the calling form, these values can be added to a parameter list. Then, the internal ID or the name of this parameter list can be added as the last argument in the call to the procedure OPEN_FORM.

As said earlier, when multiple modules are open, you can navigate to them by directly clicking one of their windows, or by choosing its name from the list of open windows in the WINDOW menu. You can also navigate between modules programmatically. As each independent module is opened, it is assigned an internal ID. The procedure NEXT_FORM navigates to the form that has the next higher ID than the current form. When the current form is the last one to be opened, NEXT_FORM will place the focus to the first form that was opened. PREVIOUS_FORM navigates to the form with the next lower ID. When PREVIOUS_FORM is invoked form the form that was activated first, the focus is place on the form that was opened last.

You can also use the procedure GO_FORM to navigate directly to a given form. This procedure may take as its argument the name of the form or its internal ID. Given the higher possibility of making a mistake when using the name of the form, the later version is preferred and considered safer and more efficient. Figure 21.1 shows the example of a procedure that navigates to a form if it is already opened, or opens it if it is not.

At the conclusion of this section, let us discuss a few things that you must be aware of when invoking independent forms with OPEN_FORM.

- Because each opened module will take a share of the system resources, you should be careful with the number of modules that are open at any one time. Educate users to maintain open only those modules that are indispensable, and close the ones that are not needed.
- OPEN_FORM is a restricted procedure which cannot be called from Query Mode.
- When the focus moves from one module to another either because the module is opened with the ACTIVATE activation mode, or because a user-initiated or programmatic navigation occurs, none of the usual POST-*object*, PRE-*object*, and WHEN-NEW-*object* triggers fire. The only triggers fired are WHEN-WINDOW-DEACTIVATED in the module that opens or initiates the navigation to the new module, and WHEN-WINDOW-ACTIVATED in the target module.

```
PROCEDURE Goto_Form (formName VARCHAR2) IS
 formID    FormModule;
BEGIN
 formID := FIND_FORM(formName);
 IF ID_NULL(formID) THEN
   OPEN_FORM(formName);
   CHECK_PACKAGE_FAILURE;
 ELSE
   GO_FORM(formID);
   CHECK_PACKAGE_FAILURE;
 END IF;
END;
```

FIGURE 21.1 Opening or navigating to modules programmatically.

- In MDI applications, the menu Window will list the titles of the windows as they are defined in each individual module. This could lead to more than one window with the same title being open and displayed in the list. For example, the windows that hold CUSTOMER block data for each of the modules MRD and ANALYZE could inadvertently be titled "Customer." In order to help your users associate windows with the module that owns them, you should include some sort of indication about the purpose of the module in the window title. Therefore, the windows in the module ANALYZE.FMB are called "Customer Revenue" and "Movie Revenue."
- The MDI frame is a common objects shared by all the modules being opened. Changes that a module makes to the MDI frame such as setting its title, remain visible until overwritten, even after the module is closed.

21.1.3 POST, COMMIT, AND ROLLBACK

Before discussing the other two ways used to call modules from existing Form Builder modules, I will shed some more light on the concepts of posting, committing, and rolling back transactions. Recall from previous discussions about transaction processing in the Oracle database that in order to mark certain points in a transaction you use savepoints. The main purpose of the savepoints is to undo or rollback only a part of the transaction, without losing all the work performed from the moment the transaction began. When interacting with the database, Form Builder uses savepoints and rollbacks on your behalf.

By default, a savepoint is issued when the Form Runtime is initially launched, each time a new form is loaded in memory using NEW_FORM or CALL_FORM, and each time the procedures POST and COMMIT_FORM are invoked.

The procedures POST and COMMIT_FORM are similar in the sense that they both write the data to the database. In the process all the default validation and commit processing of Forms occurs in identically the same manner. However, they are fundamentally different, because the data written by POST are not committed and can be rolled back. By contrast when COMMIT_FORM is issued, all the data since the beginning of the transaction, including those temporarily stored by POST are written permanently to the database.

Rollbacks can be issued when either of the procedures CLEAR_FORM, EXIT_FORM, or NEW_FORM are invoked. Each of these procedures takes an argument called `rollback_mode`. By default, the value of this argument is TO_SAVEPOINT. With this value, all the uncommitted changes in the current module, including those that are posted, will be discarded when any of the above procedures will complete. The other two values that this argument can take are NO_ROLLBACK and FULL_ROLLBACK. When you use NO_ROLLBACK, Form Builder does not perform any rollback. Only the changes in the current module that are not posted or committed will be lost at the end of the procedures mentioned above. In the case of EXIT_FORM and NEW_FORM, the data posted in the current module, and all the locks obtained by this module will be preserved even after the module is removed from memory. When the argument `rollback_mode` takes the value FULL_ROLLBACK, Form Builder wipes out all the pending changes, even those posted. The rollback occurs at the session level, rather than at the module level, which occurs when TO_SAVEPOINT is used. This means that changes made but not yet committed in the current form, and in all the other forms that called or were called by this form will be lost.

21.1.4 REPLACING MODULES WITH NEW_FORM

One of the major drawbacks of opening multiple modules using OPEN_FORMis the toll each of these modules takes on the memory available to the system. Before deciding to open a module independently, you must consider whether you can release the resources occupied by the current form. If it is the case that the users will not need to have both forms available at the same time, you can replace the old form with the new one using the procedure NEW_FORM. The general syntax of this procedure is:

```
NEW_FORM (module_name, rollback_mode, query_mode,
parameter_list);
```

The meaning and usage of the first and last of the arguments above is the same as for the procedure OPEN_FORM, explained in Section 21.1.2. When Form Builder encounters the NEW_FORM procedure, it exits the current form and launches the form `module_name`. If parametric values need to be passed from the current form to the new form, these values are placed in a parameter list.

The meaning of the argument `rollback_mode` is as explained in the previous section. Its default value is TO_SAVEPOINT, but it can take the additional values NO_ROLLBACK and FULL_ROLLBACK. By default, users will be able to query and manipulate data in this form like in any other form. If you want to restrict them to use the form only for query purposes, you can set the argument `query_mode` to QUERY_ONLY. The default value of this argument is NO_QUERY_ONLY.

When the requirements of your application allow you to replace the modules, NEW_FORM offers a good and efficient solution to the problem of building multiple-form application. However, like OPEN_FORM, this procedure is a restricted procedure that can be used only in Normal Mode.

21.1.5 CALLING MODAL MODULES WITH CALL_FORM

Using the built-in CALL_FORM to invoke another form is an option that you should consider only in very rare occasions, if at all. There are three basic reasons for this argument, as explained in the following paragraphs:

- When you use CALL_FORM to invoke another module, Form Builder keeps the current form running in the background, disabled and unavailable to the users, while running the new module. Thus, the memory resources will be used without users seeing any benefits of it.
- A certain amount of the memory allocated to a module opened with CALL_FORM is locked until that module is exited.
- In a GUI application, the only application modal windows should be dialog boxes. It is certainly not necessary and not efficient to have a whole module running as a modal form.

The general syntax of this procedure is:

```
CALL_FORM (module_name, display, switch_menu,
query_mode, parameter_list);
```

The meanings of parameters such as `module_name`, `query_mode`, and `parameter_list` are explained in Sections 21.1.2 and 21.1.4. The argument `display` can take one of the two values: HIDE and NO_HIDE. The value HIDE, which is also the default value means that Form Builder will hide the current form from the view before displaying the new called form. When the called form is exited, the background form becomes active again. If NO_HIDE is specified, the calling form remains visible, and its windows can be activated, resized, minimized, and maximized. However, any items, controls, or toolbars associated with it are disabled and not available.

The argument `switch_menu` controls whether the called form uses the menu of the calling module or its own menu. The default value of this argument is NO_REPLACE, which means that both modules will share the same menu module associated with the calling module. If this argument is set to DO_REPLACE, the menu module attached to the called form takes over and replaces the menu of the original module.

Despite the inherent disadvantages, the procedure CALL_FORM has a feature that the other two procedures discussed previously do not enjoy. CALL_FORM is not a restricted procedure, which means that it can be used equally well in Query Mode and in Normal Mode.

21.2 INTEGRATING TOOLS WITH RUN_PRODUCT

RUN_PRODUCT is a built-in procedure that allows you to invoke from Form Builder other components of the Developer family of tools. You can use this procedure to call Form Builder, Report Builder, and Graphic Builder modules, however, it is used mostly to invoke Reports and Graphics, and almost never other Forms modules.

The previous section discussed the different alternatives you have to invoke other forms from within a form module. OPEN_FORM, NEW_FORM, and CALL_FORM limit considerably the need and the use of RUN_PRODUCT to call other forms. As you will see in the following section, Graphic Builder is well integrated with Form Builder as well, through chart items and the PLL library OG. Often you would prefer to use these resources to display data graphically in your application. This leaves Oracle Reports as the primary tool invoked with RUN_PRODUCT, and Oracle Book as a distant candidate. RUN_PRODUCT can be used to invoke reports in both client/server and Forms/Reports server environments.

RUN_PRODUCT takes several arguments as input. Its general syntax is:

```
RUN_PRODUCT (product, document, commmode, execmode,
location, list, display);
```

The meaning of each argument is explained in the following paragraphs:

- **Product.** This argument represents the type of application that will be invoked. Its values can be FORMS, REPORTS, or GRAPHICS.
- **Document.** This argument specifies the name of the module to be loaded. This is the file name if the document is maintained as a file in the directory structure, or the module name if it is stored in the database. When the document argument specifies a file, you can specify its full path, or provide only the file name. In this last case, the product will look for the file in the working directory and in the default directory defined for the tool, which in general is %ORACLE_HOME%\BIN.
- **Commode.** The name of this argument is an abbreviation for communication mode, and defines when the control will return to calling form after the call to the product is issued. If the value of this argument is SYNCHRONOUS, the new application is modal with respect to the calling module. Users cannot perform any actions in the form while the called application is active. Only when this application is exited, the control returns to the calling forms. If the value of the argument `commmode` is ASYNCHRONOUS, RUN_PRODUCT issues the call to the new product and returns immediately the control to the parent form, even if the invoked application may not have been displayed completely.
- **Execmode.** The value of this argument controls the execution mode of the invoked tool. All the tools that are invoked with RUN_PRODUCT are executed either in BATCH or RUNTIME mode. All, with the exception of Form Builder modules. In the rare event you will invoke Forms with this procedure, you must always use the value RUNTIME. When the value of the argument `execmode` is set to BATCH, the invoked product is executed without the intervention of the users. A meaningful situation when you would

```
DECLARE
 param_list_id     ParamList;
 param_list_name   VARCHAR2(20) := 'Report_pl';
 sql_stat          VARCHAR2(255);

BEGIN
—Make sure that parameter list does not exist.
 param_list_id := GET_PARAMETER_LIST(param_list_name);
 IF NOT ID_NULL(param_list_id) THEN
  MESSAGE('Parameter_list '||param_list_name||' already
exists.');
  RAISE FORM_TRIGGER_FAILURE;
 END IF;

—Create the parameter list.
 param_list_id := CREATE_PARAMETER_LIST(param_list_name);
 IF ID_NULL(param_list_id) THEN
  MESSAGE('Parameter_list '||param_list_name||' cannot be
created.');
  RAISE FORM_TRIGGER_FAILURE;
 END IF;

—Build the WHERE clause.
 sql_stat := Build_Where_Clause('MAIL.SELECTED');

—Add the WHERE clause to the parameter list.
 ADD_PARAMETER(param_list_id, 'WHERE_CLAUSE',
TEXT_PARAMETER, sql_stat);

—Run the report that prints the label.
 RUN_PRODUCT(REPORTS, 'MRDLABEL', ASYNCHRONOUS,
        RUNTIME, FILESYSTEM, param_list_id, NULL);

—Destroy Parameter List
 DESTROY_PARAMETER_LIST(param_list_id);

EXCEPTION
 WHEN OTHERS THEN
  Message('Internal error occurred in WHEN-BUTTON-
PRESSED.');
  RAISE FORM_TRIGGER_FAILURE;
END;
```

FIGURE 21.2 Invoking reports with RUN_PRODUCT.

use this argument is when you want to run a report in the background, possibly send it directly to the printer. However, when calling Graphics modules, which are of a more interactive character than Reports, the value of this argument should be set to RUNTIME. In such a case, the new application is fully available to the users.

- **Location.** The setting of this argument is related to the value of the argument `document`. It can take only two values: FILESYSTEM and DB. The first value indicates that the module is stored in the file system, and the name of the file is defined in the argument document. The second value means that the module is stored in the database. In this case, document contains the name of the database module.
- **List.** This is the name or the internal ID of a parameter list with values that the calling form will pass to the invoked application. As mentioned earlier, the parameter list can either contain text string values, or record groups. Form Builder can be called only with TEXT_PARAMETER parameter lists. Another restriction that applies across the board is that when a record group is passed as a parameter list, the new product must be invoked synchronously.
- **Display.** This argument requires a value only if you are invoking an Graphics display. In this case, the value of this argument is the name of the chart item that will serve as container for the chart. When other tools are invoked, the setting of this argument does not bear a meaning.

In Chapter 17, you created a trigger associated with the push button PRINT in the block MAIL of the MRD module. This trigger builds a parameter list and calls the report MRDLABEL, which ultimately prints the labels. Figure 21.2 shows once again the contents of this trigger.

As you can see from this figure, the execution mode of the report is set to RUNTIME because the users must set the page orientation to Landscape before sending the data to the printer. You also want the control to return to the users immediately after they invoke the report. Therefore, the communication mode argument is set to ASYNCHRONOUS.

21.3 INTEGRATING FORM BUILDER WITH REPORT BUILDER

In order to provide for a better integration with Report Builder objects, the Form Builder allows you to maintain the report modules invoked from the form as objects of the form module. These objects can be invoked using the Form Builder built-in RUN_REPORT_OBJECT, rather than the generic RUN_PRODUCT discussed in the previous section. Furthermore, properties and queries that build a data block in the form module can be used to create a report directly from the

Form Builder. In this section I will explain how you create and maintain Report Builder objects in your form modules.

Report Builder objects are maintained under the node Reports of the Object Navigator. You can use any of the Navigator's commands to start the process of creating a new report object, for example, click the icon Create on the toolbar. The dialog box New Report shown in Figure 21.3 appears. The radio items in this dialog box allow you to base the report object either on an existing report module saved and stored in the file system or on a new report module that you create on the fly.

If you choose to create a new report module—by selecting the radio item Create New Report File—specify the name and location of this file in the text item Filename. You may also take advantage of structure of a data block already existing in the Form Builder module by setting the check box item Base Report on Block and entering the block name in the text item to its right. Ultimately, when you click OK to dismiss the New Report dialog box—having chosen to create a new report module—the Report Builder will display its Report Wizard. Like other wizards I have presented so far, the Report Wizard facilitates a particular development task—in this case, designing the report module. In the following paragraphs, I briefly explain the purpose of the Report Wizard's screens.

- **Report style screen.** Reports come in different styles, including Tabular, Form, Matrix, Mailing Label, and Form Letter. All of these styles are listed in this screen of the Report Wizard, as shown in Figure 21.4. Picking a style here assigns a number of attributes and properties to the layout of your report, therefore it is a good idea to become familiar with the look and feel of each style, so that you can make the appropriate choice.
- **Data screen.** This screen as shown in Figure 21.5 allows you to define the SQL statements that will query the data for your report. If you create the report based on a data block, you will not see this screen. The Form Builder automatically transfers the information about the database objects on which

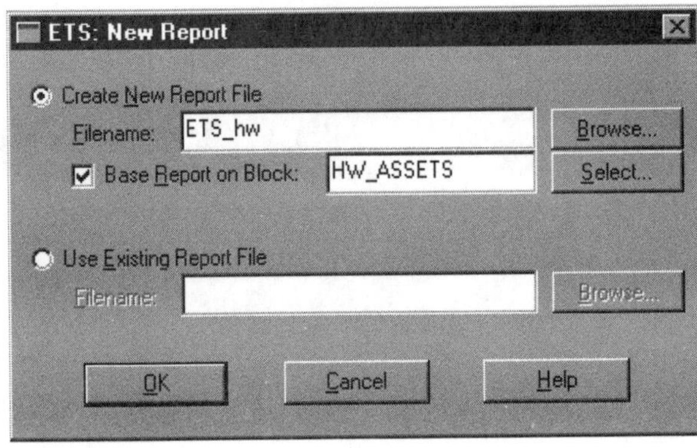

FIGURE 21.3 The New Report dialog box.

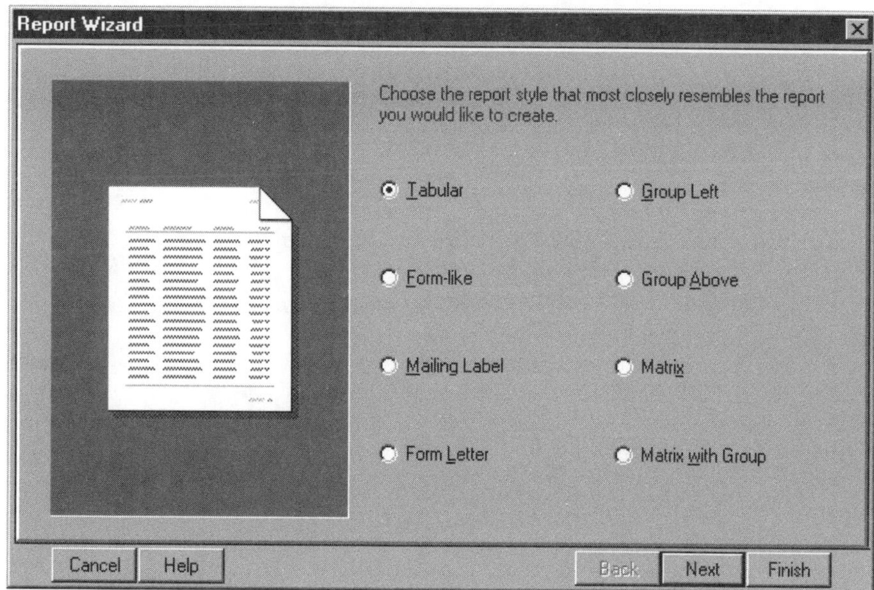

FIGURE 21.4 The Style screen of the Report Wizard.

the block is based to the Report Builder. If you are not basing the report on an existing block, then you can use this screen to type in the SQL statement, to import it from a text file saved in the file system, or build it interactively using the Developer Query Builder.

- **Fields screen.** This screen allows you to select among all the data items returned by the query those that will become displayed as fields in the report. This screen is very similar in behavior and functionality to the Block screen in the Layout Wizard of the Form Builder, therefore I will not cover it in details.
- **Formula screen.** You can use this screen to define calculated fields in your report. Figure 21.6 shows an example of how the sum of the purchase cost for all the hardware assets is defined in this screen. In order to add another calculated field to the report, you simply select it in the Available Fields list and click one of the buttons that represents an operation.
- **Display screen.** This screen is similar to the Items screen in the Form Builder's Layout Wizard, as well. It allows you to maintain the prompt, width, and height of all the fields in your report.
- **Template screen.** Report Builder modules can inherit a number of properties from templates, just as Form Builder modules do. These include color settings, fonts, and the report layout. The template screen allows you to se-

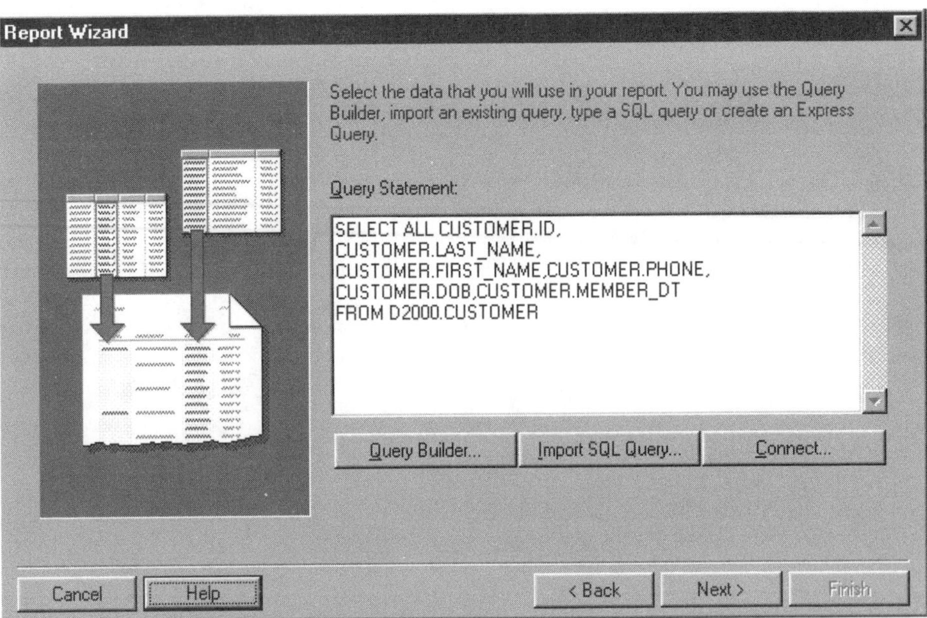

FIGURE 21.5 The Data screen of the Report Wizard.

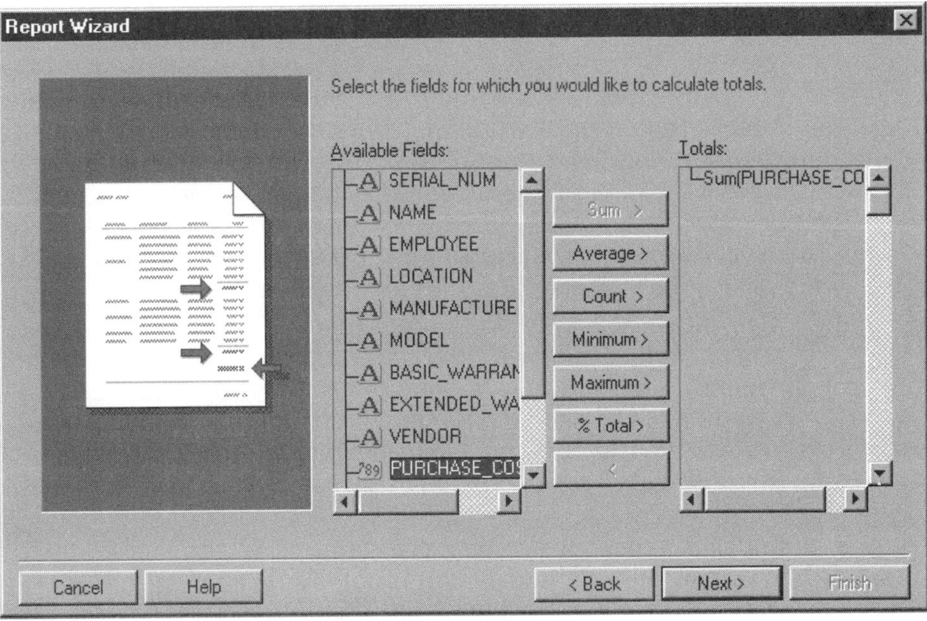

FIGURE 21.6 The Formula screen of the Report Wizard.

lect a predefined screen for your report or one that is saved as a separate module in the file system. You can also skip the template selection and create the report without one.

Once you have gone through the screens described here and clicked Finish, the Report Wizard creates the report module in the Report Builder. From that point, you can continue to refine and develop this module independently of the Form Builder module. The Form Builder, on the other hand, creates a Report object in the module's object hierarchy. You can maintain the properties of this object in the Property Palette, a copy of which is shown in Figure 21.7. The group Dev Integration contains properties that Form Builder uses to invoke the module—such as Filename, Execution Mode, and Communication Mode. The meaning of these properties is the same as of the arguments passed to the built-in RUN_PRODUCT, discussed in Section 21.2. The properties in the group Reports correspond to command line arguments that are processed by the Report Runtime engine when a report is executed. In the example shown in Figure 21.7, the report object invokes the module ETS_hw, in runtime and synchronous mode.

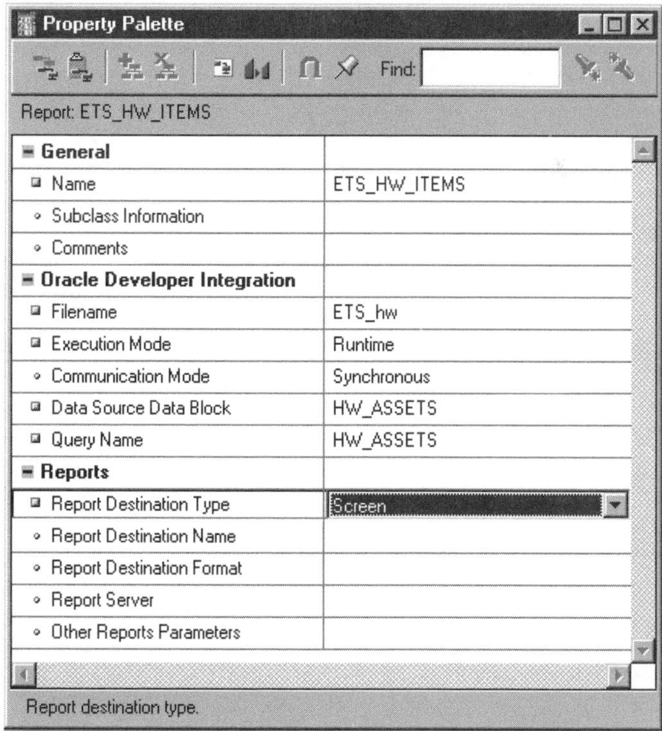

FIGURE 21.7 The properties of a Report object in the Form Builder.

This report is based on the block HW_ASSETS of the form module and its results will be displayed on the screen.

In order to activate the report referenced by the Report object, you can use a combination of the built-ins FIND_REPORT_OBJECT, ID_NULL, RUN_REPORT_OBJECT, REPORT_OBJECT_STATUS and COPY_REPORT_OBJECT_OUTPUT. Keep in mind that REPORT_OBJECT_STATUS, CANCEL_REPORT_OBJECT and COPY_REPORT_OBJECT_OUTPUT are only functional if using the Reports Server. The most important function in this group is RUN_REPORT_OBJECT, which, as the name suggests, actually runs the report module. This function takes two parameters: the first one is the name or ID of report object in the Form Builder module; the second argument is the name or ID of the parameter list handed over to the report from the form. This function returns a handle to the report in the form of an alphanumeric string. The handle is useful in cases when the report is run asynchronously. You can pass it to the function REPORT_OBJECT_STATUS, which, in turn, returns the status of the running report. Figure 21.8 shows the contents of a trigger that invokes the report whose properties were shown in Figure 21.7.

If the property Communication Mode of this report is set to "Asynchronous," you could store the report handle returned by RUN_REPORT_OBJECT to

```
DECLARE
 report_id      Report_Object;
 report_handle  VARCHAR2(30);

BEGIN
—Make sure that report object exists.
 report_id := FIND_REPORT_OBJECT('ETS_HW_ITEMS');
/* IF NOT ID_NULL(report_id) THEN
  MESSAGE('Report object ETS_HW_ITEMS does not exist.');
  RAISE FORM_TRIGGER_FAILURE;
 END IF;
*/
—Start the report.
 report_handle := RUN_REPORT_OBJECT(report_id, '');
EXCEPTION
 WHEN OTHERS THEN
  Message('Internal error occurred in WHEN-BUTTON-
PRESSED.');
  RAISE FORM_TRIGGER_FAILURE;
END;
```

FIGURE 21.8 Invoking reports with RUN_PRODUCT.

a control item or global variable and then use it to check the completion status of the report with the function REPORT_OBJECT_STATUS. In order to provide users with continuous feedback, you can store the status in a display item and use a timer to update it at regular time intervals. Figure 21.9 shows the contents of the trigger that invokes the report 'ETS_hw' revised to store the handle of the report in the control item RPT_HANDLE of block HW_ASSETS.

Notice that the last executable line of the trigger shown in Figure 21.9 creates the timer ETS_HW_TIMER which fires every second—1000 milliseconds—and that repeats itself at such intervals. Whenever the timer is activated, you want to retrieve the status of the report. The form-level WHEN-TIMER-EXPIRED is where you need to place the statement that retrieves this status. This trigger will fire each time a timer expires in your form, therefore, its code should perform the following steps:

1. Retrieve the name of the timer that just expired and caused the trigger to fire. This name is stored in the runtime property TIMER_NAME of the application.

```
DECLARE
 report_id     Report_Object;
 report_timer   Timer;

BEGIN
—Make sure that report object exists.
 report_id := FIND_REPORT_OBJECT('ETS_HW_ITEMS');
/* IF NOT ID_NULL(report_id) THEN
  MESSAGE('Report object ETS_HW_ITEMS does not exist.');
  RAISE FORM_TRIGGER_FAILURE;
 END IF;
*/
—Start the report.
 :HW_ASSETS.report_handle := RUN_REPORT_OBJECT(report_id,
'');
 report_timer := CREATE_TIMER('ETS_HW_TIMER', 1000,
REPEAT);
EXCEPTION
 WHEN OTHERS THEN
  Message('Internal error occurred in WHEN-BUTTON-
PRESSED.');
  RAISE FORM_TRIGGER_FAILURE;
END;
```

FIGURE 21.9 Invoking reports with RUN_PRODUCT.

```
DECLARE
  expired_timer  VARCHAR2(30);
BEGIN
  expired_timer:=GET_APPLICATION_PROPERTY(TIMER_NAME);
  IF expired_timer='ETS_HW_TIMER' THEN
    :HW_ASSETS.RPT_STATUS :=
REPORT_OBJECT_STATUS(:HW_ASSETS.RPT_HANDLE);
    IF :HW_ASSETS.RPT_STATUS = 'Complete' THEN
       DELETE_TIMER('ETS_HW_TIMER');
    END IF;
  END IF;
END;
```

FIGURE 21.10 The WHEN-TIMER-EXPIRED trigger that checks the status of the report.

2. Execute the appropriate logic that the timer will invoke. In the case of ETS_HW_TIMER, the logic is to retrieve the status of the report object ETS_hw and store it in the display item RPT_STATUS of the HW_ASSETS block. Since the timer ETS_HW_TIMER is a repeating one, you should be careful to delete it once it is no longer needed, that is, when the report status becomes 'COMPLETED.'

Figure 21.10 shows the contents of the WHEN-TIMER-EXPIRED trigger discussed here.

If running a report asynchronously, you can use the CANCEL_REPORT_OBJECT to cancel a long-running report, even allowing a user button to do so. The COPY_REPORT_OBJECT_OUTPUT can be used to copy a cached output from the reports server to a local file.

21.4 INTEGRATING FORM BUILDER WITH GRAPHIC BUILDER

Graphic Builder is a component of Developer that has excellent integration capabilities with Form Builder. Functionally, it complements the features provided by the Forms, that allows you to graphically display and summarize the data. Therefore, it is quite natural that Oracle puts a great amount of effort in the seamless integration of these products. There are three approaches you can take to include Graphic Builder displays in your applications.

- Implement items of your application as chart items, a special type of Form Builder items designed for integration with Graphics Builder. For a tighter integration, you can use the functionality provided by the PL/SQL library OG, supplied by Developer.

- Invoke the tool using the built-in procedure RUN_PRODUCT.
- Use the OLE Compound Documents and OLE Automation technology.

The first two options require that you create a chart item that will serve as a container where the Graphics display will reside. The integration achieved by these options is based on the features provided by Developer. One of the major advantages provided by this approach is that the integrated application you develop can be ported with no additional efforts in all the platforms where Developer tools will run. With the third approach, you still need a container to hold the Graphic Builder display, but the container in this case is an OLE Container item, rather than a chart item.

> **TIP**
>
> It is usually easier and more efficient to integrate Graphic Builder and Form Builder with one of the first two techniques listed above. The OLE server capabilities of Graphic Builder are normally used to display graphs from within other Microsoft Windows products.

The first approach will be discussed in the rest of this chapter. The second approach was discussed in detail in Section 21.2, therefore it will not be revisited again here. Simply recall that whenever you invoke a Graphic Builder display with RUN_PRODUCT, a chart item must have been created in the Form Builder, and the name of this item provided as the last argument to the procedure. The chapters in Part Five will discuss in detail the OLE technology and the integration of object classes generated by OLE application servers in Form Builder.

You will work with the module ANALYZE.FMB in which you will insert two Graphic Builder charts. The first one will display the cumulative amount of revenue collected by the video rental store for a given period of time. The revenue will be grouped by zip codes of the customers that rent the movies. The second chart will look at the revenue from a different angle. The income from video rentals will be grouped based on the ratings of the movies. Before moving to the next section, open the module ANALYZE.FMB provided with the companion software.

21.4.1 CREATING CHART ITEMS

As said earlier, in order to integrate Graphic Builder with Form Builder, you must first provide a container in the Forms which will contain the display. These containers are a distinct type of items, called chart items. As with other types of items, there are several ways to create chart items in your Form Builder module:

- Use the Chart Wizard.
- Manually create the item on the canvas in the Layout Editor.
- Specify the type of item in the Data Block Wizard, upon creation of a new data block.
- Modify the property Item Type of an existing item to 'Chart Item.'

The most simple method to create the chart item is to use the Chart Wizard, which will be discussed in the following section.

21.4.2 WORKING WITH THE CHART WIZARD

The Chart Wizard is very helpful if you want to create chart items driven by data items of an existing block. In order to invoke this wizard you need to display the canvas where the chart will be displayed and set its context to the block that will own the new item. Then, you can click the icon Chart Wizard in the Layout Editor's toolbar or click the icon Chart Item icon from the tool palette and chose the option to use the Chart Wizard in the dialog box that comes up.

Like other wizards, the Chart Wizard has a number of screens that help you complete each step in the process of defining a new chart. The first functional screen immediately after the Welcome screen is the one show in Figure 21.11.

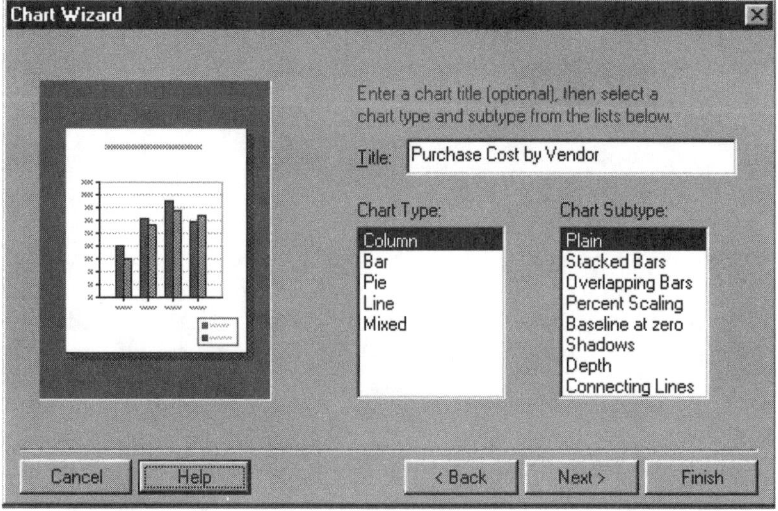

FIGURE 21.11 The Type screen of the Chart Wizard.

This screen allows you to specify a title for your chart and, most importantly, to select a type and a subtype for the new chart. The picture item to the left of the screen is updated each time you select a new type of chart to give you an idea of the layout of this type.

The next three screens of the Chart Wizard help you pick the data items that will be displayed by the chart. The Block screen displays a list of all the blocks currently defined in the module. Here you select the block that contains the items that will be graphed in the new chart. The graphs you create with the Layout Wizard are two-dimensional, therefore, after picking the block, you need to select items from this block whose data will be plotted in the abscissa (X) and ordinates (Y) axis. The Category screen is used to define the items that will populate the X axis. The distinct values of this item—returned from a query or entered in the block—become points or categories for which the values of the chart are computed and presented in the Y axis. The items for which these values are computed in each category are defined in the Value screen. Figure 21.12 shows an example of the Category screen, in which the item VENDOR is selected. If the item PURCHASE_COST is selected in the Value axis, then the graph will plot the data of this item for each vendor. Obviously, data from more than one item can be plotted in the same chart, as long as the argument for their values—VENDOR in this example—remains the same. The last screen of the Chart Wizard allows you to save the new display as a Graphic Builder module.

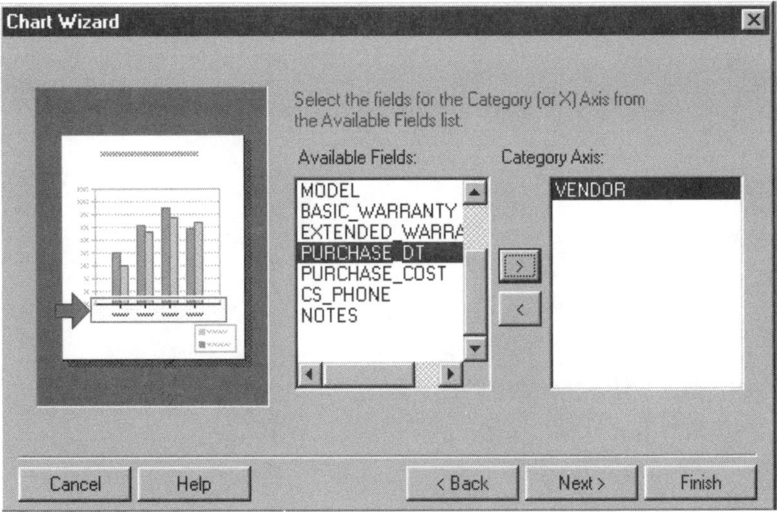

FIGURE 21.12 The Category screen of the Chart Wizard.

21.4.3 PROPERTIES OF CHART ITEMS

In cases when the charts display relationship more complex than simple mappings between data items, you can create the chart item manually in the Form Builder and associate it with a Graphic Builder module that is developed separately. In order to create a new chart item in the CUSTOMER canvas of the module ANALYZE.FMB, take these steps:

1. Display the canvas in the Layout Editor, and set the context to the block CONTROL.
2. Click the Chart Item icon from the tool palette and choose not to use the Chart Wizard.
3. Draw a square-shaped chart item to the right of the Amount column in the CUSTOMER block.
4. Double-click the newly-created item to display its Property Palette and rename it to REVENUE_BY_ZIP.
5. Arrange the layout of the canvas, so that it looks similar to Figure 21.13.
6. Perform similar steps to create the chart item REVENUE_BY_RATING in the MOVIE canvas.

While you are in the Property Palette, take a look at the properties of a chart item. Notice that chart items have the same properties in the Dev Integration group as Report objects described in Section 21.3. From the properties in the group Chart, the first two ones—Data Source X Axis and Data Source X Axis—

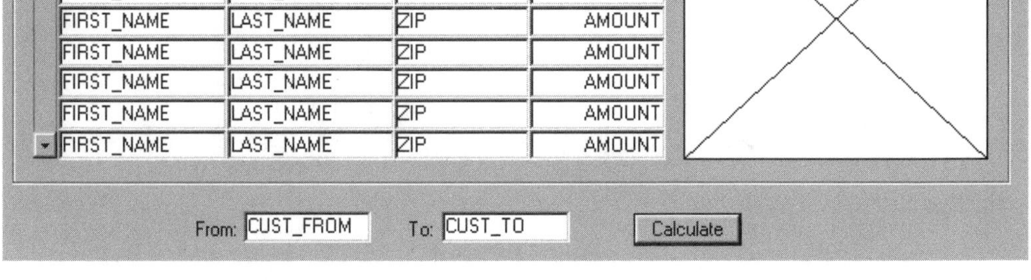

FIGURE 21.13 Layout of canvas CUSTOMER in module ANALYZE.FMB.

correspond to the columns you select in the Category and Value screen of the Chart Wizard. The other two properties—Update on Query and Update on Commit—affect the events that cause the refresh of the chart during the application's life. Both these properties are set to "Yes" by default.

Being Form Builder items, chart items have a number of other properties you can set. Such properties include Popup Menu in the Functional group, Previous Navigation Item and Next Navigation Item in the Navigation group, and a number of properties in the Physical group that control the location and dimensions of the chart item on the canvas.

Although you can specify a named visual attribute object or a background color for the chart item using properties in the Font & Color group, these properties have effect only initially, when the chart is not drawn on the form. On the other hand, you can set the text label and visual properties of the prompt using a number of properties in the groups Prompt and Prompt Font & Color. Finally, as with other Form Builder items, you can provide a string that appears a tooltip help when users move the mouse over the chart by setting the property Tooltip in the group Help.

21.4.4 THE OG PACKAGE

In order to activate Graphic Builder displays and exchange data between them and form modules in your application, you can use the PL/SQL package OG. This package is provided in the form of a PLL library together with the other software modules provided by Developer. By default, it is installed in the directory %ORACLE_HOME%\Tools\DevDem20\Demo\Forms.

The core functionality of this package is a series of program units that allow you to open and close Graphic Builder displays, exchange data with them, invoke program units defined in them, and trigger mouse events in these displays. All these program units require two arguments: `display` and `item`. They specify the file name of the chart to display and the chart item that will serve as a container for this display, respectively. Initially, the Graphic Builder module and the Form Builder chart item are associated together using the procedure OG.OPEN. Only after this step, you can use any of the other program units in the package OG. Here is a brief description of each program unit defined in the OG package:

- **OPEN.** This procedure allows you to activate an Graphic Builder display and associate it with a chart item in your form module. The general syntax of this procedure is as follows:

  ```
  OG.OPEN (display, item, clip, refresh, parameter_list);
  ```

  The arguments `clip` and `refresh` are of Boolean data type. The first one controls the way the bitmap representation of the display will populate the chart item. If it is TRUE, which is also the default value, the chart item will preserve the dimensions defined in the Form Builder and the display will be clipped if it cannot entirely fit in this item. When `clip` is FALSE, the size of the display will change at runtime to match the dimensions of the chart item. The default setting of the argument `refresh` is TRUE, and this setting updates the Graphics display upon its opening. If you set this argument to FALSE, the display presented initially is a static bitmap that may not represent the true relationship of data in the databases. Eventually, you will have to bring the display up to date using the procedure OG.REFRESH. If any values are to be passed from the Forms environment to the Graphics display, these values can be bundled in the form of a parameter list, whose name is passed on by the argument `parameter_list`.

- **CLOSE.** The specification of this procedure is:

  ```
  OG.CLOSE(display, item);
  ```

  It simply closes the Graphic Builder display associated with the chart item.

- **REFRESH.** The general syntax of this procedure is:

  ```
  OG.REFRESH(display, item, parameter_list);
  ```

  This procedure updates the pictorial representation of the display in the chart item container. If, for example, the data upon which the chart based come from a query, the query is re-executed, and the display is updated accordingly.

- **INTERPRET.** This is an important procedure because it allows you to send PL/SQL statements for execution to the Graphic Builder display. These statements can range in length and complexity from simple one-line program unit calls to full-blown PL/SQL blocks. The general syntax of this procedure is:

  ```
  OG.INTERPRET(display, item, plsql_string, refresh, parameter_list);
  ```

  The first three arguments are required, and the last two are only optionally defined. Figure 21.14 later in this section shows an example of how the `plsql_string` argument is prepared and passed to this procedure.

- **GETCHARPARAM and GETNUMPARAM.** These two functions return the value of alphanumeric or numeric parameters defined in the Graphic Builder display. The general syntax of these functions is:

  ```
  char_param_value := OG.GETCHARPARAM(display, item, display_parameter);
  ```

  ```
  num_param_value := OG.GETNUMPARAM(display, item, display_parameter);
  ```

  In both these functions, the argument `display_parameter` is the name of the parameter in the Graphic Builder display whose value you want to retrieve. This parameter must have been defined at design time. While parameter lists allow you to pass values and data from Form Builder to Graphic Builder environment, the functions GETNUMPARAM and GETCHAR-

PARAM are used to transfer data in the opposite direction. You can use them to return to the Form Builder values of parameters defined in an Graphic Builder display.

- **MOUSEDOWN.** This procedure allows you to simulate the event MouseDown on the Graphic Builder display. The primary reason for its use is to seamlessly transmit the event of clicking a chart item in Form Builder onto the Graphic Builder environment. The ultimate effect is the same as if the MouseDown event had occurred in the Graphic Builder display. The display object on which the mouse goes down becomes event-active, and receives all the mouse events until the next MouseDown event, upon which a new event-active object is defined. The general syntax of this procedure is:

  ```
  OG.MOUSEDOWN(display, item, x, y, refresh, clickcount,
  button, constrained, parameter_list);
  ```

  The first two arguments of this procedure are required; the remaining arguments are all optional. The arguments `display`, `item`, `refresh`, and `parameter_list` have the same meaning as in the other program units discussed previously. The arguments `x` and `y` represent the coordinates of the mouse when it was clicked. You need to specify these coordinates only when you want to make the display believe that the MouseDown event occurred in a location other than the actual location of the mouse. If you do not specify any of these coordinates, the current mouse coordinates stored in the system variables SYSTEM.MOUSE_X_POS and SYSTEM.MOUSE_Y_POS are used. The argument `clickcount` contains the number of times the MouseDown event occurred. In a regular click, this value is 1, in a double-click it is 2, and so on. The argument `button` is the button pressed. Its default value is 1, which denotes the left button. If it is 2, a right-click occurred. Finally, the Boolean argument `constrained` is set to TRUE only if the SHIFT key was pressed simultaneously with the MouseDown event. Its value is FALSE in all other cases.

- **MOUSEUP.** This procedure triggers the MouseUp event in an Graphic Builder display. It is very similar to the procedure MOUSEDOWN. The general syntax of this procedure is:

  ```
  OG.MOUSEUP(display, item, x, y, refresh, button, con-
  strained, parameter_list);
  ```

  Notice that in the case of this procedure, the argument `clickcount` is not required as it does not make sense in general to count the number of times the mouse button is released.

The procedures OG.MOUSEDOWN and OG.MOUSEUP provide for arguments like `clickcount`, `button`, and `constrained`, and their meaning is documented in the Form Builder documentation. However, at least in the current stage of functionality that Graphic Builder enjoys, they do not have any impact on the way mouse events are passed from Forms to Graphics displays. Graphic Builder recognizes only the following mouse events: MouseDown, MouseUp, MouseMoveDown, MouseMoveUp. Any values you provide for the arguments mentioned are ignored in the procedure MouseUpDown defined in package OG. Both OG.MOUSEDOWN and OG.MOUSEUP ultimately invoke this procedure to implement their functionality.

The following section will show the implementation of the function GETNUMPARAM from the package OG. If you examine the contents of this and other functions and procedures discussed here, you will notice that they are nothing more than a convenient API layer on top of the generic RUN_PRODUCT routine. A skillful combination of parameters in these program units prior to calling RUN_PRODUCT provides for all the added flexibility and ease of programming that OG has to offer. These parameters are passed in the form of a parameter list.

21.4.5 USING THE TOOLS_IO PACKAGE

It is interesting to open a parenthesis here and discuss TEXT_IO, another package that comes with Developer and allows you to manipulate text files. This package is used in the implementation of the functions GETNUMPARAM and GETCHARPARAM in the package OG. These functions are very similar not only in their specification, but also in the details defined in their bodies, and perform the following steps:

1. Open a temporary file for write.
2. Write to this file the value of the parameter passed as argument.
3. Close the temporary file.
4. Open the temporary file for read.
5. Read the value stored in that file to a local variable.
6. Close the temporary file.
7. Return this value to the calling environment.

The implementation of these steps is split between the Graphic Builder and the function in the OG package. The first three steps are bundled together in the form of an anonymous PL/SQL block. The function GETNUMPARAM or GETCHARPARAM builds the content for this block and passes them over to Graphic Builder for execution using the procedure OG.INTERPRET. The functions of opening, closing, writing to and reading from files are all handled by methods in the TOOLS_IO package. Figure 21.14 shows the implementation details of the function OG.GETNUMPARAM.

21.4.6 USING OG PACKAGE IN ANALYZE MODULE

In Section 21.4.3 you created two chart items that will display in graphical form summary data about the revenue of the video rental store. These graphs are im-

```
FUNCTION getnumparam
   (
      display  IN VARCHAR2,
      item     IN VARCHAR2,
      param    IN VARCHAR2
   )
   RETURN NUMBER IS

      strval VARCHAR2(255);
      tfp TEXT_IO.FILE_TYPE;
      strint VARCHAR2(255);

   BEGIN
      strint :=
         'DECLARE '                                        ||
         'tfp TEXT_IO.FILE_TYPE;'                          ||
         'BEGIN '                                          ||
         'tfp:=TEXT_IO.FOPEN(''ogtmp.dat'',''w'');'        ||
         'TEXT_IO.PUT_LINE (tfp, TO_CHAR(:' || param ||
                                                 '));'     ||
         'TEXT_IO.FCLOSE(tfp);'                            ||
         'END;';

      og.interpret (display, item, strint, FALSE);

      — *Temporary* means of getting data back
      — from Oracle Graphics.  In future releases
      — we will pass data directly.  For now,
      — we use a temporary file...
      tfp := TEXT_IO.FOPEN ('ogtmp.dat', 'r');
      TEXT_IO.GET_LINE (tfp, strval);
      TEXT_IO.FCLOSE (tfp);

      return TO_NUMBER(strval);

   END getnumparam;
```

FIGURE 21.14 Example of using components of the TOOLS_IO package.

plemented in the form of two Graphic Builder displays, provided in the companion disk in the form of binary modules BYZIP.OGD and BYRATING.OGD. Now you will integrate these displays with the chart items created previously, using program units from package OG.

The module BYZIP.OGD displays the sum generated by rental transactions between two given dates in the form of a pie chart organized by the zip code of the customers that initiated and paid for these transactions. The module BYRATING.OGD displays a similar sum in the form of a bar chart, organized by the rating categories of the movies offered for rent. Figure 21.15 shows the SQL query that is used to populate the charts BYZIP.OGD.

Figure 21.16 shows the SQL query that is used to populate the charts BYZIP.OGD.

Both displays store the range dates in the parameters `start_dt` and `end_dt`. You will pass values for these parameters when you invoke the displays from the Forms module ANALYZE.FMB. In each display a drill-down relationship is defined. In BYZIP.OGD the parameters of the drill-down relationship are defined in such a way that when users click on a slice of the pie, the zip code represented by that slice is stored in the parameter zip. In BYRATING.OGD when users will click a bar, the rating that the bar represents will be stored in the parameter `rating`.

With this information in hand, you are ready to integrate these two displays with the chart item containers REVENUE_BY_ZIP and REVENUE_BY_RATING defined in block CONTROL of module ANALYZE.FMB.

1. Attach the library OG.PLL. This is located in the directory %ORACLE_HOME%\Tools\DevDem20\Demo\Forms. Remember to place this directory in the environment variable FORMSxx_PATH if you chose to remove the path of the library.
2. Define two global variables in a PRE-FORM trigger that will store the names of the Graphics displays executables. For example:

```
:GLOBAL.byzip := 'BYZIP.OGD';
:GLOBAL.byrating := 'BYRATING.OGD';
```

```
SELECT
 SUM((RETURN_DT - RENT_DT) * DAILY_RATE) amount,
 ZIP
FROM RENTALS R, CUSTOMERS C
WHERE RENT_DT >= TO_DATE(:start_dt)
 AND RETURN_DT <= TO_DATE(:end_dt)
 AND R.CUSTOMER_ID = C.ID
GROUP BY ZIP
```

FIGURE 21.15 SQL statement that populates the display BYZIP.OGD.

```
SELECT
 SUM((RETURN_DT - RENT_DT) * DAILY_RATE) amount,
 DECODE(RATING, 1, 'G', 2, 'PG-13', 3, 'R', 4, 'NC-17')
rating
FROM RENTALS R, TAPES T, MOVIES M
WHERE RENT_DT >= TO_DATE(:start_dt)
 AND RETURN_DT <= TO_DATE(:end_dt)
 AND R.TAPE_ID = T.ID
 AND T.MOVIE_ID = M.ID
GROUP BY RATING
```

FIGURE 21.16 SQL statement that populates the display BYRATING.OGD.

3. Create a WHEN-NEW-BLOCK-INSTANCE trigger for block CUSTOMER. It should contain the following line:

   ```
   OG.OPEN   (:GLOBAL.byzip,    'CONTROL.REVENUE_BY_ZIP',
   FALSE, FALSE);
   ```

   Recall from Section 21.4.4 that these options will open the display file whose name is in `GLOBAL.byzip` and attach it to the chart item CONTROL.REVENUE_BY_ZIP. The display will be resized and will not be updated right away.
4. Create a WHEN-NEW-BLOCK-INSTANCE trigger for block MOVIE. It should contain the following line:

   ```
   OG.OPEN(:GLOBAL.byrating, 'CONTROL.REVENUE_BY_RATING',
   FALSE, FALSE);
   ```

At this point, save, compile, and run the module. You will notice that none of the displays contains their graph. This is because the queries that populate them are not executed if the `refresh` argument is FALSE. You do not want to set the `refresh` argument to TRUE in the call to OG.OPEN because you want to give the users the opportunity to enter the range dates for the analysis. The code that will populate the displays should be invoked when users enter the range dates and click the button labeled Calculate in each window.

1. Return to the Form Builder and create a WHEN-BUTTON-PRESSED trigger for the CUST_CALC button.
2. Enter the contents of this trigger as shown in Figure 21.17.
3. Create a WHEN-BUTTON-PRESSED trigger for the MOVIE_CALC button.
4. Enter the contents of this trigger similar to what is shown in Figure 21.17. In the calls to procedures ADD_PARAMETER and OG.REFRESH replace

```
DECLARE
 plist ParamList;
BEGIN
 plist := CREATE_PARAMETER_LIST('revenue');
 IF ID_NULL (plist) THEN
   MESSAGE('Cannot create parameter list.');
   RAISE FORM_TRIGGER_FAILURE;
 END IF;

 ADD_PARAMETER(plist, 'start_dt', TEXT_PARAMETER,
        TO_CHAR(:CONTROL.CUST_FROM));
 ADD_PARAMETER(plist, 'end_dt', TEXT_PARAMETER,
        TO_CHAR(:CONTROL.CUST_TO));
 OG.REFRESH(:GLOBAL.byzip, 'CONTROL.REVENUE_BY_ZIP',
plist);

 DESTROY_PARAMETER_LIST(plist);

EXCEPTION
 WHEN OTHERS THEN
   MESSAGE('Error occurred in block CUSTOMER.');
   RAISE FORM_TRIGGER_FAILURE;
END
```

FIGURE 21.17 Refreshing the contents of a chart in Form Builder.

`:GLOBAL.byzip` with `:GLOBAL.byrating` and `'CONTROL.REVENUE_BY_ZIP'` with `'CONTROL.REVENUE_BY_RATING'`.

It is clear from Figure 21.17 how you pass the range dates to the appropriate graphics display in the form of text parameters. When the procedure OG.REFRESH will be activated, these values will be passed on to the actual parameters defined in each display. Based on these values, the charts will be updated with revenues for the specified period.

You want the users to restrict the records displayed in each block by clicking areas in the display. If, for example, they click the slice of the pie chart that corresponds to zip code 22043, the block CUSTOMER should display only those customers who live in that zip code area. If users click the bar corresponding to rating category PG-13, only movies from this category should be displayed in the block MOVIE.

Recall that there is a drill-down relationship defined in each display which stores the value of the clicked slice or chart in a parameter. You want to retrieve these values in the Form Builder environment and then use them as query criteria for the respective blocks. The following steps describe how you achieve this:

1. Add the following global variables declarations to the trigger PRE-FORM:
2. Display the Property Palette for block CUSTOMER and set the property WHERE Clause in the Database group as follows:

```
:GLOBAL.zip := NULL;
:GLOBAL.rating := NULL;
```

```
ZIP = :GLOBAL.zip
```

3. Display the Properties Window for block MOVIE and set the property WHERE Clause as follows:

```
RATING = :GLOBAL.rating
```

Steps 2 and 3 ensure that the settings of the property WHERE Clause will become part of the WHERE clause in the SELECT statement that Form Builder executes to populate the blocks with data. To complete the task, you need to store the values of the zip code and rating category clicked by users in the charts in the variables `GLOBAL.zip` and `GLOBAL.rating`. This is how you store these values:

1. Create a trigger WHEN-MOUSE-CLICK for the block CONTROL.
2. Enter the contents of this trigger as shown in Figure 21.18.

Finally, save, generate and run the module to test its functionality.

```
IF :SYSTEM.MOUSE_ITEM = 'CONTROL.REVENUE_BY_ZIP' THEN
  OG.MOUSEDOWN(:GLOBAL.byzip, 'CONTROL.REVENUE_BY_ZIP');
  :GLOBAL.zip := OG.GETCHARPARAM(:GLOBAL.byzip,
             'CONTROL.REVENUE_BY_ZIP', 'ZIP');
  GO_BLOCK('CUSTOMER');
  EXECUTE_QUERY;
ELSIF :SYSTEM.MOUSE_ITEM = 'CONTROL.REVENUE_BY_RATING'
THEN
  OG.MOUSEDOWN(:GLOBAL.byrating,
'CONTROL.REVENUE_BY_RATING');
  :GLOBAL.zip := OG.GETCHARPARAM(:GLOBAL.byrating,
             'CONTROL.REVENUE_BY_RATING', 'RATING');
  GO_BLOCK('MOVIE');
  EXECUTE_QUERY;
END IF;
```

FIGURE 21.18 Retrieving values from Graphic Builder into Form Builder.

21.5 SUMMARY

This chapter discusses creating integrated Developer applications composed of several Form Builder, Report Builder and Graphic Builder modules. The most important concepts of this chapter were:

- **Creating Multiple-Form Applications**
  - Passing Values to Called Modules
  - Opening Independent Modules with OPEN_FORM
  - POST, COMMIT, and ROLLBACK
  - Replacing Modules with NEW_FORM
  - Calling Modal Modules with CALL_FORM
- **Integrating Tools with RUN_PRODUCT and RUN_REPORT_OBJECT**
- **Integrating Form Builder with Report Builder**
- **Integrating Form Builder with Graphic Builder**
  - Creating Chart Items
  - Working with the Chart Wizard
  - Properties of Chart Items
  - The OG package
  - Using the TOOLS_IO Package
  - Using OG Package in ANALYZE Module

The following table describes the software assets that were discussed in this chapter and are provided with the companion software. From the main HTML page of the software utilities provided with the book follow *Software* and *Chapter 21* to access these assets:

ASSET NAME	DESCRIPTION
CH21_1.FMB	The MRD application completed in Part III. Use this module as a starting point for the activities discussed in this chapter.
MRDMENU.PLL	The PL/SQL library MRDMENU created in Section Chapter 19.
MRDMENU_1.PLL	The MRD application invoking the ANALYZE module.
CH21_2.FMB	The MRD application invoking the MRDLABEL Report Builder module.
CH21_2.FMX	The executable version of CH21_2.FMB compiled for Win32 platforms.
MRDLABEL.RDF	The Report Builder module that prints addresses of customers in mailing labels.
MRDLABEL.REP	The executable version of MRDLABEL.RDF compiled for Win32 platforms.

ASSET NAME	DESCRIPTION
ANALYZE.FMB	The ANALYZE module that can be used as a starting point for the activities discussed in Section 21.4.6.
ANALYZE_1.FMB	The final version of the ANALYZE module with two Graphic Builder modules integrated in it.
ANALYZE_1.FMX	The executable version of ANALYZE_1.FMB compiled for Win32 platforms.
BYZIP.OGD	The Graphic Builder module that displays customer revenue by ZIP codes.
BYZIP.OGR	The executable version of BYZIP.OGD compiled for Win32 platforms.
BYRATING.OGD	The Graphic Builder module that displays movie revenue by rating codes.
BYRATING.OGR	The executable version of BYRATING.OGD compiled for Win32 platforms.

Chapter 22

DEVELOPER REUSABLE COMPONENTS

A cloak is not made for a single shower of rain.
—Italian proverb

- Overview of Developer Controls
- Calendar Control
- Hierarchy Tree Browser Control
- Wizard Control
- Summary

Developer reusable components are object groups and associated PL/SQL libraries that allow you to implement a number of GUI controls and functions in your Form Builder applications. They are provided with the Developer software together with working modules that show how their functionality will appear to the end users. This chapter walks you through the steps of implementing these controls in Form Builder modules. In particular, the focus will be on the following areas:

- Calendar control
- Hierarchy tree native control
- Wizard dialog box

First an overview of these controls and the steps you follow to integrate them in your applications.

22.1 OVERVIEW OF DEVELOPER CONTROLS

Developer controls allow you to include in Form Builder modules functionality that users of Windows applications expect and are familiar with. Such functionality includes the ability to navigate hierarchical relationships using a tree browser, the ability to make multiple selections from a text list, or the ability to complete a task by going through the steps of a wizard-style dialog box. One method to include this functionality in your forms is to use third-party software components. Chapter 29 will explain how you can take advantage of the support that Form Builder offers for COM-based components to expand your applications with Automation servers or ActiveX controls. Despite the advantages detailed in Chapter 29, the COM-based approach has the following drawbacks:

- **It works only if your application runs on Microsoft Windows.** Although the majority of desktop clients today use one of the Microsoft Windows operating systems, Form Builder applications themselves can run in a variety of other platforms, including Macintosh and Unix X-Motif. It would be nice to have the functionality of all the above-mentioned controls available in these platforms as well.
- **It works only if your application will be deployed in a client/server configuration.** If you want to deploy the application in your corporate intranet or on the Internet using Developer Forms for the Web, the COM-based controls will not be available to the end-users.
- **It requires you to be well-versed with multiple technologies.** Which is a good thing, but it's a time-consuming luxury that not too many developers and projects can afford. Furthermore, in order to integrate a third-part com-

ponent successfully, you need to understand well its methods, properties, and events. Although the OLE Importer utility—explained in Chapter 27—helps create the interface between the component and your PL/SQL environment, for a complex component, additional programming is often needed to take advantage of its functionality.

- **It may have financial implications on your application.** The third-party components you integrate in your applications will have to be licensed from the respective vendors. Depending on the application portfolio of your company and the number of users of these applications, the costs associated with these licenses may be significant. Trying to alleviate the financial burden by developing some of these controls yourself may not be a feasible alternative either. If you've tried, you know that building an ActiveX control has become easier and easier with each release of Microsoft development tools. But, building a good quality software component is an entirely different thing at remains a difficult and complex task.

Now that I have shown some reasons why you should consider using the components that Developer provides, I'll provide an overview of these components. Each component is made up of the following:

- **A number of objects that implement the user interface and data containers of the component.** These objects are grouped in object groups and can be accessed through the modules that Developer provides to demonstrate the use of the components. These modules are located in the directory %ORACLE_HOME%\Tools\Devdem\Demo\Forms. For example, the module CALENDAR.FMB contains the object group CALENDAR, which in turn contains all the data blocks, canvases, windows, property classes, and visual attribute groups required to implement the calendar component. It is a good idea to place all the object groups that implement these components in an object library module, which will serve as the container for all the Developer components—those provided by Oracle as well as those you will develop. The directory Ch22 of the companion software, contains the library COMPONENTS.OLB, which includes the components I will discuss in the rest of this chapter.
- **A PL/SQL library that implements the functionality and application logic of the component.** These libraries are provided in the same directory as the demo modules. I suggest that you copy them to your development directory to preserve the baseline version of these libraries in cases when you need to modify them. These libraries will be attached to the modules you develop, therefore, you must ensure that the environment variable FORMS60_PATH in your Registry includes the directory where they are located. The directory Ch22 of the companion software provides the libraries required to implement the components I will discuss in this chapter.

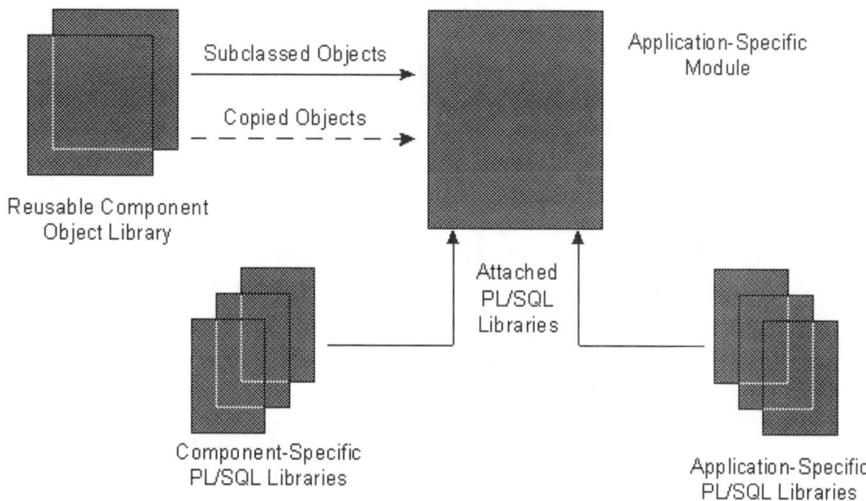

FIGURE 22.1 Architecture of a Form Builder module with reusable components.

In general, the steps to implement the Developer components in your applications are as follows:

1. Subclass or copy the object group that corresponds to your component in the desired module.
2. Attach the component PL/SQL library to your module.
3. Perform any customizations necessary to fine-tune the component for the specific module.

Figure 22.1 shows the architecture of a Form Builder module that uses Developer components. In the following sections, I will detail the steps required to implement several of these components.

22.2 CALENDAR CONTROL

Have you ever struggled to enter dates in a text item that requires you to type the date exactly in the desired format? Wouldn't it be much nicer to have a utility that allows you to browse dates, click the desired one, and place the text in the form item? This is exactly what the Developer calendar control provides. In this section I will explain how you can add this control to your forms. As a preliminary step, open one of the form modules you have worked with so far that contains a date item, for example ETS.FMB. Open the library COMPONENTS.OLB and follow these steps to add the calendar control object in the module.

1. Display the Object Library window and switch to the tab Calendar.
2. Drag the object group CALENDAR and drop it on the node Object Groups of the module. This object group contains the data blocks, items, and associated logic to implement the calendar control. It also contains the canvas, window, property classes, and a number of visual attributes that control the look and feel of the calendar control. In order to maintain a consistent interface across modules, I recommend that you subclass this object group. Therefore, click Subclass when prompted whether you want to subclass or copy the object.
3. Attach the library CALENDAR.PLL to the module. Remove the hard-coded path to this library and make sure that the directory where it resides is specified in FORMS60_PATH environment variable. This library contains the package DATE_LOV, which contains variables and methods to display the control and to store the date back to the item once the calendar is dismissed.
4. Save the module.

Now you are ready to integrate the control with your date item. Minimally, you want to place a call to the procedure GET_DATE of package DATE_LOV. Figure 22.2 shows the specification of this procedure and the following paragraphs describe the meaning of each argument:

- **display_date.** This is the date that the control will display as the current date when initially displayed. If the date item already contains a value, you

```
PROCEDURE get_date ( display_date  IN DATE,
                     return_item   IN VARCHAR2,
                     v_x_pos      IN NUMBER   := 0,
                     v_y_pos      IN NUMBER   := 0,
                     v_title      IN VARCHAR2 := 'Date
List of Values',
                     v_ok         IN VARCHAR2 := 'OK',
                     v_cancel      IN VARCHAR2 :=
'Cancel',
                     v_highlight   IN BOOLEAN  := TRUE,
                     v_autoconfirm IN BOOLEAN  := FALSE,
                     v_autoskip    IN BOOLEAN  := FALSE);
```

FIGURE 22.2 The specification for the procedure GET_DATE.

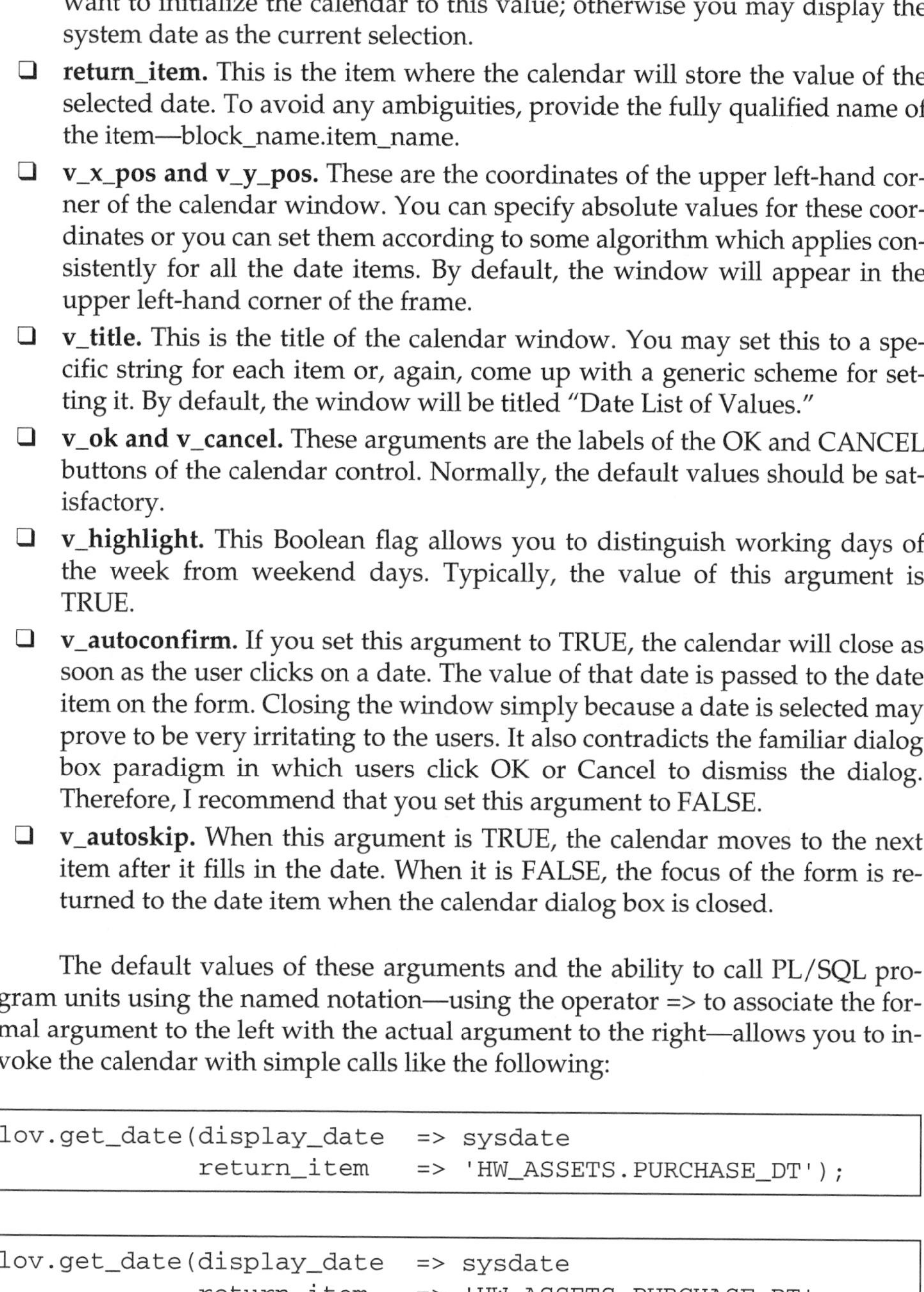

want to initialize the calendar to this value; otherwise you may display the system date as the current selection.

- **return_item.** This is the item where the calendar will store the value of the selected date. To avoid any ambiguities, provide the fully qualified name of the item—block_name.item_name.
- **v_x_pos and v_y_pos.** These are the coordinates of the upper left-hand corner of the calendar window. You can specify absolute values for these coordinates or you can set them according to some algorithm which applies consistently for all the date items. By default, the window will appear in the upper left-hand corner of the frame.
- **v_title.** This is the title of the calendar window. You may set this to a specific string for each item or, again, come up with a generic scheme for setting it. By default, the window will be titled "Date List of Values."
- **v_ok and v_cancel.** These arguments are the labels of the OK and CANCEL buttons of the calendar control. Normally, the default values should be satisfactory.
- **v_highlight.** This Boolean flag allows you to distinguish working days of the week from weekend days. Typically, the value of this argument is TRUE.
- **v_autoconfirm.** If you set this argument to TRUE, the calendar will close as soon as the user clicks on a date. The value of that date is passed to the date item on the form. Closing the window simply because a date is selected may prove to be very irritating to the users. It also contradicts the familiar dialog box paradigm in which users click OK or Cancel to dismiss the dialog. Therefore, I recommend that you set this argument to FALSE.
- **v_autoskip.** When this argument is TRUE, the calendar moves to the next item after it fills in the date. When it is FALSE, the focus of the form is returned to the date item when the calendar dialog box is closed.

The default values of these arguments and the ability to call PL/SQL program units using the named notation—using the operator => to associate the formal argument to the left with the actual argument to the right—allows you to invoke the calendar with simple calls like the following:

```
date_lov.get_date(display_date  => sysdate
                  return_item   => 'HW_ASSETS.PURCHASE_DT');
```

```
date_lov.get_date(display_date  => sysdate
                  return_item   => 'HW_ASSETS.PURCHASE_DT',
                  v_x_pos       => '200',
                  v_x_pos       => '80');
```

Now that you have seen the mechanism of how the calendar is initialized and invoked, complete the integration of the control with your form. Here are the steps you should follow to add the calendar to the date item PURCHASE_DT of the block HW_ASSETS:

1. Create a button in the block HW_ASSETS and position it immediately after the item PURCHASE_DT in the Object Navigator.
2. Subclass this button from the object DATE_LOV_BUTTON in the Calendar tab of the object library COMPONENTS.OLB. This turns the button into an iconic button with the default Form Builder icon for lists of values. Furthermore, this button contains a WHEN-BUTTON-PRESSED trigger which navigates to the date item using the built-in PREVIOUS_ITEM and invokes the default List of Values functionality of this item. The fact that this trigger uses the built-in PREVIOUS_ITEM explains why I asked you to place the button immediately after PURCHASE_DT in the Object Navigator. You could have used the other built-in GO_ITEM, but the trigger would have been tied up to a specific item and, therefore, the button class DATE_LOV_BUTTON would have lost its general-use character.
3. Arrange the layout of the canvas so that the iconic button appears next to the date item, as well.
4. Subclass the item PURCHASE_DT from the object DATE_ITEM in the Calendar tab of the object library.
5. Save and generate the form module.

Notice here that the iconic button helps make the interface more user-friendly but is not required to attach the calendar to the date item. The trigger KEY-LISTVAL that your date items inherit from the object DATE_ITEM is responsible for invoking the calendar control. This trigger is generic enough to be used with any date item and it is constructed so that the properties of the text item drive the way the calendar control is initialized. Figure 22.3 shows the contents of this trigger. There are four major steps that this trigger uses to prepare and launch the calendar window. They are described in the following paragraphs:

1. Initialize the date of the calendar. The logic of this step is simple. If the date item is null the calendar will be set to the system date; otherwise the actual date of the item will be used to initialize the control.
2. Use properties of the date item to initialize the calendar. This step uses the value of the property Tooltip Text of the item to set the title of the calendar window. If you do not set this property, the window will be called simply "Calendar." The property Automatic Skip of the item is also used to determine whether the calendar will skip to the next item when dismissed.
3. Center the calendar window on the item's window. This step gets the di-

```
DECLARE
  current_dt        DATE;
  block_item        VARCHAR2(80);
  item_canvas_name VARCHAR2(80);
  item_id           ITEM;
  cal_title         VARCHAR2(80);
  autoskip          BOOLEAN := FALSE;
  cal_view_width    NUMBER :=
GET_VIEW_PROPERTY('DATE_LOV_CANVAS', WIDTH);
  cal_view_height   NUMBER :=
GET_VIEW_PROPERTY('DATE_LOV_CANVAS', HEIGHT);
  curr_view_width   NUMBER;
  curr_view_height NUMBER;
  x                 NUMBER := 0;
  y                 NUMBER := 0;
BEGIN
  block_item := NAME_IN('SYSTEM.TRIGGER_ITEM');

— 1. Initialize the date of the Calendar.
  current_dt := TO_DATE(NAME_IN(block_item), 'DD-MON-YYYY');
  IF current_dt IS NULL THEN
    current_dt := SYSDATE;
  END IF;

— 2. Use properties of the date item to initialize the
Calendar.
  item_id := FIND_ITEM(block_item);
  cal_title := NVL(GET_ITEM_PROPERTY(item_id,
TOOLTIP_TEXT),'Calendar');
  IF (GET_ITEM_PROPERTY(item_id, AUTO_SKIP)='TRUE') THEN
    autoskip := TRUE;
  END IF;

— 3. Center the Calendar window on the item's window.
  item_canvas_name := GET_ITEM_PROPERTY(item_id, ITEM_CANVAS);
  curr_view_width  := GET_VIEW_PROPERTY(item_canvas_name,
WIDTH);
  curr_view_height  := GET_VIEW_PROPERTY(item_canvas_name,
HEIGHT);
  x := (curr_view_width - cal_view_width)/2;
  IF (x < 0) THEN x := 0; END IF;
```

FIGURE 22.3 The contents of the trigger KEY-LISTVAL of the DATE_ITEM object class.

```
  y := (curr_view_height - cal_view_height)/2;
  IF (y < 0) THEN y := 0; END IF;

– 4. Invoke the Calendar.
  DATE_LOV.GET_DATE ( display_date  => current_dt,
                      return_item   => block_item,
                      v_x_pos       => x,
                      v_y_pos       => y,
                      v_title       => cal_title,
                      v_autoskip    => autoskip);
END;
```

FIGURE 22.3 The contents of the trigger KEY-LISTVAL of the DATE_ITEM object class. (Continued)

mensions of the canvas DATE_LOV_CANVAS and those of the view in which the date item is displayed. Then the coordinates of the upper left hand corner of the calendar window are computed so that the window appears in the center if possible or along the edges of the item's window.

4. Invoke the calendar. This step passes the arguments computed in the previous steps to the procedure DATE_LOV.GET_DATE.

I will conclude this section with a brief description of the functionality of the calendar window. Figure 22.4 shows an example of this window. It displays the dates one month at a time. Use the buttons labeled '<' and '>' to navigate to the previous or next month. Use the buttons labeled '<<' and '>>' to navigate to

FIGURE 22.4 The Developer Calendar components.

the previous or next year. To select a date, simply click it on the window and click OK. Click Cancel to close the window without selecting a date.

22.3 HIERARCHY BROWSER CONTROL

The hierarchy tree browser object allows you to implement an interface similar to the Object Navigator in the Form Builder and is available as a native control. This interface is one made popular by the Windows Explorer (along with numerous other applications) and is very useful especially when navigating data organized hierarchically. Although previously available as a reusable component made of Forms objects, the new hierarchical tree control is a true native Forms item type with properties built-ins and triggers to support it. In this section I will show how you can integrate this control in your applications. The database objects I will use in this and the following two sections are shown in Figure 22.5. Here is a brief description of them:

- **COMPANIES.** This table stores the name and description of companies, as well as the name of their Chief Executive Officer (CEO).
- **PRODUCTS.** This table contains the products and services created or marketed by each company.

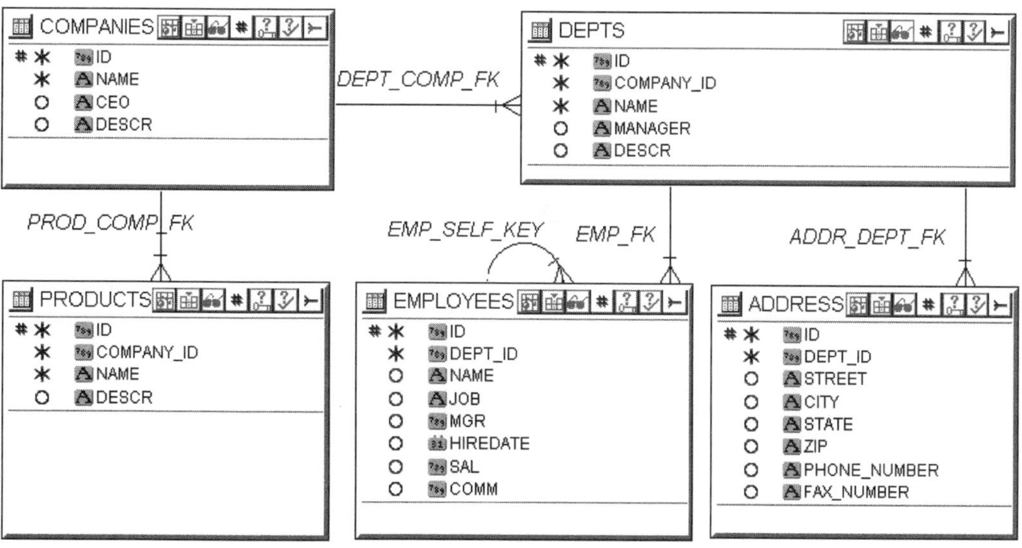

FIGURE 22.5 Database objects in the Companies database.

- ❑ **DEPTS.** This table stores the name and description of departments within a company, as well as the name of the person in charge of the department.
- ❑ **EMPLOYEES.** This table stores information about employees in each department.
- ❑ **ADDRESSES.** Each department may have multiple locations. The addresses of these locations are stored in this table.

The companion software provided with the book contain the SQL file CH22.SQL that creates and populates these objects with data.

The goal of this section is to build an interface that allows users to navigate through companies and departments in the hierarchy tree control. As a preliminary step, create a new module in the Form Builder, and subclass or copy the object group NAVIGATOR from the tab with the same name of the object library COMPONENTS.OLB. This step will provide your module with the following objects:

- ❑ Two blocks with the associated data items that implement the data interface of the hierarchy tree as well as the utilities located in its toolbars.
- ❑ A number of canvases and a window that serve as containers for the display of the navigator control.
- ❑ A number of visual attributes and property classes that allow you to customize the look and feel of the tree nodes—regular, selected, or current—and of the icons on the toolbars.

Then, attach the PL/SQL library NAVIGATE.PLL to your module. This library contains the procedures to refresh the content of the tree, expand and collapse its elements, including expanding and collapsing all their elements. The library uses the new built-in package FTREE to add/delete/modify tree elements. You can find FTREE functions documented in the Forms help system.

While there will be only one tree container in your module, you can maintain several trees in it and switch the display from one to the other as needed. Physically, the nodes of a tree form an array of records which can be created either from a query run against the database or one by one in a record group. Each node in the tree has the following five characteristic properties:

- ❑ **Initial State.** This property is set to –1 if the node is shown in collapsed state and to 1 if the node is shown expanded. If the node represents a leaf node—one that may not contain children, the State is set to 0.
- ❑ **Depth.** This property indicates the level of the node in the hierarchy tree. Nodes with Depth 1 are "root" nodes, those with Depth 2 are first-level children, and so on.
- ❑ **Label.** This is the string that will be displayed to the users at runtime. In the

case of data from the table COMPANIES, the label of the nodes could be populated using the column NAME.

- **Icon.** This allows each node to be associated with and display an icon. If set null no icon is displayed.
- **Value.** This is the data that the node represents from the application's perspective. For example, when nodes display companies, you may want to track the ID of each node as its value. This will allow you to access each company's record in other areas of the application as needed.

Note that there is no explicit property that points to the parent of a node in the hierarchy tree. This information is inferred from the settings of the properties Index and Depth of nodes. For example, a node of depth 2 is child of the first node of depth 1 with an index lower than its index. Or, differently said, a node of depth x is parent to all the nodes of depth $x + 1$ with index higher than its index and lower than the index of the next node of depth x. To clarify this explanation, Figure 22.6 shows to the left the combination of Index, Depth, and Label properties of nodes as maintained by the navigator and the hierarchical display that the users see at runtime.

The hierarchical tree control property palette contains most of the properties associated with other item types as you would expect. The properties unique to hierarchical tree control are shown in Figure 22.7. The interesting properties are allow empty branches, multi-selection allowed, show lines, show symbols, record group and data query.

The FTREE built-in package allows you to manipulate the properties and functionally of the tree control. The functions included in FTREE are:

- **ADD_TREE_DATA.** This routine copies a set of values from a record group to the tree.

```
1     Continents                    Continents
2     North America                       North America
3     U.S.A.                                    U.S.A.
3     Canada                                    Canada
3     Mexico                                    Mexico
2     South America                       South America
...                                 ...
1     Oceans                        Oceans
2     Atlantic                            Atlantic
2     Pacific                             Pacific
...                                 ...
```

FIGURE 22.6 How the Navigator control infers the parent-child relationships by combining the properties Index and Depth.

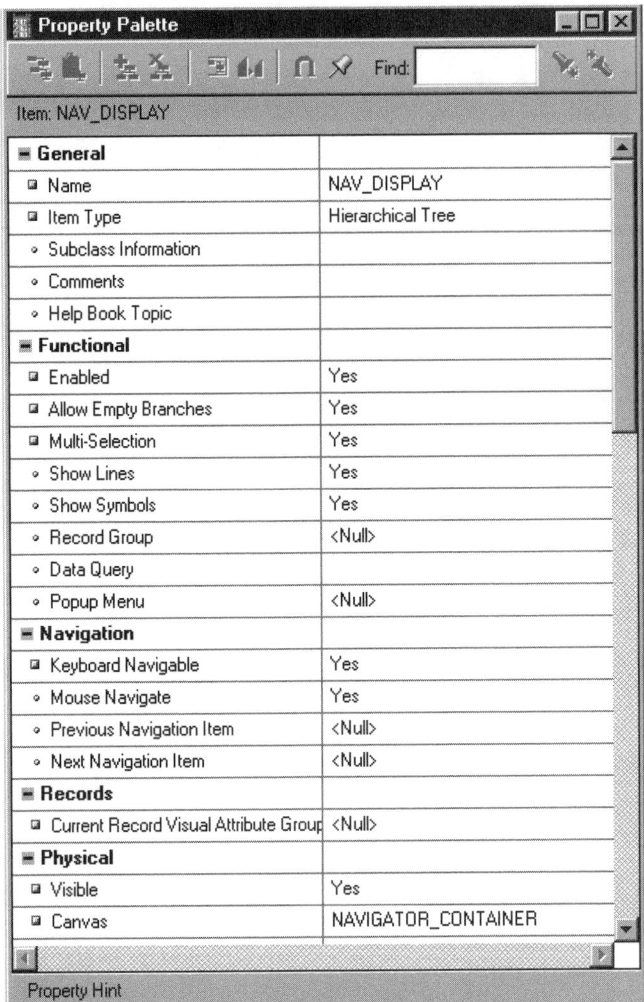

FIGURE 22.7 A property palette for a hierarchy tree control object.

- **ADD_TREE_NODE.** Adds one data element to a hierarchical tree item.
- **DELETE_TREE_NODE.** Removes a data element from a hierarchical tree.
- **FIND_TREE_NODE.** Finds the next node in the tree whose label or value matches a string.
- **GET_TREE_NODE.** Returns property values of the specified hierarchical tree.
- **GET_TREE_NODE_PARENT.** Returns the parent of the specified node.

- **GET_TREE_NODE_PROPERTY.** Returns the value of the specified property of a node.
- **GET_TREE_PROPERTY.** Returns property values for the tree.
- **GET_TREE_SELECTION.** Returns the user selected nodes. Supports single or multiple selections.
- **POPULATE_GROUP_FROM_TREE.** Populates a record group with the data from the hierarchical tree.
- **POPULATE_TREE.** Removes data already in the tree and adds the data specified by the RecordGroup or QueryText properties.
- **SET_TREE_NODE_PROPERTY.** Sets the state of a branch node.
- **SET_TREE_PROPERTY.** Sets the value of the specified tree property.
- **SET_TREE_SELECTION.** Specifies the selection of a single node.

The components of the NAVIGATE package allow you to expand and collapse tree objects and populate them with data. The following paragraphs describe the program units of this package.

- **Expand and collapse trees.** There are four program units in this category: `Expand, Collapse, Expand_All, and Collapse_All`. These routines are invoked from WHEN_BUTTON_PRESSED triggers attached to buttons in the toolbar. Users can expand and collapse selected branches of the tree.
- **Refresh trees.** The procedure `Refresh_Trees` contains the code to create and build the record group from the data in the tables COMPANIES, DEPARTMENTS, and PRODUCTS. It then sets the tree property to display the data in the record group.

Now that I have explained the internals of the navigator control, you should have no problems following the implementation steps that I will discuss below. Ultimately, you want to display in the navigator all the companies and for each company the products it creates and the departments it contains. Given the implementation of this hierarchy by the control, the following are the steps required to populate the tree with data:

1. Add a node with label "Companies" and depth 1 to the tree. This node will serve as a node type for all the company information located under it.
2. Retrieve all the companies from the database.
3. For each company add an element of depth 2 to the tree to represent the company.
4. Add a node of depth 3 to represent all the departments of the company.
5. Select all the departments for the current company.

6. For each department add a leaf element of depth 4 in the tree.
7. Add a node of depth 3 to represent all the products of the company.
8. Select all the products created by the current company.
9. For each product add a leaf element of depth 4 in the tree.

Figure 22.8 shows the procedure that implements the steps listed above, which you should create in your module. In order to complete the implementation, create a form-level WHEN-NEW-FORM-INSTANCE trigger that invokes the procedure `Refresh_Trees`, and displays the Navigator window. This trigger contains the following lines in its body:

```
– set the navigator window size
SET_WINDOW_PROPERTY('navigator', width,  255);
SET_WINDOW_PROPERTY('navigator', height, 270);
WINDOW_UTIL.RESIZE_NAV(255, 270);
– Built the Record Group and populate the tree
Refresh_Trees;
```

Finally, create a WHEN-WINDOW-RESIZED trigger that redraws the Calendar display each time its window is resized. The contents of this trigger are shown in the following lines:

```
DECLARE
      new_w   NUMBER;
      new_h   NUMBER;
BEGIN
   IF :system.event_window = 'navigator' THEN
      new_w := GET_WINDOW_PROPERTY('navigator', width);
      new_h := GET_WINDOW_PROPERTY('navigator', height);
      WINDOW_UTIL.RESIZE_NAV(new_w, new_h);
   END IF;
END;
```

At this point, save, compile, and run the module. Based on the setting of the expand/collapse status for the nodes in the procedure `Refresh_Trees`, the tree will display all the companies with the categories Departments and Product collapsed. Notice that the navigator contains fully functional icons in the vertical toolbar that allow you to expand and collapse the hierarchy tree. In addition, the controls in the vertical toolbar implement the same context list and search controls that you use in the Form Builder Object Navigator. Figure 22.8 shows an example of this control.

```
PROCEDURE refresh_trees IS
   cursor cursor_comp is
      SELECT ID,NAME FROM COMPANIES;
   cursor cursor_dept (comp_id NUMBER)is
      SELECT ID, NAME FROM DEPTS WHERE COMPANY_ID=comp_id;
   cursor cursor_prod(comp_id NUMBER) is
      SELECT ID, NAME FROM PRODUCTS WHERE COMPANY_ID=comp_id;
   i NUMBER := 1;
   v_ignore        NUMBER;
   rg_comp         RECORDGROUP;
   v_init_state    GROUPCOLUMN;
   v_level         GROUPCOLUMN;
   v_label         GROUPCOLUMN;
   v_icon          GROUPCOLUMN;
   v_value         GROUPCOLUMN;
BEGIN
   — Build a Record Group
   rg_comp := FIND_GROUP('COMP');
   IF NOT ID_NULL(rg_comp) THEN
     DELETE_GROUP(rg_comp);
   END IF;

   rg_comp := CREATE_GROUP('COMP');
—  define the columns of the record group
   v_init_state := ADD_GROUP_COLUMN(rg_comp, 'init_state',
number_column);
   v_level      := ADD_GROUP_COLUMN(rg_comp, 'level',
number_column);
   v_label      := ADD_GROUP_COLUMN(rg_comp, 'label',
char_column, 40);
   v_icon       := ADD_GROUP_COLUMN(rg_comp, 'icon',
char_column, 20);
   v_value      := ADD_GROUP_COLUMN(rg_comp, 'value',
char_column, 40);

   i := 1;
— Add root node
   ADD_GROUP_ROW(rg_comp, i);
   SET_GROUP_NUMBER_CELL(v_init_state, i, 1);
   SET_GROUP_NUMBER_CELL(v_level      , i, 1);
   SET_GROUP_CHAR_CELL  (v_label      , i, 'Companies');
   SET_GROUP_CHAR_CELL  (v_icon       , i, NULL);
```

FIGURE 22.8 Procedure that populates the navigator with data.

```
  SET_GROUP_CHAR_CELL  (v_value      , i, 'Companies');
  i := i + 1;
  FOR comp IN cursor_comp LOOP
    ADD_GROUP_ROW(rg_comp, i);
    SET_GROUP_NUMBER_CELL(v_init_state, i, 1);
    SET_GROUP_NUMBER_CELL(v_level      , i, 2);
    SET_GROUP_CHAR_CELL  (v_label      , i, comp.NAME);
    SET_GROUP_CHAR_CELL  (v_icon       , i, NULL);
    SET_GROUP_CHAR_CELL  (v_value      , i, to_char(comp.ID));
    i := i + 1;

    ADD_GROUP_ROW(rg_comp, i);
    SET_GROUP_NUMBER_CELL(v_init_state, i, -1);
    SET_GROUP_NUMBER_CELL(v_level      , i, 3);
    SET_GROUP_CHAR_CELL  (v_label      , i, 'Departments');
    SET_GROUP_CHAR_CELL  (v_icon       , i, NULL);
    SET_GROUP_CHAR_CELL  (v_value      , i, 'Departments');
    i := i + 1;

    FOR dept IN cursor_dept(comp.ID) LOOP
     ADD_GROUP_ROW(rg_comp, i);
      SET_GROUP_NUMBER_CELL(v_init_state, i, 0);
      SET_GROUP_NUMBER_CELL(v_level      , i, 4);
      SET_GROUP_CHAR_CELL  (v_label      , i, dept.NAME);
      SET_GROUP_CHAR_CELL  (v_icon       , i, NULL);
      SET_GROUP_CHAR_CELL  (v_value      , i,
           to_char(dept.ID));
      i := i + 1;
    END LOOP;

    ADD_GROUP_ROW(rg_comp, i);
    SET_GROUP_NUMBER_CELL(v_init_state, i, -1);
    SET_GROUP_NUMBER_CELL(v_level      , i, 3);
    SET_GROUP_CHAR_CELL  (v_label      , i, 'Products');
    SET_GROUP_CHAR_CELL  (v_icon       , i, NULL);
    SET_GROUP_CHAR_CELL  (v_value      , i, 'Products');
    i := i + 1;

    FOR prod IN cursor_prod(comp.ID) LOOP
      ADD_GROUP_ROW(rg_comp, i);
      SET_GROUP_NUMBER_CELL(v_init_state, i, 0);
```

FIGURE 22.8 Procedure that populates the navigator with data. (Continued)

```
        SET_GROUP_NUMBER_CELL(v_level      , i, 4);
        SET_GROUP_CHAR_CELL  (v_label      , i, prod.NAME);
        SET_GROUP_CHAR_CELL  (v_icon       , i, NULL);
        SET_GROUP_CHAR_CELL  (v_value      , i,
to_char(prod.ID));
        i := i + 1;
      END LOOP;
    END LOOP;
-   The tree will be populated by the Record Group.
    FTREE.SET_TREE_PROPERTY('navigator.nav_display'
                           , ftree.record_group, rg_comp);
END;
```

FIGURE 22.8 Procedure that populates the navigator with data. (Continued)

Figure 22.9 also shows a number of icons in the vertical toolbar which do not contain generic code but, instead, will have to be customized in each implementation of the navigator. They include the icons Open, Revert, Add, Delete, and Edit. The generic steps to implement the custom functionality are as follows:

1. Create the Form Builder objects and application logic necessary to carry out the operations. In the application you are currently building, you could create a block based on companies, for example, to create, maintain, and delete these objects.

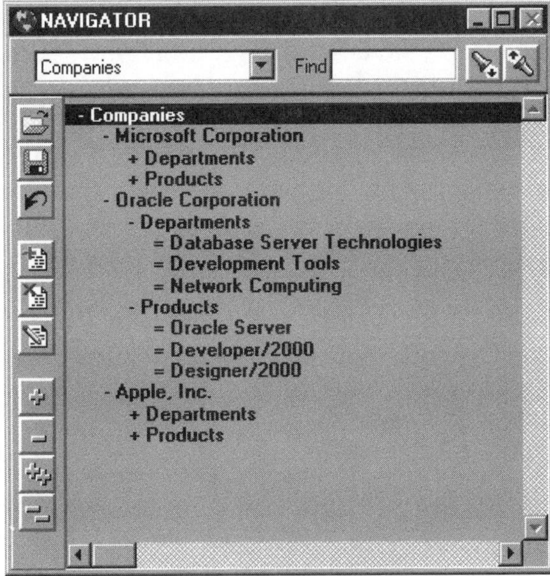

FIGURE 22.9 A view of the Developer hierarchy tree navigator.

2. Implement the functionality that understands the type of object users selected when invoking the operation. In other words, if users click Add, you need to know whether they are creating a new company, department, or product.
3. Implement the branching mechanism that applies the operation to the appropriate object type.

The module NAVIGATOR.FMB in the companion software contains a version of the module I have discussed thus far that allows users to create and maintain companies and products. The implementation is similar and consists of two data blocks based on tables COMPANIES and PRODUCTS responsible for the maintenance operations of these tables. The function `Get_Node_Type` returns the node type of the object upon which users are invoking the action—'COMP,' 'PROD,' or 'DEPT.' Figure 22.10 shows the content of this function.

At this point, the actual operation is performed upon the block COMPANIES of PRODUCTS and the tree is refreshed when the operation is completed. Figure 22.11 shows the implementation of the delete operation for company objects. Note the following features in this implementation:

- The nodes of level 1 and 3 correspond to the object types Companies, Products, and Departments. Therefore they cannot be deleted.
- For a company or product, the element value corresponds to the ID of this object. This ID is used to set the property DEFAULT_WHERE of the corresponding block so that the subsequent query can retrieve the desired object in the block.
- The advantage of using a data block based on COMPANIES and PRODUCTS is that you can use all the appropriate Form Builder built-ins—such as DELETE_RECORD or POST—to complete your task.

The delete operation can be implemented in the background and does not require any user interaction. However, the process of creating a new object or editing an existing one will typically require that you display the window or dialog box where these operations occur. In the following section, I will explain how you can implement the creation and editing of departments using the Developer Wizard component.

22.4 WIZARD CONTROL

The Wizard control allows you to implement Microsoft Windows wizards in your applications. These wizards walk the users through the process of completing processes that require a number of steps. Using this control you will imple-

```
FUNCTION Get_Node_Type (v_node ftree.node) RETURN
VARCHAR2 IS
  node_type       VARCHAR2(20);
  node_index      NUMBER;
  node_parent_idx ftree.node;
  node_depth      NUMBER;
  node_parent_value  VARCHAR2(80);
BEGIN

  node_depth :=
ftree.get_tree_node_property('navigator.nav_display',
               v_node,ftree.NODE_DEPTH);

  IF node_depth IN (1,3) THEN
    — Current node is a node type itself; nothing to
return
    node_type := NULL;
  ELSE
    node_parent_idx :=
       ftree.Get_Tree_Node_Parent('navigator.nav_display'
                                 ,v_node);
    node_parent_value :=

ftree.Get_Tree_Node_Property('navigator.nav_display'
                                    ,node_parent_idx
                                    , ftree.NODE_VALUE);
    IF node_parent_value = 'Companies' THEN
       node_type := 'COMP';
    ELSIF node_parent_value = 'Departments' THEN
       node_type := 'DEPT';
    ELSIF node_parent_value = 'Products' THEN
       node_type := 'PROD';
    END IF;
  END IF;
  RETURN node_type;
END;
```

FIGURE 22.10 Contents of function Get_Node_Type.

```
DECLARE
  node_type VARCHAR2(20);
  v_count   NUMBER;
  v_button  NUMBER;
  v_node    FTREE.NODE;
  v_depth   NUMBER;
  v_value   VARCHAR2(80);
  where_clause   VARCHAR2(80);
BEGIN
  v_count := FTREE.GET_TREE_PROPERTY('navigator.nav_display'
                                    ,ftree.selection_count);
  IF v_count < 1 THEN
    v_button := SHOW_ALERT('no_selection');
  ELSIF v_count > 1 then
    v_button := SHOW_ALERT('too_many_selection');
  END IF;

  IF v_count = 1 THEN
    v_node  :=
FTREE.GET_TREE_SELECTION('navigator.nav_display',1);
    v_depth :=
FTREE.GET_TREE_NODE_PROPERTY('navigator.nav_display'

,v_node,Ftree.NODE_DEPTH);
    IF v_depth IN (1,3) THEN
      RETURN; — Current node is a node type; cannot process
    END IF;

    v_value :=
FTREE.GET_TREE_NODE_PROPERTY('navigator.nav_display'

,v_node,ftree.NODE_VALUE);
    where_clause := 'ID='||v_value;
    node_type := Get_Node_Type(v_node);
    IF node_type = 'COMP' THEN
      SET_BLOCK_PROPERTY('COMPANIES', DEFAULT_WHERE,
where_clause);
      GO_BLOCK('COMPANIES');
    ELSIF node_type = 'DEPT' THEN
      SET_BLOCK_PROPERTY('DEPTS', DEFAULT_WHERE, where_clause);

      GO_BLOCK('DEPTS');
```

FIGURE 22.11 Example of deleting an object from the navigator.

```
    ELSIF node_type = 'PROD' THEN
      SET_BLOCK_PROPERTY('PRODUCTS', DEFAULT_WHERE,
where_clause);
      GO_BLOCK('PRODUCTS');
    END IF;
    CLEAR_BLOCK(NO_COMMIT);
    EXECUTE_QUERY;
    DELETE_RECORD;
    POST;
    REFRESH_TREES;
  END IF;
END;
```

FIGURE 22.11 Example of deleting an object from the navigator. (Continued)

ment the process of creating and maintaining departments in a three-step wizard. The module NAVIGATOR.FMB discussed at the end of the previous section contains blocks, canvases and windows that allow you to create departments, employees, and addresses in the traditional way. Here you will tie these steps together as part of a business transaction that crosses the boundaries of physical database objects. This is the list of steps to follow in order to add the Wizard component to your application:

Subclass or copy the object group Wizard from the tab Wizard of the object library COMPONENTS.OLB. This group contains all the objects required to implement the wizard, including the buttons to navigate between pages, a canvas, a window, and a visual attribute object.

1. Attach the library WIZARD.PLL to the module. This library contains the package WIZARD which exposes three methods you can use to interact programmatically with the wizard.
2. Select the canvases you want to display in the wizard and set their property Canvas Type to "Stacked."
3. Set the property Window of these canvases to "WIZ_WINDOW."
4. Set the properties Viewport Width and Viewport Height of these canvases if necessary. Upon initialization, the wizard will set these properties for all the canvases it will display, to those of the canvas with the largest viewport. Therefore, this step is needed only if you want to reduce the size of the largest canvas to that the wizard window appears with the appropriate dimensions.
5. In the appropriate program unit, invoke the function `Wizard_Begin` from the package WIZARD to display the wizard. The names of the canvases that

```
DECLARE
  started BOOLEAN := FALSE;
BEGIN
  started :=
WIZARD.Wizard_Begin('DEPTS,EMPLOYEES,ADDRESSES',
'Department Wizard', TRUE);
  IF NOT started THEN
    MESSAGE('Error initiating wizard');
    WIZARD.Wizard_Finish;
    RAISE FORM_TRIGGER_FAILURE;
  END IF;
END;
```

FIGURE 22.12 The contents of a trigger that initializes and displays the Developer Wizard component.

will make up the pages of the wizard are passed as the first argument to the function in form of comma-separated string. The title of the window is passed as the second argument. The third argument of this function is a Boolean flag that when set to TRUE causes the wizard to display page counter at the bottom of the window in the format 'Page <current page number> of <total page number>.'

6. Enhance the functionality associated with the wizard button Next, Previous, Finish, and Cancel. For the first two buttons, the wizard contains the logic to

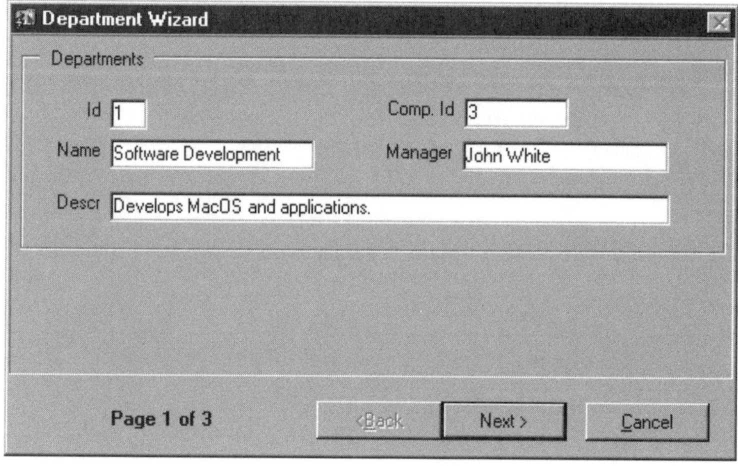

FIGURE 22.13 The implementation of the Developer Wizard component.

navigate to the appropriate page. You may want to complement this functionality with navigation to items within these pages. The Finish and Cancel operations are normally where most of the custom code is required as they handle the completion of rollback of the process implemented by the wizard.

Figure 22.12 shows the contents of a trigger that initializes and displays the Developer Wizard component.

Figure 22.13 shows the implementation of the Wizard component in the context of the application discussed in this section. The completed version of this module is provided in the companion software with the name WIZARD.FMB.

22.5 SUMMARY

The use of prepackaged software components is one of the most important success factors of rapid application development. Developer controls allow you to include in your applications functionality, such as selecting dates from a calendar control, navigate hierarchical relationships using a tree browser, making multiple selections from a text list, or the completing a task by going through the steps of a wizard-style dialog box. This chapter discussed how you integrate these controls in your applications. The most important topics of this chapter included:

- **Overview of Developer Controls**
- **Calendar Control**
- **Hierarchy Tree Browser Control**
- **Wizard Control**
- **Summary**

The following table describes the software assets that were discussed in this. From the main HTML page of the software utilities provided with the book follow the links *Software* and *Chapter 22* to access these assets:

ASSET NAME	DESCRIPTION
COMPONENTS.OLB	The object library module with the components that will be used in this chapter.
CH22_1.FMB	The Equipment Tracking System module developed in this book. Use this module to add the calendar control.

ASSET NAME	DESCRIPTION
CH22_2.FMB	The Equipment Tracking System module that implements the Developer calendar control.
CH22_2.FMX	The executable version of CH22_2.FMB compiled for Win32 platforms.
CALENDAR.PLL	The PL/SQL library that implements the functionality of the Developer calendar control.
CH22.SQL	A SQL*Plus script file that created the database objects used by the NAVIGATOR and WIZARD modules.
D2KDLSTR.PLL	A library of utilities provided by Developer Forms.
NAVIGATOR.FMB	A Form Builder module that implements the Developer hierarchy tree control.
NAVIGATOR.FMX	The executable version of NAVIGATOR.FMB compiled for Win32 platforms.
NAVIGATE.PLL	The PL/SQL library that implements the functionality of the Developer hierarchy tree control.
WIZARD.FMB	A Form Builder module that implements the Developer wizard control.
WIZARD.FMX	The executable version of WIZARD.FMB compiled for Win32 platforms.
WIZARD.PLL	The PL/SQL library that implements the functionality of the Developer wizard control.

Chapter 23

MANAGING DEVELOPER PROJECTS

For art and science cannot exist but in minutely organized particulars.
—William Blake

- Overview of the Project Builder
- Managing Projects with the Project Builder
- Customizing the Project Builder
- Delivering Projects
- Summary

A software project typically involves a number of software assets and files ranging from the requirements document to the executables deployed to the users. In order to be able to find all the pertinent facts about the project in a timely fashion, it is important to organize and group these files together. When projects are small and simple, the files associated with them are relatively few and manageable. But for large projects, such as those involving complex screens and reports, extensive database schemas, or modules of different types and languages, managing all their components manually becomes impossible. It is necessary in such situations to use a tool that allows you to create and administer projects, maintain the list of software components that are part of them, track the dependencies between these components, and package together all the components that will be delivered to the users. The tools should automate a number of these tasks and other housekeeping chores, thus allowing you to focus on more important issues where your contribution is more valuable. The Project Builder is the tool aimed at meeting the need for managing Developer projects. The Project Builder is also the topic of this chapter.

23.1 OVERVIEW OF THE PROJECT BUILDER

A full-blown Developer application may contain a number of files of different types. The most common ones are the Forms modules, both in binary and in executable format, as well as Reports, Graphics, PL/SQL library, menu, and object library modules. Other important types of files are the scripts that install the database schema—SQL, Oracle Export files, SQL*Loader scripts, and others—icons for the implementation of toolbars, help files, documentation files in different formats, applications and application extensions written in 3GL languages and their corresponding source files, and so on. The Project Builder allows you to maintain all the files of a Developer project and provides the following major functional features:

- A number of predefined types of files that you can add to your projects.
- A predefined list of actions associated with each type that allows you to perform the most important actions on these files, such as opening, editing, compiling and executing them—whenever possible. You may add metatypes that define actions that affect many types and therefore files.
- A flexible architecture that allows you add your own types of files and to define new actions against all of the file types. A Module type wizard provides a quick easy way to define new types.
- A mechanism that tracks dependencies among files of different types.
- Ability to build a project incrementally, by compiling only the objects that have changed since the last build.
- Password protection for projects.

The rest of the chapter will explain how you accomplish these and other tasks with the Project Builder.

23.1.1 LAUNCHING THE PROJECT BUILDER

To start the Project Builder you select Start | Programs | Oracle Forms & Reports 6i | Project Builder from the windows task bar. If this is the first time you are starting the tool, you will see the welcome dialog box shown in Figure 23.1. This dialog box allows you to use the Project Wizard, create a new project in the Project Navigator, or open an existing project. If you want to learn about the Project Builder, select the options Take a Quick Tour or Explore the Cue Cards. Recall that the Form Builder contains a similar welcome dialog box. It is very useful when you are starting to work with the tool and it can be easily turned off after a while by de-selecting the check box in the lower left-hand corner.

23.1.2 WORKING WITH THE PROJECT WIZARD

If you select the first option in the Welcome dialog box and click OK, the welcome page of the Project Wizard will appear. Like other Developer wizards, this wizard walks you through the steps of a specific task—in this case, creating a project. All the files that make up a project are stored in what is called the project registry. In the first screen of the Project Wizard, you can specify the file name of the project registry, as shown in Figure 23.2. In the second screen, you can specify the title for the project and top-level directory, as shown in Figure 23.3. The next screen of the wizard is used to specify the name of the developer who creates the

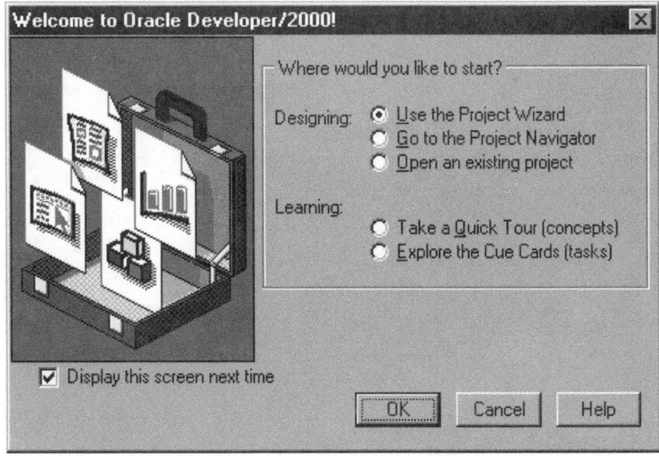

FIGURE 23.1 The Project Builder welcome window.

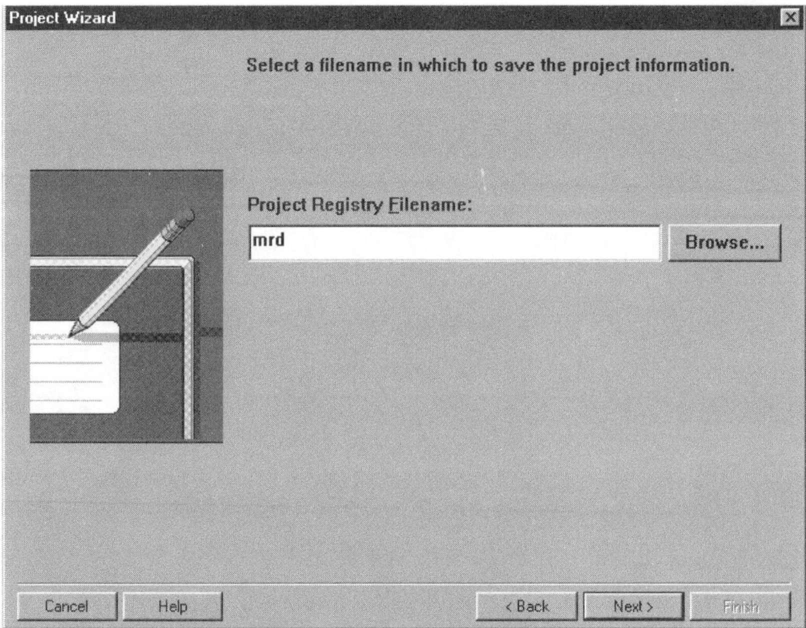

FIGURE 23.2 The first screen of the Project Wizard.

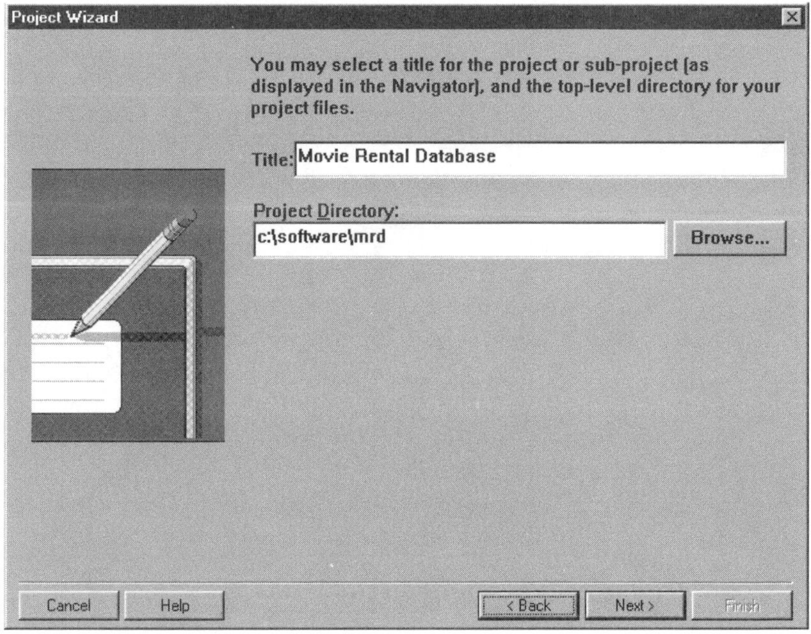

FIGURE 23.3 The second screen of the Project Wizard.

project and a brief comment about the project as shown in Figure 23.4. If all the modules in the project will share a common database connection that has already been defined in the Project Builder database, you can assign this connection to the project by selecting it from the list Connection, as shown in Figure 23.5. Alternatively, this screen allows you to create a new connection. The last screen of the Project Wizard allows you to conclude your task by simply creating the project or, in addition, to invoke a dialog box where you can select files to include in the project, as shown in Figure 23.6.

Besides accessing the Project Wizard from the Welcome dialog box, you can invoke it explicitly by issuing one of the following two commands:

- ❑ Click the icon Project Wizard on the toolbar.
- ❑ Select Tools | Project Wizard from the menu.

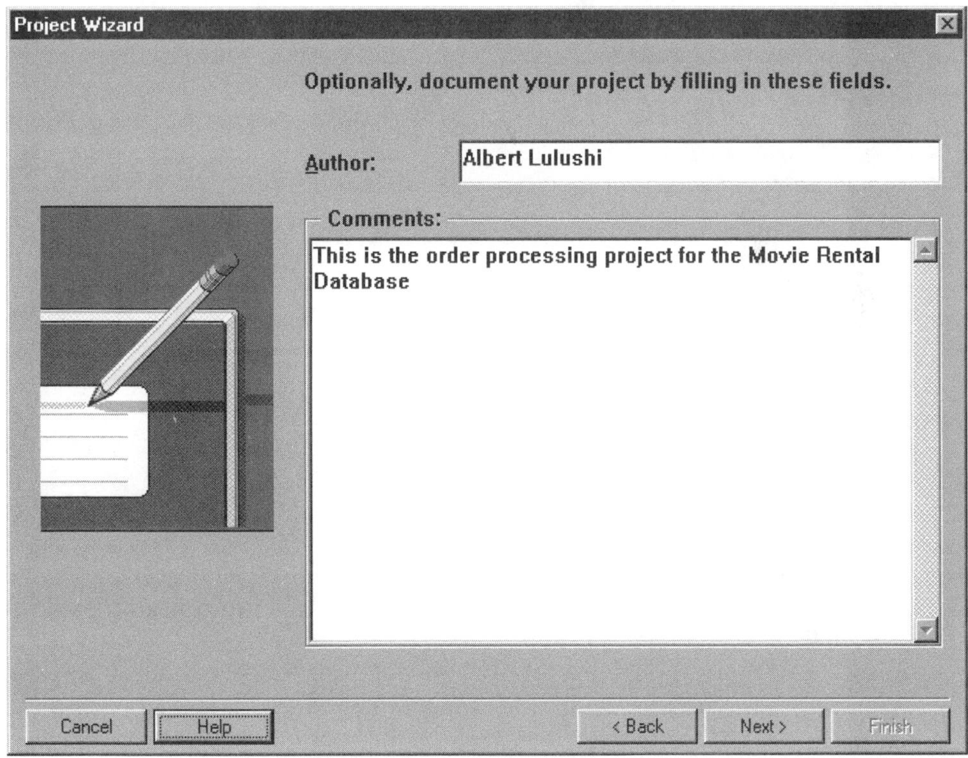

FIGURE 23.4 The third screen of the Project Wizard

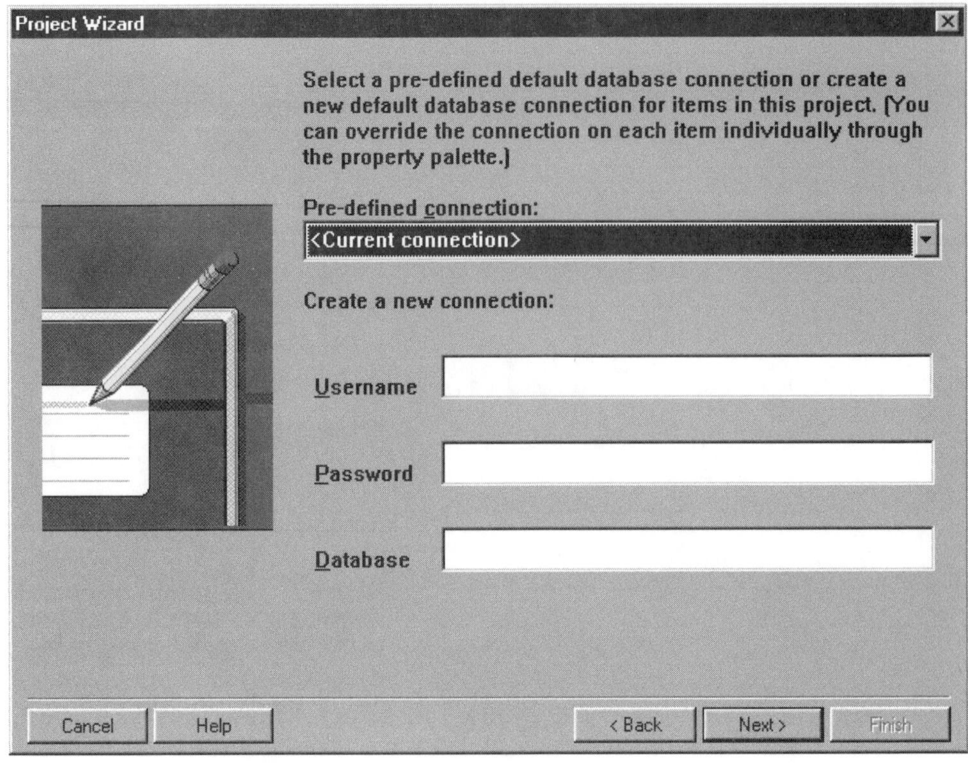

FIGURE 23.5 The fourth screen of the Project Wizard

23.1.3 COMPONENTS OF THE PROJECT BUILDER

When the Project Builder starts up, you are presented with a window similar to the one shown in Figure 23.7. This window shows the major objects of the Project Builder. An important component of Project Builder is the Navigator. As in the case of Form Builder, the Project Navigator allows you to visually maintain and traverse the relationships between Project Builder objects. There are four major groups of objects managed by the Project Navigator:

- **Global Registry.** The global registry contains a list of file types that the Project Builder recognizes across all the projects and all users. The properties of each file type, such as the icon and label to represent it and actions that can be issued against files of that type are defined in the global registry. Section 23.3.1 will provide more details about the global registry.
- **User Registry.** The user registry plays a role similar to the global registry, except that the file types created and maintained here have a more limited

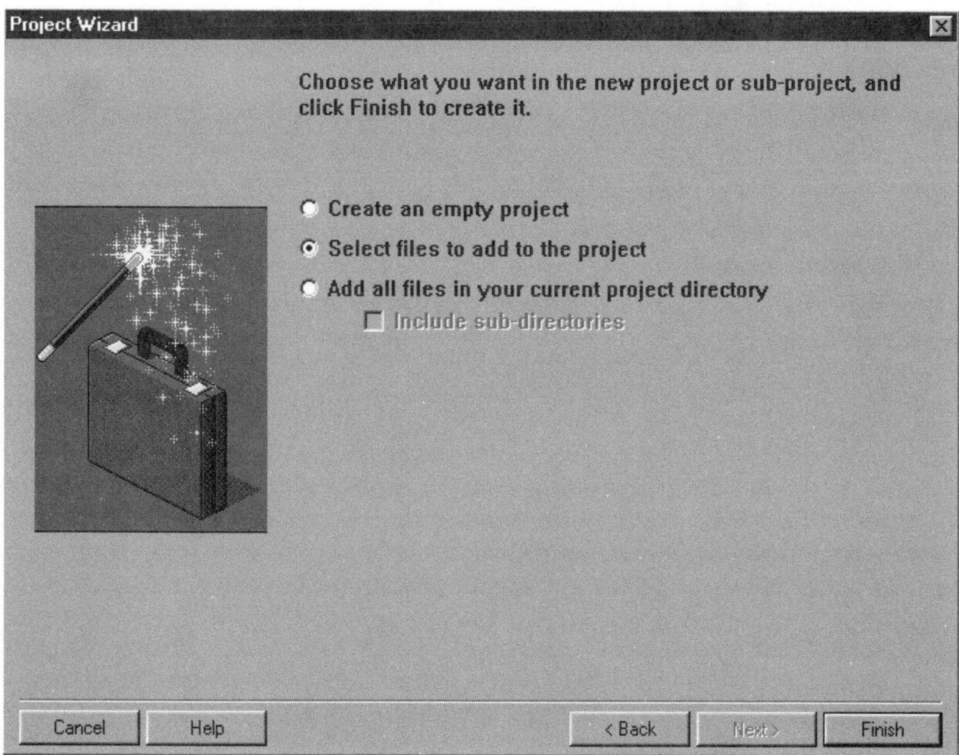

FIGURE 23.6 The fifth screen of the Project Wizard

scope. They are user-specific and may not be of value to other members of the team. Section 23.3.1 will provide more details about user registries, as well.

- **Database Connections.** A number of software components in Developer projects will interact with a database. Database connection objects allow you to maintain the user name, database name and, optionally, the password of different database accounts. By applying them to different modules you can, for example, execute these modules against different schemas.
- **Projects.** Managing projects is ultimately the goal of the Project Builder. Each project you create in the Project Navigator contains files whose types are defined in the global registry or the user registry. Based on the properties of the file type, you can invoke a number of actions on each file instance included in the project. Section 23.2 will discuss in detail the process of managing projects in the Project Builder.

Like all the other Developer tools, the Project Builder has a toolbar across its window which allows you to access the most frequent commands with a mouse-

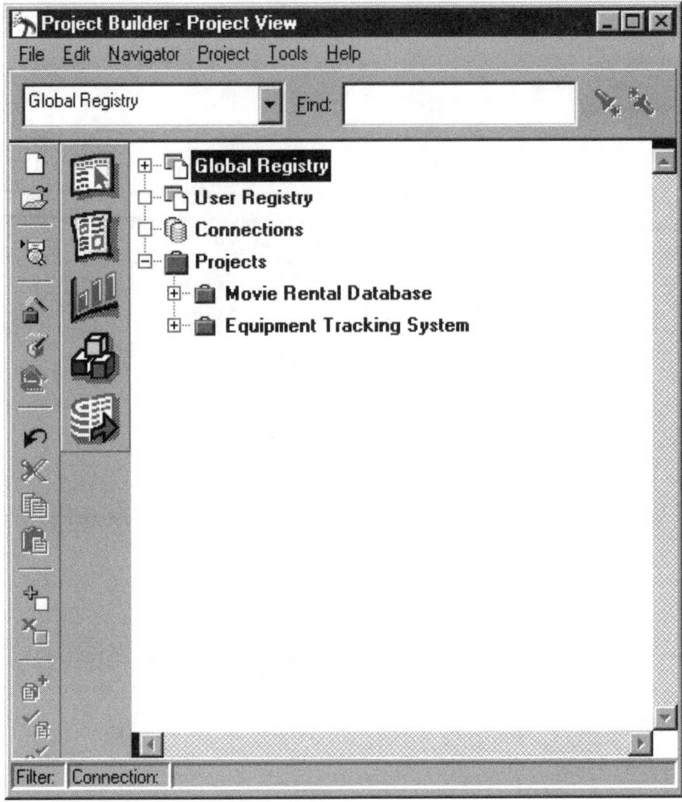

FIGURE 23.7 The Project Builder window.

click. The vertical toolbar seen in Figure 23.7 is also known as the Launch bar. Here you can dock iconic representations of executables you often launch during your Developer projects. Section 23.3.4 later in the chapter will explain how you can maintain the launch bar.

23.2 MANAGING PROJECTS WITH THE PROJECT BUILDER

Managing projects is the main purpose of using the Project Builder. This section discusses the major tasks you perform in this area, including creating projects and maintaining their properties, adding files to projects, maintaining the dependencies among files, compiling projects, and bundling projects for distribution.

23.2.1 CREATING AND MAINTAINING PROJECTS

The Project Wizard, discussed in Section 23.1.2, is one of the fastest ways to create new projects in the Project Builder. Alternatively, you can create a new project by clicking the icon New on the toolbar or selecting File | New | Project from the menu. To create a subproject for an existing project, select this project in the Navigator, and choose File | New | Subproject from the menu. You can also right-click the object and select the option New Subproject from the pop-up menu.

The information about a project is stored in a file—with the extension .UPD—called the project registry. The project files can be opened by using standard commands such as clicking the icon Open Project on the toolbar, or selecting the corresponding menu item from the File menu. The Project Builder "remembers" which projects you were working on the last time you exited the application and opens them automatically in the Navigator. To close a project, select it in the Navigator and then choose File | Close Project from the menu or press CTRL+W on the keyboard.

23.2.2 EXPORTING AND IMPORTING PROJECTS

Typically, projects that will require the use of Project Builder to manage their assets will involve a team of developers. Therefore, there will be a need to access and maintain the project file at different development machines. Copying and distributing the project registry is one way to share the information about one project across the developers. Many times this method does not offer enough control of the distribution process and cannot be implemented if the developers use different platforms. In such cases, the export and import mechanisms may be used.

The export mechanism allows you to write the information stored in the global registry, user registry, and in one or more projects to a text file, which can be easily be uploaded to any supported platform using the import mechanism. To initiate an export process, select File | Export Project... from the menu. The dialog box Export Options, shown in Figure 23.8, appears. By setting the controls in this dialog box, you can control the granularity and scope of the export operation. The following paragraphs describe the most typical settings of these options and what you can achieve with them.

If you want to export the definition of one or more file types, select them in the list Export types on the right half of the dialog box. This list presents in a unified view all the file types defined in the global registry and in the user registry, ordered alphabetically. Normal commands of text lists, such as Control+Click and Shift+Click, as well as the buttons Select All and De-select All can be used to pinpoint the types to export.

The file types can be exported separately from project entries if, in addition to the steps described above, you select the item Don't export any items from the radio group Export items. To export the definitions of one or more project entries,

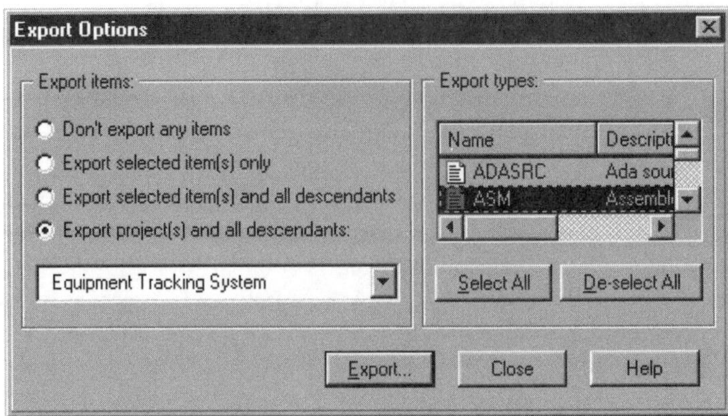

FIGURE 23.8 The Export Options dialog box.

select them in the Project Navigator before invoking the Export Options dialog box. Then select the radio button Export selected item(s) only from the radio group Export items. To export objects that depend on the selected objects, select the option Export selected item(s) and all descendants from the radio group. And finally, to export an entire project, select the option Export project(s) and all descendants and pick the name of the object from the list box.

After setting the options of the export process, you can click the button Export… to start this process. As a preliminary step, you will be prompted to specify a name and location for the export file.

Importing a project is the reverse process of exporting it. To initiate the process, you select File | Import Project… from the menu. This command invokes the dialog box Import Options shown in Figure 23.9. You can set the check boxes Import items and Import types to indicate the category of information the Import process will load from the export file. The options Override existing items

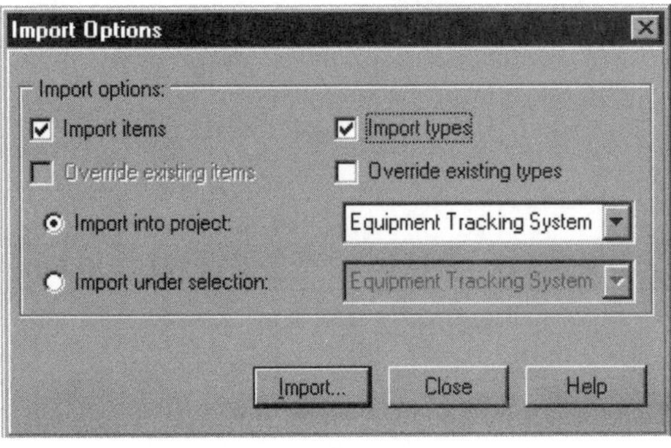

FIGURE 23.9 The Import Options dialog box.

and Override existing types can be set if you want to replace the information that currently exists in the global, user, or project registries with that coming from the export file. Finally, if you are importing project items, you need to indicate the project to which these items will be added. To add them to any of the projects currently open in the Navigator, select the radio item Import into project and select the project from the list box to its right. To add the items to any of the projects selected before the Import Options dialog box was invoked, select the radio item Import under selection and pick the project name from the list next to the radio item. After the import options are set, click the button Import.... This will invoke a standard dialog box, which allows you to select the file to import.

23.2.3 POPULATING PROJECTS WITH FILES

The process of adding files to a project is very simple and consists of the following steps:

1. Select the desired project on the Project Navigator.
2. Click the icon Add Files to Project on the toolbar. Alternatively, you can select Project | Add Files... from the menu. (You may also add entire directories with subdirectories as a subproject using Project | Add Directories.)
3. In the dialog box Add Files to Project that appears, select one or more files to be added to the project.
4. Click OK.

If the file extension corresponds to one of the types recorded in the global registry or the user registry, the file is placed under the node that represents that type in the project. For example, Form Builder modules will be added under the node Form Builder document and C files under the node C source file, as shown in Figure 23.10. Any files whose extension is not a registered type are classified under the node <Any Type>, as in the case of the file ETS.PAL in Figure 23.10. If there is a file type defined as deliverable or otherwise related to a given file type, the Project Manager will automatically add an entry for the deliverable file each time you add the source file to the project. For example, adding a Form Builder document to the project automatically creates an entry for its executable version under the node Form Builder executable. Adding a C or C++ source file will add its corresponding object and executable files, as shown in Figure 23.10.

Files from one project can be easily shared with other projects either by adding them directly to the new project or by copying or moving a file from one project to another. To move a file between projects, follow these steps:

1. Expand nodes in the Project Navigator until you select the file you want to move.

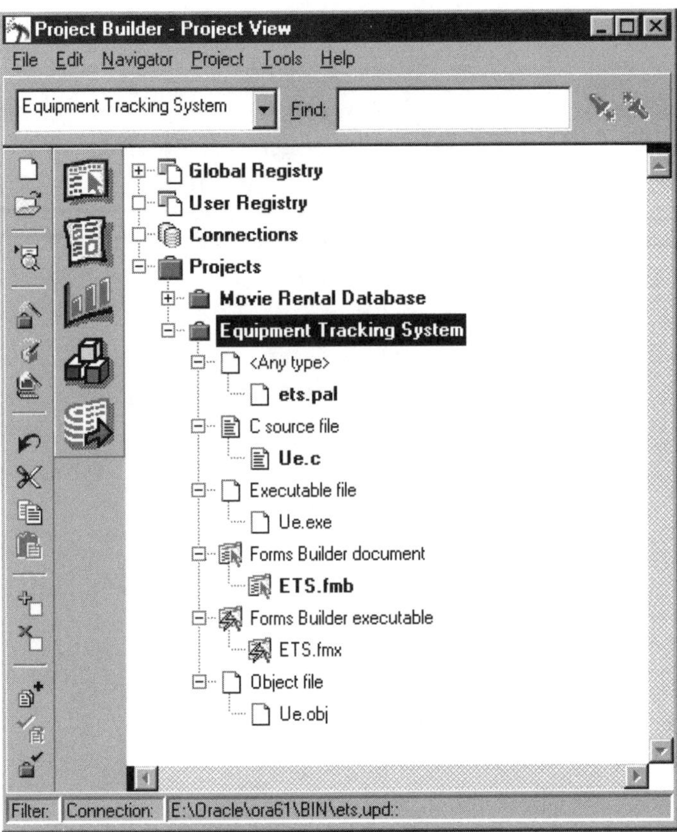

FIGURE 23.10 The representation of files in the Project Navigator.

2. Drag the file over to the new project. Alternatively, you can also cut the file and paste it in the new project.

To copy a file from one project to another, follow these steps:

1. Expand nodes in the Project Navigator until you select the file you want to move.
2. Press the Control key on the keyboard and drag the file over to the new project. Alternatively, you can also copy the file and paste it in the new project.

To remove files from a project, you simply select them in the Project Navigator and press the DELETE key on the keyboard.

By default, files in the Project Navigator are organized by file type. This is also known as the project view of the Navigator. Illustrations of the Project Navigator shown so far, such as Figure 23.10, have been in this view. The Project Navigator also allows you to display the files in a way that shows their dependency upon one another. Figure 23.11 shows the same project shown in Figure 23.10 but this time in its dependency view. Notice here how the executable ETS.FMX has the Form Builder document ETS.FMB as its dependent or how the executable UE.EXE depends on the object file UE.OBJ, which in turn depends on the C source file UE.C. Notice also how files that do not depend on any other files do not appear at all in the hierarchy tree of the Project Navigator in dependency view.

The view mode of the Project Navigator is controlled by two radio items in the Navigator menu. By selecting Project View or Dependency View from this menu, you will set the Navigator to the corresponding view mode.

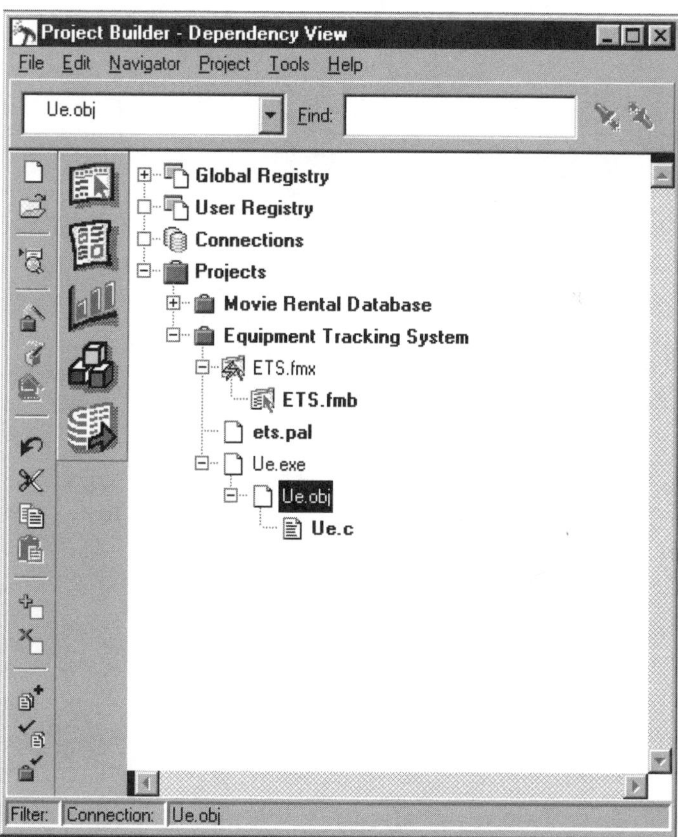

FIGURE 23.11 The Project Navigator in dependency view.

23.2.4 MAINTAINING PROPERTIES OF FILES

Files that are part of a Developer project have a number of properties which can be viewed and maintained in the Property Palette window. This window appears each time you select Property Palette from the Tools menu or the pop-up menu that appears when you right-click an object instance. Figure 23.12 shows an example of the Property Palette window. As you can see from the figure, this window is very similar in appearance and functionality to the Property Palette window of the Form Builder. The properties of files are grouped in four categories:

- **General Information.** These are general properties, such as the name, type, and size of the file, or the label that will represent it in the Project Navigator.
- **Connection.** The three properties in this group allow you to record the user name, password, and database name required to perform certain operations against the file, such as compile a Form Builder document or execute its binary version.
- **Actions.** These are actions that you can issue against the file. The number of actions is unlimited and the Project Builder provides several actions for the

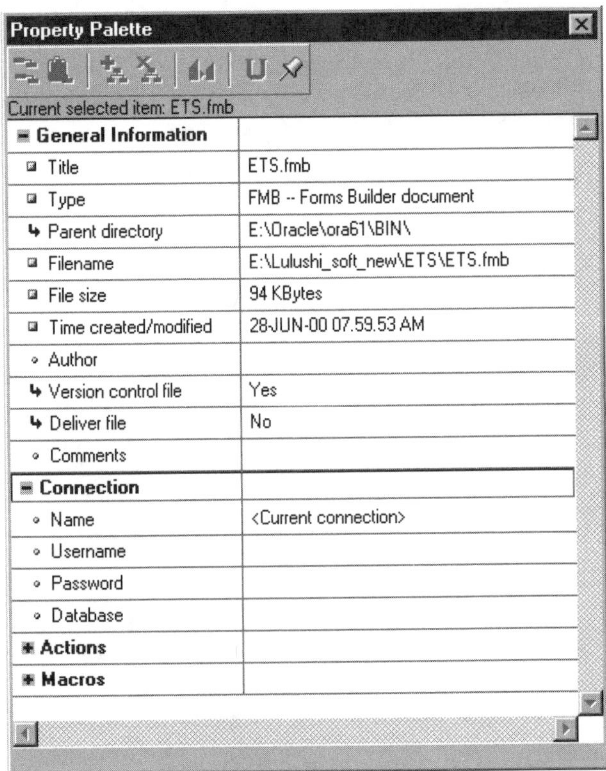

FIGURE 23.12 The Property Palette window.

predefined file types. Section 23.3.2 will discuss how you can add your own customized actions.

- **Macros.** Macros are variables used to simplify in the specification of one or more actions. When the actions are executed, the Project Builder substitutes the names of these variables with their values. Section 23.3.3 will explain how you define and use macros.

Once you include a file in a project, the Project Builder sets almost all its properties by inheriting them from the following two sources:

- **Objects in the Project Navigator.** Most of the properties of files are inherited from other objects maintained by the Project Builder. These include all the properties in the Connection, Actions, and Macros groups, as well as a number of properties in the General Information group, such as Project Directory, Author, Version control file, Deliver file, and Comments. You may apply a filter, which allows you to display only those projects or project items that meet a certain criteria.
- **Physical attributes of the file.** These properties are located in the General Information group and include Filename, File size, and Time created/modified. These properties are updated each time the corresponding attributes of the file change. I include in this category the property Title—the label that represents the file in the Project Navigator—which is initially derived from the file name.

The inheritance of properties in the Project Builder follows a well defined hierarchy. At the top of the hierarchy reside file types in the global registry, followed by file types in the user registry, the properties of the node Projects in the Navigator, the properties of each project, and, finally, the properties of each subproject, if it exists. If a property is defined at one of these levels, then any object in the levels below will inherit the same setting, unless the setting is overwritten. For example, if an action is defined for Form Builder documents in the global registry, this action will be inherited to all the Form modules in your projects. Or, if the property Author is set for the node Projects in the Navigator, then all the projects created will have the same author name. Or, if the property Project directory is set for a project, all the files added to that project will have the same setting for their Project directory. As with properties in the Form Builder Property Palette window, you can identify the inheritance level of the property by inspecting the icon associated with its name. The following are the four states that this icon can have:

- **Default setting.** This icon indicates that the property is not set for the current object or any object above it in the inheritance hierarchy.
- **Local setting.** This icon indicates that the current object is the first level in

the inheritance hierarchy where the property is set. To clear this setting and return the property to its unset state, click the icon Delete Property on the Property Palette's toolbar.

- **Inherited setting** . This icon indicates that the property's setting is inherited from its parent in the inheritance hierarchy.
- **Overwritten setting** . This icon indicates that the property is set in the level above the current level and the current setting overrides its parent. To inherit the setting of the property from its parent, click the icon Inherit on the toolbar.

23.3 CUSTOMIZING THE PROJECT BUILDER

So far, I have described how easily you can create projects and manipulate the files that are part of them. However, among the strongest features of the Project Builder are its openness and flexibility. The tool provides ways to handle the file types that you will most likely encounter in your Developer programming activity. At the same time, it offers a number of ways in which you can add new types and modify the properties of existing types. The following three sections focus on how you customize the Project Builder and, in particular, how you add new file types in the global or user registry, how you create and maintain actions and macros, and how you customize the Launch Pad.

23.3.1 MAINTAINING THE PROJECT REGISTRIES

I have referred to the global and user registries several times thus far. Now is the moment to explain exactly what they are and what to do with them. The global registry contains the definitions of all the file types that will be shared by the entire development team. Physically, these definitions are stored in the Project Builder folder (%ORACLE_HOME%\PJ60) in the file types<language_code>.upd. Here, the language code corresponds to the language for which Developer is installed. In American English installations, for example, this file would be typesus.upd. The contents of this file appear under the node Global Registry of the Project Navigator. This file, since it is distributed in every machine where the Developer software is installed, can be accessed and modified by all the users that have access to that machine, unless you use operating system features to restrict the "write" privilege of the users with project administration responsibilities.

It is a good practice to keep only one global registry file shared by all the developers for all the projects. This will add consistency to the way the teams manage projects and to the actions that they perform with the files that are part of them. However, in certain situations one or more of your developers may want to create new types for their own use, which may not necessarily apply to all the development teams. In other situations, a developer may want to override some settings established by the project administrator for a global type. In both cases, the file type definitions may be maintained in the user registry. Like the global registry, the user registry is physically stored in a file located in the folder %ORACLE_HOME%\PJ 60. The name of this file follows the pattern pjuser<language_code>.upd. In American English installations, this file is called pjuserus.upd. The contents of this file appear under the node User Registry of the Project Navigator.

Now, I will describe how you add a new file type to handle SQL files that create the database objects of your applications. There is no difference in the way you create or maintain file types in the global or user registry. As I said earlier, the only difference resides on who should change each of these registries. Therefore, the following actions could be issued against any of the registries. Here, I will assume that the new file type is being added to the user registry.

To create a new file type, right-click the appropriate registry node in the Project Navigator and then select New Type... from the pop-up menu that appears. Alternatively, you can select File | New | Type... from the menu. Both actions will invoke the Module Type Wizard, which is used to set the properties of the file type. One way to set the properties is provide values for each control in the wizard. These are the steps to set the properties of the new SQL file type:

1. Set Type to "SQL."
2. Enter a few words to describe the new file type in the text item Description. The setting of this item becomes the label of the new type in the hierarchy tree of the Project Navigator. For example, you could enter "Oracle SQL Files." At this point, the wizard should look like Figure 23.13. Click Next to continue to the next screen of the wizard.
3. Select the radio item Extension from the group Filename Format and set it to "sql." Note here that this field Pattern is already set to "{b}"—a macro that indicates the base name of the file. Typically, you will only add the extension to the format of the file, as in this case.
4. Select the radio item Textual to the right of the dialog box to indicate that the file contents are text rather than binary.
5. Set the check box Version-controlled to indicate that file of this type will be under a version control package.
6. Set the check box Deliverable to indicate that file type will be part of the project deliverables. Because SQL files are maintained and delivered under the same format, you do not need to modify the option "UPDANY—<Any type>" of the list box Deliver As. If, however, they are delivered as a different type, you should select this type from the list box Deliver As. For example, the Form Builder documents (FMB) are delivered as Form Builder executables (FMX). Now your screen should look like Figure 23.14. Click Next.
7. In the next screen, view and modify the actions defined for this type, as shown in Figure 23.15. Click Next.

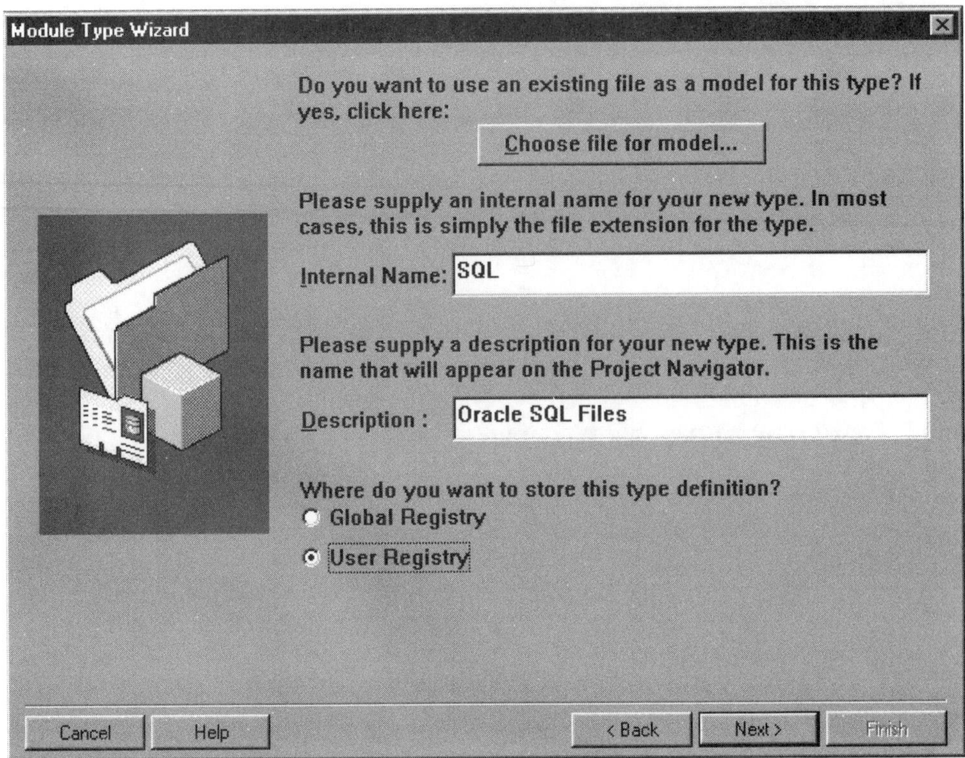

FIGURE 23.13 The first screen of the Module Type Wizard.

8. In the next screen (shown in Figure 23.16), provide a characteristic icon for the files of the new type. The Project Builder provides a number of icons, among which the SQL*Plus icon shown in Figure 23.16. If the one you want is not among these icons, you can select the check box From file and then click Browse… to find the file that contains the desired icon.

If you already have a file of the type you are defining, you can reduce a number of the steps described above. When the Module Type Wizard is displayed, click the button Choose file for model… and, in the dialog box Derive Type that appears, select the sample file. The Project Builder will derive the type, format, description, as well whether the file is text or binary. Whenever possible, it selects an icon as well.

The process of editing the properties of a file type is very similar. You simply right-click the type in the Project Navigator and select the item Edit Type… from the pop-up menu. The dialog box Add Type appears again. You can maintain all the properties here as described earlier. (The only property you can no

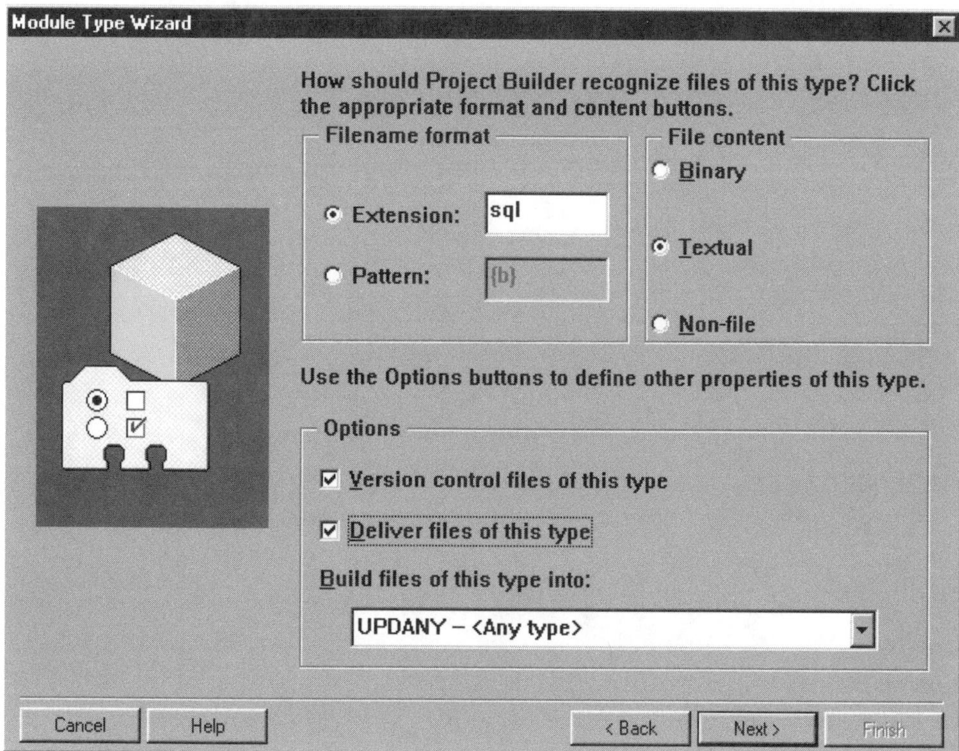

FIGURE 23.14 The second screen of the Module Type Wizard.

longer edit is Type.) As I have already mentioned, the Project Builder comes with a considerable number of predefined types in the global registry. If you want to override the properties of a global type locally, while still preserving their original settings in the global registry, you should follow this procedure.

1. Inspect the setting of the Type property in the global registry for the file you want to modify. Recall that you view this property in the Add Type dialog box.
2. Create a new type in the user registry.
3. Set the property Type of the new object to the same setting as its corresponding global type. As soon as you navigate outside this item, the Project Builder will populate the properties of the new type with the settings of the global type.
4. Override any properties as needed.
5. Click OK to save changes in the user registry.

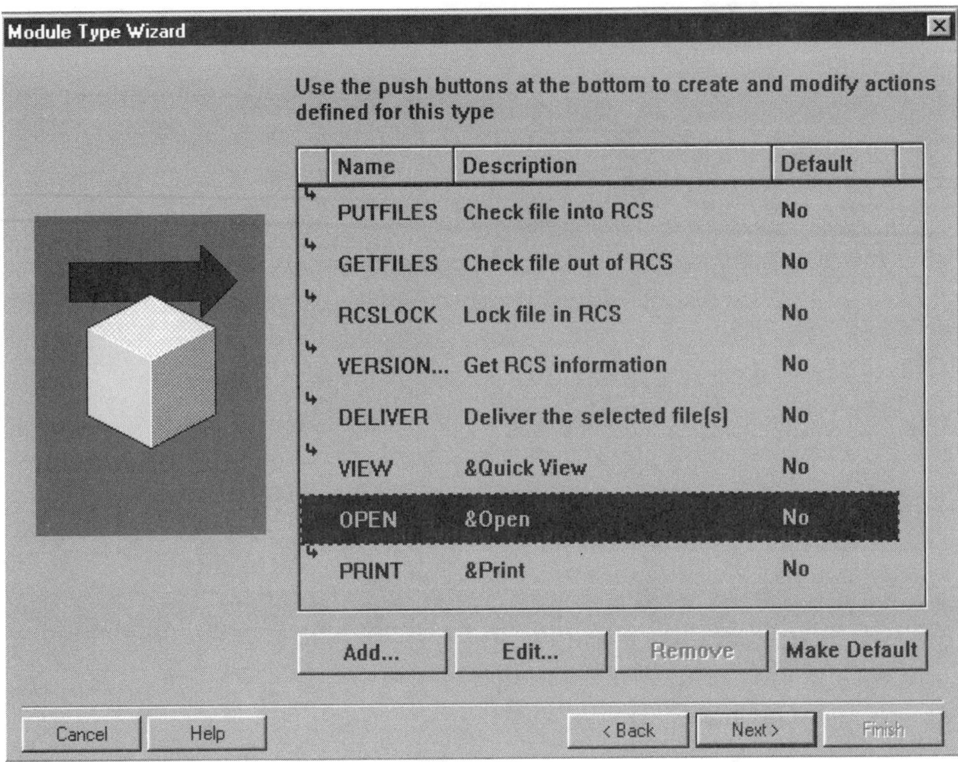

FIGURE 23.15 The third screen of the Module Type Wizard.

23.3.2 MAINTAINING ACTIONS

Actions are properties of objects that can be defined and maintained at any level in the inheritance hierarchy discussed in Section 23.2.4, from the definition of a file type in the global registry to a particular file in a project. To better explain how you add an action to an object, I will describe the process of adding the action "Run" to the SQL file type defined in the previous section. Before I begin this, let me point out that for each new type you create, the Project Builder adds automatically a number of commands. Figure 23.17 shows the list of actions defined for the SQL file type. Some of these actions, like Edit, work as they are defined. Some others, including all the source control software commands, are defined as templates which you need to edit in order to provide the actual commands. Furthermore, a number of actions, such as Edit, Check file into RCS, and Check file out of RCS, are defined in such a way that they appear in the pop-up menu when you right-click a file of the given type in the Project Navigator. You can convince yourself of this by right-clicking a SQL file and noticing the items Edit, Check In, and Check Out in its menu. These actions are inherited from the

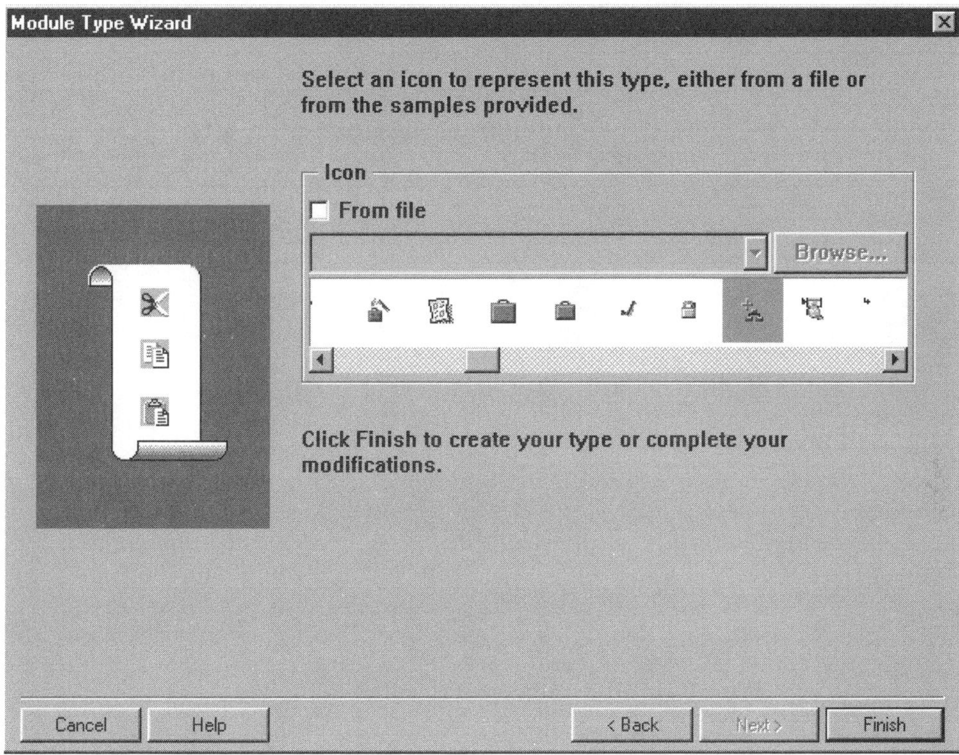

FIGURE 23.16 The fourth screen of the Module Type Wizard.

file type <Any type> in the Global Registry of the Project Builder. This is the object with which you need to work, if you want to modify the settings globally, or add a new command that will apply to all the types you create.

In order to add a new command to an object, right-click this object in the Project Navigator—for example, the file type in the Global Registry or User Registry—and choose the item Add Action… from the pop-up menu. Alternatively, you can select File | New | Action… from the menu or, in the Property Palette of the object, select the Actions group and click the icon Add Property… . Any of these commands will display the dialog box Add Action, used to define the new command. Figure 23.18 shows the settings of this dialog box if you want to add the Run command to the SQL file type. The following are the steps to set these properties:

1. Type "RUN" in the combo-box Name. If you expand this list, you will notice the other commands already defined, including GETFILES, PUTFILES, DELIVER, and VERSIONCTL.

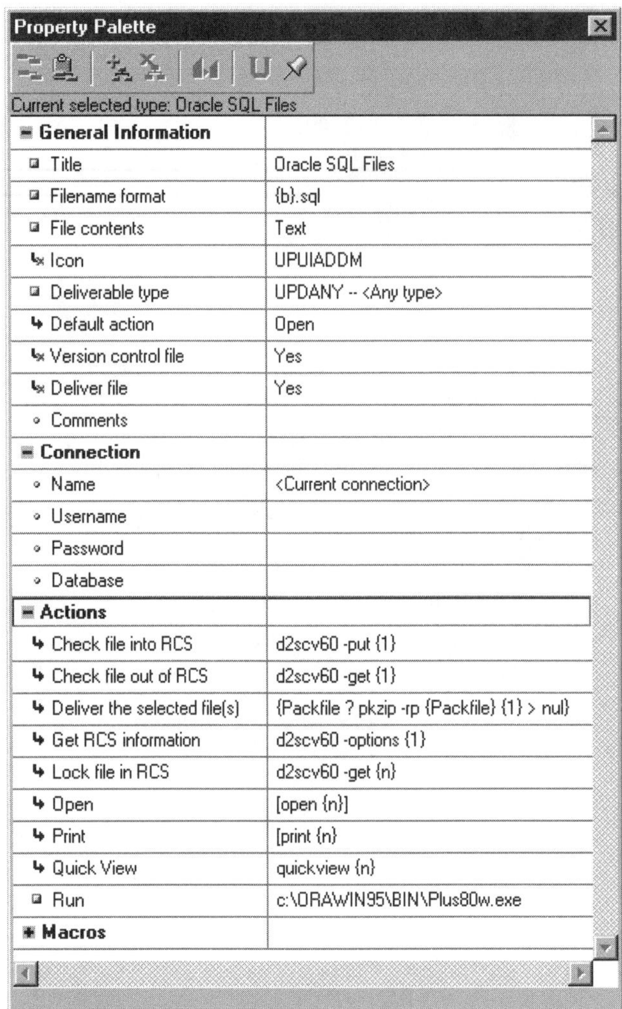

FIGURE 23.17 Actions defined automatically by the Project Builder for a new type.

2. Enter "&Run" in the text item Description. This will be the label of the item in the pop-up menu. Hence the use of the ampersand character before the letter "R," which allows you to invoke the command by pressing Alt+R on the keyboard.
3. Set the check box Add to Pop-up menu to add the new action to this menu.
4. Clear the check box Default action. If you set this check box, the action will be executed against a file when you double-click it in the Project Navigator. For file types that can be edited, such as SQL*Plus files or Form Builder documents, the default action usually is that of opening them in the editor. For

executable files, like Form Builder executables or Report Builder executables, the Run command is normally set as the default action.

At this point, you need to define the operating system command to be executed when the action is invoked. You can type it in the text box Action definition or, better yet, use the buttons Insert application… and Insert macro… as explained in the following steps to simplify your task.

5. Click Insert application… and use the dialog box Select an Application that appears to find the SQL*Plus executable file in the BIN folder of your Oracle Home directory. In the example shown in Figure 23.18, this file is C:\ORAWIN95\BIN\Plus80w.exe.
6. Type a blank space and then the character "@" in the text box Action definition.

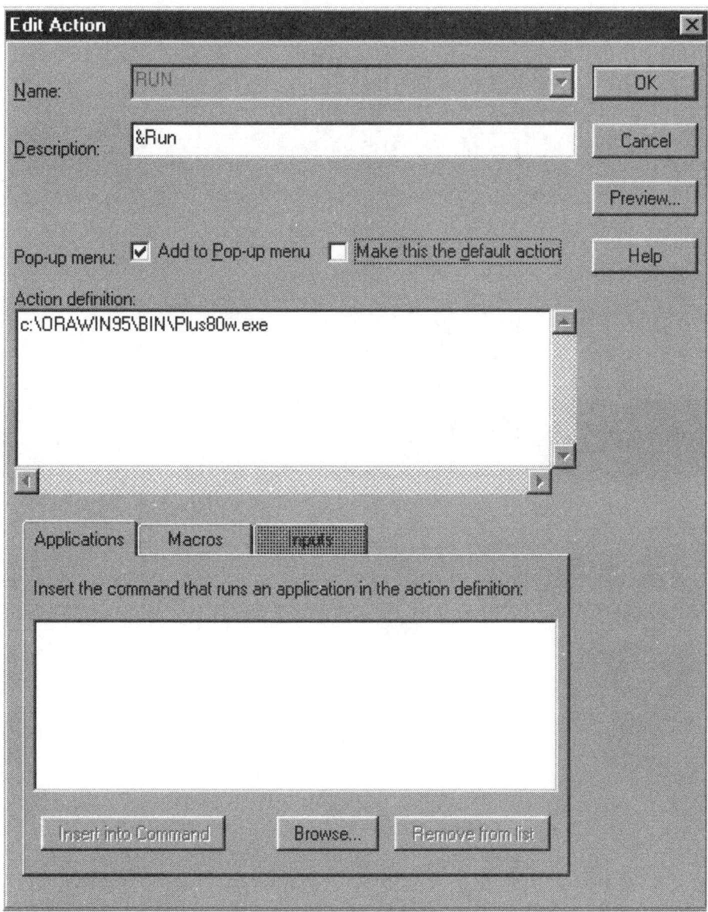

FIGURE 23.18 Setting for the Add New Action dialog box.

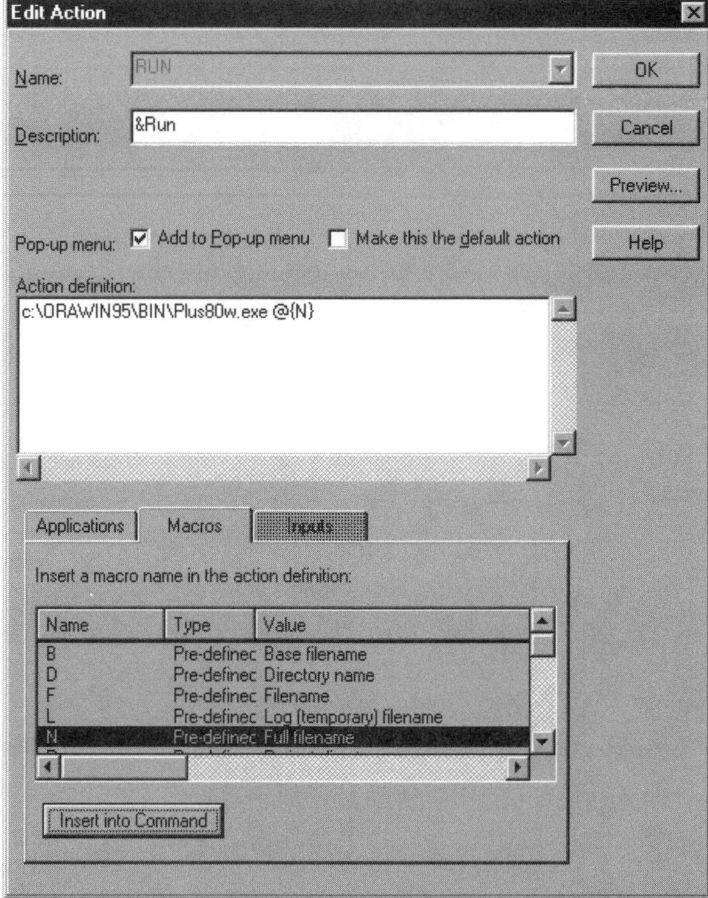

FIGURE 23.19 The Macro Tab of the New Action dialog box.

7. Click the Macro tab, select the macro N (Full Filename) and click Insert into Command. At this point, the dialog box should look like the one shown in Figure 23.19.
8. Click OK to complete the process of defining the new type.

23.3.3 MAINTAINING MACROS

The executable command for the action Run as defined in Step 5 of the previous section is tightly coupled with the installation of SQL*Plus in a specific machine. While this may be acceptable for user-defined types, it is certainly not optimal when the action needs to be executed by different users in different environments. In such cases, the commands should be defined parametrically, using variables whose values are resolved and substituted by the Project Builder when the action is invoked. These variables in Project Builder are called macros. There are three types of macros:

- **Built-in macros.** Such macros are provided by the Project Builder, their names consist of only one character—digit or letter—and they cannot be edited. One of these macros, "n," was used in the previous section to indicate the full name and location of the file. Another one, "b" is used to provide the base name of a file in the definition of the file type format, as discussed in 23.3.1. Figure 23.19 shows these and a number of other built-in macros.
- **Predefined macros.** These macros are provided by the Project Builder, as well. However, you can edit their definition if you are not satisfied with it. The predefined macros can be viewed and maintained in the Macro section of the Property Palette window for the file type <Any type> in the Global Registry. To modify the definition of a macro globally or to add a macro that applies to all the file types, you need to perform these actions against this object. Figure 23.20 shows the list of predefined macros in Project Builder.
- **Environment variables.** All the environmental variables that can be set in your operating system may be used as macros in the Project Builder. When used carefully, they may make your commands very flexible and independent of the physical configuration of your environment. For example, ORACLE_HOME is an environment variable that is always defined in Oracle installations. Using this variable as a macro allows you to refer to the location of files logically, in a way that does not depend on where these files are actually stored.
- **User-defined macros.** These are macros that you define. The macro definitions follow the same rules of inheritance discussed in Section 23.2.4.

Macros are name-value pairs that allow you to use the macro name when defining actions. When the Project Builder is about to execute the action, the name of the macro is substituted with its value. Macros can also be made to prompt the user to enter information. To distinguish the names of macros from other regular strings, they are enclosed in curled brackets. The previous section described how you can define the action of the command run to the following string:

```
C:\ORAWIN95\bin\Plus80w.exe @{n}
```

In this definition, the built-in macro "n" will be expanded when the command is invoked to the full name and location of the file. In order to make the de-

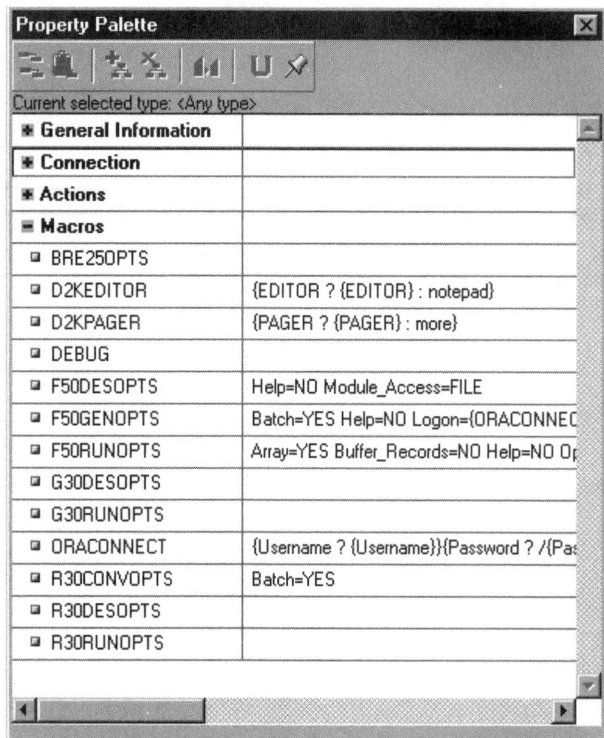

FIGURE 23.20 The pre-defined macros in the Project Builder.

finition of this action independent of the Oracle installation, replace the string above with the following one:

```
{ORACLE_HOME}\bin\Plus80w.exe @{n}
```

One important piece missing in this command is the database connection information. This way of defining the command is advantageous when you cannot predict against which database schema you will run the SQL files. Each time you execute these files, SQL*Plus will prompt you to provide the user name, password, and database name to establish the connection. However, if you know ahead of time the connection information, you would like to take advantage of it. Fortunately, the Project Builder already provides a macro that concatenates together the settings of the properties Username, Password, and Database in the Connection group, if they exist. This macro is called ORACONNECT. This is how the action definition will look now that this macro is used:

```
{ORACLE_HOME}\bin\Plus80w.exe {ORACONNECT} @{n}
```

In order to view the definition of the macro ORACONNECT, display the Property Palette of an object in the Project Navigator, expand the node Macros and double-click the macro. The dialog box Add Macro will be displayed—similar to the one discussed earlier. The following is the value of the macro ORACONNECT:

```
{Username ? {Username}}{Password ? /{Password}}{Database
? @{Database}}
```

The way this expression works is as follows:

1. If the property Username is set to a certain value, then the expression {Username ? {Username}} is set to this value.
2. If the property Password is set, the expression {Password ? /{Password}} is set to the character "/" followed by the value of Password.
3. If the property Database is set, the expression {Database ? @{Database}} is set to the character "@" followed by the value of Database.

Thus, when the settings for Username, Password, and Database are "d2000," "d2000_pwd," and "d2000_db," respectively, the macro ORACONNECT evaluates to "d2000/d2000_pwd@d2000_db"; when the Password is unset, ORACONNECT evaluates to "d2000@d2000_db"; and when Database is not set, ORACONNECT becomes "d2000/d2000_pwd."

The syntax discussed here allows you to evaluate macros conditionally. The general syntax for defining the value of a macro conditionally is:

```
{macro_name ? expression 1 : expression 2}
```

To evaluate the macro, the Project Builder checks whether the macro is defined and has an assigned value. If yes, the macro is evaluated to expression 1; otherwise, it is evaluated to expression 2. An example of the conditional definition of a macro is D2KEDITOR, another pre-defined macro whose value—in Microsoft Windows environments—is set as follows:

```
{EDITOR ? {EDITOR} : notepad}
```

This macro is used to define the default Edit command of files ({D2KEDITOR} {n}). Since the macro EDITOR is not a predefined one, the default editor files in the Project Builder will be Notepad. To make Wordpad the default editor of SQL files, you should create a new macro for the SQL type named "EDITOR" whose value is set to "write." These are the steps you need to follow in order to create a new macro:

1. Find the appropriate object in the Project Navigator where the new macro will be defined. Keep in mind the extent to which you want this macro to have effect and the inheritance rules when define this object.
2. Right-click the object and select New Macro... from the pop-up menu. You can also select File | New | Macro... from the menu or display the Property Palette of the object, select the node Macros, and click the icon Add Property... . Each of these actions displays the dialog box Add Macro shown in Figure 23.21.
3. Provide the name for the new macro in the text item Macro name.
4. Enter the value of the macro in the text box Macro definition.
5. Click OK when finished.

Just as the macros can be used to define an action, so they can be used to define another macro. To insert a macro in the text box Macro definition, click the button Add nested macro... . The same dialog box Add Macro to Definition discussed in the previous section appears, allowing you to select the name of the desired macro.

23.3.4 MAINTAINING PROJECT BUILDER PREFERENCES

The Project Builder is a tool that can be customized very easily through a number of preferences. These preferences allow you to hide or display a number of elements, such as the Launch Pad or the toolbar, set a number of project properties to default values, or maintain the structure of the Launch Pad. They are maintained in the Preferences dialog box that is displayed by selecting Tools | Preferences... from the menu. This dialog box is made up of three tabs, which are described in the following paragraphs.

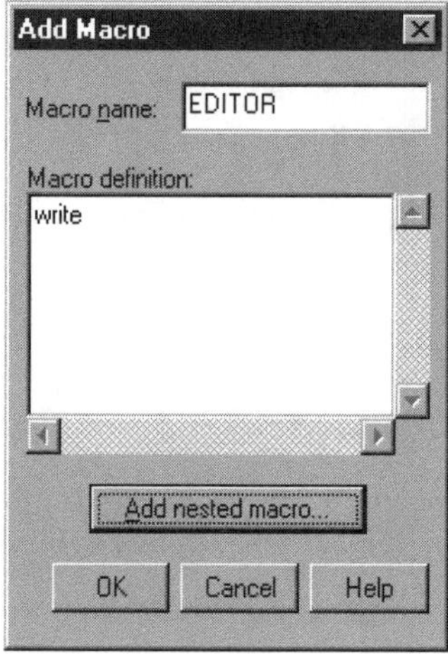

FIGURE 23.21 The Add Macro dialog box.

- **Display tab.** This tab is used to control the display of a number of items of the Project Builder, including the toolbar, the Launch Pad, the initial Welcome dialog box and the Project Wizard's Welcome tab. Figure 23.22 shows an example of this tab.
- **Project tab.** If you want assign default values to the properties Author, Username, Password, Database, and Comments of each new project you create, you can set them in the Project tab of the Preferences dialog box. Figure 23.23 shows an example of such a tab. Notice here that the list box Connection can be set to any of the database connections defined in the Project Navigator.

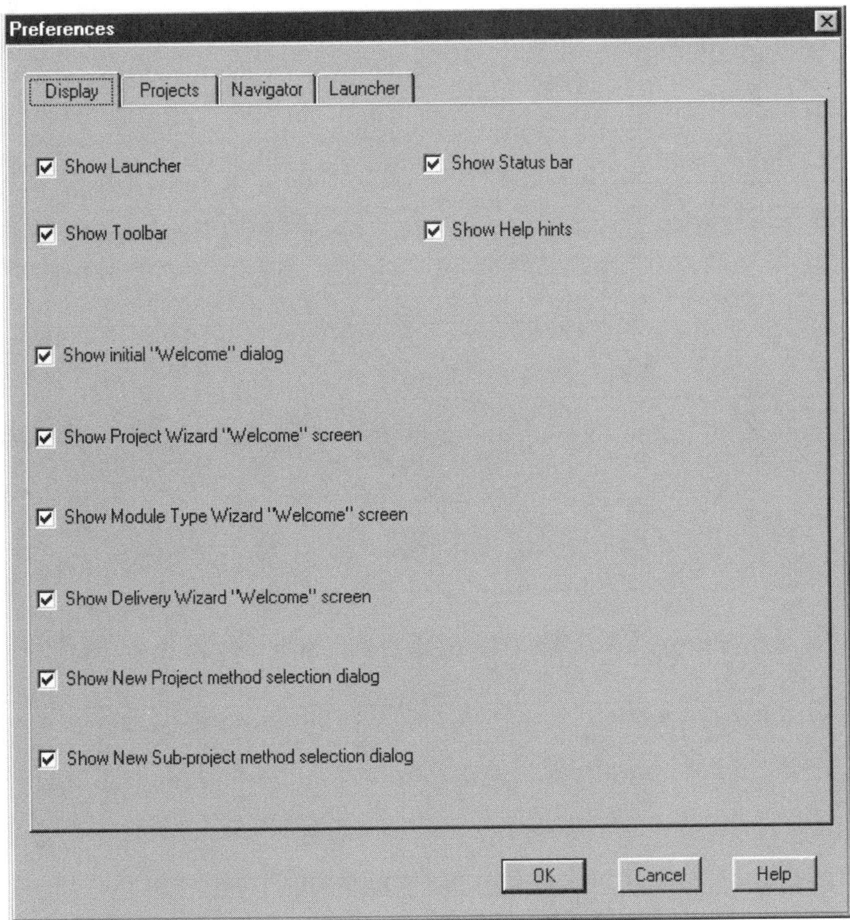

FIGURE 23.22 The Display tab of the Preferences dialog box.

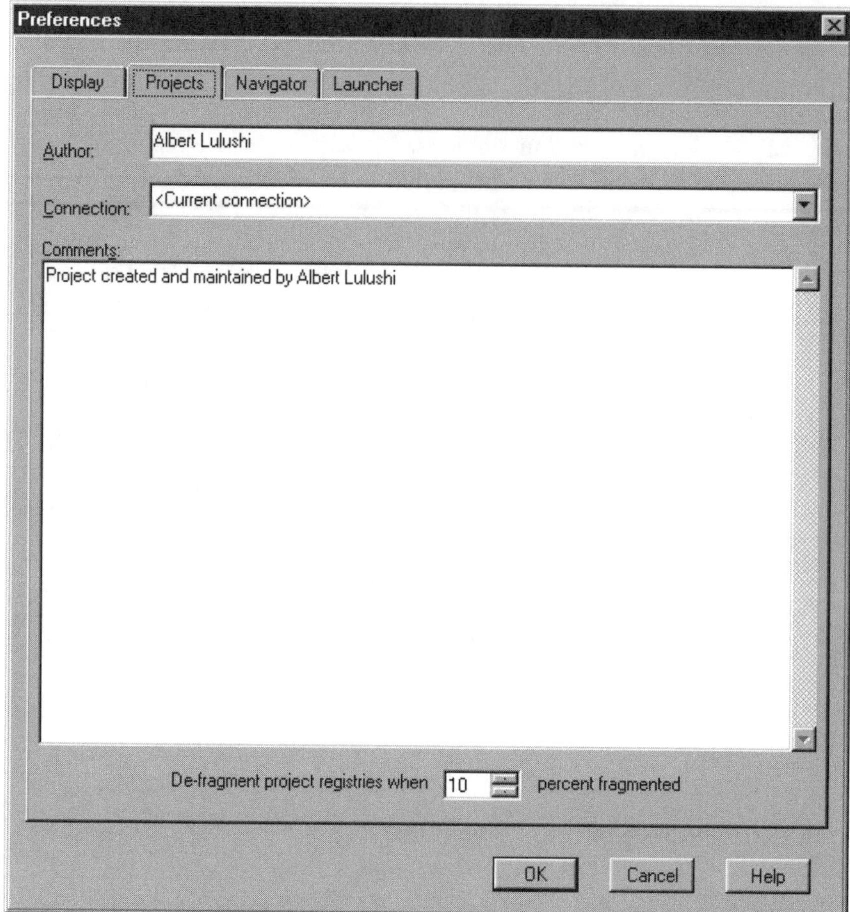

FIGURE 23.23 The Projects tab of the Preferences dialog box.

- **Navigator tab.** This tab is used to control options concerning the navigator, as shown in Figure 23.24.
- **Launcher tab.** By default, the Project Builder Launch Pad contains five icons that you can use to start the Form Builder, Report Builder, Graphic Builder, Procedure Builder, and Query Builder. The Launcher tab can be used to customize this component. Figure 23.25 shows an example of this tab.

The hierarchy tree control that occupies the left half of the Launcher tab allows you to visualize the icons in the Launch Pad. Here you can also re-sequence the items by dragging them to the desired position. By setting the radio items in

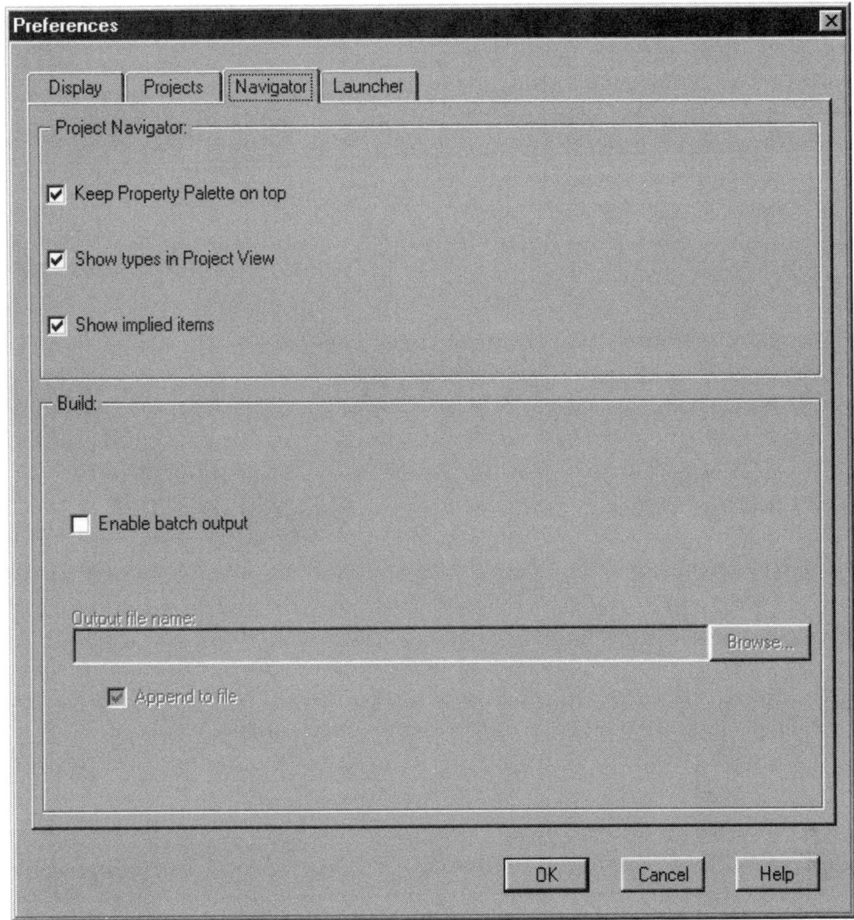

FIGURE 23.24 The Navigator tab of the Preferences dialog box.

the Display group, you can have the tools in the Launch Pad be represented with only an icon or with the icon and a text label. The options in the Layout group control the position of the Launch Pad with respect to the Project Navigator window. As you can see, this toolbar can be docked along the left side of this window—the default position—or at the top, under the toolbar, or it can be left floating around in its own window.

To create a new entry in the Launch Pad, you click the button Add...; to maintain an existing entry, select it in the hierarchy tree and click Update.... In both cases, the dialog box Edit Launcher Entry appears. This dialog box allows you to set the properties of the entry. Figure 23.26 shows this dialog box for the

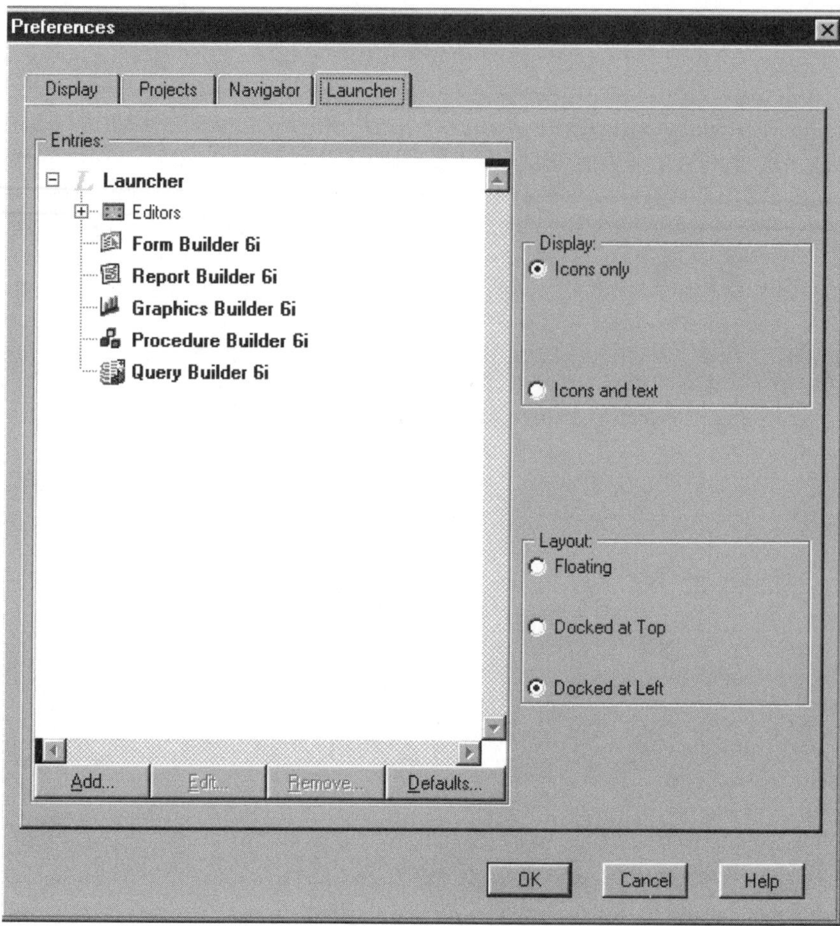

FIGURE 23.25 The Launcher tab of the Preferences dialog box.

Form Builder entry. The following paragraphs highlight the most important things to keep in mind when setting these properties.

- By default, objects in the Launch Pad are action items; they execute the command provided in the text box Command—the button Insert application... can be used to browse the file system and find the appropriate application to execute.
- If you want the entry to serve a menu item from which other options will depend, select the radio item Group instead of Item. Then, define one or

more items as members of this group by dragging them on the group object in the hierarchy tree of the Launcher tab.

- If you do not want to display an item or group, set the check box Hidden. Keep in mind that once you hide a group, all the items that depend from it will not be accessible, no matter how their Hidden property is set.
- The text item Label is used to define the entry that will identify the object in the hierarchy tree of the Launcher pad. The label appears as a pop-up hint when you move the mouse over the object in the Launch Pad. It also appears if you display the objects as icons with text—by selecting the option Icons and text in the radio group Display of the Launcher tab.
- The text item Description appears as a hint in the status bar of the Project Navigator when you move the mouse over the object.

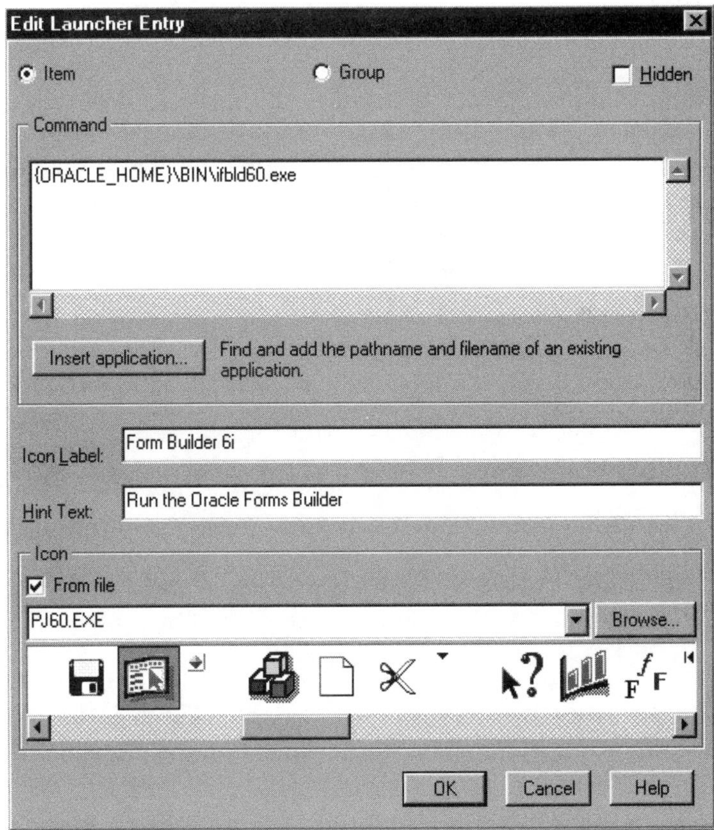

FIGURE 23.26 The Edit Launcher Entry dialog box.

- The icon defined in the group of properties at the bottom of the dialog box represents the object both in the Launch Pad and in the hierarchy tree of the Launcher tab.

As I mentioned earlier, the Launch Pad comes with a default configuration saved in the global registry. If you have modified the properties of the objects that are part of this configuration, you can always reset them to their original settings by clicking the button Sync....

23.4 DELIVERING PROJECTS

Two important tasks in the process of managing software projects are building the software components that users will execute, and bundling them for delivery. As part of maintaining Developer projects, the Project Builder provides for these two tasks. The following sections explain how you compile and bundle project for delivery.

23.4.1 COMPILING PROJECTS

In Project Builder, the process of compiling files is a special case of building the target file type from the source file type. For example, Form Builder executables (FMX files) are built from Form Builder documents (FMB files). The Project Builder creates the FMX version of the file by executing the command specified in the Build form FMB action. There are three methods of compiling files in the Project Builder:

- **Compile each file individually.** In order to compile a file individually, you need to right-click it in the Project Navigator and then select the pop-up menu item that corresponds to the action Build from <source file type>. When the name of this action is defined as "BUILD," you can invoke it by clicking the icon Compile Selection on the toolbar or by selecting Project | Compile Selection from the menu.
- **Compile projects incrementally.** In order to build a project incrementally, select the project in the Project Navigator and then click the icon Compile Incremental or select Project | Compile Incremental from the menu. During an incremental compilation, the Project Builder compiles only those files that are out of date. To determine these files, the Project Builder compares the date stamps of the source files and their targets, if they exist. If the source file is older than its binary version, the compilation occurs. The command used to compile the file is that defined for the action Build from <source file type>.
- **Compile the entire project.** To compile the entire project, simply select Project | Compile All from the menu. In this case, all the appropriate files are built, irrespective of the last time they were last compiled.

23.4.2 DELIVERING PROJECTS

The Project Builder allows you to package all the files that are defined as deliverables of a project in a compressed file that can then be transferred to each location where the project will be deployed. There is an action defined for each file type called DELIVER. The description of this action, which you will see in the Property Palette of objects is "Deliver the selected file(s)." The command executed when this action is invoked is defined as follows:

```
{Packfile ? pkzip -mrp {Packfile} {1}}
```

Recall from the discussion on macros in Section 23.3.3 that the string of this command will be empty if the macro Packfile is not defined. Therefore, one of the preliminary steps before packaging projects is to define this macro. The value of the macro Packfile is the name and location of the zipped file that will contain the project deliverables. You can hard code this name to point to a specific directory and file for each project, or you can use the built-in macros to make Packfile generic. I recommend that you define this macro at the node Projects in the Project Navigator and set its command to the following string:

```
{p}\{b}.zip
```

Thus, the deliverable version of each project will be located in the project directory—provided by the macro "p"—and its file will have the same base name as the project file, but extension ZIP.

Note also that the definition of the action BUILD shown earlier requires that PKZIP be installed and accessible in the Windows path. If this is not the case, or a different packaging utility is used, you should revise the command of this action to point to the appropriate utility.

After all the preliminary steps described above have been completed, you are ready to package a project or any file within it. To package a project, select its entry in the Project Navigator and select File | Administration | Deliver from the menu. The archive file of the project will contain zipped versions of all its components defined as deliverable.

23.5 SUMMARY

When Developer projects contain a considerable number of files and software components, maintaining them in the context of the project, without losing sight of all the dependencies and relationships among them, becomes a complicated task. Project Builder is the Developer tool that helps you create, manage, build, and package your projects. This chapter discusses the components and the functionality of the Project Builder. The principal topics of the chapter were

- **Overview of the Project Builder**
  - Launching the Project Builder
  - Working with the Project Wizard
  - Components of the Project Builder
- **Managing Projects with the Project Builder**
  - Creating and Maintaining Projects
  - Exporting and Importing Projects
  - Populating Projects with Files
  - Maintaining Properties of Files
- **Customizing the Project Builder**
  - Maintaining the Project Registries
  - Maintaining Actions
  - Maintaining Macros
  - Maintaining Project Builder Preferences
- **Delivering Projects**
  - Compiling Projects
  - Delivering Projects

Chapter 24

Developer Forms for the Web

Adapt yourself to the environment in which your lot has been cast.
—Marcus Aurelius

- What Is the Network Computing Architecture?
- Developer Forms' Three-Tier Architecture
- Implementing Developer Forms on the Web
- Special Considerations for Deploying Developer Forms on the Web
- Summary

The World Wide Web has become one of the ubiquitous technologies developed in the recent years. Nowadays, presence on the Web is required for any business entity or person that has a message to deliver or a product to sell. Software vendors have rushed to fill in the need for tools, utilities, and solutions that help businesses move their data and message on the Web. Oracle Corporation has been one of the major proponents of the Web and has positioned itself behind a new IT architecture that enables successful distributed Web-based computing. The definition of this architecture, named the Network Computing Architecture (NCA), has had its effects on traditional client/server development tools like Developer. This chapter presents an overview of NCA and then focuses on how you can take advantage of it to deploy your Developer applications on the Web.

24.1 WHAT IS THE NETWORK COMPUTING ARCHITECTURE?

Typically, software applications have functionality that can be classified in one of the following three layers:

- **Presentation services.** These services handle the interface of users with the application, present data to them as well as capturing and handling events triggered by them.
- **Business logic services.** Services in this category are mostly responsible for implementing the business rules checked or enforced by the system.
- **Data management services.** These services provide storage and retrieval mechanism for data that the application handles and presents to the users.

Looking into the history of database systems and considering what is in store for them in the future, you can identify four categories of systems.

- **Mainframe systems.** In these systems, all the data management and implementation of business rules was performed in large mainframe computers. Dumb terminals connected to these computers provided the data presentation services.
- **Early client/server systems.** These systems separated the enforcement of business rules from data management services and attached it to presentation services. The data management services now were running on a central database server. The other two services resided on client PCs, connected to the server through Local Area Networks (LANs) and, occasionally, Wide Area Networks (WANs).
- **Mature client/server systems.** These systems are distinguished from earlier ones in that the enforcement of business rules in them is partitioned between the client application and the database server. These systems are re-

lated principally to the development of robust DBMS products, such as Oracle RDBMS. Database servers in earlier client/server systems provided limited support for business rules, such as referential integrity. Current database products like Oracle7 or Oracle8 provide full support for implementation of application logic in the form of stored program units and database triggers.

- **Internet/intranet systems.** These systems reintroduce some characteristics of the mainframe systems paradigm into the new reality of the Web. In these systems, the data management services are stored in database servers networked together. The presentation services are offered by Web browsers running on PCs or Network Computers (NCs) connected to the corporate intranet and to the worldwide Internet. Some business rules are implemented in the form of canned units of code—applets, which, upon demand, are transferred from the servers to the presentation devices, where they are executed. The rest are implemented in middle-tier application servers whose primary purpose is to enforce these rules. Oracle's application server implements this middle tier using the CORBA object specification as specified by the Object Management Group (OMG), a consortium of more than 700 companies.

For the first two types of systems, computers that hosted the data played a distinct role from that of terminals or PCs through which the system was accessed. In either case, the boundaries between these roles were very well defined. Because the implementation of business rules fell either on one side or on the other side of the border, no need existed to articulate them distinctly. In mature client/server systems, the border mentioned above becomes fuzzy and more difficult to define. These systems may start out with a partitioning of functionality between clients and database servers that optimize an existing configuration. However, as the components of the system change (newer client PCs, more RAM on the server, faster network, and so on), the configuration of the system changes. In order to maintain the performance at an optimal level, you need to be able to repartition the application logic so that it takes advantage of the new configuration.

How easily this move can be achieved depends on how you defined the requirements, as well as on how you designed and developed the system. If you followed the traditional mainframe approach, you did not distinguish between user interface requirements and business rule implementation requirements. For this reason, the designers and developers often intermixed the business rule functions with the code that draws the screens or manages the windows. In order to move the business rule functionality from the client over to the server, you need to go through the code, dissect the functions, customize, and even rewrite it so that it can be stored in the database.

On the other hand, you can now identify the business rules separately; designers design it as a separate module, and developers implement it as a component in a PL/SQL library that is attached to the Developer Forms client application. To transfer the function in this case, all you need to do is drag the library object and drop it in the database server. Developer components, such as Forms, Reports, and Graphics, allow you to literally drag PL/SQL libraries or components of them and drop them in the Oracle database schema. This flexibility that they provide in partitioning the application logic is why they are often referred to as second-generation client/server tools.

Figure 24.1 represents the Developer client/server model discussed here. As you can see from this figure, the Forms Runtime engine is responsible for implementing the following services:

- **User interface services.** They include rendering text items and different GUI widgets on the screen, managing windows, menus, and dialog boxes, as well as displaying fonts and colors. The appropriate interfacing with the operating system is handled at this stage.
- **Business logic services.** They are the means to implement the business rules of the application. These services include the handling of events triggered by the user interface, the validation of data based on the properties of items, and the validation of items and records based on programmatic rules

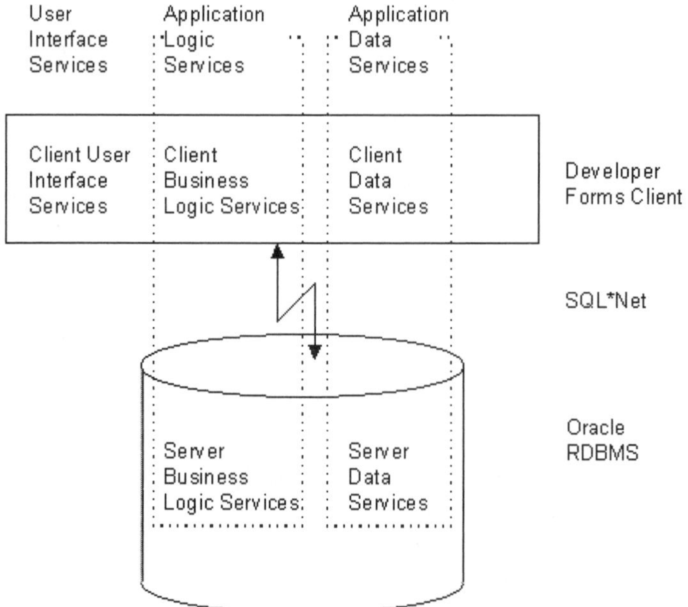

FIGURE 24.1 Representation of the Developer Client/Server Model.

defined in WHEN-VALIDATE triggers. Based on the application design, some of these services may be implemented by the database engine.

- **Data management services.** They coordinate and perform the database interaction. These services include those that manage states of records, blocks, and modules, those that interact with the database, and those responsible for trigger processing. Based on the application design some of these services may be implemented by the database engine, as well.

The client/server architecture has a number of positive features and has improved over time. However, its implementation in large-scale applications used by an extensive number of users identified a series of shortcomings in the areas of deployment, scalablity, portability, and reliability. These shortcomings led to the definition and implementation of multi-tiered architectures that have the potential to provide better solutions. These architectures move a number of functions into a middle tier, often referred to as the application logic tier. These functions include the implementation of a number of business rules, transaction management, load balancing, security services, and event logging.

As more and more multi-tiered applications were being developed, software engineers realized that a number of functions across each tier could be implemented once and then reused in multiple applications. Hence, the need for tools that offer these functions and services in such a way that they can be reused independently on the tier, platform, or programming language used to implement them. To meet this need, in 1996 Oracle Corporation introduced a comprehensive strategy to enable distributed computing, called the Network Computing Architecture (NCA). The NCA is built around the concept of software object components known as cartridges. Cartridges can be written for the presentation, application server, or database server tier and are called client, application, and data cartridges, respectively. NCA specifies the standards that a software component must meet in order to be a cartridge. As long as these standards are followed, the cartridge can be implemented in a number of programming languages, including C/C++, Java, Perl, LiveHTML, COBOL, ODBC, VRML and PL/SQL. Cartridges can communicate with one another via a virtual communication bus implemented using standard technologies such as the Inter-Cartridge exchange (ICX). ICX is a stateless protocol mirrored after HTTP that enables cartridges to exchange information via a send/request mechanism.

An NCA compliant environment provides each cartridge with a number of universal services that can be accessed and used independently of the location of the cartridge. These are services that any cartridge developer can take advantage of and include installation, administration, monitoring, security, transaction management, messaging, and queuing features. The Oracle Application Server is one product that provides this NCA compliant environment. Besides these common services, each cartridge implements its own tier-specific and cartridge-specific servers according to its specifications. Figure 24.2 shows a graphical representation of the NCA and cartridges.

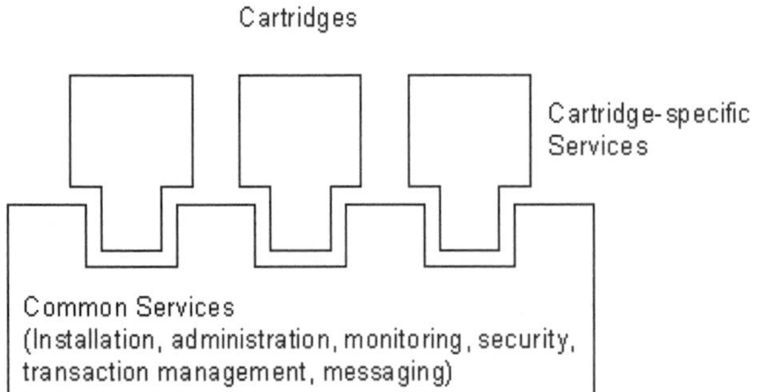

FIGURE 24.2 Graphical representation of the Network Computing Architecture.

24.2 DEVELOPER FORMS' THREE-TIER ARCHITECTURE

Developer for the Web is an enhancement of the traditional Developer tools that enables you to *deploy* applications developed with the Builder components (Form Builder, Report Builder, and Graphic Builder) on the Web. This section will describe the architecture of the Developer for the Web and focus more on the Forms component of the tool.

24.2.1 OVERVIEW OF DEVELOPER FOR THE WEB

As discussed in the previous section, the original Developer architecture followed a second-generation client/server model. In this model, the Runtime component is responsible for rendering the user interface elements, managing the application logic and interacting with the database. Developer for the Web separates the rendering of user interface elements from the Runtime component. In this model, the presentation tier is a Java-enabled Web browser or Java applet viewer; the application logic and the data management services reside in middle-tier application servers and the database engine resides in the back-end tier.

In the case of Forms applications, the presentation tier utilizes a common Java applet downloaded to or cached in the user's browser at runtime. This applet is also known as the Forms Client and is normally the same applet for all Forms applications. As users interact with the applet, different events and commands are passed to and from the middle-tier application server. This server, also known as Forms Server, has two components: listener and runtime engine. The listener component is responsible for establishing a connection between the Forms Client and the Runtime engine when the client applet is initially downloaded. The runtime engine is responsible for all the data processing, application logic execution, and interaction with the database. This engine is a modified version of the Forms Runtime in the client/server model that lacks only its user interface features. Instead, this engine generates the necessary instructions that are passed on to the Forms Client. The Forms Client then performs the graphical user interface drawing and returns user responses to the Runtime engine. Figure 24.3 presents the architecture of Web Developer Forms applications as discussed here.

In the case of Report and Graphic modules, the architecture is simpler. Reports for the Web can be generated in one of the following formats: HTML and/or Adobe Portable Document Format (PDF). Graphics for the Web are generated as HTML files. Therefore, the presentation tier of Reports and Graphics modules consists simply of the HTML browser with appropriate plugins/objects such as Adobe Acrobat Reader. The Forms Server supports the use of RUN_PRODUCT and RUN_REPORT_OBJECT so that a form can activate reports and graphics.

The communication between the Forms Client applet and the Forms Server consists of requests issued by the client in response to events triggered by users and responses sent by the server that modifies the user interface. The responses sent to the applet by the Forms Server consist of batches of instructions. The applet interprets these instructions and draws the user interface accordingly. When

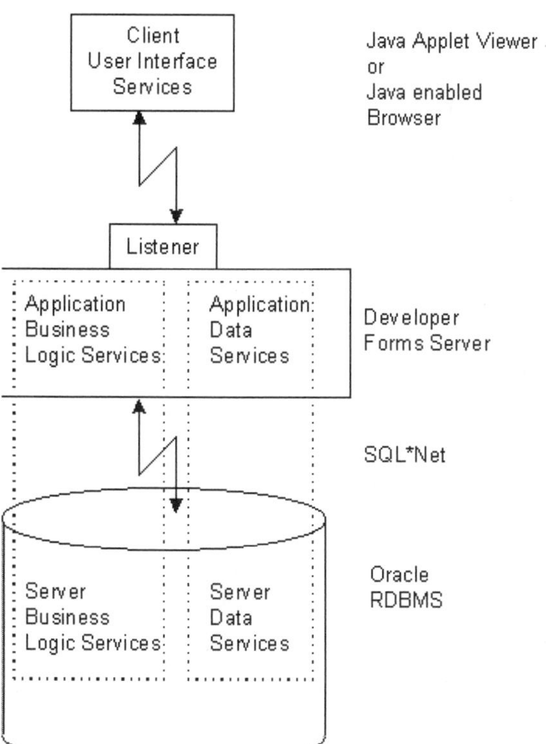

FIGURE 24.3 Architecture of Web Developer Forms applications.

necessary, the Forms Server interacts with the database server much as in the client/server model. The communication protocol between the applet and Forms Server has been optimized to avoid any unnecessary exchange of information thereby reducing the need for high-speed network connections. For example, when the user requests to display a form, the Forms Server sends the applet all the instructions necessary to render the canvas on the screen. When the user executes a query on a block, the Forms Server sends only instructions necessary to populate the items with data fetched by the query. Instructions on redrawing the canvas are not needed since they are known by the applet. Recent upgrades to the Forms Server and Forms Client have reduced network traffic using "Message diff-ing," "Smart event bundling," and a "lightweight menu bar."

24.2.2 INTERACTIONS BETWEEN TIERS

The typical configuration of the Developer for the Web applications is as follows:

- Desktop machines are deployed in the front-end. These machines are equipped with Java-enabled Web browsers or applet viewers and are used by the end-users to run the applications. Numerous client platforms are supported and certified. These include MS Windows, Sun Solaris, Apple Mac, HP-UX11 and Linux. Because of variations in the client Java Runtime Environment (JRE) within different browsers and browser revision levels, Oracle optionally provides its certified JRE called Jinitiator for Windows platforms. Jinitator is installed as a plugin or object for the client browser and when used replaces the native client JRE. Jinitiator also provides additional features such as JAR (Java Archive) file caching, incremental JAR file loading, and applet caching.
- One or more application servers reside in the middle-tier. These servers run the Web Listener and one or more Developer Server components (Forms, Reports, or Graphics). The Forms Server consists of the Forms Listener, Forms Runtime Engine, and Forms CGI (optional). Forms Server natively delivers load-balancing capabilities. Load balancing efficiently distributes client requests across system resources.
- Database server resides in the back-end tier. This is where the database runs. Typically, this is a separate computer, although it may reside in the same box as one of the application servers.

In order to start the application, the users point their browser or applet viewer to a Uniform Resource Locator (URL) string that is uniquely associated with the application. This action causes an HTML page to be downloaded from the Web server to the client desktop. Depending on the configuration of the Forms Server, this HTML page can be static or it can be built dynamically, utilizing the Forms Server Common Gateway Interface (CGI) method. (Note: Older versions of the Forms Server also supported dynamically built HTML pages but required the use of an Oracle Application Server Cartridge). Section 24.3 will discuss in more detail the ways to configure this HTML page. At this point, it is essential to know that the page contains all the information necessary to download the Forms Client applet, the port number through which the applet will communicate, the name of the module that the applet will execute, and any parameters that will be passed to this module.

> **TIP**
>
> The only functionality that the Web Server software plays in the Forms deployment on the Web is to download the HTML file pointed to by the application URL and to start the applet according to the specifications of this file. Any CGI-capable Web Server, including Oracle's WebDB listener, Oracle Applicaton Server, or Microsoft's Internet Information Services, can be used.

After the HTML page described above is downloaded, the Forms Client applet is downloaded according to the instructions in that HTML file. The applet sends a communication request along with the module name and any additional parameters specified in the HTML file to the port specified in this file. On the server end of the line, the request is received by the Forms Server Listener process. Obviously, in order to process the arriving request, this process must be up and running and listening to the same port. The role of the listener is to twofold:

- **Connect to a Forms Server process.** This can be one that already exists and is available, or one that is freshly started to handle the request. The parameters passed to the listener by the applet are handed over to the Forms Server process.
- **Return the connection information to the requesting applet.** The connection established by the Forms Server Listener into this Forms Server process is normally a direct socket connection but HTTP/1.1 and SSL has been introduced in Release 6i. The HTTP/HTTPS protocol allows the Forms Server to communicate across the firewalls which many companies use as well as offering a fully secure connection if needed. Regardless of which protocol is used, the socket information is returned by the listener to the Forms Client applet that requested it.

After the applet receives the socket information from the Forms Server Listener, it uses it to establish a direct connection to the Forms Server process started for it. From that point on, this socket is used to pass events and responses be-

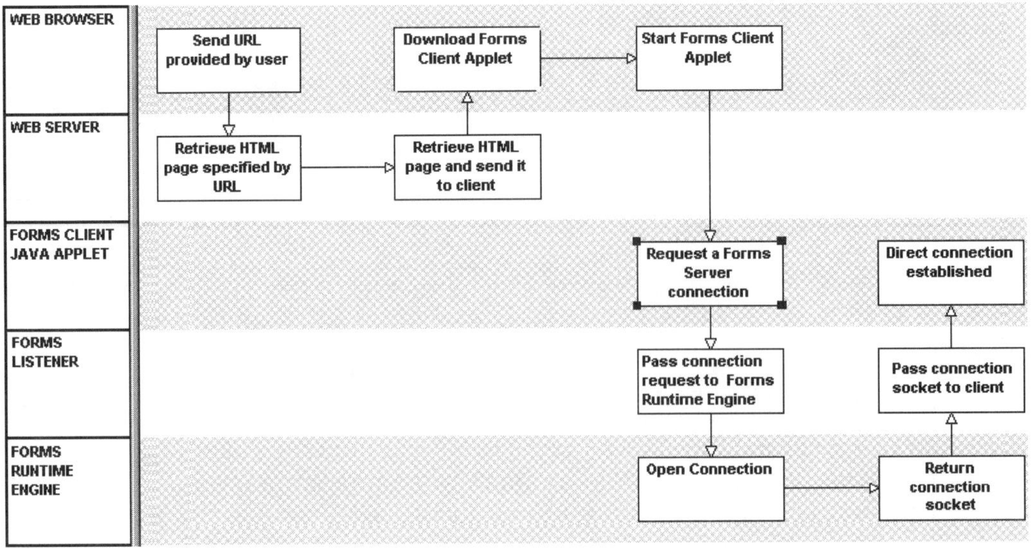

FIGURE 24.4 Process flow diagram of Developer Forms on the Web.

tween the Forms Client applet and the Forms Server process. The Forms Server expects a heartbeat signal from the Forms client periodically (normally two minutes). If this heartbeat is not received within a required amount of time (normally 15 minutes), the Forms Server assumes the client process has terminated abnormally. In this case the Forms Server cleans up the orphan process and frees the resources used. If the module requires database interaction, the Forms Server creates a SQL*Net/Net8 connection to the database server, as it normally does in the client/server implementation. Figure 24.4 shows in a diagram the steps described above and the flow of information between the different components of the Developer Web architecture.

24.3 IMPLEMENTING DEVELOPER FORMS ON THE WEB

The previous section described the architecture of Developer Forms applications deployed on the Web and the interactions between the different components of this architecture. In this section, I will discuss the steps you need to follow in order to configure the application server and to deploy the Form modules on the Web.

24.3.1 CONFIGURING THE MIDDLE-TIER APPLICATION SERVER

The first step in the process of implementing Developer Forms on the Web is to configure the middle-tier application server. Besides the basic software requirements that this machine must meet—operating system and networking software, for example—two additional requirements are specific to its use as a Developer application server.

1. It must have a CGI-capable Web server installed and running.
2. It must have the Runtime components of Developer Server.

From the hardware perspective, you need to be careful to allocate the appropriate amount of memory, as a combination of real and virtual memory. This should be sufficient to allow all the processes to run without competing for memory. These processes include the operating system, the Web server, the Forms Server, and any other processes and applications that may be running on the machine. Different factors determine the memory needed by Forms Server. Among the most important ones are the number of concurrent users and the footprint of the application itself. While there are no rigorous formulas to calculate this memory, estimates and approximations are available. For Forms 5, it is documented, for example, that in order to support an application made up of 8–10 modules each ranging in size from 100Kb to 1Mb, you need about 4Mb of RAM and three times as much free swap space for each user connected to the application. Forms Server 6i has significantly reduced the amount of memory required through improved dynamic link library sharing, middle-tier caching, and messaging layer. When using Forms Server 6i, Oracle has shown that with a medium-size application (2MB–10MB memory per user), a two CPU Intel Pentium-based NT Server with 512MB real memory and 2GB swap space can support 200 users efficiently. If the number of concurrent users is projected to be such that the memory of one application server is not sufficient, you can either upgrade the existing hardware or add additional application servers. Forms Server 6i contains logic to direct the overflow of users to the multiple servers using its load balancing capability.

After the application server's hardware and software are installed and configured, you need to deploy your application in executable format. While you can develop the modules in any platform where Form Builder can run, you need to compile the executable version (.FMX files) on the same operating system as the application server. If this is different from the development platform, you may use the Forms Generate component to generate all the files in a batch.

As I have mentioned earlier, the binary source version of Form Builder modules is portable across different platforms but the executable version is operating system specific. This means that you, for example, can develop the application on Windows NT and compile it on Sun Solaris for deployment. The look and feel of the interface of the application depends on the window managers of the underlying operating system. Therefore, modules compiled on Windows NT have a Microsoft Windows look and feel, but those same modules, when compiled on Solaris, present windows and widgets characteristic of the Motif environment. Ultimately, the operating system of your application server will also determine the GUI flavor of your applications. Oracle has attempted to standardize the appearance of Forms applications across platforms by providing Lookand-Feel and ColorScheme parameters that override some the operating system windows definitions. To create a more web-friendly user experience, the Oracle Look and Feel provides color scheme control, animated controls in user dialogs, enhanced rounded user controls, highlighting for drop down lists and support for the multiple document interface (MDI).

After the modules are generated, you need to deploy them on the application server's file system. I recommend that you place all the executables for a particular application under a directory that serves as home directory for that application. As you do so, you may need to update the values of Forms environment variables with the values of the deployment directories, which may be different from those of the development directories.

24.3.2 INSTALLING THE WEBDB LISTENER AND FORMS SERVER

The Web server is needed for the initial download of the HTML file that starts the application and Forms Client applet. It should also be able to activate a CGI executable. The Oracle Developer Installation CD provides a full out-of the-box solution that installs and configures the Forms Server and the WebDB listener on single or multiple computers. Installing the Forms Server requires a separate install step from the Forms Developer install as shown in Figure 24.5.

You may now choose whether to deploy the client/server runtimes or Forms Server for Web as shown in Figure 24.6.

The most straightforward installation choices for the WebDB listener and Forms Server are shown in Figure 24.7 through Figure 24.10.

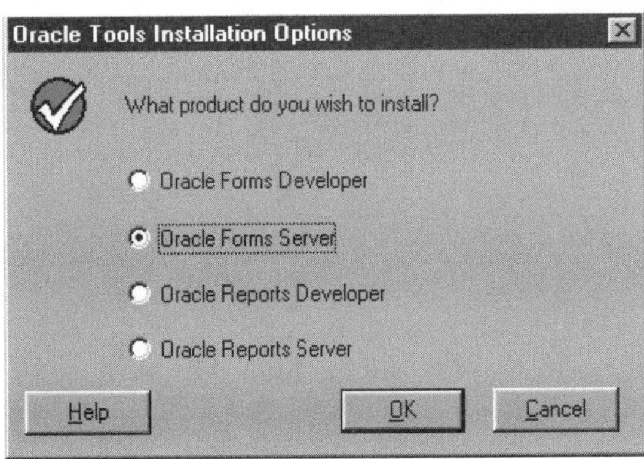

FIGURE 24.5 Choosing the Forms Server during installation.

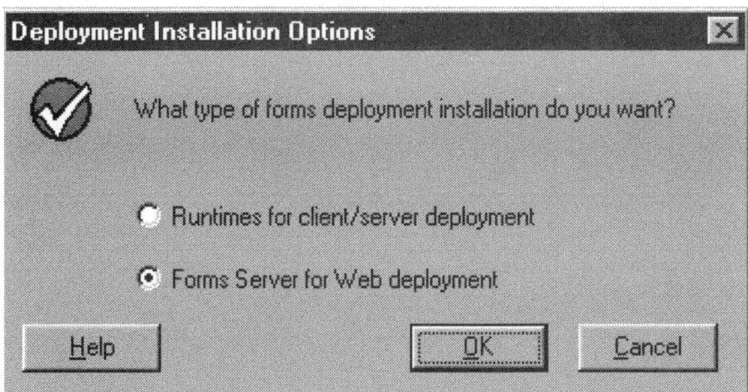

FIGURE 24.6 Choosing the deployment options during installation.

After the software installation is complete, the WebDB listener and Forms Server are automatically installed as NT services and are set to "autostart" for subsequent startups. You can now test the installation by going to Start | Programs | Oracle Forms 6i | Run a Form on the Web. This selection will start the test form in your default web browser as shown in Figure 24.11.

The Forms Server Tester allows you to start forms of your choice and control various parameters using the CGI method of starting a form. When you press Run form, the specified form is started with your chosen parameter values as shown in Figure 24.12.

This method utilizes the CGI method to activate ifcgi60.exe and passes required information to the Forms Server as parameter values. This method allows the user flexibility in activating numerous forms with varying parameters.

24.3.3 CONFIGURING THE WEBDB LISTENER

If you should need to modify the WebDB listener configuration, you can use your browser to go to

```
http://yourcomputer.yourdomain:port/webdb/admin/listener
.htm
```

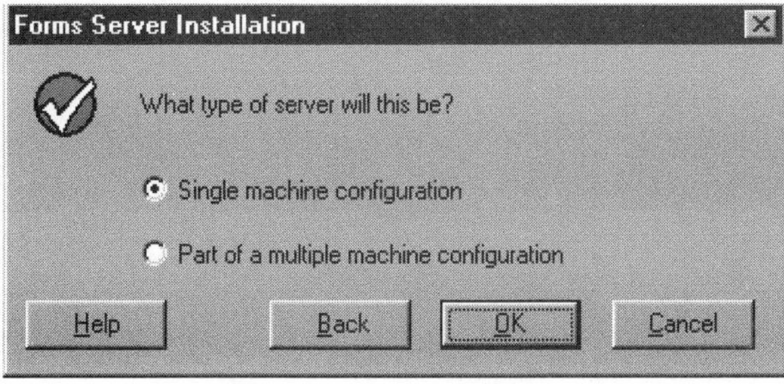

FIGURE 24.7 Single or Multiple Machine selection.

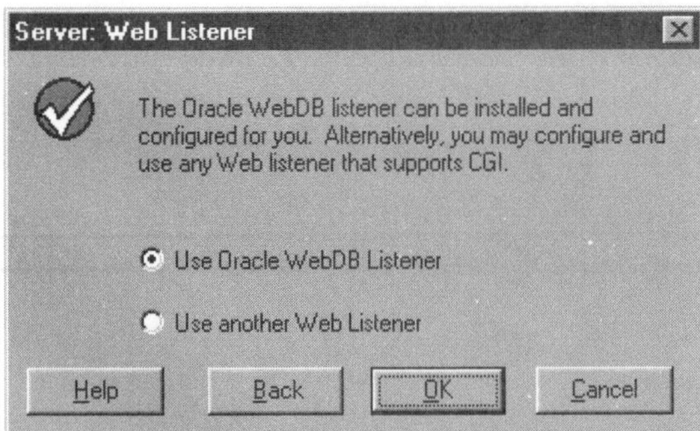

FIGURE 24.8 Choosing the WebDB Listener.

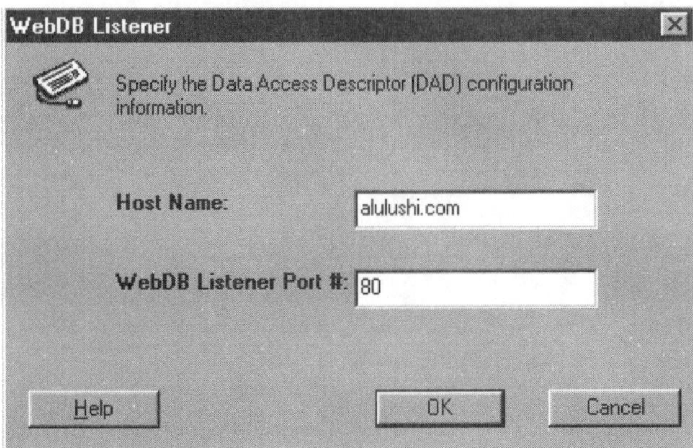

FIGURE 24.9 WebDB Listener host information.

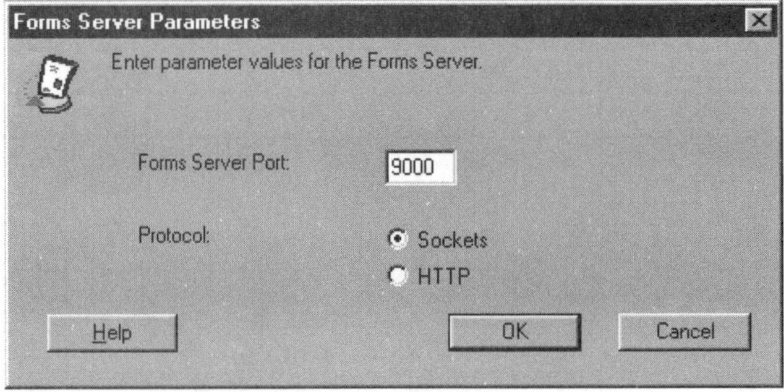

FIGURE 24.10 Forms Server Parameters.

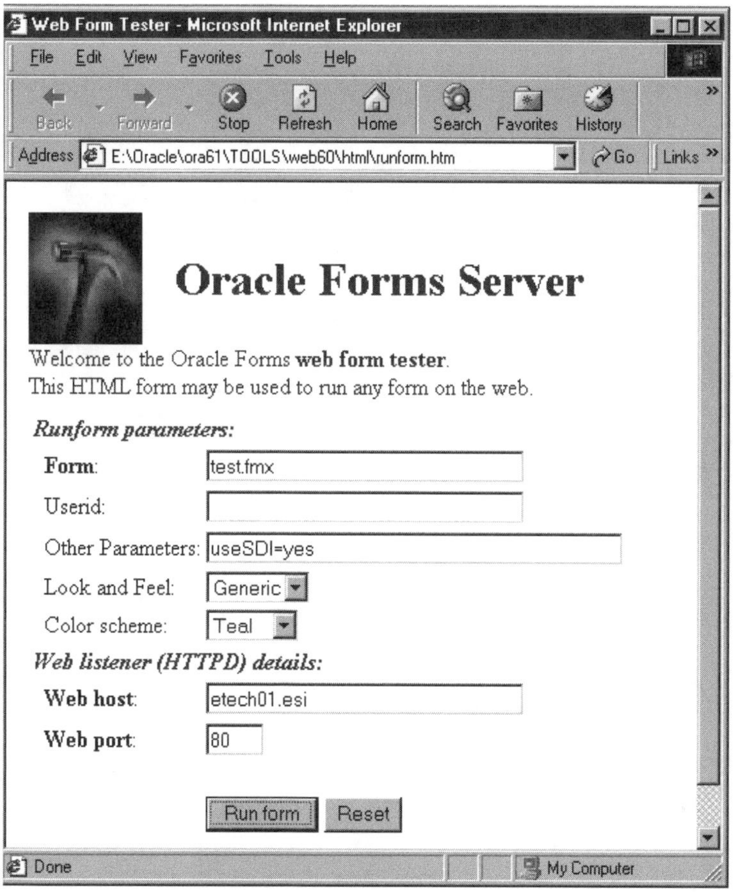

FIGURE 24.11 Forms Server Tester.

The installed listener parameters are shown in Figure 24.13 through Figure 24.16.

Should you need to modify the WebDB PL/SQL Gateway settings, you can use your browser to go to:

```
http://yourcomputer.yourdomain:port/webdb/admin_/gateway
.htm.
```

At this point, the WebDB listener is installed, configured, and started. An NT service for the Forms Server has also been created and started. The standard configuration is set up to use Jinitiator as the Java Runtime Engine.

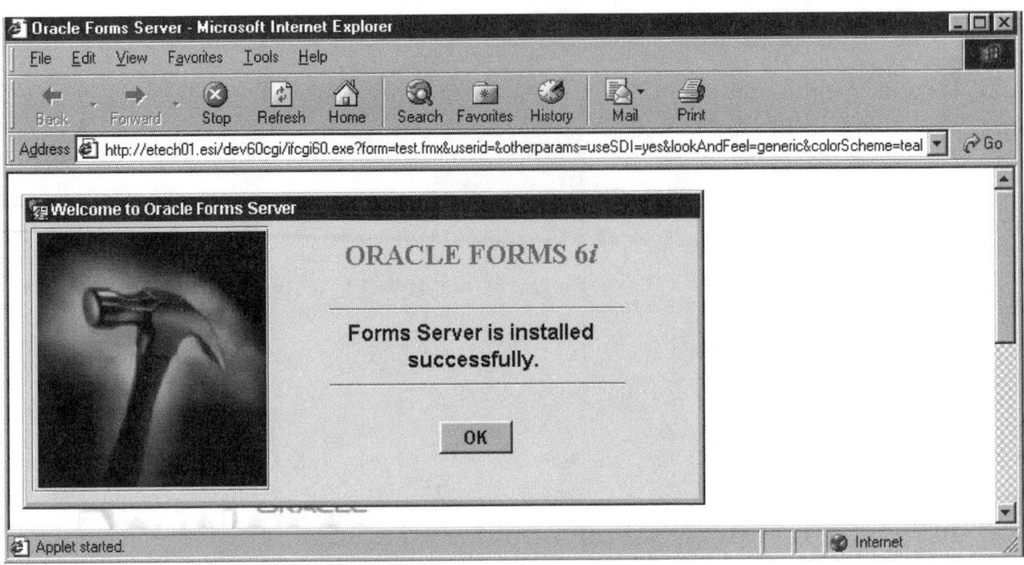

FIGURE 24.12 Forms 6i test.fmx form.

24.3.4 CONFIGURING THE IIS WEB SERVER

Since many of you may already have a Web Server running, I provide instructions in this section on how you can configure, start and shutdown one non-Oracle server, Microsoft's Internet Information Services (IIS). A utility allows you to manage the Internet-related services on Windows NT. To access this utility, select Start | Programs | Microsoft Internet Server (Common) | Internet Service Manager from the desktop toolbar. The Microsoft Internet Service Manger window appears. As shown in Figure 24.17, this window lists the Internet services for each connected server. In the situation shown in this figure, the server tiger has only the World Wide Web (WWW) server running. By selecting a service and clicking the buttons Play, Stop, and Pause on the toolbar, you can start, shut down, or temporarily disable the service.

The Web server software in its most basic form is responsible for presenting content to a user using the Web browser. This content is stored in files and directories stored on the file system of the machine where the Web server runs. The physical storage of these files and the actual structure of the directories however may be quite different from what a user perceives it to be. Virtual directories are Web server definitions that map what users see as directories on their browsers to the physical directories on the server machine. When deploying Developer applications on the Web it is a good idea to assign a dedicated virtual directory to store the HTML files that start the application modules. Through the Web server software, you can map this directory to the physical directory in which these files ac-

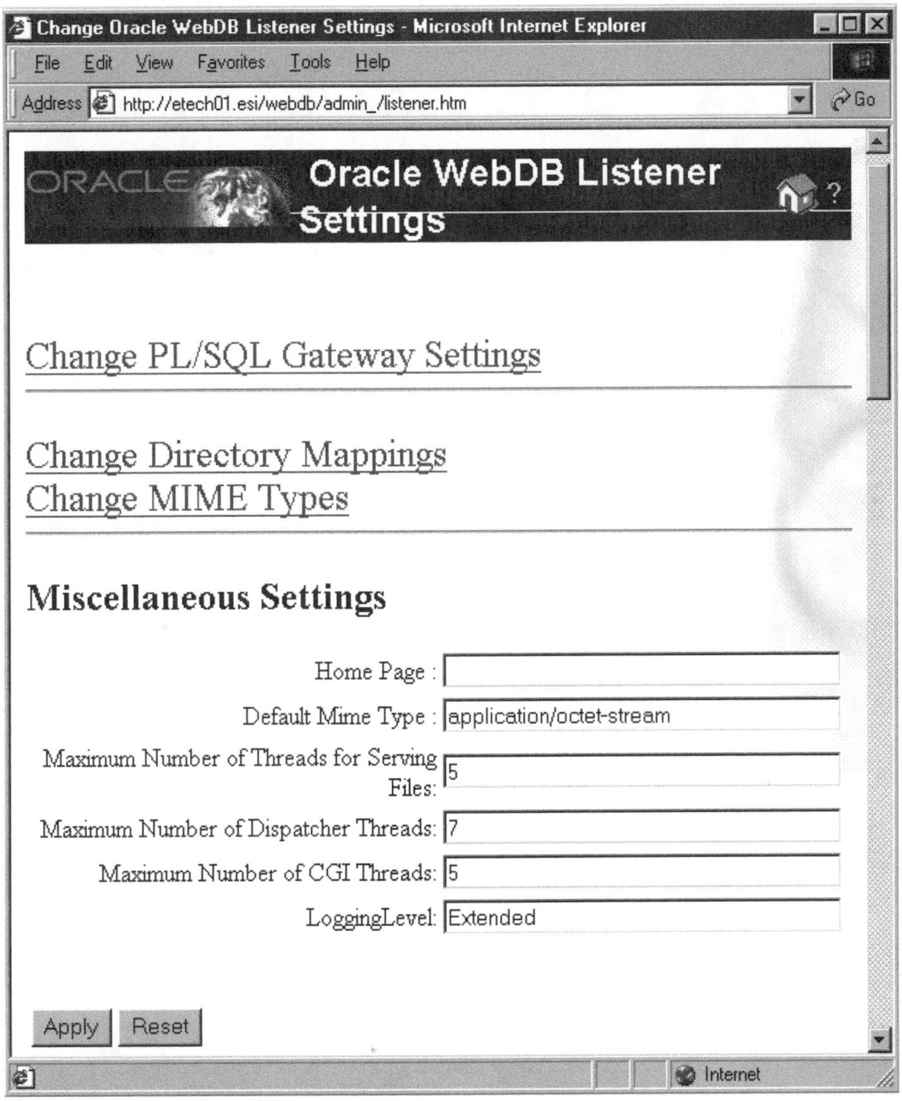

FIGURE 24.13 The first screen of the WebDB listener settings.

tually reside. Here are the steps to view the virtual directories defined on Microsoft's Internet Service Manager:

1. Select the WWW service for the desired server.
2. Select Properties | Service Properties... from the menu. The dialog box WWW Service Properties shows up.

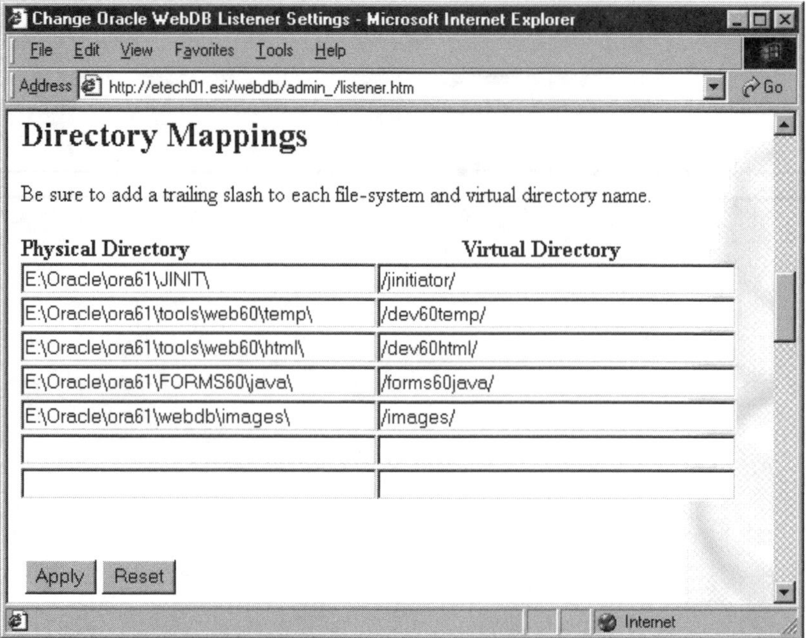

FIGURE 24.14 The WebDB Directory Mappings.

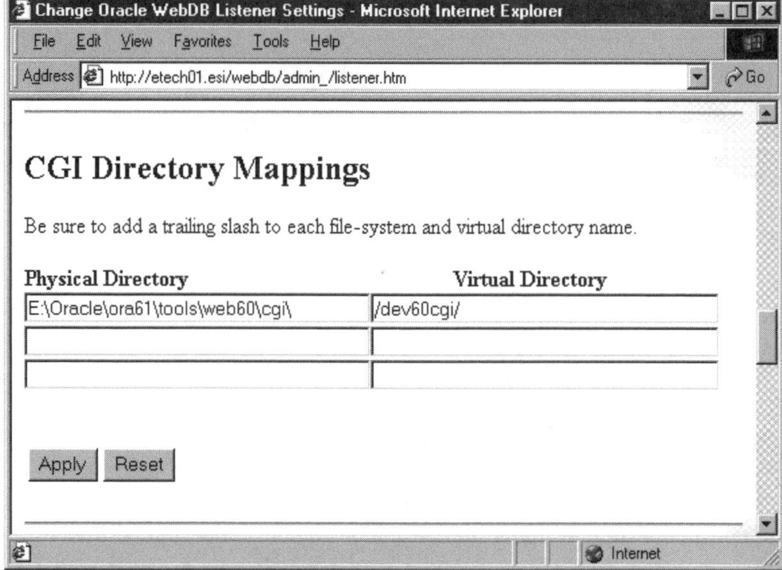

FIGURE 24.15 The WebDB CGI Directory Mappings.

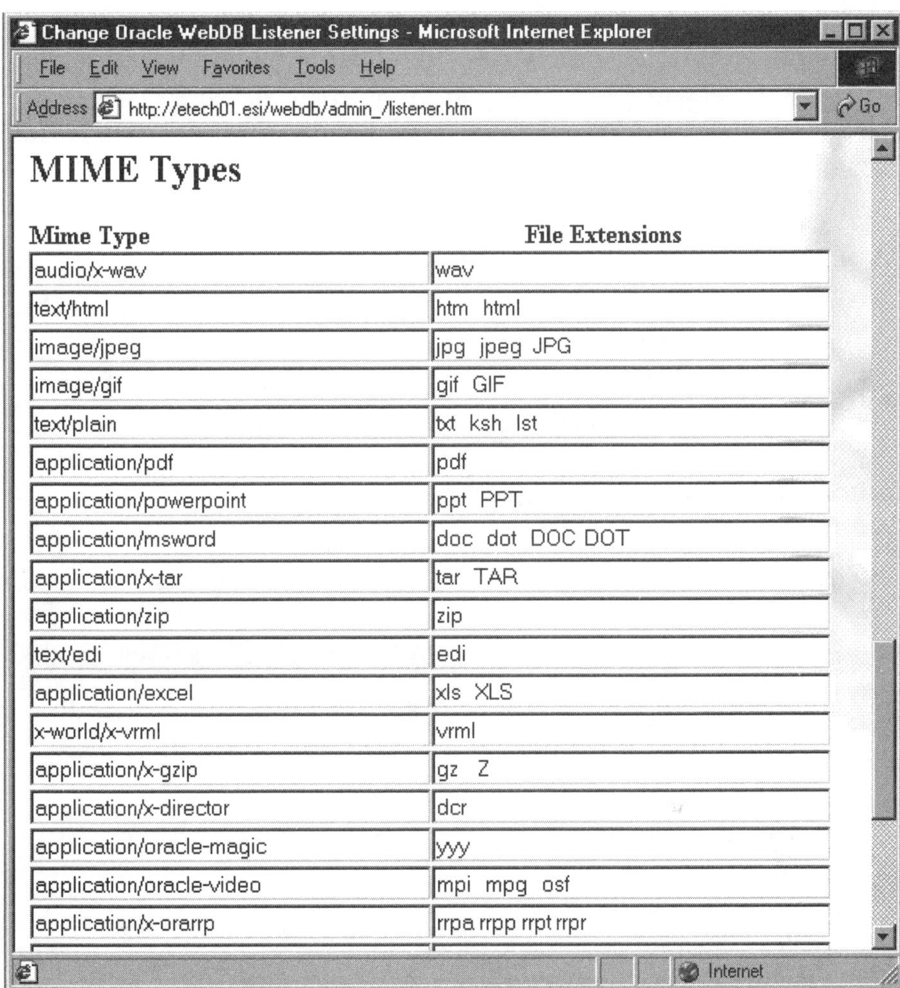

Mime Type	File Extensions
audio/x-wav	wav
text/html	htm html
image/jpeg	jpg jpeg JPG
image/gif	gif GIF
text/plain	txt ksh lst
application/pdf	pdf
application/powerpoint	ppt PPT
application/msword	doc dot DOC DOT
application/x-tar	tar TAR
application/zip	zip
text/edi	edi
application/excel	xls XLS
x-world/x-vrml	vrml
application/x-gzip	gz Z
application/x-director	dcr
application/oracle-magic	yyy
application/oracle-video	mpi mpg osf
application/x-orarrp	rrpa rrpp rrpt rrpr

FIGURE 24.16 The WebDB MIME Types.

3. Switch to the tab Directories of this dialog box. You will see a listing of all the virtual directories defined for this Web server, similar to the one shown on Figure 24.18. Notice here how the physical directory "C:\inetserv\www-root\Albert\web_code" is mapped to the virtual directory "/web_forms." If the HTML file that starts the application is called MRD.HTML and is stored under this directory, users can access it by pointing their Web browser to the URL "http://<domain_name>/web_forms/mrd.html."

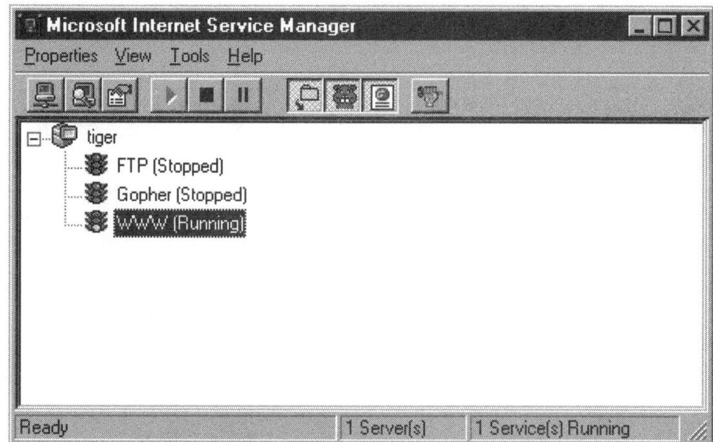

FIGURE 24.17 Microsoft Internet Service Manager.

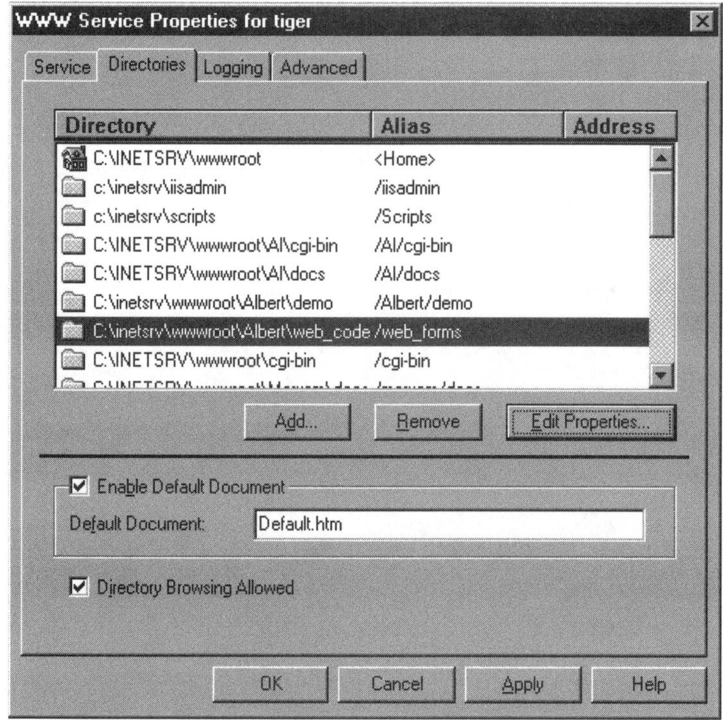

FIGURE 24.18 The WWW Service Properties dialog box.

To add a new virtual directory, click the button Add. In the Directory Properties dialog box specify the physical and virtual name of the directory as shown in Figure 24.19.

Besides defining a virtual directory for the HTML files, it is also recommended that you define the following directories:

- **Applet codebase directory.** This should point to the application server directory where the Forms Client applet searches for Java class files. Physically, this directory is at %ORACLE_HOME%\Forms60\Java, for example, C:\Orant\Forms60\Java. You can map it to a directory like "/web_forms."
- **Java archive files directories.** This should point to the directory where Java archive repository (JAR) files provided by Oracle or other sources are stored. These files are downloaded to the user's browser when the Forms Client applet is started. For each release, the JAR file provided has changed. For Forms 6i, the JAR file that Oracle provides is called f60web.jar and it is stored at %ORACLE_HOME%\Forms60\Java, for example, C:\Orant\Forms60\Java. You have mapped this directory already as the applet code-

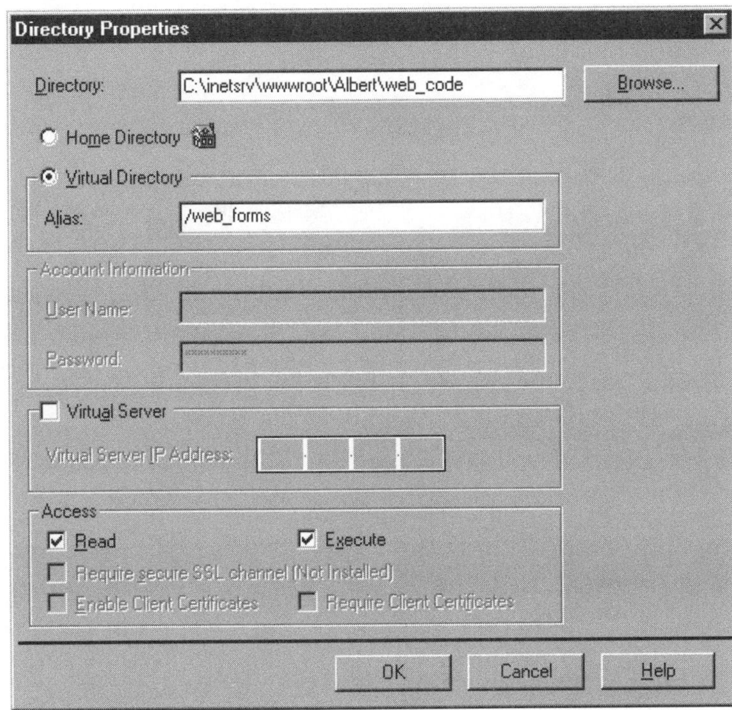

FIGURE 24.19 The Directory Properties dialog box.

base virtual directory. If you have additional JAR files stored, for example, in the directory C:\MRD\Java, you can map this directory to the virtual "/mrd_jars/."

- **Starter HTML files for running forms**. /dev60html/ should be mapped to %ORACLE_HOME%\tools\html\.
- **CGI executables.** /dev60cgi/ should be mapped to %ORACLE_HOME%\tools\web60\cgi\.
- **Jinitiator (for download).** /jinitiator/ should be mapped to %ORACLE_HOME%\jinit\.
- **Forms Temporary Files.** % ORACLE_HOME%\tools\web60\temp\.

As mentioned already, the instructions for downloading the Forms Client applet and executing a particular Form module are stored in an HTML file, located in one of the virtual directories of the Web server. The URL of this file is handed over to the users who access it from their Web browsers. This HTML file can be static or generated dynamically by either the Forms CGI method or the Oracle Application Server Cartridge method. Although still supported, the use of the Oracle Application Server has been deemphasized in favor of the WebDB listener CGI method. The Static and Forms CGI methods are covered in the following two sections. The examples in the following sections are based on the standard WebDB and Forms Server configuration.

24.3.5 STATIC IMPLEMENTATION OF WEB FORMS

In the static implementation, all of the variables in the HTML file are hard coded for your particular form. You begin by copying the file base.htm provided by Developer into the application server directory that will serve as home directory of the application. If you want to use Jinitiator, you should use the basejinit.htm file. The file base.htm is located in the directory %ORACLE_HOME%\Forms60\server. One of the most important sections of this file is the definition of the applet. Figure 24.20 shows an example of this section.

In order to turn base.htm into a useful file, you need to replace all of the variables surrounded by % with values required by your module. You may choose to remove some of the optional parameters as this example shows. The following paragraphs discuss some of the variables that you will most likely change.

- **CODEBASE.** This parameter should point to the virtual directory defined for the Applet codebase, for example, "/forms60java/." Note that, depending on the operating system, the settings of these parameters may be case-sensitive.
- **ARCHIVE.** This parameter points to one or more JAR files to be downloaded to the client when the applet is initialized. To point to the Oracle JAR

```
<!-- Forms applet definition (start) -->
<APPLET CODEBASE="/forms60java/"
        CODE="oracle.forms.engine.Main"
        ARCHIVE="%archive%"
        WIDTH="%Width%"
        HEIGHT="%Height%">

<PARAM NAME="serverPort" VALUE="%serverPort%">
<PARAM NAME="serverHost" VALUE="%serverHost%">
<PARAM NAME="connectMode" VALUE="%connectMode%">
<PARAM NAME="serverArgs"
       VALUE="module=%form% userid=%userid%
%otherParams%">
<PARAM NAME="separateFrame" VALUE="%separateFrame%">
<PARAM NAME="splashScreen"  VALUE="%splashScreen%">
<PARAM NAME="background"  VALUE="%background%">
<PARAM NAME="lookAndFeel"  VALUE="%lookAndFeel%">
<PARAM NAME="colorScheme"  VALUE="%colorScheme%">
<PARAM NAME="serverApp" VALUE="%serverApp%">

</APPLET>
<!-- Forms applet definition (end) -->
```

FIGURE 24.20 Sample applet definition section in the HTML file that launches a Forms module on the Web.

file, for example, you would set this parameter to "/forms60java/f60web.jar." To add to this the file mrd.jar, located in the virtual directory "/mrd_jars/", you would set the ARCHIVE parameter to "/forms60java/f60web.jar, /mrd_jars/mrd.jar." To reduce the form startup time, you may choose to use a smaller jar file with reduced functionality or build your own jar file. You can also package your icons/images into a jar file to be downloaded in one round trip.

- **serverPort.** This is the port number on the application server machine where the applet will send the request to connect to the Forms Server. It is important to synchronize the setting of this parameter with the port number the Forms Server Listener uses to listen to incoming requests.
- **serverArgs.** This argument is used to specify any command line parameters typically passed to the Forms Runtime. The name of the module is normally specified in this parameter. If you provide only the module name, without its location, the Forms Server will look for it in the directory %ORACLE_HOME%\BIN and in any directories specified in the environ-

ment variable FORMS60_PATH, in this sequence. If the module is not located in any of these directories, you need to provide the entire physical path and the name of the module. However, because the HTML file is downloaded to the client machines, by providing the hard-coded path to the module, you can compromise the security of the application server. If there is a default user and database connection for the application, you may save your users some typing by defining them in the setting of the serverArgs parameter. Never provide the password of the account as suggested in the template, unless you want to make this password publicly available.

- **Additional Parameters:** A number of optional parameters are supported by the Forms Server. The most important ones are:
  - connectMode="socket" or "http" or "https"
  - lookAndFeel="Oracle" or "Generic"
  - ColorScheme="teal" or "titanium" or "red" or "khaki" or "blue" or "olive" or "purple" (used if lookAndFeel="Oracle")
  - splashScreen="no" or "xxxx.gif"
  - background="no" or "xxxx.gif"
  - separateFrame="yes" or "no"
  - heartbeat=2 or xx minutes
  - webformsTitle="My_Title"

Figure 24.21 shows the example of the HTML file with the arguments of the template set to the values discussed above.

Once you create the HTML file you need to give its URL to the users so that they can access it from their browsers. There is nothing in the URL that sets it apart from URLs of other pages in your Web site. It will contain the domain name or IP address of the server, the Web server listener port (if not 80), the virtual directory where the HTML file is stored and the name of the HTML file. The following URLs serve as examples:

```
http://www.alulushi.com/web_forms/mrd.html
http://www.alulushi.com:5000/web_forms/mrd_project/start
.html
```

24.3.6 DYNAMIC IMPLEMENTATION OF WEB FORMS

The difference between the dynamic and static implementation of Web Forms resides not on their final outcome—an HTML file that downloads the Forms Client applet and executes a form—but on how they arrive at this outcome. With the static method, you need an HTML page for each combination of values for the arguments of the applet. If you need to change the values of at least one of them, for example, the port number, or module name, or user name, you have to create a new HTML page where the new values are specified. This is similar to coding

```
<!-- applet definition (start) -->
<APPLET CODEBASE="/forms60java/"
        CODE="oracle.forms.uiClient.v1_4.engine.Main"
        ARCHIVE="/forms60java/f60web.jar,
        /mrd_jars/mrd.jar"
        HEIGHT=20
        WIDTH=20>

<PARAM NAME="serverPort"
       VALUE="8001">

<PARAM NAME="serverArgs"
       VALUE="module=mrd.fmx userid=mrd_user@mrddb">

<PARAM NAME="serverApp"
       VALUE="default">

</APPLET>
<!-- applet definition (end) -->
```

FIGURE 24.21 Sample applet definition section in the HTML file that launches a Forms module on the Web.

many additional routines that compute the sum of two specific numbers. It is easy to see how you can end up with a number or routines, like Add_1_2, Add_4_9, Add_123_546, and so on. Obviously, the most elegant solution is to have only one routine Add(n, m) that returns the sum of any two numbers passed as arguments at runtime. The implementation of Forms Web CGI method allows you to achieve exactly this. With it, you define some—or all—the arguments of the Forms Client applet parametrically. The actual values of some of these parameters can be provided at runtime as query parameters in the URL request and other values come from the FORMSWEB.CFG file located in %ORACLE_HOME%\Forms60\server.

Before covering the actual HTML setup, you should understand the FORMSWEB.CFG file configuration file. To provide control of the Forms Server, this editable configuration file is installed and provides parameter values for the Forms Web CGI method. Parameters which effect all of your forms applications should be specified in FORMSWEB.CFG. Parameters specific to only one application should be defined in its HTML file or in the SPECIFIC CONFIGURATIONS section of FORMSWEB.CFG. Variables (%variablename%) can be used in FORMSWEB.CFG but must be either Oracle registry or environmental variables or the special variable %leastloadedhost%. When initially installed the FORMSWEB.CFG file is as shown in Figure 24.22:

```
; Forms Web CGI Configuration File
; ----------------------------
; This file defines parameter values used by the Forms Web CGI

; ********************************
; PARAMETER VALUES USED BY DEFAULT
; ********************************
  ; SYSTEM PARAMETERS
  ; -----------------
  ; These have fixed names and give information required by the Forms
  ; Web CGI in order to function.  They cannot be specified in the URL
    query
  ; string.  But they can be overriden in a named configuration (see
    below).
baseHTML=%FORMS60%\server\base.htm
baseHTMLJInitiator=%FORMS60%\server\basejini.htm
HTMLdelimiter=%
MetricsServerPort=9020
MetricsServerErrorURL=
  ; The next parameter specifies how to execute the Forms applet under
  ; Microsoft Internet Explorer 5.0.  Put IE50=native if you want the
  ; Forms applet to run in the browser's native JVM.
IE50=JInitiator

  ; USER PARAMETERS
  ; ---------------
  ; These match variables (e.g. %form%) in the baseHTML file. Their
    values
  ; may be overridden by specifying them in the URL query string
  ; (e.g.
    "http://myhost.mydomain.com/ifcgi60.exe?form=myform&width=700")
  ; or by overriding them in a specific, named configuration (see
    below)

  ; 1) Runform arguments:
form=test.fmx
userid=
otherparams=

  ; 2) HTML page title, attributes for the BODY tag, and HTML to add
    before and
```

FIGURE 24.22 The default FORMSWEB.CFG file.

```
  ;    after the form:
pageTitle=Oracle Forms Server
HTMLbodyAttrs=
HTMLbeforeForm=
HTMLafterForm=

  ; 3) Values for the Forms applet parameters:
width=650
height=500
separateFrame=false
splashScreen=no
    ; select default background by not specifying a value
background=
lookAndFeel=Oracle
colorScheme=teal
serverApp=default
serverPort=9000
serverHost=
connectMode=Socket
archive=f60web.jar

  ; 4) Parameters for JInitiator
    ; Page displayed to Netscape users to allow them to download
      JInitiator.
    ; If you create your own version, set this parameter to point to
      it.
jinit_download_page=/jinitiator/us/jinit_download.htm
    ; Parameters related to the version of JInitiator.
jinit_classid=clsid:093501ce-d290-11d3-a3d6-00c04fa32518
jinit_exename=jinit.exe#Version=1,1,7,27
jinit_mimetype=application/x-jinit-applet;version=1.1.7.27

; ********************************
; SPECIFIC CONFIGURATIONS
; ********************************
;  You may define your own specific, named configurations (sets of
   parameters)
;  by adding special sections as illustrated in the following
   examples.
;  Note that you need only specify the parameters you want to change.
   The
```

FIGURE 24.22 The default FORMSWEB.CFG file. (Continued)

```
;   default values (defined above) will be used for all other
    parameters.
;   Use of a specific configuration can be requested by including the
    text
;   "config=<your_config_name>" in the query string of the URL used to
    run
;   a form.  For example, to use the sepwin configuration, your could
    issue
;   a URL like "http://myhost.mydomain.com/ifcgi60.exe?config=sepwin".

; Example 1: configuration to run forms in a separate browser window
  with
;            "generic" look and feel (include "config=sepwin" in the
URL)
[sepwin]
separateFrame=True
lookandfeel=Generic

; Example 2: configuration affecting users of MicroSoft Internet
  Explorer 5.0.
;            Forms applet will run under the browser's native JVM
             rather than
;            using Oracle JInitiator.
[ie50native]
IE50=native

; Example 3: configuration forcing use of the base.htm base HTML file
  in all
;            cases (means applet-style tags will always be generated
             and
;            JInitiator will never be used).
[applet]
baseHTMLJInitiator=
```

FIGURE 24.22 The default FORMSWEB.CFG file. (Continued)

The steps required for the CGI implementation of Web Forms are as follows:

1. Modify the formsweb.cfg file to suit your requirements.
2. Create an HTML file by making a copy of base.htm and/or basejini.htm and be sure to rename the file to your desired filename. This file may be in any

directory as long as the baseHTML or baseHTMLJInitiator parameter in the formsweb.cfg contains the full physical path location.

3. Modify your HTML file as required although in most cases you will not need to modify your file.
4. Move your executable forms to the directory as defined in the registry variable FORMS60_PATH.
5. Provide users with URLs for different values of the startup parameters.

These steps will be described in the following paragraphs. FORMSWEB.CFG parameters you will probably want to initially modify include baseHTML, baseHTMLJInitiator, form, pageTitle and various Forms applet text parameters that are visible to the user. If you have a number of applications, you will probably want to include their parameters as specific named configurations under the SPECIFIC CONFIGURATIONS section to reduce the number of query parameters in the URL.

Your copy of the BASE.HTM file should initially look as shown in Figure 24.23.

Variables (%variablename%) in the base HTML file are replaced with parameter values from the formsweb.cfg file and then from any query parameters in the URL. All of the variables in your HTML file must receive a value at runtime or the Forms Server will issue an error. Since you will probably try to achive a consistent look and feel for your applications, you will probably make most modifications to the parameters in the formsweb.cfg file rather than the HTML file. If you don't want to use a parameter tag that is provided in your base.htm file, delete it. Many of the parameters in the formsweb.cfg and base.htm files are self-explanatory and will not be covered in detail here.

After moving your Forms executables to the middle tier, you can provide the user with the required URL to start the application. Your URL might be something like:

```
http://www.alulushi.com:80/dev60cgi/ifcgi60.exe?form=
myform.fmx&colorScheme=purple
```

This URL consists of the following components:

- ❑ Protocol: http
- ❑ Domain: www.alulushi.com
- ❑ Port: 80 (This is the default port number)
- ❑ Virtual CGI directory: /dev60cgi
- ❑ CGI executable file: ifcgi60.exe (The character "?" following indicates that parameters are being passed)

```
<HTML>
<!-- FILE: base.htm (Oracle Developer Forms)                    -->

<!-- This is the default base HTML file for running a form     -->
<!-- on the web using APPLET-style tags to include the         -->
<!-- Forms applet. This file will be REPLACED if you           -->
<!-- reinstall "Forms Web CGI and cartridge", so you are       -->
<!-- advised to make your own version if you want to make      -->
<!-- any modifications.  You should then set the baseHTML      -->
<!-- parameter in the Forms web CGI configuration file         -->
<!-- (formsweb.cfg) to point to your new file instead of       -->
<!-- this one.  -->

<!-- IMPORTANT NOTE: default values for all the variables      -->
<!-- which appear below (delimited by the percent character)-->
<!-- are defined in the formsweb.cfg file. It is preferable -->
<!-- to make changes in that file where possible, and leave -->
<!-- this one untouched.                                       -->

<HEAD><TITLE>%pageTitle%</TITLE></HEAD>

<BODY %HTMLbodyAttrs%>
%HTMLbeforeForm%

<!-- Forms applet definition (start) -->
<APPLET CODEBASE="/forms60java/"
        CODE="oracle.forms.engine.Main"
        ARCHIVE="%archive%"
        WIDTH="%Width%"
        HEIGHT="%Height%">

<PARAM NAME="serverPort" VALUE="%serverPort%">
<PARAM NAME="serverHost" VALUE="%serverHost%">
<PARAM NAME="connectMode" VALUE="%connectMode%">
<PARAM NAME="serverArgs"
       VALUE="module=%form% userid=%userid% %otherParams%">
<PARAM NAME="separateFrame" VALUE="%separateFrame%">
<PARAM NAME="splashScreen"  VALUE="%splashScreen%">
<PARAM NAME="background"  VALUE="%background%">
<PARAM NAME="lookAndFeel"  VALUE="%lookAndFeel%">
<PARAM NAME="colorScheme"  VALUE="%colorScheme%">
```

FIGURE 24.23 The initial BASE.HTM file.

```
<PARAM NAME="serverApp" VALUE="%serverApp%">

</APPLET>
<!-- Forms applet definition (end) -->

%HTMLafterForm%

</BODY>
</HTML>
```

FIGURE 24.23 The initial BASE.HTM file. (Continued)

- Query parameters: form=myform.fmx&colorScheme=purple. (Each parameter=value pair is separated by the character "&").

24.3.7 MAINTAINING THE FORMS SERVER LISTENER

After all the steps described in the previous sections are completed, your modules will be deployed, the Web Forms will be configured, and the users will have URLs to access the modules. The last piece to complete the puzzle is to start up the Forms Server Listener process if not already started and to ensure that is up and running throughout the time users will use the application. Recall that the Forms Server Listener is the utility that receives the initial connection request from the Forms Client applet and opens a connection to the Forms Server on behalf of this request. It then returns the socket information to the applet, which then establishs a direct communication channel with the server. You start up the Forms Server Listener by invoking an executable and, optionally, passing the port number that will be used to listen for incoming requests. If the port number is not specified explicitly, the default port 9000 will be used. Remember that this port number should correspond to the parameter serverPort of the Forms Client applet. The Forms Server can also be installed as an NT service and set to start automatically upon reboot. In Windows NT installations, the location and name of the Listener executable is %ORACLE_HOME\bin\ifsrv60.exe; in the UNIX implementation, it is %ORACLE_HOME/lib/f60srvm.exe.

The Forms Server uses the following environmental variables that you may to add or modify:

- FORMS60_PATH specifies the paths that Forms Server searches when looking for a Form to run.
- FORMS60_OUTPUT is the physical directory in which to store generated reports if your form calls Reports.

- FORMS60_MAPPING is the virtual directory pointing to the physical directory defined by FORMS60_OUTPUT.
- FORMS60_MESSAGE_ENCRYPTION (TRUE or FALSE) controls whether to encrypt Forms messages. Applies to HTTP and socket communication modes. Default is encrypted.
- FORMS60_WALLET is used for HTTPS communications mode only identify the Wallet directory location.
- FORMS60_HTTPS_NEGOTIATE_DOWN is used for HTTPS communications mode only and defaults to FALSE.
- FORMS60_REPFORMAT is the Reports output format (PDF or HTML).

To install and start the Forms Server as a service type the following:

```
ifsrv60 -install <NewFormsServerServiceName>
port=<portNum> mode=<socket/http/https>
[pool=<numOfRunforms> log=<logfilePath>
exe=<RunformexeName>]
```

After the service is started you can monitor its state and start and stop it using Start | Settings | Control Panel | Services as shown in Figure 24.23 and Figure 24.24:

You can stop the service using the NT Service Control panel. To remove an existing Forms Server service type:

```
ifsrv60 -uninstall <FormsServerServiceNameToBeRemoved>
```

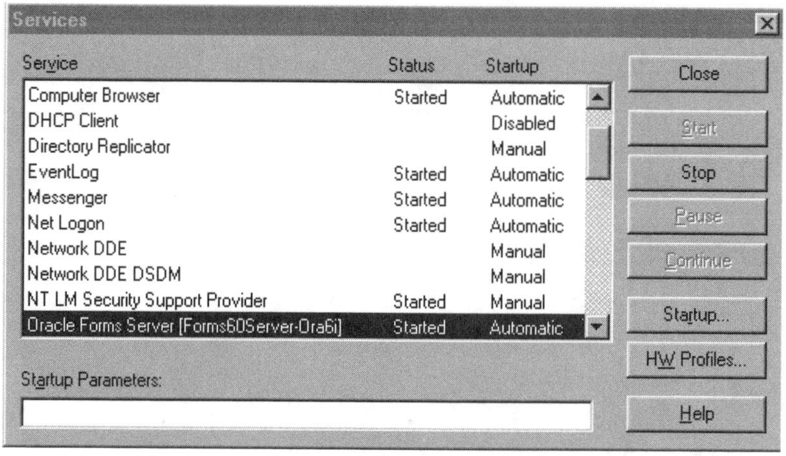

FIGURE 24.24 NT Services showing Forms Server

FIGURE 24.25 Forms Server startup type.

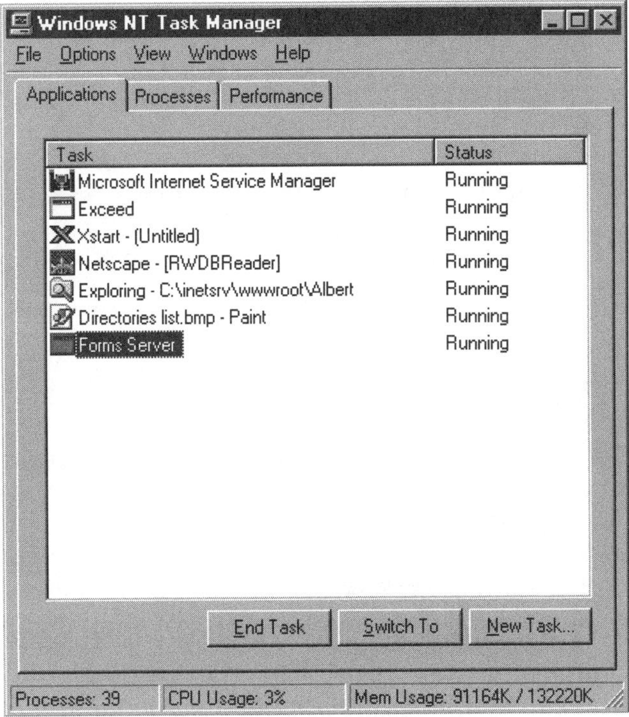

FIGURE 24.26 Using the Task Manager to monitor the Forms Server process.

A temporary Forms Server install may be started from the command line and may be stopped with the NT Task Manager. To start a temporary Forms Server instance type:

```
ifsrv60 port=<portNum> mode=<socket/http/https>
[pool=<numOfRunforms> log=<logfilePath>
exe=<RunformexeName>]
```

After the Listener is started, you can monitor its state and shut it down using the standard utilities of the operating system. In Windows NT, for example, you can use the Task Manager utility. Figure 24.25 shows how the status of Forms Server Listener will appear in this utility. To terminate this process, simply select it in the list and click End Task.

24.4 SPECIAL CONSIDERATIONS FOR DEPLOYING DEVELOPER FORMS ON THE WEB

Many Developer Forms modules are developed and deployed in the traditional client/server architecture that can be deployed on Web by simply compiling them on the application server platform. No changes are required and no special coding is necessary. However, there are Forms features and objects used very successfully in two-tier implementations—especially on Microsoft Windows platforms—that cannot or should not be used for Web deployment. This section describes such features and explains the problems they may cause in a Web deployment of your modules. The restrictions discussed here stem essentially from three reasons:

- ❑ Functionality that modifies the GUI interface of the application through calls to external resources is confined to the application server and therefore, cannot be viewed by the users in the client machines. Because of this limitation, you cannot use forms with embedded ActiveX controls or OLE Documents. You also cannot use forms that make calls to the operating system (through the Foreign Function Interface, user exits, or host commands) with requests that modify the GUI interface of the application.
- ❑ Functionality specific to the Microsoft Windows operating systems is not portable on the Web. This means that any features using DDE and OLE are not portable. The MDI interface is now supported. When implementing iconic toolbars on the Web, keep mind that the icon files must be in GIF or JPG format. By default they should be in GIF format and reside in the same directory as the HTML file. You can change the icon directory by modifying the iconpath parameter in the Registry.dat file stored in the

%ORACLE_HOME%\FORMS60\java\oracle\forms\registry\ directory. You can also change the iconextension parameter to jpg in the same file if you wish to use jpg files.

- A number of features that generate extensive network traffic may be acceptable for a local area network deployment but may drastically degrade the performance of applications on the Web. One example is all the triggers related to mouse events. Given the extensive network traffic they can generate, any PL/SQL associated with such triggers is ignored on the Web. Timers that fire frequently may overload the network traffic unnecessarily and should be kept to a minimum. Finally, image items and boilerplate images will need to be downloaded from the application server to the client, therefore they should be avoided whenever possible and, if they must be used, their sizes should be minimal.
- Since most fonts are not supported across all platforms, use standard fonts when designing your forms. The fonts you use are mapped to their Java equivalents at runtime. When a font is not available on a platform, Forms/Java attempts to use a similar font. Java uses a Font alias list defined in Registry.dat.

Although beyond the scope of this book, Forms Server now fully supports the use of HTTP and HTTPS (SSL). Using HTTPS, you can deploy Forms applications on the Internet securely with 128-bit encryption using the Oracle Wallet Manager (installed with Forms Server)

24.5 SUMMARY

Traditionally, Developer Forms have been deployed in a two-tier, client/server architecture. However, nowadays more and more companies need to deploy their software assets on the Web. The low maintenance and administration cost associated with Web applications, as well as the savings that come from a low-cost, thin client that the Web computing paradigm offers have been two powerful factors that have pushed application development in this direction. Developer for the Web is the flavor of Developer that allows you to deploy Forms, Reports, and Graphics modules on the Web. This chapter focused on the steps you need to take in order to implement and deploy Developer Forms on the Web. The major topics of this chapter included:

- **What Is the Network Computing Architecture?**
- **Developer Forms' Three-Tier Architecture**

Chapter 25

Creating Forms with Designer

The tools to him that can handle them.
—Thomas Carlyle

Designer is the Oracle Corporation's modeling, design, and application generation suite of tools that can be used very successfully to track the requirements of your system, as well as design and generate its modules. A detailed discussion of Designer is certainly beyond the scope of this book. If you are interested to learn more about it, refer to my other book, *Inside Oracle Designer/2000*, published in 1997 by Prentice Hall. In this chapter and the following one, I will only explain how Form Builder modules can be designed and generated using Designer.

Among Designer tools most directly involved with the design and generation of your applications are the Function Hierarchy Diagrammer, the Application Design Transformer, and the Design Editor. During the requirements analysis, the Function Hierarchy Diagrammer is the principal tool for modeling the requirements of your system. The Application Design Transformer converts the user interface requirements into modules, thus providing you with an initial design of your application. The Design Editor allows you to enhance and expand this initial design and to bring it to a level where you can generate fully functional software modules, ready for deployment and use. This chapter will discuss the concept and structure of modules in Designer, as well as some of the major activities you perform with modules in the Design Editor.

25.1 MODULES IN DESIGNER

Modules represent information about a front-end application recorded in the Designer Repository. The ultimate purpose of modules is to generate a software application that meets one or more user interface requirements of your system. The following sections discuss the major types of modules in Designer and methods used to populate the Repository with modules.

25.1.1 TYPES OF MODULES

The most popular way to classify modules in Designer is to group them by the language in which they will implement the user requirements of the application system. The Repository Object Navigator and the Design Navigator use a characteristic icon to denote each module type in the hierarchy tree of objects. Figure 25.1 shows a list of the principal types of modules in Designer, together with their characteristic icons.

The modules listed in Figure 25.1 represent screen or report modules. Designer also allows you to maintain menu modules and libraries of application logic objects—PL/SQL libraries. These modules are intended primarily for use in Developer applications, although they can be implemented for other environments such as the Web. In any case, Designer uses different icons for these modules, independent of the implementation language. Menus are represented by the icon and libraries are represented by the icon .

CHARACTERISTIC ICON	MODULE TYPE
	Developer Forms
	Developer Reports
	Developer Graphics
	Oracle WebServer
VB	Visual Basic

FIGURE 25.1 Characteristic icons for the principal categories of Designer modules.

25.1.2 POPULATING THE REPOSITORY WITH MODULES

One of the methods to populate the Designer Repository with module objects is to use the Application Design Transformer. This tool uses user interface requirements and information about the data model of your application system to create an initial list of candidate modules. The following steps summarize this method:

1. Capture the user interface requirements of the application.
2. Perform data modeling activities to identify the data requirements and data-related business rules of the application system.
3. Define data usages for the user interface functions.
4. Generate an initial logical database design using the Database Design Transformer.
5. Enhance and expand the logical database design in the Design Editor.
6. Create an initial module design using the Application Design Transformer.
7. Accept or reject the candidate modules according to the needs of your application.

The method described above works well in cases when you are developing a new system from scratch. At other times, information systems are developed to replace existing systems that are outdated and no longer meet the requirements of the business community. In such situations, you can recover the design of these front-end software components into application modules stored in the Repository using the Designer Recover Module Design utility. This utility allows you to convert and store in the Repository the definitions of Developer Forms and Reports modules from the file system or a database, as well as Visual Basic project files. Combined with the Recover Database Design tool, this utility provides full support for capturing the state of an application system and modifying and redesigning it. The following steps are required to recover the design of a Developer Form module in the Design Editor:

1. Select Utilities | Recover Design of | Form. The Forms Design Recovery dialog box appears.
2. In the list box Location, select the environment where the module is currently located. Since Developer Forms modules are maintained mostly in the file system, the option selected in this list is normally File.
3. Enter the name and the location of the module in the file system. You can also click Browse... to display a standard Microsoft Windows dialog box that allows you to browse the directory structure of your PC and select the module.
4. Select one of the options in the Recovery Mode radio group. By default, Recover ONLY module design is selected. If you want to also recover any program units or triggers you have built into the module, select the option Recover BOTH module design and application logic.
5. If you selected one of the first two options in the Recovery Mode radio group, enter the name of a new module in the text box Destination Module. If you are updating the application logic of an existing module in the Repository, enter the name of this module in Destination Module.
6. Set the checkbox Create on Diagram after Recovery if you want to display the module in a module diagram after the recovery process is completed.

Now the dialog box Forms Design Recovery should be similar to the one shown in Figure 25.2. In order to set the options of the process, click the button Options... to display the dialog box Forms Design Recovery Options, shown in Figure 25.3. By setting the appropriate check boxes in this dialog box, you can add notes to different module elements, you can instruct the utility to create lookup table usages for the list of values defined in the module, and you can recover the design of control blocks in addition to the design of data blocks. In this dialog box, you can also enter the name and location of a file where the utility writes a report of activities performed during the design recovery process.

After you have set the options of the recovery tool, click Start to begin the process of recovering the design of the selected module in the Repository. The Message Window of the Design Editor will display the messages generated by the process, as well as any errors or warnings encountered. When the recovery is complete, you are prompted to save the new module in the repository, to revert the changes, or to go to the Design Editor and review the changes individually. If you set the option to generate a report, you may also review this report to see a log of all the actions performed. Excerpts from such a report are shown in Figure 25.4.

Figure 25.4 shows some of the elements of a module that the Design Recovery utility creates in the Repository, based on the properties of the recovered module. These elements include the module definition itself, module components, windows, bound and unbound items, and so on. Section 25.2 provides more details about these elements.

So far, I have presented two methods of populating the Repository with modules. Both methods are automated to a good degree by Designer utilities.

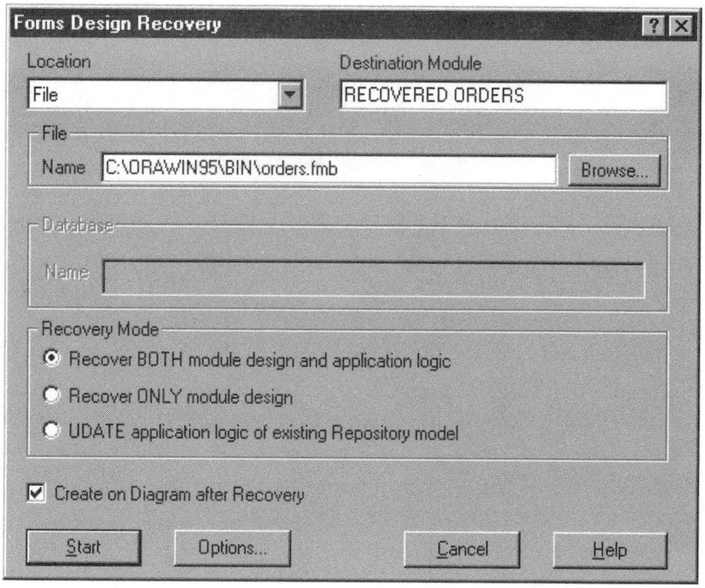

FIGURE 25.2 The Forms Design Recovery dialog box.

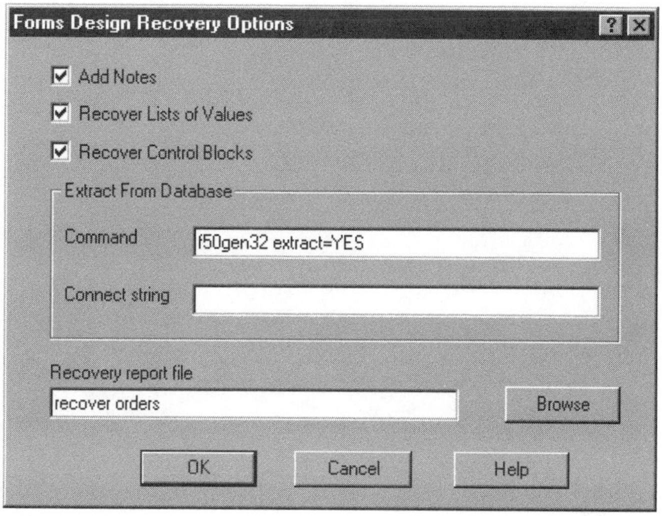

FIGURE 25.3 The Forms Design Recovery Options dialog box.

```
CREATE WINDOW - ROOT_WINDOW from
Title:Order Maintenance Form

CREATE MODULE COMPONENT - ORD1 from
Insert:True  Update:True  Query:True  Delete:True

CREATE MODULE DETAILED TABLE USAGE - ORD1 from
Table:ORDERS Type:BASE

CREATE ITEM - ORDER_NUMBER from
Column:ORDER_NUMBER Type:BASE
Display:True  Insert:True  Update:False  Query:True
Nullify:False
Display Datatype: Display Width:6 Display Height:1
Prompt:Order Number
Hint Text:The unique identifier for an order.
Order By Sequence:1
Justification:2

CREATE ITEM - CUSTOMER from
Column:CUSTOMER Type:UNBOUND
Display:True  Insert:True  Update:True  Query:True
Nullify:False
Display Datatype: Display Width:48 Display Height:1
Prompt:Customer
Hint Text:The name of the customer placing the order.
Order By Sequence:1
Justification:1
```

FIGURE 25.4 Excerpts from a report of the Forms Design Recovery utility.

When everything else fails, you can always create the modules manually in the Design Editor. Section 25.3 discusses this process.

25.2 STRUCTURE OF MODULES

You can look at the structure of a module in two ways:

- **Data view.** The elements that are part of the data view of a module describe the interaction of the modules with sources of data, such as database objects.

- **Display view.** The elements that make up the display view of a module describe the layout of the user and how the users will interact with the data elements of the module.

The Module Diagrammer component of the Design Wizard allows you to represent visually the data and display views of a module. The Design Navigator, on the other hand, maintains the objects that are part of each view under separate nodes in the hierarchy of a module. The names of these nodes are Data View and Display View. The following sections describe the module elements that are parts of each view.

25.2.1 THE DATA VIEW OF A MODULE

The data view of a module, as the name implies, represents the module elements as they appear from the database interaction perspective, without any consideration of the layout or the position of these elements. Figure 25.5 shows the major elements of this view. Each of these elements is described in the following paragraphs:

- **Module component.** Module components are groupings of data items that can be maintained, addressed, and used independently in Designer modules. A module component is characterized by the types of operations it performs on its data elements and by the way these elements are organized in the user interface. The power of the module components as design elements resides in the fact that they bundle together data items, data relationships, application logic, and layout properties. With respect to their use in modules, you can divide module components into reusable and specific module components. Reusable module components extend the concept of software reusability into reusability of design. They are module components that are designed, stored, and maintained independently of any module. When needed, these components can be included in any module that requires the functionality they offer. When the module component is used in the context of a given module, it is called a specific module component. As you progress in the design efforts of your application system, carefully identify those module components that have potential for reuse and store them as reusable components. If you do this process consistently and to a reasonable extent, you will reach a point where you will be able to create new modules by simply assembling components used by other modules, without having to go though the pain of building everything from the scratch.
- **Module component table usages.** Table usages represent the items from a database table used within a module component. A module component is not required to contain a table usage, in which case it is known as a *control*

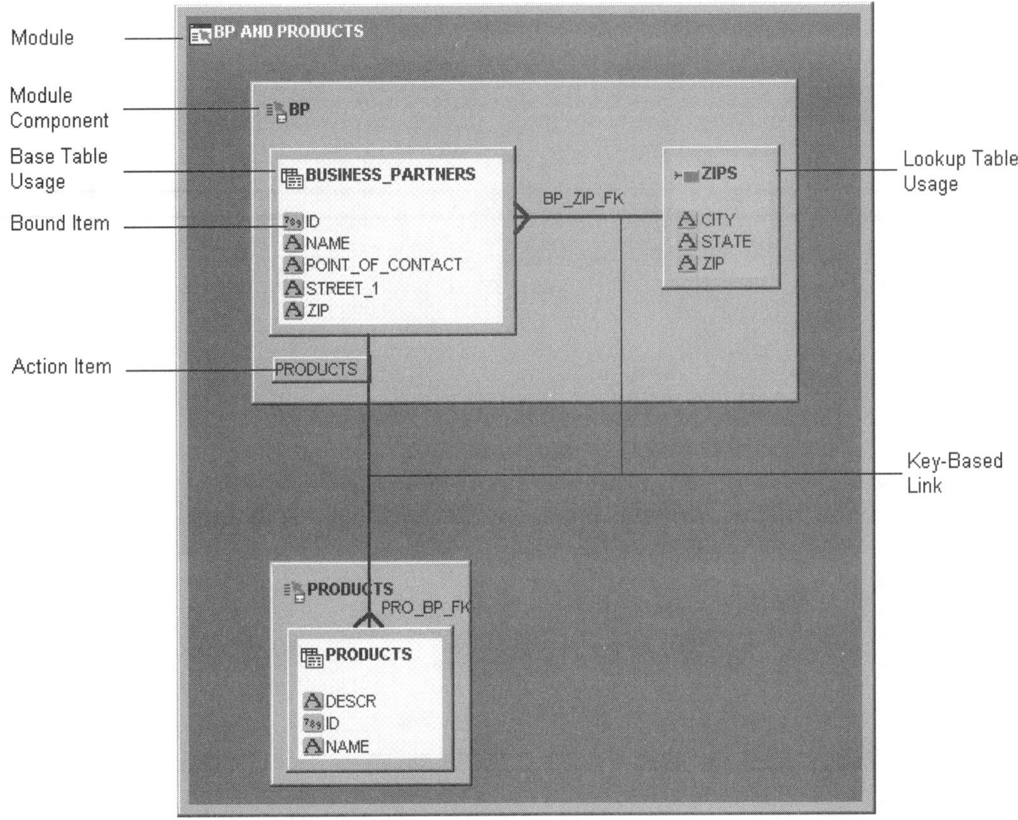

FIGURE 25.5 The major elements in the data view of a module.

module component. However, when the module component contains table usages, one of them must be a base table usage, which shapes the characteristics of the module components. It is complemented by lookup table usages, which are another type of table usages. Occasionally, and in certain types of report modules, like the Developer Reports modules, you may encounter table usages that represent nested SELECT statements or computations of SQL group functions, like SUM, COUNT, MIN, and MAX, for each record of the base table usage.

- **Module component links.** These links represent associations that module components inherit because of associations that exist between their base table usages. They are divided into key-based links and shared-data links. Key-based links are very common and occur in every type of module. They can be established between two module components as long as a foreign key constraint is defined between the underlying base table usages of these components. Shared-data links are encountered only in Developer Forms and Developer Reports modules that contain a chart component embedded in them. If the module components pass data to the chart component for graphical display, the relationship is represented by a shared-data link.

> **TIP**
>
> The data view of module diagrams also displays links between modules, like the one shown in Figure 25.5. These links are intended to visually represent the calling relationship that exists between modules in your application system. They are very typical for menu modules and less common in other types of modules. The example in Figure 25.5 shows a menu item calling a screen module.

- **Items.** Items represent containers of data used in the application system. When the items correspond to a database column, they are called *bound items.* An item whose value is not directly associated with a database column is called an *unbound item* and relates to a control item in Developer. A third category of items, *action items,* represents push buttons that allow users to perform some action implemented by the application logic associated with the item. They can also be used to implement navigational buttons to components within the module or to different modules. Bound items are owned by a module component table usage. Graphically, they are presented within the boundaries of the parent table usage. Unbound and action items on the other hand, are owned by the module component. Therefore, they are shown on data diagrams within the boundaries of the module component but outside any table usage.

25.2.2 THE DISPLAY VIEW OF A MODULE

The display view of a module displays the elements of a module from the layout and user interface perspective. Two module elements shared between the display and data views are the module component and the items. Figure 25.6 shows the display view of the same module shown in Figure 25.5 in its data view. By comparing these two figures, you can easily identify the modules and the common items between the two views. Note, however, the following difference in the way items are represented in the display view:

- Table usages of module components are not shown in display mode.
- No distinction exists between bound or unbound items in display view.
- Only the items that are displayable are shown in display view.
- The characteristic icon of each item in data view represents its data type,

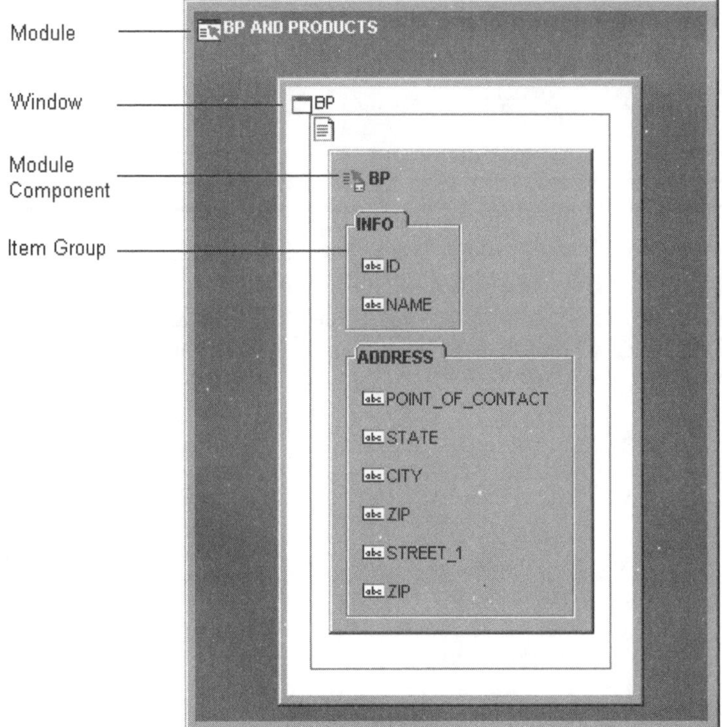

FIGURE 25.6 The major elements in the display view of a module.

such as alphanumeric, number, or date; the characteristic icon of the same item in display view represents the display type of the item, such as text item, list box, or radio group.

Two important elements of a module are present in the display view of the module. They are windows and item groups. The following paragraphs describe these elements:

- **Windows.** Windows are the GUI containers of all the displayed items of a module. A module may contain multiple windows, and a window may contain multiple module components. Windows represent different objects for different types of modules. They represent windows in Developer Forms, the entire report in Developer Reports, layers in Developer Graphics, forms in Visual Basic applications, and HTML pages in WebServer modules.
- **Item groups.** As the name implies, item groups are a way to group together different displayed items of a module component. The main purpose for bundling items in a group is so that they are considered as one layout item

by the front-end generator. They serve the purpose of displaying logically-related data items. Item groups can be laid out individually in the window, or can be stacked in the same area of the window. In the case of stacked item groups, only one group can be visible at any one moment. The principal use of stacked items is to implement tabbed property controls in your Developer Forms and Visual Basic modules.

25.2.3 MODULE APPLICATION LOGIC

Important components of a module are application logic elements that can be associated with the entire module or with elements of the module. *Application logic* is the term that encompasses the code generated by the front-end generators and the code that you associate with different elements of the module. Events and named routines are two categories of application logic objects maintained in the Design Editor. The front-end generators create events and named routines based on the properties of the modules defined in the Repository and on a number of other sources, like object libraries and templates. You have the opportunity to add your own specific programmatic structures to the ones created by the generators, by associating the code with events and named routines in the Repository. For environments like Developer Forms, Reports, and Graphics, events correspond to triggers, and named routines correspond to program units.

25.3 WORKING WITH MODULES

Section 25.1.2 provided an overview of the three methods used to populate the Designer Repository with modules and provided the general steps for performing two of them: creating modules using the Application Design Transformer and recovering the design of existing modules using the Module Design Recovery utility. In the following sections, I will discuss the process of creating and maintaining modules in the Design Editor.

25.3.1 THE MODULE APPLICATION GUIDE

The Module Application Guide is a powerful tool that guides you through the process of creating and maintaining the design of your modules. To access this guide in the Design Editor, select Tools | Application Module Guide.... The entry screen of the tool is shown in Figure 25.7. From this screen, you perform one of the following actions:

- ❑ Create and edit modules in the application system.
- ❑ Recover the design of existing modules by running the Module Design Recovery utility.

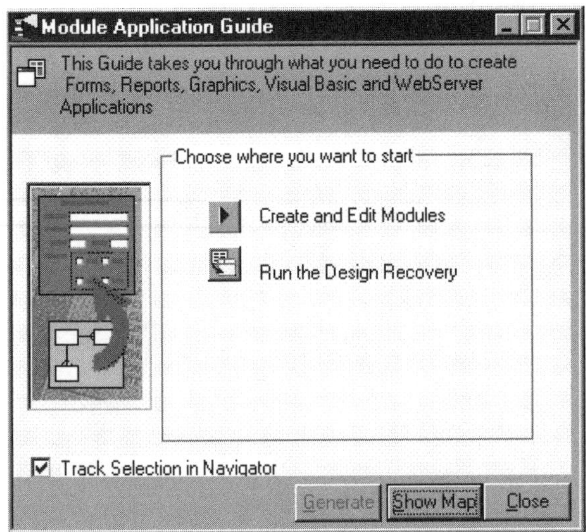

FIGURE 25.7 The entry screen of the Module Application Guide.

If you click the icon ▶, the entry screen of the guide is replaced with a screen that lists the three categories of module elements you can create and maintain in the Design Editor: Modules, Module Components, and Menus. By clicking this icon, you can move to the next level of action you can perform in this guide. The titles of the categories of objects are hyperlinks to the Designer online help for the category.

Figure 25.8 shows the screen that is displayed if you choose to proceed with the process of creating and editing modules. The list control in the center of the screen displays all the modules defined in the repository. From this screen, you can perform one of the following actions:

- Create a new module by clicking New….
- Display the properties of a module by selecting it in the list and clicking Edit…. You can also double-click to bring up the Edit Module dialog box, where these properties are maintained.
- Display a module in its module diagram by selecting it in the list and clicking Diagram….
- Delete one or more modules by selecting them in the list and clicking Delete….
- Invoke the appropriate front-end generator for a module by selecting it and clicking Generate.

Similar actions may be performed on other screens where elements of modules are displayed. Buttons like Diagram or Generate will be disabled where the context does not allow you to perform the functions that they represent. If the currently se-

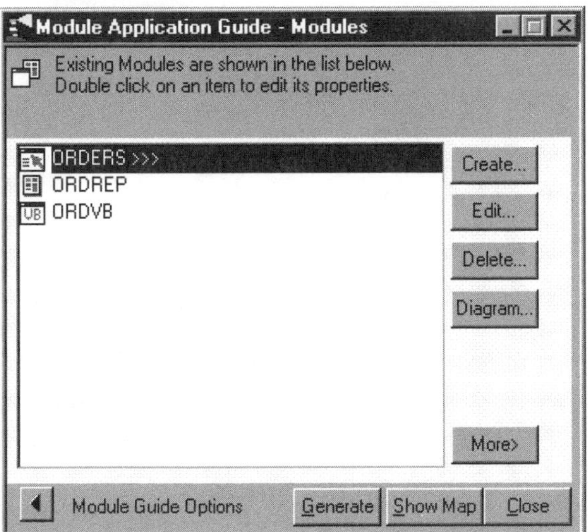

FIGURE 25.8 The Modules screen of the Module Application Guide.

lected object contains other categories of objects within its definition, its name is followed by the characters >>>, as shown in Figure 25.8 for the case of the modules ORDERS >>>. To view the categories of these objects, click the button More>. In each screen, you can click the icon to return to the previous screen of the guide.

The Module Application Guide is a very effective tool to navigate up and down the hierarchy module elements. It also provides a Map component that allows you to jump from one area of the hierarchy onto another. In order to display the map, click the button Show Map on the screen. Figure 25.9 shows the hierarchy tree representation of the module elements you can maintain in the Design Editor. Each push button on the map represents a screen of the Module Application Guide. If the button is enabled, you can navigate to its associated screen immediately, by clicking the button. If the button is not enabled, the context of the current screen is such that it does not allow navigation to that particular element. In the example shown in Figure 25.9, the nodes Data, Items, and Groups under the Reusable Component button are not enabled because the context of the guide is the modules defined in the Repository. If you switch the context to the reusable components of the application system and select one such object from the list, the nodes mentioned earlier will be enabled.

25.3.2 CREATING AND MAINTAINING MODULES

The process of creating modules is simple and, despite some differences between different types of modules, can be summarized as follows:

1. Invoke the Create Module dialog box. You can invoke this dialog by using the Module Application Guide as explained in the previous section or in a

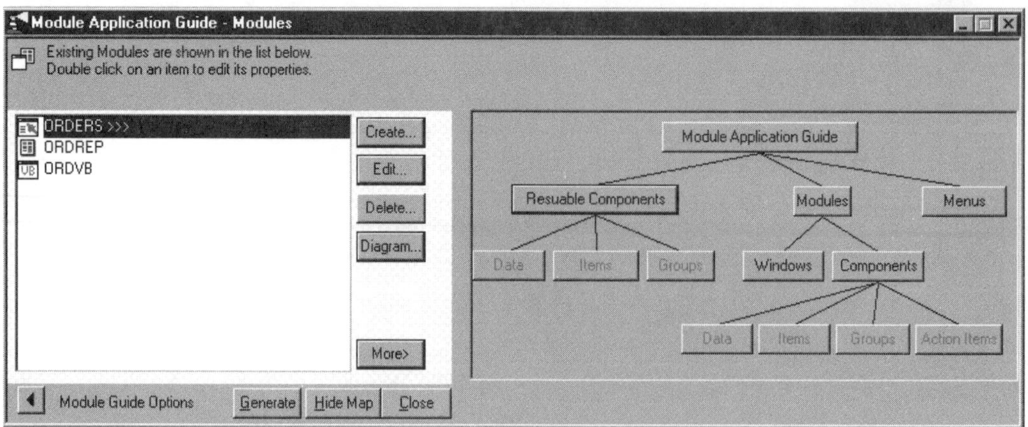

FIGURE 25.9 The Module Application Guide with the map.

more conventional way by selecting the node Modules on the tab with the same name of the Design Navigator and then clicking the icon Create.

2. Set the properties of the new module on the first tab of the dialog. Among the most important properties you set in this step are the short name and the implementation language of the module. Figure 25.10 shows an example of the settings on this tab.
3. Click Finish to complete the process.

You could also click Next to enter other properties of the new module; however, I recommend that you quickly create the modules you need to add in the application system, and then complete the definition of their properties in the Edit Module dialog box. You can invoke this dialog box by double-clicking the module in the Design Navigator, provided that the Design Editor is in the "Show Dialogs" mode. If the module is presented in a data diagram, you can display its property dialog box by double-clicking the module frame on the diagram.

The Edit Module dialog box is composed of multiple property tabs. The number of these tabs depends on the language selected to implement the module. The first tab of the Edit Module dialog box for every module type is the tab Name with the same properties and layout as Figure 25.10. In addition, every module contains a tab that allows you to associate user help about the module, and another one that allows you to associate the current module with other modules. Where appropriate, some modules, like Developer Reports and Graphics, contain a tab to enter parameters; some other modules contain a tab that allows you to maintain the title for the module, which may become the title of the report in the case of Developer Reports, the title of the HTML page in the case of Oracle WebServer, or the title of the generated form in the case of Visual Basic modules. The

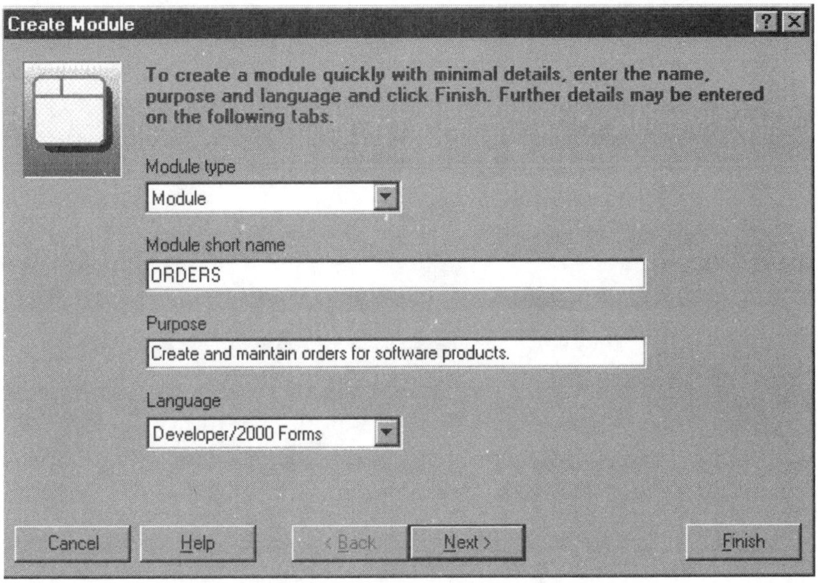

FIGURE 25.10 The Create Module dialog box.

following sections discuss the most important properties you maintain for modules.

25.3.3 MAINTAINING HELP CONTENTS

For software modules that will be deployed on Microsoft Windows platforms, such as Developer Forms, Visual Basic, and Oracle Power Objects modules, the best method to provide user help is to compile it in the form of Microsoft Help files integrated with the applications. In order to prepare for the generation of such files, you need to enter the help content as you refine the design of your application modules. The Help tab in the Edit Module dialog box allows you to associate help information with the module. Figure 25.11 shows an example of this tab.

As you can see from Figure 25.11, you enter two types of text in the Help text item of this tab. First you enter a description of the module that the users will see when they request help for the module. Then you enter the keywords to enable the search of this help page. Each keyword or phrase must be in a separate line and preceded by the characters "@@" to be recognized. In addition, you may also specify an image file that will be included in the help page for the module.

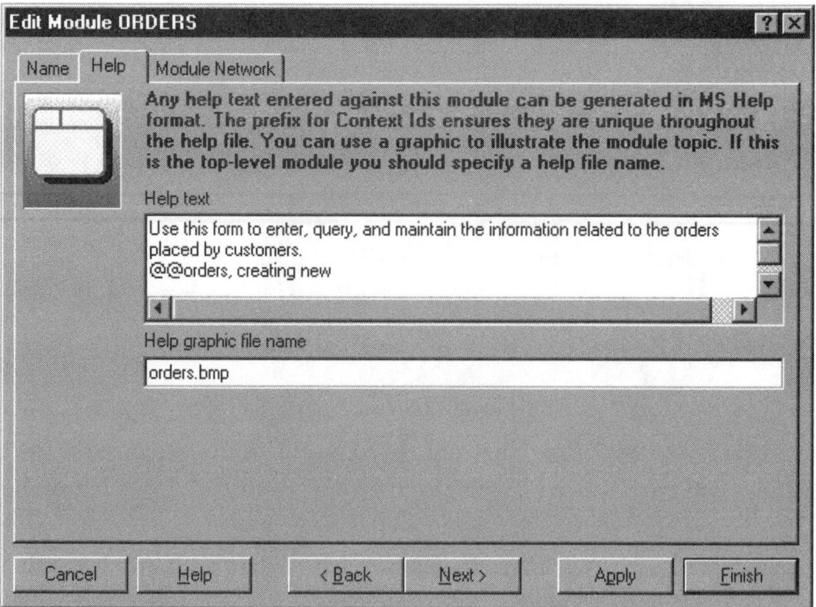

FIGURE 25.11 The Help tab of the Edit Module dialog box.

25.3.4 CREATING AND MAINTAINING MODULE ASSOCIATIONS

Various modules in the application system you develop may be associated to form what is called a module network. Menu modules, for example, may call screen or report modules, screen modules may invoke other screen or report modules, a library module may be linked to a Developer Forms module, and so on. The tab Module Network allows you to create and maintain associations of the current module with other modules. Figure 25.12 shows an example of this tab in which the library ORD_APPL_LOGIC is associated with the module ORDERS.

To create an association between the current module and an existing module, click Select Modules… and choose the desired module to link from the dialog box that appears. You can also type the name of a new module in the text item Called Modules to create a new module and association at the same time.

> **TIP**
>
> In certain circumstances, you may find very useful the ability to create new modules and associate them with the current module on the Module Network tab of the Edit Module dialog box. For example, you could use it to build the menu structure of your application with all the submenus and menu items that call the appropriate screen or report modules.

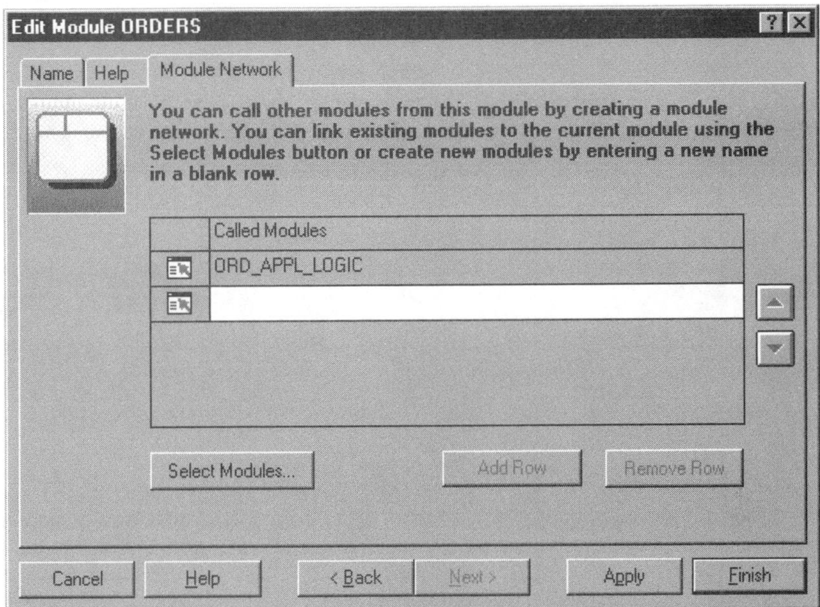

FIGURE 25.12 The Module Network tab of the Edit Module dialog box.

25.3.5 MAINTAINING MODULE ARGUMENTS

In general, you can create arguments for any of the Developer modules; however, they are mostly used in Developer Reports and Developer Graphics modules, where they are called *parameters*. The Parameters tab of the Edit Module dialog is where you can create and maintain the parameters of a report or chart module. Figure 25.13 shows an example of this tab.

To create a new parameter, click Add, and then place the cursor inside the text box Name and type the name of the parameter. In the controls to the right, you can enter the label that users will see for this parameter, pick its data type, and set the maximum length when applicable. You can inherit these last two properties from a domain already defined in your Repository. To select the domain, click the button Domain…, and choose it from the list of domains that appears.

25.3.6 COPYING MODULES

Yet another way to expand the module portfolio of your application system with new modules is to copy existing modules. In order to copy a module in the Design Editor, you need to select it in the Design Navigator and then choose Utilities | Copy. This operation brings up the Copy Objects dialog box, whose functionality was discussed in Chapter 5. In the case of modules, the Design Editor

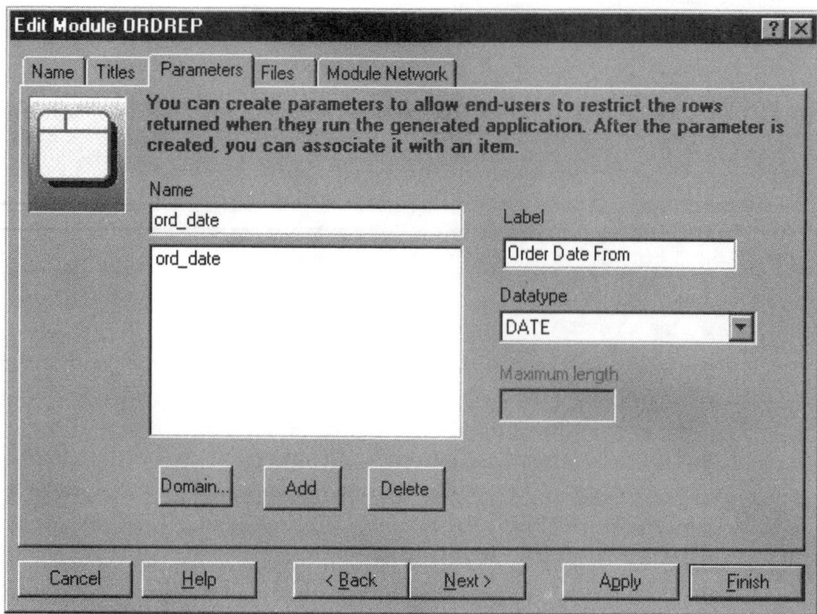

FIGURE 25.13 The Parameters tab of the Edit Module dialog box.

offers a twist to the copy procedure that allows you to recast a module implemented in one language into modules of other languages. For example, you could copy a Developer Forms module into an Oracle WebServer or Visual Basic module, and vice versa. The following are the steps you need to follow to accomplish this task:

1. Select the source module in the Design Navigator.
2. Select Utilities | Copy with New Language.... The dialog box Create As Copy appears.
3. Enter the new name of the module and select the implementation language for the new module as shown in Figure 25.14.
4. Click OK.

The process of copying a module with a new language is really advantageous in the following cases:

- When you are required to implement the module in multiple environments, for example Developer and Visual Basic. In this case, you could analyze the user requirements in a unified way and use the Application Design Transformer to create the initial module design for one language. Using the utility

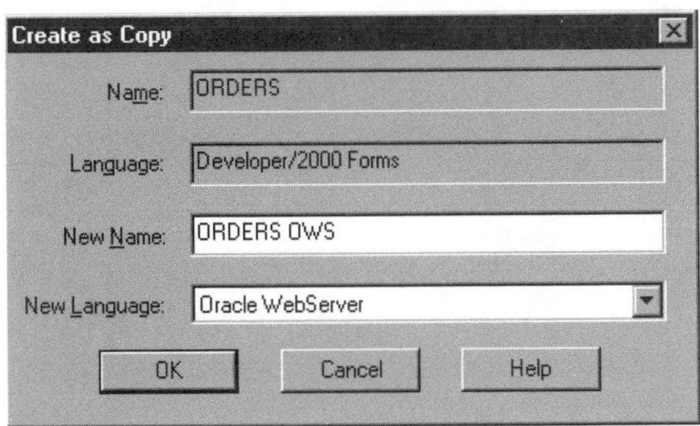

FIGURE 25.14 The Create as Copy dialog box.

described above, you could then create the modules for the second implementation language with minimal effort.

- When you are required to implement an existing application system into a new environment. In this situation, you could recover the design of the current modules, for example Developer modules, copy these modules with the new language implementation, for example Oracle WebServer, and then generate the modules in the new environment. This approach is followed quite often to Web-enable a number of client/server applications.

> **TIP**
>
> Be sure to understand that when you copy a module from one language implementation to another, inevitably, details will be lost. If, for example, you have recorded application logic in a Developer Forms module and copy it as a WebServer module, the application logic will not be carried over, due to the different event models of these tools.

25.3.7 DEVELOPER MODULE SECURITY

When designing Developer applications, you can combine the Developer Menus security roles with the Oracle database users and roles to control the access to modules invoked by the menu items. The following steps allow you to grant access for a module to a database user:

1. Expand the node that represents the user and select the node Security.
2. Click the icon Create. The dialog box Oracle User Module Accesses for Module appears (see Figure 25.15). In this dialog box, the list to the left represents the Oracle database users who do not have access to the module; the list to the right represents those users who already have access.

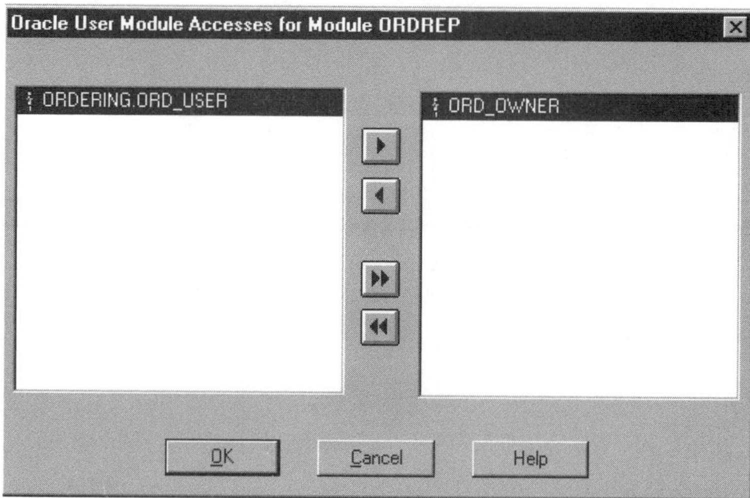

FIGURE 25.15 The Oracle User Module Accesses for Module dialog box.

3. Perform the familiar operations to move a database user from the list to the left, to the list to the right, thus effectively granting her access to the module.
4. Click OK.

Similar actions can be performed to grant access to a role. I mentioned that a condition for implementing user security rules with the method described above is that the modules should be Developer modules. In fact, modules of other types do not even have a node called Security under their hierarchy. Even for Developer modules, the following two conditions must be met in order for the generators to implement these rules:

- The module should be invoked from a menu module.
- The database user or role associations should be created not only for the module in question, but also for all the ancestor menu modules that are used to access the module.

25.4 CREATING AND MAINTAINING MODULE ELEMENTS

During the design of your application system, you will need to add new elements to modules or maintain the properties of existing ones. Like every other activity required during the application design, you can perform these actions in the Design

Navigator. However, displaying the modules in the Data Diagrammer component of the Design Editor and accessing these functions from its interface is more intuitive. The following sections discuss ways and methods to perform these tasks efficiently in module diagrams. In particular, they focus on these topics:

- ❑ Displaying modules in module diagrams.
- ❑ Creating module elements in the module diagram.
- ❑ Maintaining the properties of module elements in the module diagram.

25.4.1 DISPLAYING MODULES IN DIAGRAMS

One way to create a module diagram is to select File | New | Module Diagram… from the Design Editor's menu. The dialog box that comes up as a result of this action contains a list of all the modules defined in the Repository. To complete the action, select one of them and click OK. Another method is to expand the hierarchy tree of the Design Navigator until you see the desired module, and then right-click the module. From the pop-up menu that appears, select the item Show On Diagram.

Module diagrams in the Design Editor come in two flavors. They can show the data view or the display view of the elements of a module. In data view, the module diagram allows you to create, view, and edit module components, their table usages, including base and lookup usages, the bound items that are part of the table usages, and the unbound and action items that are part of the component. In the diagram's data view, you can also see the key-based links, the shared-data links, or the module links of a module. In order to display the data view of a module diagram, select View | Data View or click the icon Switch to Data View.

The diagram in display view is used to maintain the layout elements of the module. Although you can use it to access and maintain the properties of module components and items, the display view is used primarily to create and maintain properties of windows and item groups. To show a module diagram in display view, select View | Display View or click the icon Switch to Display View.

25.4.2 CREATING MODULE ELEMENTS

The tool palette of the Module Diagrammer offers a number of iconic tools that can be used to create the different elements that make up the module. The following paragraphs describe the steps to create each of these elements. These paragraphs will list only the minimal properties you need to set in order to create the element. The remaining properties are discussed in Sections 25.4.3 through 25.4.8.

The following elements can be created in the data view of the module diagram:

- ❑ **Module components.** To create a new module component, select the icon Create Specific Component and click the module on the diagram. In the

Create Module Component dialog box that appears, enter the name and language implementation of the component. Optionally, you may also enter a title that will be used to identify the component on the screen or the report. Click Next to move to the other tabs where you can set additional properties of the module component, or click Finish to complete the process. If you want to include a reusable component in the module, select the icon Include Reusable Component and click the module object on the diagram. In the dialog box Include Module Component that appears, select the desired component and click OK.

> **TIP**
>
> When you select one of the icons on the tool palette, you will notice that the mouse cursor will indicate the areas on the diagram where you can and cannot create the new element.

- **Table usages.** To create a new module component table usage, select the icon Create Table Usage and click inside the module component that will own this table. If the module component does not contain any table usages, this action will invoke the Create Base Table Usage dialog box. In this dialog, select the name of the base object for the component from the list of tables, views, and snapshots in the Repository, and click Finish. If the component has a base table usage defined already, the action above will invoke the Create Table Lookup Usage dialog box. This dialog box displays a list of the database objects that are referenced by a foreign key of the base table usage of the component. Select one of the objects from the list and click Finish.
- **Key-based links.** If two base table usages share a foreign key constraint, you can implement that constraint in the form of a key-based link between these usages. To create such a link, select the icon Create Links and click the parent table first and then the detail table. The link is automatically shown on the diagram.

> **TIP**
>
> The link may not necessarily go from the "One" end to the "Many" end of the foreign key constraint. You can have a link whose source is the detail record and the destination the parent record, identified by the value of the primary key that is recorded in the foreign key column of the detail record.

- **Items.** To create a bound item, select the icon Create Item and click a table usage on the diagram. In the dialog box Create Bound Item that appears, select the column on which the bound item will be based and provide the name of the new item. To create an unbound item, select the icon Create Item and click inside the module component, but outside any table usage of this component. Provide the item name and type in the dialog box Create Unbound Item and click Finish. Finally, action items can be created by selecting the icon Create Action Item and clicking the module component that will own the item. In the dialog box Create Navigation Action Item that appears, choose the type of action that the action will perform and click Finish.

The following elements are created in the display view of the module diagram:

- **Windows.** To create a window, select the icon Window and then click the module on the diagram. In order to place one or more module components in the new window, draw a rectangle on the diagram that includes these components.
- **Item groups.** To create a group of items and populate it with elements at the same time, select the items on the diagram and click the icon Create Group . In the dialog box Create Item Group that appears, enter the name and label of the item group and choose whether the item group is stacked or not.

As I mentioned earlier, the procedures described in this section allow you to simply create the elements of the module, without worrying much about properties other than what is absolutely required to insert the element in the Repository. Sections 25.4.3 through 25.4.8 describe the most important properties of these objects.

25.4.3 MAINTAINING MODULE COMPONENTS

The properties of module components are maintained in the Edit Module Component dialog box displayed when you double-click the object in the diagram or in the Design Navigator. Except for a few differences, modules implemented in different languages have common property tabs, some of which are discussed in the following paragraphs:

- **Operations.** The purpose of this tab is to allow you to specify whether the base table usage of this module will allow users to perform the four basic operations: Insert, Update, Delete, and Query. This tab is common for all the modules that are used to implement screens. For modules implemented with tools like Developer Reports and Developer Graphics, the only operation is Select, therefore this tab is not present. Figure 25.16 shows an example of the Operations tab for a Developer Forms module. Notice that for this type of module, the source and destination of data may be objects other

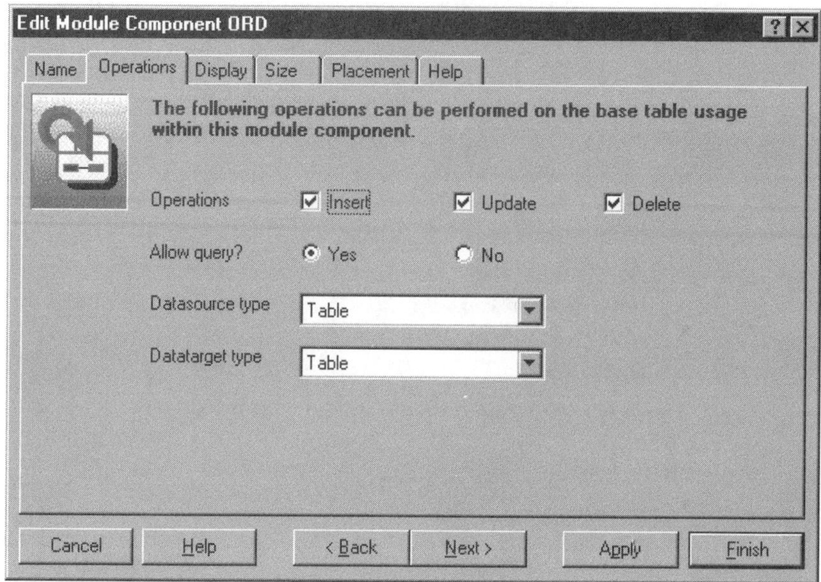

FIGURE 25.16 The Operations tab of the Edit Module Component dialog box.

than database tables. To populate the data block that corresponds to the module component, Developer allows you to query a table, or to use a stored procedure or a transactional trigger. Likewise, the changes and modifications to the data may be sent directly to the table or through a stored procedure or transactional triggers. The list boxes Datasource type and Datatarget type in Figure 25.16 allow you to specify these behaviors of the data block that will be created by the Developer Forms Generator.

- **Display.** This property tab is used primarily to define the number of records that the generated module component will accommodate on the screen or report. Usually, components with a form layout display the data one record at a time. Components that display multiple records should not display more than 5–8 records at a time, unless they occupy the entire window. Another important control on this tab is the list box Overflow Style. The setting of this control provides instructions to the front-end generators about the layout of the items they create. Two options in this list are most often used: Wrap line is used to give the data block in the generated module a form layout; Spread table is used to present the data block in tabular format, in the form of a spread table. Figure 25.17 shows an example of the Display tab.
- **Placement.** This tab essentially allows you to control what you already see in the diagram of a module: whether a module component is placed in a

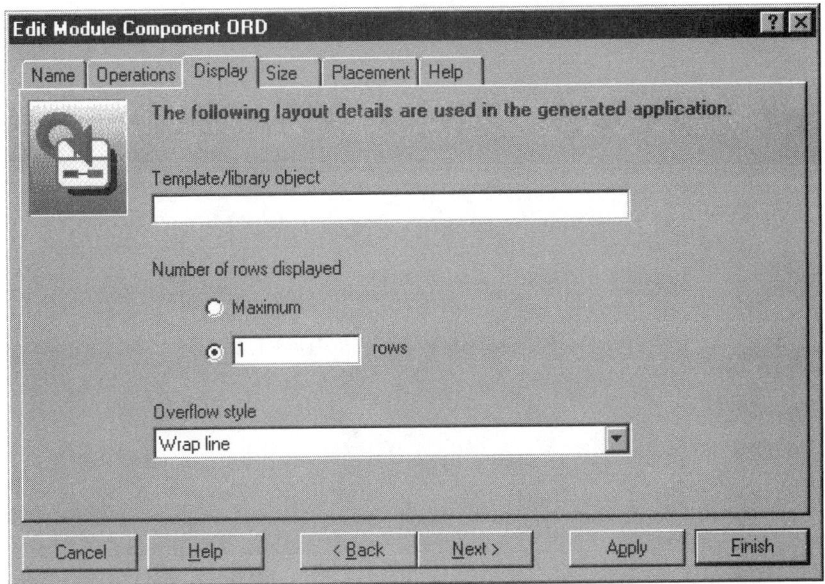

FIGURE 25.17 The Display tab of the Edit Module Component dialog box.

new window or in the same window as its predecessor. For certain environments, you can also specify the size that the module items should occupy on the screen, although letting the generators compute the values and set these properties is better.

- **Help.** This tab is used to associate context-sensitive help with the module component. What I said in Section 25.3.3 for the case of modules applies for their components as well.

25.4.4 MAINTAINING TABLE USAGES

Despite its name, the dialog box with the properties of a module component table usage is used primarily to maintain the properties of the bound items within the table. Different tabs in this dialog box allow you to include columns in the list of bound items for the table and to maintain a number of their properties, like allowed operations, display order, optionality, and so on. The following paragraphs provide some details for the most important tabs in the Edit Base Table Usage dialog box.

- **Where.** This tab is used in cases where you want to restrict the records returned to the table usage by a query. The conditions you specify in the text box become the WHERE clause of the SELECT statement that retrieves these records. If, for example, you enter *STATUS = "A"* on the Where tab of table usage ORDERS, the generated block will retrieve only active orders from the database. When set for lookup table usages, this property may also restrict the options that users may have available for setting an item.

- **Items.** The purpose of this tab is to allow you to maintain the list of items that you want to include in the table usage. You can include an item by moving it from the list Available columns into the list Selected items. For the items already included in the table usage, you can indicate whether or not you want them displayed to the users by setting or clearing the checkbox associated with each element in the list. By arranging the ranking of items in the list Selected items, you can also set their display order in the front-end module. Figure 25.18 shows an example of this tab.
- **Item Names.** This tab allows you to maintain the names of the items included in the tab module. By default, these items are named as the corresponding columns.
- **Operations.** This tab is where you check those items in the table usage that will be used to enter query criteria, that will accept data when a new record is created, and that will be updateable. By default, the usages are set based on the properties of the database columns. Columns that are part of primary keys, for example, are not updateable.

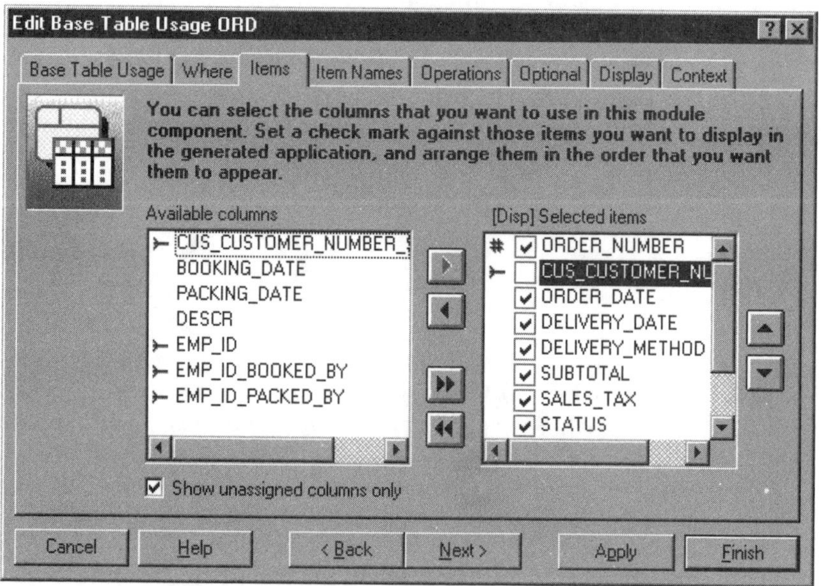

FIGURE 25.18 The Items tab of the Edit Base Table Usage dialog box.

- **Optional.** The main purpose of this tab is to identify the items for which users will have to enter data in the generated module. By default, the list Mandatory items on the right-hand side of this tab is populated with items that correspond to NOT NULL database columns. You can add to this list items from the list Optional items if the situation requires you to do so.
- **Display.** This tab captures some of the display properties of each item in the table usage, including Prompt, Display Type, Width, and Height. Like other item properties, properties of items on this tab are inherited from their corresponding columns.
- **Context.** This tab is used to identify those data items within a table usage that identify a row of data from the business and user perspective rather than from the system or database perspective. In the example shown in Figure 25.19, for example, the item NAME is the context item for the CUSTOMER table because a user identifies customers by their name. The value of their CUSTOMER_NUMBER, which is what the database uses to uniquely identify customers, may be meaningless to the users. Context items are very useful in cases where the layout of the module component is a spread table and not all the data items can be displayed simultaneously. In such a case, users may scroll to the right to view the hidden data items but still keep in front of them the context items for the record.

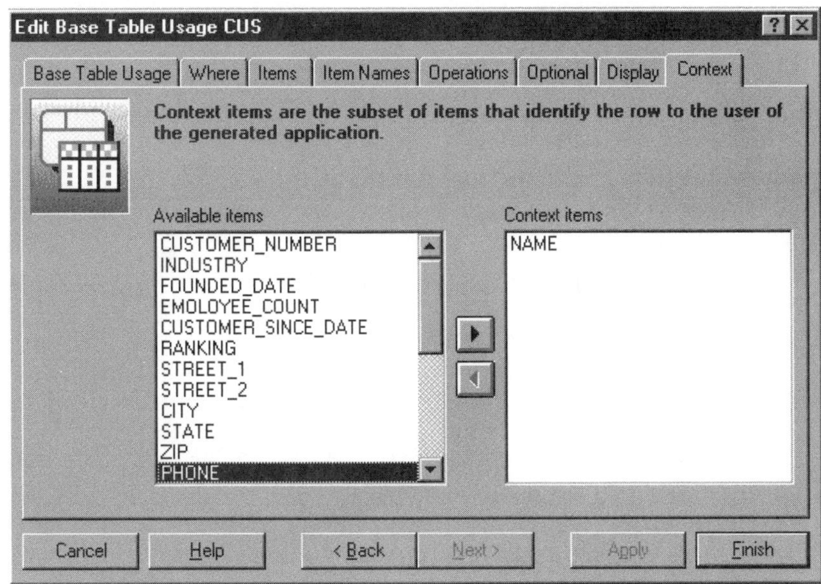

FIGURE 25.19 The Context tab of the Edit Base Table Usage dialog box.

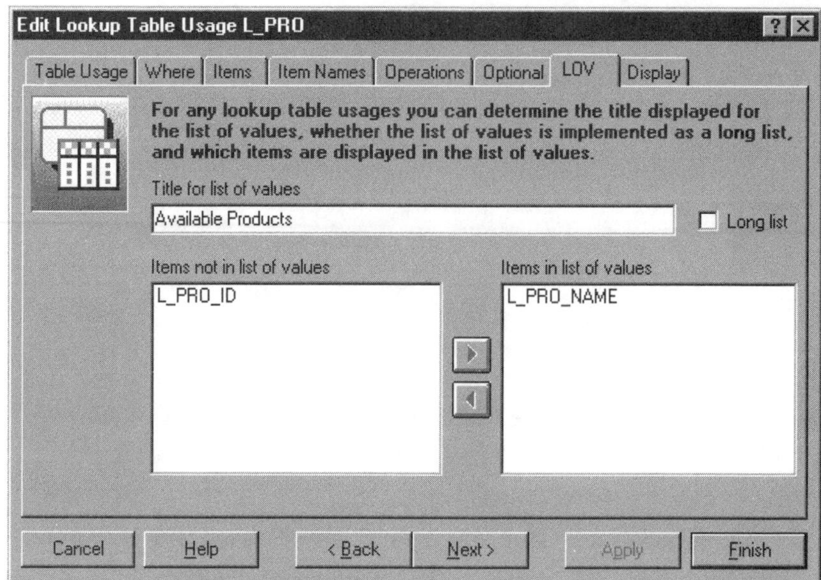

FIGURE 25.20 The LOV tab of the Edit Lookup Table Usage dialog box.

The dialog box for lookup table usages contains all the tabs described in the previous paragraphs. In addition, this dialog contains the tab LOV, which is specific for this type of table usage. Figure 25.20 shows an example of this dialog box. As you can see from the example, the LOV tab allows you to pick the items that will be displayed in the list of values—hence the abbreviation LOV. It also allows you to enter a title for the dialog box in which the list will be displayed.

25.4.5 MAINTAINING BOUND ITEMS

From the description of the property tabs of table usages presented in Section 22.4.4, you can easily see that most of the properties of bound items are maintained in the dialog box of the parent table usage. However, you may need to access the properties of items on an individual basis, especially for the purpose of fine-tuning those properties that control the GUI implementation of the item. The dialog box Edit Bound Item contains five property tabs, which are described briefly below:

- ❑ **Column.** This tab is used to maintain the name of the item, associate it with a base table column, and set the *Display* property of the item to "Yes" or "No."

- **Operations.** On this tab, you select the operations (Insert, Update, and Select) that may be performed against the item. If the module is an Oracle WebServer module, you can also indicate that the item is indexed by a policy of the Oracle ConText Cartridge. When the WebServer Generator encounters an item with the property Context set to "Yes," it customizes the query form of the module component so that it includes controls to specify full-text search criteria.
- **Definition.** This tab is used to set the data type of the item, any default values you may want to associate with the item, and whether the item is required or optional.
- **Display.** This is probably the tab you will access and modify the most, since, as the name suggests, it contains the display properties of the item. Figure 25.21 shows an example of this tab. Among the properties most frequently accessed on this tab are Display Type, which defines the type of GUI control that will represent the item; Alignment; and Format Mask. Closely related with the Display Type list box is the list box Show Meaning. This list box is set when the display type is a list box or radio group. Its setting defines the value used to represent the elements of the list or the radio buttons of the radio group. In the example shown in Figure 25.21, the item STATUS will be displayed as a drop-down list (also known as a pop-up list), and its elements will display the meaning associated with each allowed value registered against the column or the domain.

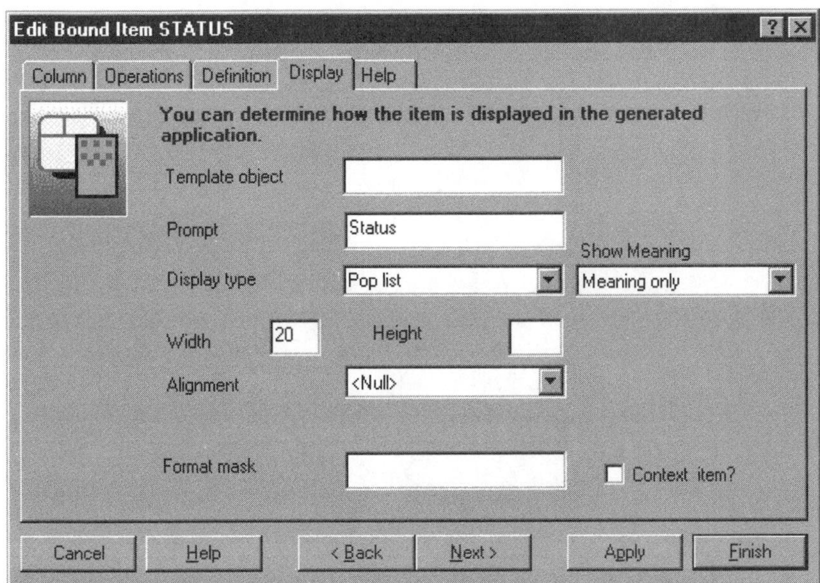

FIGURE 25.21 The Display tab of the Edit Bound Item dialog box.

- **Help.** On this tab, you can view and maintain the Hint property of the item, as well as help content that will be incorporated by the Microsoft Help Generator in the help files of the application.

25.4.6 MAINTAINING UNBOUND ITEMS

A lot of overlap exists between the bound and unbound items when it comes to the organization of their properties on the tabs. The Edit Unbound Item dialog box in fact contains the property tabs Operations, Definition, Display, and Help, which are similar in content and layout to the corresponding tabs in the Edit Bound Item dialog box. Differences exist as well, such as the fact that unbound items are not associated with any database column. Furthermore, each type of unbound item contains properties that are specific to the functionality covered by the type. The type of an unbound item is set and maintained on the Name tab, together with the name of the item. Modules implemented in different languages may contain unbound items of different types. The following paragraphs describe the types of unbound items used in Developer Forms modules and the properties associated with them.

- **Client Side Function.** These items derive their value from a function implemented in the front-end application. The statement that calls this function and passes the necessary arguments is added and maintained on the tab Client Side Function.
- **Computed.** These items derive their value from a bound item in the table usage, using one of the standard SQL group functions, like AVG, SUM, MIN, and MAX. The function and the item used to compute this value are maintained on the tab Computed.
- **Custom.** Custom items are implemented as push buttons or menu items in the generated Developer Forms module. You can enter and edit the application logic that is associated with these items on the Custom tab.
- **SQL Expression.** An unbound item of this type derives its value from the SQL expression defined on the tab with the same name. This expression may use values from one or more bound items and one or more scalar SQL functions. The difference between a SQL Expression unbound item and a computed one resides in the type of SQL functions used to derive the values (scalar versus group). When you create an unbound item, its type is by default SQL Expression. Figure 25.22 shows an example of such an item that displays the name of the customer in a friendly format. Notice at the bottom of this tab a feature that is available on other tabs as well. The list box Function allows you to select the function you want to use, and the list item contains all the bound items in the current table usage. When you set these lists, you can click Add to paste the usage of the function in the text box SQL expression, thus saving yourself some typing efforts.

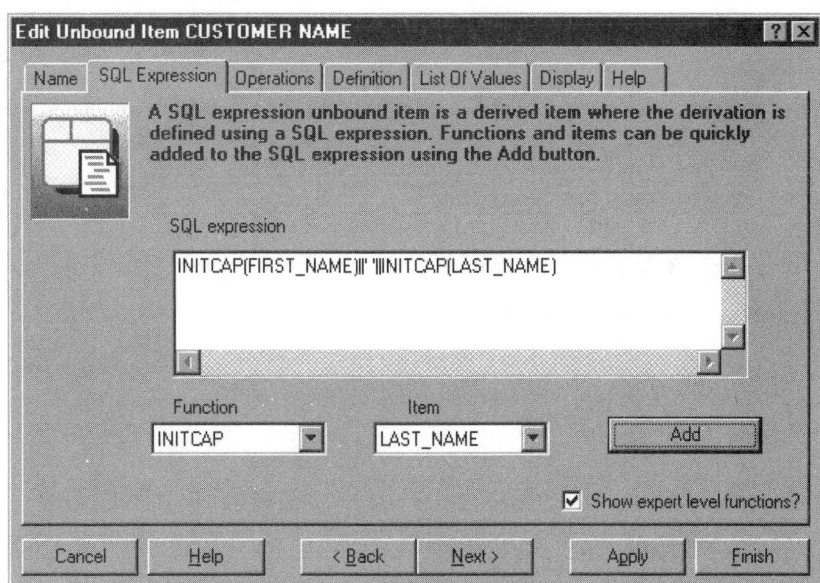

FIGURE 25.22 The SQL Expression tab of the Edit Unbound Item dialog box.

- **Server Side Implementation.** Items of this type derive their value from a PL/SQL function stored in the database server. You can maintain the name and arguments passed to this function on the tab Sever Side Implementation.

Action items are a special case of unbound items that allow you to navigate to different module components within the module or to a different module, as well as to perform any user-defined action. These items are ultimately implemented as buttons; therefore their properties that require customization are very limited. Besides the properties Name and Prompt, for navigation action items, you may need to maintain the target of their navigation. The property tab Navigation serves this purpose. As you can see from the example shown in Figure 25.23, all you need to do to set the target of the navigation is to select an object from the list of candidates and click Apply.

25.4.7 MAINTAINING ITEM GROUPS

As I explained earlier, you can create and view item groups only if the module diagram is in display mode. To bring up the dialog box of the properties for an item group, double-click the item group in the diagram or in the Design Navigator. The Edit Item Group dialog box is composed of two tabs. The first one, called

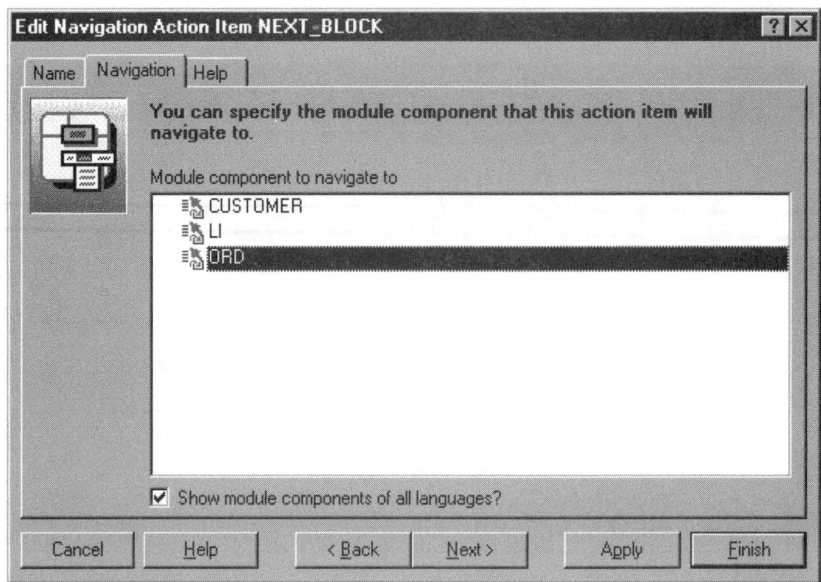

FIGURE 25.23 The Navigation tab of the Edit Navigation Action Item dialog box.

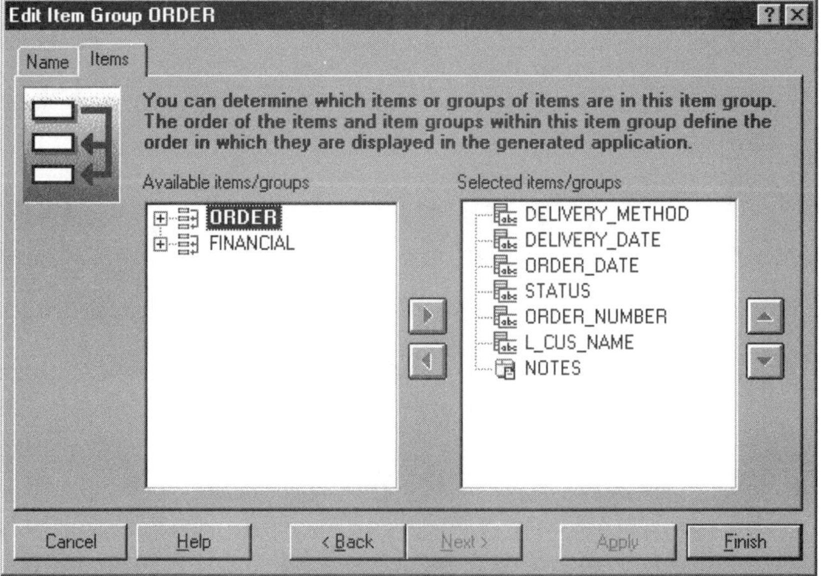

FIGURE 25.24 The Items tab of the Edit Item Group dialog box.

Name, maintains the name and prompt of the item group. The most important property on this tab is Stacked. Recall that in Developer Forms and Visual Basic, stacked item groups implement tabbed dialog boxes in the generated module.

The members of the item group are maintained on the Items tab of the Edit Item Group dialog, shown in Figure 25.24. On this tab, you can add or remove items from a group and arrange their display sequence within the group.

25.4.8 MAINTAINING WINDOWS

The number of properties of a window object are very limited, and they are grouped in two tabs of the Edit Window dialog box. The property you would edit the most on the tab Name is Window Title. As part of your goal to create user-friendly applications, carefully set the title of each window to reflect the functionality of the module components that the window contains.

The second property tab, Size, sets the position and size of the window object in the generated module. For each module and possibly across all the modules, try to minimize the variance in the dimensions of the window objects. Furthermore, if a module contains multiple windows, set the X-Position and Y-Position of these properties in such a way that when the windows are opened

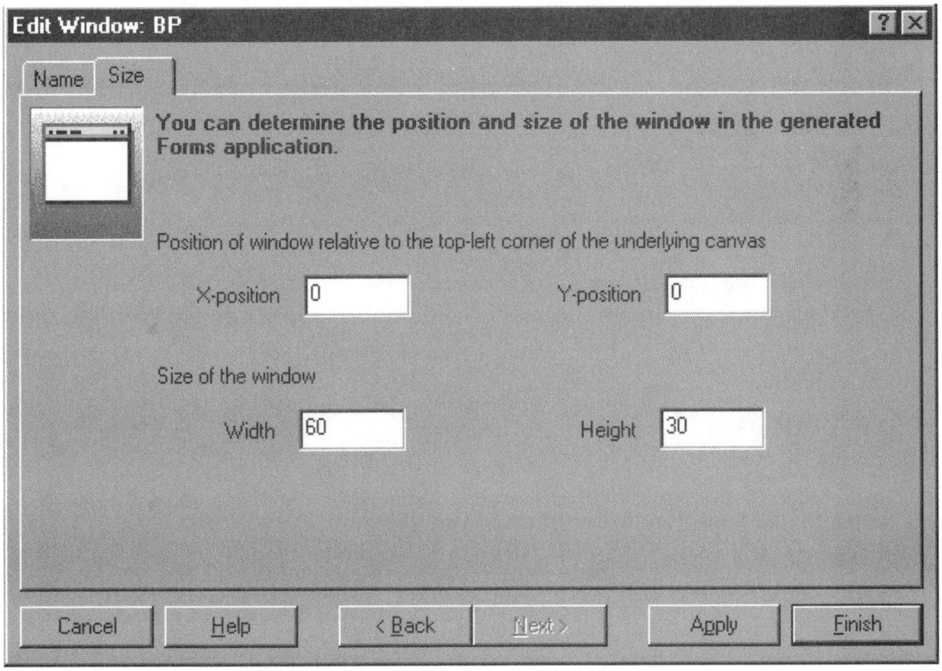

Edit Window: BP

Name | Size

You can determine the position and size of the window in the generated Forms application.

Position of window relative to the top-left corner of the underlying canvas

X-position 0 Y-position 0

Size of the window

Width 60 Height 30

Cancel | Help | < Back | Next > | Apply | Finish

FIGURE 25.25 The Size tab of the Edit Window dialog box.

initially, they are cascaded. To achieve this effect, you may set these properties to multiples of a certain number for the window objects of the module. If, for example, your module contains three windows, then the coordinates of the first window could be (0, 0), those of the second window (3, 3), and those of the last window (6, 6). Figure 25.25 shows an example of the Size tab of the Edit Window dialog box.

25.5 MODULE WIZARDS

The previous sections of this chapter described the different elements that form the architecture of a module and provided information about how you can set and maintain their properties in the Design Editor. From the information presented there, you can easily identify the following steps required to add a new component to your module:

1. Create and set the properties of the module component.
2. Add the table usages (base and lookup) to the module component.
3. Set the properties of items within the module component.
4. Define the layout and visual attributes of the module objects.

These steps may be performed by accessing the properties of the module elements in the dialog boxes and property tabs discussed in Section 25.4. Given the number of dialog boxes and tabs involved, clearly some guidance through the process is required. As in similar situations, the Design Editor provides tools and utilities that you can use to simplify and streamline the creation of new module components. These tools are:

- **Module Component Data Wizard.** This tool provides a road map for the process of creating table usages and bound items of a module component.
- **Module Component Display Wizard.** You can use this Wizard to define the interface layout of the module components.
- **Chart Wizard.** This is a utility that walks you through the steps of creating a Developer Graphics chart.

The following sections will highlight the functionality of each of these wizards.

25.5.1 THE MODULE COMPONENT DATA WIZARD

This wizard combines steps from the process of creating module components, table usages, and bound items into one activity that allows you to create a new module component and populate it with the necessary data elements. Its counterpart in the Form Builder is the Data Block Wizard. To invoke the wizard from anywhere in the Design Editor, select Tools | Module Component Data Wizard. If the context of the Editor is a module, the Wizard will create a module component for that particular module; otherwise, the Wizard will create a reusable module component. The following is a list of steps you can follow to create a module component with the Module Component Data Wizard. Each of these steps is implemented as a separate tab in the Module Component Data Wizard dialog box. You can move from one step to another by using the buttons Back and Next and, when you are ready to complete the activity, click Finish.

1. Provide a name and title for the module component; select the implementation language of this component.
2. Select the table object that will become the base table usage of the module component. The tab on which you select the table has a useful feature that allows you to create lookup table usages together with the base table usage. The control Lookup table usages on this tab displays all the tables defined in the Repository that reference the table selected in the list box Base table usage. You can expand each node in the list to display the tables that reference the table, as shown in Figure 25.26. To include a table as a lookup

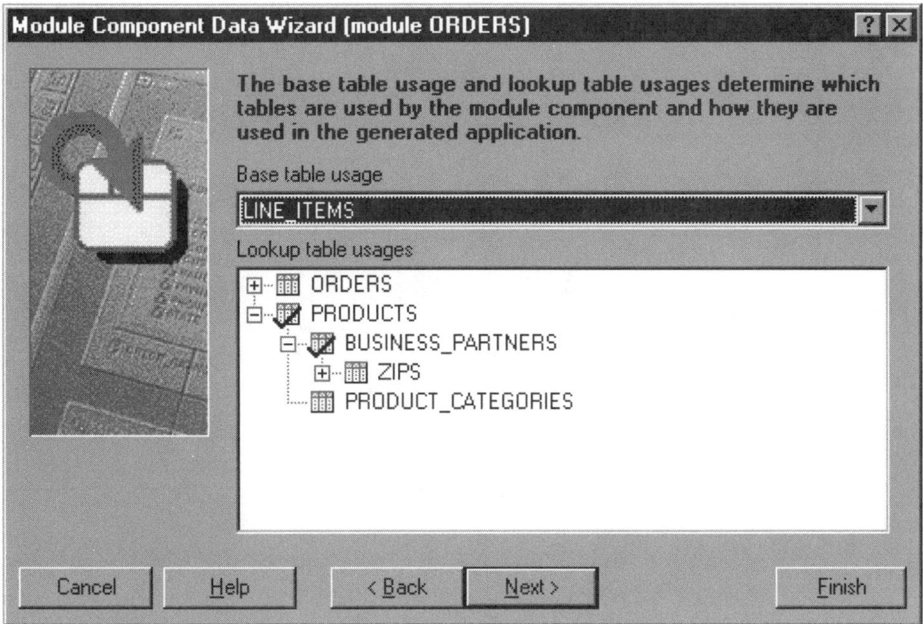

FIGURE 25.26 The Table Usage tab of the Module Component Data Wizard.

usage, click the icon associated with the table name to place a check mark across this icon.

The advantage that this tab provides is that it allows you to define nested lookup table usages. For example, with the settings of Figure 25.26, the module component will contain the base table usage LINE_ITEMS, the lookup table usage PRODUCTS that complements ORDERS, and the lookup table usage BUSINESS_PARTNERS that complements PRODUCTS. Such a combination of table usages may be useful if you want to display the name of the product and its manufacturer for each line item in an order.

3. Define the operations that users will be allowed to perform on the base table of the module component.
4. Select the columns that will be included in the base table usage. Mark those items that you want to display to the users and arrange the display order of the items.
5. Accept the default names of the items derived from the corresponding column names or provide new names.
6. Specify whether users will be able to insert, update, or query the items included in the base table usages.
7. Define which items will be optional and which ones will be mandatory in the generated module.
8. Click Finish to complete the process.

25.5.2 THE MODULE COMPONENT DISPLAY WIZARD

Whereas the Module Component Data Wizard helps you define the data elements that will become part of a module component, the Module Component Display Wizard is a power tool used to enhance the layout of the component. This wizard corresponds to the Layout Wizard in the Form Builder. You can invoke this Wizard by selecting a module component and then choosing Tools | Module Component Display Wizard. The dialog box that appears is composed of property tabs that correspond to the steps you may take to define layout and visual properties of the module component using this Wizard. These steps are listed below:

1. On the Display tab, set the number of rows displayed by the module component and the overflow style of its data items.
2. On the tab Displayed Items, maintain the list of the displayed items and their order.
3. On the tab Item Details, maintain the prompt and display type of each item. To view properties of the database column upon which an item is based, select this item and click the button Column Details. The dialog box that appears displays properties such as Column Name, Datatype, and Length.
4. On the tab Item Groups, maintain item group properties like Name, Prompt, and Stacked. You can also create a new item group on this tab.

5. On the tab Items and Groups, maintain membership properties of items in items groups. Figure 25.27 shows an example of this tab. The icons ▲ and ▼ on this tab are used to move items in and out of groups, to arrange the order of items within a group, and to arrange the order of items and item groups in the layout of the module component.
6. On the tab Context, identify the items that define the business context of the data items.
7. Click Finish to complete the process.

25.5.3 THE CHART WIZARD

This wizard allows you to create module components whose generation output becomes input for Developer Graphics. Like the other wizards discussed in the previous two sections, this wizard combines property tabs from different edit dialog boxes into one sequence of steps that facilitates the process of creating chart module components. The steps through which the Chart Wizard guides you are as follows:

1. Define the name of the new module component. Specify whether the component is a reusable component or attached to a specific module.

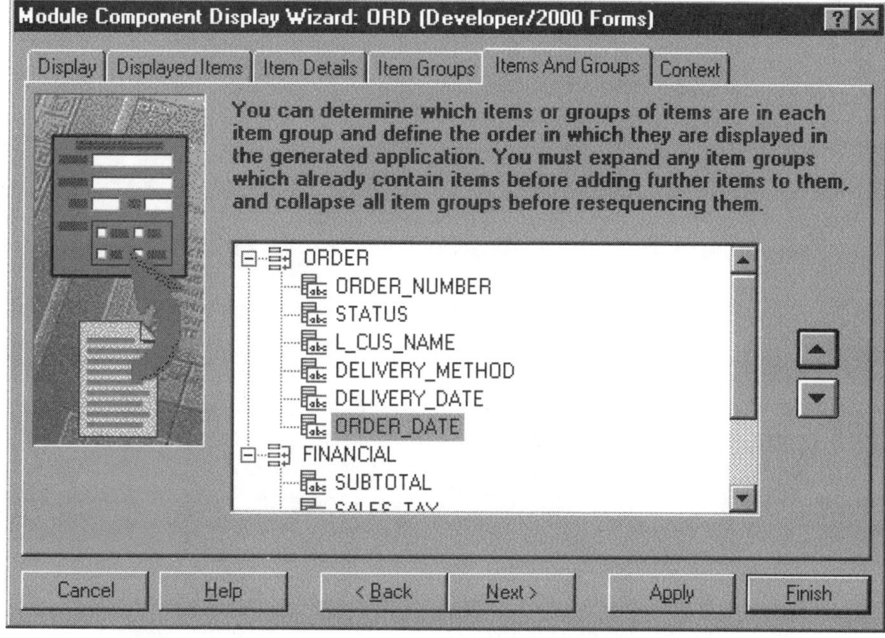

FIGURE 25.27 The Items and Groups tab of the Module Component Display Wizard.

2. Select the base table and any lookup tables that will be required by the chart. The property tab that allows you to select the table usages is the same as the one discussed in Section 25.5.1 and shown in Figure 25.26.
3. Select the columns from the base and lookup tables that will be used by the chart.
4. Create any unbound items the chart will need to display the data.
5. Select the chart style.
6. Click Finish to complete the process.

> **TIP**
>
> If the component is a specific component for a given module, you need to specify the name of the container module component and the chart item; whether this item will appear in an existing module window or in a window of its own; and whether you want to create a new chart from scratch, create a new chart that shares data with other module components, or incorporate a reusable chart component.

25.6 REUSABLE COMPONENTS

In many areas of the economy, assembling existing objects or components into higher-level objects or products is typical. In recent years, this concept has found wide acceptance in software engineering as well. The component-based development paradigm essentially means building application systems by assembling reusable components. The popularity of ActiveX and COM on one hand and Java Beans and CORBA technologies on the other has pushed the component-based development into the mainstream.

While software component technologies focus on the development and reuse of software, a higher level of thinking of components is to come up with reusable design objects—encapsulations of data structures and software module layouts that can be reused over and over in new applications. The reusable module components are the technology provided by Designer to allow you to componentize important design concepts in such a way that you can easily reuse them in different modules. You have two ways to create a reusable module component in the Design Editor:

- ❑ Use the Module Component Data Wizard. Make sure that the context is not a module when you invoke the tool.
- ❑ In the Design Navigator, switch to the tab Modules, select the node Reusable Module Components, and click the icon Create.

Reusable module components and specific components are no different as far as the way the properties are set and the elements included in them. What sets apart these two types of modules is the property Module Component Type, which is set to "Re-usable" or "Specific." You can access this property in the Property Palette of a module component. In order to include a reusable component in an existing module, you can take one of the following actions:

- In the Design Navigator, drag the reusable module component and drop it on the module where you want to add it.
- If the module is shown already in the Data Diagrammer, click the icon Include Reusable Component, and click the module in the diagram. From the list of reusable module components defined in the repository, select the component you want to add and click OK.

The properties of reusable module components included in a particular module cannot be modified. Technically speaking, these components are read-only references of the source component in the body of the module. So if you have included the same reusable module component in multiple modules, you need to modify and maintain the properties in only one place. The reference mechanism implemented by Designer will ensure that the properties are propagated to each instance. Thus, reusable module components extend the inheritance concept of object-oriented programming into the design world.

In order to break the link between a reusable module component and its use in a module, you need to switch the property Module Component Type from "Re-usable" to "Specific." To be able to do so, the reusable component must be used by only one module. When the property setting is modified, the component becomes an element of the module. Conversely, you can promote any specific module component to a reusable component by setting the property Module Component Type to "Re-usable."

As I explained earlier in the chapter, the data diagram of a module is very helpful for understanding and visualizing the elements and layout of modules. The Design Editor allows you to display reusable module components in module diagrams although these components do not represent complete modules. To display a reusable component in the Module Diagrammer, select it in the Design Editor and issue one of the following commands:

- Select Tools | Reusable Component Graphical Editor.
- Right-click the component and select the item Show On Diagram from the pop-up menu that appears.

The Diagrammer window for a reusable module component is the same as the Diagrammer for regular modules in all aspects, except that it lacks all the tools that are meaningful for modules but not for reusable components, such as the ability to create new module components or windows.

25.7 SUMMARY

The Design Editor is the environment in which you perform all the activities related to the creation, maintenance, and design of the modules in your application system. This chapter discussed how to use this Editor to perform a number of activities related to modules. The major topics of the chapter included:

- **Modules in Designer**
  - Types of Modules
  - Populating the Repository with Modules
- **Structure of Modules**
  - The Data View of a Module
  - The Display View of a Module
  - Module Application Logic
- **Working with Modules**
  - The Module Application Guide
  - Creating and Maintaining Modules
  - Maintaining Help Contents
  - Creating and Maintaining Module Associations
  - Maintaining Module Arguments
  - Copying Modules
  - Developer Module Security
- **Creating and Maintaining Module Elements**
  - Displaying Modules in Diagrams
  - Creating Module Elements
  - Maintaining Module Components
  - Maintaining Table Usages
  - Maintaining Bound Items
  - Maintaining Unbound Items
  - Maintaining Item Groups
  - Maintaining Windows
- **Module Wizards**
  - The Module Component Data Wizard
  - The Module Component Display Wizard
  - The Chart Wizard
- **Reusable Components**

Chapter 26

GENERATING DESIGNER MODULES

Give us the tools and we will finish the job.
—Sir Winston Churchill

One of the major advantages of using Designer in the software development process is its ability to generate modules based on the analysis and design information stored in the Repository. Provided that the right objects are stored in the Repository and the appropriate sequence of steps is followed, you can create functional software components from the early stages of the application design. This capability allows you to build prototype models that you can use to refine the requirements and the design of your application. As new information is gathered, the properties of objects in the Repository are updated and new and more refined modules are generated to reflect these properties. The cyclic and evolutionary approach to software development enabled by the Designer generators ultimately allows you to create applications whose functionality meets the real needs of your users. This chapter will discuss the use of Designer generators in software development projects. In particular, it focuses on the following topics:

- Repository-based software development
- The influence of preferences in the generation process
- The role of object libraries and template software modules in the generation process
- Properties of different Designer generators
- Iterative development and regeneration

26.1 REPOSITORY-BASED SOFTWARE DEVELOPMENT

In a traditional software development environment, a very clear line divides requirements analysis and application design from application development. The approach, methods, and tools used to perform the tasks in the first two categories are different from those used to complete tasks of the last category. The people who analyze requirements and design systems are often different from those who develop the software modules. The picture is quite different in an environment where Repository-based tools such as Designer are used. These tools store the information about the application in a common Repository so that it can be shared by multiple users and accessed at different stages of the software life cycle. The distinctions among analysis, design, and development are blurred. When a software engineer works on defining the properties of a function in a tool such as the Function Hierarchy Diagrammer, he or she is not only analyzing and documenting the properties of that function but also laying the foundations for the design of the module that will be created by the Application Design Transformer. Similarly, when the engineer defines the data usages and other properties of the module, he or she is also accomplishing a good part of the development of the modules in the target software package. Whereas a developer would build the module from scratch by manually creating each object, the Designer engineer simply sets a few properties of these objects in the graphical interface provided by the tools. In order to create actual software modules, he or she uses the Designer generator for the target environment.

All the front-end application generators of Designer work based on the same principles. They create code based on the properties of objects defined in the Repository and on a number of other sources. The following list describes the components used by these generators to create the software modules of your application:

- Definitions in the Repository of the data model, including tables, columns, and related properties.
- Definitions in the Repository of modules and their properties.
- Definitions in the Repository of module components, table usages, items—including bound, unbound, and action items.
- Settings of generation preferences for the particular generator. The Generator Preferences component of the Design Editor manages and accesses these settings in the Repository.
- Libraries of objects from which generated applications may inherit their properties and template modules with objects that will be included in or used by the generated modules. These are software modules usually stored as operating system files outside the Designer Repository.
- Database objects in an accessible database created based on the definition of Repository objects. These objects are not required to generate the modules, but you can compile them, where applicable, and execute them so that you can view and test their functionality.

So far in this book, you have seen how to create the data model of an application in the Repository and how to implement it in a database, how to create modules, and how to set the properties of their data usages. Sections 26.2, 26.3, and 26.4 will discuss the role of preferences, object libraries, and templates in the generation of software modules.

26.2 MAINTAINING PREFERENCES

As explained in Section 26.1, each Designer front-end generator needs, among other things, a set of preferences to create software modules from definitions of objects stored in the Repository. Designer provides default values for these preferences, which are also known as *factory settings.* They enable you to create software modules without having to set a single preference manually. In fact, during prototyping efforts, modules are often generated with the default factory preferences. However, after finalizing on the elements that will be part of a module and after establishing their properties, you can enhance the look and feel of the front-end application you develop by setting the preferences of the generator. The Design Editor provides the Generator Preferences as the tool to view and maintain preferences of its generators. The following sections will discuss properties of this tool and the different functions you can perform with it.

26.2.1 THE GENERATOR PREFERENCES

One of the following commands may be used to access the Generator Preferences:

- Click the Generator Preferences icon on the toolbar.
- Right-click the module in the Design Navigator and select Generator Preferences from the pop-up menu that appears.

At any moment in time, the Generator Preferences allow you to view and set the preferences of an application system for a particular product. To work with the preferences of a different product, select it from the list box Product. Figure 26.1 shows an example of the Generator Preferences for the Developer Forms Generator.

The Generator Preferences shares many common functions with other navigators in Designer and Developer tools. The main area of its window is taken up by a hierarchy tree where all the preferences are displayed. The nodes in the tree

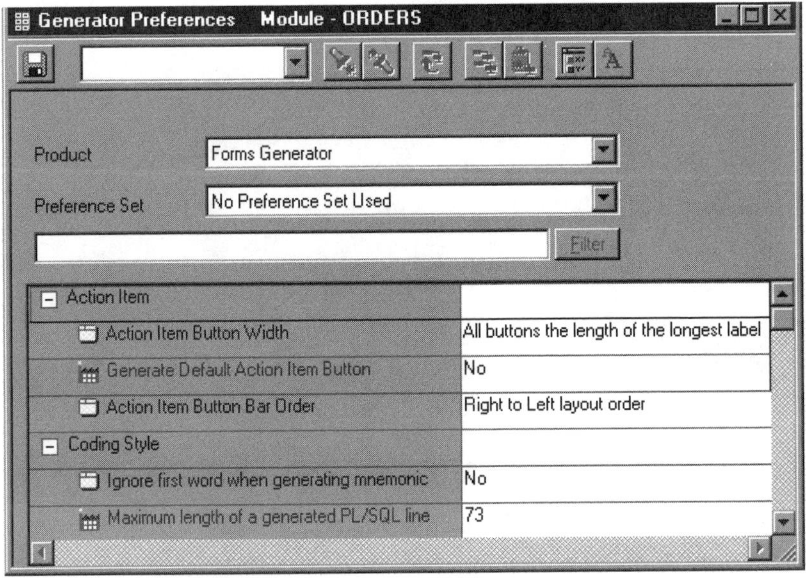

FIGURE 26.1 The Generator Preferences window.

can be expanded to display their branches or collapsed to hide the details. These nodes fall into one of the following two categories:

- **Preference type.** A preference type node serves the purpose of grouping together related preferences in order to simplify the process of viewing and accessing them. In Figure 26.1, for example, Action Item is a preference type that groups together several preferences that govern the way the generator creates action items in the modules it generates.
- **Preference.** A preference node represents the actual preference that you set and that influences the way the front-end generator creates the software modules. Preferences always belong to a preference type. Examples of preferences for the Action Item type are Action Item Button Width and Action Item Button Bar Order.

By default, the preferences displayed in the Generator Preferences window are coordinated with the objects selected in the Design Navigator. The title bar of this window always indicates the context in which the preferences are set. In the case shown in Figure 26.1, the preferences are for the module ORDERS. The check menu item Palette | Track Selection allows you to turn on or off the ability of the Generator Window to update its preferences when the focus on the Design Navigator changes.

26.2.2 MANAGING THE GENERATOR PREFERENCES

The number of individual preferences displayed in the Generator Preferences window is large. To help you locate a preference quickly, the Generator Preferences provides all the standard browsing tools found in other hierarchy tree navigators, such as expanding and collapsing the hierarchy or searching the tree for a node based on its name.

In addition to the search features described above, the Generator Preferences provide you with multiple ways to display the nodes in the hierarchy tree. The different configurations that the hierarchy tree can take allow you to view the preferences in different, more descriptive formats and to reduce the number of nodes that the tree contains. By default, the Generator Preferences displays the preferences using their name, a six-character string, which is not very mnemonic or descriptive. Indeed, names like LOVMWD and DFTLED are very difficult to associate with a meaningful preference. Therefore, you will often display the descriptions of preferences rather than their names. To do so, select View | Show Description from the menu.

By default, the Generator Preferences displays all these nodes, although in some circumstances, hiding some of the branches of the tree may be advantageous. Different options under the submenu View allow you to hide different parts of the Preferences Hierarchy window. A description of some of these options follows:

- **Hide Default Values.** This option removes from the tree the preferences with default or factory settings. Given the fact that the majority of your preferences will inherit the factory settings, you can reduce the number of nodes in the tree significantly with this option.
- **Hide Application Level Values.** This option removes from the tree all the preferences that are set at the application level, including those that maintain the factory settings. As you will see in Section 26.2.3, in most cases, you will set the preferences at this level. Therefore, this option may reduce the number of nodes in the tree significantly, as well.
- **Show Modified Values.** This option will keep in the hierarchy tree only those preferences whose factory setting is overwritten. Thus, the outcome of selecting this option is the same as that of selecting the option Hide Default Values discussed above.
- **Show All Values.** This option returns the display of preferences to its default setting by displaying all the values.

26.2.3 WORKING WITH PREFERENCES

Section 26.2.2 discussed how to search for and manage the display of preferences. In this section, you will see how to set preferences and what is involved in this process. The process of setting a preference is simple and can be performed with the following steps:

1. Select the preference in the Generator Preferences window.
2. Select a setting from the list of allowed values for the preference. Most of the preferences are set this way. For a few of them, you have to type the setting in the text box rather than pick it from a list.

As mentioned earlier, each preference comes with a default value known as its factory setting. You can always revert to the factory setting of a preference that has been modified manually by selecting the preference in the hierarchy tree and clicking the icon Inherit on the Generator Preferences toolbar.

The preference may be set for different objects in the Design Navigator. For example, the preference PLSMAX—Maximum number of items in a popup list—can be set at several levels, including Application, Module, Table, and Item. The level where you set a preference is closely related to the impact of its setting on the generated code. Setting the preference at the Item level will affect only one particular item instance; setting the property at the Module level will affect all the items within that module that will be displayed as list boxes; and setting the property at the application level will affect all the list boxes in all the modules of that application.

> **TIP**
>
> When you set a preference, the navigator precedes its label in the hierarchy tree with an icon that indicates the level where the setting occurs. The icons are the characteristic icons of the objects used by the Repository Object Navigator.

Setting preferences for different objects also implies an order of precedence used by the generators to retrieve the settings of these preferences. When creating an object, the generators use the first applicable setting of the preferences they can find. The search starts from the lowest level where the preference may be set. This can be Item when generating a text item, Item Group when generating an item group, Module Component when generating a Developer Forms block, and so on. If a preference is set at that level, the generator uses it to create the object. Otherwise, it looks at the same preference in the next level. If the preference is not set in any level, including the application level, the factory setting is used. The order in which generators look at preference settings leads to the following guidelines for setting preferences:

- ❑ Set a preference at the highest level possible in order to ensure that the generators will create applications with a consistent look and feel.
- ❑ When a preference is set at multiple levels, understand the precedence order, scope, and implications of each setting.
- ❑ Consider the process of setting preferences as an important part of the application development effort and not as a byproduct of module design efforts.
- ❑ Consider preference settings like coding standards for the software modules you generate. Document them, make them available to the development team, and override them only for well founded reasons.

26.2.4 CREATING AND MAINTAINING NAMED PREFERENCE SETS

The order in which the generators evaluate the preference settings helps you create software modules with consistent interface and functionality. Like coding standards, preference settings should apply across applications whenever possible. Using the same preferences for multiple applications will provide you with software modules with the same look and feel across the enterprise. To facilitate the process of sharing preference settings among different application systems, Designer provides a special type of object, called a *preference set.* A preference set is a group of preferences whose settings can be applied to one or more objects in one or more applications. In the Generator Preferences, you can create a preference set by following these steps:

1. Select an object in the Design Navigator and display its preferences in the Generator Preferences.
2. Select Edit | Create As Preference Set….
3. Enter the name of the new set in the dialog box Create Set As.
4. Click OK.

I prefer to create preference sets using the method described above because you can inherit all the settings and the product flavor of the preferences as you create the set. However, another method is described below:

1. Switch to the Modules tab of the Design Navigator and expand the node Preference Sets.
2. Select the node that represents the flavor for which you want to create the set.
3. Click Create.
4. Provide the name of the set in the Property Palette.
5. All the preferences in the set created with this method have the factory settings. To modify these settings, select the set in the Navigator, invoke the Generator Preferences, and set the desired preferences as described in Section 26.2.3.

26.2.5 IMPLEMENTING PREFERENCES SECURITY

Preferences are a way of enforcing coding standards in the software modules you create. Therefore, you naturally want some way of enforcing these standards by protecting preferences set at a certain level. The Generator Preferences provides two methods of preserving preference settings. The first one is intended primarily to protect users from accidentally modifying preferences of one or more instances in the Generator Preferences. In order to achieve this, follow these steps:

1. Select the object whose preferences you want to protect in the Design Navigator and switch to the Generator Preferences window.
2. Select Security | Lock Preferences.

At this point, the icon is displayed to the left of each preference to indicate that it is protected from changes. To remove the protection of preferences for an object, select the object and choose Security | Unlock Preferences. To remove the preference protections set by a user for all the objects in the application system with one command, choose Utilities | Remove Locks. Objects protected by a user remain protected for other users as well. To these users, the Generator Preferences display the characteristic lock icon in a yellow background.

Any application user may set and remove his or her own locks on preferences. The application owner or any user with administration privileges on the application can remove the protections from object instances set by other users by selecting Security | Remove All User Locks.

Another method to protect preference settings is to freeze them. This method is available only to application owners or users with administration privileges. Other users of the application system cannot modify preferences set in frozen state. The steps below allow you to freeze preferences of one or more objects in the Generator Preferences:

1. Select an object whose preferences you want to freeze in the Design Navigator and switch to the Generator Preferences window.
2. Select Security | Freeze.

The navigator displays the icon to the left of each instance to indicate that the objects are protected from changes. To unfreeze the preferences of an object, select it, switch to the Generator Preferences window, and choose Security | Unfreeze. To remove the protection from all the objects in the application system with one command, choose Security | Unfreeze All.

> **TIP**
>
> I mentioned that one of the differences between locking and freezing preferences is that any user can lock but only application administrators or owners can freeze preferences of an object. Another difference is that when freezing preferences of an object that contains dependent objects, you freeze the preferences of the dependents as well. Freezing the preferences of a module, for example, will freeze the preferences of all its components, items, and item groups. If, on the other hand, you lock the preferences of the module, you will prevent users from modifying its preferences, but they can still modify the preferences of its components and items.

26.3 OBJECT CLASS LIBRARIES

As explained in previous chapters of this book, object libraries are special Developer modules that contain one or more objects and simplify the reuse of these objects in other modules. When the Developer Forms Generator creates the new software module, it subclasses or copies objects from the libraries. The following sections will focus in these topics:

- Types of objects in an object library
- Object libraries supplied by Designer

26.3.1 TYPES OF OBJECTS IN AN OBJECT LIBRARY

Object libraries are an important source of information used by the Developer Forms Generator to create software modules. Based on the settings of the preference OLBSOC—Object Library Subclass or Copy—the generator will subclass or copy the objects included in the library. An object library used by the generator contains two major categories of objects from which the generator inherits new objects. The following paragraphs describe these categories.

- **Standard source objects.** These are special objects that you create in the object library according to predefined conventions and that are understood by the generator. These objects create objects of a particular type in the generated module.

  The name of each object tells the generator whether it is dealing with a standard source object or an implementation source. Conventionally, all the standard source objects are named according to this pattern:

  ```
  CGSO$<RecognizedKeyword>
  ```

  If the generator encounters an object whose name begins with CGSO$ but is not followed by a recognized keyword, this object is ignored altogether. Standard source objects allow you to subclass or copy all the objects of a given category from the same object. If, for example, you create an item named CGSO$DATE in the object library, all the generated items of data type DATE in the target form will inherit their properties from this item. In most cases, you can refine the inheritance of properties for the same type of object by creating new items whose name contains predefined suffixes recognized by the generator. For example, the item CGSO$DATE_MR inherits date items in multi-record blocks, CGSO$DATE_CT is used for date items in control blocks, CGSO$DATE_DO displays items, and CGSO$DATE_MD is used for mandatory date items. A combination of these suffixes may be used as well. CGSO$DATE_MR_DO, for example, is used by display date items in multi-record blocks.

  A predefined hierarchy of source objects is used by the generator to inherit the properties of the objects it creates. Figure 26.2 shows this hierarchy for the case of date items. When the generator is about to create a date item in a multi-record block, it looks in the object library for an item titled CGSO$DATE_MR. If it finds the item, it uses the item to copy or subclass the generated item. If it does not find one, it navigates up the tree shown in Figure 26.2 until it finds a source object.
- **Implementation source objects.** These are objects that are used instead of standard source objects when an object is generated. The property Template/Library Object of the element in the Repository must be set to the name of the implementation source object in the library.

```
CGSO$DEFAULT_ITEM
      CGSO$CHAR
            CGSO$DATE
                  CGSO$DATE_MR
                  CGSO$DATE_CT
                  CGSO$DATE_DO
                  CGSO$DATE_MD
```

FIGURE 26.2 A hierarchy of visual attributes recognized by the Developer Forms generator.

The standard object library provided with Designer contains a number of implementation source objects. The names of these objects begin with CGAI$, to distinguish them from implementation objects you may create. You can use these objects to create buttons that invoke the built-in Developer Forms functionality. They are used for action items and unbound items that will be displayed as buttons. The number of generator items in this category is quite large. Figure 26.3 contains only a few of these objects.

26.3.2 OBJECT LIBRARIES SHIPPED WITH DESIGNER

Designer provides a library of objects you can use in the generation of Developer Forms modules. The name of this library is OLGSTND2.OLB. By default, the library is located in the ADMIN directory of the Developer Forms Generator—%ORACLE_HOME%\CGENF50\ADMIN. This library contains all the standard source objects used by the generator and the implementation source objects discussed in the previous section. The objects are organized into six tab folders, as shown in Figure 26.4. The first five tabs organize the standard source objects (CGSO$) into groups of parent objects, those use in multi-row and data blocks,

GENERATOR OBJECT NAME	DEVELOPER FORMS BUILT-IN FUNCTIONALITY
CGAI$COMMIT	Commit
CGAI$EXIT	Exit
CGAI$ENTER_QUERY	Enter Query
CGAI$EXECUTE_QUERY	Execute Query
CGAI$COUNT_HITS	Count Query Hits
CGAI$INSERT_RECORD	Insert Record

FIGURE 26.3 Generator objects that implement Developer Forms built-in functions.

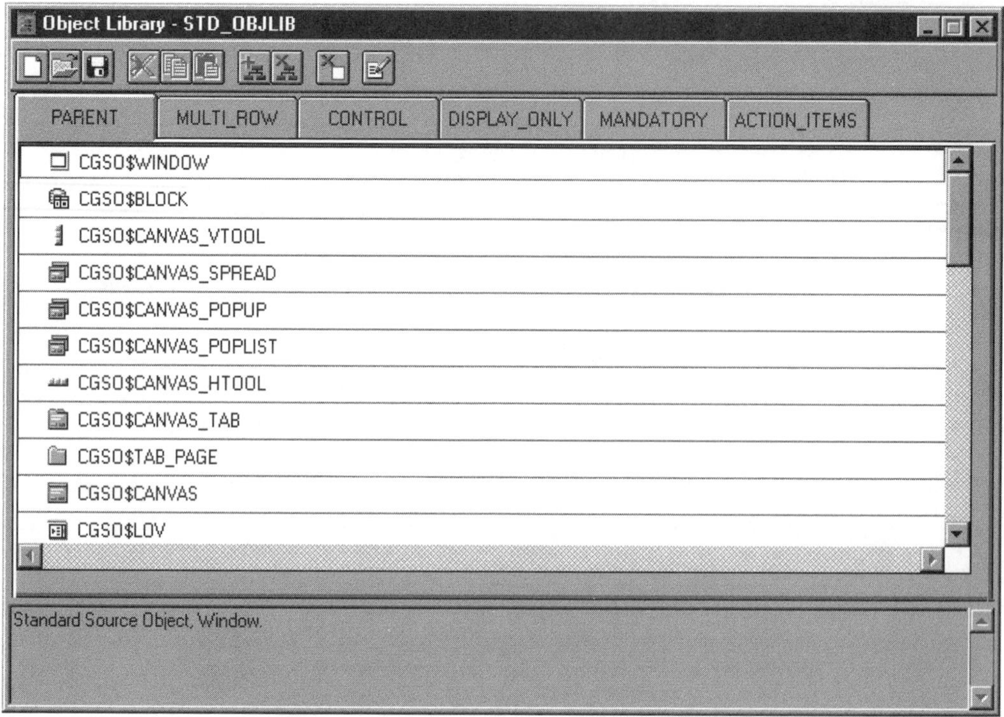

FIGURE 26.4 The Designer shipped object library.

and those that correspond to display and mandatory objects. The last tab lists the implementation source objects (CGAI$).

During the development of your application, you will find the need to customize the default object library. I recommend that you work with a copy of the library supplied by Designer. If you need to modify the properties of an existing object, perform the following actions:

1. Open the object library in the Developer Form Builder and create a new Form module.
2. Drag the object you want to modify and drop it in the appropriate location in the Form module. Notice that you need to respect the hierarchy in which the objects are stored in a Developer Forms module. For example, to be able to drop the object CGSO$DEFAULT_ITEM, a block must already exist in the module.
3. Copy the object to the new module when the Form Builder prompts whether to copy or subclass it.
4. Modify the properties of the object according to your needs.

5. Drag the object from the Form module onto the object library.
6. Choose the option to replace the existing object when prompted whether you want to replace it or not.
7. Save the object library.

If you want to add new objects to the library, I recommend that you create one or more separate tab folders and drag the new objects into these folders.

26.3.3 USING OBJECT LIBRARIES DURING GENERATION

A few preferences are set in order to point the Developer Forms Generator to the appropriate object library during the generation of your modules. These preferences are located in the Standards group and are described in the following paragraphs:

- ❑ **STOOLB—Name of Object Library for Generation.** This preference is set to OFGSTND1.OLB, which is the object library shipped with Designer. If you are using a different object library, specify its name in this preference. Note also that you can override the setting of the preference when you invoke the Developer Forms Generator, by specifying the name and location of the object library.
- ❑ **OLBSOC—Object Library Subclass or Copy.** By default, this preference is set to subclass objects. I recommend that you keep this setting in order to take advantage of the benefits that subclassing provides in Developer Forms.
- ❑ **OLBOLD—Library Keep Old Preferences.** As I mentioned earlier, the concept of object libraries was introduced with version 2.0 of Developer. The Developer Forms Generator included with version 2.0 of Designer takes advantage of these libraries to generate the modules. A number of properties that in version 2.0 are inherited from library objects were set using preferences in earlier versions of Designer. For example, all the properties of window objects were maintained through preferences in versions of Designer prior to version 2.0. Although these preferences are considered obsolete, Designer allows you to use them for backward compatibility reasons. In order to do so, set the preference OLBOLD—Library Keep Old Preferences to Yes.

> **WARNING**
>
> I recommend that you maintain the preference OLBOLD—Library Keep Old Preferences set to No and use the object libraries to implement the functionality offered by the obsolete preferences. As such, the support for these preferences will eventually be discontinued.

26.4 GENERATOR TEMPLATES

For software modules created with Developer tools, an important source of information that Designer generators use is template modules. These are Developer Forms and Developer Reports modules that reside in the file system and have a number of properties and objects that may be used in the modules you are generating. In the case of Developer Forms modules, the generator derives the names of templates from the setting of the preference STFFMB—The name of the template form, in the Standards group of preferences. In the case of Developer Reports modules, the template names are maintained in the preferences DETREP—Detail Report Template and LAYREP—Layout template. Both of these preferences are located in the Templates group of preferences.

Sections 26.4.1 through 26.4.4 will focus on the purpose and use of templates, the types of objects in a template, the Designer supplied templates, and how to customize these templates for the special needs of your applications.

26.4.1 PURPOSE AND USE OF TEMPLATES

Templates used in the generation of Developer Forms or Developer Reports modules serve primarily two purposes:

- To add objects to your modules that you cannot or do not want to specify in the Designer Repository. In this case, templates allow you to expand and customize the functionality of the generated modules. Such objects are known as *user objects.*
- To modify form-level properties.

Among the objects that you can include in the generated modules, the most important are:

- Control blocks in Developer Forms modules. A particular case of control blocks is iconic toolbars that you can attach to the MDI frame or to individual windows of your application.
- Form-level triggers common across all modules.
- Parameter forms for Developer Reports modules.
- Headers and footers in Developer Reports modules.
- Boilerplate items, such as logos or background images.

One way in which you can influence the look and feel of generated modules is to define the coordinate system and cell size for the generated modules.

For versions of Designer prior to Release 2, templates were a very important source of objects and properties for the Developer Forms Generator. They enforced application development standards, include objects recognized by the Generator and objects defined by the users include triggers and module-specific program units, and specify PL/SQL library attachments. Expanded features of Designer Release 2 have greatly diminished the role of templates in the generation of Developer Forms modules. These features include the support for control module components, the ability to attach application logic in the form of events and named routines, and the ability to define library attachments using module networks. Due to the use of object libraries by the Developer Forms Generator, the templates have also lost their role as tools to enforce standards and include user-defined objects in the generated modules.

26.4.2 TYPES OF TEMPLATE OBJECTS

Although template objects are Developer Forms and Reports modules, they are not, in general, functional modules that can be used independently. Their main purpose is to serve as containers for objects that are included in or influence the properties of generated modules. These objects are classified into two groups:

- **User objects.** These are objects for which the generator creates an identical copy in the generated module. In Developer Forms templates, they include blocks, items within blocks, triggers defined at any level, program units, attached PLL libraries, windows, and canvases. In the template module, these objects may be defined as references to other modules. In the case of Developer Reports, user objects include any objects defined in the header, trailer, or margin areas of the template module.
- **Generator objects.** These are special objects that you create in the template module according to predefined conventions and that are understood by the generator. These objects are not merely copied over to the generated module. In a general sense, they serve as a set of instructions or directives for the generator. For each of these objects that the generator encounters in the template, the generator takes a well-defined list of actions. These may include creating objects in the generated module, creating PL/SQL code, creating boilerplate text, or any combination of these.

The name of each object tells the generator whether it is dealing with a user object or a generator object. Conventionally, all the generator objects are named according to this pattern:

```
CG$<RecognizedKeyword>
```

If the generator encounters an object whose name begins with CG$ but is not followed by a recognized keyword, this object is ignored altogether. An exception to this rule is when multiple generator objects of the same type need to be created in different areas of the module. Since the object names must be unique, add some unique characters *after* the recognized keyword, to avoid any naming conflict that may arise. Generally, a sequence number, as in CG$AT_1 and CG$AT_2, refers to two instances of the generator item that store the application title. In the case of canvas generator objects in Developer Forms, the sequence appended after the recognized keyword implies an association with another object generated in the module. For example, the generator object CG$HORIZONTAL_TOOLBAR represents a toolbar canvas that will be associated with all the windows that do not have an explicit toolbar assigned to them. The generator object CG$HORIZONTAL_TOOLBAR_0 represents the toolbar associated with the first window created by the generator. The generator objects can be grouped into the following categories:

- **Objects whose content is populated from Repository information.** These generator objects when included in your modules will inherit their settings from properties of the application system and the current module stored in the Repository. These objects are usually used as boilerplate items or used to set the title bar of windows dynamically at runtime. Figure 26.5 contains some of the most common generator objects in this category. They can be used in both Developer Forms and Reports modules.
- **Objects that implement standard built-in Developer Forms functions.** These objects may create buttons that invoke the built-in Developer Forms directives. The functionality of objects in this category has been superseded by the implementation source objects in the object library supplied by Designer (CGAI$ objects).
- **Objects that serve as boilerplate text.** These objects can display information such as the date, the Oracle user running the module, the current page, and the total number of pages. Some of them, like the first two, can be used equally well in Developer Forms and Developer Reports modules. Some others, like the last two objects, are more suitable for reports than forms. Figure 26.6 shows the most representative objects in this category.

GENERATOR OBJECT NAME	SOURCE OF CONTENT
CG$AN	Application system name
CG$AT	Application title
CG$MN	Module name
CG$MP	Module purpose

FIGURE 26.5 Generator objects that derive their content from Repository information.

GENERATOR OBJECT NAME	TYPE OF TEXT GENERATED IN THE BOILERPLATE
CG$DT	Current date
CG$US	User of the module
CG$PN	Current page number
CG$PT	Total number of pages
CG$PM	Page n of m, where n is the current page number and m is the total number of pages.

FIGURE 26.6 Generator objects that implement Developer Forms built-in functions.

- **Visual attribute objects.** These objects allow you to set the visual attributes of objects in Developer Forms at the object category level. This functionality has been superseded by the concept of standard source objects. Use these objects to set not only the visual attribute properties, but also every other property of the objects.

  In order to define visual attributes of Developer Reports modules, you create text objects in the body area of the template report. The names of these objects correspond to categories of Reports objects for which you can control visual attributes. By setting the visual attributes of these objects, you instruct the Developer Reports generator to apply the same settings to the objects in the generated module. Figure 26.7 lists all the generator objects you can create in the body area of the template report and the categories of objects that inherit their visual attribute properties.

26.4.3 TEMPLATES SUPPLIED BY DESIGNER

Developer Forms and Developer Reports generators come with a number of templates that allow you to generate modules without having to define any of your

GENERATOR OBJECT NAME	OBJECTS THAT INHERIT VISUAL ATTRIBUTE PROPERTIES
CG$PROMPT	Field prompt
CG$FIELD	Field
CG$HEADER	Frame title
CG$PARAMETER	Parameter prompt
CG$SIZING	Font, font size, and font weight

FIGURE 26.7 Visual attribute generator objects used in Developer Forms.

own templates. The functionality they provide is often sufficient for the needs of the modules you develop. These templates are especially important for prototyping efforts and in rapid application development environments. The following paragraphs briefly describe the major templates used by the Developer Forms Generator.

- **OFG4PC1T.FMB.** This is the default template that the Developer Forms generator uses. It is customized for modules generated for Microsoft Windows platforms. This template includes a toolbar with some of the major Developer Forms built-ins implemented as icons on a horizontal toolbar canvas. The forms generated with this template use a real coordinate system with the inch as the unit. The MDI frame title of these forms is set to the name of the application system defined in the Repository.
- **OFG4PC2T.FMB.** This template may be used to generate modules that call other modules. Based on the network modules defined in the Design Editor, the Developer Forms generator will create buttons to navigate between forms if the OFG2PC2T.FMB template is used. In addition, modules generated with this template will inherit all the functionality of modules generated with OFG2PC1T.FMB.
- **OF4GUIT.FMB.** This template is used to generate Developer Forms modules with character coordinates intended to run primarily on non-GUI environments.

> **WARNING**
>
> The best way to handle navigation among modules is to use navigation action items in the module component from which the navigation occurs.

26.4.4 CREATING CUSTOMIZED TEMPLATES

As discussed in the previous sections, generator templates are Developer Forms and Reports modules with objects that can be included in the generated modules. Therefore, the process of creating a customized template is no more complicated than that of creating and editing a regular form or report. A copy of any of the provided templates can serve as a starting point for your custom-developed templates. You can modify them in any of the following ways:

- Add generator objects according to naming standards discussed in Section 26.4.2.
- Add user-defined objects to the template, including items, blocks, windows, and canvases.
- Add PL/SQL objects to the template, including triggers and program units.

26.5 DESIGNER FRONT-END GENERATORS

Designer provides a series of generators that allow you to create front-end software modules for different programming environments. These include generators for a series of Oracle programming tools, such as Developer Forms, Developer Reports, Developer Graphics, and Oracle WebServer. In addition, Designer allows you to generate Microsoft Help files associated with your modules, and provides a generator for MS Visual Basic projects. The process of invoking and setting the options of the Developer Forms Generator is discussed in the following sections.

26.5.1 INVOKING AND USING FRONT-END GENERATORS

In order to invoke a front-end generator, you need to select the module you want to generate in the Design Editor and perform one of the following actions:

- Select Utilities | Generate....
- Click the icon Generate on the Editor's toolbar.

Based on the implementation language of the module you selected, Designer launches the appropriate generator. In some cases, you may want to generate a module defined in one language into a different implementation language. This may be helpful, for example, in cases where you have requirements to produce data entry screens and reports with similar layout. In such cases, you can design one Developer Forms module and generate it in its native environment and as a Developer Reports module. The following actions allow you to generate a module for an implementation environment different from the one used by the module:

1. Select the module in the Design Navigator.
2. Select Utilities | Generate As... from the Editor's menu.
3. Select the target generator from the dialog box Generate Module As that appears (see Figure 26.8).
4. Click OK to invoke the selected generator.

Each generator has its own characteristic dialog box that allows you to set its properties. In principle, however, all the generators work alike. After setting the properties and options of the generator, you click Start to initiate the generation process. At this point, the Design Editor displays the Messages pane, where the principal activities of the generator are listed. Warnings issued by the generator or errors encountered in the process are listed in this pane, in blue and red letters, respectively. During the generation process, the generator may apply default

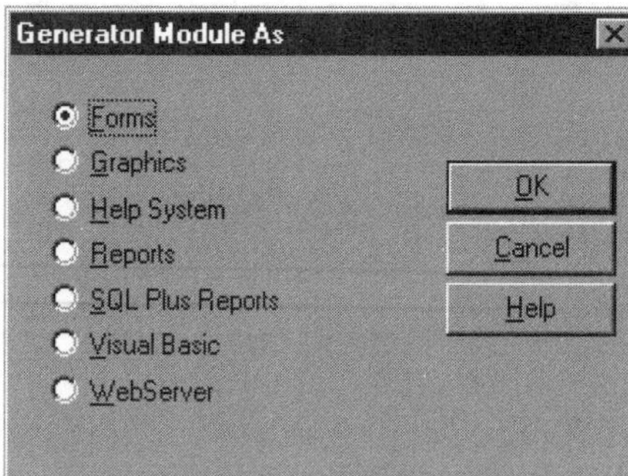

FIGURE 26.8 The Generate Module As dialog box.

settings to properties you have not set explicitly or prompt you to modify conflicting settings of other properties. If the generation is successful, you have the option to save these settings to the Repository, revert them, or view the changes and edit them individually.

If the generation process is not successful, you can use the information listed in the Messages pane to see what caused the failure and identify the module object that is responsible for it. The following actions can be performed after you place the cursor in a message line:

- Click or select Messages | Show Help on Message to get an explanation about the message.
- Click or select Messages | Go to Source of Error to place the focus in the Design Navigator on the violating object.

Other icons on the Messages pane toolbar and their corresponding items on the menu Messages may be used to copy all the contents of the pane to the Windows Clipboard, to navigate to the next or previous message, and to clear the messages from the pane.

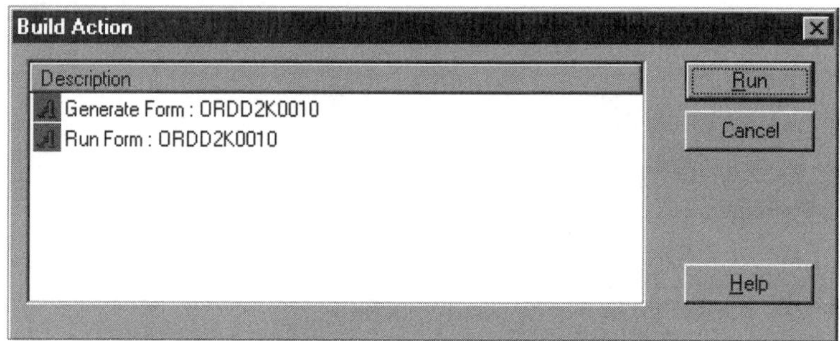

FIGURE 26.9 The Build Action dialog box.

Finally, when you set the generator options, you may decide to queue some actions of the generator in an action list. For example, you may decide to generate a Developer Forms module, and place in the queue the processes of compiling and executing the generation module. To view the contents of the queue, click on the toolbar of the Messages pane or select Messages | List Actions…. In the Build Action dialog box that appears, you can see all the processes placed in the queue. To execute one of these processes, select it and click Run. Figure 26.9 shows an example of this dialog box.

> **TIP**
>
> All the generators allow you to compile, where appropriate, and execute the generated modules right after their generation. In order for these processes to succeed, all the database objects required by the module must be installed in the development database schema. These objects include the obvious ones, like tables, views, and sequences, but also the less obvious ones, like the code control tables, the reference codes tables, the table API, and the module API.

26.5.2 DEVELOPER FORMS GENERATOR

Developer Forms generator is the most sophisticated Designer generator that creates Developer Forms, Menus, and PL/SQL library modules from properties of modules stored in the Repository. Its interface is implemented via a dialog box, called Generate Form, shown in Figure 26.10. The properties in this dialog box serve primarily the following purposes:

- **Defining the generation option.** The list box at the top of the Generation Option group of properties instructs the generator to create only forms, menus, or libraries. The check boxes in this group control whether or not the generator ignores the application logic defined in the Repository, generates the menu and any PL/SQL modules associated with the module, or generates other Forms or Reports modules that may be called from the current module. Furthermore, in cases when the module has been previously generated, you can use the checkbox Preserve Layout to instruct the generator to preserve or override the layout of the previously generated module.
- **Specifying which generation preferences to use.** By selecting one of the radio buttons in the Use Preferences radio group, you can direct the generator on which preferences to use. By default, the generator will use the module preferences as defined in the Generator Preferences. In order to enforce coding standards across multiple modules in your application, you may also use the preferences that a specific module or a named preference set. In this case, you must select the radio button Other Module or Named Set, and

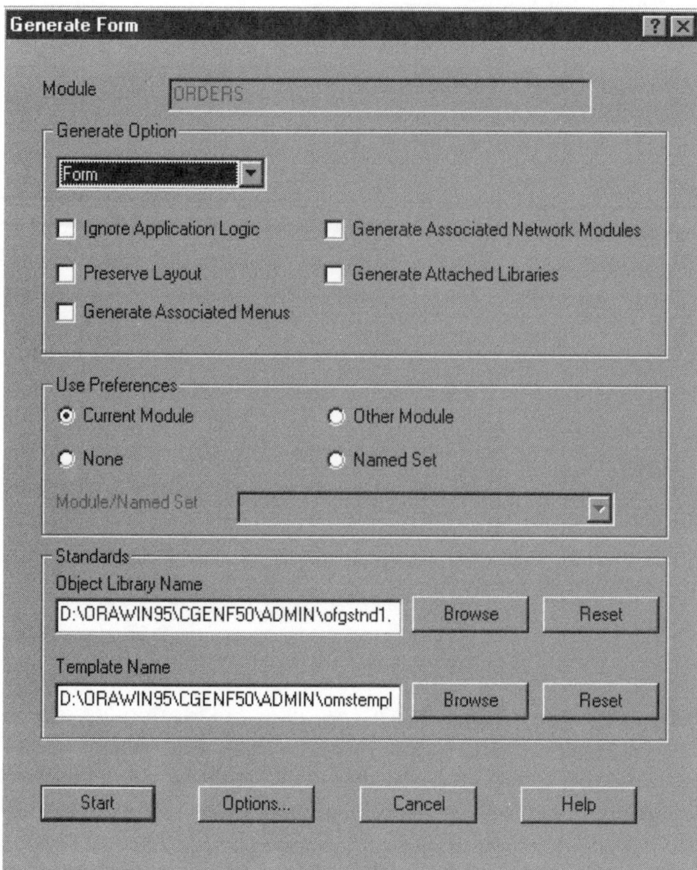

FIGURE 26.10 The Generate Form dialog box.

pick the name of the module or named set from the list box Module/Named Set. One option of generating modules, although very rarely used, is not to use any preference settings. You can achieve this by selecting the radio button None in the Use Preferences group.

- **Specifying the object library and module template used during the generation.** The options in the group Standards allow you to use the default object library and template module, as specified by the Generator preferences, or to click Browse and select a specific file yourself.

You can set a number of options, maintained in the Forms Generator Options dialog box, which influence the way the generator runs. To invoke this dialog box, click the button Options... in the Generate Form dialog box. This dialog box is composed of multiple property tabs, which will be described in the following paragraphs.

The property tabs File Option, Menu Option, and Library Option are similar in form and functionality. They are used primarily to define the location of the generated software modules of the corresponding type. By default, these modules are stored in the file system, in the subdirectory BIN of your ORACLE_HOME directory. You can specify your own directory by setting the property Destination, as shown in Figure 26.11 for the case of Forms. You may use the Browse button to navigate the directory tree and pick the desired location more easily. Developer Forms and Menus modules may be stored in an Oracle database as well. If they are, the list box Location is set to Local Database—the database where the Repository resides, or Other Database. The text box Connect String contains the user name, password, and connect string used to establish a connection to a remote database. The text items in the Commands group specify

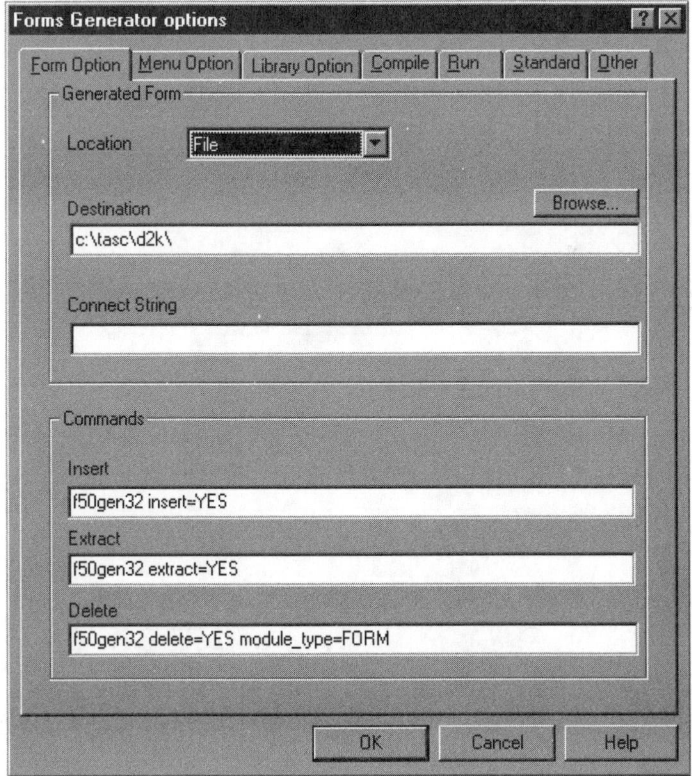

FIGURE 26.11 The Form Option tab of the Forms Generator Options dialog box.

the commands for inserting, extracting, and deleting the modules from the database.

The process of developing modules is often an iterative one, in which the design of the module is modified and the new module is generated, compiled, and executed in order to validate the changes. The Developer Forms generator provides a smooth transition among these three stages by allowing you to compile and execute a module that is successfully generated. The generator creates the software modules in binary format (.FMB or .MMB) and can compile them in executable modules (.FMX and .MMX). The Compile tab, shown in Figure 26.12, is where you set the preferences that control this process. By setting the properties in the Compile Form/Menu radio group, you can direct the generator to compile the binary module, not to compile it, or to add the compilation task to the action list. Obviously, the compiling process can initiate only if the module is generated successfully.

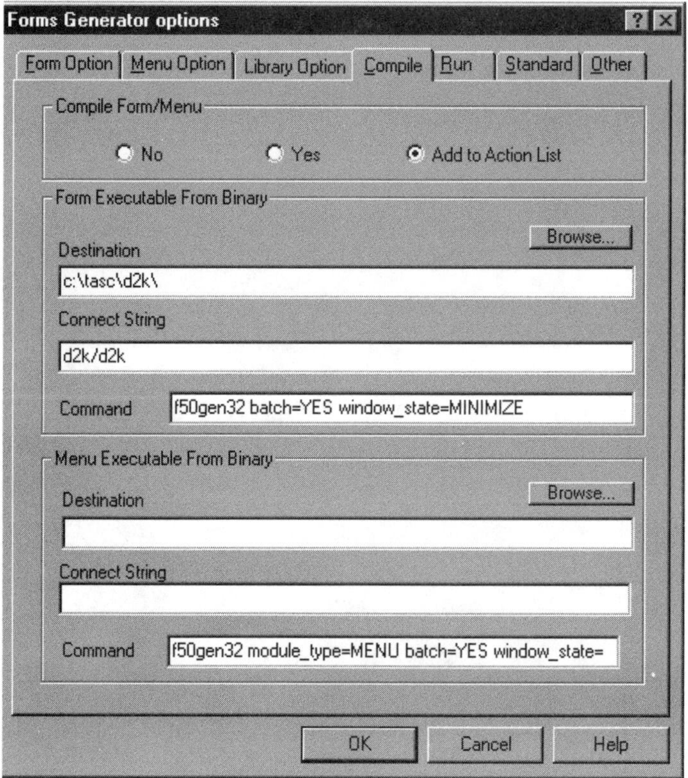

FIGURE 26.12 The Compile tab of the Forms Generator Options dialog box.

If modules will be compiled, you can specify the directory where the executables will be stored by setting the text box Destination. When generating Developer Forms modules that access database objects, these objects must exist in a given schema, and the Developer Forms Generator must have access to this schema. By default, the generator looks for these objects in the schema of the current Repository user. In general, though, this schema must not contain objects used by an application. You can use the Connect String as shown in Figure 26.12 to specify the user name, password, and connect string for the schema that contains the objects used by the application system.

Once a Forms module is successfully generated and compiled, you may choose to run its executable. The Run tab allows you to set properties that control how the generator executes the module. Depending on the selection of the radio group Run Form, the generator will stop after the generation is complete, it will run it without prompting, or it will queue the task in the action list. The generator can run a module only if it compiles it successfully. You need to provide the user

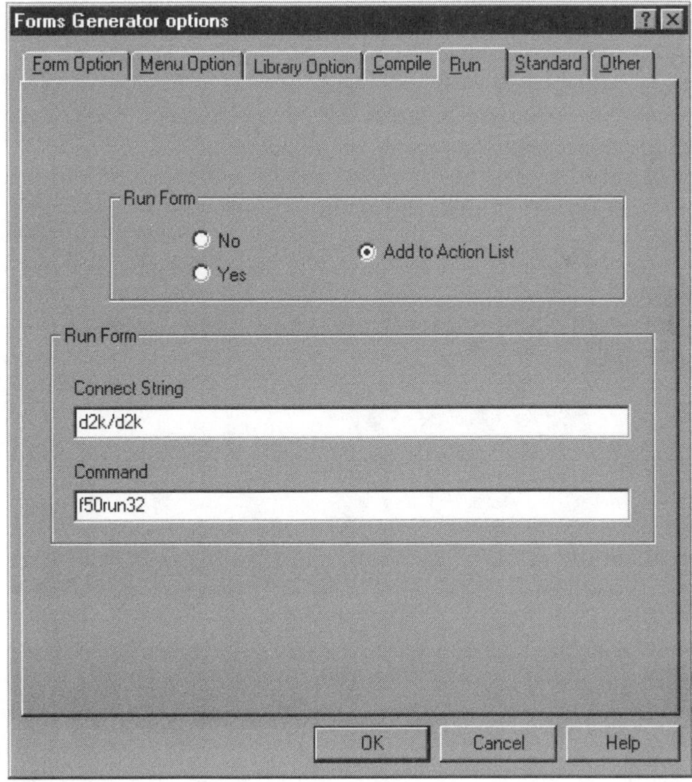

FIGURE 26.13 The Run tab of the Forms Generator Options dialog box.

name, password, and database string in the property Connect String to allow the user to connect to a database schema where all the objects used by the module exist. Figure 26.13 shows an example of the Run tab.

Figure 26.14 shows the Standard tab, used to specify the location of the template module that will be used during the generation. In general, you access this tab if you are storing the templates in a location different from the default directory. If it is another directory, its name is specified in the Path text box. If the template module is stored in the database, the properties Location, Command, and Connect String have meanings similar to the same properties on the Form Option of Menu Option tab. Be sure to note that although this tab allows you to specify the location of the template module, the name of the module itself is controlled by the preference STFFMB—the name of the template form, specified in the Standards group of preferences.

The property tab Other contains a miscellaneous group of generation properties, the most important of which is the property PLL Files Path. When set, this

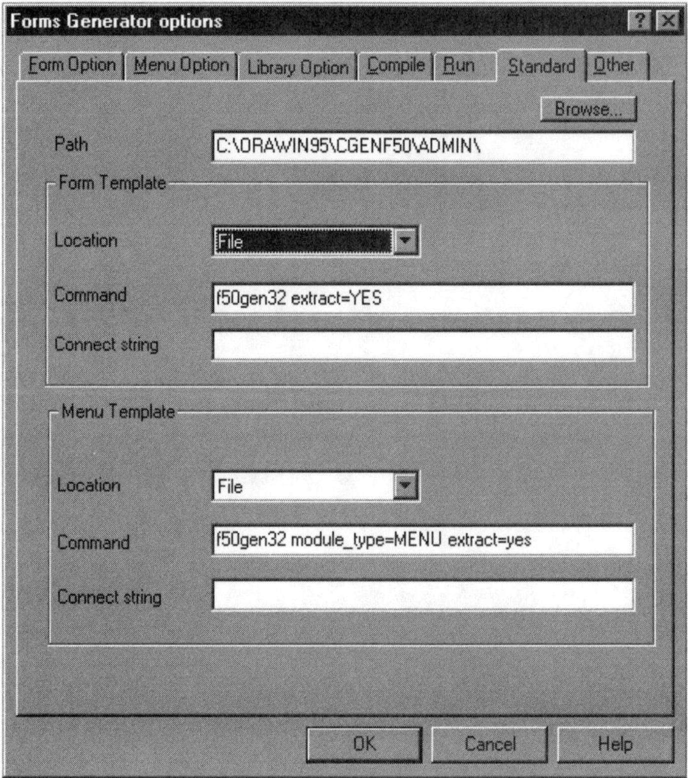

FIGURE 26.14 The Standard tab of the Forms Generator Options dialog box.

property instructs the generator where to find the PL/SQL modules that contain program units invoked by the generated forms. However, do not use this property, since the libraries will be attached with the hard-coded path, possibly resulting in problems when the software is deployed. The best way to specify the location of these libraries is to set the variable FORMS50_PATH in the client's Registry.

Despite the number of properties that can be set in the Forms Generator Options dialog box, you don't usually need to set them each time you run the generator. A number of properties, such as the destination of generated and compiled modules, location of templates, and the necessary information to connect to the appropriate database schema reflect the software environment of your application. Assuming that you have set up this environment correctly, you will have to specify these properties only once.

> **TIP**
>
> If the Developer Forms modules you are generating contain module components that require the module API packages, you need to create and install them before compiling and executing the generated module.

26.6 SUMMARY

Designer provides a number of tools that generate software modules to implement the user interface of your applications in different products and flavors, such as Developer Forms, Developer Reports, and Oracle WebServer. These tools are commonly known as front-end generators. The software modules they produce are defined by a number of components, including the properties of modules in the application system Repository, settings of preferences, and template modules. This chapter explained the relationship among these components, as well as the major properties of each front-end generator. The major topics of this chapter were:

- **Repository Based Software Development**
- **Maintaining Preferences**
  - The Generator Preferences
  - Managing the Generator Preferences
  - Working with Preferences

- Creating and Maintaining Named Preference Sets
- Implementing Preferences Security

- **Object Class Libraries**
  - Subclassing, Objects, and Object Librariers
  - Types of Objects in an Object Library
  - Object Libraries Shipped with Designer
  - Using Object Libraries During Generation

- **Generator Templates**
  - Purpose and Use of Templates
  - Types of Template Objects
  - Templates Supplied by Designer
  - Creating Customized Templates

- **Designer Front-End Generators**
  - Invoking and Using Front-End Generators
  - Developer Forms Generator

Part V

Extending Developer Applications with Microsoft Technologies

Coming together is a beginning, staying together is progress, and working together is success.

—Henry Ford

Chapter 27

Dynamic Data Exchange

Only connect! That was the whole of her sermon.
—Edward Morgan Forster

- **What Is DDE?**
- **DDE in Developer Tools**
- **Examples of DDE with Form Builder**
- **Summary**

The implementation of Form Builder in the Microsoft Windows environment provides its application with a whole variety of features used in this platform. They include exchanging data with other applications, controlling other applications from within the Forms applications, and exchanging instructions and commands from within the PL/SQL triggers and program units.

Form Builder implements the integration with other Windows applications through the support for Dynamic Data Exchange (DDE), COM-based technologies—including OLE Documents, Automation, and ActiveX Controls—and the PL/SQL interface for interacting with dynamically-linked libraries (DLL). This chapter explains the meaning of DDE and its role in the integration of MS Windows applications in general, and Form Builder with these applications, in particular. The following two chapters discuss OLE and how it is supported by the Form Builder. Chapter 30 discusses how to access members of DLL libraries of functions, and take advantage of these functions in your Form Builder applications.

27.1 WHAT IS DDE?

DDE is a set of functions defined in Microsoft Windows that allow programs to communicate between them. The communication between processes is established using shared memory resources to exchange the data between applications. Because the DDE functions are implemented at the operating system level, they are standard, and allow any two applications that follow their conventions to communicate and exchange data with each other. Because these functions can be incorporated in the programming scripts of each application, they allow programmers to automate the process of establishing connections and exchanging data among applications.

27.1.1 DDE COMPONENTS

The process that occurs when two applications are engaged in a DDE transaction is called *conversation*. For a conversation to take place, the following conditions must be met:

1. Both applications support the DDE communication protocol.
2. Both applications are running simultaneously.

Like any other conversation, the DDE conversation must be initiated by one party. The application that issues a request for communication is called the *DDE client*. The other application, that responds to such request, is called the *DDE server*. Once the DDE client initiates a conversation, it is also responsible for the agenda of the conversation. In other words, it can send data to the server, receive data from the server, ask the server to execute certain actions, or decide to terminate the conversation. The DDE server, on the other hand, is passive, and responds to incoming requests from the clients. It receives data from them, services their requests for information, or executes the commands according to their instructions.

DDE clients need a name to address the server. This name is also called the application name, and is usually the name of the .EXE file of the program. For example, for MS Excel, the file name is EXCEL.EXE and the application name is *Excel;* for MS Word, the names are WINWORD.EXE and *Winword;* for WordPerfect, the names are WPWIN.EXE and *Wpwin;* but for Lotus 1-2-3, the names are LOTUSW.EXE and *Lotus*.

The metaphor of conversation for applications that communicate using DDE extends a little further than what I said above. Like any other conversation, the DDE conversation focuses on one *topic*. When the DDE client issues a request for conversation, it must inform the DDE server about the topic that will be the subject of the conversation. The DDE mechanism in Windows divides DDE servers in several topics. Some topics are specific to the application and, therefore, are called special topics. The special topics may vary from one server application to another. However, most servers support the special topic called *system*, which, in turn, can be used to get the names of other special topics supported by the application. For DDE servers that support the MDI paradigm, each document is a topic for DDE conversation. The name of the topic in this case is the fully-qualified path of the file in which the document is saved. Suppose for example that C:\Documents\EXPENSE.XLS is the name of the Excel spreadsheet that contains your monthly expenses. If you want to access it from another application using DDE, the topic of conversation will also be C:\ Documents\EXPENSE.XLS. However, if you want to access a new spreadsheet from the client application, you would use BOOK1 as the topic of the conversation with Excel. When working with other servers, you would use the appropriate extensions and names for new documents.

It is obvious that the same client and server applications may engage simultaneously in conversations about different topics. For example, from a Form Builder application—the DDE client—you may send some data to an Excel spreadsheet—the DDE server—and receive other data from a second spreadsheet. Windows considers each combination of the DDE server and topic as a unique *channel* of communication. When the client initiates a conversation with a server about a given topic, Windows opens a DDE channel, assigns it an internal ID, and informs the DDE client about it. As long as the conversation is active, the client uses this ID, or channel, to exchange data with, or transmit commands on the topic to the server. In the example above, the first DDE channel would be established between the Forms module and the spreadsheet that will be the destination of data. The second channel would be established between the Forms module and the spreadsheet that is the source of data.

After a DDE communication channel is established, the DDE client may exchange data with the server. In the DDE context, the named objects in the server where these data elements reside are called *items*. Items can be used to receive data from clients, or to store information that can be uploaded by them during a DDE conversation. The items that can be used in DDE transactions depend of the DDE server and on the topic of conversation. For special topics such as *System*, the items will depend on the specific applications. When the topic is set on a document, the variety and number of items is larger. If the application is a spreadsheet application such as Excel, each cell can be an item. Ranges of cells and named blocks can also be items.

The fact that each cell in a spreadsheet can be accessed directly as an object places them among the DDE servers that are the easiest to use. Word processing applications are a little harder to work with, because their structure is not as fragmented in objects. However, all the major word processing packages such as MS Word, WordPerfect or AmiPro, support bookmarks, which allows you to name certain areas within a document. These bookmarks are used for navigation and cross-referencing from within the document, or as items in DDE communications.

Figure 27.1 shows graphically the components of a typical DDE conversation as described above.

27.1.2 DDE ACTIONS

Actions in a DDE conversation can originate only from the client application. As explained above, the server will only respond to the incoming requests from the clients. This division of responsibilities is reflected in the type of support that different applications offer to DDE communications. There are applications, such as

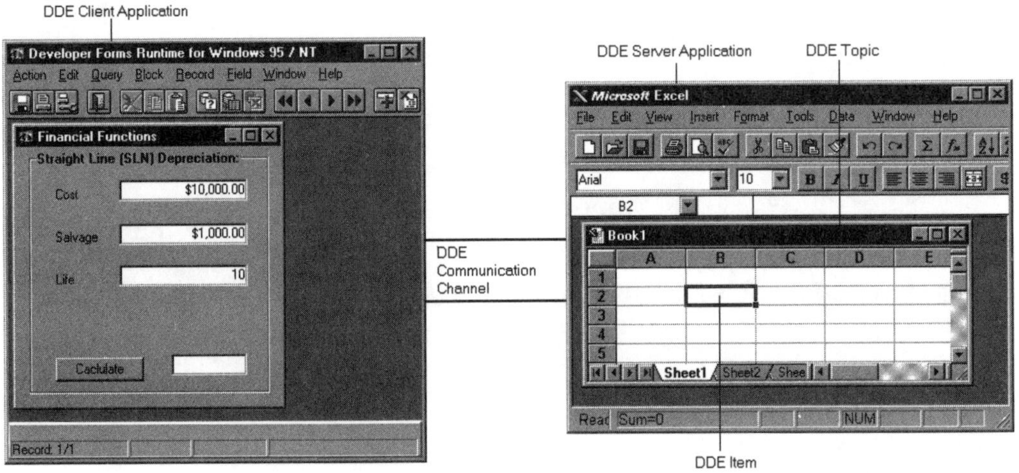

FIGURE 27.1 Components of a typical DDE conversation.

MS Word or Excel that can be DDE clients, as well as DDE servers. These applications are able to not only issue DDE commands, but also understand DDE commands that other clients send to them. There are other applications, such as Form Builder, that can behave only as DDE clients. They cannot respond to the DDE instructions sent by other applications but can initiate actions in DDE servers.

The fundamental layer of functions used in DDE communications is defined in the Dynamic Data Exchange Management Library (DDEML) included with the MS Windows software. Each client application builds an Application Programming Interface (API) layer on top of it, which brings inevitable differences in implementation from one application to the other. The way DDE is implemented in Form Builder, for example, is different from that of MS Excel. However, each client application supports at least five basic operations in its implementation of DDE. These are *Initiate, Request, Poke, Execute,* and *Terminate.*

Assuming that both the client and server applications are running, a DDE communication channel must be established between them, before any exchange of data can occur. The process that establishes this channel is called Initiate. During the initiation process, the client application "agrees" with the server application on a particular topic about which they will converse during the session.

After the communication channel is established, the client and the server may exchange data. The action through which the client application receives data from the server is called Request. The operation through which data is sent from the client to the server is called Poke. The DDE client may also instruct the server to perform certain actions. The commands for these actions are transmitted during the Execute operation.

Finally, when the DDE conversation is completed, the Terminate action is used to close the communication channel.

Many DDE clients applications provide for two operations, *Advise* and *Unadvise,* that are used to detect any changes in the data stored by the server application. The Advise operation is a message sent to the client application whenever a change occurs in the server application. This message may trigger the necessary actions to be taken when such changes occur, such as sending the new data from the server to the client. The Unadvise command is used to end the Advise operation.

27.2 DDE IN DEVELOPER TOOLS

As I mentioned earlier, Form Builder can play only the client part in a DDE communication transaction. This is true with all the other Developer components, including Report Builder and Graphic Builder. The DDE functionality in all these tools is implemented using a common interface provided by the package DDE. This package allows you to access DDE servers from within PL/SQL triggers and program units. Although this section and the rest of this chapter will focus on the usage of the DDE package with Form Builder, the concepts discussed here apply to other members of Developer family as well.

27.2.1 PROGRAM UNITS IN THE DDE PACKAGE

The DDE package contains five program units that provide for the five fundamental processes in every DDE communication.

- **INITIATE.** This is a function that establishes a communication channel between the Form Builder module and a DDE topic on the server application. The function returns the internal identifier that Windows assigns to the channel. This identifier can be used to funnel data through the channel from the Forms module to the server and vice versa.
- **REQUEST.** This is a procedure that places data from an item in the server into a buffer declared in the PL/SQL program unit. The data can then be accessed from this buffer and used in the Forms application.
- **POKE.** This is a procedure that sends data from the Forms module to an item in the DDE server application.
- **EXECUTE.** This is a procedure used to send a command over to the server. The command must be a valid command recognizable by the server. Most of the DDE server support their own programming languages, that allow creation of macros or subprograms. For example, all the MS Office tools have some dialect of Basic as their programming language. EXECUTE allows you to invoke these macros or subroutines from within Form Builder.
- **TERMINATE.** This procedure closes the DDE communication channel that was opened with INITIATE.

When using the procedures REQUEST, POKE, and EXECUTE, Form Builder expects a confirmation message back from the server that acknowledges the receipt of the command. All these procedures take a parameter that allows you to tell Form Builder how long to wait for the acknowledgment, before deciding that the procedure failed. The value of this time-out parameter is specified in milliseconds, and it defaults to 1000 milliseconds. If the default value is used, Forms will issue the data exchange request or command to the server. If the server has not responded within one second, Forms will raise the appropriate exception, informing the calling program that the instruction failed.

As mentioned above, DDE communication between two applications may occur only if both applications are running. The DDE package enables you to launch an application that is not currently running in order to exchange data with it through the DDE Bridge. The function APP_BEGIN may be used in this case. This function returns an internal identifier for the application. If an application started with APP_BEGIN is running and you want to place the focus of Windows on it, the procedure APP_FOCUS can be used. This procedure takes as a parameter the internal ID assigned to the application by APP_BEGIN. Finally, if you want to close an application started with APP_BEGIN, you can invoke the procedure APP_END, which takes as parameter the internal ID of the application.

27.2.2 DATA FORMATS

For the data exchange operations (Request and Poke), the procedures REQUEST and POKE will also need to know the format of the data to transfer. As explained earlier, Form Builder uses the underlying operating system DDE functions and procedures to carry out the processes. Therefore, these data formats must either be the predefined MS Windows data types, or user-defined formats registered with MS Windows.

The MS Windows predefined data formats are part of a number of global constants, described in the Windows API documentation. They are also defined as constants in the package DDE, which allows you to use them in the DDE operations from within Form Builder. The numeric value of these constants can be accessed through the function GETFORMATNUM. Furthermore, this function can be used to register a new user-defined format. If you know the value of the format, and want to retrieve its name in the form of a character string, you may use the function GETFORMATSTR.

The companion software includes a small application, called FORMATS.FMB that allows you to inspect the names and values of the pre-defined MS Windows data formats, and to create new ones. This application consists of a text list that you can use to scroll the data formats currently available. For the

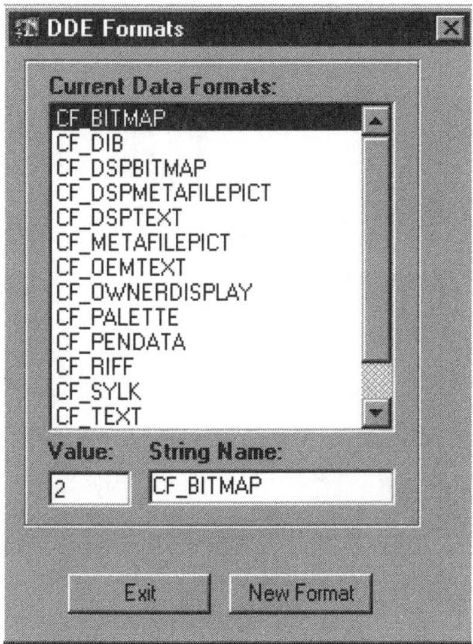

FIGURE 27.2 Data formats defined in the Form Builder DDE package

current list element, the numeric value and the name of the format are displayed on the side. Figure 27.2 shows the dialog box where this list is displayed.

Follow these steps if you want to create a new data format:

1. Click the button New Format. You will see that the fields Value and String Name will be cleared.
2. Click inside the item String Name and enter the name of the new format.
3. Press ENTER when done. You will see the numeric value that MS Windows will assign to the new format displayed in the Values item. The new format is added to the end of the list.

If you inspect the contents of the trigger WHEN-LIST-CHANGED attached to the text list, you will see the following lines:

The first statement retrieves the value of the format for the current element

```
:FORMATS.VALUE := DDE.GETFORMATNUM (:FORMATS.FORMAT);
:FORMATS.TEXT := DDE.GETFORMATSTR(DDE.
    GETFORMATNUM(:FORMATS.FORMAT));
```

of the list. The second statement retrieves the string name of this format based on its numeric value. The contents of the trigger WHEN-VALIDATE-ITEM attached to the item FORMATS.TEXT are as follows:

```
:FORMATS.VALUE := DDE.GETFORMATNUM(:FORMATS.TEXT);
Add_List_Element('FORMATS.FORMAT', 1, :FORMATS.TEXT,
TO_CHAR(:FORMATS.VALUE));
```

It is clear here that the value generated by MS Windows for the new item is generated first and then inserted at the beginning of the list.

Although the data type conversion functions are available in the DDE package, it is very unlikely that you will ever need to use them in your application. The reason for this statement is that with DDE, applications can exchange data only in the text format. Therefore, in all the POKE and REQUEST statements you will write, the data format will be CF_TEXT.

27.2.3 EXCEPTIONS IN THE DDE PACKAGE

Besides the functions and data formats discussed in the previous two sections, the DDE package contains a series of predefined exceptions that allow you to handle several situations and errors in the DDE transactions you will program.

Some of these exceptions can be raised by specific program units; others are raised as a result of failures in memory or in the MS Windows DDE layer.

The application support function APP_BEGIN can raise the exception DDE_APP_FAILURE if the application specified as the parameter of the function cannot be launched. The other two functions of the same group, APP_FOCUS and APP_END, raise the exception DDE_APP_NOT_FOUND if the application ID passed as a parameter does not correspond to a currently running application.

If the function INITIATE fails to establish a communication channel between Form Builder and the server, the exceptions DDE_INIT_FAILED or DMLERR_NO_CONV_ESTABLISHED may be raised.

If Form Builder issues a data exchange instruction or command against the server using REQUEST, EXECUTE, or POKE, and the time-out interval specified in these procedures expires without the server acknowledging the request, the following exceptions may be raised: DMLERR_DATAACKTIMEOUT, DMLERR_EXECACKTIMEOUT, or DMLERR_POKEACKTIMEOUT.

If any of the parameters passed to the previous routines is not specified correctly, the following exceptions may be raised: DDE_PARAM_ERR, DMLERR_INVALIDPARAMETER, or DMLERR_NOTPROCESSED.

If the server is busy when the DDE operation request is sent, the exception DMLERR_BUSY is raised; if the server application terminates before servicing the operations, the exception DMLERR_SERVER_DIED is raised.

The data type translation function GETFORMATSTR can raise the exception FMT_NOT_FOUND if the format number supplied as a parameter does not exists. The other function of this category, GETFORMATNUM, can raise the exception FMT_NOT_REG if the string name of the format passed as parameter is not a pre-defined MS Windows format, or cannot be registered as a user-defined format.

Finally, all the program units may raise the generic errors DMLERR_MEMORY_ERROR, and DMLERR_SYS_ERROR.

You must handle these exceptions in the program units you create, in order to ensure that the DDE commands will either complete successfully, or terminate gracefully in case an error occurs.

27.3 EXAMPLES OF DDE WITH FORM BUILDER

This section presents and discusses several examples of communication between Form Builder and other Windows applications. It will start with an example that uses Excel as DDE server. Then, you will see how MS Word can be used as a server. In the last part, you will make Form Builder interact with the Windows Program Manager through DDE.

For each instance, you will use a separate Forms application. The templates for these applications are provided with the companion software. They contain the block and data items for each application and their layout in the canvas. The names of the modules are DDEEXCL.FMB, DDEWORD.FMB, and DDEPROG.FMB. In the rest of the chapter you will add the DDE communication functionality to these templates. The final versions of these applications are also provided for you to consult. These files are DDEEXCLF.FMB, DDEWORDF.FMB, and DDEPROGF.FMB, respectively.

Despite the different functionality of each module, some general steps will be followed in each of them. These steps are:

1. Start the DDE server.
2. Establish a communication channel between the Form Builder and a topicin the application server.
3. Perform the necessary DDE operations.
4. Terminate the DDE communication.
5. Shut down the DDE server launched in Step 1.

These steps, especially Steps 2 to 4, may be repeated several times during the life of the Forms module.

27.3.1 INTEGRATING FORM BUILDER WITH SPREADSHEETS

The integration of Form Builder applications with spreadsheet packages such as Excel is probably the most fruitful way of using the DDE technology with Form Builder. Each spreadsheet is organized hierarchically in sheets, rows, and columns. Their cells are fully qualified by specifying the names of the objects above. These cells, on the other hand, are items with which you exchange data during a DDE conversation. Thus, spreadsheets have a large number of items that you can reference or exchange data with in your applications. Another advantage of exchanging data with spreadsheets is their excellent support for a variety of functions such as financial, mathematical, trigonometric, and statistical functions. By establishing a communication channel between Form Builder and one of these spreadsheets, you increase by orders of magnitude the ability to compute and analyze the data stored in the database.

In the module DDEEXCL.FMB, you will implement two financial functions from MS Excel. The first one can be used to compute the straight-line depreciation of an asset for a given period of time. The second one can be used to return the periodic payment for an annuity based on constant payments and a constant interest rate over a given period of time. Start the Form Builder, and open the module DDEEXCL.FMB. This module has only one canvas, which looks like Figure 27.3.

A quick inspection of the contents of this module will reveal that all three blocks of this module are control blocks. The left half of the screen contains the items of block SLN, which will be used to compute the straight-line depreciation of an asset. COST will be used to enter the initial value of the asset. SALVAGE will contain the value of the asset at the end of the depreciation period. The number of periods over which the asset will be depreciated will be entered in the item LIFE. As an example, if you pay $3,000 to purchase a computer for your home business, and, for tax purposes, intend to depreciate 90 percent of its value over 4 years, you could set COST to 3000, SALVAGE to 300, and LIFE to 4. Then click the push button Calculate. This button will invoke the Excel function that will calculate the depreciation and will store it in the display item DEPRECIATION.

The right half of the screen contains the items of block PMT, where you will compute the periodic payment for an annuity. The first two items store the interest rate in percentage points. The ANNUAL_RATE item is provided for convenience, since rates usually are defined in these terms. However, the formula for the payment will use the monthly percentage rate that is computed and stored in the item RATE. NUM_YEARS is the life of the annuity in years. Based on the value entered here, the number of periods, or months, in the life of the annuity is computed and stored in the item NPER. The check item TYPE is used to specify the type of payment for the annuity. If the box is checked, the payment is made at the beginning of the month. If the box is not checked, the annuity is paid at the end of the month. The items PV and FV are used to provide the present value of the annuity, and its final value at the end of the payment period. The button CALCULATE invokes the Excel function PMT, which calculates and stores in item PAYMENT the periodic payment for the annuity based on the data entered. As an example, to calculate how much you will have to pay for a mortgage of $150,000, at a fixed rate of 8% APR, payable in 30 years, you should set ANNUAL_RATE to 8, NUM_YEARS to 30, PV to 150000, FV to 0, and click the button Calculate.

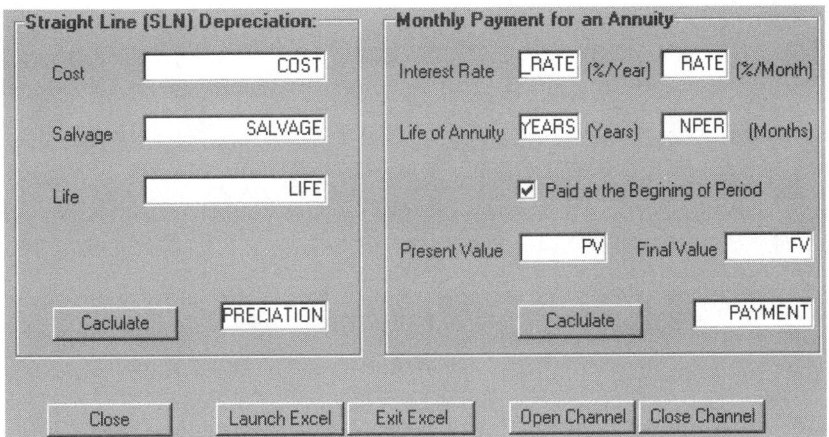

FIGURE 27.3 Layout of a Forms application that interacts with Excel using DDE.

Finally, this module contains five push buttons, horizontally aligned at the bottom, which belong to the block CONTROL. The first one to the left closes the application. The next two buttons to the right start and terminate Excel. The fourth button establishes a communication channel with Excel, and the last one closes it (see Figure 27.3).

In this module, you will need to access the application ID that Windows assigns to Excel when started from several program units. Likewise, the internal ID assigned to the communication channel when established will be used in several triggers and program units. These internal IDs will be stored in two global variables, called `GLOBAL.application_id`, and `GLOBAL.channel_id`. Declare these variables in a PRE-FORM trigger and assign the NULL value to both of them.

Now, add the necessary triggers to the push buttons in the module's button palette as described in the following paragraphs.

1. Create a WHEN-BUTTON-PRESSED trigger for the item LAUNCH and enter the statements shown in Figure 27.4 in the body of the trigger. The statements shown in this figure assume that Excel is installed in the directory C:\MSOffice\Excel. If your environment differs provide the appropriate location of EXCEL.EXE. As you can see from this figure, when the application is launched for the first time, its ID is stored in the global variable

```
DECLARE
 appl_name  VARCHAR2(255);
BEGIN
 IF :GLOBAL.application_id IS NOT NULL THEN
   MESSAGE('Application is already running.');
 ELSE
   appl_name := 'C:\MSOffice\Excel\EXCEL.EXE';
   :GLOBAL.application_id := DDE.APP_BEGIN(appl_name,
DDE.APP_MODE_NORMAL);
 END IF;
EXCEPTION
 WHEN DDE.DDE_APP_FAILURE THEN
   MESSAGE('Could not launch application for DDE
operations.');
   RAISE FORM_TRIGGER_FAILURE;
 WHEN OTHERS THEN
   MESSAGE('Error: '||TO_CHAR(SQLCODE)||' '||SQLERRM);
   RAISE FORM_TRIGGER_FAILURE;
END;
```

FIGURE 27.4 Launching a DDE server application.

GLOBAL.application_id. This avoids repeated startups of the server application when an instance has been started previously and is available for use. Notice that the application is started in Normal mode. To start it minimized or maximized, the parameter DDE.APP_MODE_NORMAL in DDE.APP_BEGIN should be replaced with DDE.APP_MODE_MINIMIZED or DDE.APP_MODE_MAXIMIZED.

2. Create the WHEN-BUTTON-PRESSED trigger for button CLOSE, and enter the statements shown in Figure 27.5 in its body. The only statement that may require some clarification in this figure is the use of the procedure DDE.APP_FOCUS to make Excel the current application before terminating it. When you send data over to Excel items, they will be stored temporarily in a new document. When DDE.APP_END instructs the application to terminate, Excel will prompt you to save the modified document. The prompt will not be visible normally, unless Excel is given the Windows focus.

   Note that when the server application is terminated, Windows will no longer recognize its internal ID, or the ID of any DDE channel that was established with the application. Therefore you must set to NULL the global variables that store these ID values in the application.

```
DECLARE
 application_id   PLS_INTEGER;
BEGIN
 IF :GLOBAL.application_id IS NULL THEN
   MESSAGE('Cannot terminate an instance that is not
initiated by this application.');
 ELSE
   application_id := TO_NUMBER(:GLOBAL.application_id);
   DDE.APP_FOCUS(application_id);
   DDE.APP_END(application_id);
   :GLOBAL.application_id := NULL;
   :GLOBAL.channel_id := NULL;
 END IF;
EXCEPTION
 WHEN DDE.DDE_APP_NOT_FOUND THEN
   MESSAGE('Could not find application for DDE
operations.');
   RAISE FORM_TRIGGER_FAILURE;
 WHEN OTHERS THEN
   MESSAGE('Error: '||TO_CHAR(SQLCODE)||' '||SQLERRM);
   RAISE FORM_TRIGGER_FAILURE;
END;
```

FIGURE 27.5 Terminating a DDE server application.

3. Create the trigger WHEN-BUTTON-PRESSED for the button EXIT_FORM. The contents of this trigger are very similar with the trigger discussed in the previous step. In fact, the DECLARE and EXCEPTION parts of these triggers are identical. In the execution part, you should end the instance of Excel that may have been started previously, and then invoke the built-in procedure EXIT_FORM.
4. Create the trigger WHEN-BUTTON-PRESSED for button OPEN_CHANNEL. This trigger invokes DDE.INITIATE to establish a communication channel with Excel. The topic of conversation will be "BOOK1," which is the document that Excel opens by default when it is started. Figure 27.6 provides the necessary details to implement this trigger.

   This trigger checks first for a communications channel that may already exist. It assumes that Excel is not available if it is not started from within your application. This means that although the users may be working with Excel on their own, the trigger will not take advantage of the instance that they are already running. To complete the functionality it is designed to perform, this application should launch its own duplicate instance of Excel instead. This is certainly a draw back inherent in the way DDE is designed

```
BEGIN
 IF :GLOBAL.channel_id IS NOT NULL THEN
   MESSAGE('Communication channel already established.');
 ELSIF :GLOBAL.application_id IS NULL THEN
   MESSAGE('Application must be launched first.');
 ELSE
  :GLOBAL.channel_id := DDE.INITIATE('EXCEL', 'BOOK1');
 END IF;
EXCEPTION
 WHEN DDE.DDE_INIT_FAILED THEN
   MESSAGE('Could not initialize DDE communication
channel.');
   RAISE FORM_TRIGGER_FAILURE;
 WHEN DDE.DMLERR_NO_CONV_ESTABLISHED THEN
   MESSAGE('Could not establish DDE communication
channel.');
   RAISE FORM_TRIGGER_FAILURE;
 WHEN OTHERS THEN
   MESSAGE('Error: '||TO_CHAR(SQLCODE)||' '||SQLERRM);
   RAISE FORM_TRIGGER_FAILURE;
END;
```

FIGURE 27.6 Establishing a DDE communication channel.

to work. The computer resources will not be used efficiently. However, from a data security perspective, it may be considered an advantage as well, because it protects the documents that the users may be editing in the other instance from accidental modifications.

5. Create the trigger WHEN-BUTTON-PRESSED for button CLOSE_CHANNEL. The content and functionality of this trigger are similar to those described above. This trigger simply checks that a DDE communications channel is open, and, if so, invokes DDE.TERMINATE procedure to close it. Figure 27.7 shows the details of this trigger.

So far, you have implemented the functionality that starts Excel, establishes the communication channel between Excel and Forms, terminates this channel, and closes Excel. In order to complete the functionality of the application, you must create the PL/SQL program units that transfer the data from Forms items to Excel cells, invoke the functions SLN and PMT in Excel, and return the results of these functions to Form Builder. Create a function, called `Calc_SLN`, and enter its specifications as shown in Figure 27.8.

This function takes as parameter the communication channel ID established previously, and the numeric arguments required to compute the straight-line depreciation. The first three statements in the execution part of the function transfer the data from the input arguments of the function to Excel cells. Note the fact that these data are all converted to text strings before handed over to the DDE.POKE function for transmission.

```
DECLARE
 channel_id   PLS_INTEGER;
BEGIN
 IF :GLOBAL.channel_id IS NULL THEN
   MESSAGE('No communication channels are open at this
time.');
 ELSE
   channel_id := TO_NUMBER(:GLOBAL.channel_id);
   DDE.TERMINATE(channel_id);
   :GLOBAL.channel_id := NULL;
 END IF;
EXCEPTION
 WHEN OTHERS THEN
   MESSAGE('Error: '||TO_CHAR(SQLCODE)||' '||SQLERRM);
   RAISE FORM_TRIGGER_FAILURE;
END;
```

FIGURE 27.7 Terminating a DDE communication channel.

```
FUNCTION Calc_SLN (channel_id PLS_INTEGER,
                   cost       NUMBER,
                   salvage    NUMBER,
                   life       NUMBER)
RETURN NUMBER IS
 return_value VARCHAR2(1024) := NULL
BEGIN
 DDE.POKE(channel_id, 'R1C1', TO_CHAR(cost),
DDE.CF_TEXT, 1000);
 DDE.POKE(channel_id, 'R1C2', TO_CHAR(salvage),
DDE.CF_TEXT, 1000);
 DDE.POKE(channel_id, 'R1C3', TO_CHAR(life),
DDE.CF_TEXT, 1000);
 DDE.POKE(channel_id, 'R1C4', '=TEXT(SLN(A1, B1, C1),
0.00)', DDE.CF_TEXT, 1000);

 DDE.REQUEST(channel_id, 'R1C4', return_value,
DDE.CF_TEXT, 1000);

 RETURN(TO_NUMBER(return_value));
EXCEPTION
 WHEN OTHERS THEN
   MESSAGE('Error: '||TO_CHAR(SQLCODE)||' '||SQLERRM);
   RAISE FORM_TRIGGER_FAILURE;
END;
```

FIGURE 27.8 Calculating the straight-line depreciation of an asset.

The fourth POKE statement is similar in structure to the previous three ones. It does little more than sending a stream of characters from the form to the spreadsheet. This string however, is different from the previous three. It is not just raw data, but contains a command that will direct Excel to compute the SLN function and format the outcome. The SLN function will take as arguments the data stored earlier in cells A1, B1, and C1. Note that when you send data over, these items are referred to as R1C1, R1C2, and R1C3, but in order to refer to the contents of these cells in Excel, you must use the notations A1, B1, and C1.

The value computed by the function SLN must be returned to the form through the DDE communication channel. Therefore, it must be in text format. This is the reason why the Excel data conversion function TEXT is called after the

SLN function, and before the DDE.REQUEST function transfers the result back to the form module.

Now create the trigger WHEN-BUTTON-PRESSED for button CALCULATE in the block SLN. The contents of this trigger should be as shown in Figure 27.9.

This trigger checks first that a DDE communication channel is established, and then invokes the function `Calc_SLN` with values entered in the items of block SLN as arguments. The properties of these items are set to ensure that the arguments passed to the function will be valid ones. For example, the property Required is set to "Yes" and the property Lowest Allowed Value is set to "0." This means that before the trigger shown in Figure 27.9 is activated, non-negative numbers must be entered in the text items of block SLN. In general, you should check for the validity of the arguments before sending the data over to Excel for computation.

There is no conceptual difference in the way you calculate the monthly payments for an annuity. Without repeating the detailed discussion above, Figure 27.10 presents the contents of function `Calc_PMT`. This function is called from the trigger WHEN-BUTTON-PRESSED associated with the button PMT.CALCULATE. Figure 27.11 shows the contents of this trigger.

After you enter these last two program units, save and compile the form. Make sure to use it in order to answer the questions posed at the beginning of the section. You will find, for example, that over the next four years, you can depreciate your $3,000 computer by $675 every year. The monthly payments for your 30-year, fixed 8% APR, $150,000 mortgage will be $1,093 per month if you pay at the beginning of the month, but $1,101 per month if you pay at the end of it. Notice

```
DECLARE
 channel_id PLS_INTEGER;
BEGIN
 IF :GLOBAL.channel_id IS NOT NULL THEN
   channel_id := TO_NUMBER(:GLOBAL.channel_id);
   :SLN.DEPRECIATION := Calc_SLN(channel_id, :SLN.COST,
                                  :SLN.SALVAGE, :SLN.LIFE);
 ELSE
   MESSAGE('A communication channel must be established
first.');
 END IF;
END;
```

FIGURE 27.9 Calling the function Calc_SLN.

```
FUNCTION Calc_PMT (channel_id PLS_INTEGER,
                   rate       NUMBER,
                   nper       NUMBER,
                   pv         NUMBER,
                   fv         NUMBER,
                   type       NUMBER)
RETURN NUMBER IS
 return_value VARCHAR2(1024) := '';
BEGIN
 DDE.POKE(channel_id, 'R1C1', TO_CHAR(rate), DDE.CF_TEXT,
1000);
 DDE.POKE(channel_id, 'R1C2', TO_CHAR(nper), DDE.CF_TEXT,
1000);
 DDE.POKE(channel_id, 'R1C3', TO_CHAR(pv),  DDE.CF_TEXT, 1000);
 DDE.POKE(channel_id, 'R1C4', TO_CHAR(fv),  DDE.CF_TEXT, 1000);
 DDE.POKE(channel_id, 'R1C5', TO_CHAR(type), DDE.CF_TEXT,
1000);
 DDE.POKE(channel_id, 'R1C6', '=TEXT(PMT(A1, B1, C1, D1, E1),
0.00)', DDE.CF_TEXT, 1000);

 DDE.REQUEST(channel_id, 'R1C6', return_value, DDE.CF_TEXT,
1000);

 RETURN(TO_NUMBER(return_value));
EXCEPTION
 WHEN OTHERS THEN
   MESSAGE('Error: '||TO_CHAR(SQLCODE)||' '||SQLERRM);
   RAISE FORM_TRIGGER_FAILURE;
END;
```

FIGURE 27.10 Calculating the periodic payment for an annuity.

that the value calculated will be a negative number, to indicate that this is cash that will flow away from you for the annuity term.

You can use the PMT block for a variety of other purposes. Suppose for example that your heir will go to college in 10 years, and you want to have $100,000 saved for her Law degree by then. Your local municipal bonds offer a 6% return on the investment and you want to see how much you need to save every month to reach your goal. In the block PMT, set ANNUAL_RATE to 6, NUM_YEARS to 10, PV to 0, FV to 100000, and click the push button Calculate. You will see that you will need to send $607 at the beginning of each month to your investor.

```
DECLARE
 channel_id PLS_INTEGER;
BEGIN
 IF :GLOBAL.channel_id IS NOT NULL THEN
   channel_id := TO_NUMBER(:GLOBAL.channel_id);
   :PMT.PAYMENT := Calc_PMT(channel_id, :PMT.RATE/100,
:PMT.NPER,
                     :PMT.PV, :PMT.FV, :PMT.TYPE);
 ELSE
   MESSAGE('A communication channel must be established
first.');
 END IF;
END;
```

FIGURE 27.11 Invoking function Calc_PMT.

> **TIP**
>
> Using this formula, you can see yet another convincing proof of the power of the compound interest (interest earned on interest) that often goes unnoticed. Had you started saving ten years ago, when your baby was born, the monthly sum you had to contribute to your savings would have been only $215. To reach the $100,000 objective with the same amount of monthly investment, but starting today, ten years late, you have to guarantee a steady rate of return of 23 percent for the next ten years.

27.3.2 INTEGRATING FORM BUILDER WITH WORD PROCESSORS

Spreadsheets provide a high number of items that can be used as data containers in DDE transactions. This feature originates from the highly structured organization of these applications. Word processing packages such as MS Word, WordPerfect, or AmiPro, given their nature, have a smaller number of objects loosely organized inside their documents. Therefore, when word processors are used as server applications in DDE transactions, is the number of choices you have for items is limited.

Nevertheless, as you will see in this section, these applications can be used successfully to expand the functionality of Form Builder applications. The most popular combination of word processors and database packages is the creation of form letters. Form letters are documents based on a template, which differ from each other in a limited number of points. For example, the video store discussed in this book may need to send reminders to customers who fail to return their videos on time. The content and format of each letter will be similar to the one shown in Figure 27.12.

Certain data in this letter will reflect information that is already stored in the database such as the customer name and address or the title of the movie. It would certainly be nice if you could spare the account representatives the effort of typing all these data elements for each letter they send out.

In order to implement the transfer of data from the form module to the letter template, some items must exist or be defined in the document. Word processing applications use bookmarks as DDE items. Bookmarks are markers of certain areas of text in the document. Every word processor provides for ways to create bookmarks. For example, in MS Word you would take the following steps:

VIDEO RENTAL STORE

8123 Lincoln Avenue
Falls Church, VA 33334-2121

March 30, 1998

Michelle Johnson
123 North Main Street
Apt 309
Falls Church, VA 20129-3453

Dear Michelle :

This is a reminder about the movie *The Piano*, which is now over 30 days past due. If there is a problem with the video tape, please call me at once so we can correct it.

Thank you for your business and for your prompt attention to this matter.

Sincerely,

Robert S. Walker

Account Representative

P.S. If you have already returned the movie, please accept our thanks and disregard this notice

FIGURE 27.12 Typical form letter that can be produced by integrating Form Builder with word processors.

1. Select the text that will be marked.
2. Choose Edit | Bookmark from the menu. The Bookmark dialog box will appear (see Figure 27.13).
3. Type the new name in the Bookmark Name field.
4. Press Add button to create the new bookmark.

Figure 27.13 also shows the bookmarks that are created in the template document LETTER.DOC. This document is provided with the companion software and will be used in this section in combination with the Form Builder module DDEWORD.FMB. The bookmarks are ordered by their location in the document. If the contents of Figure 27.13 are compared with the template document shown in Figure 27.12, it is not difficult to identify the location of each bookmark. You can also open the document LETTER.DOC and press F5 to go to any bookmark you want. Further more, you can have Word display the bookmarks inside square brackets by following these steps.

1. Chose Tools | Options... from the MS Word menu. The Options dialog box appears.
2. Select View tab.
3. In the Show group, check the check box item Bookmarks and then click the OK button.

As it was the case with the module in the previous section, DDEWORD.FMB contains a template of the form to which you will add the DDE functionality. The layout of the items in this module is shown in Figure 27.14.

All the data items in this block are query-only, and can be used to retrieve the name and address of the customer, and the title of the movie that the customer has failed to return. The text item TEMPLATE, at the bottom of the window is where the location of the letter template document is stored. The information entered here will be used to open the template when MS Word is initially

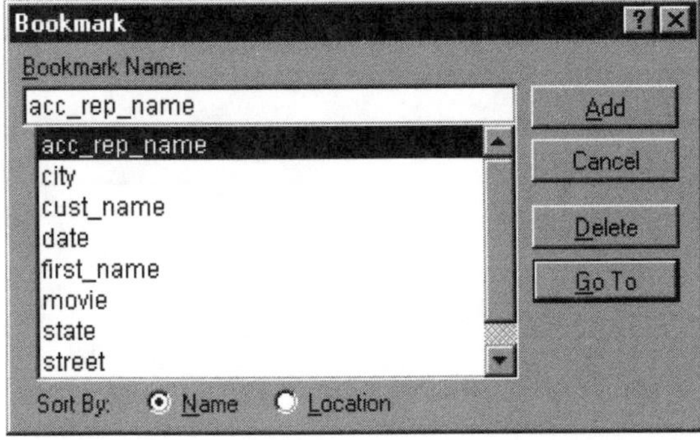

FIGURE 27.13 MS Word Bookmark dialog box.

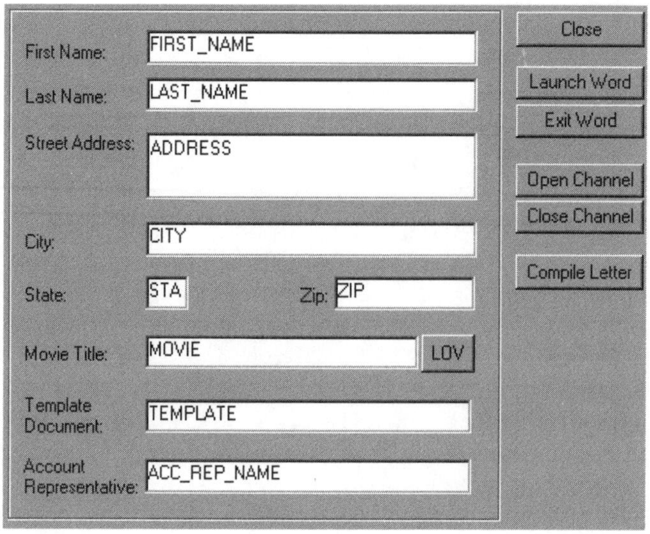

FIGURE 27.14 Layout of a Forms application that interacts with MS Word using DDE.

launched, and will also serve as a topic of conversation when the DDE communication channel will be established. The text item ACC_REP_NAME will be used to send the name of the account representative to the Word document.

The functionality attached to the first five push buttons is almost identical to the functionality attached to these buttons in the module DDEEXL.FMB. The only changes that should be made in order to reflect the new type of DDE server are as follows:

1. In the WHEN-BUTTON-PRESSED for button LAUNCH, the name of the application is defined by the command below:

   ```
   appl_name := 'C:\MSOffice\WINWORD\WINWORD.EXE'||:CUS-
   TOMER.TEMPLATE;
   ```

2. In the WHEN-BUTTON-PRESSED for button OPEN_CHANNEL the DDE communication channel is initialized with this statement:

   ```
   :GLOBAL.channel_id := DDE.INITIATE ('WINWORD', :CUS-
   TOMER.TEMPLATE);
   ```

CAUTION

In the module DDEWORD.FMB, as in DDEEXCL.FMB, the location of WINWORD.EXE is hardcoded. You must ensure that you use the right path for your environment.

These triggers are already included in the module DDEWORD.FMB, and you may inspect them on your own if you have any questions regarding their functionality. Here the focus will be on the trigger associated with the button COMPILE. When this trigger is executed, it initially performs some minor arrangements and formatting of the data queried in the CUSTOMER block. Then it passes these data elements to the procedure `Compile_Letter`, which will ultimately send them to the MS Word document, and display the letter to the user. The contents of this procedure are shown in Figure 27.15.

You can see from this figure how the function DDE.POKE is used to transfer the data from the Form Builder environment to the MS Word document items. These items are addressed using the bookmark names defined in the template document.

TIP

Each Word document has three bookmarks built in its structure. Their names are `\doc`, `\startofdoc`, and `\endofdoc`. The first bookmark represents the entire document. If, for example, you want to transfer the contents of a document in an Form Builder item, you would use the following statement:

```
DDE.REQUEST (channel_id, '\doc', buffer_name,
DDE.CF_TEXT, 1000);
```

The other two bookmarks represent the beginning and the end of the document, respectively, but do not actually contain any data. Consider for example the following statement:

```
DDE.POKE (channel_id, '\startofdoc', 'At the
beginning of document.', DDE.CF_TEXT, 1000);
```

This statement will add the string in quotes at the begging of the document, but will not overwrite any existing data. The bookmark `\startofdoc` itself will remain to the left of the new string, at the beginning of the document.

Besides these bookmarks, Word sets and updates a number of other predefined bookmarks, which are documented in the on-line help under topic *Predefined Bookmarks.* Note the important fact that these built-in bookmarks must be preceded by the "\" character in order to be recognized by MS Word.

```
PROCEDURE Compile_Letter (channel_id  PLS_INTEGER,
                          date   VARCHAR2,
                          cust_name     VARCHAR2,
                          street        VARCHAR2,
                          city   VARCHAR2,
                          state         VARCHAR2,
                          zip           VARCHAR2,
                          first_name  VARCHAR2,
                          movie         VARCHAR2,
                          acc_rep_name VARCHAR2) IS
BEGIN
 DDE.POKE(channel_id, 'date',         date,         DDE.CF_TEXT, 1000);
 DDE.POKE(channel_id, 'cust_name',    cust_name,    DDE.CF_TEXT, 1000);
 DDE.POKE(channel_id, 'street',       street,       DDE.CF_TEXT, 1000);
 DDE.POKE(channel_id, 'city',         city,         DDE.CF_TEXT, 1000);
 DDE.POKE(channel_id, 'state',        state,        DDE.CF_TEXT, 1000);
 DDE.POKE(channel_id, 'zip',          zip,          DDE.CF_TEXT, 1000);
 DDE.POKE(channel_id, 'first_name',   first_name,   DDE.CF_TEXT, 1000);
 DDE.POKE(channel_id, 'movie',        movie,        DDE.CF_TEXT, 1000);
 DDE.POKE(channel_id, 'acc_rep_name', acc_rep_name, DDE.CF_TEXT, 1000);
EXCEPTION
 WHEN OTHERS THEN
   MESSAGE('Error: '||TO_CHAR(SQLCODE)||' '||SQLERRM);
   RAISE FORM_TRIGGER_FAILURE;
END;
```

FIGURE 27.15 Transferring data to MS Word through a DDE communication channel.

The only thing that is left now to complete the task is to create the WHEN-BUTTON-PRESSED trigger for button COMPILE. In this trigger, before issuing the call to the procedure `Compile_Letter`, you need to prepare some of its arguments, so that they match the format of the data elements in the template letter. For example, you will retrieve the SYSTEM date and convert it in the format `Month DD, YYYY` which is more appropriate in a business letter than the default `DD-MON-YYYY` format. You will also concatenate the first and last names of the customer.

After the procedure `Compile_Letter` sends the data to the MS Word document, the users should have the ability to do any last minute editing and send the letter to the printer. Therefore the last statement of the trigger sets the focus of Windows on the MS Word document. Figure 27.16 shows the contents of this trigger.

```
DECLARE
 appl_id      PLS_INTEGER;
 channel_id   PLS_INTEGER;
 date         VARCHAR2(50);
 cust_name    VARCHAR2(60);
BEGIN
 IF :GLOBAL.channel_id IS NOT NULL THEN
   channel_id := TO_NUMBER(:GLOBAL.channel_id);
   SELECT TO_CHAR(SYSDATE, 'Month DD, YYYY') INTO date FROM DUAL;
   cust_name := :CUSTOMER.FIRST_NAME||' '||:CUSTOMER.LAST_NAME;

   Compile_Letter(channel_id, date, cust_name, :CUSTOMER.ADDRESS,
                  :CUSTOMER.CITY, :CUSTOMER.STATE, :CUSTOMER.ZIP,
                  :CUSTOMER.FIRST_NAME, :CUSTOMER.MOVIE,
                  :CUSTOMER.ACC_REP_NAME);

   appl_id := TO_NUMBER(:GLOBAL.application_id);
   DDE.APP_FOCUS(appl_id);
 ELSE
   MESSAGE('A communication channel must be established first.');
 END IF;
END;
```

FIGURE 27.16 Trigger that transfers data from Form Builder to MS Word.

27.3.3 CONTROLLING OTHER PROGRAMS FROM WITHIN FORM BUILDER

The examples presented in the previous two sections show how Form Builder modules can exchange data with other applications. In this section, you will see how to send commands from form modules to another application using a DDE communication channel.

For the DDE to work, both the client and the server applications must be up and running at the same time. However, there is one server application that is always running as long as Windows is running. This is the Windows shell program, also known as the Program Manager. By establishing a DDE communication channel between Form Builder and the Program Manager, you will be able to send commands and directives to the Windows shell from within Forms.

In this section, you will use the module DDEPROG.FMB, which contains only five push buttons aligned horizontally. The first three of these buttons, labeled Close, Open Channel, and Close Channel, have a similar functionality as their counterparts in the modules discussed in the previous sections. Note that in this case, you do not need push buttons to launch or terminate the DDE server, since this server, the Program Manager, will be available during the life of our application.

For the Windows Program Manager, both the Service and the Topic of conversation are called PROGMAN. Recall that they are required to initiate a communication link through DDE. Therefore, the statement that establishes this link in the WHEN-BUTTON-PRESSED trigger of the Open Channel button is as follows:

```
:GLOBAL.channel_id := DDE.INITIATE ('PROGMAN',
'PROGMAN');
```

In the triggers associated with the other two buttons, Create and Delete, you will send some commands to the Program Manager. Among the most frequently used commands with the Program Manager are `CreateGroup`, `AddItem`, `DeleteItem`, `ShowGroup`, and `DeleteGroup`. These commands are issued primarily by installation utilities, in order to create the necessary program groups and items to access the applications. Here you will access them form within Form Builder using the DDE functionality. The discussion has practical importance, because you can follow the same approach to create your own installation utility, as a tool in the cumbersome process of deploying an application to environments that are not configured consistently.

As mentioned earlier the function DDE.EXECUTE allows you to send a command string to the server application through the DDE communication channel. This command string is enclosed in single quotes and may contain one or more commands recognizable by the server. Each command must be enclosed in square brackets. For example, to create a program group called Chapter 27, you could use the following statement:

```
DDE.EXECUTE (channel_id, '[CreateGroup(Chapter 27)]',
1000);
```

If, on the other hand, you want to send the instruction to create the group together with that to show the group, you would use the following statement:

```
DDE.EXECUTE (channel_id, '[CreateGroup(Chapter 27)]
[ShowGroup(Chapter 27, 1)]', 1000);
```

As you can see from these statements, the function `CreateGroup` takes the name of the group to be created as the only argument. This name will become the label that will be displayed in Programs menu of the Windows Start menu or in the title bar of the group's window. The function `DeleteGroup` takes only the group name as a parameter as well. This function deletes a group from the Program Manager.

The function `ShowGroup` takes two parameters. The first one is the name of the group to be displayed. The second parameter is the mode in which the window of the group is set when the function is executed. The values of this parameter range from 1 to 8. When values 1, 2, and 3 are used, the window will be displayed in Normal, Minimized, and Maximized mode, respectively.

In the module DDEPROG.FMB you will enable users to create a program group called Chapter 27 and add program items to it. These program items will open the MS Word document that served as a letter template in the previous section. They will also run the modules DDEEXCL.FMB and DDEWORD.FMB. Other program items could be added to this group as well. The function `AddItem` is used to add a program item to the current program group. Let us discuss briefly this function, before moving to the actual implementation of its functionality in the trigger.

The function `AddItem` may take up to eight parameters. The description and sequence of these parameters is as follows: `Command Line`, `Description`, `Icon Source File`, `Icon Index`, `X Position`, `Y Position`, `Working Directory`, `Shortcut Key`. You may realize that this is the same information that you provide in the Program Item Properties dialog box when you create a new program item from the Program Manager.

The `Command Line` is the statement that will be executed when the icon of the item will be double-clicked. `Description` will be the label that will go underneath the icon of the program item in its parent program group. `Icon Source File` is the file that contains the icon for the item. Since this file may contain several icons, the `Icon Index` allows you to pick the one you want. `X Position` and `Y Position` are the initial coordinates of the program item icon in the window of the parent program group. The `Working Directory` is the directory where the files of the program item are located and where new files will be created. The `Shortcut Key` is a combination of the CTRL, SHIFT, or ALT keys, usually CTRL+ALT, with a character from the keyboard that allows you to switch to the application when it is running or to launch it from the Program Manager.

Now you are ready to create the WHEN-BUTTON-PRESSED triggers for buttons CREATE and DELETE. Figure 27.17 shows the contents of the first trigger. The first call to DDE.EXECUTE creates the program group called Chapter 27. The second call creates a program item that will open the MS Word document C:\MRD\LETTER.DOC. The description for this program item is Letter Template. Its icon will be drawn from the MS Word executable file. The horizontal position for the icon will be 30, and the working directory of the program will be C:\MSOffice\Winword. The next two EXECUTE statements create two additional program items for modules DDEEXCL.FMX and DDEWORD.FMX. Finally, after the program groups are added, the `ShowGroup` command is issued to display the new program group in normal mode.

```
DECLARE
 channel_id PLS_INTEGER;
BEGIN
  IF :GLOBAL.channel_id IS NOT NULL THEN
    channel_id := TO_NUMBER(:GLOBAL.channel_id);
    DDE.EXECUTE(channel_id, '[CreateGroup(Chapter 27)]', 1000);
    DDE.EXECUTE(channel_id, '[AddItem(winword c:\mrd\letter.doc,
                Letter Template, c:\MSOffice\Winword\winword.
                exe, , 30, ,
                c:\MSOffice\Winword)]', 1000);
    DDE.EXECUTE(channel_id, '[AddItem(f50run32.exe c:\forms
                             \ddeexcl.fmx,
                Forms & Excel, f50run32.exe, , 110, ,
                c:\orawin\bin)]', 1000);
    DDE.EXECUTE(channel_id, '[AddItem(f50run32.exe c:\forms
                             \ddeword.fmx,
                Forms & Word, f50run32.exe, , 190, ,
                c:\orawin\bin)]', 1000);
    DDE.EXECUTE(channel_id, '[ShowGroup(Chapter 27, 1)]', 1000);
  ELSE
    MESSAGE('A communication channel must be established first.');
  END IF;
END;
```

FIGURE 27.17 Executing Program Manager commands from Form Builder.

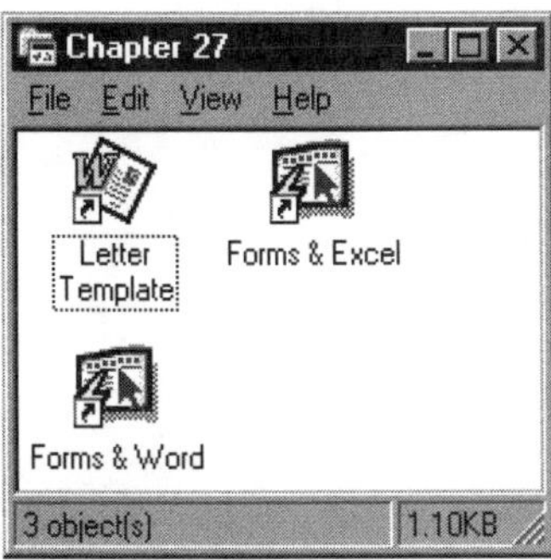

FIGURE 27.18 Program group and program items created from Form Builder.

Depending on your environment, the actual directory names that you will use in the trigger may be different, but the approach is the same. Notice that you may choose not to specify some parameters in the `AddItem` program. However, if other parameters that follow them are specified, you must maintain their position with an empty space. In the statements Figure 27.17, although the icon index or vertical position parameters are not specified, an empty space followed by a comma is used to represent them. The empty space is not needed for the shortcut key parameters because there are no other parameters specified after it.

The trigger attached to button DELETE will be very similar to the trigger discussed above. The only difference is that all the DDE.EXECUTE statements there are replaced by the following line:

```
DDE.EXECUTE (channel_id, '[DeleteGroup(Chapter 27)]',
1000);
```

When you are finished with the editing of both triggers, save, generate and run the module DDEPROG.FMB. Click the Open Channel button to initiate a conversation with the Program Manager. Click the button Create to create the program group with the program items discussed above. The picture you should see will be similar to Figure 27.18. If you do not want to keep this program group in your desktop, return to the module DDEPROG.FMB and click the button Delete to remove it from the Program Manager.

27.4 SUMMARY

This chapter discussed one of the earliest Windows technologies for data sharing and exchange between applications: Dynamic Data Exchange or DDE. Among major concepts explained here were:

- **What Is DDE?**
  - DDE Components
  - DDE Actions
- **DDE in Developer Tools**
  - Program Units in the DDE Package
  - Data Formats
  - Exceptions in the DDE Package
- **Examples of DDE with Form Builder**
  - Integrating Form Builder with Spreadsheets
  - Integrating Form Builder with Word Processors
  - Controlling Other Programs from within Form Builder

The following table describes the software assets that were discussed in this chapter. From the main HTML page of the companion software follow the links *Software* and *Chapter 27* to access these assets:

ASSET NAME	DESCRIPTION
FORMATS.FMB	A Form Builder module that allows you to inspect the names and values of data formats defined in the DDE package.
FORMATS.FMX	The executable version of FORMATS.FMB compiled for Win32 platforms.
DDEEXCEL.FMB	A Form Builder module that will be integrated with Microsoft Excel using DDE. Use this module as starting point for the activities discussed in Section 27.3.1.
DDEEXCEL_1.FMB	The final version of DDEEXCEL.FMB with all the activities discussed in Section 27.3.1.
DDEEXCEL_1.FMX	The executable version of DDEEXCEL_1.FMB compiled for Win32 platforms.
DDEWORD.FMB	A Form Builder module that will be integrated with Microsoft Word using DDE. Use this module as starting point for the activities discussed in Section 27.3.2.
DDEWORD_1.FMB	The final version of DDEWORD.FMB with all the activities discussed in Section 27.3.2.
DDEWORD_1.FMX	The executable version of DDEWORD_1.FMB compiled for Win32 platforms.
LETTER.DOC	A Microsoft Word document that serves as a template for the form letters created in Section 27.3.2.
DDEPROG.FMB	A Form Builder module that will be integrated with Windows Program Manager using DDE. Use this module as starting point for the activities discussed in Section 27.3.3.

ASSET NAME	DESCRIPTION
DDEPROG_1.FMB	The final version of DDEPROG.FMB with all the activities discussed in Section 27.3.3.
DDEPROG_1.FMX	The executable version of DDEPROG_1.FMB compiled for Win32 platforms.

Chapter 28

COM-Based Technologies

If there's one thing a computer is good at,
it's helping you combine diverse elements.
—Michael Hawley

The Component Object Model (COM) is a technology standard that enables the integration and reusability of different software components in one application. This chapter and the following discuss a number of its aspects and how they relate to applications that you develop with Form Builder. This chapter, in particular, focuses on one of the earlier implementations of COM, the OLE Documents technology, which allows the creation of compound documents through the linking or embedding of objects.

28.1 WHAT IS COM?

COM and DCOM—its extension for distributed computing—form the foundation upon which the architecture, and the fortunes, of a number of software products are build. It has become ubiquitous in the Microsoft Windows environments and its being extended at a furious pace to a number of other environments, including Mac and several implementations of UNIX operating systems. This section presents a brief history of COM and its major concepts.

28.1.1 HISTORY OF COM

Reviewing the history of COM is like reviewing the history of Microsoft's several versions and implementation of Windows operating systems. Each major technological achievement in these operating systems aimed at enabling users to share and reuse data and software components is also a milestone in the road towards COM or in the process of implementing COM. The following paragraphs describe the evolution of these achievements:

- **The Windows Clipboard.** You may also call this the Stone Age approach to share data between applications running on Windows. The clipboard serves as the temporary placeholder of data copied from and application source. These data can be pasted in one or more target applications, provided they understand and accept the type of data help in the clipboard.
- **Dynamic Data Exchange (DDE).** DDE was the first attempt to link two applications in such a way that one could use the functionality of the other or reflect the changes that occur in the other dynamically. DDE was a protocol that each application vendor would follow in order to extend their product to become DDE clients or DDE servers. As explained in the previous chapter, the major drawback of DDE is that it requires the DDE server application to be running—thus being resource-intensive—and is difficult to program. DDE is still used, however as the lowest-common denominator protocol for exchanging data between applications.
- **Object Linking and Embedding (OLE) 1.0.** OLE 1.0 introduced a document-centric computing paradigm by expanding the facilities of the Win-

dows clipboard to hold more than just raw data from an application and using DDE as a means of communicating between applications. The clipboard now would hold either raw data copied by the user or the reference to a file containing the data. In association with this content, the clipboard would record information that would allow Windows to launch the application responsible for editing the content, as well as a visual representation of this information. When users would paste the clipboard content onto another application, this content would be either embedded—if raw data was stored in the clipboard—or linked—if a file reference was stored instead—in the target document. Hence the term object linking and embedding. The details of object linking and embedding and how it changes the way users approach editing and maintenance of content will be discussed in the rest of this chapter.

- **Object Linking and Embedding (OLE) 2.0.** OLE 2.0 was a reimplementation of OLE 1.0 from the ground up, conceived, designed and released in 1992 to 1993. While it preserved the object linking and embedding functionality of its predecessor—a hit in the end-user community by that time—the architecture of OLE 2.0 was radically different from that of OLE 1.0. The whole DDE dependency was thrown away and the newly devised standard—COM—was used to implement the interactions between the applications. Once this shift occurred, Microsoft engineers realized that the new architecture allowed them to extend OLE far and beyond the creation of compound documents. Bonus features that came along were the implementation of structured storage, in-place editing, cross-application drag-and-drop, and OLE Automation.

  Microsoft's 32-bit Windows systems (NT 3.51, NT 4.x, and 95) were released at the same time or soon after the release of OLE 2.0. Along with them was released a 32-bit version of OLE 2.0 which addressed some of the scalability and performance problems of its 16-bit counterpart. The 32-bit implementation was built upon a more robust and streamlined version of COM, with an even more flexible architecture that enables new pieces and components can be added to the picture without requiring any revisions of it. At this point, Microsoft started promoting OLE as its principal technology for the integration of software components. The numbering of OLE was dropped, to signify that there will be no OLE 3, 4, or 5. The term OLE did no longer refer simply to object linking and embedding. It was rather seen as a code name identifying a whole range of technologies built upon the COM standard.

- **OLE Controls.** A clear example of the flexible architecture of COM are OLE controls—software components built upon COM long after the specifications of COM were finalized. OLE controls, also known as OCX controls, implement and extend the features of Visual Basic Controls (VBXs) in the COM and 32-bit environments. They expose their properties and methods through COM interfaces. OCX controls can exist only in the context of another application. This application implements a container object where the control is dropped. The application communicates with the OCX control through the container. The container can inspect the properties of OCX control and invoke its methods through the COM interface that the control exposes. The control itself exposes COM interfaces to allow it to handle events generated within the OCX control.

- **ActiveX.** This term was coined and used as part of the 180-degree turn towards Internet that Microsoft undertook in late 1995–early 1996. It represents the Microsoft technologies that enable users to turn the content displayed in static Web pages into active documents—hence the "Active" part of ActiveX. It includes technologies such as Compound Documents, Controls, Automation, and a number of other "Active" technologies—hence the "X" part of ActiveX. After the dust of the marketing campaign settled, it became clear that these were fundamentally the same COM-based technologies previously known with the OLE prefix. The most notable difference was in the specification of ActiveX Controls. They are leaner and smaller versions of the OCX controls, which are not only simple and faster to develop, but also quicker to download from the Web.
- **DCOM.** Distributed COM specifies the standards for integrating software components that live in different physical machines in the network. DCOM has been part of the COM architecture from the beginning, although developers could not take advantage of it until its implementation in a network operating system, such as Windows NT. Microsoft and other companies, such as DEC and Software AG, have worked to port COM and DCOM to operating systems other than Windows.

Figure 28.1 summarizes the relationship between COM/DCOM and the different technologies based upon them.

28.1.2 THE NEED FOR COM

In several software-engineering books, the metaphor of building a house is used to describe the process of developing software applications. In both cases, clients get together with the construction team to explain to them what they want and how it should look. Design plans are created, which clients eventually sign off on, and the construction process begins. During this process users may inspect the progress of work, may require some new features or drop some previous requirements. At the end of it, users get the keys to the house, the constructors pocket the money, and everybody lives happy thereafter.

For all its didactic advantages, the metaphor is not exactly correct, especially if you consider it in the reverse direction. Think for a minute of constructing a house in the same fashion many software systems are built today. First of all you make sure to fence a territory large enough to contain several houses like the

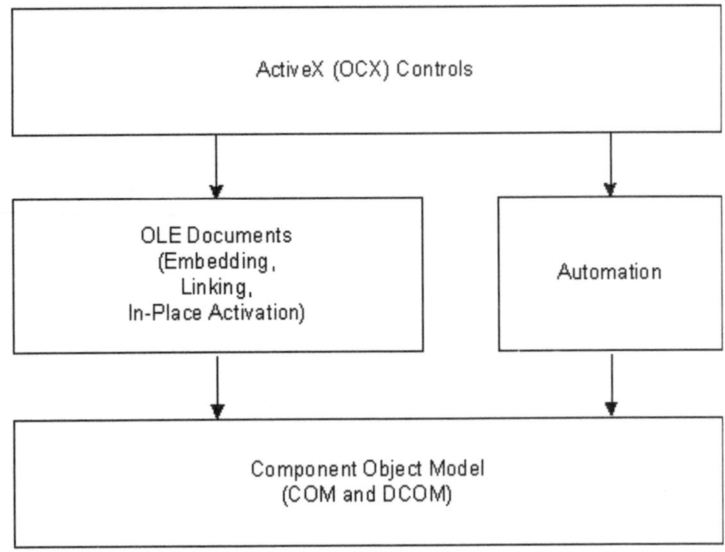

FIGURE 28.1 Relationship between COM-based technologies.

one you will build. You will be wasting some resources, but, hey, users must pay for them if they want an efficient house. Then, you place "No Trespassing" signs all over the fence, so that nobody else wanders in your territory. If somebody is able to obtain a pass to visit your compound, you will constantly keep an eye, probably a leash, on them, just in case. Then off to the real job of building the house!

You break the job in several tasks, subtasks, steps and substeps, and divide your resources so that the project is completed on time. Some of your people are responsible for producing nails of all sizes. After they are done with this, they will switch to the production of light bulbs. Another team will be responsible for the production of bricks, and door knobs. Yet another one will take care of the tiles, faucets, and glass. You have meticulously covered everything, and count on your teams to finish on time, so that the real construction can begin. When this day arrives, your people become carpenters, brick layers, painters, electricians, etc. Some of them move on to building the furniture, and others to decorating the house. A few others are responsible for putting together instructions on how to go from one room to another, on how to turn the oven on, on how to adjust the air temperature, etc.

Then the day when your project is completed arrives and you hand the keys over to your clients, together with a list of disclaimers and known problems with the house. If they ever want to rearrange the furniture in the living room, they should be aware that this will affect the heat pump in the basement. They cannot invite more that five guests per night and you are not to be held responsible for that. The paintings in the kids room are nailed to the wall and should not be removed, otherwise the roof may leak. And the list may go on like this.

If houses were really built this way, we would all be living in monolithic, Flintstone-type houses, too cold in winter, too hot in summer, far and isolated from each other. But we have constructed houses for centuries and we have learned to do better than that. Today we divide the work and specialize in certain aspects of the process. Hardware equipment and tools are produced by hardware companies. Construction materials are made by some other type of companies. Building contractors purchase these materials and equipment according to the customer demand, and provide skilled workers, brick layers, plumbers, electricians, etc., to actually build the house. Furniture, decorations, and appliances for the house can be purchased from yet another group of companies. What is more important, we can customize and add to our houses the features we want. We can all go to the store, buy furniture packaged so that it fits in the trunk of the car, and bring it back home. A list of a few instructions and drawings is sufficient to put the piece of furniture together in a matter of minutes.

Unfortunately, many software systems encountered today are built and continue to be built like monolithic applications, that limit the functionality and the ability of users to integrate them with other applications. The challenge facing the information technology world is to transform the application development from a process in which everything is done from scratch, into a process where software engineers, and even end-users, put together pieces of pre-made software objects into fully-fledged and fully-functional applications. These components can be purchased independently from manufacturers that specialize in their production and testing, much like we buy nails or paint in our local hardware store.

COM is the framework that allows the integration of these software objects into one application. COM provides the protocol that enables products made by different vendors to communicate and exchange information with each-other. This protocol is defined at the binary, or machine language level, and is not dependent on any programming language. This means that the COM framework will accommodate objects created with procedural and object-oriented languages alike, as long as these objects contain the necessary binary information.

28.1.3 COMPONENT SOFTWARE TECHNOLOGY

COM is not an application development environment. It is rather an architecture that integrates object-based software services. A number of these services are provided by the COM framework; additional customized services may be created and added to the framework. Every application that follows the COM protocol may use any of these services, no matter who developed them and when, where and how they were developed. In other words, the fact that Form Builder conforms to the COM standards allows you to use any of the services provided by other COM service providers such as word processing, spreadsheets, graphics, sound, and video. Thinking in terms of the metaphorical house, COM tells you what are the standard jacks to install. These very same standards are followed by electrical appliances manufacturers. This ensures that you will be able to plug and use anywhere around the house a VCR, a TV set, a stereo, or an iron. COM brings to software engineering common sense standards established long ago in other industries.

On the other hand, COM is an extendible architecture of services. As new services become available, they can replace or be added to existing ones without affecting the rest of the application that uses them. When a new version of the word processor embedded in the Forms application becomes available, all you will need to do is install the new version, without having modify the form module itself. Just like when replacing the ten-year old TV set with a home entertainment center, you simply plug the new equipment in an existing jack, without having to rewire the electrical circuits of the house.

Each COM service is provided by a particular application called the server. For example word processing is a service that may be provided by applications such as MS Word or WordPerfect. The service contains one or more software components. For example, MS Word has a text editing component, a drawing component, a chart editing component, etc. These components are made up of one or more objects. Word.Basic, for example, is an object that is part of the text editing component of MS Word. Each object has several attributes, properties and methods associated with it. Semantically related methods and features are bound together in groups called interfaces. COM ensures communication between services through their interfaces. COM cannot and does not allow access to internal or private variables of an object. The only way to access the service is by going through its interface.

The COM interface consists of the prototypes of its methods and the protocol for their use and it is not tied to the implementation of these methods. The interfaces are actually implemented by COM classes, which are responsible for producing, or instantiating COM objects that expose these interfaces. This means that once you define and register an interface with your system, you are advertising the availability, layout, and functionality of a type of objects to other applications can use. These applications do not need to know how and in what language you implement the COM class corresponding to this interface.

Remember that all this is done at binary level and is language independent. Thus, COM extends the object-oriented paradigm from the source code language-dependent level to the machine language level. Objects normally developed with object-oriented tools remain isolated until COM features are added to them. Their interaction with other objects is limited within the boundaries of the application a part of which they are. When these objects become part of a COM software component, some, or all of their functionality is exposed to the other components through the interfaces. These interfaces allow components to be plugged into other applications that may have been developed in an entirely different programming environment, from a different vendor.

28.1.4 CLIENTS AND SERVERS

COM-based technologies use the concepts of client and server like other technologies in the computer world. The client is an application that requests and uses the services of another application. The server is the one who provides these services. COM, as the fundamental layer these technologies, ensures the integration between clients and servers. Based on this model, when a client requests a service, it is really asking to interface with the component of a server. All the available components with which the client can interface are registered during the installation process of their respective software packages in the registry database of the machine. The client will pick from this database the component to interface with, or rather an internal class identifier (CLSID) of this component. This unique identifier points to the COM class that implements the interface. This class starts the server application, instantiates a new copy of the object in memory, and return to the client an interface pointer for the object. Recall that in the COM terminology the interface is a set of methods used to access, modify, or act upon an object. This means that this interface pointer will expose to the client all the functionality of the server.

Suppose for example that you want to add text editing services to your Form Builder application. You have to query the registry database for word processors installed in your machine. When you pick one, say MS Word, you are sending its unique internal class identifier to the COM mechanism of Windows. This mechanism uses this CLSID to retrieve from the registry information about the directory in which Word is installed and how to start it up. Windows uses this information to start the server, and instantiate a Word object. The pointer to this new instance of Word is returned to Forms, which uses it to access all the functionality that this application provides.

28.1.5 THE WINDOWS REGISTRY

The Registry is a centralized database shared by the Windows operating systems and all the applications installed in your machine. Its contents are updated and maintained by Windows and change as programs are installed on the machine. You can also view or edit its contents using the Registry Editor. Before you proceed, note that for all its importance as a centralized repository of your machine, the Registry is not a well-protected database. Toying with it, without knowing what exactly you are doing may cause severe problems with your applications or the entire operating system. Therefore be careful as you proceed through this section and be especially careful not to delete or modify any entries. To invoke this editor in Windows 95, click the Start button in your Windows task bar, select

Run… and type *regedit* in the Open dialog box that appears. (In Windows NT, the command to type is *regedt32*.)

The entries in the Registry are organized hierarchically in keys and subkeys. The hierarchy of these keys can be browsed in the left pane of the Registry Editor. Each key usually has one default value displayed in the right pane of the Registry Editor. The area of the Registry used by COM is all under the key HKEY_CLASSES_ROOT. The subkeys under this category can be divided in the following groups:

- **File extensions.** This area of the Registry stores all the file extensions that different applications register. These are listed first under the key HKEY_CLASSES_ROOT. Figure 28.2 shows the entries in my Registry for the file extension .doc. The default value of the file extension points to the application used by default to view or edit files with that extension. In the example shown in Figure 28.2, this application is MS Word, although as you can see, .doc files can be edited by WordPad as well. Launching the application to edit the files with associated extensions may not necessarily use COM services. However, when they are used, the value associated with the extension in the Registry points to the programmatic ID of the editing application.
- **Programmatic IDs (ProgIDs).** ProgIDs are user-friendly identifiers of the COM servers. They are listed alphabetically in under the key HKEY_CLASSES_ROOT after the file extensions. Their names usually follow the convention <Program>.<Component>.<Version> as in Word.Document.6 or WordPad.Document.1; the version number is dropped in order to enable applications to use the latest version of this component. Figure 28.3 shows the ProgID entries for Microsoft Word (version-independent, version 6, and version 8). Normally, under a progID entry, programs register information such as the default icon that objects of that type will use on the desk-

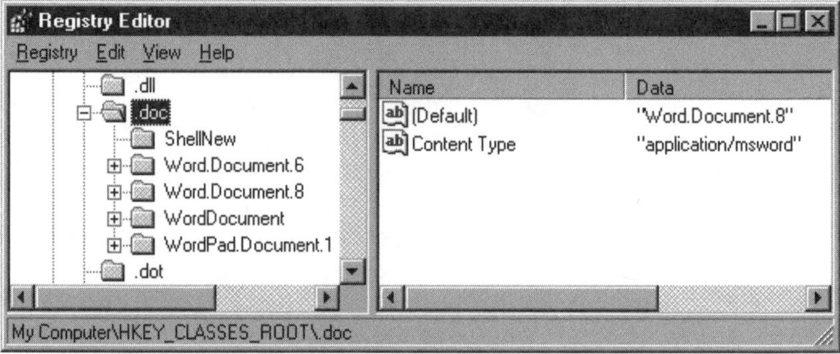

FIGURE 28.2 File extension information in the Registry Editor.

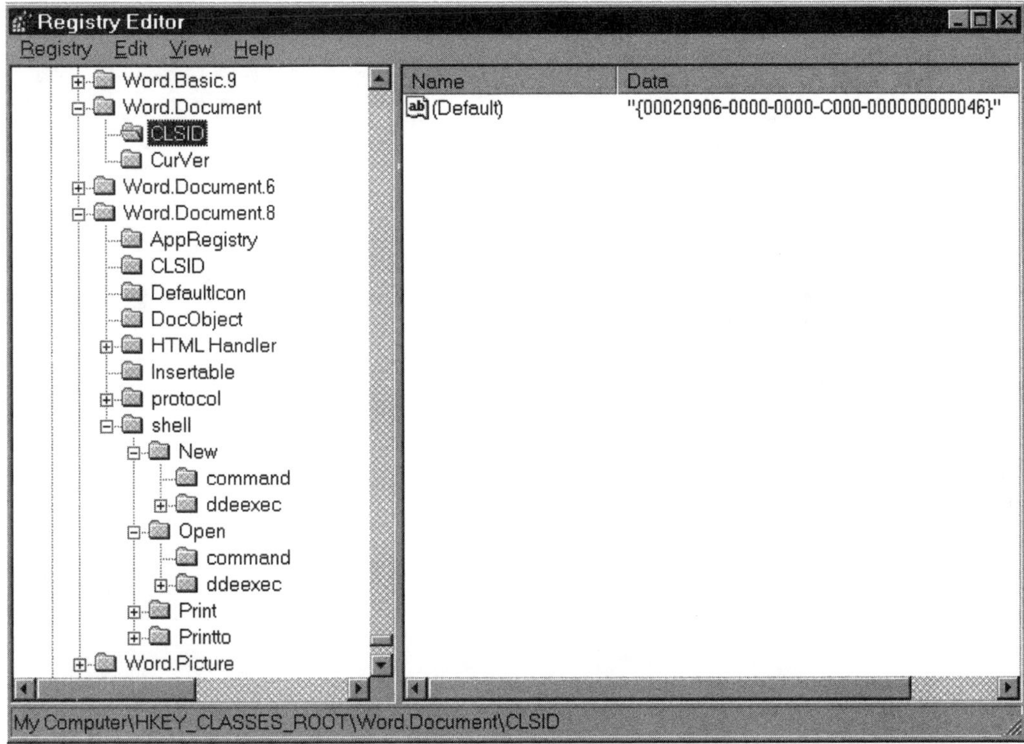

FIGURE 28.3 ProgID information in the Registry Editor.

top or actions that can be launched from the Explorer or the desktop, such New, Open, or Print, in the case of Word documents. An important value for COM-based components is the id of the COM class responsible for generating objects of this type, stored in the CLSID key. The CLSID for Word 6.0 in Figure 28.3 is {00020900-0000-0000-C000-000000000046}.

- **COM Class IDs (CLSID).** The identifiers for all the COM classes installed in your machine are located under the key CLSID HKEY_CLASSES_ROOT. Figure 28.4 shows an example of the subkeys for the Microsoft Word Document CLSID installed in my machine. Note the LocalServer32 item which points to the path where MS Word is currently installed, C:\Program Files\Microsoft Office\Office\WINWORD.EXE. This is where Windows will search for the server to activate during COM processes. Figure 28.4 contains other nodes such as DefaultIcon or Verb whose meaning will be discussed in the coming sections. Note also the last node, VersionIndependent-ProgID, which identifies the server Word Basic. This server generates Word objects that will be used in Automation processes discussed in Chapter 29.

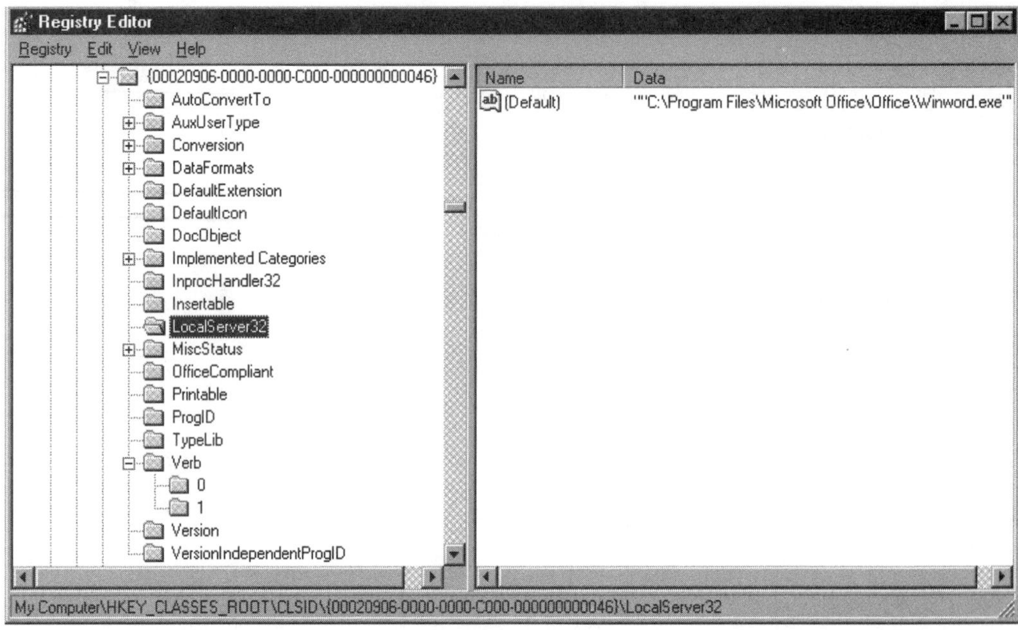

FIGURE 28.4 The subkeys for Microsoft Word Document CLSID.

28.2 OLE DOCUMENTS TECHNOLOGY

OLE Documents is a significant part of COM-based technologies that handles the process of creating and managing compound documents. Specifically, it deals with the embedding or linking of objects from OLE servers in the body of OLE client applications. As I explained in Section 28.1.1, compound documents initially were text processing files where users needed to insert drawing, pictures, spreadsheets, or, in general, data from other applications. The existing capabilities of Windows such as Clipboard operations, were not sufficient to meet these needs. Often, during the Cut and Paste actions, data were lost. In the cases when the operation was successful, meaningful data such as rows and columns from a spreadsheet, were replaced by pictures in metafile or bitmap format, where most of the original content of data was lost. Object Linking and Embedding, OLE 1, was born to address some of these problems. OLE 2 was the effort to fix the flaws of the original design, and extend the original architecture of OLE by basing it upon COM. The extension was such that it now supports a whole range of other COM-based technologies, such as Property Pages, drag-and-drop, OLE Automation and OLE controls. Therefore, the original functionality of OLE—creating and maintaining compound documents—is now represented by what the technology called OLE Documents.

The meaning of documents has changed as well. Today a compound document does not have to be a file produced with a text editor. Any application that implements the client side of the OLE Documents technology enables itself to store and manipulate objects creates by any OLE server. The support of Form Builder for this technology makes it possible to create front-end applications that provide not only strong database features, but also the functionality and features of numerous other applications. The COM concept of code reusability at the binary level allows you to use the inventive work of other programmers as if it was yours, without violating any of their intellectual property rights. Furthermore, the support of the Oracle Server database large object (LOB) data type columns provides you with a way to permanently and dynamically bind text, pictures, multi-media, and other types of files, with the record structures in which you organize the data. The following sections discuss how to implement linking and embedding of OLE components in Form Builder applications.

28.2.1 THE COMPOSERS APPLICATION

In this part, you will work with the application COMPOSER.FMB while different components of object linking and embedding are explained. This is a simple two-block form, whose layout is shown in Figure 28.5. The module is provided in the directory CH26 of the companion software.

The block COMPOSER contains biographical information about composers such as name, date of birth, death and nationality. The block WORK contains a listing of works from these composers. Both these blocks correspond to database tables with the same names. As you see in the picture, the original template of the application contains ample free space to the right of both blocks. You will fill this

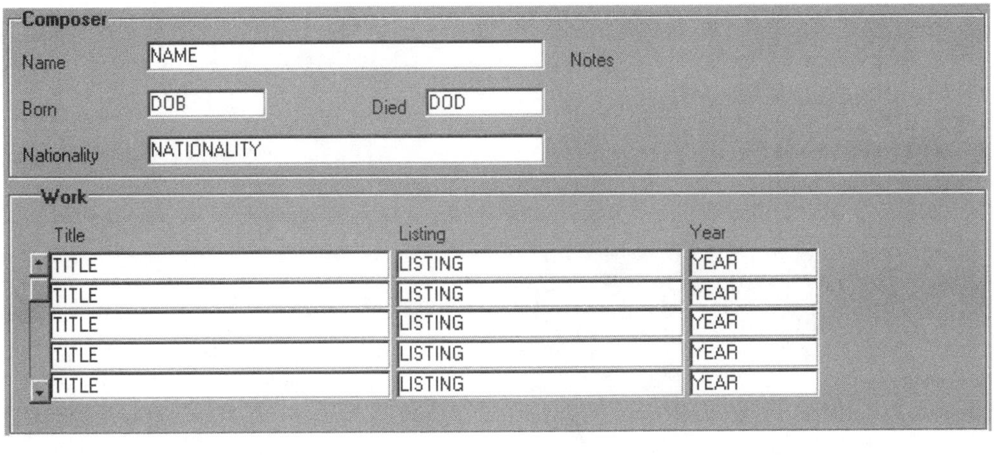

FIGURE 28.5 Layout of the module COMPOSER.FMB.

space in the following sections with two OLE containers. These items will allow you to store at runtime biographical information about composers and samples of their music in the database. The information can be queried, viewed, played, and edited like any other data element in the form module.

As a preliminary step, open the module COMPOSER.FMB in the Form Builder, compile, and run it to become familiar with the kind of data that the tables contain.

28.2.2 OLE CONTAINERS IN FORM BUILDER

In this section, you will create an OLE container in the COMPOSER block that will help users store samples of works from different composers in the database. Follow these steps to create the item:

1. Open the canvas COMPOSER in the Layout Editor and set the context to the block COMPOSER.
2. Click the icon OLE Container in the tool palette and create the OLE container in the space to the right of the text label Notes in this block.
3. Double-click the newly created item to display its Property Palette. You will see that the Item Type property for the item is set to "OLE Container."
4. Set the name of the item to "BIOGRAPHY."

While you still are in the Property Palette, let us discuss the properties of OLE container items in the Functional group.

- ❑ **OLE Class.** By default, this property is not set, which means that you in the Form Builder, or your users at runtime can insert OLE objects from any

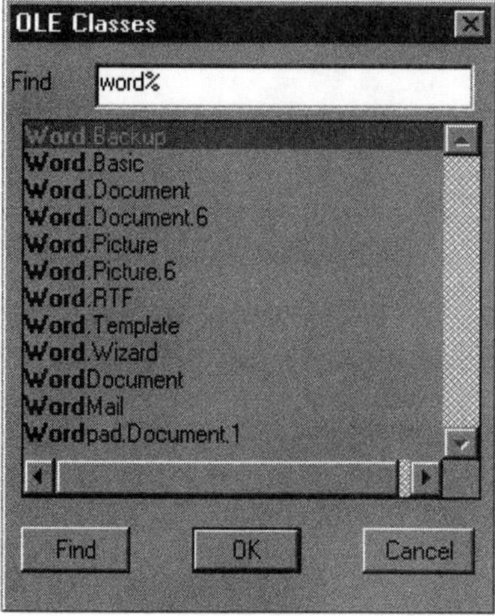

FIGURE 28.6 The OLE Classes dialog box.

class registered in the machine. If you want to restricts the contents of the container to only one particular class, double-click this property in the Property Palette for the item. A dialog box will appear listing all the OLE classes currently installed in your machine (see Figure 28.6). You can use the automatic reduction features of similar list of values dialog boxes to pinpoint the desired class. If, for example, you select Word.Document from the list, the only objects that can be inserted in the container will be Microsoft Word documents produced by this class. As you can see, you can either restrict the contents of the item to be OLE objects from one class only, or you cannot restrict them at all.

- **OLE Activation Style.** The setting of this property controls how you in the Form Builder, or the users at runtime will activate the object in the OLE container. The default setting is "Double-Click." If you want the object to become active as soon as the focus moves on it, set the property to "Focus-in." If the setting of this property is "Manual," you can activate the object only by selecting an item from the popup menu displayed when you right-click the object.
- **OLE In-place Activation.** This property is set to "Yes" by default. This allows you to activate the object within the borders of the OLE container in the form. If you want to activate the objects in a window of its own, different from the window in which your application is running, set this property to "No." Section 28.3 will discuss this property in more detail. Closely related with this setting is also the property OLE Inside Out Support, which will be discussed in that section as well.
- **OLE Tenant Types.** This property defines the type of objects that reside within the OLE container. If you want the OLE container in your form to host any of these types of objects, set its OLE Tenant Types property to "Any." This is also the default setting. If you do not want any objects to reside in the container, set the property to "None." This is not a particularly useful setting. If the container should host only embedded or linked objects, set the property to "Embedded" or "Linked." In the case when the object was previously linked and the link is broken, the property OLE Tenant Types is set to "Static." This will display only an image metafile of the object previously linked. Finally, to embed an OLE control in the container, set the property to "Control." Embedding and linking objects will be discussed in the remaining sections of this chapter and the next chapter will cover OLE controls and ActiveX controls.
- **Show OLE Tenant Type.** When this property is set to "Yes," as it is by default, it is supposed to indicate the type of object that resides in the container. However, this setting does not have any visual effects on the borders of the OLE container item.
- **OLE Tenant Aspect.** This property controls the way the OLE object is displayed within the container. By default, this property is set to "Content,"

which means that the content of the object will be displayed inside the container according to the setting of property OLE Resize Style. If OLE Tenant Aspect is set to "Icon," the container will represent the OLE object as an icon. This setting should be coordinated with the way the object is created, in the Insert dialog box, which you will discuss in the following sections. The property can also be set to "Thumbnail Preview," which offers a reduced version of the object.

- **OLE Resize Style.** This property controls how the object is displayed inside the container. "Scale" is the default setting, and means that the object the object will be reduced or enlarged as necessary to fit the container. This setting is mostly used for pictures and bitmaps. If the setting is "Clip," the object will be cropped to fit the size of the container as defined in the Form Builder. If the setting is "Initial," it is the container that will be resized to fit the size of the OLE object. However this is done only when the object is initially created. Subsequent retrievals of the object do not change the dimensions of the container. If you want the container to adjust its size so that it fits the object in any situation, set the property to "Dynamic."
- **Show OLE Popup Menu.** This property controls the ability of the OLE object to respond to the right-click event with a pop-up menu. By default, this property is set to "Yes."
- **OLE Popup Menu Items.** In order to see the items in the pop-up menu of the OLE object, double-clicking the property OLE Popup Menu Items. The OLE Menu dialog box will appear (see Figure 28.7). By default, all the items in the list are displayed in the pop-up menu, however you can manipulate the display and enable status of these objects by setting and clearing the corresponding check boxes in the dialog box. The availability of the menu items is also determined by the object and clipboard contents. For example, if there is nothing copied in the clipboard, the item Paste will be disabled. The last item in the list, labeled Object, will never appear as such as runtime. This label will be replaced by the name of the actual object you will store in the container.

FIGURE 28.7 The OLE Menu dialog box.

> **TIP**
>
> From all the properties of OLE containers discussed here, OLE Popup Menu Items is the only one that can be manipulated programmatically, as well as in the Form Builder. You can use the built-ins GET_ITEM_PROPERTY and SET_ITEM_PROPERTY to retrieve and set its settings as you would do for any other property. The runtime name of this property is POPUPMENU_CONTENT_ITEM.

28.2.3 EMBEDDING OBJECTS IN FORM BUILDER

In the COMPOSER.FMB module, you will implement the item BIOGRAPHY as an OLE container that will store embedded objects. First size its dimensions in the Layout editor to a rectangle that fills the empty space left to the right of the other data items in the block COMPOSER. Then, set the property OLE Tenant Types to "Embedding," OLE In-place Activation to "No," and OLE Resize Style to "Clip." Finally, save and compile the module.

Now, run the module to see how you would work with the new OLE container in the form from a user's perspective. Query the COMPOSER block for composer Franz Liszt and follow these steps to embed its biography:

1. Move the mouse pointer over the OLE container created previously, and right click. The pop-up menu for OLE items is displayed. If you had nothing copied in the clipboard, you will notice that only the Insert Object... item in this menu is enabled. Otherwise, Paste and Paste Special... will also be enabled.
2. Select Insert Object... from the pop-up menu. The Insert Object dialog box will appear (see Figure 28.8). In this dialog box, you can select the type of object to insert in the container from the text list. The contents of this list are determined by the setting of OLE Class property in the Designer, and by the OLE classes currently stored in the Windows registry. Because you did not set the OLE Class property for this item, Windows is showing all the OLE objects that are currently installed in the machine.
3. Scroll down the list and select the object type Microsoft Word Document. You will notice that the message in the Result text box will change according to the object currently selected.
4. Click OK.

At this point two things may happen. If MS Word is not running, Windows will launch it and create a new document window with the title Document in Unnamed. If you were working with Word previously, the application will be acti-

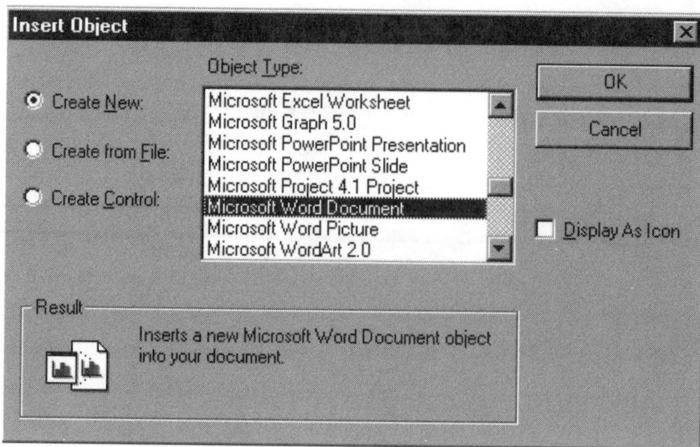

FIGURE 28.8 The Insert Object dialog box.

vated and the same new document window will be created. The MS Word File menu is also slightly different from what you see normally. The following are some of the major differences:

- The menu item Close now appears as Close and Return to Unnamed. By selecting this item, you will close the window and return to the Forms application. MS Word will prompt you to save any changes you may have made.
- The menu item Save is now replaced by Update. The normal Save operation in MS Word now updates the Form container item with the contents of the document. The command Save As… now becomes Save Copy As….
- The menu item Save All is replaced by Save and Update All. When you select this item, MS Word will save any open file documents, and will update any OLE container with the data from their corresponding documents.

The Forms application has slightly changed as well. If you switch to it, you will notice that the OLE container item that you are editing in Word is displayed with diagonal lines across it. This is an indicator that the object is being edited. The rest of the application is in its normal state and you can continue to enter and edit data in the other items. However, you should keep in mind how Form Builder processes its transactions. For example, if in the middle of editing the Biography in a Word document, you return to Forms and navigate to another record in the COMPOSER block, Forms will simply disconnect its link with MS Word, which in turn will close the window without saving any of the new changes.

In the MS Word document that represents the notes for Liszt enter the text shown in Figure 28.9. Select File | Close and Return to Unnamed from the Word menu.

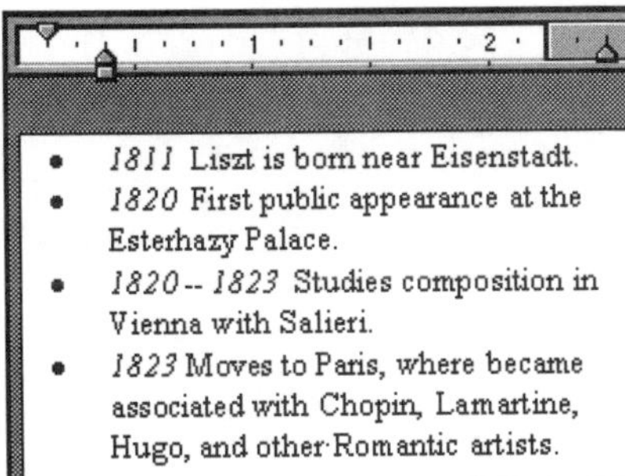

FIGURE 28.9 Editing an embedded OLE document.

Figure 28.9 purposely shows the horizontal ruler for the document. As you can see, the width of the document is reduced so that the entire lines fit inside the OLE container in the Forms module. The left margin is also shifted right, so that the bullets do not appear attached to the left border of the container. All these are cosmetic changes due to the fact that the container will clip the document and display only the upper left hand corner that fits in the OLE container. The changes are intended to make the document readable without requiring the users to access Word in edit mode to see its contents.

In the case described above, you created the embedded Word document from scratch. It is also possible to create it based on an existing file. Query the record for Chopin in the block and follow the first two steps described previously to insert a MS Word object in the Notes container. In the Insert Object dialog box (see Figure 28.8), click the radio button Create from File. The dialog box will be transformed as shown in Figure 28.10.

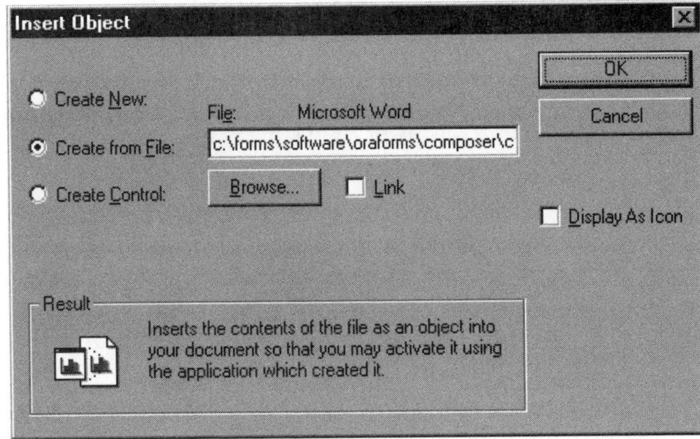

FIGURE 28.10 Insert Object dialog box with the Create from File option checked.

The OLE object classes in Figure 28.6 are now replaced by a text item where you can specify the name of the file that you want to embed. The following steps are required to complete the task:

1. Click the Browse... button to display a standard dialog box that allows you to select the file you want to embed.
2. Select the file CHOPIN.DOC located in the same directory where the module COMPOSER.FMB is installed. When you select this file, Windows queries the Registry database for the ProgID that corresponds to the file extension. Once the ProgID is retrieved, its associated OLE class ID is queried, The information defined for this CLSID is passed to Form Builder, which will prepare its container to store the new object.
3. Click OK.

28.2.4 CONVERTING EMBEDDED OBJECTS

The problem you tried to solve when creating the document for the first record applies to the second one as well. The document contained in the file CHOPIN.DOC is a normal size document, and only the upper left part of it appears inside the container. In fact, unless the documents you will embed have only a few lines, you will always be faced with the problem of the actual size of the document being larger than the actual size of the container. You can alter the setting of OLE Resize Style property, however, none of the other alternatives offers a problem-free solution. "Scale" will proportionally reduce the dimensions of the document to a point where its contents are no longer legible. As I said earlier, this setting is more appropriate with pictures and graphics. If the object contains text, the letters will be scrambled and will overlap each other in the scaling process. The other two settings, "Dynamic" and "Initial," which size the container according to the dimensions of the document, are not desirable if you expect the document to be large. A full-page or multi-page document will cover other items in the form.

One solution, which should always be considered for large-size objects, is to display them as icons. As a user, you can do this by following these steps.

1. Right-click the OLE object to display its pop-up menu. Note that the last item of this menu, by default called Object, now is called Document Object to reflect the type of object embedded.
2. Select Document Object from the pop-up menu. Another smaller menu appears.
3. Select Convert..., which is the last item in the menu. The Convert dialog box appears (see Figure 28.11).

The current type of object is displayed in the upper part of this window. The Object Type list box in the center of the dialog displays the types to which the

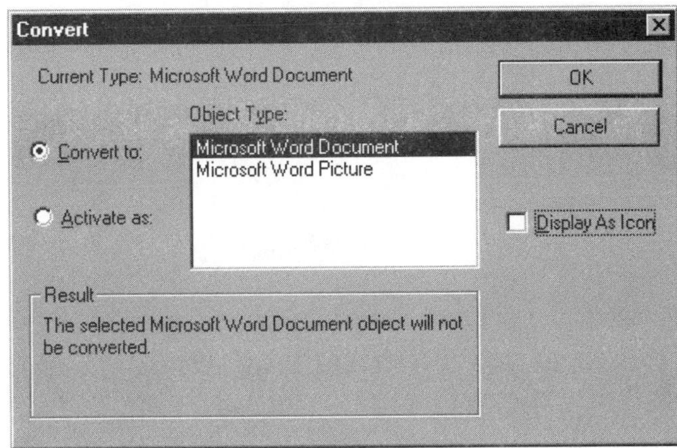

FIGURE 28.11 The Convert dialog box.

current object could be possibly converted. In the example shown in Figure 28.11, MS Word files can be converted in Microsoft Word Picture—a metafile Windows representation of the contents of the file. If you select the first radio button, the object will be converted from a Word document to Windows Picture file. If you select the second button, the object will be activated as a Windows Picture file. This is a very important advantage provided by the OLE mechanism. It allows you to create and embed data with one class, and view the data with every other compatible OLE class. The fact that MS Word was used to create notes for these two composers does not prevent users who have these classes installed in their desktops from viewing and manipulating these data. The OLE functionality will ensure that the appropriate conversions occur, just as when file documents are converted from one tool to the others.

To display the embedded object as an icon, check the check box Display as Icon to the right of the dialog. As soon as you do this, one of the MS Word icons will be displayed, with the label Document displayed underneath. Notice also that the message to in the text box in the lower part of the window will change to reflect the fact that the object will now be displayed as an icon. Click the push button Change Icon... to display the Change Icon dialog box (see Figure 28.12).

In this dialog box, the radio button Current displays the icon currently selected in the previous dialog. The default icon, the file that contains the icon and its position inside the file are also displayed. Where is this information stored? If you look back at Figure 28.4, which contains the registration information for MS Word in the Windows Registry, you will see that there is an entry there, called DefaultIcon. This key points to the file name and position for the icon. If you want to change the default setting, pick one of the available icons in the WINDWORD.EXE file, or click the push button Browse... to search for another icon file in the directory tree.

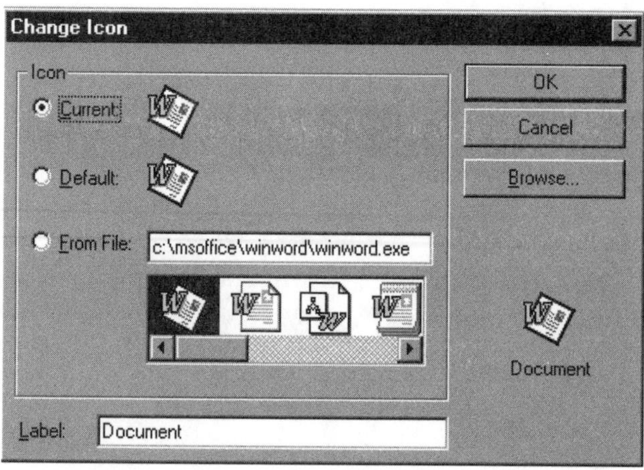

FIGURE 28.12 The Change Icon dialog box.

After you select the icon and click OK in both dialog boxes, you will return back to the form. Now the embedded object is represented only by the icon you have chosen.

If you expect all the objects that will be embedded in a container to be too large to fit inside the container, you may want to set their display status to an icon from the Designer. You can do this by setting their OLE Tenant Aspect property to 'Icon.' This will not guarantee that the objects will be displayed as such though. Users must still choose to display the object as an icon when creating the object. They do this by checking the check box Display as Icon in the Insert Object dialog box (see Figure 28.8 and Figure 28.10).

28.2.5 VERBS OF EMBEDDED OBJECTS

In the previous section, I asked you to display the pop-up menu and then the submenu associated with its last item, Document Object. Besides the option Convert Object, this submenu contains two other items, which are knows as the verbs of the OLE object. These verbs represent the interface that the OLE object exposes to client applications, or, in other words, actions that can be performed on the object.

Usually every embedded object has a verb called Edit, which allows you to modify the contents of the object in the server application. Then, most of the document-based OLE servers offer an Open verb, which opens the documents. These two verbs are synonymous for embedded objects. Multimedia servers such as MS Video for Windows or Wave Sound have a verb called Play, which allows you to play the contents of the object. When the OLE server is installed, together with other information, it also registers its verbs with the Windows Registry. It is here that you can look up the verbs supported by any application. Looking back at Figure 28.2, you can see that the verbs for MS Word are Edit and Open. Figure

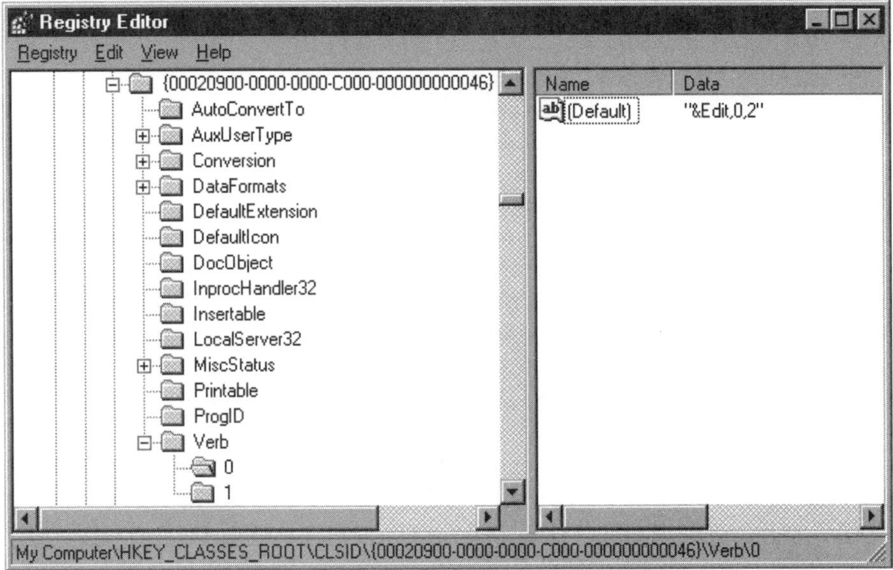

FIGURE 28.13 The Verbs for an OLE class.

28.13 shows the contents recorded in the Registration Database for the application Quick Time Movie Player by Apple Computer, Inc.

The verb that is listed first is the action that the will be executed when the OLE object is double-clicked in the container.

28.3 IN-PLACE ACTIVATION OF EMBEDDED OBJECTS

In all the examples you have worked with so far, the OLE server applications are displayed in their own windows, separate from the Forms application that invoked them. In a sense, the focus in this approach is placed on the application. When users work with the form module, they are in an Form Builder window; when they need to edit the biographical notes for some composer, they switch to MS Word. Although this is the way the software tools work internally, there is no reason why this should be imposed on the users. They would be more interested to work with an application that is centered around one document and does not require switching back and forth between different windows.

One of the great improvements provided by the reimplementation of OLE using COM is the ability to bring all the necessary functionality for editing an embedded object inside the OLE container of the document. The approach is very elegant, because instead of asking users to go to the OLE server to edit the application, the internal negotiation between the client and the server, all based on the COM standards, brings the application to the user. This extended functionality of embedded objects is called in-place activation.

Recall from Section 28.1.1 how ActiveX replaced OLE in the Microsoft vocabulary due primarily to a marketing drive. For similar reasons, the name of in-place activation was changed several times. The original name, *in situ editing,* was found to be too academic. For fear that not too many programmers would grasp the meaning of the Latin word, it was changed to *in-place editing*. However, since the COM framework was much wider than just editing compound documents, the term *editing* was replaced with *activation*. Then, in the euphoric move to place a visual in front of everything, the term was changed to *Visual Editing*(™). The trademark was obtained for the new name as well. Therefore, depending on who you talk to, and what kind of literature you read, you may encounter all of these terms.

In order to enable an OLE container item for in-place activation, you must set its OLE In-place Activation property to "Yes." Do so for the item BIOGRAPHY in the block COMPOSER. In addition, rearrange the items in this block, so that they look like Figure 28.14.

The reason for this rearrangement is to enlarge the dimensions of the OLE container. Now that the editing will be in-place, Word will enlarge or reduce the view of the document proportionally with the width of the container. As shown in Figure 28.14, the document will be displayed approximately at normal size. But if you reduce the width of the item to half, the view of the document will be only 50 percent. This will make it very hard to see the characters being typed. Remember that this will not affect the way characters look after the editing is completed, only while Word is active.

After these arrangements, save, generate, and execute the form. For any record, double-click the OLE container. You will notice that the OLE container will yield to a MS Word document in which you can enter your notes. Pay attention to the fact that the Form Builder menu is now replaced by the MS Word menu and toolbars. For all purposes, you are in Word, just as before, except that now you do not have to do the editing in another window.

FIGURE 28.14 The block COMPOSER after the rearrangement.

The container now is surrounded by a hatched border line. As you move the mouse over the border you will see it change shape to indicate that you can move the container around the window, or you can resize it to your needs. The position and dimensions will be valid only while you are editing. As soon as you click outside the hatched border, the container will return to its original size and the text you entered will be displayed inside of it.

Notice that the Word menu for this type of embedded object is a little different from what you are used to seeing. The main difference is that the File submenu disappears altogether. It is assumed that the client application will perform all the actions that normally go under this menu. While for other applications this may not be a drawback, in Forms, this fact will not allow you, for example, to print the contents of the document directly to the printer, which you could do in other cases.

Another difference is that all the items in the View menu that allow you to control the view size of the document are disabled. This is also true for the Zoom Control drop-down list box in the toolbar. This is the reason why you had to size the item in the Form Builder, so that the view offered is one with which users can work comfortably.

If you have more than one embedded object with the property OLE In-place Activation set to 'Yes,' by default, the editing window can be active for each of them at the same time. This is because the property OLE Inside-Out Support is set to "Yes." If you want the window of an object to be deactivated even if users activate the editing window of another object, set this property to "No."'

28.4 LINKING OBJECTS IN FORM BUILDER

As you were working through the examples discussed in the previous sections, you probably experienced some performance problems during the update and retrieval of records, especially if you are accessing the database across a busy network. The reason is the amount of data that was associated with each embedded object that you inserted in the database. Although you entered only a few lines in the biographical notes of the composers, Form Builder had to store all the native data required to instruct the embedded objects to start themselves up the next time you will need to edit them. This is how the embedding is designed to work.

In a compound document, embedding objects from other application servers, will increase the size of the file to which the document is saved. This eventually could lead to problems, because larger the size of the file, longer it will take the application to open and load it into memory. It is easier to reach the critical point where deterioration of the performance becomes noticeable if the file is loaded in a file server. It is even easier to reach this point when a third processing party—the database server—is added to the picture.

In order to alleviate the burden of the application, linking of objects should be considered as a serious alternative. Functionality-wise there is no difference between linking and embedding. The container treats the objects equally, by executing the same code, no matter whether they are linked or embedded. The only difference is that an embedded object, as discussed earlier, encapsulates within itself all the data, whereas the data for a linked object reside elsewhere, in a file. The object stored in the client container is just a pictorial representation of the data, with a pointer to the location of the file where the rest of the data resides.

TIP

These pointers, called monikers, are not what is normally understood when the term is used in programming languages such as C or C++. They are not as simple as the name of the file where the data is stored either. The normal file name is just a string of characters. An application does not know what to do with it, unless some additional instructions accompany it. The monikers are COM constructs that encapsulate names with instructions on what to do with these names. These instructions primarily direct the moniker to find the object with that name and to return a pointer to the interface, or the set of methods, that that object offers to the outside world. Moniker itself is a British slang for nickname.

In this section, you will link some of the records of works of composers with 60-second samples of these works. The sound files were recorded using the standard Windows Sound Recorder and can be played using the Microsoft's Media Player or any other application that support the feature.

Start by creating a container in the WORK block where these samples will be stored.

1. Set the context of the Layout Editor to the block WORK.
2. Click the OLE Container icon in the tool palette, and create the OLE container to the right of the YEAR column. You will see that the Form Builder will create five objects, one for each displayed record in the block.
3. Double-click the newly created item to display its Property Palette.
4. Set the name of the item to WORK and the property Number of Items Displayed in the Records group to "1."

Now, set some of the Functional properties of the item according to your situation.

1. Set the property OLE Class to "mplayer," or any other sound playing application that you have installed in your machine. This is with the way you used the OLE objects in the previous sections. There you could enter any type of data for the composer, such as a document with biographical data, a

portrait in picture format, or a video clip. Here, you are narrowing the scope of objects to only sound objects.

2. Set the property OLE Tenant Type to "Linked." Users can link the files even if this property is set to "Any," but this setting would not prevent them from embedding these files. You must avoid embedding especially for multi-media files which are quite large.
3. Set the property OLE Tenant Aspect to "Icon." This is how you would normally display objects such as sound or video clips.
4. Return in the Layout Editor and set the dimensions of the container to a size appropriate to display an icon.

Save, generate and run the module to use the new functionality from a user's perspective.

1. Query the record for Franz Liszt, and click on the record that represents its third etude after Paganini, also known as La Campanella. The theme of this etude comes from the third movement of Paganini's second violin concerto, also known as "La Campanella." In that movement, you can hear the sound of a little bell that accompanies the music in the background. In Italian, the word for a small bell is *campanella*.
2. Right-click the OLE container and choose Insert Object... from the pop-up menu. The Insert Object dialog box appears. This looks very similar to the one shown in Figure 28.10. However, if you read carefully the contents of the text box at the bottom of the window and compare them with Figure 28.10, you can realize the different context in which you are operating now. While in the previous sections you were embedding object to the OLE container, here only a picture of the file will be inserted, and a link will be established between this picture and the file itself.
3. Click Browse... and locate the file LISZT03.WAV stored in the same directory as the module COMPOSER.FMB.
4. Check the Display As Icon check box.
5. Click OK to return to the Forms application.

At this point, you can double-click the icon to listen to the music. You can also select the verb Play from the pop-up menu. If you select the verb Edit, the application server will run, and the sound file will be loaded, so that you can edit it.

Pay attention to an item in the pop-up menu which was disabled when you were working with embedded objects, but is enabled now. This is Links... . Select it and you will see the Links dialog box similar to Figure 28.15.

The central area of this dialog repeats the information displayed at the bottom. The Source is the name and location of the file linked to the OLE object. The

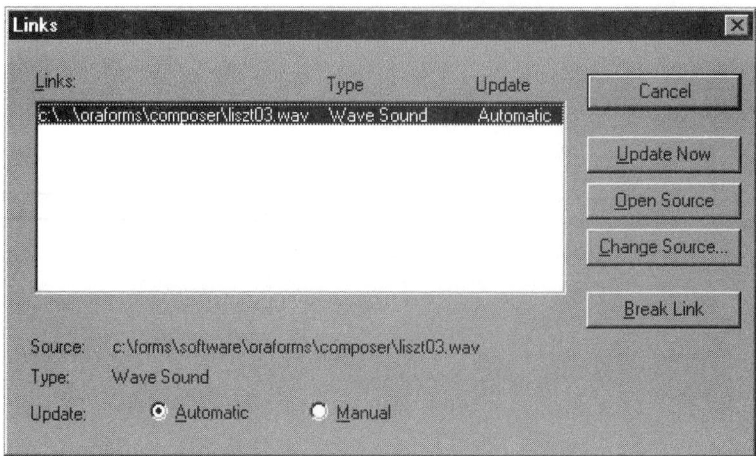

FIGURE 28.15 The Links dialog box.

Type corresponds to the OLE class that produced the object. The update mode by default is Automatic. This means that whenever the contents of the file change, the modifications will be seen immediately and automatically by the OLE container. If the radio item Manual is checked instead, the only way to update the OLE container is to click the button Update Now in the Links dialog box.

In this dialog box, you can also change the file linked with the OLE container by clicking the Change Source... button. A standard dialog box will be displayed which you can use to search for the new file. If you want to launch the server application, click the button Open Source. This will also close the Links dialog box. Note that this action is equivalent to selecting Edit from the pop-up menu of the OLE object.

Finally, if you click the button Break Link, the link between the OLE container and the file will be disrupted. You will be left with just a static picture of the object, and any editing functionality will be lost. In this case only the icon would remain after you break the link. If the object is an Excel graph, what remains after the link with the source file is broken, is just a pictorial representation of the chart, with no data or editing capabilities behind it.

28.5 LINKING AND EMBEDDING IN THE LAYOUT EDITOR

When you define an Form Builder item as an OLE container, you can use all of the features discussed so far from the Layout Editor, as well as at runtime. You should be cautious about how you use the functionality, though. Linking or embedding an object in the Layout Editor is similar to setting the Default Value property for a normal item. Whenever a new record is created, its OLE container will be populated with the object that you stored there at design time. This may result in objects being saved unnecessarily in the database.

However, you can use this functionality to see the effects of different settings for the properties of the OLE items. You can also size the containers to the right dimensions. For example, in Section 28.3, several objects were embedded in the BIOGRAPHY item until the right size of the object was found.

28.6 MANIPULATING COMPOUND DOCUMENTS PROGRAMMATICALLY

On some occasions, you may want to modify the default interface provided by the OLE functionality, in order to make the application more robust, or to protect the data from unwarranted modifications. In the example discussed in the previous section, users are free to edit and modify the contents of the records files at their will. In a corporate-wide application, only authorized users may have the privilege to edit such data. The rest of the users who create links to these files, should be able to view the data, or play the recording in this case, but not modify them.

Form Builder provides a number of built-in functions and procedures that allows you to control programmatically the interaction between the OLE client and OLE server applications. In this section, you will use some of these built-ins to create an interface such that users can link sound files to the OLE containers, play these files, or break the links at their will. However, they will be forbidden from editing these files.

Continue to work with the module COMPOSER.FMB, and with the block WORK in particular, by following these steps:

1. Display the Property Palette for the OLE container item WORK.
2. Make sure that the property OLE Tenant Type is still set to "Linked," OLE Class to "mplayer," and OLE Tenant Aspect to "Icon."
3. Set the OLE Activation Style property to "Manual." This will prevent users from activating the object by double-clicking or placing the focus in the item.
4. Double-click the property OLE Popup Menu Items to display the OLE Menu dialog box as shown in Figure 28.7.
5. Select the last item in the list, called Object, and clear the check box Enable.

With these settings, you have left the users only the possibility to insert objects from one specific class—Mplayer. By disabling the Object menu item, you are not allowing them to access the verbs of these objects. This way you are blocking globally their interface with the object, so that you can take control and grant them access only to the functionality you want.

Give the users back the ability to play the sound files.

1. Create a push button in the block WORK.
2. Set its Name and Label to "Play," and set its Number of Items Displayed property to "1."
3. Size the button and place it below the OLE container on the canvas.
4. Create a WHEN-BUTTON-PRESSED trigger for the button, and enter in the body of the trigger the statements shown in Figure 28.16.

In the first group of statements in the trigger, the internal ID of the item is retrieved. Then, the function SERVER_ACTIVE is used to check whether the server application is currently running or not. This function returns a Boolean value of TRUE if the server is running and FALSE if not. This value is stored in the variable `running`.

Immediately after the call to function SERVER_ACTIVE, you check if an error occurred or not. The reason for this check is that the users may be trying to play an item that is not inserted yet. In this case, the call to the previous function will generate the error message "FRM-41344: OLE object not defined for WORK in the current record." In the trigger, this error message is followed with an instruction on what to do to insert an object.

If the server is not running, the function ACTIVATE_SERVER will start it up. This function establishes a bridge between the OLE container and the server application. The function CLOSE_SERVER has the reverse effect of breaking this connection.

The function GET_VERB_COUNT returns the number of verbs defined for the object. Since this number is returned in a character format, you convert it to numeric format in order to use it as the upper bound for a loop that will search for the verb *Play* in the list of available verbs. Inside the loop, the function GET_VERB_NAME is used to retrieve the name of the verb based on the index value. When the verb Play is found, the procedure EXEC_VERB is used to actually invoke the action that this verb represents. This is equivalent to selecting the verb from the pop-up menu of the OLE object.

The final version of the application is provided with the companion software under the name COMPOSER_1.FMB.

In version 4.5 of Forms, the functions and procedures discussed here were part of the built-in package FORMS_OLE. For backward compatibility they are still supported, although you will not be able to see this package listed under the node Built-in Packages of the Object Navigator. In the new modules you develop, you should use the built-in program units discussed here rather than those from the package FORMS_OLE.

```
DECLARE
 container_id      ITEM;
 container_name    VARCHAR2(60):='WORK.WORK';
 running           BOOLEAN;
 verb_count        VARCHAR2(10);
 verb              VARCHAR2(50);
BEGIN
 container_id := FIND_ITEM(container_name);
 IF ID_NULL(container_id) THEN
   MESSAGE('Item '||container_name||' does not exist.');
   RAISE FORM_TRIGGER_FAILURE;
 END IF;

 running := SERVER_ACTIVE(container_id);
 IF NOT FORM_SUCCESS THEN
   MESSAGE('Right-click the icon above button Play and
       select Insert Object... from the menu.');
   RAISE FORM_TRIGGER_FAILURE;
 END IF;
 IF NOT running THEN
   ACTIVATE_SERVER(container_id);
 END IF;

 verb_count := GET_VERB_COUNT(container_id);
 FOR i IN 1..TO_NUMBER(verb_count) LOOP
   verb := GET_VERB_NAME(container_id, i);
   IF UPPER(verb) = 'PLAY' THEN
    EXEC_VERB(container_id, i);
    EXIT;
   END IF;
 END LOOP;
EXCEPTION
 WHEN OTHERS THEN
  MESSAGE('Error: '||TO_CHAR(SQLCODE)||'--'||SQLERRM);
  RAISE FORM_TRIGGER_FAILURE;
END;
```

FIGURE 28.16 Manipulating OLE objects programmatically.

28.7 SUMMARY

This chapter discussed COM-based technologies and how they apply to the development of Form Builder applications. The first part of it was an overview of COM, and the second part explained the use of OLE Documents in Form Builder. Important topics in this chapter were:

- **What Is COM?**
  - History of COM
  - The Need for COM
  - Component Software Technology
  - Clients and Servers
  - The Windows Registry
- **OLE Documents Technology**
  - The Composers Application
  - OLE Containers in Form Builder
  - Embedding Objects in Form Builder
  - Converting Embedded Objects
  - Verbs of Embedded Objects
- **In-Place Activation of Embedded Objects**
- **Linking Objects in Form Builder**
- **Linking and Embedding in the Layout Editor**
- **Manipulating Compound Documents Programmatically**

The following table describes the software assets that were discussed in this chapter. From the main HTML page of the software utilities provided with the book follow the links *Software* and *Chapter 28* to access these assets:

ASSET NAME	DESCRIPTION
COMPOSERS.FMB	A Form Builder module that allows you to understand the object linking and embedding features of Developer Forms.
COMPOSERS_1.FMB	The final version of the COMPOSERS module with the linked and embedded objects discussed in this chapter.
COMPOSERS_1.FMX	The executable version of COMPOSERS_1.FMB compiled for Win32 platforms.
CHOPIN.DOC	A Microsoft Word file that may be embedded or linked in the COMPOSERS application.
LIST03.WAV	A sound file that may be linked in the COMPOSERS application.

Chapter 29

AUTOMATION AND ACTIVEX CONTROLS

Give me where to stand, and I will move the earth.
—Archimedes (said in reference to the lever—
the world's first automaton and control)

Chapter 28 offered an overview of the COM-based technologies as a whole, and focused on OLE Documents, which is an important component of these technologies. You learned how to use OLE container items in Form Builder and integrate them with OLE server applications. As it was emphasized in that chapter, COM today provides much more functionality than mere creation of compound documents through linking and embedding.

An area that is being explored intensively and offers a great perspective is the Automation technology, a set of protocols and constructs that allows creation of universal applications that access and use features from an array of other applications with the goal to facilitate and automate processes that otherwise would require the human intervention. The first part of this chapter will discuss how Automation can be implemented in the Form Builder environment.

Another area where COM promises to offer a lot is the creation and use of OCX and ActiveX controls. Their advent in the computing world is quite recent, and is another proof of the extendible architecture of COM. OCX and ActiveX controls did not exist when COM was designed, however, they fit perfectly well in the framework of objects and interfaces defined by COM. The second half of this chapter focuses on the support that Form Builder offers for these controls.

29.1 AUTOMATION

The modern workplace today relies heavily on the utilization of software products for the purpose of facilitating and substituting several tedious and labor-intensive tasks such as document editing, financial calculations, plotting of charts and graphs, or storage and retrieval of data. In each area, several applications have distinguished themselves as being full of features, which are easy to learn, access and use. However, despite the strong capabilities that each individual package offers, much to be desired is left on their integration and cooperation.

Imagine for a second the activities of a payroll office in a typical enterprise today. Periodically, its staff must download data from a database where all the employees log their time onto a spreadsheet package, where several complicated computations are made, charts are drawn, and financial analysis of the company's welfare is done. Then, some of these data may go to a printer where paychecks for the employees are printed. Someone working on the monthly report for the company's executives needs to cut and paste some charts. Yet another person sends notification messages by e-mail to certain employees whose records may need some verification and supplemental information. Lo and behold, it is a busy hive of working bees, running around to keep the company healthy and prosperous.

Unfortunately, too much of this energy may be wasted on tasks of a secondary nature such as figuring out how to transfer the data across applications, ensuring that the right data elements are available when people need them, and preventing unauthorized persons from accessing data. Today there exists the technology to automate a considerable amount of these tasks at the software level. This technology is Automation, an important component of the COM-based technologies. At different points in time, this technology has been known as OLE Automation or ActiveX Automation. In this chapter I will simply refer to it as Automation.

Automation is a set of standard interfaces and data types designed to enable applications to exchange data with each other and to drive their respective components programmatically. Automation makes possible the use of the native language of an application to control and manipulate other applications. In the scenario presented above, if all the individual applications support Automation, it is possible to write a script in any of them, that would download the data from the database, format and calculate the spreadsheet, create the necessary charts, paste them in the monthly report, send the paychecks to the printer, and send the e-mail messages to the employees that must be notified. The entire human interface can be encapsulated in this program unit. Thus the computers will do what they are good at, and the humans will be relieved to do more creative and productive work.

Automation is based on the concepts of *automation objects* and *automation controllers*. The automation objects are COM objects that have a special type of interface, which displays all their methods, properties and arguments to the outside environment. This interface, called *dispatch interface*, or *dispinterface*, assigns a unique identifier, known as dispID, to each member function or property of the object. An outside application that can access the automation object through its class identifier CLSID, can also use the dispinterface to query the dispIDs provided by the object. Each method or property can then be invoked based on this identifier. On the other side of the equation stand the automation controllers. They provide programmers with language structures that can be used to access the properties and execute the methods of automation objects. The automation controllers use the dispID to access the properties of an object or to invoke its methods.

Automation is a very important technological standard, because it allows applications to use their own native language scripts to drive any other application that implements the dispinterface according to this standard.

29.2 AUTOMATION IN FORM BUILDER

Form Builder, and all the other Developer tools, are automation controller applications. You can create program units in PL/SQL that drive any automation object such as a word processor, or a spreadsheet, or a drawing package. This functionality is provided by the package OLE2, which comes with these tools. The following section discusses the contents of this package, and in Sections 29.2.2

and 29.2.3 you will use it to implement Automation features in some sample Form Builder applications.

29.2.1 OLE2 PACKAGE

The OLE2 package provides a small number of data types and program units, which are generic enough to allow you to control any automation object. The following paragraphs describe the components of the OLE2 package you will most likely use in your programming activities.

Each automation object in Form Builder is represented and accessed by a variable of data type OLE2.OBJ_TYPE. You can create an object from scratch by using the function CREATE_OBJ. This function takes as argument the name of an OLE class installed in your machine. The Windows registry is queried with this name, the class identifier CLSID is retrieved, and this information is used to start the server application and create a new object instance of the specified class. The function returns a pointer to that object. If an OLE container already exists in the Form Builder and an object is linked or embedded in it as explained in the previous chapter, you can achieve the same functionality by using the built-in function GET_INTERFACE_POINTER. After you have finished work with the automation object, you can use the procedure RELEASE_OBJ to release all the system resources that the object is using.

As I said in the previous section, once the automation controller, obtains a handle to the automation object, the dispinterface of the object will reveal all its properties and methods. You can use four functions of the OLE2 package to get different properties of the object. Depending on the data type of the property—numeric, alphanumeric, Boolean, or a COM object—the functions GET_NUM_PROPERTY, GET_CHAR_PROPERTY, GET_BOOL_PROPERTY, and GET_OBJ_PROPERTY, return the values of these properties, or a pointer to the COM object in the last case. If you want to set the property of an object, use the procedure SET_PROPERTY to pass the new value to the property.

Four members of the OLE2 package are used to invoke the object's methods. If the method is a procedure, the procedure INVOKE is used. When the method is a function that returns a number, alphanumeric string, or another automation object, the functions INVOKE_NUM, INVOKE_CHAR, and INVOKE_OBJ are used respectively.

Each of the program units for accessing the properties and methods of an automation object take as parameters the pointer to the object and the name of the property or method. Any parameters that may be required are passed in the form of an argument list. Argument lists are special objects of data type OLE2.LIST_TYPE. They can be created with the function CREATE_ARGLIST, which returns an internal identifier for the list. Arguments are added with the procedure ADD_ARG. The order of the arguments must be exactly as required by the method. Finally, when the list is no longer needed, its resources can be returned to the available pool by invoking the procedure DESTROY_ARGLIST.

29.2.2 OLE AUTOMATION WITH SPREADSHEETS

In this and the following section you will use the OLE Automation features of Form Builder to implement the functionality created in Chapter 27 using DDE communication channels. The template modules that you will work with in this section are called OLEEXCL.FMB and OLEWORD.FMB. The finished versions of these modules, which contain the features you will implement in this section are provided with the names OLEEXCL_1.FMB and OLEWORD_1.FMB.

Start the Form and open the module OLEEXCL.FMB. The canvas layout of this module is shown in Figure 29.1. The layout is similar with that of module DDEEXCL.FMB. The main difference is that in OLE Automation, you do not need any communication channel like in DDE. This is the reason why in this module there is only one button to launch Excel, and another one to close it, but no buttons to open or close a channel. For the same reason, the PRE-FORM trigger declares only one global variable `GLOBAL.application_id`.

The trigger WHEN-BUTTON-PRESSED for the button Launch Excel will create an OLE Automation object from the class Excel.Application—which, as described in the previous chapter, refers to the most current version of the application installed in your environment. A pointer to the automation object will be stored in the global variable `GLOBAL.application_id`. Obviously, if the object already exists, a new one will not be instantiated. Create the trigger and enter its contents as shown in Figure 29.2.

Now, create a WHEN-BUTTON-PRESSED trigger for the button Exit Excel. This trigger will invoke the procedure OLE2.RELEASE_OBJ to free up the resources taken by the object. The variable `GLOBAL.application_id` will also be set to NULL. The contents of this trigger are shown in Figure 29.3.

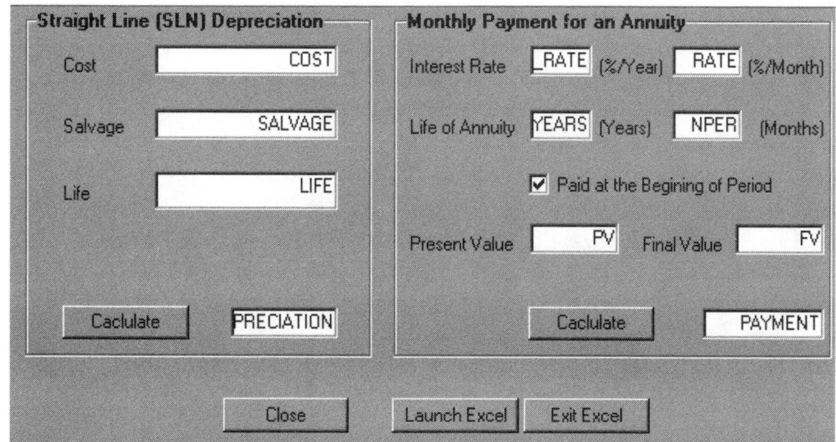

FIGURE 29.1 Layout of module OLEEXCL.FMB.

```
DECLARE
 appl_name VARCHAR2(255) := 'EXCEL.APPLICATION';
BEGIN
 IF :GLOBAL.application_id IS NOT NULL THEN
   MESSAGE('Application is already running.');
 ELSE
   :GLOBAL.application_id := OLE2.CREATE_OBJ(appl_name);
 END IF;
EXCEPTION
 WHEN OTHERS THEN
   MESSAGE('Error: '||TO_CHAR(SQLCODE)||' '||SQLERRM);
   RAISE FORM_TRIGGER_FAILURE;
END;
```

FIGURE 29.2 Initializing an Excel OLE Automation object.

The trigger for the button Close is very similar to the one shown in Figure 29.3. In this trigger you should still check to see if the automation object is created by the application. If this is the case, you discard it using the procedure RELEASE_OBJ. Then you invoke EXIT_FORM to terminate the application.

In the triggers WHEN-BUTTON-PRESSED for the buttons Calculate in both blocks, you should ensure first that the automation object is already initialized. Then you call the functions `Calc_SLN` and `Calc_PMT`, whose return values pop-

```
DECLARE
 application_id  PLS_INTEGER;
BEGIN
 IF :GLOBAL.application_id IS NULL THEN
   MESSAGE('Cannot terminate an instance that is not
   initiated by this application.');
 ELSE
   application_id := TO_NUMBER(:GLOBAL.application_id);
   OLE2.RELEASE_OBJ(application_id);
   :GLOBAL.application_id := NULL;
 END IF;
EXCEPTION
 WHEN OTHERS THEN
   MESSAGE('Error: '||TO_CHAR(SQLCODE)||' '||SQLERRM);
   RAISE FORM_TRIGGER_FAILURE;
END;
```

FIGURE 29.3 Deleting an OLE Automation object.

ulate the items SLN.DEPRECIATION and PMT.PAYMENT, respectively. The arguments passed with these functions are the interface pointer to the Excel spreadsheet object and the values entered in the text item of the respective blocks. The property Required is set to "Yes" for all these items, therefore you will not have to check whether they are NULL before calling the functions. Figure 29.4 shows the contents of trigger WHEN-BUTTON-PRESSED for button Calculate in block SLN.

Figure 29.5 shows the contents of trigger WHEN-BUTTON-PRESSED for button Calculate in the block PMT.

Now, create the functions `Calc_SLN`, and `Calc_PMT`. Because of the similarities between these functions, it is sufficient to show only one of them in detail, and leave the implementation of the second function to you. Figure 29.6 shows the contents of function `Calc_SNL`.

The first part of this function creates an argument list, and adds to it the three input arguments that will be passed to the Excel function SLN. Then the function GET_NUM_PROPERTY is used to return the value that function SLN computes based on the arguments in the list. This is also the value returned from the function `Calc_SLN`. At the end of this function, the argument list is destroyed, in order to free the resources it occupies. The function `Calc_PMT` will differ only in the number of arguments added to the argument list, and in the fact that the Excel function PMT is used instead of SLN.

Save, generate, and run the module in order to see its new functionality.

29.2.3 AUTOMATION WITH WORD PROCESSORS

Now open the module OLEWORD.FMB, which you will use to transfer data from the Oracle database to an MS Word form letter. The module DDEWORD.FMB discussed in Chapter 27 supported a similar functionality. However, as you will

```
DECLARE
 application_id PLS_INTEGER;
BEGIN
 IF :GLOBAL.application_id IS NOT NULL THEN
   application_id := TO_NUMBER(:GLOBAL.application_id);
   :SLN.DEPRECIATION := Calc_SLN( application_id,
                                  :SLN.COST,
                                  :SLN.SALVAGE,
                                  :SLN.LIFE);
 ELSE
   MESSAGE('The application must be started first.');
 END IF;
END;
```

FIGURE 29.4 Invoking function Calc_SLN.

```
DECLARE
 application_id PLS_INTEGER;
BEGIN
 IF :GLOBAL.application_id IS NOT NULL THEN
   application_id := TO_NUMBER(:GLOBAL.application_id);
   :PMT.PAYMENT := Calc_PMT(application_id,
   :PMT.RATE/100, :PMT.NPER,
                             :PMT.PV, :PMT.FV,
                             :PMT.TYPE);
 ELSE
   MESSAGE('The application must be started first.');
 END IF;
END;
```

FIGURE 29.5 Invoking function Calc_PMT.

```
FUNCTION Calc_SLN ( application_id PLS_INTEGER,
                    cost           NUMBER,
                    salvage        NUMBER,
                    life           NUMBER)
RETURN NUMBER IS
 arg_list           OLE2.LIST_TYPE;
 return_value       NUMBER;
BEGIN
 arg_list := OLE2.CREATE_ARGLIST;
 OLE2.ADD_ARG(arg_list, cost);
 OLE2.ADD_ARG(arg_list, salvage);
 OLE2.ADD_ARG(arg_list, life);

 return_value := OLE2.GET_NUM_PROPERTY(application_id,
 'SLN', arg_list);
 OLE2.DESTROY_ARGLIST(arg_list);

 RETURN(return_value);
EXCEPTION
 WHEN OTHERS THEN
   MESSAGE('Error: '||TO_CHAR(SQLCODE)||' '||SQLERRM);
   RAISE FORM_TRIGGER_FAILURE;
END;
```

FIGURE 29.6 Using OLE Automation to calculate the straight-line depreciation of an asset.

see here, the functionality you can add using the Automation technology is much more powerful and transparent for the user than in the DDE approach.

Chapter 27 discussed in detail the template letter that will be used in this application. In a nutshell, several bookmarks are defined in the document. Each of these bookmarks will be populated with data from the record of the current customer, when the letter will be compiled. This is how much functionality you implemented in Chapter 27. If users of that application want to perform any action with the document such as printing, saving it to a file for record-keeping purposes, or running the spell checker, they have to switch to the MS Word window and do it there. You will see here how easy it is to incorporate this functionality inside the Forms application, using the OLE2 package.

Figure 29.7 shows the layout of the module OLEWORD.FMB. The contents of the WHEN-BUTTON-PRESSED trigger for button Launch Word are almost the same as what Figure 29.2 shows. The only difference is that here the application name is Word.Basic instead of Excel.Application. The triggers for buttons Exit Word and Close are exactly the same as in the module OLEEXCL.FMB. All three triggers are provided in the template module OLEWORD.FMB.

The only thing left to discuss is the trigger that actually compiles the letter. In this trigger you will implement more functionality than you did in the DDE application, simply because the Automation mechanism allows you to access all the functions of MS Word, and every other server application, with great ease

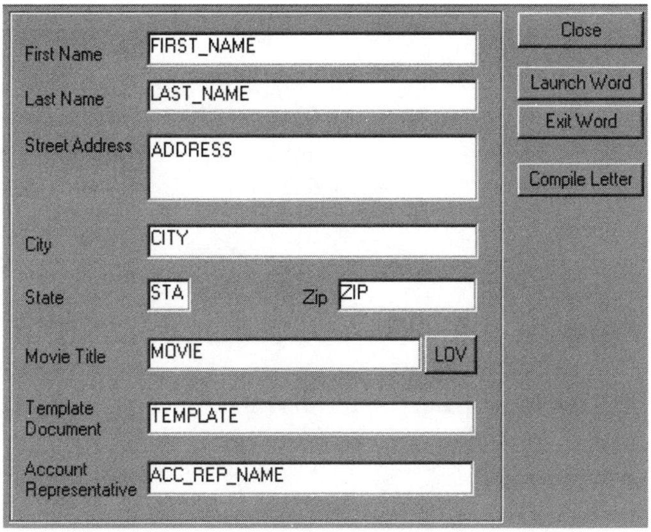

FIGURE 29.7 The layout of module OLEWORD.FMB.

and simplicity. Specifically, these are the actions that will be taken when the users press the Compile Letter button:

1. The trigger will check if the application is already started, and will continue processing only if this is the case.
2. The trigger will retrieve the current system date, and will concatenate the first and last names of the customer. These two steps are the same as in the DDE application.
3. The trigger will calculate the name of a file, where this letter will be saved. The directory will be the same where the template is saved; the extension of the file will be *.doc*; the name of the file will be the string formed by concatenating the last name with the first name. For example, if the template is retrieved from C:\FORMAPPS\LETTER.DOC, and the customer name is Michelle Johnson, the form letter for her will be saved as C:\FORMAPPS\JohnsonMichelle.DOC.
4. The trigger will open the template file from the location provided by the user.
5. The bookmarks defined in this file will be replaced with data provided in the items of block CUSTOMER.
6. The file will be saved under the new name.
7. The file will be sent to the printer.
8. The file will be closed.

As you can see from these steps, despite some tricks done initially to render user-entered data in an appropriate form, the core functionality of this trigger is issuing MS Word commands from PL/SQL. For the sake of simplicity, uniformity and reusability of the code, you should group these functions in a PL/SQL library which can be attached to the OLEWORD.FMB module, and any other module where you will need to add this functionality in the future. These are the steps to create this library and its program units:

1. In the Object Navigator create a new library module and name it OLEWORD.PLL.
2. Create a package specification program unit called WORD, with contents as shown in Figure 29.8.
3. Create the package body of WORD and declare a variable of data type OLE2.OBJ_TYPE, called `appl_id`. Initialize the variable to the value of `GLOBAL.application_id` using the following statement:

```
appl_id OLE2.OBJ_TYPE:= TO_NUMBER(NAME_IN('GLOBAL.ap-
plication_id'));
```

```
PACKAGE WORD IS
 PROCEDURE File_Open (file VARCHAR2);
 PROCEDURE File_Save_As (file VARCHAR2);
 PROCEDURE File_Print;
 PROCEDURE File_Close;
 PROCEDURE Replace_Bookmark (bookmark VARCHAR2, content
 VARCHAR2);
END;
```

FIGURE 29.8 PL/SQL package for OLE Automation with MS Word.

Recall that in other Developer modules you must reference global variables indirectly.

4. Create the body for procedure `File_Open`. The contents of this procedure are shown in Figure 29.9. It calls the MS Word FileOpen method using the OLE2 procedure INVOKE.
5. Create the body for procedure `File_Save_As`. The only difference between this and the previous procedure is it invokes the Word method FileSaveAs instead of FileOpen.
6. Create the body for procedure `File_Print` containing the following line:

   ```
   OLE2.INVOKE(appl_id, 'FilePrint');
   ```
7. Create the body for procedure `File_Close` containing the following line:

   ```
   OLE2.INVOKE(appl_id, 'FileClose');
   ```
8. Finally, implement the body of procedure `Replace_Bookmark`, as shown in Figure 29.10.

```
PROCEDURE File_Open (file VARCHAR2) IS
 arg_list OLE2.LIST_TYPE;
BEGIN
  arg_list := OLE2.CREATE_ARGLIST;
  OLE2.ADD_ARG(arg_list, file);
  OLE2.INVOKE(appl_id, 'FileOpen', arg_list);
  OLE2.DESTROY_ARGLIST(arg_list);
END;
```

FIGURE 29.9 Opening a MS Word file using OLE Automation.

```
PROCEDURE Replace_Bookmark (bookmark VARCHAR2,
                    content VARCHAR2) IS
 arg_list OLE2.LIST_TYPE;
BEGIN
  arg_list := OLE2.CREATE_ARGLIST;
  OLE2.ADD_ARG(arg_list, bookmark);
  OLE2.INVOKE(appl_id, 'EditGoTo', arg_list);
  OLE2.DESTROY_ARGLIST(arg_list);

  arg_list := OLE2.CREATE_ARGLIST;
  OLE2.ADD_ARG(arg_list, content);
  OLE2.INVOKE(appl_id, 'Insert', arg_list);
  OLE2.DESTROY_ARGLIST(arg_list);
END;
```

FIGURE 29.10 Replacing bookmarks in MS Word using OLE Automation.

CAUTION

There is a caveat that you should be aware of in the procedure Replace_Bookmark. Given the way bookmarks are implemented in Word, overwriting their previous contents with new data will erase them as named objects in the document. This means that any of the customer-specific files generated by OLEWORD.FMB will not contain the bookmarks. For a get-around to this problem, and for many other great tips on integrating Windows applications using DDE and OLE, you may reference *Making Windows Applications Work Together,* by Rob Krumm (M&T Books, 1994).

At this point, compile and save the module OLEWORD.PLL, and attach it to your form. Now, you are ready to create the body of the trigger WHEN-BUTTON-PRESSED for button Compile Letter. Recall that in this trigger you want to save each new document to a file named after the customer to whom the letter is sent. The name of this file can be easily created by concatenating the last name with the first name. Getting the directory path from the definition of the letter template entered by the users is a little trickier. First you should get the position of the last back-slash character "\" in the template name. For this, you can use the function INSTR with the following parameters:

```
last_slash_pos := INST(:CUSTOMER.TEMPLATE, '\', -1, 1);
```

Recall from Chapter 11 that these parameters make INSTR return the position of the first occurrence of character "\" in the string stored in CUSTOMER.TEMPLATE, starting from the end of the string (the reason for setting the third argument to –1).

Then, you can use SUBSTR to return the part of :CUSTOMER.TEMPLATE from the first character to the character in the position defined in the previous step. This string will be the directory where the new file will be stored. You can also provide users with a text item in the form, similar to TEMPLATE, where they themselves can specify the directory where the new file will be located. Better yet, as you will see in the following chapter, you can allow them to browse the file system hierarchy with one of the standard Windows dialog boxes.

Figure 29.11 shows the detailed implementation of this trigger.

As you can see from the examples discussed in this and the previous section, Automation offers you great possibilities to make the most out of the investment made in different software packages. Integrating these products with the Form Builder applications is also a very straightforward and easy process. In fact, the main difficulty you may encounter is not as much in the actual PL/SQL code you write, as in finding the names of the native functions you should use, and the parameters they take. This obviously requires programming skills not just in Form Builder, but also in the third-party products you will decide to integrate. There are several ways to overcome this difficulty. One would be to expand the development team with people that have solid experience with these tools. The users' community—people that use the word processing, spreadsheet, and graphic applications every day—would provide you with some surprisingly good experts on the subject. Ask them to share with you the toolbox of macros and utilities they may have created over the years.

Another way is to take advantage of the large variety of books written on Windows applications that cover their programming macro languages. Then, if you are one of those do-it-yourself personalities, you may want to take a plunge in the on-line documentation that each of these tools provides. The content page for each application that supports programming usually contains a section that provides references and examples for each function and procedure supported by the tool. For example, in MS Word this section is called *WordBasic Reference;* in Excel it is called *Microsoft Excel Visual Basic Reference.*

Finally, you can use the functions you want to reference from Form Builder in the native environment and record the session in the form of a macro. This macro then can be inspected to identify which functions were called and how their parameters were passed. Figure 29.12, for example, shows the macro that was used to identify the functions needed in the OLEWORD.FMB module. The names of the functions in this figure are highlighted for the sake of clarity.

As you can see from this figure, the number of arguments for some of these functions such as FileOpen, FileSaveAs, or FilePrint, may be overwhelming at times. However, only a few of them are required. The remaining arguments can maintain their default values.

```
DECLARE
 date            VARCHAR2(50);
 cust_name       VARCHAR2(60);
 work_dir        VARCHAR2(144);
 new_file        VARCHAR2(60);
 last_slash_pos  NUMBER;
BEGIN
 IF :GLOBAL.application_id IS NULL THEN
   MESSAGE('The application must be started first.');
   RAISE FORM_TRIGGER_FAILURE;
 END IF;
 SELECT TO_CHAR(SYSDATE, 'Month DD, YYYY') INTO date FROM DUAL;
 cust_name := :CUSTOMER.FIRST_NAME||' '||:CUSTOMER.LAST_NAME;

 new_file := :CUSTOMER.LAST_NAME||:CUSTOMER.FIRST_NAME;
 last_slash_pos := INSTR(:CUSTOMER.TEMPLATE, '\', -1, 1);
 work_dir := SUBSTR(:CUSTOMER.TEMPLATE, 1, last_slash_pos);
 new_file := work_dir||new_file;

 Word.File_Open(:CUSTOMER.TEMPLATE);
 Word.Replace_Bookmark('date',          date);
 Word.Replace_Bookmark('cust_name',     cust_name);
 Word.Replace_Bookmark('street',        :CUSTOMER.ADDRESS);
 Word.Replace_Bookmark('city',          :CUSTOMER.CITY);
 Word.Replace_Bookmark('state',         :CUSTOMER.STATE);
 Word.Replace_Bookmark('zip',           :CUSTOMER.ZIP);
 Word.Replace_Bookmark('first_name',    :CUSTOMER.FIRST_NAME);
 Word.Replace_Bookmark('movie',         :CUSTOMER.MOVIE);
 Word.Replace_Bookmark('acc_rep_name', :CUSTOMER.ACC_REP_NAME);
 Word.File_Save_As(new_file);
 MESSAGE('File saved in: '''||UPPER(new_file)||'''.');
 Word.File_Print;
 Word.File_Close;
END;
```

FIGURE 29.11 Transferring data from Form Builder to MS Word using Automation.

```
Sub MAIN

FileOpen .Name = "LETTER.DOC", .ConfirmConversions = 0,
.ReadOnly = 0, .AddToMru = 0, .PasswordDoc = "", .PasswordDot =
"", .Revert = 0, .WritePasswordDoc = "", .WritePasswordDot = ""

EditGoTo .Destination = "date"
Insert "November 12, 1995"

FileSaveAs .Name = "JOHNSONM.DOC", .Format = 0, .LockAnnot = 0,
.Password = "", .AddToMru = 1, .WritePassword = "",
.RecommendReadOnly = 0, .EmbedFonts = 0, .NativePictureFormat =
0, .FormsData = 0

FilePrint .AppendPrFile = 0, .Range = "0", .PrToFileName = "",
.From = "", .To = "", .Type = 0, .NumCopies = "1", .Pages = "",
.Order = 0, .PrintToFile = 0, .Collate = 1, .FileName = ""

FileClose

End Sub
```

FIGURE 29.12 MS Word macro used to locate WORD.BASIC methods used in OLEWORD.FMB.

29.3 SOFTWARE COMPONENTS

In everyday life, we constantly use devices, big and small, to perform certain actions or to control the performance and execution of others. Although today we are surrounded by a myriad of electronic devices and buttons, we have used controls for a long time. In fact, the history of the humanity can be seen as a constant evolution of our abilities to refine these devices, and make them take us to new heights and achievements. Nobody knows the genius who first invented the wheel, or the lever, but without him or her, wonders such as the Great Pyramids would not exist. The industrial revolution was generated and nourished by the eagerness of people to replace manual labor with mechanical devices. The information revolution, of which we are experiencing just the beginning, is replacing such mechanical devices with automated tools that can be controlled by a panel full of buttons, switches, and keys. We are so used to these controls and devices in our life so much that we never notice most of them until they breakdown: the door knob does not turn, the elevator button will not work, or the remote control is broken.

The revolution that graphical user interface environments brought in the computing industry was to build graphical screens based on the metaphor of the controls that we use every day. The GUI designers rightly assumed that people, used to pushing buttons to request service in hotel rooms or to switching light buttons on and off, would also feel comfortable working with applications that offer similar controls to perform their functions.

Originally, the types of controls used in the software industry were limited to push buttons, radio buttons, check boxes, list boxes, scroll bars, spin boxes, and a few others. Visual Basic introduced the powerful technique of integrating custom-made controls with applications developed with it. These controls were referred to as Visual Basic Extension, or VBXs for short. They allowed developers to include in their applications the functionality—properties, methods, and events—of objects developed by third-party vendors.

The Component Object Model architecture used the initial idea behind VBX controls in a whole new and radical way. This architecture enables building entire applications—not just the GUI—out of COM components. While applications developed traditionally are monolithic in nature, applications developed based on software components are made of a framework or an application bus in which different components are plugged. These components are chunks of functionality typically designed, developed, and tested by third party vendors. The components are delivered in binary format and expose their functionality in the form of interfaces, according to standards defined by COM. As long as these interfaces do not change, a component can be replaced with a newer version, or a totally different component without affecting the application or requiring any modifications to it. Figure 29.13 shows graphically the difference between monolithic applications and those build using a software component architecture.

The following paragraphs list some of the most important advantages that the component-based paradigm introduces in software engineering:

- **Encapsulation.** Components encapsulate and hide the implementation details of their functionality from applications using them. Thus, they bring in the software industry the remarkable advances that areas of technology are

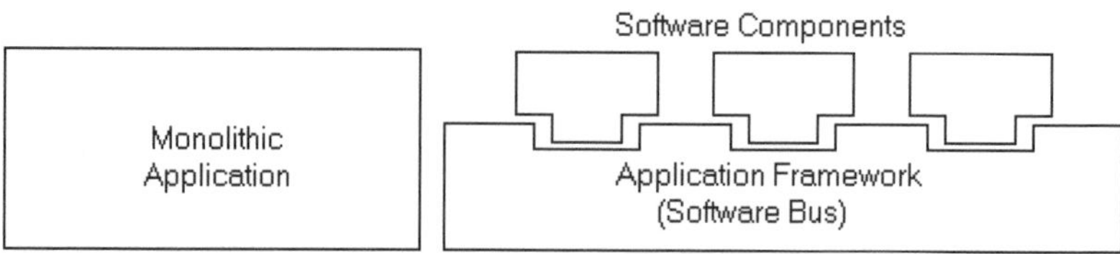

FIGURE 29.13 Graphical representation of monolithic and component-based applications.

experiencing. Imagine for a minute the car you drive, for example. You sit in comfortable seats, turn on the ignition key, switch gears and drive. You turn the wheel, press the gas or brake pedals, press a button to turn the lights on, and so on. A great deal of things must happen so that each of these operations may occur. However, you are shielded from all the details. All you have and need is a panel where each of these functions is represented by a switch, a button, or a control, which you use to get the car going. Software components promise to bring exactly that in software systems. They encapsulate a large number of services, properties and methods, which are exposed to the other software programs to use and benefit from.

- **Rapid Application Development.** Software components introduce the assembly-line paradigm in software engineering. In this paradigm, a number of 'software component' companies focus in the development and mass production of software components. Consumers purchase these components—exactly what they need and in the desired quantity—and assemble them in frameworks to create applications that meet their business needs. The popularity and success of this approach in a number of other business disciplines ensures that it will be very successful in software engineering as well. Furthermore, it allows you to build software solutions on time and within budget—one of the paramount promises of RAD.
- **Software maintenance.** Software components allow you to use the plug-and-play paradigm in software engineering. If a component needs to be updated or replaced, you can easily do it without having to touch the rest of the application. Thus, an application built based on components is much easier to maintain in the long run.
- **Distributed computing.** The fact that a software component exposes its services while hiding the implementation details provides a lot of flexibility in the partitioning of the application. You can easily move a local component onto the network and replace it with a *thin* component that serves as the mediator between the remote component and the other components. Figure 29.14 shows how the software component architecture facilitates distributed computing. Initially, the application A is implemented using the local components B and C. Then, the component C is moved to the network. This component is replaced by another component C′ that implements the same interface as C, but is very thin on functionality. The sole purpose of C′ is to forward the requests across the network to C, which performs the actual processing. Because the interface of C and C′ are identical, no changes are required in the application A.

Currently, there are two major implementations of software component architecture: ActiveX controls, based on COM, and Java Beans, based on Java. ActiveX controls are more popular but limited to platforms where COM and DCOM are implemented—primarily Microsoft Windows. Java Beans are components

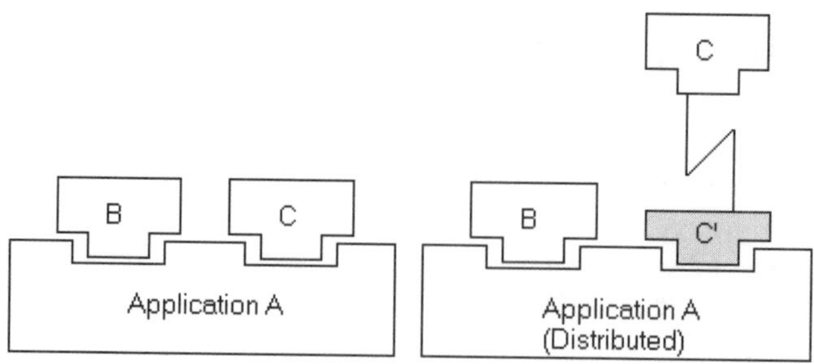

FIGURE 29.14 The software component architecture facilitates distributed computing.

that run wherever a Java Virtual Machine is implemented but are a more recent development, therefore not as widespread as ActiveX controls. Discussing these two technologies in detail, and comparing them, is definitely nor a subject of this book. Therefore, I will focus simply on the support that Form Builder provides for ActiveX controls.

29.4 ACTIVEX CONTROLS

This section will discuss how to integrate ActiveX controls in your Form Builder applications. I will guide you through a number of activities that will highlight the key items you need to know about these controls.

29.4.1 OVERVIEW OF ACTIVEX CONTROLS

As I have explained, VBX controls were the first effort to introduce the software component model to Windows (Visual Basic) programming. Despite the popularity among application developers, the design of VBXs was not free of errors and hasty decisions. However, it was not until Microsoft embarked in the journey to create a 32-bit operating system that they realized that this design contained major flaws. In fact VBXs would not migrate well, if at all, in the new operating systems. Therefore, new designs were put needed. By this time though, the COM standards were well established. The newest components added to the technology were the OLE controls. They are at the top of the other COM technologies in the sense that they build on them, especially on OLE Documents, In-place Activation, and OLE Automation. To maintain the analogy with their distant relatives, the OLE controls are referred to as OCX controls. OCX controls were bulky initially and required a number of interfaces to be implemented. This made their physical size too large to be used in Internet applications. Thus, a leaner type of controls were designed and named ActiveX controls. ActiveX controls are required to implement only one interface that allows client applications to discover any other interfaces implemented by the control. From a strict technical perspective, ActiveX controls are OCX controls but not all OCX controls are ActiveX controls. However, because Form Builder handles these two types of controls identically, I will consider them the same and refer to them as ActiveX controls.

ActiveX controls are objects packaged in binary format that encapsulate properties and methods in a way that is easier for the users to access. ActiveX controls cannot live independently but must be stored inside a container in the client application. Form Builder provides a special type of items that serve as ActiveX containers. Each ActiveX control is characterized by its properties, events, and methods. Properties are named attributes of the control, which govern its appearance and functionality. Events are actions that the control is programmed to recognize. Such events can be triggered externally—for example, when users click an area of the control—or internally, by programmatically changing the state of a control or some of its properties. Methods are program units such as functions and procedures that act upon the control.

29.4.2 PROPERTIES OF ACTIVEX CONTROL ITEMS

In Form Builder, ActiveX controls are a special type of items that share many common characteristics with other items. They can be used to enter, retrieve and manipulate data from the database. In addition, they can also be used to provide a better and friendlier interface to the applications. The following are several ways to create an ActiveX control item in a form:

- Click the ActiveX Control iconic button in the Layout Editor's tool palette and draw the control on the canvas.
- Set the type of item to ActiveX Control in the Items tab of the Data Block Wizard, upon creation of a new base table block.
- Set the property Item Type of an existing item to "ActiveX Item."

The new ActiveX control is an empty container on the canvas. It will not come to life until an actual control is attached to it from the file system. Storing the control is very similar to embedding or linking a document. The following are the steps you need to follow:

1. Right-click the container and select Insert Object… from the menu. The dialog box Insert Object appears. This dialog is the same one used in the previous chapter to pick the document to link or embed in the OLE container. Except that when invoked from ActiveX container objects, only the option Create Control is enables, as shown in Figure 29.15.
2. Select the ActiveX control to embed.
3. Click OK.

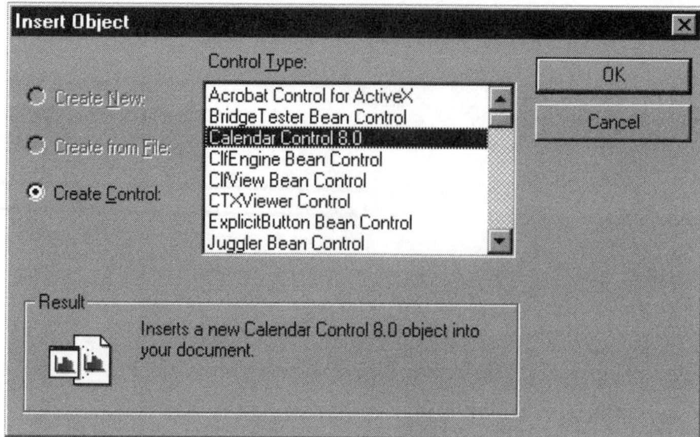

FIGURE 29.15 The Insert Object dialog box for ActiveX containers.

At this point, the control is embedded in the container. Note that a control can be embedded in the container at design time or at runtime, following the same actions described above. Embedding it at design time presents users with an application that is instantiated and ready to use. The application is more protected from errors due to the incompatibility of the control users may embed in the container at runtime with what your application code expects.

By double-clicking a control in its container you will display its Property Palette. Notice that the Functional group contains only four properties specific to ActiveX controls:

- **OLE Class.** This property has the same meaning as in the case of OLE containers, discussed in the previous chapter. It allows you to restrict the choice of controls that can be embedded in the container to only one class. Then, at design time or at runtime, the container will support only controls from the specified class.
- **Control Properties.** The setting of this property is always a button which, when clicked, displays the property maintenance interface provided by the control, if there is one. Each control has its own unique properties that can be set using this interface. These properties allow you to set the control in its initial state.
- **About Control.** This property is also a button which, when clicked, displays information about the control that typically goes in an About dialog box. The control must contain a method that displays this dialog; otherwise it will not be displayed. A well-written control should always expose the About method and associated dialog box.

- **Control Help.** Clicking this property launches the online help for the control if one is provided. A well-documented control should always come with online help, describing at minimum the properties, methods and events of the control.

29.4.3 MANIPULATING ACTIVEX CONTROLS PROGRAMMATICALLY

Placing an ActiveX control in the container is just the beginning. In order to take full advantage of its functionality, you need to interact with it—activate its methods, set its properties, trap and handle the events that the control raises. Form Builder makes it very easy to interact with the ActiveX control from your PL/SQL program units. It provides a utility—OLE Importer—that automatically builds a PL/SQL wrapper around ActiveX controls. This wrapper consists of packages whose methods can be used for the following two purposes:

- They can be called from other PL/SQL blocks to invoke methods and set properties of the ActiveX control.
- Their body can be expanded to implement the functionality activated by events within the package.

In order to invoke the OLE Importer, you should select Program | OLE Importer... from the menu. The dialog box Import OLE Library Interfaces appears (see Figure 29.16). In this dialog box, scroll down the OLE Classes list until you find the class that corresponds to the ActiveX control you want to interact with. The list boxes below the OLE Classes list display the interfaces that the control has implemented to expose the methods and events. By selecting the interfaces in these lists and setting the check boxes Methods and Properties below you can create the following PL/SQL packages:

- A PL/SQL package that implements only the interface to all the methods of the control. To achieve this, select the desired interface in the list Method Packages, set the check box Methods, and clear the check box Properties. The package created will be named according to the template <OLE Class Name>_M_<Interface>. In the example shown in Figure 29.16, the package name will be `MSCAL_M_Icalendar`.
- A PL/SQL package that implements only the interface to all the properties of the control. To achieve this, select the desired interface in the list Method Packages, clear the check box Properties, and clear the check box Properties. The package created will be named according to the template <OLE Class Name>_P_<Interface>. In the example shown in Figure 29.16, the package name will be `MSCAL_P_Icalendar`. A principle of good software component programming is to prevent client applications from modifying the properties of a control directly. Instead, Get and Set methods are provided

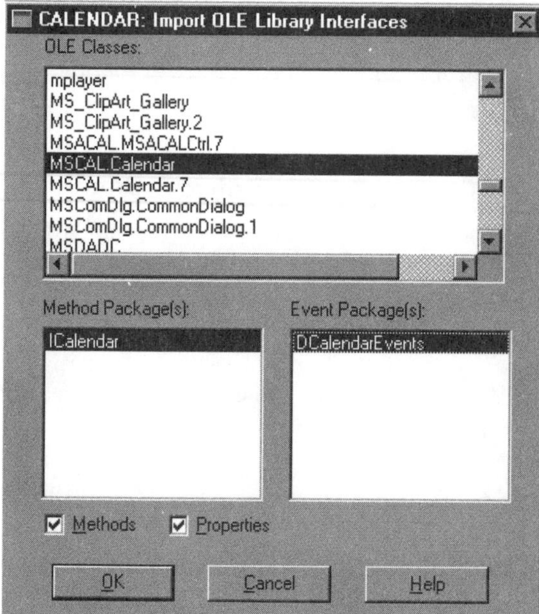

FIGURE 29.16 The Import OLE Library Interfaces dialog box.

for each property to read and write the value of this property. Although ActiveX controls do not enforce this convention, a professionally written control will almost never expose its properties publicly. Thus, this package will most likely be empty.

- A PL/SQL package that implements the interface to both methods and properties of the control. For this, select the interface name in the list Method Packages and set both Methods and Properties check boxes. The package created in this case will be named after the OLE class and the interface, as in `MSCAL_P_Icalendar`.
- A PL/SQL package that allows you to react to any event triggered by the control. The name of this package will be <OLE Class Name>_<Interface>_EVENTS. The package generated for the calendar control shown in Figure 29.16 is `MSCAL_Calendar_EVENTS`.
- A PL/SQL package that defines subtypes for the control and its interfaces. This package has only the specification type, is always generated, and it's named following the template <OLE Class Name>_CONSTANTS, as in `MSCAL_CONSTANTS`.

Once the packages described above have been created you are ready to interact with the control programmatically. To invoke a method of the control, identify its corresponding PL/SQL wrapper in the appropriate package and call it from your PL/SQL code as you would call the method of any other PL/SQL package. All these methods take as the first argument the interface pointer to the ActiveX control. In the Form Builder, this pointer is stored in a variable of data type OLEObj and is retrieved using the following statement:

```
OLEObj_Variable :=
:ITEM('BlockName.ActiveXContainerName').interface;
```

Responding to an event from the control is a little trickier. For each event, the EVENTS package generated by the OLE Importer contains a PL/SQL procedure. Figure 29.17 shows the contents of one such procedure generated when users click the object. Form Builder, through its ActiveX container, is responsible for listening to the control embedded in the container. When the event Click occurs in the control, the container automatically calls the corresponding procedure in the EVENTS package. If you want to handle the event, replace the NULL statement with the desired logic. A handle to the control is passed through the argument interface in case you need to read the state of the control or invoke another method of it. If you do not expand the body of the procedures in the EVENTS package, the control will still trigger the container each time the events occur, but the Form Builder application will not react to these events.

29.4.4 ACTIVEX CONTROLS IN FORM BUILDER— THE CALENDAR CONTROL

In this section, I will explain how you can integrate in your applications the calendar control that comes with Microsoft Office. As in other occasions, you will start with a template form provided with the companion software, named CALENDAR.FMB. The layout of this module is shown in Figure 29.18. This is a list of the functionality you will add to this module:

1. Add the ActiveX control in the CALENDAR container.
2. Call methods that retrieve the value of the currently selected date in the control and store it in text items.

```
PROCEDURE /* Click */ EVENT4294966696(interface OleObj) IS
BEGIN
  NULL;
END;
```

FIGURE 29.17 A typical procedure generated by the OLE Importer to handle the event of an ActiveX control.

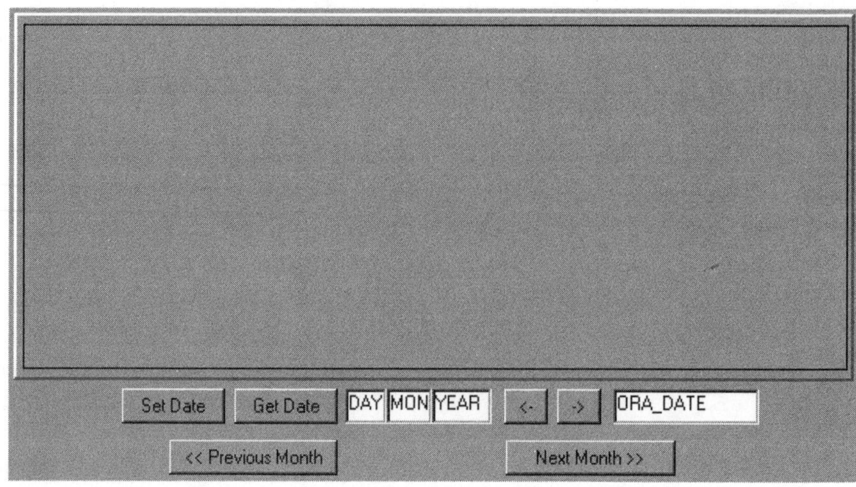

FIGURE 29.18 The initial layout of the CALENDAR.FMB module.

3. Call methods that set select a new day in the calendar based on the value entered in text items.
4. Handle the Click event of the control in the way that the date selected in the control is stored in the form's text items.

In preparation for the integration, insert the control in the container and create the PL/SQL packages that will handle the interface between them. The following steps allow you to accomplish this goal:

1. Right-click the ActiveX container item and select Insert Object... from the pop-up menu.
2. Select the Calendar control in the dialog box Insert Object, as shown in Figure 29.15.
3. Click OK. You will see that the component is inserted in the container with the current date selected.
4. Display the Property Palette of the control and double-click the property Control Properties. The dialog box Calendar Properties appears (see Figure 29.19). There are a number of properties that you can set in the three tabs of this control to configure the display of the control.
5. Customize the settings of properties for the control. Click Apply to see the effect of the changes without closing the dialog box. Click OK when finished setting the properties.
6. Select Program | OLE Importer... from the menu to display the dialog box Import OLE Library Interfaces.

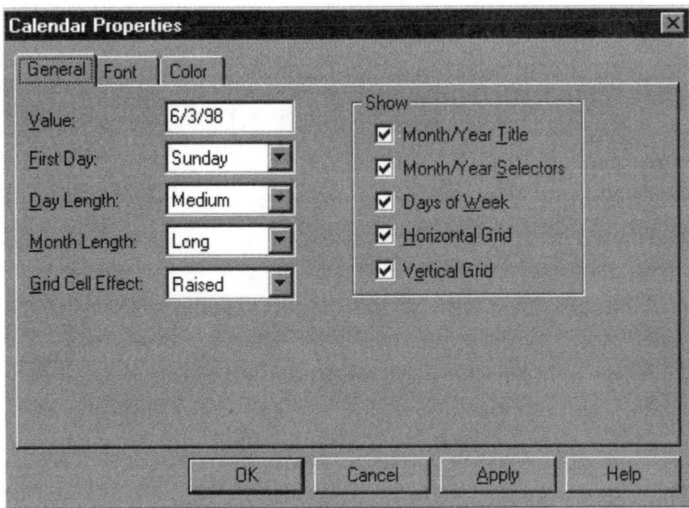

FIGURE 29.19 The Calendar Properties dialog box.

7. Select MSCAL.Calendar from the list OLE Classes, ICalendar from the list Method Packages, and DCalendarEvents from the list Event Packages. Leave the check boxes Methods and Properties selected. At this point, the dialog box Import OLE Library Interfaces will look like Figure 29.16.
8. Click OK to have the OLE Importer create the packages MSCAL_CONSTANTS, MSCAL_Calendar_EVENTS, and MSCAL_ICalendar.

Now, you want to create a WHEN-BUTTON-PRESSED trigger attached to the button Get Date which stores the values returned by the methods Day, Month, and Year of the control into the items DAY, MONTH, and YEAR of the CALENDAR block. Figure 29.20 shows the contents of this trigger. Notice how it stores the interface to the control to an OLEObj variable first, and then I invoke the desired methods. Reading the values of the form items and passing them to

```
DECLARE
  Cal_Control OLEObj;
BEGIN
  Cal_Control := :ITEM('CALENDAR.CALENDAR').interface;
  :CALENDAR.DAY := MSCAL_ICalendar.Day(Cal_Control);
  :CALENDAR.MONTH := MSCAL_ICalendar.Month(Cal_Control);
  :CALENDAR.YEAR := MSCAL_ICalendar.Year(Cal_Control);
END;
```

FIGURE 29.20 Getting the date value from the Calendar control.

the control is almost the symmetrical process. Figure 29.21 shows the contents of the WHEN-BUTTON-PRESSED trigger of button Set Date that implements this functionality.

Implementing the triggers associated with the buttons Previous Month and Next Month is even simpler. You should use the framework of the trigger shown in Figure 29.21. Except that instead of invoking the procedures Day, Month, and Year, you should invoke the procedures PreviousMonth and NextMonth of package MSCAL_ICalendar. These procedures require no arguments other than the interface pointer.

To finish up, write the code that responds to the Click event in the calendar control and stores the clicked date in the form items. This code should be implemented in the procedure that corresponds to this event in the EVENTS package created by OLE Importer. Figure 29.22 shows the contents of this procedure. As you can see, this procedure is very similar to the trigger shown in Figure 29.20, except that here the interface to the ActiveX control is passed as an argument in the procedure and, therefore, there is no need to retrieve it.

As mentioned earlier, you do not need to call this procedure explicitly; when the event occurs in the ActiveX control, the Form Builder container receives its ID—4294966696, in this case—and calls the corresponding procedure from the EVENTS package. By default, the event procedures are restricted in the sense that you cannot have logic there that changes the navigation focus of the form. If you need to take actions, such as moving to a different item or block, in response to the ActiveX control events, create a ON-DISPATCH-EVENT trigger at the block or form level and dispatch the desired event in a non-restricted mode, using the built-in procedure DISPATCH_EVENT. Figure 29.23 shows the content of an ON-DISPATCH-EVENT trigger that dispatches the Click event in the Calendar control in unrestricted mode and every other event in the default mode.

The following items should be noted in the implementation of this trigger:

- ❑ The event ID generated by the control should correspond to the event you want to handle. Use the EVENTS package created by the OLE Importer to find this number.

```
DECLARE
  Cal_Control OLEObj;
BEGIN
  Cal_Control := :ITEM('CALENDAR.CALENDAR').interface;
  MSCAL_ICalendar.Day(Cal_Control, :CALENDAR.DAY);
  MSCAL_ICalendar.Month(Cal_Control, :CALENDAR.MONTH);
  MSCAL_ICalendar.Year(Cal_Control,:CALENDAR.YEAR);
END;
```

FIGURE 29.21 Setting the date value of the Calendar control.

```
PROCEDURE /* Click */ EVENT4294966696(interface OleObj) IS
BEGIN
  :CALENDAR.DAY := MSCAL_ICalendar.Day(interface);
  :CALENDAR.MONTH := MSCAL_ICalendar.Month(interface);
  :CALENDAR.YEAR := MSCAL_ICalendar.Year(interface);
END;
```

FIGURE 29.22 Handling the Click event in the Calendar control.

- You do not call the procedure to handle the event in the ON-DISPATCH-EVENT trigger. You simply forward the event to the same mechanism that handles it in the default case.
- The ELSE clause is important because without it Forms will ignore any other events generated by this or any other ActiveX control in the module.

29.4.5 CONVERTING THE DATA

In the example discussed in Section 29.4.4, the three methods of the Calendar control stored the date in three form items—DAY, MONTH, and YEAR. Obviously, for a complete integration with the Form Builder environment, you want to convert these three items in one value of Oracle's DATE data type. Figure 29.24 shows the statement that concatenates the three values and converts them into a DATE item. The reverse functionality is obviously desired, as well. Figure 29.25 shows how you could strip an Oracle date in its default format and store it three separate items that can be passed on to the Calendar control.

In order to help you converting data, Developer provides a package called D2Kconv in the PL/SQL library d2kconv.pll. Like other utilities, this library is located in the directory %ORACLE_HOME%\Tools\Devdem20\Demo\Forms. The package D2Kconv contains the functions described in the following paragraphs:

```
IF :SYSTEM.CUSTOM_ITEM_EVENT = 4294966696 THEN
  FORMS4W.DISPATCH_EVENT(RESTRICTED_ALLOWED);
ELSE
  FORMS4W.DISPATCH_EVENT(RESTRICTED_FORBIDDEN);
END IF;
```

FIGURE 29.23 Dispatching events in restricted and non-restricted mode.

```
:CALENDAR.ORA_DATE :=    TO_DATE(:CALENDAR.DAY||'/'||
                         :CALENDAR.MONTH||'/'||
                         :CALENDAR.YEAR, 'DD/MM/YYYY');
```

FIGURE 29.24 Converting values retrieved from the Calendar control into a DATE item.

- **Expr_to_Number.** This function takes as an argument an alphanumeric expression—for example, ((5*4)-10)/13) and returns its computed numeric value. The following line shows an example of this function. It assumes that users type in an expression like the one shown earlier in the item INPUT and it returns the computed value in the item OUTPUT:

```
BEGIN
   :Control.Output :=
D2Kconv.Expr_to_Number(:Control.Input);
EXCEPTION
  WHEN VALUE_ERROR THEN
    MESSAGE('Value cannot be computed. Please reenter. ');
END;
```

- **String_to_Date.** This function takes as argument a date stored in an alphanumeric string, one or more formats in which the date may be stored, and the delimiting character that separates these formats. The function returns the value of the date in the Oracle DATE data type. The following example shows how you can covert the date loaded as an alphanumeric string of multiple formats from a legacy system into the standard Oracle DATE format:

```
BEGIN
   :MOVIE.RENT_DT :=
D2Kconv.String_to_Date(:MOVIE.LEGACY_DT,
                        'DD/MM/YYYY, 'DD/MON/YYYY);
EXCEPTION
  WHEN VALUE_ERROR THEN
    MESSAGE('Date cannot be converted. ');
END;
```

```
:CALENDAR.DAY    := TO_NUMBER(TO_CHAR(:CALENDAR.ORA_DATE,'DD'));
:CALENDAR.MONTH  := TO_NUMBER(TO_CHAR(:CALENDAR.ORA_DATE,'MM'));
:CALENDAR.YEAR   :=
TO_NUMBER(TO_CHAR(:CALENDAR.ORA_DATE,'YYYY'));
```

FIGURE 29.25 Splitting a DATE item into values passed to the Calendar control.

29.5 SUMMARY

This chapter continued the discussion of implementing COM-based technologies in Form Builder applications initiated in the previous chapter. The focus of this chapter was the use of Automation and ActiveX controls in such applications. The most important concepts discussed here were:

- **Automation**
- **Automation in Form Builder**
  - OLE2 Package
  - OLE Automation with Spreadsheets
  - Automation with Word Processors
- **Software Components**
- **ActiveX Controls**
  - Overview of ActiveX Controls
  - Properties of ActiveX Control Items
  - Manipulating ActiveX Controls Programmatically
  - ActiveX Controls in Form Builder—The Calendar Control
  - Converting the Data

The following table describes the software assets that were discussed in this chapter. From the main HTML page of the software utilities provided with the book follow the links *Software* and *Chapter 29* to access these assets:

ASSET NAME	DESCRIPTION
OLEEXCEL.FMB	A Form Builder module that will be integrated with Microsoft Excel using OLE Automation services. Use this module as starting point for the activities discussed in Section 29.2.2.

ASSET NAME	DESCRIPTION
OLEEXCEL_1.FMB	The final version of OLEEXCEL.FMB with all the activities discussed in Section 29.2.2.
OLEEXCEL_1.FMX	The executable version of OLEEXCEL_1.FMB compiled for Win32 platforms.
OLEWORD.FMB	A Form Builder module that will be integrated with Microsoft Word using OLE Automation services. Use this module as starting point for the activities discussed in Section 29.2.3.
OLEWORD_1.FMB	The final version of OLEWORD.FMB with all the activities discussed in Section 29.2.3.
OLEWORD_1.FMX	The executable version of OLEWORD_1.FMB compiled for Win32 platforms.
LETTER.DOC	A Microsoft Word document that serves as a template for the form letters created in Section 27.2.3.
CALENDAR.FMB	A Form Builder module that will incorporate an ActiveX calendar control. Use this module as starting point for the activities discussed in Section 29.4
CALENDAR_1.FMB	The final version of CALENDAR_1.FMB with all the activities discussed in Section 29.4.
CALENDAR_1.FMX	The executable version of CALENDAR_1.FMB compiled for Win32 platforms.

Chapter 30

FOREIGN FUNCTION INTERFACE

Skilled in the works of both languages.

—Horace

- Types of Foreign Functions
- Sample Foreign Functions
- User Exit Interface
- PL/SQL Foreign Function Interface
- Summary

Another important add-on functionality provided by Form Builder, besides DDE and COM-based integration, is the utilization of modules created with Third Generation Languages (3GL) tools such as C, FORTRAN, and COBOL. The functions and procedures in these modules can be accessed in the form of user exits and foreign functions interface directly from PL/SQL. This chapter will discuss the process of creating and accessing C functions, and most importantly, Windows Software Development Kit (SDK) functions both from user exits and the PL/SQL foreign functions interface.

30.1 TYPES OF FOREIGN FUNCTIONS

In MS Windows foreign functions can be accessible only if they are bundled in a Dynamic Link Library (DLL) file. Therefore, any programming language or compiler that can create DLL can also be used to write a library of foreign functions that will be used from Form Builder. Based on whether they access the Oracle database independently and the implementation, foreign functions are grouped in the following categories:

- **Non-Oracle foreign functions.** This category includes those foreign functions that are implemented using purely native language constructs. These functions do not contain any Oracle call interface (OCI) or precompiler structures—hence the name of the category. These functions are written using the compiler of the host language and you cannot access any of the Form Builder variables and items, or the Oracle database.
- **Oracle Call Interface (OCI) functions.** This category includes functions that access the Oracle database independently using the OCI libraries. While allowing you to access the Oracle Server database, OCI functions cannot access variables in the Form Builder or other development tools. Therefore, they are rarely used in Form Builder applications.
- **Oracle Precompilers functions.** This category includes functions written using one of Oracle's precompiler utilities. These functions have access to either the Form Builder variables or the Oracle database; therefore they are among the most popular foreign functions.

In Oracle Precompiler functions, you can combine valid syntactic constructs of the host language with SQL statements, PL/SQL blocks, and Form Builder variables. The precompiler interprets these files and produces source files that contain only host-language statements. All SQL or PL/SQL statements are converted to their equivalents in the host language. You can compile and link this file as you would normally do with any other file. For example, you use the Pro*C/C++ precompiler to create an Oracle Precompiler function for C or C++. This function is saved in a file with the extension .PC. When Pro*C processes this file, it checks for the accuracy of SQL and PL/SQL statements contained therein. If no errors are encountered, a file with the extension *.c* is produced at the end of the process. This file then can be passed to the C compiler for normal compilation and linking processing.

The Oracle Precompiler functions can use any of the host-language statements. In addition, they can execute any SQL statement by preceding it with the keywords EXEC SQL. To execute Oracle Precompiler options that are not standard SQL commands, you prefix them with the keywords EXEC ORACLE.

Another important set of statements used in precompiler functions are those that transfer data, context information, and messages between Form Builder items or variables and host-language variables. These statements are EXEC TOOLS GET, EXEC TOOLS SET, EXEC TOOLS MESSAGE, EXEC TOOLS GET CONTEXT, and EXEC TOOLS SET CONTEXT.

The statement EXEC TOOLS GET is used to pass values from Form Builder variables such as items, parameters, global and system variables to variables in the 3GL program. The statement EXEC TOOLS SET sets a Form Builder variable to a value currently stored in the host-language variable. EXEC TOOLS MESSAGE allows you to send a message from the foreign function to the Form Builder environment. Finally, the statements EXEC TOOLS SET CONTEXT and EXEC TOOLS GET CONTEXT are used to maintain certain values globally, across calls of foreign functions, much in the same way global variables in Form Builder preserve values across program units. EXEC TOOLS SET CONTEXT is used to associate the desired value with a context name, and EXEC TOOLS GET CONTEXT is used to retrieve the value previously stored in a context variable.

30.2 SAMPLE FOREIGN FUNCTIONS

In this chapter, I will use several C functions to discuss their implementation in user exit interfaces and PL/SQL foreign functions interface. This section describes the contents of these functions, and in the rest of the chapter you will create a DLL library that contains these functions. This library will be used to access these functions from within Form Builder. The samples of this chapter were compiled using Microsoft Visual C++ 5.0. If you are using a different compiler, you should use the appropriate instructions for creating DLL projects; however, you will not have to modify any of the source code files.

The following is a description of the contents of the C files contained in the companion diskette that you will use in this chapter.

30.2.1 MODULES UEERROR.H AND UEERROR.C

The module UEERROR.H is a header file that contains the definition of Failure, Fatal and Success codes that other functions will return. It also contains the declaration for a function that will display an error message to the Form Builder users, if this is necessary.

The module UEERROR.C contains the function that displays an error message that is raised by one of the other functions. The contents of this function are shown in Figure 30.1.

There are three functions from the Windows SDK toolkit that are used in function `UEError`. The following paragraphs cover each of them:

- The function `wsprintf` formats the characters in the third argument according to the specifications in the format-control string, specified by the second argument. The formatted character is stored in the buffer provided by the first argument. In your case, you are formatting the title and the text of the error message as character strings.
- The function `MessageBox` creates and displays a message box window. The first argument in this function is the handle of the window that will be the parent of the dialog box. The following two arguments contain respectively the text and the title of the message box. The last argument defines the style of the dialog box. In this case, the message box will contain a stop-sign icon and one OK button to dismiss it. The function returns the numeric value of the button that was pressed to dismiss the dialog box.
- The function `GetActiveWindow` is used to return the handle of the window that is the active windows when the message box is created. This also serves as the parent window for the new message box. You may also set this parameter to NULL.

```
#include <windows.h>

#include "ueerror.h"


void UEError ( LPSTR messageTitle, LPSTR messageText )
{
  char text[200],
     title[80];

  wsprintf (title,"%s",messageTitle);
  wsprintf (text,"%s",messageText);

  MessageBox ( GetActiveWindow(),text,title,MB_ICONSTOP);
}
```

FIGURE 30.1 C function that displays a message box.

The example shown in Figure 30.1 can also serve as a template for implementing your own customized message boxes. Recall that Form Builder uses alerts to display messages to the users. However, in order to use some standard Windows dialog boxes, you may call directly the Windows SDK function `MessageBox`. If, for example, you set the last parameter to MB_ICONQUESTION | MB_YESNOCANCEL, the message box will display a questions mark icon (which cannot be obtained by alerts), and three buttons: Yes, No, and Cancel.

30.2.2 MODULE HELP.C

This file contains the definitions for the functions `WinHelpIndex`, `WinHelpContents`, `WinHelpQuit`, `WinHelpSearchOn`, and `WinHelpContext`. Figure 30.2 shows the contents of the function `WinHelpIndex`. Given the similarity between the contents of this function with the remaining four functions, they will not be discussed in this section.

Fundamentally, all these functions invoke the Windows SDK function `WinHelp`. Their differences come from different values of the arguments passed to this function. The meaning of these values and arguments is documented in any book that covers the Windows SDK and in the on-line help that comes with programming tools such as Visual Basic, or Microsoft Visual C++.

The input argument of this function will be a string like the one shown here:

```
WinHelpIndex file=c:\example\helpfile.hlp
```

The function `strtok` is used to parse the string in different tokens. In the first call, this function scans the argument `inputArgs` until it reaches the first blank space. The pointer to this string is returned to the variable `Parameter`. The successive call reads the next token from the string `inputArg`, until the character "=" is found. This token must be the keyword 'FILE' for the processing to continue. Another call to `strtok` returns the string up to the first empty space is found, which is also the name of the help file passed as the input argument. Note that to retrieve any other tokens after the first one, the first argument to `strtok` must be NULL.

After the name of the file is parsed, the function `OpenFile` is used to check for the existence of the file. When this function is invoked with the flag OF_EXIST, Windows opens and closes the file without affecting any of its attributes. If the file does not exist, the function returns the value -1, in which case, you inform the user about the invalid file name.

Finally, when you are sure about the existence of the file, the Windows function `WinHelp` is invoked. This function start the Windows Help engine in different configurations, depending on the arguments passed. The first argument is a handle to the window that is requesting help. The second is a pointer to the name of the file to be opened. The last two arguments are used in combination to specify the type of help to be displayed and other additional data required to dis-

```
#include <windows.h>
#include <string.h>
#include <stdio.h>
#include <stdlib.h>

#include "ueerror.h"


/*
** user_exit('WinHelpIndex file=c:\example\helpfile.hlp');
**      Opens the help file at the "Index"
*/
int WinHelpIndex(inputArgs)
  char    *inputArgs;
{
  HWND     hParentWin;
  OFSTRUCT of;
  HANDLE   hFile;
  char    *fileName, *Parameter;

  char    errorTitle[80] = "Error in User Exit WinHelpIndex";
  char    invalidFile[80] = "Invalid WinHelp File Name.";
  char    invalidFileParameter[100] = "Invalid FILE Parameter.";

  Parameter = strtok(inputArgs," ");
  Parameter = strtok(NULL,"=");

  if ( strcmp(strupr(Parameter),"FILE")==0 )
     fileName = strtok(NULL," ");
  else
  {
     UEError(errorTitle, invalidFileParameter);
     return FATAL_ERR;
  }

  hFile = OpenFile((LPSTR)fileName,&of,OF_EXIST);

  if ( hFile != -1 ) // OpenFile returns -1 if unsuccessful
```

FIGURE 30.2 C function that invokes Windows Help utility.

```
    {
       hParentWin = GetActiveWindow();
       WinHelp(hParentWin,(LPSTR) fileName,HELP_INDEX,NULL);
    }
    else
    {
       UEError(errorTitle, invalidFile);
       return FATAL_ERR;
    }

    return SUCCESS;
} /* WinHelpIndex */
```

FIGURE 30.2 C function that invokes Windows Help utility. (Continued)

play it. In the case shown in Figure 30.2, the parameter HELP_INDEX will open the topic "Index" defined within the help file.

The function `WinHelpContents` invokes `WinHelp` with the parameter HELP_CONTENTS, which displays the Help contents topic as defined in the [OPTIONS] section of the Help project file.

The function `WinHelpQuit` invokes `WinHelp` with the parameter HELP_QUIT. This instructs the Help engine that Help is no longer needed for the application that opened it. Windows closes the Help file and, if no other applications are using Help, it dismisses the Help engine.

For all these functions, the fourth parameter is not needed; therefore it is set to NULL. For the remaining two functions however, this parameter is used. In the function `WinHelpSearchOn`, the statement that calls `WinHelp` is as in the following line:

```
WinHelp(hParentWin,(LPSTR) fileName,HELP_KEY, (DWORD)
(LPSTR) Parameter);
```

The argument HELP_KEY instructs `WinHelp` that help is requested on the string contained in the `Parameter`. If there is exactly one topic that matches this string, this topic is displayed. Otherwise the Search dialog box is displayed to allow users to select the appropriate topic.

In the function `WinHelpContext`, the function `WinHelp` is invoked as follows:

```
WinHelp(hParentWin,(LPSTR) fileName,HELP_CONTEXT,
(DWORD) numericContext);
```

In this case, the parameter HELP_CONTEXT informs `WinHelp` to display Help for the topic identified by the context number contained in the fourth parameter. This number must have been defined in the [MAP] section of the Help project file.

Obviously, in these functions, an additional step is required to parse the fourth parameter. For a detailed description of these functions, refer to module HELP.C provided in directory Ch28 of the companion disk.

30.2.3 MODULE FILENAME.PC

This file contains the definition of the function `GetFileName`, which makes use of another Windows SDK function, `GetOpenFileName`, to display a dialog box similar to Open or Save, which will allow users to browse the directory structure, search for a file, and return its name to a Form Builder item. Figure 30.3 shows the details of this function. The steps performed by this function are described below:

1. Initialize and set data items such as the title of the dialog box, or the error message.
2. Use the function `GetSystemDirectory` to retrieve the current system directory. This will be the initial directory displayed by the dialog box.

```
#include <windows.h>
#include <string.h>
#include <commdlg.h>
#include <memory.h>

#include "ueerror.h"

int GetFileName ( LPSTR szBuffer )
{
  HWND       hParentWin;
  OPENFILENAME ofn;
  char       szDirName[256], szFile[256], szFileTitle[256];
  UINT       i, cbString;
  char       chReplace,  /* string separator for szFilter */
         szFilter[256]  = "All Files (*.*)|*.*|",
         dialogTitle[80] = "Get File Name\0";
```

FIGURE 30.3 C function that displays a standard Open dialog box.

```
  /* Get the system directory name, and store in szDirName */
  GetSystemDirectory(szDirName, sizeof(szDirName));
  szFile[0] = '\0';

  cbString = lstrlen(szFilter);
  chReplace = szFilter[cbString - 1]; /* retrieve wildcard */
  for (i = 0; szFilter[i] != '\0'; i++) { /* Replace wildcard
  with '\0' */
     if (szFilter[i] == chReplace)
     szFilter[i] = '\0';
  }

  hParentWin = GetActiveWindow();

  /* Set all structure members to zero. */
  memset(&ofn, 0, sizeof(OPENFILENAME));

  /* Initialize structure members. */
  ofn.lStructSize = sizeof(OPENFILENAME);
  ofn.hwndOwner = hParentWin;
  ofn.lpstrFilter = szFilter;
  ofn.nFilterIndex = 1;
  ofn.lpstrFile= szFile;
  ofn.nMaxFile = sizeof(szFile);
  ofn.lpstrFileTitle = szFileTitle;
  ofn.nMaxFileTitle = sizeof(szFileTitle);
  ofn.lpstrInitialDir = szDirName;
  ofn.Flags = OFN_SHOWHELP | OFN_PATHMUSTEXIST |
  OFN_FILEMUSTEXIST;
  ofn.lpstrTitle = dialogTitle;

  if (GetOpenFileName(&ofn))
           lstrcpy (szBuffer,ofn.lpstrFile);
  else   {
     *szBuffer=0;
    return FATAL_ERR;
  }
     return SUCCESS;
}
```

FIGURE 30.3 C function that displays a standard Open dialog box. (Continued)

3. Replace the wildcard—by convention this is the last character of szFilter—with the NULL character "\0." For example, if the variable szFilter is initialized to "All Files (*.*)|*.*|", at the end of the FOR loop, its value will be "All Files (*.*)\0*.*\0".
4. Get the handle of the current window that will serve as the parent for the Get File Name dialog box.
5. Clear and initialize the structure ofn, based on the data prepared in the previous steps.
6. Invoke the function GetOpenFileName which takes the structure ofn and uses it to populate the components of the dialog box. If the user selects a file from the dialog box, this function returns a non-zero value and stores the name of the file in the lpstrFile member of the structure. This string is placed in the buffer that will store the name of the selected file.

As you can see from Figure 30.3, the function GetFileName stores the name of the file selected by users in the buffer szBuffer which is passed as an argument to this function by the calling environment. In order to make this value available to Form Builder, you must transfer it from this buffer to a variable in Forms. The function ReturnFileName serves this purpose. Because this function will access Forms items, the Oracle Pro*C Compiler must be used. This function is contained in the file FILENAME.PC, as well, and is shown in details in Figure 30.4.

As you can notice, this function parses the input argument string in a similar fashion as the WinHelp functions discussed previously. Note however that the variables that will be used in the SQL statement are declared in a separate DECLARE section, bounded by the EXEC SQL BEGIN DECLARE and EXEC SQL END DECLARE statements. Furthermore, you should also notice that PL/SQL variables of VARCHAR data type are structures of two components. After you precompile the file FILENAME.PC, you can open the module FILENAME.C generated by the Pro*C precompiler. You will see, for example, that the precompiler has replaced the declaration:

```
VARCHAR FormsItemName[256];
```

with the statements:

```
struct {
unsigned short len;
unsigned char arr[256];
} FormsItemName;
```

In the rest of the function, you can reference both components of this structure. As you can see from Figure 30.4, the component FormsItemName.arr is

```
int ReturnFileName(inputArgs)
 char *inputArgs;
{
 char *Parameter, szBuffer[256], *itemName,
 errorTitle[80] = "Error in User Exit RetrieveFileName\0",
 invalidItemParameter[80] = "Invalid Parameter. ITEM was
expected.\0",
 errorMsg[80] = "Cannot invoke the Get File Name dialog
box.\0";

 EXEC SQL INCLUDE SQLCA;

 EXEC SQL BEGIN DECLARE SECTION;
    VARCHAR fileName[256];
    VARCHAR FormsItemName[256];
 EXEC SQL END DECLARE SECTION;

 Parameter = strtok(inputArgs," ");
 Parameter = strtok(NULL,"=");

 if ( strcmp(strupr(Parameter),"ITEM")==0 )
    itemName = strtok(NULL," ");
 else {
    UEError(errorTitle, invalidItemParameter);
    return FATAL_ERR;
 }

 if ( GetFileName ( szBuffer ) == SUCCESS ) {
    strcpy(FormsItemName.arr, itemName);
    FormsItemName.len = strlen( itemName );
    strcpy(fileName.arr, szBuffer);

    EXEC TOOLS SET :FormsItemName VALUES (:fileName);
 }
 else {
    UEError(errorTitle, errorMsg);
    return FATAL_ERR;
 }

 return SUCCESS;
} /* ReturnFileName */
```

FIGURE 30.4 Pro*C file that passes values to Form Builder variables.

where the contents of the variable reside. The component `FormsItemName.len` holds the number of characters currently stored in the first component.

30.3 USER EXIT INTERFACE

In order to access the above functions from a user exit in Form Builder, a dynamic link library must be built to contain these and a few other functions. In this section you will create this library and the user exits calls step by step. If you have Pro*C installed in your machine, precompile the module FILENAME.PC. The output of this process will be the module FILENAME.C, which contains only C statements. This module is provided in the case you do not have access to the Pro*C software.

As a preliminary step, create a separate directory, where all the C functions will be placed and the DLLs will be created. Name this directory UE_CH30.

30.3.1 IAPXTB CONTROL STRUCTURE

IAPXTB is a tabular structure of pointers to the functions of a given DLL library that can be accessed from user exits. When Form Builder is installed, two templates of this structure are provided in the directory %ORACLE_HOME%\FORMS50\USEREXIT. The first one, UE_XTB.C, contains a sample IAPXTB structure with only one function. The second template, UE_XTBN.C, contains only an empty structure, with no functions declared. Each line in the structure should follow the format shown below:

```
"Function_Name", CFunctionName, XITCC,
```

The string included in the double quotes contains the name with this the user exit will invoke the function. The second variable is the name of the function as defined in the host language module. The third variable is a reference to the programming language in which this function is created. XITCC denotes the C language, XITCOB denotes COBOL, XITFOR denotes FORTRAN, and so on.

In your case, the IAPXTB structure is defined in the module UE_CH30.C, which you should copy from the module provided with the companion software in the directory UE_CH30. The contents of this function are shown in Figure 30.5.

The first part of this module declares functions that are contained in other modules. The central part of it is taken by the IAPXTB structure;. Note that the IAPXTAB structure does not contain every function of the library, but only those functions that you will need to access from user exits.

The first line of this module is a statement that includes the header file UE.H. This file is found in the %ORACLE_HOME%\FORMS50\USEREXIT directory and must be copied in the directory UE_CH30, as well.

```
#include "ue.h"

extern ReturnFileName();
extern WinHelpIndex();
extern WinHelpContents();
extern WinHelpQuit();
extern WinHelpSearchOn();
extern WinHelpContext();

/* Define the user exit table */
extern  exitr iapxtb[] = { /* Holds exit routine pointers
*/
      "ReturnFileName", ReturnFileName, XITCC,
      "WinHelpIndex",  WinHelpIndex,  XITCC,
      "WinHelpContents", WinHelpContents, XITCC,
      "WinHelpQuit",   WinHelpQuit,   XITCC,
      "WinHelpSearchOn", WinHelpSearchOn, XITCC,
      "WinHelpContext", WinHelpContext, XITCC,
   (char *) 0, 0, 0     /* zero entry marks the end */
}; /* end iapxtb */
```

FIGURE 30.5 Contents of IAPXTB user exit structure.

30.3.2 CREATING THE DLL FILE

Now you are ready to create the new dynamic link library file.

1. Launch the Microsoft Visual C++ compiler.
2. Choose File | New... from the menu. The New dialog box is displayed with the tab Project selected (see Figure 30.6).
3. Set the Project name to UE_CH30.
4. Select Win32 Dynamic-Link Library in the list box as the type of project to create.
5. Edit the location of the new project files is desired.
6. Click OK.

The new project is created in the Microsoft Developer Studio. Now add the files that will be part of this project by following these steps:

1. Select Project | Add to Project | Files… from the menu. The dialog box Insert Files into Project appears (see Figure 30.7).
2. Select the files discussed earlier as shown in Figure 30.7.
3. Click OK. All the files will be added to the project.

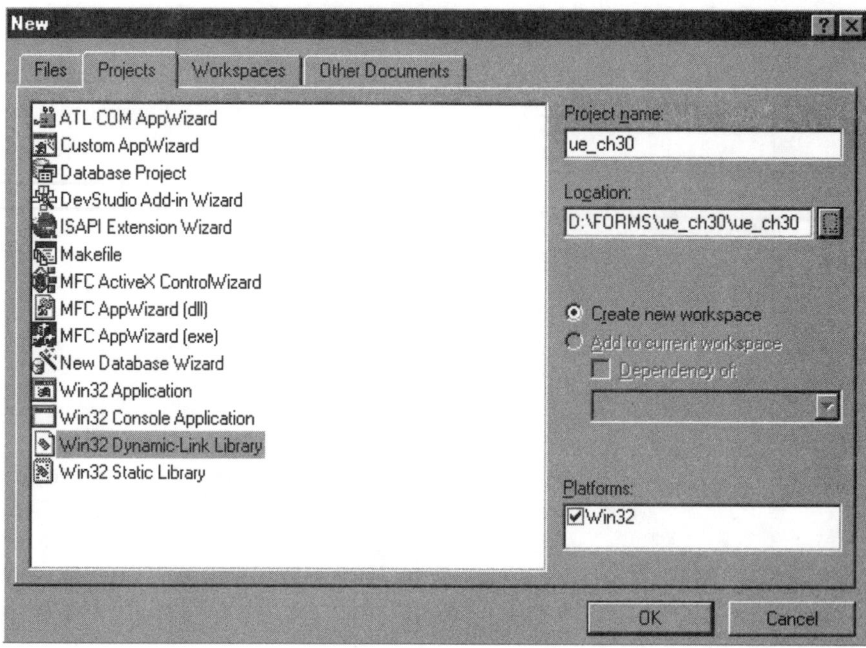

FIGURE 30.6 Microsoft Visual C++ New Project dialog box.

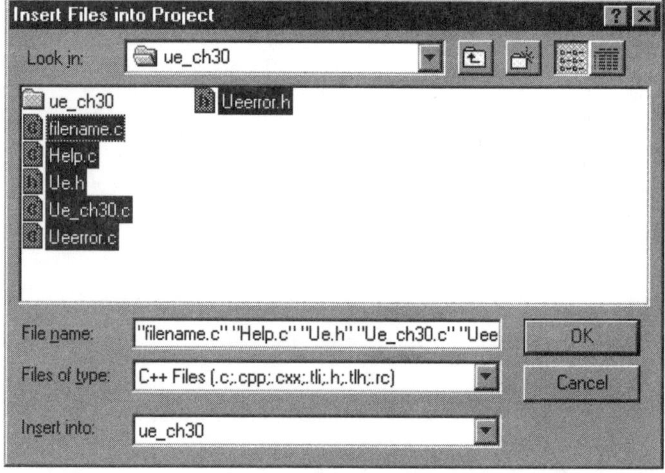

FIGURE 30.7 Microsoft Visual C++ Edit Makefile dialog box.

Recall that the file FILENAME.C is created by the Oracle Pro*C Precompiler. In order to be able to link these files successfully, you should add to the project the libraries SQLLIB18.LIB and SQXLIB18.LIB. You can find these libraries in the subdirectory \FORMS60\USEREXIT of your ORACLE_HOME directory. The directory %ORACLE_HOME%\FORMS60\USEREXIT contains some other files that you must include every time you create a user exit DLL. These files are UEZ.OBJ, and F50R32.LIB. Form Builder records in the F50XTB.DEF file the export statements for functions that it uses to assess other user exit functions that you create. These statements must not be changed. The steps to add these additional files to the project are very similar to those for adding the C and header files described earlier.

When all the files described above are added to the project, choose Project | Build UE_CH30.DLL, or Project | Rebuild All from the menu to compile, link and build the dynamic link library.

30.3.3 DEPLOYING THE USER EXIT DLL

By default, Form Builder will recognize user exits defined in the library F50XTB32.DLL located in the directory %ORACLE_HOME%\BIN. One way to deploy the library built in the previous section is to rename it to F60XTB32.DLL, and move it to that directory. This will obviously overwrite any functions that you may have previously linked in the file F50XTB32.DLL. Especially for large applications, with a significant number of user exits, it is not recommended that all the foreign function be packed in the default DLL. Besides resource contention problems that may arise when a sizable DLL is loaded in the memory, you may also experience problems if multiple users access the library at the same time.

The other, more elegant approach is to bundle together related functions in separate DLLs, and to add the locations of these files in the definition of the environment variable FORMS50_USEREXIT. This variable is defined in the Windows Registry. Spreading the foreign functions across multiple DLLs, provides for a more flexible application that will utilize better the systems resources, and will be easier to maintain and upgrade in the future.

In order to be able to follow the examples in the following section, you must make the new DLL available to the Form Builder user exits, in any of the two ways described above.

30.3.4 CALLING USER EXITS IN FORM BUILDER

Now, you are ready to invoke the user exits created in the previous sections in the Form Builder applications you have worked with in this book. You can use the functions that invoke the Windows Help engine to add MS Windows help to these applications. As an example, you will integrate the file MRD.HLP with the application Movie Rental Database. This file is provided together with the other MRD application modules in the companion software. I assume here that you have copied it in the working directory of the MRD application, for example C:\MRD.

First, start by adding the call to the user exit from the Help menu item and the Help iconic button in the toolbar. The PL/SQL code executed from both these places is `Click_Button('HELP')`. Therefore you should edit this function in the PLL module MRDMENU.PLL.

1. Start the Form Builder and open the PLL module MRDMENU.PLL.
2. Open the procedure Click_Button in the PL/SQL editor.
3. Enter the following statement in the PL/SQL editor for menu item Contents:

   ```
   USER_EXIT('WinHelpContents FILE=MRD.HLP');
   ```
4. Compile and save the library module.

Now, open the form module MRD.FMB, also provided under the name CH30.FMB in the companion software and add user exit calls to the Windows Help utility. Recall that there is a Help button defined in the windows CUSTOMER, MOVIE, RENTAL, and MAIL. In order to add context-sensitive help to your application you should create a WHEN-BUTTON-PRESSED trigger for each of them. The triggers should contain the following statement:

```
USER_EXIT('WinHelpContext FILE=MRD.HLP CONTEXT= i');
```

In this statement, *i* is the context number that has been associated with each particular Help topic in the [MAP] section of the Help project file MRD.HPJ. The following is a list of the context numbers for the principal windows of the application.

```
Customer      1
Movie         2
Rental        3
Mail          4
```

Save and generate the form module and run it to see the newly added Help functionality.

Now, integrate the functionality to browse the directory tree in search of a file. There are several forms that would benefit from such functionality. The module OLEWORD.FMB that you used in Chapter 27, for example, requires the use of a template form for the customer letter. You could improve the functionality of this module, by allowing users to search for the file that contains this template.

1. Open the module OLEWORD.FMB in the Designer.
2. In the Layout Editor create a push button labeled Browse... and place it to the right of the data item TEMPLATE.

3. Create a WHEN-BUTTON-PRESSED trigger for this button. Enter the following statement in the body of the trigger:

```
USER_EXIT('ReturnFileName ITEM=CUSTOMER.TEMPLATE');
```

4. Save, generate and run the module to test the newly added functionality.

To conclude this section, I will also add that the built-in procedure USER_EXIT, may take as a second argument an error message that is returned to Form Builder in case the call to the foreign function fails. Form Builder considers the call to a user exit like a call to any of its built-in program units, in the sense that no errors raised within the foreign function are passed to the calling environment. You can use the functions FORM_SUCCESS, FORM_FATAL, and FORM_FAILURE to check the outcome of a user exit routine. For example, the following lines represent a template for calling foreign functions from user exits in Form Builder:

```
USER_EXIT('ForeignFunctionName Arguments','Error
message');
IF NOT FORM_SUSSESS THEN
  /* Call to foreign function failed. */
END IF;
```

30.4 PL/SQL FOREIGN FUNCTION INTERFACE

Traditionally, Form Builder applications have been able to invoke and use foreign functions through user exits. Since version 4.5, Form Builder has allowed developers to access these functions directly from PL/SQL, by using the components of the ORA_FFI package. In order to be able to use this package, the foreign functions must be C functions bundled in a dynamic-link library, static library, or any executable application, created by you or by a third-party vendor. The arguments they take must be compatible with PL/SQL data types.

30.4.1 COMPARING USER EXITS WITH THE PL/SQL FOREIGN FUNCTION INTERFACE

In order to access a foreign function from the PL/SQL, you must imitate the interface of this function with a PL/SQL function. This feature, under certain circumstances makes the PL/SQL interface more advantageous and flexible than the user exits.

A drawback of the user exits is that you must create and link at least the IAPXTB structure together with the other functions that you want to access. If these functions are located in third-party API modules, you will generally have to create a functional layer in the 3GL target language, in order to be able to compile and link these functions together in one DLL that can be addressed by the user exits. This means that you must switch repeatedly between PL/SQL programming and 3GL programming. The configuration of the application will also become more difficult to maintain in track, because of the number of additional files that need to be maintained. (Recall how many files you had to edit, compile, and link in the user exit examples in the previous sections.)

Another drawback of the user exit interface to foreign functions is that user exits written in straight C cannot directly return values to the Form Builder variables. In the example of function `ReturnFileName` discussed earlier, you were able to return the file name chosen by the user only by using Oracle Precompiler statements. Although Pro*C is easy to learn and similar to C, the fact remains that you add to the system complexity by choosing to implement the function through a user exit.

Furthermore, recall that in order to invoke foreign functions from user exits, these foreign functions must be in a dynamic-link library. Furthermore, you must build the front-end IAPXTB matrix and often a layer of C functions on top of the existing DLL function. None of these is required when you access the functions through the PL/SQL interface. The member functions of the package ORA_FFI are all you will need to integrate foreign functions from any source in your Form Builder applications. The remainder of this chapter will provide details about the components of this package and will show you how to use these components to create the foreign functions interface manually.

Finally, Oracle Corporation provides a tool—Foreign Function Interface Generator—that facilitates enormously the task of building a PL/SQL interface to any DLL library. The last section of this chapter will describe the tool and show you how to use it to automate the process of creating this interface.

30.4.2 ORA_FFI PACKAGE

The ORA_FFI package contains data types, functions, procedures, and exceptions that are used in order to access foreign functions from PL/SQL program units.

Three types of special objects are used in the PL/SQL interface to foreign functions: libraries, functions, and pointers. Libraries represent the dynamic-link library, the static library, or the executable file that contains the foreign functions that will be accessed. In PL/SQL program units the libraries are addressed through handles, which are objects of ORA_FFI.LIBHANDLETYPE data type. Similarly, member functions of these libraries are accessed through handles of type ORA_FFI.FUNCHANDLETYPE. In rare occasions, you may need to implement unspecified pointers in your programs, similar to the void pointer in C. To obtain such variables, you must declare them of ORA_FFI.POINTERTYPE data type.

The following statement declares the variable `lh_User` as a library handle:

```
lh_User ORA_FFI.LIBHANDLETYPE;
```

The following statement declares the variable `fh_WinHelp` as a function handle:

```
fh_WinHelp ORA_FFI.FUNCHANDLETYPE;
```

The following statement declares the variable `dwData` as a pointer:

```
dwData ORA_FFI.POINTERTYPE;
```

The data type ORA_FFI.POINTERTYPE is in reality a record structure with only one element in it called *handle*. This element is of NUMBER data type, which limits the use of these pointers. The following statements assigns the value 5 to the variable `dwData`:

```
dwData.handle := 5;
```

The package ORA_FFI provides three functions that allow you to check if a library is currently loaded in memory, to load it if this is not the case, or to unload it when no longer needed. The function FIND_LIBRARY takes as an argument the name of a library and returns a handle to it, if the library is previously loaded. Otherwise, this function raises the exception ORA_FFI.FFI_ERROR. The function LOAD_LIBRARY takes as parameter the directory and the name of the library. If the library file is located in the current system directory, or in a directory that is included in the PATH environment variable, you may set the directory argument to NULL, and provide simply the library name. The function loads the library and returns a handle to it. If the loading process is not successful the function returns NULL. When you are finished using the functions in a library, you may want to unload it, in order to release the system resources it occupies. Use the procedureUNLOAD_LIBRARY for this purpose. This procedure takes as argument the handle of the library to be unloaded.

Figure 30.8 shows sample code that registers the Windows library USER.EXE and the user exitlibrary that you developed in the previous sections.

The library USER.EXE is located in the directory \WINDOWS\SYSTEM, which is always accessible to Windows. This is the reason why you do not need to specify the directory in the function that loads this library. On the other hand, the directory must be specified in the second case, assuming that the directory C:\FORMS\USEREXIT is not in the path. Note how the directory name must be terminated with the back slash character "\."

Once the library is loaded, all its member functions become available for you to use. As a preliminary step though, you must initialize them. Initializing a function is a process that involves the following three steps:

1. Register the function using REGISTER_FUNCTION. This function takes as arguments the library handle where the foreign function is located, the

```
BEGIN
 lh_USER := ORA_FFI.FIND_LIBRARY('USER.EXE');
EXCEPTION WHEN ORA_FFI.FFI_ERROR THEN
 lh_USER := ORA_FFI.LOAD_LIBRARY(NULL,'USER.EXE');
END;
BEGIN
 lh_UE_CH25 := ORA_FFI.FIND_LIBRARY('UE_CH25.DLL');
EXCEPTION WHEN ORA_FFI.FFI_ERROR THEN
 lh_USER :=
ORA_FFI.LOAD_LIBRARY('C:\FORMS\USEREXIT\','UE_CH25.DLL');
END;
```

FIGURE 30.8 Loading DLL libraries with ORA_FFI procedures.

name of the function, and the calling standard used by the function. The value of the last argument can be either ORA_FFI.PASCAL_STD for functions that follow the Pascal/FORTRAN naming and calling standards, or ORA_FFI.C_STD for those functions that follow the C naming and calling standards.

2. Use the procedure REGISTER_PARAMETER to register the type of each argument of the function. This procedure takes as arguments the handle to the function and the C data type of the function argument being registered. The values that the second argument may take are presented in Figure 30.9.
3. Use the procedure ORA_FFI.REGISTER_RETURN to register the return type of the foreign function. This procedure is very similar to the procedure ORA_FFI.REGISTER_PARAMETER. It takes as first argument the handle of the function, and as second argument the C data type that will be returned by the function.

TIP

When C or C++ declarators (functions, arrays, and pointers) are preceded by the keyword __pascal, the compiler uses the Pascal naming and calling convention. The Pascal naming convention requires that all names be converted to uppercase. It also requires that the function remove its parameters from the stack before returning to the caller. The Pascal calling convention is widely used nowadays. Most of the Win32 API functions and the interfaces of a majority of non-Microsoft tools follow this standard. Therefore, this is also known as the standard calling convention.

> When the names of variables or functions are preceded by the keyword __cdecl, the compiler is instructed to follow the C naming and calling conventions. The C naming conventions require that the names of variables and functions be preceded by an underscore character, and the case-sensitivity be maintained. The C calling convention requires that the calling program be responsible for removing the arguments of a function from the stack.
>
> The C naming and calling conventions are the default. Therefore, unless you use the keyword __pascal, all the variables and functions you use in your programs will follow these conventions.

In the general case, all the above steps must be performed in order to properly initialize a foreign function. However, depending on the type of function being initialized, Step 2 or Step 3 may not be necessary. If, for example, the function does not take any arguments, you may skip Step 2. If the function return type is void, thus the function is a procedure, you do need to register a return type, therefore, the Step 3 may be skipped. Figure 30.10 shows examples of initialization of three functions from the Windows SDK USER library.

The first group of statements registers the functions `WinHelp`, the types of arguments, and its return type. The second group of statements registers the procedure `SetWindowText`, and the data types of its two arguments. This procedure sets the title of the window whose handle is passed in the first argument to the character string contained in the second argument. Finally, the last two state-

SPECIFIED VALUE	CORRESPONDING C DATATYPE
ORA_FFI.C_CHAR	char
ORA_FFI.C_CHAR_PTR	char *
ORA_FFI.C_SHORT	short
ORA_FFI.C_SHORT_PTR	short *
ORA_FFI.C_INT	int
ORA_FFI.C_INT_PTR	int *
ORA_FFI.C_DOUBLE	double
ORA_FFI.C_DOUBLE_PTR	double *
ORA_FFI.C_LONG	long
ORA_FFI.C_LONG_PTR	long *
ORA_FFI.C_FLOAT	float
ORA_FFI.C_FLOAT_PTR	float *
ORA_FFI.C_DVOID_PTR	void *

FIGURE 30.9 Mapping of argument types to C data types.

```
fh_WinHelp :=
ORA_FFI.REGISTER_FUNCTION(lh_USER,'WinHelp',ORA_FFI.PASCAL_STD);
ORA_FFI.REGISTER_PARAMETER(fh_WinHelp,ORA_FFI.C_INT);
ORA_FFI.REGISTER_PARAMETER(fh_WinHelp,ORA_FFI.C_CHAR_PTR);
ORA_FFI.REGISTER_PARAMETER(fh_WinHelp,ORA_FFI.C_INT);
ORA_FFI.REGISTER_PARAMETER(fh_WinHelp,ORA_FFI.C_DVOID_PTR);
ORA_FFI.REGISTER_RETURN(fh_WinHelp,ORA_FFI.C_INT);

fh_SetWindowText :=
ORA_FFI.REGISTER_FUNCTION(lh_USER,'SetWindowText',ORA_FFI.PASCA
L_STD);
ORA_FFI.REGISTER_PARAMETER(fh_SetWindowText,ORA_FFI.C_INT);
ORA_FFI.REGISTER_PARAMETER(fh_SetWindowText,ORA_FFI.C_CHAR_PTR);

fh_GetActiveWindow :=
ORA_FFI.REGISTER_FUNCTION(lh_USER,'GetActiveWindow',ORA_FFI.PAS
CAL_STD);
ORA_FFI.REGISTER_RETURN(fh_GetActiveWindow,ORA_FFI.C_INT);
```

FIGURE 30.10 Different cases of C functions initialization.

ments register the function `GetActiveWindow` and its return type. This function does not take any arguments, and returns a handle to the window that is currently active.

I will conclude this section by mentioning the function ORA_FFI.IS_NULL_PTR. You can use this function to check if any library handle, function handle, or pointer is NULL. In such a case, the function returns the Boolean value TRUE; otherwise it returns the value FALSE.

30.4.3 IMPLEMENTING THE PL/SQL FOREIGN FUNCTION INTERFACE

In this section, you will create a PL/SQL interface to several functions from the Windows USER.EXE library. Some of these functions such as `WinHelp`, `GetActiveWindow`, and `SetWindowText`, were introduced in the previous section, where you learned how to register them, their parameter types, and return data type. In addition to these, you will also use the function `MessageBox`, to display quickly and easily message boxes, without going through Form Builder alerts. For a detailed description of the use of these functions, and their parameters, you should consult the Windows SDK documentation that comes with compilers such as Microsoft Visual C++ or Visual Basic.

The module you will work with in this section is called PLSQLFFI.FMB and is provided in the companion software. This is a one-block form that can display message boxes and Windows Help using the Windows SDK functions mentioned above. The layout of this form is presented in Figure 30.11.

In the left half of the window you will be enter the title, text, and style of the message box that will be displayed. In the second half you can enter the name of the help file, the command, and additional data, if required by the command. For the items STYLE and COMMAND, the lists will help you choose the appropriate value of the parameter. In the rest of this section you will create the triggers and program units that will display the message box and the help file according to the specified parameters.

The program units that will carry out this functionality will be encapsulated in a package. Because this package will implement the foreign function interface with the library USER.EXE, its name will be FFI_USER. Start the development activity by creating the specification for this package.

1. Launch the Form Builder Designer, and open the module PLSQLFFI.FMB.
2. Create a package specification called FFI_USER.
3. Enter the contents of the package specification as shown in Figure 30.12.

Defining these functions, their return types, number of arguments and the data type for each argument is as easy as looking up the definition of the corresponding functions in the Windows SDK documentation. Figure 30.13, in fact shows the definitions of these functions in the Windows library.

An important difference is that the data types of arguments and the return type of the functions in the package FFI_USER are PL/SQL data types. Given that the other program units in the Form Builder application will access these functions only through the package specification interface, you guarantee that they will not have to rely on any implementation details of these functions.

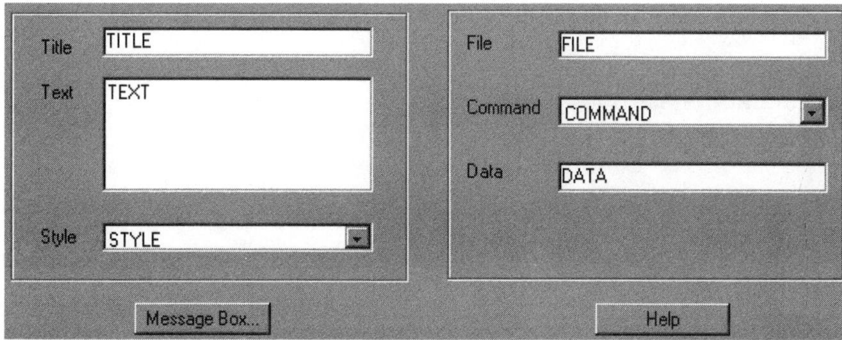

FIGURE 30.11 Layout of module PLSQLFFI.FMB.

```
PACKAGE FFI_USER IS
 FUNCTION WinHelp (hwnd IN PLS_INTEGER,
  lpszHelpFile IN OUT VARCHAR2,
  fuCommand IN PLS_INTEGER,
  dwData IN OUT VARCHAR2)
 RETURN PLS_INTEGER;

 FUNCTION GetActiveWindow
 RETURN PLS_INTEGER;

 FUNCTION MessageBox ( hwndParent IN PLS_INTEGER,
  lpszText IN OUT VARCHAR2,
  lpszTitle IN OUT VARCHAR2,
  fuStyle IN PLS_INTEGER)
 RETURN PLS_INTEGER;
END;
```

FIGURE 30.12 Specification for package FFI_USER.

When creating the program units for the body of this package you should follow these steps:

1. Declare variables that will store the handle to the foreign functions library and the foreign functions that will be used from that library.
2. Load the C library, and register the functions, their return type, and the data

```
BOOL WinHelp(hwnd, lpszHelpFile, fuCommand, dwData)
 HWND hwnd;    /* handle of window requesting help          */
 LPCSTR lpszHelpFile; /* address of directory-path string   */
 UINT fuCommand;      /* type of help                       */
 DWORD dwData;        /* additional data                    */

HWND GetActiveWindow(void)

int MessageBox(hwndParent, lpszText, lpszTitle, fuStyle)
 HWND hwndParent;     /* handle of parent window            */
 LPCSTR lpszText;     /* address of text in message box     */
 LPCSTR lpszTitle;    /* address of title of message box    */
 UINT fuStyle;        /* style of message box               */
```

FIGURE 30.13 Definitions of the Windows functions in the USER.EXE Library.

types of all their parameters. This should be done in the execution part of the package body.

3. For each function in the package specification, create a subordinate function, whose only purpose is to associate the C foreign function, or rather its handle, with the PL/SQL data types and return type of the function.
4. Create the body of each function declared in the package specification. The ultimate purpose of this function is to issue a call to the subordinate function created in the previous step. This function then, will bind the data passed as arguments with the C function through the function handle. The foreign function will be executed, and will return a value to the PL/SQL environment.

The previous section explained how you can implement the first two steps. You simply declare the desired variables using the data types defined in the package ORA_FFI. Then, you use the necessary functions from this package to load the library and register the foreign functions, their arguments, and their return values. In order to do this in your case, create a package body, name it FFI_USER, and enter its contents as shown in Figure 30.14. Be aware that the package shown in this figure is not complete yet and will not compile successfully at this point.

Now you are ready to create the functions that will implement the interface of the package. These functions should be created in the declaration part of the package body, immediately after the statements that declare the handle variables to the library and the foreign functions.

Figure 30.15 contains the details of the functions that are needed to implement the interface with the `WinHelp` function.

First, the subordinate function `icd_WinHelp` is declared. This is very similar with the `WinHelp` function declared in the package specification. It returns the same type of data, and takes the same arguments as this function. One important difference to point out is that the function `icd_WinHelp` takes as its first argument the handle to the foreign function registered previously. Another significant difference with PL/SQL program units you have seen so far is that this function is passed for execution to the component of Form Builder that interfaces with C libraries. The PRAGMA directive instructs the compiler to execute this branching.

CAUTION

The only argument that you may change in the PRAGMA INTERFACE statement is the middle one that specifies the function name. The first and the third arguments must be exactly as shown in Figure 30.15 for all the cases.

```
PACKAGE BODY FFI_USER IS
 lh_User ORA_FFI.LIBHANDLETYPE;
 fh_WinHelp ORA_FFI.FUNCHANDLETYPE;
 fh_GetActiveWindow ORA_FFI.FUNCHANDLETYPE;
 fh_MessageBox ORA_FFI.FUNCHANDLETYPE;

/* Function declarations will go here. */

BEGIN
 BEGIN
  lh_USER := ORA_FFI.find_library('USER.EXE');
 EXCEPTION WHEN ORA_FFI.FFI_ERROR THEN
  lh_USER := ORA_FFI.load_library(NULL,'USER.EXE');
 END;

 fh_WinHelp :=
 ORA_FFI.REGISTER_FUNCTION(lh_USER,'WinHelp',ORA_FFI.PASCAL_STD);
 ORA_FFI.REGISTER_PARAMETER(fh_WinHelp,ORA_FFI.C_INT);
 ORA_FFI.REGISTER_PARAMETER(fh_WinHelp,ORA_FFI.C_CHAR_PTR);
 ORA_FFI.REGISTER_PARAMETER(fh_WinHelp,ORA_FFI.C_INT);
 ORA_FFI.REGISTER_PARAMETER(fh_WinHelp,ORA_FFI.C_DVOID_PTR);
 ORA_FFI.REGISTER_RETURN(fh_WinHelp,ORA_FFI.C_INT);

 fh_GetActiveWindow :=

ORA_FFI.REGISTER_FUNCTION(lh_USER,'GetActiveWindow',ORA_FFI.PAS
CAL_STD);
 ORA_FFI.REGISTER_RETURN(fh_GetActiveWindow,ORA_FFI.C_INT);

 fh_MessageBox :=

ORA_FFI.REGISTER_FUNCTION(lh_USER,'MessageBox',ORA_FFI.PASCAL_S
TD);
 ORA_FFI.REGISTER_PARAMETER(fh_MessageBox,ORA_FFI.C_INT);
 ORA_FFI.REGISTER_PARAMETER(fh_MessageBox,ORA_FFI.C_CHAR_PTR);
 ORA_FFI.REGISTER_PARAMETER(fh_MessageBox,ORA_FFI.C_CHAR_PTR);
 ORA_FFI.REGISTER_PARAMETER(fh_MessageBox,ORA_FFI.C_INT);
 ORA_FFI.REGISTER_RETURN(fh_MessageBox,ORA_FFI.C_INT);
END;
```

FIGURE 30.14 Declaring and initializing the functions in package FFI_USER.

```
FUNCTION icd_WinHelp (funcHandle IN
ORA_FFI.FUNCHANDLETYPE,
 hwnd IN PLS_INTEGER,
 lpszHelpFile IN OUT VARCHAR2,
 fuCommand IN PLS_INTEGER,
 dwData IN OUT VARCHAR2)
RETURN PLS_INTEGER;
PRAGMA INTERFACE(C,icd_WinHelp,11265);

FUNCTION WinHelp (hwnd IN PLS_INTEGER,
 lpszHelpFile IN OUT VARCHAR2,
 fuCommand IN PLS_INTEGER,
 dwData IN OUT VARCHAR2)
RETURN PLS_INTEGER IS
 rc PLS_INTEGER;
BEGIN
 rc := icd_WinHelp(fh_WinHelp, hwnd, lpszHelpFile,
fuCommand, dwData);
 RETURN (rc);
END ;
```

FIGURE 30.15 Using the PRAGMA directive to bind PL/SQL variables with foreign functions.

The statements in the body of function `WinHelp` are self-explanatory. The main purpose of this function is to bind the arguments with the foreign function handle by issuing a call to the function `icd_WinHelp`, which. in turn, will call the foreign function. For the sake of simplicity, the statements shown in Figure 30.15 assume that all the arguments are valid. You may place other statements in the body of these functions to ensure that the appropriate data is passed along, or that any errors that may occur are trapped and handled.

The process of creating the functions `GetActiveWindow` and `MessageBox` is entirely similar. The contents of these functions are shown in Figure 30.16.

At this point you are ready to create the WHEN-BUTTON-PRESSED triggers for push buttons MESSAGE and HELP. Both these triggers will ultimately call the functions `MessageBox` and `WinHelp` from the package FFI_USER. Since both these functions require a window handle as their first parameter, the function `GetActiveWindow` is invoked prior to each of the other two functions. The first block of code in Figure 30.17 shows the contents of the trigger attached to the Help button. The second block of code contains the trigger attaches to the Message Box... button.

By carefully examining the functions shown in this chapter, you will notice that all the variables that will correspond to C pointer types are declared as IN

```
FUNCTION icd_GetActiveWindow (funcHandle IN
ORA_FFI.FUNCHANDLETYPE)
RETURN PLS_INTEGER;
PRAGMA INTERFACE(C,icd_GetActiveWindow,11265);

FUNCTION GetActiveWindow
RETURN PLS_INTEGER IS
 rc PLS_INTEGER;
BEGIN
 rc := icd_GetActiveWindow(fh_GetActiveWindow);
 RETURN (rc);
END ;

FUNCTION icd_MessageBox(funcHandle IN
ORA_FFI.FUNCHANDLETYPE,
 hwndParent IN PLS_INTEGER,
 lpszText IN OUT VARCHAR2,
 lpszTitle IN OUT VARCHAR2,
 fuStyle IN PLS_INTEGER)
RETURN PLS_INTEGER;
PRAGMA INTERFACE(C,icd_MessageBox,11265);

FUNCTION MessageBox (hwndParent IN PLS_INTEGER,
 lpszText IN OUT VARCHAR2,
 lpszTitle IN OUT VARCHAR2,
 fuStyle IN PLS_INTEGER)
RETURN PLS_INTEGER IS
 rc PLS_INTEGER;
BEGIN
 rc :=
icd_MessageBox(fh_MessageBox,hwndParent,lpszText,lpszTitle,
fuStyle);
 RETURN (rc);
END ;
```

FIGURE 30.16 Accessing Windows SDK functions with ORA_FFI.

OUT variables. This allows Forms to treat these parameters as initialized variables, for which the appropriate memory is already allocated. If the default mode of the parameters (IN) is used, these parameters act like constants inside the body of the functions. In order for the subsequent call to the foreign function to work, you must declare a local variable, assign it the value of the parameter, and pass

```
DECLARE
 rc PLS_INTEGER;
 hwnd PLS_INTEGER;
 command PLS_INTEGER := :WINHELP.COMMAND;
BEGIN
 hwnd := FFI_USER.GetActiveWindow;
 rc := FFI_USER.WinHelp (hwnd, :WINHELP.FILE, command,
:WINHELP.DATA);
END;
```

```
DECLARE
 rc PLS_INTEGER;
 hwnd PLS_INTEGER;
 style PLS_INTEGER := :WINHELP.STYLE;
BEGIN
 hwnd := FFI_USER.GetActiveWindow;
 rc := FFI_USER.MessageBox (hwnd, :WINHELP.TEXT,
:WINHELP.TITLE, style);
END;
```

FIGURE 30.17 Calling foreign functions from PL/SQL triggers.

this local variable to the foreign function. Figure 30.18 shows an example of the function `WinHelp` implemented with IN parameters.

30.4.4 THE FOREIGN FUNCTION INTERFACE GENERATOR

In addition to the Form Builder software, Oracle Corporation optionally ships a module that reduces significantly the programming effort and minimizes the possibility of errors when creating a PL/SQL interface to foreign functions. The Foreign Function Interface Generator (FFIGen) application allows you to specify in one unified screen the name of the PL/SQL package to be created, the DLL library that contains the foreign functions, and each function to be included in the package with information about its arguments and return datatype. The information you provide is stored in database tables and is used to generate a .PLL file that contains the PL/SQL package that interfaces with the foreign functions in the specified DLL.

FFIGen application has three components:

1. FFIGEN.SQL contains the SQL statements that create the application tables and insert the necessary data to generate the package WINSAMPLE used in another Form Builder demo.

```
FUNCTION WinHelp (hwnd IN PLS_INTEGER,
 lpszHelpFile IN VARCHAR2,
 fuCommand IN PLS_INTEGER,
 dwData IN ORA_FFI.POINTERTYPE)
RETURN PLS_INTEGER IS
 hwnd_l PLS_INTEGER := hwnd;
 lpszHelpFile_l VARCHAR2(144) := lpszHelpFile;
 fuCommand_l PLS_INTEGER := fuCommand;
 dwData_l VARCHAR2(1028) := dwData;
 rc PLS_INTEGER;
BEGIN
 rc := i_WinHelp(fh_WinHelp, hwnd_l, lpszHelpFile_l,
fuCommand_l, dwData_l);
 RETURN (rc);
END;
```

FIGURE 30.18 Interfacing with foreign functions with IN arguments.

2. FFIGEN.FMB contains the binary code for the form of FFIGen.
3. FFIGEN.MMB contains the binary code for the menu of FFIGen.

In the remaining part of this section, you will use the FFIGen application to generate the package FFI_USER which you created manually in the previous section. First, launch the application and create the necessary database objects:

1. Double-click the program item created above. The Form Builder Logon dialog box appears.
2. Specify the username, password, and database connection string in the Login dialog box. If the logon is successful and the FFIGen database objects do not exist in the schema you specify, the dialog box Foreign Function Demo Setup will appear (see Figure 30.19).
3. Click Create Tables button to create the FFIGen application tables. In this case, the script FFIGEN.SQL is executed. Alternatively, you may elect to run this script form SQL*Plus prior to invoking FFIGen for the first time.

After the logon and the installation of database objects are successful, you will see the Foreign Function Interface Generator Demo window. This window contains information about the package WINSAMPLE. In the following steps you will insert the information required to generate the package FFI_USER.

1. Click in the Package Name item, under WinSample and enter `FFI_USER`.
2. Click inside Dynamic Link Library Name item and enter `USER.EXE`.

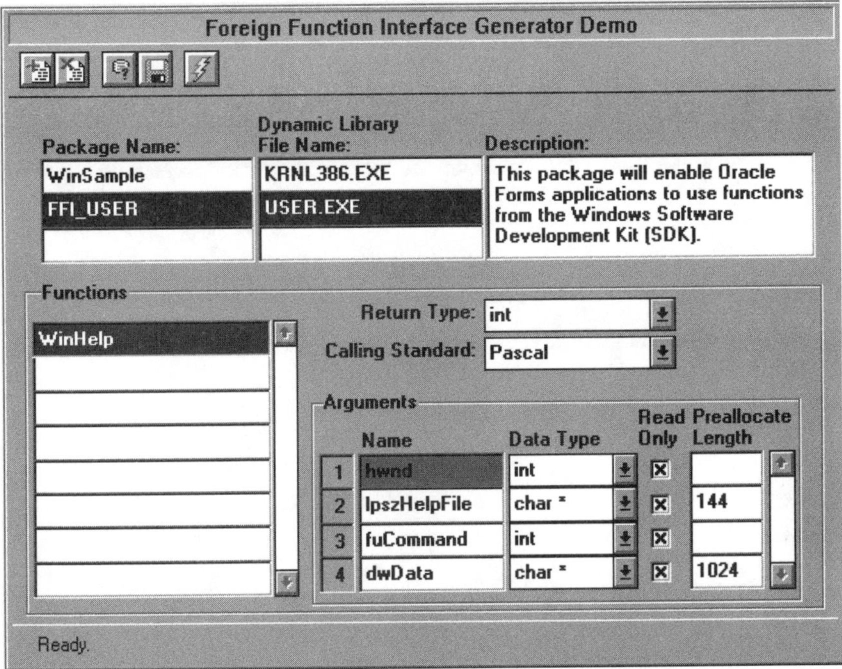

FIGURE 30.19 Foreign Function Demo Setup dialog box.

3. Click inside Description item and enter comments for this package.
4. Click in the Functions block and enter the information for function `WinHelp`, its return type, and arguments as shown in Figure 30.20.
5. Click under the function `WinHelp`, save the changes when prompted, and enter the information for function `GetActiveWindow`. As discussed earlier in the chapter, this function does not take any arguments, its return type is `int`, and the calling standard is `Pascal`.
6. Click under the function `GetActiveWindow`, and enter the information for function `MessageBox` as shown in Figure 30.21.
7. Click the Save icon to save the changes.
8. Click the Generate icon to create the library FFI_USER.PLD in the working directory.

You should always check the checkbox Read Only for IN arguments. For IN OUT or OUT variables this checkbox should not be checked. Furthermore, if the function will return some value to an argument, you must allocate enough space to that argument to hold the value. You do this by entering a value in the Preallocate Length field.

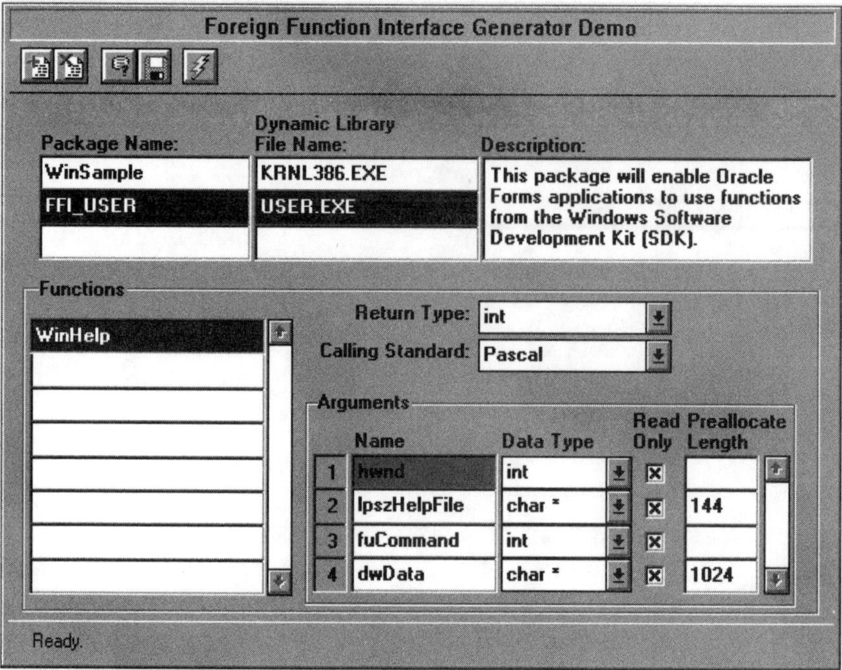

FIGURE 30.20 Foreign Function Interface Generator window.

These steps are equivalent to the tedious manual coding effort described in Section 0.[au: pls provide cross-reference] They result in a library that can be used in the module PLSQLFFI.FMB. Since FFI_USER.PLD is the text version of this library, you must convert it to .PLL format before attaching it to the form PLSQLFFI.FMB. These are the steps to perform this conversion:

FIGURE 30.21 Specifications for GetActiveWindow function.

1. Launch the Form Builder if it is not already running.
2. Select File | Administration | Convert... from the menu. The Convert dialog box appears (see Figure 30.22).
3. Specify the settings in the Convert dialog box as shown in Figure 30.22. Use the Browse utility to search for FFI_USER.PLD in the working directory of FFIGen application.
4. Click Convert. The text file FFI_USER.PLD is converted into the PLL file FFI_USER.PLL.
5. Open FFI_USER.PLL in the Designer and select File | Compile... from the menu. The library should compile without errors.
6. Save FFI_USER.PLL in the same directory as PLSQLFFI.FMB.
7. Attach the library FFI_USER.PLL to PLSQLFFI.FMB and use the components of package FFI_USER.

This is a quick and very effective way to create a package that provides you with a large amount of functionality. It is recommended that you use the FFIGen application whenever you need to create a PL/SQL interface to foreign functions. If you need to customize the contents of some of the functions or document your functions, you can edit the components of the generated package, but you will not have to do the heavy-duty programming prone to inconsistencies and errors required to manually develop this package.

30.4.5 GENERATING FOREIGN FUNCTION INTERFACE PACKAGES FROM PROCEDURE BUILDER

The ORA_FFI package contains a procedure that is not mentioned so far in this discussion. Its name is GENERATE_FOREIGN, and can be used only in the Oracle Procedure Builder environment. After you load the C library and register all the functions and arguments that you want to use, you can invoke this procedure to create a PL/SQL package that will govern the PL/SQL interface with these functions. In this section, you will perform the steps to accomplish this.

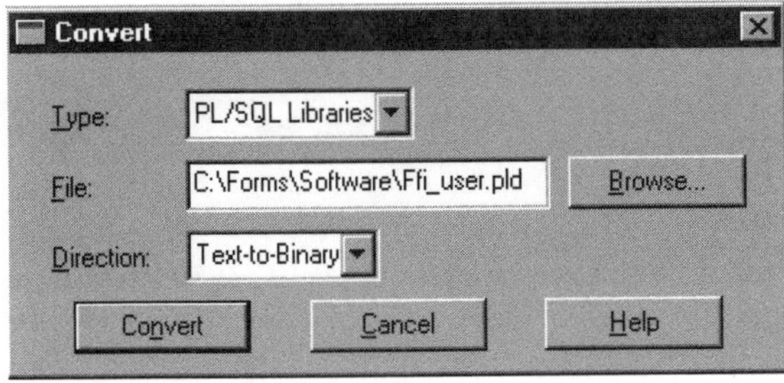

FIGURE 30.22 Convert dialog box.

1. Launch the Oracle Procedure Builder.
2. Choose File | Load... from the menu. The Load Program Unit dialog box will appear.
3. Click the Browse... button if necessary to select the file FFI_USER.TXT located under the same directory as the module CH30.FMB.
4. Click Load.

You will see that a procedure called FFI_USER is created when the file is loaded. If you display the contents of this procedure in the PL/SQL editor, you will notice that its body contains the type declarations and statements shown in Figure 30.14. To complete the process of creating the package, follow these steps:

1. Enter the following lines at the end of the procedure, and compile it when done:

```
ORA_FFI.GENERATE_FOREIGN (lh_USER);
ORA_FFI.UNLOAD_LIBRARY (lh_USER);
```

2. Choose Tools | PL/SQL Interpreter... from the menu. The PL/SQL Interpreter window becomes the active window.
3. At the PL/SQL> prompt enter the following command:

   ```
   .EXECUTE PROC FFI_USER
   ```

If you switch back to the Navigator, you will see that two new objects are created: the package specification FFI_USER, and package body FFI_USER. This is a fully functional package that you can put in a library, attach to any module and use in your applications.

This method is certainly better than manual coding of the foreign function interface, but should be considered only if you cannot obtain the FFIGen application. Besides the fact that it still requires programming of the initialization part of the package, the package that it generates still requires editing for readability and documentation purposes. For example, an inspection of the package generated with this method will show that the arguments to the functions are named arg0, arg1, and so on, which are not very meaningful and should be clarified.

30.5 SUMMARY

This chapter discussed the use of functionality developed in 3GL languages and compiled in the form of Dynamic Loadable Libraries from within Form Builder. It explained two ways to access these functions: through user exits and using the PL/SQL foreign function interface. Important concepts in this chapter were:

- **Types of Foreign Functions**
- **Sample Foreign Functions**
  - Modules UEERROR.H and UEERROR.C
  - Module HELP.C
  - Module FILENAME.PC
- **User Exit Interface**
  - IAPXTB Control Structure
  - Creating the DLL file
  - Deploying the User Exit DLL
  - Calling User Exits in Form Builder
- **PL/SQL Foreign Function Interface**
  - Comparing User Exits with the PL/SQL Foreign Function Interface
  - ORA_FFI Package
  - Implementing the PL/SQL Foreign Function Interface
  - The Foreign Function Interface Generator
  - Generating Foreign Function Interface Packages from Procedure Builder

The following table describes the software assets that were discussed in this chapter. From the main HTML page of the software utilities provided with the book follow the links *Software* and *Chapter 30* to access these assets:

ASSET NAME	DESCRIPTION
UEERROR.H and UERROR.C	Header and C file that displays an error message to the users.
HELP.C	C file with functions that invoke the Windows Help utility.
FILENAME.PC	Pro*C file that implements a function that returns the name of a file to a Form Builder item.
FILENAME.C	The C version of FILENAME.PC created by the Oracle Pro*C precompiler.
UE_CH30.C	C file with the IAPXTB structure used in Chapter 30.
UE_CH30.DLL	Dynamic-link library used in Chapter 30.
MRD.HLP	Windows Help file for the MRD application.
MRDMENU.PLL	A version of the MRDMENU PL/SQL library that invokes Windows help using a user exit call.
CH30_1.FMB	The MRD module developed in previous chapters.
CH30_2.FMB	The MRD module with user exit calls added.
CH30_2.FMX	The executable version of CH30_2.FMB compiled for Win32 platforms.
OLEWORD.FMB	The OLEWORD module created in Chapter 29 with user exit calls added.

ASSET NAME	DESCRIPTION
OLEWORD.FMX	The executable version of OLEWORD.FMB compiled for Win32 platforms.
PLSQLFFI.FMB	A Form Builder module that will be used to implement PL/SQL Foreign Function Interface calls.
PLSQLFFI_1.FMB	The final version of PLSQLFFI with Foreign Function Interface calls.
PLSQLFFI_1.FMX	The executable version of PLSQLFFI_1.FMB compiled for Win32 platforms.
FFI_GEN.SQL	SQL*Plus script that creates the database objects required by the FFIGen application.
FFI_GEN.FMB	A Form Builder module that facilitates the creation of PL/SQL wrappers around DLL libraries.
FFI_GEN.FMX	The executable version of FFI_GEN.FMB compiled for Win32 platforms.
FFI_GEN.MMB	The Form Builder menu module that accompanies FFI_GEN.FMB.
FFI_GEN.MMX	The executable version of FFI_GEN.MMB compiled for Win32 platforms.
FFI_USER.PLD	The text version of the PL/SQL library FFI_USER, as created by the FFIGen utility.
FFI_USER.PLL	The PL/SQL library FFI_USER, converted from FFI_USER.PLD.
FFI_USER.TXT	Text file with the definition of the procedure used in Section 30.4.5.

INDEX